THE COLLECTED WORKS OF
SAMUEL TAYLOR COLERIDGE · 9

AIDS TO REFLECTION

General Editor: KATHLEEN COBURN
Associate Editor: BART WINER

THE COLLECTED WORKS

1. Samuel Taylor Coleridge, from a portrait
painted by an unidentified artist about 1826
Highgate Literary and Scientific Institution; reproduced by kind permission

THE COLLECTED WORKS OF

Samuel Taylor Coleridge

Aids to
Reflection

EDITED BY

John Beer

ROUTLEDGE

✤ BOLLINGEN SERIES LXXV
PRINCETON UNIVERSITY PRESS

THIS EDITION
OF THE WORKS OF
SAMUEL TAYLOR COLERIDGE
IS DEDICATED
IN GRATITUDE TO
THE FAMILY EDITORS
IN EACH GENERATION

CONTENTS

---

[1] The Contents page of *AR* (1831) also indicated two subdivisions to this section: "On the Duty and Advantage of Cultivating the Power and Habit of Reflection" (pp "1–14", i.e. *Int Aph I–XIX* below) and "Prudence, Morality and Religion interdistinguished" (pp "15–30", i.e. *Int Aph XX–XXXII*). These titles were not carried forward into the 1831 text itself, which continued to indicate all the aphorisms, as in 1825, simply as "Introductory Aphorisms".

LIST OF ILLUSTRATIONS

[1] For a discussion of this painting and its provenance see E. W. Nye "A Portrait of the Sage at Highgate" *The Wordsworth Circle* xiii (1982) 231–2.

EDITOR'S FOREWORD:
PLAN OF THIS EDITION;
ACKNOWLEDGMENTS

*A*ids to Reflection presents a variety of challenges to its editor. It was the central piece of writing in Coleridge's later career, yet, as explained more fully in the Editor's Introduction below, it came into being half by accident, having begun as a more modest scheme. In a volume to be entitled "The Beauties of Archbishop Leighton" he had planned to offer his readers the experience of exposure to a saintly seventeenth-century divine in whose mind thought and devotion were so intimately associated as to offer a total vision of the world more compelling than could be attained by use of the reasoning powers alone. As the work grew into the more ambitious *Aids to Reflection* the range of its reference became correspondingly extended: sometimes he would write in a strain of homely wisdom, sometimes make a scholarly point, sometimes address major questions of theology. As a result the book is often more like a piece of "work in progress" as Coleridge summons up successive topics and presents his latest thinking in relation to them.

Since in doing so he drew upon the fruits of a lifetime's reading, annotation of the volume that resulted must necessarily range very extensively, covering not only the works he was turning to while writing his volume but others that he had read years before. One aim of such annotation is to discover the degree to which, working across the whole range of contemporary knowledge and claiming to make his own contribution in a number of fields, his conclusions were justifiable in terms of what was known in his own time, as well as in ours. The fact that *Aids to Reflection* is a nodal document in his later writing makes such extended annotation desirable also as an aid to understanding his other work during the last period of his life. In view of this larger relevance attention is drawn in the notes to discussions by other scholars of important points, even though for obvious reasons such coverage cannot hope to be exhaustive.

In certain instances the relevance of the thought and knowledge opened up by a single word or phrase, though important for an understanding of Coleridge's work as a whole, extends well beyond the particular matter under discussion. In such cases it has proved desirable to examine the issues involved in "Excursus Notes", printed in an appendix, where the discussions are made available to those who are interested.

A further complication is created by the fact that the volume was itself a piece of editing by Coleridge—his presentation of Leighton and some other seventeenth-century authors—and that the main text he was dealing with, Leighton's commentary on the First Epistle of Peter, was also, in one sense, an editorial enterprise. We are in the unusual position of being able to examine not only how Coleridge dealt with the task of editing another author's work but how he did so when that work itself consisted of commentary on a further text. The materials for such a study are present in the notes and will be found also in a number of the appendixes.

Among the interests that run through this particular volume is Coleridge's concern with language. Thinking about religion meant reflecting not only on the words which it employs, but on ordinary speech as well. In the introductory section, particularly, he recurs to questions of etymology, claiming that to trace the history of a particular word will often throw unexpected light upon some abiding human concern. This archaeological enterprise was not a matter of excavating dead forms: Coleridge was concerned to show that words were living entities, and that their life was always in growth. His delight in inventing words, prominent in earlier years, had lost little of its former impetus, moreover: readers of the notes will observe how often his use of a word is the first or only example recorded in the *Oxford English Dictionary*.

The editing has also involved investigating the actual production of the volume. Coleridge's dealings with the printer were more demanding than would nowadays be tolerated. Part of the setting-up was undertaken directly from marginal annotations by him in the original volumes of Leighton, part from additional transcripts and notes which he supplied separately. The main annotated volumes have survived but the manuscript material is only partially extant; it seems that after his death the Gillmans, with whom he had been living, sometimes gave away pages of it to friends as mementos. While some long sections of the surviving text were retained together, later to be acquired by the British Museum, other short pieces are now scattered through libraries all over the world. All known examples are reproduced in an appendix to the present volume. The printer's proof has disappeared, apart from a single sheet, but that sheet, as is explained in the Editor's Introduction below, throws considerable light upon the early stages of the printing. After the volume was published, moreover, Coleridge wrote copious annotations in some of the volumes which he presented to others—more indeed than in any other of his works. As much of this material as has been tracked down to date is reproduced in the textual and editorial notes and in Appendix D below.

Coleridge's enthusiasm for the seventeenth-century divines took him to some recondite places, so that it becomes necessary to explore minute points of theology. As always, however, his major enterprise was the difficult one of reconciling the wisdom of the old with the insights of the new, tracing ancient roots while also responding to modern energies. Once discovered, his sources often throw further light on these processes.

It is now many years since the production of a collected edition of Coleridge's work was first planned, and I have had the privilege of being included among the editors from the first stages. In the early days the enthusiasm of Rupert Hart-Davis carried the editors through doubts and difficulties, to be followed in due course by the sustaining encouragement given by Jack Barrett, Vaun Gilmour, and others associated with the Bollingen foundation and the Princeton University Press. Among the latter, Elizabeth Powers deserves special mention for her continuing commitment to the edition. The guiding spirit throughout has of course been that of Kathleen Coburn, who was willing to add to the labours of producing the *Notebooks* those of looking after this even more ambitious project. It was a happy experience to draw upon her advice and help over so many years and a great sadness when in September 1991 the ill health that had for the last few years forced her to withdraw into the background was followed by her death. The debt owed to her by all the editors of the edition has been incalculable.

As the work has progressed, also, editors have acknowledged a steadily increasing debt to the Associate Editor, Bart Winer. With his unrivalled experience from previous volumes he was always at hand to assist successive editors with suggestions for possible further notes and to point out cases where an annotation might need to be looked at again. His unexpected death early in 1989 was a bitter blow; but it is a source of limited consolation that he had by then solved most of the complex problems of presentation that arose in the edition as a whole. Fortunately for the present volume, one of the most difficult to organise for publication, he had also been able to see the first major version and had copy-edited most of the typescript at the time of his death. While the volume necessarily lacks some touches that he would have provided in the last stages, the amount of work he had done on it renders it another monument to his skills. The work he put in has been supplemented at proof stage by John Waś.

An equally great debt is owed to the work of Lorna Arnold, the adviser to the edition on matters involving the classics. Coleridge's great interest in etymology at the time of this volume meant that he was more than usually attentive to the histories of the words he was using—including those in Latin and Greek. The editor needs to be able not only to make clear the correct position according to etymologists of the present day but to convey what Coleridge's contemporaries would have thought at a time when such questions were open to fertile speculation. Lorna Arnold has also been able to bring the knowledge acquired from her previous editing—particularly of the later volumes of the *Notebooks* and of the *Philosophical Lectures*—to the philosophical and theological discussions called for here. In a large number of cases she has been able to improve my notes on such matters, sometimes transforming them out of all recognition. Her hand is particularly detectable in some of the Excursus Notes.

In view of the fact that Coleridge was now calling on thirty years' reading and writing, it has been a particular benefit to be able to undertake the main editing of this volume at a point when a number of important works on his earlier thinking have appeared, including those of J. Robert Barth, Thomas McFarland, and Elinor Shaffer—who have also been happy to share their fuller knowledge with me. In the same way I was privileged to exchange views and information with the late Earl Leslie Griggs over a number of years, particularly during the time when he was working on the relevant volumes of the *Letters*. It was a memorable experience to work for many years with George Whalley, who asked me to share the editing of the annotations on Robert Leighton for the *Marginalia*, so that work on *Aids to Reflection* could be aligned with that on its most important single source. His death in 1983 was a particularly sad blow, for he had set his individual stamp on Coleridge studies, providing by his unfailing courtesy and elegant writing a model for the rest of us. To Heather Jackson, who has taken over the editing of the *Marginalia* since George Whalley's death, I owe equally large debts—particularly, again, with regard to the annotations on Leighton. As a co-editor in the edition as a whole I have continually received from her more than I have been able to give. My gratitude is further due to others who have been editing relevant volumes and have been generous of their time in dealing with my queries or raising points of mutual interest: I think particularly of Reg Foakes, Robin Jackson, Jim Mays, the late Barbara Rooke, and Carl Woodring.

It has not always been possible to track citations to their original source—particularly when, as sometimes happened, Coleridge was relying on an imperfect memory—and I shall be delighted to hear from anyone who recognises a source for any of those where it has been necessary to acknowledge temporary defeat at the time of going to press. Among those who have already earned my gratitude, Geoffrey Day was able to throw light on *insania amabilis*, Nick Penny on the blindness of Cupid, and Myles Burnyeat on the *sorites*. In the field of theology I have been able to draw on the expertise of Paul Avis, Daniel Hardy, Douglas Hedley, David Jasper, and Alister McGrath, and for the history of science on that of Trevor Levere and Desmond King-Hele. Marian Hobson and Ralph Leigh were helpful on points of French language and literature; others who have provided information on specific points include Peter Allen, John Chapple, Tim Chilcott, Stephen Clark, John Drew, Howard Erskine-Hill, Anthony Harding, Mary Jacobus, Brian Mastin, Mary Anne Perkins, Christopher Ricks, Paul Stanwood, and John Woolford. I am also grateful to others who replied promptly and helpfully to my queries: Owen Chadwick, Nicholas de Lange, Peter Dronke, Susan James, Paul Magnuson, Edwin W. Marrs, Jr, Jeremy Maule, Henry Merlen, Leon Pompa, Quentin Skinner, the late Gordon Rupp, Anthony W. Shipps, and Keith Thomas. It is a particular pleasure to acknowledge the help of members of my own college, including Henry Chadwick (who pointed me to important possible sources in Augustine and Waterland), Hugh Dacre, Caroline Moore (who solved several queries, from sources as diverse as Pliny and Indian religion), Roderick Munday, Ted Kenney, and Philip Pattenden. Jim McCusick kindly provided additional information on word-coinages by Coleridge as recorded in the *Oxford English Dictionary*.

Eric Nye drew my attention to an uncollected letter of Coleridge's to William Blackwood, and Mary Anne Perkins to a hitherto unknown annotated copy of *Aids to Reflection* now in her possession, about which she was able to provide detailed information. Among the libraries whose staffs have given me assistance must be mentioned first and foremost the British Library (including the Students' Room and Newspaper Room), Cambridge University Library and the library of Victoria College, Toronto—including those who over the years have staffed the Coleridge Room there and in particular Freda Gough. In addition I should like to thank the librarians and staff of the following institutions for answering queries and making materials available to me: the Bodleian Library; the English Faculty Library, Cambridge; Eton College Library; Trinity College Library, Hartford, Connecticut; the Highgate Literary and Scientific Institution; the Houghton Library at Harvard; Leeds University Library; the Lilly Library, Indiana University; Liverpool University Library; London University Library; Manchester Public Libraries; Manchester University Library; Peterhouse Library; the Pierpont Morgan Library; Reading University Library; the John Rylands Library; the Library of the Royal College of Surgeons of England; the Bailey/Howe Library, University of Vermont; the Wisbech and Fenland Museum; Yale University Library.

For permission to reproduce the portrait of Coleridge used as the frontispiece, grateful acknowledgments are due to the Highgate Literary and Scientific Institution; for permission to reproduce the title-page of the copy of the 1825 edition presented to Dr Keate, to the Provost and Fellows of Eton College. For permission to reproduce the annotations on various copies of the 1825 edition the edition is indebted to the Berg Collection, the New York Public Library, the Pierpont Morgan Library, Yale University Library, the British Library, Mrs N. F. D. Coleridge, and Mary Anne Perkins. For permission to reproduce manuscript fragments in their possession it is indebted to the British Library, Harvard University Library, the Osborn Collection in Yale University Library, Cornell University Library, the Fales Collection in New York University Library, the University of Iowa Library, Penn State University Library, and Victoria College Library, Toronto.

For an original collation of the 1825 and 1831 texts of *Aids to Reflection* I am grateful to Mary Firth and for expert and painstaking help in an extended checking of textual notes to the keen eye of Lyndeth Vasey. The typing, often of tortuously presented manuscripts, has been undertaken patiently and accurately by Hazel M. Dunn and Maureen Ashby. A final word is due to my wife, since although the editing of the volume has been by no means a continuous process it has been a presence, at least in the background, throughout our married life. Her patience has been exemplary.

Peterhouse, Cambridge   JOHN BEER

EDITORIAL PRACTICE, SYMBOLS, AND ABBREVIATIONS

A S EXPLAINED in the Editor's Introduction below, the copy-text used here is that of the second edition, published in 1831, which was the one followed for later nineteenth-century editions, and all variations between the texts of 1825 and 1831 are recorded in the Textual Notes to the present volume. Fortunately the differences between the two texts on a large scale are not so great as to cause much confusion. In general the aim has been to reproduce the texts of both as exactly as possible. In accordance with the practice of the *Collected Works* generally, accents in Greek, French, and Italian are, where appropriate, normalised. The original readings are recorded in the textual notes. In the extracts from Coleridge's own manuscript writings on the other hand, and in the extracts from the 1825 edition reproduced in Appendix G, the Greek accents or lack of them are reproduced exactly. In all cases Greek abbreviations are regularised and Greek ligatures (only) are expanded. Page-references in Coleridge's text are adjusted to the pagination of the present edition.

Coleridge's footnotes are indicated by symbols (*, †, etc) and are printed full measure. The editor's footnotes are numbered and (when not too brief) are printed in double columns. The order of the editor's footnotes follows (perhaps Coleridgian) logic: i.e. it is assumed that when the text contains an asterisk or a dagger the reader then turns from text to note and then goes back again. The editor's footnotes, which are sometimes notes on Coleridge's footnotes, follow that order. Thus the footnote indicators within the text may leap from 1 to 5, notes 2–4 being notes on Coleridge's footnotes. Textual notes at the foot of the page, preceding the editor's footnotes, are designated by superior letters (a–b, etc) and are ordered as they occur on the page. They take account of the 1825 edition, its List of Corrections and Amendments, and the further amendments made by Coleridge to copies of it he annotated. Where the words EDITOR, LEIGHTON, *et sim* are recorded they are to be understood as appearing full right in the 1825 text.

IMPORTANT NOTE: Page-numbers of the 1825 edition are incorporated into the Textual Notes. References from *AR* (1825), as given in other volumes of the *Collected Coleridge*, can easily be found by looking through those notes, therefore. Page-numbers in *AR* (1831) normally vary by only a few pages from those in *AR* (1825), which can thus be used as a rough guide in locating their place in the *CC* text.

Coleridge manuscripts, where quoted, are printed literatim, including cancellations, except that "it's", "its' ", "your's", and "yours' " have been standardised to "its" and "yours" unless appearing so in a published version. The following symbols are also used in quoting from mss (with "wild" as an example):

[wild]	A reading supplied by the editor.
[?wild]	An uncertain reading.
[?wild/world]	Possible alternative readings.
⌐wild⌐	A tentative reading (owing to obliterations, torn paper, etc).
[. . .]	An illegible word or phrase.
⟨wild⟩	A later insertion by Coleridge.

Strokes, dashes, and other symbols are Coleridge's.

The editions referred to in the editor's footnotes are, when they are known, those that Coleridge used. Exceptions are made in the case of some writers for whom such editions, found only in a few libraries, are unavailable to most readers, but for whom the standard modern editions may be readily available.

ABBREVIATIONS

(Place of publication is London, unless otherwise noted.)

AR (1825)	S. T. Coleridge *Aids to Reflection* (1825). Later editions (see App H) indicated similarly by date.
AR (1825) Corr	"Corrections and Amendments", a list of Errata on pp xv–xvi of *AR* (1825).
AV	The "Authorised Version"—or "King James Version" —of the Bible, in modern orthography.
Barth	J. R. Barth, SJ *Coleridge and Christian Doctrine* (Cambridge, Mass 1969).
BCP	*The Book of Common Prayer and Administration of the*

	Sacraments and other rites and ceremonies of the Church according to the use of the Church of England.
Beer CPI	J. B. Beer *Coleridge's Poetic Intelligence* (1977).
Beer CV	J. B. Beer *Coleridge the Visionary* (1959).
BL (1817)	S. T. Coleridge *Biographia Literaria; or Biographical Sketches of My Literary Life and Opinions* (2 vols 1817).
BL (1847)	S. T. Coleridge *Biographia Literaria* ed H. N. and Sara Coleridge (2 vols 1847).
BL (1907)	S. T. Coleridge *Biographia Literaria . . . with his Aesthetical Essays* ed J. Shawcross (2 vols Oxford 1907).
BL (CC)	S. T. Coleridge *Biographia Literaria* ed James Engell and W. Jackson Bate (2 vols London & Princeton 1983) = *CC* VII.
Bl Mag	*Blackwood's Edinburgh Magazine* (Edinburgh 1817–1980).
BM	British Library, Reference Division, formerly ''British Museum Library''.
Boulger	J. D. Boulger *Coleridge as Religious Thinker* (New Haven, Conn 1961).
B Poets	*The Works of the British Poets* ed Robert Anderson (13 vols Edinburgh & London 1792–5; vol XIV 1807).
Bristol LB	George Whalley ''The Bristol Library Borrowings of Southey and Coleridge'' *Library* IV (Sept 1949) 114–31.
C	Samuel Taylor Coleridge.
C&S	S. T. Coleridge *On the Constitution of the Church and State, According to the Idea of Each* (1829, 2nd ed 1830).
C&S (CC)	S. T. Coleridge *On the Constitution of the Church and State* ed John Colmer (London & Princeton 1976) = *CC* X.
C&SH	George Whalley *Coleridge and Sara Hutchinson and the Asra Poems* (1955).
Carlisle LB	Carlisle Cathedral Library Borrowings 1801–2.
CC	*The Collected Works of Samuel Taylor Coleridge* general editor Kathleen Coburn (London & Princeton 1969–).
CH	*Coleridge: The Critical Heritage* ed J. R. de J. Jackson (1970).
CIS (1840)	S. T. Coleridge *Confessions of an Inquiring Spirit* ed H. N. Coleridge (1840). To appear in *SW&F (CC)*.
CL	Charles Lamb.
CL	*Collected Letters of Samuel Taylor Coleridge* ed Earl Leslie Griggs (6 vols Oxford & New York 1956–71).

C Life (C)	E. K. Chambers *Samuel Taylor Coleridge* (Oxford 1938).
C Life (G)	James Gillman *The Life of Samuel Taylor Coleridge* (vol I only pub, 1838).
CM (CC)	S. T. Coleridge *Marginalia* ed George Whalley (London & Princeton 1980–) = *CC* XII.
CN	*The Notebooks of Samuel Taylor Coleridge* ed Kathleen Coburn (New York, Princeton, & London 1957–).
Conc	"Conclusion" to the present edition, pp 383–410 below.
C Pantheist	Thomas McFarland *Coleridge and the Pantheist Tradition* (Oxford 1969).
CRB	*Henry Crabb Robinson on Books and Their Writers* ed Edith J. Morley (3 vols 1938).
CR (*BCW*)	*Blake, Coleridge, Wordsworth, Lamb, etc. being Selections from the Remains of Henry Crabb Robinson* ed Edith J. Morley (Manchester 1922).
CRD	*Diary, Reminiscences, and Correspondence of Henry Crabb Robinson* ed Thomas Sadler (2 vols 1872).
C 17th C	*Coleridge on the Seventeenth Century* ed R. F. Brinkley (Durham, NC 1955).
C Talker	R. W. Armour and R. F. Howes *Coleridge the Talker* (Ithaca, NY 1949).
CW	*The Complete Works of S. T. Coleridge* ed W. G. T. Shedd (7 vols New York 1853).
DC	Derwent Coleridge.
DeQ	Thomas De Quincey.
DeQ Works	*The Collected Writings of Thomas De Quincey* ed David Masson (14 vols Edinburgh 1889–90).
Diels	Hermann Diels *Die Fragmente der Vorsokratiker* ed Walther Kranz (3 vols Zurich 1972).
DNB	*Dictionary of National Biography* (1885–).
Duffy	*Coleridge's American Disciples: the Selected Correspondence of James Marsh* ed J. J. Duffy (Amherst, Mass 1943).
DW	Dorothy Wordsworth.
DWJ	*Journals of Dorothy Wordsworth* ed Ernest de Selincourt (2 vols 1941).
EB	*Encyclopaedia Britannica* (11th ed 29 vols Cambridge 1910–11).
EC	Edward Coleridge
Ed Rev	*The Edinburgh Review* (Edinburgh & London 1802–1929).

EHC	Ernest Hartley Coleridge
EM	*Encyclopaedia Metropolitana* (26 vols 1845).
Enc RE	*Encyclopaedia of Religion and Ethics* ed J. Hastings (13 vols Edinburgh 1908–26).
EOT (CC)	S. T. Coleridge *Essays on His Times in "The Morning Post" and "The Courier"* ed David V. Erdman (3 vols London & Princeton 1978) = *CC* III.
Friend (CC)	S. T. Coleridge *The Friend* ed Barbara E. Rooke (2 vols London & Princeton 1969) = *CC* IV.
G Mag	*The Gentleman's Magazine* (1731–1907).
HC	Hartley Coleridge.
HC Poems	*Poems by Hartley Coleridge, with a memoir of his life by his brother* [Derwent Coleridge] (2 vols 1851).
HCR	Henry Crabb Robinson.
HEHL ms	MS 8195, "On the Divine Ideas", at Henry E. Huntington Library and Art Gallery, San Marino, California: part of the *Op Max ms* (see below).
HNC	Henry Nelson Coleridge.
H Works	*The Complete Works of William Hazlitt* ed P. P. Howe (12 vols 1930–4).
Int Aph	"Introductory Aphorisms: On the duty and advantage of cultivating the power and habit of Reflection" in the present edition, pp 11–42 below.
IS	*Inquiring Spirit: A New Presentation of Coleridge from His Published and Unpublished Prose Writings* ed Kathleen Coburn (1951; rev ed Toronto 1979).
JDC	James Dykes Campbell.
JEGP	*Journal of English and Germanic Philology* (Urbana, Ill 1903–).
JHI	*Journal of the History of Ideas* (New York 1940–).
L&L	*Coleridge on Logic and Learning* ed Alice D. Snyder (New Haven & London 1929).
L&S	H. G. Liddell and R. Scott *A Greek–English Lexicon* (1843; 9th ed Oxford 1940).
LCL	Loeb Classical Library.
Lects 1795 (CC)	S. T. Coleridge *Lectures 1795: On Politics and Religion* ed Lewis Patton and Peter Mann (London & Princeton 1971) = *CC* I.
Lects 1808–1819 (CC)	S. T. Coleridge *Lectures 1808–1819: On Literature* ed Reginald A. Foakes (2 vols London & Princeton 1984) = *CC* VI.
Leighton COPY A	*The Expository Works and Other Remains of Archbishop*

	Leighton, some of which were never before printed. Revised by Philip Doddridge, D.D. With a preface by the Doctor (2 vols Edinburgh 1748). *CM (CC)* III.
Leighton COPY B	*The Genuine Works of R. Leighton, D.D. Archbishop of Glasgow: with a preface by Philip Doddridge, D.D.* A new edition, with corrections and additional letters. To which is now prefixed, the life of the author, by the Rev. Erasmus Middleton (4 vols 1819). *CM (CC)* III.
Leighton COPY C	*The Whole Works of Robert Leighton, D.D. some time Bishop of Dunblane, afterwards Archbishop of Glasgow.* A new edition, carefully corrected. To which is prefixed a memoir of the author, by George Jerment, D.D. (4 vols 1820). BM c 126 h 1. *CM (CC)* III.
LL	*The Letters of Charles Lamb to Which Are Added Those of His Sister Mary Lamb* ed E. V. Lucas (3 vols 1935).
LL (M)	*The Letters of Charles and Mary Lamb* ed Edwin W. Marrs, Jr (Ithaca, NY 1975–).
Logic (CC)	S. T. Coleridge *Logic* ed J. R. de J. Jackson (London & Princeton 1980) = *CC* XIII.
LR	*The Literary Remains of Samuel Taylor Coleridge* ed H. N. Coleridge (4 vols 1836–9).
LRR	"Lectures on Revealed Religion" in *Lects 1795 (CC)*.
LS	S. T. Coleridge *A Lay Sermon, Addressed to the Higher and Middle Classes, on the Existing Distresses and Discontents* (1817).
LS (CC)	S. T. Coleridge *Lay Sermons* [being *The Statesman's Manual* and *A Lay Sermon*] ed R. J. White (London & Princeton 1972) = *CC* V.
M Chron	*The Morning Chronicle* (1769–82).
Migne *PG*	*Patriologiae cursus completus . . . series Graeca* ed J. P. Migne (162 vols Paris 1857–1912).
Migne *PL*	*Patriologiae cursus completus . . . series Latina* ed J. P. Migne (221 vols Paris 1844–64).
Misc C	*Coleridge's Miscellaneous Criticism* ed T. M. Raysor (1936).
MLN	*Modern Language Notes* (Baltimore 1886–).
Mor Aph	"Moral and Religious Aphorisms" in the present edition, pp 69–132 below.
MP	*Modern Philology* (Chicago 1903–).
M Post	*The Morning Post* (1702–1937).
Mrs C	Sara Coleridge née Fricker (wife of C).
N	Notebook of Samuel Taylor Coleridge (numbered or otherwise denominated) in ms. References given by folio.

N&Q	*Notes and Queries* (1849–).
NED	S. T. Coleridge *Notes on English Divines* ed Derwent Coleridge (2 vols 1853).
NF⁰	Coleridge's folio notebook, now in the Henry E. Huntington Library.
NLS	S. T. Coleridge *Notes and Lectures upon Shakespeare and Some Other Old Poets and Dramatists with Other Literary Remains* ed Sara Coleridge (2 vols 1849).
NTP	S. T. Coleridge *Notes, Theological, Political and Miscellaneous* ed Derwent Coleridge (1853).
NYPL	New York Public Library.
ODCC	*Oxford Dictionary of the Christian Church* ed F. L. Cross (1957; 2nd ed 1974).
OED	*The Oxford English Dictionary being a corrected reissue . . . of ''A New English Dictionary on Historical Principles''* (12 vols Oxford 1970).
Omniana	*Omniana, or Horae otiosiores* ed Robert Southey [with articles by C] (2 vols 1812).
Op Max ms	MSS of Coleridge's ''Opus Maximum'', mss VCL S MS 28–9, vols numbered according to Alice Snyder's scheme in *L&L* xii (with older numbering in brackets). See also *HEHL ms* above.
Phil Trans RS	*The Philosophical Transactions of the Royal Society* (1665–1886).
PL	John Milton, *Paradise Lost*. (See also Migne above.)
P Lects (1949)	*The Philosophical Lectures of Samuel Taylor Coleridge* ed Kathleen Coburn (London & New York 1949).
P Lects (CC)	*The Philosophical Lectures of Samuel Taylor Coleridge* ed Owen Barfield and Kathleen Coburn = *CC* VIII.
PML	The Pierpont Morgan Library, New York.
PMLA	*Publications of the Modern Language Association of America* (Baltimore 1889–).
Pref	Coleridge's ''Preface'' in the present editon, pp 5–10 below.
Prel Sp Aph	''Elements of Religious Philosophy, preliminary to the Aphorisms on Spiritual Religion'' in the present edition, pp 133–43 below.
Prelude (1959)	1805 and 1850 versions of *The Prelude* in William Wordsworth *The Prelude, or Growth of a Poet's Mind* ed Ernest de Selincourt, rev Helen Darbishire (Oxford 1959).
''Prometheus''	S. T. Coleridge ''On the *Prometheus* of Aeschylus: An Essay . . . read at the Royal Society of Literature, May 18, 1825'', first printed in *Transactions of the Royal So-*

	ciety of Literature II (1834) 384–404 and to appear in *SW&F (CC)*.
Prud Aph	"Prudential Aphorisms" in the present edition, pp 45–53 below.
PW (1829)	*Poetical Works* (3 vols 1829).
PW (EHC)	*The Complete Poetical Works of Samuel Taylor Coleridge* ed E. H. Coleridge (2 vols Oxford 1912).
PW (JDC)	*The Poetical Works of Samuel Taylor Coleridge* ed J. D. Campbell (1893).
QR	*The Quarterly Review* (1809–1952).
Rees Cyclopaedia	Abraham Rees *The Cyclopaedia; or, Universal Dictionary of arts, sciences and literature* (39 vols 1819).
Refl Mor	"Reflections respecting Morality" in the present editon, pp 55–65 below.
RS	Robert Southey.
RSL	Royal Society of Literature.
RX	John Livingston Lowes *The Road to Xanadu* (Boston 1927, rev 1930).
SB	*Studies in Bibliography* (Charlottesville, Va 1949–).
SC	Sara Coleridge (daughter of C, and wife of HNC).
SC Memoir	*Memoir and Letters of Sara Coleridge* ed Edith Coleridge (2 vols 1873).
SH	Sara Hutchinson
Sh C	*Coleridge's Shakespearean Criticism* ed. T. M. Raysor (2 vols 1930; rev ed 2 vols 1960).
SIR	*Studies in Romanticism* (Boston, Mass 1961–).
S Letters (Curry)	*New Letters of Robert Southey* ed Kenneth Curry (2 vols New York & London 1965).
S Life (CS)	*Life and Correspondence of Robert Southey* ed C. C. Southey (6 vols 1849–50).
S Life (Simmons)	Jack Simmons *Southey* (1945).
SM	S. T. Coleridge *The Statesman's Manual: or, The Bible, the Best Guide to Political Skill and Foresight. A Lay-Sermon Addressed to the Higher Classes of Society* (1816).
SM (CC)	S. T. Coleridge *The Statesman's Manual* in *LS (CC)* above.
Sp Aph A	"Aphorisms on Spiritual Religion" in the present edition, pp 145–53 below.
Sp Aph B	"Aphorisms on that which is indeed Spiritual Religion" in the present edition, pp 155–410 below.
SW&F (CC)	S. T. Coleridge *Shorter Works and Fragments* ed H. J.

	Jackson and J. R. de J. Jackson (2 vols London & Princeton, in press) = *CC* xi.
Tennemann	W. G. Tennemann *Geschichte der Philosophie* (11 vols Leipzig 1798–1819). C's annotated copy in BM (C 43 e 24): *CM (CC)* v.
TL (1848)	S. T. Coleridge *Hints Toward the Formation of a More Comprehensive Theory of Life* ed Seth B. Watson (1848).
TT (1836)	*Table Talk of Samuel Taylor Coleridge* ed H. N. Coleridge (rev ed 1836). Cited as part of *TT (CC)*.
TT (CC)	*Table Talk* ed Carl R. Woodring (London & Princeton 1990) = *CC* xiv.
VCL	Victoria College Library, University of Toronto.
Watchman (CC)	S. T. Coleridge *The Watchman* ed Lewis Patton (London & Princeton 1970) = *CC* ii.
W Prose	*The Prose Works of William Wordsworth* ed W. J. B. Owen and J. W. Smyser (3 vols Oxford 1974).
WPW	*The Poetical Works of William Wordsworth* ed Ernest de Selincourt and Helen Darbishire (5 vols Oxford 1940–9).
WW	William Wordsworth.

CHRONOLOGICAL TABLE
1772–1834

1772 (21 Oct) Birth of C at Ottery St Mary, Devonshire, to the Rev John and Ann (Bowden) Coleridge, youngest of their 10 (and John's 14) children

George III king (1760–1820)
Wordsworth two years old
Scott one year old
Swedenborg d
M Post begun

1774

Southey b
Priestley discovers oxygen

1775

American War of Independence
C. Lamb b
Jane Austen b

1776

(4 Jul) US Declaration of Independence
Adam Smith *Wealth of Nations*
Gibbon *Decline and Fall* (–1788)

1778 C to Ottery Grammar School

Hazlitt b
Rousseau and Voltaire d

1779

Hume *Dialogues concerning Natural Religion*
Johnson *Lives of the Poets* (–1781) (as prefaces)

1780 (Nov) Death of brother William

Gordon Riots

1781 (6 Oct) Death of C's father

Lessing d
Kant *Critik der reinen Vernunft*
Schiller *Die Räuber*
Rousseau *Confessions* (–1788)

1782 (Spring) In London with John Bowden (Jul) Enrolled at Christ's Hospital, Hertford
(Sept) Christ's Hospital, London (to 1791); to meet C. Lamb, G. Dyer, T. F. Middleton, R. Allen, J. M. Gutch, Le Grice brothers

Priestley *Corruptions of Christianity*

1783

(3 Sept) Treaty of Versailles between Britain, France, and USA
(19 Dec) Pitt's first ministry (–1801)
Blake *Poetical Sketches*
J. G. Eichhorn *Einleitung ins Alte Testament* completed

1784 Brother George graduates from Pembroke College, Oxford

Samuel Johnson d

1785	Walks wards of London Hospital with brother Luke	DeQ b
		Paley *Principles of Moral and Political Philosophy*
		Cowper *The Task* and *John Gilpin*
1786		American Constitution drafted
		Mozart *The Marriage of Figaro*
1787	(Apr) Death of brother Jack in India	Thomas Taylor's *Concerning the Beau-*
	First contribution to Boyer's *Liber Au-reus*	*tiful* (from Plotinus) initiates his Neoplatonist translations
1788	(Feb) Brother James marries Frances Duke Taylor	Byron b
		Hutton *New Theory of the Earth*
	(early summer) Elected Grecian; meets Evans family	Kant *Critik der praktischen Vernunft*
		Crowe *Lewesdon Hill*
1789	(Summer) Visits Ottery after 7 years	Washington first President of USA
	Introduced to Bowles's *Sonnets* by Middleton	(14 Jul) Fall of Bastille: French Revolution
	Spends much of year 1789–90 in school sick-ward	Blake *Songs of Innocence*
		Erasmus Darwin *The Botanic Garden* (–1791)
1790	(Feb) Death of brother Luke	Burke *Reflections on the Revolution in France*
	(26 Jul) C's first published poem (in *The World*)	Bruce *Travels to Discover the Source of the Nile*
		Mozart *Così fan tutte*
1791	(12 March) Death of sister Ann	(2 Mar) John Wesley d
	(Oct) Jesus College, Cambridge, Exhibitioner, Sizar, Rustat Scholar; to meet W. Frend, S. Butler, Porson, C. Wordsworth, Wrangham	(Jul) Anti-Jacobin riots at Birmingham; Priestley's house attacked.
		Paine *Rights of Man* (–1792)
		Boswell *Life of Johnson*
		Mackintosh *Vindiciae Gallicae*
		Mozart *The Magic Flute*
1792	Death of brother Francis in India: C hears news a year later	Shelley b
		(22 Sept) Fr Republic proclaimed
	Wins Browne medal with Greek Sapphic *Ode on the Slave Trade*; poem read at Commencement (3 Jul)	Pitt's attack on the slave-trade
		Fox's Libel Bill
		Rogers *Pleasures of Memory*
	(Summer) visits Ottery and praises WW's poetry in Exeter	Wollstonecraft *Rights of Woman*
1793	(Jan) One of four placed first for Craven Studentship (awarded to youngest) (May)	(21 Jan) Louis XVI executed
		(1 Feb) France declares war on England and Holland
	Attends Cambridge trial of Frend	(Mar–Dec) Revolt of La Vendée
	(Summer) Greek *Ode on Astronomy* fails to win Browne medal	(June) Reign of Terror begins
		(16 Oct) Marie Antoinette executed
	(25 Jul) First poem in *Morning Chronicle*	(16 Oct) John Hunter d
		Godwin *Political Justice*
	(2 Dec) Enlists in 15th Light Dragoons as Silas Tomkyn Comberbache	Wordsworth *An Evening Walk* and *Descriptive Sketches*
		Kant *Religion innerhalb der Grenzen der blossen Vernunft*
1794	(9 Apr) Returns to Cambridge	(23 May) Suspension of Habeas Corpus

(Jun) Sets out with Joseph Hucks; meets RS in Oxford and plans pantisocracy; Welsh tour

(Aug–Sept) Joins RS and Burnett in Bristol; meets Thomas Poole, engaged to Sara Fricker

(Sept) To London and Cambridge; with RS publishes *The Fall of Robespierre* (Cambridge); *Monody on Chatterton* published with *Rowley Poems* (Cambridge)

(Dec) To London; sonnets in *M Chron*; "noctes Atticae" with Lamb at Salutation and Cat

(24 Dec) *Religious Musings* begun

"Glorious First of June"

(28 Jul) Robespierre executed; end of Terror

(Oct–Dec) State Trials: Hardy, Tooke, and Thelwall acquitted of charge of high treason

Paine *Age of Reason* (–1795)

Paley *Evidences of Christianity*

Radcliffe *Mysteries of Udolpho*

Blake *Songs of Experience, Europe, Book of Urizen*

E. Darwin *Zoonomia* (–1796)

J. G. Fichte *Über den Begriff der Wissenschaftslehre*

1795 (Jan) RS brings C back to Bristol; lodgings with RS, Burnett; meets Joseph Cottle

(Late Jan–Feb) Political Lectures

(Feb) *A Moral and Political Lecture* published

(May–Jun) Lectures on Revealed Religion

(16 Jun) Lecture on Slave-Trade Portrait by Peter Vandyke

(Aug) Quarrel with RS; pantisocracy abandoned; meets WW in Bristol

(4 Oct) Marriage to Sara Fricker

(26 Nov) Lecture on the Two Bills

(3 Dec) *Conciones ad Populum* published

(Dec) *An Answer to "A Letter to Edward Long Fox"* and *The Plot Discovered* published; *The Watchman* planned

(3 Jan) Josiah Wedgwood d

(19 May) Boswell d

(13 Jun) T Arnold b

(Jun–Jul) Quiberon expedition

(26 Sept) WW and DW to Racedown

(5 Oct) Bonaparte disperses Paris mob

(31 Oct) Keats b

(Nov) Directory begins

(6 Nov) Treason and Convention Bills introduced

(4 Dec) Carlyle b

(18 Dec) Two Acts put into effect

M. G. Lewis *Ambrosio, or the Monk*

Blake *Book of Los, Song of Los, Book of Ahania*

Goethe *Wilhelm Meister*

1796 (9 Jan–13 Feb) Tour to Midlands and north to sell *The Watchman*; meets Erasmus Darwin, Joseph Wright (painter)

(1 Mar–13 May) *The Watchman* in ten numbers

(16 Apr) *Poems on Various Subjects*

(19 Sept) Birth of Hartley C; reconciliation with RS

(31 Dec) *Ode to the Departing Year* in *Cambridge Intelligencer*; move to Nether Stowey completed

(Jul) Robert Burns d

(Sept) Mary Lamb's violent illness

(Nov) Catherine of Russia d

England treating for peace with France

Threats of invasion of England

Jenner performs first smallpox vaccination

Burke *Letters on a Regicide Peace*

Dr Thomas Beddoes *Essay on the Public Merits of Mr Pitt*

Lewis's novel reissued as *The Monk*

1797 (Mar) WW at Stowey

(Jun) C at Racedown

(Jul) DW, WW, and Lamb at Stowey; DW and WW to Alfoxden House

(Jul–Sept) *Poems, to Which Are Now Added, Poems by Charles Lamb and Charles Lloyd*

Pitt proposes to finance the renewed war against France by increasing taxes.

(Feb) Bank of England suspends cash payments

(Apr–Jun) Mutinies in British Navy

(26 May) Grey's motion for Parliamen-

(14 Oct) *Osorio* finished; C visits Bowles.

("Fall of the year") *Kubla Khan* composed

(13–16 Nov) Walk with Wordsworths to Lynton; *Ancient Mariner* begun

(Nov) C engaged by *M Post*

(Dec) poetry in *M Post*, inc *Visions of the Maid of Orleans*

tary Reform defeated

(9 Jul) Burke d

(17 Oct) France and Austria sign peace treaty

(Nov) Frederick William II of Prussia d; Frederick William III begins rule

(20 Nov) *Anti-Jacobin, or Weekly Examiner* begins

Schelling *Ideen zur Philosophie der Natur*

Radcliffe *The Italian*

1798 (2 Jan) First prose definitely by C appears in *M Post*

(Jan) C's Unitarian sermon at Shrewsbury heard by Hazlitt; Wedgwood £150 annuity accepted

(Feb) *Frost at Midnight*

(Mar) *Ancient Mariner* completed

(Apr) *The Recantation* (later *France: An Ode*); *Fears in Solitude*

(14 May) Birth of Berkeley C

(c 20 May–11 Jun) Hazlitt visits Stowey

(Sept) *Lyrical Ballads* published

(19 Sept) WW, DW, Chester, and C to Hamburg; (21) meets Klopstock; (30) to Ratzeburg

(Feb–Oct) Irish uprising

(Spring) Swiss cantons suppressed

(12 Jun) Malta taken by French

(Jul) Bonaparte invades Egypt

(9 Jul) *Anti-Jacobin* last number

(1–2 Aug) Battle of the Nile: Nelson's victory

Lloyd *Edmund Oliver*

Malthus *Essay on the Principles of Population*

Bell introduces Madras system of education into England

Fichte *System der Sittenlehre*

1799 Stuart buys *Courier*

(10 Feb) Death of Berkeley C; news reaches C c 6 Apr

(12 Feb) C to University of Göttingen

(May) Ascent of Brocken

(29 Jul) In Stowey again

(Sept) Devon walking tour with RS

(Oct) Nitrous oxide experiments with Humphry Davy in Bristol

(26 Oct) Meets Sara Hutchinson

(Oct–Nov) Walking tour of Lakes from Sockburn, with WW

(10 Nov) C receives Stuart's invitation to work in London

(27 Nov) Arrives in London

(4 Dec) C and Davy visit Godwin

(c 20 Dec) DW and WW to Town End (later Dove Cottage)

(Jan) First attempt at vote for Union defeated in the Irish Parliament

(Apr) Newspaper Act

(25 Jul) Bonaparte drives Turks from Aboukir

(29 Aug) Pope Pius VI d as prisoner at Valence, France

(8 Oct) Bonaparte suddenly appears in France

(9 Nov) Bonaparte first consul under new constitution

Royal Institution founded

Schiller *Piccolomini* and *Wallensteins Tod* published

1800 (Jan–6 Apr) *M Post* reporter and leaderwriter; translating *Wallenstein* at Lamb's

(2 Mar) Mrs C leaves London

(Mar) C at Pentonville with Lamb; offered proprietary share in *M Post*, declines offer

(6 Apr–4 May) At Grasmere with WW; *Wallenstein* completed 20 Apr, pub soon after

(18 Jan) Debate over Union in Dublin

(3 Feb) Fox returns to Parliament

(Feb) Bill for Union passed

(Mar–Apr) Pius VII Pope

(Apr) Commons approves bill for Union

(25 Apr) Cowper d

(14 Jun) Battle of Marengo

(Aug) Union of Great Britain and Ireland

(May–Jun) In Stowey and Bristol
(24 Jul) Move to Greta Hall, Keswick
(14 Sept) Birth of Derwent C
(Sept–Oct) Superintends printing of *Lyrical Ballads* (2nd ed)

(5 Sep) Malta falls to English after long siege.
Burns *Works* ed Currie
Davy *Researches . . . concerning Nitrous Oxide*
Schelling *System der Transzendentalen Idealismus*

1801   (Jan) *Lyrical Ballads* (1800) published; prolonged illnesses
(21 Jan) C returns to London
(Jul–Aug) At Gallow Hill and Middleton with MH and SH, reading in Durham Cathedral Library
(15 Nov) To London; writing for *M Post*
(28 Dec–c 19 Jan) At Stowey

Davy lecturer at Royal Institution
(Jan) Evangelicals begin monthly *Christian Observer*
(Mar) Pitt resigns over Catholic Emancipation: Addington ministry (–1804)
(2 Apr) Battle of Copenhagen
(Jul) Bonaparte signs Concordat with Pope
Treaty of Luneville; Austria makes peace; French gains in Germany

1802   (21 Jan–Mar) In London; attends Davy's lectures at Royal Institution; writing for *M Post*; to Gallow Hill
(From 19 Mar) At Greta Hall; severe domestic discord
(4 Apr) 1st version of *Dejection* as "A Letter to — [Sara Hutchinson]"
Suspects "radical difference" from WW in opinions respecting poetry
(1–9 Aug) Lakes tour and Scafell climb; (late Aug) visit by Lambs
(Sept–Jan) Writing for *M Post*
(4 Oct) *Dejection* ode in *M Post*
(Nov) Three-day visit to London
(Nov-Dec) Tour of South Wales with Tom and Sally Wedgwood
(23 Dec) Birth of Sara C

(25 Mar) Peace of Amiens
(18 Apr) Erasmus Darwin d
(8 May) Bonaparte life consul
(4 Oct) WW marries Mary Hutchinson
(Oct) French army enters Switzerland
Fox encounters Bonaparte at his levee in Paris
Ed Rev founded
Cobbett's *Weekly Political Register* started (–1835)
Paley *Natural Theology*
Spinoza *Opera* ed Paulus (1802–3)
Bentham's *Civil and Penal Legislation* introduces theory of Utilitarianism
Lamb *Charles Woodvil*
Scott *Minstrelsy of the Scottish Border* begun

1803   (Jan–Mar) in West Country with Wedgwoods, Poole; with Lamb in London; makes will
(Jun) *Poems* (1803)
(summer) Visits by Hazlitt, Beaumonts, and S. Rogers to C in Lakes; Hazlitt's portrait of C
(Jul–Aug) "The Men and the Times" in *M Post*
(15–29 Aug) Scottish tour with DW and WW
(29 Aug–15 Sept) Continues Scottish tour alone
(15 Sept) Returns to Keswick
(Sept–Oct) Plans to write "my metaphysical works, as *my Life, & in* my Life"
(20 Dec) To Grasmere on way to London

(Jan) Charles Erskine elected cardinal
(Feb) Act of Mediation in Switzerland
(30 Apr) Louisiana bought by US from France
(18 May) Official declaration of war against France.
(25 May) Emerson b
(Sept) Emmet's execution in Ireland
Cobbett starts *Parliamentary Debates* (later Hansard)
Chatterton *Works* ed RS and Cottle
Malthus *Essay on . . . Population* (2nd ed)

1804   (Jan) Ill at Grasmere
(14 Jan) To London; portrait by Northcote

(6 Feb) Priestley d
(12 Feb) Kant d
(14 Feb) King George becomes ill

(Feb–Mar) Writes for *Courier*
(27 Mar) To Portsmouth
(9 Apr–18 May) In convoy to Malta
(Jul) Under-secretary to Alexander Ball, British High Commissioner at Malta
(Aug–Nov) Sicily, ascent of Etna; stays with G. F. Leckie

(Mar) Code Napoleon
(Apr) Collapse of Addington's administration; 2nd Pitt ministry (–1806)
(16 May) Napoleon Emperor
(12 Dec) Spain declares war on Britain
J. C. Eichhorn *Einleitung in das Neue Testament*

1805 (18 Jan) Appointed Acting Public Secretary in Malta
(5 Feb) John Wordsworth drowned in loss of *Abergavenny*: news reaches C 31 Mar
(Sept–Nov) In Sicily
(mid-Nov) To Naples
(Dec) Calabria, Naples again
(25 Dec) Sets out for Rome

(Apr) Third Coalition against France.
(9 May) Schiller d
(26 May) Napoleon King of Italy
(10 Jul) T. Wedgwood d
(17 Oct) Napoleon's victory at Ulm
(21 Oct) Trafalgar
(2 Dec) Austerlitz
Hazlitt *Principles of Human Action*
Knight *Principles of Taste*
Scott *Lay of the Last Minstrel*
RS *Madoc*
Beethoven *Fidelio*

1806 (18 Jan) In Rome, meets W von Humboldt and L. Tieck, stays with Washington Allston at Olevano
(Mar) Meets Angelica Catalani
(18 May) To Florence, Pisa
(23 Jun) Sails from Leghorn
(17 Aug) Lands in England; London, job-hunting; letters on theological issues
(26–8 Oct) In Kendal with Wordsworths and SH
(30 Oct–7 Dec) Keswick, determined on separation from Mrs C
(21 Dec) Joins Wordsworths and SH at Coleorton; (26) crisis of jealousy

(23 Jan) Pitt d; (Feb) "Ministry of All the Talents" under Grenville (–1807)
(Apr) British blockade begins
(6 Aug) Holy Roman Empire ends
(26 Aug) Palm executed
(13 Sept) Fox d
(14 Oct) Napoleon's victory at Jena
(Nov) Berlin Decrees begin Continental System
Arndt *Geist der Zeit* (–1818)

1807 (Jan–Apr) At Coleorton; (late Jan) hears WW read *Prelude*, writes *Lines to William Wordsworth*
(Apr 4) To London with Wordsworths; discusses plans for 2–vol collection of poems with Longman
(Jun) To Stowey with family; remains till Sept alone
(Jul) Meets DeQ in Bridgewater
(Sept–Nov) In Bristol and Stowey
(23 Nov) To London; thoughts of rewriting *Osorio*

(Feb) Napoleon attacks Russia
(Mar) Portland ministry (–1809)
(25 Mar) Abolition of slave-trade
(Apr) WW *Poems in Two Volumes*
(Jul) Peace of Tilsit
(Aug) Truce between Russia and Turkey
(2–5 Sept) British fleet bombards Copenhagen
(Dec) Peninsular War begins
RS *Letters from England by Don Espriella; Specimens of the Later English Poets*
C. and M. Lamb *Tales from Shakespeare*
Hegel *Phänomenologie des Geistes*
Crabbe *The Parish Register*
Byron *Hours of Idleness*

1808 C translates and revises Arndt *Geist der Zeit*

Bell–Lancaster controversy
Joseph Bonaparte made king in Spain

(13 Jan–Jun) In rooms at *Courier* office, Strand; lectures at Royal Institution on Poetry and Principles of Taste; illness
(Feb–Mar) WW in London
(May) Wordsworths move to Allan Bank, Grasmere
(Jun) To Clarkson at Bury St Edmunds
(Jul) Review of Clarkson's *History of the Abolition of the Slave-Trade* in *Ed Rev*
(Aug) Leeds and the north
(1 Sept) Arrives at Allan Bank
(5 Sept) to Keswick with WW
(7 Sept) To Allan Bank; instructs Mrs C to send his books
(Nov) First Prospectus of *The Friend* issued at Kendal

(1 May) Hazlitt marries Sarah Stoddart
(21 Aug) Wellington's victory at Vimeiro
(30 Aug) Convention of Cintra
(14 Nov) Arrival of British troops under Moore in Salamanca
(23 Nov) Spanish armies routed
(Dec) Napoleon invades Spain
(4 Dec) Madrid reoccupied by French
(24 Dec) Dr T. Beddoes d. Dalton *New System of Chemical Philosophy* (–1810) and publication of atomic theory
Lamb *Specimens of English Dramatic Poets*
Scott *Marmion*
John and Leigh Hunt begin *Examiner*
Goethe *Faust* pt I

1809 (1 Jun–15 Mar 1810) *The Friend* in 27 numbers plus supernumerary
(7 Dec–20 Jan 1810) "Letters on the Spaniards" in *Courier*

(Jan) Sir John Moore d at Corunna; victories in the Peninsula
(Feb) *Quarterly Review* founded
(9 Mar) Byron *English Bards and Scotch Reviewers*
(23 Mar) Holcroft d
(May) Napoleon captures Vienna
WW *Convention of Cintra* pamphlet
(21 Sept) Canning–Castlereagh duel
(Oct) Perceval ministry (–1812)
(14 Oct) Peace of Schönbrunn
(20 Oct) Alexander Ball d in Malta
A. W. Schlegel *Vorlesungen über dramatische Kunst und Literatur* (–1811)

1810 (Mar) SH leaves Grasmere for Wales
(15 Mar) *The Friend* last number
(May–Oct) At Keswick
(16–18 Oct) To London; Montagu precipitates WW–C quarrel; with Morgans in Hammersmith
(Nov) Meets HCR at Lamb's and other houses; personal association begins

(Mar) Battle over admission of press to House of Commons
(May) Whig reform bill to extend franchise defeated
(21 Jun) Burdett released from Tower
(Jul) Napoleon annexes Holland
(Dec) George III generally recognised as insane
WW *Guide to the Lakes*
Mme de Staël *De l'Allemagne* (tr 1813)
Scott *Lady of the Lake*
RS *Curse of Kehama*
Crabbe *The Borough*

1811 (Mar–Apr) Miniature painted by M. Betham; meets Grattan
(20 Apr) First table talk recorded by JTC
(May–Sept) Regular contributions to *Courier*
(18 Nov–27 Jan 1812) Lectures on Shakespeare and Milton at Scot's Cor-

(5 Feb) Prince of Wales made Regent
(18 Jun) Debate on Catholic Emancipation ("Catholic claims")
(27 Jun) Lord Stanhope introduces bill to make banknotes legal tender
(Nov) Bread riots in Nottingham
(Nov) Luddite uprisings begin

poration Hall, attended by Collier, Byron, Rogers, HCR

(Dec) George Dawe bust of C

(25 Nov) Dr Marsh addresses University of Cambridge concerning Bible Society

Shelley *Necessity of Atheism, St Irvine*

Jane Austen *Sense and Sensibility*

1812 (Jan–May) Essays in *Courier*

(Feb–Mar) Last journey to the Lakes to collect copies of *Friend*

(Apr) With the Morgans, Berners Street, Soho

(Apr–Jul) WW in London

(May–Jun) Lectures on drama in Willis's Rooms; portrait by Dawe

(May) Lamb and HCR patch WW quarrel

(14 May) C writes obituary on Perceval for *Courier*

(4 Jun) Catharine Wordsworth d

(Jun) *The Friend* reissued

(3 Nov–26 Jan 1813) Belles Lettres lectures in Surrey Institution

(Nov) Half Wedgwood annuity withdrawn; RS and C *Omniana*

(1 Dec) Thomas Wordsworth d

(Mar) Wellington captures Badajos

(11 May) Spencer Perceval assassinated in House of Commons by John Bellingham

(Jun) Lord Liverpool forms cabinet

(Jun) US Congress approves war against Britain

(22 Jun) Napoleon enters Russia

(Oct–Dec) Retreat from Moscow

(18 Dec) Napoleon reaches Paris

Combe *Tour of Dr Syntax in Search of the Picturesque*

Byron *Childe Harold* cantos i and ii

Davy *Elements of Chemical Philosophy*

1813 (23 Jan) *Remorse* opens at Drury Lane and runs 20 nights

(1 May) Wordsworths move to Rydal Mount

(summer) Morgan's financial affairs deteriorating; he escapes to Ireland by Oct

(autumn) Meets Mme de Staël

(Oct–Nov) Lectures in Bristol on Shakespeare and education, in Clifton on Milton and poetry

(Dec) Mary Morgan and Charlotte Brent at Ashley nr Bath

(winter) illness and spiritual crisis at Bath and Bristol

(21 Jun) Vittoria: Wellington's victory

(Jul–Aug) Peace Congress at Prague fails

(10 Aug) Austria declares war on Napoleon

(Sept) RS Poet Laureate

(Oct) Wellington enters France

(autumn) Switzerland, Holland, Italy, Rhineland, Spain, Trieste, Dalmatia freed of French rule

Leigh Hunt imprisoned for libel (–1815)

RS *Life of Nelson*

Northcote *Memoirs of Reynolds*

Jane Austen *Pride and Prejudice*

Shelley *Queen Mab*

1814 (Apr) Lectures at Bristol on Milton, Cervantes, Taste; lecture on French Revolution and Napoleon; under medical care of Dr Daniel for addiction and suicidal depression; first enthusiasm for Leighton and annotations in *Expository Works* (1748)

(26–7 Apr) Corresponds with Cottle on his condition

(1 Aug) *Remorse* performed in Bristol

(Aug–Sept) Allston portrait of C and Bristol exhibition; essays "On the Principles of Genial Criticism" pub

(Sept) At Ashley Cottage, joint tenant

(1 Jan) Invasion of France by Allies

(Mar) Allied forces reach Paris

(9 Mar) Castlereagh obtains four-power pact against separate negotiations.

(22 Mar) Ministers decide against further negotiations with Bonaparte

(11 Apr) Napoleon abdicates

(30 May) Napoleon exiled to Elba; restoration of the Bourbons; First Treaty of Paris

(Sept–Jun 1815) Congress of Vienna

(24 Dec) Peace of Ghent signed by Britain and US

with Morgan
(autumn) Visits P. C. Methuen
(20 Sept–10 Dec) Letters "To Mr. Justice Fletcher" in *Courier*
(Nov) Acquires Field *Of the Church*
(c 5 Dec) Moves with Morgans to Calne, Wilts "at a Mr Page's, Surgeon"

Inquisition re-established in Spain
WW *Excursion*
Scott *Waverley*
Cary's *Dante* completed
Jane Austen *Mansfield Park*

1815 (Apr–May) C to collect his poems with a new "preface". Receives 1815 ed of WW's *Poems*
(May) HC to Merton Coll. Oxford
(Jun) *Remorse* performed at Calne
(summer) HC at Calne for Long Vacation
(Jul–Sept) Extends preface into an "Autobiographia literaria"
(Aug–Sept) Printing of *BL* with *Sibylline Leaves* begins at Bristol

(Feb) Napoleon escapes from Elba, returns to France
(Mar–Jun) The Hundred Days
(6 Apr) Allies mobilise vs Napoleon
(18 Jun) Waterloo
Restoration of Louis XVIII
(Oct) Napoleon from Plymouth to St Helena
(20 Nov) Second Treaty of Paris
WW *Poems* of 1815; *The White Doe of Rylstone*
Scott *Guy Mannering*

1816 (Feb) Grant from Literary Fund, gift from Byron
(Mar) To London; illness
(10 Apr) Sends *Zapolya* to Byron
(15 Apr) Accepted as patient and housemate by James Gillman, Surgeon, Moreton House, Highgate
(25 May) *Christabel, Kubla Khan and The Pains of Sleep*; renews acquaintance with J. H. Frere
(Sept–Nov) At Muddiford: friendship with H. J. Rose begins
(Nov–Dec) Composes *Theory of Life* (pub 1848)
(Dec) *Statesman's Manual* pub
Antagonistic reviews of C, attributed to Hazlitt, in *Examiner* (Jun, Sept, Dec) and *Ed Rev* (Dec)

(Feb) Byron *Siege of Corinth*
(24 Apr) Byron's departure from England
(21 Jun) Motion for relief of Roman Catholics rejected in Lords
(7 Jul) Sheridan d
Parliamentary Committee on Education of the Poor
(2 Dec) Spa Fields Riot
Shelley *Alastor and Other Poems*
Peacock *Headlong Hall*
Maturin *Bertram*
J. H. Frere ms tr of Aristophanes
Jane Austen *Emma*
Scott *Antiquary, Old Mortality*
Cuvier *Le Règne animal*

1817 (Mar) Second *Lay Sermon* pub
(14 and 16 Apr) *Remorse* revived
(13 Jun) Meets L. Tieck at house of new acquaintance, Joseph Henry Green
(Jul) *Biographia Literaria, Sibylline Leaves* pub
(autumn) At Littlehampton, meets Henry Francis Cary; association with C. A. Tulk begins
(Nov) *Zapolya* pub; C's tr of Hurwitz's *Hebrew Dirge* for Princess Charlotte

(13 Feb) RS *Wat Tyler*
(4 Mar) Habeas Corpus suspended
(4 Mar) *Cobbett's Political Register* reduces price to 2d
(27 Mar) Sidmouth Circular on libels
(Apr) *Blackwood's Magazine* founded as *Edinburgh Monthly Magazine*
(18 Jul) Jane Austen d
(18 Dec) 'Immortal evening' at Haydon's
Elgin Marbles purchased by Govt and put in BM
Hazlitt *Characters of Shakespeare's Plays*
Ricardo *Principles of Political Economy*

1st American ed of *BL*
Keats *Poems*
Moore *Lalla Rookh*

1818 (Jan) "Treatise on Method" pub in *Encyclopaedia Metropolitana*
(Jan) Meets Thomas Allsop
(27 Jan–13 Mar) 14 lectures on principles of judgment, culture, and European literature
(9 Feb) *Zapolya* at Surrey Theatre for 10 nights.
(Apr) Two pamphlets supporting Peel's Bill against exploitation of child labour. Meetings with J. H. Green begin
(summer) Portrait by Thomas Phillips
(Nov) *The Friend* (3-vol ed)
Drawing by C. R. Leslie
(Dec–Mar 1819) Alternating lectures: 14 Dec–29 Mar, 14 on History of Philosophy; 17 Dec–28 Jan, 6 on Shakespeare, 11 Feb–25 Mar, 7 on Shakespeare, Milton, Dante, Spenser, Cervantes

(28 Jan) Habeas Corpus restored, not again suspended
(1 Jun) Parliamentary motion for universal suffrage and annual parliaments defeated
(Jun) Westmorland election
Keats *Endymion*
Jane Austen *Northanger Abbey, Persuasion*
(Aug) *Bl Mag* and *QR* attacks on Keats
Hallam *Middle Ages*
Hazlitt *Lectures on the English Poets*
Lamb *Collected Works* (vol II dedicated to C)
Peacock *Nightmare Abbey*
Scott *Heart of Midlothian*
Mary Shelley *Frankenstein*

1819 (Mar) Financial losses from bankruptcy of publisher Rest Fenner
(29 Mar) Last lecture
(11 Apr) Meets Keats in Millfield Lane
(14) HC elected probationary Fellow of Oriel
(spring) More on child labour, Bill passes Lords. Begins occasional contributions to *Bl Mag* (–1822)
Gillman acquires Leighton *Genuine Works*
(13 Dec) First record of conversation by Allsop
B. W. Procter meets C at Lamb's

(May) Grattan's Motion for Relief of Roman Catholics defeated
(Jun) Grey's Bill to abolish Declaration against transubstantiation defeated
(16 Aug) Peterloo massacre
WW *Peter Bell* and *The Waggoner*
Scott *Ivanhoe*
Byron *Don Juan* (–1824)
Shelley *The Masque of Anarchy*
Schopenhauer *Die Welt als Wille und Vorstellung*

1820 (Mar) Letter on renewed plans for Great Work
(May) HC refused renewal of Fellowship at Oriel; C intervenes unsuccessfully through summer
(summer) Green becomes surgeon to St Thomas' Hospital
(Aug) Green acting as weekly amanuensis to record C's work on Old and New Testament
(Oct) DC to St John's Cambridge
(1820–1) Writings for HC, later to become part of "*Prometheus*"

(29 Jan) George III d; accession of George IV
Cato Street Conspiracy
(Feb) Parliament dissolved
(Summer) Christopher W Master of Trinity Coll. Cambridge
Revolution in Spain and Portugal
(Aug–Nov) Trial of Queen Caroline
Godwin *Of Population*
Keats *Lamia . . . and Other Poems*
Lamb *Essays of Elia* in *London Magazine* (–1823)
Shelley *Prometheus Unbound etc*
RS *Life of Wesley*
WW *The River Duddon*

1821 (8 Jan) "Getting regularly on" with

(Feb) Plunkett's Motion for Relief of

"Logic", devoting Sundays with Green to "Assertion of . . . Religion" (Apr–May) Projects 3 Letters to C. A. Tulk MP on Catholic Question
(8 Jun) George C fails to visit Highgate
(Jun) HC excluded from Montagu's house
(Nov) Invitation to lecture in Dublin declined
HNC essay on C in *Etonian*

Roman Catholics passed by Commons, rejected in Lords (Apr)
(23 Feb) Keats d in Rome
(5 May) Napoleon d
Greek War of Independence
DeQ "Confessions of an English Opium Eater" in *London Magazine*
Hazlitt *Lectures on Elizabethan Drama*
Mill *Elements of Political Economy*
RS *A Vision of Judgment*
Schleiermacher *Der christliche Glaube* 1st ed (–1822)

1822 (18 Jan) Proposes "Beauties of Archbishop Leighton" to Murray, who sends him *Whole Works* (1820)
(Jan) Dictating "Logic" to C. B. Stutfield and J. Watson
(25 Feb) Announces weekly select class on philosophical subjects for young men
(spring) SC's tr of Martin Dobrizhoffer *An account of the Abipones*
(Jun–Jul) DC seriously ill at Highgate
Julius Hare becomes tutor at Cambridge
(8 Oct) Describes "four griping and grasping sorrows" of his life
(Oct–13 Nov) At Ramsgate
(6 Nov) Meets Liverpool and Canning there
(29 Dec) First record of table talk made by HNC

(30 Apr) Canning's Catholic Peers Bill carried in Commons, rejected in Lords
(8 Jul) Shelley d
(12 Aug) Castlereagh's suicide
(Sept) Canning Foreign Secretary
(Nov–Dec) Faction-fights between Orangemen and Catholics in Ireland
(24 Dec) M. Arnold b
Congress of Verona
Byron *The Vision of Judgment*
Grattan *Speeches*
Shelley *Hellas*
Blanco White *Letters from Spain*
WW *Ecclesiastical Sonnets*

1823 (3 Jan–5 Mar) Mrs C and SC at Highgate
(21 Mar) HNC's diary claims secret engagement to SC
(Jun) Meets W. E. Channing
(Jul) Meets Edward Irving
(Jul) Murray declines "Beauties of Leighton"; offered as *AR* to Taylor and Hessey (8 Aug); accepted by 15th
(Sept) Reading for prefatory Life of Leighton; proposes to seek admission to BM through Sir Humphry Davy
(Oct–10 Nov) At Ramsgate; receives proofs; meets SH again
(Nov, before 10th) Gillmans move to 3 The Grove; C's attic study
(11 Nov) Declines invitation to lecture at Leeds
(Dec) Accident to Mrs Gillman; "forge-hammer sound" in his ear

(Apr) Plunkett's Motion for Relief of Roman Catholics abandoned for lack of support
Establishment of Catholic Association in Dublin (May); in London (Jun)
War between France and Spain
Hazlitt *Liber Amoris*
RS *History of the Peninsular War*

1824 (24 Jan) DC takes pass degree at Cambridge; to become schoolmaster
(c 26 Jan) DC visits on way from Cam-

(9 Jan) John Thurtell hanged
(30 Mar–1 May) Green's first lectures as Professor of Anatomy

bridge; C alarmed by his religious opinions

(18 Feb) SC "everything the fondest and most ambitious Parent could pray for"

(18 Feb) *AR* has been "growing and new-forming itself" under his hand

(by 24 Feb) "Comfortable letter" from DC

(Mar) Elected Royal Associate, Royal Society of Literature, with annuity of 100 guineas

(late Mar) Misunderstanding with Gillmans; C withdraws till 7 Apr

(Jun) Carlyle calls at Highgate

(Sept) JTC becomes editor of *QR* (–Oct 1825)

(Oct–Nov) At Ramsgate

(19 Apr) Byron d aiding Greeks

Foundation of London Mechanics' Institution

Repeal of Combination Acts

Cary tr *The Birds of* Aristophanes

Godwin *History of the Commonwealth of England* (–1828)

RS *The Book of the Church*

Landor *Imaginary Conversations*

Scott *Redgauntlet*

1825 (15 Apr) Dr Prati calls on C and introduces Vico's work to him

(6 May) Six Disquisitions on religious subjects promised to publisher, J. A. Hessey

(10 May) Proposes three lectures in connection with projected London University; (17) gives up plan

(18 May) "*Prometheus*" delivered before RSL

(c 25 May) *Aids to Reflection* pub; Bp of London expresses favourable opinion

(30 Jun) Partnership of Taylor and Hessey dissolved,

(Jul) Blanco White visits C

(Sept) Henry Gillman to Eton after C's coaching

(Oct–Nov) At Ramsgate

(Nov) Corrects proofs of Hurwitz's *Hebrew Tales*

(Feb–May) Burdett's Motion for the Relief of Roman Catholics passed in Commons, defeated in Lords

(May) Liverpool's speech on Coronation Oath; quoted with approval by Canning

(Aug) Frere arrives in England

First railway, Stockton to Darlington, opened

Brougham *Practical Observations upon the Education of the People*

Hazlitt *The Spirit of the Age*

Mill *Essays on Government* (–1828)

C. Butler *Book of the Roman-Catholic Church*

Blanco White *Poor Man's Preservative Against Popery* and *Practical and Internal Evidence Against Catholicism*

1826 (spring) Intensive work on Daniel and Apocalypse

(summer) Long periods with Frere

(Sep) Frere obtains promise of sinecure of £200 from Liverpool for C

(11 Oct–14 Dec) At Ramsgate

(29 Oct) DC ordained deacon

(late Oct) Henry Gillman removed from Eton

(Dec) Occupies his renovated book-room on return to Highgate

C disturbed by Irving's wild theories

C visits H. F. Cary at BM

General Election with Corn Laws and Catholic Emancipation as main issues

England sends troops to Portugal

First Atlantic crossing under steam

HNC *Six Months in the West Indies*

Turner *History of Henry VIII*

RS *Vindiciae Ecclesiae Anglicanae*

Blanco White *A Letter to Charles Butler*

1827 (4 Feb) J. A. Heraud's first visit

(7 Feb) Sir George Beaumont d leaving £100 to Mrs C

(Feb) Lord Dudley & Ward intending to

(17 Feb) Liverpool seized with paralysis and forced to resign

(Mar) Burdett's Bill rejected in Commons; Canning PM

speak to Liverpool on C's behalf
(May) Hears Thomas Chalmers preach;
  (10) Chalmers calls at Highgate; C's
  serious illness; visit from Poole
(15 Jul) DC ordained priest
(Oct–22 Nov) At Ramsgate
(6 Dec) DC marries Mary Pridham

(26 Mar) Beethoven d
(8 Aug) Canning d
(12 Aug) Blake d
(31 Aug) Goderich ministry
University of London founded
Hallam *Constitutional History*
J. C. and A. Hare *Guesses at Truth*
Irving tr of *The Coming of Messiah*
Keble *Christian Year*
A. and C. Tennyson *Poems by Two Brothers*

1828 (12 Jan) Death of George C
(22 Apr) Fenimore Cooper meets C
(21 Jun–7 Aug) Netherlands and Rhine
  Tour with Dora and WW
J. C. Young, T. C. Grattan meet C
(18 Aug) Bacchanal party at Reynolds's
  with Hook, Lockhart, and Jerdan
(Jun–Jul) *Poetical Works* (3 vols)
John Sterling first visits Highgate
Hyman Hurwitz appointed Professor of
  Hebrew, London University, with support from C
(Oct–Nov) At Ramsgate
(17 Oct) Derwent Moultrie C b
(11 Nov) Hurwitz *Introductory Lecture*
A. H. Hallam and Monckton Milnes call
  at Highgate

(Jan) Wellington administration
(Apr) Russia goes to war with Turkey
(May) Repeal of Test and Corporation
  Acts
(May–Jun) Burdett's Bill for Relief of
  Roman Catholics passed in Commons, rejected in Lords
(Aug) Peel and Wellington correspond
  over Catholic question
(Sept) T. Arnold Headmaster of Rugby
(4 Dec) Lord Liverpool d
F. D. Maurice editing *Athenaeum*,
  Sterling contributing
Brougham *A Speech on the Present
  State of the Law of the Country*
Hazlitt *Life of Napoleon* (–1830)

1829 (Jan–Feb) Refuses to sign Petition
  against Catholic Emancipation
(Mar) W. P. Wood visits C
(spring) Illness delays writing of *C&S*
(May) *Poetical Works* (2nd ed)
(14 July) Lady Beaumont d leaving C
  £50, which he sends to Sara C for HC
(28 July and 1 Aug) John Wheeler visits
  C
(summer) Onset of severe intermittent illnesses
(3 Sept) SC marries her cousin HNC;
  Poole visits Highgate
(17 Sept) C revises will
(Sept) Mrs C leaves Greta Hall for good
W. B. Donne reports that C talks of recasting his "Aids"
American ed of *AR*, ed J. Marsh
HNC and SC living in Holborn area
(Dec) *On the Constitution of the Church
  and State* pub

(Jan) King agrees to discussion of
  Catholic Emancipation in Cabinet
(Feb–Mar) Bill passed to suppress
  Catholic Association
(10 Mar) 1st reading in Commons of
  Catholic Relief Bill
(10 Apr) 3rd reading in Lords passed
(13 Apr) George IV gives reluctant assent
(spring) A. H. Hallam's ref to C in
  poem *Timbuctoo*
(29 May) Sir Humphry Davy d
(Nov) Visit of Cambridge Conversazione Club members to Oxford with
  enthusiasm for C's ideas
Thomas Arnold *Sermons*
Hurwitz *Elements of the Hebrew Language*
RS *Sir Thomas More*
[Isaac Taylor] *Natural History of Enthusiasm* (May)

1830 (Apr) Republication of *The Devil's Walk*
  as "by Professor Porson"; reissued in
  autumn as by C and RS
(c Apr) *On the Constitution of the Church
  and State* (2nd ed)

Reform agitation
(25 Jun) Death of George IV; accession
  of William IV
(Jul) Revolution in France
(Nov) Grey ministry

(3 May) Chalmers visits C again
(4 Jun) John McVickar visits C
(Jun) HNC and SC settle in Hampstead
(2 Jul) Codicil to will concerning HC
(18 Sept) Hazlitt d
(7 Oct) Herbert C b
(winter) Last meetings with WW

Greece independent
Comte *Cours de philosophie positive*
Lyell *Principles of Geology*
Tennyson *Poems, chiefly Lyrical*

1831 *Aids to Reflection* (2nd ed)
(May) Emma Willard visits C
(May) RSL annuity withdrawn; C refuses personal grant of £200 from Grey, claiming devotion to principle, not party politics
(23 Sept) J. S. Mill, Henry Taylor, James Stephen visit C
Comments on Parliamentary Reform in *Table Talk*.
American ed of *The Friend* ed J. Marsh

(1 Mar) Lord John Russell introduces Reform Bill in Commons
(23 Apr) Dissolution of Parliament
(Sept–Oct) Second Reform Bill passes Commons, rejected by Lords
(14 Nov) Hegel d
(12 Dec) Third Reform Bill introduced
British Association founded
J. S. Mill *The Spirit of the Age*
Hurwitz *Etymology and Syntax*
Walsh *Popular Opinions on Parliamentary Reform*

1832 Legacy of £300 from Steinmetz
(20 Mar) W. R. Hamilton's first visit
(summer) Thomas McLellan visits C
(9 Aug) Attends christening of Edith C (b 2 Aug)
(29 Sept) HCR brings W. S. Landor to C
(Sept) Portrait by Moses Haughton
(? this year) Harriet Martineau visits C

(3 Feb) Crabbe d
(22 Mar) Goethe d
(May) Grey resigns; Wellington fails to form ministry; Grey recalled
(6 Jun) Bentham d
(7 Jun) Reform Bill becomes law
(21 Sept) Scott d
Green *Address Delivered in King's College*
Martineau *Illustrations of Political Economy* (–1834)
Park *Dogmas of the Constitution*

1833 HC's *Poems*, dedicated to C
(24–9 Jun) At Cambridge for meetings of British Association
(Jul) At Ramsgate
(5 Aug) Emerson calls at Highgate
(Sept) Visit to C by correspondent of *New York Observer*
HC's *Biographia Borealis (Northern Worthies)*

(14 Jul) Keble's sermon on "National Apostasy"
(25–9 Jul) "Hadleigh Conference" at H. J. Rose's Rectory; Oxford Movement initiated
Tracts for the Times (Newman *et al*) begin
Thomas Arnold *Principles of Church Reform*
Carlyle *Sartor Resartus*
Lamb *Last Essays of Elia*
Browning *Pauline*

1834 (Mar–Aug) *Poetical Works* (3rd ed) 3 vols published separately
(Apr) Instructs Hurst to dispose of his share in eds of *AR* and *C&S*
(30 Jun) Viscount Adare visits C and reports to Hamilton
(25 July, 6.30 a.m.) Death of C at Highgate followed by autopsy
(2 Aug) Funeral: C immured in vault in Highgate Churchyard.

(Feb) New Poor Law
(18 Feb) Augustus Hare d
(Apr) Petition to admit Dissenters to Cambridge degrees
(23 Dec) Malthus d
(27 Dec) Lamb d
Tolpuddle martyrs
Bentham *Deontology*

EDITOR'S INTRODUCTION

*A*ids to Reflection, which began life as a simple proposal by Coleridge to reprint the best passages of a seventeenth-century divine accompanied by comments of his own, became in the making a much more complex work—so much so that when it was published he found himself obliged to comment on the changes it had undergone since he returned the proofs of the first pages to the printer. Characteristically, his explanation took the form of an organic simile:

> In the bodies of several species of Animals there are found certain Parts, of which neither the office, the functions, nor the relations could be ascertained by the Comparative Anatomist, till he had become acquainted with the state of the Animal before birth.[1]

Some of the changes, he explained, had taken place as a result of his own reflections while compiling the work, supplemented by "conversation with men of eminence in the Literary and Religious Circles"; but it is clear that the complexity of its composition is also due to processes that had been in motion long before it was ever conceived. *Aids to Reflection* represented an attempt on his part to hand on as directly as possible the fruits of his own spiritual experiences in a work that would be acceptable to the general educated public, but those spiritual experiences, however simple they might seem in their essence, could not be separated from his previous intellectual and psychical development. When Coleridge tried to comment on a passage, his straightforward and immediate response was likely to become involved with issues and questions that had stirred him all his life. By degrees, therefore, the volume began to present itself as a preliminary version of the work on religion which he had been planning for more than twenty years. It could not take the place of the projected "Assertion of Religion", the work in which he hoped to establish his position at length and philosophically, but it brought forward some of the issues in that work which he felt to be urgent in the intellectual life of his own time and which lay close to the heart of his own concerns. In order to understand its form, then, it is necessary to take some account of his earlier thinking.

---

[1] *AR* (1825) "Advertisement": see App G(a) below.

The Development of Coleridge's Religious Thought

Even during the years when Coleridge was a Unitarian, his religious thinking was disturbed by intellectual conflict. Discussing his state when he was living at Stowey, he sums up his religious dilemma at that time as follows in *Biographia Literaria*: "For a very long time indeed I could not reconcile personality with infinity; and my head was with Spinoza, though my whole heart remained with Paul and John."[2] During this period, which lasted at least until his journey to Malta in 1804, his metaphysical speculations were particularly spurred on by discussions with Wordsworth, Godwin, Tom Wedgwood, and other radical intellectuals: many of the investigations described in his notebooks represent attempts to explore connexions between the "nature" that was revealed in the external world, and the "nature" that worked in the human unconscious through dreams and abnormal mental phenomena.

There were times, indeed, when his thought seemed to be verging on pure Spinozism, but he was never a pantheist. Throughout the period there are evidences of a continuing devotion to the Christian religion in some form. While exploring the implications of nature as far as they led him he was trying (as the account in the *Biographia* states) to find an intellectual position that would also embody the thinking of St Paul and St John. The names are not simply representative, moreover. Years later he would write that he had found a greater authority in their writings than in those of the other Apostles—including the first three Gospels.[3] To St Paul he looked for doctrines based on the conviction of man's sin and unworthiness before God; to St John for the doctrine (unfolded in the fourth Gospel) that showed the workings of the Creative Word as an essential part of the whole divine process. The great tradition in Christian thinking, so far as he was concerned, was that which had continued to affirm, and endeavoured to reconcile, the thinking of these two great figures. By following it he might hope to bring together the sense of his own failings and shortcomings with his continuing belief that his career as a creative writer and thinker was also morally significant.

The first indication that he might be hoping to present the results of his labours in a prose work is in a notebook entry of 1802 which gives a list of projected writings:

1. On Popery. 2. Luther & Lutheranism, Calvin & Calvinism (with Zwinglius).

---

[2] *BL* ch 10 *(CC)* I 201.
[3] See letters of 1826: *CL* VI 552, 556. C seems later to have given greater promi-nence to Luke than to Matthew and Mark: see e.g. ibid 784.

3. Presbyterians & Baxterians in the time of Charles 1 and 2nd—George Fox—
& Quakerism/ Socinians & Modern Unitarians.[4]

Another such list a year later included a revised version of this scheme as the ninth proposal:

Revolutionary Minds, Thomas Aquinas, Scotus, Luther, Baxter as represent. of the English Presbyterians & as affording a place for the Church of England—Socinus, G. Fox.—[5]

In this later scheme the emphasis is laid on minds rather than on movements. Luther and Baxter, figures whom Coleridge continued to honour throughout his career, retain equal importance in each; Quakerism and Unitarianism, however, have receded into a brief mention of George Fox and Socinus, while the (apparently disparaging) reference to "Popery" has been replaced (following Coleridge's sympathetic reading in the scholastic tradition at that time) by mention of Aquinas and Scotus, minds now seen to be important for his own sense of Christian metaphysics.

"Revolutionary Minds" remained one project among many; even in 1803 his ultimate plan was to write a great work "On Man, and the probable Destiny of the Human Race, followed & illustrated by the Organum vere Organum, & philosophical Romance to explain the whole growth of Language . . ."[6] Such a work, however, would require many years' labour, and was planned to appear late in his life; the important work of the decade under discussion was *The Friend*, a periodical in which his main aim was to establish a position of responsibility, of regard for principle, which chimed with the views of Wordsworth at the time, and in which religious thinking was one strand among many. First and foremost *The Friend* was a work addressed to men of goodwill everywhere, and had the political, intellectual, and social condition of the times as its central concern.

Coleridge's religious speculations, which had continued, emerge with particular distinctness in several letters to George Fricker and to Thomas Clarkson, written during the autumn of 1806. In one of these he recorded the change in his beliefs that had taken place since 1798:

I was for many years a Socinian; and at times almost a Naturalist, but sorrow, and ill health, and disappointment in the only deep wish I had ever cherished,

---

[4] *CN* I 1181.
[5] *CN* I 1646.
[6] Ibid. The Latin title means "Organ that is truly an Organ". In 1803 (*CL* II 947) C gives the alternative "or an *Instrument* of practical Reasoning in the Business of real Life"; in 1828 (*CL* VI 773) "or Logic in it's living uses, for the Senate, the Pulpit, the Bar . . .".

forced me to look into myself; I read the New Testament again, and I became fully convinced, that Socinianism was not only not the doctrine of the New Testament, but that it scarcely deserved the name of a religion in any sense.

The ". . . mode of defending Christianity, adopted by Grotius first; and latterly, among many others, by Dr. Paley"[7] had, he thought, increased the number of infidels:

. . . never could it have been so great, if thinking men had been habitually led to look into their own souls, instead of always looking out, both of themselves, and of their nature. If to curb attack, such as yours on miracles, it had been answered:—Well, brother! but granting these miracles to have been in part the growth of delusion at the time, and of exaggeration afterward, yet still all the doctrines will remain untouched by this circumstance, and binding on thee. Still must thou repent and be regenerated, and be crucified to the flesh; and this not by thy own mere power; but by a mystérious action of the moral Governor on thee; of the Ordo-ordinians, the Logos, or Word. Still will the eternal filiation, or Sonship of the Word from the Father; still will the Trinity of the Deity, the redemption, and the thereto necessary assumption of humanity by the Word, "who is with God, and is God," remain truths: and still will the vital head-and-heart FAITH in these truths, be the living and only fountain of all true virtue. Believe all these, and with the grace of the spirit consult your own heart, in quietness and humility, they will furnish you with proofs, that surpass all understanding, because they are felt and known; believe all these I say, so as that thy faith shall be not merely real in the acquiescence of the intellect; but actual, in the thereto assimilated affections; then shalt thou KNOW from God, whether or not Christ be of God. But take notice, I only say, the miracles are extra essential; I by no means deny their importance, much less hold them useless, or superfluous. Even as Christ did, so would I teach; that is, build the miracle on the faith, not the faith on the miracle.[8]

Coleridge was to retain for the rest of his life the set of convictions recorded here, including the insistence that some kinds of evidence could be furnished only by belief. George Fricker evidently protested against his playing down of the doctrine of redemption, since in his next letter he explained that they did not constitute the whole of his faith, but comprised such

. . . as a clear Head & honest Heart assisted by divine Grace might in part discover by self-examination and the light of natural conscience, & which *efficiently* & *practically* believed would prepare the way for the *peculiar Doctrine* of Christianity, namely Salvation by the Cross of Christ. I meant these doctrines as the Skeleton, to which the death & Mediation of Christ with the supervention of the Holy Ghost were to add the Flesh, and Blood, Muscles, nerves, & vitality.—

[7] Letter to George Fricker 4 Oct 1806: *CL* II 1189.

[8] Ibid 1189–90. The text is from Cottle; C presumably wrote *ordinans* without a second "i": cf *Sp Aph B II* at n 49 below, and *CN* IV 4728 f 2.

He continued, however:

> God of his goodness grant, that I may arrive at a more living Faith in these last, than I now feel. What I now feel is only a very strong *presentiment* of their Truth and Importance aided by a thorough conviction of the hollowness of all other Systems. Alas! my moral being is too untranquil, too deeply possessed by one lingering passion after an earthly good withheld—& probably withheld by divine goodness—from me, to be capable of being that, which it's own 'still small voice' tells me, even in my dreams, that it ought to be, yet of itse[lf] cannot be.[9]

The "earthly good withheld" was presumably that of reciprocated human love—figured for him at the time in the possibility of marrying Sara Hutchinson; the presence and encouragement of Wordsworth, meanwhile, held before him intellectual ideals of a mainly secular kind. When Sara finally withdrew and Wordsworth seemed no longer sympathetic towards his larger enterprises he had been left in a state of emotional aridity, leading gradually into spiritual crisis.

At the end of 1813 he suffered a week of severe illness, in which (to quote his own account) ". . . tho' driven up and down for seven dreadful Days by restless Pain, like a Leopard in a Den, yet the anguish & remorse of Mind was worse than the pain of the whole Body.—O I have had a new world opened to me, in the infinity of my own Spirit!"[10] To another correspondent he described that new world in greater detail:

> . . . You have no conception of what my sufferings have been, forced to struggle and struggle in order not to desire a death for which I am not prepared.—I have scarcely known what sleep is, but like a leopard in its den have been drawn up and down the room by extreme pain, and restlessness, worse than pain itself.
>
> O how I have prayed even to loud agony only to be able to pray! O how I have felt the impossibility of any real *good will* not born anew from the Word and the Spirit! O I have seen far, far deeper and clearer than I ever saw before the ground of pernicious errors! O I have seen, I have felt that the worst offences are those against our own souls! That our souls are infinite in depth, and therefore our sins are infinite, and redeemable only by an infinitely higher infinity; that of the Love of God in Christ Jesus. I have called my soul infinite, but O infinite in the depth of darkness, an infinite craving, an infinite capacity of pain and weakness, and excellent only as being passively capacious of the light from above. Should I recover I will—no—no may God grant me power to struggle to become *not another* but a *better man*—O that I had been a partaker with you of the discourse of Mr Robt Hall! But it pleased the Redeemer to appoint for me a sterner, tearfuller, and even more eloquent preacher, if to be impressive is to be eloquent. O God save me—save me from myself. . . .[11]

The crisis had persisted throughout the spring of 1814, when Cole-

---

[9] Letter to Fricker 9 Oct 1806: *CL* II 1192.
[10] Letter to Mrs J. J. Morgan 19 Dec 1813: *CL* III 463.
[11] Letter to Thomas Roberts c 19 Dec 1813: *CL* III 463–4.

ridge visited Bristol and was stung by a letter from Joseph Cottle, who had just discovered the extent of his drug addiction and urged him to rouse himself. Coleridge replied that this was like asking a man paralysed in both arms to rub them briskly together. Cottle wrote a further letter immediately, urging him to pray, to which he replied the same day:

> O I do pray inwardly to be able to *pray*; but indeed to pray, to pray with the faith to which Blessing is promised, this is the reward of Faith, this is the Gift of God to the Elect. O if to feel how infinitely worthless I am, how poor a wretch, with just free will enough to be deserving of wrath, & of my own contempt, & of none to merit a moment's peace, can make a part of a Christian's creed; so far I am a Christian—.[12]

In another letter to Cottle at this time, however, he discussed the question of prayer in a less agonised manner, declaring that Christians expected ". . . no outward or sensible Miracles from Prayer—It's effects and it's fruitions are spiritual, and accompanied (to use the words of that true *Divine*, Archbishop Leighton) 'not by Reasons and Arguments; but by an inexpressible kind of Evidence, which they only know who have it.' "[13] In the remainder of the letter he described further the wretchedness of his own condition and his desire to have himself put under some kind of permanent supervision.

The mention of Leighton in that letter indicates something of the extent to which his writings were assisting Coleridge's fight for spiritual survival at this time. In the same month he wrote in the copy of his major work that William Brame Elwyn had lent him,

> Surely if ever Work not in the sacred Canon might suggest a belief of Inspiration, of something more than human, this it is. When Mr Elwyn made this assertion, I took it as an hyperbole of affection, but now I subscribe to it seriously & bless the Hour that introduced me to the knowlege of the evangelical apostolical Archbishop Leighton.[14]

In later notes he was to develop an image of Leighton's commentary on the First Epistle of Peter as being a true reverberation from the inspiration of the Gospels—"Next to the inspired Scriptures, yea, and as the *vibration* of that once struck hour remaining on the Air . . ."[15] If this sense of a timeless truth speaking to him was comforting, however, it could also be alarming. When Leighton wrote "If any one's Head or

---

[12] Letter to Cottle 26 Apr 1814: *CL* III 478.
[13] 27 Apr 1814: *CL* III 478–9, citing Leighton COPY A I 83; cf *CM (CC)* III 509.
[14] Note on Leighton COPY A flyleaf: *CM*

(CC) III. For title-page details of COPY A see Abbreviations under Leighton.
[15] *CN* IV 4867 (Jan 1822). Cf letter to John Murray 18 Jan 1822, quoted at n 36 below.

Tongue should grow apace, and all the rest stand at a Stay, it would certainly make him a Monster'', Coleridge recognised the picture guiltily and wrote down repeated cries for mercy.[16] When Leighton wrote of a sick man that ''. . . the Kindness and Love of God is then as seasonable and refreshing to him, as in Health, and possibly more'', Coleridge wrote in the margin: ''To the regenerate; but to the conscious Sinner a Source of Terrors insupportable''—and then, perhaps aware that he had just written a capital S and a capital T, he continued, ''S. T. C. i.e. Sinful, Tormented Culprit.''[17] Yet he was also sustained by Leighton's assurances concerning the grace of God. On a passage concluding ''. . . though I saw, as it were, his Hand lifted up to destroy me, yet from that same Hand would I expect Salvation'', he wrote: ''Bless God O my soul! for this sweet and strong Comforter. The Honey in the Lion.''[18] On the sentence ''. . . such an Assent as this, is the peculiar Work of the Spirit of God, and is certainly saving Faith'', he commented, ''Lord I believe! help thou my unbelief. My natural reason acquiesces. I believe enough to *fear*—& grant me the Belief that brings sweet Hope.''[19]

Coleridge warmed particularly to the presence, amid Leighton's warnings and assurances, of a strong imaginative sense that linked with his own. Above all he came to admire the chastity of Leighton's imagination: ''. . . a *subdued*ness, a self-checking Timidity, in his Colouring, a sobering silvery-grey Tone over all . . . by this sacrifice, however, of particular effects giving an increased permanence to the impression of the Whole, and wonderfully facilitating it's soft and quiet *Illapse* into the very recesses of our Conviction''.[20] He seems also to have felt that such writing sprang from the impersonal element of the author's nature. This was a feature equally of his great admiration for Luther, whose doctrine of justification by faith relied likewise not on a self-conscious personal response, but on a more impersonal acceptance within the depths of one's being.

For the rest of 1814 Leighton's star continued in the ascendant. Coleridge visited the estate of Paul Cobb Methuen near Bath as a guest that autumn; years later his son Thomas was to recall how in 1814–16 he had marvelled at his ''. . . familiarity with Leighton and kindred religious authors''. ''From the rich, and spiritually speaking, jewelled pages of Leighton, he would repeat ample passages.''[21] Yet little of this enthusi-

---

[16] Note on Leighton COPY A I 213: *CM (CC)* III.
[17] Ibid 219: *CM (CC)* III.
[18] Ibid 75: *CM (CC)* III.
[19] Ibid 82: *CM (CC)* III.
[20] Letter to Murray 18 Jan 1822, quoted more fully at n 36 below: *CL* v 199.
[21] *C Talker* 304, 310.

asm passed directly into his published writings of the following period, and the copy he had annotated probably went back to its owner at an early stage.

During the remainder of 1814 and well into 1815, nevertheless, Coleridge continued to think about theological questions and to read theological works. In November he touched on Jeremy Taylor's views on original sin and acquired Richard Field's *Of the Church*.[22] He discussed Edward Williams's views on modern Calvinism in the following spring and, a little later in 1815, miracles.[23] For him to be thinking about such matters was not, as we have seen, new. In the 1809–10 *Friend*, for instance, a long passage (which was to be introduced into *Aids to Reflection*) was devoted to the question of the Fall, and of the rôle of the will.[24] In that passage, however, there had been no mention of Arminius and Calvin; his new interest was evidently connected with a reading of Williams's *Defence of Modern Calvinism* (1812), probably after his discovery of Leighton and shortly before a letter to R. H. Brabant of March 1815 in which he went on to discuss Williams's *Essay on the Equity of Divine Government*:

My remarks on the larger work I have written on slips of Paper, which you will find at the pages to which they refer: with the exception of my opinion de toto which I incautiously wrote on the blank Leaf at the Beginning. But if it should be improper to send it back to the owner thus, you can take it out and with a few Drops of Gum-water replace it to advantage with a leaf of better paper.—If Dr W's Opinions be indeed those of the Modern Calvinists collectively, I have taken my last Farewell of *Modern* Calvinism. It is in it's inevitable consequences Spinosism, not that which Spinosism, i.e. the doctrine of the Immanence of the World in God, might be improved into, but Spinosism with all it's Skeleton unfleshed, bare Bones and Eye-holes, as presented by Spinoza himself. In one thing only does it differ. It has not the noble honesty, that majesty of openness, so delightful in Spinoza, which made him scorn all attempts to varnish over fair consequences, or to deny in words what was affirmed in the reasoning.—I said, in one thing only. O I did injustice to thee, Spinoza!—Righteous and gentle Spirit, where should I find that iron Chain of Logic, which neither man or angel could *break*, but which falls of itself by dissolving the rock of Ice, to which it is stapled—and which thou in common with all thy contemporaries & predecessors didst mistake for a rock of adamant?* Where shall I find the hundred deep and solemn Truths, which as so many Germs of Resurrection to Life and a glorified Body will make, sooner or later, "the dry Bones Live?"—

That I am not mischarging Dr Williams, you would be convinced in ten minutes by merely turning to Spinoza's three Letters, (especially the second) to

---

[22] Letter to John Kenyon 3 Nov 1814: *CL* III 540–2; inscription in Richard Field *Of the Church* (1635): *CM (CC)* II 686.
[23] Letter to Brabant 13 Mar 1815: *CL* IV

553 (see also below at n 26); note of May 1815: *CN* III 4249.
[24] *Friend (CC)* II 279–81; cf *Prel Sp Aph* below.

Blyenburgh.—But Spinoza never was guilty of such an evasion, as that we were responsible Beings to God, as a *Judge*, because he does not act on the will, but only the Heart, or Nature—which however the Will *cannot* but follow—He knew too well, that Causa causae causa causati.[25] You might as well cut the Rope that suspended a hanging Scaffolding, and pretend that the man in it fell and broke his Limbs of his own accord—for you never pushed him—you did not even touch him.—No! Spinoza tells his Correspondent plainly—"The difference between us is, that you consider Actions in relation to God, as *a Judge*—and if I did the same, I could not evade your consequences, but should myself exclaim—Why yet findeth he fault, seeing we do nothing but what he himself forced us to do? seeing that in truth we do nothing but it is he worketh in us both to will and to do? But I do not contemplate God as a Judge, or attribute any human Qualities or offices to him, but regard him as the Eternal Source of necessary Causes."—Now this is fair Dealing at least.—

So much for theological Metaphysics! . . .[26]

---

* viz. God as an *Object*, forgetting that an Object as much presupposes a Subject, as a Subject does an Object. Spinoza's is a World with one Pole only, & consequently no Equator. He had commenced either with the natura naturata, as the Objective Pole, or at the "I per se I" as the Subjective Pole—he must necessarily in either case have arrived at the Equator, or Identity of Subject and Object—and thence instead of *a God*, = the one only Substance, of which all finite Things are the modes and accidents, he would have revealed to himself the doctrine of The Living God, having the Ground of his own Existence within himself, and the originating Principle of all dependent Existence in his Will and Word.

The intellectual stability that he had achieved from his reflections on Leighton also helped give space and opportunity for creative works such as *Biographia Literaria*, *Zapolya*, and the *Lay Sermons*, together with new editions of his poems and *The Friend*. The next clear stage in the relationship came in 1819, when James Gillman, in whose house he had been living for three years, bought a copy of Leighton's *Genuine Works*, an edition which, issued first in 1805 with Philip Doddridge's preface and a life by Erasmus Middleton, contained not only the Commentary on 1 Peter but the rest of his surviving works. The comments which Coleridge wrote in this volume survive only in manuscript transcripts by John Watson and Sara Coleridge; they represent a further stage in Coleridge's relationship to Leighton, however, which has been obscured by the fact that when they were printed after his death, in *Literary Remains* IV, they were run together with the earlier annotations. Examined as a separate sequence, their specific character is clearer. In 1814 Leighton had been an immediate presence, the inspired man speaking to Coleridge directly across the years. In the new sequence, by contrast, the

---

[25] "The cause of the cause is the cause of the thing caused": for C's use in *AR* see

below, *Sp Aph B Xb* n 11.
[26] *CL* IV 548–9.

quality of Leighton's inspiration is taken for granted and Coleridge's concern becomes more theological. His first, very important note shows him grappling with a key doctrine of Christianity: that of the atonement for sin made by Christ and the mode of its effect on human beings. Unlike some Christians, who were unhappy with such a doctrine as a whole, and sought to modify its implications, Coleridge (whatever he might have thought at an earlier stage in his life) had now become convinced that such doctrines could not ". . . be denied or explained away without removing (as the modern Unitarians) or (as the Arminians) unsettling and undermining the foundation of the Faith".[27] It was therefore his aim to reaffirm such doctrines while still managing to allow for the disquiets that some Christians might feel concerning some of its possible implications. He could not, like the Unitarians, simply disregard the doctrine as part of a mistaken mystification that had taken place in the Church; nor could he, like the later Arminians, oppose the Calvinist doctrines of election—at least if (as in the later developments of Arminianism as typified by Grotius) that opposition led to an assertion of man's free will so powerful that it seemed to set it in the power of human beings whether or not they chose to be saved from sin. Yet this did not mean, either, that he accepted Calvinism itself—though, as with Arminianism, it was *modern* Calvinism that attracted his hostility. In a letter concerning proposed lectures on theological questions he had set out his problem and his fear of alienating the audience by offending both opposing parties:

. . . Now on the subject proposed I must of *moral* necessity deliver opinions that would bring down a Swarm from opposite Hives—. The so called moderate Grotian and Paleyan Divines and *thus almost all who will hear me* who have formed their notions of Christian Evidence from the Writers of this School I must offend by the proof that the Church of England and the great Founders of the Reformation held these opinions as scarcely less than heretical pravity, or half way between Popery and Pelagianism and even Socinianism—and that I am decisively and earnestly of the same opinion.
The ⟨modern⟩ Calvinists I should offend bitterly by proving that Calvin would have cried: Fire & Faggot, before he had read 100 pages of Dr Williams's Modern Calvinism—and by declaring my conviction that it would be difficult to say which stand at the greatest Distance from Luther, Calvin, our Whitaker, Field, &c., the hodiernal Evangelicals or their Antagonists with Mr Mant at their head. Above all, the Missionary Society—how would they recoil from the assertion, that Go ye into all nations, &c means nothing more, than/ Preach the Gospel indifferently to ⟨Jews and Gentiles—⟩ all that will hear you, in whatever part of the Roman Empire the Hearer may have been . . .[28]

[27] Annotation on Leighton COPY B I 9–13: *CM (CC)* III. For title-page details of COPY B (the *Genuine Works* of 1819) see

Abbreviations under Leighton.
[28] Fragment of a letter pasted into Kant *Die Religion innerhalb der Grenzen der*

Other notes on the 1819 Leighton show Coleridge more ready to criticise him than before, while retaining reverence and delight for him at his best: "Oh! were it not for my manifold infirmities, whereby I am so all unlike the white-robed Leighton, I could almost conceit that my soul had been an emanation from his!"[29] In his notebooks and letters, meanwhile, he was continuing to explore theological themes more generally and still working on the thoughts of St John and St Paul, protagonists respectively of the Word and the Will. A feature of Leighton's writing that had appealed particularly to him was his ability to bring together these themes quite effortlessly, speaking of the inward light in a way that accorded with Christian Platonism while also affirming the depravity of man and his need for redemption.

Recognition of the complete infirmity of his own will had driven him more forcibly towards the affirmations of St Paul concerning the transcendence of God and the inability of sinful man to approach him by way of his own reason and volition alone; yet continuing awareness of his own intelligential powers drew him to reflect on the possibility that inner revelation could also be ministered to by propitious circumstances. In an undated note on Kant's *Religion*, discussing the mode by which the unmediated act of God in redemption might take place, he referred to this other possibility as a kind of complementary mode:

. . . The will then may be acted on . . . by shocks of Sickness forcing the attention backward in upon the state of our collective consciousness;—&c. &c. (See that fine Sonnet, entitled Sin, p 37 of Herbert's Temple)—Why not then an influence of influences from the Son of God with the Spirit of God, acting directly on the Homo Νουμενον, as well as thro' the Homo Phænomenon? This would make a just distinction between Grace to Redemption, and Providential Aids—the direct action on the Noumenon would be the Grace, the Call—the influence on the Noumenon thro' the Homo phænomenon by the pre-arrangement of outward or bodily circumstances would be, as they are commonly called in pious language, Providences.—[30]

The reference to the rôle of sickness in preparing a propitious state of mind and the allusion to Herbert's *Sin* (quoted also in *Biographia Literaria*[31]) are relevant to the production of *Aids to Reflection*, in which both appear; the reference to "Providential Aids" may also have helped the formulation of the title.

The work which he was annotating, Kant's *Religion innerhalb der Grenzen der blossen Vernunft*, also had its part to play in the germinat-

blossen Vernunft (Königsberg 1794) between 210 and 211: *CM (CC)* III 308–9. Cf *P Lects* (1949) 446–7.

[29] Note on Leighton COPY B III 63: *CM*

(CC) III.

[30] Note on Kant *Religion* +2–+4, referring to p 297: *CM (CC)* III 312–13.

[31] *BL* ch 19 *(CC)* II 95–6.

ing process. Kant discusses such terms as "virtue" (*Tugend*) and "prudence" (*Klugheit*).[32] He puts the case for a "reflective" (*reflectirend*) faith in contradiction to the alternatives of fanaticism (*Schwärmerei*), superstition (*Aberglaube*), illumination (*Illuminatismus*), and thaumaturgy (*Thaumaturgie*).[33] More importantly, his concern with the rôle of Will in relation to sin and redemption was evidently a stimulus to Coleridge's thinking; indeed, as Elinor Shaffer has pointed out, some later sections of *Aids to Reflection* can be read as covertly offering an alternative to Kant's views on these questions, with Coleridge invoking Kant's concept of "transcendental reflection", as elaborated in the *Critik der reinen Vernunft*, to provide a new solution for the problems raised in his treatise on religion.[34]

At first, however, Coleridge's plans for a new work were less ambitious, and his proposed title different. Since giving his Lectures on the History of Philosophy in 1819, Coleridge had been turning his thoughts more and more to his projected "Assertion of Religion",[35] a work calling for extensive thought and complex construction. Meanwhile, however, his friends (and especially James Gillman) seem to have been anxious to see another work from the press: an offering to serve the needs of the current hour, including those connected with the doubts and uncertainties of the younger generation.

If he was to satisfy the urgings of his friends and the needs of his contemporaries yet still give attention to the "Assertion of Religion" a book that would not be too demanding of his time was called for. What more natural, then, than that he should turn back to the work which had made such a strong impression upon him in the time of his own spiritual need? If Leighton's commentary on St Peter had held out such valuable admonitions and assurances to him, why should he not help make them available to others who were in need? But if so, what was needed was not a new edition of the work as such (two new editions had recently been published) but a persuasive presentation of Leighton's best thoughts together with interpretative comments.

Coleridge set out his project to John Murray on 18 January 1822. Since his letter includes various points later to be taken up in the final work it will bear quoting in full:

Dear Sir
If not with the works, you are doubtless familiar with the name of that "*wonderful man*" (for such, says Doddridge, I must deliberately call him) Arch-

[32] Kant *Religion* 67, 70.
[33] Ibid 63–4.
[34] Elinor S. Shaffer "Metaphysics of Culture: Kant and Coleridge's *Aids to Re-* flection" *JHI* xxxi (1970) 199–218.
[35] See e.g. his letter to Allsop 26 Nov 1820: *CL* v 119–20.

bishop Leighton. It would not be easy to point out another name, which the eminent of all parties, Catholic and Protestant, Episcopal and Presbyterian, Whigs and Tories, have been so unanimous in extolling. "There is a spirit in Archbishop Leighton, I never met with in any human writings; nor can I read many lines in them without impressions which I could wish always to retain"—observes a Dignitary of our Establishment and F.R.S. eminent in his day both as a Philosopher and a Divine. In fact, it would make no small addition to the size of the volume, if as was the fashion in editing the Classics, we should collect the eulogies on his writings passed by Bishops only and Church Divines, from Burnet to Porteus. That this confluence of favorable opinions is not without good Cause, my own experience convinces me. For at a time, when I had read but a small portion of the Archbishop's principal Work, when I was altogether ignorant of it's celebrity, much more of the peculiar character attributed to his writings (that of making and leaving a deep impression on Readers of all classes) I remember saying to Mr Southey—"that in the Apostolic Epistles I heard the last Hour of Inspiration striking, and in Arch. Leighton's Commentary the lingering *Vibration* of the Sound." Perspicuous, I had almost said transparent, his style is *elegant* by the mere compulsion of the Thoughts and feelings, and in despite, as it were, of the writer's wish to the contrary. Profound as his Conceptions often are, and numerous as the passages are, where the most *athletic* Thinker will find himself tracing a rich vein from the surface downward, and leave off with an unknown depth for to morrow's delving—yet there is this quality peculiar to Leighton—unless we add Shakespear—that there is always a sense on the very surface, which the simplest may understand, if they have head and heart to understand any thing. The same or nearly the same, excellence characterizes his Eloquence. Leighton had by nature a quick and pregnant Fancy: and the august Objects of his habitual Contemplation, and their remoteness from the outward senses; his constant endeavour to see or to bring all things under some point of Unity; but above all, the rare and vital Union of Head and Heart, of Light and Love, in his own character;—all these working conjointly could not fail to form and nourish in him the higher power, and more akin to Reason—the power, I mean, of Imagination. And yet in his freest and most figurative passages there is a *subdued*ness, a self-checking Timidity, in his Colouring, a sobering silvery-grey Tone over all; and an experienced eye may easily see where and in how many instances Leighton has substituted neutral tints for a strong Light or a bold Relief—by this sacrifice, however, of particular effects giving an increased permanence to the impression of the Whole, and wonderfully facilitating it's soft and quiet *Illapse* into the very recesses of our Conviction, Leighton's happiest ornaments of style are made to appear as efforts on the part of the Author to express himself *less* ornamentally—more plainly.

Since the late alarm respecting Church Calvinism and Calvinistic Methodism (—a cry of Fire! Fire! in consequence of a red glare on one or two of the windows, from a bonfire of Straw and Stubble in the Church-yard, while the Dry Rot of virtual Socinianism is snugly at work in the Beams and Joists of the venerable Edifice—) I have heard of certain gentle Doubts and Questions as to the Archbishop's *perfect* Orthodoxy—some small speck in the Diamond which had escaped the quick eye of all former Theological Jewellers from Bishop Burnet to the outrageously Anti-methodistic Warburton. But on what grounds I cannot even conjecture—unless it be, that the Christianity which Leighton teaches contains the doctrines peculiar to the Gospel as well as the Truths common to it with the (so called) Light of Nature or Natural Religion—that he dissu[a]des students and the generality of Christians from all attempts at explaining the Mysteries of Faith by *notional* and metaphysical speculations, and rather by a heavenly life and temper to obtain a closer view of these Truths, the *full* Sight and Knowledge of which it is in Heaven only that we shall possess. He further advises them in speaking of these Truths to prefer scripture-language; but since something more than this had been made necessary by the restless spirit of Dispute, to take this *"something more"* in the precise terms of the Liturgy and Articles of the established Church.—Enthusiasm? Fanaticism?—Had I to recommend an Antidote, I declare on my conscience that above all others it should be Leighton. And as to *Calvinism*, L's exposition of the scriptural sense of Election ought to have prevented the very [?suspicion].

You will long ago, I fear, have [?been asking yourself,] To what does all this tend?—Briefly then—I feel strongly persuaded—perhaps because I strongly wish it—that The Beauties of Archbishop Leighton selected and methodized, with a (*better*) Life of the Author, i.e. a biographical and critical Introduction or Preface, and Notes—would make not only a useful but an interesting POCKET VOLUME—. 'Beauties' in general are objectionable works—injurious to the original Author, as disorganizing his productions—pulling to pieces the well-wrought *Crown* of his glory to pick out the shining stones—and injurious to the Reader, by indulging the taste for unconnected & for that reason unretained single Thoughts—till it fares with him as with the old Gentleman at Edinburgh, who eat six *Kittiwakes* by way of *whetting* his appetite—whereas (said he) it proved quite the contrary: I never sat down to a dinner with so little!—But Leighton's principal Work—that which fills two Volumes and a half of the 4— being a Commentary on St Peter's Epistles, verse by verse, and varying of course, in subject, &c with almost every paragraph, the Volume, I propose, would not only bring together his finest passages, but these being afterwards arranged on a principle wholly independent of the accidental place of each in the original Volumes, and guided by their relative bearings, it would give a connection or at least a propriety of *sequency*, that was before of necessity wanting.— It may be worth noticing, that the Editions, both the one in Three, and the other in Four, Volumes are most grievously misprinted & otherwise disfigured.— Should you be disposed to think this worthy your attention, I would even send you the Proof *transcribed*, sheet by sheet, as it should be printed, tho' doubtless, by sacrificing one Copy of Leighton's Works, it might be effected by references to Volume, page, and line—I having first carefully corrected the Copy.—Or should you think another more likely to execute the plan better or that another name would better promote it's sale—I should by no means resent the preference—nor feel any mortification, for which the having occasioned the existence of such a Work tastefully selected & judiciously arranged would not be sufficient compensation for,

dear Sir, your obliged

S. T. Coleridge.

P.S. Might I request the favor of a single Line in answer?[36]

---

[36] *CL* v 197–200. The "Dignitary" was Gilbert Burnet, who wrote a eulogy of Leighton in *History of His Own Time* (1724) 134–9.

Murray wrote back to Coleridge encouragingly and evidently offered him a copy of Leighton's *Whole Works* (edited by George Jerment, 1820) to work from, since Coleridge wrote again on 26 January:

Your suggestion entirely coincides with my purpose. I waited indeed only to know that you did not decline it primâ facie—to have proposed the same myself. There is a Copy of Leighton's Works here; but it is not my own—nor would it be proper for me to use it as such. I will therefore embrace your offer of sending me your Copy—which I doubt not, I shall be able to send back with the passages marked, and with a sufficient numeration of the order in which I intend them to stand, and specimens of the Headings, to enable you to form a tolerably correct fore-judgement of the contents and appearance of the Volume.—A few inaccuracies and slovenly combinations, I think, may be silently corrected where they chance to interfere with the effect of a passage otherwise eminently interesting—and I had some thoughts of adjoining, as a sort of appendix, some short biographical and critical notice of that every way interesting class of Writers, before and immediately following Thomas à Kempis, whose works and labors were the powerful and most effective Pioneers of the Reformation—with some short specimens from the very rare Works of J. Tauler which were with difficulty procured for me in Germany last year—& which thoroughly bear out the high character, which I once heard Klopstock give of them—[37]

The fate of the "Beauties of Leighton" soon became caught up in a further proposal that John Murray should become the publisher of Coleridge's philosophical works, and a version of the *Logic* was apparently submitted to him. These initiatives resulted in disappointment, however. More than a year later, on 7 July 1823, Coleridge wrote to Charlotte Brent that he had been

. . . always at the West End of the Town—and mostly dancing attendance on a proud Bookseller, & I fear, to little purpose—weary enough of my existence, God knows! and yet not a tittle the more disposed to better it at the price of Apostasy or Suppression of the Truth.—If I could but once get off the two Works, on which I rely for the Proof that I have not lived in vain, and had these off my mind, I could then maintain myself well enough by writing for the purpose of what I got by it . . .[38]

Shortly afterwards he was to report puzzlement as to Murray's intentions concerning the acceptance of any of his works. As far as "The Beauties of Leighton" was concerned, he wrote to C. A. Tulk,

The case is this. On the Day, I dined with you, I had called in Albermarle Street with the Volumes of Archbishop Leighton's Works, with the several passages, I had considered as the characteristic Beauties of his Writings, marked in the side Margins, and my own Notes in the blank space at the top and bottom of the

---

[37] *CL* v 205. For title-page details of COPY C (the Jerment edition) see Abbreviations under Leighton.
[38] Ibid 280.

Page—and having waited an hour or so & the young Gentleman in attendance informing [me] that there was no chance of Mr Murray's coming for that day, I wrote a few lines stating the proposed title, and scheme of the little Volume, and intimated that I should call again on the Friday following at two o'clock. I did so. Bur Mr Murray was not at home to me; but had left a note, declining the publication on a ground, which he knew as well when the Proposal was first made by me & to a certain degree encouraged by him—namely, the existence of a Reprint of Leighton's Works—and entreated my Acceptance of the Copy, which he had sent me, for the purpose of selecting from it—[39]

Undeterred, Coleridge now submitted the planned volume to Taylor and Hessey. In a letter of 8 August 1823 he again set out his reasons for admiring Leighton and gave an account of the volume as he planned it:

Dear Sirs

I have the honor of agreeing with all the thinking Men, with whom I have conversed, in their objection to "Beauties" of this or that writer, taken as a *general* Rule. In the greater number of cases, these collections of striking and shewy passages without any connection given in lieu of that which had been destroyed is almost as injurious to the Original, as the taking out of the Lights of a Titian or a Correggio & presenting them apart from the Shades would be, considered as a specimen of the Picture. And it is in fact no less injurious to the Reader, and one of the most effective recipes for depraving his Taste and weakening his memory.—But if, as in all cases, there are any exceptions to this Rule, the Works of Archbishop Leighton form one of the strongest. I need not enlarge to *you* on the high and peculiar Merits of Leighton—on his persuasive and penetrating eloquence, or the fine Fancy and profound Reflection which seem trying to hide themselves in the earnest simplicity and if I may so express myself, in the cordiality and *conversing*ness of his style and manner. The point, on which I mainly rest as to my present purpose, is this: that from the nature and necessity of his principal work, (A commentary on the 1 Epistle of St Peter, Text by Text) the most important and valuable Lights of these precious Volumes present themselves to the Reader in a far more *un-* or rather *dis*-connected manner, than they would in the Work, I have in view: so much so indeed, that I was first led to take it in hand from the observations of several, to whom I had strongly recommended the original Volumes, that from the abrupt transitions from one subject to other and wholly different, and the continual interruptions of the thread of Interest as well as of Thought had prevented them, some from continuing the perusal, and more from reading him with the satisfaction, they would otherwise have received—.

Now the Volume, I have prepared, will be best described to you by the proposed Title—

Aids to Reflection: or Beauties and Characteristics of Archbishop Leighton, extracted from his various Writings, and arranged on a principle of connection under the three Heads, of 1. Philosophical and Miscellaneous. 2. Moral and Prudential. 3. Spiritual—with a Life of Leighton & a critique on his writings and opinions—with Notes throughout by the Editor.

[39] Ibid 282 (July 1823).

I have marked out all the passages intended for Extraction in my Copy of Leighton's Works—which, if you think the proposal worth attending to in the first instance, I would leave with you—tho' you are well aware, how much more favorable Impression the passages would make, arranged and in sequence, with the necessary additions, or completions, & the occasional substitutions of a word or phrase when the words in the original have acquired by association & change of fashion a mean or ludicrous sense. Will you do me the favor of letting me know your opinion either by my friend or by a Line addressed to me at Highgate?—In the mean time I remain,

> dear Sirs, | with sincere respect | Your obliged Servt.
>
> S. T. Coleridge

To
    Messrs. Taylor and Hesse

P.S. The volume, I should propose, would be a small pocket octavo (Fool's cap, I believe, they call the size, I mean) of about 300 pages: which, I can with truth aver, w[ill] contain the greater portion of all in the 4 thick miserably misprinted Volumes that is peculiarly and characteristically Leighton's Mind and Genius— & give to nine Readers out of ten a much truer, livelier, and more retainable Idea than they would form from their own reading of the Works themselves, even on the assumption that their patience held out so far.[40]

This letter seems to mark the point at which the final title for the work was adopted, since the previous letter quoted was still referring to "the characteristic Beauties" of Leighton's writings; two years later, moreover, looking back on the event, he remembered Murray as ". . . declining the publication of the proposed Life [& Be]auties of Arch-bishop Leighton".[41] The new title, indeed, may have been partly prompted by his own reference to the "fine Fancy and profound Reflection" that seemed to be "trying to hide themselves" in Leighton's other qualities. The reply from Taylor and Hessey was evidently swift and satisfactory, since by 16 August he was thanking them for it and giving a businesslike account of his plans. He also asked if they could procure works by Laud and Leighton for him:[42] the plan for a "Life of Leighton & a critique on his writings and opinions" was now uppermost in his mind. It was indeed to dominate his work during the later part of 1823. Another letter of the time (probably to a bookseller) makes a further request for works on Laud, Leighton, Burton, and others, along with Archbishop Spottiswood's *History of the Church and State of Scotland*.[43] By September 1823 he was writing to Hessey that he had collated "Spottis-

---

[40] Ibid 289–91.
[41] Ibid 438. Given his growing reservations about Paleyan theology, it is possible that the original title "The Beauties of Archbishop Leighton" was conceived partly as a response to that of W. Reid's selection *The Beauties of Paley* (1810).
[42] Ibid 294.
[43] Ibid 295.

wood, Heylin, Prynne, Wharton, Burnet, Hacket &c'',[44] and we know
that he borrowed from Sion College Library Gilbert Burnet's *Memoires*,
*The History of the Troubles and Tryal of . . . William Laud, Wrote by
himself*, *The Second Volume of the Remains of . . . William Laud* and
Charles Kirkpatrick Sharpe's edition, from manuscript, of James Kirk-
ton's *The Secret and True History of the Church of Scotland from the
Restoration to the year 1678*.[45] Evidence of work towards the "Life"
survives both in marginal comments on some of the relevant volumes
and in various manuscript drafts, particularly in the Egerton manuscripts
in the British Library.[46] Eventually the project of writing such an introductory life and critique was to be abandoned, but the work he did for it
was not without its effect on the final volume, where some of the historical instances cited seem to spring from his reading of these and related
works.

The scheme as first presented to Taylor and Hessey was a simple one,
designed to be realised in print by the end of the year. In the event the
volume did not appear until nearly two years later and on the way various changes took place. On occasion, as a result, type was left set up for
long periods. Sheets were normally printed off once the final proof-read-
ing was complete, moreover, and so put beyond the possibility of
change while Coleridge was writing the later part of the work. Although
no one could be blamed for this Coleridge felt a natural sense of frustra-
tion, which he expressed in the "Advertisement" he wrote as the work
finally went to press. Some features of the completed work, certainly,
cannot be understood unless we consider both the technical problems
that arose and the changes in Coleridge's conception of what he was
doing.

First Work for the 1825 Edition

Coleridge's first problem as he began to prepare copy for the printer was
that of producing large quantities of material which included long extracts from another writer. In his first letter to Murray he had pronounced
himself ready to transcribe everything but had also pointed out that "by
sacrificing one Copy of Leighton's works" the task could be accomplished more economically, since then only "references to Volume,
page and line" would be needed. Murray's gift of the 1820 edition of

---

[44] Ibid 300–1.
[45] In Sept: *CM (CC)* II xvi, *CN* IV
4990n.
[46] I.e. in MS Egerton 2801, part of the

miscellaneous collection sold by EHC to
the BM in the 1880s. See also e.g. *CL* v
299–301. Coleridge's work towards it will
form part of *SW&F (CC)*.

the *Whole Works* enabled him to carry out the latter plan; he did not at that time foresee the problems that would be created when proofs based on this edition were sent to Highgate, where he had only the differently paginated edition of the 1819 *Genuine Works* to check them against.

As he marked and annotated the copy of Leighton given him by Murray, the plan described to Taylor and Hessey in August was probably the one in his mind, since a list of references on the end flyleaf of volume IV includes, apart from those for "Life of Leighton", several for "P.", "M.", and "S": i.e. the sections 1–3 that he had detailed in his letter.[47] These could stand for the "Prudential", "Moral and Religious", and "Spiritual" sections of the final volume, but it seems more likely that they stood for the "Philosophical and Miscellaneous", "Moral and Prudential", and "Spiritual" of the earlier scheme: the one extract indicated by "P." seems marginally more fitted to "Philosophical and Miscellaneous", while one of those indicated by "M." was eventually included in the "Prudential" section of the 1825 edition; if that section had already existed in Coleridge's mind when he made the extract he could be expected to have written "P." rather than "M." at that point.

In pursuit of his plan to send the whole work as quickly as possible to Taylor and Hessey, Coleridge devoted a good deal of his time initially to the "Life of Leighton". On 16 August 1823 he wrote:

The Leighton may be put to the Press *immediately* if you please—I wish only to learn from you, what number of pages you would consider as the advisable limit, and what proportion the Life and Critique should make. Would 50 pages for this latter be too much—? Of course, it will be the elucidations from little known Writers of that age, and biographical sketches of the Men with whom Leighton was condemned to act, that will carry the Life to this extent—and it will therefore be no difficult, tho' from the beauty or curiosity of the quotations an unwilling, task to shorten it. But I should be much obliged to you, if you could procure for me the Loan of Archbishop Laud's Works, including his Diary or private Journal. And (from Williams's or the Dissenters' Library?) the Zion's Plea of Leighton's Father, with the small Tract containing the Detail of his Sufferings and those of his Companions, Burton &c.—I saw this latter once at Sir G. Beaumont's near Ashby de la Zouch—and a work of deeper interest I never read.—[48]

On 9 September he reported further progress on the "Life":

I find that my apology for the Life of Leighton—which I believe, whether from vanity or on good grounds to *deserve* as a yet more appropriate tho' less expedient Title that of—The first impartial and philosophical Account & Explanation of the Conflict between the Protestant Hierarchy (from Edward VI to the

[47] *CL* IV 290; cf note on Leighton COPY C IV ⁺1: *CM (CC)* III.　　[48] *CL* IV 294.

Revolution) and the Puritans of England with the Presbyterians in Scotland—which how especially it is the vital Center of the History of England might be presumed even from the unexampled interest felt by all ranks in the first Series of Sir Walter Scott's Novels—I find, I say (you must forgive my hasty *parentheses* in my letters, & I will take [care] that you shall find few to be forgiven in my future publications) that the Life &c will occupy a full half of the Volume—. I think it right to apprize you of this—that if you see any objection as to the saleability of the Book, it may be altered—which however can only be done by retaining only the abstract of the main events of Leighton's Life which, however, I could give only as an Abstract from the Lives prefixed to the several Editions of his Works, not worthy to be called even an Apology for a Life—or such an apology as the fragments of a dry Caterpillar Skin could be for the Life of the Butterfly.—

Now all my Materials are both ready, and arranged, save only a spot of terra incognita which I hope to colonize out of Woodrow's History of the Church—to which, but of far less Likelihood, I may add the *"Bibliographia Scoticana"*.—But the former I *must* have looked thro' before I dare publish my Life—well aware of the immense importance of the Advice given me in the inclosed Note from that worthy & enlightened man, the Revd. Joseph Hughes, the Secretary of the Brit. & For. Bible Society. In my laborious Collation of Spottiswood, Heylin, Prynne, Wharton, Burnet, Hacket &c I have had reason to congratulate myself on the having submitted to the Task.—Now Woodrow's Work (in two Volumes Folio) is, Mr Irving assures me, a common book in Scotland—and he was surprized at his disappointment in not being able to procure it for me from any of his Scottish Acquaintance and Church-members in London—Neither is it or the Bibliographia Scoticana, in Sion College or in Dr Williams's Library in Red Cross Street—. I should be much obliged to you to have it enquired whether it is in the London Institution Library—. I trust that it will, at all events, be in the British Museum, & have this morning written to Sir H. Davy to be admitted, as a Reader there—. If not, my last resource must be to procure it by Mr Irving's means from Scotland.—But should it be in any of the London Catalogues, and could be purchased for any tolerable price (for instance, not exceeding five guineas) I would gladly have the sum put to my Account—if the Loan of it for a fortnight could not be obtained—and so too (but with less anxiety) the Book entitled, Bibliographia Scoticana.—[49]

"I shall not go to the Sea side till I have the whole of the 'Aids to Reflection' ready for the Printer," he continued. This was over-optimistic, but his publishers were now convinced that the work was well advanced. On Thursday, 9 October, Hessey wrote to Taylor: "Mr Coleridge has been with me again today with his Title and Preface, and on Saturday the whole will be in my hands. It will be a delightful Book and will be sure to sell well."[50]

On the following Monday, 13 October, Coleridge was by the sea at Ramsgate, but only part of the work was by then with the publisher.

---

[49] Ibid 299–300. It is not clear when the planned "Life" was dropped.

[50] Edmund Blunden *Keats's Publisher* . . . (1936) 143.

That part of it had by then been delivered seems clear from a letter from Hessey to Taylor seven days later, which includes the statement "Here is also a second sheet of Mr Coleridge's book".[51] Coleridge must have received proofs quickly, also, since when he wrote to Hessey on 6 November he was insisting that he had been ". . . busily and anxiously employed" since their last meeting.[52] A week later he referred to a proof sheet that had been sent on to him at Ramsgate.[53]

The course of production cannot be determined with complete exactitude on present evidence but it seems clear that by early October Coleridge had left material with the printer taking the volume into the "Moral" section (however that section was further defined): that is, enough for about sixty-four pages or four signatures. There are various possibilities here: he might have left all that material, together with volumes I and IV of Leighton, with Hessey on 11 October (probably on his way to Ramsgate), or sent it to him then—or he might have left part of the material earlier and even perhaps have picked up a first signature at that meeting. At all events, it seems clear that he did not actually see a proof to study it until after his last call on Hessey (whether that was on 9 or 11 October). In the November letter he wrote:

As soon as I saw the Proof, I was struck with the apprehension of the disorderly and heterogeneous appearance which the Selections intermixed with my own comments &c would have—I had not calculated aright on the relative quantity of the one and the other—and the more I reflected, the more desirable it appeared to me to carry on the promise of the Title Page (*Aids* to reflection) systematically throughout the work—But little did I anticipate the time and trouble, that this *rifacciamento* would cost me—[54]

Later in the letter he also proposed a change in format:

I leave it to your better Judgement; but it strikes me, that by printing the Aphorisms *numerically* with interspace, as I have written them—thus—

Aphorism I

Then the title or heading of it, if any: and then the passage itself, would be so very much the best way, as to make it worth while—and instead of the (Leighton, Vol. I. p. —) at the *end*, simply to have an L. either thus

Aphorism V. L.

or before the first word of the aphorism, on the same line with it.

L. A reflecting mind &c—

and when it is not Leighton's, to put either E. (Editor's) or nothing.—

[51] *The Keats Circle* ed H. E. Rollins (Cambridge, Mass 1965) II 452.
[52] *CL* v 306.
[53] Ibid 308.
[54] Ibid 306.

In those Aphorisms in which part only is Leighton's, they might be marked L. E.

On the address sheet there also appeared a sketch for the same notation:

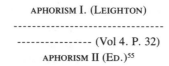

APHORISM I. (LEIGHTON)

---------------- (Vol 4. P. 32)

APHORISM II (ED.)[55]

If, as Earl Leslie Griggs suggests, this is in Hessey's handwriting, we may further surmise that the latter sketched this out as a way of dealing with Coleridge's suggestion and that subsequently (perhaps at the meeting on 11 November promised in Coleridge's letter) it was further modified to the final format, in which neither brackets nor page-references to Leighton appear.

From this letter it is clear that the division into aphorisms was a late innovation, the original submission having been at least partly in continuous prose, and that only after some consideration had Coleridge decided on a new method of arrangement, isolating the quotations into separate sections to be entitled "Aphorisms" and writing "Comments" on them where appropriate. With these he interspersed Aphorisms of his own.

The term "aphorism" deserves attention. As with "Beauties", the aphoristic method was one which he himself had sometimes criticised in the past: in *Biographia Literaria*, for example, he had attacked the popular philosophy introduced by "certain immethodological aphorising Eclectics".[56] Yet it could be seen to offer a convenient way of dealing with a writer such as Leighton, much of whose best work had been presented not systematically but in the course of commentary on another text. And if the length of the aphorisms in part of *Aids to Reflection* is startling to those who recall Pascal or La Rochefoucauld, they can find Coleridge's main justification—and no doubt his inspiration as well—in the work of Bacon, who had organised his *Novum Organum* into "Aphorismi", which, while not as long as the most extended discussions in *Aids to Reflection*, were often much longer than aphorisms of the normal kind.

The wisdom of adapting the mode throughout the work is nevertheless debatable; there are places, in the first section at least, where the reader who is willing to ignore the headings may find that various of the successive paragraphs read better as the continuous prose in which they

[55] Ibid 306–7.   [56] *BL* ch 12 *(CC)* i 292.

were originally written. The distinction between comment and aphorism is not always clear, moreover—particularly since aphorisms of Coleridge's are also, sometimes, followed by "Comments".

The fragments of manuscript (j) and (k) printed in Appendix B below throw further light on the original printing. A passage originally marked by the printer to appear on page "42" was eventually printed on page 37 of the first edition; a passage marked to begin signature "D" on page "49" appeared on page 42. This indication that the original proofs took up more pages is explained by a further piece of evidence,[57] a single page of proof surviving evidently from among those corrected by Coleridge at Ramsgate. While this used the same typeface it was set in a smaller format than that adopted for the 1825 edition. The decision to have more words on the page may have been taken to accommodate the changes now proposed by Coleridge.

Throughout this first proof, apparently, the extracts from Leighton were set in inverted commas, the reference to the 1820 edition being given at the end. The surviving portion opened in the middle of a passage later used for Aphorism 12 of the Prudential Aphorisms, on pages 45–6 of *AR* (1825): ". . . or hurried hither and thither . . .", and had at the end the reference: "LEIGHTON, vol. iv, p. 268".

Next came the passage "There is a settled friendship, nay, . . . to HIMSELF." with the reference: "Leighton, p. 274, 275". This is marked in the margin "Aph. 13"—which is where it is in *AR* (1825), on page 46. Then followed "And if we seriously consider this subject but a little", down to ". . . peaceable than . . ." (at which point the proof breaks off). In the proof this is deleted; in *AR* (1825) it appears on page 37 as Prudential Aphorism 8. Leighton's Latin and Greek footnotes, which had been reproduced in full by the printer, were marked for deletion in the proof and do not appear in *AR* (1825). On both pages the words "Aids to Reflection" appear as running heading, whereas in *AR* (1825) the words appear, in larger type, on the left-hand page only, the right hand carrying the name of the current section.

This proof contains further pieces of valuable information. The two pages are numbered 57 and 58; this evidence that at least four signatures had been printed off in October is further reinforced by a statement in Coleridge's letter of 4 November: "If it were feared, that there is too much matter—all the extracts from l. 2 of p. 52, viz. Aphorisms 12, 13, 14, 15, might be omitted." In point of fact these aphorisms did appear in 1825, on pages 45–8, again suggesting that problems of space were

---

[57] Reproduced as Illustration 5 to the present volume.

one reason for enlarging the format from the "pocket" size, originally proposed by Coleridge and used in the proof, to the size used in the edition as finally published. The proof confirms that the printer was taking text directly from Leighton, since the notes cancelled by Coleridge would not have been included in a transcription by him; its successive extracts in inverted commas also help to suggest why Coleridge was disturbed when he first saw the proof, his actual work on it witnessing to some of the shifting around which he undertook as a result.

Further light on the original state of the proofs is given by the appearance of page 2 in the 1825 edition, where the first paragraph of the passage from Leighton is included in inverted commas, repeated at the beginning of each line. Since this is the only occasion where this happens in the whole of the 1825 edition it may be supposed that a feature from the original printing was through an oversight perpetuated. As will be seen from the text of the present edition,[58] it was not changed in 1831.

We can also learn something of the original form of the copy from a number of the manuscripts for the early sections that are reproduced in Appendix B below. As it happens, none of these intermesh with extracts from Leighton's text; it seems likely that Coleridge indicated the latter by way of references on slips for the printer to work from, as he does on one or two manuscripts for later sections. They confirm, however, that Coleridge originally wrote much of his work in continuous prose; there is also evidence of some work towards the eventual numbering of the aphorisms once they had been so designated. In one case (BM MS Egerton 2801 f 165^v, App B (j) below) the successive paragraphs are numbered "7" and "8". In the final version paragraph 7 appears under the title Aphorism VII, but after this there appears as Aphorism VIII the paragraph noticed above as deleted from page "54" of the original proof sheet. The paragraph marked "8" in the manuscript then appears as a "Comment" to that aphorism. Some parts of the manuscript, then, already contained numbered paragraphs, thus providing an embryonic version of the aphorism form finally decided upon.

One final source of evidence concerning the copy as originally submitted and used by the printer may be mentioned. On page 22 of volume ɪ of Coleridge's 1820 Leighton a handwritten "F" and the number "65" appear in pencil in the gutter: the only occasion when such a mark is made in these volumes. The number evidently corresponds to the paging of *Aids to Reflection*; in the 1825 edition it marks the point where a line begins on page 64 and close examination suggests that that line has been

---

[58] See *Int Aph IV*, below.

brought up into the page at that point, the gap between that and the line above being rather narrow. "F", then, indicates the new signature (F) that was to begin with page 65.

The existence of this mark is significant for a further reason. In *AR* (1825) the extracts from Leighton which form the first two sections are all taken from volume IV of Leighton, while those which make up "Moral and Prudential Aphorisms" are all taken from volume I. While all these are marked for the printer at the places in question, none is given a number. The Aphorism that begins just before page 65, and in which the mark occurs, also signals a development in this respect: as well as being marked in pencil it is numbered in ink "M.5" (corresponding to its number in the 1825 edition). From then on all extracts are numbered in ink.

All this evidence would suggest that Coleridge's first submission to the publisher took the form of continuous prose of his own in manuscript, coupled with detailed references to the passages from Leighton which he wished to be printed. The printer set these up in proof down to the end of page 64, marked the place where he left off, and sent them back to Coleridge at Ramsgate together with volume IV of Leighton. Coleridge's next move would then be signalled by the following letter, sent probably just before the one of 6 November quoted earlier:

> Having an opportunity of trusting them to a young friend on whom I can rely for delivering them to your own hand, I have sent the more important MSS, in the first instance—while the books, corrected proofs, and all that belongs to the Work, the Essay on the Life, Character, & Times of Leighton not included, will be forwarded *per Coach* on Thursday Night—unless an old Highgate Neighbor should decide on returning to Town by the Saturday Morning's Steam-vessel, which I shall know before Thursday—
>
> You will then see the causes of my silence & in part at least, the rewards of the delay—.[59]

In the meantime, we may further suppose, Coleridge had not only altered the proofs that had been sent to him, but marked up volume I of Leighton for the remainder of the "Moral and Religious" Aphorisms, numbering them throughout. What went back to Hessey on 6 November, therefore, consisted of corrected proofs for signatures B to E (in the old format) accompanied by copy taking the work to the end of the Moral and Religious Aphorisms. The printer then revised the format of the volume into a larger page to accommodate Coleridge's extra material, ending signature E roughly where he had done before. The new copy

[59] *CL* v 305–6.

that was then set up provided as many sheets again, taking the volume up to page 128. In view of Coleridge's statement in the letter of 6 November that he would return "the conclusion of the last Division (Spiritual & Philosophical)" with the next proofs,[60] it might be supposed that he had included some of this section also with his copy; but this is by no means clear. The last sentence of "Moral and Religious Aphorisms" promises that an aphorism by Leighton will ". . . commence the Aphorisms relating to Spiritual Religion"; this statement does not square with the beginning of the next section, which is devoted to Henry More. Nor was the section called "Spiritual and Philosophical" when it was printed. It is possible, however, that the section entitled "Elements of Religious Philosophy, preliminary to the Aphorisms on Spiritual Religion", up to the break on page 139, was sent with the November packet of copy.[61] All such matters, however, are caught up in the question of further revisions that ensued. By now it was Coleridge's conception of the work as a whole that was causing his main problems.

COLERIDGE'S DEVELOPING CONCEPTION OF *Aids to Reflection*

From the first, Coleridge's changes were more than just a matter of improving typographical elegance. In his opening pages he had devoted a good deal of his discussion to the importance of language: he had emphasised the need to give attention to the exact derivations and meanings of words and had tried to suggest ways in which (as he put it in his preface) they were not "THINGS" but "LIVING POWERS". Once this was comprehended, even apparently commonplace expressions could be transformed into new lustre, while the act of reflection would cease to be regarded as a mechanical process and come to be appreciated for its illuminating power. Yet he felt the difficulty of conveying all this to the reader and seems to have feared that the adoption of continuous prose would encourage over-swift reading of sentences where the meaning was highly concentrated. The aphoristic method had the advantage that it held up specific statements as successive points of focus for the reader's meditation, making a superficial reading more difficult. He could again find justification in Bacon, who had praised the aphorising method in *The Advancement of Learning* on the grounds, first, that ". . . it tries the writer, whether he be light and superficial in his knowledge, or solid"; secondly, that ". . . as actions in common life are dispersed,

---

[60] Ibid 306.   [61] See above, pp lxi–lxii.

and not arranged in order, dispersed directions do best for them"; and thirdly, that aphorisms, ". . . representing only portions and as it were fragments of knowledge, invite others to contribute and add something in their turn".[62]

As has been noted above, the early work on the volume resulted in a change in the ordering of the contents, from the three sections proposed in August 1823: "1. Philosophical and Miscellaneous. 2. Moral and Prudential. 3. Spiritual", towards those of the volume as it finally appeared: Introductory Aphorisms; Prudential Aphorisms; Reflections respecting Morality; Moral and Religious Aphorisms; Elements of Religious Philosophy, preliminary to the Aphorisms on Spiritual Religion; Aphorisms on Spiritual Religion; Aphorisms on that which is indeed Spiritual Religion; and Conclusion.

The new ascent via "Introductory", "Prudential", and "Moral and Religious" led more naturally to the same, "Spiritual", section; the intervening "Reflections respecting Morality" and "Elements of Religious Philosophy" suggest a further attempt to convey a continuous overall argument, raising the reader's mind from the realm of the prudential to that of moral principle and so, via the inculcation of religious philosophy, to a true understanding of spiritual religion. In spite of this, however, Coleridge's method of compilation in these early sections became increasingly "mechanical" after the introductory aphorisms—at least in the sense that the extracts from Leighton's writing appeared in the same order as in the original.

Examination of the annotated volumes in the British Library elucidates Coleridge's method of working. He went through the volumes marking, and sometimes annotating, the chosen passages, and then produced further slips (some of which survive) to provide further comments and give instructions to the printer. The books and slips went together to the printing-house, where the sheets were then set up. The fact that the order of aphorisms in the early sections usually corresponds to the

---

[62] Bacon "De Augmentis" vi 2: *Works* ed J. Spedding et al (1860) iv 450–1 (cf 85). Reflecting on the history of the mode in a review of Arthur Helps *Thoughts in the Cloister and the Crowd* (1835) John Stuart Mill cited in addition to Bacon Thucydides, Aristotle, and Quintilian among classical writers and in later times Pascal, La Rochefoucauld, Burke, and Goethe. Although he discussed works by Coleridge he apparently overlooked the use of the term in *AR*: "Aphorism: Thoughts in the Cloister and the Crowd" (1837) *Collected Works* ed J. M. Robson and J. Stillinger (Toronto 1981–) i 419–29.

C's re-examination of the role of language (which, as will be mentioned later, was one of the most influential elements in *AR* for its early Victorian readers) is a central theme in ch 7 of Stephen Prickett's *Wordsworth and Coleridge: The Poetry of Growth* (Cambridge 1970) and in his *Romanticism and Religion* (Cambridge 1976).

order in which they appeared in the original may represent a concession to the needs of the compositor, who thus needed only to turn to the next passage each time, not to search out a new reference. Since the order was that provided by commentary on a biblical text, the sense of a developing discourse was here necessarily reduced, being sustained largely by Coleridge's own interspersed comments; in the "moral and religious" section these become rarer. When they do occur, however, they are often longer, keeping alive the sense of a continuing discussion.

In these discourses Coleridge's aim was to present Leighton's passages to a reader whom he conceived of as accepting the need for morality but not convinced of any necessary link between morality and religion. He was particularly concerned with the term "spirit", which was to figure centrally in the final section and to become the subject of a long discourse in "Moral and Religious Aphorisms" (after Aphorism VI).[63] Coleridge had long been disturbed not only by the rationalist movements of eighteenth-century theology—including Deism and Unitarianism—but by the more rational apologists for Anglicanism, such as Paley, who by their emphasis on "evidences" for religion seemed in danger of adopting a method of argument which, if pursued logically within terms set by human sense-experience, might lead the enquirer out of religion rather than into it. At the same time he was equally disturbed by writers such as Swift, Samuel Butler, and Warburton, who by their savage satire on those people (often members of small dissenting religious sects) who pretended to "Gifts of the Spirit" might discourage *any* sense of the working of the Spirit and so in the end undermine the basis of Christianity itself.

Coleridge's method of defence here is to go back to the basic nature of *being* in humans; it is of the essence of the Spirit, he contends, that it cannot be known directly by human consciousness. When the term "spirit" is used in the Bible, it tends to be qualified by reference to some particular moral gift: we hear of "the spirit of meekness", "the spirit of righteousness", and so on. The Bible does not speak of the Spirit directly in such contexts, because it cannot be known directly; its working through particular moral gifts, on the other hand, may be immediately experienced. And such workings are still a supernatural process, which should not be ignored in favour of rational proofs derived from the workings of nature. The mistake of those who claim special possession by the spirit lies not in what they are claiming (which may be true) but in their assurance that they can know directly what is in fact ultimately

---

[63] See *Mor Aph VI* (Comment), below.

unknowable, for it is revealed, if at all, only in the depths of the unconscious, at a level to which human rational enquiry can never penetrate. The human being who is convinced of the need for a moral basis to human life should not feel discouraged from exploring the possibility that such a spiritual element exists, but should approach that possibility with the humility called for by awareness that if it does it can never be known directly.

One of the few aphorisms in this section which is wholly Coleridge's, rather than Leighton's or a blend, stresses the need for such a humble spirit. After Leighton's assertion that "dubious questioning is a much better evidence, than that senseless deadness which most take for believing", Coleridge offers an injunction of his own: "Never be afraid to doubt, if only you have the disposition to believe, and doubt in order that you may end in believing the Truth", followed by an aphorism that was to become famous:

He, who begins by loving Christianity better than Truth, will proceed by loving his own Sect or Church better than Christianity, and end in loving himself better than all.[64]

This asseveration, which foreshadows a tradition in Victorian thinking summed up in Tennyson's

There lives more faith in honest doubt,
Believe me, than in half the creeds[65]

did not in Coleridge's thinking allow for the diverse paths into which later thinkers would be led by following such "honest doubt". On the contrary, it was germane to his position that anyone who followed his injunction was bound to reach the same conclusion as himself. As he was to put it in a subsequent discussion, "I assume a something, the proof of which no man can *give* to another, yet every man can *find* for himself. If any man assert, that he *can* not find it, I am *bound* to disbelieve him! I cannot do otherwise without unsettling the very foundations of my own moral Nature."[66]

In further support of his object in the present section, Coleridge draws on an analogy with natural phenomena. In his comment on Aphorism VI he compares the interaction between the air and the "vital energy" of the lungs in breathing to suggest the necessary relationship between human will and the moral universe, with which it must interact in order to produce good actions. This argument against moral self-sufficiency is

---

[64] *Mor Aph XXV*, below.
[65] Tennyson *In Memoriam* xcvi 11.
[66] "Elements of Religious Philosophy", *Prel Sp Aph*, below.

followed by another, drawn from even more basic principles of nature:
". . . in the World we see every where evidences of a Unity, which the
component parts are so far from explaining, that they necessarily pre-
suppose it as the cause and condition of their existing *as* those parts: or
even of their existing at all."[67]

A similar "antecedent Unity" is traced in the moral universe, a "One
universal Presence, a One present to all and in all" within the "great
Community of *Persons*".[68] The "one Life" idea is thus brought from
its quasi-pantheist status in *The Eolian Harp*[69] to a more orthodox version—which still suggests an essential benevolence in nature. Something of the same kind is to be found in an account, first written on the
pages of Leighton, of the moral qualities to be discerned in the various
gradations of being through nature: ". . . the filial and loyal Bee; the
home-building, wedded, and divorceless Swallow; and above all the
manifoldly intelligent Ant Tribes . . ." Who, asks Coleridge, could
look at these without perceiving ". . . the Shadow of approaching Humanity"? Each rank of creatures, moreover, "as it ascends in the scale
of Creation leaves death behind it or under it": the metal at the height
of its being crystallises into a semblance of vegetation, vegetation in its
blossom and flower seems impatient of the fixedness that differentiates
it from the butterfly that in other ways resembles it.[70]

At a swift first reading, this might well seem an evolutionary account
of the development of nature by which each ascending mode of living
creatures, emerging at a new stage in time, represents a closer approach
to man, with signs of a corresponding ascent towards the best in human
nature. Such a benevolent evolutionism (which indeed had a place in
pre-Darwinian thinking) was not, however, a part of Coleridge's purpose; indeed, for some years he had been attacking the ". . . absurd
notion . . . of Man's having progressed from an Ouran Outang state—
so contrary to all History, to all Religion, nay, to all Possibility . . ."[71]
(The last point no doubt had to do with contemporary acceptance of the
biblical time-scheme, which left little or no time for such a development.) Instead, Coleridge pictures the ascent through the scale of creation not as a process accomplished through development in time but as
inherent in the swift unfolding of the creation described in Genesis, in
the ". . . teeming Work-days of the Creator".[72] Coleridge was writing

[67] *Mor Aph VI* below at n 6.
[68] Ibid, remainder of paragraph.
[69] See below, *Int Aph IX* n 1.
[70] Annotation on Leighton COPY C II 52–
8: *CM (CC)* III. Cf *Mor Aph XXXVI* n 7 below.
[71] Letter to WW 30 May 1815: *CL* IV
574–5.
[72] *Mor Aph XXXVI* at n 7, below.

for a public still dominated by the idea of a guiding providence which had not only created all things but had also set here and there in the creation signs of the moral ascendancy that man was meant to achieve as the head of the scale. As a whole, the account becomes a comment on a single sentence of Leighton's: "It must be a higher good to make you happy." Coleridge uses arguments from analogy and from human experience to suggest the existence of an absolute ground behind all man's moral strivings, the readership to which he is addressing himself being, above all, that select group of individuals ". . . whose inward State, though disquieted by Doubts and oftener still perhaps by blank Misgivings, may, nevertheless, betoken the commencement of a Transition from a not irreligious Morality to a Spiritual Religion".[73] What that "Spiritual Religion" was like, would be, as he several times intimated, the concern of the final section, which was to be the crown of the work.

THE SPIRITUAL APHORISMS

As Coleridge considered the nature of spiritual experience the question that increasingly engaged his mind was that of redemption. The presupposition that sin could be followed quite simply by repentance and a turning to God, claiming a forgiveness already promised, seemed to him inadequate: it was certainly one which his own experience made questionable.

Coleridge's first plan for the Spiritual Aphorisms seems to have been that a discussion of the question of redemption on these lines (still drawing on extracts from Leighton and comments of his own) would have been followed by further quotations from and comments on passages in Leighton which described the nature of the spiritual life more generally. Traces of the work that had already been carried out for the section survive in the volumes of Leighton now in the British Library, where several extracts are marked out with the designation "Sp" or "Spir"; in some cases verbal alterations had already been made. Some other passages which are sidelined or marked off as aphorisms would no doubt have been considered for possible inclusion.

There are hardly any comments in the margins of these unused passages, but in one or two cases Coleridge has already heightened the imagery towards a grander effect. The most striking is the following, which in Leighton reads:

---

[73] Conclusion to *Mor Aph XX*, below.

No wonder, then, that the Apostle, having stirred up his Christian brethren, whatsoever be their estate in the world, to seek to be rich in those jewels of faith, and hope, and love, and spiritual joy, and then, considering that they travel amongst a world of thieves and robbers,—no wonder, I say, that he adds this, advises them to give those their jewels in custody, under God, to this trusty and watchful grace of godly fear . . .

Coleridge writes:

Substitute—Is a Man rich in the precious Gems of Faith, and Hope, and Love, and Spiritual Joy, all set in the virgin gold of Innocence—& dare we wonder, that he is admonished to appoint godly Fear, as the trusty Warden of the Jewel Office? Seeing too, that they are Crown-jewels given in pledge—& which the Sovereign of Heaven will redeem with eternal Bliss![74]

Despite the existence of such preliminary work, however, hardly any of the extracts chosen were to appear among the "Aphorisms on Spiritual Religion" in the volume as printed. Indeed, of the thirty aphorisms in those sections only eight were from Leighton at all, the rest being either from Coleridge's other favourite divines or his own.

To the reader of *Aids to Reflection* in the final form there may indeed appear to be something strange about the transition from the Moral and Religious section to the Spiritual one. At the end of the former, Coleridge concludes his remarks on redemption with the words "But the Reflections of our evangelical Author on this subject will appropriately commence the Aphorisms relating to Spiritual Religion."[75] When one turns the page, one finds a section, "Elements of Religious Philosophy, preliminary to the Aphorisms on Spiritual Religion", followed several pages later by another, entitled "Aphorisms on Spiritual Religion". These sections one might expect from the preceding comments to be the last (particularly since Coleridge has just invited the reader to "the third and last Division of the work"). The new section does not begin with the promised aphorism, however, but is ended abruptly after seven pages of text, to be followed by "Aphorisms on that which is indeed Spiritual Religion". This section, on the other hand, *does* begin with the aphorism on the subject of redemption that had been marked out of Leighton as "Spir. Aph. 1" (the only extract marked as a Spiritual Aphorism which is also numbered). It is reasonable to conclude that this aphorism was the one mentioned on page 127 and that between Coleridge's promise and his fulfilment of it on page 152 a change of his plans had taken place.

---

[74] Note on Leighton COPY C I 124–5: *CM* (*CC*) III.   [75] Conclusion to *Mor Aph L*, below.

The evidence from which the reasons for such a reworking can be inferred is somewhat difficult to disentangle. There were various practical problems, to be mentioned in a later section, which delayed his work. The event most likely to have affected Coleridge's thinking about the contents of his volume, however, was a visit from his son Derwent on his way from Cambridge, which took place on 25 or 26 January 1824. The account of his intellectual position that he gave his father alarmed him. Writing to Tulk on the 26th he exclaimed, "O what a Place of Poisons that University of Cambridge is—Atheism is quite the *Ton* among the Mathematical Geniuses, Root and Branch Infidelity!"[76] To George Skinner at Cambridge he wrote on 17 February that he had been ". . . more mortified by the shallowness than frightened by the profligacy and wickedness" of Derwent's creed, ascribing it to vanity and comparing it to the "sterile fluency" of a sand torrent, which looks and sounds like water to strangers at a distance;[77] a passage on the relationship between intellectual and moral beliefs that then followed was subsequently used for *Aids to Reflection*. By 24 February he had received a "comfortable Letter" from Derwent which he found reassuring[78] and two years later Derwent was to be ordained into the Church of England. The jolt that Coleridge had experienced, however, coming as it did in the wake of severe disappointments with Hartley, may well have given a further impulse to produce work which would be genuinely helpful to young men in need of intellectual guidance. For whatever reason, the spiritual aphorisms marked up in his copy of Leighton were discarded in favour of others more suitable for opening extended discussion of particular religious doctrines.

Coleridge was not without intellectual difficulties of his own, meanwhile. His original plan seems to have been that the passage from the Moral and Religious section to the Spiritual one would have involved a simple "through the looking-glass" transition. Whereas the former had been written for those who were ready to pass from a "not irreligious Morality" to a "Spiritual Religion",[79] they now would be addressed rather from the standpoint of one who had made that crossing. The crucial point concerning the transcendent nature of redemption would first be made with the aid of Leighton, whose eloquent passages on the blessings surrounding those who had passed into a spiritual religion would provide a fitting series of discourses to end the work. The putting together of the two elements was not altogether easy, however, since it

---

[76] *CL* v 327. DC had graduated with a pass degree on 24 Jan.
[77] Ibid 330–1.
[78] Letter to Skinner: ibid 340.
[79] Conclusion to *Mor Aph XX*, quoted earlier at n 73.

called for a reasoned account of the redemption—which was something Coleridge had always found it difficult to arrive at. As he put it in a note on Luther's *Table Talk*:

I will here record my experience. Ever when I meet with the doctrine of Regeneration and Faith and Free Grace simply announced—*"So it is"*—then I believe; my Heart leaps forth to welcome it. But as soon as an explanation or reason is added, such explanations, namely and reasonings as I have any where met with— then my Heart leaps back again, recoils—and I exclaim, Nay! Nay! but not *so*.[80]

His presentation of Leighton's thoughts involved him in a similar dilemma. Unless he were simply to present those thoughts straightforwardly and without comments, leaving them to work on the reader directly, he must offer explanations and reasonings. And he could not sidestep the issue of redemption, since it had been central to his original encounter with Leighton and its effect on his own religious attitude.

Coleridge himself left a clue to the growth of the last section when he referred to part of his comment on the second aphorism as having been ". . . the first marginal Note I had pencilled on Leighton's Pages, and thus (remotely, at least), the occasion of the present Work".[81] The reference seems to be to a long note in Gillman's copy, dealing with Leighton's development of the text "Elect, according to the foreknowledge of God the Father, through sanctification of the Spirit, unto obedience, and sprinkling of the blood of Jesus Christ."[82] Coleridge's note there sets out his already quoted conviction that the doctrines in question ". . . cannot be denied or explained away without removing (as the modern Unitarians) or (as the Arminians) unsettling and undermining the foundation of the Faith"; it goes on to acknowledge that they are, under certain presentations, morally offensive. Nevertheless he contends that to evolve a modified position, as the Arminians do, is of no service; rather it should be recognised that to draw out logical consequences of *any* kind is inappropriate in this case, since the truths in question ". . . are *transcendent*, and have their *evidence*, if any, *in* the *Ideas* themselves, and for the *Reason*". Such truths are not primarily addressed to the Intellect, ". . . but are substantiated *for us* by their correspondence to the wants, cravings, and interests, of the Moral Being, for which they were given, and without which they would be devoid of all meaning". Coleridge is reverting to his insistence on the difference in kind of such truths from those which can be mediated either by image

---

[80] Note of 25 Sept 1819 on Luther *Colloquia Mensalia* (1652) 226: *CM (CC)* III 752–3.

[81] *Sp Aph B II* n 22, below.

[82] Note on Leighton COPY B I 9–13: *CM (CC)* III.

("the seeking after which is *Superstition*") or sensation ("the watching for which is *Enthusiasm* and the conceit of its presence Fanatical Distemperature"). He concludes with a text that is central to one element in all that he is saying: "Do the will of the Father and ye shall *know* it."[83]

The doctrinal position set out in that note, which in *Aids to Reflection* is stated again in the paragraphs following the statement quoted, preserves the link with Leighton, who is seen as having reached a position of such assurance and as wisely dwelling on the spiritual and practical effects of the doctrines he is discussing rather than on the difficulties of treating them in logical terms. The discussion proceeds at some length, since Coleridge feels it to touch on other doctrines, such as that of the Trinity; he reverts to his exposition of his doctrine of the Ideas and concludes with a strong assertion that all things involved in "Faith" are "Derivatives from the practical, moral, and spiritual Nature and Being of Man".[84]

This emphasis on the practical is still more evident in the first of the Spiritual Aphorisms, which in Coleridge's first manuscript version was limited to a single sentence: "Where, if not in Christ, is the Power that can persuade a Sinner to return, that can *bring home a Heart to God?*" Coleridge here fashions a forceful rhetorical question out of what was in Leighton a more simple assertion: ". . . there is nothing but the power of Christ alone, that is able to effect this, to persuade a sinner to return, to bring home a heart to God"; he thus places the emphasis even more firmly on human insufficiency. Dwelling on the phrase "in Christ" (which is his and not in Leighton), he includes in its meaning "spiritual Truth", the knowledge of which ". . . is of necessity immediate and *intuitive*". But he insists that the will of man is also involved and attacks the modern Calvinism which ". . . represents a Will absolutely passive".[85]

Coleridge's dominant insistence on the fact of redemption here recalls the drama and directness of his original reaction to Leighton in 1814. And that in turn helps direct attention to the fact that his chief concern is with the nature of man's response. This is equally evident in his next annotations of Gillman's copy, where his various distinctions sometimes involve limited criticism. When Leighton writes, ". . . all evil actions come forth from the heart, which is there all one with the soul; and therefore this purifying begins there, *makes the tree good that the fruit*

---

[83] Ibid.
[84] Below, Conclusion to *Sp Aph B II*.
[85] *Sp Aph B I* at n 5, below.

may be good", Coleridge comments (perhaps picking up the organic metaphor): ''We must distinguish the Life and the Soul; tho' there is a certain Sense in which the Life may be called the Soul . . .'' and goes on to explore the relation between reason and spirit.[86] He also takes Leighton to task for not distinguishing between the kind of belief that is involved in the ''ordinary and scientific sense'' and the faith in the truth ''in Christ'': ''. . . belief is implied in faith; but faith is not necessarily implied in belief''.[87] When Leighton then begins discussing some biblical texts that include analogies with natural phenomena, Coleridge comes back to a favourite distinction of his:

. . . in order to secure a safe and Christian interpretation to these and numerous other passages of like phrase and import in the Old Testament it is of highest concernment that we should distinguish the Personëity or Spirit as the Source and principle of personality, from the person itself as the particular product at any one period and as that which cannot be evolved or sustained but by the Co-Agency of the System and circumstances in which the individuals are placed.[88]

The importance for him of this distinction between personality and ''personëity'' is further elucidated in another annotation on Gillman's copy:

. . . the main and most noticeable difference between Leighton and the modern Methodists is to be found in the uniform *Self*ishness of the latter Not do you wish to love God? Do you love your neighbour?—Do you think O how near and lovely must Christ be or but are you certain that Christ has saved you, that he died for *you*—you—you—you yourself on to the end of the Chapter—this is Wesleys *Doctrine*.[89]

Coleridge's point is that the emphasis on ''you yourself'' continually invokes conscious personality instead of calling on the deeper resources that lie in less self-conscious areas of the being. One of Leighton's virtues, in his eyes, had lain in his power to admonish and assuage at this deeper level. The doctrine of redemption was one that had always given Coleridge trouble—for while he suffered acutely at times from states of guilt, he could not always reconcile those states with the Christian scheme. On the one hand his rational powers objected to some of the implications of the doctrine of the atonement, on the other he found that his own attempts to rid himself of guilt by simple acts of will directed towards the Christian saviour were a disastrous failure. In Leighton he encountered something less hectic: a voice that spoke in simple authority

---

[86] Note on Leighton COPY B I 157: *CM (CC)* III.
[87] Note ibid 158: *CM (CC)* III.
[88] Note ibid 170: *CM (CC)* III.
[89] Note ibid III 204: *CM (CC)* III.

and to which he could attend without immediately finding himself caught up into mazes of critical thinking and personal self-doubt. That voice, speaking to personëity rather than to personality, had offered him a lifeline at a crucial moment.

The experience of those years, when he had had (in his own words) ". . . a new world opened to me, in the infinity of my own Spirit",[90] lies behind the "Aphorisms on Spiritual Religion". It gave him a sense of certainty about the doctrine of redemption and a confident authority in commending it to others. And so as the final section of the work unfolds the standpoint is indeed changed, but more subtly. The attempt to present Christianity from a reasonable point of view continues, but interinvolved with arguments of that kind is a form of persuasion based on Coleridge's confidence concerning what will be found in the actual experience of Christianity. When we hear now of "Aids" they are ". . . all the supernatural Aids vouchsafed and conditionally promised in the Christian Dispensation"; yet as soon as they have been mentioned Coleridge can insist from this new vantage-point that the human will has its part to play: ". . . not *by* the Will of man alone; but neither *without* the Will". He proceeds to develop the position which he had been formulating after his first encounter with Leighton, arguing for the free will of man ". . . however enslaved by sin he may be" rather than for its absence. His position he believes to have been that of Luther and Calvin alike: it is the later Calvinists such as Dr Williams and Jonathan Edwards who have failed to preserve the necessary distinction between a free will that is totally enslaved and a lack of any free will at all.[91]

For his second comment, the origins of which have already been discussed above, Coleridge chooses a passage from Leighton that includes a carefully worded mention of man's election: the doctrine of Election above all, he believes, illustrates his contention that one should not apply to the workings of God the processes of logic which are applicable to finite matters. As a doctrine derived from the moral being, it should be treated in moral terms. The individual needs to look for the marks of election in himself, not to speculate about the nature of election from God's point of view. Taken thus, the doctrine ". . . is in itself a necessary inference from an undeniable fact—necessary at least for all who hold that the best of men are what they are through the grace of God".[92] To take logical argument further is inappropriate and dangerous, just as it would be for a reasoner to deduce from the fact that God was eternal

---

[90] *CL* III 463–4, quoted above, p xlv.
[91] See below, *Sp Aph B I* at nn 5ff.
[92] See below, *Sp Aph B II* at n 36.

and immutable that the creation of the universe was impossible, or possible only through some special means.

In the course of this argument address to an audience slightly different from that supposed in the "Moral and Religious Aphorisms" is again apparent. "I suppose the person, with whom I am arguing, already so far a Believer, as to have convinced himself, both that a state of enduring Bliss is attainable under certain conditions; and that these conditions consist in his compliance with the directions given and rules prescribed in the Christian Scriptures."[93] At the same time he admits that for most believers not trained in the schools the justification for their beliefs will lie in doctrines they accept through their own experience, not through a process of reasoning. The rôle of reason, therefore, is ultimately a negative one: it is to determine that the doctrine does not contradict any universal principle. In the same way (as he points out in his comment on the third aphorism) that same faculty is bound to test whether the ideas presented to it have an ascertainable meaning; he gives an example of a possible statement, relating to the doctrine of transubstantiation, to which no meaning could be ascribed.[94]

A further step brings him to the assertion that whereas ancient philosophy could speak only to those who were already fit recipients of it, and so was a light only to itself, Christianity, by cleansing the heart, the moral nature, restores the intellect itself to its proper clarity. This leads him naturally to an aphorism of his own that calls for a child-like humility at the start of the search for truth, followed by a statement of the doctrines of Christianity which he believes to be peculiar to it. His argument from experience is then invoked as the leading idea. To the questions "How can I comprehend this?" and "How is this to be proved?" his answers are, respectively, "Christianity is not a Theory, or a Speculation; but a *Life*" and "TRY IT".[95] Above both sense and reason stands faith, which is in a position (in Leighton's words) to correct "the errors of natural Reason judging according to Sense".[96] But in order to understand the full implications of this statement and to prevent the twin evils of "ultra-fidianism" (as in Sir Thomas Browne's famous assertion that there were not impossibilities enough in religion for an active faith) and "minimi-fidianism" (which amounts to the picking and choosing of beliefs to suit the understanding of the believer) Coleridge finds it necessary to set out, once again, a distinction which has over the years become central to his moral thinking.[97]

---

[93] See below, *Sp Aph B II*, after n 30.
[94] See *Sp Aph B III* below, at nn 2–3.
[95] See below, *Sp Aph B VII* at n 26.
[96] See *Sp Aph B VIII* (Aphorism), below.
[97] See *Sp Aph B VIIIa* and *VIIIb*.

REASON AND UNDERSTANDING

The nature of the distinction between Reason and Understanding had by now been a subject of intense and continuing thought for about twenty years. Coleridge had discussed it as early as 1806 in reply to a query from Thomas Clarkson, aligning the terms with the Greek *noumena* and *phaenomena* and referring to the understanding as ". . . that Faculty of the Soul which apprehends and retains the mere notices of Experience".[98] All such notices, by contrast, as were "characterized by UNIVERSALITY and NECESSITY" were the work of the Reason. He had continued: "Reason is therefore most eminently the Revelation of an immortal soul, and it's best Synonime—it is the forma formans, which contains in itself the law of it's own conceptions." In this brief discussion Coleridge had stated the core of his distinction in a form which, as he must already have known, differed from Kant's by making reason explicitly ". . . the Revelation of an immortal soul". In *The Friend* three years later he made a threefold discrimination, distinguishing between sense, as comprising ". . . all that Man is in common with animals, in *kind* at least", understanding, as ". . . the faculty of thinking and forming *judgements* on the notices furnished by the Sense, according to certain rules existing in itself", and pure Reason as ". . . the power by which we become possessed of Principle . . . and of Ideas, (N.B. not images) as the ideas of a point, a line, a circle, in Mathematics; and of Justice, Holiness, Free-Will, &c. in Morals".[99] A year later, when he came to write down his Confession of Faith in a notebook, reason was being used in a more emphatically moral sense: "Reason, or a Law of Right and Wrong, which uniting with my sense of moral responsibility constitutes the voice of Conscience". This led him to the duty of believing in a God who was, correspondingly, ". . . a Being in whom Supreme Reason and a most holy Will are one with an infinite Power". By now he had come to complement his sense of the pure Reason by the moral demands of human nature: the doctrine of the Trinity, for instance, he believed to be ". . . a necessary *Idea* of my speculative Reason", but it acquired the "Reality" that made it a necessary object of belief only through the fact of man's redemption.[100]

Subsequent years saw Coleridge finding support for his sense of the distinction in earlier English writers. By the time that he composed the *Biographia*, he was drawing attention to the correspondence with his own position to be found in Raphael's lines to Adam in *Paradise Lost* describing how as the spirits of life are sublimed they

---

[98] *CL* II 1198.
[99] *Friend* 28 Sept 1809 *(CC)* II 104.
[100] *CN* III 4005 (3 Nov 1810).

> give both life and sense,
> Fancie and understanding, whence the Soule
> Reason receives, and reason is her being,
> Discursive, or Intuitive; discourse
> Is oftest yours, the latter most is ours,
> Differing but in degree, of kind the same.[101]

Milton's view of reason evidently seemed closer to his sense of its constitutive power than did that of Kant, who had carefully avoided any such conclusion: his own version of the distinction, he could now maintain, was ". . . encouraged and confirmed by the authority of our genuine divines, and philosophers, before the revolution".[102] Clearly, however, it was the Platonic sense of reason as an indwelling light that they supported rather than the equally important distinction between two powers, as advocated by Kant and himself.

It may have been the organic element in Milton's lines that drew Coleridge towards further speculation about the rôle of animal instinct in elucidating his distinction. When he took up residence at the house of James Gillman, this was evidently a theme of discussions with his host. In a letter to him late in 1816 he proposed to examine the implications of his thinking primarily in their relation to life, seen as at once individuation and universality.[103] (He was still, evidently, exploring the implications of his old formulation, "every Thing has a Life of it's own, & . . . we are all *one Life*".[104]) In a copy of *The Statesman's Manual* which he presented to Gillman (then or later), he drew attention to the twofold nature of reason and of understanding. At the "theoric or intellective" level reason was "The contemplation of *immediate* truths", whereas understanding was "The power of generalizing the motives of the Sense"; at the practical level Reason was "The power of determining the Will by Ideas, as *Ultimate* Ends", whereas understanding was "The faculty of selecting and adapting means to *proximate* ends—i.e. such *ends* as in their turn become means." In this second, practical sense, understanding was ". . . the same faculty as the intelligent *Instinct* in the Dog, Beaver, Elephant, Ant, &c"; it became human understanding ". . . by its co-existence in one and the same Subject with the Reason and the Free Will".[105] The point about instinct can be found developed further in the 1818 *Friend*, where he maintained that ". . . many animals possess a share of Understanding, perfectly distin-

---

[101] *PL* v 485–90.
[102] *BL* ch 10 *(CC)* I 173.
[103] Letter of 10 Nov 1816: *CL* IV 688–90.

[104] *CL* II 864.
[105] *SM (CC)* 60–1 (n 2). One of the annotations on this copy is dated 1830.

guishable from mere Instinct'', citing the intelligence of individual dogs, or, in a more general fashion, the maternal instincts of animals and the cell-building aptitudes of bees.[106]

Coleridge continued to work at the question. In his marginal annotations on Tennemann's *Geschichte der Philosophie* reason appears in its negative form as the source of Principles and in its positive as an indwelling light: "Gerson's & St Victore's Contemplation is in my System = *Positive* Reason, or R. in her own sphere as distinguished from the merely *formal* & Negative Reason, R. in the lower sphere of the Understanding. The + R. = Lux [Light]: − R. = Lumen a Luce [Illumination from the Light]."[107] In a letter to Tulk of February 1821, meanwhile, he differentiated three levels of the power corresponding to the understanding in human beings as it was manifested in animals: vital power, ". . . the power, by which *means are adapted* to proximate ends", instinct, "the power *which adapts* means to proximate ends", and understanding, "the power which adapts means to proximate ends according *to varying circumstances*". It is at the last level that animal and insect behaviour approaches more closely to human understanding: he adduces the behaviour of ants as recorded by Pierre Huber. This kind of behaviour, however, still differs from that by which human beings make inferences and deductions. That belongs to the sphere of reason.[108]

One further development, associated with the need to give a moral dimension to reason by associating it with the human will, is Coleridge's insistence that the understanding is also to be associated with St Paul's φϱόνημα σαϱκός, "the wisdom of the flesh". This was a point he made repeatedly in letters, notes, and marginalia, including several dated in 1819.[109] While reiterating the connection between understanding and animal powers, it brings out the negative implication of that link, for the understanding is here seen as akin to the serpent, which was "the most subtle of the beasts of the field" and which, according to Genesis, seduced mankind to sin.

The fuller range of his thinking about the understanding emerges in another discussion, to be found in the Opus Maximum manuscript. This makes clear the manner in which its status varies in his eyes: when "irradiated" by the reason it is enabled to operate in its noblest fashion; when it remains "unsubordinated", on the other hand, it is no more than servant of the flesh:

---

[106] *Friend (CC)* I 154–61.
[107] Annotation on Tennemann VIII [ii]: *CM (CC)* V.
[108] *CL* V 136–8.
[109] See below, *Sp Aph B Xb* n 31.

The reason & its objects are not things of reflection, association, or *discourse*; the latter word used as opposed to intuition, a use frequent & established in our elder writers, thus Milton "discursive or intuitive". Reason does not indeed necessarily exclude the finite, whether in time or in space, in figure or in number, because it includes them eminenter. Thus the prime mover of the material universe was affirmed in the elder philosophy to contain all motion as its cause, but not to be or suffer motion in itself. The reason is not the faculty of the finite. The faculty of the finite is that, which reducing the confused impressions of sense to its own essential forms, to quantity, quality, relation, & inclusively to the forms of action reaction, cause & effect, &c &c, thus raises the materials furnished by the senses & sensations into objects of reflection i.e. renders them capable of being reflected on, & thus makes experience possible. Without this faculty the man's representative power would be a delirium, a mere chaos & scudding-cloudage of shapes, and it is therefore most appropriately called the understanding or sub-stantiative faculty. Our elder metaphysicians down to Hobbes inclusively named it ⟨in its logical exercise⟩ likewise discourse, discursus discursio, from its mode of action as not staying at any one object, but running as it were from this to that to abstract, generalize, classify &c. Now when this faculty is employed in the service of the reason to bring out the necessary & universal truths contained in the infinite into distinct contemplation by means of the pure acts of the imagination ex. gr. in the production of the forms of space and time extracted from all corporeity or of the inherent forms of the understanding itself abstractly from the consideration of particulars—processes which constitute the science of geometry, numeral mathematics, universal logic, & pure metaphysics—in this case the discursive faculty becomes what our Shakspeare, with equal felicity & precision, entitles "discourse of reason".

It is evident then that the reason as the irradiative power of the understanding, and the representative of the infinite* i.e. the boundless, judges the understanding as the faculty of the finite, and cannot without grievous error be judged by it. When this is attempted, where the understanding in its synthesis with the personal will, usurps the supremacy of the reason, or affects to supersede the reason, it is then what St Paul calls φρονημα σαρκος the mind of the flesh σοφια του κοσμου τουτου the wisdom of this world &c. . . . The result then of this our third subdivision is: The reason is super-finite, and in this relation it hath for its antagonist the unsubordinated understanding, the φρονημα σαρκος, or MIND OF THE FLESH.[110]

* *Infinite*:–that is sine finibus, not having, or essentially incapable of having outlines; not bounded, or boundable from without. The reader must be on his guard not to substitute for this, the proper and scientific sense of infinite, the popular meaning of infinite, viz. what is immeasureably vast.

The interacting of these strands of thought is also to be found in the passages on Reason and Understanding in *Aids to Reflection*, the fullest of all Coleridge's discussions of the subject. In particular, he reproduces in full certain passages of Huber describing the extraordinary persistence of insects in working on towards the realisation of a plan, despite all

[110] *Op Max ms* B3 ("II") 9–12.

attempts by a human experimenter to disrupt the process. Such behaviour exhibits best the ". . . power which adapts means to proximate ends according *to various circumstances*", but even so, Coleridge again insists, it does not rise above ". . . the faculty judging according to sense". A schematic version of the distinction follows, in which the understanding is characterised as discursive and extra-referrent, being the faculty of reflection, whereas reason is seen as fixed and self-referrent, being the faculty of contemplation. Understanding involves three acts: attention, abstraction, and generalisation; the speculative reason, on the other hand, is to be defined either as ". . . the source of necessary and universal Principles, according to which the Notices of the Senses are either affirmed or denied" or as ". . . the Power by which we are enabled to draw from particular and contingent Appearances universal and necessary conclusions". In either case it is to be seen as different in kind from the Understanding.[111]

So far in this discussion Coleridge has omitted the positive side of the nature of Reason as an indwelling light. That affirmation is reserved for a long footnote, in which he contends that a truth can often emerge from the understanding only in the disguise of two contradictory conceptions, each of which is partially true. The reason, however, penetrates the contradiction and embraces the truth, which could not otherwise be comprehended. This reason is identified (in an adaptation of St John's formulation) as "The Light that lighteth every man's individual understanding".[112]

Coleridge remains aware that the common failure of human beings to make this distinction might be seen as an argument against its truth: if it is indeed universal, why are human beings so unprepared to accept its nature and working? The solution to the problem will lie partly in the moral dimension, still to be discussed, but he also believes that there is a more immediate answer, which lies in the nature of human upbringing. "In Wonder all Philosophy began"; if we take this so literally as to trace the roots of philosophy to the childhood sense of wonder we must recognise that such an origin is in one sense inimical to the interests of reason, since a human being's beliefs and convictions, rooted in so rich a soil, may come to be taken so much for granted that the mind is not properly prepared for the rational objections later to be encountered in a civilisation founded on the understanding. If the spontaneity of the original wonder has by then been frozen, that which might have borne the fruits

---

[111] *Sp Aph B VII* at n 30 to end of *VIIIb*, below.   [112] *Sp Aph B VIIIb* at n 66, below.

of true philosophy will be left barren. To counter this threat, the human being must be taught to assign such arguments to their proper sphere, that of the understanding, and grasp that the doctrines most importantly in question do not belong to it. Once their true nature comes to be seen (as the aphorism on which he is commenting asserts) the philosophy that began in wonder will end in an act of adoration.[113]

By now, the main points of the distinction between reason and understanding had been set out, but the further association of reason with the moral sense, which was to provide a central link with the forthcoming discussion of original sin, had hardly been mentioned. Before Coleridge could reach it, a gap occurred in his composition.

ORIGINAL SIN AND REDEMPTION

After Spiritual Aphorism IV, on wonder and philosophy, Coleridge had written not his customary "Comment" but "Thoughts Suggested by the Preceding Aphorism"; when he eventually came to write the comment itself he began by referring to an ". . . interim of depression and disqualification"[114] since the preceding pages had been composed, during which he heard to his pleasure that the Professor of Anatomy at the Royal College of Surgeons had adopted his distinction between reason and understanding for his opening lectures. The Professor was Coleridge's old friend Joseph Henry Green, who gave his first lectures from 30 March to 1 May 1824.

Up to this point, as we have seen, Coleridge had been deploying in succession his major arguments in defence of the Christian faith, culminating in the distinction between understanding and reason. The way was now at last clear for him to turn from that to original sin and redemption: yet he may have felt that the transition (despite his ability to identify the understanding with St Paul's "wisdom of the flesh") was not proving as easy as he had hoped, particularly since his distinction seemed to be carrying so little conviction among those to whom he had explained it. In such circumstances, Green's adoption of the distinction in his lectures would naturally have been greeted, as Coleridge put it, ". . . with a delight and an interest, that I might . . . call medicinal". To see his biological examples supported by a leading scientist in such a public setting was to feel that he was not labouring in vain. And the lectures enabled him now to produce further examples in illustration of his point that instinctive behaviour was the equivalent of "understand-

---

[113] *Sp Aph B IX* (Aphorism) below.　　　　[114] *Sp Aph B IX* at n 22, below.

ing" in human beings, understanding ". . . differing in *degree* from Instinct and *in kind* from Reason". Such a distinction, he reiterated, was important in removing obstacles to ". . . an intelligent Belief of the *peculiar* Doctrines of the Gospel".[115]

The most debatable of those doctrines was that of original sin, to which Coleridge now turned. His opening aphorism was a passage on the subject from Jeremy Taylor; for the first time in the volume, significantly, his succeeding comment raised questions instead of simply endorsing and developing the views expressed. He also found it necessary to draw attention to the need to develop, in appropriate circumstances, a negative use of reason: nothing, in other words, should be a matter of faith that was contrary to it. In the case of the doctrine of election he had been able to avoid such use by arguing that some of the more extreme traditional statements were forms of catachresis; but there were occasions, he believed, when it needed to be brought into service. As he had already put it in the 1818 edition of *The Friend*, Christian teachers must be ready to teach ". . . the articles of prevenient and auxiliary grace" and ". . . the necessity of being born again to the life from which our nature had become apostate", but ". . . they must not seek to make the mysteries of faith what the world calls *rational* by theories of original sin and redemption borrowed analogically from the imperfection of human law-courts and the coarse contrivances of state expedience".[116] In *The Friend* he had also criticised a passage from Jeremy Taylor concerning hereditary guilt which drew a questionable analogy with King David's displeasure at Michal's misconduct and his consequent decision not to spare her innocent sons.[117] A point he had made in less than a page there is now developed at considerable length.[118] The idea of hereditary guilt strikes him as repugnant to the moral sense: in human terms the judgment that because Adam, endowed with many virtues, sinned, his whole progeny should not only be deprived of his virtues, but also punished throughout eternity, can hardly be considered just. Coleridge himself avoids the need to make such a judgment by tracing the sources of sin not to an event in time but to a mystery out of time. Sin is eternal, not as having existed since an event that took place in the beginning of human history, but in a more absolute sense. Using reason in a similar way Coleridge then reproduces a passage from Field's *Of the Church* concerning the nature of Christ's atonement for the sins of man, on which he had written a similar criticism in a marginal note, here

---

[115] *Sp Aph B IX* at n 47, below.
[116] *Friend (CC)* I 432–3.

[117] Ibid 433–4 (on 2 Sam 21.8–9).
[118] *Sp Aph B X*.

expanded into a long disquisition.[119] Since the idea that Christ could atone for sins by reason of his own sinlessness is seen to be unjust within human terms it must be repugnant to the moral sense. To pay a debt of money for another can be regarded as making complete restitution, but for one person to substitute for another in atonement for a crime against humanity would not in the field of earthly conduct be acceptable. Such analogies, he concludes, are to be taken not as adequate descriptions of Christ's work but as affective metaphors, giving to humankind some indication of the largeness of the act involved, an act which—like the spirit—is incomprehensible in itself, comprehensible only in its effects. The important fact lies in the result of that work: a being is born again to spiritual life, so escaping the spiritual death which can (if allowed) work as an equally active principle of corruption.

At this point Coleridge seems once again to feel the need for further discussion and justification: a riddling paragraph[120] hints that in a more technical disquisition he would here develop a distinction between two kinds of will, linked to a discrimination between the absolute God who cannot be known by human beings and the God whom they can address as Father. He goes no further, however, declaring that to do so would take him not only beyond the purposes of his present book but also, probably, beyond the comprehension of most of his readers. Instead he turns back to Jeremy Taylor for eloquent assertions of the chief doctrines of Christianity, including a revealed faith that ". . . the Soul of Man does not die; that though things were ill here, yet to the good who usually feel most of the evils of this life, they should end in honor and advantages".[121] (Coleridge chooses a minimal statement of this doctrine that avoids any discussion of heaven and hell.)

Finally he broaches a question already adumbrated in his discussion: that of baptism, the ceremony by which the new life is to be transmitted to new members of the Church. He returns for the last time to Leighton, who in a comment on the preaching of John the Baptist dwells briefly on the relationship between baptism and preaching as a significant combination, ". . . the Word unfolding the Sacrament, and the Sacrament sealing the Word", and then goes on to speak of the light which informs both word and sacrament.[122]

The question of baptism had already been raised in the aphorism from Field,[123] which began with a reference to the Roman Catholic doctrine that sins committed after baptism were ". . . not so remitted for Christ's sake". Leighton's account is to be taken up as a safe guide to such ques-

---

[119] *Sp Aph B XIX.*
[120] Ibid at nn 79–83.
[121] See *Sp Aph B XXIII* below.

[122] See *Sp Aph B [XXIV]*, 1st paragraph.
[123] *Sp Aph B XIX*, 1st paragraph.

tions. Coleridge recalls an occasion when he had been asked for advice by a Baptist friend who had married a member of the Anglican Church. He had urged that baptism served two great purposes, responded to in the Anglican Church by the twofold practice of admission through infant baptism followed by confirmation at years of discretion—the importance of the second being witnessed to in the fact that it was to be undertaken only by a bishop. The Baptist practice answered to only one of those purposes; yet he could not believe that difference on a matter such as this warranted a step so drastic as schism from the main body of the Church. He concludes with a quotation from a work by William Wall followed by his own marginal comment on it, made in 1816. In a note he adds that he had intended to treat the question of the eucharist in the same way, but now plans to produce a small supplementary volume on that, together with the articles on faith and the philosophy of prayer. So end the Spiritual Aphorisms.

This might seem an abrupt way to conclude such an important series of discussions. Coleridge would no doubt have replied that he had now provided a series of "aids to reflection" which could be applied to most religious issues—whether or not discussed in his volume. And while the marginal note of his own with which he concludes the section may seem a little perfunctory, that is partly because it is printed in small type. The tribute to the Church of England as the ". . . *most* Apostolic Church" that forms its final sentence, employing as it does an organic metaphor whereby the Church's imperfections are viewed as spots in the sun which do not impede its virtue from reaching the crops beneath, could in one sense be seen as a majestic rounding off of his argument in the section as a whole. The small type in which it is printed may, in fact, have been no more than a printer's device to conserve space.

Any truncated effect in the final pages of the Spiritual Aphorisms is further compensated for by Coleridge's Conclusion. Here he turns to survey his own work as a whole and to look at possible objections—particularly to what might be thought of as its "mysticism". His views, he urges, are based upon an interpretation of the fourth Gospel which he challenges others to question. He then goes on to define his own attitude to mysticism in terms of his old paradigm which dismissed alike those, such as the Socinians, who worshipped "light" alone, and those, such as the Methodists, who worshipped "heat" alone. (He himself had looked for an ideal sun, uniting heat and light).[124] In the case of mysticism, those who worship the light alone are the enthusiastic mystics, such as Jakob Böhme (or, in a higher degree, Fénelon); those who wor-

[124] *CN* I 367, 1233.

ship the heat alone, who press their vision on everyone else, are the fanatics. The latter are not further identified at this point; instead, Coleridge presses home his argument that although individual mystics may be deluded the truths *behind* their assertions are not thereby compromised. Seeking the motives for the more sweeping charges that are levelled against such people, he finds them to lie in a disguised materialism—for so he is bound to describe the "corpuscular philosophy" current in the age. Against this he poses the emergence of a new and more hopeful "dynamic" philosophy, returning human beings to a sense of the wonder inherent in all organic processes, including those by which plants transmute air and water into grass or leaves—while oxen and elephants, by ". . . an Alchemy still more stupendous", change *these* products, indifferently, into "the pulpy Brain, or the solid Ivory". He points also to the Cartesian analysis of bodies and space, which in his view transforms the world into a ". . . lifeless Machine whirled about by the dust of its own Grinding", and contends that Kepler and Newton, by expelling the Cartesian vortices, made necessary the presupposition of an active power in the universe.[125] In their logic, however, this had simply engendered as a next step the assumption that God was both law and law-giver—so that the creator became a kind of *Anima mundi*: ". . . not only . . . a necessary but . . . a *necessitated* Being".[126] Such an inference prompts his celebrated attack on the idea of "evidences of Christianity"; instead of attempting to make such appeals to the understanding, it is necessary to rouse humanity to a sense of need, so that all that is left out of Christianity by such a scheme—the holiness of God, the divine hatred of sin—will be appreciated once more. And it is on *this* ground, he once again insists, that he finds himself forced (despite admiration for his achievement) to object so strenuously to the teachings of William Paley. Finally he rounds on the unthinking among his readers, urging them to use their intellectual powers in an effort to grasp truths which may otherwise seem too arcane for them. Once again in this volume—and for the last time—assertion and affirmation are supplemented by the call for an open-minded, heuristic approach.

THE QUESTION OF REFLECTION

The Conclusion, particularly Coleridge's attempts to place mystics and fanatics in relation to the truth by his parable of the travellers who per-

---

[125] *Conc* at nn 36–71.   [126] *Conc* at nn 82–3.

ceive a visionary landscape, but without the equipment necessary to appreciate its true nature, exhibits a complexity which inheres in *Aids to Reflection* as a whole and which is neatly encapsulated within the keyword of its title. In its more straightforward sense "reflection" is one of the commonest words in eighteenth-century thought. For some readers, particularly in France, the word had acquired an adverse colouring from Rousseau, who had written ". . . allowing that Nature intended we should always enjoy good health, I dare almost affirm that a State of Reflection is a State against nature, and that the man who meditates is a depraved Animal."[127] From the first Coleridge's use involved an implicit rejection of such claims and a development of the positive valuation that had been inherent in the English moral tradition. In 1793 he had praised Mary Evans for possessing ". . . a mind acute by Nature, and strengthened by habits of Reflection"; in the Allegoric Vision that formed part of his 1795 Lectures on Revealed Religion, the ideal figure of Religion appeared as one whose countenance ". . . displayed deep Reflection animated by ardent Feelings".[128] The value of the word, as is evident even in these early examples, was that it could be used both as an abstract word to describe a mental process and as an image invoking metaphors of religious and moral illumination. This double sense, which can be traced in Plato, Plotinus, Proclus, and Aquinas,[129] had passed into the writings of their English admirers. In Butler's *Sermons at the Rolls Chapel*, for instance (which he praised to Hazlitt in 1798),[130] Coleridge would have found the following:

There is a Principle of Reflection in Men, by which they distinguish between, approve, and disapprove their own Actions. We are plainly constituted such sort of Creatures as to reflect upon our own Nature. . . . This Principle in Man, by which he approves or disapproves his Heart, Temper, and Actions, is Conscience . . .[131]

If he also read John Norris's *Theory of the Ideal World* he would have come across a passage still closer to the position to be developed in his early sections:

[127] J.-J. Rousseau *Discours . . . de l'Inégalité* (1750–4) tr as *A Discourse upon the Origin and Foundation of the Inequality among Mankind* (1768) 27.

[128] *CL* I 51, *Lects 1795 (CC)* 91.

[129] In an unpublished paper for the Modern Languages Association "Reflection in Locke and Coleridge" (1986), to which I am indebted at this point, Robert Griffin draws attention to the imagery of bending back in the original etymology of "reflec-

tion" and traces the history of the word in earlier philosophy, citing Plato *Republic* 518c, *Timaeus* 37A and 77B–C, Plotinus *Ennead* 5.3.1, Proclus *Elements of Theology* prop 168, and Aquinas *Summa Theologica* 1.85.2.

[130] "My First Acquaintance with Poets" *H Works* XVII 113.

[131] Joseph Butler *Fifteen Sermons Preached at the Rolls Chapel* (1726) 13–14.

. . . there is but here and there a Man that *reflects*, that turns himself to himself, and carefully and attentively observes what's doing in his own Mind, and considers the various workings of that intellectual Principle which is the Dignity and Excellency of his Nature, that sets him above the Beasts, and but little lower than the Angels. This is but dry Entertainment to the generality even of studious and curious Men, they would rather study Books than Things, and any thing rather than their own Minds, by which means it comes to pass that when they know almost every thing besides, they live in a deep ignorance of themselves, like those that have travell'd most parts of the World, and yet are Strangers to their own Country.

Norris also spoke of the existence of the "Intelligible . . . World", wherein ". . . the Allwise and Almighty God, as in a fair intelligible Mirrour contemplated the Natural World before he made it. . . ."[132] Such language connects naturally to Coleridge's preoccupation with the phenomena of physical reflection, as in *Frost at Midnight*, where

> . . . lakes, and sandy shores, beneath the crags
> Of ancient mountain

and clouds, ". . . Which image in their bulk both lakes and shores | And mountain crags", set up a complex interplay of reflections and imagings; these are presented by the poet as a part of

> The lovely shapes and sounds intelligible
> Of that eternal language, which thy God utters . . .[133]

By 1801 he was describing natural reflections in his notebooks. On one occasion in 1802 he studied the reactions of Hartley when presented with the reflection of a landscape in a looking-glass and then, in the evening, analysed minutely the effect of seeing the interior of the room in which he was working reflected on the window and at the same time superimposed upon the nightscape beyond. In 1803 he asked himself (vainly, as it turned out), "The Soul within the Body, can I in any way compare this to the Reflection of the Fire seen thro' my window on the solid Wall, seeming of course within the solid wall, as deep within as the distance of the Fire from the Wall?"[134]

At one level, these observations formed part of a continuing dialogue with Wordsworth, who gives various kinds of visual reflection an important role in his poetry, including the remembered image of Peele Castle, steadfast in the water through many summer days, and memories

---

[132] John Norris *An Essay Towards the Theory of the Ideal or Intelligible World* (1701–4) II 121–2; I 26.

[133] *PW* (EHC) I 242.
[134] *CN* I 923, 1737.

from his youth of the experience of skating "across the image of a star",
or, most important of all, of occasions when a reflected scene,

> With all its solemn imagery, its rocks,
> Its woods, and that uncertain Heaven, receiv'd
> Into the bosom of the steady Lake

would "enter unawares into his mind".[135] Wordsworth, too, was fascinated by the possibilities of finding psychological analogies in the power
of reflection to merge together and reconcile two different sets of imagery. Coleridge, however, could pursue the implications further, into
philosophy, since they provided an instrument with which to turn
Locke's arguments against his own conclusions. In 1801 he drew attention to the latter's definition of "Ideas of Reflection" as ". . . those,
which the mind gets by reflecting on it's own operations within itself".[136] If the mind had such a power it might well provide a means of
approach to the innate ideas that Locke had tried to banish from philosophy.

By this time he may also have been familiar with the crucial rôle assigned by Herder to "reflection" [*Reflexion*] in the evolution of language among human beings as establishing their difference from the
beasts:

Man manifests reflection when the force of his soul acts in such freedom that, in
the vast ocean of sensations which permeates it through all the channels of the
senses, it can, if I may say so, single out one wave, arrest it, concentrate its
attention on it, and be conscious of being attentive. He manifests reflection
when, confronted with the vast hovering dream of images which pass by his
senses he can collect himself into a moment of wakefulness and dwell at will on
one image, can observe it clearly and more calmly, and can select in it distinguishing marks for himself so that he will know that this object is this and not
another.[137]

Whether or not he knew this passage, in 1806 he set out a division
among animated beings more subtle than Herder's, making three
classes: "those . . . whose consciousness exists in higher minds",
"those who are conscious of *a* continuousness, but . . . are not endued

[135] "Eleglac Stanzas" *WPW* IV 258–6; *Prelude* (1959) 1805 vn I 477, v 410–13. The 1850 vn reads "reflex of a star".

[136] Letter to Wedgwood 18 Feb 1801: *CL* II 680, citing Locke's *Essay on the Human Understanding* II ch i 4.

[137] J. G. Herder *Abhandlung über den Ursprung der Sprache* (1772) tr J. H. Moran and A. Gode (New York 1966) 115–16. For C's general knowledge of Herder see *CM (CC)* II 1048–9; cf also *Prel Sp Aph* n 7 below. Ernst Cassirer links Herder's "reflection" here to Leibniz's "apperception" and Kant's "synthesis of recognition": *The Philosophy of Symbolic Forms* (New Haven, Conn 1953) I 152–3.

with reflex Faculties'', and those who, ''. . . tho' not conscious of the whole of their continuousness, are yet both conscious of *a* continuousness, & make that the object of a reflex consciousness''. He continued:

> And of this third Class the Species are infinite; and the first or lowest, as far as we know, is Man, or the human Soul. For Reflexion seems the first approach to, & shadow of, the divine Permanency; the first effort of divine working in us to bind the Past and Future with the Present, and thereby to let in upon us some faint glimmering of that State in which Past, Present, and Future are co-adunated in the adorable I AM.[138]

This is one of Coleridge's most revealing accounts of what he meant by reflection and what he hoped for from it, containing ideas which continued to work in his mind. In a note of the following year, the concept of reflection was developed through a memory of the sun seen apparently suspended in a Mediterranean sky:

> The Sky, o rather say, the Æther, at Malta, with the Sun apparently suspended in it, the Eye seeming to pierce beyond, & as it were, behind it—and below the ætherial Sea, so blue, so ⟨a⟩ zerflossenes Eins, the substantial Image, and fixed real Reflection, of the Sky—O I could annihilate in a deep moment all possibility of the needlepoint pinshead System of the *Atomists* by one submissive Gaze! Λογος ab *Ente*—at once the ~~essential~~ existent Reflexion, and the Reflex Act—at once actual and real—therefore, filiation not creation/ Thought *formed not fixed*—the molten *Being* never cooled into a *Thing*, tho' begotten into the vast adequate Thought. Est, Idea, Ideatio—*Id*—inde, ноc et *illud*. Idea—*atio*, seu *actio* = Id: iterum, ⟨Hoc + Id, & then⟩ Id + Ea (i.e. Coadunatio Individui cum Universo per Amorem) = Idea: Idea + actio = Ideatio, seu αγιον πνευμα, which being transelemented into we are mystically united with the *Am*—Ειμι—.[139]

Here again, reflection is closely associated with the nature of Being, the relation of sky and sea being so intimately interwoven as to be like the relationship between parent and child, ''filiation not creation'': as a result reflection becomes a key to an understanding of the nature of the Word, or Logos.

In the years that followed natural imagery would be used more warily, but the central valuation of reflection would remain. As he first developed his ideas in *The Friend*, for instance, it came in to help his chief argument there. Early in the 1809 edition he spoke of some of the problems involved in knowledge:

> Conclusions drawn from facts which subsist in perpetual flux, without definite

---

[138] Letter to Clarkson 13 Oct 1806: *CL* II 1197.

[139] *CN* II 3159 (var). For explanations of the German, Latin, and Greek terms see *CN* II 3159n.

place or fixed quantity, must always be liable to plausible objections, nay, often to unanswerable difficulties; and yet having their foundation in uncorrupted feeling are assented to by mankind at large, and in all ages, as undoubted truths.[140]

In revising the work for the 1812 edition he added a further point:

Such are all those facts, the knowledge of which is not received from the senses, but must be acquired by reflection; and the existence of which we can prove to others, only as far as we can prevail on them to *go into themselves* and make their own minds the Object of their stedfast attention.[141]

Neither passage was taken into the 1818 *Friend*, but in the meantime he had dwelt further on the general questions involved. Human beings were increasingly learning to think critically, whether or not this was desirable, and the result of trying to prevent such developments would simply be to foster the wrong uses of reflection. It was a mistake to think that the ''Peace of Nations'' could be re-established by excluding the people from knowledge: ''O! never, never! Reflections and stirrings of mind, with all their restlessness, and all the errors that result from their imperfection, from the *Too much*, because *Too little*, are come into the world.''[142] On the contrary, reflection was something to be encouraged for its own sake. In a letter of 1814, he had claimed that he could stand against any of his contemporaries for ''. . . usefulness in the excitement of reflection, and the diffusion of original or forgotten, yet necessary and important truths and knowledge'';[143] and in an annotation on an Appendix to *The Statesman's Manual*, claiming that its object was ''. . . to fix the true meaning of the Terms, Reason, Understanding, Sense'', he wrote of it as

. . . a string of Hints and Materials for Reflection/ The Object too was ⟨to⟩ rouse and stimulate the mind—to set the reader a thinking—and at least to obtain entrance for the question, whether the ⟨truth of the⟩ Opinions in fashion is quite so certain as he had hitherto taken for granted—rather than to establish the contrary by a connected chain of proofs and arguments.[144]

The necessary distinction had been pursued through *Biographia Literaria*, where recollection of his early presentiment that ''. . . all the products of the mere *reflective* faculty partook of DEATH''[145] is followed

---

[140] *Friend (CC)* II 6–7.
[141] Ibid II 7n. For an application to the idea of Self of his doctrine that ''nothing can become an object of consciousness but by reflection, not even the things of perception'' see *Op Max ms* B2 (''III'') 49ff, quoted Elinor S. Shaffer ''Iago's Malignity Motivated'' *Shakespeare Quarterly* (1968) XIX 197.
[142] *SM (CC)* 39.
[143] Letter to Wade 3–4 May 1814: *CL* III 487.
[144] *SM (CC)* 114n.
[145] *BL* ch 9 *(CC)* I 152.

later by the assertion that pure philosophy must be referred to as the "transcendental philosophy" to distinguish it

> . . . both from mere reflection and *re*-presentation on the one hand, and on the other from those flights of lawless speculation which abandoned by *all* distinct consciousness, because transgressing the bounds and purposes of our intellectual faculties, are justly condemned, as *transcendent*.[146]

The emphasis is on "mere". The *true* activity of "reflection", on the other hand, is presented in a lecture of 1818, in which he argues that Art begins where there is a "congruity of the animal impression with the reflective Powers of the mind". In true art, "the *essence* must be mastered—the natura naturans, & this presupposes *a bond* between *Nature* in this higher sense and the soul of Man—" Within Nature acting on her own, by contrast, "there is no reflex act—but the same powers without reflection, and consequently without Morality".[147]

In the *Biographia Literaria*, again, there occurs the well-known assertion that ". . . the best part of human language, properly so called, is derived from reflection on the acts of the mind itself", and Kant's method is located as commencing ". . . at the point of reflection"[148]— a method to which Coleridge himself resorts in the *Logic*, when he comes to explore the discursive powers of the mind. "It was . . . determined," he writes there, "that we should confine our inquisition, to the data presented to us by *reflection*, and *as* they appear to us in the act of reflecting."[149] Reflection is here used in its more technical sense, and always associated with the understanding; but there is a clear presumption that such work is preparatory to that which will lead towards the truths revealed by intuition. The further depth inherent in the word is hinted at in his reference to Leighton's "fine Fancy and profound Reflection";[150] it emerges explicitly in the ninth aphorism of the volume, in which Coleridge writes of life as the "one universal soul" that is common to all organised bodies, but then asserts that human beings, by contrast, are inhabited by a soul "having its life in itself", as expressed in the biblical text "And man became a living soul". To perceive the existence of this "*proper being*", this "*house not built with hands*",

> Nothing is wanted but the eye, which is the light of this house, the light which is the eye of this soul. This *seeing* light, this enlightening eye, is Reflection. It

---

[146] Ibid ch 12 i 237.
[147] *Lects 1808–1819 (CC)* ii 220–1 (from *CN* iii 4397).
[148] *BL* ch 17 *(CC)* ii 54; ch 9 i 154.
[149] *Logic (CC)* 245. Cf his critique of the *Naturphilosophen* for not recognising the need of this discipline: annotation on Herder *Kalligone, CM (CC)* ii 1066–7.
[150] See above, p lvi.

is more, indeed, than is ordinarily meant by that word; but it is what a *Christian* ought to mean by it, and to know too, whence it first came, and still continues to come—of what light even this light is *but* a reflection. This, too, is THOUGHT . . .[151]

The imagery here continues a central strain that had been more common in the early notebooks, taking up the imagery from Plotinus which was echoed in John Smith's ". . . as the Eye cannot behold the Sun . . . unless it be *Sunlike* . . . so neither can the Soul of man behold God . . . unless it be *Godlike* . . ."[152] The ideal state, the issuing forth from the soul of

> A Light, a Glory, and a luminous Cloud
> Enveloping the Earth!

which he had envisaged for Sara Hutchinson in the first version of *Dejection: an Ode*,[153] had seemed to him to have been embodied in some of the supreme experiences described by Wordsworth in *The Prelude*:

> . . . moments awful,
> Now in thy inner life, and now abroad,
> When power streamed from thee, and thy soul received
> The light reflected, as a light bestowed . . .[154]

The peculiar sense of interfusion in nature that resulted from such a state, an intuition of permanent illumination in the midst of flux, was one which would continue to preoccupy him, particularly when he noticed images appropriate to it within the phenomena of nature herself. In a notebook of 1802, for example, he wrote: "Quiet stream, with all its eddies, & the moonlight playing in them, quiet as if they were Ideas in the divine Mind anterior to the Creation—".[155] As late as 1828, three years after *Aids to Reflection*, some lines in *The Picture* describing how the waves in the stream dart off and reunite to "join | In deep embrace" were altered to read:

> And see! they meet,
> Each in the other lost and found: and see
> Placeless, as spirits, one soft water-sun
> Throbbing within them, heart at once and eye![156]

This presence of the image-making poet in the thinker is further to be traced in Coleridge's favourite image of the sun caught in a fountain, which he used both for the achievement of a good man and for the

---

[151] See *Int Aph IX*, below.
[152] John Smith *Select Discourses* (1660) 2, cited *CN* II 2164.
[153] *CL* II 798.
[154] *PW* (EHC) I 404–5.
[155] *CN* I 1154 (var).
[156] *PW* (EHC) I 373.

Church itself.[157] The "fontal light" of an idea was an image still being used in the year before his death.[158]

Coleridge's sense of the need to be responsive to the ". . . master light of all our seeing" (Wordsworth's phrase in the Immortality Ode) had been developed in *The Friend*. In all cases where the "master-light" is missing, ". . . the reflective mind avoids Scylla only to lose itself on Charybdis"; ". . . that grand prerogative of our nature, A HUNGRING AND THIRSTING AFTER TRUTH", is after truth ". . . that must be found within us before it can be *intelligibly* reflected back on the mind from without, . . . the master-light . . . recommended by whatever is of highest authority with the venerators of the ancient, and the adherents of modern philosophy".[159] In *Aids to Reflection* it finally comes into its own. Sun-imagery is used explicitly in Introductory Aphorism XXIX: "Awakened by the cock-crow (a sermon, a calamity, a sick bed, or a providential escape), the Christian pilgrim sets out in the morning twilight, while yet the truth . . . is below the horizon", the further subtlety involved in the idea of an inward sun, to which reflection needs to become exposed, having been exhibited eight pages before, in Aphorism XX, where Coleridge writes, of the sublime ". . . intention to form the human mind anew after the DIVINE IMAGE", "The very intention, if it be sincere, is a ray of its dawning."

Coleridge's most detailed and intricate account of the operation of reflection as the "irradiative power" of reason has already been quoted in the previous section from the "Opus Maximum" manuscripts; his conception of the manner in which reflection may act as a guide to the recognition of religious truth is set out in a note made two years later:

27 Oct 1827 Ramsgate.

When the Ideas rise up within me as independent growths of my Spirit, and I then turn to the Epistles of Paul and John, and to the Gospel of the latter, these seem a looking-glass to me in which I recognize the same truths as the reflected Images of my Ideas . . .[160]

PROBLEMS OF COMPOSITION, 1823–1825

While the reasons for Coleridge's delay in completing *Aids to Reflection* after his first submissions of copy were ultimately intellectual, the work, he said, "growing and new-forming itself" under his hand as he thought

---

[157] *Friend (CC)* I 103; *C&S (CC)* 55, 214.

[158] *TT* 15 May 1833 *(CC)* I 384 (1836 vn II 229); see also N 36 f 74ᵛ and e.g. *Op Max*

[159] *Friend (CC)* I 468, 495.

[160] See above at n 110; the ms note of 1827 is also in VCL.

ms B2 ("III") 48.

further about some of the issues it raised,[161] he was also dogged by practical difficulties. The proofs from the early submissions were not returned very promptly to the publisher. The removal of the Gillmans from one house to another in November disrupted his facilities for study, an accident which incapacitated Mrs Gillman for a time in December distressed him considerably, and a "forge-hammer" sound in his ear which began just afterwards was still troubling him, though decreasingly, in January.[162] (The appearance from another publisher of a volume of selections from Leighton apparently similar to the one he himself was compiling had earlier caused anxiety until he laid hands on a copy and found it to be very different.[163]) After describing Mrs Gillman's accident and his malady in a letter to Hessey apologising for the delay in returning proofs and promising new material, he continued:

And the attempt to look out or compare any thing in the mechanical part of the work (for instance, the finding out the places in Mr G's Edition of Leighton, corresponding to those in my own) has a worse effect than writing itself—. I must therefore intreat you to go on with the printing—. With the inclosed (and the *numbers*, & names of the Pages, &c for the remainder of the Spiritual Aphorisms, which you will have on Monday, there being nothing more to be composed) you will have matter enough for some three weeks at least—. And tho' it grieves me that I cannot send you the biographical Essay, being really unable to put the different *Parts* together—yet I feel the necessity of making a full stop for a *week* & without attempting as I have day after day been doing, to effect what is not in my power—. Let the worst come, the materials of the Essay are all in existence, & if Medicine, Starving, and doing nothing do not bring me round in the course of six or eight days, I will get Mr Carey or some other literary Friend to put them together for me—You may rely in the mean time for the Proofs being corrected & returned without an hour's further delay—[164]

This letter, probably sent in late December, draws attention to some of the technical problems that Coleridge had been facing: in particular, the need to correct proofs from Gillman's 1819 edition, since presumably the relevant volumes of the marked-up 1820 edition were still at the printers. Perhaps that edition had recently been returned, since Coleridge is now promising to send on the numbers and names of the Spiritual Aphorisms, along with the page-numbers; or perhaps he had already made notes for these but needed to find the corresponding pages in Gillman's copy. It also raises questions. What was the "inclosed" that he was sending on this occasion? If we assume that the "Elements of Re-

[161] *CL* v 333.
[162] Ibid 319–20, 322, etc.
[163] W. Wilson *Selections from the Works of Archbishop Leighton, to which is* prefixed *a brief sketch of his life* (1824); *CL* v 302.
[164] *CL* v 320.

ligious Philosophy'' up to page 139 had been sent in previously the new material may well have included the remainder of that introduction and the ''Aphorisms on Spiritual Religion''. There is good supporting evidence for this in the fact that an extract from Henry More used in this section, followed by a comment which forms the basis of Coleridge's in *Aids to Reflection*, appears in the notebooks at this time, being dated by the editor to December 1823 (see Spiritual Aphorism A III, below). If so, the material sent to Hessey in December included some of the manuscript material in the British Museum manuscript Egerton 2801 (Appendix B below): namely folios 174ᵛ, 174, 175, 175ᵛ, 176, 176ᵛ, 177, 177ᵛ and 265. In their manuscript form these were numbered as pages 3 to 11; pages 1 and 2, now lost, would have begun at the beginning of page 143 or 142; when the sheet on which they were written was lost, page 11 also perhaps became detached.

As a numbered sequence, these sheets were presumably submitted together; and they may or may not then have been accompanied by the pages in Egerton 2801 numbered there as folios 178, 178ᵛ, 179, 179ᵛ. This is a particularly interesting sequence, since it was originally headed ''Aphorisms on Spiritual Religion'', the word ''Preliminary'' being later added above it and then deleted with the rest. The sequence had been numbered as pages 7 to 10, and we may suppose that it had then run straight on from the manuscript which concluded the Moral and Religious Aphorisms (to page 127) but that Coleridge either withheld it or withdrew it while he gave further thought to the section. The first page of it has been altered from an earlier state by the deletion of the words ''(says Leighton)'' and the insertion of ''Aphorism I''; it also carries a reference to a passage to be printed from volume ɪɪ (where it is in fact marked up as ''Spir. Aph. 1''); as has been remarked earlier, it would fall readily into sequence with the last sentence of the Religious and Moral and Religious Aphorisms. So we may assume that these pages, and perhaps more, were already written at the time when Coleridge submitted that section in early November, but were held back by him while he inserted various pieces of preparatory matter.

These pages, which took the printing to page 155 of the 1825 text, were renumbered 11 to 14 and may have been included in the December packet or sent later; in either case their numbering is slightly anomalous, since page 11 was already in existence (Eg 2801 f 265).

There is one small objection to the chronology proposed here, which is that in the 1825 edition pages 147 to 148 carry a footnote devoted to the case of John Thurtell, the hanged murderer who was found to have had a pronounced bump of benevolence. Since he was hanged on 9 January 1824 and his case discussed in a medical journal a week later, this footnote must date, at earliest, from the second half of January.

There is no sign of this footnote in the manuscript fragments, however, and the most likely explanation is that Coleridge added it in proof. As it happens later copy for a passage in the middle of page 163 in *AR* (1825) is marked by the printer as having originally begun signature M on page 161. This also would suggest that some additional matter had been added to the previous signature while in proof.

The next evidence we have concerning the chronology of the printing events comes in a letter to Hessey which is unfortunately undated. It runs as follows:

Monday afternoon—

Dear Sir

I feel a more than selfish gratification in being able to announce to you, that during the last week my Health had made such progress that yesterday, for the first time, I was able to venture out—& walked to my friend, Mr Charles Lamb's, concerning whose illness I had suffered much anxiety, and returned by the stage, without finding myself the worse for it—I think, therefore, that I can now promise you a *straight going on*—without delays. I shall send off every other day the remaining *copy*—& am ready for the *Proofs*, as soon as they are ready.—

In the next work (the Elements of Discourse) I must make a bargain with the Printers or Compositors, that the Initial Letters shall be printed as in the MS.— When Adjectives are used substantively, as the Beautiful, the Good; or Substantives are used that in other places are participles, as the Being, a capital is necessary. In the present work it is not of so much importance—& I shall make no corrections that are not absolutely required in order to perspicuity.—

The inclosed III and IV Aphorism, with a Vth, consisting of a beautiful passage from a Sermon of Hooker's, the transcript of which I have mislaid—& am afraid of losing the Post if I stay to look it up—is the whole additional matter— the rest are Leighton's or my own—& the *numbers*, pages, &c—will be sent off as soon as I can get thro' with the collation—the Edition, I have, being differently paged from that at the Printer's—I am obliged to conclude abruptly—
Your obliged
S. T. Coleridge[165]

Griggs dated this letter tentatively 19 January 1824, on the grounds that in a letter on the 23rd Lamb wrote to Barton about having been ill for "many weeks" and also mentioned *Aids to Reflection*: "Coleridge's book is good part printed, but sticks a little for *more copy*. It bears an unsaleable Title, Extracts from Bishop Leighton, but I am confident there will be plenty of good notes in it, more of Bishop Coleridge than Leighton, I hope, for what is Leighton?"[166]

[165] Ibid 323–4. [166] *LL* II 416.

This evidence is not conclusive. Lamb's account of *Aids to Reflection* is not particularly well informed, his version of the title being apparently out of date, and he could have gathered what was currently happening to the volume in a number of ways: he had been in touch with Crabb Robinson during the preceding period, for instance. It may also be noted that a month later Coleridge wrote to the Secretary of the London Institution that ". . . such is and for a long time has been the state of my Health, that for the last six or eight months it has prevented me from accepting a single invitation from my oldest Friends or nearest Neighbors, and that I have never once spent an evening abroad".[167] Aphorisms III and IV of "Indeed Spiritual" (if they are what was included with the letter quoted above) appear on pages 180 to 185 of the 1825 edition, so that they form part of signature N. On the first page of that signature (177), however, there begins a footnote containing part of a "letter to a Friend" which is clearly identifiable with Coleridge's letter to George Skinner dated 17 February 1824.[168] If we accept Griggs's date, or one close to it, therefore, we have to assume that this footnote, again, was added in proof.

The matter cannot easily be settled; however, it is probably simplest to conclude that this letter dates from late January or early February, in view of its insistence that the rest of the volume will consist of aphorisms from Leighton or himself; by 18 February he was giving his account of the work as ". . . growing and new-forming itself under my hand" and saying that in the course of printing it had become ". . . an original work almost".[169] This suggests that the idea of using sources other than Leighton was by then gaining ground. One point which *is* clear is that Hessey accepted Coleridge's points concerning capital letters, since from this point onwards the text corresponds much more closely to the manuscript in this respect.

Another letter to Hessey of the period should perhaps be placed after the one just discussed rather than before as in *Collected Letters*:

> Grove, Highgate—
> Thursday Afternoon.

Dear Sir

I have no other way of accounting for the detention of the inclosed Sheet, but that it having been drawn off on fine Paper, I had been led to suppose that the whole Number had been drawn off—the more readily, that with the exception of the omission of the word, raises, in p. 144, there was nothing that absolutely required further correction. The few corrections made by me in the proof were intended for my own copy, ex. gr. p. 135—and tho' the insertion would improve

---

[167] *CL* v 339. See also above, p lxxiii, and below, pp cvi–cvii.

[168] Ibid 331.

[169] Ibid 336.

the §§ph., I am by no means desirous to have it done, if it cannot be done without displacing the type or other trouble.—The stop after the Vocative Case, Lucili! (Ita dico, Lucili! SACER instead of Ita dico: Lucilî SACER) is of more importance.—By the bye, of the Sheets printed off I possess B, C, D, E, F, G, I.—but not H. 97–112.—

But in the sheet M.—p. 161 of the former proof, and p. 163 of the proof inclosed, there must have been some oversight, whether mine or the printer's I know not, and therefore hold myself bound to suppose the former. A Slip was written by me, to be inserted, instead of the bewildering long and entangled Sentence—& I *feel positive* that I put it into the Proof & sent it off. But as experience has long ago taught me not to confound the *feeling* of POSITIVE-NESS with the *sense* of *certainty*, but rather to consider the former as a strong presumption that there is no ground for the latter, but that my fancy, in some odd way blending with a *sensation* of Memory, has been playing me a trick—therefore, tho' I can no where find the said Slip among my Scraps, I conclude that it is a blunder of my own making. I found the beginning of a first Copy of the Slip, which I have completed so as to make sense, and this I have inclosed—in case, the true Simon Sly should not turn up at the Printer's.

And yet when I look over the proof as it now is, omitting only l. 10, I become doubtful whether my meaning is not rendered sufficiently clear.—You will greatly oblige me, my dear Sir! if you will compare the two—and if *you* think the superior clearness of the Slip inclosed will make it worth while to unsettle the type, you will, of course, have it substituted. But if not, I shall be content with the present, omitting the 10th line, and put the—after "Consequences"—

respectfully | your obliged

S. T. Coleridge[170]

If we assume that the letter previously discussed was submitting copy for signature N, it was almost certainly sent before this one, since signature M has now had time to pass into a second proof.

The next letter to Hessey in *Collected Letters* is as follows:

Wednesday Noon

Dear Sir

God be praised! I have here inclosed the last of the manifoldly and intricately altered and augmented Proofs—and I venture to assure you, that the Copy you will receive the day after tomorrow will be a fair specimen of all that will follow—and that there shall be no further delays on my part—except only what I cannot help, that I take more than twice the time in correcting a proof, and in fact in every mode and appurtenance of Composition, than Writers in general—partly, no doubt, from the state of my health, but in part likewise from the distressing activity and if I may use such a phrase, the excessive *productivity* of my mind.—

respectfully | and truly your | obliged

S. T. Coleridge[171]

For obvious reasons this letter is extremely hard to date. The reference

---

[170] Ibid 320–1. For the changes on *AR*   [171] Ibid 323.
(1825) 163 see below, App B(s).

to Coleridge's poor health would suggest a date in January or February, however, and if these were really ". . . the last of the manifoldly and intricately altered and augmented Proofs", they might have been proofs of signature L or M, since we know from the letter quoted immediately before that certain alterations had made it necessary to insert two pages at the beginning of M. If so, it must precede that letter.

There are one or two further pieces of evidence which help to support the chronology outlined above. On page 223 of the 1825 edition, towards the end of signature P, Coleridge related the word "Name" to the Latin "nomen" and the Greek "νουμενον"; in a letter of 26 January 1824 he declares to Tulk that νουμενον ". . . taken subjectively, and distinctly, is the *Nomen*, or Noun . . ." This collocation of words is a favourite one with Coleridge, however; more striking is the relationship between Aphorism IX, beginning on page 228 of the 1825 edition, and the notebook in which it is drafted, where the relevant entry is dated by the editor to late February 1824.[172] This also helps to suggest that after a period of intellectual activity in March, signalled by the letters of the time and his rereading of Kant, John Smith, and Luther, his temporary withdrawal from Highgate towards the end of March matched the beginning of a break in composition recorded on page 234.

FINAL WORK, 1824–1825

The next important indicator of chronology in the 1825 edition is the passage already quoted from page 234, in which Coleridge speaks of an ". . . interim of depression and disqualification" since the preceding pages were composed, during which he heard that in his lectures the present Professor of Anatomy at the Royal College of Surgeons had adopted his contradistinction of understanding from reason. Joseph Henry Green's first lectures were delivered from 30 March to 1 May; page 234 can hardly have been composed before they began and was probably not written before mid-April at the earliest.

The period of "depression and disqualification" to which Coleridge refers may well be connected with a series of events which involved his having left the Gillman household for about ten days from late March to early April, and resided with the Allsops. There was clearly an estrangement of some kind, connected possibly with a discovery that he was continuing to obtain supplies of opium. Mrs Gillman also mentioned in a letter to Coleridge that her husband was ". . . much hurt about your

---

[172] See below, *Sp Aph B IX* n 1.

Book not being out'', which suggests that Coleridge's new changes in *Aids to Reflection* had led to tension in the relationship. Coleridge himself may well have been dismayed by the fact that Southey's *Book of the Church*, which he had looked forward to seeing reviewed alongside *Aids to Reflection*,[173] was already out while his own writing hung fire. At all events, a reconciliation took place, and on 7 April Gillman fetched him back to the house;[174] on the 12th Coleridge wrote to Wordsworth, ''I must now set to work with *all* my powers and thoughts to my Leighton, and then to my logic, and then to my *opus maximum!*'' From this point onwards, however, his letters carry few references to the work, which up till then had been mentioned frequently. One may speculate that the reconciliation with Gillman included a new agreement with the printers whereby they accepted an extended time-scheme for the production of the remainder, after which he set to work to produce the last section of the work (still amounting to one-third of the whole) at a slower pace.

Whether page 234, which occurs in signature Q, was composed in April or later, it is likely that letter 1383 in *Collected Letters*, dated tentatively by Griggs in March 1824, was written later still, since it refers to the end of page 256, the last page of signature R, as part of a proof which had recently been returned to his publisher. The letter runs:

Dear Sir

In the last Proof sent to Fleet Street I omitted to insert the word ''*not*'' on the last page, & I believe, nearly the last period. I mean to say, that even Taylor's meaning is not clear. Be so good as to insert the words ''not quite'' before ''clear''. You would oblige me likewise by hinting the number of pages, which it is desirable this Work should consist of. The title, of course, must be altered for one more truly characteristic of the Work in it's present state—Something to this purpose perhaps—

Aids to Reflection in the formation of fixed Principles, prudential, Moral and religious, illustrated by extracts from Leighton—& other eminent Divines.

But of this in a future letter.

S. T. C.—[175]

Griggs's reason for dating this in March was presumably that in another letter, written to George Skinner on 22 March, he wrote:

. . . from the great over-balance of the original writing I have changed the Title to Aids to Reflection &c, illustrated by Aphorisms & select passages extracted from our Elder Divines, and chiefly from Archbishop Leighton—[176]

---

[173] *CL* v 306. The Bp of London, who had received his copy of *The Book of The Church* by mid-February, wrote to RS to express his appreciation: *S Letters* (Curry) II 263. Later he read *AR*: see n 214 below.

[174] *CL* v 346–8; 354.

[175] *CL* v 344. It is the subtitles C is changing here, not the main title: see the letter quoted above at n 40.

[176] Ibid 345.

It is not necessary to assume that the two statements were made at the same time, however; Coleridge was presumably giving thought to the exact form of the subtitles over a longer period. (The form eventually chosen, ". . . illustrated by Select Passages from our Elder Divines, especially from Archbishop Leighton", was, it is true, closer to that in the letter to Skinner, but that is not conclusive evidence.)

Number 1383 is the last surviving letter to Hessey until February 1825, which may be further evidence that a new agreement had been reached with him in the spring of 1824, allowing production of the volume to proceed slowly and steadily from that time on. On page 246 there is a reference to John Smith, whose *Select Discourses* he had annotated on 6 and 8 March (in Tulk's copy); from 251 to 287 a long discussion of Jeremy Taylor on original sin, drawing on annotations in his own copy; on pages 294 to 295 a passage from Luther (whose work he had annotated on 16 March 1824); and from 309 to 333 a discussion of Field on redemption (again drawing on earlier work). There is no strong evidence (internal or external) of the date of actual composition, however, until pages 323 to 325, where a long footnote includes an extract from *Baldwin's London Weekly Journal* for 4 December 1824, referring to the trial of Henry Fauntleroy, which Coleridge had been discussing as early as 2 November, a month before.[177] (The footnote may of course have been added in proof.) It is particularly noticeable that during his stay at Ramsgate that year, which lasted from early October to late November, he wrote ten long letters to Gillman, yet the only reference to work on *Aids to Reflection* comes in a single paragraph on 23 November:

I shall come back, a free man: as far as books and publishers are concerned— and please God, I will starve, rather than send a sheet to the press or make any promise of so doing, till the whole Work, thoroughly revised and corrected, is sent along with it.—[178]

One should perhaps infer from this that Coleridge had hoped to complete the volume at Ramsgate, but that both he and Gillman were by now avoiding direct reference to the subject. It is not in fact until the following year that clues to his progress occur again in the text and letters. On page 336, at the end of signature Y, he refers to what "must be at most a venial heterodoxy in 1825". To Samuel Mence on 12 January 1825 he wrote:

I am aware of few subjects more calculated to awake a deep [and] at once practical and speculative interest in a philosophic mind than the analogies between organic (I might say, organific) Life and Will. The Facts both of Physi-

---

[177] Ibid 392.   [178] Ibid 397.

ology and Pathology lead to one and the same conclusion—viz. that in some way or other the Will is the obscure *Radical* of the Vital Power.—My dear Sir! am I under the inebriation of Self-conceit? I trust, not.—Yet there are not half a dozen men in the world of my acquaintance, to whom I should dare utter the sentiment, which I now confess to *you*—that there are *Libraries* of Works from infra-duodecimos to Ultra-folios on the two great Moments of the Christian Faith, ORIGINAL Sin (i.e. Sin, as the *Source* of sinful actions) and Redemption; that the *Ground*, and this the *Superstructure*, of Christianity.—And yet (it is my persuasion that) only not every thing is yet to be said! In the article of Redemption, Metaphors have been obtruded as the Reality: and in all the Mysteries subordinate to Redemption, Realities have been *exinanized* into Metaphors. Luther indeed was a mighty Wrestler: and the very *Halt* on the Thigh bears witness of the Manfulness of his Struggles. But Luther had no Elisha to succeed him.—[179]

The connexion of the first part of this with the reference to original sin and redemption as the ". . . two great moments of the Christian Religion" ("*that* the Ground, *this* the Superstructure of our faith") on page 301 of the 1825 edition, and the link between ". . . realities have been *exinanized* into Metaphors" here and ". . . realities will be evaporated into metaphors" (again in relation to the mysteries of redemption) on page 294, followed there by a quotation from Luther, may suggest that Coleridge was reading proofs of signature U, in which they both occur, at this time. (On page 372 he was also to use his favourite description of Luther as "a mighty Wrestler" in connexion with Irving.)

On 10 February Coleridge wrote to Allsop that he ". . . had Proofs to correct and a passage of great nicety to add . . ."; he also complained that he was ". . . almost incapacitated from thinking of and doing any thing as it ought to be done" by Mrs Gillman's ". . . restless and *interrogatory* anxieties", which meant that he must either enter into a "mock-indifference of a Quarrel" or suffer himself to be ". . . fidget-watched and 'are you going on?—what are you doing now? is this for the Book?' &c &c, precisely as if I were Henry at his Lesson."[180] On 16 February he wrote to Hessey that he was very anxious for some proofs, concluding "The remaining Copy is ready—and whenever wanted, will be sent by return of Post"; on the same day he wrote to Dunn, putting off a debt (presumably for a supply of laudanum) with the words "The last sheet of my work is now going to the Press".[181] A letter on 8 April includes the words ". . . when I have . . . got my 'Aids to Reflection' out of the Press"; in letters of 15 and 26 April it was ". . . on the eve of publication".[182] In an undated letter he returned a proof

[179] Ibid 406.
[180] Ibid 411.
[181] Ibid 414.
[182] Ibid 427–8.

with a volume of Paley that was needed for the final two pages (403–4) of the volume and asked for the return of his old *Friend* and Wall on Baptism, which had been used for pages 372–5.[183] (The request for return of the *Friend* was repeated on 12 May.[184]) At some point in the final stages he decided not to include the letters on the inspiration of the Scriptures which he had been composing (and which were to appear eventually after his death as *Confessions of an Inquiring Spirit*), proposing them to Hessey for separate publication, along with others on Faith, the Eucharist, Prayer, the Hebrew Prophets, and the Church; on 5 May he was waiting for the return of the proof of his "Advertisement", which concluded with a recommendation of Hurwitz's *Hebrew Tales* in a paragraph which was on second thoughts to be withdrawn in a letter of 17 May.[185] By 12 May he was still rewriting a passage in the "Conclusion" to make up for a packet which had been lost;[186] about the same time he submitted the mottos from Marinus and Vico, asking for them to appear on a surviving blank page at the beginning.[187] (A letter to Gioacchino de' Prati of 14 May records that he is "more and more delighted with G. B. Vico".[188]) On 19 May he wrote, "My Book will be *out*, on Monday next" (i.e. on 23 May): he was hoping to have a copy ready by the 20th so that he could present it to the Bishop of London.[189] On the 23rd he wrote to Hessey, "Of course, as soon as a few Copies can be made ready, I shall be glad to receive them—".[190] On 1 June he sent a copy to Prati, on the 6th one to Southey, on the 13th one to J. T. Coleridge.[191]

In the *London Monthly Literary Advertiser* for 10 May 1825 *Aids to Reflection* was announced as "published", but that statement is not to be interpreted literally. The earliest date at which it is likely to have been issued was that mentioned by Coleridge, 23 May; it was certainly out by 1 June. On the evidence at present available, it is hard to get closer to the date of actual publication.

FURTHER WORK ON THE FIRST EDITION OF
Aids to Reflection, 1825–1828

The publication of *Aids to Reflection* came as a relief to its author. "Coleridge is better (was, at least, a few weeks since) than he has been

---

[183] Ibid 431–2.
[184] Ibid 450.
[185] Ibid 433–5, 438–41, 450–1, 457.
See also below, *Sp Aph B [XXIV]* at n 95.
[186] Ibid 450, 452.
[187] Ibid 445.

[188] Ibid 454.
[189] Ibid 462.
[190] Ibid 465.
[191] See App E, Copies 1, 2, and 3, below.

AIDS TO REFLECTION

IN THE

FORMATION OF A MANLY CHARACTER

ON THE SEVERAL GROUNDS OF

PRUDENCE, MORALITY, AND RELIGION:

ILLUSTRATED BY

SELECT PASSAGES FROM OUR ELDER DIVINES, ESPECIALLY FROM ARCHBISHOP LEIGHTON.

BY S. T. COLERIDGE.

This makes, that whatsoever here befalls,
You in the region of yourself remain,
Neighb'ring on Heaven: and that no foreign land.

DANIEL.

LONDON:

PRINTED FOR TAYLOR AND HESSEY,

93, FLEET-STREET;

AND 13, WATERLOO-PLACE, PALL-MALL.

1825.

2. *Aids to Reflection* (1825). Title-page of a copy
presented to Dr Keate, Headmaster of Eton, in July 1825
Eton College Library; reproduced by kind permission

for years," wrote Lamb in August. "His accomplishing his book at last has been a source of vigour to him."[192] As he had made clear in his "Advertisement", however, Coleridge was not satisfied with the final form that his work had taken. The fact that sheets had been printed off as the work progressed meant that it would have been impossible to alter anything in the early part even had he been able to spare the further effort and time: as a result the first half of the book contained a high proportion of quotations from Leighton, and Coleridge's own ideas were not developed in extended form until the second half. In November 1824 he had written ruefully to Gillman that he would never again submit a work to the press until he had the whole manuscript complete.[193] At the time of publication all he could do in the way of revision was to include a slip containing "Corrections and Amendments" and to annotate copies for individual friends so as to elucidate his purpose further.

His letters to them make clear the varying topics which he thought each would find of interest. To Daniel Stuart, with his interest in public affairs, he wrote:

The conviction respecting the character of the Times, expressed in the COMMENT on Aph. vi. p. 147, contains the Aim & Object of the whole Book. I venture to direct your notice particularly to the Note, p. 204–207, to the Note to p. 218, and to the sentences respecting Common Sense in the last 12 lines of p. 252, and the CONCLUSION, p. 377.[194]

In a copy for Edward Coleridge he enclosed his note on the distinction between Deed and Act and discussed in particular the question of Original Sin; he also mentioned clergymen who had paid tribute to the value of his views as a ". . . perpetual comment on the Writings of Paul, and John" and, more particularly, Blanco White's appreciation of the preliminary essay to the Aphorisms on Spiritual Religion (pages 130 to 140) and of ". . . the Disquisitions on Original Sin & Redemption, with that on the Diversity of Reason & Understanding".[195] Sending a copy to Derwent the following January he wrote:

I do not want you to read the Aids to Reflection thro', till you can sit down to it with calmness & in leisure. But one thing I *do* wish—viz. that before I see you, you would run your eye over the pages, which I have marked down overleaf.

The passages in question were as follows:

(1) The Preface. (2) P. 4. *note*. (3) p. 14–17. (4) 26, *note*. Defin. of *Prudence*,

---

[192] Letter to Southey 19 Aug 1825: *LL* III 23.

[193] See above, n 178.

[194] Letter of ?8 Jul 1825: *CL* v 475. See also App E, Copy 4, below.

[195] Ibid 478–82 (and App E, Copy 6).

generally.—40, 41. Def. of Pleasure & Happiness. (5) 51–56. (6) *67–71. Definition of Nature*. See p. 73. (7) 81–82.—(8) 111–112.—116–121. (9) 131–135. 154. (10) 159–162. 176, 177.—Lastly, 229–233.—[196]

These references carry only a few correspondences to the passages marked by Coleridge in the text itself. He evidently wished now to draw Derwent's particular attention to some key passages concerning the relation between reason and religion so that he could discuss with him the main arguments involved; the passages cited stop short of the long discussions of original sin. In letters to others he developed more generally some points raised in the book but the only further specific reference came in May 1827, when he told Cary: "I can conscientiously repeat every syllable of the Nicene Creed, and likewise of that which I am modest enough to think no bad Supplement for individual Catechumens, the Confessio Fidei in p. 189–191 of 'the Aids to Reflection' . . . ".[197]

His notebooks, meanwhile, contained references to various topics in the 1825 edition. At different times he referred to the following pages: 240, § 2, on the relation between Instinct and Understanding;[198] 338–9 on ". . . a Socinian Spirit among the Clergy";[199] 226 on ". . . the characteristic Test of an Idea";[200] 189–91 on ". . . my inward Creed, as a Christian";[201] the note to 55 on the sacramental nature of marriage;[202] 262 on the relation between Reason and Will;[203] notes to 191, 184, and 364 on Superstition;[204] 224 on words as products of the Understanding;[205] and 209 (cf 251n and 263–4) on the conception of Spirit.[206] A long note on Baptism which he wrote in 1828 appears in Appendix D (d) below.

Coleridge's most intricate work on the text of his volume, however, took the form of annotations to volumes which he presented to his friends. The textual apparatus of the present edition gives an account of these annotations; as will be seen, the pattern varied from time to time and from copy to copy. Many simply represent attempts to clarify the sense by small verbal changes, but on some matters Coleridge aimed at a more extended clarification. A note which appeared in three of the first few copies to be annotated represented a further attempt to bring out more fully the distinction between the Understanding and the Reason by showing how it worked at both speculative and practical levels; another,

---

[196] Ibid vi 537 and n (and App E, Copy 7).

[197] Ibid 684.

[198] *CN* iv 5209 f 20 (and see ibid 5210 f 21ᵛ on Reason and Understanding).

[199] Ibid 5213.

[200] Ibid 5216.

[201] Ibid 5243 f 33.

[202] Ibid 5348 f 37ᵛ.

[203] Ibid 5377 f 47.

[204] Ibid 5398 f 75ᵛ.

[205] Ibid 5406 f 88ᵛ.

[206] Ibid 5443 f 97ᵛ.

in all four of these copies, developed his view of sin by way of a distinction between criminal Deed and wicked Act, bringing out the importance of the latter in his eyes.[207] Further single copies contained additional long notes, some of which were included in the 1831 edition and therefore form an integral part of the main text in the present edition.[208]

Coleridge could also console himself with the thought that any deficiencies of the work could be made good in his *Opus Maximum*. Writing to J. T. Coleridge on 8 May 1825, he pointed out that he had "touched on the Mystery of the Trinity only in a *negative* way", demonstrating that the doctrine "involves nothing contrary to Reason . . ." "But," he went on,

> the positive establishment of the Doctrine (i.e. of the Trinity) as involved in the Idea, God—together with the *Origin* of EVIL, as distinguished from Original Sin (on which I *have* treated at large) and the Creation of the visible World—THESE as absolutely requiring the habit of abstraction, and *severe Thinking*, I have reserved for my larger Work—of which I have fin[ished] the first Division, namely, the Philosophy of the Christian Creed, or Christianity true in *Idea*. The 2nd. Division will be—Xty true in *fact*—i.e. historically. The third & last will be—Xty true in *act*—i.e. morally & spiritually.[209]

In a notebook entry of the same month he set out a scheme of the difference between Reason and Understanding corresponding to that in the annotated copies, concluding,

> A more positive *insight* into the true character of Reason, and a greater evidentness of its diversity from the Understanding, might be given—but then it must be *synthetically* and *genetically*. And this I have done in my larger work, in which I commence with the Absolute, and from thence deduce the Tri-unity, and therein the substantial Reason (Λογος) as the ὁ ὤν—ὁ πρωτογενὴς.[210]

In the letter to J. T. Coleridge he further claimed that with the exception of the positive proof of the Trinity, the Origin of Evil, and the Creation, *Aids to Reflection* and its six planned supplementary Disquisitions contained a complete system of internal evidences.

The extent of his readership was more difficult to determine. By November he was reflecting on the poor prospects of issuing his major works, given "the unsaleableness of all that have been published", while in an annotation on Southey's *Life of Wesley* he began by attributing the incomprehension of certain readers to "the manner, and even the obtruded purpose of the Friend or the Aids to Reflection", going on

---

[207] For details see App D below.
[208] See also App H below.

[209] *CL* v 444.
[210] *CN* IV 5210; cf 5215.

to develop the point at some length.[211] At times, on the other hand, he would feel sufficiently encouraged to believe that he had been successful in his aim of reaching more than one section of the reading public. Two years after the volume's publication he would divide his readers into two kinds:

> For as many as are wanting either in leisure or inclination, or belief of their own competency to go further—from the miscellaneous to the systematic—that volume is a whole, and for them the whole work. While for others these disquisitions form the drawbridge, the connecting link, between the disciplinary and preparatory rules and exercises of reflection, and the system of faith and philosophy of S.T.C.[212]

THE EARLY RECEPTION IN ENGLAND[213]

As might be expected, enthusiasm for Coleridge's new volume was expressed first among his immediate circle of friends and acquaintances: he was encouraged to receive praise from his nephew John Taylor Coleridge while the volume was going through the press, and once it was out Sir George and Lady Beaumont brought it to the attention of the Bishop of London, who expressed a "MOST favorable opinion".[214] Joseph Blanco White, a former Roman Catholic priest from Spain who had converted to the Church of England and become a friend of Southey's, acquired a copy and went to Highgate to see Coleridge, who was delighted to discover that he already had the work ". . . at his fingers' ends".[215] Later Coleridge was able to refer to his own publisher John Taylor as ". . . himself a literary man, whom the Aids to Reflection had restored to Christianity and the doctrines of the Church".[216] (The influence evidently remained, since in a letter to his brother James on 18 March 1827 Taylor wrote of his enthusiasm for Leighton: "Next to the Bible I sho[d] deem it the wisest Book in our Language".[217])

---

[211] *CL* v 509 (cf *CN* iv 5257); annotation on Southey *Life of Wesley* (Oxford 1820) ii 166: *CM (CC)*.

[212] *SM (CC)* 73n (note of 1827).

[213] For some of the information in this section and the concluding one I am particularly indebted to C. R. Sanders *Coleridge and the Broad Church Movement* (Durham, NC 1942) and W. B. Elliott "The Uses of Coleridge" (unpub PhD thesis, University of London 1978).

[214] See letter to EC of 19 May 1825: *CL* v 462, and ibid 475, 481. The Bp of London at this time was William Howley, who

was translated to Canterbury in 1828. See also a reference in *AR* (1825) COPY F: *Sp Aph B VII* n 4, below.

[215] *CL* v 481. Blanco White later gave a copy to Tom Mozley at Oriel College, Oxford, and urged him to read it: he acknowledged his gratitude in *Reminiscences of Oriel College and the Oxford Movement* (1882) i 61–2. Blanco White was mentioned by C in *AR*; his copy still survives. See below, *Sp Aph B XXIIIb* at n 30 and App E 201.

[216] Letter to EC 27 Jul 1826: *CL* vi 592.

[217] Bakewell MSS, quoted by Tim Chil-

Older friends of Coleridge were less drawn to the work. In reply to a request for advice on philosophical studies Southey wrote to Henry Taylor on 31 December 1825:

> With regard to metaphysics I know nothing, and therefore can say nothing. Coleridge I am sure knows all that can be known concerning them; and if your friend can get at the kernel of his "Friend" and his "Aids to Reflection", he may crack peach-stones without any fear of breaking his teeth.[218]

To J. G. Lockhart two days later he wrote:

> I understood from John Coleridge that Heraud had written a paper upon the *Aids to Reflection* by S. T. C. which was very ably written—but over laboured and too much like the book itself, yet capable of being made a good thing.[219]

If there is any record of Lamb's response it is to be found in an amused question to Coleridge; one of Lamb's friends, Hone, meanwhile, described the volume as "a proper brain-cracker", while another, Elton, borrowed the volume from the publisher and returned it next day, saying (as Lamb reported to Coleridge) that "20 years before, when he was pure, he thought as you do now, but that he now thinks as you did 20 years ago".[220] Wordsworth, in his only reference, conveyed an impression of the volume as "rather to have been a collection of marginal notes which Coleridge made in the books from which the aphorisms are taken, than any settled writing on the subjects, and to have been published by the request of Friends".[221] There is little evidence that Wordsworth had seriously grappled with it, however; his sympathy with Coleridge's general aims, on the other hand, is exhibited in such statements as his reference in the 1850 *Prelude* to

> Reason and her pure
> Reflective acts to fix the moral law
> Deep in the conscience . . .[222]

Crabb Robinson, who was familiar with the underlying issues, was more enthusiastic: on first dipping into it on 3 July 1825 he wrote, "It is a book most pregnant of thought and most generative also. It surpasses

---

cott *A Publisher and His Circle* (1972) 176.

[218] *S Life* (CS) v 240.

[219] *S Letters* (Curry) II 299–300.

[220] CL's query (see *Mor Aph XV* n 5 below) and the remark by Charles Abraham Elton (1778–1853) are in *LL* III 8. For Lamb's friendship with William Hone (1780–1842), radical-thinking bookseller,

see F. W. Hackwood *William Hone: His Life and Times* (1912) 266–81; and, for C's knowledge of him, *CL* IV 814–15, v 9. C reports Hone's comment on *AR* in the long annotation on Southey *Life of Wesley*, cited above at n 211, which it helped to prompt.

[221] H. Alford *Life, Journal and Reminiscences* (1874) 62.

[222] *Prelude* (1850 vn, 1959) III 83–5.

any of Coleridge's writings in intelligible, and at the same time interesting, matter."[223] Continuing it nearly a year later he described it as ". . . a book of great talent but of strange singularities. His religion that of the vulgar, his philosophy his own."[224] In his journal for the year he wrote:

> In May I was engaged reading Coleridge's *Aids to Reflexion*, that beautiful *composition*, in the special sense of being compounded of the production of the Scotch Archbishop *Leighton* & himself. I compared it to an ancient statue, said to be made of ivory & gold, likening the portion belonging to the Abp. to the ivory, & that of the poet to the gold. Coler. somewhere admits that, musing over Leighton's text, he was not always able to distinguish what was properly his own from what was consciously derived from his master. J. J. Taylor quotes this & hints that this might be the case with St. John in his old age when writing his Gospel. On first reading these *Aids*, I remarked that his, Coleridge's philosophy was his own, his religion that of the vulgar. This [is] in my journal. Might I not more truly have said that Col. was not unwilling in one publication to write both *eso*terically & *exo*terically? I also at first considered this as an attempt to express Kantian principles in the English language & adapt it to popular religious sentiment.[225]

On finishing it, he had described it as "A book which excited feelings that will probably never ripen and doubts that will remain unsolved."[226] His continuing interest is demonstrated by the fact that in 1829 he gave it as a parting present to Victor Benecke, with whom he had been staying in Heidelberg, and in 1830 sent from Florence for a copy.[227]

Coleridge did not expect good notices in the press, since he believed that Jeffrey of the *Edinburgh Review* was determined to "cut up" whatever he published, and that Gifford of the *Quarterly* also disliked him. John Taylor Coleridge, he thought, was likely to feel inhibited by family ties from reviewing him in the latter.[228] In the event neither journal noticed the book; the reviews that did appear were not, however, very encouraging. An unsigned notice in the *British Review* was simply dismissive; a review in the *British Critic* for October 1826, though longer and more considered, was still adversely critical.[229] While expressing a sense of obligation for ". . . the various lights thrown by his writings upon the excellence and the beauty of the Christian scheme", it criticised him for the intricacy and obscurity of his writings, and proceeded to attack some of his detailed statements. The long poetical passage about the scale of creation, which concludes "All things strive to as-

[223] *CRB* i 322.
[224] Ibid 335.
[225] CR *(BCW)* 87–8.
[226] *CRB* i 336.
[227] See H. Marquardt *Henry Crabb Robinson und seine deutschen Freunde* (2 vols

Göttingen 1964, 1967) ii 289 and *CRB* iii 853.
[228] *CL* v 475. See also C's notebook entry of 1 Nov, *CN* iv 5257.
[229] Both are reprinted in *CH* 485–513.

cend, and ascend in their striving. And shall man alone stoop?'', was attacked as ''neither fact nor argument, and, therefore, not adapted for students in Theology''. Coleridge's various discussions of reason and understanding and of doctrines such as the Redemption were criticised on the grounds that practical piety would lead more surely to the truths for which he was contending: ''. . . we want sound practical piety, content to form itself upon the model of the faith once delivered to the Saints, and looking for no other guide. In the christian philosophy there is nothing exoteric;[230] there is not one language for the learned, and another for the vulgar.'' Finally the writer took exception to Coleridge's criticisms of Paley for suggesting that a future state could not be proved except by ''. . . the teacher who testifies by miracles that his doctrine comes from God''.[231] (Coleridge may have been making too much out of a single statement here, but the author of the review seems not to have noticed that he was not casting doubts on Paley's general orthodoxy but expressing a fear that statements such as the one quoted might help justify others who *were* unorthodox in this way.)

Such magazines were addressed to the orthodox, who felt no need for support of Coleridge's kind, and feared rather that such appeals to human reason, even if that reason were being redefined, might do more harm than good. The article by Heraud to which Southey alluded, and which had presumably been offered to J. T. Coleridge's *Quarterly Review*, did not appear, but in 1832, when the second edition had appeared, he reviewed it very favourably.[232] In the meantime *Aids to Reflection* had begun to find an audience, particularly among young men who were becoming conscious of the difficulty of holding Christian beliefs within the new intellectual climate that was beginning to emerge. As with Crabb Robinson, and as in America, those who knew what was going on in Germany were most likely to appreciate the significance of what Coleridge was doing, but this audience seems not at first to have been in London. Carlyle, who had presumably heard about the book during his visits to Highgate in 1824, did not apparently know when the book was published: a letter to Crabb Robinson in April 1826 includes in a postscript the query, ''What has become of Coleridge and his book of *Aids*?''[233] It was in Cambridge, and particularly in Trinity College, that its reputation first spread. The fact that Christopher Wordsworth, William's brother, was a clergyman and Master of Trinity may have had

---

[230] The word ''esoteric'' may have been intended here.

[231] See below, *Sp Aph B XXIIIa* n 3.

[232] *Frazer's Magazine* v (1832) 585–97:

CH 585–608.

[233] *The Collected Letters of Thomas and Jane Welsh Carlyle* ed C. R. Sanders and K. J. Fielding (Durham, NC 1970) IV 82.

something to do with this; the fact that Julius Hare, an admirer of Coleridge's thought, was tutor there certainly did. Hare, whose knowledge of German thought and literature was unusual in England at that time, had attended Coleridge's Shakespeare lectures, and had already been strongly affected by his writings, especially *The Friend*, when he was brought back to the college at Whewell's invitation in 1822. He shared Coleridge's belief that young men should learn to think for themselves, and conveyed an enthusiasm for his writing—which he was also to express in his contributions to *Guesses at Truth*, first published in 1827—to the young men with whom he came into contact.

Among these John Sterling, who became Hare's curate later at Herstmonceux and whose works Hare collected posthumously with a biography, was particularly attracted. Writing to Hare in 1836, he said, "To Coleridge I owe *education*. He taught me to believe that an empirical philosophy is none, that Faith is the highest Reason, that all criticism, whether of literature, laws, or manners, is blind, without the power of discerning the organic unity of the object."[234] According to Hare, he was an early admirer of *Aids to Reflection*; he went on to seek out its author at Highgate and when Coleridge died he was permitted, at his own request, to be one of those who accompanied the body to the grave.[235] He was also a member of the Cambridge Apostles, several of whom spoke up on behalf of the early Romantic poets, including Coleridge, at the Union. His own liking for the Romantics was limited, however. When an expedition set out to bear the gospel of Shelley to Oxford, he refused to join it, declaring that though he had respect for Shelley's genius he distrusted his thought, which he believed to be founded on a mistake. He continued:

I scarcely hold fast by anything but Shakspeare, Milton and Coleridge and I have nothing serious to say to any one but to read the "Aids to Reflection in the formation of a *Manly* Character"—a book the more necessary now to us all because except in England I do not see that there is a chance of any *men* being produced any where.[236]

In 1832, writing to Richard Chenevix Trench from abroad, he reported that he had ". . . read the 'Aids to Reflection' again and again, and with ever new advantage".[237]

---

[234] Julius Hare "Sketches of the Author's Life" in Sterling *Essays and Tales* (1848) I xv.

[235] Letter of SC 5 Aug 1834: *CL* VI 993.

[236] Letter to J. W. Blakesley 25 Nov [1829] (Blakesley MSS) quoted by Peter Allen *The Cambridge Apostles: The Early Years* (Cambridge 1978) 90–1.

[237] Letter of 31 Aug 1832, *Richard Chenevix Trench Archbishop: Letters and Memorials* ed Maria Trench (2 vols 1888) I 119.

Sterling's interest was shared by others of the Apostles. "Coleridge and Wordsworth were our principal divinities, and Hare and Thirlwall were regarded as their prophets," wrote Charles Merivale.[238] In late 1829 William Donne wrote to Trench that "Coleridge *talks* of writing upon prophecy, and recasting the 'Aids' ".[239] By the following summer Trench, in turn, was sending a copy of the volume to his future wife:

A book accompanies this letter, which, if you will thoughtfully peruse it, will place you among those more exalted thoughts and feelings, which alone can be your permanent abiding-place. The latter half of the "Aids" is far the most important, beginning with the axioms on Spiritual Religion. It is full of hard sayings, but they are worth revolving often. Indeed, I believe it impossible for one mind to communicate to another a great truth *all at once*, however by humility and earnestness that mind may be prepared to receive it. It must take root, and grow and expand like a seed cast in the earth, before it can attain its full dimensions. This, I doubt not, you have often felt when reading St. John or St. Paul. I wish I could have presented you with a copy of Coleridge's book, but it is out of print, and not to be obtained. This copy, however, you may keep as long as you please, and do not think of returning it, at least till you see me next.[240]

Trench had a long interview with Coleridge in 1832, describing him afterwards as "the old man eloquent"[241]—a quotation from Milton also adapted by Hallam for the figure based on Coleridge in his poem "Timbuctoo".[242] Hallam, too, seems to have known the later writings well: in addition to citation of Coleridge's views concerning ". . . the mischief a writer does by confounding the distinct senses of words"[243] his work includes apparent echoes of phrases such as "behind the veil",[244] "the abysmal secrets of personality",[245] and "the Absolute, the ὁ 'Ωv" as terms for the ultimate nature of God.[246]

Sterling, meanwhile, was evidently claiming that Coleridge had established a religious position from which it was possible for a sceptically educated young man of his time to seek ordination in the Church. James Spedding wrote of Sterling in August 1834:

He seems to think that no man can have any moral effect on society unless he write himself reverend: and that every body is at liberty (& therefore under a

---

[238] Charles Merivale *Autobiography and Letters* ed J. A. Merivale (Oxford 1898) 98.

[239] *Richard Chenevix Trench* I 42. See also below at n 308.

[240] Ibid 75.

[241] Ibid 123–4, citing Milton *Sonnet X. To the Lady Margaret Ley* line 8.

[242] See *The Writings of Arthur Hallam* ed T. H. Vail Motter (New York 1943) 42–3, quoted below, n 387.

[243] Ibid 193. Cf below, *Prud Aph I* n 4.

[244] Ibid 83. Cf below, *Sp Aph B XXIIIb* n 40.

[245] Ibid 211. Cf below, *Sp Aph B XIX* n 80.

[246] Ibid 204. Cf *Sp Aph B XVIII* n 30 below and *C&S (CC)* 182.

moral obligation) to profess orthodox opinions *as they are, by the orthodox in this generation, expounded,*—as long as he can expound them to himself, *either in that or any other manner*, so as to satisfy his reason.

Spedding did not, however, feel that in his present moral and spiritual state he himself could safely give up ". . . the poor strength of sincerity and an honest mouth";

In the mean time by way of giving myself a last chance and justifying the pretensions of my organisation I have possessed myself of the Aids to Reflection, and am in deliberate progress through them—but I sadly fear without any increased disposition to admire and accept. I shall give them however a fair trial . . .[247]

He did not seek ordination, and Sterling himself seems to have become less sure of his position after a time: he relinquished his curacy (while retaining his orders) in the following year, and later expressed privately some disenchantment with Coleridge.[248] By then, however, the work was coming to be well known in England, while in America its success had been even more striking.

JAMES MARSH'S EDITION OF 1829 AND THE AMERICAN RECEPTION[249]

American intellectuals had first become aware of Coleridge as a prose writer through the publication of *Biographia Literaria* and the *Lay Sermons*, but early reviewers found the metaphysical element in his writing

---

[247] Letter to W. H. Thompson 29 Aug 1834: Thompson MSS, quoted by Peter Allen *Cambridge Apostles* 169 (omitted line kindly provided by Professor Allen).

[248] See long letter to his mother of July 1844, quoted by A. K. Tuell *John Sterling* (New York 1941) 261–3. Sterling must have been particularly disturbed by the long exposure of the unacknowledged borrowings from Schelling in *Biographia Literaria* made by J. F. Ferrier in an unsigned article for *Bl Mag* XLVII (1840) 287–99: this made the previous defence mounted by Sterling's tutor and friend J. C. Hare in the *British Magazine* VII (1835) 15–27 look flimsy. SC's more sympathetic examination of the question in her own edition of *BL*, where the evidence was fully set out, followed three years after his letter.

[249] For some of the information in this section I am indebted to the following sources: Joseph Torrey's "Memoir" in his edition of *The Remains of the Rev. James Marsh D.D.* (Burlington, Vt 1843, 2nd ed New York 1845); *Coleridge's American Disciples: the Selected Correspondence of James Marsh* ed J. J. Duffy (Amherst, Mass 1973); P. Carafiol "James Marsh's American Aids to Reflection: Influence through Ambiguity" *New England Quarterly* XLIX (1976) 27–45; Anthony J. Harding "James Marsh as Editor of Coleridge" in *Reading Coleridge* ed W. B. Crawford (Ithaca, NY 1979) 223–51 and "Coleridge and Transcendentalism" in *The Coleridge Connection* ed. R. Gravil and M. Lefebure (1990) 233–53; and P. H. Huff "Coleridge and Classic American Criticism" (unpub PhD thesis, University of London 1977).

cloudy and obscure: his reputation as a poet continued for some years to be the chief source of his fame there. It was the American publication of *Aids to Reflection* in 1829 that was the decisive event in establishing respect for him as a thinker.

The first editor of *Aids to Reflection* in America was James Marsh, President of the University of Vermont, and well known to historians of education for having reformed the courses of study there so as to encourage students to think for themselves:

> The great object of education then undoubtedly is to develope in the subject of it and to call forth into conscious and active exercise the powers of the mind both intellectual and moral. . . . by unfolding the powers of an individual's mind we do in fact not only communicate necessarily those departments of science and literature which are made use of as instruments for effecting that purpose but we give him the most important of all knowledge, the knowledge of himself. We awaken the latent principles of his being into conscious existence.[250]

As will be seen from these statements in the address to the Corporation of the University of Vermont, the ideals of the new curriculum not only echoed Coleridge's belief in the importance of awakening the powers of the mind but followed his conviction that to do so would be to arouse ". . . the latent principles of [one's] being", which would in turn reveal themselves as the true springs of knowledge and morality.

Marsh had not only been disturbed by the deadening effect of educational methods which aimed simply at producing rote-learning of knowledge, but had become anxious that the expansion of knowledge that was taking place during his lifetime should not lead to a disjunction between science and belief. Although he had not followed Coleridge's intellectual course to its fullest extent, he was sufficiently drawn by the study of nature to be fascinated by accounts of Coleridge's dealings with pantheism. As he read *Biographia Literaria*, however, his interest in Coleridge's description of the way in which he skirted the "sandy deserts of unbelief" had been succeeded by an attraction to Coleridge's insistence on the importance of experience in religious thinking. As Anthony Harding has pointed out, that fascination reached its climax when he came to Coleridge's argument that the division commonly made between "knowing" and "being" resulted from an exclusion or misunderstanding of intelligence itself. If it were once perceived that the intelligence of man and the intelligence by which the world was ordered were, at the deepest level, the same, such a division—and indeed the need for it— would disappear.[251] Coleridge's further claim that since knowing and

[250] Address to the Corporation of the University of Vermont 25 Mar 1827: Duffy 61–2.   [251] Harding "Marsh as Editor of Cole-

being were at the deepest level inseparably linked, introspection and the cultivation of religious experience would automatically bring belief in its train was equally attractive to Marsh.[252]

Reading *Biographia Literaria* had thus prepared Marsh for the positions set forth in *Aids to Reflection*, his encounter with which in 1826 impressed him still further. The book struck him as a powerful storehouse of arguments against the intellectual assumptions of the time. It was particularly relevant to America, moreover, since Coleridge's contentions, which were directed equally against the Unitarians and the extreme Calvinists, could be directly applied to the state of affairs in New England, where the dominating Unitarian ideas of Harvard were countered in neighbouring theological colleges by teaching that followed Jonathan Edwards's attempts to blend Calvinism with Lockean philosophy.[253] (Edwards's teachings were in fact the subject of specific comment in *Aids to Reflection*.) There were further factors to attract Marsh's interest. Dartmouth College, which he had attended from 1813 to 1817, had then been in a state of religious ferment, while at Andover Theological Seminary he had come into contact with Moses Stuart, a professor who was unusually conversant with the current intellectual state of Germany. The interest in Kant and other German philosophers which, along with an awareness of German biblical criticism, had been aroused in him at that time had taken Marsh away from the orthodoxy that Stuart continued to profess. German philosophy in itself had not been sufficient to help him in his intellectual struggles, however. Like Wordsworth he had been oppressed by the apparent power of determinism in human affairs; as with him, also, the study of Euclid accompanied his sense of despair.[254] In this predicament Coleridge's philosophy, and its emphasis on the importance of religious experience, had been timely; and when he read *Aids to Reflection* he became convinced that the work ought to be put into the hands of his fellow-countrymen as soon as possible. For the resulting American edition he wrote an introduction that dwelt particularly on its virtues as providing a proper metaphysical grounding for Christian religion. Unitarians and modern Calvinists, for all their differences, shared a common allegiance to the philosophy of Locke and his successors which Coleridge's distinction between reason and understanding, properly understood, should lead them to question.

---

ridge" pp 225, 228, citing Torrey's "Memoir" in *Remains* p 114; cf *BL* ch 9 *(CC)* I 143.

[252] Harding "Marsh as Editor" pp 227–8, quoting C's "Credidi, ideóque intellexi, appears to me the dictate equally of Philosophy and Religion": *BL* ch 24 *(CC)* II 244.

[253] Duffy 15–24.

[254] Torrey "Memoir" in *Remains* p 20; *Prelude* (1850 vn, 1959) XI 275–333.

The impression is sometimes given that Coleridge had misunderstood Kant's distinction between reason and understanding and that Marsh followed his misunderstandings, thus helping to propagate false conceptions of it among later American writers. As far as Coleridge is concerned, the facts of the case are rather more complex, as we have seen above. When he addressed himself directly to Kant's text he had no difficulty in following his arguments or reproducing his various distinctions. At the same time, however, he thought that Kant had been held back, perhaps through prudence or timidity, from making further affirmations concerning the status of reason, by which the rôle of reason became constitutive rather than regulative. Such affirmations he believed to be inherent in the writings of earlier thinkers such as Bacon and Leighton—even though they themselves would not have drawn the distinction in quite the same terms; he also attempted to identify Leighton's "... faculty judging according to sense" with Kant's conception of the understanding, while acknowledging elsewhere that Leighton had not made out the distinction fully.[255] Henry A. Pochmann has examined Marsh's position in relation to these complexities.[256] The Preliminary Essay suggests that whereas he too had made an earlier study of Kant in the original he was now attracted by Coleridge's suggestions that the fullest and most valuable accounts of the reason were to be found in the English seventeenth-century writers, and so was willing to adopt an interpretation of the distinction that followed those lines. Whether he ever believed Kant himself to have gone so far is not clear; certainly his letters to Coleridge suggest that he was looking for further guidance. In his first, after expressing appreciation of Coleridge's work, he expressed a desire to hear more:

The German philosophers, Kant and his followers, are very little known in this country, and our young men who have visited Germany have paid little attention to that department of study while there. I cannot boast of being wiser than others in this respect, for though I have read a part of the works of Kant it was under many disadvantages, so that I am indebted to your own writings for the ability to understand what I have read of his works and am waiting with some impatience for that part of your works which will aid more directly in the study of those subjects of which he treats.[257]

By the time that he wrote the essay which he prefixed to his American edition of *The Friend* (published in 1831) he was quite clear as to the difference involved in Coleridge's thinking:

I shall . . . merely take the occasion to remark, that his system is by no means,

---

[255] See below, *Sp Aph B VIIIa* n 32.
[256] Henry A. Pochmann *German Culture in America* (Madison, Wis 1961) 134–8.
[257] Duffy 80 (letter of 23 Mar 1829).

as some have alleged, essentially the same with that of Kant. . . . He differs from him, as Cudworth and More and the Platonizing divines of the same age generally would have differed, and as some of the most eminent German philosophers, as well as Tholuck and other evangelical divines, of the present day, differ from him in their philosophical and theological views.[258]

As the previous quotation indicates, Marsh was also aware of remaining questions which he hoped Coleridge would resolve in his promised works. He also received enquiries about these works from others, and after Coleridge's death wrote first to James Gillman and then to Joseph Henry Green about the likelihood of their posthumous publication.[259] Henry Nelson Coleridge sent him the *Literary Remains* as they were published, but these were not what he was primarily seeking; in 1839 Green wrote to him that the "full development" of Coleridge's system of philosophy had not been accomplished, and that he was now doing his best to make up the deficiency by writing a work of his own.[260]

As early as 1830 Marsh had planned a second edition of *Aids to Reflection*, the first having sold quickly, and on hearing of Coleridge's planned new edition had written asking for copies.[261] Coleridge did not reply, however, and the plan languished. Marsh was probably held back in addition, first by a hope that the "Elements of Discourse" and "Assertion of Religion" would appear, enabling him to elucidate Coleridge's position further, and then in later years by the news that Henry Nelson Coleridge was himself working on a new edition of *Aids to Reflection*. This, the fourth edition, turned out in the event to add little of importance, but Marsh was no doubt flattered to find his own essay included in it.[262]

After the publication of this new edition in 1839 there was an unexpected development. In that year a new American reprint appeared from the New York publisher Swords, Stanford and Company, in which Marsh's Preliminary Essay was replaced with one by Professor John McVickar of Columbia College.[263] This began with an explanation of the need for a new preface by someone who was ". . . untrammelled by the conditions of a self-constituted ministry, and the fetters of an incongruous metaphysical creed".[264] Marsh's preface, it was also claimed, presenting as it did an ". . . unqualified eulogium of Coleridge and his opinions", was ". . . an unsafe guide for young and enthusiastic minds".[265] This in turn prompted an anonymous piece in the *Vermont*

[258] *The Friend* ed J. Marsh (Burlington, Vt 1831) vi.
[259] Duffy 212, 221–2.
[260] Duffy 220.
[261] Duffy 108.

[262] See below, App H.
[263] See below, ibid, for details.
[264] McVickar's ed (ibid) x.
[265] Ibid ix.

Chronicle for 1 January 1840, drawing attention to the omission of Marsh's essay in the new edition and asking whether the question of copyright had had anything to do with it; if so the author was being deprived of his just reward.[266] Marsh himself wrote to H. N. Coleridge, expressing a hope that "Mr. Coleridge's friends" would not be persuaded that he had sought to pervert Coleridge's views to ". . . narrow and sectarian uses".[267] The development was not quite so unscrupulous as it may at first sight seem, since surviving correspondence makes it clear that Swords, Stanford and Company had first sought Marsh's permission to use his own essay and that he had declined (perhaps because he was planning a new reprint of his own).[268] His apprehension now was evidently caused less by the appearance of the new essay as such than by McVickar's statement that a decision had been taken to "drop" his essay and by the fact that the title-page carried Pickering's name as well as those of Swords and Stanford—which suggested that it was being issued simultaneously in London and had become the authorised English edition. A letter from H. N. Coleridge shortly afterwards was reassuring: "Mr Pickering's name is usurped in the title page, neither he nor I having any knowledge of the publication . . . . I should not agree with any denial of your having rendered a great service to the cause of sound philosophy as involved in the principles taught by Mr Coleridge."[269] Meanwhile, Marsh had proceeded to a reissue of his own edition and essay. From this his own notes were now excluded—presumably because they had largely consisted of quotations from other works by Coleridge that had been inserted to elucidate various points in *Aids to Reflection*; these had now been made redundant by publication of the works involved.

It is not clear whether McVickar's assertion that Marsh's essay had been "dropped" for the reasons he gave would have had the support of the publishers or whether he had simply taken it upon himself to make the claim. He was certainly no adversary to *Aids to Reflection*, even if his attitude to it was fundamentally different. In 1830 he had visited Coleridge with Edward Irving, at which time he had been struck by Coleridge's eloquence and powers of thought, yet carried away an impression of him ". . . rather as a brilliant meteor flashing forth dark light, than as a steadfast luminary, by whose guidance Christians might safely walk".[270] Since his death, however, Coleridge's stature had risen in his estimation, partly owing to the fact that he now appeared ". . . in his

---

[266] Quoted Harding "Marsh as Editor" p 250.

[267] Letter of 20 Jan 1840: Duffy 223.

[268] Letter of 18 Jul 1839: Duffy 222.

[269] Letter of 1 Apr 1840: Duffy 230.

[270] *AR* ed McVickar (1839) xii.

works, and in his works alone'', which revealed him as a foremost
thinker ''. . . for his profound insight into the laws of our moral and
spiritual being, and his clear, eloquent, and Christian exposition of the
truths and duties that flow from them''.[271]

McVickar's presentation of Coleridge in his Preliminary Essay was
not, like Marsh's, of an exciting new guide for those who were seeking
to reconcile reason and revelation, but of an eloquent reproclaimer of
truths that had always been present in the Church of England, having
been dimmed only by the lesser insights of later thinkers, inside and
outside the Church. There were points on which he disagreed with Coleridge, of course: three, which he identified, were his ''. . . allegorized
view of the historical circumstances of the fall of man'', his ''. . . defective argument and unjustifiable admissions on the subject of Infant
Baptism'', and, ''most striking of all'', his ''. . . false and dangerous
estimate, of perhaps the moral worth, certainly the spiritual teaching of
. . . Edward Irving''.[272] For the rest he saw Coleridge as one of the most
eloquent and persuasive advocates that the Anglican Church had found
in recent times.

Although his reading of *Aids to Reflection* was responsive to the de-
votional flavour of its style, which recommended it as proper reading
for Episcopalians, McVickar angered Marsh's friends by implying that
it could only be properly understood and interpreted by orthodox Angli-
cans. It is true that Coleridge had been anxious not to assist the Dissenters, but the positions he was setting forth were bound to excite a wider
interest. McVickar went further, moreover, asserting that Marsh's preface was ''. . . mainly occupied in justifying Coleridge and his philosophy against objections which have no place except on the Calvinistic
scheme of Divinity''—which, along with his statement that his prede-
cessor was trying to ''. . . reconcile Coleridge with Calvinism'', made
Marsh appear to be himself a modern Calvinist.[273] George Allen, a former student of Marsh's, leapt to his defence in a series of sarcastic articles in *The Churchman* in 1840 and had little difficulty in showing that
such statements misrepresented Marsh's position.[274]

McVickar's preface does not totally merit Allen's scorn, however.
Rather, it draws attention to the ambiguity of what Coleridge had been
doing. When McVickar attacked Marsh's affirmation that ''. . . we can
have no right views of Theology till we have right views of the human
mind'' as inculcating ''. . . a false and dangerous principle, viz. that

[271] Ibid xiii.
[272] Ibid xx.
[273] Ibid vii.

[274] *The Churchman* x (14, 21, and 28
Mar, 4, 11, and 18 Apr 1840) Nos 1–6. See
also Duffy 228–9, 232–3.

some system of metaphysical philosophy is essential to soundness in Christian doctrine'',[275] he was, as Allen pointed out, ignoring statements in Coleridge's own work on which such a position could legitimately be based; yet it is equally true that on this question Coleridge himself might ultimately have taken McVickar's part or at least shown sympathy. The fact is that he was trying at one and the same time to be Anglican and universal, to reconcile traditional doctrines with a position in metaphysics that would support them. As a result his work could, according to one's presuppositions, be read either generally, as an apologia for Christianity that might show the way out of a contemporary impasse, or, more specifically, as an attempt, which even a Tractarian might applaud, to reinfuse spirituality into Anglicanism.

In the event, both editions were reprinted in America at the time, but McVickar's continued to be reprinted until 1872, whereas Marsh's edition lapsed after his death in 1842. H. N. Coleridge's inclusion of Marsh's preface in the English editions up to the sixth, on the other hand, ensured it a continuing prominence, and when Marsh's pupil W. G. T. Shedd, publishing his *Collected Works of Coleridge* in 1857, set *Aids to Reflection*, preceded by Marsh's essay, at the beginning of the first volume, this helped further to establish it as the foremost American commentary—a position which was fortified at the end of the century by its being reprinted on both sides of the Atlantic in the Bohn editions.

Meanwhile Coleridge's work had been awakening interest elsewhere in North America. In a letter to H. N. Coleridge of 16 July 1840 Marsh reported Coleridge's widespread influence: ''His views indeed are taught ex cathedra only here [i.e. in Vermont] but in all our Colleges and Theological schools his works are read and have a daily increasing influence.''[276]

The exact extent of that influence is not altogether easy to determine now. In 1842 Emerson noted in his journal a report from Edward Washburn at Andover that ''whole shelvesful'' of *Aids to Reflection* were being sold there yearly to the students.[277] This, however, may have reflected the special conditions there, since Leonard Woods and Moses Stuart had fought a stubborn rearguard action against Coleridge's ideas, which had meanwhile become a rallying-point for younger Congregationalists. Woods, at least, had allowed himself to be won over in some respects.[278] Elsewhere, the volume's reputation was spread by pupils of

[275] *AR* ed McVickar (1839) vii–viii.
[276] Duffy 233.
[277] Duffy 8.

[278] Carafiol ''Marsh's American *Aids to Reflection*'' 32–5.

Marsh such as George Allen at Newark, Delaware. Sometimes, however, an enthusiasm for Emerson might be enough to awaken a young man's interest in the volume. In the 1880s Moncure Conway, an early American enthusiast for Hegel, was to recall how he had carried in his saddle-bag and studied Marsh's edition of *Aids to Reflection* during his years as a Methodist circuit-rider in Ohio.[279] Horace Bushnell, the Congregationalist theologian, constructed his whole position on the volume.[280]

Marsh's hope of finding a sympathetic readership for *Aids to Reflection* among the Unitarians was not to be fulfilled, on the other hand—which was hardly surprising, perhaps, in view of the comments on them to be found in the text. A few men such as Carl Follen at Harvard and R. H. Dana, Sr, were moved by Coleridge's arguments for a more spiritual religion, but the only prominent Unitarian to express real enthusiasm was William Ellery Channing, who visited Coleridge at Highgate in June 1823 and claimed that he owed more to him than to any other philosophical thinker.[281]

In general, most religious writers in America treated Coleridge's views with considerable respect and admiration. Many, nevertheless, found doctrines with which to disagree. His views on the doctrine of atonement, for example, caused divergence of opinion: Thomas P. Smith had written to Marsh that they were "admirable and unanswerable", but Leonard Woods at Andover had found them "defective" and Charles Hodge declared that if ". . . the death of Christ produced its effects by operating a subjective change in us" this must amount to ". . . changing the whole system of the Gospels, as it has been commonly understood".[282] Although he acknowledged that Coleridge was not a Unitarian, and had come to this belief by a quite different route, the belief itself was identical with that held by Unitarians. More often, however, it was a particular attitude, a disposition of the spirit, that caught the imagination of readers—particularly if their introduction to it was mediated by Marsh's Essay. As late as 1929 John Dewey, giving an address in Vermont to commemorate the centenary of the American edition, spoke of Marsh as one who had ". . . wished to use scholarship

[279] Lloyd D. Easton *Hegel's First American Followers* (Athens, Ohio 1966) 126, cited Duffy 8. Conway later ran a humanist sect at South Place Institute in Finsbury, which the young Nathaniel Wedd, later to be a Cambridge Apostle and E. M. Forster's tutor, joined for a time: Paul Levy *Moore: G. E. Moore and the Cambridge Apostles* (Oxford 1981) 119.

[280] See M. B. Cheney *Life and Letters of Horace Bushnell* (New York 1880) 208, 499.

[281] Elizabeth Peabody *Reminiscences* (Boston 1880) 75.

[282] Duffy 123, 107, 116.

and philosophy to awaken his fellowmen to a sense of the possibilities that were theirs by right as men, and to quicken them to realize these possibilities in themselves'', his transcendentalism having been ''. . . the outer form congenial in his day to that purpose''.[283] When Dewey was presented with a copy of *Aids to Reflection* at a birthday party late in his life and asked if it reminded him of anything, he replied, ''Yes, I remember very well that this was our spiritual emancipation in Vermont. Coleridge's idea of the spirit came to us as a real relief, because we could be both liberal and pious; and this *Aids to Reflection* book, especially Marsh's edition, was my first Bible.''[284]

It was some of the Transcendentalists themselves who had given Coleridge's ideas their widest currency in the United States. Here again the influence exercised by *Aids to Reflection* varied considerably, being greatest on those who belonged to what has been called the ''mystical'' wing—Bronson Alcott, for example: ''[In 1833] I was looking around for the origin of the human powers. . . . It was Coleridge that lifted me out of this difficulty. The perusal of the 'Aids to Reflection', the 'Friend', and the 'Biographia Literaria' at this time gave my mind a turn towards the spiritual . . .''[285] ''Were I to name any modern 'master' '', he wrote elsewhere, ''it would be him.''[286] According to Odell Shepard, Alcott's voluminous notes in his own copy demonstrated the continuing stimulus of the work: ''Four years after the first perusal he was reading it for the fifth time, and fifty years later it was still on the list of his annual reading.''[287]

Those who founded the Transcendental Club in 1836 acknowledged a debt to Coleridge's writings, supplemented by some of Carlyle's earlier essays: Frederic Henry Hedge had written a favourable review of Coleridge in the *Christian Examiner* for 1833;[288] George Ripley's enthusiasm for Coleridge's inspiration was qualified only by criticism of his ''. . . want of philosophical clearness and precision''.[289] James Freeman Clarke, a younger man, was perhaps the most explicit:

[283] John Dewey ''James Marsh and American Philosophy'' *JHI* II (1941) 131–50.

[284] Corliss Lamont *Dialogue on John Dewey* (New York 1959) 15–16.

[285] A. Bronson Alcott *Ralph Waldo Emerson, Philosopher and Seer: an Estimate of His Character and Genius* (Boston 1888) 47. (Cf also p 27.)

[286] *The Journals of Bronson Alcott* ed O. Shepard (Port Washington, NY 1966) 471. (See also pp 32 and 67.) Shepard's note to p 32 points out that Alcott read *AR* before he knew Emerson, having perhaps been encouraged to do so by W. E. Channing.

[287] Odell Shepard, *Pedlar's Progress: The Life of Bronson Alcott* (Boston 1937) 159.

[288] F. H. Hedge ''Coleridge's Literary Character'' *Christian Examiner* XIV (1833) 108.

[289] George Ripley ''Introductory Notice'' to *Specimens of Foreign Standard Literature* (1838).

. . . something within me revolted at all . . . attempts to explain soul out of sense. . . . So I concluded I had no taste for metaphysics and gave it up, until Coleridge showed me from Kant that though knowledge begins *with* experience it does not come *from* experience. Then I discovered that I was born a transcendentalist . . .[290]

Other transcendentalists, by contrast, had little time for Coleridge's ideas.[291] When those ideas were approved, moreover, it was often in a simplified form. When Thoreau quoted from *Aids to Reflection* it was on the love of God: "He that loves, may be sure that he was loved first", and the first quotation from the book to be copied out by Emerson, in a notebook of 1827, was, significantly, the phrase "All things strive to ascend & ascend in their striving."[292] When Marsh's edition came out two years later Emerson read it with great interest: late in 1829 he was listing various works that Coleridge mentioned there and he wrote in January that he had read ". . . Coleridge's Friend with great interest; Coleridge's Aids to Reflection with yet deeper".[293] He visited James Marsh in 1831[294] and Coleridge himself in 1833, leaving an account of his conversation.[295] In 1834, when he was continually exalting the intuitions of reason (regarding its gestures as "graceful & majestic" by comparison with those of the understanding, which were "quick & mean"),[296] he wrote to his brother, ". . . let me ask you do you draw the distinction of Milton Coleridge & the Germans between Reason & Understanding. I think it is a philosophy itself."[297] The remainder of the 1834 letter shows that his idea of Reason was at once semi-mystical and undiscriminating. But although in 1835 he could write of Carlyle as "one of the best, and since Coleridge is dead, I think, the best thinker of the age", in 1836 he said of Coleridge's work in a lecture, "the Aids to Reflection, though a useful book I suppose, is the least valuable".[298]

[290] James Freeman Clarke *Autobiography, Diary and Correspondence* ed E. E. Hale (Boston 1891) 39.

[291] Cf e.g. R. D. Habich *Transcendentalism and the Western Messenger* (Cranbury, NJ and London 1985), discussing the spread of Transcendentalism in the Ohio Valley, in which the name of Coleridge does not appear anywhere.

[292] H. D. Thoreau *Journal* ed E. H. Witherell et al (Princeton, NJ 1981) I 222; *The Journals and Miscellaneous Notebooks of Ralph Waldo Emerson* ed W. H. Gilman and A. R. Ferguson (Cambridge, Mass 1964) VI 38.

[293] Ibid III 164–5; *The Letters of Ralph Waldo Emerson* ed R. L. Rusk (New York 1939) I 291.

[294] R. L. Rusk *Life of Ralph Waldo Emerson* (1949) 154.

[295] *C Talker* 360; cf *Journals and Miscellaneous Notebooks of Ralph Waldo Emerson* ed A. R. Ferguson IV 401–10.

[296] Ibid IV 299.

[297] Emerson *Letters* I 412–13, 432.

[298] *The Early Lectures of Ralph Waldo Emerson* ed S. W. Whicher and R. E. Spiller (Cambridge, Mass 1966) I 379. A lecture on George Fox a year earlier, on the other hand (ibid I 168), had contained the assertion that religion could not in the end be transmitted: "It must be lived. It cannot

As a Unitarian, he would have found Coleridge's devotion to Anglicanism an unacceptable accretion to the ideas he valued in *The Friend*.

Peter Carafiol adduces such facts in favour of his argument that *Aids to Reflection* was influential in the United States partly through a further ambiguity: the orthodox could welcome the support of its spirituality (even if they found it heterodox and perhaps dangerous) while the Transcendentalists, mining Coleridge's doctrine of the mind's ability to derive spiritual knowledge from its own depths and disregarding his efforts in behalf of orthodoxy, could arrive at a position in which they no longer needed to believe in Christian doctrines.[299] Carafiol even goes so far as to assert that Marsh was alone in being able to combine Coleridge's radical philosophy with his allegiance to a historical orthodoxy.[300]

Such transcendentalist developments of Coleridge's ideas were not in harmony with his own later thinking. Already, some years before, he had attacked views that ignored the fullness of his own position. When John Wheeler, Marsh's friend, visited him in 1829, he had criticised Dr Channing's Unitarian opinions and insisted on the importance of the doctrine of the Trinity, as saving human beings ". . . from Pantheism on the one hand and idolatry on the other" and as ". . . the only possible way of harmonizing the contradiction that exists between spirit and matter, and the tendency of the mind to run into the extreme of spirituality and materialism".[301] (The doctrine of the Trinity, it will be recalled, had not been discussed as such in *Aids to Reflection*, being reserved for separate treatment in the uncompleted Opus Maximum.)

The Transcendentalists, who in any case were captivated by the power of Coleridge's imagination rather than by the subtlety of his ideas, would not have understood his concern for orthodoxy. Emerson was more inclined to treat Coleridge's reason as identifiable with what he had had to say about the imagination, maintaining that Coleridge's churchmanship was "perfectly separable" from his criticism.[302] Patricia Huff, who draws attention to this statement, expounds Emerson's position further as aligning itself with Coleridge's doctrine of imagination to no more than a limited extent: "In literary terms, his attempt to graft the Coleridgean imagination onto monism led him to put great emphasis on

---

be writ"—a sentiment close to C's in *AR*: see below, *Sp Aph B VII* at n 26; *Conc* at n 87.

[299] Carafiol "Marsh's American *Aids to Reflection*" 32–5.

[300] Ibid 45.

[301] *C Talker* 360. For transcripts of the whole of Wheeler's record see John Beer

"Transatlantic and Scottish Connections" *The Coleridge Connection* ed R. Gravil and M. Lefebure (1990) 331–6 and, var, *TT (CC)* II 429–33.

[302] Patricia H. Huff "Coleridge and Classic American Criticism" (unpub thesis, University of London 1977) 318.

perception, and almost none at all on the specifics of artistic making." As she also points out, Edgar Allan Poe complemented Emerson's position by drawing out the element in Coleridge's doctrine that dwelt on the creative power of the imagination: "Poe is as convinced of the artist's need for absolute control over his materials, as Emerson is of the artist's obligation to yield himself to his vision and allow that greater power to shape the medium through him."[303] (One might perhaps say that Poe is preoccupied with the secondary imagination, Emerson with the primary—which he aligned with the transcendental Reason.) Emerson's position was based on the distinction between reason and understanding, particularly as expounded in works such as *The Friend*. Poe, by contrast, was more interested in Coleridge's imaginative works, and went so far as to say that Coleridge's "Genevieve" (i.e. *Love*) was a poem in which he ". . . aided Reflection to better purpose" than in his prose manual.[304]

Whatever Coleridge thought about the specific uses to which his ideas were being put, however, he could not help but be gratified by the amount of attention *Aids to Reflection* and other such works were receiving on the other side of the Atlantic. Shortly before his death he told Richard Monckton Milnes and Arthur Hallam that they should go there if they had the opportunity. "I am known there. I am a poor poet in England, but I am a great philosopher in America."[305]

COLERIDGE'S WORK TOWARDS A NEW EDITION, 1825–1831

Even while *Aids to Reflection* was going through the press ideas for further publication had been growing out of Coleridge's work on it. At a late stage he had offered his series of letters on the interpretation of the Scriptures to fill out the volume, only to be told by the publisher that they would take up too much room. A disquisition on Baptism was then included in the volume, as the last of his "aphorisms"; in the course of this he wrote of a similar piece on the Eucharist which, "together with the Articles on Faith and the philosophy of Prayer", he was deferring to form "a small supplementary Volume". A few pages later he referred to an Essay on the Church and a series of letters on "the right and the superstitious use and estimation of the Bible" which, together with the

[303] Ibid 318, 320.
[304] Poe "American Prose Writers. No 2: N. P. Willis" *Broadway Journal* (18 Jan 1845): *Works* (New York 1902) xii 37, cited Huff 327. See also A. J. Bate "Edgar Allan Poe: A Debt Repaid" *The Coleridge Connection* ed R. Gravil and M. Lefebure (1990) 255.
[305] T. W. Reid *The Life, Letters and Friendships of Richard Monckton Milnes* (1890) ii 432.

full version of the dialogue between "Nous and Antinous", were planned to appear in a small volume by themselves. Soon afterwards, in May 1825, he offered to Hessey the first five, along with another, "On the Hebrew Prophets & the prophetic Gift. (not more than four pages.)", for publication either as a supplement to *Aids to Reflection* or as a separate volume, to be entitled *Six Disquisitions*, devoted to the various topics.[306] The offer was not taken up, perhaps because Coleridge's publishers were already in financial difficulties, but the scheme remained active in his mind. On 19 January he wrote to H. N. Coleridge, ". . . certain strong motives have engaged me in sending to the press immediately the supplementary disquisitions requisite for the completion of 'the Aids of Reflection' . . ."; three weeks later he mentioned his "Essay on the Philosophy of Prayer" as if it were completed, adding that illness had prevented him from sending his disquisitions to the press; and on 27 February he wrote to William Blackwood about such a scheme, planned apparently with a reprint of *Aids to Reflection* as the first volume, as if it had been more or less accepted for publication by him. Nothing further is known of the Blackwood's project; the fact that Hessey had mislaid the letters on the Scriptures and did not find them again until June may have been a decisive factor in thwarting publication at that time. In the event the disquisition on the Church was issued separately and those of the others that were ready were set aside, to be published after his death.[307]

Coleridge's plans then came to take the form of a "rifacimento" of *Aids to Reflection* on the lines of the one formerly produced for the 1818 edition of *The Friend*. William Donne's 1829 statement, ". . . Coleridge *talks* of writing upon prophecy, and recasting the 'Aids' ", has already been quoted.[308] The plan had been afoot the previous year, when Coleridge wrote to Hyman Hurwitz, asking him to discover from John Taylor whether or not the first edition was out of print, and continued, "I have been strongly urged to re-publish the Aids to Reflection, considerably improved".[309] In a draft agreement with John Taylor which was sent to the publisher Thomas Hurst for advice in January 1829 he men-

---

[306] *Sp Aph B [XXIV]* at n 95, below; *Conc* at nn 17, 18, below; *CL* v 434–5 and nn.

[307] See *CL* vi 542, 556, 788n; and Eric W. Nye "Coleridge and the Publishers: Twelve New Manuscripts" *MP* LXXXVII (1989) 64–5, printing an uncollected ms letter of 24 Feb 1826 from C to Blackwood in which he promises to complete the vol-

ume for publication by mid-March. For more on the Disquisitions see *Sp Aph B [XXIV]* n 95 and *Conc* nn 17, 18, below. Those parts that were completed, apart from *C&S*, will be included in *SW&F (CC)*.

[308] See above, n 239.

[309] Letter of 21 Nov 1828: *CL* vi 773.

tioned three works: the "Rinfacciamento of the Aids to Reflection", the "System of the Faith and Philosophy of S. T. C." in two volumes, and a "Volume on the Power and Use of Words". Coleridge explained that the first would be ". . . an almost entire *Rinfacciamento*, or Re-construction of the Aids to Reflection, as a Second Edition, newly arranged & with large Editions (*sic*)".[310] (The other two were also mentioned in the draft agreement.) Further points in the letter suggest a hope on his part that Hurst might take on the publication himself and offer better terms, which was what eventually happened; in February, however, he was still planning to send the work to Taylor, while complaining of ailments and a resulting depression so completely incapacitating that he had been ". . . compelled to suspend the task".[311]

Before the work could be completed, in any case, he became preoccupied by a desire to develop into a pamphlet his ideas on the nature of the Church, the subject being of topical interest; as this work, *On the Constitution of the Church and State*, came to fruition the 1829 edition of the *Poetical Works* was also passing through the press. His health at this time continued to be subject to sudden periods of deterioration and when he wrote to Hurst in September 1829 enclosing the proofs and remaining copy for *On the Constitution of the Church and State*, he was worried by problems that had arisen during the printing, leaving a ragged effect. Reaffirming a former resolution ". . . never to send a Work to the Press till it has received my last Finish, and till some Friend has undertaken to revise and correct the Proofs for me", he continued: "If I can contrive with honor to transfer my Aids to Reflection &c, my Nephew & now Son-in-law, Henry Nelson Coleridge, whose Chambers are in Lincoln's Inn Square, No. I., has undertaken to do this for me."[312] In the following August, 1830, a letter to Hurst contained the following postscript:

P.S. You may if you like & continue to wish it have the first half of the Aids to Reflection, on the understood condition that you shall have the second as soon as it is actually required, whether I have or have not made the additions or rather substitutions which I meditate, and which consisting almost wholly of transcription from MSS, my health only has prevented—This is the best compromise that in the present uncertainty and restiveness of my *Beast*-body I can make between my desire to improve the Book and my anxiety not to worry or disappoint you or your Printer.

S. T. C.[313]

The publisher presumably accepted this plan, since by 1 December

---

[310] Letter of 19 Jan 1829: ibid 780–2 and nn.
[311] Ibid 786.
[312] Ibid 819.
[313] Ibid 845.

AIDS TO REFLECTION

IN THE

FORMATION OF A MANLY CHARACTER

ON THE SEVERAL GROUNDS OF

PRUDENCE, MORALITY, AND RELIGION:

ILLUSTRATED BY

SELECT PASSAGES FROM OUR ELDER DIVINES, ESPECIALLY FROM
ARCHBISHOP LEIGHTON.

BY S. T. COLERIDGE, ESQ., R.A., R.S.L.

> This makes, that whatsoever here befalls,
> You in the region of yourself remain,
> Neighb'ring on Heaven: and that no foreign land.
> DANIEL.

SECOND EDITION.

LONDON:
HURST, CHANCE, & CO., ST. PAUL'S CHURCH-YARD.

1831.

3. *Aids to Reflection* (1831). Title-page

Coleridge was answering H. N. Coleridge's queries concerning a "Corrected Copy" which he had evidently passed on to him. From this letter it is clear that in that copy (which has since disappeared) he had deleted all the headings that assigned the authorship to Leighton, other authors, or himself, and that this had led to problems in the main text where, for example, references to "the Archbishop" that sometimes survived were no longer clear. To Henry he now wrote,

> As to your questions, I am somewhat puzzled for an answer, not having the Corrected Copy. The best that suggests itself to my mind, is to substitute "Leighton" for "the Arch-bishop", in the few instances of formal quotation—: and to leave all the rest to be explained in the preface—For my object, God knows! being to convey what appeared to me truths of infinite concernment, I thought neither of Leighton nor of myself—but simply of *how* it was most likely they should be rendered intelligible and impressive—The consequence of this was, that in so many aphorisms, taken in the main, from Leighton, I had so modified them, that a *contra*-distinction of these from my own was deceptive.— In the preface, I shall state plainly the Leightonian Origin & still remain[ing] *ingrediency*—and I assure you, that I have quite confidence enough in your taste & judgement to give you a Chart Blanch for any amendments in the style—[314]

The result of this policy, as E. L. Griggs points out,[315] was to replace a phrase such as "The Editor and Annotator of the present Volume" by "The Author of the present Volume"; "Reflections by the Editor", similarly, became "Reflections by the Author".

The effects were not altogether happy, since while many references to Leighton and other sources remained in the text, the relationship between the work of Coleridge and such authors was now disguised in ways that could easily confuse the reader. Although passages from Leighton had sometimes been modified, a large number had been quoted more or less verbatim from the original. Coleridge's intention of dealing with the matter by stating plainly in his preface the ". . . Leightonian Origin & still remain[ing] *ingrediency*" was not fulfilled, moreover; on the contrary, the 1825 Advertisement, in which the relationship to Leighton had been made reasonably clear, was now dropped in favour of an address "To the Reader" derived from a note that Coleridge wrote in the copy of *Aids to Reflection* (COPY D) that he presented to Daniel Stuart.

The problem created by these omissions arose partly from the dropping of the original plan to produce a full-scale revision of the 1825 edition and partly, perhaps, from Coleridge's long-standing tendency to underestimate the extent of contributions from others once they had been

[314] Ibid 848–9.   [315] Ibid 849n

incorporated in his own work. Another important factor, however, was the transfer of authority to his nephew, who evidently did not immediately perceive (as Coleridge himself might have done) the confusion which was being created, and who could not know that Coleridge's unacknowledged borrowings were to become a sensitive issue after his death. By the time that he came to compile the fourth edition of 1839, on the other hand, he had evidently become aware of such problems, and restored the original attributions. From then on this usage became standard except in Thomas Fenby's editions of 1873 onwards, where the third edition was used as copy-text[316] and as a result attributions of authorship were once again omitted from the headings.

The only other piece of evidence to have survived from work on the second edition is a letter to his nephew early in 1831. H. N. Coleridge had presumably pointed out that the contents page from the 1825 edition needed to be revised to take account of the new form of the opening pages; he also had a problem concerning the "Synoptical Summary" of the argument concerning reason and understanding, originally intended for insertion in the 1831 text at the appropriate point, and evidently either omitted in the proofs or left out deliberately by Coleridge in the hope that he could extend what he had written there. Coleridge wrote to him as follows:

Introductory Aphorisms
on the duty and advantage of cultivating the power and habit of reflection
                                                                    P. 1–14
Prudence, Morality, and Religion inter-distinguished   P. 15
Prudential Aphorisms &c—

My dear Henry
    I find myself too ill, too low, and by the frequent *subsultus* of muscle & seemingly of the whole trunk too painfully interrupted, to be able to finish what I had planned & begun—
    Just let the omitted part be added at the end—and substitute or rather insert the above in the CONTENTS Page—[317]

His instructions for the Contents page were carried out, but with one small error. The phrase "Introductory Aphorisms" was cut off from the rest of the heading and given a separate page reference "1"; the rest was then printed with the anomalous further reference "1–14" as in the copy furnished by Coleridge. The "Synoptical Summary" ("the omitted part") was duly added as an "Appendix" on a separate, tipped-in page "EE" at the end of the text (after the sheet with the printer's name on it) and was subsequently reprinted as an appendix in later editions.

[316] The third edition contains some small typographical differences from the second, which Fenby follows.
[317] Ibid 853.

In the end the alterations from the 1825 edition were not on a large scale. The most important consisted in the omission of the Advertisement, together with several sections from the Introductory and Prudential Aphorisms and from the Reflections respecting Morality. These passages, which are reproduced in Appendix G below, amount to some fifteen pages of the original text, of which about nine were originally from Leighton; it is unclear whether several others, which concerned the relationship with Leighton's text, were excised by Coleridge or by his nephew. The fact that there are no omissions beyond page 58 suggests that Coleridge wearied fairly soon of his revising and failed to excise as much of Leighton as he had originally intended.

Long additions to the 1825 text were even rarer: apart from the appendix already mentioned two pages of "Corollaries" were added to Aphorism XV in the Moral and Religious Aphorisms: these correspond with a long note originally written in a copy of *Aids to Reflection* (COPY F) presented to Edward Coleridge. (That note may have been transcribed (incorrectly); more probably it was already in the "Corrected Copy" sent to HNC.) Many other notes which survive in the annotated copies (including COPY F) were not, meanwhile, carried over into the 1831 publication, and only a very limited number of the detailed small revisions found their way there: indeed, even the list of "Corrections and Amendments" printed in the 1825 edition was not used in its entirety.

Although offering a distinct advance on that of 1825, then, the text of the 1831 edition is still not ideal, particularly since it may contain a few small unauthorised changes made by H. N. Coleridge, acting under his "Chart Blanch"; without access to the "Corrected Copy" which Coleridge passed to him it is impossible to be sure, but careful reading suggests that the initiative passed to him more fully in the later pages. Yet it remains distinctly the better text for later readers, not only because it is the one that had Coleridge's final approval but because he made significant alterations, particularly in the early pages, which represent his most considered thoughts on the subjects he was dealing with there.

The new edition was advertised in *Bent's Monthly Literary Advertiser* for June 1831, and presumably issued at about that time.

THE LATER ENGLISH RECEPTION

The steady growth in the English reputation of Coleridge's prose writings, and particularly of *Aids to Reflection*, owed a good deal to the efforts not only of John Sterling, who from 1827 was living and writing in London and who, as mentioned earlier, visited Coleridge at Highgate, but of his friend Frederick Denison Maurice, who, while not having met

Coleridge, had preceded Sterling in enthusiasm for the writings. When he went up to Trinity College in 1823 he was already familiar with his work; he was elected to the Apostles shortly afterwards and was soon defending "Coleridge's metaphysics and Wordsworth's poetry" against the dominant utilitarian thinkers of the time[318]—indeed, he was largely responsible for a change in the nature of their discussions. In 1830 Arthur Hallam declared that Maurice had created the spirit, though not the form, of the club and four years later he was toasted as its "author" (in these terms) by the members at their annual dinner.[319]

Maurice's enthusiasm for Coleridge early made itself felt beyond the confines of Cambridge. Before he left he had helped found the *Metropolitan Quarterly Magazine* in London and by 1828 was writing for and then editing the *Athenaeum*, where he and Sterling constantly championed Coleridge's thought. He praised his distinction between reason and understanding, calling him ". . . the first of living English philosophers" and ". . . the greatest of critics".[320] He also greeted the collection that Julius Hare had compiled with his brother, *Guesses at Truth*, which included several quotations from Coleridge, as the most delightful book to have appeared in England for a long time, ". . . with the exception of Coleridge's 'Aids to Reflection' ".[321] His brief stay in Oxford from 1829 to 1830 enabled him to spread his enthusiasm for Coleridge in person there also.

Maurice never became a slavish disciple of Coleridge's. He felt that his occasional lack of respect for facts was a "great defect";[322] nor did he claim him to be a great systematic thinker. The point of *The Friend*, however, lay not in proclaiming a system but in initiating the reader into "a way of seeking";[323] the *Biographia Literaria*, similarly, presented a man groping after truth. His obligations to *Aids to Reflection*, which he felt to be of the same order, he believed to be "more deep and solemn". He also contended that the book's so-called "obscurity" was much exaggerated:

I have heard the simplest, most child-like men and women express an almost rapturous thankfulness for having been permitted to read this book, and so to understand their own hearts and their Bibles, and the connexion between the one and the other, more clearly.[324]

---

[318] Frederick Maurice *The Life of Frederick Denison Maurice* (1884) I 176.

[319] Ibid 56, 110, 165.

[320] *Athenaeum* 8 Mar 1828 p 289n; 30 Jul 1828 p 623. Cited Sanders 188, 189.

[321] *Athenaeum* 6 Aug 1828 pp 641–2

and n. Sanders 189.

[322] F. Maurice I 203.

[323] Dedication to *The Kingdom of Christ* (1842) x–xi.

[324] Ibid xv–xviii.

If the book had given, and would always give, offence to many, that was due not to its theories, but to its practical character. Those who followed Rousseau and who believed that a man who was a slave to his passions could also be a very right and true man would be repelled by its ". . . manly denunciation of the sentimental school'', while those who called simply for decency of conduct would be repelled by his object of drawing his readers from the study of mere worldly and external morality ". . . to that which concerns the heart and the inner man'':

> But here, again, he is so unfortunate, that those who have turned ''heart-religion'' into a phrase—who substitute the feelings and experiences of their minds for the laws to which those feelings and experiences may, if rightly used, conduct us—will be sure to regard him as peculiarly their enemy.

It is, he goes on, precisely because so many have tried these varying philosophies and wearied of them that the volume ". . . has found its way into so many studies, and has gained access to so many hearts''.[325]

Maurice admitted that Coleridge might not have approved of all the views expressed in his own work, yet he believed that there was one idea above all that they had in common: the question, namely—which he believed to be crucial for his own generation—whether there was ". . . a Universal Society for man as man''. In his own approach he had been indebted to Coleridge

> for shewing me a way out of the dreadful vagueness and ambition which such a scheme as this involves, for leading me not merely to say, but to feel, that a knowledge of The Being is the object after which we are to strive, and that all pursuit of Unity without this is the pursuit of a phantom.[326]

The nature of Coleridge's influence on Maurice rendered it diffusive in effect: in *The Kingdom of Christ*, for instance, he acknowledged debts to *The Statesman's Manual* and *On the Constitution of the Church and State*.[327] The particular importance to him of *Aids to Reflection*, nevertheless, re-emerges years later, in his *Moral and Metaphysical Philosophy*, when, writing of Coleridge's plan to write a great work in which he would set out his philosophy completely and systematically, he commented that he could not regret the fact that it had not been completed:

> There would have been a contradiction in it in Coleridge's case which there was not in either of the others [Hegel's work in Germany and Cousin's in France]. A system of ontology must be contained in a book; the Word of Wisdom is a living teacher speaking to men. . . . The real *Logo-Sophia* of Coleridge is contained in his *Lay Sermons* . . . [and] in his *Aids to Reflection*, wherein he awak-

---

[325] Ibid xviii–xix.   [327] Ibid xix–xx.
[326] Ibid xxiv.

ens young men to ask themselves whether that divine Wisdom is not speaking to *them* . . . whether there is not a will in them which can only be free when it is obeying the motions of a higher Will.[328]

The visit of the party from the Cambridge Conversazione Club to Oxford in the autumn of 1829 to support a motion in favour of Shelley and against Byron has already been mentioned. The members seem to have brought tidings of Coleridge also (Hallam had recently visited Coleridge and written the admiring account based on him in "Timbuctoo"). Gladstone entertained Hallam and Monckton Milnes to breakfast a day or two after the debate and sat with them all the morning: in the evening he wrote in his diary, "With respect to the Cambridge philosophy I am not altogether enchanted—I should like more time to judge . . ." Two days later he began reading Coleridge's *Friend*.[329] Hallam and Milnes may also have drawn the Oxford men's attention to the recent arrival of Maurice, who shortly afterwards joined Gladstone's Essay Society and was soon elected to its presidency.

A number of other chance factors assisted the spread of Coleridge's ideas in Oxford at this time. Maurice had recruited Derwent Coleridge among his contributors to the *Metropolitan Quarterly Magazine* a year or two earlier.[330] Derwent had been ordained and was now teaching at a school in Helston, Cornwall. A neighbouring clergyman with whom he became friendly, Thomas Fisher, was rector of Roche and a tutor to boys of the Acland family.[331] Thomas Dyke Acland (the 11th baronet) went up to Oxford in 1827; in 1829 both brothers became founder members of Gladstone's Essay Society.[332] Thomas wrote in his journal for 1830: "In regard to my own mind the chief thing has been the introduction to Coleridge (The Friend), read and not understood in the Long Vacation, addled over in the ensuing term and also Biographia Literaria; no good effect yet exhibited but rather conceit as having a new power and being above the Scotchmen."[333] He also mentioned that through the Essay Society he had had an introduction to F. D. Maurice and that he had read Plato with him.[334] On 12 February 1831 he acquired a copy of *Aids to Reflection*[335] and read it; a few months later he was able to record some moral improvement in his journal, ascribing it to various factors "But

---

[328] Maurice *Moral and Metaphysical Philosophy* (2 vols 1872) II 670.
[329] Diary entries for 28 and 30 Nov 1829: *The Gladstone Diaries* ed M. R. D. Foot and H. C. G. Matthew (Oxford 1968) 270–1.
[330] Peter Allen *The Cambridge Apostles* 36.

[331] A. H. D. Acland *Memoir and Letters of the Right Honourable Sir Thomas Dyke Acland* (1902) 6–9.
[332] Ibid 23–4.
[333] Ibid 24–5.
[334] Ibid 31.
[335] Ibid.

more than all human means, Coleridge's Aids to Reflection and my mother's letter . . .''.[336] By the end of the year he had delivered a piece on Coleridge to the Club; in later years he was to describe his "Spiritual Philosophy" as having been ". . . the breath of life to young men".[337]

In the meantime Acland had begun to study with Newman, and to be drawn towards the ideas of those who were to become leaders of the Tractarian movement.[338] When he began to press Coleridge's claims on Newman, however, he found him at first resistant—partly, it seems, on account of the fact that Coleridge was not living with his wife.[339] Newman was always in fact to insist that Coleridge's ideas had had no effect upon the early growth of the Tractarian movement (E. B. Pusey, who had read *Aids to Reflection* by 1828, was not associated with it in its first stages).[340] In 1835, however, stirred perhaps by comments on Coleridge after his death, he finally came to his work. A note of 29 March in that year runs:

> During this Spring, from Christmas down, Acland lending me some of Coleridge's works I have *for the first time* read parts of them—and am surprised how much I thought mine, is to be found there. I believe at Froude's in 1831 I carelessly looked into the Idea of Church and State—and had read two or three sentences in Jemima's Aids to Reflection.[341]

Newman's more favourable opinion of Coleridge is reflected not only in direct comments but in quotations from his work. In the *Grammar of Assent*, for example, he quoted as an example of "informal inference" Coleridge's inference from our dissatisfaction with the objects of our bodily senses that

> . . . there is something in the human mind which makes it know that in all finite quantity, there is an infinite, in all measures of time an eternal; that the latter are the basis, the substance of the former; and that, as we truly are only as far as God is with us, so neither can we truly possess, that is, enjoy our being or any other real good, but by living in the sense of his holy presence.[342]

Newman evidently found the conclusion congenial, yet could not regard

[336] Ibid 25.

[337] Ibid 54, 41.

[338] He knew Newman by 1829 (ibid 29), but the acquaintance ripened slowly.

[339] Harold Anson *Looking Forward* (1938) 63.

[340] *The Letters and Diaries of John Henry Newman* ed C. S. Dessain and Thomas Gornall, SJ (31 vols 1961–) xxx 91, xxxi 7. For Pusey's knowledge, see below, *Prel Sp Aph* n 15. It may also be noted that the host to the important Hadleigh Rectory Conference in 1833 was Hugh James Rose (1795–1838), who had corresponded enthusiastically with C as a young man and received from him annotated copies of the 1812 and 1818 *Friend*: see e.g. *CL* IV 669–71, 684–7, 881–2, and *Friend (CC)* II 388, 391.

[341] Newman, diary 29 Mar 1835, *Letters and Diaries* v 53.

[342] See below, *Mor Aph XII* n 3.

the argument as one which would—or should—be accepted by the ordinary reader. "Does not the author rightly number it among his 'aids' for our 'reflection', not instruments for our compulsion?" The worth of the passage would be secured only by a reader with a good preparation in mental discipline, appreciation of religious ideas, and a perspicacity and steadiness of intellectual vision.[343] There is further evidence of Coleridge's influence in Oxford during the subsequent period: R. W. Church, who was there from 1836 to 1838 reading for an Oriel Fellowship, wrote, ". . . there is something in Maurice, and his master Coleridge, which wakens thought in me more than any other writings almost: with all their imputed mysticism they seem to me to say plain things as often as most people".[344] In his memoirs, Mark Pattison wrote in a similar vein:

Early in 1837 I had fallen under the influence of Coleridge. I got all of his books that I could; they had not then been reprinted, and were difficult to procure. The *Aids to Reflection* especially dominated me. The vague mysticism in which he loves to veil himself had a peculiar charm for me. Led on by Coleridge I had read Augustus Schlegel, and I certainly had fallen away from Baconian principles, and passed under the first influences of a realistic philosophy. It so happened that I could not have handled the Oriel philosophy paper in a way to meet the views of the examiners, but for this strong infusion of Coleridgian metaphysics.

When he contributed to *Essays and Reviews*, he praised the "new impulse and . . . new direction" that Coleridge had given to theology but was more hostile to his revival of older doctrines.[345]

A further tributary to the current came by way of Thomas Arnold at Rugby, who had been a fellow of Oriel from 1816 to 1820 and was a keen admirer of Coleridge, sometimes reading his works with his older pupils.[346] There is some evidence in the early writings of Arthur Hugh Clough that he had come under the influence of them, probably while still at Rugby.[347] In 1840, when he was in his last undergraduate year at Balliol, a contemporary described a wine-party in Clough's rooms

---

[343] *An Essay in Aid of a Grammar of Assent* (1870) 297–8.

[344] *Life and Letters of Dean Church* ed M. C. Church (1895) 17.

[345] Mark Pattison *Memoirs* (1885) 164–5; "Tendencies of Religious Thought in England, 1688–1750": *Essays and Reviews* (1860) 263–4, 315–18. Pattison took an uncautious statement in the *AR* Preface (p 6 below) to entail the belief that the Athanasian Creed was "THE PERFECTION OF HUMAN INTELLIGENCE"; C, however,

would not have been likely to agree: cf *TT* (*CC*) II 433.

[346] For Arnold's praise of C in 1835–6 see A. P. Stanley *Life and Correspondence of Thomas Arnold* (12th ed 1881) I 374 (on *TT*), II 23, 50 (on *LR*).

[347] For a reconstruction of the mediation of C's ideas to Clough via Thomas Arnold, see Robindra K. Biswas *Arthur Hugh Clough: Towards a Reconsideration* (Oxford 1972) 17–18, drawing on an unpub PhD dissertation by R. M. Gollin.

where "The conversation soon became general, and turned shortly to Wordsworth and from him to S. T. Coleridge and the *Aids to Reflection*."[348] J. C. Shairp, who went up to Balliol in that year and came to know Clough, and who later wrote about the volume and about Coleridge more generally,[349] was to be in his turn a major influence on Shadworth Hodgson, author of *The Philosophy of Reflection* (1878).[350] In 1841 Frederick Temple, who was later to become Archbishop of Canterbury but who was then at Balliol reading mathematics, wrote to his sister,

> I have been reading Coleridge a good deal lately and I can hardly tell how much I admire him; I have a sort of feeling, however, that this admiration cannot last long. Reading him excites me so much that I can hardly do anything else after it; I am obliged never to read it except just before I am going to walk. What a wonderful power of conversation he must have had; no subject seems to have baffled him.

Temple then proceeded to develop a foundation for Christian faith, based on inner response to the truths to be found in the Bible, which seems to have owed a considerable debt to his reading of Coleridge. Later he corresponded about him with his son William, who was also to become Archbishop of Canterbury, and who as a young man had become fascinated by his ideas, along with those of Kant and Bacon.[351] William Temple's thought, from *Mens Creatrix* (1917) to *Readings in St John's Gospel* (1939–40), shows strong affinities with some of the ideas expressed in *Aids to Reflection*; so far as he himself quoted from Coleridge in these later works, however, it was normally from the poetry, which he read for its thought along with that of Wordsworth, Tennyson, and Browning. It is unlikely that he would have been exposed to Coleridge's ideas directly when he went up to Oxford at the end of the century: G. D. Boyle, the Dean of Salisbury, producing his *Recollections* in 1895, wrote,

> . . . the influence of Coleridge is not what it used to be in the days when I first knew Oxford as an undergraduate, when tutors were in the habit of recommending *The Friend* and *Aids to Reflection* to such of their pupils as were reading for honours.[352]

Boyle had gone up to Exeter College in 1847.

[348] G. G. Bradley, quoted in W. Knight *Principal Shairp and his friends* (1888) 49.

[349] See J. C. Shairp *Studies in Poetry and Philosophy* (Edinburgh 1868) 224–31, etc.

[350] Hodgson's volume was dedicated to "Samuel Taylor Coleridge, my father in philosophy, not seen but beloved".

[351] E. G. Sandford *Frederick Temple, An Appreciation* (1907) 23–4, 72, 232, 290–3.

[352] G. D. Boyle *Recollections of the Very Rev. G. D. Boyle, Dean of Salisbury* (1895) 81.

In England, as in America, *Aids to Reflection* could be interpreted, and so exercise influence, in more than one way. While its import was seen by some as encouraging a more liberal-minded approach to religion and so as providing an important statement in support of the Broad Church Movement, others found in its doctrines the basis for a truer and fuller Catholicism. Aubrey de Vere, an early enthusiast for the volume, is a good example: moving from acceptance of Coleridge's organicism, he learnt from him, according to his biographer, "to view religion, and especially Christianity, as the expression of the universal mind of regenerate man—as something resting on wider and deeper experiences than belong to the life of one individual—and as in some inadequate manner the partial reflection of the infinite mind of God".[353] Associating that "universal mind" with an ideal Catholicism that had always been present in the Church, he was brought naturally into the Tractarian position (and may well have been in Carlyle's mind when he associated Coleridge's teaching with the fathering of "Puseyisms"[354]). In 1841 he became friendly with Sara Coleridge,[355] who had also come to associate her father's teachings with a High Church position and was about to publish her essay "On Rationalism" as an appendix to her husband's edition of *Aids to Reflection*.[356] Unlike her, DeVere eventually followed Newman to Rome; he never lost his veneration for Wordsworth and Coleridge, however, nor did he believe that there was any essential contradiction between the teachings of the three. As far as he was concerned, Newman was simply making explicit what had been implicit in their writings—particularly Coleridge's distinction between understanding and reason.[357]

In Cambridge, meanwhile, the ideas of Coleridge had continued to be disseminated among the Apostles, who remained closely in touch with their former members, but it is not clear that his influence spread far in the university at large. By the time that Julius Hare took a living at Herstmonceux in 1832, Sterling and Maurice had already left Cambridge, so that there was no one to carry on the tradition directly. When Charles

---

[353] Wilfrid Ward *Aubrey de Vere: A Memoir* (1904) 22–3 (cf 8, 11–14 including the anecdote of the young lady who read *Aids to Reflection* between breakfast and luncheon and "thought it a very pleasant book—found nothing difficult in it").

[354] See below, at n 374. For de Vere's acquaintance with Carlyle see Ward 78–80 etc.

[355] Ward 66 and index.

[356] See below, App H. For her early reaction to *AR* see *Memoir and Letters of Sara Coleridge* ed Edith Coleridge (2 vols 1873) I 31.

[357] After calling on Newman in Edgbaston on one occasion, de Vere went on to visit C's grave at Highgate and WW's haunts in the Lake District: Ward 20. For Understanding and Reason see pp 174–80.

Kingsley (who had been a pupil at Helston School, where Derwent Coleridge was headmaster) went up to Magdalene College in 1838, he was not elected to the Apostles and seems not to have known *Aids to Reflection* until (by contrast with Trench) his future wife, Fanny Grenfell, introduced him to the volume (along with Carlyle's *French Revolution*) in 1841.[358] Although Kingsley is sometimes thought of as a Coleridgian, the main influence came to him via Maurice, whose *Kingdom of Christ* he read at about the same time.

Coleridge's chief later advocate in Cambridge was in fact to be F. J. A. Hort, another of Thomas Arnold's pupils, who graduated in 1850 and was elected to the Apostles the year after. He, like Kingsley, acknowledged a deep debt to Maurice and no doubt imbibed from him further interest in Coleridge—coupled with Maurice's sense of his unreliability as to matters of fact. While he was by no means uncritical of Coleridge's theology, suspecting an underlying tendency to Sabellianism,[359] he remained a warm admirer. To an Oxford undergraduate who wrote asking for help with the thirty-nine articles of the Church of England he recommended *Aids to Reflection* on original sin: "It is quite unhistorical, and rambling and discursive in the extreme, but it is a book to be read again and again."[360] In 1856 he published a long piece on Coleridge[361] (still regarded as one of the best accounts of his thought), in the course of which he was careful to distinguish the purposes of *Aids to Reflection* as (in Coleridge's own later words) ". . . the disciplinary and preparatory rules and exercises of reflection"[362] from the "system of faith and philosophy" that he had hoped to present elsewhere; he took issue with some of the views which he found expressed, but defended Coleridge against any charge of having denied the doctrines of original sin and the atonement: ". . . the reverse is the case".[363]

As an undergraduate Hort had been taught by the slightly older Brooke Foss Westcott, who became his great friend and collaborator. On 25 March 1849 Westcott wrote in his journal: "Today I begin Coleridge's *Aids* seriously. Still I feel at starting a kind of prejudice, not against the book, but against the man; because he seems to have done so little compared with what he was able to have done." No more about that reading is recorded in the published journals, but as he passed through a crisis of doubt in subsequent months he evidently found the

[358] *Charles Kingsley: his Letters and Memories of his Life* ed F. E. Kingsley (2 vols 1877) I 53.

[359] A. F. Hort *Life and Letters of F. J. A. Hort* (2 vols 1896) I 136.

[360] Ibid II 329.

[361] F. J. A. Hort "Coleridge" in *Cambridge Essays* II (Cambridge 1856) 294–351.

[362] *SM (CC)* 73n.

[363] Hort "Coleridge" 324, 343.

ideas in it, and in Coleridge's biblical criticism, sustaining. On 20 May he wrote, "I cannot but feel that the N.T. 'finds' me; and that with its deepest mysteries—but as mysteries, not dogmas"; on 24 July "Faith is an intuition".[364] His stress on the importance of a sense of "mystery" is still evident in *The Gospel of Life* (1892), by which time it included the mysteries revealed in the work of scientists such as Darwin and Clerk Maxwell. His urgings that education should awaken the sense of mystery and his delight in contradictions on the ground that the attempt to resolve them brought one into that realm may well indicate his most important debt to Coleridge, who made the same point in a footnote near the end of Spiritual Aphorism B VIII. The enthusiasm exhibited in *Aids to Reflection* for the ideas promulgated in the Fourth Gospel—particularly that of the incarnation of God in the Word, or Logos—as being central to Christianity may equally have provided a vital stimulus for the devotion given to them, and to the text of that Gospel, by Westcott, Hort, and their collaborator J. B. Lightfoot.

In London, interest in Coleridge's ideas had been sustained partly by those who, after coming across them in Cambridge, had propagated them in London journals of the 1820s: it was then that Maurice had edited the *Metropolitan Quarterly Magazine*, followed by his work with Sterling for the *Athenaeum*. In *Fraser's Magazine* J. A. Heraud wrote about them in a series of articles which included his 1832 review of *Aids to Reflection*.[365] P. G. Patmore, friend of Hazlitt and Lamb, bequeathed a respect for Coleridge to his son Coventry, who was to describe how in his youth the intellectual questioning of his faith had been removed by a study of Butler's *Analogy*, and how

> . . . the moderating lessons of experience were aided by much reading of Scripture, and, among other books, by Coleridge's "Aids to Reflection"—which I got almost by heart—the "Pilgrim's Progress", Leighton's "Sermons", Taylor's "Holy Living", and other books having a more practical tendency than most of those with which I began my studies of religion.[366]

[364] A. Westcott *Life and Letters of Brooke Foss Westcott* (2 vols 1903) I 111–12. C's statement concerning the Bible that "whatever *finds* me, bears witness for itself that it has proceeded from a Holy Spirit . . ." is in Letter I of *CIS* (1840), his insistence on the centrality of intuition in e.g. *Sp Aph B I* at n 4. Westcott's citation, in *An Introduction to the Study of the Gospels* (1860) 8, of the saying "Plotinus thanked God that he was not tied to an immortal body" in almost the exact form in which it appears in *AR, Mor Aph XI*, suggests that he had the work readily to hand.

[365] For these and many other articles on C by Heraud see *Samuel Taylor Coleridge: an Annotated Bibliography of Criticism and Scholarship* ed R. Haven, W. Crawford et al (2 vols Boston, Mass 1976–83).

[366] Basil Champneys *Memoirs and Correspondence of Coventry Patmore* (2 vols 1901) II 48–9. Cf his letter to H. S. Sutton 26 Feb 1847: "what religion I have . . . I have drawn . . . mainly from the Bible, interpreted by that mental eye which I have acquired by long and laborious study of the writings of Coleridge": ibid II 144.

John Ruskin, Sr, was also an admirer of Coleridge and may well have been moved by the volume.[367] His son, who was interested more by the poetry, wrote in his diary for 6 February 1843, ". . . read some of Coleridge's *Friend*, which gives one a higher notion of him than even his poetry"; there is reason to believe that he also read *Aids to Reflection*,[368] but Coleridge's general encouragement of a nobler view of human beings than that available from recent philosophy had in any case come to him already by way of his father. Others in London who acknowledged a debt to Coleridge were F. F. Barham, the Alist,[369] J. W. Marston, the playwright and critic,[370] James Hinton, the surgeon,[371] and Shadworth Hodgson, the philosopher.[372]

There were always some who, like Newman, registered reservations about Coleridge's religious thinking. Arthur Hugh Clough, noted among his contemporaries for his strong sense of the actual, was writing by 1841:

I should like much to have heard Carlyle's complaints against Coleridge. I keep wavering between admiration of his exceedingly great perceptive and analytical power and other wonderful points and inclination to turn away altogether from a man who has so great a lack of all reality and actuality.[373]

---

[367] For evidence indicating such an interest see *The Ruskin Family Letters* ed Van Akin Burd (2 vols Ithaca, NY 1973) I xxix.

[368] *The Diaries of John Ruskin* ed Joan Evans and J. H. Whitehouse (3 vols Oxford 1956–9) I 242. Ruskin's mention of C's praise for Baxter's "Life" three weeks later (II 245) suggests a reading of *Aids to Reflection*, in which C praises a "golden passage" in his "Life" (i.e. *Reliquiae Baxterianae* ed M. Sylvester) which includes the assertion that Catholics may under some circumstances be saved: "And I can never believe that a man may not be saved by that religion, which doth but bring him to the Love of God and to a heavenly mind and life." The sentence is quoted below, *Sp Aph B VIIIa* at n 24, and italicised by C.

[369] F. F. Barham (1808–71). *A Memorial of Francis Barham*, edited by Isaac Pitman (1873), contains "Lecture on the Life and Doctrines of Coleridge" by Barham, followed by "Alism"; both are written in the phonetic alphabet.

[370] J. W. Marston (1819–90). In a leading article on "the state and prospects of Genius" in *The Psyche* ed Marston et al, I No 1 (8 Jun 1839) 9, appears the statement

"Coleridge, Wordsworth and others, who have represented the outward as the type of higher antecedencies, are the heralds of an advent which we may call the Universal Poetic Dispensation." This is followed by a quotation from "Dejection: An Ode".

[371] James Hinton (1822–75). Writing to his future wife in 1850, he promised that they would look over Coleridge together, asserting of *AR*, "No book ever had a greater influence on the development of my mind": Ellice Hinton *Life and Letters of James Hinton* (1878) 40. He later joined the Metaphysical Society, which included Tennyson and Maurice among its members.

[372] Shadworth Hodgson (1832–1912), also a member of the Metaphysical Society, was particularly influenced by Coleridge's work on the relationship between subject and object (see e.g. below, *Sp Aph B II* at nn 53–72). For his book *The Philosophy of Reflection* (1878) see also above, n 350.

[373] Letter to J. N. Simpkinson: *The Correspondence of Arthur Hugh Clough* ed F. L. Mulhauser (2 vols Oxford 1957) I 106.

When Carlyle came to present his "complaints" in polished form in the *Life of John Sterling* (1851), the effects were hardly favourable to Coleridge's reputation. Not only was the advocate of a "manly character" depicted as himself a broken-down figure, but his religious thought was being blamed by Carlyle for the ". . . strange Centaurs, spectral Pusey-isms, monstrous illusory Hybrids, and ecclesiastical Chimeras,—which now roam the Earth in a very lamentable manner!"[374] Yet the chapter as a whole makes clear how difficult Carlyle found it to keep a proper balance between the laudable and reprehensible qualities in Coleridge: within much that was mistaken from his own point of view he could discern the workings of an intelligence that commanded his admiration.

This divided viewpoint was evident also in Matthew Arnold's comments. If he praised the "stimulus of his continual effort" he must immediately insert the astonishing parenthesis "—not a moral effect, for he had no morals—" before resuming, "his continual instinctive effort, crowned often with rich success, to get at and to lay bare the real truth of his matter in hand".[375] Twenty years later, nevertheless, he was still praising " 'the great Coleridgean position', that Christianity rightly understood, is identical with the highest philosophy, and that, apart from all questions of historical evidence, the essential doctrines of Christianity are necessary and eternal truths of reason". Despite a continuing disparagement of Coleridge's moral weakness he believed this to be one of the crucial ideas for his time: "it is true, it is deeply important, and by virtue of it Coleridge takes rank, so far as English thought is concerned, as an initiator and founder". It was, indeed, "henceforth the key to the whole defence of Christianity".[376]

A more potent check to the reputation of *Aids to Reflection* came as the ideas of Darwin and Wallace helped to subvert the sense of a moral hierarchy in nature which was, for thinkers such as Arnold, the most attractive feature of Coleridge's thinking; the development of biblical criticism meanwhile had proceeded well beyond Coleridge's positions.[377] Those who were most swayed by such ideas were henceforward likely to direct their praise rather to Coleridge's achievements in literary criticism. A good example of such an attitude may be found in William Hale White (who, however, was particularly influenced by Carlyle's ac-

---

[374] Thomas Carlyle *The Life of John Sterling* (1851) 80.

[375] "Joubert" in *Essays in Criticism* (1865) 223.

[376] "A Comment on Christmas" (1885) reprinted in *St Paul and Protestantism* (1887): *Complete Prose Works* ed R. H. Super (Ann Arbor, Mich 1960–77) x 226–7.

[377] Particularly those expressed in *CIS*, published posthumously in 1840. See *SW&F (CC)*

count of Coleridge in the *Life of Sterling*, which he edited with an introduction[378]). In 1893 he wrote to his son:

> The Aids to Reflection are not Coleridge's best work. They are too theological. There is a seductive side to him against which it is always necessary to be on one's guard. "The procreator of strange Centaurs, spectral Puseyisms, monstrous illusory hybrids and ecclesiastical chimeras" was the immortal verdict of Carlyle and it is *true*. I like Coleridge best when he gets away from the Vernunft and Verstand and the Logos and his mediated German metaphysics. One arrowy word on a play of Shakespeare has more Vernunft in it to me than all his Kantian-Schellingian disquisitions on the faculty itself.[379]

Although there were no new editions as such after 1867, however, the volume continued to appear: it was issued in Bohn's Library, where it remained in print for many years; an edition by Thomas Fenby (Liverpool, 1873) was also reprinted several times. There was evidently a continuing popular audience for the work, even if that now expressed itself less readily in print. The unveiling of the bust of Coleridge in Westminster Abbey in 1885 was the occasion of some favourable references—particularly, in connection with the generosity displayed by American donors, to its popularity in the United States.[380] John Tulloch, surveying early nineteenth-century religious thought in the same year, and praising *Aids to Reflection*, especially for its sense of religion as a living body of thought, declared, "It is a book which none but a thinker on Divine things will ever like. It is such a book as all such thinkers have prized."[381] Thomas Walker (1822–98), a former editor of the *Daily News*, wrote

> In a blessed hour I met with the 'Aids to Reflection,' and having read it patiently I said, 'Now I know what "man being made in the Image of God" means; here is not only a pool of fresh water but a living spring'. I have kept up the habit of re-reading the 'Aids' yearly ever since.[382]

In 1904 Dr Wace, the Dean of Canterbury, speaking at the Church Congress at Liverpool, referred to it as ". . . a book he would like to see more read".[383] The book continued to be reprinted until 1915; after the First World War, however, there were to be no further reprints apart from small ones in facsimile, noted in Appendix H below.

---

[378] See W. Hale White ("Mark Rutherford") preface to Carlyle *Life of John Sterling* (World's Classics Oxford 1907).

[379] W. Hale White, letter to his son John 16 Oct 1893, quoted (var) Wilfred Stone *Religion and Art of William Hale White* (Stanford, Calif 1954) 65–6n.

[380] Lucy E. Watson *Coleridge at High-gate* (1925) 96.

[381] John Tulloch *Movements of Religious Thought in Britain during the Nineteenth Century* (1885) 9.

[382] Letter to Lucy Watson, quoted *Coleridge at Highgate* 98.

[383] Report in *The Guardian* 7 Oct 1904, cited ibid 99.

In the mid-nineteenth century the elements in *Aids to Reflection* which were thought to be particularly valuable varied considerably from one person to another; so much, at least, is suggested by the elements in it which were chosen for quotation and approval. Sterling looked to the book to provide the basis for a reasoned acceptance of orthodoxy by young clergymen unsure of their position; Maurice was impressed by its central ideas as offering a key to the founding of a Universal Society. Hort, who praised ". . . five golden pages on the confusion of sensibility with morality",[384] also found particular value in the section on original sin and atonement; Mill approved the implied injunction to love Truth if necessary more than Christianity itself.[385] For Trench, future author of *The Study of Words*, the remarks on the importance of attending to language and its history were of particular importance;[386] his friend Hallam admired Coleridge's power to lead human thought to ". . . Being's dim foundations".[387] Newman, as we have seen, was moved by Coleridge's inference from our dissatisfaction with objects of the senses that ". . . there is something in the human mind which makes it know that in all finite quantity, there is an infinite, in all measures of time an eternal . . ."—even though he felt that such insights could properly be fostered only within the discipline of the Church. Coventry Patmore was evidently impressed by the more practical argument that Christianity, as a way of life, must be tried if its truth were to be tested: he devoted a whole essay to the point.[388]

The more common ground of admiration, however, was Coleridge's emphasis on the need for a "spiritual" religion which could replace positions based simply on prudence or "evidences of religion" without falling into "enthusiasm": here Broad Churchmen and High Churchmen could assent and unite in eulogy. In this respect the main impact of the book was felt during the thirty or forty years following its publication. Hort, in fact, not only praised these qualities in the book, but saw its teachings, with their emphasis on freedom, as having offered a way forward better than that of the more authoritarian theologies to which writers such as Carlyle thought them to have contributed:

---

[384] "Coleridge" *Cambridge Essays* II 336.

[385] Reprinted in John Stuart Mill *Dissertations and Discussions* (1859) I 458–9: see below, *Int Aph XXV*.

[386] See *Study of Words* (1851) v, and cf below, C's note to *Int Aph XII*.

[387] See lines 160–71 of his poem *Timbuctoo*, based according to his note on

"conversations with that 'good old man, most Eloquent' Samuel Coleridge": *Writings of Arthur Hallam* ed T. H. Vail Motter (New York 1943) 42–3 and above, at nn 242–6.

[388] Coventry Patmore "Christianity an Experimental Science" in *Religio Poetae Etc.* (1893) 38–45.

The prodigious changes which have taken place in the last forty years render much of the *Aids to Reflection* very perplexing to those who forget the time when it was written. Because the Warburtonian doctrine, that all language respecting direct spiritual influences is purely metaphorical, is scarcely intelligible to us now, we must not forget that in the first quarter of the century it was almost an axiom of orthodoxy, and its denial identified with fanatical Methodism. To denounce it with all his might, and at the same time to clear the truth from the spurious additions of the Methodists, was one of the great purposes of Coleridge's life. To Wesley himself, or his professed followers, or the corresponding movement within the Church, it was impossible that he should feel any repugnance, except in so far as they attempted to vilify and uproot more ancient truths of which they knew nothing. This characteristic of his writings and conversation had however other effects: it compelled sundry thoughtful men to recognise the fact that a belief in spiritual influences, and the tremendous power which may thereby be exercised, are no prerogatives of any one type, least of all a thoroughly modern type, of Christianity, that they have at least an equal affinity with the most genuine elements of old English tradition. The outward fruits of that conviction constitute a no less conspicuous than important part of the history of the last twenty-five years, and therefore are known to the whole world; but the world does not recognise how a spirit of freedom originated and still animates a movement, which bears upon its surface such innumerable results of an altogether opposite and reactionary kind, and is itself too palpably capable of ministering to a hateful spiritual bondage.[389]

Not long after Hort wrote these words the influence of the volume began to be more diffused and scattered, partly as a result of the forces mentioned earlier. Their effect on the intellectual climate can be traced in Walter Pater's article "Coleridge's Writings", published ten years later,[390] for example. Pater was singularly well equipped to attempt a critical re-evaluation of Coleridge, being temperamentally attuned to his poetic sensibility yet aware of the growth of evolutionary and relativist thinking. He acknowledged the important contribution that Coleridge's biblical criticism, published in 1840 as *Confessions of an Inquiring Spirit*, had made towards the growth of liberal theology and deplored the damage to his reputation incurred among some of the orthodox through the posthumous publication of such views. In his more conservative writings, on the other hand, Pater traced as a fatal flaw his striving to establish an Absolute. The history of recent thought, he believed, had shown that only the relative could now count: in consequence he devalued those of Coleridge's works in which he worked for the establishment

---

[389] "Coleridge" *Cambridge Essays* II 346–7.
[390] *Westminster Review* NS XXIX (1866) 106–32. Parts of this article, lightly revised, along with the consideration of Coleridge's poetry contributed to *The English Poets* ed T. H. Ward (1880) IV 102–14, formed the essay "Coleridge" in *Appreciations* (1889).

of fixed principles. *Aids to Reflection*, for example, displayed for him "Archbishop Leighton's vague pieties all twisted into the jargon of a spiritualistic philosophy": "it is only here and there that the poorer matter becomes vibrant, is really lifted by the spirit".[391]

Elsewhere in his article he displays more insight into Coleridge's general arguments than such comments might suggest, perceiving not only the ways in which they related to Schelling's transcendentalism but the common antecedents of both thinkers in Greek thought.[392] He was evidently attracted by the "faint glamour of the philosophy of nature" to be traced in Coleridge's thinking as a whole, the "idea of a subtle winding parallel, a 'rapport' in every detail, between the human mind and the world without it, laws of nature being so many transformed ideas". The very principle of organisation in *Aids to Reflection*, ranging upwards through the three supposed ranges of man's reflective life—Prudence, Morality, Religion—owed much, he thought, to Schelling's principle that "the explanation of every phase of life is to be sought in that next above it".[393] But when Coleridge went on to draw his analogy between the principle of organisation in the flower and that in human beings[394] and attempted to validate religious belief on its basis, Pater parted company, seeing in his arguments something "too like the exploded doctrine of final causes".[395]

So long as Coleridge was not trying to establish firm religious conclusions of this kind, Pater could recognise in him a fellow-labourer, for despite his conviction that religious expression of the passion for perfection in terms harking back to writers such as Augustine was "no longer congruous with the culture of the age" he believed that that culture could not go very far before the "religious graces" reappeared in it "in a subtilized intellectual shape".[396] Coleridge might have failed in Pater's eyes through his lack of the Greek spirit, with "its engaging naturalness, simple, chastened, debonair", but by reason of his manifest "hunger for eternity" and all that that brought with it he was still to be "ranked among the interpreters of one of the constituent elements of our life".[397]

Pater no doubt spoke for many in the late nineteenth century who in the face of Darwinism clung to the idea that the religious spirit, or the life of the soul, was evolving through time, as being closer to acceptable contemporary language than Coleridge's insistence that the upward spiralling form of the spirit had shown no development in history, being

[391] "Coleridge's Writings" 112, 116.
[392] Ibid 118–19.
[393] Ibid 121, 124.
[394] See *Mor Aph VI* below at n 7.
[395] "Coleridge's Writings" 125.
[396] Ibid 126.
[397] Ibid 132.

essentially permanent and timeless. Attempts to re-establish old truths on such a basis seemed to them outdated. Others in turn believed that the eternal truths of Christianity could not be defended by such whole-sale accommodations to the new thinking, so that *Aids to Reflection* continued to have its admirers: Coleridge's moral insistences, in particular, remained attractive to those who were disturbed by the amoral implications of a thoroughgoing relativism. In the twentieth century Basil Willey was to attest, like Dewey and many before him, to the abiding qualities of the work.[398]

In recent years, and with the growing availability of Coleridge's writings as a whole, it has become possible to see each of his works in a larger perspective, and to recognise more fully the subtlety of his underlying enterprise in trying to reconcile old and new ways of apprehending human existence. *Aids to Reflection* is a particularly important volume for those who wish to understand the full significance of his thought. While it is a central document in helping to explain how one who in his early days had been so radical and innovative as an "inquiring spirit" could also have come to be known to subsequent generations as an eloquent and timely defender of the Christian faith, it also points to fundamental issues. Coleridge's early efforts to understand the new position of human beings in a universe that was being increasingly interpreted from a materialist point of view had stimulated ideas and speculations that were still at work in his later religious enquiries—enquiries turning back again and again to the rôle of the "spiritual" in such a universe.

Some of the questions involved were to remain crucial for subsequent thinkers, including immediate successors such as Maurice, Trench, and Newman: the possibility of building and sustaining a moral society, the nature of language as an expression of the human spirit, the need to find a true ground for human fidelity. The relevance of the volume is not confined to the nineteenth century, however, since the basic issue that underlies such concerns has not ceased to exercise reflective minds: on a world scale, indeed, the tension between views of human nature based on fidelity to the past and those looking to an exploratory scepticism has become if anything more marked during the present century. It is Coleridge's intelligent and subtle exploration of the contradictions involved, along with his attempts—with varying degrees of success—to resolve them, that gives continuing life to the discussions in his pages and is the ultimate justification for an intricate and extensive editing of his work.

---

[398] See e.g. *Nineteenth Century Studies*   (1972) 212–35, 257.
(1949) 31–8; *Samuel Taylor Coleridge*

AIDS TO REFLECTION

IN THE

FORMATION OF A MANLY CHARACTER

ON THE SEVERAL GROUNDS OF

PRUDENCE, MORALITY, AND RELIGION:

ILLUSTRATED BY

SELECT PASSAGES FROM OUR ELDER DIVINES, ESPECIALLY FROM ARCHBISHOP LEIGHTON.

BY S. T. COLERIDGE, ESQ., R.A., R.S.L.[1]

> This makes, that whatsoever here befalls,
> You in the region of yourself remain,
> Neighb'ring on Heaven: and that no foreign land.
> DANIEL.[2]

SECOND EDITION

---

[1] In a letter to his publisher 7 May 1825, shortly before publication, C discussed whether he should add letters after his name: "Again: what do you think? *Ought*

I to attach ROYAL ASSOCIATE of the R. S. L.?—I have no fondness for this Bashaship with *one Tail*—(My Brother-in-law has, at least a dozen queues.) neither for the Title, nor for the Thing . . .'': *CL* v 435–6. The letters here did not appear in *AR* (1825) but were added in both eds of *C&S* (1829, 1830) and in the 2nd ed of *AR* (1831).

² The first two lines are slightly adapted from a poem described as ''incomparable'' by C in 1804 (*CN* II 2224 f 85ᵛ): Samuel Daniel *To the Lady Margaret, Countess of Cumberland* st x lines 1–2 (lines 73–4): *Poetical Works* (2 vols 1781), C's annotated ed, II 354 (in *B Poets* IV 205):

> Which makes, that whatsoever here befals,
> You in the region of yourself re-main . . .

The last line is unidentified and may well be C's own addition: it may e.g. represent poetic transformation of a sentence from Böhme that concludes pt 1 of William Law *The Spirit of Prayer* (2 pts 1749–50): ''O how great a Triumph is there in the Soul when [Christ] arises in it! then a Man knows, as he never knew before, that he is a Stranger in a foreign Land.'' See *Conc* n 9, below. In BM MS Egerton 2801 f 262ᵛ C proposed as a motto for *AR* the following lines:

> What Soul so e'er in any language can
> Speak Heaven like his, is my Soul's Countryman.

These are from Richard Crashaw *An Apology for the Precedent Hymn* in *B Poets* IV 322 (in which ''his'' reads ''hers''); they had been copied correctly in N 19 in 1807: *CN* II 3013 and n.

TO THE READER[1]

FELLOW-CHRISTIAN![a] the wish to be admired,[b] as a fine Writer,[c] held a very subordinate place in the *Author's* thoughts and feelings in[d] the composition of this Volume. Let then its comparative merits and demerits, in respect of style and stimulancy[e] possess a proportional weight, and no more, in determining *your* judgment[f] for or against its contents. Read it *through:*[g] then compare the state of your mind,[h] with the state[i] in which your mind was,[j] when you first opened the Book. Has it led you to reflect? Has it supplied or suggested fresh subjects for reflection? Has it given you any new information? Has it removed any obstacle[k] to a lively conviction of your responsibility[l] as a moral agent?[m] Has it solved any [n]difficulties, which[o] had impeded your faith as a Christian? Lastly, has it increased your power of thinking connectedly? Especially[p] on the Scheme[q] and purpose of the Redemption by Christ? If it have done none of these things, condemn it aloud as worthless: and strive to compensate for your own loss of time,[r] by preventing others from wasting theirs.[s] But if your conscience dictates an affirmative answer to all or any of the preceding questions, declare this too aloud, and endeavour[t] to extend my utility.[u]

---

[a] COPY D: Fellow-Christian!   [b] COPY D: admired   [c] COPY D: Writer
[d] COPY D: on   [e] COPY D: stimulancy,   [f] COPY D: judgement
[g] COPY D: *thro'*:   [h] COPY D: mind   [i] COPY D: state,
[j] COPY D: was   [k] COPY D: obstacles   [l] COPY D: responsibility,
[m] COPY D: Agent?   [n–o] COPY D: difficulties that   [p] COPY D: Especially,
[q] COPY D: scheme   [r] COPY D: time   [s] COPY D: theirs!
[t] COPY D: endeavor   [u] COPY D adds at right: S. T. Coleridge

---

[1] This passage appears, with differences in punctuation, etc, in *AR* (1825) COPY D, presented to Daniel Stuart and apparently sent to him before 8 Jul 1825 (see *CL* v 474–5). C probably retained a transcript of his own, which he used when it was first printed here in 1831, replacing the longer ''Advertisement'' which had appeared in 1825 (see App G(a) below). (The leaves [+]1 to [+]4 in COPY D containing the passage have been removed from the volume in the BM and placed in a separate folder.)

3

^aΟὕτως πάντα πρὸς ἑαυτὴν ἐπάγουσα, καὶ συνηθροισμένη ψυχὴ αὐτὴ^b εἰς αὐτήν^c, ῥᾷστα καὶ μάλα βεβαίως μακαρίζεται.

MARINUS[1]

Omnis divinae atque humanae eruditionis elementa tria, NOSSE, VELLE, POSSE: quorum *principium* unum^d MENS, sive SPIRITUS; cujus *Oculus* est RATIO; cui *lumen* praebet DEUS.

Vita di G. B. VICO, p. 50[2]

---

^a AR (1825): Follows "Preface"   ^b AR (1825, 1831): αὐτη
^c AR (1825): αὐτὴν ; AR (1831) αὐτην   ^d AR (1825): unam ; COPIES D, G: unum

[1] These mottoes were added at the latest possible time before publication, after the Preface and Contents page and on p xiv of AR (1825), the one blank page still available (letter to Hessey c 10 May 1825: CL v 445). The first is a free adaptation from Marinus De vita Procli. C had it in Proclus In Platonis theologiam ed (with Latin tr) A. Portus (Hamburg 1618). "So a soul, collecting all things to itself, and itself gathering itself together, most easily and surely becomes blessed." Thomas Taylor's tr, adapted as indicated, gives the meaning of the original in Marinus: "And thus the soul of this blessed man, having collected itself from all parts and retiring into [itself], [used to depart] after a manner from [the] body; while it yet appeared to be contained in [it]": The Life of Proclus by Marinus in Philosophical and Mathematical Commentaries of Proclus on the First Book of Euclid's Elements (2 vols 1792) I 18. Joseph Henry Green had given In Platonis theologiam (1618) to C in 1820, and C had immediately noted from it a number of mottoes, though not this one: CN IV 4744, 4746. He had earlier owned and annotated the Thomas Taylor volume, which is now in the BM. See also below, Sp Aph B II n 29.

[2] C used the 6th ed of Giambattista Vico Principi di scienza nuova (3 vols Milan 1816), which he began reading on 2 May 1825: CN IV 5204 and n. See M. H. Fisch

"The Coleridges, Dr. Prati and Vico" MP XLI (1943) 113. The 1816 text, copied almost exactly in N 20 (CN IV 5204), runs "Omnis divinae, atque humanae eruditionis Elementa tria, Nosse, Velle, Posse: quorum principium unum Mens; cuius oculus ratio, cui aeterni veri lumen praebet Deus . . .": "Vita di G. B. Vico" Scienza I 50–1; tr "All divine and human learning has three elements: knowledge, will and power, whose single principle is the mind, with reason for its eye, to which God brings the light of eternal truth": Vico Autobiography tr M. H. Fisch and T. G. Bergin (Ithaca, NY 1944) 156. C has altered this to read "mind, or spirit" and to omit "of eternal truth" at the end. For Vico see also CN IV 5205–9, 5211, 5219, 5231, 5232, and nn; CL v 454. B. Croce Bibliografia Vichiana (Naples 1947) I 520 misdates C's first reading of Vico and so supposes that the body of AR was influenced by Vico.

In AR (1839), after C's death, a third motto was added by HNC and included in subsequent editions: "Naturam hominis hanc Deus ipse voluit, ut duarum rerum cupidus et appetens esset, religionis et sapientiae. Sed homines ideo falluntur, quod aut religionem suscipiunt omissa sapientia; aut sapientiae soli student omissa religione; cum alterum sine altero esse non possit verum. LACTANTIUS"; from Divinae institutiones 3.11; tr W. Fletcher

4

^aPREFACE

AN Author has three points to settle: to what sort his Work belongs, for what Description of Readers it is intended, and the specific end or object, which it is to ^banswer. ^cThere is indeed a preliminary Interrogative respecting the end which the Writer himself has in view, whether the Number of Purchasers, or the Benefit of the Readers. But this may be safely passed by; since where the book itself or the known principles of the writer do not supersede the question, there will seldom be sufficient strength of character for good or for evil, to afford much chance of its being either distinctly put or fairly answered.^d

I ^eshall proceed therefore to state^f as briefly as possible the intentions of the present volume in reference to ^gthe three first-mentioned, viz. *What? For Whom? and For what?*^h

I. WHAT? The answer is contained in the Title-page. It belongs to the class of *didactic* Works. Consequently, those who neither wish instruction for themselves,ⁱ nor assistance in instructing others, have no interest in its contents. *Sis Sus, sis Divus: Sum* CALTHA, *et non tibi spiro!*[1]

^a AR (1825): p [v]

^b COPY F: answer. *What*? for *Whom*? & *for* What?

^{b-h} COPY G: answer. WHAT? for WHOM? and FOR what? Under these three heads, therefore, I shall endeavor to state as briefly as possibly the nature and purpose of the present volume.

^{c-d} COPY F: "There is . . . answered." is ringed around, with note: "To be printed as a *Note*, at the bottom of the page."

^{e-f} COPY F: shall state

^{g-h} COPY F: these.

ⁱ AR (1825): p vi (selves,)

The Works of Lactantius (2 vols Edinburgh 1871): "God willed this to be the nature of man, that he should be desirous and eager for two things, religion and wisdom. But men are mistaken in this, that they either undertake religion and pay no attention to wisdom, or they devote themselves to wisdom alone, though the one cannot be true without the other."

[1] "*Be you a Pig, be you a God: I am* CALTHA, *and do not breathe for you!*" A favourite motto with C; an exact source for

this dactylic hexameter line has not been traced, but cf his note concerning the pig and marjoram in Erasmus' "Abstine Sus! non tibi spiro", from his *Colloquia (Convivium religiosum): Opera* (Leiden 1707) I 674B (*CN* II 3181 and n), as well as *Friend (CC)* II 41n (10 Aug 1809): "Sus apage! Haud tibi spiro", and *BL* ch 12 *(CC)* I 235, in which a "good and learned man" is substituted for the pig. The editor of *The Friend* cites also a herbal of Camerarius and the title-page of Sir Philip Sidney *The*

II. For whom? *Generally*, for as many in all classes as wish for aid in disciplining their minds to habits of reflection—for all who, desirous of building up a manly character in the light of distinct consciousness, are content to study the principles of moral Architecture on the several grounds of prudence, morality and religion. And lastly, for all who feel an interest in the Position, I have undertaken to defend—this, namely, that the Christian Faith (*in which I include every article of belief and doctrine professed by the first Reformers in common*) is the Perfection of Human Intelligence: an interest sufficiently strong to insure[a] a patient attention to the arguments brought in its support.

But if I am to mention any particular class or description of Readers, that were prominent in my thought during the composition of the volume, my Reply must be: that it was *especially* designed for the studious Young at the close of their education or on their first entrance into the duties of manhood and the rights[b] of self-government. And of these, again, in thought and wish I destined the work (the latter and larger portion, at least) yet more particularly to Students intended for the Ministry; *first*, as in duty bound, to the members[c] of our two Universities: *secondly*, (but only in respect of this mental precedency *second*) to all alike of whatever name, who have dedicated their future lives to the cultivation of their Race, as Pastors, Preachers, Missionaries, or Instructors of Youth.

III. For what? The Worth of the Author is estimated by the ends, the attainment of which he proposed to himself by the particular work: while the Value of the Work depends on its fitness, as the Means.[2] The Objects of the present volume are the following, arranged in the order of their comparative importance.

1. To direct the Reader's attention to the value of the Science of

---

[a] *AR* (1825): ensure   [b] copy d: Duties [not necessarily in C's hand]
[c] *AR* (1825): p vii (bers)

Countesse of Pembrokes Arcadia (1593), for the words "Non tibi spiro" associated with a picture of a pig and and a herb. *Friend (CC)* i 41n. *Caltha* appears in classical authors as a sweet-smelling yellow flower, but is now the botanical name of the unscented marsh marigold. The pig's dislike for marjoram was mentioned by Lucretius *De rerum natura* 6.794 and, as proverbial, by Aulus Gellius *Noctes Atticae* preface § 19.

[2] For the distinction between worth and value see, in 1810, *Friend (CC)* ii 350–1 (cf i 556, 440); in 1811, *EOT (CC)* ii 320; *LS (CC)* 74, 189, 211, and *C&S (CC)* 168. The longest discussion is in *P Lects* Lect 12 (1949) 364, in which C gives the example of a malicious stabbing that results by chance in a cure as an act of value without worth and associates the distinction with Kant. Cf *Grundlegung zur Metaphysik der Sitten* (Riga 1797) esp p 77. C's copy is in the BM.

Words, their use and abuse (see *Note, p.*[a] 17) and the incalculable advantages attached to the habit of using them appropriately, and with a distinct knowledge of their primary, derivative, and metaphorical senses. And in furtherance of this Object I have neglected no occasion of enforcing the maxim, that to expose a sophism and to detect the equivocal or double meaning of a word is, in the great majority of cases, one and the same thing. Horne Tooke entitled his celebrated work, [b]Ἔπεα πτερόεντα,[3] Winged Words: or Language, not only the *Vehicle* of Thought but the *Wheels*. With my convictions and views, for ἔπεα I should substitute λόγοι, *i.e.*,[c] Words *select* and *determinate*, and for πτερόεντα ζώοντες[d], i.e. *living* Words.[4] [e]The *Wheels* of the intellect I admit them to be; but such as Ezekiel beheld in "the visions of God" as he sate among the Captives by the river of Chebar.[5] "Whithersoever the Spirit was to go, the Wheels went, and thither was their Spirit to go: *for the Spirit of the living creature was in the wheels also.*"[6]

[a] *AR* (1825): p.
[b-c] *AR* (1825): No accents or breathings in the Greek
[d] *AR* (1825): *i. e.*,
[e] *AR* (1825): p viii

[3] John Horne Tooke Ἔπεα πτερόεντα; *or, The Diversions of Purley* vol I 1st ed 1786 (C used this at Cambridge in Jan 1792: J. C. C. Mays "Coleridge's Borrowings from Jesus College Library 1791–4" *Transactions of the Cambridge Bibliographical Society* VIII—1981–6—567); enlarged 2nd ed 1798; vol II 1st ed 1805 (the projected vol III was never published: Tooke burned the ms). C sent for the 1798 ed before leaving for Germany (letter of 18 Sept 1798: *CL* I 417) and dined with Tooke after his return (*CL* I 559). He wanted Godwin to write a book on the power of words in which he would "*philosophize* Horn Tooke's System": *CL* I 625. Despite his respect for Tooke's book, and his description of Tooke as a "clear-headed old man", he found "a sort of charletannery in his manner" (*CL* I 559–60)—an opinion developed thirty years later in the phrase "that clearness which is founded on shallowness": *TT* 7 May 1830 *(CC)* I 117–21 (1836 vn, dated 7 and 8 May 1830, II 82–5). For possible debts to Horne Tooke's etymologies see e.g. *CN* III Index 1.

[4] Many years before, in his fifth lecture of 1811–12, C said that Horne Tooke's book might in his judgment have been "much more fitly called *Verba Viventia*, or 'living words' for words are the living products of the living mind & could not be a due medium between the thing and the mind unless they partook of both": *Lects 1808–1819 (CC)* I 273. The phrase ἔπεα ζώοντα appears also e.g. in a notebook entry of 1814 *(CN* III 4237) in which this idea is developed, in an annotation on Böhme *Works—CM (CC)* I 606—and in *C&S (CC)* 166, 184. For λόγοι ζώοντες cf Plato *Phaedrus* 276A: ". . . λόγον ζῶντα καὶ ἔμψυχον . . ."—the "living and breathing word" (or rather speech) of one who knows, of which the written word is a mere image and reminder; cf also Acts 7.38: λόγια ζῶντα, "the lively oracles" of God. See, in addition, App I, Excursus Notes 1, "Logos and related words", and 4, "Coleridge on Nous and Logos".

[5] Ezek 1.1.

[6] Ezek 1.20 (var). C is probably transcribing the quotation directly from *SM*, in which it varies in exactly the same ways, including the omission of "and the wheels were lifted up over against them": *SM (CC)* 29. The association of the mysterious

2. To establish the *distinct* characters of Prudence, Morality, and Religion: and to impress the conviction, that though the second requires the first, and the third contains and supposes both the former; yet still Moral Goodness is other and more than Prudence, or the Principle of Expediency; and Religion more and higher than Morality. For this distinction the better Schools even of Pagan Philosophy contended. (*See pp.* 40–2).

3. To substantiate and set forth at large the momentous distinction between REASON and Understanding.[7] Whatever is achievable[a] by the UNDERSTANDING for the purposes of worldly interest, private or public, has in the present age been pursued with an activity and a success beyond all former experience, and to an extent which equally demands my admiration and excites my wonder. But likewise it is, and long has been, my conviction, that in no age since the first dawning of Science and Philosophy in this Island have the Truths, Interests, and Studies that especially belong [b]to the REASON, contemplative or practical, sunk into such utter neglect, not to say contempt, as during the last century. It is therefore one main Object of this Volume to establish the position, that whoever transfers to the understanding[c] the primacy due to the Reason, loses the one and spoils the other.

4. To exhibit a full and consistent Scheme of the Christian dispensation,[d] and more largely of all the *peculiar* doctrines of the Christian Faith; and to answer [e]all the objections[f] to the same, that do not originate in a corrupt Will rather than an erring Judgment;[g] and to do this in a manner intelligible for all who, possessing the ordinary advantages of education, do in good earnest desire to form their religious creed in the light of their own convictions, and to have a reason for the faith which

---

[a] *AR* (1825): atchievable
[b] *AR* (1825): p ix
[c] *AR* (1825): Understanding
[d] *AR* (1825): Dispensation,
[e–f] COPY G: all objections
[f] *AR* (1825): Objections
[g] *AR* (1825): Judgement;

---

wheels with living creatures is constant throughout Ezekiel's descriptions of them (Ezek 1.15–21 and 10.1–19), assisting C's anti-mechanistic argument. *SM* explains his point further: there the wheels are associated not with "words" but with "symbols", "harmonious in themselves, and consubstantial with the truths, of which they are the *conductors*. . . . The truths and the symbols that represent them move in conjunction and form the living chariot that bears up (for *us*) the throne of the Divine Humanity": *LS (CC)* 19.

[7] See esp *Sp Aph B VIIIb* and C's Appendix below; also App D(a) for versions of an extended annotation on the distinction, including one at this point in COPY A.

they profess. There are indeed Mysteries, in evidence of which no reasons can be *brought*. But it has been my endeavor[a] to show, that the true solution of this problem is, that these Mysteries *are* Reason, Reason in its highest form of Self-affirmation.

Such are the special Objects of these "Aids to Reflection." Concerning the general character of the work, let me be permitted to add the few following sentences. St. Augustine, in one of his Sermons, discoursing on a high point of Theology, tells his auditors[b]—Sic accipite, ut mereamini intelligere. Fides enim debet praecedere intellectum, ut sit intellectus fidei praemium*.[8] Now without a certain portion of gratuitous and (as it were) *experimentative* faith in the Writer, a Reader will scarcely give that degree of continued attention, without which no *didactic* Work worth reading can be read to any wise or profitable purpose. In *this* sense, therefore, and to *this* extent, *every* Author, who is competent to the office he has undertaken, may without arrogance repeat St. Augustine's words in his own right, and advance a similar claim on similar grounds. But I venture no farther than to imitate the sentiment at a humble distance, by avowing my belief that He, who seeks *instruction* in the following pages, will not fail to find *entertainment* likewise; but that whoever seeks entertainment only will find neither.

READER!—You have been bred in a land abounding with men, able in arts, learning, and knowledges manifold, this man in one, this in another, few in many, none in all. But there is one art, of which every man [c]should be master, the art of REFLECTION.[9] If you are not a *thinking* man, to what purpose are you a *man* at all? In like manner, there is one knowl-

---

* TRANSLATION. *So* receive this, that you may deserve to understand it. For the faith ought to precede the Understanding, so that the Understanding may be the reward of the faith.

[a] *AR* (1825): endeavour   [b] *AR* (1825): p x   [c] *AR* (1825): p xi

---

[8] Augustine was preaching on John 10.30: "I and my Father are one." C transcribed the passage in a notebook entry of 1807 (*CN* II 3133) from the 57th sermon *De verbis Domini* (Sermon CXXXIX: Migne *PL* XXXVIII 770), where it begins "Sic accipite, sic credite, ut mereamini . . ." Transcribed also in BM MS Egerton 2801 f 260. C's interest in Isa 7.9 in the Septuagint version ("Unless you believe you will not understand") and in St Augustine's variations on it was shown also in *CN* III 3888 and IV

4611, in *BL* ch 24 *(CC)* II 244, and in the 1818 *Friend: Friend (CC)* I 427, and in annotations on Böhme *Works* and on Chillingworth *Works*: *CM (CC)* I 605, II 29. See also Barth 48. For Isa 7.9 see also below, *Mor Aph VI* n 29, and the paragraph in *Sp Aph B V* at nn 5, 6, and 7. "Experimentative" below is *OED*'s first example.

[9] For the growth of this idea in C's mind see above, Editor's Introduction, pp lxxxviii–xcvi.

edge, which it is every man's interest and duty to acquire, namely, SELF-KNOWLEDGE: or to what end was man alone, of all animals, endued[a] by the Creator with the faculty of *self-consciousness?* Truly said the Pagan moralist, E coelo descendit, Γνῶθι Σεαυτόν[b].[10]

But you are likewise born in a CHRISTIAN land: and Revelation has provided for you new subjects for reflection, and new treasures of knowledge, never to be unlocked by him who remains self-ignorant. Self-knowledge is the key to this casket; and by reflection alone can it be obtained. Reflect on your own thoughts, actions, circumstances, and—which will be of especial aid to you in forming a *habit* of reflection,—accustom yourself to reflect on the words you use, hear, or read, their birth, derivation[c] and history. For if words are not THINGS, they are LIVING POWERS,[11] by which the things of most importance to mankind are actuated, combined, and humanized. Finally, by reflection you may draw from the fleeting facts of your worldly trade, art, or profession, a science permanent as your immortal soul; and make even these subsidiary and preparative to the reception of spiritual truth, "doing as [d]the dyers do, who having first dipt their silks in colors[e] of less value, then give them the last tincture of crimson in grain."[12]

S. T. COLERIDGE[13]

---

[a] *AR* (1825): indued
[b] *AR* (1825, 1831): Σέαυτον
[c] *AR* (1825): derivation,
[d] *AR* (1825): p xii
[e] *AR* (1825): colours

[10] "Know thyself" was one of the two mottoes reputedly inscribed in the temple at Delphi. C's quotation is from Juvenal *Satires* 11.27, tr "From heaven descends the 'Know thyself' ". Cf *BL* chs 12, 24 *(CC)* I 252, II 240 (C's note) and *SM (CC)* 79. In 1832 he made it the motto of a sombre poem, *Self-knowledge*, in which he asked "What is there in thee, Man, that can be known?" and concluded "Ignore thyself, and strive to know thy God!": *PW* (EHC) I 487.

[11] See n 4 above, and *CL* v 228 (1822) on Words as "Spirits and Living Agents that are seldom misused without avenging themselves".

[12] For the general process of "double-dyeing" see Pliny *Natural History* 9.136–41. No closer source has been traced. For C's interest in dyeing, and particularly "mordants" that fix the colour, see *CN* III 3606n, 4301, *CM (CC)* II 496, *Friend (CC)* I 463, and *BL* ch 18 *(CC)* II 71.

[13] A pencilled note by C in COPY E, p ⁻1, reads: "Four Species of Prudence 1. an evil Prudence; 2. a commendable Prudence; 3. a wise Prudence; 4. a holy Prudence. p. 23." For another version see below, *Int Aph XXIX* n 1.

^aAIDS TO REFLECTION

INTRODUCTORY APHORISMS

APHORISM I^b

^cIn philosophy equally as in poetry it is the highest and most useful prerogative of genius to produce the strongest impressions of novelty, while it rescues^d admitted truths from the neglect caused by the very circumstance of their universal admission.[1] Extremes meet.[2] Truths, of all others the most awful and interesting, are too often considered as *so* true, that they lose all the power of truth, and lie bed-ridden in the dormitory of the soul, side by side with the most despised and exploded errors.

APHORISM IIe

There is one sure way of giving freshness and importance to the most *common-place* maxims—that of *reflecting* on them in direct reference to our own state and conduct, to our own past and future being.

---

^a *AR* (1825): p 1
^b *AR* (1825): EDITOR.
^{c-d} *AR* (1825) Corr: It is the prerogative of Genius to produce novel impressions from familiar objects: and seldom can philosophic genius be more usefully employed than in thus rescuing, &c.
^e *AR* (1825): EDITOR.

---

[1] The first two sentences may be traced to a notebook entry of Apr 1805 (*CN* II 2535), which was then used for *The Friend* 14 Sept 1809, in which the whole of this first aphorism is to be found var: *Friend (CC)* II 74, cf I 110. The third sentence appears again in *SM (CC)* 25 and *Op Max ms* B2 ("III") 131. For the power of genius to produce impressions of novelty in poetry see also the account of WW in *BL* ch 14 *(CC)* II 5–7.

[2] This, C's favourite proverb, was used by him in the *M Post* as early as 28 Jan 1800: *EOT (CC)* I 138; it is cited in a letter to Sotheby 26 Aug 1802 (*CL* II 857) and again, with examples, in a note of 11 Dec 1803 (*CN* I 1725). See also *CN* II 2066, III 3400, 3405, IV 4830, *EOT (CC)* II 336 (cf I cxliv), *Friend (CC)* I 110 and n 5, *LS (CC)* 133, *C&S (CC)* 96, *CM (CC)* I 518.

*a*APHORISM III*b*

To restore a common-place truth to its first *uncommon* lustre, you need only *translate* it into action. But to do this, you must have *reflected* on its truth.

APHORISM IV*c1*

"It is the advice of the wise man, 'Dwell at home,' or, with yourself;[2] "and though there are very few that do this, yet it is surprising that the "greatest part of mankind cannot be prevailed upon, at least to visit "themselves sometimes; but, according to the saying of the wise "Solomon, *The eyes of the fool are in the ends of the earth.*"[3]

A reflecting mind, says an ancient writer, is the spring and source of every good thing. ("*Omnis boni principium intellectus cogitabundus.*")[4] It is at once the disgrace and the misery of men, that they live without fore-thought. *d*Suppose yourself fronting a mirror.*e* Now*f* what the objects*g* behind you are to their*h* images*i* at the same apparent*j* distance before you,*k* such is Reflection to Fore-thought. *l*As a*m* man with-

---

a *AR* (1825): p 2

b *AR* (1825): EDITOR.

c *AR* (1825): LEIGHTON.

d-e Added in 1831. *AR* (1825) Corr: Suppose yourself . . . a glass mirror. ; COPY A: Suppose your self . . . a glass mirror. ; COPIES C & D: Suppose yourself . . . a Glass Mirror. ; COPY G: Reads as 1831.

f *AR* (1825): But ; Corr, COPIES A, C, D, G: Now

g *AR* (1825) Corr: Objects

h *AR* (1825): the ; Corr, COPIES, A, C, D, G: their

i *AR* (1825) Corr: *images*

j Added in 1831. *AR* (1825) Corr, COPIES A, C, D, G: apparent

k *AR* (1825): you in a looking-glass, ; Corr, COPIES A, G: you, ; COPY D: you:

l-m COPIES C, D, E, F, G: A

---

[1] The first paragraph is reprinted almost exactly from Leighton's *Theological Lectures* No XXIV: "Before the Communion": Leighton COPY C IV 348–9, in which C marked the whole passage in ink. See *CM (CC)* III. The second paragraph is excursive from the next sentence in Leighton, which begins: "It is the peculiar property of the human mind, and its signal privilege, to reflect upon itself; yet we, foolishly neglecting this most valuable gift . . .". In *AR* (1825) the use of inverted commas in the first paragraph (as here) and the appearance of the sign "ED." at the end (by comparison with the normal "L. & ED." at the head) suggest that both paragraphs survive,

not fully standardised, from the first proof (see above, Editor's Introduction, at nn 57–8).

[2] Cf Persius 4.52: "tecum habita". The commentators quote Aristotle *Nicomachean Ethics* 9.4.5 (1166ᵃ23–4); Horace *Satires* 2.7.112.

[3] Prov 17.24.

[4] Both quotation and translation are from Leighton COPY C IV 191 and n (shortly before the second sentence used for *Aph VIII*, below). For "reflecting" Leighton's unidentified translator reads "thoughtful"; he refers to "the ancients" rather than "an ancient writer". A source has not been found.

out Fore-thought scarcely deserves the name of a man, so[a] Fore-thought without Reflection is but a metaphorical phrase for the *instinct* of a beast.[b]

APHORISM V[c]

As a fruit-tree is more valuable than any one of its fruits singly, or even than all its fruits of a single season, so the noblest object of reflection is the mind itself,[1] by which we reflect:

[d]And as the blossoms, the green, and the ripe, fruit, of an orange-tree are more beautiful to behold when on the tree and seen as one with it, than the same growth detached and seen successively, after their importation into another country and different clime; so is it with the manifold objects of reflection,[2] when they are considered principally in reference to the reflective power, and as part and parcel of the same. No object, of whatever value our passions may represent it, but becomes *foreign* to us, as soon as it is altogether unconnected with our intellectual, moral, and spiritual life. To be *ours*, it must be referred to the mind either as motive, or consequence, or symptom.

APHORISM VI[e]

He [f](says Archbishop Leighton)[g][1] who teaches men the principles and precepts of spiritual wisdom, before their minds are called off from foreign objects, and turned inward upon themselves, might as well write his instructions, as the sybil wrote her prophecies, on the loose leaves of trees, and commit them to the mercy of the inconstant winds.

---

[a] COPIES C, D, E, F, G: ; and   [b] *AR* (1825): ED.
[c] *AR* (1825): EDITOR.   [d] *AR* (1825): p 3
[e] *AR* (1825): LEIGHTON.   [f-g] Added in 1831

[1] For further examples of C's thinking in this "organic" strain see J. S. Hill *Imagination in Coleridge* (1978) Index s.v. "organic".

[2] *AR* (1825) COPY E adds a note at this point: "Even in the higher order of Intellects, great and momentous is the difference between those who reflect on their Thoughts in relation to Things, and those who habitually contemplate Things in relation to Thoughts. Each is at length transfigured into its ultimate purpose. In the former class, the Thoughts gradually sensualize: in the latter, Things light up into Symbols and become more and more intellectual. The sensual Veil of the *Phænomenon* loses its opacity, and the *Substance* the Numen or το νουμενον, shines thro'."

[1] C here paraphrases from Leighton's Introduction to his *Theological Lectures*: see Leighton COPY C IV 190 (not marked at this point): App A(a) below.

In order to learn we must *attend:* in order to profit by what we have learnt, we must *think*—i.e.[b] reflect. He only thinks who *reflects.*[*c]

It is a matter of great difficulty, and requires no ordinary skill and address, to fix the attention of men [e]on the world within them, to induce them to study the processes and superintend the works which they are themselves carrying on in their own minds; in short, to awaken in them both the faculty of thought† and the inclination to exercise it. For alas! the largest part of mankind are nowhere greater strangers than at home.

* The indisposition, nay, the angry aversion to *think*, even in persons who are most willing to *attend*, and on the subjects to which they are giving studious *attention*,—*ex. gr.*, Political Economy, Biblical Theology, Classical Antiquities, and the like,—is the phenomenon that forces itself on my notice afresh, every time I enter into the society of persons in the higher ranks. To assign a *feeling* and a determination of their *will*, as a satisfactory reason for embracing or rejecting this or that opinion or belief, is of ordinary occurrence, and sure to obtain the sympathy and the suffrages of the company. And yet to *me*, this seems little less irrational than to apply the nose to a picture, and to decide on its genuineness by the sense of smell.

† *Distinction between Thought and Attention.*[2]—By THOUGHT is here meant the voluntary reproduction in our own minds of those states of consciousness, or (to use a phrase more familiar to the religious reader) of those inward experiences, to which, as to his best and most authentic documents, the teacher of moral or religious truth refers us. In ATTENTION, we keep the mind *passive:*[3] In THOUGHT, we rouse it into activity. In the former, we submit to an impression—we keep the mind steady in order to *receive* the stamp. In the latter, we seek to *imitate* the artist, while we ourselves make a copy or duplicate of his work. We may learn arithmetic, or the elements of geometry, by continued attention alone; but *self*-knowledge, or an insight into the laws and constitution of the human mind,[f] and

[a] *AR* (1825): EDITOR.
[b] *AR* (1825): i. e.
[c] Footnote added in 1831
[d] *AR* (1825): L. & ED.
[e] *AR* (1825): p 4 begins with "(especially of young men*)", with footnote: "So Leighton says: my own experience would rather have suggested the contrary remark."
[f] *AR* (1825): mind

[1] Another paraphrase and development from Leighton COPY C IV 190–1. See App A(b), below, in which the middle part appears simply as "It is the advice of the Psalmist, that we should *converse much with ourselves*" (referring presumably to Ps 4.4: "commune with your own heart upon your bed, and be still").

[2] The first and last sentences of this paragraph are based closely on a discussion of thought and attention in *The Friend* 11 Jan 1810, associated with a note of 3 Jan 1810: *Friend (CC)* II 277, *CN* III 3670. In

The Friend, however, C dwells on the effort involved in both activities; here his emphasis is on the passivity of attention. The latter idea had been developed in the meantime in *Logic*, in which his hesitation in describing attention as an "act" is ascribed partly to the fact that it is a feature of the brute creation, where "we have no sufficient ground for assuming that this takes place . . . by any energy of the percipient power itself": *Logic (CC)* 60.

[3] The creative relationship between active and passive powers is illustrated by the

APHORISM IX[a]

Life is the one universal soul,[1] which,[b] by virtue of the enlivening
BREATH, and the informing WORD, all organized bodies have in common, each *after its kind*. This, therefore, all animals possess, and man
as an animal. But, in addition to this, God transfused into man a higher
gift, and specially imbreathed:—even a [c]living (that is, self-subsisting)
soul, a soul having its life in itself. [d]"And man became a living soul."[e][2]
He did not merely *possess* it, he *became* it.[3] It was his proper *being*, his
truest *self, the* man *in* the man. None then, not one of human kind, so
poor and destitute, but there is provided for him, even in his present
state, *a house not built with hands.*[4] Aye, and spite of the philosophy
(falsely so called) which mistakes the causes, the conditions, and the
occasions of our becoming *conscious* of certain truths and realities for
the truths and realities themselves—a house gloriously furnished. Nothing is wanted but the eye, which is the light of this house, the light which
is the eye of this soul. This *seeing* light, this *enlightening* eye, is Reflection.[5]*[f] It is more, indeed, than is ordinarily meant by that word; but it

---

the *grounds* of religion and true morality, in addition to the effort of attention requires the
energy of THOUGHT.

* The *"Dianoia"* of St. John, I. Ep. v. 20, inaccurately rendered "Understanding" in
our translation. To exhibit the full force of the Greek word, we must say, "a power of
discernment by Reason."[6]

[a] *AR* (1825): EDITOR.
[b] *AR* (1825): which
[c] *AR* (1825): p 5
[d-e] COPY F: underlined, with "Gen. 2.7" in the margin (not in C's hand)
[f] Footnote added in 1831

---

image of a water-insect in *BL* ch 7 *(CC)* I
124. See also below, *Refl Mor* n 4.
   [1] The "universal soul" (a concept available to C in early years from Virgil and the
Greeks, e.g., and later from Bruno) was
used as a term for God in the early speculations on animated life as a series of wind-
harps, played on by an intellectual breeze,
that went into C's verse drafts for *The Eolian Harp* (1795): "Thus *God* would be the
Universal Soul. . . ."; see *PW* (EHC) II
1022. The relationship between "anima"
(soul) and "animation" remained a lifelong preoccupation. In the 1809 *Friend* the
substitution by modern physiologists of
"vital power" (*vis vitae*) for soul was approved, to be later censured as "imperfect
and in part erroneous" in an annotated
copy of 1816: *Friend (CC)* II 75 and n. See
also lectures in 1811–12: *Lects 1808–1819*

(CC) I 314, 457. In the present (more orthodox) aphorism C looks to the term "living soul" to point the essential difference
between human beings and the rest of "animated nature". "Each after its kind": cf
"after his kind", Gen 1.11, 12, 21, 24, 25.
   [2] Gen 2.7. Cf a later comment on John
Asgill *A Collection of Tracts*: *CM (CC)* I
126.
   [3] By contrast, C maintains of genius that
"the Man of Genius *has*, not *is*, a Genius":
comment on an aphorism by Schlegel in
Athenaeum: *CM (CC)* I 149.
   [4] 2 Cor 5.1: "a house not made with
hands". C's ms for the remainder of this
aphorism, from "of our becoming . . .", is
reproduced in App B(a) below.
   [5] See Editor's Introduction, above, at nn
158–60.
   [6] 1 John 5.20: "And we know that the

is what a *Christian* ought to mean by it, and to know too, whence it first came, and still continues to come—of what light even this light is *but* a reflection. This, too, is THOUGHT; and all thought is but unthinking that does not flow out of this, or tend towards it.

APHORISM X[a]

Self-superintendence! that any thing should overlook itself! Is not this a paradox, and hard to understand? It is, indeed, difficult, and to the imbruted sensualist a direct contradiction: and yet most truly does the poet exclaim,

> ——Unless *above* himself he can
> Erect himself, how mean a thing is man![1]

[b]APHORISM XI[c]

An hour of solitude passed in sincere and earnest prayer, or the conflict with, and conquest over, a single passion or "subtle *bosom* sin,"[1] will teach us more of thought, will more effectually awaken the *faculty*, and form the *habit*, of reflection, than a year's study in the schools without them.[d]

[a] *AR* (1825): EDITOR.
[b] *AR* (1825): p 6
[c] *AR* (1825): EDITOR.
[d] COPY F, added: "Ps iv.4." (not in C's hand)

Son of God is come, and hath given us an understanding, that we may know him that is true, and we are in him that is true, even in his Son Jesus Christ." Διά-, equivalent to English "through", may also imply distinction or separation; -νοια is cognate with νοῦς or reason. C's point is best brought out in his pastiche of Wisd of Sol 7 in *SM*, characterising reason as "substantiated and vital", "one only, yet manifold, overseeing all, and going through all understanding": *SM (CC)* 69 and n 2. Cf. also ibid 97 on "discourse of reason". Διάνοια is usually translated "mind" in AV —"understanding" only in Eph 1.18 and here. Cf also *CN* IV 4796 on Gen 8.21, in which Septuagint διανοηθείς (AV "said in his heart") is related by C to "the δια NOY of Heraclitus" and "The Logos";

and Epigraph to *Sp Aph A* n 2 below.
[1] The original reads "poor" for "mean". Daniel *To the Lady Margaret, Countess of Cumberland* XII lines 7–8: *Poetical Works* (2 vols 1718) II 354; in *B Poets* IV 205. Quoted, in this form, below in *AR, Mor Aph XXXVI* at n 18, *P Lects* (1949) 394, and *CN* IV 4711 f 131ᵛ; and, correctly, in *Friend (CC)* I 100 and comment on Leighton COPY C I 11–15: *CM (CC)* III. Quoted correctly by WW *Excursion* IV 330–1: *WPW* V 119. (For another quotation from the poem see above, title-page at n 2.) C's ms for this aphorism is transcribed in App B(b) below.
[1] "One cunning bosom-sin". George Herbert *Sin* line 14: *The Temple* (1673) i 38. See below, *Int Aph XIX* n 3 and *Sp Aph B VII* 28.

APHORISM XII[a]

In a world, [b]the opinions of which[c] are drawn from outside shows, many things may be *paradoxical*, (that is, contrary to the common notion) and nevertheless true: nay,[d] paradoxical,[e] *because* they are true. How should it be otherwise, as long as the imagination of the Worldling is wholly occupied by surfaces, while the Christian's thoughts are fixed on the substance, that which *is* and abides, and which, *because* it is the substance*, the outward senses cannot recognize. Tertullian had good reason for his assertion, that the simplest Christian (if indeed a Christian) knows more than the most accomplished irreligious philosopher.[3]

[f]COMMENT[4]

Let it not, however, be forgotten, that the powers of the understanding and the intellectual graces are precious gifts of God; and that every

* *Quod stat subtus*,[1] that which stands *beneath*, and (as it were) supports, the appearance. In a language like ours, where so many words are derived from other languages, there are few modes of instruction more useful or more amusing than that of accustoming young people to seek for the etymology, or primary meaning, of the words they use.[2] There are cases, in which more knowledge of more value may be conveyed by the history of a *word*, than by the history of a campaign.

[a] *AR* (1825): EDITOR.
[b-c] *AR* (1825): whose opinions
[d] COPY C: they may be paradox,
[e] Added in 1831
[f] *AR* (1825): p 7

[1] An important point for C: cf his discussion in *Op Max ms* B3 ("II") 10–11 (see above, Editor's Introduction, p lxxxii), where he describes the work of raising "the materials furnished by the senses & sensations" into "objects of reflection" as being "appropriately called the understanding or sub-stantiative faculty". In *Sp Aph B [XXIV]* below at n 47 C defines superstition as "the *sub*stantiation of things that stand *over*"; cf *Sp Aph B IV* at n 8. For further discussions see *CN* IV 4679, 4739, 4843 f 117ᵛ, 5222 † 85ᵛ, 5418, and 5422, *CM (CC)* I 145, 469, 524. C's ms for this note is transcribed in App B(c) below.

[2] Cf *The Friend* 10 Aug 1809: "The best and most forcible sense of a word is often that, which is contained in its' Etymology": *Friend (CC)* II 44 (C's note). For some lists of words treated by C in this fashion see e.g. *C&S (CC)* 13 n 2 and Indexes to *Logic (CC)* and present volume, s.v. "etymology". See also below, *Sp Aph B IX* n 28 and refs.

[3] Cf Tertullian *Apologeticus adversus gentes pro Christianis* 46: Migne *PL* I 508–9.

[4] At this point C seems to have picked up his *Lay Sermon* for a discussion of the rôle of intellect in religion. A passage from which several subsequent aphorisms are drawn refers to religion as "that sincere, that entire interest, in the undivided faith of Christ which demands the first-fruits of the whole man, his affections no less than his outward acts, his understanding equally with his feelings": *LS (CC)* 175. The first sentence here is related to that statement, while the last follows one at the foot of the same page (see next note).

Christian, according to the opportunities vouchsafed to him, is bound to cultivate the one and to acquire the other. Indeed, he is scarcely a Christian who wilfully neglects so to do. What says the apostle? Add to your faith *knowledge,* and to knowledge *ᵃmanly energy:ᵇ⁵* for this is the proper *ᶜrendering* of ἀρετήν,*ᵈ* and not virtue, at least in the present and ordinary acceptation of the word.*ᵉ*

APHORISM XIII*ᶠ*[1]

Never yet did there exist a full faith in the Divine Word (by whom *light,* as well as immortality, was brought into the world,) which did not expand the intellect, while it purified the heart: which did not multiply the

---

* I am not ashamed to confess that I dislike the frequent use of the word virtue, instead of righteousness, in the pulpit: and that in prayer or preaching before a Christian community, it sounds too much like *Pagan* philosophy. The passage in St. Peter's epistle*ᵍ* is the only scripture authority that can be pretended for its use,⁶ and I think it right, therefore, to notice that it rests either on an oversight of the translators, or on a change in the meaning of the word since their time.

ᵃ⁻ᵇ COPY F: underlined, with "Pet.2. c. 1. v. 5." in the margin (not in C's hand)
ᵇ *AR* (1825): *energy,* (ἀρέτην) ; *AR* (1831) is misaccented similarly
ᶜ⁻ᵈ *AR* (1825): rendering,
ᵉ *AR* (1825): word*.
ᶠ *AR* (1825): EDITOR.
ᵍ *AR* (1825): epistle,

---

⁵ Cf *LS (CC)* 175–6 (immediately following the passage used for Comment to *Aph XIII,* below): "Or again: if to believe were enough, why are we commanded by another Apostle, that, 'besides this, giving all diligence we should add to our faith manly energy and to manly energy *knowledge!*' " C is there closer to the word order of 2 Pet 1.5 but there also substitutes "manly energy" for the AV "virtue", explaining his alteration in a note to RS's copy of *LS*, "αρετη, strangely mistranslated in our Testament by the unmeaning Generalissimo, 'Virtue' ". (See the *CC* footnote and below, following note.) C's preoccupation with "manliness", which finds its way into the final title of *AR,* was earlier associated with his love for SH and envy of WW. Cf *The Picture* line 107: *PW* (EHC) I 372; *Letter to Sara Hutchinson* line 140: *Poems* ed J. Beer (1963) 275; *CN* II 3148 ff 45ᵛ–6. Cf also the sleep of "the manly effective *Will*" in *CN* II 2086 f 40.

⁶ In its earliest appearances in Greek literature (applied by Homer to the conduct of his heroes), the word seems to have approximately the meaning C suggests. He presumably connected it with Ἄρης (Mars) and ἄρρην (male). If C were right "virtue" (from *vir,* man) would be exactly parallel (cf *Sp Aph B V* n 8, where C refers to this note). He accepts the corruption of the meaning of the Latin word but not of the Greek one. Many etymologists, then and now, take the "proper", i.e. the non-transferred, etymological, or primary meaning to be "fittingness", however. Ἀρετή appears about four times in the NT, so that its meanings can be established only approximately, by context; at 2 Pet 1.3 there is in any case an uncertainty in the text.

¹ From a passage in *LS (CC)* 175 immediately following the sentence quoted in *Int Aph XII* n 4, above. C follows closely, changing "mind" to "understanding".

aims and objects of the understanding, while it fixed and simplified those of the desires and passions*.

^aCOMMENT⁴

If acquiescence without insight; if warmth without light; if an immunity from doubt, given and guaranteed by a resolute ignorance; if the habit of *taking for granted* the words of a catechism, remembered or forgotten; if a mere *sensation* of positiveness substituted (I^b will not say,^c for the *sense* of *certainty;*^{d5} but)^e for that calm assurance, the very means and conditions of which it supersedes; if a belief that seeks the darkness, and yet strikes no root, immoveable as the limpet from the rock, and, like the limpet, fixed there by mere force of adhesion;^f if these suffice to make men Christians, in what sense could the apostle affirm that believers receive, not indeed worldly wisdom, that comes to nought, but the

* The effects of a zealous ministry on the intellects and acquirements of the laboring^g classes are not only attested by Baxter,[2] and the Presbyterian divines, but admitted by Bishop Burnet, who, during his mission in the west of Scotland, was "amazed to find a poor commonality so able to argue," &c.[3] But we need not go to a sister church for proof or example. The diffusion of light and knowledge through this kingdom, by the exertions of the Bishops^h and clergy, by Episcopalians and Puritans, from Edward VI. to the Restoration, was as wonderful as it is praiseworthy, and may be justly placed among the most remarkable facts of history.

^a *AR* (1825): p 8
^b *AR* (1825): —I
^c *AR* (1825): say
^d *AR* (1825): *certainty,*
^e *AR* (1825): but—
^f *AR* (1825): adhesion;—
^g *AR* (1825): labouring
^h *AR* (1825): bishops

[2] "Some of the Poor men did competently understand the Body of Divinity, and were able to judge in difficult controversies": Baxter *Reliquiae Baxterianae* ed M. Sylvester (1695) 85. Cf *Logic (CC)* 20.

[3] See Gilbert Burnet *History of His Own Time* (2 vols Dublin 1724, 1734) i 293 (part of the account of Leighton's conferences with the Presbyterians in 1670): "We were indeed amazed to see a poor commonalty so capable to argue upon points of government, and on the bounds to be set to the power of Princes in matters of religion: Upon all these topicks they had texts of scripture at hand; and were ready with their answers to any thing that was said to them."

[4] Again from *LS (CC)* 175. C inserts "mere" before "sensation" and omits "intelligible" before "sense"; he also leaves out two instances from his final questioning: Jesus' pronouncing it a sign and miracle that the Gospel was preached to the poor (Matt 11.5, Luke 4.18, 7.22) and St Paul's saying that every Christian receives "the Spirit that searcheth all things, yea the deep things of God himself" (1 Cor 2.10).

[5] A favourite distinction of C's, particularly in 1807–9: see *CN* ii 3095, *CL* iii 49, *Friend* 1 Jun 1809 *(CC)* ii 7 (cf 76n). Cf also Barth 48–9. C's ms for the remainder of this paragraph is transcribed in App B(d) below.

wisdom of God, *a*that we might*b* *know and comprehend* the things that are freely given to us of God?*6* On what grounds could he denounce the sincerest *fervor* of spirit as *defective*, where it does not likewise bring forth fruits in the UNDERSTANDING?*7*

APHORISM XIV*c1*

In our present state, it is little less than impossible *d*that the affections should be kept constant to an object which gives no employment to the understanding, and yet cannot be made manifest to the senses. The exercise of the reasoning and reflecting powers, increasing insight, and enlarging views, are requisite to keep alive the substantial faith in the heart.

APHORISM XV*e1*

In the state of perfection, perhaps, all other faculties may be swallowed up in love, or superseded by immediate vision; but it is on the wings of the CHERUBIM, *i.e.*,*f* (according to the interpretation of the ancient Hebrew doctors,) the *intellectual* powers and energies,*2* that we must first be

---

a–b *AR* (1825): *that we might*
c *AR* (1825): EDITOR.
d *AR* (1825): p 9
e *AR* (1825): EDITOR.
f *AR* (1825): i. e.

---

6 "Now we have received, not the spirit of the world, but the spirit which is of God; that we might know the things that are freely given to us of God": 1 Cor 2.12.

7 At this point in *LS (CC)* 175 C explained his reference by a footnote quoting 1 Cor 14.20 as (var): "Brethren! be not children in understanding: howbeit, in malice be ye children, but in understanding be men."

1 In *LS (CC)* 180, C discussed the simplicity of truth in Christianity, and drew attention to the difficulty of certain parts of the Bible, continuing, "But it is impossible that the affections should be kept constant to an object which gives no employment to the understanding. The energies of the intellect, increase of insight, and enlarging views, are necessary to keep alive the substantial faith in the heart." C's ms for this passage, from "keep alive" to "strong and" in *Aph XV* (Comment), is transcribed

in App B(e) below.

1 The source is again *LS*, after an intervening sentence, "They are the appointed fuel to the sacred fire": *LS (CC)* 180–1. The *LS* version does not include the phrase "or superseded by immediate vision"; it reads: "the powers and efforts of the Intellect" for "the *intellectual* powers and energies" and "poor Mortals" for "imperfect mortals"; and concludes with a fuller version of the Psalm quotations, while excluding the gloss on "broad". There are also minor variations.

2 The cherubim were allegorised in various forms by the early Fathers. The interpretation that they stood for intellectual powers, which is used by Didymus of Alexandria, Jerome, and Augustine, apparently derives from Philo, who makes the term equivalent to ἐπίγνωσις καὶ ἐπιστήμη πολλή (mighty knowledge and understanding): *Life of Moses* 3.8. See *Enc RE* III 510a,

borne up to the "pure empyrean."[3] It must be seraphs, and not the hearts of imperfect mortals, that can burn unfuelled and self-fed.[4] *Give me understanding*, (is the prayer of the Royal Psalmist),[a] and I shall observe thy law with my *whole* heart.[5]—Thy law is exceeding *broad*[6]—that is, comprehensive, pregnant, containing far more than the apparent import of the words on a first perusal. It is my *meditation* all the day.[7]

COMMENT[8]

It is worthy of especial observation, that the Scriptures are distinguished from all other writings pretending to inspiration, by the strong and frequent recommendations of knowledge, and a spirit of inquiry. Without reflection, it is evident that neither the one can be acquired nor the other exercised.

[b]APHORISM XVI[c]

The word *rational* has been strangely abused of late times. This must not, however, disincline us to the weighty consideration, that thought-

[a] *AR* (1825): Psalmist)
[b] *AR* (1825): p 10   [c] *AR* (1825): EDITOR.

512b. The cherubim were also a focus of controversy in the eighteenth century, following the assertion by John Hutchinson (1674–1737) that three of their faces, the bull, lion, and eagle, signified the persons of the Trinity, and the fourth, man, was thus an emblem of humanity taken into the trinitarian essence. See Hutchinson *Works* (12 vols 1747–9) esp vols VI and VII (cited approvingly in J. Parkhurst *Hebrew and English Lexicon*—2nd ed 1778—290–308). C endorsed his interpretation of the cherub in the 1818 *Friend: Friend (CC)* I 502 and nn. Hutchinson also records (VI 387) that "Cherub among the more antient Hebrews signified *Power*". C's assertion may therefore be linked back to a speculation that the relationships in the Trinity provided the key to the inner workings of the intelligential powers in man; cf Beer *CV* 77–81.

[3] *PL* III 56–8:

Now had th' Almighty Father from above,
From the pure Empyrean where he sits
High thron'd above all highth, bent

down his eye . . .

[4] Cf C's note on John Oxlee *The Christian Doctrines of the Trinity and Incarnation Considered and Maintained on the Principles of Judaism* (1815) I 41–2: ". . . the Seraphim were no less symbolic Images than the Cherubim—": *CM (CC)* III 1089. For possible sources of C's interest in seraph lore see Beer *CV* 72f, 127–8, 164, 179.

[5] Ps 119.34.
[6] Ps 119.96.
[7] Ps 119.97.
[8] The first sentences echo both *Friend* and *SM*, which quotes it: "It is highly worthy of observation, that the inspired writings received by Christians are distinguishable from all other books pretending to Inspiration . . . in their strong and frequent recommendations of Truth. I do not here mean Veracity, which cannot but be enforced in every Code which appeals to the religious principle of Man; but Knowledge": *Friend (CC)* II 70–1 (I 104); *SM (CC)* 47–8.

fulness, and a desire to rest[a] all our convictions on grounds of right reasoning,[b] are inseparable from the character of a Christian.

APHORISM XVII[c]

A reflecting mind is not a flower that grows wild, or comes up of its own accord. The difficulty is indeed greater than many, who mistake quick recollection for thought, are disposed to admit; but how much less than it would be, had we not been born and bred in a Christian and Protestant land, the fewest of us are sufficiently aware. Truly may we, and thankfully ought we to, exclaim with the Psalmist: The entrance of thy words *giveth* light; it giveth understanding even to the simple.[1]

APHORISM XVIII[d1]

Examine the journals of our zealous missionaries, I will not say among the Hottentots or Esquimaux, but in the highly *civilized*, though fearfully *uncultivated*,[2] inhabitants of ancient India. How often, and how feelingly, do they describe the difficulty of rendering the simplest chain of thought intelligible to the ordinary natives, the rapid exhaustion of their whole power of attention, and with what distressful effort it is exerted while it lasts![3] Yet it is among these that [e]the hideous practices

> [a] *AR* (1825): ground ; Corr, COPY G: rest
> [b] *AR* (1825): reason,
> [c] *AR* (1825): EDITOR.
> [d] *AR* (1825): EDITOR.
> [e] *AR* (1825): p 11

[1] Ps 119.130.
[1] Quoted from *The Friend* (1818), which differs from the first version of 10 Aug 1809: *Friend (CC)* I 55–6 (II 49). For "ancient India" *Friend* reads "Hindostan"; for "reflect" "*think*", etc. The first part of the passage is based on a note of 1809, when C was reading missionary accounts (esp William Carey's) in *Periodical Accounts Relative to the Baptist Missionary Society* (Clipstone 1800): *CN* III 3511. See n 4, below.
[2] The terms of his distinction between "civilized" and "cultivated" seem to have come into focus for C in 1818. It figures twice in the "Essays on Method" for *The Friend* and in the second lecture on the history of philosophy (28 Dec 1818), in which it is applied to ancient Egypt and (as here)

India: *Friend (CC)* I 494, 500; *P Lects* (1949) 110. See *C&S (CC)* 42–3 and n for further discussion.
[3] Carey occasionally touches upon such matters, e.g. "Their poverty of words to express religious ideas is amazing; all their conversation being about earthly things": *Periodical Accounts* I 203–4; cf also *CN* III 3505, 3507. There may be other sources closer to C's point. In 1821–2 he had copied into a notebook an account of the Californian Indians by Kotzebue which included the author's comment, "The Missionaries assured us, it was difficult to instruct them, on account of their stupidity; but I believe these gentlemen do not give themselves much trouble about it": *CN* IV 4841.

of self-torture chiefly prevail. O if folly were no *easier* than wisdom, it being often so very much more *grievous*, how certainly might these unhappy slaves of superstition be converted to Christianity! But, alas;[a] to swing by hooks passed through the back,[4] or to walk in shoes with nails of iron pointed upwards through the soles[5]—all this is so much less *difficult*, demands so much less exertion of the will than to *reflect*,[6] and by reflection to gain knowledge and tranquillity!

COMMENT

It is not true, that ignorant persons have no notion of the *advantages* of truth and knowledge. They confess, they see and bear witness to these advantages in the conduct, the immunities, and the superior powers of the possessors. Were they attainable by pilgrimages the most toilsome, or penances the most painful, we should assuredly have as many pilgrims and self-tormentors in the service of true religion, as now exist under the tyranny of papal or Brahman superstition.[7]

[a] *AR* (1825): alas!

[4] In the 1809 notebook entry (*CN* III 3511) this was prompted immediately by Carey's narrative (*Periodical Accounts* I 173–4). C may also have recalled the plate facing p 110 in J. G. Stedman *Narrative of a Five Years' Expedition* (1796) I; but see Mary Lynn Johnson "Coleridge's Prose and a Blake Plate in Stedman's *Narrative* . . ." *The Wordsworth Circle* XIII (1982) 36–8. Carey also refers (I 197) to "falling on spikes of iron, dancing with threads or bamboos thrust through their sides", etc.

[5] This draws on an account by Mr Thomas (*Periodical Accounts* I 29) of a man on the Malabar coast who wished to make atonement for sin and was directed "to drive in spikes through his sandals, and on these spikes he was to place his naked feet, and walk about 480 miles". On hearing a missionary preach "The blood of Jesus Christ cleanseth from all sin", he threw off his sandals and cried, "This is what I want!" C knew this from an article in *QR* I (1809) 215, which he cited in a note on [James Sedgwick] *Hints . . . on the Nature and Effect of Evangelical Preaching* (4 pts 1808–10) iii 31–4: *LR* IV 356, *CM (CC)* IV. For both hooks and spikes see also *P Lects* Lect 8 (1949) 251, where the editor's

note refers to J. A. Dubois *Description of the . . . People of India . . .* (1817) 414. C annotated this book at some point: *CM (CC)* II 339–49.

[6] The original notebook entry (*CN* III 3511) reads, more idiosyncratically, "than to think, and to become by a habit of action what we thinking know to be our IDEA".

[7] In the case of Roman Catholic penances, C was no doubt thinking of flagellation, a form of penance particularly common from the eleventh to the fourteenth century. See "Flagellants" in *Enc RE* VI and references. So far as Indian religion is concerned he may be recalling Thomas Maurice *Indian Antiquities* (7 vols 1793–1806) v, in which ". . . the Horrible Penances of the Indian Devotees are detailed" (title-page), including growing nails through hands, holding arms above the head until they fuse, wearing huge iron collars and spike-lined shoes, remaining suspended from trees, and staring into the sun for years on end (pp 1053–78). C may also have had in mind suttee, the institution whereby a widow could elect to destroy herself by burning after her husband's death. See J. Z. Holwell *A Review of the Original Principles, Religious and Moral,*

APHORISM XIX[a]

In countries enlightened by the gospel, however, the most formidable and (it is to be feared) the most frequent impediment to men's turning the mind inward upon themselves, is that they are afraid of what they shall find there. There is an aching hollowness in the bosom, a dark cold speck at the heart,[1] an obscure and boding sense of a somewhat, that must be kept *out of* [b]*sight* of the conscience; some secret lodger, whom they can neither resolve to eject or retain.*[c]

* The following sonnet was extracted by me from Herbert's Temple, in a work long since out of print,[2] for the purity of the language and the fulness of the sense. But I shall be excused, I trust, in repeating it here for higher merits and with higher purposes, as a forcible comment on the words in the text.

Graces vouchsafed in a Christian land.[3]

Lord! with what care hast thou begirt us round!
Parents first season us. Then schoolmasters
Deliver us to laws. They send us bound
To rules of reason. Holy messengers;
Pulpits and Sundays; sorrow dogging sin;
Afflictions *sorted;* anguish of all sizes;
Fine nets and stratagems to catch us in!
Bibles laid open; millions of surprizes;[d]
Blessings beforehand; ties of gratefulness;
The sound of glory ringing in our ears:
Without, our shame; within, our consciences;
Angels and grace; eternal hopes and fears!
Yet all these fences, and their whole array,
One cunning BOSOM-SIN[e] blows quite away.

[a] *AR* (1825): EDITOR.
[b] *AR* (1825): p 12
[c] *AR* (1825): retain*.
[d] *AR* (1825): surprises;
[e] *AR* (1825): BOSOM SIN

---

of the Ancient Bramins (1779) 87–101. C's ms for this passage, from "see and bear witness" to the first word of *Aph XIX*, is transcribed below in App B(f).

[1] Cf C's comment on himself: ". . . even in boyhood there was a cold hollow spot, an aching in that heart, when I said my prayers—that prevented my entire union with God—that I could not *give up*, or that would not give *me* up—as if a snake had wreathed around my heart, and at this one point its Mouth touched at & in-breathed a weak incapability of willing it away": *CN* IV 5275. Cf K. Coburn *The*

Self-Conscious Imagination (1974) 11–12.

[2] C's annotated copy was *The Temple* (1673), in which he singled out this poem as "a good sonnet": *CM (CC)* II 1035. See also *BL* ch 19 *(CC)* II 95–6 and n, in which it is again quoted, and the note on Kant *Religion innerhalb der Grenzen der blossen Vernunft* (Königsberg 1794) 2–4, quoted above, Editor's Introduction, at n 30.

[3] The text is that of the poem *Sin: The Temple* (1673) i 37–8 (see also above, *Int Aph XI* n 1, and below, *Sp Aph B VII* 28). In *BL* it is called *The Bosom Sin*.

COMMENT

Few are so obdurate, few have sufficient strength of character, to be able to draw forth an evil tendency or immoral practice into distinct *consciousness*, without bringing it in the same moment before an awaking *conscience*.[4] But for this very reason it becomes a duty of conscience to form the mind to a habit of distinct consciousness. An unreflecting Christian walks in twilight among snares and pitfalls! He entreats the *a*heavenly Father not to lead him into temptation, and yet places himself on the very edge of it, because he will not kindle the torch which his Father had given into his hands, as a means of prevention, and lest he should pray too late.

APHORISM XX[b]

Among the various undertakings of men, can there be mentioned one more important, can there be conceived one more sublime, than an intention to form the human mind anew after the DIVINE IMAGE?[1] The very intention, if it be sincere, is a ray of its dawning.

The requisites for the execution of this high intent may be comprised under three heads; the prudential, the moral, and the spiritual:

APHORISM XXI[c]

First, *d*RELIGIOUS PRUDENCE*e*—What this*f* is, will be best explained by its effects and operations. *g*PRUDENCE in the service of RELIGION*h*

a *AR* (1825): p 13
b *AR* (1825): EDITOR.
c *AR* (1825): EDITOR.
d–e *AR* (1825): PRUDENCE. ; Corr: PRUDENCE, *religious* Prudence, I mean; a prudence in the service of religion. N. B. ; *What Prudence is in itself and independent of religion*, is explained p. 26, in the note to Aph. XXXI. ; COPY C: PRUDENCE:—*Religious* Prudence, I mean: or Prudence in the service of Religion. ; COPY D agrees (var) adding: *What Prudence is, generally taken, see explained* in p. 26. Note to Aph XXXI ; COPY E (not in C's hand) and COPY F agree (var) with COPY D
f COPY G: Religious Prudence
g–h *AR* (1825): It

[4] The relationship between conscience and consciousness, conscience being seen as a central light to consciousness, is a recurrent theme in C's writings. See e.g. his note on a copy of *The Friend*: ". . . Consciousness itself, that Consciousness of which all reasoning is the varied modification, is but the Reflex of the Conscience, when most luminous, and too often a fatuous vapor, a warmthless bewildering Mockery of Light exhaled from its corrup-tion or stagnation": *Friend (CC)* I 523n. For conscience as "the sole fountain of certainty" see C's "Confessio Fidei" of 3 Nov 1810: *CN* III 4005 f 4ᵛ. For more on conscience and consciousness see *CN* III 3231 and a passage in the Opus Maximum mss, both of which are quoted and discussed further in Boulger 121–4. See also Barth 27–31, 98–9, 109–10, 114.

[1] Cf Gen 1.27. C may be recalling this precise phrase from his reading of Blake's

consists*[a1]* in the prevention or abatement of hinderances and distractions; and consequently in avoiding, or removing, all such circumstances as, by diverting the attention of the workman, retard the progress and hazard the safety of the work. It is likewise (we deny not) a part of this unworldly prudence, to place ourselves as much and as often as it is in our power so to do, in circumstances[2] directly favorable*[b]* to our great design; and to avail ourselves of all the *positive* helps and furtherances which these circumstances afford. But neither dare we, as Christians, forget whose and under what dominion *[c]*the things are, quae nos *circumstant*, i.e. that *stand around* us. We are to remember, that it is the *World*[3] that constitutes our outward circumstances; that in the form of the World, which is evermore at variance with the Divine Form (or idea),*[d]* they are cast and moulded; and that of the means and measures which *[e]*the same*[f]* prudence requires in the forming anew of the Divine Image in the soul, the far greater number suppose the World at enmity with our design. We are to avoid its snares, to repel its attacks, to suspect its aids and succours:*[g]* and even when compelled to receive them as allies within our trenches, *[h]*we are*[i]* to commit the outworks alone to their charge, and

[a] *AR* (1825): consists then
[b] *AR* (1825): favourable
[c] *AR* (1825): p 14
[d] *AR* (1825): idea)
[e-f] Added in 1831
[g] *AR* (1825): succours,
[h-i] *AR* (1825): yet

Songs of Innocence and of Experience in Feb 1818, when the poem of this title was one of three to win his highest mark of approval: *CL* IV 837. C's ms for the next paragraph and *Aph XXI* to "next greater" is transcribed below in App B(g).

[1] In earlier years C was more concerned to distinguish prudence, pursued as an end in itself, from religion, as in his note of 1810, *CN* III 3955 and n (and cf 3293). See also *Friend* (1809–10) *(CC)* II 18, 72, 82, 85.

[2] Having in 1795 believed (following Pistorius) that "vice originates not in the man, but in the surrounding circumstances", *Lects 1795 (CC)* 12, 40, 217n, C retained a lifelong interest in "circumstances": see e.g. Indexes s.v. in *EOT (CC), Friend (CC),* and *LS (CC).* See also "the clear light of circumstance flashed | Upon an Independent Intellect" in WW's

Borderers lines 1495–6: *WPW* I 187, and its reuse in *The Prelude* (1850) XI 243–4.

[3] *AR* (1825) COPY G inserts a note at this point: "The World, Worldliness—what these words mean in Scripture? The duty of withdrawing from the World, is it of perpetual Obligation? Or did it arise out of circumstances peculiar to the first Christians, and cease to bind when these ceased to exist? If the duty remains the same, has not the change of circumstances induced a corresponding change in the *way* of performing it? These questions I have endeavored to answer in a particular Dialogue, I am now preparing for the Press, suggested by the effects produced on the minds of several innocent and accomplished Young Women by certain Professors, who ground the Morality of the Monks on the Divinity (or rather, Diablery) of the Manicheans."

to keep them at a jealous distance from the citadel. The powers of the world are often *christened*, but seldom christianized. They are but *proselytes of the outer gate;*[a4] or, like the Saxons of old, enter the land as auxiliaries, and remain in it as conquerors and lords.

APHORISM XXII[b]

The rules of prudence in general, like the laws of the stone tables, are for the most part prohibitive. *Thou shalt not* is their characteristic formula: and it is an especial *part* of *Christian* prudence that it should be so. Nor would it be difficult to bring under this head, all the social obligations that arise out of the relations of the present life, which the sensual understanding (τὸ φρόνημα τῆς Σαρκός[c1], Romans viii. 6.) is of itself able to discover, and the performance of which, under favorable[d] worldly circumstances, the merest [e]worldly [f]self interest,[g] without love or faith, is sufficient to enforce; but which Christian Prudence[h] enlivens by a higher principle, and renders symbolic and sacramental. (Ephesians v. 32.)[2]

COMMENT[i]

This then, [j]under the appellation of prudential requisites,[k] comes first[l] under [m]consideration: and may be regarded as[n] the [o]shrine and frame-

---

[a] *AR* (1825): *gate:*
[b] *AR* (1825): EDITOR.
[c] *AR* (1825, 1831): Σαρκὸς
[d] *AR* (1825): favourable
[e] *AR* (1825): p 15
[f-g] *AR* (1825): self-interest,
[h] *AR* (1825): prudence
[i] COPY C in margin: Substitute from the Corrections and Amendments. [i.e. *AR* (1825) Corr]
[j-k] *AR* (1825) Corr: comprizing the PRUDENTIALS of religion, ; COPY G: comprising the PRUDENTIALS of Religion,
[l] *AR* (1825) Corr: *first*
[m-n] *AR* (1825) Corr: consideration. *Next* follow the MORAL requisites. If in the *first* we have ; COPY G: consideration. *Next* follow the MORAL Requisites. In the *first* we have
[o-p] *AR* (1825) Corr, COPIES F (var) & G (var): *shrine* and *frame-work*

[4] A ''proselyte of the gate'' was one who did not submit to all the ordinances of the law, especially to circumcision, or participate in all the privileges of an Israelite (*OED*). According to F. W. Farrar, the term was later than St Paul: *St. Paul* (2 vols 1879) I 139.
[1] For other translations by C of this phrase see *CM (CC)* I 358–9n. See also below, *Sp Aph B Xa* nn 31, 33, 41.
[2] Eph 5.30-2: ''For we are members of his body, of his flesh, and of his bones. For this cause shall a man leave his father and mother, and shall be joined unto his wife, and they two shall be one flesh. This is a great mystery: but I speak concerning Christ and the church.''

work[p] [a]for the[b] Divine image,[c] into which the [d]worldly human[e] is to be [f]transformed. We[g] are [h]next to[i] bring out the [j]Divine Portrait itself, the[k] distinct features of its countenance, as a sojourner among men; its benign aspect turned towards its fellow-pilgrims, the extended arm, and the hand that blesseth and healeth.

APHORISM XXIII.[l]

The outward service (Θρησκεία[m]*) of ancient religion, the rites, ceremonies and ceremonial vestments of the [n]old law, had morality for their substance. They were the *letter*, of which morality was the *spirit;* the

---

* See the epistle of St. James, c. i. v. 26, 27,[o] where, in the authorized version, the Greek word θρησκεία[p] is falsely rendered *religion:* whether by mistake of the translator, or from the intended sense having become obsolete, I cannot decide.[1] At all events, for the English reader of our times it has the effect of an erroneous translation. It not only obscures the connexion of the passage, and weakens the peculiar force and sublimity of the thought, rendering it comparatively flat and trivial, almost indeed tautological, but has occasioned this particular verse to be perverted into a support of a very dangerous error; and the whole epistle to be considered as a *set-off* against the epistles and declarations of St. Paul, instead of (what in fact it is)[q] a masterly comment and confirmation of the same. I need not inform the religious reader, that James, c. i. v. 27,[r] is the favourite text and most boasted authority of those divines[2] who represent the Redeemer of the world as little more than a moral reformer, and the Christian faith as a code of ethics, differing from the moral system of Moses and the prophets by an additional motive; or rather, by the additional strength and clearness which the historical fact of the resurrection has given to the same motive.

[a-b] *AR* (1825) Corr: for that ; COPY G: of that
[c] *AR* (1825) Corr: Image, ; COPY G: Image
[d-e] *AR* (1825) Corr: Wordly-human ; COPY G: Worldly
[f-g] *AR* (1825) Corr, COPY G: transformed; in the *second*, we
[h-i] *AR* (1825) Corr, COPY G: to
[j-k] *AR* (1825) Corr: *Portrait itself*—the ; COPY E: portrait itself, the ; COPIES D, F, G: Portrait itself—the
[l] *AR* (1825): EDITOR.
[m] *AR* (1825, 1831): Θρησκέια
[n] *AR* (1825): p 16
[o] *AR* (1825): 27.
[p] *AR* (1825, 1831): θρησκέια
[q] *AR* (1825): is),
[r] *AR* (1825): 27.

---

[1] James 1.26–7: "If any man among you seem to be religious, and bridleth not his tongue but deceiveth his heart, this man's religion is vain. Pure religion and undefiled before God and the Father is this, to visit the fatherless and widows in their affliction, and to keep himself unspotted from the world." The point concerning θρησκεία is developed also in annotations on Field, *CM (CC)* II 655, and on Luther *Colloquia Mensalia*, Epistle Dedicatory: *LR* IV 4, *CM (CC)* III; and in *CN* IV 5398 f 75ᵛ (cf 4839 f 123 and n). See also J. C. Hare, *Mission of the Comforter* (2nd ed 1850) Note B.

[2] I.e. the Unitarians: see next note.

enigma, of which morality was the *meaning*. But morality itself is the service and ceremonial (cultus exterior, θρησκεία[a]) of the Christian religion. The scheme of grace and truth that *became** through Jesus

> * The Greek word ἐγένετο, unites in itself the two senses of *began to exist* and *was made to exist*.[3] It exemplifies the force of the *middle voice*, in distinction from the verb reflex. In answer to a note on John i. 2.,[b] in the Unitarian[c] version of the New Testament,[4] I think it worth noticing, that the same word is used in the very same sense by Aristophanes in that famous parody on the cosmogonies of the Mythic poets, or the creation of the finite, as delivered, or supposed to be delivered, in the Cabiric or Samothracian mysteries, in the Comedy of the Birds.
>
> ───────γένετ᾽ Οὐρανός, Ὠκεανός[d] τε
> Καὶ Γῆ.[5]

> [a] *AR* (1825): θρησκέια   [b] *AR* (1825): 2.   [c] *AR* (1825): unitarian
> [d] *AR* (1825): ἐγένετ᾽ Ὀυρανος, Ω᾽κεανός ; *AR* (1831): γένετ᾽ Ὀυρανὸς, Ω᾽κεανός

[3] C's meaning here is compressed. The word ἐγένετο appears six times in the first 17 verses of St John's Gospel; AV translations include "made" in v 14, "And the Word was made flesh, and dwelt among us . . . full of grace and truth", and "came" in "grace and truth came by Jesus Christ", v 17. C looked for a consistent meaning—and one that would rule out a Unitarian interpretation (see next n). He made many attempts to define its precise implications in biblical contexts. The meanings he gives here are not characteristic of the middle voice (and γίγνομαι—later γίνομαι—has tenses variously in active, middle, and passive form without noticeably affecting the meaning). Reflexivity *is* one meaning of the middle, and is found in C's note on Daniel Waterland *The Importance of the Doctrine of the Holy Trinity* (1734) 259 (*LR* IV 251–2, *CM—CC*—v), in which he implied that the correct translation of John 1.14 was "he caused himself to become flesh". Below in *AR* (see *Conc* n 14) C settled for the AV version: "The Word was made flesh". For another note on the question of Christ's begetting see his annotation on Leighton COPY C IV 10–11: *CM (CC)* III.

[4] *The New Testament, in an Improved Version, upon the Basis of Archbishop Newcome's New Translation: with a Corrected Text, and Notes Critical and Explanatory* ed Thomas Belsham was first published in London in 1808. Belsham's note (p 201) on John 1.3 (not 2), which is clearly of crucial importance for Unitarians, reads: " 'All things were made by him, and without him was not any thing made that was made.' Newcome: who explains it of the creation of the visible material world by Christ, as the agent and instrument of God. See his notes on ver. 3 and 10. But this is a sense which the word εγενετο will not admit. Γινομαι occurs upwards of seven hundred times in the New Testament, but never in the sense of *create*. It signifies in this gospel, where it occurs fifty-three times, to be, to come, to become, to come to pass: also, to be done or transacted. . . . All things in the christian dispensation were done by Christ, i.e. by his authority, and according to his direction; and in the ministry committed to his apostles, nothing has been done without his warrant. . . ."

[5] Aristophanes *The Birds* 701–2. But Aristophanes here tells how "Heaven, Ocean, and Earth came into being" as a result of the mingling of all things by Love. He draws on various cosmogonies, including the Orphic. C believed that the mysteries of the Cabiri of Samothrace were the oldest, introduced to Greece by the Phoenicians, and that they were the source of the Orphic, Eleusinian, and other mysteries, teaching a physiotheism that contained dim memories of the divine revelation given to the Hebrews. Cf C's annotation on

Christ, the faith that *looks* down into* the perfect law of liberty, [a]has "light for its *garment:*"[11] its very [˙]*robe*[b] is righteousness."[12]

* James c. i. v. 25. Ὁ[c] δὲ παρακύψας εἰς νόμον τέλειον τὸν τῆς ἐλευθερίας.[6] The Greek word, parakupsas, signifies the incurvation or bending of the body in the act of *looking down into;* as, for instance, in the endeavour to see the reflected image of a star in the water at the bottom of a well. A more happy or forcible word could not have been chosen to express the nature and ultimate object of reflection, and to enforce the necessity of it, in order to discover the living fountain and spring-head of the evidence of the Christian faith in the believer himself, and at the same time to point out the seat and region, where alone it is to be found. Quantum *sumus, scimus.*[7] That which we find within ourselves, which is more than ourselves, and yet the ground of whatever is good and permanent therein, is the substance and life of all other knowledge.

N.B. The Familists of the sixteenth century,[8] and similar enthusiasts of a[d] later date, overlooked the essential point, that it was a *law*, and a law that involved its own end (τέλος[e]), a *perfect law (τέλειος)* or law that perfects and completes itself; and therefore, its obligations are called, in reference to human statutes, *imperfect* duties, i.e. incoercible from without. They overlooked that it was a law that *portions out* (Νόμος *from* νέμω *to allot, or make division of*[9]) to each man the sphere and limits[f] within which it is to be exercised—which as St. Peter notices of certain profound passages in the writings of St. Paul, (2 Pet. c. iii. v. 16.) οἱ ἀμαθεῖς καὶ ἀστήρικτοι [g]στρεβλοῦσιν, ὡς καὶ τὰς λοιπὰς γραφάς,[h] πρὸς τὴν ἰδίαν αὐτῶν ἀπώλειαν.[10]

> [a] *AR* (1825): p 17
> [b] *AR* (1825): "*robe*
> [c] *AR* (1825): 'Ο
> [d] Added in 1831
> [e] *AR* (1825, 1831): τελος
> [f] *AR* (1825): limits,
> [g-h] *AR* (1825, 1831): στρεβλοῦσιν, ὡς καὶ τὰς λοίπας γραφὰς,

---

G. S. Faber *Mysteries of the Cabiri*, in which he refers to this passage if not to *Sp Aph B Xb*, at n 63, below: *CM (CC)* II 582–3. Cf also *P Lects* Lects 2, 11 (1949) 89, 322–3 (the latter passage not recognised in 1949 as relating to the Cabiri), and *Int Aph XXXI* n 3, below.

[6] "But he that looketh into the perfect law, the law of liberty . . ." (AV). Cf notes of 1810 and 1811 (*CN* III 3743, 4065) and of 1826 (*CN* IV 5347), also *Op Max ms* B3 ("II") 119. For the image of the law of liberty as the "inward Sun" see *Mor Aph XV* n 12, below. The text is an important one for C in *AR*: see also *Int Aph XXIX* n 1, *Sp Aph B XII* n 3 and *XV* n 9 below; also *Int Aph XXIX* n 20 below and further refs there for the phrase νόμος αὐτόνομος.

[7] "As much as *we are, we know*." C's italicisations stress the point that he is trying to make: i.e. that we come to know by coming to be. Cf *LS (CC)* 78, in which the phrase is preceded by the statement ". . . as Truth is the correlative of Being, so is

the act of Being the great organ of Truth", and *BL* chs 9, 8 *(CC)* I 142–3 and n, 132–3 and n, and Index s.v. "knowing". To "be" in this sense is to relate oneself to the Divine "Being": see N Q f 4 (*CN* v): "Never shall we be able to comprehend ourselves ⟨better than we might⟩, but we may learn what is of far more worth and importance, to *know* ourselves better. *Sis* ut *scias*! Scire et [?esse], ⟨sciendi et essendi⟩ eadem est norma. [*Be* in order that you may *know*! . . . The norm of being and knowing is the same.] The more we become normal in this respect the clearer and more distinct is the Image of God in [?esse] of him who eternally affirmeth, I Am, and that eternal Act begetteth the Being who is the Fullness of Beings. . . ." The phrase "what we are we know", cited in a letter of 1830 by R. C. Trench *Letters and Memorials* ed M. Trench (2 vols 1888) I 53, may well derive from C, whom he admired: see above, Editor's Introduction, at nn 237 and 239–41. Emerson cited the Latin in reverse as

COMMENT

Herein the apostle places the pre-eminency, the peculiar and distinguishing excellence, of the Christian religion. The ritual is of the same kind, (ὁμοούσιον)[13] though not of the same order, with the religion *a*itself. It is*b* not arbitrary or conventional, as types and hieroglyphics are in relation to the things expressed by them; but inseparable, consubstantiated (as it were), and partaking therefore of the same life, permanence, and intrinsic worth with its spirit and principle.[14]

*c*APHORISM XXIV*d*

Morality is the body, of which the faith in Christ is the soul—so far indeed an*e* earthly body, as it is adapted to our*f* state of warfare on earth,

a–b *AR* (1825): itself—   *c* *AR* (1825): EDITOR.
d *AR* (1825): p 18   *e* *AR* (1825): its ; COPY G: the
f *AR* (1825): its ; COPY G: the

"Quantum scimus sumus" at a time when he was taking notes from *AR*: see *Journals and Miscellaneous Notebooks of Ralph Waldo Emerson* ed A. R. Ferguson (Cambridge, Mass 1964) III 164.

[8] The Familists, or Family of Love, were founded by Henry Nicholas (or Niclas or Niklaes, c 1502–c 1580), who "taught an anabaptist mysticism entirely without dogmatism, yet of exalted ideals. . . . He held himself and his elders to be impeccable, and the license which they claimed for themselves in this respect gained for them the [unfounded] reputation of 'libertines' ": *DNB*. In his *Theological Works* (1708) Henry More attacked Nicholas, principally for setting himself up as a prophet as great as Christ himself: see esp 171–88. C's annotated copy in the BM includes annotations on pages (180, 259, and 372–3) where Nicholas is being attacked. See *CM (CC)* III 926–7 and, for extracts used below in *Prel Sp Aph* and *Sp Aph A*, below, App A(c) to (g); cf also *CN* IV 5068.

[9] C's etymology is sound here, but the choice between the derived meaning and the primitive is presumably determined by the point he wishes to make.

[10] ". . . they that are unlearned and unstable wrest as they do also the other scriptures, unto their own destruction" (AV). *AR* (1825) COPY G has a note at this point (added by DC to *AR* —1854—15n): "For a rational Agent the Obligation of a Law is

co-eval and commensurate with the perception of its Lawfulness. Only on this ground is he a *Moral* Agent: in this consists the *possibility* of any *Morality* at all. The mind can scarcely conceive a grosser absurdity, than to separate the Law and the Obligation, to seek the source and seat of the one in the *divine* of our nature, and of the other in the *beast*."

[11] "O Lord my God . . . who coverest thyself with light as with a garment": Ps 104.1–2. C's hostility to the phrase "a Robe of Light", *CM (CC)* II 544, involves a distinction from the less literal image here.

[12] See Isa 61.10, quoted below, *Sp Aph B [XXIV]* n 33.

[13] The Greek word ὁμοούσιος ("of the same substance") was most familiar from its introduction into the "Nicene Creed" to settle the controversy with the Arians, who denied the divinity of Christ; but it was earlier used, e.g. by Eusebius of Caesarea, to say what the Platonic ideas were *not* in relation to God, and by Plotinus (*Enneads* 4.7.10) to express the consubstantiality of the soul with the divine.

[14] The discussion here is closely related to C's view of the symbol; particularly that it "always partakes of the Reality which it renders intelligible": *SM (CC)* 30. See e.g. *P Lects* Lect 8 (1949) 260–1, a note on Donne *LXXX Sermons*: *CM (CC)* II 279–80, and *CN* IV 4831–2. Cf also Barth 171.

and[a] the appointed form and instrument of communion[b] with the present world; yet not "terrestrial," nor of the world, but a celestial body,[1] and capable of being transfigured from glory to glory,[2] in accordance with the varying circumstances and outward relations of its moving and informing spirit.[3]

APHORISM XXV[c]

Woe to the man, who will believe neither power, freedom, nor morality; because he no where finds either entire, or unmixed with sin, thraldom and infirmity. In the natural and intellectual realms, we distinguish what we cannot separate; and in the moral world, we must distinguish *in order to* separate.[1] Yea, in the clear distinction of good from evil the process of separation commences.

COMMENT

It was customary with religious men in former times, to make a rule of taking every morning some text, or aphorism*, for their occasional med-

---

* In accordance with a preceding remark, on the use of etymology in disciplining the youthful mind to thoughtful habits, and as consistent with the title of this work, "Aids[d] to Reflection,"[e] I shall offer no apology for the following and similar notes:

Aphorism, determinate position, from the Greek, ap, from; and horizein, to bound[f] or limit; whence our horizon.—In order to get the full sense of a word, we should first present to our minds the visual image that forms its primary meaning. Draw lines of different colours round the different counties of England, and then cut out each separately, as in the common play-maps that children take to pieces and put together[2]—so that each district can

---

[a] COPY G: and is
[b] *AR* (1825): its communion ; COPY G: communion
[c] *AR* (1825): EDITOR.
[d] *AR* (1825): 'Aids
[e] *AR* (1825): Reflection,'
[f] *AR* (1825): bound,

---

[1] "There are also celestial bodies, and bodies terrestrial: but the glory of the celestial is one, and the glory of the terrestrial is another": 1 Cor 15.40. In this chapter St Paul continues to develop the differences caused by the resurrection from the dead: "It is sown a natural body; it is raised a spiritual body", etc.

[2] "But we all, with open face beholding as in a glass the glory of the Lord, are changed into the same image from glory to glory . . .": 2 Cor 3.18.

[3] An unfinished ms draft by C for the preceding paragraphs (i.e. *Aphs XXIII* and *XXIV* without C's notes) is transcribed below in App B(h).

[1] See below, *Aph XXVI* n 1.

[2] Dissected maps for teaching geography were invented by John Spilsbury in the early 1760s and were the first form of jigsaw puzzle. See Linda Hannas *The English Jigsaw Puzzle 1760–1890* (1972) 13–20 and illustrations.

itation *a*during the day, and thus to fill up the intervals of their attention to business. I do not point it out for imitation, as knowing too well, how apt these self-imposed rules are to degenerate into superstition or hollowness:[4] or I would have recommended the following as the first exercise.

APHORISM XXVI*b*

It is a dull and obtuse mind, that must divide in order to distinguish; but it is a still worse, that distinguishes in order to divide.[1] In the former, we may contemplate the source of superstition and *idolatry; in the latter, of schism, heresy†, and a seditious and sectarian spirit‡.

---

be contemplated apart from the rest, as a whole in itself. This twofold act of circumscribing, and detaching, when it is exerted by the mind on subjects of reflection and reason, is to *aphorize*, and the result an *aphorism*.[3]

* Τὸ Νοητὸν διηρήκασιν εἰς πολλῶν Θεῶν Ἰδιότητας*c*.—*Damasc. de Myst. Egypt;*[2] *i.e.* They *divided* the intelligible into many and several individualities.

† From *d*αἴρεσις.[3] Though well aware of its formal and apparent derivation from *haireo*, I am inclined to refer both words to *airo*, as the primitive term, containing the primary visual image: and therefore should explain *haeresis*, as*e* a wilful raising into public notice, an uplifting (for display) of any particular opinion differing from the established belief of the church at large, and making it a ground of schism, *i.e.* division, from schizein, to cut off—whence our "scissars" is supposed to have been derived.[4]

‡ I mean these words in their large and philosophic sense in relation to the *spirit*, or

a AR (1825): p 19
b AR (1825): EDITOR.
c AR (1825): Τὸ Νόητον διρήκασιν εἰς πολλῶν Θεῶν Ἰδιοτήτας ; AR (1831): Τὸ Νόητον διηρήκασιν εἰς πολλῶν Θεῶν Ἰδιοτήτας
d-e AR (1825): αἴρεσις,

[3] See above, Editor's Introduction at n 56. Earlier in his career C had used "aphorising" as a pejorative term: cf his quotation from Milton on "aphorising Pedantry" in *CN* I 108; his phrase "immethodical aphorising Eclectics" in ch 12 of *BL (CC)* I 292, and "aphorising for aphorising sake" in a note on *Athenaeum: CM (CC)* I 141.

[4] C's ms for the passage from this word to "same moment" in *Aph XXVIII* (excluding his notes) is transcribed below in App B(i).

[1] AR (1825) COPY F has a note at this point: "i.e. that distinguishes in matters of *opinion* in order to divide *persons*, thus converting innocent difference into discord and alienation". COPIES C, D, and E have

similar shorter notes. Cf *The Friend* 28 Sept 1809: "Distinct notions do not suppose different *things*. When we make a threefold distinction in human nature, we are fully aware, that it is a distinction not a division . . . Nevertheless, it is of great practical importance that these distinctions should be made and understood . . .": *Friend (CC)* II 104n (I 177n); *BL*, ch 14 (*CC*) II 11: "The office of philosophical disquisition consists in just *distinction*; while it is the priviledge of the philosopher to preserve himself constantly aware, that distinction is not division"; note on Marcus Aurelius *Conversation*: "The understanding the difference between Division & Distinction is the first step in the Solution of the seeming Contradictions concerning

^aAPHORISM XXVII^b

Exclusive of the abstract sciences, the largest and worthiest portion of our knowledge consists of *aphorisms:* and the greatest and best of men is but an *aphorism.*

APHORISM XXVIII^c

On the prudential influence which the fear or foresight of the *consequences* of his actions, in respect of his own loss or gain, may exert on a newly converted Believer.

---

originating temper and tendency, and not to any one mode under which, or to any one class, in or by which, it may be displayed. A seditious spirit may (it is possible, though not probable)^d exist in the council-chamber of a palace as strongly as in a mob in Palace-Yard;[5] and a sectarian spirit in a cathedral, no less than in a conventicle.

  ^a *AR* (1825): p 20   ^b *AR* (1825): EDITOR.   ^c *AR* (1825): EDITOR.   ^d *AR* (1825): probable,)

Individuality & final Co-adunation . . .'': *CM (CC)* I 175; cf also *CN* II 3154.

[2] C first used this quotation in the 1797 version of *Religious Musings* as a note to the lines ''. . . melting into day | What floating mists of Idolatry | Broke and misshap'd the Omnipresent Sire.'' The note disappeared from the 1834 ed: *PW* (EHC) I 110n. The 1831 text here inserts the first eta (omitted in 1825) but without its iota subscript and fails to correct the accents on the second and seventh words. (The versions in successive eds of the *Poems* were unaccented.) The source has been identified by Ian Wylie (*Young Coleridge and the Philosophers of Nature* —Oxford 1989— 12–13, 24 and n) as from Damascius (born c 480) and as evidently found by C in Ralph Cudworth *Intellectual System of the Universe* ch 4 § xxxviii (2nd ed 1743) I 461, a work he borrowed from the Bristol Library from 15 May to 1 Jun 1795 and again from 9 Nov to 13 Dec 1796: *Bristol LB* 120, 124; see also Indexes to *CN* I and *Lects 1795 (CC)*. This edition augments Cudworth's reference to ''Damas de princ [i.e. De primis principiis] MS'' by adding a location: the published text in J. C. Wolf *Anecdota* (3 vols 1722–4) III 260. Cudworth states that the statement quoted here was ''particularly noted concerning the Egyptians'' by Damascius, which helps to explain how C assigned to it in 1797 a title, ''de Myst Aegypt.'', belonging in fact to a work by Iamblichus, *De mysteriis Aegyptorum*, which he had asked Thelwall to purchase for him a few months earlier, in Nov 1796: *CL* I 262.

[3] The two verbs αἴρω—earlier ἀείρω— (I raise) and αἱρέω (I take, or I choose) are easily confused in some of their inflections and sometimes overlap in meaning. More recent etymologists have made various suggestions as to their derivation but find no reason to connect the two roots. John Parkhurst, however, in *A Greek and English Lexicon to the New Testament* (1769 and many subsequent eds) does derive αἱρέω from αἴρω.

[4] HNC omitted this last clause in *AR* (1839). ''Scissors'' is ultimately derived from Latin *caedere*, ''to cut'', but it owes the initial *sc* and the double *s* to an etymological confusion with the Latin verb *scindere*, ''to split'', which is cognate with σχίζειν. In C's day it was still generally accepted that Latin was derived from Greek.

[5] Presumably St James's Palace, a common focus of popular demonstrations: see e.g. G. Rudé *Wilkes and Liberty* (Oxford 1962) 181; cf *EOT (CC)* I cli, III 252–3, and *CN* IV 4772.

PRECAUTIONARY REMARK.—We meddle not with the dispute respecting *conversion*, whether, and in what sense, necessary in all Christians. It is sufficient for our purpose, that a very *large* number of men even in Christian countries *need* to be converted, and that not a few, we trust, have been. The tenet becomes fanatical and dangerous, only when rare and extraordinary exceptions are made to be the general rule;—when what was vouchsafed to the apostle of the Gentiles by especial grace, and for an especial purpose, viz. a conversion *begun and completed in the same moment, *ᵃis demanded or expected of all men, as a necessary sign and pledge of their election. Late observations have shown, that under many circumstances the magnetic needle, even after the disturbing influence has been removed, will keep wavering, and require many days before it points aright, and remains steady to the pole.[2] So is it ordinarily with the soul, after it has begun to free itself from the disturbing forces of the flesh and the world, and to convert† itself towards God.

APHORISM XXIX[b]

Awakened by the cock-crow,[c] (a sermon, a calamity, a sick bed, or a providential escape),[d] the Christian pilgrim sets out in the morning twi-

---

* Whereas Christ's other disciples had a breeding under him, St. Paul was *born* an apostle; not carved out, as the rest, by degrees and in course of time, but a *fusile* apostle, an apostle poured out and cast in a mould. As Adam was a perfect man in an instant, so was St. Paul a perfect Christian. The same spirit was the lightning that melted, and the mould that received and shaped him.—Donne's Sermons—*quoted from memory.*[1]

† From the Latin, *convertere*—*i.e.* by an act of the WILL *to turn towards* the true pole, *at the same time* (for this is the force of the prepositive *con*) that the understanding is convinced and made aware of its existence and direction.

ᵃ *AR* (1825): p 21
ᵇ *AR* (1825): EDITOR.
ᶜ *AR* (1825): cock-crow
ᵈ *AR* (1825): escape)

[1] Donne Sermon XLVI: *LXXX Sermons* (1640) 460: "In this sense especially doth S. *Paul* call himslf *Abortivum*, a person borne out of season, That whereas Christ's other Disciples and Apostles, had a breeding under him, and came first *ad Discipulatum*, and then *ad Apostolatum*, first to be Disciples, and after to be Apostles, S. *Paul* was borne a man, an Apostle, not carved out, as the rest in time; but a fusil Apostle, an Apostle poured out, and cast in a Mold; As *Adam* was a perfect man in an instant, so was S. *Paul* an Apostle, as soone as Christ tooke him in hand." C cited this pas-sage in 1814–15: see T. A. Methuen "Retrospect of Friendly Communication with the Poet Coleridge" *Christian Observer* XLV (1845) 261; *TT (CC)* II 349. For the lightning imagery see next n and *CM (CC)* III 477–8. C's ms for the last words of his footnote is transcribed below in App B(i).

[2] For further discussion of C's interest in magnetism and magnetic imagery see Beer *CPI* 81–7 and *CV* 155. Cf also C's early notebook entry: "It is not true that men always go gradually from good to evil or evil to good. Sometimes a flash of lightning will turn the magnetic poles": *CN* I 432.

light, while yet the truth (the νόμος τέλειος ὁ τῆς ἐλευθερίας)[1] is below the horizon. Certain necessary *consequences* of his past life and his present undertaking will be *seen* by the refraction of its light: more will be apprehended and conjectured. The phantasms that had[a] predominated during the hours of darkness, are still busy. [b]Though they no longer present themselves, as distinct Forms, they yet remain as[c] formative Motions in the Pilgrim's [d]soul, unconscious of its own activity and overmastered by its own workmanship. Things take the signature of Thought.[2] The shapes of the recent dream become a *mould* for the objects in the distance; and these again give an outwardness and a sensation of[e] reality to the Shapings[f] of the Dream. The Bodings[g] inspired [h]by [i]the long habit[j] of selfishness, and self-seeking cunning, though [k]they are now commencing the process of their purification[l] into that fear which is the *beginning* of wisdom,[3] and [m]which, as such, is[n] ordained to be our guide and safeguard, till the sun of love, the perfect law of liberty,[4] is fully arisen—these Bodings[o] will set the fancy at work, and haply, for a time, transform the mists of dim and imperfect knowledge into determinate superstitions.[5] But in either case, whether seen clearly or dimly,

[a] *AR* (1825): had not ; Corr, COPIES A, C, D, F, G: had

[b-c] *AR* (1825): No longer present, as Forms, they will yet exist as moulding and

[d-e] *AR* (1825): Soul. The Dream of the past night will transfer its shapes to the objects in the distance, while the objects give outwardness and ; COPY D has an * after the first "objects", with a note: "to real objects"

[f] *AR* (1825): shapings

[g] *AR* (1825): fears ; COPY G: Forebodings

[h] *AR* (1825): p 22

[i-j] *AR* (1825): long habits

[k-l] *AR* (1825): now purifying

[m-n] Added in 1831

[o] *AR* (1825): fears ; COPY G: forebodings ; COPY H: Dreads and self-centered forebodings

[1] *AR* (1825) COPY H has a note at this point: "The perfect (that is, self-perfecting) Law of Liberty: from the Ep. of St. James. This exists, where the Individual finds a sufficient *motive* for obedience to the Law in the perception of its rightfulness: in short, where the *Reason* acts as Motive. *Honor* carried into the *whole* of a man's conduct, & in *all* his relations the Law of Honor would be the same with the Apostle's 'perfect Law' of Liberty. The *Gentleman* resents the supposition that he needs any outward motive to act as a man of Honor—." The reference is to James 1.25. Cf C's footnote to *Int Aph XXIII* and n 6, above. For the arousing effect of material shocks see above, p li.

[2] For the relation between thoughts and

things, a favourite theme of C's, see e.g. his 1809 account in *The Friend* of Luther's vision of the devil, in which "*Thoughts* . . . shape and condense themselves into Things, into Realities!": *Friend (CC)* II 120, the account of the composition of *Kubla Khan*, in which "images rose up" before him "as things": *PW* (EHC) I 296; and *TT* 29–30 Aug 1827 *(CC)* I 94 (1836 vn, dated 30 Aug, II 71).

[3] "The fear of the Lord is the beginning of wisdom": Ps 111.10. See also next n.

[4] *AR* (1825) COPY H has a note at this point: "The *Fear* of the Lord is the *Beginning* of Wisdom but perfect Love shutteth out Fear". The further reference is to 1 John 4.18: "perfect love casteth out fear".

[5] For C's imagery of sun and mist see

whether beheld or only imagined, the *consequences,*[a] contemplated in their bearings on the individual's inherent* desire of happiness and dread of pain,[b] become *cmotives:* and (unless all distinction in the words be done away with, and either prudence or virtue be reduced to a superfluous synonyme, a redundancy in all the languages of the civilized

---

* The following extract from Leighton's Theological Lectures, sect. II.[6] *d*may serve*e* as a comment on this sentence:

f"The human mind, however stunned and weakened by the fall, still retains some faint idea of the good it has lost; a kind of languid sense of its misery and indigence, with affections suitable to these obscure notions. This at least is beyond all doubt and indisputable, that all men wish well to themselves; nor can the mind divest itself of this propensity, without divesting itself of its being. This is what the schoolmen mean,*g* when in their manner of expression they say, that "the will (*mem.* voluntas, *not* arbitrium)[7] is carried towards happiness not simply as *will*, but as *nature*."

I venture to remark that this position, if not more *certainly*, would be more *evidently* true, if instead of *beatitudo*, the word *indolentia* (*i.e.* freedom from pain, negative happiness)[8] had been used. But this depends on the exact meaning attached to the term *self*, of which more in another place.[9] One conclusion, however, follows inevitably from the preceding position, viz. that this propensity can never be legitimately made the *principle* of morality, even because it is no part or appurtenance of the moral will; and because the proper object of the moral principle, is to limit and control this propensity, and to determine in what it *may* be, and in what it *ought* to be*h* gratified; while it is the business of philosophy to instruct the understanding, and the office of religion to convince the whole man, that otherwise than as a *regulated*, and of course therefore a *subordinate*, end, this propensity, innate and inalienable though it be, can never be realized or fulfilled. Τὸν Δέσποιναν ποθοῦντα ἀσπάζεται ἡ Θεράπαινα.*i*[10]

a AR (1825): *consequences*

b AR (1825): pain

c AR (1825): p 23

d–e AR (1825): cannot be introduced more to the purpose than

f AR (1825): 'The

g AR (1825): mean

h AR (1825): be,

i AR (1825): Τὴν . . . Θεράπαινας.

Beer *CV*; for this example, 153–4 and n. Cf also 1809 *Friend (CC)* ɪɪ 72 (ɪ 106); *EOT (CC)* ɪɪ 405; *Lects 1808–1819 (CC)* ɪ 268; and N 47 ff 44ᵛ–5 (*CN* v).

[6] Leighton COPY C ɪᴠ 194–5 ("sect. II" should have read "Lect. II"): *CM (CC)* ɪɪɪ. Leighton's longer original for the first two sentences is printed in the editor's note.

[7] This parenthesis is C's own, drawing upon Leighton's original Latin given in the footnote: "In beatitudinem fertur voluntas". See below, App I Excursus Note 18 "Two Words for 'Will' ".

[8] See previous n. This was the classical meaning, e.g. in Cicero *Tusculan Disputations* 2.4, a discussion of synonyms for happiness.

[9] Presumably in the Opus Maximum. Cf the extracts on the Self quoted from the ms of that work by Elinor S. Shaffer "Iago's Malignity Motivated: Coleridge's Unpublished 'Opus Magnum' " *Shakespeare Quarterly* xɪx (1968) 195–203.

[10] "The Handmaiden greets the man who yearns for [her] Mistress" (i.e. philosophy and other ancillary disciplines instruct our understanding while underneath we are yearning for our reason to be illuminated). The 1825 reading Τὴν for Τὸν would suggest a translation of "a man" rather than "the man". The Greek (for which no source has been found) was omitted from *AR* (1839) onwards. For Nature as "Handmaid" of God see *CN* ɪᴠ 4843.

world), these motives, and the acts and forbearances directly proceeding from them, fall under the head of PRUDENCE, as belonging to one or other of its four*a* very distinct *b*species.[11]

I. It*c* may be a prudence, that stands in opposition to a higher moral life, and tends to preclude it, and to prevent the soul from ever arriving at the hatred of sin for its own exceeding sinfulness (*Rom.* vii. 13):[12] and this is an EVIL *d*PRUDENCE.

II. Or*e* it may be a *neutral* prudence, not incompatible with spiritual growth: and to this we may, with especial propriety, apply the words of our Lord, "What is not *against* us is for us."[13] It is therefore an innocent, and (being such) a proper, and COMMENDABLE PRUDENCE.

III.*f* Or it may lead and be subservient to a higher principle than itself. The mind and conscience of the individual may be reconciled to it, in the foreknowledge of the higher principle, and with a yearning towards it that implies a foretaste of future freedom. The enfeebled convalescent is reconciled to his crutches, and thankfully makes use of them, not only because *g*they are necessary for his immediate support, but likewise, because they are the means and conditions of EXERCISE; and by exercise, of establishing, *gradatim paulatim*,[14] that strength, flexibility, and almost spontaneous obedience of the muscles, which the idea and cheering presentiment of health hold out to him. He finds their *value* in their present necessity, and their *worth* as they are the instruments of finally superseding it.[15] This is a faithful, a WISE PRUDENCE, having, indeed, its birth-place in the world, and the *wisdom of this world* for its father;*h* but naturalized[16] in a better land, and having the wisdom*i* from above

a *AR* (1825): three ; COPIES C, D, E, F, G: four
b–c *AR* (1825): species. It ; COPIES E, F, G, H: species. §It
d–e *AR* (1825): PRUDENCE. Or ; COPIES G, H: PRUDENCE. §Or
f Added in 1831; COPY G: §Or
g *AR* (1825): p 24
h *AR* (1825): Father;
i *AR* (1825): Wisdom

[11] *AR* (1825) COPY H has a note at the foot of the page: "Four sorts of Prudence. 1. an evil. 2. an innocent and commendable— 3 a wise— & 4 a holy Prudence." Cf above, *Pref* n 13.

[12] "Was then that which is good made death unto me? God forbid. But sin, that it might appear sin, working death in me by that which is good; that sin by the commandment might become exceeding sinful."

[13] Luke 9.50: "He that is not against us is for us."

[14] "By steps, little by little".

[15] For the worth/value distinction see above, *Pref* n 2.

[16] For an early use of this word see the lines in *Religious Musings* describing how the passions of the Elect are "enrobed with Light, and naturalised in Heaven": *PW* (EHC) I 112–13. The lines are quoted in the 1818 *Friend* as "Made pure by Thought, and naturalized in Heaven": *Friend (CC)* I 271 and n.

for its Sponsor and Spiritual Parent. To steal a dropt feather from the spicy nest of the Phoenix,[17] (the fond humor,[a] I mean, of the mystic divines and allegorizers of Holy Writ,)[b18] it is the *son of Terah from Ur of the Chaldees*, who gives a tithe of all to the King of Righteousness, without father, without mother, without descent,[19] (Νόμος αὐτόνο-μος[c]),[20] and receives a blessing on the remainder.

IV.[d] Lastly, there is a prudence that co-exists with morality, as morality co-exists with the spiritual life: a prudence that is the organ of both, as the understanding is to the reason and the will, or as the lungs are to the heart and brain. This is A HOLY PRUDENCE, the steward faithful and discreet, (οἰκονόμος πιστὸς καὶ[e] φρόνιμος,[21] Luke xii. 42), the[f]"eldest servant"[g22] in the family of faith, *born in the house*,[23] and "made[h] the ruler over his lord's household."[i24]

Let not then, I entreat you, my purpose be misunderstood; as if, in *distinguishing* virtue from prudence, I wished to divide the one from the other. [j]True morality is hostile to that prudence only, which is preclusive

---

[a] *AR* (1825): humour,
[b] *AR* (1825): Writ)
[c] *AR* (1831): αὐτονόμος
[d] Added in 1831; COPY G: §Lastly,
[e] *AR* (1825, 1831): πίστος καὶ
[f-g] *AR* (1825): 'eldest servant'
[h] *AR* (1825): 'made
[i] *AR* (1825): household.'
[j] *AR* (1825): p 25

---

[17] Cf Crashaw *On a Foule Morning, being then to take a journey* lines 20–2:

. . . he will throw
A fragrant breath suck'd from the spicy
nest
O th' precious Phoenix, warm upon her
Breast.

B Poets IV 732. Cf *Poetical Works* ed L. C. Martin (Oxford 1957) 182.

[18] Cf *C&S (CC)* 122 n 3: "some of the mystic divines, in their fond humour of allegorizing . . .".

[19] The son of Terah was Abram (or Abraham): Gen 11.31. On his return from the slaughter of Chedorlaomer he was met by Melchizedek, king of Salem, who offered him bread and wine and received in return a tithe of his spoil: Gen 14.18–20. He is treated as a forerunner, or type, of Christ in Heb 5.6, 10; 6.20, and 7, in which (7.3) he is described as "without fa-

ther, without mother, without descent". See *Sp Aph B XIX* n 50 and *XXIIIb* n 42, below. Since Melchizedek means "king of righteousness" and "king of Salem" means "king of peace" (cf *CN* IV 5384 and n) later writers could find further allegorical justification for their typological interpretation.

[20] As C translates it in *"Prometheus"*: "a law containing its law in itself": *LR* II 346 (cf 353), *SW&F (CC)*. For the full implications of this Kantian phrase see *Mor Aph XV* n 12 below.

[21] ". . . faithful and wise steward".

[22] Cf Abraham's "eldest servant": Gen 24.2.

[23] "Abram . . . armed his trained servants, born in his own house": Gen 14.14. Cf Gen 15.3, 17.12, 13, 23, 27; Lev 22.11; Eccl 2.7.

[24] Luke 12.42 again.

of true morality. The teacher, who *subordinates* prudence to virtue, cannot be supposed to *dispense* with it; and he who teaches the proper connexion of the one with the other, does not depreciate the lower in any sense; while by making it a link of the same chain with the higher, and receiving the same influence, he raises it.

*a*In general, Morality may be compared to the Consonant, Prudence to the Vowel. The former cannot be *uttered* (reduced to practice) but by means of the latter.*b*25

*c*APHORISM XXX*d*

What the duties of MORALITY are, the apostle instructs the believer in full, *e*comprising them under the two heads of negative and positive. Negative,*f* to keep himself pure from the world; and positive,*g* beneficence from*h* loving-kindness, *i.e.* love of his fellow-men (his kind) as himself.[1]

APHORISM XXXI*i*

Last and highest, come the *spiritual*, comprising all the truths, acts and duties that have an especial reference to the Timeless, the Permanent, the Eternal: to the sincere love of the True, as truth; *j*of the Good, *as* good: and of God as both in one. It comprehends the whole ascent from uprightness (morality, virtue, inward rectitude) to *godlikeness*, with all the acts, exercises, and disciplines of mind, will, and affection, that are requisite or conducive to the great design of our redemption from the form of the evil one, and of our second creation or birth in the divine image*.

* It is worthy of observation, and may furnish a fruitful subject for future reflection, how nearly this scriptural division coincides with the Platonic, which, *commencing* with the prudential, or the habit of act and purpose preceeding*k* from enlightened self-interest,

a–b *AR* (1825): For the longer passage in 1825 (with footnote) see App A
c *AR* (1825): p 26
d *AR* (1825): EDITOR.
e–f *AR* (1825): reducing them under two heads: negative
f COPY G: negative, viz.
g COPY G: positive, viz.
h *AR* (1825): with sympathy and
i *AR* (1825): EDITOR.
j *AR* (1825): truth,
k *AR* (1825): proceeding

25 This sentence replaces a paragraph and note in *AR* (1825) on the Logos, reprinted below in App A(b).

[1] C is presumably thinking of James 1.27, cited above: see *Int Aph XXIII* n 1.

a(qui animi imperio, corporis servitio, rerum auxilio, in proprium sui commodum et sibi providus utitur, hunc esse *prudentem* statuimus)*b1* *ascends* to the moral, *i.e.* to the *purifying* and *remedial* virtues:*c* and seeks its *summit* in the imitation of the Divine nature.[2] In this last division, answering to that which we have called the Spiritual, Plato includes all those inward acts and aspirations, waitings, and watchings, which have a growth in god-likeness for their immediate purpose, and the union of the human soul with the Supreme Good as their ultimate object. Nor was it altogether without grounds that several of the Fathers[3] ventured to believe that Plato had some dim conception of the necessity of a Divine Mediator, whether through some indistinct echo of the patriarchal faith, or some rays of light refracted from the Hebrew prophets through a Phoenician medium,*d* (to which he may possibly have referred in his phrase, θεοπαράδοτος σοφία,[4] the wisdom delivered

a–b AR (1825): [qui . . . statuimus],

c AR (1825): virtues;

d AR (1825): medium

[1] "One who uses the command of the mind, the subservience of the body, and the assistance of material goods for his own personal benefit and in making provision for himself—that man we define as prudent." The Latin as a whole may be C's own; "animi imperio, corporis servitio magis utimur" is found in Sallust *Bellum Catilinae* 1.2.

[2] A copy formerly in the possession of Barron Field (see below, App E(c) 202) has a note, not in C's hand, at this point: "To philosophize is to know, to love and to imitate God. *Plato*." Cf Augustine on Plato in *City of God* 8.5. For a prudential attitude to morality in Plato see e.g. *Republic* 339B, *Protagoras* 358B, or *Gorgias* 474B; for the imitation of God *Theaetetus* 176B.

[3] The early Fathers, concerned to justify Christian theology to both Jews and pagans, often went to exaggerated lengths to find anticipations of incarnation, crucifixion, and resurrection, of a Redeemer and Mediator, in the OT, and echoes of the OT and anticipations of the NT in Plato. Cf Justin Martyr *Apology* 1.60, deriving Plato *Timaeus* 36B (which describes the Demiurge as putting the universe together in the form of a cross) from Num 21.8, and Clement of Alexandria *Stromateis* 5.13, pointing out that the sufferings of the just man in *Republic* 362E "all but predict the economy of Salvation". The editors of *P Lects (CC)* refer, in a note on the passage cited below as (1949) 129, to Thomas Gray *Works* (2 vols 1814) II 322–3 on *Alcibiades II* 150D–151A: "When will that time arrive, Socrates, and who will be my instructor? . . . He who cares about you." Gray,

whose comments on Plato C annotated, and used in preparing *P Lects*, remarked that "some Christian writers would give a very extraordinary turn to this . . . as though Plato meant to prove the necessity of a Revelation"; he also pointed out that 1 Pet 5.7 used the same Greek phrase. See also *P Lects* Lect 3 (1949) 125: "when Plato teaches another doctrine [than pantheism] he expressly says it was a wisdom derived from the Gods, which had been received from the barbarous nations, whom, in another place, he calls the Holy Nations". No convincing source has yet been found for this. Later, C is even more specific about yearnings for and anticipations of a "Being to instruct" or "Realizer" on the part of Plato and Socrates: ibid Lects 3 and 4, pp 129, 169.

For C's own finding of rays in Greek religion refracted from patriarchal faith through a Phoenician medium see *Int Aph XXIII* n 5 above. Cf also his "Confession of Faith" in 1810: "My reason convinces me, that no other mode of redemption is conceivable, and, as did Socrates, would have yearned after the Redeemer . . .": *CN* III 4005 f 5.

[4] For connections with Plato see n 3, above. For σοφία θεοπαράδοτος see also *SM (CC)* 95 and n, in which the editor suggests that C may have had in mind particularly Berkeley *Siris* § 301 (with θεοπαράδοτος φιλοσοφία for σοφία). L&S give Damascius *De principiis* 311 as a reference for C's exact phrase: this part of the work was not published till 1889; cf *Int Aph XXVI* n 2 above. C had earlier (1805) echoed Samuel Horsley's use of the word θεο-

It may be an additional aid to reflection, to distinguish the three kinds severally,[1] according to the faculty to which each corresponds, the faculty or part of our human nature which is more particularly its organ. Thus: the prudential corresponds to the sense and the understanding; the moral to the heart and the conscience; the spiritual to the will and the reason, *i.e.* to the finite will reduced to harmony with, and in subordination to, the reason, as a ray from that true light which is both reason and will, universal reason, and will absolute.*ᶜ*[2]

---

from God), or by his own sense of the mysterious contradiction in human nature between the will and the reason, the natural appetences and the no less innate law of conscience (*Romans II*. 14, 15),[5] we shall in vain attempt to determine. It is not impossible that all three may have cooperated in partially unveiling these awful truths to this plank from the wreck of paradise thrown on the shores of idolatrous Greece, to this Divine Philosopher,

> Che in quella schiera andó piú presso al segno
> Al qual aggiunge, a chi dal cielo e dato.
>
> *Petrarch, Del Triunfo della Fama, Cap. III. l.* 5, 6.[6]

ª *AR* (1825): p 27   *ᵇ* *AR* (1825): EDITOR.
ᶜ *AR* (1825): For an additional passage here in *AR* (1825), p 28, see App G(c)

παράδοτος (*CN* II 2445) and had probably still earlier observed Cudworth's use of it, particularly in the context of the corruption by the later Platonists of the "theology of divine tradition" in the "Chaldaean Oracles" (on which see *CN* III 4424, 4446–7, and nn): Cudworth *True Intellectual System of the Universe* (1743) 292, 294, 548, 555, 627. The word does not occur in Plato, nor, indeed, earlier than Proclus (412–85), apparently. Cf also *Op Max ms* B3 ("II") 59, where C refers to Heraclitus and Plato, "who both referr'd for their actual faith to a Σοφια Θεοπαραδοτος", and *CM (CC)* II 1123 (on Homer).

[5] "For when the Gentiles, which have not the law, do by nature the things contained in the law, these, having not the law, are a law unto themselves: Which shew the work of the law written in their hearts, their conscience also bearing witness, and their thoughts the mean while accusing or else excusing one another".

[6] "[Plato there I saw,] who of them all came closest to the goal | Whereto by Heaven's grace man may attain": tr E. H. Wilkins *Triumphs of Petrarch* (Chicago, Ill

1962) 85. In 1819 C had quoted these lines in a marginal note, criticising Gray's interpretation of Plato by inserting "ma non quel Plato" (but not that Plato): *CM (CC)* II 868, using *NLS* text. They were prefixed by the editor to Gray's "Some Account of the Dialogues of Plato and of His Epistles with Notes": *Works* ed Thomas Mathias (2 vols 1814) II 293, and C had presumably copied them from there. (The reading there is "Che in", whereas all three editions of Petrarch that C is known to have read or owned—see *CN* III 3360n and *CM (CC)* IV—read "Che'n". C's reference to the title in this form—except the misspelling of "Trionfo" and his line-numbers—could have come from any of these, but not from Gray. The accents, including one on *è*, are all grave, in all four printed versions.)

[1] By the time he wrote this paragraph C had finally determined the threefold ordering of his volume: see Editor's Introduction, above, at n 47.

[2] Cf *BL* ch 7 *(CC)* I 116 and n 3. Three brief paragraphs which follow here in *AR* (1825) are reprinted below in App G(c).

^aPRUDENTIAL APHORISMS[1]

^a *AR* (1825): p 29 (p 30 blank)

[1] This section includes some of the rare remodelling that C undertook for the 1831 ed. (See App G below, and especially (d) to (e), in which the 1825 version of the changed passages behind the first two paras will be found reprinted.)

*PRUDENTIAL APHORISMS

———

[c]WITH respect to any final aim or end, the greater part of mankind[d] live at hazard. They have no certain harbour in view, nor direct their course by any fixed star. But to him that knoweth not the port to which he is bound, no wind can be favourable; neither can he who has not yet determined at what mark he is to shoot, direct his arrow aright.

[e]It is not, however, the less true,[f] that there is a proper object to aim at; and if this object be meant by the term happiness, (though I think that not the most appropriate term for a state, the perfection of which consists in the exclusion of all *hap* (*i.e.* chance)),[g] I assert that there is such a thing as human [h]happiness, as *summum bonum*, or ultimate good.[i][j]What this is, the Bible alone shows clearly and certainly, and points out the

[a] *AR* (1825): p 31

[b] *AR* (1825): L & ED.

[c-d] *AR* (1825): For the larger version in *AR* (1825) see App G(d)

[e] *AR* (1825): p 32

[e-f] *AR* (1825): I assert, then,

[g] *AR* (1825): chance), and should greatly prefer the Socratic *Eupraxy*, as expressing the union of well-being and well-doing,) ; *AR* (1831) has no second parenthesis

[h-i] *AR* (1825): happiness. This is indeed implied in the belief of an infinitely wise Author of our being.

[i] *AR* (1825): Aph II from Leighton follows; see App G(d)

[j] *AR* (1825): APHORISM III. LEIGHTON. §What

[1] The first paragraph is from Leighton's *Theological Lectures* No III "On the Happiness of Man": Leighton COPY C IV 198, reprinted at greater length in 1825. The first sentence of the next paragraph takes its point of departure from Leighton COPY C IV 200: "We assert, then, that there is such a thing as human felicity", then takes in his own ms comment on Leighton's use of the term: "An unhappy use of the term Happiness for that which excludes all Hap.—Good—Blessedness, Eupraxy": *Prud Aph II* n 8. Cf also *Op Max ms* B2 ("III") 42: "Hap originally designated not mere chance but a fortunate chance as is the case with the word Fortune itself and our own anglo-saxon Luck". In the reference to the *summum bonum*, not present as such in 1825, C encapsulates two sentences in Leighton COPY C IV 201 (= *Aph II* in 1825). The final three sentences are from Leighton COPY C IV 201 (= *Aph III* in 1825). All Leighton passages are in *CM (CC)* III.

way that leads to the attainment of it. This is that which prevailed with St. Augustine to study the Scriptures, and engaged his affection to them. "In Cicero, and Plato, and other such writers," says he, "I meet with many things acutely said, and things that excite a certain warmth *ᵃof emotion, but in none of them do I find these words, *Come unto me, all ye that labour, and are heavy laden, and I will give you rest**.*"*ᵇ²

COMMENT*ᶜ³*

Felicity, *in its proper* sense, is but another word for fortunateness, or happiness; and I can see no advantage in the improper use of words, when proper terms are to be found, but, on the contrary, much mischief. For, by familiarizing the mind to *equivocal* expressions, that is, such as may be taken in two or more different meanings, we introduce confusion of thought, and furnish the sophist with his best and handiest tools. For the juggle of sophistry consists, for the greater part, in using a word in one sense in the premise, and in another sense in the conclusion. We should accustom ourselves to *think*, and *reason*, in precise and stedfast*ᵈ* terms; even when custom, or the deficiency, or the corruption of the language will *ᵉnot permit the same strictness in speaking. The mathematician finds this so necessary to the truths which he is seeking, that his science begins with, and is founded on, the definition of his terms. The botanist, the chemist, the anatomist, &c., feel and submit to this necessity at all costs, even at the risk of exposing their several pursuits to the ridicule⁴ of the many, by technical terms, hard to be remembered, and alike quarrelsome to the ear and the tongue. In the business of moral and religious reflection, in the acquisition of clear and distinct conceptions of our duties, and of the relations in which we stand to God, our

---

* Apud Ciceronem et Platonem, aliosque ejusmodi scriptores, multa sunt acute dicta, et leniter calentia, sed in iis omnibus hoc non invenio, *Venite ad me*, &c. (Matt. xii. 28.)

ᵃ *AR* (1825): p 33
ᵇ *AR* (1825): For Aphs IV and V (pp 33–5) from LEIGHTON see App G(e)
ᶜ *AR* (1825): APHORISM VI. EDITOR.
ᵈ *AR* (1825): steadfast
ᵉ *AR* (1825): p 36

² St Augustine *Confessions* 7.21, 27, quoting Matt 11.28. Leighton's translator has "wittily" for "acutely" and "things that have a moderate tendency to move the passions" for "things that excite a certain warmth of emotion", but in a footnote he also gives the Latin original, which includes "acute" and "lene calentia" for these phrases: C has gone back to the Latin and translated it a little more exactly.

³ This "Comment" appeared as *Aphs VI* and *VII* in *AR* (1825).

⁴ C's ms for the 1825 version of the following passage, down to the first three words of *Aph II* (as yet untitled in the ms), is transcribed below in App B(j).

neighbour, and ourselves, no such difficulties occur. At the utmost we have only to rescue words, already existing and familiar, from the false or vague meanings imposed on them by carelessness, or by the clipping[5] and debasing misusage of the market. And surely happiness, duty, faith, truth, and final blessedness, are matters of deeper and dearer interest for all men, than circles to the geometrician, or the characters of plants to the botanist, or the affinities and combining principle of the elements of bodies to the chemist, or even than the mechanism (fearful and wonderful[6] though it be!) of the perishable Tabernacle[7] of the Soul can be to the anatomist. Among the *aids to* reflection, place the following maxim prominent: let distinctness in expression advance side by side with distinction in thought.[8] For one useless subtlety in our elder divines and moralists, I will produce ten sophisms of equivocation in the writings of our modern preceptors: and for one error *ᵃ*resulting from excess in *distinguishing* the indifferent, I would show ten mischievous delusions from the habit of *confounding* the diverse. Whether*ᵇ* you are reflecting for yourself, or reasoning with another, make it a rule to ask yourself the precise meaning of the word, on which the point in question appears to turn; and if it may be (*i.e.* by writers of authority *has been*) used in several senses, then ask which of these the word is at present intended to convey. By this mean, and scarcely without it, you will at length acquire a facility in detecting the *quid pro quo*.[9] And believe me, in so doing you will enable yourself to disarm and expose four-fifths of the main arguments of our most renowned irreligious philosophers, ancient and modern. For the *quid pro quo* is at once the rock and*ᶜ* quarry, on and with which the strong-holds of disbelief, materialism, and (more pernicious still) epicurean morality*ᵈ* are built.

ᵃ *AR* (1825): p 37
ᵇ *AR* (1825): APHORISM VII. EDITOR. §Whether
ᶜ COPY G: and the
ᵈ *AR* (1825): morality,

[5] The mutilation of coins by removing metal from their edges was a profitable fraud from the Middle Ages onwards.

[6] "I am fearfully and wonderfully made": Ps 139.14.

[7] This term (referring particularly to the temporary dwellings and place of worship set up by the Israelites while journeying through the wilderness) is used for the body in 2 Cor 5.1, 4 and 2 Pet 1.13, 14. It replaces the ms "Organ": see App B(j).

[8] Cf C's Preface and *Int Aph XII* n 2 above, and C's note at *Sp Aph B IX* n 29 below. The need to avoid confused terms is the theme of an extract from Daniel Sennert, which C used in a note of 1801/2 (*CN* I 1000C), as a motto for the third Bristol essay "On the Principles of Genial Criticism" (1814): *BL* (1907) II 228, and again in *BL* ch 16 *(CC)* 31. Cf C's annotation on C. J. Blomfield *Charge: CM (CC)* I 533. The present sentence is underlined, not necessarily by C, in *AR* (1825) COPY F.

[9] "Something for something", i.e. a substitution the falseness of which invalidates an argument. Cf *Logic (CC)* 217 and *CN* IV 5100.

If we seriously consider what religion is, we shall find the saying of the wise king Solomon to be unexceptionably true: *Her ways are ways of pleasantness, and all her paths are peace.*²

Doth religion require any thing of us more than that we live *soberly, righteously, and godly in this present world?*³ Now what, I pray, can be more pleasant or peaceable than these? Temperance is always at leisure, *ᵇ*luxury always in a hurry: the latter weakens the body and pollutes the soul, the former is the sanctity, purity, and sound state of both. It is one of Epicurus's fixed maxims, "That life can never be pleasant without virtue."*ᶜ⁴*

COMMENT

In the works of moralists, both Christian and Pagan, it is often asserted (indeed there are few common-places of more frequent recurrence) that the happiness even of this life consists solely, or principally, in virtue; that virtue is the only happiness of this life; that virtue is the truest *pleasure*, &c.

I doubt not that the meaning, which the writers intended to convey by these and the like expressions, was true and wise. But I deem it safer to say,*ᵈ* that in all the outward relations of this life, in all our outward conduct and actions, both in what we should *ᵉ*do, and in what we should abstain from, the dictates of virtue are the very same with those of *ᶠ*self-interest, tending *to*, though they do not proceed *from*, the same point. For*ᵍ* the outward object of virtue being the greatest producible sum of

---

ᵃ *AR* (1825): VIII. LEIGHTON.

ᵇ *AR* (1825): p 38

ᶜ For the continuation in *AR* (1825), see App G(f)

ᵈ *AR* (1825): say, nor do I doubt that in diverting men from sensual and dishonest courses it will often be expedient to say,

ᵉ *AR* (1825): p 39

ᶠ⁻ᵍ *AR* (1825): self-interest; that though the incitements of virtue do not proceed *from* the same point, yet they tend *to* the same point with the impulses of a reflecting and consistent selfishness; that

---

¹ From Leighton's *Theological Lectures* No XIX "That Holiness is the Only Happiness on Earth": Leighton COPY C IV 319–20 (= *Aph VIII* in 1825). Leighton is contending that "virtue, or . . . piety, which is absolutely the sum and substance of all virtues and all wisdom, is the only happiness of this life . . .". He continues: "And if we seriously consider this subject but a little, we shall find the saying of the wise

king Solomon concerning this wisdom, to be unexceptionably true . . .". The remainder is quoted word for word: see *CM (CC)* III.

² Prov 3.17.

³ Titus 2.12.

⁴ *Letter to Menoecus* in Diogenes Laertius *Lives of the Philosophers* 10.132. For the continuation of this aphorism in 1825 see below, App G(f).

happiness of all men,[5] it must needs include the object of an intelligent self-love,[6] which is the greatest possible happiness of one individual; for what is true of all, must be true of each. Hence, you cannot become better, (*i.e.* more virtuous), but you will become happier: and you cannot become worse, (*i.e.* more vicious), without an increase of misery (or at the best a proportional loss of enjoyment) as the consequence. If the thing were not inconsistent with our well-being, and known to be so, it would not have been classed as a *vice*. Thus what in a *ᵃdisordered and enfeebledᵇ* mind is called prudence, is the voice of nature in a healthful state: as is proved by the known fact, that the prudential duties, (*i.e.* those actions which are commanded by virtue *because* they are prescribed by prudence), the animals fulfil by natural instinct.

The pleasure that accompanies or depends on a healthy and vigorous body will be the consequence and reward of a temperate life and habits of active industry, whether this pleasure were or were not the chief or only determining *motive* thereto. Virtue may, possibly, add to the pleasure a good of another kind, a higher good, perhaps, than the worldly mind is ᶜcapable of understanding, a spiritual complacency, of which in your present sensualized state you can form no idea. It may *add*, I say, but it cannot detract from it. Thus the reflected rays of the sun that give light, distinction, and endless multiformity to the mind, affordᵈ at the same time the pleasurable sensation of *warmth* to the ᵉbody.

Ifᶠ then the time has not yet come for any thing higher, act on the maxim of seeking the most pleasure with the least pain: and, if only you do not seek where you yourself *know* it will not be found, this very pleasure and this freedom from the disquietude of painᵍ may produce in you a state of being directly and indirectly favorableʰ to the germination and up-spring of a nobler seed. ⁱIf it be true, that men are miserable because they are wicked, it is likewise true, that many men are wicked because they are miserable. Health, cheerfulness, and easy circum-

---

ᵃ⁻ᵇ *AR* (1825): enfeebled and disordered

ᶜ *AR* (1825): p 40

ᵈ *AR* (1825): give

ᵉ⁻ᶠ *AR* (1825): body. If

ᵍ *AR* (1825): pain, existing in conjunction with their immediate causes and necessary conditions, and with the other almost certain consequences of these causes, (for instance, the advantages of good character, the respect and sympathy of your neighbours, sense of increasing power and influence, &c.)

ʰ *AR* (1825): favourable

ⁱ Added in 1831

---

[5] For Mill's approval of this statement see below, n 7.

[6] For a subsequent disquisition on this theme see *CN* ɪv 5209 (May 1825). For other discussions of the rôle of self-love see *LS* (*CC*) 186–7, 1818 *Friend* (*CC*) ɪ 424–7, and *P Lects* Lect 4 (1949) 154–5.

stances, the ordinary consequences of Temperance and Industry, will at least leave the field clear and open, will tend to preserve the scales of the judgment even: while the consciousness of possessing the esteem, respect and sympathy of your neighbours, and the sense of your own increasing power and influence, can scarcely fail to give a tone of dignity to your mind, and incline you to hope nobly of your own Being. And thus[a] they[b] may prepare and predispose you to the sense and acknowledgment of a principle, differing not merely in degree but in *kind* from the faculties and instincts of the higher and more intelligent species of animals, (the ant, the beaver, the elephant), and which principle is therefore your proper humanity. And on this account and with this view alone may certain modes of pleasurable or *agreeable* sensation, without confusion of terms, be honored[c] with the title of refined, intellectual, ennobling pleasures.—For Pleasure (and happiness in its proper sense is but the [d]continuity and sum-total of the pleasure which is allotted or happens to a man,[7] and hence by the Greeks called εὐτυχία[e], *i.e.* goodhap, or more religiously εὐδαιμονία[f], *i.e.* favorable[g] providence)[8]— Pleasure, I say, consists in the harmony between the specific excitability of a living creature, and the exciting causes correspondent thereto. Considered therefore exclusively in and for itself, the only question is, quantum? not[h] quale?[9] *How much on the whole?* the contrary, *i.e.*[i] the pain-

---

[a] Added in 1831   [b] *AR* (1825): They   [c] *AR* (1825): honoured
[d] *AR* (1825): p 41   [e] *AR* (1825): ευτύχια
[f] *AR* (1825): εὐδαιμόνια   [g] *AR* (1825): *i. e.* favourable
[h] *AR* (1825): not,   [i] *AR* (1825): *i. e.*

[7] John Stuart Mill mentioned this and a preceding comment (above, n 5) in his essay on C in the *London and Westminster Review* xxxiii (1840) 297 (reprinted *Dissertations and Discussions*—1859—i 459), as sentiments of which "even a utilitarian can have little complaint to make".

[8] C has taken up again the point made in his earlier interpolation into Leighton's text: see *Prud Aph I* n 1, prompted by footnotes in Leighton copy c iv 196–7 which give the Greek words "commonly used to express happiness or felicity" as μακαριότης and εὐδαιμονία and quote the sentence " Ἡ εὐδαιμονία ἡδονὴ ἀμετάβλητός [Happiness is uninterrupted pleasure]". C would have in mind that τύχη corresponds to "chance", or "hap", in English, whereas εὐδαιμονία by derivation implies the benign influence of a divine power, a δαίμων. Cf *Op Max ms* B2 ("III") 43–5, where, having defined happiness as "the aggregate of fortunate chances" and catalogued such "circumstances" of man as all "prizes in the lottery of life", C continues: "The more reflecting who reject alike the notions of chance and of fate are accustomed to express the same meaning by the words 'favorable providence'. And even so in the greek the epicurean would express our happiness by μακαριοτης, the stoic or platonist by ευδαιμονια."

For attempts to desynonymise other words for happiness see *CN* iii 3558 and 4422 (cf *P Lects* Lect 3—1949—140–1) and an annotation on Tennemann ii 50–5: *CM (CC)* v.

[9] "How much?" not "of what quality?"

ful and disagreeable, having been subtracted. The quality is a matter of *taste:* et de *gustibus* non est disputandum.[10] No man can judge for another.

This, I repeat, appears[11] to me a safer language than the sentences quoted above,[a] (that virtue alone is happiness; that happiness consists in virtue, &c.),[b] sayings which I find it hard to reconcile with other positions of still more frequent occurrence in the same divines, or with the declaration of St. Paul: "If in this life only we have hope, we are of all men most miserable."[c12]

[d]At all events, I should rely far more confidently on the converse, viz. that to be vicious is to be *miserable*. Few men are so utterly reprobate, so imbruted by their vices, as not to have some lucid, or at least quiet and sober, intervals; and in such a moment, *dum desaeviunt irae*,[13] few can stand up unshaken against the appeal to their own experience—what have been the wages of sin?[14] what has the devil done for you? What sort of master have you *found* him?[15] Then let us ask in befitting *detail*, and by a series of questions that ask no loud, and are secure against any *false*, answer, urge home the proof of the position, that to be vicious is to be wretched: adding the fearful corollary, that if even in the body,

---

[a] *AR* (1825): above ; COPY D: before quoted
[b] *AR* (1825): &c.)
[c] For the continuation of the passage in *AR* (1825) see App G(g)
[d] *AR* (1825): p 42

---

[10] "And there can be no disputing concerning *tastes*". Proverbial. Cf *Mor Aph XXVI* n 2 below. C's ms for the following passage, from "disputandum" to "which it" in the penultimate paragraph, as it appeared in *AR* (1825) *Prud Aph VIII*, is transcribed below in App B(k).

[11] For "This, I repeat, appears" *AR* (1825) COPIES D and E (var) read: "~~The when not~~ Whereever it is desirable to act~~ing~~ on men of loose and unsettled principles by motives of selfish prudence, ⟨this mode, as specified ~~as given~~ in the last two pages⟩—this appeal to ~~mere~~ the principle of Self-love accompanied, as it is, with the express declaration that it is appealed to only as a Proxy or Locum-tenens, tolerated during the absence or minority of the rightful Principle—appears." See also n 12 below. COPY F deletes only "This" and reads: "If in any case we may attempt to influence the mind by motives of selfish

Prudence, this line of argument, as pursued in the two preceding pages, this appeal to the principle of Self-love accompanied with an express declaration, that it is tolerated only as a Proxy during the absence or minority of the rightful Principle—this,".

[12] 1 Cor 15.19 reads "hope in Christ" for "hope", which suggests that C did not have the text in front of him. *AR* (1825) has two further sentences in this paragraph, re-written in COPIES D and E: see below, App G(g) and textual notes.

[13] "While their passions die down". Cf Lucan *De bello civili* [*Pharsalia*] 5.303–4: ". . . nec dum desaeviat ira | Exspectat" (nor did he wait until their rage should die down).

[14] "For the wages of sin is death": Rom 6.23.

[15] "No man can serve two masters . . . . Ye cannot serve God and mammon": Matt 6.24, Luke 16.13.

which as long as life is in it can never be *wholly* bereaved of pleasurable sensations, vice is found to be misery, what must it not be in the world to come? There, where even the *crime* is no longer possible, much less the gratifications that once attended it—where nothing of vice remains but its guilt and its misery—vice must be misery itself, all and utter misery.[16]—So best, if I err not, may the motives of prudence be held forth, and the impulses of self-love be awakened, in alliance with truth, and free from the danger of confounding two[a] things (the Laws of Duty, I mean, and the Maxims of Interest)[17] which it deeply concerns us to keep distinct, inasmuch as this distinction and the faith therein are essential to our moral nature, and this again the ground-work and pre-condition of the spiritual state, in which the Humanity strives after God-liness and, in the name and power, and through [b]the prevenient and assisting grace, of the Mediator, will not strive in vain.

[c]The *advantages* of a life passed in conformity with the precepts of virtue and religion, and in how many and various respects they recommend virtue and religion, even on grounds of prudence, form a delightful subject of meditation, and a source of refreshing thought to good and pious men. Nor is it strange if, transported with the view, such persons should sometimes discourse on the charm of forms and colors[d] to men whose eyes are not yet *couched;*[18] or that they occasionally seem to invert the relations of cause and effect, and forget that there are acts and determinations of the will and affections, the *consequences* of which may be plainly foreseen, and yet cannot be made our proper and primary *motives* for such acts and determinations, without destroying or entirely

---

[a] Added in 1831
[b] *AR* (1825): p 43
[c] *AR* (1825): APHORISM IX. EDITOR.
[d] *AR* (1825): colours

---

[16] Cf C's letter to his brother George 2 Apr 1807: ". . . perfect . . . Self-knowlege may be among the spiritual punishments of the abandoned . . .": *CL* III 6. For this and several similar passages see Barth 191–3.

[17] This distinction may owe something to Kant, who, however, in his *Grundlegung zur Metaphysik der Sitten* (Riga 1797) (tr T. K. Abbott *Fundamental Principles of the Metaphysics of Morals*—1907—35–6) makes a more complex distinction, first between the "practically good", which determines the will by

means of the conceptions of reason, and the "pleasant," which influences the will by means of merely subjective causes, then, in a footnote, between "taking an interest" and acting "from interest": in the first case interest is allied with duty, in the second not. "Pre-condition is *OED*'s first example of the word.

[18] To remove a cataract from the eye by inserting a needle. *OED* cites DeQ's 1839 description of DW's effect on WW: "She it was . . . that first *couched* his eye to the sense of beauty": *DeQ Works* II 239. Cf also *BL* ch 2 (1907) I 27fn.

altering the distinct nature and character of the latter.[19] Sophron is well informed that wealth and extensive patronage will be the consequence of his obtaining the love and esteem of Constantia.[20] But if the foreknowledge of this consequence were, and were *found out* to be, Sophron's main and determining motive for seeking this love and esteem; and if Constantia were a woman that merited, or was capable of feeling, either one or the other; would not Sophron find (and deservedly too) aversion and contempt in their stead? Wherein, if not in this, [a]differs the friendship of worldlings from true friendship? Without kind offices and useful services, wherever the power and opportunity occur, love would be a hollow pretence. Yet what noble mind would not be offended, if he were thought to value the love for the sake of the services, and not rather the services for the sake of the love?[b][21]

APHORISM III[c]

Though prudence in itself is neither virtue nor spiritual holiness, yet without prudence, or in opposition to it, neither virtue nor holiness can exist.

APHORISM IV[d]

Art thou under the tyranny of sin? a slave to vicious habits? at enmity with God, and a skulking fugitive from thy own conscience? O, how idle the [e]dispute, whether the listening to the dictates of *prudence* from prudential and self-interested motives be virtue or merit, when the *not* listening is guilt, misery, madness, and despair! The best, the most *Christianlike* pity thou canst show, is to take pity on thy own soul. The best and most acceptable service thou canst render, is to do justice and show mercy to *thyself*.[f][1]

---

[a] *AR* (1825): p 44
[b] For the continuation in *AR* (1825) see App G(h)
[c] *AR* (1825): X. EDITOR.
[d] *AR* (1825): XI. EDITOR.
[e] *AR* (1825): p 45
[f] For Aphs XII–XV from Leighton, which follow in *AR* (1825) (pp 45–8), see App G(i)

[19] For another meditation on this theme see *CN* II 2210.
[20] Sophron, in Henry More's *Divine Dialogues* (1688), represents "The Sober and wary man." Like Constantia (constancy) it is a name that appears more than once in eighteenth-century literature.
[21] A further paragraph follows here in *AR* (1825), reprinted below in App G(h).
[1] The remaining aphorisms of this section in *AR* (1825) are reprinted below in App G(i).

*ᵃ*REFLECTIONS,

MORAL AND RELIGIOUS APHORISMS

———

I. On Sensibility

II. On the Morals, as theoretically distinguishable both from the Prudential
and the Religious Character*ᵇ*[1]

ᵃ *AR* (1825): p 19
ᵃ⁻ᵇ *AR* (1825): REFLECTIONS RESPECTING MORALITY.

[1] In *AR* (1825) this section was not sub-divided and was entitled simply "Reflections respecting Morality"; the second section indicated here was not included as such in *AR* (1831). It is likely that when C removed from the 1825 version the conclud-ing paragraphs of this section, reproduced in App G(j) below, he intended to enlarge it, perhaps also transferring discussion from *Int Aph XXIX* and *XXX* above, but then omitted to do so. "Morals" is presumably a misprint for "Moral".

^aON SENSIBILITY^b1

If Prudence, though practically inseparable from Morality, is not to be confounded with the Moral Principle; still less may ^cSensibility, *i.e.*^d a constitutional quickness of Sympathy with Pain and Pleasure,[2] and a keen sense of the gratifications that accompany social intercourse, mutual endearments, and reciprocal preferences,^e be mistaken, or deemed a Substitute^f for either.^g ^hSensibility isⁱ ^jnot even a^k sure pledge^l of a

---

^a *AR* (1825): p 51 (p 50 blank)
^{a–b} *AR* (1825): REFLECTIONS RESPECTING MORALITY.
^{c–d} COPIES G & H: Sensibility (*i. e.*
^e COPIES G & H: preferences)
^f COPY G: Substitute,
^g COPIES C, D, E, F, H: it.
^{h–i} *AR* (1825): They are ; COPY D: Sensibility is ; COPY G: It is
^{j–l} COPIES C, D, E, F, H: no sure pledge even
^k Added in 1831; COPY G: a
^l *AR* (1825): pledges ; COPY G: pledge

---

[1] As will be seen from the passage in *The Watchman* which C uses in an adapted form later in this section (see n 5, below), his suspicion of "sensibility" was of long standing. It echoes Dr Johnson's comments: e.g. "You will find these very feeling people are not very ready to do you good. They *pay* you by *feeling*": James Boswell *Life of Johnson* ed G. B. Hill, rev L. F. Powell (6 vols Oxford 1934–50) II 95. See also R. Voitle *Samuel Johnson the Moralist* (Cambridge, Mass 1961) esp 26–32, 50–4, 130–1. C was also wary of Jacobinism appearing as "refined SENSIBILITY and PHILANTHROPY"—*EOT (CC)* II 384—and of the tendency of "universal benevolence" to "deaden the affections, and extinguish the generous sensibilities of the heart" as with Rousseau, who "delegated the care of his children to the Public Hospital": ibid II 330. Yet he was drawn towards the cult as well: cf his (only semi-

ironic) "Bless thee, Man of Genius and Sensibility!" in a letter of Jul 1794: *CL* I 92. For many examples of this tension see e.g. *EOT (CC)* and *Friend (CC)* Indexes s.v. "sensibility".

[2] Compare DeQ's description of DW's "excessive organic sensibility", the "glancing quickness of her emotions", and her "exceeding sympathy": "The pulses of light are not more quick . . . than were the answering and echoing movements of her sympathizing attention." *DeQ Works* II 239. Cf *Prud Aph II* n 18, above. For an account of C's own paradoxical sensibility, which "shrank from mere uneasiness like a child, and bore the preparatory agonies of his death-attack like a martyr", see *TT* (1835) Preface: *TT (CC)* II 28 (and cf Index s.v. "sensibility"). The position is complicated by the fact that C in middle life often "sought refuge from his own sensibility" (*Friend—CC—*II 187), suffering from a

57

GOOD HEART,[3] though among the most common meanings of that many-meaning and too commonly misapplied expression.

So far from being either Morality, or one with the Moral Principle, it[a] ought not even to[b] be placed in the same rank with Prudence. For Prudence is at least an offspring of the Understanding; but Sensibility (the Sensibility, I mean, here spoken of), is for the greater part a quality of the nerves, and a result of individual bodily temperament.

Prudence is an *active* Principle, and implies a sacrifice of Self, though only to the same Self *projected*, as it were, to a distance. But the very term Sensibility, [c]marks its *passive* nature;[4] and in its mere self, apart from Choice and Reflection, it proves little more than the coincidence or contagion of pleasurable or painful Sensations in different persons.

Alas! how many are there in this over-stimulated age, in which the occurrence of excessive and unhealthy sensitiveness is so frequent, as even to have reversed the current meaning of the word, [d]*nervous*.[5] How[e] many are* there whose sensibility prompts them to remove those evils

* This paragraph is abridged from the Watchman, No. IV. March 25, 1796;[6] respecting which the inquisitive Reader may consult my "Literary Life."[f7]

> [a] *AR* (1825): they ; COPIES D, E, F, H: it ; COPY G: Sensibility
> [b] Added in 1831
> [c] *AR* (1825): p 52
> [d-e] *AR* (1825): nervous,—how
> [f] *AR* (1825): Life."   S. T. C

"morbid state of the moral Being", one symptom of which was "an excessive sensibility and strange cowardice with regard to everything that is likely to affect the Heart" (letter to Lady Beaumont 15 Apr 1810: *CL* III 287), yet also (from a quite different angle) regarded sensibility as a crucial element in the life process: see e.g. *C&S (CC)* 179–81, *TL* (1848) 84, and below, *Mor Aph XXXVI* n 6.

[3] Cf Sir John Hawkins's identification of Henry Fielding as "the inventor of the cant phrase, goodness of heart, which is every day used as a substitute for probity, and means little more than the virtue of a horse or dog": *Life of Johnson* (1787) 215.

[4] The harmful effects of a habitual passivity are a constant theme of C's. Cf *The Friend* 26 Oct 1809: "It cannot but be injurious to the human mind never to be called into effort and the habit of receiving pleasure without any exertion of thought, by the mere excitement of curiosity and

sensibility, may be justly ranked among the worst effects of habitual novel reading": *Friend (CC)* II 150 (I 20). By contrast, ". . . a mind . . . roused and awakened" cannot be "brooded on by mean and indistinct emotion": *BL* ch 15 *(CC)* II 22. For the healthful interplay of activity and passivity see above, *Int Aph VIII* n 3.

[5] At this time the primary meaning of "nervous" was still "sinewy", "vigorous" (see *OED*). However, the modern sense of the word, which had made its way into the language by way of terms such as "nervous disorders", was also well established, at least in colloquial usage. Cf Johnson's letter to Mrs Thrale 24 Nov 1783: "A tender, irritable, and as it is not very properly called, a nervous constitution", and other examples in *OED*.

[6] *The Watchman* had used slightly stronger language: "There is observable among the Many a false and bastard sensibility that prompts them to remove those

alone, which by hideous spectacle or clamorous outcry are present to their senses and disturb their selfish enjoyments. Provided the dunghill is not before their parlour window, they are well contented to know that it exists, and perhaps as the hotbed on which their own luxuries are reared. Sensibility is not necessarily Benevolence. Nay, by rendering us tremblingly alive to trifling misfortunes, it frequently prevents it, and induces an effeminate Selfishness instead,

> ———— pampering the coward heart,
> With feelings all too delicate for use.
>
> Sweet are the Tears, that from a Howard's eye
> Drop on the cheek of one, he lifts from earth:
> And He, who works me good with unmoved face,
> Does it but half. He chills me, while he aids,
> My Benefactor, not my Brother Man.
>
> But even this, this *cold* benevolence,[a]
> Seems Worth, seems Manhood, when there rise before me
> [b]The sluggard Pity's vision-weaving tribe,[c]
> Who sigh for wretchedness[d] yet shun the wretched,[e]
> Nursing in some delicious solitude,[f]
> Their slothful[g] Loves and dainty Sympathies.
> [h]*Coleridge's Poetical Works, Vol. I. p.* 229[i][8]

Lastly, where Virtue is, Sensibility is the ornament and becoming

---

[a] COPIES C, D, E, F: beneficence, ; COPY G: beneficence
[b] *AR* (1825): p 53
[c] *AR* (1825): Tribe,
[d] *AR* (1825): Wretchedness
[e] COPIES C, D, E, F, G: Wretched,
[f] *AR* (1825): Solitude
[g] *AR* (1825): Slothful ; COPIES C, D, E, F, G: slothful
[h–i] *AR* (1825): *Sibylline Leaves,* p. 180.

---

evils and those evils alone, which by hideous spectacle or clamorous outcry are present to their senses, and disturb their selfish enjoyments. . . . Provided the dunghill be not before their parlour window, they are well content to know that it exists, and that it is the hot-bed of their pestilent luxuries. . . . Sensibility is not Benevolence. Nay, by making us tremblingly alive to trifling misfortunes, it frequently prevents it, and induces effeminate and cowardly selfishness": *Watchman (CC)* 139. The passage was reproduced more fully (var) in *Omniana* (1812) II 204. Cf the anecdote of the girl with a ". . . half-famished sickly Baby" in a letter of 6 Jul 1794 (*CL* I 83–4), and "Lecture on the Slave-Trade" 17 Jun 1795: ". . . true Benevolence is a rare Quality among us. Sensibility indeed we have to spare—what novel-reading Lady does not over flow with it . . .": *Lects 1795 (CC)* 249.

[7] *BL* ch 10 *(CC)* I 179–87 and nn.

[8] *Reflections on Having Left a Place of Retirement* lines 47–59 (var): *PW* (1829) I 229. Cf *PW* (EHC) I 107. First published in *Monthly Magazine* II (Oct 1796) 712.

Attire of Virtue. On certain occasions it may almost be said to *become**
Virtue. But Sensibility and all the amiable Qualities may likewise become, and too often *have* become, the pandars of Vice and the instruments of Seduction.[12]

So must it needs be with all qualities that have their rise only in *parts*
and *fragments* of our nature. A man of warm passions may sacrifice half
his estate to rescue a friend from Prison;[a] for he is naturally sympathetic,
and the more social *part* of his nature happened to be uppermost. The
same man shall afterwards exhibit the same disregard of money in an
attempt to seduce that friend's Wife or Daughter.

All the evil achieved by Hobbes and the whole School of
Materialists[13] will appear inconsiderable,[b] if it be compared with the
mischief effected and occasioned by the sentimental Philosophy of
STERNE, and his numerous[c] Imitators. The vilest appetites and the most

---

* There sometimes occurs an apparent *Play* on words, which not only to the Moralizer,
but even to the philosophical Etymologist, appears more than a mere Play.[9] Thus in the
double sense of the word, *become*. I have known persons so anxious to have their Dress
become them, so *totus in illo*,[10] as to convert it at length into their proper self, and thus
actually to *become* the Dress. Such a one, (safeliest spoken of by the *neuter* Pronoun), I
consider as but a suit of *live* finery.[d] It is indifferent whether we say—It *becomes* [e]He, or,
He[f] *becomes* it.[11]

[a] *AR* (1825): Prison:

[b] *AR* (1825): inconsiderable

[c] *AR* (1825): p 54 (merous)

[d] *AR* (1825): Finery.

[e-f] COPIES D, E, F: Henry, or Henry ; COPY G: FLORUS, or, FLORUS

[9] For other cases where the pun is "the
buffoon Brutus concealing Brutus, the
Consul" see C's note on Böhme *Works* and
the editor's n 2: *CM (CC)* I 610.

[10] "Entirely in that". A very common
tag, with C and with others. Cf Horace *Satires* 1.9.2: "nescio quid meditans nuga-
rum, totus in illis"; tr H. R. Fairclough
(LCL 1926): "musing on some trifle or
other, and wholly intent thereon".

[11] *AR* (1825) COPY F has a note by C at
this point: "It may serve to elucidate this
remark, which many will, perhaps, condemn as a subtlety bordering on a play of
words, if I refer to the not unfrequent
Transfer of our sense of personal identity
(τοῦ Ἐγω) to alien forms, and sometimes
even to Images of inanimate Objects,
which now and then takes place in our
Dreams. S. T. C."

[12] Cf "Sterne . . . makes the best dis-

positions of our nature the pandars & Con-
diments for the basest": Lect 9 of 1818:
Lects 1808–1819 (CC) II 174.

[13] ". . . by Hobbes and others of the
materialists, compulsion and obligation
were used indiscriminately; but the distinction of the two senses is the condition of all
moral responsibility": annotation on Walter Birch *Sermon on . . . Infidelity and Enthusiasm*: *CM (CC)* I 495–6. Cf *P Lects*
Lect 5 (1949) 174 and 200, *BL* ch 4 *(CC)* I
87n and n 1, *Logic (CC)* 123. HNC pointed
out that the term "obligation" was not
used by Hobbes in his *Treatise on Liberty
and Necessity—BL* (1847) I 84–5n—but
the editors of *BL (CC)* I 87n locate usages
in *Philosophical Rudiments Concerning
Government and Society* (1651; later
known as *De Cive*) 25, etc. C borrowed *De
Cive* from the Carlisle Cathedral library in
1801.

remorseless inconstancy towards their objects, acquired the titles of *the Heart, the irresistible Feelings, the too tender Sensibility;*[a] and if the Frosts of Prudence, the icy chains of Human Law[14] thawed and vanished at the genial warmth of Human *Nature,* who *could help it? It was an amiable Weakness!*[15]

About this [b]time, too,[c] the profanation of the word[d] Love, rose to its height. The French Naturalists, Buffon and others,[16] borrowed it from

[a] *AR* (1825): *Sensibility:*
[b-c] *AR* (1825): time too
[d] *AR* (1825): word,

[14] C's image of the chain probably involves a satirical glance at the deathly constraints imposed by Hobbes's logic. Cf the remark reported by Methuen "Retrospect of Friendly Communications with the Poet Coleridge": "Hobbes . . . fancied the first link of his chain was fastened to a rock of adamant; but it proved to be a rock of ice": *Christian Observer* XLV (May 1845) 260. C was referring presumably to *Leviathan* (1651) pt 2 ch 21 § 108, in which Hobbes discusses "the Actions which men voluntarily doe: which, because they proceed from their will, proceed from *liberty*; and yet, because every act of mans will, and every desire, and inclination proceedeth from some cause, and that from another cause, in a continuall chaine, (whose first link is in the hand of God the first of all causes,) proceed from *necessity*. So that to him that could see the connexion of those causes, the *necessity* of all mens voluntary actions, would appear manifest." Cf also *CN* IV 4786 f 124 and C's question (apostrophising Spinoza): ". . . where should I find that iron Chain of Logic, which neither man or angel could *break*, but which falls of itself by dissolving the rock of Ice, to which it is stapled—and which thou in common with all thy contemporaries & predecessors didst mistake for a rock of adamant?": letter of 10 Mar 1815: *CL* IV 548 and n.

[15] C was perhaps more critical of the "Imitators" than of Sterne himself, whom he admired as a humorist, reprehending only the *underlying* moral tendency of his work. See Lect 9 of 1818: *Lects 1808–1819 (CC)* II 174–7. Cf n 12, above. "Sterne's morals are bad—but I don't think they can do much harm to any one

whom they would not find bad enough before": *TT* 17 Aug 1833 *(CC)* I 425 (1836 vn, dated 18 Aug, II 254). See also his insistence that love is "yet an act of the will—and that too one of the *primary* & therefore . . . ineffable Acts". Otherwise, "I know not how we could attach Blame & Immorality to Inconstancy when ⟨it is⟩ confined to the Affections,—⟨& sense of Preference—⟩ Either therefore we must brutalize our notions with Pope . . . or dissolve & thaw away all bonds of morality by the inevitable Shocks of an irresistible Sensibility with Sterne": *CN* III 3562.

[16] Annotating an observation that elephants had no "particular seasons of love" (*Encyclopaedia Londinensis* VI—1810), C wrote, "This detestable use of the word 'love' was introduced by the French; and is a good instance of the filthiness of mock-modesty": *CM (CC)* II 527 and n. A good example of the French tradition C objects to can be found in the work of J. O. de la Mettrie (1709–51), with his polemically materialist interpretation of nature. For his conception of love see e.g. *L'Art de jouir* (1751). The reference to Georges Buffon (1707–88) and to sentimental fiction suggests that C may be recalling a passage at the end of ch 8 "des sens en general" in the section "De l'homme" in Buffon's *Histoire naturelle,* which tries to recreate the experience of a human being entering the world and discovering sensuous experience for the first time. The climax of his exploration comes when he finds himself with another human being: " 'By the touch of my hand I found her to be animated; expression and vivacity darted from her eyes and impressed my soul, and love served to complete that happiness which was begun

the sentimental Novelists:[a] the Swedish and English Philosophers took the contagion;[17] and the Muse of Science condescended to seek admission into the Saloons of Fashion and Frivolity, *rouged* like a[b] Harlot, and with the Harlot's wanton leer.[18] I know not how the Annals of Guilt

[a] *AR* (1825): Novellists:
[b] *AR* (1825): an

in the individual, and every sense was gratified in its full variety' '': Buffon *Natural History* tr J. S. Barr (10 vols 1797) IV 190, a free translation of the original, *De l'homme* (1749) ed M. Duchet (Paris 1971) 218. For more on C's view of the French and love see *CN* III 4015, *CM (CC)* II 73, *BL* ch 21 *(CC)* II 117.

[17] In his *Loves of the Plants* (1789) 183–4 Erasmus Darwin cited a Swedish observer, "M. Haggren, Lecturer in Natural History", on the flashing of certain plants, in connexion with his lines about *Tropaeolum* (136–7), in which the male–female ration is 8 to 1:

Eight watchful swains along the lawns
    of night
With amorous steps pursue the virgin-
    light . . .

(C took over Haggren's observation when he reproduced part of Darwin's account, verbatim, in a note to *Lines Written at Shurton Bars*: *PW*—EHC—I 99–100. See *RX* 464–5.)

The prime Swedish figure was Linnaeus, who introduced the system of botanical classification by sexual characteristics that Darwin versified. For an example of the impact see the notice of John Russel in Anthony Pasquin (John Williams) *Memoirs of the Royal Academicians* (1796) 128: "In the last exhibition Mr. RUSSEL laboured to soar above himself in a design for a frontispiece to an Illustration of the Sexual System; it involved the bust of *Linnaeus*. At the pedestal was a Cupid, indicting the following expressive and explanatory lines with his arrow—

Ah! let not the oppressive huge *Savoy*
Touch the soft fibres of yon *female
    Plant*,
(Like *Polypheme* on *Galatea*'s breast;)
Such premature embraces I abhor.
Oh! let the vegetable Maid alone,

Nor watch her at the coming on of eve,
When she would naked lave amid the
    dew.

"I must take this occasion to express my complete disapprobation of the unqualified uses which are momentarily made of the ingenuity of the philosophic Swede. Would it not offend both Gods and men, to behold an F.R.S. crawling, in the blaze of day, upon his hands and feet, through the mazes of a flower garden, to operate as the he-bawd to an *Auricula*, or peep up the petti-coats of a *Tulip*, to ascertain the gender?—It must be extremely mortifying to the *Vegetable World* to know, that, after hiding their amours so many thousand years, they are now subject to the impertinent curiosity of every prying Naturalist, in the face of heaven; and that an impassioned *Turnip* cannot pay his devoirs to an *Artichoke*, or a *Crab-tree* to a *Gooseberry-bush*, but there are a thousand microscopes directed to the scene; not merely to discover, but most indelicately to aggrandize, that exertion which, according to my liberal opinion, should be considered as mystic, and held as sacred!''

[18] *AR* (1825) COPY G has a note at this point: "Ex. gr. Kean's Letters to M[rs] Cox." Edmund Kean's liaison with the wife of Alderman Cox was a matter of considerable notoriety in 1823–5: see *Cox versus Kean: Fairbairn's Edition of the Trial Between Robert Albion Cox, Esq. and Edmund Kean for Crim. Con. Including the Curious Love Letters &c &c* (1825), and particularly Kean's letter of 2 Aug 1822 (p 19): "O God, Charlotte, how I love you. If such a feeling is a crime, why are we given it? I did not seek it. The power that will condemn has placed you in my way; the same inspiring hand that framed my better qualities pointed to you as the object of my love—my everlasting love . . . every day shoots up some unexpected tendrill round

could be better forced into the service of Virtue, than by such a Comment on the present paragraph, as would be afforded by a selection from the sentimental correspondence produced in Courts of Justice within the last thirty years, fairly translated into the true meaning of the words, and the actual Object and Purpose of the infamous *a*Writers.

Do*b* you in good earnest aim at Dignity of Character? By all the treasures of a peaceful mind, by all the charms of an open countenance, I conjure you, O youth! turn away from those who live in the Twilight between Vice and Virtue. Are not Reason, Discrimination, Law, and deliberate Choice, the distinguishing Characters of Humanity? Can *c*aught, then,*d* worthy of a human Being,*e* proceed from a Habit of Soul, which would exclude all these and (to borrow a metaphor from Paganism) prefer the den *f*of Trophonius[19] to the Temple and Oracles of the God of Light?[20] Can any thing *manly*, I say, proceed from those, who for Law and Light would substitute shapeless feelings, sentiments, impulses, which as far as they differ from the vital workings in the brute animals,*g*[21] owe the difference to their former connexion with the proper Virtues of Humanity; as Dendrites derive the outlines, that constitute their value above other clay-stones, from the casual neighborhood and pressure of the Plants, the names of which they assume![22] Remember, that Love itself in its highest earthly Bearing, as the ground of the marriage union,*h becomes Love by an inward FIAT[29] of the Will, by a com-

---

* It might be a mean of preventing many unhappy Marriages, if the youth of both sexes had it early impressed on their minds, that Marriage[23] contracted between Christians is a

---

a–b AR (1825): Writers. Do *c–d* AR (1825): aught then
e AR (1825): Being *f* AR (1825): p 55
g AR (1825): animals *h* AR (1825): union*,

---

the root of my affections, and you—little witch—you have so entangled it, that nothing but an earthquake can disperse them.''

[19] The ''den'' of Trophonius was an underground oracle. C used the image ironically for his own philosophy in the letter to himself in *BL* ch 13 *(CC)* I 302 (cf the similar passage in *P Lects* Lect 9—1949—269). In *P Lects* Lect 2 (1949) 105 he mentioned the charmed sleep and the proverbial melancholy of those who consulted the oracle, as phenomena related to animal magnetism. All the details he uses are to be found in John Potter *Archaeologia Graeca* bk II ch 10 (1697–8 and many subsequent eds). See *CL* VI 843 for C's knowledge of this in his schooldays. Potter quotes Pau-

sanias and Plutarch among others.

[20] Apollo, whose oracles (notably the one at Delphi) were commonly regarded as of supreme authority.

[21] *AR* (1825) COPY F has a note: ''*See p. 254*.'' (i.e. p 263–4n, below).

[22] A dendrite is a stone or mineral with a tree- or moss-like marking. *OED* cites Chambers *Cyclopaedia* (1728) s.v.: ''In some dendrites, the figures, or signatures, penetrate quite through.'' Cf *CM (CC)* II 1185 and *CN* IV 4677.

[23] For a concurrent meditation on the nature of marriage see C's notebook entry of Dec 1823 or Jan 1825: *CN* IV 5097. J. R. Barth (Barth 180–1n) suspects some subsequent vacillation on the sacramentality of

pleting and sealing *ᵃ*Act of Moral Election, and lays claim to permanence only under the form of DUTY.*ᵇ*³⁰

---

true and perfect Symbol or Mystery; that is, the actualizing Faith being supposed to exist in the Receivers, it is an outward Sign co-essential with that which it signifies, or a living Part of that, the whole of which it represents. Marriage,*ᶜ* therefore, in the Christian sense (Ephesians v. 22*ᵈ*–33),²⁴ as symbolical of the union of the Soul with Christ the Mediator, and with God through Christ, is perfectly a *sacramental* ordinance, and not retained by the Reformed Churches as one of THE Sacraments, for two reasons; first, that the Sign is not *distinctive* of the Church of Christ, and the Ordinance not peculiar nor owing its origin to the Gospel Dispensation; secondly, it is not of universal obligation, not a means of Grace enjoined on all Christians. In other and plainer words, Marriage does not contain in itself an open Profession of Christ, and it is not a Sacrament of the *Church*, but only of certain Individual Members of the Church. It is evident, however, that neither of these Reasons affect or diminish the *religious* nature and dedicative force of the marriage Vow, or detract from the solemnity of the Apostolic Declaration: THIS IS A GREAT MYSTERY.²⁵

The interest*ᵉ* which the state *ᶠ* has in the appropriation of one Woman to one Man, and the civil obligations therefrom resulting, form an altogether distinct consideration. When I meditate on the words of the Apostle, confirmed and illustrated as they are, by so many harmonies in the Spiritual Structure of our proper Humanity, (in the image of God, male

ᵃ *AR* (1825): p 56
ᵇ For the continuation in *AR* (1825) of pp 56–8, see App G(j)
ᶜ *AR* (1825): Marriage
ᵈ *AR* (1825): 22,
ᵉ *AR* (1825): interest,
ᶠ *AR* (1825): State

---

marriage: in Apr 1826 (*CN* IV 5348) C referred back to this footnote, pointing out that while it distinguishes a symbol or mystery from a ceremony it does not determine the distinctive character of a symbol that is likewise a sacrament: "I therefore retract the position that 'Marriage——is perfectly a *sacramental* Ordinance' . . . In order for Marriage to be a Sacrament, the substantiative act must be *spiritual*, i.e. an act of the Soul corresponding to an Act of the Divine Spirit, and as it were the medium thro' which the gracious influence of the latter is conveyed to the Believer, and not merely a *moral* Act—." The rest of the 1826 notebook entry defined his position further. He did not amend the 1825 footnote in 1831, however, and in a note of 1827 referred approvingly to the fact that St Paul "so profoundly calls Marriage a great Mystery, or Sacramental Symbol" (N 35 f 41: *CN* v). See also his note on Sir Thomas Browne *Religio Medici: CM (CC)* I 751, Barth 181n—which lists some further references by C to marriage—and his

letter of 1821: *CL* v 152–8.

²⁴ This passage on the duties of husbands and wives to one another contains the verse "This is a great mystery: but I speak concerning Christ and the church" (5.32). See also above, *Int Aph XXII* n 2, and below, *Sp Aph B Xb* n 61.

²⁵ In *AR* (1825) COPY F C inserted a note at this point: "It may be well to inform the English Reader that this is the same word as Sacrament, the latter being the rendering of the Apostle's *musterion* (mystery) in the Latin Vulgate." The point is not clear-cut, however, since in other places the Vulgate translates μυστήριον by "mysterium"; and the English "sacrament" might be said to translate only one sense of "sacramentum", which also has several meanings. C explored the relationship between the two words further in a note of 25 Feb 1826 on Rev 17.5: *CM (CC)* I 472. In Apr 1826 he gave a definition of sacrament that he thought "far more to the purpose than that which is implied in the Note to p. 55 of 'Aids to Reflection' ": "A Sacrament is a

and female created he the Man),[26] and then reflect how little claim so large a number of legal cohabitations have to the name of Christian Marriages—I feel inclined to doubt[a] whether the plan of celebrating Marriages universally by the [b]Civil Magistrate,[c] in the first instance, and leaving the *religious* Covenant[d] and sacramental Pledge to the election of the parties[e] themselves, adopted during the Republic in England,[27] and in our own times by the French Legislature,[f] [28] was not *in fact*, whatever it might be in intention, *reverential* to Christianity. At all events, it was their own act and choice, if the Parties made bad worse by the profanation of a Gospel Mystery.

[a] *AR* (1825): doubt,
[b–c] *AR* (1825): civil magistrate,
[d] *AR* (1825): Covenant,
[e] *AR* (1825): Parties
[f] COPY D: Legislature—it seems to be doubtful, I say, whether this plan

Symbol or Mystery consisting of a sensible Sign and a *spiritual* Substantive Act'': *CN* IV 5348. Cf n 23, above.

[26] Gen 1.27: ''So God created man in his own image, in the image of God created he him; male and female created he them.''

[27] By Act of Parliament (24 Aug 1653) only marriages solemnised before a justice of the peace were declared lawful. W. H. Hutton *The English Church from the Accession of Charles I to the Death of Anne* (1903) 160.

[28] On 20 Sept 1792 the Assembly ''ended its months of discussion on the subject and placed the register of births, marriages and deaths in the hands of secular authorities'': G. Lefebvre *The French Revolution from Its Origins to 1793* tr E. M. Evanson (1962) 245.

[29] ''Let it come to pass''. For C the ''aweful Fiat'' of the divine creation in Gen 1 (*CL* IV 545), that of the sun rising to ''create'' a landscape with its light (''the silent Fiat of the uprising Apollo'') used as an analogue of artistic creation (Lect 1 of 17 Dec 1818: *Lects 1808–1819—CC*—II 263) and the comparison of the coming of true love (the ''day-spring'': cf *Religious Musings* lines 415–19: *PW*—EHC—I 125) to the rising of the sun (''no man who had never watched for the rise of the Sun, could

understand what I mean'': *CL* III 304) formed an important nexus of images and ideas, which is evidently at work here also. The word ''Fiat'' is used portentously both by Böhme in *Aurora* (see e.g. xx 42 and xxvi 11: *Works* ed G. Ward and T. Langcake—1764–81—I 200, 257) and by William Law: e.g. ''Love is the great Creating Fiat that brought forth every Thing, that is distinct from God'' (*The Spirit of Prayer—* 1749–50—pt ii 81). See Beer *CV* 33, 264; *CPI* 46–7 and n, 98–9, 182.

[30] *AR* (1825) COPY H has a note at this point: ''However true it is, that it is but a poor security for the performance of an Act, that the Man knows, he *ought* to do so in any particular case: it is no less true, that taking the world at large, the thought, *I ought to do so*, when accompanied with the knowlege that the Society, in which we live, is agreed & knows, that I ought to do it . . .''. The rest of the note is cut away. A long passage followed here in *AR* (1825), elaborating C's aims. It was perhaps omitted because it promised a further discussion of ''Prudence, namely, as it flows out of Morality, and Morality as the natural Overflowing of Religion'', which was not fulfilled in the completed text. It is reprinted in App G(j), below.

^aMORAL AND RELIGIOUS

APHORISMS

^a *AR* (1825): p 59 (p 60 blank)

*ᵃMORAL AND RELIGIOUS APHORISMS

WHAT the Apostles were in an extraordinary way befitting the first annunciation of a Religion for all Mankind, this all Teachers of Moral
Truth, who aim to prepare for its reception by calling the attention of
men to the Law in their own hearts, may, without presumption, consider
themselves to be,ᶜ under ordinary gifts and circumstances;ᵈ namely,
Ambassadors for the Greatest of Kings, and upon no mean employment,
the great Treaty of Peace and Reconcilement betwixt him and Mankind.

Though Divine Truths are to be received equally from every Minister
alike, yet it must be acknowledged that there is something (we know not
what to call it) of a more acceptable reception of those whichᶠ at first
were the means of bringing men to God, than of ᵍothers; like the opinion
some have of physicians, whom they love.

ᵃ *AR* (1825): p 61
ᵇ *AR* (1825): LEIGHTON.
ᶜ *AR* (1825): be
ᵈ *AR* (1825): circumstances:
ᵉ *AR* (1825): LEIGHTON.
ᶠ *AR* (1825): who
ᵍ *AR* (1825): p 62

---

¹ From Leighton COPY C I 5, much altered: *CM (CC)* III. C seems to have
changed it in proof, which may explain
why in *AR* (1825) the ascription at the head
was to Leighton alone. All the Moral
Aphorisms, except L, are drawn from
Leighton's *Commentary on 1 Peter*.
¹ From Leighton COPY C I 6, which reads
"of those who" for "of those which": *CM
(CC)* III.

APHORISM III[a1]

The worth and value of Knowledge is in proportion to the worth and value of its object. What, then, is the best knowledge?

The exactest knowledge of things, is, to know them in their causes; it is then an excellent thing, and worthy of their endeavours who are most desirous of knowledge, to know the best things in their highest causes; and the happiest way of attaining to this knowledge, is, to possess those things, and to know them in experience.

APHORISM IV[b1]

It is one main point of happiness, that he that is happy doth know and judge himself to be so. This being the peculiar good of a reasonable creature, it is to be enjoyed in a reasonable way. It is not as the dull resting of a stone, or any other natural body in its natural place; but the knowledge and consideration of it is the fruition of it, the very relishing and tasting of its sweetness.

REMARK

As in a Christian Land we receive the lessons of Morality in connexion with the Doctrines of Revealed Religion, we cannot too early free the mind from prejudices widely spread, in part through the abuse, but far more from ignorance, of the true meaning of [c]doctrinal Terms, which, however they may have been perverted to the purposes of Fanaticism,[2] are not only scriptural, but of too frequent occurrence in Scripture to be overlooked or passed by in silence. The following extract, therefore, deserves attention, as clearing the doctrine of Salvation, in connexion with the divine Foreknowledge, from all objections on the score of Morality, by the just and impressive view which the Archbishop here gives of those occasional revolutionary moments, that *Turn of the Tide* in the mind and character of certain Individuals, which (taking a religious course, and referred immediately to the Author of all Good) were in his

[a] *AR* (1825): L. & ED.
[b] *AR* (1825): LEIGHTON.
[c] *AR* (1825): p 63

[1] From Leighton COPY C I 14: *CM (CC)* III. The first paragraph is by C.
[1] From Leighton COPY C I 21: *CM (CC)* III.
[2] For C's concern to protect doctrinal terms against fanaticism see also below, pp 72, 78, 85, 173, 389–90 and nn, and App I Excursus Note 22 "Coleridge on Enthusiasm and Fanaticism".

day, more generally than at present, entitled EFFECTUAL CALLING.[3] The theological interpretation and the philosophic validity of this Apostolic Triad, Election, Salvation, and Effectual Calling, (the latter being the intermediate),[a] will be found among the[b] Comments on the Aphorisms of Spiritual Import. For our present purpose it will be sufficient if only we prove, that the Doctrines are in themselves *innocuous*, and may be both held and taught without any practical ill-consequences, and without detriment to the moral frame.[4]

APHORISM V[c1]

Two Links of the Chain (viz. Election and Salvation) are up in heaven in God's own hand; but this middle one (i.e. Effectual Calling) is let down to earth, into the hearts of his children, and they laying hold on it have sure hold on the other two: for no [d]power can sever them. If, therefore, they can read the characters of God's image in their own souls, those are the counterpart[e] of the golden characters of His love, in which their names are written in the book of life. Their believing writes their names under the promises of the revealed book of life (the Scriptures) and thus ascertains them, that the same names are in the secret book of life which God hath by himself from eternity. So that finding the stream of grace in their hearts, though they see not the fountain whence it flows, nor the ocean into which it returns, yet they know that it hath its source in their eternal election, and shall empty itself into the ocean of their eternal salvation.[2]

If *election, effectual calling* and *salvation* be inseparably linked together, then, by any one of them a man may lay hold upon all the rest, and may know that his hold is sure; and this is the way wherein we may

---

[a] *AR* (1825): intermediate)
[b] *AR* (1825): the Editor's
[c] *AR* (1825): LEIGHTON.
[d] *AR* (1825): p 64
[e] *AR* (1825): counter-part

[3] The phrase is used in the *Shorter Catechism* (1648) for "the work of God's Spirit, whereby . . . he doth persuade and enable us to embrace Jesus Christ": *OED* s.v. "effectual".

[4] In *AR* (1825) COPY F EC noted at the end of this aphorism, "To be read again & again."

[1] From Leighton COPY C I 20–1, 22–3:

CM (CC) III.

[2] From "yet they know" to here C is condensing Leighton's "yet they know that it hath its source, and shall return to that ocean which ariseth from their eternal election, and shall empty itself into the ocean of their eternity of happiness and salvation". For the last metaphor see also below, p 540 at n 26.

attain[a] and ought to seek, the comfortable assurance of the love of God. Therefore *make your calling sure*, and by that, your *election*; for that being done, this follows of itself. We are not to pry immediately into the decree, but to read it in the performance. Though the mariner sees not the *pole-star*, yet the needle of the compass which points to it, tells him which way he sails: thus the heart that is touched with the loadstone of divine love, trembling with godly fear, and yet still looking towards God by fixed believing, interprets the fear by the love *in* the fear,[3] and tells the soul that its course is heavenward, towards [b]the haven of eternal rest. He that loves[c] may be sure he was loved first; and he that chooses God for his delight and portion, may conclude confidently, that God has chosen him to be one of those that shall enjoy him, and be happy in him for ever; for that our love and electing of him is but the return and repercussion of the beams of his love shining upon us.

Although from present unsanctification, a man cannot infer that he is not *elected*; for the decree may, for part of a man's life, run (as it were) underground; yet this is sure, that that estate leads to death, and unless it be broken, will prove the black line of reprobation. A man hath no portion amongst the children of God, nor can read one word of comfort in all the promises that belong to them, while he remains unholy.

REMARK[4]

In addition to the preceding, I select the following paragraphs as having no where seen the term, Spirit, the Gifts of the Spirit, and the like, so effectually vindicated from the sneers of the Sciolist[5] on the[d] one hand, and protected from the perversions of the Fanatic on the other. In these paragraphs the Archbishop at once shatters and precipitates[6] the only draw-bridge between the fanatical and the orthodox doctrine of Grace, and the Gifts of the Spirit. In Scripture the term[e] Spirit, as a power or

[a] *AR* (1825): attain,
[b] *AR* (1825): p 65
[c] *AR* (1825): loves,
[d] *AR* (1825): Added in 1831
[e] *AR* (1825): term,

[3] Leighton COPY C reads "points at the love of election"; C's "interprets the fear by the love *in* the fear" attempts a more psychological interpretation.

[4] The text of this "Remark", from "at once shatters", is taken, with trivial alterations, from C's marginal comment on the next passage he quotes, from Leighton COPY C I 23–6. See *CM (CC)* III.

[5] "Superficial pretender to knowledge": *OED*. Cf *LS (CC)* 94, 168: *BL* ch 3 *(CC)* I 57; *C&S (CC)* 21 and n, 67–8, 218.

[6] C is evidently using the word in the sense of "casts down" rather than either of its two other main senses.

property seated in the human soul, never stands singly, but is always *specified* by a genitive case following; this being a*ᵃ* Hebraism instead of the adjective which the Writer would have *ᵇ*used if he had *thought*, as well as *written*, in Greek.⁷ It is "the Spirit of Meekness" (a meek Spirit), or "the Spirit of Chastity," and the like.⁸ The moral Result, the specific Form and Character in which the Spirit *manifests* its presence, is the only sure pledge and token of its presence;*ᶜ* which is to be, and which safely may be, inferred from its practical effects, but of which an *immediate* knowledge or consciousness is impossible; and every pretence*ᵈ* to such knowledge is either hypocrisy or fanatical delusion.

APHORISM VI*ᵉ*[1]

If any pretend that they have the Spirit, and so turn away from the straight rule of the Holy*ᶠ* Scriptures, they have a spirit indeed, but it is a fanatical spirit, the spirit of delusion and giddiness;*ᵍ* but the Spirit of God, that leads his children in the way of truth, and is for that purpose sent them from Heaven*ʰ* to guide them thither, squares their thoughts and ways to that rule whereof it is author, and that word which was inspired by it, and sanctifies them to obedience. *He that saith I know him, and keepeth not his commandments, is a liar, and the truth is not in him.* (1 John ii. 4.)

Now this Spirit which sanctifieth, and sanctifieth to obedience, is within us the evidence of our election, and the earnest of our salvation. And whoso are not sanctified and led by this Spirit, the Apostle tells us what is their condition: *If any man have not the Spirit of Christ, he is none of his.*² The stones which are *ⁱ*appointed for that glorious temple above, are hewn, and polished, and prepared for it here; as the stones

---

ᵃ AR (1825): an
ᵇ AR (1825): p 66
ᶜ AR (1825): presence:
ᵈ AR (1825): Pretence
ᵉ AR (1825): LEIGHTON.
ᶠ AR (1825): holy
ᵍ AR (1825): gıddıness:
ʰ AR (1825): heaven
ⁱ AR (1825): p 67

---

⁷ The usage is associated with the lack of adjectives in Hebrew. For another example see below, *Sp Aph B [XXIV]* at n 42.
⁸ For "the Spirit of Meekness" see 1 Cor 4.21, Gal 6.21. "The Spirit of Chastity" is not in the Bible, but there are many further NT examples of the form.
¹ From Leighton COPY C I 23: *CM (CC)* III.
² Rom 8.9.

were wrought and prepared in the mountains, for building the temple at *Jerusalem.*[3]

COMMENT[4]

There are many serious and sincere Christians who have not attained to a fulness[a] of knowledge and insight, but are well and judiciously employed in preparing for it. Even these may study the master-works of our elder Divines with safety and advantage, if they will accustom themselves to translate the theological terms into their *moral* equivalents; saying to themselves—This may not be *all* that is meant, but this *is* meant, and it is that portion of the meaning, which belongs to *me* in the present stage of my progress. For example: render the words, sanctification of the Spirit, or the sanctifying influences of the Spirit, by[b] Purity in Life and Action from a pure Principle.[5]

[c]He needs[d] only reflect on his[e] own experience to be convinced, that the Man makes the *motive*, and not the motive the Man. What is a strong

[a] *AR* (1825): fullness
[b] *AR* (1825): by,
[c–d] *AR* (1825): He need ; Corr: We need
[e] *AR* (1825) Corr: our

[3] See 1 Kgs 5.13–18.

[4] *AR* (1825) COPY D has a note here: "This Comment to p. 82 is as it were the Vestibule to all the Reasoning in this Volume: and to these pages therefore the Reader's attention is especially directed. To afford them a re-iterated and studious perusal will be afterwards found good *Economy* of his Time and Effort. S. T. C."; COPY E followed with small variations. The version in COPY F is as follows: "N.B. This Comment, from p. 67 to p. 82, may be regarded as the Vestibule to all the Reasoning in the remainder of the Volume. The *first* step to a rational Faith is the clear understanding of the sense attached to the word, *Spirit*, as that which is not included in *Nature*. The NEXT step is the conviction, that if there be aught spiritual actually existing, the Will must be the Spiritual part of our Humanity. And the last, or entrance into the Temple, is the persuasion of the actual existence of both—viz. of the Spiritual, as contra-distinguished from the Natural, and of a Will; and that this latter is the *Spirit* of a Man.

(Matth. XII. 45)
To these pages, therefore, the Reader's attention is especially directed—a thoughtful & re-iterated Perusal will be found an *economic* management of his Time and Effort. S. T. C.
[*On p 69:*] P.S. To the preceding Mss Note I may add, that the vagueness of men's conceptions respecting Spirit, Spirits, &c—the too often superstitious and almost always indistinct & at the same time inappropriate notions attached to the term—is the ground of false Divinity throughout—and the Bane of rational Faith, which dies now into Superstition, and now into Materialism."

[5] Matthew Arnold's view of religion develops the idea outlined here, taking in the Church's festivals as well. The incarnation e.g. is "a homage to the virtue of pureness", Lent "a homage to the virtue of self-control": "A Comment on Christmas" *Complete Prose Works* ed R. H. Super (Ann Arbor, Mich 1960–77) x 234.

motive to one man, is no motive at all to another. If, then, the man determines the motive, what determines the Man—to a good and worthy act, we will say, or a virtuous Course of Conduct? The intelligent Will, or the self-determining Power? True, *in part* it is; and therefore the Will is pre-eminently the *spiritual* Constituent in*[a]* our Being. But will any reflecting man admit, that his own Will is the only and sufficient determinant of *[b]*all he *is*, and all he does? Is nothing to be attributed to the harmony of the system to which he belongs, and to the pre-established Fitness of the Objects and Agents, known and unknown, that surround him, as acting *on* the will, though, doubtless, *with* it likewise? a process, which the co-instantaneous yet reciprocal action of the Air and the vital Energy of the Lungs in Breathing may help to render intelligible.

Again: in the World we see every where evidences of a Unity, which the component parts*[c]* are so far from explaining, that they necessarily pre-suppose it as the cause and condition of their existing *as* those parts: or even of their existing at all. This antecedent Unity, or Cause and Principle of each Union, it has since the time of Bacon and Kepler been customary to call a law.*[d]6* This Crocus, for instance: or any other Flower, the Reader may have in sight or choose to bring before his fancy. That the root, stem, leaves, petals, &c.,*[e]* cohere to one plant, is owing to an antecedent Power or Principle in the Seed, which existed before a single particle of the matters that constitute the *size* and visibility of the Crocus, had been attracted from the surrounding Soil, Air, and

---

[a] *AR* (1825): n
[b] *AR* (1825): p 68
[c] *AR* (1825): Parts
[d] *AR* (1825): Law.
[e] *AR* (1825): &c.

---

[6] In his discussion of "Method" for the 1818 *Friend* C proposed that the two kinds of relationships in which objects may be contemplated are those of law and theory. His discussion of the first, *Friend (CC)* I 458–63, as operating where "the relation of the parts to each other and to the whole is predetermined by a truth originating in *the mind*", is preceded by an epigraph from Bacon *De augmentis scientiarum* bk VI ch 2: *Works* (4 vols 1740) I 165–6 (var) asserting the need to attend to the "roots" of sciences as well as their "trunks". For Bacon's use of the word "law" see e.g. *Novum organum* bk II § 5: ". . . naturae . . . leges fundamentales et communes quae constituunt formas": *Works* (1740) I 315; tr: "the fundamental and universal laws of nature that constitute the forms [*alternatively,* the ideas, *as C might translate it*]". See also *C&S (CC)* 13 and n and for Bacon more generally *Sp Aph B VIIIa* nn 27–31 below. The main intellectual enterprise of Johannes Kepler (1571–1630), from his first publication, the *Mysterium cosmographicum* (1596), to *Harmonice mundi* (1619), which announced his third law of planetary motion (he did not himself use the term "law" in this connexion), was a Pythagorean attempt to find the mathematical principles on which, as he confidently believed, the universe must function. See also below, *Conc* n 64.

Moisture. Shall we turn to the Seed? Here too the same necessity meets us. An antecedent Unity (I speak not of the parent plant, but of an agency antecedent in the order of operance, yet remaining present as the conservative and reproductive Power) must here too be supposed.[7] Analyse the Seed with the finest tools, and let the Solar Microscope[8] come in aid of your *a*senses, what do you find? Means and instruments, a wondrous Fairy-tale of Nature, Magazines of Food, Stores of various sorts, Pipes, Spiracles,[9] Defences—a House of many Chambers, and the Owner and Inhabitant invisible! Reflect further on the countless millions*b* of Seeds of the same Name, each more than numerically differenced from every other: and further yet, reflect on the requisite harmony of all surrounding Things, each of which necessitates the same process of thought, and the coherence of all of which to a System, a World, demands its own adequate Antecedent Unity, which must therefore of necessity be present *to* all and *in* all, yet in no wise excluding or suspending the individual Law or Principle of Union in each. Now will Reason, will common*c* Sense, endure the assumption, that *d*in the material and visible system,*e* it is highly reasonable to believe a Universal

---

a *AR* (1825): p 69　　*b* *AR* (1825): Millions　　*c* *AR* (1825): Common

d-e Added in 1831; *AR* (1825) Corr: in the *material and visible* System ; COPY C: in the material & visible system ; COPIES D, E, F: in the material and visible System ; COPY G: in the material and visible system

---

[7] The present passage is referred back to in connexion with a reference to the "productive *form* of the plant" in *C&S (CC)* 180. The implications of the principle of growth are a favourite Coleridgian theme: see e.g. *SM (CC)* 72–3 and S. Prickett *Coleridge and Wordsworth: the Poetry of Growth* (Cambridge 1970) esp ch 7.

[8] A microscope in which an object was illuminated by the sun's rays, reflected into and concentrated by a lens fixed in a window-shutter; the magnified image was further reflected and projected on to a suitable surface. In an annotation on Samuel Pepys *Memoirs* ed Lord Braybrook (2 vols 1825) 72–3, C referred to the experiments with it by Agnes Ibbetson, and to her contributions to W. Nicholson's *Journal of Natural Philosophy, Chemistry, and the Arts*: *CM (CC)* IV. In a paper in the number for Sept 1810, entitled "On the Structure and Growth of Seeds", XXVII 1–17, Mrs Ibbetson described the minute organisation of seeds in terms not unlike those which C used in the next sentence. For extravagant

praise of Mrs Ibbetson see *CN* IV 4842 and for Gustavus Katterfelto and his claims in 1782 to show through his solar microscope the insects he alleged to be causing a current influenza epidemic, see *CM (CC)* I 519 and n, III 9, and *CN* IV 5207, 5334 f 32; cf also *Omniana* II 5.

[9] This use of "spiracle" for a breathing-pore in a plant is rare, according to *OED*. C was perhaps drawn to it by his interest in the beneficent significance of breathing as a universal phenomenon. See his discussion in *C&S (CC)* 21, which mentions the spiracula of insects, and M. H. Abrams's account in "Coleridge and the Romantic Vision of the World" *Coleridge's Variety* ed J. Beer (1974) 128–30 and nn. C also referred to the benign effects of the "great Spiracles made by earthquakes & volcanos", no doubt echoing Erasmus Darwin *Botanic Garden* (1791) Note (1) but also, possibly, Bp Lavington *Enthusiasm of Methodists* (1749) II 120 (see also below, n 23): *CN* III 3802 and n.

Power, as the cause and pre-condition of the harmony of all particular Wholes, each of which involves*a* the working Principle of its own Union*b*—that it is reasonable, I say, to believe this respecting the Aggregate of *Objects*, which without a *Subject* (*i.e.c* a sentient and intelligent Existence) would be purposeless; and yet unreasonable and even superstitious or enthusiastic to entertain a similar Belief in relation to the System of intelligent and self-conscious Beings, to the moral and personal World? But if in *this* *d*too, in*e* the great Community of *Persons*, it is rational to infer*f* One universal Presence, a One present to all and in all, is it not most irrational to suppose that a finite Will can exclude *g*it?

Whenever,*h* therefore, the Man is determined (*i.e.i* impelled and directed) to act in harmony of inter-communion, must not something be attributed to this allpresent*j* power as acting *in* the Will? and by what fitter names can we call this than the*k* LAW, as empowering; THE WORD, as informing; and THE SPIRIT, as actuating?

What has been *l*said here*m* amounts (I am aware) only to a negative Conception; but this is all that is required for a Mind at that period of its growth which we are now supposing, and as long as Religion is contemplated under the form of Morality. A *positive* Insight belongs to a more advanced stage: for spiritual truths can only spiritually be discerned.[10] This we know from Revelation, and (the existence of spiritual truths being granted) Philosophy is compelled to draw the same conclusion. But though merely negative, it is sufficient to render the union of Religion and Morality *conceivable*; sufficient to satisfy an unprejudiced Inquirer, that the spiritual Doctrines of the Christian Religion are not at war with the reasoning Faculty, and that if they do not run on the same Line (or Radius) with the Understanding, yet neither do they cut or cross it. It is sufficient, in short, to prove, that some distinct and consistent meaning may be attached to the assertion of the learned and philosophic Apostle, that "the Spirit beareth witness with our spirit"—*i.e.n* with *the Will*, as the Supernatural in Man and the Principle of our Personality—

---

a COPY G: contains in itself likewise
b *AR* (1825): Union, in the material and visible System— ; Corr, COPIES C, D, E, F, G: Union—
c *AR* (1825): i. e.
d-e COPIES C & F: too, if in ; COPY G: too—if in
f *AR* (1825): infer a
g-h *AR* (1825): it? Whenever, [p 70 begins with "Whenever,"]
i *AR* (1825): i. e.
j *AR* (1825) all-present
k *AR* (1825): THE
l-m *AR* (1825): here said
n *AR* (1825): i. e.

[10] See 1 Cor 2.13–14 and below, pp 146n, 278fn, 324n, 407n.

of that, I mean, by which *a*we are responsible Agents; *Persons*, and not merely living *Things**.[11]

It will suffice to satisfy a reflecting mind, that even at the porch and threshold of Revealed Truth there is a great and worthy sense in which we may believe the Apostle's assurance, that not only doth "the Spirit aid our infirmities;"[12] that is, *act on* the Will by a predisposing influence *from without*, as it were, though in a spiritual manner, and without suspending or destroying its freedom (the possibility of which is proved to us in the influences of Education, of providential Occurrences, and, above all, of Example) but that in regenerate souls it may act *in* the will; that uniting and becoming one† with our will *b*and spirit,*c* it may "make intercession for us;" nay, in this intimate *d*union taking upon itself the form of our infirmities, may intercede for us "with groanings that cannot be uttered."[14] Nor is there any danger of Fanaticism or Enthusiasm as

---

* Whatever is comprised*e* in the Chain and Mechanism of Cause and Effect, of course *necessitated*, and having its necessity in some other thing, antecedent or concurrent—this is said to be *Natural*; and the Aggregate and System of all such things is NATURE. It is, therefore, a contradiction in terms to include in this the Free-will, of which the verbal definition is—that which *originates* an act or state of Being. In this sense,*f* therefore, which is the sense of St. Paul, and indeed of the New Testament throughout, Spiritual and Supernatural are synonymous.

† Some distant and faint *similitude* of this, that merely as a similitude may be innocently used to quiet the Fancy, provided it be not imposed on the understanding as an analogous fact or as identical in kind, is presented to us in the power of the Magnet to awaken and strengthen the magnetic power in a bar of Iron, and (in the instance of the compound Magnet) acting in and with the latter.[13]

---

a *AR* (1825): p 71
b–c *AR* (1825): or spirit
d *AR* (1825): p 72
e *AR* (1825): comprized
f *AR* (1825): sense

---

[11] Rom 8.16. As early as 1795 C announced his intention of attacking "things" rather than "persons"; for the more refined distinction here see the 1809 *Friend*: "Every Man is born with the faculty of Reason: and whatever is without it, be the Shape what it may, is not a Man or PERSON but a THING. Hence the sacred Principle . . . the Principle indeed, which is the *ground-work* of all Law and Justice, that a Person can never become a Thing": *Friend (CC)* II 125 (cf I 189–90). Cf *EOT (CC)* II 393n–4, III 235 and n (note of 1832), *BL* ch 10 *(CC)* I 205, *TT* 17 Dec 1831 *(CC)* I 260 (1836 vn, dated 18 Dec, II

153–4), *C&S (CC)* 15–16, N 44 ff 75–6 (c 1830: *CN* v), and below, *Sp Aph B XIX* n 69.

[12] Rom 8.26. C cited this in a more personal context, *CN* II 2437.

[13] A compound magnet is one that has been "armed" by being capped, cased, or set in iron and steel, so that the two elements mutually reinforce their magnetic power. See Rees *Cyclopaedia* s.v. magnetism, armed. For C's more general interest in magnetism see Beer *CPI* 82–7.

[14] Rom 8.26. See also the discussion and references in Barth 149.

the consequence of such a belief, if only the attention be carefully and earnestly drawn to the concluding words of the sentence (Romans*ᵃ* viii. v. 26);*ᵇ* if only the due force and *full* import be given to the term *unutterable* or *incommunicable*, in St. Paul's use of it. In this, the strictest and most proper use of the term, it signifies, that the subject, of which it is predicated, is something which I *cannot*, which from the nature of the thing it is impossible that I should, communicate to any human mind (even of a person under the same conditions with myself) so as to make it *in itself* the object of his direct and immediate consciousness. It cannot be the object of *my own* direct and immediate Consciousness; but must be *inferred*. Inferred it may be *from* its workings;*ᶜ* it cannot be perceived *in* them. And, thanks to God! in all points in which the knowledge is of high and necessary concern to our moral and religious welfare, from the *Effects* it may safely be inferred by us, from the Workings it may be assuredly known; and the Scriptures furnish the clear and unfailing Rules for directing the inquiry, and for drawing the conclusion.

If any reflecting mind be surprised that the aids of the Divine Spirit should be deeper than our Consciousness can reach, it must arise from the not having attended sufficiently to the nature and necessary limits of human Consciousness. For the same impossibility *ᵈ*exists as to the first acts and movements of our own will—the farthest back our recollection can follow the traces, never leads us to the first foot-mark—the lowest depth that the light of our Consciousness can visit even with a doubtful Glimmering, is still at an unknown distance from the Ground: and so, indeed, must it be with all Truths, and all modes of Being that can neither be counted, colored,*ᵉ* or delineated. Before and After, when applied to such Subjects, are but allegories, which the Sense or Imagination supplies*ᶠ* to the Understanding. The Position of the Aristoteleans, Nihil in intellectu quod non prius in sensu, on which Mr. Locke's Essay is grounded, is irrefragable: Locke erred only in taking half the truth for a whole Truth.[15] Conception is consequent on Perception.[16] What we cannot *imagine*, we cannot, in the proper sense of the word, conceive.

ᵃ *AR* (1825): Romans,
ᵇ *AR* (1825): 26.);
ᶜ *AR* (1825): workings:
ᵈ *AR* (1825): p 73
ᵉ *AR* (1825): coloured,
ᶠ *AR* (1825): supply

---

[15] "There is nothing in the mind that was not previously in the senses". For the origin of C's knowledge of this principle in a joke by Boyer, who, he said, translated it, "You must flog a Boy before you can make him understand", see his annotation on Baxter *Reliquiae Baxterianae*: *CM (CC)* I 354 and n. He quoted the principle (which

I have already given one definition of Nature.[17] Another, and differing from the former in words only, is this: Whatever is representable in the forms of Time and Space, is Nature. But whatever is comprehended in Time and Space, is included in the Mechanism of Cause and Effect. And conversely, whatever, by whatever means, has its principle in itself, so far as to *originate* its actions, cannot be contemplated in any of the forms of Space and Time—it must, therefore, be considered as *Spirit* or *Spiritual* by a mind in that stage of its Developement which is here supposed, and which we have agreed to understand under the name of Morality, or the Moral State: for *a*in this stage we are concerned only with the forming of *negative* conceptions, *negative* convictions; and by *spiritual* I do not pretend to determine *what* the Will *is*, but what it is *not*—namely, that it is not Nature.[18] And as no man who admits a Will at all, (for we may safely presume that no man *b*not meaning*c* to speak figuratively, would call the shifting Current of a stream the WILL* of the River), will suppose it *below* Nature, we may safely add, that it is super-natural; and this without the least pretence to any positive Notion or Insight.

> * "The River windeth at his own sweet will."
> *Wordsworth's exquisite Sonnet on Westminster-bridge at Sun-rise.*[19]

But who does not see that here the poetic charm arises from the known and felt *impropriety* of the expression, in the technical sense of the word *impropriety*, among Grammarians?

a AR (1825): p 74

b-c AR (1825): meaning ; COPY A: unless he mean ; Corr, COPIES C, D, F: not meaning ; Corr has as alternative: *for* meaning, *read* except he meant

had become a tag in European philosophy as a result of Aristotle *De anima* 427^{b}16; 432^{a}78) as "notorious" in the first philosophical letter to the Wedgwoods 18 Feb 1801 (*CL* II 680), in which (following Leibniz in this and other points) he related it to his critique of Locke's philosophy (see also *CN* IV 5133 f 99). Below, in *Sp Aph B VIIIb* at n 30, as also in *BL* ch 9 *(CC)* I 41, *P Lects* Lect 13 (1949) 383, and *Logic (CC)* 226, C quoted Leibniz's crucial addition as "praeter ipsum intellectum" ("except the mind itself"). Cf *Nouveaux Essais sur l'entendement humain* bk II ch 1 § 2: Leibniz *Œuvres philosophiques* (1765) 67; also a letter of Leibniz to F. G. Bierling in Leibniz *Opera omnia* ed L. Dutens (6 vols Geneva 1768) v 359, in which the passage to be quoted in *SM (CC)* 30n immediately follows. In both passages the wording is "nisi ipse intellectus"—with the same meaning. *Nouveaux Essais* (written

in 1704 but first published 1765) is not included in Dutens's ed, for which see *Sp Aph B VIIIa* n 10 below.

[16] See the distinctions between Sensation, Perception, Intuition, Conception, Notion, and Idea in *SM (CC)* 113, which includes the statements: "A PERCEPTION immediate and individual is = an INTUITION. The same, mediate, and by means of a character or mark common to several things is = a CONCEPTION."

C's list there is based upon, but not identical with, a similar scheme in Kant *Critik der Reinen Vernunft* (Leipzig 1799) 376–7 (tr Kemp Smith—1933—314). C's copy in the BM is sidelined from p 378 to p 380: *CM (CC)* III.

[17] Perhaps referring to the discussion at n 6.

[18] Cf C's annotation on Böhme *Works*: *CM (CC)* I 605 and n.

[19] *Composed upon Westminster Bridge,*

Now Morality accompanied with Convictions like these, I have ventured to call *Religious* Morality. Of the importance I attach to the state of mind implied in these convictions, for its own sake, and as the natural preparation for a yet higher state and a more substantive knowledge, proof more than sufficient, perhaps, has been given in the length and minuteness of this introductory Discussion, and in the foreseen risk which I run of exposing the volume at large to the censure which every work, or rather which every writer, must be prepared to undergo, who, treating of subjects that cannot be seen, touched, or in any other way made matters of outward sense, is yet anxious both to attach to,[a] and to convey a distinct meaning[b] by,[c] the words he makes use of—the censure of being dry, abstract, and (of all qualities most scaring and opprobrious to the ears of the present generation) *metaphysical;*[d] though how it is possible that a work not *physical*, that is, employed on Objects known or believed on the evidence of [e]the senses,[f] should be other than *meta-physical*, that is, treating on Subjects, the evidence of which is not derived from the Senses, is a problem which Critics of this order find it convenient to leave unsolved.[20]

The Author[g] of the present Volume, will, indeed, have reason to think himself fortunate, if this be all the Charge! How many smart quotations, which (duly cemented by personal allusions to the Author's supposed Pursuits, Attachments, and Infirmities), would of themselves make up "A Review" of the Volume, might be supplied from the works of Butler, Swift,[h] and Warburton.[21] For instance: "It may not be amiss to inform the Public, that the Compiler of the Aids to Reflection, and Commenter on a Scotch Bishop's platonico-calvinistic commentary on St. Peter, belongs to the Sect of the *Aeolists*, whose fruitful imaginations lead them into certain notions, which although in appearance *very unaccountable, are not without their mysteries and their meanings;* fur-

---

[a] Added in 1831
[b] *AR* (1825): p 75 (ing)
[c] *AR* (1825): to
[d] *AR* (1825): *metaphysical:*
[e-f] *AR* (1825): senses, ; Corr: Sense, ; COPIES A, D, E: the senses,
[g] *AR* (1825): Editor and Annotator
[h] *AR* (1825): Swift

September 3, 1802, line 12. WW's line reads: "the river glideth at his own sweet will": *WPW* III 38.

[20] C explores this point also in 1817, *CL* IV 790, and in an annotation to the 1818 *Friend: (CC)* I 440n.

The title "Metaphysics" was originally applied to the 13 books of Aristotle's works (those on ontology) which came after (μετά) the Physics. From an early time, however, the meaning of the word was transferred to denote, as here, the science of things transcending what is physical or natural.

[21] For Butler and Warburton see below, nn 23, 24.

nishing plenty of Matter for such, *whose converting Imaginations dispose them to reduce all things into* TYPES; *who can make* SHADOWS, *no thanks to the Sun; and then mould them into* SUBSTANCES, *no thanks to Philosophy; whose peculiar ªTalent lies in fixing* TROPES *and* ALLEGORIES *to the* LETTER, *and refining what is* LITERAL *into* FIGURE *and* MYSTERY.''—Tale of the Tub, Sectᵇ* xi.²²

And would it were my lot to meet with a Critic, who, in the might of his own Convictions, and with arms of equal Point and Efficiency,ᶜ from his own Forge, would come forth as my Assailant; or who, as a friend to my purpose, would set forth the objectionsᵈ to the matter and pervading Spirit of these Aphorisms, and the accompanying Elucidations. Were it my task to form the mind of a young man of Talent, desirous to establish his opinions and belief on solid principles, and in the light of distinct understanding,—ᵉI would commence his theological studies, or, at least, that most important part of them respecting the aids which Religion promises in our attempts to realize the ideas of Morality, by bringing together all the passages scattered throughout the Writings of Swift and Butler,²³ that bear on Enthusiasm, Spiritual Operations, and pretences to the Gifts of the Spirit, with the whole train of New Lights, Raptures, Experiences, and the like. For all that the richest Wit, in intimate union with profound Sense and steady Observation, can supply on these topics,ᶠ is to be found in the works of these Satirists; though unhappily alloyed with much that can only tend to pollute the Imagination.

Without stopping to estimate the degree of caricature in the Portraits sketched by these bold Masters, and without attempting to determine in how many of the Enthusiasts, brought forward by them in proof ᵍof the influence of false Doctrines, a constitutional Insanity, that would probably have shown itself in some other form, would be the truer Solution, I would direct my Pupil's attention to one feature common to the whole

ᵃ *AR* (1825): p 76
ᵇ *AR* (1825): Sect.
ᶜ *AR* (1825): Efficiency
ᵈ *AR* (1825): Objections
ᵉ *AR* (1825): understanding,
ᶠ *AR* (1825): Topics,
ᵍ *AR* (1825): p 77

²² From Swift *Tale of a Tub* § xi (1704) 195–6. C transcribed and adapted parts of this passage into a notebook in late 1823 (*CN* IV 5041); that transcription is evidently being used here, since he has lost sight of the fuller statement in the original, which is given in the editor's note to *CN* IV 5041.

²³ Samuel Butler (1612–80), whose *Hudibras* (1663–78) and other writings contain various passages of this kind. C was fond of making brief comments on Butler's satire: see *C 17th C* 614–17 and *Misc C* Index s.n. Butler.

Group—the pretence, namely, of possessing, or a Belief and Expectation grounded on other men's assurances of their[a] possessing, an immediate Consciousness, a sensible Experience, of the Spirit in and during its operation on the soul. It is not enough that you grant them a consciousness of the Gifts and Graces infused, or an assurance of the Spiritual Origin of the same, grounded on their correspondence with the Scripture *Promises*, and their conformity with the *Idea* of the divine Giver. No! They all alike, it will be found, lay claim (or at least look forward) to an inward perception of the Spirit itself and of its operating.

Whatever must be misrepresented in order to be ridiculed, is in fact *not* ridiculed; but the thing substituted for it. It is a Satire on something else, coupled with a Lie on the part of the Satirist, who knowing, or having the means of knowing the truth, chose to call one thing by the name of another. The Pretensions to the Supernatural, *pilloried* by Butler, sent to Bedlam by Swift, and (on their re-appearance in public) *gibbetted* by Warburton,[24] and *anatomized* by Bishop Lavington,[25] one and all have *this* for their essential character, that the Spirit is made the immediate Object of Sense or Sensation. Whether the Spiritual Presence and Agency are supposed cognizable by[b] indescribable Feeling or[c] unimaginable Vision [d]by some specific visual energy; whether seen, or heard, or touched, smelt[e] and tasted—for in those vast Store-houses of fanatical assertion, the volumes of Ecclesiastical History and religious Auto-biography, Instances are not wanting even of these[f] three latter extravagancies;[26]—[g]this variety in the mode may render the several pre-

[a] COPY D: *their*
[b] *AR* (1825): by an
[c] *AR* (1825): or in
[d] *AR* (1825): p 78
[e] *AR* (1825): smelt,
[f] *AR* (1825): the
[g] *AR* (1825): extravagancies—

[24] William Warburton (1698–1779), bp of Gloucester. In 1810 C paid attention to his view of the supernatural, as expressed in his discourse *Julian* (1750), and planned "a heavy censure on Warburton, & the character of that *suspicious* Prelate": *CN* III 3802–8 and nn. He also set forth his long-standing idea (relevant here) that "The great difficulty of attacking all Superstition is this—that the superstitious ground their faith in certain aweful & profound Truths imperfectly caught hold of—glimpsed—the full understanding of which is the most arduous effect of the most ex-

panded & potent Intellect": *CN* III 3808.

[25] George Lavington (1684–1762), bp of Exeter, wrote *The Enthusiasm of Methodists and Papists Compared* (1749) and *The Moravians Compared and Detected* (1755), the latter annotated by C: *CM (CC)* III. See also above, n 9.

[26] For St Catherine of Genoa's unusual experiences of touch and smell see F. von Hügel *The Mystical Element of Religion* (1908) I 178–81. (Taste is also mentioned in the *Vita e dottrina de S. Caterina*—1551, 13th ed Geneva 1847—106, but probably erroneously: Hügel I 180n.) St

tensions more or less offensive to the *Taste*; but with[a] the same Absurdity for the *Reason*, this being derived from a contradiction in terms common and radical to them all alike, the assumption of a something essentially supersensual, that is nevertheless the object of Sense, *i.e. not* supersensual.[27]

Well then!—for let me be allowed still to suppose the Reader present to me, and that I am addressing him in the character of Companion and Guide—the positions recommended for your examination not only do not involve, but they[b] exclude, this inconsistency. And for aught that hitherto appears, we may see with complacency the Arrows of Satire feathered with Wit, weighted with Sense, and discharged by a strong Arm, fly home to their mark. Our conceptions[c] of a possible Spiritual Communion, though they are but negative, and only preparatory to a faith in its actual existence, stand neither in the Level or in[d] the Direction of the Shafts.

If it be objected, that Swift and Warburton did not choose openly to set up the interpretations of later and more rational Divines against the decisions of their own Church, and from *prudential* considerations did not attack the doctrine *in toto:*[e] that is *their* concern (I would answer), and it is more charitable to think [f]otherwise. But we are in the silent school of Reflection, in the secret confessional of Thought. Should we "*lie* for God," and that to our own Thoughts? They indeed, who dare do the one, will soon be able to do the other. So did the Comforters of Job:[28] and to the Divines, who resemble Job's Comforters, we will leave both attempts.

[a] COPY C: leaves ; COPIES D, E: leave
[b] Added in 1831
[c] *AR* (1825): Conceptions
[d] *AR* (1825): Added in 1831
[e] *AR* (1825): toto:
[f] *AR* (1825): p 79

Teresa of Avila related how once when she ended a visitation from a devil by sprinkling holy water the sisters who afterwards arrived smelt an unpleasant smell like brimstone, though she herself did not: *The Works of the Holy Mother S[t] Teresa of Jesus* (3 pts 1675, 1669) pt i 220, a work annotated by C. According to his biographer, Henry More related that his urine "had naturally the Flavour of Violets in it" and "his breast and body, especially when very Young, would of themselves . . . send forth flowry and Aromatic Odours from them": R. Ward *Life of the Learned and Pious Dr Henry More* . . . (1710) 123–4. When RS quoted the anecdote of More's urine in *Omniana* (1812) ii 147, C wrote in the margin of one copy, "Q[y]. Had not the philosophic Divine been eating Asparagus?": *CM (CC)* iii 1075.

[27] See below, *Sp Aph B Xb* n 23.

[28] See Job's words to the comforters: "Will you speak wickedly for God? and talk deceitfully for him?": Job 13.7, cited *Friend (CC)* i 39; also Job 42.7: ". . . the Lord said to Eliphaz the Temanite, My

But (it may be said), a possible Conception is not necessarily a true one; nor even a probable one, where the Facts can be otherwise explained. In the name of the supposed Pupil I would reply—That is the very question I am preparing myself to examine; and am now seeking the Vantage-ground where I may best command the Facts. In my own person, I would ask the Objector, whether he counted the Declarations of Scripture among the Facts to be explained. But both for myself and my Pupil, and in behalf of all rational Inquiry,[a] I would demand that the Decision should not be such, in itself or in its effects, as would prevent our becoming acquainted with the most important of these Facts; nay, such as would, for the mind of the Decider, preclude their very existence. *Unless ye believe*, says the Prophet, *ye cannot understand*.[29] Suppose (what is at least possible) that the facts should be consequent on the belief, it is clear that without the belief the materials, on which the understanding is to exert itself, would be wanting.

The reflections that naturally arise out of this last remark, are those that best suit the stage at which we last halted, and from which we now recommence our [b]progress—the state of a *Moral* Man, who has already welcomed certain truths of Religion, and is inquiring after other and more special Doctrines: still however as a Moralist, desirous indeed to receive them into combination with Morality, but to receive them as its Aid, not as its Substitute. Now, to such a man I say; Before you reject the Opinions and Doctrines asserted and enforced in the following Extract from Leighton,[c] and before you give way to the Emotions of Distaste or Ridicule, which the Prejudices of the Circle in which you move, or your own familiarity with the mad perversions of the doctrine by Fanatics in all ages, have connected with the very words, Spirit, Grace,

---

[a] *AR* (1825): Enquiry,
[b] *AR* (1825): p 80
[c] *AR* (1825): our eloquent Author,

---

wrath is kindled against thee, and against thy two friends: for ye have not spoken of me the thing that is right, as my servant Job hath''. Cf *The Friend* 8 Feb 1810: ''. . . fear-ridden and thence angry Believers, or rather *Acquiescents*, would do well to reperuse the Book of Job, and observe the sentence passed by the All-just on the Friends of the Sufferer, who had hoped, like venal advocates, to *purchase* the favour of Deity by uttering Truths, of which in their own hearts they had neither convic-tion nor comprehension'': *Friend (CC)* II 312 (I 280).

[29] C alludes to Isa 7.9 in the Septuagint version. In *The Statesman's Manual* he quoted the Greek: see *SM (CC)* 97 and n, drawing attention to Schleiermacher's quotation of it in his work on Heraclitus in *Museum der Alterthumswissenschaft*, used elsewhere in *SM*. For Augustine's frequent citation of the text see above, *Pref* n 8, and esp *CM (CC)* I 605n.

Gifts, Operations, &c.,[a] re-examine the arguments advanced in the first pages of this Introductory Comment, and the simple and sober View of the Doctrine, contemplated in the first instance as a mere Idea of the Reason, flowing naturally from the admission of an infinite omnipresent Mind as the Ground of the Universe. Reflect again and again, and be sure that you *understand* the Doctrine before you determine on rejecting it. That no false judgments,[b] no extravagant conceits, no practical ill-consequences need arise out of the Belief of the Spirit, and its possible communion with the Spiritual Principle in Man, can[c] arise out of the *right* Belief, or are compatible with the Doctrine truly and scripturally explained, Leighton, and almost every single Period in the Passage here transcribed from him, will suffice to convince you.

On the other hand, reflect on the consequences of [d]rejecting it. For surely it is not the act of a reflecting mind, nor the part of a Man of Sense to disown and cast out one Tenet, and yet persevere in admitting and clinging to another that has neither sense nor purpose, that does not *suppose* and rest on the truth and reality of the former! If you have re-solved that all belief of a divine Comforter present to our inmost Being and aiding our infirmities, is fond and fanatical—if the Scriptures promising and asserting such communion are to be explained away into the action of circumstances, and the necessary movements of the vast machine, in one of the circulating chains of which the human Will is a petty Link—in what better light can Prayer appear to you, than the groans of a wounded Lion in his solitary Den,[30] or the howl of a Dog with his eyes on the Moon?[31] At the best, you can regard it only as a transient bewilderment of the Social Instinct, as a social Habit misapplied! Unless indeed you should adopt the theory which I remember to have read in the writings of the late Dr. Jebb,[32] and for some supposed beneficial re-

---

[a] *AR* (1825): &c.
[b] *AR* (1825): judgements,
[c] *AR* (1825): or *can*
[d] *AR* (1825): p 81

---

[30] For a different use of this image, in relation to the leopard, see the letters of 1813 quoted above, Editor's Introduction, at nn 10–11.

[31] C and the Wordsworths were interested in other versions of this phenomenon; see *DWJ* 27 Jan 1798: "The manufacturer's dog . . . howls at the murmur of the village stream", and Sir Leoline's mastiff bitch howling to the chimes of the clock: *Christabel* lines 6–13: *PW* (EHC) I 216.

For possible links with animal magnetism (a reference to which follows here) see Beer *Wordsworth in Time* (1979) 120–2.

[32] See John Jebb *Works, Theological, Medical, Political, and Miscellaneous* (2 vols 1787) II 164–5: "Prayer, philosophically considered, may, by altering the affections of the mind, put me into that state, according to which, the course of divine providence renders me capable of blessings: popularly considered, i.e. in the ef-

action of Praying on the Prayer's own Mind, should practise it as a species of *Animal-Magnetism* to be brought about by a wilful eclipse of the Reason, and a temporary *make-believe* on the part of the Self-magnetizer![33]

At all events, do not pre-judge a Doctrine, the utter rejection of which must oppose a formidable obstacle to your acceptance of Christianity itself, when the Books, from which alone we can learn what Christianity is and *a*what it*b* teaches, are so strangely written, that in a series of *c*the most concerning points, including (historical facts expected) all the *peculiar* Tenets of the Religion, the plain and obvious meaning of the words, that in which they were understood by Learned and Simple for at least sixteen centuries,*d* during the far larger part of which the language was a living language, is no sufficient guide to their actual sense or to the Writer's own Meaning! And this,*e* too, where the literal and

---

a–b *AR* (1825): Added in 1831
c *AR* (1825): p 82
d *AR* (1825): Centuries,
e *AR* (1825): this

---

fect, and as a secondary affection, it is to be supposed as working an alteration in the mind of God, our creator, governor, and judge. This seems to be the case. July 1773, but it cannot be worthily performed, unless the latter idea prevails at the time.'' C referred back to this theory in a letter to Mrs Aders 23 Jan 1826: *CL* VI 545. John Jebb (1736–80) wrote a pamphlet on representation that interested Josiah Wedgwood: see letter of 20 May 1780, *Letters of Josiah Wedgwood* ed K. E. Farrar (1903–6) II 574–6; it may have been through him that C became acquainted with Jebb's works. See also below, *Mor Aph L* n 8, *Sp Aph B XXII* n 2.

[33] Animal magnetism, or Mesmerism, was a subject of great interest in Europe at the end of the eighteenth century following the work of Anton Mesmer (1734–1815). C's interest in hypnotic powers is apparent in the first version of *The Ancient Mariner*: see e.g. lines 362–5: *PW* (EHC) II 1040. J. F. Blumenbach, the leading physiologist, whose lectures C had attended in Göttingen in 1798–9, refused to believe even in the phenomenon. In 1800 C deleted the more overt references to animal magnetism from his poem, and it was not, apparently,

until he learned that Blumenbach had retracted his scepticism in 1817 that his interest was fully reawakened: *Friend (CC)* I 59n. In 1830 he recorded that his mind was ''in a state of philosophical doubt'' on the subject: *TT* 31 Mar 1830 *(CC)* I 96–7 and nn (1836 vn, dated 30 Apr, II 78), a point amplified towards the end of a note on RS *Life of Wesley* (Oxford 1820) I 301–5 *(CM—CC)*: ''Nine years has the subject of zoo-magnetism been before me. I have traced it historically, collected a mass of documents . . . have never neglected an opportunity of questioning eye-witnesses . . . and I remain where I was . . . without having advanced an inch backward or forward . . .''. The annotation concludes with a remark made to him by L. C. Treviranus: ''I have seen what I am certain I would not have believed on *your* telling; and in all reason, therefore, I can neither expect nor wish that you should believe on *mine*''. See R. Darnton *Mesmerism and the End of the Enlightenment in France* (Cambridge, Mass 1968) and Beer *CPI* 73, 220–3, 279, 285–6. Although fascinated by a phenomenon that brought out the mystery in nature, C was clearly also concerned at its possible pantheistic implications.

received Sense involves nothing impossible[a] or immoral, or contrary to reason. With such a persuasion, Deism would be a more consistent Creed. But, alas! even this will fail you. The utter rejection of all present and living communion with the Universal Spirit impoverishes Deism itself, and renders it as cheerless as Atheism, from which indeed it would differ only by an obscure impersonation of what the Atheist receives unpersonified,[b] under the name of Fate or Nature.

APHORISM VII[c][1]

The proper and natural Effect, and in the absence of all disturbing or intercepting forces, the certain and sensible accompaniment of Peace (or Reconcilement) with God, is our own inward Peace, a calm and quiet temper of mind. And where there is a consciousness of earnestly desiring, and of having sincerely striven after the former, the latter may be considered as a *Sense* of its presence. In this case, I say, and for a soul watchful, and under the discipline of the Gospel, the Peace with a man's self may be the medium or organ through which the assurance of his Peace with God is conveyed.[2] [d]We will not therefore condemn this mode of speaking, though we dare not greatly recommend it. Be it, that there is, truly and in sobriety of speech, enough of just Analogy in the subjects meant, to make this use of the words, if less than proper, yet something more than metaphorical; still we must be cautious not to transfer to the Object the defects or the deficiency of the Organ, which must needs partake of the imperfections of the imperfect Beings to whom it belongs. Not without the co-assurance of other senses and of the same sense in other men, dare we affirm that what our Eye beholds, is verily there to be beholden.[e] Much less may we conclude negatively, and from the inadequacy,[f] or [g]the suspension,[h] or [i]from any other affection of[j] Sight infer the non-existence, or departure, or changes of the Thing itself. The

---

[a] *AR* (1825): impossible,
[b] *AR* (1825): unpersonified
[c] *AR* (1825): L. & ED.
[d] *AR* (1825): p 83
[e] *AR* (1825): beheld.
[f] *AR* (1825): inadequacy
[g–h] *AR* (1825): suspension
[i–j] *AR* (1825): affections of the

[1] From "This Peace which we have . . ." C is following Leighton closely, though omitting almost a page between paragraphs. See Leighton COPY C I 29–30: *CM (CC)* III. The part previous to this consists of C's marginal comment at the same point in COPY C, lightly revised. See *CM (CC)* III.

[2] The marginal comment here continues: ". . . and the Organ, as it were, of its spiritual Perception". In the line above, "or organ" is an addition made in the 1825 text to compensate for this omission.

Chamelion*ᵃ³* darkens in the shade of him who*ᵇ* bends over it to ascertain its colors.*ᶜ* In like manner, but with yet greater caution, ought we to think respecting a tranquil habit of*ᵈ* inward life, considered as a spiritual *Sense*, as the Medial*ᵉ* Organ in and by which our Peace with God, and the lively Working of his Grace on our Spirit, are perceived by us. This Peace which we have with God in Christ, is inviolable; but because the sense and persuasion of it may be interrupted, the soul that is truly at peace with God may for a time be disquieted in itself, through weakness of faith, or the strength of temptation, or the darkness of desertion, losing sight of that grace, that love and light of God's countenance, on which its tranquillity and joy depend. *Thou didst hide thy face*, saith David, *and ᶠI was troubled.*⁴ But when these eclipses are over, the soul is revived with new consolation, as the face of the earth is renewed and made to smile with the return of the sun in the spring; and this ought always to uphold Christians in the saddest times, viz. that the grace and love of God towards them depends*ᵍ* not on their sense, nor upon any thing in them, but is still in itself, incapable of the smallest alteration.

A holy heart that gladly entertains grace, shall find that it and peace cannot dwell asunder; while an ungodly man may sleep to death in the lethargy of carnal presumption and impenitency; but a true, lively, solid peace he cannot have. *There is no peace to the wicked, saith my God*, Isa. lvii. 21.

APHORISM VIII*ʰ¹*

WORLDLY HOPES

Wor[l]dly*ⁱ* hopes are not living, but lying hopes; they die often before us, and we live to bury them, and see our own folly and infelicity in

---

ᵃ *AR* (1825): Camelion
ᵇ *AR* (1825): that
ᶜ *AR* (1825): colours.
ᵈ *AR* (1825): of the
ᵉ *AR* (1825): medial
ᶠ *AR* (1825): p 84
ᵍ *AR* (1825): depend
ʰ *AR* (1825): LEIGHTON.
ⁱ *AR* (1825): Worldly

³ Although this spelling is not unknown (it was used e.g. by Bacon), C's alteration of the 1825 spelling "camelion" probably reflects uneasy awareness that that traditional spelling was in his time beginning to give way, particularly among scientists, to the modern "chameleon".

⁴ Ps 30.7.
¹ From Leighton COPY C I 35–6. See *CM (CC)* III for original text and C's alterations. In the first line Leighton reads "lying hopes, and dying hopes"; later "this hope" for "the lively Hope . . . Portion".

trusting to them; but at the utmost, they die with us when we die, and can accompany us no further. But the lively Hope, which is the Christian's Portion, answers expectation to the full, and much beyond it, and deceives no way but in that happy way of far exceeding it.

A *living hope*, living in death itself! The world dares say no more for its device, than *Dum spiro spero*;[2] but the children of God can add, by virtue of this living hope, *Dum expiro*[a] *spero*.[3]

[b]APHORISM IX[c1]

THE WORLDLING'S FEAR

It is a fearful thing when a man and all his hopes die together. Thus saith Solomon of the wicked, Prov. xi. 7.[d] When he dieth, then die his hopes; (many of them *before*, but at the utmost *then**, all of them;) but *the righteous hath hope in his death*, Prov. xiv. 32.

APHORISM X[e1]

WORLDLY MIRTH

As he that taketh away a garment in cold weather, and as vinegar upon nitre, so is he that singeth songs to a heavy heart, Prov. xxv. 20. Worldly mirth is so far from curing spiritual grief, that even worldly

---

* One of the numerous proofs against those who with a strange inconsistency hold the Old Testament to have been inspired throughout, and yet deny that the doctrine of a future state is taught therein.[2]

---

[a] *AR* (1825): *exspiro*
[b] *AR* (1825): p 85
[c] *AR* (1825): LEIGHTON.
[d] *AR* (1825): 7.,
[e] *AR* (1825): L. & ED.

---

[2] "While I live (breathe) I hope". Traditional motto.
[3] "While I die (breathe my last) I hope".
[1] From Leighton COPY C I 36: *CM (CC)* III.
[2] C's footnote here corresponds to his own annotation at the foot of the page in Leighton COPY C I 36, which continues with a sentence later cancelled: "I grieve to hear that this Warburtonian Whimsy is in great favor and acceptance with many of our Church Dignitaries." See *CM (CC)* III.

The prime reference is to Warburton *The Divine Legation of Moses Demonstrated, on the Principles of a Religious Deist, from the Omission of a Doctrine of a Future State of Reward and Punishment in the Jewish Dispensation* (2 vols 1738–41).

[1] For the first paragraph see Leighton COPY C I 38–9: *CM (CC)* III. The second paragraph, which may have been intended as a "Comment", is probably referred to in C's footnote to Leighton at this point as to be found on "page 10, Slip III"; the latter has since disappeared.

grief, where it is great and takes deep root, is not allayed but increased by it. A man who is full of inward heaviness, the more he is encompassed about with mirth, it exasperates and enrages his grief the more; like ineffectual weak physic, which removes not the humor,*a* but stirs it and makes it more unquiet. But spiritual joy is seasonable for all estates: in prosperity, it is pertinent to crown and sanctify all other enjoyments, with this which so far surpasses them; and in distress, it is the only *Nepenthe*,[2] the cordial of fainting *b*spirits: so, Psal. iv. 7.*c He hath put joy into my heart.* This mirth makes way for itself, which other mirth cannot do. These songs are sweetest in the night of distress.

There is something exquisitely beautiful and touching in the first of these similies:*d* and the second, though less pleasing to the imagination, has the charm of propriety, and expresses the transition with equal force and liveliness. A Grief of recent birth is a sick Infant that must have its medicine administered in its milk,*e* and sad Thoughts are the sorrowful Heart's natural food. This is a Complaint that is not to be cured by opposites, which for the most part only reverse the symptoms while they exasperate the Disease—or like a Rock in the Mid Channel of a River swoln by a sudden rain-flush from the mountains,*f* which only detains the excess of Waters from their proper Outlet, and makes*g* them foam, roar, and eddy. The Soul in her desolation hugs the sorrow close to her, as her sole remaining garment: and this must be drawn off so gradually, and the garment to be put in its stead so gradually slipt on and feel so like the former, that the Sufferer shall be sensible of the change only by the refreshment. The true Spirit of Consolation is well content to detain the tear in the eye, and finds a surer pledge of its success in the smile of Resignation that dawns through that, than in the liveliest shows of a forced and alien exhilaration.

*h*APHORISM XI*i*[1]

Plotinus thanked God, that his Soul was not tied to an immortal Body.

---

a AR (1825): humour, *b AR* (1825): p 86
c AR (1825): 7, *d AR* (1825): similes:
e AR (1825): Milk, *f AR* (1825): mountain,
g AR (1825): make *h AR* (1825): p 87
i AR (1825): EDITOR.

---

[2] From *nēpenthēs*, the adjective used at *Odyssey* 4.221 to describe the drug which "banishes grief or trouble" from the mind: *OED*.

[1] Leighton COPY C I 41: *CM (CC)* III— attributed in *AR* (1825) to "EDITOR". Cf Augustine on Plotinus in *City of God* 9.11.

APHORISM XII*a*

What a full Confession do we make of our dissatisfaction with the Objects of our bodily senses, that in our attempts to express what we conceive the Best of Beings, and the Greatest of Felicities to be, we describe by the exact Contraries of all, that we experience here—the one as *In*finite, *In*comprehensible, *Im*mutable, &c.,*b* the other as *in*corruptible, *un*defiled, and that passeth *not* away.[1] At all events, this Coincidence, say rather, Identity of Attributes,*c* is sufficient to apprize us, that to be inheritors of Bliss we must become the children of God.[2]

This Remark of Leighton's is ingenious and startling. Another, and more fruitful, perhaps more solid, inference from the fact would be, that there is something in the human mind which makes it know (as soon as it is sufficiently awakened to reflect on its own thoughts and notices), that in all finite Quantity there is an Infinite, in all measures of Time an Eternal; that the latter are the basis, the substance, the true and abiding *reality* of the former; and that as we truly *are*, only as far as God is with us, so neither can we truly *possess* (*i.e.* enjoy) our Being or any other real Good, but by living in the sense of his holy presence.[3]

A Life of Wickedness is a Life of Lies;*d* and an *e*Evil Being, or the Being of Evil, the last and darkest mystery.[4]

---

a *AR* (1825): L. & ED.
b *AR* (1825): &c.
c *AR* (1825): Attributes
d *AR* (1825): Lies:
e *AR* (1825): p 88

---

[1] This sentence is based very loosely indeed on Leighton COPY C I 41. It is an elaboration of Leighton's central remark (on 1 Pet 1.3–4) that "as divines say of the knowledge of God which we have here, that . . . we know rather what He is not than what He is, infinite, incomprehensible, immutable, &c., so it is of this happiness, this inheritance . . . It is by privatives . . . that we describe it, and we can go no further, than this,—*Incorruptible, undefiled, and that fadeth not away.*"

[2] This sentence was probably prompted by a remark by Leighton (I 46): "It is doubtless a great contentment to the children of God, to hear of the excellencies of the life to come . . .".

[3] This paragraph takes the reader away from Leighton. The idea that "there is something in the human mind which makes it know" the infinite in the finite, the eternal in the temporal, is C's comment on the "inheritance incorruptible". Cf *BL* ch 24 *(CC)* II 234 on "Eternity revealing itself in the phaenomena of Time" and *SM (CC)* 49: "The Bible alone contains a Science of *Realities*: and therefore each of its Elements is at the same time a living GERM, in which the Present involves the Future, and in the Finite the Infinite exists potentially." For J. H. Newman's guarded approval of C's statement here, see Editor's Introduction above, at n 343.

[4] C's ms for the preceding two paragraphs from "more fruitful", his direction for *Aph XIII*, and his ms for *Aph XIV* to "*product* (*i.e.* the" in the second paragraph are transcribed below in App B(l).

APHORISM XIII[a][1]

THE WISEST USE OF THE IMAGINATION

It is not altogether unprofitable; yea, it is great wisdom in Christians to be arming themselves against such temptations as may befal them hereafter, though they have not as yet met with them; to labor[b] to overcome them before-hand, to suppose the hardest things that may be incident to them, and to put on the strongest resolutions they can attain unto. Yet all that is but an imaginary effort; and therefore there is no assurance that the victory is any more than imaginary too, till it come to action, and then, they that have spoken and thought very confidently, may prove but (as one said of the Athenians) *fortes in tabula*,[2] patient and courageous in picture or fancy; and, notwithstanding all their arms, and dexterity in handling them by way of exercise, may be foully defeated when they are to fight in earnest.

APHORISM XIV[c]

THE LANGUAGE OF SCRIPTURE

The Word of God speaks to men,[d] and therefore it speaks the language of the Children of Men.[1] This just and pregnant Thought was suggested to Leighton by Gen. xxii. 12.[2] The same Text has led the Editor to unfold and expand the Remark.—On moral subjects, the Scriptures speak in the language of the Affections [e]which they excite in us; on sensible objects, neither metaphysically, as they are known by superior intelligences; nor theoretically, as they would be seen by us were we placed in the Sun;[3] but as they are represented by our human senses in our

[a] *AR* (1825): LEIGHTON.
[b] *AR* (1825): labour
[c] *AR* (1825): EDITOR.
[d] *AR* (1825): Men,
[e] *AR* (1825): p 89

[1] From Leighton COPY C I 55 *CM (CC)* III.

[2] Source untraced.

[1] This sentence is from Leighton COPY C I 55: *CM (CC)* III.

[2] After the first sentence, Leighton (COPY C I 55) continues: "thus, Gen. xxii. 12, *Now I know that thou fearest God, seeing thou hast not withheld thy son, thine only son from me*". C quotes this text below: see n 6.

[3] Cf *Religious Musings* lines 105–14: *PW* (EHC) I 113, in which the poet says, of him who "feeds and saturates his constant soul" with the truth that the "one Mind" is "Love",

> From himself he flies,
> Stands in the sun, and with no partial gaze
> Views all creation . . .

This refers in turn to the angel who stood

present relative position.[4] Lastly, from no vain, or worse than vain, Ambition of seeming "to walk on the Sea" of Mystery in my way to Truth, but in the hope of removing a difficulty that presses heavily on the minds of many who in Heart and Desire are believers, and which long pressed on my own mind, I venture to add: that on *spiritual* things, and allusively to the mysterious union or conspiration of the Divine with the Human in the Spirits of the Just, spoken of in Romans, vii.[a] 27,[b5] the Word of God attributes the language of the Spirit sanctified to the Holy One, the Sanctifier.

Now the Spirit in Man (that is, the Will) knows its own State in and by its Acts alone: even as in geometrical reasoning the Mind knows its constructive *faculty* in the *act* of constructing, and contemplates the act in the *product* (*i.e.* the mental figure or diagram) which is inseparable from the act and co-instantaneous.

Let the Reader join these two positions: first, that the Divine Spirit acting *in* the Human Will is described as *one with* the Will so filled and actuated: secondly, that our actions are the means, by which alone the Will becomes assured of its own state: and he will understand, though he may not perhaps adopt [c]my suggestion, that the Verse, in which God *speaking of himself*, says to Abraham, *Now I know* that thou fearest God, seeing thou hast not withheld thy Son, thy only Son, from me[6]— may be more than merely *figurative*. An *accommodation* I grant; but in the *thing expressed*, and not altogether in the Expressions. In arguing with Infidels, or with the weak in faith, it is a part of religious Prudence, no less than of religious Morality, to avoid whatever looks *like* an evasion. To retain the literal sense, wherever the harmony of Scripture permits, and reason does not forbid, is ever the honester, and nine times in ten, the more rational and pregnant interpretation. [d]The contrary plan is an easy and approved way of *getting rid* of a difficulty; but nine times in ten a bad way of solving it. But alas! there have been too many Com-

---

^a COPY C: viii.
^b AR (1825): 27.,
^c AR (1825): p 90
^{d–e} Added in 1831

---

in the sun, Rev 19.17, and to Satan's meeting there in *PL* III 547–70 with the angel Uriel.

[4] For discussion of this sentence in the context of C's "semidualism" see Boulger 117.

[5] A slip for Rom 8.27, which reads: "And he that searcheth the hearts knoweth what is the mind of the Spirit, because he maketh intercession for the saints according to the will of God." Cf also Rom 15.16: ". . . being sanctified by the Holy Ghost", and Heb 12.23: ". . . the spirits of just men made perfect". The slip was corrected by C in a further amendment to the "Corrections and Amendments" list in *AR* (1825) COPY C, but overlooked in 1831.

[6] See above, n 2.

mentators who are content not to understand a text themselves, if only they can make the reader believe that they do.[e]

Of the Figures of Speech in the Sacred[a] Volume, that are only Figures of Speech, the one of most frequent occurrence is that which describes an effect by the name of its most usual and best known cause:[7] the passages, for instance, in which Grief, Fury, Repentance, &c., are attributed to the Deity. But these are far enough from justifying the (I had almost said[b] dishonest) fashion of metaphorical Glosses, in as well as out of the Church; and which our fashionable Divines have carried to such an extent, as, in the doctrinal part of their Creed, to leave little else but Metaphors. But the reader[c] who wishes to find this latter subject, and that of the Aphorism, treated more at large, is referred to Mr.[d] Southey's Omniana, Vol. II. p. 7–12;[f][8] and to the Note in p. 62–67,[g] of the Author's[h] second Lay-Sermon.[9]

_[i]APHORISM XV[j][1]

THE CHRISTIAN NO STOIC

Seek not altogether to dry up the stream of Sorrow, but to bound it, and keep it within its banks. Religion doth not destroy the life of nature, but

---

[a] *AR* (1825): sacred
[b] *AR* (1825): said.
[c] *AR* (1825): Reader
[d] Added in 1831
[f] *AR* (1825): 12.
[g] *AR* (1825): 67.
[h] *AR* (1825): Editor's
[i] *AR* (1825): p 91
[j] *AR* (1825): L. & ED.

---

[7] *AR* (1825) COPY D has a note at this point: "See p. 197–200, and 311–328, where the Biblical Student will find this most fruitful Canon of Interpretation explained at large, and exemplified." Also in COPY E, with "pages" for "p." and no comma after "large". See below, pp 204–6, 318–34.

[8] *Omniana* II 7–12 begins during a piece entitled "Pelagianism". A new paragraph there opens "I am firmly persuaded, that no doctrine was ever widely diffused, among various nations through successive ages, and under different religions (such as is the doctrine of original sin, and redemption . . .), which is not founded either in

the nature of things or in the necessities of our nature. . . ." On p 12 (in the next section, "The Soul and its Organs of Sense") the bottom paragraph concerns the relationship between "whatever is common to all languages" and a universal consciousness.

[9] *LS* (1817) 62–7n: *(CC)* 181–4n. C's footnote is about the manner in which the Bible is read by Unitarians.

[1] From Leighton COPY C I 56–7: *CM* *(CC)* III. The first paragraph follows Leighton closely, except that C substitutes "Religion" for Leighton's "Grace" and omits several lines between "are on them" and "Where there is no feeling". The second paragraph is C's own.

adds to it a life more excellent; yea, it doth not only permit, but requires some feeling of afflictions. Instead of patience, there is in some men an affected pride of spirit suitable only to the doctrine of the *Stoics* as it is usually taken. They strive not to feel at all the afflictions that are on them; but where there is no feeling at all, there can be no patience.

Of the sects of ancient philosophy the Stoic *ª*is, perhaps,*ᵇ* the nearest to Christianity. Yet even to this sect*ᶜ* Christianity is fundamentally opposite. For the Stoic attaches the highest honor*ᵈ* (or rather, attaches honor*ᵉ* *solely*) to the person that acts virtuously in spite of his feelings, or who has raised himself above the conflict by their extinction; while Christianity instructs us to place small reliance on a Virtue that does not *begin* by bringing the Feelings to a conformity with the Commands of the Conscience. Its especial aim, its characteristic operation, is to moralize the affections. The Feelings, that oppose a right act, must be wrong feelings.*ᶠ* The *act*, indeed, whatever the Agent's *feelings* might be, Christianity would command: and under certain circumstances would both command and commend it—commend it, as a healthful*ᵍ* symptom in a sick Patient; and command it, as one of the ways and means of changing the feelings,*ʰ* or*ⁱ* displacing them by calling up the opposite.

*ʲ*COROLLARIES TO APHORISM XV²

I. The more *consciousness* in our Thoughts and Words, and the less in our Impulses and general Actions, the better and more healthful the state both of head and heart. As the Flowers from an Orange Tree in its time of blossoming, that burgeon forth, expand, fall and are momently re-

---

ᵃ⁻ᵇ *AR* (1825): is, doubtless, ; COPY C: has been held ; COPIES D & E: has been deemed
ᶜ Added in 1831
ᵈ *AR* (1825): honour
ᵉ *AR* (1825): honour
ᶠ *AR* (1825): Feelings.
ᵍ *AR* (1825): p 92 (ful)
ʰ *AR* (1825): Feelings,
ⁱ COPY C: or of
ʲ⁻ᵏ Added in 1831: see n 2 and App D(c) below

² The whole of this section was added for the 1831 ed. It constitutes an important meditation upon the relationships between, on one hand, consciousness and the head, and, on the other, unconsciousness and the heart. An original ms version appears in *AR* (1825) COPY F p ii and is reproduced below in App D(c). Another version, in an unidentified hand, is tipped into N Q, to form f 2–2ᵛ: *CN* v; it does not seem to have been used for *AR* (1831). Some of the readings in COPY F (noted below) are better and suggest that C was not exercising a close editorial control here in 1831.

placed,[3] such is the sequence of hourly and momently[4] Charities in a pure and gracious soul. The modern Fiction which depictures[5] the son of Cytherea with a bandage round his eyes,[6] is not without a spiritual meaning. There is a sweet and holy Blindness in Christian LOVE, even as there is a blindness of Life, yea and of Genius too in the moment of productive Energy.[7]

II. Motives are symptoms of weakness, and supplements for the deficient Energy of the living PRINCIPLE, the LAW within us. Let them then be reserved for those momentous Acts and Duties, in which the strongest and best balanced natures must feel themselves deficient, and where Humility, no less than Prudence, prescribes Deliberation. We find a similitude of this, I had almost said a remote analogy, in Organized Bodies. The lowest class of Animals or Protozoa, the Polypi for instance, have

---

[3] C may be imperfectly remembering a description of the magnolia tree in William Bartram *Travels through North and South Carolina, etc* (1792) 159: "Its thick foliage of a dark green colour, is flowered over with large milk-white fragrant blossoms, on long slender elastic peduncles, at the extremities of its numerous branches, from the bosom of the leaves, and renewed every morning; and that in such incredible profusion, that the tree appears silvered over with them. . . ." For C's knowledge of Bartram see *RX* 513–14.

[4] Cf *Kubla Khan* line 19: ". . . momently was forced": *PW* (EHC) I 297. For the word as adjective, see below, *Sp Aph B Xb* n 50.

[5] For this word cf C's note to "Satyrane's Letters" III on the power of German to condense meaning by forming compounds: "It tends to make their language more picturesque; it *depictures* images better": *Friend (CC)* II 241–2n.

[6] C is presumably using the term "modern" in the sense that opposes it to "ancient" and "mediaeval". The tradition of blindfold Cupid had been well known since at least the fourteenth century and was drawn on by painters such as Piero della Francesca, Lucas Cranach the Elder, and Titian. For a full account and illustrations see E. Panowsky "Blind Cupid" in *Studies in Iconology* (New York 1939) 95–128. In 1805 C produced an allegorical explanation of the blinding of Cupid: *CN* II 2588. Shortly after *AR* was published in 1825 Lamb wrote to C, ". . . by the way what is your Enigma about Cupid? I am Cytherea's son, if I understand a tittle of it" (*LL* III 8). The reference to "Cytherea's son" suggests that he was thinking of this passage rather than one of the other references to Cupid in the volume: if so, he must have seen a copy of *AR* (1825) which was annotated with the note on which this passage in *AR* (1831) was based: see note 2 above and J. Beer "Lamb, Elton and Coleridge's 'Enigma about Cupid' " *Charles Lamb Bulletin* NS 71 (Jul 1990) 246–8.

[7] The ms note in *AR* (1825) COPY F continues: "Ειργασται: ιδε δ' αυ· εστι γαρ αγαθον" ("It is made: and behold; for it is good"). Cf Gen 1.31: "And God saw everything that he had made, and behold, it was good". C's Greek here is quite different, however, from the Septuagint version, in which the verb is ἐποίησε (aorist). C would here be stressing, by using the Greek perfect tense in εἴργασται, the instantaneous working of the productive energy of genius. The same word is used, to the same effect, in *CM (CC)* II 1107 and *CN* IV 5394, of the timeless certainty of the fulfilment of prophecy; in *CL* V 214 (in English translation) of Medea's decision to kill her children; and similarly in his notes on Greek grammar, written c 1824: *SW&F (CC)*.

neither brain nor nerves.[8] Their motive powers are all from without. The Sun, Light,[9] the Warmth, the Air are their Nerves and Brain. As life ascends, nerves appear; but still only as the conductors of an *external* Influence; next are seen the knots or Ganglions, as so many Foci of *instinctive* Agency, that imperfectly imitate the yet wanting *Center*. And now the Promise and Token of a true Individuality are disclosed; both the Reservoir of Sensibility and the imitative[10] power that actuates the Organs of Motion (the Muscles) with the the the net-work of conductors, are all taken inward and appropriated; the Spontaneous rises into the Voluntary, and finally after various steps and a long Ascent, the Material and Animal Means and Conditions are prepared for the manifestation of a Free Will, having its Law within itself and its motive in the Law—and thus bound to originate its own Acts, not only without but even against alien Stimulants.[11] That in our present state we have only the Dawning of this inward Sun (the perfect Law of Liberty)[12] will sufficiently limit and qualify the preceding Position if only it have been allowed to produce its twofold consequence—the excitement of Hope and the repression of Vanity.[k13]

[8] Cf Lamarck on polyps: ". . . on ne retrouve en eux ni cerveau, ni moelle longitudinale, ni nerfs, ni organes particuliers pour la respiration, ni vaisseaux pour la circulation des fluides, ni ovaire pour la génération . . . Les *polypes* étant éminemment irritables, ne se meuvent que par des excitations extérieures et étrangères à eux"; tr "One finds in them neither brain, nor parenchyma, nor nerves, nor specific organs for breathing, nor ducts for the circulation of fluids, nor ovary for generating. . . . Polyps, being eminently irritable, do not move except through excitations exterior and foreign to them": J.-B.-P.-A. Lamarck *Philosophie zoologique* (Paris 1809) I 202–3, 206.

[9] The COPY F reading "Sun-light" is better here.

[10] COPY F reads "Initiative", which gives better sense.

[11] COPY F reads "against the influence of alien Stimulants".

[12] Cf *Int Aph XXIII* n 6 above and refs there. Before the phrase, COPY F inserts "νομος αυτονομος" [i.e. an autonomous law, a law governed by free will]. The phrase, untraced in ancient sources, is reminiscent of statements by Kant, e.g. "What else, then, can the freedom of the will be but autonomy [Autonomie], that is, the property of the will to be a law to itself": *Grundlegung der Metaphysik der Sitten* (Riga 1797) 98; tr T. K. Abbott in *Kant's Critique of Practical Reason and Other Works on the Theory of Ethics* (1889) 65–6. In identifying "the perfect law of liberty" with an equivalent of "Autonomie" or "Will" C is adapting the Kantian ethic and giving it a theological foundation. Above, he applies the Greek phrase to Melchizedek, who in the NT is treated as anticipating Christ: see above, *Int Aph XXIX* n 20 and refs. In 1825, in "*Prometheus*", C equated the phrase with idea and with reason both theoretical and practical: *LR* II 346, 353; cf 351, 356. In 1830 in N 46 f 16 (*CN* V), paraphrasing John 1.17 as "The Law came by Moses, Grace and Truth by Jesus Christ", he equated it with Truth. For similar treatment of moral law below, see *Sp Aph B X, XII*, and *XV*.

[13] HNC, *AR* (1843), comments: "The reader is referred, upon the subject of this remarkable paragraph, to Mr Joseph Henry Green's Recapitulatory Lecture, p. 110,

APHORISM XVI[a1]

As excessive eating or drinking both makes the body sickly and lazy, fit for nothing but sleep, and besots the mind, as it clogs up with crudities the way through which the spirits should pass*, bemiring them, and making them move heavily, as a coach in a deep way; thus doth all immoderate use of the world and its delights wrong the soul in its spiritual condition, makes it sickly and feeble, full of spiritual distempers and inactivity, benumbs the graces of the Spirit, and fills the soul with sleepy vapors,[b] makes it grow secure and heavy in spiritual exercises, and obstructs the way and motion of the Spirit of God, in the soul. Therefore, if you would be spiritual, healthful, and vigorous, and enjoy much of the consolations of Heaven, be sparing and sober in those of the earth, and what you abate of the one, shall be certainly made up in the other.

[c]APHORISM XVII[d1]

INCONSISTENCY

It is a most unseemly and unpleasant thing, to see a man's life full of ups and downs, one step like a Christian, and another like a wor[l]dling;[e] it cannot choose but both pain himself and mar the edification of others.

The same sentiment, only with a special application to the maxims

---

*[2] Technical phrases of an obsolete System will yet retain their places, nay, acquire universal currency, and become sterling in the language, when they at once represent the feelings, and give an apparent solution of them by visual images easily managed by the Fancy. Such are many terms and phrases from the *Humoral* Physiology[3] long exploded, [f]but which[g] are far more popular than any description would be from the Theory that has taken its place.

[a] *AR* (1825): LEIGHTON.
[b] *AR* (1825): vapours,
[c] *AR* (1825): p 93
[d] *AR* (1825): L. & ED.
[e] *AR* (1825): worldling;
[f-g] *AR* (1825): yet ; COPY C: which yet

Vital Dynamics, 1840;—a volume of singular worth and importance.'' See also below, App C.

[1] The aphorism comes from Leighton COPY C I 110–11: *CM (CC)* III. C follows Leighton almost exactly.

[2] This footnote is taken from C's note to Leighton COPY C I 110–11, with minor corrections of expression: *CM (CC)* III.

[3] For antecedents to this use of ''humoral'' see *OED*, in which the present usage is also cited.

[1] The first paragraph is from Leighton COPY C I 119: *CM (CC)* III. This follows Leighton exactly, apart from the reading ''wordling'', a misprint from the ''worldling'' of Leighton and *AR* (1825).

and measures of our Cabinet and Statesmen, has[a] been finely expressed by a sage Poet of the preceding Generation, in lines which no Generation will find inapplicable or superannuated.

> God and the World we worship both together,
>   Draw not our Laws to Him, but His to ours;
> Untrue to both, so prosperous in neither,
>   The imperfect Will brings forth but barren Flowers!
> Unwise as all distracted Interests be,
> Strangers to God, Fools in Humanity:
> Too good for great things, and too great for good,
> While still "I dare not" waits upon "I wou'd."[2]

APHORISM XVII. CONTINUED[b3]

THE ORDINARY MOTIVE TO INCONSISTENCY

What though the polite man count thy fashion a little odd and too precise, it is because he knows nothing above that model of goodness which he hath set himself, and therefore approves of nothing beyond it;[c] he knows not God, and therefore doth not discern and esteem what is most like Him. When courtiers come down into the country, the common home-bred people [d]possibly think their habit strange; but they care not for that, it is the fashion at court. What need, then, that Christians should be so tender-foreheaded, as to be put out of countenance because the world looks on holiness as a singularity? It is the only fashion in the highest court, yea, of the King of Kings himself.

APHORISM XVIII[e1]

SUPERFICIAL RECONCILIATIONS, AND THE SELF-DECEIT IN
FORGIVING

When, after variances, men are brought to an agreement, they are much

---

[a] *AR* (1825): had
[b] *AR* (1825): LEIGHTON.
[c] *AR* (1825): it:
[d] *AR* (1825): p 94
[e] *AR* (1825): LEIGHTON.

[2] An adaptation of Fulke Greville *A Treatie of Warres* sts 66–7: *Certaine Learned and Elegant Workes* (1633) 82, which is given in *PW* (EHC) II 1115. The fourth line there reads "Amid their owne desires still raising feares"; the last line is not Greville but adapted by C from *Macbeth* I vii 44. The passage was used as a motto for the second *Lay Sermon*: see *LS* *(CC)* 120 and n, which also includes a note by C on the passage.

[3] From Leighton COPY C I 122: *CM (CC)* III. C follows Leighton exactly, except that he reads "Christian" for "the godly". The "continuity" is of theme, not of Leighton's text.

[1] From Leighton COPY C I 148: *CM (CC)* III.

subject to this, rather to cover their remaining malices with superficial verbal forgiveness, than to dislodge them, and free the heart of them. This is a poor self-deceit. As the philosopher said to him, who being ashamed that he was espied by him in a tavern in the outer room, withdrew himself to the inner, he called after him, "That is not the way out,*a* the more you go that way, you will be the further in!"[2] So when hatreds are upon admonition not thrown out, but retire inward to hide themselves, they grow deeper and stronger than before; and those constrained semblances of reconcilement are but a false healing, do but skin the wound over, and therefore it usually breaks forth worse again.

APHORISM XIX*b*[1]

OF THE WORTH AND THE DUTIES OF THE PREACHER

The stream of custom and our profession bring us to the Preaching of the Word, and we sit out our hour *c*under the sound; but how few consider and prize it as the great ordinance of God for the salvation of souls, the beginner and the sustainer of the Divine life of grace within us! And certainly, until we have these thoughts of it, and seek to feel it thus ourselves, although we hear it most frequently, and let slip no occasion, yea, hear it with attention and some present delight, yet still we miss the right use of it, and turn it from its true end, while we take it not as *that ingrafted word which is able to save our souls.*d* James i. 21.

Thus ought they who preach to speak the word; to endeavor*e* their utmost to accommodate it to this end, that sinners may be converted, begotten again, and believers nourished and strengthened in their spiritual life; to regard no lower end, but aim steadily at that mark. Their hearts and tongues ought to be set on fire with holy zeal for God and love to souls, kindled by the Holy Ghost, that came down on the apostles in the shape of fiery tongues.

a *AR* (1825): out;
b *AR* (1825): LEIGHTON.
c *AR* (1825): p 95
d *AR* (1825): *souls,*
e *AR* (1825): endeavour

[2] "Very neat was the remark made by Diogenes to a young man, who being seen at a tavern, fled for refuge within. 'The farther you flee inside,' said he, 'the more you are in the tavern.' ": Plutarch "De perfectibus in virtute" 11: *Moralia* 82c–D, tr F. C. Babbitt (LCL 1927). According to Plutarch *Moralia* 847F, and Diogenes Laertius 6.34, the young man was Demosthenes the orator.

[1] From Leighton COPY C I 171–2: *CM (CC)* III. C follows Leighton almost exactly, apart from an initial alteration necessitated by extraction from its context. This he makes in ms in COPY C, writing in the title also.

And those that hear, should remember this as the end of their hearing, that they may receive spiritual life and strength by the word. For though it seems a poor despicable business, that a frail sinful man like yourselves should speak a few words in your hearing, yet, look upon it as the way wherein God communicates happiness to those who believe, and works that believing unto happiness, alters the whole frame of the soul, and makes a new creation, as it begets it again to the inheritance of glory. Consider it thus, which is its true notion; and then, what can be so precious?

*^a*APHORISM XX*^b*[1]

The difference is great in our natural life, in some persons especially; that they who in infancy were so feeble, and wrapped up as others in swaddling clothes, yet, afterwards come to excel in wisdom and in the knowledge of sciences, or to be commanders of great armies, or to be kings: but the distance is far greater and more admirable, betwixt the small beginnings of grace, and our after perfection, that fulness of knowledge that we look for, and that crown of immortality which all they are born to, who are born of God.

But as in the faces or actions of some children, characters and presages of their after-greatness have appeared (as a singular beauty in Moses's face, as they write of him,[2] and as Cyrus was made king among the shepherds' children with whom he was brought up, &c.[3]) so also, certainly, in these children of God, there be some characters and evidences that they are born for Heaven by their new birth. That holiness and meekness, that patience and faith which shine in the actions and sufferings of the saints, are characters of their Father's image, and show their high original, and foretel their glory to come; such a glory as doth not only surpass the world's thoughts, but the thoughts of the children of God themselves. 1 John iii. 2.

---

^a *AR* (1825): p 96
^b *AR* (1825): LEIGHTON.

---

[1] From Leighton COPY C I 175–6: *CM (CC)* III. C follows Leighton, apart from omitting, after "betwixt", the phrase ". . . the weakness of these *new-born babes*", which he deleted also in COPY C.

[2] Josephus, describing Moses' childhood, states that he was of divine form (μορφῇ θεῖον) and so beautiful that passers-by stood transfixed to look at him and labourers left their work to steal a glance: *Jewish Antiquities* 2.9.6–7.

[3] The story is told in Herodotus *Histories* 1.113ff.

COMMENT[a]

This Aphorism would, it may seem, have been placed more fitly in the Chapter following.[4] In placing it here, I have been determined by the following Convictions:[b] 1. Every State, and consequently that which we have described as the State of Religious Morality, which is not progressive, is dead or retrograde. 2. As a pledge of this progression, or, at least, as the form in which the propulsive tendency shows itself, there are certain Hopes, Aspirations, Yearnings, that, with more or less of consciousness, rise and stir in the Heart of true Morality as naturally as the Sap in the full-formed Stem of a Rose flows towards the Bud, within which the Flower is maturing.[5] 3. No one, whose own experience authorizes him to confirm the truth of this statement, can have been conversant with the Volumes of Religious Biography, can have perused (for instance) the Lives of Cranmer, Ridley, Latimer, Wishart, Sir Thomas More, Bernard Gilpin, Bishop Bedel, or of Egede, Swartz, and the Missionaries of the Frozen World,[6] without an occasional conviction, that these men lived under extraordinary influences, which[c] in each instance and in all ages of the Christian aera bear the same characters, and both

---

[a] *AR* (1825) Corr, inserted as heading: "On an intermediate state, or state of *transition* from Morality to Spiritual Religion."

[b] *AR* (1825): p 97 (victions:)

[c] *AR* (1825): that

---

[4] C seems still to be thinking of his main series of Spiritual Aphorisms as "the next chapter". See Editor's Introduction, above, at n 75 and onwards.

[5] An interesting variant on C's more common images of moral growth as from chrysalis to butterfly. See below, App I Excursus Note 2 "Psyche as butterfly and soul".

[6] All the figures mentioned were renowned for single-minded integrity and disregard of self. Lives of Hugh Latimer (c 1485–1555), Thomas Cranmer (1489–1556), and Nicholas Ridley (c 1500–55) appeared in Foxe's *Book of Martyrs* (1563) and were reprinted, along with a ms life of Sir Thomas More (1478–1535) and Bp Carleton's life of Bernard Gilpin (1517–83), in Christopher Wordsworth *Ecclesiastical Biography* (6 vols 1818). Accounts of George Wishart (c 1513–46), Scottish reformer, may be found in Foxe, in John Knox *History of the Reformation in Scotland* (1586–7), and in Robert Lindsay of

Pitcottie *Chronicles*, published from old mss by J. G. Dalyell (Edinburgh 1814). Gilbert Burnet wrote a *Life* of William Bedell (1517–1642), bp of Kilmore and Ardagh (C annotated an edition of 1685); the mention of the "Missionaries of the Frozen World" probably refers to David Cranz *The History of Greenland* (2 vols 1767), which, entirely devoted to the Greenland missions from I 279 onwards, contains an account of Hans Egede (1686–1758) and his determination to bring Christianity to the Greenlanders (I 279–366). (C knew of this work earlier and cited it in a note to *The Destiny of Nations* line 110: *PW*—EHC—I 135; see *RX* 94–101 and cf *CM*—CC—I 431 and n.) For Christian Friedrich Swartz (1725–98), the great German missionary to India, see the *Remains* (2nd ed 1826) and H. Pearson *Memoirs of . . . the Reverend Christian Frederick Swarz* (2 vols 1834), with a preface taking note of some earlier accounts.

in the accompaniments and the results evidently refer to a common origin. And what can this be? is the Question that must needs force itself on the mind in the first moment of reflection on a phenomenon so interesting and apparently so anomalous. The answer is as necessarily contained in one or the other of two assumptions. These influences are either the Product of Delusion (Insania Amabilis,[7] and the Re-action of disordered Nerves), or they argue the existence of a *a*Relation to some real Agency, distinct from what is experienced or acknowledged by the world at large, for which as not merely *natural* on the one hand, and yet not assumed to be *miraculous** on the other, we have no apter name than *spiritual.*[8] Now if neither analogy justifies nor the moral feelings permit the former assumption; and we decide therefore in favor*b* of the Reality of a State other and higher than the mere Moral Man, whose Religion†

---

* In check of fanatical pretensions, it is expedient to confine the term *miraculous*, to cases where the *Senses* are appealed to*c* in proof of something that transcends, or*d* can be*e* part of*f* the Experience derived from the Senses.

† For let it not be forgotten, that Morality, as distinguished from Prudence, implying (it matters not under what name, whether of Honor,*g* or Duty, or Conscience, still, I say, implying), and being grounded in, an awe of the Invisible and a Confidence therein beyond (nay occasionally in apparent contradiction to) the inductions of outward Experience, is essentially religious.[9]

---

a *AR* (1825): p 98

b *AR* (1825): favour

c *AR* (1825): to,

d COPIES C & D: and

e *AR* (1825): be a ; COPY C: be no ; COPY D: form no

f COPIES C & D: of,

g *AR* (1825): Honour,

[7] The phrase is used by Horace (*Odes* 3.4.6) in connexion with poetic inspiration and three times by Robert Burton in *The Anatomy of Melancholy* (1651): "Democritus to the Reader", 1.2.2.6, and 1.2.3.14. Tr "an Amiable Madness".

[8] The first of C's attempts in this work to redefine the nature of the spiritual. See Editor's Introduction, above, pp lxvi–lxxviii.

[9] *AR* (1825) COPY C has a note here: "In plainer words, Religion and Morality have the same Root—viz. the Awe of the Invisible, and the disposition of unconditional Obedience to the unconditional Commands of the Invisible Principle. This is what a Gentleman means when he says, His *Honor* dictates this or that: and would resent as an insult ~~any~~ the question—*Why* do you comply with the dictates of your

Honor?" The note in COPY D reads: "In plainer words, the common Root both of Morality and of Religion is the Awe of the Invisible and Supersensual, i.e. of the Reason in the Conscience, and in the disposition of the Will to receive its dictates as *unquestionable*, and entitled to an unconditional Obedience. *Why do you do this?* My Honor dictates it. If the Querist rejoined—But why do you blindly follow your *Honor*?—the Gentleman either resents the Question as an insult, or turns away from the Querist with scorn or disgust.

When the Invisible is sought for by means of the Fancy in the World *without*, and the Awe ⟨is⟩ is transferred to imaginary Powers (Dæmons, Genii, &c) or to sensible objects (*Fetisches, Gri Gris,* Saints'

consists in Morality, has attained under these convictions; can the existence of a *transitional* state appear other than probable? or that these
very Convictions, when accompanied by correspondent dispositions and
stirrings of the Heart, are among the Marks and Indications of such a
state? And thinking it not unlikely that among the Readers of this Volume, there may be found some Individuals, whose inward State, though
disquieted by Doubts and oftener still perhaps by blank Misgivings,[10]
may, nevertheless, betoken the commencement of a Transition *[a]*from a
not irreligious Morality to a Spiritual Religion, with a view to their interests I placed this Aphorism under the present Head.

APHORISM XXI[b1]

The most approved teachers of wisdom, in a human way, have required
of their scholars, that to the end their minds might be capable of it, they
should be purified from vice and wickedness. And it was Socrates's custom, when any one asked him a question, seeking to be informed by
him, before he would answer them, he asked them concerning their own
qualities and course of life.

APHORISM XXII[c1]

KNOWLEDGE NOT THE ULTIMATE END OF RELIGIOUS PURSUITS

The Hearing and Reading of the Word, under which I comprize theological studies generally, are alike defective when pursued *without* increase

[a] *AR* (1825): p 99
[b] *AR* (1825): LEIGHTON.
[c] *AR* (1825): L. & ED.

Images, Relics, &c) the Man becomes a
Phantast in the one case and superstitious
in the other.—The *Idea* of God is contained
in the Reason: and the *Reality* of this Idea
is a Command of the Conscience. Yet by
placing even this out of ourselves, as if it
existed in Space, we change it into an
Idol.'' A grigri (or greegree) is "an African
charm, amulet, or fetish'': *OED*. COPY E
has a note that is a variation of that in COPY
D.
   [10] Cf WW's Immortality Ode line 45:
WPW IV 283.
   [1] From Leighton COPY C I 182: *CM (CC)*
III. C reproduces the two sentences exactly,
but in COPY C he deleted, and here omits,

an intervening sentence describing how
". . . the philosopher judges young men
unfit hearers of moral philosophy, because
of the abounding and untamedness of their
passions, granting that, if those were composed and ordered, they might be admitted''.
   [1] The first sentence, which is C's own,
may have been prompted by Leighton's
comment (I 187) on the desire of the word:
"The ear is indeed the mouth of the mind,
by which it receives the word . . . but meat
that goes no further than the mouth, you
know, cannot nourish.'' For the remainder
see Leighton COPY C I 187–8: *CM (CC)* III.
C follows Leighton exactly.

of Knowledge, and when pursued chiefly *for* increase of Knowledge. To seek no more than a present delight, that evanisheth with the sound of the words that die in the air, is not to desire the word as meat, but as music, as God tells the prophet Ezekiel of his people, Ezek. xxxiii. 32. *And lo, thou art unto them as a very lovely song of one that hath a pleasant voice, and can play well upon an instrument; for they hear thy words, and they do them not.* To desire the word for the increase of knowledge, although this is necessary and commendable,[a] and, being rightly qualified, is a part of spiritual accretion, yet, take it as going no further, it is not the true end of the word. Nor is the venting of that knowledge in speech and frequent discourse of the word and the divine truths that are in it; which, where it is governed with Christian prudence, is not to be despised, but commended; yet, certainly, the highest knowledge, and the most frequent and skilful speaking of the word, severed from the growth here mentioned, misses the true end of the word. If any one's head or tongue should grow apace, and all the rest stand at a stay, it would certainly make him a monster; and they are no other, who are knowing and discoursing Christians, and grow daily in that respect, but not at all in holiness of heart and life, which is the proper growth of the children of God. Apposite to their case is Epictetus's comparison of the sheep; they return not what they eat in grass, but in wool.[2]

APHORISM XXIII[b1]

THE SUM OF CHURCH HISTORY

In times of peace, the Church may dilate more, and build as it were into breadth, but in times of trouble, it arises more in height; it is then built upwards;[c] as in cities where men are straitened, they build usually higher than in the country.

[d]APHORISM XXIV[e1]

WORTHY TO BE FRAMED AND HUNG UP IN THE LIBRARY OF EVERY THEOLOGICAL STUDENT

Where there is a great deal of smoke, and no clear flame, it argues much moisture in the matter, yet it witnesseth certainly that there is fire there;

---

[a] *AR* (1825): p 100 (able,)   [b] *AR* (1825): LEIGHTON.
[c] *AR* (1825): upwards: [d] *AR* (1825): p 101   [e] *AR* (1825): L. & ED.

[2] Epictetus *Enchiridion* 46.
[1] From Leighton COPY C I 205: *CM (CC)* III. C follows Leighton exactly.

[1] For the first paragraph see Leighton COPY C I 226: *CM (CC)* III. C follows Leighton exactly, except that after "ques-

and therefore dubious questioning is a much better evidence, than that senseless deadness which most take for believing. Men that know nothing in sciences, have no doubts. He never truly believed, who was not made first sensible and convinced of unbelief.

Never be afraid to doubt, if only you have the disposition to believe, and doubt in order that you may end in believing the Truth. I will venture to add in my own name and from my own conviction the following:

APHORISM XXV*al*

He, who begins by loving Christianity better than Truth, will proceed by loving his own Sect or Church better than Christianity, and end in loving himself better than all.

APHORISM XXVI*b1*

THE ABSENCE OF DISPUTES, AND A GENERAL AVERSION TO RELIGIOUS CONTROVERSIES, NO PROOF OF TRUE UNANIMITY

The boasted Peaceableness about questions of Faith too often proceeds from a superficial Temper, and not *c*seldom from a supercilious Disdain

---

a AR (1825): EDITOR.
b AR (1825): L. & ED. (1831 printed XXIV)
c AR (1825): p 102

---

tioning'' he omits the phrase ''. . . of a man concerning himself'', which he deleted also in COPY C. The second paragraph is by C.

¹ Taken from a note of Oct 1823 by C: *CN* IV 5026. Quoted approvingly by Mill in his article in the *London and Westminster Review* XXXIII (1840) 266–7 (reprinted *Dissertations and Discussions*—1859—I 408). The seed for the thought may well have been St Augustine *De Trinitate* bk III § 2 preface (Migne *PL* XLII 869): "Just as I do not desire my reader to be my devoted [i.e. uncritical] admirer, so I do not wish my critic to be devoted to himself. The former I wish not to love me more than the Catholic faith. The latter I wish not to love himself more than the Catholic truth."

¹ This aphorism was originally intended to be No XXX: see Leighton COPY C I 411–12: *CM (CC)* III. C evidently saw that it came more naturally after his discussion of

doubt in *Aphs XXIV* and *XXV*, acting as a corrective to one possible misreading of them. It was presumably moved and added to at proof stage, since the intervening passages in Leighton remain marked with their original numbering. C begins by a large rewriting of Leighton's sentiments, which read: ''. . . in some this peaceableness about religion arises from a universal unbelief and disaffection; and that sometimes comes of the much search and knowledge of debates and controversies in religion. Men having so many disputes about religion in their heads, and no life of religion in their hearts, fall into a conceit that all is but juggling, and that the easiest way is, to believe nothing; and these agree with any, or rather with none. Sometimes it is from a profane supercilious disdain of all these things; . . .''. After the first three sentences, he follows Leighton's text exactly to the end of the first paragraph, but leaves

of whatever has no marketable use or value, and from indifference to Religion itself. Toleration is a[a] Herb of spontaneous growth in the Soil of Indifference; but the Weed has none of the Virtues of the Medicinal Plant, reared by Humility in the Garden of Zeal. Those, who regard Religions as matters of Taste, may consistently include all religious differences in the old Adage, De gustibus non est disputandum.[2] And many there be among these of Gallio's temper, who *care for none of these things*, and who account all questions in religion, as he did, but matter of words and names.[3] And by this all religions may agree together. But that were not a natural union produced by the active heat of the spirit, but a confusion rather, arising from the want of it; not a knitting together, but a freezing together, as cold congregates all bodies, how heterogeneous soever, sticks, stones, and water; but heat makes first a separation of different things, and then unites those that are of the same nature.

Much of our common union of minds, I fear, proceeds from no other than the aforementioned causes, want of knowledge, and want of affection to religion. You that boast you live conformably to the appointments of the Church, and that no one hears of your noise, we may thank the ignorance of your minds for that kind of quietness.

The preceding Extract is particularly entitled to our serious reflections, as in a tenfold degree more applicable to the present times than to the age in which it was [b]written. We all know, that Lovers are apt to take offence and wrangle on occasions that perhaps are but trifles, and which assuredly would appear such to those who regard Love itself as Folly. These Quarrels may, indeed, be no proof of Wisdom; but still, in the imperfect state of our Nature the entire absence of the same, and this too on far more serious provocations, would excite a strong suspicion of a comparative indifference in the Parties who can love so coolly where they profess to love so well.[4] I shall believe our present religious Tolerancy to proceed from the abundance of our charity and good sense, when

a AR (1825): an
b AR (1825): p 103

out a paragraph and the opening phrase of the next (omitted in COPY C from the passages marked for inclusion) before following Leighton's text exactly again to the end of his second paragraph.

[2] "There can be no disputing concerning tastes". Cf *Prud Aph II* n 10 above.

[3] See Acts 18.12–17.

[4] Cf C's observation in 1821, "Quarrels of anger ending in tears are favourable to love in its *spring tide, as plants are found to grow very rapidly after a thunderstorm with rain*": [Thomas Allsop] *Letters, Conversations and Recollections of S. T. Coleridge* (2 vols 1836) II 20; *TT (CC)* II 378.

I see proofs that we are equally cool and forbearing as Litigants and political Partizans.

THE INFLUENCE OF WORLDLY VIEWS (OR WHAT ARE CALLED A MAN'S PROSPECTS
IN LIFE), THE BANE OF THE CHRISTIAN MINISTRY

It is a base, poor thing for a man to seek himself;[b] far below that royal dignity that is here put upon Christians, and that priesthood joined with it. Under the Law, those who were squint-eyed were incapable of the priesthood: truly, this squinting toward our own interest, the looking aside to that, in God's affairs especially, so deforms the face of the soul, that it makes it altogether unworthy the honor[c] of this spiritual priesthood. Oh! this is a large task, an infinite task. The several creatures bear their part in this; the sun [d]says somewhat, and moon and stars, yea, the lowest have some share in it; the very plants and herbs of the field speak of God; and yet, the very highest and best, yea all of them together, the whole concert of Heaven and earth, cannot show forth all His praise to the full. No, it is but a part, the smallest part of that glory, which they can reach.

DESPISE NONE: DESPAIR OF NONE

The Jews would not willingly tread upon the smallest piece of paper in their way, but took it up; for possibly, said they, the name of God may be on it. Though there was a little superstition in this, yet truly there is nothing but good religion in it, if we apply it to men. Trample not on any; there may be some work of grace there, that thou knowest not of. The name of God may be written upon that soul thou treadest on; it may be a soul that Christ thought so much of, as to give His precious blood for it; therefore despise it not.

---

[a] *AR* (1825): LEIGHTON.
[b] *AR* (1825): himself:
[c] *AR* (1825): honour
[d] *AR* (1825): p 104
[e] *AR* (1825): LEIGHTON.

[1] From Leighton COPY C I 261: *CM (CC)* III. Apart from punctuation, C follows Leighton exactly.

[1] From Leighton COPY C I 311–12: *CM (CC)* III. C follows Leighton exactly.

APHORISM XXIX[a1]

MEN OF LEAST MERIT MOST APT TO BE CONTEMPTUOUS, BECAUSE MOST IGNORANT AND MOST OVERWEENING OF THEMSELVES

Too many take the ready course to deceive themselves; for they look with both eyes on the failings and defects of others, and scarcely give their good qualities [b]half an eye, while[c] on the contrary, in themselves, they study to the full their own advantages, and their weaknesses and defects, (as one says), they skip over, as children do their hard words in their lesson, that are troublesome to read; and making this uneven parallel, what wonder if the result be a gross mistake of themselves!

APHORISM XXX[d1]

VANITY MAY STRUT IN RAGS, AND HUMILITY BE ARRAYED IN PURPLE AND FINE LINEN

It is not impossible that there may be in some an affected pride in the meanness of apparel, and in others, under either neat or rich attire, a very humble unaffected mind: using it upon some of the aforementioned engagements, or such like, and yet, the heart not at all upon it. *Magnus qui fictilibus utitur tanquam argento, nec ille minor qui argento tanquam fictilibus*, says Seneca: Great is he who enjoys his earthenware as if it were plate, and not less great is the man to whom all his plate is no more than earthenware.[2]

APHORISM XXXI[e1]

OF THE DETRACTION AMONG RELIGIOUS PROFESSORS

They who have attained to a self-pleasing pitch of civility or formal religion, have usually that point of presumption with it, that they make

[a] *AR* (1825): LEIGHTON.
[b] *AR* (1825): p 105
[c] *AR* (1825): while,
[d] *AR* (1825): LEIGHTON.
[e] *AR* (1825): L. & ED.

[1] From Leighton COPY C I 313: *CM (CC)* III. After substituting "Too many" for "They", C follows Leighton exactly.

[1] From Leighton COPY C I 398: *CM (CC)* III. Apart from punctuation, C follows Leighton exactly.

[2] Seneca *Letters* 5.6.

[1] From Leighton COPY C II 3–5: *CM (CC)* III. The first paragraph follows Leighton exactly. The second is from a lost ms slip that C wrote out to incorporate his wide deviation from Leighton's text, which runs: "'[Detraction] spreads and infects secretly and insensibly, is not felt but in the

their own size the model and rule to examine all by. What is below it, they condemn indeed as profane; but what is beyond[a] it, they account needless and affected preciseness: and therefore are as ready as others to let fly invectives or bitter taunts against it, which are the keen and poisoned shafts of the tongue, and a persecution that shall be called to a strict account.

The slanders, perchance, may not be altogether forged or untrue: they may be the implements, not the inventions, of Malice. But they do not on this account escape the guilt of Detraction. Rather, it is characteristic of the evil spirit in question, to work by the advantage of real faults; but these stretched and aggravated to the utmost. IT IS NOT EXPRESSIBLE HOW DEEP A WOUND A TONGUE SHARPENED TO THIS WORK WILL GIVE, WITH NO NOISE AND A VERY LITTLE WORD. This is the true *white* gun-powder,[2] which the dreaming Projectors of silent Mischiefs and insensible Poisons sought for in the Laboratories of Art and Nature, in a World of Good; but which was to be found, in its most destructive form, in "the World of Evil, the Tongue."

APHORISM XXXII[b1]

THE REMEDY

All true remedy must begin at the heart; otherwise it will be but a mountebank cure, a false imagined conquest. The weights and wheels are *there*, and the clock strikes according to their motion. Even he that speaks contrary to what is within him, guilefully contrary to his inward conviction and knowledge, yet speaks conformably to what is within him in the temper [c]and frame of his heart, which is double, *a heart and a heart*, as the Psalmist hath [d]it. Psalm[e] xii. 2.

[a] *AR* (1825): p 106 (yond)
[b] *AR* (1825): LEIGHTON.
[c] *AR* (1825): p 107
[d-e] *AR* (1825): it, Psal.

---

effects of it; and it works either by calumnies altogether forged and untrue, of which malice is inventive, or by the advantage of real faults, of which it is very discerning, and these are stretched and aggravated to the utmost. It is not expressible how deep a wound a tongue sharpened to this work will give, with a very little word and little noise,—*as a razor*, as it is called in Psal. lii. 2., which with a small touch cuts very deep . . .".

[2] "White powder" was a supposed kind of gunpowder that exploded without noise. See *OED* ("White" 10), which cites Beaumont and Fletcher *The Honest Man's Fortune* II i and Nathaniel Lee *The Princess of Cleve* II ii.

[1] From Leighton COPY C II 7–8: *CM (CC)* III. Except for the substitution of "All true remedy" for "It", C follows Leighton's text exactly.

APHORISM XXXIII[a][1]

It is an argument of a candid ingenuous mind, to delight in the good name and commendation of others; to pass by their defects, and take notice of their virtues; and to speak and hear of those willingly, and not endure either to speak or hear of the other; for in this indeed you may be little less guilty than the evil speaker, in taking pleasure in it, though you speak it not. He that willingly drinks in tales and calumnies, will, from the delight he hath in evil hearing, slide insensibly into the humor[b] of evil speaking. It is strange how most persons dispense with themselves in this point, and that in scarcely any societies shall we find a hatred of this ill, but rather some tokens of taking pleasure in it; and until a christian[c] sets himself to an inward watchfulness over his heart, not suffering in it any thought that is uncharitable, or vain self-esteem, upon the sight of others' frailties, he will still be subject to somewhat of this, in the tongue or ear at least. So, then, as for the evil of guile in the tongue, a sincere heart, *truth in the inward parts*,[2] powerfully redresses it; therefore it is expressed, Psal. xv. 2, *That speaketh the truth from his heart*; thence it flows. Seek much after this, to speak nothing with God, nor men, but what is the sense of a single unfeigned heart. O sweet truth! excellent but rare sincerity! he that *loves that truth within*,[3] and who is [d]himself at once THE TRUTH and THE LIFE,[4] He alone can work it there! Seek it of him.

It is characteristic of the Roman Dignity and Sobriety, that, in the Latin, *to* [e]*favor* with[f] *the* tongue (favere lingua[g])[5] means[h] *to be silent*. We say, Hold your tongue! as if it were an injunction, that could not be

---

[a] *AR* (1825): L. & ED.
[b] *AR* (1825): humour
[c] *AR* (1825): Christian
[d] *AR* (1825): p 108
[e-f] *AR* (1825): *favour*
[g] *AR* (1825): linguæ
[h] *AR* (1825): means,

---

[1] For the first paragraph see Leighton COPY C II 9: *CM (CC)* III. C reads "He that willingly drinks in tales and calumnies, will . . ." for Leighton's "And this is a piece of men's natural perverseness, to drink in tales and calumnies; and he that doth this, will readily . . ." and "evil hearing" for his "hearing". C also inserts the words ". . . and who is himself at once THE TRUTH and THE LIFE, He". The second paragraph is taken exactly from C's own marginal note on a sentence of Leigh-

ton's: "He that spares speech, *favours his tongue* indeed, as the Latin phrase is, '*favere linguae*'; not he that looses the reins and lets it run": COPY C II 11: *CM (CC)* III.
[2] Ps 51.6. See next note.
[3] Alluding perhaps to Ps 51.6: "Behold, thou desirest truth in the inward parts . . ." and to 1 John 1.8, 2.4, etc.
[4] John 14.6: ". . . I am the way, the truth, and the life . . .".
[5] *AR* (1825) follows Leighton in reading "favours his tongue" and "linguae". The

carried into effect but by manual force, or the pincers of the Forefinger and Thumb! And verily—I blush to say it—it is not Women and Frenchmen⁶ only that would rather have their tongues bitten than bitted,⁷ and feel their souls in a strait-waistcoat, when they are obliged to remain silent.

APHORISM XXXIV*ᵃ¹*

ON THE PASSION FOR NEW AND STRIKING THOUGHTS

In conversation seek not so much either to vent thy knowledge, or to increase it, as to know more spiritually and effectually what thou dost know. And in this way those mean despised truths, that every one thinks he is sufficiently seen in, will have a new sweetness and use in them, which thou didst not so well perceive before (for these flowers cannot be sucked dry), and in this humble sincere way thou shalt *grow in grace and in knowledge*² too.³

ᵃ AR (1825): LEIGHTON.

---

alterations here suggest an unease on the part of C or HNC. The expression is much more common with *linguis* (plural) and well known from Horace *Odes* 3.1.2: "Odi profanum vulgus et arceo: | favete linguis". There, because *favere* regularly "governs" the dative, and because dative and ablative plural are identical in Latin, the meaning could be either "favour your tongues" or "be favourable with your tongues"; it is only such rare examples as "Ore favete" in Virgil *Aeneid* 5.71 (unambiguously ". . . with your mouth[s]") that prove that the case is ablative. The words were spoken before a sacred rite and were in effect an injunction to keep silence, to ensure that no words of ill omen would vitiate the sacrifice. The common use of "favour" in Leighton's and C's time in the sense of "spare", "go easy with", especially applied to horses, would have facilitated their misapprehension. On 8 Feb 1826 C replied, to what seems to have been an adverse comment of EC's: "The remark on *Favere linguae* is Leighton's, tho' not the inference—I dare say, you are right; tho' for a *moral*, Leighton's may pass. But the whole §§ph. might be omitted without loss—it is but a *witticism*": *CL* VI 566. The

paragraph was nevertheless retained in later editions.

⁶ For C's views on Frenchmen see also e.g. *CN* II 2598, *BL* ch 21 *(CC)* II 117. Otto Jespersen enjoyed C's quip when he came on it in *OED*: see *Growth and Structure of the English Language* (9th ed Oxford 1967) 158–9.

⁷ The metaphor in "bitted" was also presumably prompted by Leighton's sentence, quoted in n 1, above.

¹ From Leighton COPY C II 12–13: *CM (CC)* III. C substitutes "In conversation" for Leighton's "in these discourses", but otherwise follows the text exactly.

² 2 Pet 3.18.

³ *AR* (1825) COPY C has a note here: "This Aph. deserves to be written in letters of Gold." COPY D has a longer note: "This Aph. worthy to have been the Keep-sake from a Dying Saint to the Child of his Prayers. The Editor had not then read Leighton's Works, but he had experienced the truth and value of this Maxim, when he began THE FRIEND. 'Long after the completion of what is ordinarily called a Learned Education, I discovered a new world of intellectual profit opening ⟨on⟩ me—not from any new opinions but lying,

APHORISM XXXV*ᵃ*[1]

THE RADICAL DIFFERENCE BETWEEN THE GOOD MAN AND THE VICIOUS MAN

The godly man hates the evil he possibly by temptation hath been drawn to do, and loves the good he is *ᵇ*frustrated of, and, having intended, hath not attained to do. The sinner, who hath his denomination from sin as his course, hates the good which sometimes he is forced to*ᶜ* and loves that sin which many times he does not, either wanting occasion and means, so that he cannot do it, or through the check of an enlightened conscience possibly dares not do; and though so bound up from the act, as a dog in a chain, yet the habit, the natural inclination and desire in him, is still the same*ᵈ* the strength of his affection,*ᵉ* is carried to sin. So in the weakest *sincere* Christian, there is that predominant sincerity and desire of holy walking, according to which he is called a *righteous person*, the Lord is pleased to give him that name, and account him so, being upright in heart, though often failing.

Leighton adds, "There is a Righteousness of a higher strain." I do not ask the Reader's full assent to this position: I do not suppose him as yet prepared to yield it. But thus much he will readily admit, that here, *if* any where, we are to seek the fine Line which, like stripes of Light in Light, distinguishes, not divides, the summit of religious Morality from Spiritual Religion.

"A Righteousness (Leighton continues)*ᶠ* that is not *in* him, but *upon* him. He is *clothed* with it." This, Reader! is the controverted Doctrine, so warmly asserted and so bitterly decried under the name of "IMPUTED RIGHTEOUSNESS."[2] Our learned Archbishop,[3] you see, adopts it; and it

ᵃ AR (1825): L. & ED.
ᵇ AR (1825): p 109
ᶜ AR (1825): to do,
ᵈ AR (1825): same,
ᵉ AR (1825): affection
ᶠ AR (1825): continues),

---

as it were, at the root of those which I had been taught during childhood in my Catechism and Spelling-book.' FRIEND, V. I. p. 15." The note in COPY E, not in C's hand, differs only in accidentals; similarly with the passage from *The Friend*, in which the only verbal difference is "in" for "during": *Friend (CC)* I 15 (II 276). For "imputed righteousness" see below, *Aph XXXV* n 8.

[1] The first paragraph is from Leighton COPY C II 25: *CM (CC)* III. C follows Leighton exactly, except that he substitutes "*sincere* Christian" for "godly man" in the last sentence of the first paragraph.

[2] Leighton's text reads: "There is a righteousness of a higher strain, upon which his salvation hangs; that is not *in* him, but *upon* him; he is clothed with it; but this other kind, which consists of sin-

is on this account principally, that by many of our leading Churchmen his Orthodoxy *ᵃhas been more than questioned, and his name put in the List of proscribedᵇ Divines, as a Calvinist. That Leighton attached a definite sense to the words above quoted, it would be uncandid to doubt; and the general Spirit of his Writings leads me to presume that it was compatible with the eternal distinction between *Things* and *Persons*, and therefore opposed to *modern* Calvinism.⁴ But what it was, I have not (I own) been able to discover. The sense, however, in which I think he *might* have received this doctrine, and in which I avow myself a believer in it, I shall have an opportunity of showing in another place.⁵ My present Object is to open out the Road by the removal of prejudices, so far at least as to throw some disturbing *Doubts* on the secure *Taking-for-granted*, that the peculiar Tenets of the Christian Faith asserted in the Articles and Homilies of our National Church are in contradiction to the Common Sense of Mankind.⁶ And with this view, (and not in the arrogant expectation or wish, that a mere *ipse dixit*⁷ should be received for argument) I here avow my conviction, that the doctrine of IMPUTED Righteousness, rightly and scripturally interpreted, is so far from being either *irrational* or *immoral*, that Reason itself prescribes the idea in order to give a *meaning* and an ultimate Object to Morality; and that the Moral Law in the Conscience demands its reception in order to give reality and substantive existence to the idea presented by the Reason.⁸

ᵃ *AR* (1825): p 110
ᵇ *AR* (1825): prescribed ; COPIES A (pencil) & D: proscribed

---

cerity, and of true and hearty, though imperfect, obedience, is the righteousness here meant, and opposed to evil doing.'' Leighton does not actually use the term ''imputed righteousness'' here.

³ I.e. Leighton.

⁴ C's association of ''*modern* Calvinism'' with the treating of persons as things (for which see above, *Mor Aph VI* n 11) can be associated with his reading of two works by Edward Williams in 1815. Such thinking, he asserted, was ''in its inevitable consequences Spinosism'', though without the ''noble honesty'' and ''majesty of openness'' that were so delightful in Spinoza himself. See Editor's Introduction at n 26, above, and, for modern Calvinism and Williams, *Sp Aph B I* n 7, below. For C on Spinozism see *Conc* n 52, below.

⁵ Presumably in his planned ''Assertion of Religion'': see Introduction to *Sp Aph B*,

n 3, below.

⁶ The preceding sentence appears also, as a statement of C's object in writing *AR* as a whole, in a letter to George Skinner of 24 Feb 1824: *CL* v 340. It may have been copied from the proofs of this passage: see above, Editor's Introduction at n 168.

⁷ ''He himself said''. ''An unproved assertion resting on the bare authority of some speaker'': *OED*. Cf Cicero's disapproval of those Pythagoreans who traditionally justified themselves with the words ''He himself said it'', '' 'he himself' being Pythagoras'': *De natura deorum* 1.5.10; tr H. Rackham (LCL 1933).

⁸ For a discussion of C's interpretation of ''imputed righteousness'' see Barth 150–1, citing N 50 f 47 (1831–2) (*CN* v) and *TT* 8 Jun 1833 *(CC)* I 386 (1836 vn II 232).

*a*APHORISM XXXVI*b1*

Your blessedness is not,—no, believe it, it is not where most of you
seek it, in things below you. How can that be? It must be a higher good
to make you happy.

COMMENT[2]

Every rank of Creatures, as it ascends in the scale of Creation,[3] leaves
Death behind it or under it. The Metal at its height of Being seems a
mute Prophecy of the coming Vegetation, into a mimic semblance of
which it crystallizes.[4] The Blossom and Flower, the Acme*c* of Vegetable
Life, divides into correspondent Organs with reciprocal functions, and
by instinctive motions and approximations seems impatient of that fix-
ure, by which it is differenced in kind from the flower-shaped Psyche,
that flutters with free wing above it.[5] And wonderfully in the insect
realm doth the Irritability, the proper seat of Instinct, while yet the na-
scent Sensibility is subordinated thereto—most wonderfully, I say, doth
the muscular Life in the Insect, and the musculo-arterial in the Bird,
imitate and typically rehearse the adaptive U[n]derstanding, yea, and the

a *AR* (1825): p 111
b *AR* (1825): LEIGHTON.
c *AR* (1825): Acmè

[1] From Leighton COPY C II 52: *CM (CC)*
III. C follows Leighton exactly.
[2] The whole of this comment is taken
from C's marginal note at this point in
Leighton. See COPY C II 52–8: *CM (CC)* III.
A parallel, yet diverse, discussion may be
found in a notebook entry of 1819, *CN* IV
4517. In 1823 (Jul–Sept) C also meditated
on the question of ascent through the natural creation: *CN* IV 4984 and n: the editor
notes that he was annotating a relevant
book, Steffens *Caricaturen des Heiligsten*
(2 vols Leipzig 1819, 1821), in Jun 1823.
A note on Baxter *Reliquiae Baxterianae*
throws light on the status of reflection in
this scale: "Nature in her ascent leaves
nothing behind: but at each step subordinates & glorifies. Mass, Chrystal, Organ,
sensation, sentience, reflection": *CM (CC)*
I 299. See also *Friend (CC)* I 517 and n,
CL VI 599, *CN* IV 5182. But C was careful
to distinguish his belief in an evolving *idea*
in nature, pointing upward to humanity,
from the theory that there had been an ac-

tual evolution *in time* from the lower animals to humanity, a notion he resisted: see
P Lects Lect 7 (1949) 239, *CL* III 574–5
and VI 723; also BM MS Egerton 2801 ff
15, 17, quoted by A. D. Snyder "Coleridge on Giordano Bruno" *MLN* XLII
(1927) 427–36, and BM Add MS 34225 ff
151–2, both to appear in *SW&F (CC)*. See
also G. R. Potter "Coleridge and the Idea
of Evolution" *PMLA* XL (1925) 379–97,
J. H. Muirhead *Coleridge as Philosopher*
(1930) 130–6, Craig Miller "Coleridge's
Concept of Nature" *JHI* XXV (1964) 77–
96, H. W. Piper *The Active Universe*
(1962) 222–6, and Barth 135–7 and 137n.
[3] ". . . this is one proof of the essential
vitality of nature, that she does not ascend
as links in a suspended chain, but as the
steps in a ladder . . .": *TL* (1848) 41.
[4] For crystallisation in the scale of life
see ibid 47.
[5] See below App I Excursus Note 2
"Psyche as butterfly and soul".

moral affections and charities*a* of man.*b6* Let us carry ourselves back, in spirit, to the mysterious Week, the teeming Work-days of the Creator: as they rose in vision before the eye of the inspired Historian *c*"of the*d* Generations of the Heaven and the Earth, in the days that the Lord God made the Earth and the Heavens."*7* And who that hath watched their ways with an understanding*e* heart, *f*could, as the vision evolving, still advanced towards him,*g* contemplate the filial and loyal Bee*8*; the home-building, wedded, and divorceless Swallow*9*; and above all the manifoldly intelligent* Ant tribes, with their Commonwealths and Confed-

* See Huber on Bees, and on Ants.*h*

---

a *AR* (1825): Charities,
b *AR* (1825): Man.
c–d *AR* (1825): of "the
e *AR* (1825): p 112 (derstanding)
f–g *AR* (1825): could ; COPY D: and now beheld in spirit the fair Procession advancing toward him, could ; COPY E: and now . . . him could ; COPY F: could as the populous Vision advanced in long evolving line toward him
h *AR* (1825): footnote in italics

[6] For an extended discussion of sensibility and irritability see *TL* (1848) 75–86. At the outset C mentions Erasmus Darwin; his first speculations on the subject were probably prompted by *Zoonomia* (2 vols 1794–6) (see also below, *Sp Aph B IX* n 39). Darwin believed that the primal form of all life was a "living filament" that was moved by alternate processes of irritability and sensibility. C related in *Friend (CC)* I 470 how he was moved by reading Darwin to speculate that the relationship between the vegetable and animal worlds was one not of resemblance but of contrast, the links being most evident at the lowest level, where insects and flowers meet in an interdependent relationship. In *TL* he developed the point further, suggesting (74–5) that whereas the vegetable world is the exponent of reproduction the animal and insect worlds are exponents, respectively, of sensibility and irritability. In the insect the muscular life is predominant, with the sensibility subordinate, and it is only at the level of the animal that sensibility (manifested originally in molluscs and snails) assumes an important rôle. In the latter case, however, with the exception of "that estimable philanthropist, the dog" and perhaps the horse and elephant, the union of all three qualities provides analogies of "our vices, our fol-

lies, and our imperfections": ibid 84. It is to the insects and birds, therefore, that C turns for traits akin to human understanding, along with human affections and charities. See *CN* IV 4719 and 4886 for detailed physiological speculations and N 47 ff 16*v*–17*v* (*CN* V, quoted *CM—CC—*II 689) for a development of the spiritual application. "Musculo-arterial" is *OED*'s only example.
[7] Gen 2.4 (var).
[8] C may be recalling François Huber *New Observations on the Natural History of Bees* (Edinburgh 1806) 240, on the conduct of bees towards the old queen: "Always accustomed to respect fertile queens, they do not forget what they owe her; they allow her the most uncontrouled liberty." Pierre Huber *Natural History of Ants* (1820) 359 also mentions the bees' "affection and solicitude for the young of their common mother". For C's interest in François and Pierre Huber, and his failure to distinguish between them, see also below, *Sp Aph B VIIIb* nn 16, 18, 21, 23.
[9] Cf *CM (CC)* II 938. For a contemporary reference to the faithful swallow, see the lyric "Es kehret der Maien . . .", part of the cycle "An die ferne Geliebte" by Alois Jeitteles which was set to music by Beethoven in 1816. *OED* gives C's use here of "divorceless" as its only example.

eracies, their Warriors and Miners, the Husbandfolk, that fold in their tiny flocks on the honeyed Leaf, and the Virgin Sisters,[a] with the holy Instincts of maternal[b] Love, detached and in selfless purity[10]—and not say to himself, Behold the Shadow of approaching Humanity, the Sun rising from behind, in the kindling Morn of Creation! Thus all lower Natures find their highest Good in semblances and seekings of that which is higher and better.[11] All things strive to ascend, and ascend in their striving.[12] And shall man alone stoop?[13] Shall his pursuits and desires, the *reflections* of his inward life, be like the reflected Image of a Tree on the edge of a Pool, that grows downward, and seeks a mock heaven in the unstable element beneath it,[14] in neighbourhood with the slim water-weeds and oozy bottom-grass that are yet better than itself and more noble,[15] in as far as Substances that appear as Shadows are

[a] *AR* (1825): Sisters
[b] *AR* (1825): Maternal

[10] Pierre Huber discusses "Insects that live in Republics" (ch 12 pp 346–78), "The Wars of Ants" (ch 5 pp 178–204), miner ants (288–95), ants' tending of pucerons as food-transmitters (210–37), and the sterile females which look after the young (89–93). W. Kirby and W. Spence mention some of these phenomena, describing aphides as the "milch cattle" of ants: *Introduction to Entomology* (4 vols 1815–26) II 87. For the latter work see also below, *Sp Aph B VIIIb* nn 17, 18, 21. "Husbandfolk" here is not in *OED*. "Selfless" is its first example.

[11] C's principles of individuation are promulgated at large in *TL* (1848) 42–3.

[12] Cf the account of the "whole chain of being" in *TT* 8 Jul 1827 *(CC)* I 82 (1836 vn, dated 9 Jul, II 86).

[13] Cf the discussion, in a notebook entry of 1818 (*CN* III 4378) used in *P Lects* Lect 8 (1949) 249, of ascent through creation, which mentions the instincts of the butterfly in laying its eggs on ". . . the particular Sort of Leaf that is fitted to sustain the Caterpillar" and concludes: ". . . and is it in Man, the sole magnificent Temple in the world of visible Existence, and is it in the Holy of Holies of this Temple, that is, in the moral & rational part of Humanity, that Nature tells her first and only Lie?—Impossible". For these closing phrases see also *CN* III 4438, IV 4692 f 21ᵛ, and below,

Sp Aph B XXIIIb at n 25.

[14] Verbal reminiscences here may echo WW's description of his "mimic hootings" to the owls in boyhood, where, "when pauses of deep silence mocked my skill",

 the visible scene
Would enter unawares into my mind . . .

including

 . . . that uncertain heaven, received
Into the bosom of the steady lake

MS JJ in *The Prelude* (1959) 639–40; cf *Prelude* (1805) v 404–13. For C's praise of these lines, sent to him by WW in 1798, see *CL* I 452–3.

[15] C seems to be partially recalling his image of the well at Over Stowey, where ". . . the images of the weeds which hung down from its sides, appeared as plants growing up, straight and upright, among the water weeds that really grew from the Bottom" (*CN* II 2557), an image there related to the relationship between the happy man's ideas and impressions—which relationship is, however, subsequently discussed in terms of shadows and substances (see letter to Clarkson 13 Oct 1806: *CL* II 1194–5). The shift from psychological to moral emphasis over the years is typical of C's development.

preferable to Shadows mistaken for Substance![16] No! it must be a higher good to make you happy. While you labor[a] for any thing below your proper Humanity, you seek a happy Life in the region of Death.[17] Well saith the moral Poet—

> Unless above himself he can
> Erect himself, how mean a thing is man![18]

[b]APHORISM XXXVII[c][1]

There is an imitation of men that is impious and wicked, which consists in taking a[d] copy of their sins. Again, there is an imitation which though not so grossly evil, yet[e] is poor and servile, being in mean things, yea, sometimes descending to imitate the very imperfections of others, as fancying some comeliness in them; as some of Basil's scholars, who imitated his slow speaking, which he had a little in the extreme, and could not help.[2] But this is always laudable, and worthy of the best minds, to be *imitators of that which is good*,[3] wheresoever they find it; for that stays not in any man's person, as the ultimate pattern, but rises to the highest grace, being man's nearest likeness to God, His image and resemblance, bearing his[f] stamp and superscription,[4] and belonging peculiarly to Him, in what hand soever it be found, as carrying the mark of no other owner than Him.

[a] *AR* (1825): labour
[b] *AR* (1825): p 113
[c] *AR* (1825): LEIGHTON.
[d] *AR* (1825): the
[e] *AR* (1825): yet,
[f] *AR* (1825): His

[16] I.e. both the shadows of Plato's cave and Bacon's *idola*: see C's note on Leighton COPY B III 68: *CM (CC)* III and n.
[17] From St Augustine: "Seek what you are seeking, but it is not to be found where you are seeking it. You seek for a happy Life in the Region of Death: It is not there." *Confessions* 4.12.2 (tr 1739) 103.
[18] Daniel *To the Lady Margaret, Countess of Cumberland* XII lines 7–8. In sending forward his marginal note to be printed C evidently forgot that he had already used this favorite quotation of his in *AR*: see above, *Int Aph X* and C's footnote at n 1.
[1] From Leighton COPY C II 53: *CM (CC)*

III. After "resemblance" C omits a parenthesis by Leighton—"(and so, following the example of the saints in holiness, we look higher than them, and consider them as receivers, but God as the first owner and dispenser of grace,)"; otherwise the text follows COPY C exactly.
[2] The source of this anecdote about St Basil the Great (c 330–79) is untraced.
[3] 1 Pet 3.13.
[4] Cf Matt 22.20: "Whose is this image and superscription?", used by C himself as ". . . the superscription and the image", when describing WW's perceptive vision of humanity in *BL* ch 22 *(CC)* II 150.

APHORISM XXXVIII[a1]

Those who think themselves high-spirited, and will bear least, as they speak, are often, even by that, forced to bow most, or to burst under it; while humility and meekness escape many a burden, and many a blow, always keeping peace within, and often without too.

APHORISM XXXIX[b1]

Our condition is universally exposed to fears and troubles, and no man is so stupid but he studies and projects for some fence against them, some bulwark to [c]break the incursion of evils, and so to bring his mind to some ease, ridding it of the fear of them. Thus[d] men seek safety in the greatness, or multitude, or supposed faithfulness of friends; they seek by any means to be strongly underset this way;[e] to have many, and powerful, and trust-worthy friends. But wiser men, perceiving the un-safety and vanity of these and all external things, have cast about for some higher course. They see a necessity of withdrawing a man from externals, which do nothing but mock and deceive those most who trust most to them; but they cannot tell whither to direct him. The best of them bring him *into himself*, and think to quiet him so;[f] but the truth is, he finds as little to support him there; there is nothing truly strong enough within him, to hold out against the many sorrows and fears which still from without do assault him. So then, though it is well done, to call off a man from outward things, as moving sands, that he build not on them, yet, this is not enough; for his own spirit is as unsettled a piece as is in all the world, and must have some higher strength than its own, to fortify and fix it. This is the way that is here taught, *Fear not their fear, but sanctify the Lord your God in your hearts*;[2] and if you can attain this latter, the former will follow of itself.

---

[a] *AR* (1825): LEIGHTON.
[b] *AR* (1825): LEIGHTON.
[c] *AR* (1825): p 114
[d] *AR* (1825): Thus,
[e] *AR* (1825): way,
[f] *AR* (1825): so,

[1] From Leighton COPY C II 57: *CM (CC)* III.
[1] From Leighton COPY C II 75–6: *CM (CC)* III. C omits a long passage after his first sentence but otherwise follows Leighton exactly.
[2] 1 Pet 3.15.

APHORISM XL*a*1

WORLDLY TROUBLES IDOLS

The too ardent Love or self-willed Desire of Power, or Wealth, or Credit in the World, is (an Apostle has assured us) Idolatry.[2] Now among the words or synonimes*b* for Idols, in the Hebrew Language, there is one that in its primary sense signifies *Troubles* (Tegirim),[3] other two that signify *Terrors* (Miphletzeth and Emim).[4] And so it is certainly. All our Idols prove so to us. They fill us with nothing but anguish and Troubles, with cares and fears, that are good for nothing but to be fit punishments of the Folly, out of which they arise.

APHORISM XLI*c*1

ON THE RIGHT TREATMENT OF INFIDELS

A regardless contempt of infidel writings is usually the fittest answer; *Spreta vilescerent.*[2] But where the holy profession of Christians is likely to receive either the main or the indirect blow, and a word of defence may do any thing to ward it off, there we ought not to spare to do it.

Christian prudence goes a great way in the regulating of this. Some are not capable of receiving rational answers, especially in Divine things; they were not only lost upon them, but religion dishonored*d* by the contest.

Of this sort are the vulgar Railers at Religion, the foul-mouthed Beliers of the Christian Faith and History.[3] Impudently false and slander-

---

a *AR* (1825): LEIGHTON.
b *AR* (1825): p 115 (nimes)
c *AR* (1825): L. & ED.
d *AR* (1825): dishonoured

[1] From Leighton COPY C II 80–1: *CM (CC)* III. C refashions the text at this point in COPY C: the first two sentences (transposing the original order) are rewritten separately, as a marginal note, and the remainder (originally a sentence between them) is repunctuated to form several sentences.
[2] See Col 3.5, together with St Paul's many references to "the world".
[3] Leighton's spelling is "Tigrim": he cites Isa 45.16.
[4] Leighton cites 1 Kgs 15.13 and Job 15.25.
[1] The first two paragraphs are from Leighton COPY C II 82–6: *CM (CC)* III. Leighton's sentence runs: "Did they [the

reproaches cast upon the saint] rest in their own persons a regardless contempt of them were usually . . ." C deletes in COPY C the remainder of the first sentence in his second paragraph, which there reads: "this; for holy things are not to be cast to dogs".
[2] "Being disregarded they would become of no account". Source untraced, but *vilesco* is a favourite word of St Augustine's.
[3] This paragraph and its footnote are both taken from C's note at the point. For the original see Leighton COPY C II 82–6: *CM (CC)* III. C made minor changes both in the ms and in proof.

ous Assertions can be met only by Assertions of their impudent and slanderous falsehood: and Christians will not, must not condescend to this. How can mere Railing be answered by them who are forbidden to return a railing answer? Whether or on what provocations such offenders may be punished or coerced on the score of Incivility, and *ᵃ*Ill-neighbourhood, and for*ᵇ* abatement of a Nuisance, as in the case of other Scolds and Endangerers of the public Peace, must be trusted to the Discretion of the civil Magistrate. Even then, there is danger of giving them importance, and flattering their vanity, by attracting attention to their works, if the punishment be slight:*ᶜ* and if severe, of spreading far and wide their reputation as Martyrs, as the smell of a dead dog at a distance is said to change into that of Musk.[4] Experience hitherto seems to favour the plan of treating these Bêtes puantes and *Enfans ᵈde Diable*,*ᵉ5* as their four-footed Brethren, the *Skink* and *Squash*,*ᶠ6* are treated* by the Amer-

---

* About the end of the same year (says Kalm), another of these Animals (Mephitis Americana) crept into our cellar; but did not exhale the smallest scent, *because it was not disturbed. A foolish old Woman, however, who perceived it at night, by the shining, and thought, I suppose, that it would set the world on fire, killed it: and at that moment its stench began to spread.*[7]

We recommend this anecdote to the consideration of sundry old Women, on this side of the Atlantic, who*ᵍ* though they do not wear the appropriate garment, are worthy to sit in their committee-room, like Bickerstaff in the Tatler, under the canopy of their Grandam's Hoop-petticoat.[8]

> *ᵃ* AR (1825): p 116
> *ᵇ* AR (1825): for the
> *ᶜ* AR (1825): slight;
> *ᵈ⁻ᵉ* AR (1825): de Diable,
> *ᶠ* AR (1825): Squash,
> *ᵍ* AR (1825): who,

[4] C's early note about such phenomena was slightly different: "A dunghill at a distance sometimes smells like musk, & a dead dog like elder-flowers": *CN* I 223 (c Jun–Sept 1797). The editor gives references to *RX* 10, *Omniana* (1812) I 304, in which the version is as here, and *TT* (1836) 4 Jan 1823. (The remark does not appear in the ms of *TT*, however; HNC inserted it from C's notebook: *TT—CC*—II 38 and n.)

[5] Peter Kalm *Travels into North America* tr J. R. Forster (3 vols Warrington 1760–71) I 273, commenting on the smell of the (English) polecat or (American) skunk, continues: "The *French* in *Canada*, for the same reason call it *Bete puante* or stinking animal, and *Enfant du Diable* or child of the devil."

[6] Obsolete forms of "skunk" and "musquash", or muskrat. *OED*, s.v. "squash", cites Goldsmith *Natural His-*

tory (1774) III 380: "But the smell of our weasels, and ermines, and polecats, is fragrance itself when compared to that of the squash and skink, which have been called the Polecats of America."

[7] Goldsmith ibid 385 gives a version of Kalm's account that differs from C's only in omitting the Latin name, and mentioning a "foolish" woman and the "shining of its eyes". Kalm's account, *Travels* I 277, is twice as long and specifies "the cook" rather than a "woman". C's further details, which are not in either account, suggest the use of a source that drew on both.

[8] Bickerstaff held a court in his house to condemn the fashionable hoop-petticoat, and a specimen petticoat was hoisted above the court as a canopy "not unlike the Cupola of St *Paul's*": *Tatler* No 116, 3–5 Jan 1709/10.

ican Woodmen, who turn their backs upon the fetid Intruder, and make appear not to see him, even at the cost of suffering him to regale on the favourite viand of these animals, the brains of a stray goose or crested Thraso[9] of the Dunghill.[10] At all events, it is degrading to the majesty, and injurious to the character of Religion, to make its safety the plea for their punishment, or at all to connect the name of Christianity with the castigation of Indecencies that [a]properly belong to the Beadle, and the perpetrators of which would have equally deserved his Lash, though the Religion of their fellow-citizens, thus assailed by them, had been that of Fo or[b] Juggernaut.[c11]

On the other hand,[12] we are to answer every one that *inquires a reason,*[13] or an account; which supposes something receptive of it. We ought to judge ourselves engaged to give it, be it an enemy, if he will hear; if it gain him not, it may in part convince and cool him; much more, should it be one who ingenuously inquires for satisfaction, and possibly inclines to receive the truth, but has been prejudiced by false misrepresentations of it.

APHORISM XLII[d1]

PASSION NO FRIEND TO TRUTH

Truth needs not the service of passion; yea, nothing so disserves it, as

[a] *AR* (1825): p 117
[b] *AR* (1825): or of
[c] *AR* (1825): Jaggernaut.
[d] *AR* (1825): LEIGHTON.

[9] A braggart, from the captain in Terence's *Eunuch.*

[10] Possibly suggested by linkage with the notebook entry quoted above in n 4.

[11] Two words ("beadle", "lash") may echo *King Lear* IV vi 164–5. Some of C's detailed knowledge of Fo, whose name is Chinese for Buddha, may derive from George Staunton *An Authentic Account of an Embassy . . . to the Emperor of China* (1797), which described the extreme superstition of the common Chinese in their devotions to Fo (II 99–103). DeQ referred to Staunton's account of Fo in "The English Mail Coach" (1849): *DeQ Works* XIII 275–7. C had first referred to Fo in a lecture of 1795, drawing on Volney: *Lects 1795 (CC)* 183 and n. See also C's annotation on J.C.A. Heinroth *Lehrbuch der Anthropologie: CM (CC)* II 1022–3 and *EOT (CC)* II

344. For an eye-witness account of the Juggernaut, including the human sacrifices made to it, see Claudius Buchanan *Christian Researches in Asia* (Cambridge 1811) 17–35. In *Friend (CC)* I 99 C mentioned the "blood of thousands poured out under the wheels of Jaggernaut".

[12] C here returns to Leighton COPY C II 86, there directing the printer back to p 82, in which he substitutes "On the other hand" for Leighton's "But" and then (for 1825) follows the text exactly.

[13] Cf 1 Pet 3.15.

[1] From Leighton COPY C II 87–90: *CM (CC)* III. For Leighton's "It" C substitutes its antecedent "Truth" and at the beginning of the second paragraph omits a sentence: "Divine things are never to be spoken of in a light perfunctory way, but with a reverent, grave temper of spirit; and for

passion when set to serve it. The *Spirit of truth*[2] is withal the *Spirit of meekness*.[3] The Dove that rested on that great Champion of truth, who is The Truth itself,[4] is from Him derived to the lovers of truth, and they ought to seek the participation of it. Imprudence makes some kind of Christians lose much of their labor,[a] in speaking for religion, and drive those further off, whom they would draw into it.

The confidence that attends a Christian's belief makes the believer not fear men, to whom he answers, but still he fears his God, for whom he answers, and whose interest is chief in those things he speaks of. The soul that hath the deepest sense of spiritual things, [b]and the truest knowledge of God, is most afraid to miscarry in speaking of Him, most tender and wary how to acquit itself when engaged to speak of and for God.[*c]

---

* To the same purpose[5] are the two following sentences from Hilary:

Etiam quae *pro* Religione dicimus, cum grandi metu et disciplinâ dicere debemus.—Hilarius de Trinit. Lib. 7.[6]

Non relictus est hominum eloquiis de Dei rebus alius quam Dei sermo.—Idem.[7]

The latter, however, must be taken with certain *Qualifications* and *Exceptions*: as when any two or more Texts are in apparent contradiction, and it is required to state a Truth that comprehends and reconciles both, and which, of course, cannot be expressed in the words of either. Ex. gr. the filial subordination (*My Father is greater than I*[8]), in the equal Deity (*My Father and I are one*[9]).

---

[a] *AR* (1825): labour,
[b] *AR* (1825): p 118
[c] *AR* (1825): God*.

---

this reason, some choice is to be made both of time and persons." C's words "a Christian's belief" are substituted for Leighton's "this hope".

[2] John 14.17, 15.26, 16.13, 1 John 4.6.

[3] 1 Cor 4.21; Gal 6.1. Cf C's asseveration of 1 Mar 1796: "I trust . . . that I shall write what I believe to be the Truth in the spirit of meekness": *Watchman (CC)* 14; cf 194, 195n, 197–8.

[4] John 1.32. C had himself stressed Christ's meekness in his Bristol lectures: *Lects 1795 (CC)* 66, 162, 352, and in his 1796 *Religious Musings* lines 22–3: *Poems* ed Beer (1963) 65.

[5] The whole of this footnote comes from a marginal note by C in Leighton COPY C II 87–90: *CM (CC)* III.

[6] This and the next quotation appear in a notebook of 1807, in which they are in reverse order. There the next quotation is correctly assigned by C to *De Trinitate* 7; the present one is marked "Id.", but was not traced to Hilarius by the editor: *CN* II 3098 and n. A further search has failed to reveal its source: it was probably taken by C from a secondary work that he was reading in 1807. Tr "Even the things we say *on behalf of* Religion we ought to say with great reverence and respect."

[7] Hilarius *De Trinitate* 7.38; tr Stephen MacKenna *Saint Hilary of Poitiers: The Trinity* (Fathers of the Church; New York 1954) 266: "Human language has been left with no other choice than to express the things of God in the words of God."

[8] John 14.28.

[9] John 10.30 ("I and my Father are one").

APHORISM XLIII[a1]

ON THE CONSCIENCE

It is a fruitless verbal Debate, whether Conscience be a Faculty or a Habit. When all is examined, Conscience will be found to be no other than *the mind of a man, under the notion of a particular reference to himself* and his own actions.

COMMENT

What Conscience is, and that it is the ground and antecedent of human (or *self-*) consciousness, and not any modification of the latter, I have shown at large in a Work announced for the Press, and described in the Chapter following.[2] I have selected the preceding Extract as an Exercise for Reflection; and *because* I think [b]that in too closely following Thomas à[c] Kempis,[3] the Archbishop has strayed from his own judgment.[4] The Definition, for instance, seems to say all, and in fact says nothing; for if I asked, How do you define the *human mind?* the answer must at least *contain*, if not consist of, the words, "a mind capable of *Conscience.*" For Conscience is no synonime of Consciousness, nor any mere expression of the same as modified by the particular Object. On the contrary, a Consciousness properly human (*i.e. Self*-consciousness), with the sense of moral responsibility, presupposes the Conscience, as its antecedent Condition and Ground.[5] Lastly, the sentence, "It is a fruitless

[a] *AR* (1825): LEIGHTON.
[b] *AR* (1825): p 119
[c] *AR* (1825): a

[1] See Leighton COPY C II 93: *CM (CC)* III. Leighton's version of the first sentence is: "It is a fruitless verbal debate, whether Conscience be a faculty or habit, or not." C omits three sentences between this and the second.

[2] The "Assertion of Religion" (i.e. Opus Maximum)—introd to *Sp Aph B* below at n 3—rather than the "Elements of Discourse"—*Sp Aph B II* n 69, *VII* n 30 below—in which the conscience is not discussed at length. For discussion of conscience in the Opus Maximum see Barth 109–10 and L. Lockridge *Coleridge the Moralist* (Ithaca, NY 1977) 124–5.

[3] Leighton's point, that it is "better . . . to have this supernatural goodness of conscience, than to dispute about . . . it", is in

line with one of the sentences omitted by C, in which Thomas à Kempis is quoted: "Malo scire compunctionem quam scire ejus definitionem" (tr: "I would sooner feel the prick of conscience than know its definition"): *Imitation of Christ* 1.6.

[4] C here begins to follow his marginal note in Leighton COPY C II 93, which originally began: "This and the preceding §ph. in which L. follow[s] Thomas a Kempis, are scarcely worthy of his Candour: for the letter of this particular Definition . . .".

[5] In BM MS Egerton 2801 f 252 C refers to this ". . . aphorism on the equivocal meaning of the term, Consciousness" in explaining "the identity or co-inherence of Morality and Religion, as the Transcendent containing both *in* one and *as* one, that

verbal Debate,'' is an assertion of the same complexion with the contemptuous Sneers at Verbal Criticism by the contemporaries[a] of Bentley.[6] In questions[b] of Philosophy or Divinity, that have occupied the Learned and been the subjects of many successive Controversies, for one instance of mere Logomachy[7] I could bring ten instances of *Logodaedaly*,[8] or verbal Legerdemain, which have perilously confirmed Prejudices, and withstood the advancement of Truth, in consequence of the neglect of *verbal debate, i.e.* strict discussion of Terms. In whatever sense, however, the term Conscience may be used, the following Aphorism is equally true and important. It is worth noticing, likewise, that Leighton himself in a following page (vol. ii. p. 97), tells us, that A good Conscience is the *Root* of a good Conversation: and then quotes from St. Paul a text, Titus i. 15,[9] in which the Mind and the Conscience are expressly distinguished.[10]

[c]APHORISM XLIV[d]1

THE LIGHT OF KNOWLEDGE A NECESSARY ACCOMPANIMENT
OF A GOOD CONSCIENCE

If you would have a good conscience, you must by all means have so

[a] *AR* (1825): Contemporaries
[b] *AR* (1825): Questions
[c] *AR* (1825): p 120
[d] *AR* (1825): LEIGHTON.

which our elder Divines meant by the Seed of Election in the Soul, and which S[t] Paul calls the Root''. For further discussion of conscience as the finer form of consciousness, see Lockridge *Coleridge the Moralist* 120–30.

[6] In the age of Porson, the second of the great English ''verbal critics'', the force of C's allusion would be recognised by his readers. The attacks on Richard Bentley (1662–1742) and C's knowledge of them are discussed below in App I Excursus Note 3 '' 'Sneers at Verbal Criticism by the contemporaries of Bentley' ''.

[7] A contention about words. The first usage given in *OED* is dated 1569; it also cites C's ''disputatious word-catcher or logomachist'' in *LR* IV 272 as its first English example of that form. For the present point see C's note of c 1820 (*CN* IV 4767) and *Logic (CC)* 120–1 and 124; cf also C's annotation on Chillingworth *Works: CM (CC)* II 38 and *Friend (CC)* I 437.

[8] Cf the seventeenth-century word ''logodaedalus''; and see both words in *OED*. C distinguished ''logomachy'' from ''logodaedaly'' in 1820–1, *CN* IV 4767, and in the *Logic* turns to Pierre Bayle's work to show ''how easily a man of an acute, quick, and discursive intellect in his eagerness to detect logomachy falls himself into the more dangerous fault of logodaedalism . . .'': *Logic (CC)* 124 and n.

[9] Titus 1.15: ''Unto the pure all things are pure: but unto them that are defiled and unbelieving is nothing pure; but even their mind and conscience is defiled.''

[10] Leighton COPY C II 97: ''The *mind and conscience being defiled*, as the Apostle speaks, Tit i. 15, doth defile all the rest: it is a mire in the spring; although the pipes are cleansed, they will grow quickly foul again.''

[1] From Leighton COPY C II 94: *CM (CC)* III. C follows Leighton exactly.

much light, so much knowledge of the will of God, as may regulate you, and show you your way, may teach you how to do, and speak, and think[a] as in His presence.

APHORISM XLV[b][1]

YET THE KNOWLEDGE OF THE RULE, THOUGH ACCOMPANIED BY AN ENDEAVOR[c] TO ACCOMMODATE OUR CONDUCT TO THIS RULE, WILL NOT OF ITSELF FORM A GOOD CONSCIENCE

To set the outward actions right, though with an honest intention, and not so to regard and find out the inward disorder of the heart, whence that in the actions flows, is but to be still putting the index of a clock right with your finger, while it is foul, or out of order within, which is a continual business, and does no good. Oh! but a purified conscience, a soul renewed and refined in its temper and affections, will make things go right without, in all the duties and acts of our calling.[d]

APHORISM XLVI[e]

THE DEPTH OF THE CONSCIENCE

How deeply seated the conscience[f] is in the human Soul[g] is seen in the effect which sudden Calamities produce[h] on guilty men, even when unaided by any determinate notion or fears of punishment after death. The wretched Criminal, as one rudely awakened from a long sleep, bewildered with the new light, and half recollecting, half striving to recollect, a fearful something, he knows not what, but which he will recognize as soon as he hears the name, already interprets the calamities into *judgments*, Executions of a Sentence passed by an *invisible* Judge; as if the vast Pyre of the Last Judgment were already kindled in an unknown Distance, and some Flashes of it, darting forth at intervals beyond the rest, were flying and lighting upon the face of his Soul. The calamity may consist in loss of Fortune, or Character, or Reputation; but

[a] *AR* (1825): think,
[b] *AR* (1825): LEIGHTON.
[c] *AR* (1825): ENDEAVOUR
[d] *AR* (1825): callings.
[e] *AR* (1825): EDITOR.
[f] *AR* (1825): Conscience
[g] *AR* (1825): Soul,
[h] *AR* (1825): p 121 (duce)

[1] From Leighton COPY C II 97: *CM (CC)* III. C follows Leighton exactly.

you hear no *regrets* from him. Remorse extinguishes all Regret; and Remorse is the *implicit* Creed of the Guilty.[1]

APHORISM XLVII[a1]

God hath suited every creature He hath made with a convenient good to which it tends, and in the obtainment of which it rests and is satisfied. Natural bodies have all their own natural place, whither, if not hindered, they move incessantly till they be in it; and they declare, by resting there, that they are (as I may say) where they would be. Sensitive creatures are carried to seek a sensitive good, as agreeable to their rank in being, and, attaining that, aim no further. Now, in this is the excellency of Man, that he is made capable of a communion with his Maker, and, because capable of it, is unsatisfied without it: the soul, being [b]cut out (so to speak) to that largeness, cannot be filled with less. Though he is fallen from his right to that good, and from all right desire of it, yet, not from a capacity of it, no, nor from a necessity of it, for the answering and filling of his capacity.

Though the heart once gone from God turns continually further away from Him, and moves not towards Him till it be renewed, yet, even in that wandering, it retains that natural relation to God, as its centre, that it hath no true rest elsewhere, nor can by any means find it. It is made for Him, and is therefore still restless till it meet with Him.[2]

It is true, the natural man takes much pains to quiet his heart by other things, and digests many vexations with hopes of contentment in the end and accomplishment of some design he hath; but still the heart misgives. Many times he attains not the thing he seeks; but if he do, yet he never attains the satisfaction he seeks and expects in it, but only learns from that to desire something further, and still hunts on after a fancy, drives his own shadow before him, and never overtakes it; and if he did, yet it is but a shadow. And so, in running from God, besides the sad end, he carries an interwoven punishment with his sin, the natural disquiet and

---

[a] *AR* (1825): L. & ED.

[b] *AR* (1825): p 122

[1] A theme of C's early drama *Osorio*, later retitled *Remorse*. For C on Unitarian attitudes to remorse, and a reply to him in 1817 in the *Monthly Repository*, see *LS (CC)* 182, 255, and, for the important distinction between regret and remorse (including their relation to free will), a lecture of 1808, *Lects 1808–1819 (CC)* I 63–4 and

P Lects Lect 12 (1949) 364. *CN* IV 4846 is highly relevant.

[1] For the first four paragraphs see Leighton COPY C II 116–18: *CM (CC)* III. C omits one paragraph between his own third and fourth and alters the punctuation slightly.

[2] Cf St Augustine *Confessions* 1.1 and see Barth 188–9.

vexation of his spirit, fluttering to and fro, and *finding no rest for the sole of his foot;* the *waters* of inconstancy and vanity *covering the whole face of the earth.*[3]

These things are too gross and heavy. The soul, the immortal soul, descended from heaven, must either [a]be more happy, or remain miserable. The Highest, the Increated Spirit, is the proper good, *the Father of spirits,*[4] that pure and full good which raises the soul above itself; whereas all other things draw it down below itself. So, then, it is never well with the soul, but when it is near unto God, yea, in its union with Him, married to Him: mismatching itself elsewhere, it hath never any thing but shame and sorrow. *All that forsake Thee shall be ashamed,* says the Prophet, Jer. xvii. 13; and the Psalmist, *They that are far off from thee shall perish.* Psalm[b] lxxiii. 27. And this is indeed our natural miserable condition, and it is often expressed this way, by estrangedness and distance from God.

The same sentiments are to be found in the works of Pagan Philosophers and Moralists. Well then may they be made a Subject of Reflection in our days. And well may the pious Deist, if such a character now exists, reflect that Christianity alone both teaches the way, and provides the means, of fulfilling the obscure promises of this great Instinct for all men, which the Philosophy of boldest Pretensions confined to the sacred Few.

APHORISM XLVIII[c1]

A CONTRACTED SPHERE, OR WHAT IS CALLED RETIRING FROM THE BUSINESS
OF THE WORLD, NO SECURITY FROM THE SPIRIT OF THE WORLD

The heart may be engaged in a little business,[d] as much, if thou watch it not, as in many and great affairs. [e]A man may drown in a little brook or pool, as well as in a great river, if he be down and plunge himself into it, and put his head under water. Some care thou must have, that thou mayest not care. Those things that are thorns indeed, thou must make a hedge of them, to keep out those temptations that accompany sloth, and

---

[a] *AR* (1825): p 123
[b] *AR* (1825): Psal.
[c] *AR* (1825): LEIGHTON.
[d] *AR* (1825): business
[e] *AR* (1825): p 124

[3] Gen 8.9.
[4] Heb 12.9.
[1] See Leighton COPY C II 199: *CM (CC)*

III. Leighton's text begins: "Thy heart may be engaged in thy little business . . .".

extreme want that waits on it; but let them be the hedge: suffer them not to grow within the garden.

APHORISM XLIX[a][1]

ON CHURCH-GOING, AS A PART OF RELIGIOUS MORALITY, WHEN
NOT IN REFERENCE TO A SPIRITUAL RELIGION

It is a strange folly in multitudes of us, to set ourselves no mark, to propound no end in the hearing of the Gospel. The merchant sails not merely that he may sail, but for traffic, and traffics that he may be rich. The husbandman plows not merely to keep himself busy, with no further end, but plows that he may sow, and sows that he may reap with advantage. And shall we do the most excellent and fruitful work fruitlessly,— hear only to hear, and look no further? This is indeed a great vanity, and a great misery, to lose that labour, and gain nothing by it, which, duly used, would be of all others most advantageous and gainful: and yet all meetings are full of this.[b]

[c]APHORISM L[d][1]

ON THE HOPES AND SELF-SATISFACTION OF A RELIGIOUS MORALIST, INDEPENDENT
OF A SPIRITUAL FAITH—ON WHAT ARE THEY GROUNDED?

There have been great disputes one way or another, about the merit of good works; but I truly think they who have laboriously engaged in them have been very idly, though very eagerly, employed about nothing, since the more sober of the schoolmen themselves acknowledge there can be no such thing as meriting from the blessed God, in the human, or, to speak more accurately, in any created nature whatsoever: nay,[e] so far from any possibility of merit, there can be no room for reward any otherwise than of the sovereign pleasure and gracious kindness of God; and the more ancient writers, when they use the word merit, mean noth-

---

[a] *AR* (1825): LEIGHTON.

[b] *AR* (1825): this!

[c] *AR* (1825): p 125

[d] *AR* (1825): LEIGHTON.

[e] *AR* (1825): nay

[1] See Leighton COPY C II 211–12: *CM (CC)* III. Apart from adding the dash after "fruitlessly", C follows Leighton's text exactly.

[1] See "Meditations on Psalm CXXX", Leighton COPY C II 440–1: *CM (CC)* III. C follows Leighton exactly.

ing by it but a certain *correlate* to that reward which God both promises and bestows of mere grace and benignity. Otherwise, in order to constitute what is properly called merit, many things must concur, which no man in his senses will presume to attribute to human works, though ever so excellent; particularly, that the thing done must not previously be matter of debt, and that it be entire, or our own act, unassisted by foreign aid; it must also be perfectly good, and it must bear an adequate proportion to the reward claimed in consequence of it. If all these things do not concur, the act cannot possibly amount to merit. Whereas I think *a*no one will venture to assert, that any one of these can take place in any human action whatever. But why should I enlarge here, when one single circumstance overthrows all those titles: the most righteous of mankind would not be able to stand, if his works were weighed in the balance of strict justice; how much less then could they deserve that immense glory which is now in question! Nor is this to be denied only concerning the unbeliever and the sinner, but concerning the righteous and pious believer, who is not only free from all the guilt of his former impenitence and rebellion, but endowed with the gift of the Spirit. "For the time *is come* that judgment must begin at the house of God: and if *it* first *begin* at us, what shall the end *be* of them that obey not the Gospel of God? And if the righteous scarcely be saved, where shall the ungodly and the sinner appear?" 1 Peter,*b* iv. 17, 18. The Apostle's interrogation expresses the most vehement negation, and signifies that no mortal, in whatever degree he is placed, if he be called to the strict examination of Divine Justice, without daily and repeated forgiveness,*c* could be able to keep his standing, and much less could he arise to that glorious height. "That merit," says Bernard, "on which my hope relies, consists in these three things; the love of adoption, the truth of the promise, and the power of its performance."[2] This is the threefold cord which cannot be broken.[3]

---

a *AR* (1825): p 126
b *AR* (1825): Peter
c *AR* (1825): forgiveness

[2] Leighton's editor gives his Latin in a footnote: "Meritum, cui innititur spes mea tribus hisce consistit, charitate adoptionis, veritate promissionis, et potestate redditionis." This seems to be a conflation from St Bernard of Clairvaux *Pro Dominica VI post Pentecosten sermo* 3.6 and his *Ma-nuale* (wrongly attributed to St Augustine) 23.1: Migne *PL* CLXXXIII 344 and XL 961.

[3] Leighton is again quoting St Bernard's sermon (see note 2): "Hic est funiculus triplex qui difficile rumpitur." See Eccles 4.12 for the biblical original.

COMMENT

Often have I heard it said by advocates for the Socinian[a] Scheme[4]—
True! we are all sinners; but even in the Old Testament God has promised Forgiveness on Repentance. One of the Fathers (I forget which)[5]
supplies the Retort—True! God has promised pardon[b] on Penitence: but
has he promised Penitence on Sin?—He that repenteth shall be forgiven:
but where is it said, He that sinneth shall repent? But Repentance, perhaps, the Repentance required in Scripture, *the Passing into a new mind*,
into a new and contrary Principle of Action, this METANOIA,[*c6] is in the
Sinner's own power? at his own liking?[d] He has but to open his eyes to
the sin, and the Tears are close at hand to wash it away!—Verily, the
exploded tenet[e] of *Transubstantiation* is scarcely at greater variance with
the common Sense and Experience of Mankind, or borders more closely
on a contradiction in terms, than this volunteer *Transmentation*,[7] this
Self-change, as the easy† means of Self-salvation! But the reflections[f]
of our evangelical Author on this subject will appropriately commence
the Aphorisms relating to Spiritual Religion.

* Μετάνοια,[g] the New Testament word, which we render by Repentance, compounded
of μετά,[h] *trans*, and νοῦς,[i] *mens*, the Spirit, or practical Reason.

† May I without offence be permitted to record the very appropriate title, with which
a stern Humorist *lettered* a collection of Unitarian Tracts?—"Salvation made easy; or,
Every Man his own Redeemer."[8]

> [a] *AR* (1825): p 127 (cinian)
> [b] *AR* (1825): Pardon
> [c] *AR* (1825): METANOIA*,
> [d] *AR* (1825): Liking?
> [e] *AR* (1825): Tenet
> [f] *AR* (1825): Reflections
> [g] *AR* (1825): Μετανοια ; *AR* (1831): Μετανοιὰ,
> [h] *AR* (1825): μετα ; *AR* (1831): μετὰ,
> [i] *AR* (1825): νους,

[4] I.e. Unitarianism: cf below, *Sp Aph B
VIII* nn 8, 11, 13, 18 and refs there. Its doc-
trines were traced back to those of Socinus
(Fausto Paolo Sozzini, 1539–1604): see
Enc RE s.v. "Socinianism".

[5] Untraced.

[6] The word appears also in a note on
Leighton COPY C II 152–5: *CM (CC)* III as
well as in e.g. *CN* IV 4824, 5270, *CM (CC)*
III 477 and annotations on Jeremy Taylor:
NED I 278, 298: *CM (CC)* v.

[7] A change of the mind, or mental conversion. See *CN* IV 4824, where it is related
to the metamorphosis of the butterfly, and
5270 f 6. *OED*'s first example of this Latin-
based equivalent of the Greek μετάνοια is
dated 1647.

[8] The second part of this joking title
might well have been someone's satire on
the Unitarian John Jebb's *Every Man His
Own Priest: a Series of Papers: Works*
(1787) III 159–258. For Jebb see above,
Mor Aph VI n 32.

^aELEMENTS

OF

RELIGIOUS PHILOSOPHY,

PRELIMINARY TO THE

APHORISMS ON SPIRITUAL RELIGION

---

^a *AR* (1825): p 129 (128 blank)

*a*PHILIP saith unto him: Lord *show* us the Father, and it sufficeth us. Jesus saith unto him, He that hath seen me hath seen the Father: and how sayest thou then, *Show* us the Father? Believest thou not, that I am in the Father and the Father in me? And I will pray the Father and he shall give you another Comforter, even the *Spirit* of Truth: whom the world *cannot* receive, because it seeth him not, neither knoweth him. But ye know him (for he dwelleth *with* you and *shall* be *in* you). And in that day ye shall know that I am in my Father, and ye in me,*b* and I in you. John xiv. 8, 9, 10, 16, 17, 20.[1]

a *AR* (1825): p 130
b *AR* (1825): me

[1] Extracts, selected from the verses mentioned, are almost exactly faithful to the AV text. The italicising does not follow AV.

^aPRELIMINARY

═══

IF there be aught *Spiritual* in Man, the Will must be such.
If there be a Will, there must be a Spirituality in Man.
I suppose both positions granted. The Reader admits the reality of the power, agency, or mode of Being expressed in the term, Spirit; and the actual existence of a Will. He sees clearly, that the idea of the former is necessary to the conceivability of the latter; and that, vice versâ, in asserting the *fact* of the latter he presumes and instances the truth of the former—just as in our common and received Systems of Natural Philosophy, the Being of imponderable Matter is assumed to render the Lodestone intelligible, and the Fact of the Lode-stone adduced to prove the reality of imponderable Matter.[1]

In short, I suppose the Reader, whom I now invite to the third and last Division of the work, already disposed to reject for himself and his human Brethren the insidious title of "Nature's noblest *Animal*,"[2] or ^bto retort it as the unconscious Irony of the Epicurean Poet on the animalizing tendency of his own philosophy. I suppose him convinced, that there is more in man than can be rationally referred to the life of Nature

---

^a *AR* (1825): p 131   ^b *AR* (1825): p 132

[1] The theory of imponderable matter was one of the versions of Newtonianism deriving from the 31st query to the *Opticks*. For the relationship between imponderable matter and magnetism in the eighteenth century see R. Fox *The Caloric Theory of Gases from Lavoisier to Regnault* (Oxford 1971) 15–19. C probably discussed such questions with Davy, whose first paper, "Essay on Heat, Light, and the Combinations of Light, with a New Theory of Respiration" (1799), dealt with some of them. For C's own views see also T. H. Levere *Poetry Realized in Nature* (Cambridge 1981) 146ff. C here contends for the spiritual validity of a line of reasoning not unlike that ridiculed by Hobbes at the physical level: ". . . The Schools will tell you out of Aristotle, that the bodies that sink downwards, are *Heavy*; and that this Heaviness is it that causes them to descend: But if you ask what they mean by *Heavinesse*, they will define it to bee an endeavour to goe to the center of the Earth . . .": *Leviathan* pt 4 ch 46 (1651) 374–5.

[2] Cf Sir Thomas Browne *Hydriotaphia, Urne-Buriall* in *Works* (1659) II 46, "man is a noble animal . . .", quoted *CN* III 4373. C's annotated copy (unmarked at this point) is in NYPL: see *CM (CC)* I 760–99.

135

and the mechanism of Organization; that he has a will*a* not included in this mechanism; and that the Will is in *b*an especial and pre-eminent sense*c* the spiritual part of our Humanity.

Unless then we have some distinct notion of the Will, and some acquaintance with the prevalent errors respecting the same, an insight into the nature of Spiritual Religion is scarcely possible; and our reflections on the particular truths and evidences of a Spiritual State will remain obscure, perplexed, and unsafe. To place my Reader on this requisite Vantage-ground, is the purpose of the following Exposition.

We have begun, as in geometry, with defining our Terms; and we proceed, like the Geometricians, with stating our POSTULATES;[3] the difference being, that the Postulates of Geometry *no* man *can* deny, those of Moral Science are such as no *good* man *will* deny. For it is *not* in our power to disclaim our Nature, as *sentient* Beings; but it *is* in our power to disclaim our Nature*d* as *Moral* Beings.*e* It is possible (barely possible, I admit) that a man may have remained ignorant or unconscious of the Moral Law within him: and a man need only persist in disobeying the Law of Conscience to *make* it possible for himself to deny its existence, or to reject and repel it as a phantom of Superstition. Were it otherwise, the Creed would stand *f*in the same relation to Morality as the Multiplication Table.

This then is the distinction of Moral Philosophy—*not* that I begin with one or more *Assumptions:* for this is common to *all* science; but—that I assume a something, the proof of which no man can *give* to another, yet every man may *find* for himself. If any man assert, that he *can* not find it, I am *bound* to disbelieve him! I cannot do otherwise without unsettling the very foundations of my own moral Nature. For I either find it as an *essential* of the Humanity *common* to Him and Me: or I have not *found* it at all, except as an Hypochondriast finds *Glass* Legs.[4] If, on the

a AR (1825): Will
b-c COPY C: a pre-eminent and especial sense [with figs 1–4 over the words to indicate the order]
d AR (1825) Corr, COPY C: Prerogative
e AR (1831): Beings,
f AR (1825): p 133

[3] A key term for C: see *BL* ch 12 *(CC)* I 247–50, and cf *Friend (CC)* II (Jan 1810) 279, *CN* III 3802 (May 1810): "All reasoning commences with a *Postulate*, i.e. an *act*", and *Friend (CC)* I (1818) 115. Cf also below, *Sp Aph B Xb* at n 69. Given the strong relationship between geometry and astronomy at this time, it is legitimate to infer a connexion between the postulates here and Kant's two great objects of reverence: "Der bestirnte Himmel über mir und das moralische Gesetz in mir" [tr, after T. K. Abbott 1879, "the starry heavens above me and the moral law within me"]: *Critik der praktischen Vernunft* (Riga 1788) 288.

[4] This example is also used in *The Friend*, the editor noting a probable source

other hand, he *will* not find it, he excommunicates himself. He forfeits his *personal* Rights, and becomes a *Thing: i.e.* one who may rightfully be *employed*, or *used* as a* means to an end, against his will, and without regard to his *ª*interest. All*b* the significant objections of the Materialist and Necessitarian are contained in the term,*c* Morality, all the Objections of the Infidel in the term,*d* Religion! *e*The very terms, I say, imply a something *granted*, which the Objection supposes *not* granted. The term *presumes f* what the objection*g* denies, and in denying *presumesh* the contrary. For it is most important to observe, that the Reasoners on *both* sides commence by taking something for granted, our Assent to which they ask or demand: i.e. both set off with an Assumption in the form of a Postulate. But the Epicurean assumes what according to himself he neither is nor can be under any *obligation* to assume, and demands what he *can* have no *right* to demand: for *he* denies the reality of *all* moral Obligation, the existence of *any* Right. If he use the *words*, Right and Obligation, he does it deceptively, and means only Compulsion and Power.[6] To overthrow the Faith in aught higher or other

---

* On this principle alone is it possible to justify *capital*, or *ignominious* Punishments (or indeed any punishment not having the reformation of the Criminal, as *one* of its objects). Such Punishments, like those inflicted on Suicides, must be regarded as *posthumous:* the wilful extinction of the moral and personal life*i* being, for the purposes of punitive Justice, equivalent to a wilful destruction of the natural Life. If the speech of Judge Burnet[5] to the Horse-stealer (You are not hanged for stealing a Horse; but, that Horses may not be stolen) can be vindicated at all, it must be on *this* principle; and not on the all-unsettling scheme of *Expedience*, which is the anarchy of Morals.

a–b AR (1825): interest. §All

c COPY A: *term,*

d COPY A: *term,*

e AR (1825): p 134

f AR (1825): *pre*sumes

g AR (1825): Objection

h AR (1825): *pre*sumes

i AR (1825): Life

---

in John Webster *The Displaying of Supposed Witchcraft* (1677) 34: ". . . a famous Poet at Amsterdam did believe that his Buttocks were of glass . . .": *Friend (CC)* ɪ 321 and n 4. C's annotated copy is in the BM. The phenomenon is mentioned also in *CN* ɪɪɪ 3886 (the editor noting a closer possible source in the *Cabinet; or Monthly Report of Polite Literature* for Nov 1807—ɪɪ 216—citing Van Swieten's *Commentaries on Boerhaave*); in *Omniana* 174; and in BM MS Egerton 2801 f 60ᵛ. Cf also the "straw legs of the Hypochondrist": *CN* ɪɪɪ 3605.

[5] Judge Burnet is Thomas Burnet (1694–1753). In *The Friend*, however, C quotes this simply as an "old adage", *Friend (CC)* ɪ 79 (ɪɪ 60), the editor citing George Savile, Marquis of Halifax "Of Punishment": *A Character of King Charles the Second: and Political . . . Thoughts and Reflections* (1750) 114: "Men are not hang'd for stealing Horses, but that Horses may not be stolen." The whole passage in *The Friend* is relevant to the discussion here.

[6] C has Hobbes chiefly in mind: see above, *Refl Mor* n 13.

than Nature and physical Necessity, is the very purpose of his argument. He desires you only to *take for granted*, that *all* reality is *in*cluded in Nature, and he may then safely defy you to ward off his conclusion—that *nothing* is *ex*cluded!

But as he cannot morally demand, neither can he rationally expect, your Assent to this premiss:[a] for he cannot be ignorant, that the best and greatest of Men have devoted their lives to the enforcement of the contrary,[b] that the vast majority of the [c]Human race[d] in all ages and in all nations have believed in the contrary; and that there is not a Language on Earth, in which he could argue, for ten minutes, in support of his scheme,[e] without sliding into words and phrases, that imply the contrary. It has been said, that the Arabic [f]has a thousand names for a Lion;[7] but this would be a trifle compared with the number of superfluous words and useless Synonimes that would be found in an Index Expurgatorius[8] of any European Dictionary[g] constructed on the principles of a consistent and strictly consequential Materialism!

The *Christian* likewise grounds *his* philosophy on assertions; but with the best of all *reasons* for making them—viz. that he *ought* so to do. He asserts what he can neither prove, nor account for, nor himself comprehend; but with the strongest of *inducements*, that of understanding thereby whatever else it most concerns him to understand aright.[9] And yet his Assertions have nothing in them of Theory or Hypothesis; but are in immediate reference to three ultimate *Facts;* namely, the Reality of the LAW OF CONSCIENCE; the existence of a RESPONSIBLE WILL, as the subject of that law; and lastly, the existence of EVIL[10]—of Evil essentially such, not by accident of outward circumstances, not derived from

---

[a] *AR* (1825): premise:
[b] *AR* (1825): contrary;
[c-d] *AR* (1825): human Race
[e] *AR* (1825): scheme
[f] *AR* (1825): p 135
[g] COPY C: Dictionary, that should be

---

[7] C is perhaps here misremembering a passage from J. G. Herder *Über den Ursprung der Sprache* (1772): ". . . among the fifty words which the Arabs have for the lion, among the two hundred which they have for the snake, or the eighty for honey and the more than a thousand which they have for the sword . . ." (tr A. Gode—New York, 1966—153).

[8] The Index Expurgatorius, established after the Council of Trent (1545–63), listed passages to be expunged from works oth-

erwise permitted.

[9] C is here developing his earlier insight that religion "must have a moral origin" and his subsequent deductions; see *BL* ch 10 *(CC)* I 202–3. For further discussion of the relationship between conscience and reason see the opening paragraph to *Sp Aph B VIIIb* and n 4, below, and Barth 25–31, 120–1 and nn.

[10] For this list, with "Free-agency" replacing "the LAW OF CONSCIENCE", see *Friend (CC)* II 279.

its physical consequences, nor*a* from any cause, out of itself. The first is a Fact of Consciousness; the second a Fact of Reason necessarily concluded from the first; and the third a Fact of History interpreted by both.[11]

Omnia exeunt in mysterium, says a Schoolman:[12] *i.e. There is nothing, the absolute ground of which is not a Mystery.* The contrary were indeed a contradiction in terms: for how can that, which is to explain all things, be susceptible of an explanation? It would be to suppose the same thing first and second at the same time.

If I rested here, I should merely have placed my *b*Creed in direct opposition to that of the Necessitarians, who assume (for observe *both* Parties begin in an *Assumption*, and cannot do otherwise) that motives act on the Will, as bodies act on bodies; and that whether mind and matter are essentially the same or essentially different, they are both alike under one and the same law of compulsory Causation. But this is far from exhausting my intention. I mean at the same time to oppose the Disciples of SHAFTESBURY[13] and those who, substituting one Faith for another, have been well called the pious Deists of the last Century,[14] in order to distinguish them from the Infidels of the present age, who *persuade* themselves, (for the thing itself is not possible) that they reject all Faith. I declare my dissent from these too, because they imposed upon themselves an *Idea* for a Reality: a most sublime Idea indeed, and so necessary to human Nature, that without it no Virtue is conceivable; but still an Idea! In contradiction to their splendid but delusory Tenets, I profess a deep conviction that Man was and is a *fallen* Creature,[15] not by accidents of bodily constitution, or any other cause, which *human* Wisdom in a course of ages might be supposed capable of removing; but diseased

---

a *AR* (1825): or
b *AR* (1825): p 136

[11] From this point, and for the next four paragraphs, C reproduces a long passage from *The Friend* (1810) that had not been incorporated into the 1818 *rifacimento*: *Friend (CC)* II 279–81. Variants consist largely of past tenses changed into present, from "is far" onwards.

[12] "All things go out into mystery". This Latin phrase appears also in *The Friend (CC)* II 279, C continuing with his *id est*, as here. A source is not traced.

[13] Anthony Ashley Cooper, 3rd Earl of Shaftesbury (1671–1713).

[14] E.g. Anthony Collins (1676–1729),

Thomas Woolston (1670–1733), Thomas Chubb (1679–1747), John Toland (1670–1722), and Matthew Tindal (c 1653–1733). For Collins see *Friend (CC)* I 426.

[15] For an early version of this belief see his letter to George Coleridge 10 Mar 1798: *CL* I 397. C was praised by E. B. Pusey for having given on the present page (136) of *AR* (1825) "seasonable advice to those, who think that in the reception of Christianity the intellect alone is concerned": *Historical Enquiry into the . . . Theology of Germany* (2 vols 1828–30) I 53n.

in his *Will*, in that Will which is the true and only strict synonime of the word, I, or the intelligent Self. Thus at each of these two opposite Roads (the Philosophy of Hobbes and that of Shaftesbury), I have placed a directing Post, informing my Fellow-travellers, that on neither of these Roads can they see the Truths to which I would direct their attention.

But the place of starting was at the meeting of *four* *ª*Roads, and one only was the right road. I *ᵇ*proceed, therefore,*ᶜ* to preclude the opinion of those likewise, who indeed agree with me as to the moral Responsibility of Man in opposition to Hobbes and the Anti-Moralists, and that He was[16] a fallen Creature, essentially diseased, in opposition to Shaftesbury and the Misinterpreters of Plato; but who differ from me in exaggerating the diseased *weakness* of the Will into an absolute privation of all Freedom, thereby making moral responsibility, not a mystery *above* comprehension, but a direct contradiction, of which we do distinctly comprehend the absurdity. Among the consequences of this Doctrine, is that direful one of swallowing up all the attributes*ᵈ* of the supreme Being in the one Attribute of infinite Power, and thence deducing that Things are good and wise because they were created, and not created through Wisdom and Goodness. Thence too the awful Attribute of *Justice* is explained away into a mere right of absolute *Property;* the sacred distinction between Things and Persons is erased; and the selection of Persons for Virtue and Vice in this Life, and for eternal Happiness or Misery in the next, is represented as the result of a mere *Will*, acting in the blindness and solitude of its own Infinity.[17] The Title of a Work written by the great and pious Boyle is "Of the Awe, which the human Mind owes to the supreme Reason."[18] This, in the language of these gloomy Doctors, must be translated into—"the horror, which a Being capable of eternal Pleasure or Pain is compelled to feel at the idea of an infinite

---

ª *AR* (1825): p 137
ᵇ⁻ᶜ *AR* (1825): proceed therefore
ᵈ *AR* (1825): Attributes

[16] Retention of *The Friend*'s past tense (cf n 11 above) may be an oversight.

[17] At some date before 30 Jan 1826 (see *CL* vi 549) C sent to EC a copy of Philip Skelton *The Complete Works* (6 vols 1824), now in the BM. This contains (on pp ⁻4 to ⁻3, referring to iv 249) an annotation on ". . . those who dare misappropriate Calvin's words, that 'God's absolute *Will* is the only rule of his justice;'—thus dividing the divine attributes. (See Aids to Reflection p. 137.) Yet Calvin himself distinguishes the hidden from the revealed God, even as the Greek Fathers distinguished the θελημα Θεου, the absolute *Ground* of all Being, from the βουλης της του Θεου, as the Cause and disposing Providence of all Existence.—": *CM (CC)*. For the latter distinction see below, *Sp Aph B Xa* n 37, *XIX* n 82; for that between things and persons, above, *Mor Aph VI* n 11.

[18] Robert Boyle *Of the High Veneration Man's Intellect Owes to God; Peculiarly for His Wisedom and Power* (1685).

Power, *a*about to inflict the latter on an immense majority of human Souls, without any power on their part either to prevent it or the actions which are (not indeed its causes but) its assigned *signals*, and preceding links of the same iron chain!"*b*19

Against these Tenets I maintain, that a Will conceived separately*c* from Intelligence is a Non-entity, and a mere Phantasm of Abstraction;20 and that a Will, the state of which does in *no sense* originate in its own act, is an absolute contradiction. It might be an Instinct, an Impulse, a plastic Power, and, if accompanied with consciousness, a Desire; but a Will it *could* not be! And this *every* Human Being *knows* with equal *clearness*, though different minds may *reflect* on it with different degrees of *distinctness;* for who would not smile at the notion of a Rose *willing* to put forth its Buds and expand them into Flowers? That such a phrase would be deemed a *poetic* Licence proves the difference in the things: for all metaphors are grounded on an apparent likeness of things essentially different.21 I utterly disclaim the idea, that any *human* Intelligence, with whatever power it might manifest itself, is *alone* adequate to the office of restoring health to the Will: but at the same time I deem it impious and absurd to hold, that the Creator would have *given* us the faculty of Reason, or that the Redeemer would in so many varied forms of Argument and Persuasion have *appealed* to it, if it had been either totally useless or wholly impotent. Lastly, I find all these several Truths reconciled and united in the belief, that the *d*imperfect human understanding can be effectually exerted only in *subordination* to, and in a dependent *alliance* with, the means and aidances supplied by the all-perfect and supreme Reason; but that under these conditions it is not only an admissible, but a necessary, instrument of ameliorating both ourselves and others.

---

a *AR* (1825): p 138   *b* *AR* (1825): chain!
c *AR* (1825): separate   *d* *AR* (1825): p 139

19 For the chain image see above, *Refl Mor* n 14.

20 Cf *C&S (CC)* 123: "Now the spirit of a man, or the spiritual part of our being, is the intelligent Will . . .".

21 Cf C's assertion "It cannot . . . be denied that in all *likeness* a *difference* is involved", followed by discussion, *Logic (CC)* 11, and his aside on "the necessary inadequacy of every metaphor (*simile non est idem*, or as we say, no likeness goes on all fours) . . .": ibid 132. For the latter saying see *CN* iv 5097 f 9, *C&S (CC)* 86,

and Abraham Tucker *The Light of Nature Pursued* (3 vols in 9 1768) i 1.61 (C's copy is in VCL); also, in the form "no simile quadrates" or "squares", *Logic (CC)* 143, *CM (CC)* ii 552, 17. C normally discussed metaphor in relation to allegory: see e.g. *SM (CC)* 30, *LS (CC)* 133n, and *Lects 1808–1819 (CC)* ii 99–101, *CN* iv 4832; and cf Webster *Displaying of Supposed Witchcraft* (1677) 140–2, a volume annotated by C: see *Sp Aph B Xa* n 33 below. A long sentence intervenes at this point in the 1809 *Friend: Friend (CC)* ii 280–1.

We may now proceed to our reflections on the *Spirit* of Religion. The first three or four Aphorisms I have selected from the Theological Works of Dr. Henry More, a contemporary of Archbishop Leighton's, and like him, holden[a] in suspicion by the Calvinists of that time as a Latitudinarian and Platonizing Divine, and who[b] probably, like him, would have been arraigned as a Calvinist by the Latitudinarians (I cannot say, Platonists) of this Day, had the suspicion been equally groundless. One or two the Editor has ventured to add from his own Reflections. The purpose, however, is the same in all—that of declaring, in the first place, what Spiritual Religion is *not*, what is *not* a Religious Spirit, and what are *not* to be deemed influences of the Spirit. If after these Disclaimers the Editor shall without proof be charged by any with renewing or favoring[c] the errors of the *Familists*,[22] *Vanists*,[23] *Seekers*,[24] *Behmenists*,[25] or by whatever other names Church History records the poor bewildered Enthusiasts, who in the swarming[26] time of our Republic turned the facts of the Gospel into allegories, and superseded the written Ordinances of Christ by a pretended Teaching and sensible[d] Presence of the Spirit, he appeals against them to their own consciences, as wilful Slanderers. But if with proof, I have in these Aphorisms signed and sealed my own Condemnation.

"These things I could not forbear to write. For *the Light within me*, that is, *my Reason* and *Conscience*, does assure me, that the Ancient and

------

[a] *AR* (1825): held   [b] Added in 1831
[c] *AR* (1825): favouring   [d] *AR* (1825): p 140 (ble)

[22] See above, *Int Aph XXIII* n 8.
[23] Disciples of Sir Henry Vane the younger (1613–62), who was in turn a follower of Anne Hutchinson and Böhme. See Edward Hyde, 1st Earl of Clarendon *History of the Rebellion and Civil Wars in England* bk XVI (3 vols 1705) III 924 and n 25, below.
[24] Members of a seventeenth-century English movement with roots in Reformation Germany who thought that the visible Church was devoid of real authority and spiritual power and that the true Church must therefore be sought elsewhere. They were assimilated by the early Quakers. See Gilbert Burnet *History of His Own Time* (1724) I 164 and next note.

[25] A minor mystical group led by John Pordage (1607–81), Jane Leade (1623–1704), and Francis Lee (b 1661). Its fortunes culminated in the formation of the Philadelphia Society. Rufus M. Jones, in *Enc RE* IX 102b, describes them as "visionary, confused and lacking some of Boehme's best characteristics". See also C's notes on Behmenism in Baxter *Reliquiae Baxterianae* (1696): *CM (CC)* I 296–7. Baxter, I 75–9, referred to and described five sects: 1. The *Vanists*; 2. The *Seekers*; 3. The *Ranters*; 4. The *Quakers*; 5. The *Behmenists*.
[26] Cf the German *Schwärmen*: see below, *Conc* at n 22.

Apostolic Faith according to the *historical* Meaning thereof, and in the *literal* sense of the Creed, is solid and true: and that *Familism* in its fairest form and under whatever disguise, is a smooth Tale to seduce the simple from their Allegiance to Christ.''

HENRY MORE's Theological Works, p. 372[27]

<hr />

[27] Adapted from Henry More *An Explanation of the Grand Mystery of Godliness*, in *Theological Works* (1708) 372. C adds the words ''. . . and in the *literal* sense of the Creed'' while omitting others, such as More's description of Familism as ''. . . a mere Flam of the Devil''. For More's full text see App A(c), below.

^aAPHORISMS

ON

SPIRITUAL RELIGION

^a *AR* (1825): p 141

*a*And here[1] it will not be impertinent to observe, that what the eldest Greek Philosophy entitled *the Reason* (ΝΟΥΣ)[2] and *Ideas*, the philosophic Apostle names *the Spirit* and *Truths spiritually* discerned:[3] while to those who in the pride of Learning or in the over-weening meanness of modern Metaphysics decry the doctrine of the Spirit in Man and its possible communion with the Holy Spirit,[4] as *vulgar* enthusiasm; I submit the following Sentences from a Pagan Philosopher, a Nobleman and a Minister of State—"Ita dico, Lucilî! SACER INTRA NOS SPIRITUS SEDET, malorum bonorumque nostrorum observator et custos. Hic prout a nobis tractatus est, ita nos ipse tractat. BONUS VIR SINE DEO NEMO EST." SENECA.[5]

a *AR* (1825): p 142

[1] The whole of this passage is taken, with a few alterations, from the conclusion to an entry in N 30 of Dec 1823 on the nature of reason: *CN* IV 5089 ff 48ᵛ–49. C wrote it while composing *AR*, but probably saw the entry in its entirety as belonging rather to the "Assertion of Religion": see below, introd to *Sp Aph B* n 3.

[2] To C the eldest Greek philosophy meant Pythagoras (6th century B.C.) and Heraclitus (whose work is dated c 500 B.C.). On ideas in Pythagoras see e.g. *P Lects* Lect 2 (1949) 107–9. In his annotations on Tennemann I 107 and 120 C remarked that the numbers of Pythagoras "were evidently the same as the Ideas of Plato". For his belief that the *nous* and the ideas of ancient wisdom were a foreshadowing of St Paul's "Spirit", and their relation to *logos*, see below, App I Excursus Note 4 "Coleridge on Nous and Logos".

[3] 1 Cor 2.12, 14: "Now we have received, not the spirit of the world, but the spirit which is of God; that we might know the things that are freely given to us of God. . . . But the natural man receiveth not the things of the Spirit of God: for they are foolishness unto him: neither can he know them, because they are spiritually discerned." See above, p 77.

[4] Cf a note in N 30, written before 12 Dec 1823: "The general doctrine of the Spirit inculcated by Seneca—& the resemblance of the passage to that of Sᵗ Paul's in Ephes [cf Eph 3.6, 5.9]—not improbably the occasion of the Legend respecting the intercourse & acquaintanceship between the Apostle & the Philosopher . . .": *CN* IV 5072. C was probably reading Tennemann V 163 on Seneca, "the passage" being that quoted below. Tennemann quotes this, but does not make the comparison with St Paul.

[5] See previous note. Tennemann began, as C does not, with the striking sentence "Prope est a te Deus, tecum est, intra est": Seneca *Letters* 41; tr R. M. Gummere (LCL 1917–25): "[God is near you, he is with you, he is within you.] This is what I mean, Lucilius: a holy spirit dwells within us, one who marks our good and bad deeds and is our guardian. As we treat this spirit, so we are treated by it. Indeed, no man can be good without the help of God."

APHORISMS ON SPIRITUAL RELIGION

APHORISM I*ᵇ¹*

EVERY one is *to give a reason of his faith;* but Priests and Ministers more punctually than any, their province being to make good every sentence of the Bible to a rational inquirer*ᶜ* into the truth of these Oracles.² Enthusiasts find it an easy thing to heat the fancies of unlearned and unreflecting Hearers; but when a sober man would be satisfied of the *Grounds* from whence they speak, he shall not have one syllable or the least tittle of a pertinent Answer. Only they will talk big of THE SPIRIT, and inveigh against *Reason* with bitter Reproaches, calling it carnal or fleshly, though it be indeed no soft flesh, but enduring and penetrant steel, even the sword of the Spirit, and such as pierces to the Heart.

APHORISM II*ᵈ¹*

There are two very bad things in this resolving of men's Faith and Prac-

---

ᵃ *AR* (1825): p 143
ᵇ *AR* (1825): H. MORE.
ᶜ *AR* (1825): enquirer
ᵈ *AR* (1825): H. MORE.

¹ Adapted from Henry More *An Explanation of the Grand Mystery of Godliness*, in *Theological Works* (1708) 368. Among the changes C's phrase about how enthusiasts "heat the fancies" of their hearers (a phrase from More's next paragraph) replaces More's "Any inferiour Fellow may talk and prate Phrases and make Faces, but when . . ." and C inserts after "steel" the phrase ". . . even the sword of the Spirit". For the original text see App A(d), below.

² From 1 Pet 3.15: ". . . be ready always to give an answer to every man that asketh you a reason of the hope that is in you . . .", thus linking with the passages

of Leighton's commentary on this verse that provided *Aphs XXXIX–XLII* in the previous section.

¹ Adapted from More *Theological Works* (1708) 368. C substitutes "Faith and Practice" for More's "Matters" and continues his sentence after "Understandings" by adapting some lines from earlier in the paragraph. The effect is to play down More's polemic against enthusiasts (including his argument that magistrates ought to act against them) and bring out his arguments in favour of reason. For the original text see App A(e), below.

147

tice into *the immediate suggestion* of a Spirit not acting on our Understandings, or rather into the illumination of such a Spirit as they can *ª*give no account of, such as does not enlighten their reason or enable them to render their doctrine intelligible to others. First, it defaces and makes useless that part of the Image of God in us, which we call REASON: and secondly, it takes away that advantage, which raises Christianity above all other Religions, that she dare appeal to so solid a faculty.

APHORISM III^{b1}

It is the glory of the Gospel Charter and the Christian Constitution, that its Author and Head is the Spirit of Truth, Essential Reason as well as Absolute and Incomprehensible Will. Like a just Monarch, he refers even his own causes to the Judgment of his high Courts.—He has his King's Bench in the Reason, his Court of Equity in the Conscience; *that* the Representative of his Majesty and universal Justice, *this* the nearest to the King's heart, and the Dispenser of his particular Decrees. He has likewise his Court of Common Pleas in the Understanding, his Court of Exchequer in the Prudence. The Laws are *his* Laws. And though by Signs and Miracles he has mercifully condescended to interline here and there with his own hand the great Statute-book, which he had dictated to his Amanuensis, Nature; yet has he been graciously pleased to forbid our receiving as the *King's* Mandates aught that is not stamped with the Great Seal of the Conscience, and countersigned by the Reason.

ª *AR* (1825): p 144
b *AR* (1825): EDITOR.

[1] In N 30 C wrote the following note (dated 1823 by the editor of *CN*) on the last sentence of the passage from More p 368 that was then adapted into *Sp Aph A 1*, above: "This is the glory of Christianity, that it is the Spirit of Truth—and therefore appeals to Reason, as a lawful Monarch appeals to or refers his causes to his own high Courts, among which the Court of Conscience is the highest in dignity & nearest to the throne—but the Court of Reason is the King's Bench, to which the Chancery sends for the previous determinations of the Facts as to the Understanding in his Court of Common Pleas, to the Prudence in his Court of Exchequer—The Laws are his Laws—both the common and the *written* & is graciously pleased to command the Subject to receive no Mandates as the King's which are not countersigned by the Reason, and have not received the Great Seal of the Conscience—": *CN* IV 5066. C's rewriting adds the reference to "Absolute and Incomprehensible Will" and to "Signs and Miracles" as interlineations of the statute-book dictated to God's amanuensis, Nature. His ms for *Aph III* (from "Charter and the Christian") and the last two paragraphs of *Aph VI* (Comment), together with a promise to send transcripts of the intervening passages from More, is transcribed below in App B(m).

^{*a*}APHORISM IV¹

ON AN UNLEARNED MINISTRY, UNDER PRETENCE OF A CALL OF THE SPIRIT,
AND INWARD GRACES SUPERSEDING OUTWARD HELPS

Tell me, Ye high-flown *Perfectionists,* Ye Boasters of the *Light within* you, could the highest perfection of your inward Light ever show to you the History of past Ages, the state of the World at present, the Knowledge of Arts and Tongues, without Books or Teachers? How then can you understand the Providence of God, or the age, the purpose, the fulfilment of Prophecies, or distinguish such as have been fulfilled from those to the fulfilment of which we are to look forward? How can you judge concerning the authenticity and uncorruptedness of the Gospels, and the other sacred Scriptures?^{*b*} And how without this knowledge can you support the truth of Christianity? How can you either have, or give a reason for the faith which you profess? This *Light within,* that loves darkness,^{*c*} and would exclude those excellent Gifts of God to Mankind, Knowledge and Understanding, what is it but a sullen self-sufficiency within you, engendering contempt of Superiors, pride and a Spirit of Division, and inducing you to reject for yourselves and to undervalue in others the *Helps without,* which the Grace of God has provided and appointed for his Church—nay, to make them grounds or pretexts of your dislike or suspicion of Christ's Ministers who have ^{*d*}fruitfully availed themselves of the Helps afforded them?—HENRY MORE

APHORISM V¹

There are Wanderers, whom neither pride nor a perverse humor^{*e*} have led astray; and whose condition is such, that I think few more worthy of a man's best directions. For the more imperious Sects having put such unhandsome vizards on Christianity, and the sincere Milk of the *Word*²

---

^{*a*} *AR* (1825): p 145
^{*b*} *AR* (1831) has: Sciptures?
^{*c*} *AR* (1825): Darkness,
^{*d*} *AR* (1825): p 146
^{*e*} *AR* (1825): humour

¹ Adapted from More *Theological Works* (1708) 369. C follows More closely for the first sentence and a half, then largely expands and paraphrases, picking up only one or two phrases, such as "*Light within*" and "*Helps without*". For the original text see App A(f), below.

¹ Adapted from More *Theological Works* (1708) 372–3. In an annotation on these pages C takes issue with More for attacking the Quakers undiscriminatingly: *CM (CC)* III. For the original text see App A(g), below.
² 1 Pet 2.2.

having been every where so sophisticated by the humors[a] and inventions of men, it has driven these anxious Melancholists to seek for *a Teacher* that cannot deceive, the Voice of the *eternal* Word within them; to which if they be faithful, they assure themselves it will be faithful to them in return. Nor would this be a groundless Presumption, if they had sought this Voice in the Reason and the Conscience, with the Scripture articulating the same, instead of giving heed to their Fancy and mistaking bodily disturbances, and the vapors resulting therefrom, for inspiration and the teaching of the Spirit.—HENRY MORE

APHORISM VI[1]

When every man is his own end, all things will come to a bad end. Blessed were those days, when every man thought himself rich and fortunate by the good success of the public wealth and glory. We want public Souls, we want them. I speak it with compassion:[b] there is no sin and abuse in the world that affects my thought so much. Every man thinks, that he is a whole Commonwealth in his private Family. Omnes quae sua sunt quaerunt. All seek their own.[2]—BISHOP HACKET'S Sermons, p. 449

COMMENT

Selfishness is common to all ages and countries. In all ages Self-seeking is the Rule, and Self-sacrifice the Exception. But if to seek our private advantage in harmony with, and by the furtherance of, the public prosperity, and to derive a portion of our happiness from sympathy with the prosperity of our fellow-men—if this be Public Spirit, it would be morose and querulous to pretend that there is any want of it in this country and at the present time. On the contrary, the number of "public Souls"[c] and the general readiness to contribute to the public good, in science and in religion, in patriotism and in philanthropy, stand prominent* among

---

* The very marked, *positive* as well as comparative, magnitude and prominence of the Bump, entitled BENEVOLENCE *(see Spurzheim's Map of the Human Skull)* on the head of

[a] *AR* (1825): humours
[b] *AR* (1825): p 147 (sion:)
[c] *AR* (1825): souls"

[1] From John Hacket *A Century of Sermons* (1675) 449. C follows Hacket almost exactly. C wrote an annotation on this page, though not on this passage: *CM (CC)*
II 922. For the original text see App A(h), below.
[2] Hacket then gives the reference, Phil 2.21.

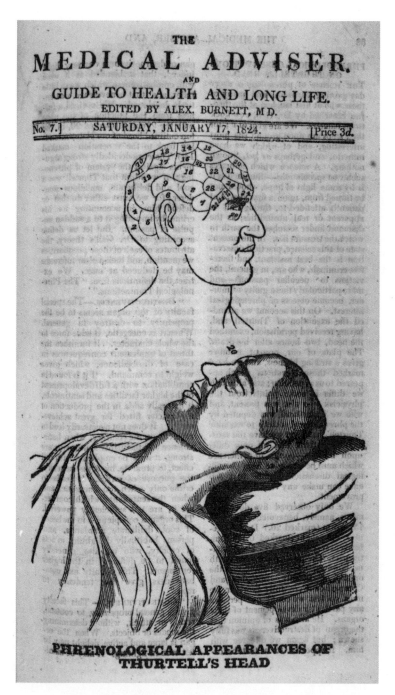

THE
MEDICAL ADVISER,
AND
GUIDE TO HEALTH AND LONG LIFE.
EDITED BY ALEX. BURNETT, M.D.

No. 7.]   SATURDAY, JANUARY 17, 1824.   [Price 3d.

PHRENOLOGICAL APPEARANCES OF THURTELL'S HEAD

4. Front page of *The Medical Adviser* 17 Jan 1824, which included
a phrenological account of the head of John Thurtell, murderer

the characteristics of this and the preceding*ᵃ* generation. The habit of referring Actions and Opinions to fixed laws; Convictions rooted in Principles; Thought, Insight, System;—these, had the good Bishop lived in our times, would have been his Desiderata, and the theme of his Complaints. "We want *thinking* Souls, we *want them.*"

---

the late Mr. John Thurtel, has woefully*ᵇ* unsettled the faith of many ardent Phrenologists, and strengthened the previous doubts of a still greater number into utter disbelief.[3] On MY mind this fact (for a *fact* it is) produced the directly*ᶜ* contrary effect; and inclined me to suspect, for the first time, that there may be some truth in the Spurzheimian Scheme. Whether future Craniologists may not see cause to *new-name* this and one or two other of these convex gnomons, is quite a different question. At present, and according to the present use of words, any such change would be premature: and we must be content to say, that Mr. Thurtel's Benevolence was insufficiently modified by the unprotrusive and unindicated Convolutes of the Brain, that secrete honesty and common-sense. The organ of Destructiveness was indirectly *potentiated*ᵈ⁴ by the absence or imperfect development*ᵉ* of the Glands of Reason and Conscience, in this "*unfortunate Gentleman!*"

ᵃ *AR* (1825): p 148 (ceding)   *ᵇ* *AR* (1825): wofully
ᶜ *AR* (1825): direct   *ᵈ* *AR* (1825): *potenziated*
ᵉ *AR* (1825): developement

[3] John Thurtell (1794–1824) was the centre of a celebrated trial (6–7 Jan 1824) at which he was convicted of murdering William Weare, a solicitor who, he believed, had cheated him out of money at cards. He is said to have designed his own gallows and was executed at Hertford on 9 Jan 1824 (cf Lamb's letter to Barton that day: *LL* II 413–14). His body was dissected by John Abernethy and the skull preserved at the Royal College of Surgeons. *The Medical Adviser and Guide to Health and Long Life* for 17 Jan 1824 carried an illustration of Thurtell's head on its front cover with a Spurzheimian diagram above it. (See Illustration 4 to the present ed.) In an article overleaf entitled "Phrenological Observations on Mr. Thurtell's head" benevolence was to be developed there, whereas destructiveness, which according to the phrenologists should be "conspicuous in the heads of cool, deliberate murderers", was very slight. (See also ibid 140–1.)

Spurzheim's diagram of the human skull, printed as frontispiece to his *Physiognomical System of Drs. Gall and Spurzheim* (1815), locates the bump of benevolence at the front of the top of the skull (see pp 409–10 there). C read this in 1815 and found it "below criticism": *CL* IV 613. He was rather more respectful in the 1818 *Friend (CC)* I 415. Spurzheim later visited him at Highgate and said that his organ of locality was unusually developed but his organ of ideality or imagination wanting or evanescent (BM MS Egerton 2800 f 188: *IS* 416)—a finding that caused considerable amusement in the company. See letter of 18 May 1825: *CL* v 460–1, *CN* IV 4763, 5194, and *TT* 24 Jun 1827, 24 Jul 1830 *(CC)* I 75–6 and n, 183–4; 1836 vns II 64 (with HNC's n) and 116 (dated 29 Jul and quoting *AR* in n). According to *Friend (CC)* I 415n, Spurzheim visited C at Highgate in 1824 and took a cast of his face; no source is given for this further information. "Unprotrusive" and "unindicated" below are *OED*'s first examples.

⁴ The 1825 reading preserves C's original spelling "potenziate", as in *BL* ch 12, in which he said that he had "even hazarded the new verb potenziate with its derivatives in order to express the combination or transfer of powers": *BL (CC)* I 287. So in several notes of 1818–19: *CN* III 4418 f 13ᵛ, 4426, 4486 f 47, and on Baxter *Reliquiae Baxterianae*: *CM (CC)* I 344. The

This and the three preceding Extracts will suffice as precautionary Aphorisms. And here again, the Reader may exemplify the great advantages to be obtained from the habit of tracing the *proper* meaning and history of Words. We need only recollect the common and idiomatic phrases in which the word "Spirit" occurs in a physical or material sense (ex. gr. fruit has lost its *spirit* and flavor),[a] to be convinced that its property is to improve, enliven, actuate some other thing,[5] not to[b] constitute a thing in its own name.[6] The enthusiast may find one exception to this where the material itself is called[c] *Spirit*. And when he calls to mind, how *this* spirit acts when taken *alone* by the unhappy persons who in their first exultation will boast that it is Meat, Drink, Fire, and Clothing to them, all in one—when he reflects, that its properties are to inflame, intoxicate, madden, with exhaustion, lethargy, [d]and atrophy for the Sequels—well for him, if in some lucid interval he should fairly put the question to his own mind, how far this is *analogous* to his own case, and whether the Exception does not confirm the Rule. The *Letter* without the Spirit killeth;[7] but does it follow, that The Spirit is to kill the Letter? To kill that which it is its appropriate office to enliven?

However, where the Ministry is not invaded, and the plain sense of the Scriptures is left undisturbed, and the Believer looks for the sugges-

---

[a] *AR* (1825): flavour),
[b] *AR* (1825): to be or
[c] COPY C: named
[d] *AR* (1825): p 149

---

form "potentiate", as here, is also found in *LR* IV 137 and *NLS* (1849) I 94: the change may have been made by HNC, preferring the Latinate form to the German. In this form the term was taken up by C's admirers Julius Hare and J. H. Green (see entries s.v. "potentiate" and "potentiation" respectively in *OED*) and passed into currency. See *CM (CC)* I 344n.

[5] Among possible sources for C's use of "actuate" here is Henry More's *Apology* in *A Modest Enquiry into the Mystery of Wickedness* (1664) 498: "The Soul is a Spirit that actuates the natural Body."

[6] *AR* (1825) COPY C has a note here: "As the human Understanding = λόγος ὁ ἐν ἑκαστῳ [the word in each individual] is a Faculty of the Man, not a Subsistent of the Ens *per se*: so is the Spirit an Energy not a Soul. The Self-subsistence of the ⟨Divine⟩ Logos (Λογος προς θεόν ['The Word . . . with

God' in John 1.1—though C objected to the translation 'with', believing the Greek to mean 'the utmost proximity without confusion': *TT* 7 Jan–13 Feb 1823 *(CC)* I 34–6 (1836 vn, dated 6 Jan 1823, II 40–1); see also *CM (CC)* II 598] = the Identity of Reason and Understanding, or the *Substantial* Reason) and of the ⟨Holy⟩ Spirit is the proper and exclusive ~~attribute~~ prerogative of the Godhead. The Reason and the Spirit of the ~~Father~~ Supreme Mind are consubstantial therewith, and not merely Attributes. This is the sense and purpose of the Nicene Creed: in any finite Being the pretence is presumption. S. T. C." With this note of C's cf that in *Sp Aph B VII* n 31, below. On the word λόγος see also *Pref* n 4, above, and App I Excursus Notes 1 and 4, below.

[7] Cf 2 Cor 3.6: ". . . for the letter killeth, but the spirit giveth life".

tions of the Spirit only or chiefly in applying particular passages to his own individual case and exigencies; though in this there may be much weakness, some Delusion and imminent Danger of more, I cannot but join with Henry More in avowing,[8] that I feel knit to such a man in the bonds of a common faith far more closely, than to those who receive neither the Letter[a] nor the Spirit, turning the one into metaphor and oriental hyperbole, in order to explain away the other into the influence of motives suggested by their own understandings, and[b] realized by their own strength.

---

[a] *AR* (1825): Letter,
[b] COPY C: and to be

[8] In his original ms C intended to introduce here a portion (from "for my own part" to "more confirmed Christians than ever") of the passage from More 372–3 on which *Aph V*, above, is based. See BM MS Egerton 2801 f 175, transcribed in App B(m) below, and (for the More passage) App A(c), below, Instead, he provided words of his own.

^aAPHORISMS

ON THAT

WHICH IS INDEED SPIRITUAL RELIGION

IN the selection of the Extracts that form the remainder of this Volume and of the Comments affixed, the Author^b had the following Objects principally in view. First, to exhibit the true and scriptural meaning and intent of several Articles of Faith, that are rightly classed among the Mysteries and peculiar Doctrines of Christianity. Secondly, to show the perfect rationality of these Doctrines, and their freedom from all just Objection when examined by their proper Organs,^{c1} the Reason and Conscience of Man. Lastly, to exhibit from the Works of Leighton,[2] who perhaps of all our learned Protestant^d Theologians best deserves the title of a spiritual Divine, an instructive and affecting picture of the contemplations, reflections, conflicts, consolations and monitory experiences of a philosophic and richly-gifted mind, amply stored with all the knowledge that Books and long intercourse with men of the most discordant characters could^e give, under the convictions, impressions, and habits of a Spiritual Religion.

^a *AR* (1825): p 150
^b *AR* (1825): Editor
^c *AR* (1825): Organ,
^d *AR* (1825): protestant
^e *AR* (1825): can

[1] *AR* (1825) COPY C has a note in the margin at "Organs": "Qu" [for "Query"].

[2] *AR* (1825) COPY C has a line in margin alongside the last sentences of the first paragraph, with a note: "See the Advertisement at the head of the Volume. I still cherish the hope of being enabled to publish the extracts, I have made, from L. with others from Baxter and from Divines to whose Writings the English Reader is a stranger—as being composed in Latin, German, Italian and Spanish. And I purpose to arrange the whole into a sequence, under the title of The inward Life and Growth of a Christian. S. T. C." C is recognising the fact that Leighton is not represented in the last section on the scale promised here. For an account of the "extracts, I have made," from Leighton see Editor's Introduction, above, at nn 73–5 and *CM (CC)* III.

*a*To obviate a possible disappointment in any of my Readers, who may chance to be engaged in theological studies, it may be well to notice, that in vindicating the peculiar tenets of our Faith, I have not entered on the Doctrine of the Trinity, or the still profounder Mystery of the Origin of Moral Evil—and this for the reasons following: 1. These Doctrines are not (strictly speaking) subjects of *Reflection*, in the proper sense of this word: and both of them demand a power and persistency of Abstraction, and a previous discipline in the highest forms of human thought, which it would be unwise, if not presumptuous, to expect from any, who require *"Aids* to Reflection," or would be likely to seek them in the present Work. 2. In my intercourse with men of various ranks and ages, I have found the far larger number of serious and inquiring Persons little,*b* if at all,*c* disquieted by doubts respecting Articles of Faith, that are simply above their comprehension. It is only where the Belief required of them jars with their *moral* feelings; where a Doctrine in the sense, in which they have been taught to receive it, appears to contradict their clear notions of Right and Wrong, or to be at variance with the divine Attributes of Goodness and Justice; that these men are surprised, perplexed, and alas! not seldom offended and alienated. Such are the Doctrines of Arbit[r]ary Election and Reprobation; the Sentence to everlasting Torment by an eternal and necessitating Decree; vicarious Atonement, and the necessity of the Abasement, Agony and ignominious Death of a most holy and meritorious Person, to appease*d* the wrath of God. Now it is more especially for such Persons, unwilling sceptics,*e* who believing earnestly ask help for their unbelief,[3] that this Volume was compiled, and the Comments written: and therefore, to the Scripture Doctrines, *intended* by the above-mentioned, my principal attention has been directed.

But lastly, the whole Scheme of the Christian Faith, including *all* the Articles of Belief common to the Greek and Latin, the Roman and the Protestant Churches,*f* with the threefold proof, that it is *ideally, morally,* and *historically* true, will be found exhibited and vindicated in a proportionally larger Work,[4] the principal Labor*g* of my Life since Manhood, and which I am now preparing for the Press under the title, Assertion of

a *AR* (1825): p 151
b *AR* (1825): little
c *AR* (1825): all
d *AR* (1825): p 152 (pease)
e *AR* (1825): Sceptics,
f *AR* (1825): Church,
g *AR* (1825): Labour

[3] Mark 9.24. See *Sp Aph B XVIII* n 13 below for C's uses in 1814.

[4] Evidently the Opus Maximum, which he now sees as tackling on a larger scale

Religion, as necessarily *involving* Revelation; and of Christianity, as the only Revelation of permanent and universal validity.[5]

APHORISM I[a1]

Where, if not in Christ, is the Power that can persuade a Sinner to return, that can *bring home a Heart to God?*

Common mercies of God, though they have a leading faculty to repentance, (Rom. ii. 4.) yet, the rebellious heart will not be led by them. The judgments of God, public or personal, though they ought to drive us to God, yet the heart, unchanged, runs the further from God. Do we not see it by ourselves and other sinners about us? They look not at all towards Him who smites, much less do they return; or [b]if any more serious thoughts of returning arise upon the surprise of an affliction, how soon vanish they, either the stroke abating, or the heart, by time, growing hard and senseless under it! Leave Christ out, I say, and all other means work not this way; neither the works nor the word of God sounding daily in his ear, *Return, return.*[2] Let the noise of the rod speak it too, and both join together to make the cry the louder, *yet the wicked will do wickedly,*[3] Dan. xii.[c] 10.

COMMENT

By the phrase "in Christ," I mean all the supernatural Aids vouchsafed and conditionally promised in the Christian Dispensation: and among

[a] *AR* (1825): LEIGHTON.

[b] *AR* (1825): p 153

[c] *AR* (1831): xi.

---

questions discussed in *AR*, along with others deliberately omitted there. See *CN* IV 5210 f 21ᵛ (May 1825) and a letter to J. T. Coleridge 8 May 1825: *CL* v 444, both quoted above in the Editor's Introduction, at nn 210 and 209.

[5] C's ms for the preceding introductory paragraphs is transcribed below in App B(n); a fragmentary draft, probably associated with the "Assertion of Religion", in App B(o). An outline for the latter work is also in the BM (MS Egerton 2801 ff 202–3) and will appear in *SW&F (CC)*.

[1] See Leighton COPY C II 120–1: *CM (CC)* III. C begins by reworking the sentence that precedes the passage marked for extraction: "And there is nothing but the power of Christ alone, that is able to effect this, to persuade a sinner to return, to bring home a heart unto God." He also omits a sentence after "under it", adapting the opening of the next accordingly. His ms for the Aphorism and Comment (with directions for the extracts from Leighton) is transcribed below in App B(p). All the Leighton passages among the Spiritual Aphorisms are drawn from his *Commentary on 1 Peter.*

[2] Cf Ps 90.3 and St Augustine *Confessions* 4.12.

[3] Dan 12.10 (var). The 1825 reference, used here for the *CC* text, corresponds to Leighton's, which is correct.

them the Spirit of Truth, which the world cannot receive, were it only that the knowledge of *spiritual* Truth is of necessity immediate and *intuitive*[4]*:* and the World or Natural Man possesses no higher intuitions than those of the pure *Sense*, which are the subjects of *Mathematical* Science. But *Aids,* observe! Therefore, not *by*[a] Will of man alone: but neither *without* the Will. The doctrine of modern Calvinism[b][5] as laid[c] down by Jonathan Edwards[6] and the late Dr. Williams,[7] which represents a Will absolutely passive, clay in the hands of a Potter, destroys

[a] *AR* (1825): by the

[b] *AR* (1825): Calvinism,

[c] *AR* (1825): layed

[4] The "intuitive" is a key term for Coleridge. In a notebook entry used for the 1809 *Friend*, the distinguishing feature of Christianity was that it found "the very end and final Bliss of the glorified Spirit" in "an intuitive Beholding of Truth in its eternal and immutable Source": *CN* III 3592. It is often considered by him in terms of the scholastic distinction between the intuitive and the discursive: in 1810 he commented on Kant's use of the two terms: see *CN* III 3801; cf also below, *Sp Aph B VIIIb* n 10, which includes uses in previous writers such as Shakespeare and Milton. Although admiring Kant's account of intuition as manifested in the apprehension of geometric truths, he believed the Kantian use to be limited to that sphere, i.e. the sphere of time and space: see *BL* ch 12 *(CC)* I 289 and n. His own version, closely associated with his conception of Reason, or Nous (see Epigraph to *Sp Aph* above and App I Excursus Note 4 below), had already been developed in *The Friend, LS,* and *Logic* (see Indexes to *CC* volumes). Important references in *AR* can be found in *Sp Aph B VIIIb* at n 62, where "*Intuition* or *immediate Beholding*" is juxtaposed with and distinguished from the "reflective and discursive Faculty", *Xa* at n 29, where the Nous, as distinguished from the Logos, is "Intuitive Reason, the Source of Ideas and ABSOLUTE Truths", and *Xb* at n 36, where "generalizing", as a function of understanding, is set against "the Power of *intuitive . . . knowledge*". The intuitions of the "enlightened conscience" are compared with those of the mathematician in an annotation on COPY F, recorded in *Sp Aph*

B II n 23; in *Sp Aph B IX*, at n 19, likewise, C refers to "the Superior Courts of Conscience and intuitive Reason". The phrase "inward Beholding" is attributed to Hooker in *Sp Aph B VIIIb* at n 28.

[5] See above, Editor's Introduction, at n 26, and *Mor Aph XXXV* n 4.

[6] Jonathan Edwards (1629–1712), American Congregational divine. C's copy of his *Careful and Strict Inquiry into the Modern Prevailing Notions of That Freedom of Will, Which Is Supposed to Be Essential to Moral Agency . . .* (5th ed 1790) is in VCL. In a notebook entry of 1823 he says of Edwards that "his World is a *Machine*": *CN* IV 5077. Cf *C&S (CC)* 17; see also below, n 8.

[7] Edward Williams (1750–1813). C discussed his *Defence of Modern Calvinism* (1812) and *Essay on the Equity of Divine Government* (1809) in letters of 10 and 13 Mar 1815 to R. H. Brabant (from whom he had borrowed them). See *CL* IV 547–9, 552–3. Some ms notes on the *Essay*, sent to Dr Brabant, were published in the *Westminster Review* XCIII (1870) 349–54: *SW&F (CC).* In an annotation on Leighton COPY C I 88–94: *CM (CC)* III, C denied that his dislike of rational defences of the "divine authority of the Scriptures" made him "an upholder of that 'Modern Calvinism', which with all due respect to the late Dr Williams, its Archaspistes [chief shield-bearer: cf *CN* IV 4755] I am persuaded that Calvin himself would have welcomed with an Anathema Maranatha." (For the last term see below, *Sp Aph B [XXIV]* n 58.) Cf *C&S (CC)* 135 and n 1 and *CM (CC)* II 801.

all Will, takes away its essence and definition, as effectually as in say-ing—This Circle is square—I should deny the figure to be a circle*a* at all. It was in strict consistency therefore, that these Writers supported the Necessitarian Scheme, and made the relation of Cause and Effect the Law of the Universe,*b* subjecting to its mechanism the moral World no less than the material or physical. It follows, that all is Nature. Thus, though few Writers use the term Spirit more frequently, they in effect deny its existence, and evacuate the term of all its proper meaning. With such a system not the Wit of Man nor all the Theodices ever framed by human ingenuity before and since the attempt of the celebrated Leib-nitz,[8] can reconcile the Sense of Responsibility, nor the fact of the dif-ference *in kind* between REGRET AND*c* REMORSE.[9] The same compulsion of Consequence drove the Fathers of Modern (or Pseudo-) Calvinism to the origination of Holiness in Power, of Justice in right*d* of Property, and whatever other outrages on the common sense and moral feelings of Mankind they have sought to cover, under the fair name of *Sovereign Grace.*[10]

I will not take on me to defend sundry harsh and inconvenient Ex-pressions in the Works of Calvin. Phrases equally strong and assertions*e* not less rash and startling are no rarities in the Writings of Luther: for Catachresis[11] was the favourite Figure of Speech in that age. But let not the opinions of either on this most fundamental Subject be confounded

a AR (1825): Circle
b AR (1825): p 154 (verse,)
c AR (1825): and
d AR (1825): Right
e AR (1825): Assertions

[8] Leibniz *Essais de Théodicée sur la Bonté de Dieu, la liberté de l'homme et l'origine du mal* (1710). C's form of the word—the only example cited by *OED*—appears also in an annotation on Leibniz *Theodicee* (Hanover & Leipzig 1763) I ii 134: *CM (CC)* III 505. C planned to make notes on this for his ''Consolations'' as he travelled to Malta in 1804, *CN* II 1993, and so evidently had a copy of it in some form then. For his ownership of a French version and his annotation of a German translation (Hanover & Leipzig 1763) said to have been DeQ's see *CN* II 1993n and *CM (CC)* III 503. In a note of Dec 1823 he wrote: ''I have not read Jonathan Edwards' notorious Tract, the Benevol. of God demonstrated in the Eternity of Hell Torments [i.e. *The Eternity of Hell's Torments* (1788)]; & am

ignorant of the principles on which his po-sition is grounded. But I suspect that they are *Leibnitzian*, or a Theodicee on the hy-pothesis of a *best possible* World'': *CN* IV 5077 and n.

[9] See above, *Mor Aph XLVI* n 1.

[10] In mentioning this Calvinistic term C has in mind Edward Williams *Essay on the Equity of Divine Government and the Sov-ereignty of Divine Grace* (1809) (see above, n 7), where it is discussed in ch 4, ''A View of Sovereign Grace''; the (partly misplaced) sections are printed on pp 291–301, 141–55, and 385–415. Williams pays particular attention there to the relation be-tween liberty and necessity.

[11] For this term see below, *Sp Aph B XVIII* n 38.

with the new-England[a] System, now entitled Calvinistic. The fact is simply this. Luther considered the Pretensions to Free-will *boastful*, and better suited to the budge Doctors of the Stoic Fur,[12] than to the Preachers of the Gospel, whose great theme[b] is the Redemption of the Will from Slavery; the restoration of the Will to perfect Freedom being the *end* and consummation of the [c]redemptive Process, and the same with the entrance of the Soul into Glory, *i.e.* its union with Christ: "GLORY" (John xvii. 5.) being one of the names of the Spiritual Messiah.[13] Prospectively to this we are to understand the words of our [d]Lord. "At[e] that day ye shall know that I am in my father,[f] and ye in me,"[g] John xiv. 20: the freedom of a finite will being possible under this condition only, that it has become one with the will of God.[14] Now as the difference of a captive and enslaved Will, and *no* Will at all, such is the difference between the *Lutheranism* of Calvin and the Calvinism of Jonathan Edwards.[15]

APHORISM II[h1]

There is nothing in religion farther out of Nature's reach, and more re-

[a] *AR* (1825): New-England
[b] *AR* (1825): Theme
[c] *AR* (1825): p 155
[d-e] *AR* (1825): Lord, At
[f] *AR* (1825): Father,
[g] *AR* (1825): me,
[h] *AR* (1825): LEIGHTON. ; COPY C: LEIGHTON & EDITOR.

[12] Milton *A Mask* . . . ("Comus") line 707.
[13] John 17.5 reads: "And now, O Father, glorify thou me with thine own self with the glory which I had with thee before the world was." Despite the reference to God's name in the next verse, C's use of this passage is open to the objection that, taken by itself, it suggests a quality rather than a name of the Messiah. It seems to be backed by a complex train of thought, taking in the "glory of the Lord" that filled the tabernacle in Exod 40.43, the use of the same term in a Messianic context in Isa 40 ("The glory of the Lord shall be revealed", v 5), and the fact that "Wisdom" (related by C to the Logos, or Word, and so to Christ) is described in the Apocrypha as "an influence from the Glory of the Almighty" (Wisd of Sol 7.27: see *Sp Aph B VIIIb* at n 13 below). For more on the word "name" and its connotations see *Sp Aph B*

II n 45 and *VIIIb* nn 48 and 52, below.
[14] C is drawing on other ideas in St John's Gospel, e.g. ". . . ye shall know the truth, and the truth shall make you free" (8.32), which he used as a motto for *The Watchman—Watchman (CC)* 3 and n—and Jesus' aspiration: "I in them and thou in me, that they may be made perfect in one" (17.23), Cf also *BCP* Morning Prayer, Second Collect: ". . . whose service is perfect freedom", and the frequent injunctions to do the will of God, or of the Father, in the NT. It should be noted, however, that though the idea of being "one" is in St John's Gospel, C's introduction of the will into that idea has no precise authority there.
[15] For the deleted opening to a new paragraph here on the will as the spiritual part of our humanity see below, App B(p).
[1] Although C draws on Leighton at the beginning and end of this aphorism, he

mote from the natural man's liking and believing, than the doctrine of Redemption by a Saviour, and by a crucified Saviour. It is comparatively easy to persuade men of the necessity of an amendment of conduct:[a] it is more difficult to make them see the necessity of Repentance in the *Gospel* sense, the necessity on[b] a change in the *principle* of action; but to convince men of the necessity of the Death of Christ is the most difficult of all. And yet the first is but varnish and white-wash without the second; and the second but a barren notion without the last. Alas! of those who admit the doctrine in words, how large a number evade it in fact, and empty it of all its substance and efficacy, making the effect the efficient cause, or attributing their election to Salvation to a [c]supposed Foresight of their Faith, Obedience. But it is most vain to imagine a faith in such and such men, which[d] being foreseen by God, determined him to elect them for salvation: were it only that nothing at all is *future*, or can have this imagined *futurition*, but *as* it is decreed, and *because* it is decreed by God so to be.

COMMENT

No impartial person, competently acquainted with the History of the Reformation, and the works of the earlier Protestant[e] Divines at home

---

[a] *AR* (1825): conduct;
[b] *AR* (1825): of
[c] *AR* (1825): p 156
[d] *AR* (1825): which,
[e] *AR* (1825): protestant

---

adapts and expands much more than in the Moral Aphorisms. It seems likely that he turned to Gillman's copy, COPY B, and transcribed from that, particularly since the following comment (see n 2, below) is drawn from his marginal comment in that volume. It may well be that COPY C I was still at the printer when he made the transcription. The first two sentences correspond to Leighton COPY C I 11, but there form part of a much longer passage, which is sidelined throughout. Cf *CM (CC)* III. The original reads (in COPY B I 11–12): "There is nothing in religion further out of nature's reach, and out of its liking and believing, than the doctrine of redemption by a Saviour, and a crucified Saviour, by Christ, and by his blood, first shed on the cross in his suffering, and then sprinkled on the soul by his Spirit. It is easier to make

men sensible of the necessity of repentance and amendment of life, (though that is very difficult,) than of this purging by the sprinkling of this precious blood." C avoids references to the sprinkling of blood (which form part of the text in 1 Peter that Leighton is discussing), and his next two sentences are only loosely connected with the ensuing discussion; his final one, however, is based on Leighton's: "It is most vain to imagine a foresight of faith in men, and that God in the view of that, as the condition of election itself, as it is called, has chosen them: for, 1. Nothing at all is *futurum*, or can have that imagined *futurition*, but *as* it is, and *because* it is decreed by God to be . . .". This sentence, on I 20 in COPY B, is not marked in COPY C (I 19), which reads "of that faith" for "of that".

and abroad, even to the close of Elizabeth's reign, will deny that the Doctrines of Calvin on Redemption and the natural state of fallen Man, are in all essential points the same as those of Luther, Zuinglius, and the first Reformers[a] collectively.[2] These Doctrines have, however, since the re-establishment of the Episcopal Church at the return of the second Charles, been as generally* exchanged[b] for what is commonly entitled

---

* At a period, in which Doctors Marsh[3] and Wordsworth[4] have, by the Zealous[c] on one side, been[d] charged with Popish[e] principles on account of their *Anti-bibliolatry*,[5] and the sturdy Adherents of the doctrines common to Luther and Calvin, and the literal interpreters

> [a] *AR* (1825): reformers
> [b] *AR* (1825): p 157 (changed)
> [c] *AR* (1825): Zealots
> [d] *AR* (1831) has: being
> [e] *AR* (1825): popish

[2] For this and the next sentence cf C's note on Leighton COPY B I 9–13: *CM (CC)* III (where he adds Knox and Cranmer to U. Zwingli—1484–1531—and other reformers). It seems likely that he had this annotation in front of him: it also provided a point of departure for other comments in *AR*.

[3] Herbert Marsh (1757–1839), bp of Peterborough, published a translation of J. D. Michaelis *Introduction to the New Testament* (4 vols Cambridge 1793–1801). The 1801 volumes also contained his own "Dissertation on the Origin and Composition of the Three First Canonical Gospels" (see *CN* IV 5323 and n). C borrowed the 1793 vols from the Bristol Library in Jun 1795: *Bristol LB* 121. In May 1820 his nephew W. H. Coleridge brought him Marsh's *The Authenticity of the New Testament*, just published, which he appraised in a letter to J. H. Green on 25 May (*CL* v 46), expressing a preference for external evidence taken from the nature of man in a manner that looks forward to *AR*.

Marsh attacked the Calvinistic Evangelicals within the established Church as well as the nonconformists in opposing the Bible Society's policy of publishing the Bible without notes or commentary, and particularly without the *Book of Common Prayer*.

More recently the ill feeling caused by his intransigent attitude had been increased by his attempt to root out Evangelicals from his diocese by insisting that his clergy answer his "eighty-seven questions", known as "a trap to catch Calvinists". See *CM (CC)* II 913n. For other passages where

C distinguishes between the "modern Calvinists" and the true followers of Luther and Calvin see *Mor Aph XXV* and cf Introduction to *Sp Aph B*, and *Sp Aph B* I above. See also *C&S (CC)* 159–60 and n.

[4] Christopher Wordsworth (1774–1846), youngest brother of WW and Master of Trinity College, Cambridge, from 1820, wrote, similarly, *Reasons for Declining to Become a Subscriber to the British and Foreign Bible Society*, of which three editions were published in 1810. His *Six Letters to Granville Sharpe, Esq., Respecting His Remarks on the Uses of the Definitive Article in the Greek Text of the New Testament* (1802) supported the interpretation of various NT passages as implying the divinity of Christ. C discussed the *Six Letters* in *CL* II 820–1 and III 282–4 and annotated them, *CM (CC)* v; cf also *CN* III 3935 f 69 and, for a full account of the controversy, III 3275n.

[5] *OED* cites this as the sole example of "anti-bibliolatry"; "bibliolatry" has an earlier provenance. See also HCR's diary for 17 Jan 1812: "Coleridge argued strongly in favour of the Bible Society, and I did not remind him of the phrase he had made use of to me: Bibliolatry . . .": *CRB* I 59; and, in connexion with Edward Irving, the entry for 15 Jun 1826, *CRD* II 330. The word was previously used by Lessing: see his piece among the anti-Goeze writings of 1778 entitled "Bibliolatrie": *Sämmtliche Schriften* (30 vols Berlin etc 1784–94) VI (Leipzig 1791) 57–8. C's annotated copy is in the BM.

Arminianism,[13] but which, taken as a complete and explicit Scheme of Belief, it would be both historically and theologically more accurate to

of the Articles and Homilies, are,[a] (I wish I could say, altogether[b] without any fault of their own) regarded by the Clergy generally as virtual Schismatics, Dividers *of*, though not *from*, the Church, it is serving the cause of charity to assist in circulating the following instructive passage from the Life of Bishop Hackett[6] respecting the disputes between the Augustinians, or Luthero-Calvinistic[c] Divines and the Grotians of his Age: in which controversy (says his Biographer) he, Hackett,[d] "was ever very moderate."

"But having been bred under Bishop Davenant[7] and Dr. Ward[8] in Cambridge, he was addicted to their sentiments. Archbishop Usher would say, that Davenant understood those controversies better than ever any man did since St. Augustin. But he (Bishop Hackett) used to say, that he was *sure* he had *three* excellent men of his mind in this controversy.[e] 1. *Padre Paolo*[f] (Father Paul)[9] whose letter[g] is extant in[h] Heinsius, *anno* 1604.[10] 2. *Thomas Aquinas.* 3. St[i] Augustin. But besides and above them all, he believed in his Conscience that St[j] Paul was of the same mind likewise. Yet at the same time he would profess, that he disliked no Arminians, but such as revile and defame every one who is *not so:* and he would often commend Arminius himself for his excellent Wit and Parts, but only tax his want of reading and knowledge in Antiquity. And he ever held, it was the foolishest thing in the world to say the Arminians were *popishly* inclined, when so many Dominicans and Jansenists were rigid followers of Augustin in these points: and no less foolish to say that the *Anti-Arminians*[k] were Puritans or Presbyterians,[l] when *Ward*, and *Davenant*, and Prideaux,[11] and Brownrig,[12] those stout Champions for Episcopacy, were decided Anti-Arminians: while Arminius himself was ever a Presbyterian. Therefore he greatly commended the moderation of our Church, which extended equal Communion to both."

[a] *AR* (1825): are
[b] *AR* (1825): *altogether*
[c] *AR* (1825): Luthero-calvinistic
[d] *AR* (1825): Hacket,
[e] *AR* (1825): controversy,
[f] *AR* (1825): *Paulo*
[g] *AR* (1825): Letter
[h] *AR* (1825): to
[i] *AR* (1825): St.
[j] *AR* (1825): St.
[k] *AR* (1825): *Anti-arminians*
[l] *AR* (1825): Presbyterians

[6] By T. Plume, prefixed to John Hacket *A Century of Sermons* (1675) xliii–xliv. Quoted in part in *CM (CC)* II 913, with an annotation by C including the words: ". . . Could Bishop Marsh ever have read this striking §ph?" For the original text see App A(i) below: C's alterations are largely stylistic; the 1825 reading "to Heinsius" is the correct one. See also *Sp Aph B Xb* n 39 below.

[7] John Davenant (1576–1641), bp of Salisbury.

[8] Samuel Ward (d 1643), Master of Sidney Sussex College, Cambridge.

[9] Paolo Sarpi (1552–1623), Venetian

scholar and Church reformer.

[10] Daniel Heinsius (1580–1665), Dutch scholar. The text in Hacket is given in *CM (CC)* II 913; and see C's annotation 913–14 and n 5[1].

[11] John Prideaux (1578–1650), bp of Worcester.

[12] Ralph Brownrig (1592–1659), bp of Exeter.

[13] I.e. the doctrine of Jacobus Arminius (1560–1609), who rejected the Calvinist doctrine of absolute predestination or election. For an early ironic reference see a notebook entry of Oct 1803: "Excess of Calvinism produced Arminianism, and

call *Grotianism*, or Christianity according to Grotius.[14] The change was not, we may readily believe, effected without a struggle. In the Romish Church this latitudinarian System, patronized by the Jesuits, was manfully resisted by Jansenius,[15] Arnauld,[16] and Pascal;[17] in our own Church by the Bishops Davenant, Sanderson,[18] Hall,[19] and the Archbishops[a] Usher,[20] and Leighton: and in the latter half of the preceeding[b] Aphorism

[a] *AR* (1825): p 158 (bishops)
[b] *AR* (1825): preceding

those not in excess *must* therefore be Calvinists!'": *CN* I 1565. See also C's annotations on Kant (quoted Editor's Introduction at n 30 above); on RS's *Life of Wesley* (Oxford 1820) I 216–18, *CM (CC)* v; and on Baxter *Reliquiae Baxterianae*: *CM (CC)* I 346, 351, 358–60 and nn; also *Friend (CC)* I 434, *C&S (CC)* 134–5, and *Sp Aph B XVII* nn 12, 14 below.

[14] Hugo Grotius (1583–1645), Dutch jurist. In the theological conflict in Rotterdam between Calvinists and Arminians Grotius sided with the Arminians or Remonstrants and suffered severely for his attempts at reconciliation. C's hostility to him may derive originally from Lessing. Cf C's letter to RS 2 Sept 1802: "Before the time of Grotius's de Veritate Christiana no *stress* was lay'd on the judicial law-cant kind of evidence for Christianity which had been so much in Fashion/ & Lessing very sensibly considers Grotius as the greatest Enemy that Xtianity ever had": *CL* II 861; cf II 1189. See also annotation on K. F. Bahrdt *Glaubens-Bekenntniss*: *CM (CC)* I 199–200 and n, *CN* II 2640 and n, III 3893 and nn, and *CN* IV Index s.n. Grotius. Similar references to him occur below: see *Sp Aph B XIX* n 99, *Conc* n 99; at the same time he is cited as an authority: see *Sp Aph B VII* n 16.

[15] Cornelius Jansen (1585–1638), bp of Ypres, followed St Augustine in believing that the natural will was by itself perverse and incapable of good. Although his doctrines were analogous to Calvin's, he rejected justification by faith, maintaining that conversion could come about only through the Roman Catholic Church. C referred to "the austere ethics, and unbending theology of Jansenism" in his "Letters to Mr. Justice Fletcher" of 1814: *EOT*

(CC) II 382.

[16] Antoine Arnauld (1612–94), Jansenist theologian, attacked the Jesuits in several tracts and was as a result condemned by the Sorbonne in 1656. C read about him in 1804 in Pascal's *Lettres provinciales* (see *CN* II 2133, 2134, 2136, and next note, below) and admired his work on the Eucharist: see below, *Conc* n 16.

[17] Blaise Pascal (1623–62), mathematician, physicist, and moralist. His most famous works in the last-named field were his *Lettres provinciales* (1656–7) on divine grace and the Jesuits' ethical code, published in reply to the attacks on Arnauld (see previous note), and his *Pensées* (1670). In 1799 (*CL* I 478) C quoted approvingly from the latter in French (out of Jacobi: see *Friend—CC*—II 7–8n). After hearing Lady Beaumont express enthusiastic admiration for him he obtained a tetraglot copy of the *Lettres provinciales* (Cologne 1684) from RS in Sept 1803 and read it with delight: *CL* II 994. Two months later he mentioned Pascal in connexion with his belief that "great men may err *wildly*, yet not be mad": *CN* I 1647. He took the tetraglot copy to Malta, annotated it, and used it for learning Italian: *CN* II 2133–6. It is now in VCL: see *CM (CC)* IV. Pascal, Madame Guyon, and Molière were exempted from his anti-Gallicism in a notebook entry of 1805: *CN* II 1598. *Lettres provinciales* was praised again in 1829: *C&S (CC)* 115.

[18] Robert Sanderson (1587–1663), bp of Lincoln.

[19] Joseph Hall (1574–1656), bp of Norwich.

[20] James Ussher (1581–1656), abp of Armagh.

the Reader has a *specimen* of the *reasonings* by which Leighton strove to invalidate or counterpoise the *reasonings* of the innovators.[a]

Passages of this sort are, however, of rare occurrence in Leighton's works. Happily for thousands, he was more usefully employed in making his Readers feel, that the Doctrines in question, *scripturally treated, and taken as co-organized parts of a great organic whole,* need no such reasonings. And better still would it have been, had he left them altogether for those, who severally detaching the great Features of Revelation from the living Context of Scripture, do by that very act destroy their life and purpose. And then, like the Eyes of the Aranea prodigiosa*, they become clouded microscopes, to exaggerate and distort all the other parts and proportions.[21] No offence then will be occasioned, I trust, by the frank avowal that I have given to the preceeding[b] passage a place among the Spiritual Aphorisms for the sake of the Comment: the following Remarks[c] having been the first original[d] Note I had pencilled on Leighton's Pages, and thus (remotely, at least), the occasion of the present Work.[22]

---

* The gigantic Indian Spider. See Baker's Microscopic Experiments.

---

[a] *AR* (1825): Innovators.
[b] *AR* (1825): preceding
[c] *AR* (1825): Remark
[d] *AR* (1825): marginal

---

[21] Henry Baker (1698–1774) describes how, desiring to see with the eyes of a giant spider, he cut them out carefully and set each in a pinhole made through a piece of card. "Their magnifying power was very great, and had they been taken from a Spider newly dead, I have Reason to believe they would have given me much Pleasure: but having been drying for some Years, they had contracted a Cloudiness that prevented Objects being seen through them with any tolerable Distinctness": *Employment for the Microscope* (1753) 413–14. Cf *Logic (CC)* 223 on the microscopic eye of the fly.

[22] The next paragraph takes its point of departure from a note on Leighton COPY C I 7, a passage marked with a pencil line in which Leighton locates the wisdom of a Christian as being ". . . when he can solace himself . . . with the comfortable assurance of the love of God, that he hath called him to holiness, given him some measure of it, and an endeavour after more;

and by this may he conclude, that he hath ordained him unto salvation". C commented: "Leighton most wisely avoids all metaphysical views of Election relatively to God; and confines himself to the practical—to the doctrine as it must bear on every Man who thinks at all.—": *CM (CC)* III. When C speaks of ". . . the following Remarks" as having been "the first original Note I had pencilled on Leighton's Pages", however, he is probably thinking of his first note in COPY B: a long comment on vol I in which he develops a similar approach at length. See *CM (CC)* III. If this "first original Note" was "(remotely, at least) the occasion of the present Work", it is more likely to have been the one made in Gillman's copy than that in COPY C, which was obtained when the work was already well planned. (See Editor's Introduction, above, at nn 81–3.)

BM MS Egerton 2801 f 171[v] seems to mark a further step in C's thinking: this is headed (probably later) "Spiritual Apho-

Leighton, I observed, throughout his inestimable Work, avoids all metaphysical views of Election, relatively to God, and confines himself to the Doctrine in its relation to Man: and in that sense too, in which every Christian may judge who strives to be sincere with his *a*own heart. The following may, I think*b* be taken as a safe and useful Rule in religious inquiries. Ideas, that derive their origin and substance from the *Moral* Being, and to the reception of which as true *objectively* (*i.e.* as corresponding to a *reality* out of the human mind) we are determined by a *practical* interest exclusively,[23] may not, like theoretical or speculative Positions, be pressed onward into all their possible *logical* conse-

---

a *AR* (1825): p 159
b *AR* (1825): think,

---

rism II L" and continues: "Vol. I. p. 9, 10 | Comment. Leighton gives an example in this passage well worthy the attention and imitation of all Ministers of the Gospel. Here (and indeed throughout his work) he avoids all metaphysical Views of Election . . .". The passage (presumably designed originally to appear as a "Comment" on an extract to have been reproduced from COPY B I 9–10) then continues as here down to "legitimate", after which a long passage is cancelled and replaced by one beginning on f 169. See App B(q) and (r) below.

[23] *AR* (1825) COPY F has a long note at this point: "The reason is obvious. Ideas (*vide* p. 226) can only be expressed in inadequate terms, *improprie* and by *accomodation*. And all the objects of religious Faith are necessarily *ideas*—i.e. neither Objects of Sense nor Conceptions generalized from sensible Objects. Now to draw full and literal conclusions from known inadequate and mixt premises is false Logic as well as bad Divinity. Example—the Prescience of God shall be the Term of the Premise. If a modern Calvinist concludes from this the necessity & coercive pre-determination of the Actions fore-known, we must remind him that in God omniscient there is neither *Præ* nor *Post*—that Prescience is a term of accomodation. Our, or the imperfect expression of an Idea for the interests and at the dictate of the Moral Being—and that the moment the Conclusion passes beyond the demands, and against the interests and intuitions of the Moral Be-

ing, the baser alloy mixt with in the expression in order to its being minted by the human Understanding, the portion of anthropomorphism, introduced as the husk and vehicles of the Idea, betrays itself.— This is excellently set forth in the Church Article on Predestination. For the superior Minds the remedy, or rather the Preventive, lies in the contemplation of the Idea itself; but for the Many the only, but likewise the Ssufficient, Safe-guard is provided in the maxim, that, ⟨as⟩ revealed truths cannot contradict each other—the words or texts, that express a truth which from the limits & constitution of our Understanding we are can only apprehend imperfectly, and in part (*I Corinth. XIII. 12.*) must have their interpretation determined & qualified by those such texts, which as express doctrines, which by the Light of Reason in the Conscience we *are* capable of understanding fully; and the certain truth of which is known with the *highest evidence*. For the intuitions (i.e. immediate truth revelations) of the enlightened Conscience, are to the Spiritual Man and even to the Moralist, what the Intuitions, or necessary forms, of Sense are to the Mathematician—the ne plus ultra, with which whatever does cannot be brought into harmony, or compatibility at least, must be false. See p. 334, 335. [i.e. pp 340–2, below]. S. T. C." The "Church Article" is "Of Predestination and Election", No XVII in *BCP*. For intuition see *Sp Aph B I* n 4 above.

quences.*^a The Law of Conscience, and not the Canons of discursive Reasoning, must decide in such cases. At least, the latter have^b no validity, which the single *Veto* of the former is not sufficient to nullify. The most pious conclusion is here the most legitimate.

It is too seldom considered, though most worthy of consideration, how far even those Ideas or Theories of pure Speculation, that bear the same name with the Objects of Religious Faith, are indeed the same. Out of the principles necessarily presumed in all discursive Thinking, and which being, in the first place^c *universal*, and secondly, antecedent to every particular exercise of the Understanding, are therefore referred to the Reason, the human Mind (wherever its powers are sufficiently developed, and its attention strongly directed to speculative or theoretical inquiries,) forms certain Essences, to which for its own purposes it gives a sort of notional *Subsistence*. Hence they are called *Entia rationalia:*²⁴ the conversion of which into *Entia realia*, or real Objects, by aid of the Imagination, has in all times been the fruitful Stock of empty Theories, and mischievous Superstitions, of surreptitious Premisses^d and extravagant Conclusions. For as these substantiated Notions were in many instances expressed by the same terms, as the objects of religious Faith; as in most instances they were applied, though deceptively, to the explanation of real experiences; and lastly, from the gratifications, which the pride and ambition of man received from the supposed extension of his Knowledge and Insight; it was too easily forgotten or overlooked, that the stablest and most indispensable of these notional Beings were but the necessary *forms* of Thinking, taken abstractedly: and that like the breadthless Lines, depthless Surfaces, and perfect Circles of Geometry, they subsist wholly and solely in and for the Mind, that contemplates them. Where the evidence of the Senses fails us, and beyond

---

* May not this just and excellent Rule be expressed more intelligibly, (to a mathematician at least), thus:—Reasoning from *finite* to *finite*, on a basis of truth, also, reasoning from *infinite* to *infinite*, on a basis of truth, will always lead to truth, as intelligible as the basis on which such truths respectively rest. While, reasoning from *finite* to *infinite;* or from *infinite* to *finite;* will lead to apparent absurdity, although the basis be true: and is not *such* apparent absurdity, another expression for "truth unintelligible by a *finite* mind?''

^a *AR* (1825): Footnote added in 1831
^b *AR* (1825): has
^c *AR* (1825): place,
^d *AR* (1825): Premises ; p 160 begins (mises)

²⁴ "Beings of the reason'', or, as C has it below, "notional Beings''. Cf *Logic (CC)* 298: "therefore, out of the mind, every generic idea is a nonentity, hence said by the old logicians to have their beings in thought, *entia rationis*''; "real Beings'': cf ibid 240–1 and C's note on pp 68–9; also *CM (CC)* III 43.

the precincts of sensible[25] experience, there is no *Reality* attributable to any Notion, but what is given to it by Revelation, or the Law of Conscience, or the necessary interests of Morality.

Take an instance;

It is the office, and,[a] as it were, the instinct of Reason to bring a unity into all our conceptions and several knowledges. On this all system depends;[b] and without this we could reflect connectedly neither on nature nor[c] our own minds. Now this is possible only on the assumption or hypothesis of a ONE as the ground and cause of the Universe, and which in all succession and through[d] changes is the subject neither of Time nor[e] Change. The ONE must be contemplated as Eternal and Immutable.[26]

[f] Well! the Idea, which is the basis of Religion, commanded by the Conscience and required by Morality, contains the same truths, or at least Truths that can be expressed in no other terms; but this Idea presents itself to our mind with additional Attributes, and these too not formed[g] by mere Abstraction and Negation—with the Attributes of Holiness, Providence, Love, Justice, and Mercy. It comprehends, moreover, the independent (*extra-mundane*) existence and[h] personality of the supreme ONE, as our Creator, Lord, and Judge.

The hypothesis of a *one* Ground and Principle of the Universe (necessary as an *hypothesis;* but having only a *logical* and *conditional* necessity) is thus raised into[i] the Idea of the LIVING GOD, the supreme Object of our Faith, Love, Fear, and Adoration. Religion and Morality do indeed constrain us to declare him Eternal and Immutable. But if from the Eternity of the Supreme Being a Reasoner should deduce the impossibility of a Creation; or conclude with Aristotle, that the Creation

---

[a] *AR* (1825): and

[b] *AR* (1825): depends:

[c] *AR* (1825): or

[d] *AR* (1825): through all

[e] *AR* (1825): or

[f] *AR* (1825): p 161

[g] COPY D: formed (like those of the *ens rationale* or hypothetic ONE above-mentioned)

[h] COPIES C & D: and the

[i] COPY D: into (or rather, *exchanged for*)

---

[25] BM MS Eg 2801 f 169ᵛ has a footnote here referring the reader to "the Chapter on Faith in the 'Assertion of Religion' ": see App B(r) below.

[26] C's terminology here resembles that of Plotinus, e.g. in *Enneads* 3.8, entitled "Nature, Contemplation, and the One", and in 6.9, "On the Good, or the One", in which the One is described (6.9.3) as existing "before all form was, before movement and before rest; for these pertain to being and are what make it many" (tr A. H. Armstrong—LCL 1966–88). C owned and annotated the edition of Plotinus, with M. Ficino's Latin translation, published at Basle in 1580: *CM (CC)* IV.

was co-eternal;[27] or, like the latter[a] Platonists, should turn Creation into *Emanation*,[28] and make the universe proceed from Deity, as the Sun-beams[b] from the Solar Orb;—or if from the divine Immutability he should infer, that all Prayer and Supplication must be vain and supersti-tious: then however evident and logically necessary such conclusions may appear, it is scarcely worth our while to examine, whether they are so or not. The Positions themselves *must* be false. For were they true, the Idea would lose the sole ground of its *reality*. It would be no longer the Idea intended [c]by the Believer in *his* premiss[d]—in the Premiss,[e] with which alone Religion and Morality are concerned. The very subject of the discussion would be changed. It would no longer be the God,[f] in whom we *believe;* but a stoical FATE, or the superessential[29] ONE of Plo-tinus, to whom neither Intelligence, nor[g] Self-consciousness, nor[h] Life, nor[i] even *Being* can[j] be attributed; nor[k] lastly, the World itself, the in-divisible one and only substance (*substantia una et unica*)[30] of Spinoza,

[a] *AR* (1825): later
[b] *AR* (1825): Sunbeams [1831 hyphenates]
[c] *AR* (1825): p 162
[d] *AR* (1825): premise
[e] *AR* (1825): Premise,
[f] *AR* (1825): God,
[g] *AR* (1825): or
[h] *AR* (1825): or
[i] *AR* (1825): or
[j] *AR* (1825): dare
[k] *AR* (1825): or

[27] A point made by e.g. Thomas Stanley *History of Philosophy* (1701) 250; Cud-worth *True Intellectual System of the Uni-verse* ch 4 § 24 (1743) 414, 417; and by Leighton in his Lecture XI "Of the Crea-tion of the World": COPY C IV 255.

[28] On emanation, including the compar-ison with the sun's rays, cf Plotinus *Enne-ads* 1.7.1, 5.1.6, 5.3.12, 6.9.9. The suc-cessors of Plotinus interposed more and more emanations between the One and the material universe. Leighton dismisses em-anation much more briefly, COPY C IV 256. See next note.

[29] Cf *Enneads* 6.8.14 in which the One is described as "primarily itself and super-essentially (ὑπερόντως) self". The word "super-essential" was used by Thomas Taylor repeatedly as the exact Latin-based equivalent of ὑπερούσιος, found in Proclus *Elements of Theology* 115 and 119, which is appended to his *Commentaries . . . on*

the *First Book of Euclid* (see also p 4 n 1, above). Plotinus stripped the One suc-cessively of all attributes in *Enneads* 6.9. Leighton COPY C IV 334–6 discusses this "negative" way to knowledge of God, slightly misquoting the Plotinus phrase.

[30] This precise form is not traced in his work, but in the early propositions of the *Ethics* (e.g. 1 prop x) Spinoza used the term "unica substantia". In 1830 C claimed that Spinoza in his last letter began to suspect his premise: "His Unica Sub-stantia is in fact a mere Notion, a *subject* of the Mind, and no *object* at all": *TT* 31 Mar *(CC)* I 98 (1836 vn, dated 30 Apr, II 77). If C is referring to Spinoza's letter to Albert Burgh of Dec 1675, the last in *Opera post-huma* (1677), see Spinoza *Opera quae su-persunt omnia* ed H. E. G. Paulus (2 vols Jena 1802–3) (HCR's copy of which, with C's annotations, is in Manchester College, Oxford) I 695–700, he is presumably think-

of which all Phaenomena, all particular and individual Things, Lives, Minds, Thoughts, and Actions are but modifications.

Let the Believer never be alarmed by Objections wholly speculative, however plausible on speculative grounds such objections may appear, if he can but satisfy himself, that the *Result* is repugnant to the dictates of Conscience, and irreconcilable with the interests of Morality. For to baffle the Objector we have only to demand of him, by what right and under what authority he converts a Thought into a Substance, or asserts the existence of a real somewhat corresponding to a Notion not derived from the experience of his Senses. It will be of no purpose for him to answer, that it is a *legitimate* Notion. The *Notion* may have its mould in the understanding; but its realization must be the work of the FANCY.

A reflecting Reader will easily apply these remarks to the subject of Election, one of the stumbling stones in the ordinary conceptions of the Christian Faith, to which the Infidel points in scorn, and which far better *a*men pass by in silent perplexity. Yet surely, from mistaken conceptions of the Doctrine. I suppose the person, with whom I am arguing, already so far a Believer, as to have convinced himself, both that a state of enduring Bliss is attainable under certain conditions; and that these conditions consist in his compliance with the directions given and rules prescribed in the Christian Scriptures. These rules he likewise admits to be such, that, by the very law and constitution of the human mind, a full and faithful compliance with them cannot but have *consequences*, of some sort or other. But these *consequences* are moreover distinctly described, enumerated, and promised in the same Scriptures, in which the Conditions are recorded; and though some of them may be apparent to God only, yet the greater number *b*of them*c* are of such a nature that they cannot exist unknown to the Individual, in and for whom they exist. As little possible is it, that he should find these consequences in himself, and not find in them the sure marks and the safe pledges, that he is at the time in the right road to the Life promised under these conditions. Now I dare assert, that no such man, however fervent his charity, and however deep his humility, may be, can peruse the records of History

a AR (1825): p 163
b-c Added in 1831

ing of Spinoza's statement: ". . . I do not presume that I have found the best Philosophy, but I know that I think [it] the true one. If you ask me how I know this, I shall answer, in the same way that you know that the three angles of a triangle are equal to two right angles" (tr A. Wolf *Correspon-* *dence of Spinoza*—1928—352). This declaration, with its resemblance to Kant, might suggest that Spinoza was thinking noumenally; but he might well have replied that in his letter he was making an epistemological point only. See also below, *Conc* n 52.

with a reflecting spirit, or "look round the world" with an observant eye,[31] and not find himself compelled to admit, that *all* men are *not* on the right Road. He cannot help judging, that even in Christian countries Many, a fearful Many! have not their faces turned toward it.

*a*This then is a*b* mere matter of fact. Now comes the question. Shall the Believer, who thus hopes on the appointed *grounds* of Hope, attribute this distinction exclusively to his own resolves and strivings? or if not exclusively, yet primarily and principally? Shall he refer the first movements and preparations to his own Will and Understanding, and bottom his claim to the Promises on his own comparative excellence? If not, if no man dare take this honor*c* to himself, to whom shall he assign it, if not to that Being in whom the Promise originated,*d* and on whom its Fulfilment depends? If he stop here, who shall blame him? By what argument shall his reasoning be invalidated, that might not be urged with equal force against any essential difference between Obedient and Disobedient, Christian and Worldling? that would not imply that both *sorts* alike are, in the sight of God, the Sons of God by adoption? If he stop here, I say, who shall drive him from his position? For thus far he is practically concerned—this the Conscience requires, this the highest interests of Morality demand. It is a question of Facts, of the Will and the Deed, to argue against which on the abstract notions and possibilities of the speculative Reason,*e* is as unreasonable, as an attempt to decide a question of Colors*f* by pure Geometry, or to unsettle the classes and specific characters of Natural History by the Doctrine of Fluxions.[32]

But if the Self-examinant will abandon this position, and exchange

---

a *AR* (1825): p 164   *b* Added in 1831
c *AR* (1825): honour   *d* *AR* (1825): originated
e *AR* (1825): Reason   *f* *AR* (1825): Colours

[31] This quotation originally came at the end of a long and very complex sentence, including a footnote referring to *The Friend*, which C changed in proof: *CL* v 321. See below, App B(s) and (t).

The quotation ("look around the world" in the ms) and the word "observant" suggest echoes in C's mind of Pope *Essay on Man* ep III lines 7–8:

Look round our World: behold the chain of Love
Combining all below and all above . . .

of Johnson's *Vanity of Human Wishes* 1–2:

Let observation with extensive view
Survey mankind from China to Peru . . .

and Cowper's *Expostulation* lines 126–7:

. . . let the Muse look round
From east to west no sorrow can be found . . .

If so he is also taking up the sombre overtones in other parts of those poems. The "road" metaphor that follows in *AR* is a favourite with Johnson and Cowper.

[32] Used as a name for the Newtonian calculus: see *OED* s.v. "Fluxions". 'Self-examinant' below is the only example in *OED*.

the safe circle of Religion and practical Reason for the shifting Sand-wastes and *Mirages* of *a*Speculative Theology; if instead of seeking after the *marks* of Election in himself he undertakes to determine the ground and origin, the possibility and mode of election*b* itself *in relation to God;*—in this case, and whether he does it for the satisfaction of curiosity, or from the ambition of answering those, who would call God himself to account, why and by what right certain Souls were born in Africa instead of England? or why (seeing that it is against all reason and goodness to choose a worse,*c* when being omnipotent He*d* could have created a better) God did not create Beasts Men, and Men Angels? or why God created any men but with pre-knowledge of their obedience, and*e* left any occasion for Election?—in this case, I say, we can only regret, that the Inquirer had not been better instructed in the nature, the bounds, the true purposes and proper objects of his intellectual faculties,[33] and that he had not previously asked himself, by what appropriate Sense, or Organ of Knowledge, he hoped to secure an insight into a Nature which was neither an Object of his Senses, nor a part of his self-consciousness!*f* [34] and so leave him to ward off shadowy Spears with the

a   *AR* (1825): p 165
b   *AR* (1825): Election
c   *AR* (1825): worse
d   *AR* (1825): he
e   *AR* (1825) Corr: and why he
f   *AR* (1825): Self-consciousness!

[33] Other statements by C suggest that he thought the ignorance of "the objects of the intellectual faculties" in the case of election to be associated with a false idea of eternity: "All the sophistry of the pre-destinarians rests on the false notion of Eternity as a sort of Time antecedent to Time. It is timeless, present with & in all times"—annotation on Bunyan *Pilgrim's Progress*: *CM (CC)* I 825. Cf *CM (CC)* II 728, 729, 735, 741 and *CN* IV 4644 f 26.

For a meditation in 1809 on the idea of time as, where the Supreme Being is concerned, "the ⟨self-⟩sacrifice which Truth makes to Conception", see *CN* III 3575. The idea that the priority of the Absolute is logical rather than temporal is an important topic in the Opus Maximum: see the accounts of the mss in J. H. Muirhead *Coleridge as Philosopher* (1930) 112–13 and Barth 87–8. Waterland makes a similar point in relation to the Father and the Son: *A Vindication of Christ's Divinity* (1719)

141: "A *priority of nature*, not of Time, or *Duration* . . ."; see also Berkeley *Siris* § 362, quoted App I Excursus Note 4 below. The origin of evil is seen as a timeless event in a notebook entry of 1822, *CN* IV 4909 f 79ᵛ, and in an annotation on Böhme, *CM (CC)* I 684–5, quoted below, *Sp Aph B Xa* n 41; redemption is viewed in similar terms in N 41 (1829–30) f 36ᵛ (*CN* v): "What Jesus did in time, and all the Elect each in time and numerically, that Christ did αχρονως [timelessly], inclusively of all by an *elevant* Act—the former being the manifestation of the latter . . .". See Barth 122–4 for other references and a fuller discussion; also, for a similar discussion in relation to baptism, N 37 ff 80–78ᵛ (*CN* v), quoted below, App D(c). In the context of *AR* it is noteworthy that "the taking Eternity as a *sort* of Time" was a defect he identified in the reasoning of Leighton; also: *CN* IV 4853.

[34] *AR* (1825) COPY D inserts at this point:

shadow of a Shield, and to retaliate the nonsense of Blasphemy with the Abracadabra of Presumption. He that will fly without wings must fly in his dreams: and till he awakes, will not find out, that to fly in a dream is but to dream of flying.[35]

Thus then the Doctrine of Election is in itself a necessary inference from an undeniable fact—necessary at least for all who hold that the best of men are what they are through the grace of God. In relation to the [a]Believer it is a *Hope*, which if it spring out of Christian Principles, be examined by the tests and nourished by the means prescribed in Scripture, will become a *lively*, an *assured* Hope,[36] but which cannot in this life pass into *knowledge*, much less certainty of fore-knowledge. The contrary belief does indeed make the article of Election both tool and parcel of a mad and mischievous fanaticism. But with what force and clearness does not the Apostle confute, disclaim, and prohibit the pretence, treating it as a downright contradiction in terms! See Romans, viii. 24.[37]

But though I hold the doctrine handled as Leighton handles it (that is practically, morally, *humanly*) rational, safe, and of essential importance, I see many* reasons resulting from the peculiar circumstances,

---

* *Exempli gratia*: at the date of St. Paul's Epistles,[b] the (Roman) World may be resembled to a Mass in the Furnace in the first moment of fusion, here a speck and there a spot of the melted Metal shining pure and brilliant amid the scum and dross. To have received the *name* of Christian was a privilege, a high and distinguishing favor.[c38] No wonder therefore, that in St. Paul's writings the words, Elect and Election, often, nay, most[d] often,[e]

> [a] *AR* (1825): p 166
> [b] *AR* (1825): Epistles
> [c] *AR* (1825): favour.
> [d] COPY D: *most*
> [e] *AR* (1825): often ; COPY D: often,

"If these remonstrances make no impression, and the chivalrous Champion '*pruriens in pugnam*' is bent on overwhelming all unbelievers by a full exposition of the Divine Counsels—what can a sober Man do but smile or sigh . . .''. Cf Martial 3.58.11: ''. . . prurit in pugnam'' (''he is eager for the conflict''), found by C in Reimarus in 1804 and Anglicised to describe the ''hot-blooded Paddy'': *CN* II 2333.

[35] For other examples of wish-fulfilment in dreams see *CN* I 44 (and *N&Q* ccxviii—1973—45–6) and *CL* I 173.

[36] 1 Pet 1.3; Heb 6.11; Acts 17.31, etc.

[37] AV: ''For we are saved by hope: but hope that is seen is not hope: for what a man seeth, why doth he yet hope for?''

[38] C's assertion receives reinforcement from the fact that the collective name of ''Christian'' was in NT times apparently used only by outsiders (Acts 11.26, 26.28, 1 Pet 4.16). St Paul addressed his letters to ''those called *to be* saints'' (κλητοὶ ἅγιοι), Rom 1.7, 1 Cor 1.2; to the church (ἐκκλησία) of God, or of Galatia, etc, 2 Cor 1.1, Gal 1.2, Eph 1.1, 1 Thess 1.1, 2 Thess 1.1; to ''the saints and faithful brethren'', Col 1.2; and the author of 1 Pet to ''the strangers [of Asia Minor] . . . elect'': 1 Pet 1.1–2 (the subject of Leighton's commentary in this aphorism). See also *TT* 19 May 1830 *(CC)* I 142–3 and nn; II (1836 vn, dated 25 May) 96.

under *a*which St. Paul preached and wrote, why a discreet Minister of the Gospel should avoid the frequent use of the *term*, and express the *meaning* in other words perfect*b* equivalent and equally scriptural: lest in *saying* truth he might convey error.[41]

---

mean the same as *eccalumeni,c* ecclesia, i.e. those who have been *called out* of the World: and it is a dangerous perversion of the Apostle's word to interpret it in the sense, in which it was used by our Lord, viz. in *opposition to the Called*. (Many are *called* but few *chosen*).[39] In St. Paul's sense and at that time the Believers collectively formed a small and select number; and every Christian, real or nominal, was one of the Elect. Add too, that this ambiguity is increased by the accidental circumstance, that the *kyriak*, Aedes *Dominicae*, Lord's House, *Kirk;* and Ecclesia, the sum total of the Eccalûmeni, *evocati, Called-out;* are both rendered by the same word Church.[40]

a *AR* (1825): p 167
b *AR* (1825): perfectly
c *AR* (1825): *eccalûmeni,*

[39] Matt 20.16, 22.14. C was not writing with NT Greek fresh in his mind. The only derivative of ἐχχαλέω (I call out) used there is ἐχχλησία (AV "church"). The word had long been established in secular Greek in the sense especially of a democratic assembly, and occurs frequently in the Septuagint (AV "congregation"). There is no sign that biblical writers were particularly conscious of the specific sense which C found so significant—and which was stressed by Richard Field and Jeremy Taylor (*CM—CC*—II 654 textus, *C&S—CC*—45 n 1). The word corresponding to "called" as a verbal adjective is, as in Rom 8.28, χλητός; the verb is χαλέω, as in Rom 8.29, 30; "elect" in AV regularly corresponds to ἐχλεχτός, which is derived from ἐχλέγομαι, regularly translated "choose".

Of St Paul's central pronouncements on predestination, Rom 28–30 e.g. mentions "calling"; in Eph 1.4–5 "God has chosen us . . . that we should be holy (ἁγίους)". He nowhere is found distinctly to oppose the "called" to the "elect". There is justification, therefore, for C's feeling that the translators' choice of "elect", a more specifically technical term than "chosen", was unfortunate.

[40] The last point is used in a notebook entry of 1815 (*CN* III 4252) and developed more fully in another of Dec 1823 (*CN* IV 5082): "In England the Liturgic & Cere-monial, in one word, τα χυριαχα, the *Church*, were uppermost in the minds of the men in power—in Scotland, the *Preaching*, the *Calling*, the *Church*—as answering to the *Ecclesia*; the εχχαλουμε-νοι—In England the Church or Kirk according to its etymology—in Scotland the Kirk by a metaphorical rendering . . .". In the notebook entry C goes on to use (as in *CN* IV 5020—Oct 1823) the coined word "enclesia" to denote the first sense; to enforce the present point by distinguishing it from "ecclesia" then becomes a favourite theme of his writings: see annotation on Skelton *Works* III 397: *LR* IV 278 (*CM—CC*); letter of c 16 May 1825: *CL* v 455; *CN* IV 5020, 5082, 5084, 5263, 5395; *CM* *(CC)* II 1139–40, 1142–3 (1824–6), I 529 and n (1830), and II 943 (1833). For central discussions see *C&S (CC)* 45–6 and n, 125 and n. In 1823 C distinguished in Kantian terms between the belief in a Theocracy, "Ecclesia *Phænomenon*", and in a symbolic religious gathering, "Ecclesia Noumenon": *CN* IV 5039. For "eccalumeni" see *TT (CC)* I 142.

[41] For further discussions of the problem of speaking truth while conveying error see *Friend* 10 Aug 1809 *(CC)* II 45–6, *BL* ch 9 *(CC)* I 157, and a notebook entry of 1805: *CN* II 2397. In *CN* II 2397n the editor draws attention to a relevant passage in Godwin *Political Justice* (3rd ed 1797) I 328. Cf also *CN* IV 4707.

Had my purpose been confined to one particular Tenet, an apology might be required for so long a Comment. But the Reader will, I trust, have already perceived, that my Object has been to establish a general Rule of interpretation and vindication applicable to *all* doctrinal Tenets, and especially to the (so called) Mysteries of the Christian Faith: to provide a *Safety-lamp*[42] for religious inquirers. Now this I find in the principle, that all Revealed Truths are to be judged of by us, as far as they are possible subjects of human Conception, or grounds of Practice, or in some way connected with our moral and spiritual Interests. In order to have a reason *for* forming a judgment on any given article, we must be sure that we possess a Reason, by and according to which a judgment may be formed. Now in respect of all Truths, to which a *real* independent existence is assigned, and which yet are not contained in, or to be imagined under, any form of Space or Time, it is strictly demonstrable, that the human Reason, considered abstractly as the source of positive[a] *Science* and theoretical *Insight*, is *not* such a Reason. At the utmost, it has only a *negative* voice. In other words, nothing can be allowed as true for the human Mind, which directly contradicts this Reason. But even here, before we admit the existence of any such [b]contradiction, we must be careful to ascertain, that there is no equivocation in play, that two different subjects are not confounded under one and the same word. A striking instance of this has been adduced in the difference between the notional ONE of the Ontologists, and the Idea of the Living God.

But if not the abstract or speculative Reason, and yet a Reason there must be in order to a Rational Belief—then it must be the *Practical* Reason of Man,[43] comprehending the Will, the Conscience, the Moral Being with its inseparable Interests and Affections—that Reason, namely, which is the Organ of *Wisdom*, and (as far as Man is concerned) the Source of living and actual Truths.

[a] COPY D: formal
[b] *AR* (1825): p 168

[42] C's old friend Humphry Davy (see also below, *Conc* n 37) invented the safety-lamp in 1815.

[43] C's schedule of the faculties in *Omniana* II 13–14 Includes "the will, or practical reason" as well as "the speculative reason". The use of these terms echoes Kant, who, near the end of his unpaginated preface to *Grundlegung zur Metaphysik* (Riga 1797) (tr T. K. Abbott—1907—7–8), observed that he had already examined "pure speculative reason" in his *Critik der reinen Vernunft* (1781) and now intended to publish a metaphysics of morals, for which the only foundation was the critical examination of a "pure practical reason". In that work, *Critik der praktischen Vernunft* (1788), the "practical reason" was in important respects identified, as here, with the will. See also *BL* ch 9 *(CC)* I 154n, quoting C's denial, in an annotation on Schelling, that Kant meant to indicate "two *Persons* or *Beings*" by his distinction, "but only that what we could not *prove* by one train of argument, we might by another".

From these premisses[a] we may further deduce, that every doctrine is to be interpreted in reference to those, to whom it has been revealed, or who have or have had the means of knowing or hearing the same. For instance: the Doctrine that there is no name under Heaven, by which a man can be saved, but the name of Jesus.[44] If the word here rendered *Name*, may be understood (as it well may, and as in other texts it must be) as meaning the Power, or originating Cause,[45] I see no objection on the part of the Practical Reason to our belief of the declaration in its whole extent. It is true universally or not true at all. If there be any redemptive Power not contained in the Power of Jesus, then Jesus is not *the* Redeemer: not the Redeemer of the *World*, not the Jesus (i.e. Saviour[46]) of Man*kind*. But if with Tertullian and Augustin we make the [b]Text assert the condemnation and misery of all who are not Christians by Baptism and explicit Belief in the Revelation of the New Covenant[47]—then I say, the doctrine is true *to all intents and purposes*. It is true, in every respect, in which any practical, moral, or spiritual Interest or End can be connected with its truth. It is true in respect to every man who has had, or who might have had, the Gospel preached to him. It is true and obligatory for every Christian Community and for every individual Believer, wherever the opportunity is afforded of spreading the *Light* of the Gospel,[c] and making *known* the name of the only Saviour and Redeemer. For even though the uninformed Heathens

[a] *AR* (1825): premisses
[b] *AR* (1825): p 169
[c] *AR* (1825): Gospel

[44] See Acts 4.12.

[45] Among the texts C might have had in mind are Ps 8.1: "O Lord our Lord, how excellent is thy name in all the earth!", followed by a meditation on the Creation, and John 17.5–6, where Jesus reflects on the glory he had with the Father "before the world was" and continues "I have manifested thy name unto the men which thou gavest me out of the world . . ." Cf too C's annotation on J. Taylor *Liberty of Prophesying* sect xviii: Σύμβολον Θεολογικόν, *or a Collection of Polemicall Discourses* (1674) 1063: ". . . in the great Form of Baptism [Mat 28.19] the words are not εν ονοματι [AV "in the name"]; but εις ονομα [into the name] & many learned men have shown that they may mean *into the power* or influence of the Father, Son, & H. Spirit": *LR* III 288; *CM (CC)*. For more on the relationship between *nomen* and *numen*

see below *Sp Aph B VIIIb* n 52, where C's text cites also Ps 20.1: ". . . the name of the God of Jacob defend thee."

[46] Although the etymology has been disputed, the interpretation of the Hebrew name "Jesus" as meaning "saviour" is of longstanding provenance, appearing in Matt 1. 21: "thou shalt call his name JESUS: for he shall save his people from their sins".

[47] C is apparently combining the points that baptism is undertaken "in the name of the Father and of the Son and of the Holy Ghost", and that Tertullian and Augustine insisted on the necessity of baptism for salvation. For Tertullian this was accompanied by encouragement of late baptism: see below *Sp Aph B [XXIV]* n 28, while for Augustine it made infant baptism desirable: ibid nn 49, 63, 64.

should *not* perish, the *guilt* of their Perishing will attach to those who not only had no certainty of their safety, but who are*[a]* commanded to *act* on the supposition of the contrary. But if, on the other hand, a theological Dogmatist should attempt to persuade me, that this Text was intended to give us an historical knowledge of God's future Actions and Dealings—and for the gratification of our Curiosity to inform us, that Socrates and Phocion,[48] together with all the Savages in the*[b]* Woods and Wilds of Africa and America, will be sent to keep company with the Devil and his Angels in everlasting Torments—I should remind him, that the purpose of Scripture was to teach us our duty, not to enable us to sit in judgment on the souls of our fellow creatures.

One other instance will, I trust, prevent all misconception of my meaning. I am clearly convinced, that *[c]*the scriptural and only true* Idea of God will, in its development, be found to involve the Idea of the Trinity.[50] But I am likewise convinced, that previously*[d]* to the promulgation of the Gospel the Doctrine had no claim on the Faith of Mankind: though it might have been a legitimate Contemplation for a speculative philosopher, a Theorem in Metaphysics valid in the Schools.

I form a certain notion in my mind, and say: this is what *I* understand by the term, God. From books and conversation I find, that the Learned generally connect the same notion with the same word. I then apply the Rules, laid down by the Masters of Logic, for the involution and evolution of Terms, and prove (to as many as agree with me in my premisses)*[e]* that the Notion, God, involves the Notion, Trinity. I now pass out of the Schools, and enter into discourse with some friend or neighbour, unversed in the *formal* sciences, unused to the process*[f]* of Abstrac-

---

* Or (I might have added) *any* Idea which does not either identify the Creator with the Creation; or else represent the Supreme Being as a mere impersonal Law*[g]* or *Ordo ordinans*,[49] differing from the Law of Gravitation only by its *universality*.

---

[a] *AR* (1825): were
[b] *AR* (1825): the untravelled
[c] *AR* (1825): p 170
[d] *AR* (1825): previous
[e] *AR* (1825): premises)
[f] *AR* (1825): processes
[g] *AR* (1825): LAW

[48] Athenian general and statesman. He was, like Socrates, a virtuous victim of popular disfavour. Irreproachable in private life, incorruptible, loyal, prudent, moderate, he was put to death as a traitor after a military defeat in 418 b.c., aged over eighty. For more see Plutarch's *Lives*.

[49] "Ordering order". Cf above, Editor's Introduction at n 8.

[50] For a discussion of the following passage in the context of C's ideas about the Trinity see Barth 98–9 and ch 4 generally. For the word "Tri-unity" see *SM (CC)* 62 and n, and *OED*, s.v.

tion, neither Logician nor*a* Metaphysician; but sensible and single-minded, "an Israelite indeed,"[51] trusting in "the Lord God of his Fathers, even the God of Abraham, of Isaac, and of Jacob."[52] If I speak of God to *him*, what will *he* understand me to be speaking of? What does he mean, and suppose me to mean, by the word? An Accident or Product of the reasoning faculty, or an Abstraction which the human Mind forms*b* by reflecting*c* on its own thoughts and forms of thinking? No. By God he understands me to mean an existing and self-subsisting reality*,

* I have elsewhere remarked on the assistance which those that labor*d* after distinct conceptions would receive from the re-introduction of the terms *objective* and *subjective, objective and subjective reality*, &c. as substitutes for *real* and *notional*, and to the exclusion of the false antithesis between *real* and *ideal*.[53] For the Student in that noblest of the Sciences, the Scire teipsum,[54] the advantage would be especially great.†*e* The few sentences that follow, in illustration of the terms here advocated, will not, I trust, be a waste of the Reader's Time.

The celebrated Euler having demonstrated certain properties of Arches, adds: "All experience is in contradiction to this; but this is no reason for doubting its truth." The words *sound* paradoxical; but mean no more than this—that the mathematical properties of Figure and Space are not less certainly the properties of Figure and Space because they can never be perfectly realized in wood, stone, or iron.[56] Now this assertion of Euler's might be

† See the *"Selection from Mr. Coleridge's Literary Correspondence,"f* in Blackwood's Ed. Magazine, for October,*g* 1821, Letter ii. p. 244–253,[55] which, however, should any of my Readers take the trouble of consulting, he must be content with such parts as he finds intelligible at the first perusal. For from defects in the MS., and without any fault on the part of the Editor, too large a portion is so printed that the man must be equally bold and fortunate in his conjectural readings who can make out any meaning at all.

a *AR* (1825): or
b *AR* (1825) Corr: makes
c *AR* (1825): p 171 (ing)
d *AR* (1825): labour
e *AR* (1825): great*.
f *AR* (1825): *Correspondence"*
g *AR* (1825): October

[51] "Behold an Israelite indeed, in whom is no guile!" Jesus' words of Nathanael, John 1.47. Used by C of his own father: see letter of 16 Oct 1797: *CL* I 355 and *C Life* (G) 4.
[52] This biblical formulation is first used by God to Moses in the incident of the burning bush: Exod 3.6. See also below, *Sp Aph B XXIIIa* n 24.
[53] See "On the philosophic import of the Words, OBJECT and SUBJECT" *Bl Mag* x (Oct 1821) 244–53: *SW&F (CC)*. Cf C's associated letters to Blackwood, *CL* v 165–71 and nn.
[54] "Know thyself". A favourite tag of

C's: he normally quotes the Greek version Γνῶθι σεαυτόν as found in Juvenal *Satires* 11.27. See above, *Pref* n 10, and *PW* (EHC) I 486. Cf also *BL* ch 24 *(CC)* II 240n.
[55] See n 53, above.
[56] The meaning is clearer in the 1818 *Friend*, in which C includes, between "this" and "but", the words ". . . sed potius fidendum est analysi" ("but one must believe the analysis rather"), followed by his paraphrase, "*i.e.* but this is no reason for doubting the analysis". It also reads "entirely transferred to material bodies" for ". . . perfectly realized in wood, stone,

expressed at once, briefly and simply, by saying, that the properties in question were *subjectively* true, though not objectively—or that the Mathematical Arch possessed a *subjective reality*, though incapable of being realized *objectively*.

In like manner if I had to express my conviction, that Space was not itself a *Thing*, but a *mode* or *form* of perceiving, or the inward ground and condition in the Percipient, in consequence of which Things are seen as outward and co-existing, I convey this at once by the words, Space is *subjective*, or Space is real in and for the *Subject* alone.

If I am asked, why not say in and for the *mind*, which every one would understand? I reply: we know indeed, that all minds are Subjects; but are by no means certain, that all Subjects are Minds. For a Mind is a Subject that knows itself, or a Subject that is its own Object.[57] The inward principle of Growth and individual Form in every Seed and Plant is a *Subject*, and without any exertion of poetic privilege Poets may speak of the *Soul* of the Flower.[58] But the man would be a Dreamer, who otherwise than poetically should speak of Roses and Lilies as *self-conscious* Subjects. Lastly, by the assistance of the terms, Object and Subject, thus used as correspondent Opposites, or as Negative and Positive in Physics (ex. gr. Neg. and Pos. Electricity) we may arrive at the distinct import and proper use of the strangely misused word, Idea. And as the Forms of Logic are all borrowed from Geometry (Ratiocinatio *discursiva* formas suas sive *canonas* recipit ab *intuitu*),[59] I may be permitted to elucidate my present meaning. Every Line may be, and by the ancient Geometricians *was*, considered as a point *produced*, the two extremes being its poles, while the Point itself remains in, or is at least represented by, the midpoint, the Indifference of the two poles or correlative opposites. Logically applied, the two extremes or poles are named Thesis and Antithesis:[60] thus in the line

we have T = Thesis, A = Antithesis, and I = Punctum Indifferens sive *Amphoteri-*

or iron'': *Friend (CC)* I 476. The editor of *The Friend* could not find a precise locus for the remark in the writings of Leonhard Euler (1707–83), the Swiss mathematician and physicist; it may represent an imprecise recollection of Euler's point that the sky is seen as an arch by everyone in spite of all demonstrations that this is purely an optical effect: *Letters to a German Princess* tr H. Hunter (2 vols 1795) II 297. This would chime with other psychological speculations by C on the relationship between subjective and objective states in the mind and throw light on his line ''For the blue sky bends over all'': *Christabel* line 331: *PW* (EHC) I 226. See Beer *CPI* 82–9 for further discussion of this issue, together with the possible relevance to it of the discussion of ''double touch'' that appears shortly afterwards in Euler's book.

[57] *AR* (1825) COPY G has a note at this point, reproduced by DC in *AR* (1854) 133: ''Nay, the distinction of has an important function in Science: as supplying the clearest and simplest definition of Life as distin-

guished from Mind: viz. MIND is a Subject that *has* its Object in itself: Life a Subject endued with the tendency to *produce* an Object for itself; and *the Finding* of itself therein, is Sensation—*Empfindung*. How do you *find* yourself?—''

[58] For C's interest in the principle of growth and individual form see also *SM (CC)* 72–3 and *C&S (CC)* 179–81, and discussions in Beer *CPI* 53–7, etc.

[59] ''*Discursive* ratiocination receives its forms or *canons* from intuition''. In *Logic (CC)* 48, 231, 247 C distinguishes ''discursive'' knowledge, obtained from the understanding, from ''intuitive'' knowledge, given by ''the sense'' (as distinct from ''the senses''); see *Logic* Index s.v. ''intuition'' for further discussions and *Sp Aph B I* n 4 above for further instances in *AR*.

[60] For more on C's theory of polarity (based primarily on magnetism) and its sources and analogues in *Naturphilosophie* see Owen Barfield *What Coleridge Thought* (1972) 30–40; Levere *Poetry Realized in Nature* 108–14, Raimonda Modi-

cum,[61] which latter is to be conceived as *both* in as far as it may be *either* of the two former. Observe: not both at the same time in the same relation: for this would be the *Identity* of T and A, not the *Indifference*. But so, that relatively to A,[a] I is equal to T, and relatively to T it becomes = A.[62] [b]For the purposes of the universal *Noetic*, in which we require Terms of most comprehension and least specific import, might not the Noetic Pentad be,—

	1. Prothesis.	
2. Thesis.	4. Mesothesis.	3. Antithesis.
	5. Synthesis.	

	= Prothesis.	
	Sum.	
Thesis.	Mesothesis.	Antithesis.
Res.	Agere.	Ago, Patior.
	Synthesis.	
	Agens.[63]	

i.e. 1. Verb Substantive = Prothesis, as expressing the *identity* or co-inherence of Act and Being.

2. Substantive = Thesis, expressing Being. 3. Verb = Antithesis, expressing Act. 4. Infinitive = Mesothesis, as being either Substantive or Verb, or both at once, only in different relations; as τὸ βαπτίζειν ᾽Αχιλῆα ἐν Στυγὶ οὐκ ἐδύνατο σώζειν τὸν ῞Ηρωα ἀπὸ τοῦ θνήσκειν.[64] Here βαπτίζειν is a Substantive and the Nom. Case in relation to the verb ἐδύνατο; and a Verb active in relation to (i.e. governing) the Accusative Case ᾽Αχιλῆα. 5. Participle = Synthesis.[c] Thus in Chemistry Sulphuretted Hydrogen is an Acid relatively

---

[a] *AR* (1825): A
[b-c] Added in 1831

---

ano *Coleridge and the Concept of Nature* (1985) 138–48. For a larger and more widely ranging discussion see Thomas McFarland *Romanticism and the Forms of Ruin* (Princeton 1981) 289–341.

[61] "The Point that is Indifferent, partaking of Both Characters." *Amphotericum* is formed from ἀμφότερος, "both". *OED* gives 1849 for its first example of the Greek-derived "amphoteric", but C used it earlier: see *CN* IV 4942 and n, 5171, and BM MS Egerton 2801 f 139ᵛ of c 1817: *SW&F (CC)*.

[62] The following passage, including the diagram, was added in 1831. When he published the table-talk of 18 Mar 1827 HNC adverted to this note (in an insertion not in his original ms version) while introducing C's application of the pentad to the parts of speech. See *TT (CC)* II 58–9 and I 69 n 2. By 1831 C had apparently written out at least five schemes, incorporating or adding adjectives and adverbs, as he did in the version reported in *TT (CC)*. Closest to the version here are those in a letter to Hyman Hurwitz of Sept 1829 (*CL* VI 816–18),

in an annotation on *Quarterly Journal of Foreign and British Medicine* I (1818–19) 33, preserved in a transcript in VCL and published in *NTP* 401–5 (*CM—CC*—IV), and —in context as well as form—a note prefixed to Irving *Sermons* expressing a wish that Irving could be persuaded to spend a day contemplating it (*CM—CC*—III). Cf also *CN* IV 4644 f 27–27ᵛ (perhaps of 1820) and N 26 f 151ᵛ–151 (dated 3 Mar 1824): noted at *CN* IV 5135, but to be published in *SW&F (CC)*. See also next note.

[63] The Latin words mean, respectively,

	I am	
thing	to act	I act, undergo
	acting	

[64] Literally: "To dip Achilles in the Styx could not save the hero from to die". A translation into Greek of Edmund Spenser *The Ruins of Time* lines 428–9, quoted by C as "For not *to dip* the Hero in the lake | Could save the son of Thetis from *to die*" in the *Quarterly Journal of . . . Medicine* annotation cited in n 62 above. Cf, besides the Irving annotation and notebook

to the more powerful Alkalis, and an Alkali relatively to a powerful Acid. Yet one other remark, and I pass to the question. In order to render the constructions of pure Mathematics applicable to Philosophy, the Pythagoreans, I imagine, represented the Line as *generated*, or, as it were, radiated, by a Point not contained in the Line but independent, and (in the language of that School) transcendent to all production, which it caused but did not partake in.[65] *Facit, non patitur.*[66] This was the Punctum invisibile, et presuppositum:[67] and in this way the Pythagoreans guarded against the error of Pantheism, into which the later schools fell. The assumption of this Point I call the logical PROTHESIS. We have now therefore four Relations of Thought expressed: *viz.* Prothesis, or the identity of T and A, which is neither, because in it, as the transcendent of both, both are contained and exist as one. Taken *absolutely*, this finds its application in the Supreme Being alone, the Pythagorean TETRACTYS;[68] the INEFFABLE NAME, to which no Image dare be attached; the Point, which has no (real) Opposite or Counter-point, &c.[69] But *relatively* taken and inadequately, the germinal power of every seed (see p. 75) might be generalised[a] under the

---

[a] *AR* (1825): generalized

---

entries also cited there, *CN* IV 4644 f 28, and *Logic (CC)* 17 and n, in which the editor traces the quotation to James Harris *Hermes: Works* (2 vols 1801) I 305n, illustrating the use of the infinitive as a verbal noun. Harris translates only "to die" (more appropriately as τοῦ θανεῖν) into Greek.

[65] C's interest in this aspect of Pythagoras may date from earlier years, when he read William Enfield *The History of Philosophy . . . Drawn up from Brucker's Historia Critica Philosophiae* (2 vols 1791), which he borrowed from the Bristol Library in Mar 1795: *Bristol LB* 119. In Enfield's account of Pythagoras (I 384), "The Monad, or Unity, is that quantity, which being deprived of all number, remains fixed . . . It is the fountain of all number", the generative pattern corresponding to that used here. See also *P Lects* Lect 2 (1949) 109, quoted below (n 68), in which C insisted on the deeper significance of Pythagoras' geometrical observations, and more especially *C&S (CC)* 180, in which ". . . the great fountains of pure Mathesis, the Pythagorean and Platonic Geometricians", are seen as describing ". . . the production or self-evolution, of the point into the circle".

[66] "It *does*, it does not *undergo*".

[67] "The invisible and presupposed Point".

[68] "On this plan (Pythagoras) founded the grand system of the Deity as the *Monas*; not as the one, but as that which without

any numbers and perfectly distinct from numbers was yet the ground, and by its will, the cause of all numbers; and in the manifestation of the Godhead he represented it by the famous triad three, while the world as a dim reflex of that was his God in the tetrameter or the four": *P Lects* Lect 2 (1949) 108–9. The sense of the last clause appears to be that the fourfold process that produces the world is a "dim reflex" of the one in the Deity. According to two schemes of the tetractys in C's notebooks of 1818 the higher form leads from Absolute God, via Son and Spirit, to its synthesis, "Father", who "images what in God only absolutely is"; the lower from the Absolute "Heaven" via "Chaos" and Chaos "impregned" to its synthesis "The World": *CN* III 4427, 4449 f 29ᵛ. See also *CN* IV 4784 (1820–1). An account of the tetractys appears in Thomas Stanley *History of Philosophy* (1701) 382 (cf n 70 below). For representations of it as grounded in "an absolute Idea *pre*supposed in all intelligential acts", which is related to "the eternal Fountain or Source of Nature", see annotations on Baxter *Reliquiae Baxterianae* and on Böhme *Works: CM (CC)* I 347–8, 562–3.

[69] I.e. that of Absolute God. C may have in mind that Pythagoras was said to have derived his tetractys from the tetragrammaton, the four-charactered name of God, too holy to be pronounced by the Jews, and, following a mediaeval misunderstanding, rendered by AV as Jehovah.

relation of Identity. 2. Thesis or Position. 3. Antithesis, or Opposition.[70] 4. Indifference. (To which when we add the Synthesis or Composition, in its several forms of Equilibrium, as in quiescent Electricity; of Neutralization, as of Oxygen and Hydrogen in Water; and of Predominance, as of Hydrogen and Carbon with Hydrogen,[a] predominant, in pure alcohol;[b] or of Carbon and Hydrogen, with the comparative predominance of the Carbon, in Oil; we complete the five most general Forms or Preconceptions of Constructive Logic.)[c]

And now for the Answer to the Question, What is an IDEA, if it mean neither an Impression on the Senses, nor a definite Conception, nor an abstract Notion? (And if it does mean either of these, the word is superfluous: and while it remains undetermined which of these is meant by the word, or whether it is not *which you please*, it is worse than superfluous. See the STATESMAN'S MANUAL, Appendix *ad finem*).[71] But supposing the word to have a meaning of its own, what does it mean? What is an IDEA? In answer to this I commence with the *absolutely* Real[d] as the PROTHESIS; the *subjectively* Real as the THESIS; the *objectively* Real as the ANTITHESIS: and I affirm, that Idea is the INDIFFERENCE of the two—so namely, that if it be conceived as in the Subject, the Idea is an Object, and possesses Objective Truth; but if in an Object, it is then a Subject[e] and is necessarily thought of as exercising the powers of a Subject. Thus an IDEA[f] conceived as subsisting in an Object becomes a LAW; and a Law contemplated *subjectively* (in a mind) is an Idea.[72]

In the third and last Section of my "Elements of Discourse;"[73] in which (after having in the two former sections treated of the Common or Syllogistic Logic,[g] the science of

[a] *AR* (1825): Hydrogen

[b] *AR* (1825): Alcohol,

[c] *AR* (1825): Logic).

[d] *AR* (1825): Real,

[e] *AR* (1825): Subject,

[f] COPY G: IDEA (the power of Gravity, for instance)

[g] *AR* (1825): Logic—

[70] The idea of an opposite necessarily involves duality. There can be no opposite to the absolute One (to be distinguished from the numeral one). Cf C's annotation on Stanley *History of Philosophy* (1701) 403: "One and *the One* must be carefully distinguished. The Monad is Prothetic—one Thetic, | one Antithetic = 2 | one Synthetic = 3": *CM (CC)*, and his assertion that when Pythagoras grasped that "in numbers considered philosophically there was a perpetual reference to an unity that was yet infinite, and yet that in each number there was an integral or individual that still contained in its nature something progressive" his famous "Eureka" sprang from "a sense of certainty that denied the opposite": *P Lects* Lect 2 (1949) 108. Cf also *CN* IV 5103.

[71] See *SM (CC)* 100–3. C's engagement with the "Idea" was associated with his growing devotion to the "spiritual platonic old England" (see his note of 1805, *CN* II 2598) and remained an essential element in his thinking to the end. See *C&S (CC)* 64–5, in which the *SM* passage is repeated as

part of the general aim to discuss the constitution of Church and State "according to the Idea of Each". (Ibid 12) Cf also *BL* ch 5 *(CC)* I 96–8n. The Indexes to *Friend (CC), LS (CC), Logic (CC),* and *C&S (CC)* s.v. "idea" indicate the pervasiveness of this theme and act as a guide to particular discussions in those works.

[72] Cf *Friend (CC)* I 491–2 and *C&S (CC)* 13.

[73] The "Elements of Discourse", referred to again below (see *Sp Aph B VII* n 30), was the unpublished ms now known as *Logic*. For a full account of its development see *Logic (CC)* xxxix–li. Although referred to in C's "Preface" and once or twice in the text (ibid 52, 57, 76, 100), the third section, or "organon", has not survived and was presumably not composed. In a letter of 29 Oct 1833, that section is said to be on logic as ". . . the Discipline, and Evolution of Ideas"—to be followed immediately by the "Disqui[si]tion on God, Nature, and Man", which is the Opus Maximum proper: *CL* VI 967.

a real and personal Being—*a*even the *Person*, the I AM, who sent Moses to his Forefathers in Egypt.[74] Of the actual existence of *b*this divine Person he has the same historical assurance as of theirs; confirmed indeed by the Book of Nature, *c*as soon and as far as that stronger and better Light has taught him to read and construe it—confirmed by *d*it,*e* I say, but not derived from it. Now by what right can I require this Man (and of such men the great majority of serious Believers consisted, previously*f* to the Light of the Gospel) to receive a *Notion* of mine, wholly alien from his habits of thinking, because it may be logically deduced from another Notion, with which he was almost as little acquainted, and not at all concerned? Grant for a moment, that the latter (i.e. the Notion, with which I first set out) as soon as it is combined with the assurance of a corresponding Reality becomes identical with the true and effective Idea of God! Grant, that in thus *realizing* the Notion I am warranted by Revelation, the Law of Conscience, and the interests and necessities of my Moral [B]eing!*g* Yet by what authority, by what inducement, am I

---

legitimate *Conclusions;* and the Critical Logic, or the Criteria of Truth and Falsehood in all *Premisses)h* I have given at full my scheme of Constructive Reasoning, or "Logic as the Organ of Philosophy," in the same sense as the Mathematics are the Organ of Science; the Reader will find proofs of the Utility of this Scheme, including,*i* the five-fold Division above-stated, and numerous examples of its application. Nor is it only in Theology that its importance will be felt, but equally, nay in a greater degree, as an instrument of Discovery and universal Method in Physics, Physiology, and Statistics. As this third Section does not pretend to the forensic and comparatively popular character and utility of the parts preceding, one of the Objects of the present Note is to obtain the opinions of judicious friends respecting the expedience of publishing it, in the same form, indeed, and as an Annexment to the "Elements of Discourse," yet so as that each may be purchased separately.

---

a *AR* (1825): p 172   *b* *AR* (1825): p 173   *c* *AR* (1825): p 174
d *AR* (1825): p 175   *e* COPIES C & D: the Book of Nature,
f *AR* (1825): previous   *g* 1831 misprints: Reing!
h *AR* (1825): *Premisses)*   *i* *AR* (1825): including

---

[74] See Exod 3.14: "And God said unto Moses, I AM THAT I AM: and he said, Thus shalt thou say unto the children of Israel, I AM hath sent me unto you." This verse was clearly important to C in the evolution of his philosophy of being: cf e.g. ". . . the eternal act of creation in the infinite I AM" (*BL* ch 13—*CC*—I 304); his statement of 3 Nov 1812: "Did philosophy commence with an IT IS, instead of an I AM, Spinoza would be altogether true" (*CRB* I 112); and his insistence on the soul's being as posterior to its existence (*CN* III 3593). Cf also *CL* VI 562 (1826): "Remember that the Personality of God, the living I AM, was the distinctive of the Hebrew Faith". For an extended discussion see McFarland *C Pantheist* esp ch 2.

entitled to attach the same reality to a second Notion, a Notion drawn from a Notion.[a] It is evident, that if I have the same Right, it must be on the same grounds. Revelation must have assured it, my Conscience required it—or in some way or other I must have an *interest* in this belief.[75] It must *concern* me, as a moral and responsible Being. Now these grounds were first given in the Redemption of Mankind by Christ, the Saviour and Mediator: and by the utter incompatibility of these offices with a mere Creature. On the doctrine of Redemption depends the *Faith*, the *Duty*,[b] of believing in the Divinity of our Lord. And this again is the strongest Ground for the reality of that Idea, in which alone [c]this Divinity[d] can be received[e] without breach of the[f] faith in the unity of the Godhead. But such is the Idea of the [g]Trinity. Strong[h] as the motives are that [i]induce me to defer the full discussion of this great Article of the Christian Creed, I cannot withstand the request of several Divines, whose situation and extensive services entitle them to the utmost deference, that I should so far deviate from my first intention as at least to indicate the point on which I stand, and to prevent the misconception of my purpose: as if I held the doctrine of the Trinity for a truth which Men could be called on to believe by mere force of reasoning, independently of any positive *Revelation*. In short, it had been reported in certain circles, that I considered this doctrine as a demonstrable part of the Religion of Nature. Now though it might be sufficient to say, that[j] I regard the very phrase *"Revealed* Religion" as a pleonasm, inasmuch as a religion not revealed is, in my judgement,[k] no religion at all;[76] I have no objection to announce more particularly and distinctly what I do and what I do not maintain on this point: provided that in the following paragraph, with this view inserted, the reader will look for nothing more than a plain *statement* of my Opinions. The grounds on which they rest, and the arguments by which they are to be vindicated, are for another place.

I hold then, it is true, that all the (so called) Demonstrations of a God either prove too little, as that from the Order and apparent Purpose in

---

[a] *AR* (1825): Notion?
[b] COPY D: *Duty*
[c-d] COPY C: the faith in this Divinity ; COPIES D & E: the faith in the Divinity of the Redeemer
[e] COPY C: professed
[f] COPY G: the no less necessary
[g-h] COPY G: Trinity. §Strong
[i] *AR* (1825): p 176
[j] *AR* (1825): this ; Corr: that
[k] *AR* (1825): judgment,

[75] See below, *Sp Aph B V* n 4.
[76] C had used the phrase less hesitat-ingly when he gave his LRR at Bristol: *Lects 1795 (CC)* 83ff.

Nature; or too much, *viz.* that the World is itself God; or they clandestinely involve the conclusion in the premisses,[a] passing off the mere analysis or explication of an Assertion for the Proof of it,—[b]a species of logical legerdemain not unlike that of the Jugglers at a Fair, [c]who putting into their mouths what seems to be a walnut, draw out a score yards of [d]Ribbon—as in[e] the Postulate of a First Cause. And lastly, in[f] all these Demonstrations [g]the Demonstrators[h] presuppose the Idea or Conception of a God without being able to authenticate it, i.e. to give an account whence they obtained it. For it is clear, that the Proof first mentioned and the most natural and convincing of all (the Cosmological I mean,[i] or that from the Order in Nature) presupposes the Ontological—i.e. the proof of a God from the necessity and necessary *Objectivity* of the Idea.[77] *If* the latter[j] can assure us of a God as an existing Reality, the former[k] will go far to prove his Power, Wisdom, and Benevolence.[78] All

---

[a] *AR* (1825): Premises,

[b] COPY D: it—

[c] *AR* (1825): p 177

[d-e] *AR* (1825) Corr: Ribbon. On this sophism rest the pretended "Demonstrations of a God" grounded on ; COPY D: Ribbon. An instance of this sophistry I find in those Reasoners, who commence their promised Proof with ; COPY E: [as COPY D but has "Sophistry" and omits comma after "Reasoners"]

[f] Added in *AR* (1825) Corr and *AR* (1831); COPY C: that in

[g-h] Added in 1831; *AR* (1825) Corr: the Authors ; COPIES C, D, E, F: the Demonstrators

[i] *AR* (1825): mean

[j] COPY F: Ontological

[k] COPY F: Cosmological

---

[77] At the foot of *AR* (1825) COPY G pp 176–7 C has written a note which refers to the preceding sentence:

"† The position is/ as b : A :: c : X. bc being the two products and AX the producent Causes—i.e. As a watch to the Human Intelligence, so the world to the Divine Intelligence. The Sceptic objects that neither the Products nor the Producents are ejusdem generis [of the same kind] consequently not subjects of Analogy: A existing only as A + y; and X as X − y.

X y d may differ from Z − y d; namely by y: and yet we may reason by analogy from X to Z: thus: E F G are products of X by force of d—therefore it may be presumed, that H I J similar in kind to E F G are products of Z by virtue of d ~~and X is to Z y d~~. But if y were the necessary condition of d, d is precluded by − y and ~~from~~ between X y d ~~to~~ and Z − y − d there is no analogy. X = Man y = finiteness d = in-

telligence Z = God − y = Infinity."

[78] For the Unitarian's view of Deity as "Power, Intelligence, and Benevolence" see *LS (CC)* 183n. *AR* (1825) COPY G has a long note here, inserted (var) by DC in *AR* (1854) 139: "When the cosmological Proof goes farther, viz. to prove the *existence* of a Supreme Being, it proceeds on an Analogy questionable in both* its factors. First, the Sceptic impugns the conclusion from things *made* to things that *grow*, (from a Watch to a Sun-flower), or to things that have no known Beginning (the Metals for instance—) and likewise the inference from the cause of the *composition* of a Whole to the cause of the existence of ⟨its⟩ ultimate particles—as a μεταβασις εις αλλο γενος [transition into another kind—see below, *Sp Aph B VIIIb* n 26].—And again—he objects that the *difference* ~~between~~ of the known ~~and~~ from the inferred

* viz—the Products and the Productors

this I hold.[79] But I also hold, that this Truth, the hardest to demonstrate, is the one which of all others least needs to be demonstrated; that though there may be no conclusive demonstrations[a] of a good, wise, living,[b] and personal God, there are so many convincing [c]reasons for it,[d] within and without—a grain of sand[e] sufficing, and a whole universe at hand to echo the decision!—that for every mind not devoid of all reason, and desperately conscience-proof, the Truth which it is the least possible to prove, it is little less than impossible not to believe! only indeed just so much short of impossible, as to leave some room for the will and the moral election, and thereby to keep it a truth of Religion, and the possible subject of a Commandment.[*f]

* In a letter to a Friend[80] on the mathematical Atheists of the French Revolution, La

> [a] COPIES C & F: *demonstrations*
> [b] *AR* (1825): living
> [c–d] COPIES C & F: *reasons* for the belief,
> [e] COPY C: wheat
> [f] *AR* (1825): commandment*.

Agent, viz. the finiteness of Man ~~and~~ contrasted with the infinitity of God, is the condition and co-efficient cause of that Intelligence in ~~Man~~ the former, which is to constitute the similarity. Consequently, the supposed Analogy fails in ~~the~~ its *positive* Ingredient, i.e. the ⟨Point of⟩ Likeness. It is *no* Analogy. You ~~reason~~ infer (Spinoza might say) from intelligence in a Finite Being, as the cause of a Time-piece, ~~so~~ an intelligence in an infinite Being as the cause of a World. But ~~this~~ very intelligence, ⟨from which you draw this inference,⟩ is wholly conditioned, and in part constituted, by that Finiteness. To invalidate this plea, we must refer to an *Idea* of Intelligence, having its evidence in itself; and which must be shewn to be the necessary Suppositum and Antecedent of the Intelligence, our Conception of which is generalized from the Understandings of Men. We must assert an intelligence that neither supposes nor requires a Finiteness by imperfection—i.e. Reason.—But in this attempt we pass out of the Cosmological Proof, the Proof a posteriori and from the Facts, into the Ontological or the Proof a priori and from the Idea.

S. T. Coleridge

[79] The watch image in the previous note suggests that Paley's reasoning is under attack here. For this and other points see below, App I Excursus Note 5 "Coleridge on the Cosmological Proof".

[80] See his letter to George Skinner of 17 Feb 1824: "As to the great question itself—I have only this to say, that the man who can have *no assurance* of a God that does not rest on an apodictic proof, even tho' it should be susceptible of strictest demonstration that such a proof is incompatible with the nature of the truth to be proved and equally incompatible with all purposes of this truth relatively to the human Being—such a man I say is not in a state to be reasoned with on any subject. If like Mr Austin he further denies the *fact* of a law of conscience or any obligation directly resulting therefrom I should be puzzled what to answer. I could not without a contradiction address him as a moral Being—or else I should admonish him that as an honest man he ought to *advertize* it as a Cavete omnes! scelus sum [Beware everyone! I am a scoundrel]—and being an honest man myself, I ought not to advise him by way of prudence and for his own sake to keep his naturam monstrosam [monstrous nature] to himself, lest I should help him on with a *Wrap-rascal* and furnish him with a Mask.—": *CL* v 331. For "Mr Austin" see n 82, below.

*a*On this account I do not demand of a *Deist*, that he should adopt the doctrine of the Trinity. For he might very well be justified in replying, that he rejected the doctrine, *not* because it could not be *demonstrated*, nor yet on the score of any incomprehensibilities and seeming contradictions that might be objected to it, as knowing that these might be, and in fact had been, urged with equal force against a personal God under any form capable of Love and Veneration; *but* because he had not the same theoretical necessity, the same interests and instincts of Reason for the one hypothesis as for the other. It is not enough, the Deist might justly say, that there is no cogent reason why I should *not* believe the Trinity: you must show me some cogent reason why I *should*.

But the case is quite different with a Christian, who *b*accepts the Scriptures as the Word of God, yet refuses his assent to the plainest declarations of these Scriptures, and explains away the most express texts into metaphor and hyperbole, *because* the literal and obvious in-

---

Lande[81] and others, or rather on a young man of distinguished abilities, but an avowed and proselyting Partizan of their Tenets,[82] I concluded with these words: "The man who will believe nothing but by force of demonstrative evidence (even though it is strictly demonstrable that the demonstrability required would countervene all the purposes of the Truth in question, all that render the belief of the same desirable or obligatory) is not in a state of mind to be reasoned with on any subject. But if he further denies the *fact* of the Law of Conscience, and the essential difference between Right and Wrong, I confess, he puzzles me. I cannot without gross inconsistency appeal to his Conscience and Moral Sense, or I should admonish him that, as an honest man, he ought to *advertise* himself, with a Cavete omnes! Scelus sum [Beware everyone! I am a scoundrel]. And as an honest man myself, I dare not advise him on prudential grounds to keep his opinions secret, lest I should make myself his accomplice, and *be helping him on with a Wrap-rascal.*"[83]

a AR (1825): p 178   *b* AR (1825): p 179

[81] Although now remembered as an astronomer, Joseph Jerome Le Français de La Lande (1732–1807) also achieved notoriety in his own day for the propagation of atheist views. In 1793 he delivered a speech at the Pantheon, with the red cap on his head, against the existence of God. In 1805 he published a Supplement to the *Dictionary of Atheists* by Silvain Mareschal, in which he endeavoured to prove that there was no Deity; Bonaparte ordered him to publish no more, and he submitted. See A. Chalmers *General Biographical Dictionary* (1815) xix 467–70; cf also *CN* iv 5114 and 5413 and nn.

[82] I.e. Charles Austin (1799–1874), who was, along with Thomas Babington Macaulay (1800–59), one of DC's under-

graduate friends. (C's concern about these two was expressed earlier in the letter quoted from in n 80 above: *CL* v 330–1; cf *CN* iv 5113 and Editor's Introduction, p lxxiii above.) As an ardent and paradoxical exponent of Bentham's doctrines he was to win high praise from John Stuart Mill (*Autobiography*—1873—ch 3, pp 76–9). In 1822 he surprised friends, familiar with his heterodox opinions, by winning the Hulsean prize for an essay on Christian evidence; he went on to become a brilliant lawyer. For a fuller account see *DNB*.

[83] A loose overcoat or greatcoat. For the joke see also *CL* iv 837 and "Verses Trivocular" (Jan 1828): *PW* (EHC) ii 985. C's "countervene" here is *OED*'s only example.

terpretation is (according to *his* notions) absurd and contrary to reason. *He* is bound to show, that it is so in any sense, not equally applicable to the texts asserting the Being, Infinity, and Personality of God the Father, the Eternal and Omnipresent ONE, who *created* the Heaven and the Earth. And the more is he bound to do this, and the greater is my right to demand it of him, because the doctrine of Redemption from Sin supplies the Christian with motives and reasons for the divinity of the Redeemer far more *concerning* and coercive *subjectively*, i.e. in the economy of his own Soul, than are all the inducements that can influence the Deist *objectively*, i.e. in the interpretation of Nature.

Do I then utterly exclude the speculative Reason from Theology? No! It is its office and rightful privilege to determine on the *negative* truth of whatever we are required to believe. The Doctrine must not *contradict* any universal principle: for this would be a Doctrine that contradicted itself. Or*ᵃ* Philosophy? No. It may be and has been the servant and pioneer of Faith by convincing the mind, that a Doctrine is cogitable, that the soul can present the *Idea* to itself; and that *if* we determine to contemplate, or *think* of, the subject at all, so and in no other form can this be effected. So far are both Logic and Philosophy to be *ᵇ*received and trusted.⁸⁴ But the *duty*, and in some cases and for some persons even the *right*, of thinking on subjects beyond the bounds of sensible*ᶜ* experience; the grounds of the *real* truth; and *Life*, the *Substance*, the *Hope*, the *Love*, in one word, the *Faith:ᵈ* these are Derivatives from the practical, moral, and spiritual Nature and Being of Man.

APHORISM III

That Religion is designed to improve the nature and faculties of Man, in order to the right governing of our actions, to the securing the peace and progress, external and internal, of Individuals and of Communities, and lastly, to the rendering us capable of a more perfect state, entitled the kingdom of God, to which the present Life is *probationary*—this is a Truth, which all who have truth only in view, will receive on its own evidence. If such then be the main end of Religion altogether (the improvement namely of our nature and faculties), it is plain, that every Part of Religion is to be judged by its relation to this main end. And

---

ᵃ COPY F: Or do I exclude
ᵇ *AR* (1825): p 180
ᶜ COPY F: *sensible*
ᵈ *AR* (1825): *Faith;*

⁸⁴ See Barth 45–7 and ch 2 generally.

since the Christian Scheme is Religion in its most perfect and effective
Form, a revealed Religion, and therefore, in a *special* sense proceeding
from that Being who made us and knows what we are, of*ᵃ* course therefore adapted to the needs and capabilities of Human Nature; nothing can
be a part of this holy faith that is not duly proportioned to this end.—
Extracted with slight alterations from Burnet's Preface to Vol. ii. *of the
History*ᵇ *of the Reformation*¹

^cCOMMENT

This Aphorism should be borne in mind, whenever a theological *Resolve*
is proposed to us as an article of Faith. Take, for instance, the Determinations passed at the Synod of Dort, concerning the Absolute Decrees
of God in connexion with his Omniscience and Fore-knowledge.² Or
take the decision*ᵈ* in the Council of Trent on the difference*ᵉ* between the
two kinds of Transubstantiation, the one in which both the Substance
and the Accidents are changed, the same matter remaining—as in the
conversion of Water to Wine at Cana:*ᶠ* the other, in which the Matter
and the Substance are changed, the Accidents remaining unaltered, as
in the Eucharist—this latter being Transubstantiation *par eminence!*³ Or

> *ᵃ* COPY F: & of
> *ᵇ* *AR* (1825): *Hist.*
> *ᶜ* *AR* (1825): p 181
> *ᵈ* *AR* (1825): Decision
> *ᵉ* *AR* (1825): Difference
> *ᶠ* *AR* (1825): Cana;

¹ From Burnet *The History of the Reformation of the Church of England* (2 vols
1683, Dublin 1730) II preface p xviii. C's
version expands it considerably, bringing
in, among other things, the reference to the
present life as probationary and religion as
". . . adapted to the needs and capabilities
of Human Nature". For the original, see
App A(j) below. In a note on II i sig b C
comments adversely on the defence of the
Reformation in Burnet's Preface: *CM (CC)*
I 834.
² The synod of Dort (1618–19), consisting of eighty-four Reformed divines, fifty-
eight of them Dutch, provided the final answer of orthodox Calvinists to the Arminian Remonstrants. Concerning the doctrine
that God ". . . by a mere arbitrary act of
His will, without the least respect or view
to any sin, has predestined the greatest part
of the world to eternal damnation" it af-

firmed that the Reformed Churches ". . .
not only do not acknowledge, but even de-
test with their whole soul" such doctrines:
Enc RE III 869b–870a, quoting E.F.K.
Muller *Symbolik* (Leipzig 1896) lviii–lxiv.
³ The Council of Trent (1545–63). At
Session CIII (Oct 1551) the doctrine of transubstantiation was affirmed and the Lutheran, Calvinist, and Zwinglian doctrines
of the Eucharist repudiated. HNC quoted
some of the relevant canons (*AR* 5th ed—
1843—139n). For C's view of transubstantiation see also *C&S (CC)* 106 and Barth
177–8, referring to notes on Donne *LXXX
Sermons*: *CM (CC)* II 281–2; William Sher-
lock *Vindication of the Doctrine of the
Trinity* (1690) 4: *CM (CC)* v; Jeremy Taylor *The Real Presence* § x and *Liberty of
Prophesying* § xviii in Σύμβολον Θεολογικόν (1674) 225, 1061: *CM (CC)* v.

rather take the still more tremendous Dogma, that it is indispensable to a saving Faith carefully to distinguish the one kind from the other, and to believe both, and to believe the necessity of believing both in order to Salvation! For each or either of these *extra-scriptural* Articles of Faith the preceding Aphorism supplies a safe criterion. Will the belief tend to the improvement of any of my moral or intellectual faculties? But before I can be convinced that a Faculty will be *improved*, I must be assured that it *exists*. On all these dark sayings, therefore, of Dort or Trent, it is quite sufficient to ask, by what *faculty, organ,* or *inlet* of knowledge, we are to assure ourselves[a] that the words *mean* any thing, or correspond to any object out of our own mind or even in it: unless indeed the mere craving and striving to think *on*, after [b]all the materials for thinking have been exhausted, can be called an *object*. When a number of trust-worthy Persons assure me, that a portion of Fluid which they saw to be Water, by some change in the Fluid itself or in their Senses, suddenly acquired the Colour, Taste, Smell, and exhilarating property of Wine, I perfectly understand what they tell me, and likewise by what faculties they might have come to the knowledge of the Fact. But if any one of the number not satisfied with my acquiescence in the Fact, should insist on my believing, that the *Matter* remained the same, the Substance and the Accidents having been removed in order to make way for a different Substance with different Accidents, I must entreat his permission to wait till I can discover in myself any faculty, by which there can be presented to me a Matter distinguishable from Accidents, and a Substance that is different from both. It is true, I have a faculty of Articulation;[c] but I do not see that it can be *improved* by my using it for the formation of words without meaning, or at best, for the utterance of Thoughts, that mean only the act of so thinking, or of trying so to think. But the end of Religion is the improvement of our Nature and Faculties. Ergo, &c. Q. E. D. I sum up the whole in one great practical Maxim. The Object of *religious* Contemplation, and of a truly Spiritual Faith, IS[d] THE WAYS OF GOD TO MAN.[4] Of the Workings of the Godhead, God himself has told us, My Ways are not as your Ways, nor my Thoughts as your Thoughts.[5]

a AR (1825): ourselves,
b AR (1825): p 182
c AR (1825): articulation;
d AR (1825): is

[4] Milton *PL* I 26: "And justifie the wayes of God to men". C's "man" is the word that appears more frequently in Milton's poem.

[5] "For my thoughts are not your thoughts, neither are your ways my ways, saith the Lord. For as the heavens are higher than the earth, so are my ways higher than your ways, and my thoughts than your thoughts": Isa 55.8–9.

*a*APHORISM IV

THE CHARACTERISTIC DIFFERENCE BETWEEN THE DISCIPLINE OF THE ANCIENT
PHILOSOPHERS AND THE DISPENSATION OF THE GOSPEL

By undeceiving, enlarging, and informing the Intellect, Philosophy sought to purify, and to elevate the Moral Character. Of course, those alone could receive the latter and incomparably greater Benefit, who by natural capacity and favorable*b* contingencies of Fortune were fit Recipients of the former. How small the number, we scarcely need the evidence of History to assure us. Across the Night of Paganism, Philosophy flitted on, like the Lantern-fly*c* of the Tropics, a Light to itself, and an Ornament, but alas! no more than an ornament, of the surrounding Darkness.[1]

Christianity reversed the order. By means accessible to all, by inducements operative on all, and by convictions, the grounds and materials of which all men might find in themselves, her first step was to cleanse the *Heart*. But the benefit did not stop here. In preventing the rank vapors*d* that steam up from the corrupt *Heart*,[2] Christianity restores the *Intellect* likewise to its natural clearness. By relieving the mind from the distractions and importunities of the unruly passions, she improves the *quality* of the Understanding: while at the same time she presents for its contemplations,*e* Objects so great and so bright as cannot but enlarge the Organ, by which they are contemplated.[3] The Fears, the Hopes, the Remembrances, *f*the Anticipations, the inward and outward Experience, the belief*g* and the Faith, of a Christian,*h* form of themselves a philosophy*i* and a Sum of Knowledge, which a Life spent in the Grove of Academus,[4]

a *AR* (1825): p 183
b *AR* (1825): favourable
c *AR* (1825): Lanthorn-fly
d *AR* (1825): vapours
e *AR* (1825): contemplations
f *AR* (1825): p 184
g *AR* (1825): Belief
h *AR* (1825): Christian
i *AR* (1825): Philosophy

[1] For a similar, but not identical, night-fly image see *CN* II 2890 (Oct 1806).

[2] The literal basis of the metaphor is in older medical theory, where such vapours ascending to the brain were most often associated with the stomach; *OED* cites e.g. William Beveridge *Sermons* (1729) I 332: "Those malign vapours which by reason of over-much eating are exhaled from the stomach into the head". For a wider and more satirical use of the same imagery see

Swift *Tale of a Tub* § ix ad init.

[3] C refers back to the preceding two sentences here in a note on Blanco White *Poor Man's Preservative Against Popery* (1825), on the rôle of ". . . stillness and genial tranquillity" in revealing ". . . the clearness and evidency of grounds and reasons in all matters not scientifically demonstrable": *CM (CC)* I 508–9.

[4] A grove sacred to Academus in Athens, near which Plato had a house and gar-

or the "painted Porch,"[5] could not have attained or collected. The result is contained in the fact of a wide and still widening CHRISTENDOM.

Yet I dare not say, that the effects have been proportionate to the divine wisdom of the Scheme. Too soon did the Doctors of the Church forget that the *Heart*, the *Moral* Nature, was the beginning[a] and the end;[b6] and that Truth, Knowledge, and Insight were comprehended in its expansion. This was the true and first apostasy—when in Council and Synod the divine Humanities of the Gospel gave way to speculative Systems, and Religion became a Science of Shadows under the name of Theology, or at best a bare Skeleton of Truth, without life or interest, alike inac[c]essible and unintelligible to the majority of Christians. For these therefore there remained only rites and ceremonies and spectacles, shows and semblances. Thus among the learned the substance of things hoped for (Heb. xi. 1.)[7] passed off into *Notions;* and for the Unlearned the surfaces of Things became *Substance. The Christian world was for centuries divided into the Many, that did not think at all, and the Few who did nothing but [c]*think*—both alike *unreflecting*, the one from defect of the *Act*, the other from the absence of an *Object*.

APHORISM V

There is small chance of Truth at the goal where there is not a[d] child-like Humility at the Starting-post.

COMMENT

Humility is the safest Ground of Docility: and Docility the surest Promise of Docibility.[1] Where there is no working of Self-love in the heart

---

* Virium et proprietatum, quae non nisi de *Sub*stantibus predicari possunt, formis *super*stantibus Attributio, est SUPERSTITIO.[8]

---

[a] *AR* (1825): Beginning
[b] *AR* (1825): End;
[c] *AR* (1825): p 185
[d] Added in 1831

---

den and where he opened his school of philosophy. It was recurrently a centre of Platonic philosophy until the time of Justinian (483–565).

[5] This porch, portico, or "stoa", in Athens, gave its name to Stoicism, first taught there by Zeno of Citium.

[6] Cf *CL* II 961; *Friend (CC)* I 524; *BL* chs 1, 7 *(CC)* 13, 17, 122.

[7] "Now faith is the substance of things hoped for, the evidence of things not seen."

[8] "The attribution of powers and properties, which can be predicated only of *Sub*stances, to forms that stand *above*, is SUPERSTITION." For substance see also *Int Aph XII* n 1 above. C's present note is repeated and amplified below, *Sp Aph B [XXIV]* at n 47.

[1] "Teachability". This is the last English usage recorded in *OED*.

that secures a leaning beforehand; where the great Magnet of the Planet is not overwhelmed or obscured by partial masses of Iron in close neighbourhood to the Compass of the Judgment, though hidden or unnoticed; there will this great Desideratum be found of a child-like Humility. Do I then say, that I am to be influenced by *no* interest?*ª* Far from it! There is an Interest of Truth: or how could there be a Love of Truth? And that a love of Truth for its own sake, and merely as Truth, is possible, my Soul bears witness to itself in its inmost recesses. But there are other interests*ᵇ*—those of Goodness, of Beauty, of Utility. It would be a sorry proof of the Humility I am extolling, were I to ask for Angel's*ᶜ* wings to overfly² my own Human Nature. I exclude none of these. It is enough if the *"lene clinamen,"*³ the gentle Bias, be given by no interest that concerns myself other than as I am a Man, and included in the great Family of mankind;*ᵈ* but which does therefore especially concern me, because being a common Interest of *all* men it must needs *ᵉ*concern the very *essentials* of my Being, and because these essentials, as existing in *me*, are especially intrusted to my particular charge.

Widely different from this social and truth-attracted Bias, different both in its nature and its effects, is the Interest connected with the desire of *distinguishing* yourself from other men, in order to be distinguished by them. Hoc revera*ᶠ est inter* te et veritatem.⁴ This Interest does indeed stand between thee and truth. I might add between thee and thy own soul. It is scarcely more at variance with the love of truth than it is unfriendly to the*ᵍ* attainment that deserves that name*ʰ*. By your own act you have appointed the *ⁱ*Many as*ʲ* your Judges and Appraisers: for the anxiety to be admired is a loveless passion, ever strongest with regard to those by whom we are least known and least cared for, loud on the

<hr>

ª AR (1825): Interest?
ᵇ AR (1825): Interests
ᶜ AR (1825): Angels'
ᵈ AR (1825): Mankind;
ᵉ AR (1825): p 186
ᶠ AR (1825): reverâ
ᵍ COPIES C & G: every
ʰ COPY C: *name* [in pencil, perhaps not STC]
ⁱ⁻ʲ COPY G: Many

² "Outsoar". See *OED* s.v.
³ Lucretius 2.292 has "exiguum clinamen" ("a little bias" or "a slight swerve"), describing the movement of atoms in Epicurus' system. The present expression is used metaphorically in Sept 1825: *CN* IV 5240 f 29. C applied the term "epicurean clinamen" to Baxter's conciliatory approach to his adversaries: *CM (CC)*

I 307 and n.
⁴ "This indeed *is between* thee and truth." C alluded elsewhere in this way to the relationship between the Latin impersonal verb meaning "it is between", hence "it concerns", and the English verb and noun "interest"; see e.g. *CN* I 1720, *CM (CC)* I 140.

Hustings, gay in the Ball-room, mute and sullen at the family Fireside. What you have acquired by patient thought and cautious discrimination, demands a portion of the same effort in those who are to receive it from you. But Applause and Preference are things of Barter; and if you trade in them, Experience will soon teach you that there are easier and less unsuitable ways to win golden judgments than by at once taxing the patience and humiliating the self-opinion of your judges. To obtain your end, your words must be as indefinite as their Thoughts: and how vague and general these are even on objects of Sense, the few who at a mature age have seriously set about the discipline of their faculties, and have honestly *taken stock*, best know by recollection of their own state. To be *a*admired you must make your auditors believe at least that they understand what you say; which, be assured, they never will, *b*under such circumstances,*c* if it be worth understanding, or if you understand your own soul. But while your prevailing motive is to be compared and appreciated, is it credible, is it possible, that you should in earnest seek for a knowledge which is and must remain a hidden Light, a secret Treasure? Have you children, or have you lived among children, and do you not know, that in all things, in food, in medicine, in all their doings and abstainings they must believe in order to acquire a reason for their belief? But so is it with religious truths for all men. These we must all learn as children. The ground of the prevailing error on this point is the ignorance, that in spiritual concernments to believe and to understand are not diverse things, but the same thing in different periods of its growth.[5] Belief is the seed, received into the will, of which the Understanding or Knowledge is the Flower, and the thing believed is the fruit. Unless ye believe (saith the Prophet) ye cannot understand:[6] and unless ye be humble as children, ye not only *will* not, but ye *can*not believe. Of such therefore is the Kingdom of Heaven.[7] Yea, blessed is the calamity that makes us humble: though so repugnant thereto is our nature, in our present state, that after a while, it is to be feared, a second and sharper calamity would be wanted to cure us of our pride in having become so humble.

Lastly, there are among us, though fewer and less in fashion than

---

[a] *AR* (1825): p 187
[b-c] Added in 1831

[5] See also the quotation from Augustine above, *Pref* n 8, and Barth 47–8.
[6] See above, *Mor Aph VI* n 29.
[7] A conflation of two texts: Matt 18.3–4: ". . . Except ye be converted, and become as little children, ye shall not enter into the kingdom of heaven. Whosoever therefore shall humble himself as this little child, the same is greatest in the kingdom of heaven."; Mark 10.14 (cf Luke 18.16): "Suffer the little children to come unto me, and forbid them not: for of such is the Kingdom of God."

among our ancestors, Persons who, like *ª*Shaftesbury,[8] do not belong to "the herd of Epicurus,"[9] yet prefer a philosophic Paganism to the morality of the Gospel. Now it would conduce, methinks, to the child-like Humility, we have been discoursing of, if the use of the term, Virtue, in that high, comprehensive, and *notional* sense in which it was used by the ancient Stoics, were abandoned, as a relic of Paganism, to these modern Pagans: and if Christians restoring the word to its original import, viz. Manhood or Manliness,[10] used it exclusively to express the quality of Fortitude; Strength of Character in relation to the resistance opposed by Nature and the irrational Passions to the Dictates of Reason; Energy of Will in preserving the Line of Rectitude tense and firm against the warping forces and treacheries of Temptation. Surely, it were far less unseemly to value ourselves on this moral Strength than on Strength of Body, or even Strength of Intellect. But we will rather value *it* for ourselves: and bearing in mind the old adage, Quis custodiet ipsum Custodem?[11] we will value it the more, yea, then only will we allow it true spiritual *Worth,* when we possess it as a gift of *Grace,* a boon of Mercy undeserved, a fulfilment of a free *Promise* (1 Corinth. x. 13.)[12] What more is meant in this last paragraph, let the venerable HOOKER say for me in the following.*ᵇ*

APHORISM VI[1]

What is Virtue but a Medicine, and Vice but a Wound? Yea, we have so often deeply wounded ourselves with Medicine, that God hath been fain to make *ᶜ*wounds medicinable; to secure*ᵈ[2]* by Vice where Virtue hath stricken; to suffer the just man to fall, that being raised he may be taught

---

ª *AR* (1825): p 188
ᵇ *AR* (1825): following
ᶜ *AR* (1825): p 189
ᵈ *AR* (1825): cure

[8] See above, *Prel Sp Aph* n 13.
[9] Horace *Epistles* 1.4.15–16; tr H. R. Fairclough (LCL 1926): "As for me, if you want a laugh, you will find me in fine fettle, fat and sleek, a hog from Epicurus' herd."
[10] See above, *Int Aph XII* nn 5–6.
[11] "Sed quis custodiet ipsos custodes?": Juvenal *Satires* 6.347; tr "But who will guard the guards themselves?" C converts them into the singular.
[12] "There hath no temptation taken you but such as is common to man: but God is faithful, who will not suffer you to be tempted above that ye are able; but will with the temptation also make a way to escape, that ye may be able to bear it."
[1] Hooker *Works* (1682) 521. Reprinted below, App A(k). C makes minor changes, mostly of style, throughout; he also inserts the words "*tripped up*". His penultimate sentence replaces Hooker's ". . . but those Crystal tears wherewith my sin and weakness was bewailed, have procured my endless joy . . .".
[2] The 1825 reading "cure" (as in Hooker) seems correct here.

what power it was which upheld him standing. I am not afraid to affirm it boldly with St. Augustine, that Men puffed up through a proud Opinion of their own Sanctity and Holiness received^a a benefit at the hands of God, and are assisted with his Grace when with his Grace they are *not* assisted, but permitted (and that grievously) to transgress.³ Whereby, as they were through over-great Liking of themselves supplanted (*tripped up*), so the dislike of that which did supplant them may establish them afterwards the surer. Ask the very Soul of PETER, and it shall undoubtedly itself make you this answer: My eager protestations made in the glory of my spiritual strength, I am ashamed of. But my shame and the Tears, with which my Presumption and my Weakness were bewailed, recur in the songs of my Thanksgiving. My Strength had been my Ruin, my Fall hath proved my Stay.⁴ *Sermon on the Nature of Pride*, HOOKER'S Works, p. 521

APHORISM VII^{b1}

The Being and Providence of One Living God, Holy, Gracious, Merciful, the Creator and Preserver of all things, and a Father of the Righteous; the Moral Law in its 1² utmost height, breadth^c and purity; a State of Retribution after Death; the 2 Resurrection of the Dead:^{d} and a Day of Judgment—all these were known and received by the Jewish People, as established^e Articles of the National Faith, at or before the Proclaiming of Christ by the Baptist.³ They are the ground-work of Christianity, and essentials in the Christian Faith, but not its characteristic and pecu-

---

^{a} *AR* (1825): receive ^{b} *AR* (1825): EDITOR.
^{c} *AR* (1825): breadth, ^{d} *AR* (1825): Dead;
^{e} *AR* (1825): p 190 (blished)

³ John Keble, in his edition of Hooker *Works* (3 vols Oxford 1833, rev R. W. Church and F. Paget 1888) III 609, cites Augustine *De civitate Dei* 14.13; tr P. Levine (LCL 1966): "I dare say too that it is useful for the proud to fall into some patent and obvious sin by which they may become displeased with themselves after they had already fallen by being pleased with themselves. Peter was in a healthier state when he was displeased with himself and wept than when he was pleased with himself and too confident."
⁴ See e.g. Matt 16.13–19, Luke 22.54–62, Acts 2.14–40.

¹ Cf *CN* IV 5243 (c Sept 1825): "My ⟨inward⟩ Creed, as a Christian, remains without substraction or addition as it stands in the Aids to Reflection—189–91": i.e. the whole of this aphorism. Cf Barth 100–2 and nn on C and the Creeds.
² C inserts note indicators "1" and "2" here, corresponding to his notes below, pp 199–200, 201–2.
³ On Jewish belief in retribution after death, and in a Day of Judgment, see W.O.E. Oesterley and T. H. Robinson *Hebrew Religion: Its Origin and Development* (1937) 386–94.

liar Doctrines: except indeed as they are confirmed, enlivened, realized and brought home to the *whole Being* of Man, Head, Heart, and Spirit, by the truths and influences of the Gospel.

Peculiar to Christianity[4] are:

I. The belief that a Means of Salvation has been effected and provided for the Human Race by the incarnation of the Son of God in the person of Jesus Christ; and that his Life on earth, his Sufferings, Death, and Resurrection,[a] are not only proofs and manifestations, but likewise essential and effective parts of the great redemptive Act, whereby also the Obstacle from the corruption of our Nature is rendered no longer insurmountable.

II. The belief in the possible appropriation of this benefit by Repentance and Faith, including the Aids that render an effective Faith and Repentance themselves possible.

III. The belief in the reception (by as many as "shall be Heirs of Salvation")[5] of a living and spiritual Principle, a Seed of Life capable of surviving this natural life, and of existing in a divine and immortal State.

IV. The belief in the awakening of the Spirit[b] in them that truly believe, and in the communion of the Spirit, thus awakened, with the Holy Spirit.

[c]V. The belief in the accompanying and consequent gifts, graces, comforts, and privileges of the Spirit, which acting primarily on the heart and will,[d] cannot but manifest themselves in suitable works of Love and Obedience, i.e. in right acts with right affections, from right principles.

----

[a] *AR* (1825): Resurrection
[b] *AR* (1825): Spirit* [Footnote reads: "* *See* pp. 68–72."]
[c] *AR* (1825): p 191
[d] *AR* (1825): will

----

[4] A note in C's hand pasted to the front endpaper of *AR* (1825) COPY J is reported to read: "In p. 190–91 will be found my Creed as a Christian, digested into seven articles. [It] may be entitled, the Coleridgian Septar[ian] Creed." COPY F has a note here: "An eminent Prelate has been pleased to express his particular approbation of this Septarticular *Confessio Fidei*." The "eminent Prelate" was presumably William Howley (1766–1848), then bp of London, whom C met through Sir George and Lady Beaumont on 20 May 1825 and to whom he presented a copy of *AR*: *CL* v 452, 456, 462. He learned from Lady Beaumont that the bishop had ". . . expressed a MOST favorable Opinion" of the work. See the letter to EC accompanying COPY F 15 Jul 1825: *CL* v 481 (and cf 475, 484), also p cx above.

[5] Heb 1.14: "Are they not all ministering spirits, sent forth to minister for them who shall be heirs of salvation?"

VI.[a] Further, as Christians, we are taught, that these WORKS are the appointed signs and evidences of our FAITH; and that, under limitation of the power, the means, and the opportunities afforded us individually, they are the rule and measure, by which we are bound and enabled to judge, of *what* spirit we [b]are.

VII. All these, together[c] with the doctrine[d] of[e] the Fathers re-proclaimed[f] in the everlasting Gospel, we receive in the full assurance, that God beholds and will finally judge us with a merciful consideration of our infirmities, a gracious acceptance of our sincere though imperfect strivings, a forgiveness of our defects through the mediation, and a completion of our deficiences by the perfect righteousness, of the Man Christ Jesus, even the Word that was in the beginning with God, and who, being God, became Man for the redemption of Mankind.

COMMENT

I earnestly entreat the Reader to pause awhile, and to join with me in reflecting on the preceding Aphorism. It has been my aim throughout this work to enforce two points: 1. That MORALITY arising out of the Reason and Conscience of Men, and PRUDENCE, which in like manner flows out of the Understanding [g]and the natural Wants and Desires of the Individual, are two distinct things.[h] 2. That Morality with Prudence as its instrument has, considered abstractedly, not only a value but a *worth* in itself. Now the question is (and it is a question which every man must answer for himself) [i]"From what you know of yourself; of your own Heart and Strength; and from what History and personal Experience have led you to conclude of mankind generally; dare you *trust* to it? Dare *you* trust to it? To *it*, and to it alone? If so, well! It is at your own risk. I judge you not. Before Him, who cannot be mocked,[6] you stand or fall.[7] But if not, if you have had too good reason to know, that

----

[a] Added in COPIES E & F and in *AR* (1831)

[b-c] *AR* (1825): are: and all these ; Corr and COPY G are: and all these together ; COPY E: are: and ⟨VII⟩ all, these⟨, together⟩ ; COPY H: as 1831

[b-f] COPY C: are: and all these, together with the doctrines of the Fathers re-proclaimed ; COPY F: are. [*At top of page* "'A fresh §graph: and insert"'] Lastly, all these doctrines, together with the faith of the Patriarchs reproclaimed &

[d] *AR* (1825) Corr, COPIES E, F, H: doctrines

[e] Added in *AR* (1825) Corr, COPY G, and *AR* (1831)

[g] *AR* (1825): p 192

[h] *AR* (1825): things;

[i] *AR* (1825): quotation marks unclosed: see n 12 below

----

[6] Gal 6.7: "God is not mocked".

[7] "Who art thou that judgest another man's servant? to his own master he standeth or falleth": Rom 14.4.

your heart is deceitful[8] and your strength weakness: if you are disposed to exclaim with Paul—the Law indeed is holy, just, good, spiritual; but I am carnal, sold under sin: for that which I do, I allow not; and what I would, that *ª*I do*ᵇ* not![9]—in this case, there is a Voice that says, Come unto *me:* and I will give you rest.[10] This is the Voice of Christ: and the Conditions, under which the promise was given by him, are that you believe *in* him, and believe his words. And he has further assured you, that *if* you do so, you will obey him.[11] You are, in short, to embrace the *Christian* Faith as your Religion—those Truths which St. Paul believed *after* his conversion, and not those only which he believed no less undoubtingly while he was persecuting Christ, and an enemy of the Christian Religion. With what consistency could I offer you this volume as Aids to Reflection,*ᶜ* if I did not call on you to ascertain in *ᵈ*the first instance what these truths are? But these I could not lay before you without first enumerating certain other points of belief, which though truths, indispensable truths, and truths comprehended or rather pre-supposed in the Christian Scheme, are yet not *these* Truths. (1 John v. 17.)[12]

While doing this, I was aware that the Positions, in the first paragraph of the preceding Aphorism, to which the numerical *marks*[13] are affixed, will startle some of my Readers. Let the following sentences serve for the notes corresponding to the marks:

1 Be you holy: even as God is holy.[14]—What more does he require of thee, O man! than to do justice, love mercy, and walk humbly with the

ª⁻ᵇ AR (1825): do I
ᶜ AR (1825): Reflection
ᵈ AR (1825): p 193

[8] Jer 17.9: "The heart is deceitful above all things, and desperately wicked . . .''.

[9] "Wherefore the law is holy, and the commandment holy, and just, and good. . . . For we know that the law is spiritual: but I am carnal, sold under sin. For that which I do I allow not: for what I would, that I do not; but what I hate, that do I'': Rom 7.12, 14–15.

[10] Matt 11.28: "Come unto me, all ye that labour and are heavy laden, and I will give you rest.'' Cf above, *Prud Aph I* and n 2.

[11] These statements are less an exact rendering of particular texts than an extrapolation from the Gospels, notably St John: e.g. ''. . . He that heareth my word, and believeth on him that sent me, hath everlasting life'' (5.24); ''. . . ye believe in God, believe also in me'' (14.1); ''. . . If a man love me, he will keep my words: and my Father will love him, and we will come unto him, and make our abode with him'' (14.23), etc.

[12] Cf John 1.17: "For the law was given by Moses, but grace and truth came by Jesus Christ.'' See also below, *Sp Aph B XXIIIb* at n 47. The movement of C's thought in the whole paragraph here is indicated by the fact that the quotation marks opened near the beginning are never closed.

[13] See above, n 2.

[14] A conflation of Lev 19.2: ''. . . Ye shall be holy: for I the Lord your God am holy'' (cited 1 Pet 1.16, and cf Lev 11.44, 45; 20.7, 26) with Matt 5.48: ''Be ye therefore perfect, even as your Father which is in heaven is perfect''.

Lord thy God?[15] To these summary passages from Moses and the Prophets (the first exhibiting the closed, the second the expanded, Hand of the Moral Law) I might add the Authorities of Grotius and other more orthodox and not less learned Divines, for the opinion, that the Lord's Prayer was a *selection,*[16] and the famous Passage (The Hour is now coming, John v. 28, 29.)[17] a *citation* by our Lord from the Liturgy of the Jewish Church. But it will be sufficient to remind the reader, that the apparent difference between the prominent *moral* truths of the Old and those of the New Testament results from the latter having been written in Greek; while the conversations recorded by the Evangelists took place in Hebrew or Syro-chaldaic. Hence it happened that where our Lord cited the original text, his Biographers substituted the Septuagint Version, [a]while our English Version is in *both* instances immediate and literal—in the Old Testament from the Hebrew Original, in the New Testament from the freer Greek Translation.[b][18] The text, "I give you a new commandment,"[19] has no connection[c] with the present subject.

[a] *AR* (1825): p 194

[b] *AR* (1825): Thus in the Text, Love your Neighbour as yourself, *Neighbour* in our New, and *Stranger* in our Old Testament represent one and the same Hebrew word. ; Corr enjoins: The readers *generally* are intreated to strike out the sentence comprised in lines 4–7 of p. 194, containing a mistaken assertion; the result of exhausted attention. ; COPIES A, C, F, G delete the sentence; COPY D deletes "Hebrew word"; COPY E had a slip pasted over the sentence, later removed

[c] *AR* (1825): connexion

[15] "He hath shewed thee, O man, what is good; and what doth the Lord require of thee, but to do justly, and to love mercy, and to walk humbly with thy God?" Mic 6.8. See also below, *Sp Aph B Xb* n 73.

[16] "Docent autem nos ea quae Hebraeorum libris ab aliis sunt citata, non tam formulam hanc à Christo suis verbis conceptam, quam in eam congestum quicquid in Hebraeorum precibus erat laudabile: sicut & in admonitionibus passim utitur notis eo saeculo proverbiis"; tr: "Quotations by others from Hebrew books show us, however, that this formula was not conceived by Christ in his own words, but rather that into it was collected whatever was praiseworthy in the prayers of the Hebrews. So, too, in his admonitions he very often uses proverbs current at that time": Grotius, commenting on Matt 6.9: *Annotationes in Libros Evangeliorum* (2 vols Amsterdam 1641, Paris 1644) I 142. Annotating Taylor Σύμβολον Θεολογικόν 22, *CM (CC)* v, C cites Lightfoot, also, as a source of this view: see J. Lightfoot on Matt 6.9 in 1658:

Whole Works (1822–5) XI (1824) 142.

[17] ". . . for the hour is coming, in the which all that are in the graves shall hear his voice, And shall come forth; they that have done good, unto the resurrection of life; and they that have done evil, unto the resurrection of damnation." Some affinities between this section of St John's Gospel and rabbinical tradition are noted by H. Odeborg *The Fourth Gospel* (Uppsala & Stockholm 1929) 190–216; in 1671 Lightfoot had related it to the "dry bones" vision of Ezek 37: *Whole Works* XII 287–8.

[18] *AR* (1825) has another sentence here: "Thus in the Text, Love your Neighbour as yourself, *Neighbour* in our New, and *Stranger* in our Old Testament represent one and the same Hebrew word." At the head of the *"Corrections and Amendments"* (1825 p xv), however, C writes: "The Readers *generally* are intreated to strike out" this sentence, ". . . containing a mistaken assertion; the result of exhausted attention." See textual note.

[19] "A new commandment I give unto

2 There is a current mistake on this point likewise, though this article of the Jewish Belief is not only asserted by St. Paul,[20] but is elsewhere spoken of as common to the Twelve Tribes.[21] The mistake consists in supposing the Pharisees to have been a distinct *Sect,* and in strangely over-rating the number of the Sadducees.[22] The former were distinguished not by holding, as matters of religious belief, articles different from the Jewish Church at large; but by their pretences to a more rigid orthodoxy, a more scrupulous performance. They were, in short (if I may dare use a phrase which I dislike as profane and denounce as uncharitable), the *Evangelicals* and strict *Professors* of the Day. The latter, the Sadducees, whose opinions much more nearly resembled those of the *Stoics* than the Epicureans (a remark that will appear paradoxical to those only who have abstracted their notions of the Stoic Philosophy from Epictetus,[23] Mark Antonine,[24] and certain brilliant inconsistencies

you, That ye love one another; as I have loved you, that ye also love one another'': John 13.34. C may be remembering that the commandment ''. . . thou shalt love thy neighbour as thyself'' appears also in the OT: Lev 19.18.

[20] Cf Acts 23.6–8: ''But when Paul perceived that the one part were Sadducees, and the other Pharisees, he cried out in the council, Men and Brethren, I am a Pharisee, the son of a Pharisee: of the hope and resurrection of the dead I am called in question. And when he had so said, there arose a dissension between the Pharisees and the Sadducees: and the multitude was divided. For the Sadducees say that there is no resurrection, neither angel, nor spirit: but the Pharisees confess both.'' St Paul's discussion of the resurrection of the body, in 1 Cor 15.35–54, throws some doubt on his acceptance of the doctrine in its most literal interpretation. See also n 21.

[21] Acts 24.14–15 and 26.6–8 also show Paul affirming his own belief in the resurrection of the dead and attributing it to contemporary Jews, the ''twelve tribes''. For the Twelve Tribes in this sense see *CM (CC)* II 832 and cf James 1.1. The question of the after-life in Jewish belief is discussed by W. O. E. Oesterley and T. H. Robinson *Hebrew Religion: Its Origin and Development* (1937) 17–19, 243–53, and 352–65.

[22] The Pharisees and Sadducees first ap-

peared under these names after the Maccabean struggle in the second century B.C. The Pharisees were a more popular party, based on the synagogues; the Sadducees, or high-priestly party, were associated with the Temple. The differences between them go back further, however: ibid 364–5, 406–7. C discusses the Sadducees in detail in a letter to William Lisle Bowles of 24 Mar 1815: *CL* IV 558. He cites as authority the ''*Univ. History*'', i.e. G. Sale, G. Psalmanazar, A. Bower, and others *An Universal History from the Earliest Account of Time to the Present* (23 vols 1736–65), which has a section on them. See also *P Lects* Lect 7 (1949) 237 and n, p 423, referring to Josephus *Antiquities of the Jews* 13.10.6, 12.5.9, and 18.1.3.

[23] Epictetus (c 50–130) shared the general Stoic belief in the possibility of achieving virtue and wisdom by one's own efforts and in the reabsorption of the soul after death into God or the soul of the world, though *Enchiridion* 15 was interpreted by some as an allusion to rewards for the virtuous after death.

[24] Marcus Aurelius Antoninus (121–80) similarly rejected the idea of personal immortality. See *Conversation with Himself* 4.15, 4.21, 5.13, each quoted in part in *CM (CC)* I 174–5, 178; C's comments there, however (cf *CM—CC*—I 179), show him eager to read Christian truths into the emperor's words.

of Seneca),[25] were a handful of rich men, *romanized* Jews, not more numerous than Infidels among us, and holden[a] by the People at large in at least equal abhorrence. Their great argument was: [b]that the Belief of a future State of rewards and punishments injured or destroyed the purity of the Moral Law for the more enlightened Classes, and weakened the influence of the Laws of the Land for the People, the vulgar Multitude.

I will now suppose the Reader to have thoughtfully re-perused the Paragraph containing the Tenets peculiar to Christianity, and if he have his religious principles yet to form, I should expect to overhear a troubled Murmur: How can I comprehend this? How is this to be proved? To the first question I should answer: Christianity is not a Theory, or a Speculation; but a *Life*. Not a *Philosophy* of Life, but a Life and a living Process. To the second: TRY IT.[26] It has been eighteen hundred Years in existence: and has one Individual left a record, like the following? [c]"I tried it; and it did not answer. I made the experiment faithfully according to the directions; and the result has been, a conviction of my own credulity." Have you, in your own experience, met with any one in whose words you could place full confidence, and who has seriously affirmed, "I have given Christianity a fair trial. I was aware, that its promises were made only *conditionally*. But my heart bears me witness, that I have to the utmost of my power complied with these conditions. Both outwardly and in the discipline of my inward acts and affections, I have performed the duties which it enjoins, and I have used the means,

---

a *AR* (1825): held
b *AR* (1825): p 195
[c–d] *AR* (1825, 1831) encloses by [ ], replaced here by " " (twice)

---

[25] See C's note ibid I 174: "As to Seneca, nothing can be gathered from his Witticisms . . . Seneca's Head was not capable of a System—his mind was discontinuous—a moral wit". For a more respectful attitude to Seneca, on the other hand, see the epigraph to *Sp Aph A* above, and nn 4, 5. Cf also *P Lects* Lect 6 (1949) 219 for the Stoics' "endless doubts respecting immortality".

[26] Boulger 113–15 notes several parallels to this statement, of which the most persuasive is *CIS* (1840) 60–2. John Smith (1618–52), whose *Select Discourses* (1660) C read and annotated (see *CN* II 2164–7, *CM—CC—*v, and below, *Sp Aph B VIIIa* n 16, *Xa* nn 12, 13), follows a not dissimilar argument in them: e.g. (p 451)

". . . let us endeavour to live more in a real practice of those Rules of Religious and Holy living commended to us by our ever-Blessed Lord and Saviour: So shall we know Religion better, and knowing it love it, and loving it be still more and more ambitiously pursuing after it . . .". In these and other passages (e.g. p lv), which draw explicitly on John 7.17, "If any man will do his will, he shall know of the doctrine, whether it be of God", Smith's language is less boldly challenging, however, emphasising rather the need to practise virtue. For Emerson's more Coleridgean view see Editor's Introduction above, n 298. C uses a similar argument from experience, this time concerning the inspiration of the Scriptures, in *CN* III 3440.

*a*which it prescribes. Yet my Assurance of its truth has received no increase. Its promises have not been fulfilled: and I repent me of my delusion!''*d* If neither your own experience nor the History of almost two thousand years has presented a single testimony to this purport; and if you have read and heard of many who have lived and died bearing witness to the contrary: and if you have yourself met with some *one,* in whom on any other point you would place unqualified trust, who has on his own experience made report to you, that "he is faithful who promised, and what he promised he has proved himself able to perform:''[27] is it bigotry, if I fear that the Unbelief, which prejudges and prevents the experiment, has its source elsewhere than in the uncorrupted judgment;*b* that not the strong free Mind, but the enslaved will,*c* is the true original Infidel in this instance? It would not be the first time, that a treacherous Bosom-Sin[28] had suborned the Understandings of men to bear false witness against its avowed Enemy, the right though unreceived Owner of the House, who had long *warned it out,*[29] and waited only for its ejection to enter and take possession of the same.

I have elsewhere in the present Work, though more at large in the "Elements of Discourse,''*e*[30] which, God permitting, will follow it, explained the difference between the Understanding and the Reason, by Reason meaning exclusively the speculative or scientific Power so called, the Nous or Mens*f*[31] of the Ancients. And wider still is the distinction between the Understanding and the Spiritual Mind. But no Gift

---

a *AR* (1825): p 196
b *AR* (1825): judgement;
c *AR* (1825): Will,
e *AR* (1825): Discourse''
f COPY D: Mens or rather the Λόγος ἐν καθολῳ as distinguished from the Λόγος ὅ ἐν ἑκάστῳ

---

[27] A conflation of Heb 10.23: ''. . . he is faithful that promised'', and Rom 4.21 (of Abraham's assurance concerning God): ''And being fully persuaded that, what he had promised, he was able also to perform.''

[28] From Herbert: see above, *Int Aph XI* n 1 and *XIX* n 3.

[29] ''Warn out'': to give a person notice to leave his employment or tenancy. Obs. *OED.*

[30] See above, *Sp Aph B II* n 73. Although the distinction between reason and understanding is presupposed throughout the *Logic,* however, the discussion of its nature is rather brief. See *Logic (CC)* 67–

70. The editor draws attention (p 169) to a fuller discussion in the "Divine Ideas" ms: *HEHL ms* HM 8195.

[31] *AR* (1825) COPY D is emended to continue: ''or rather the Λόγος ἐν καθολῳ, as distinguished from the Λόγος ὅ ἐν ἑκαστῳ'' (the ''Word in the whole'', as distinguished from the ''Word in each''). C regularly used an unrecorded adjectival κάθολος instead of the invariable adjectival καθόλου. See also below, *Sp Aph B VIIIb* n 14 and *Xa* n 27. IN COPY E the addition is copied by someone not familiar with Greek. See below, App I Excursus Note 4 ''Coleridge on Nous and Logos''.

of God does or can ^acontradict any other Gift, except by misuse or misdirection. Most readily therefore do I admit, that there can be no contrariety between Revelation and the Understanding; unless you call the fact, that the Skin, though sensible of the warmth of the Sun, can convey no notion of its figure^b or its joyous light, or of the ^ccolors, which it^d impresses on the clouds, a contrariety between the Skin and the Eye; or infer that the cutaneous and the optic nerves *contradict* each other.

But we have grounds to believe, that there are yet other Rays or Effluences from the Sun, which neither Feeling nor Sight can apprehend, but which are to be inferred from the effects.[32] And were it even so with regard to the Spiritual Sun,[33] how would this contradict the Understanding or the Reason? It is a sufficient proof of the contrary, that the Mysteries in question are not *in the direction* of the Understanding or the (speculative) Reason. They do not move on the same line or plane with them, and therefore cannot contradict them. But besides this, in the Mystery that most immediately concerns the Believer, that of the birth into a new and spiritual life, the common sense and experience of mankind come in aid of their faith. The analogous facts, which we know to be true, not only facilitate the apprehension of the facts promised to us, and expressed by the same words in conjunction with a distinctive epithet; but being confessedly not less incomprehensible, the certain *knowledge* of the one disposes us to the *belief* of the other. It removes at least all objections to the truth of the doctrine derived from the ^emysteriousness of its subject. The Life, we seek after, is a mystery; but so both in itself and in its origin is the Life we have. In order to meet this question, however, with minds duly prepared, there are two preliminary inquiries^f to be decided; the first respecting the *purport*, the second respecting the *language* of the Gospel.

ᵃ AR (1825): p 197
ᵇ AR (1825): figure,
ᶜ⁻ᵈ AR (1825): colours, it
ᵉ AR (1825): p 198
ᶠ AR (1825): enquiries

[32] C is presumably referring to the discovery of infra-red rays by William Herschel, described in *Philosophical Transactions of the Royal Society* xc (1800) 284–92. He mentioned this paper in a letter to Davy 4 May 1801: *CL* ii 727. Cf *CN* iv 5241 f 31–31ᵛ: "The Eye itself, it may well be, would have been weak and blear, had it [? not] been strengthened & nourished by the Light and other invisible eradiations of the Sun".

[33] Cf Cudworth *True Intellectual System of the Universe* (1743) 744: ". . . even those philosophic Theists, who maintained . . . *the eternity of human minds and souls*, together with the worlds, did notwithstanding, assert their essential dependence upon the *Deity*, like that of the lights upon the sun; as if they were a kind of eternal effulgency, emanation or eradiation from an eternal sun." For C's borrowings of Cudworth at Bristol in 1795–6 see above, *Int Aph XXVI* n 2.

First then of the *purport*, viz. what the Gospel does *not*, and what it *does* profess to be. The Gospel is not a system of Theology, nor a Syntagma[34] of theoretical propositions and conclusions for the enlargement of speculative knowledge, ethical or metaphysical. But it is a History, a series of Facts and Events related or announced. These do indeed[a] involve, or rather I should say they at the same time *are*, most important doctrinal Truths; but still *Facts* and Declaration of *Facts*.

Secondly of the *language*. This is a wide subject.[35] But the point, to which I chiefly advert, is the necessity of thoroughly understanding the distinction between *analogous*, and *metaphorical* language.[36] *Analogies* are used in aid of *Conviction*: Metaphors,[b] as means of *Illustration*. The language is analogous, wherever a thing, power, or principle in a higher dignity is expressed by the same thing, power, or principle in a lower but more known form.[c] Such, for instance, is the language of John iii. 6. *That which is born of the Flesh, is Flesh; that which is born of the Spirit, is Spirit*. The latter half of the verse contains the fact *asserted;* the former half the *analogous* fact, by which [d]it is rendered intelligible. If any man choose to call this *metaphorical* or figurative, I ask him whether with Hobbs[37] and Bolingbroke[38] he applies the same rule to the

[a] *AR* (1825): indeed,
[b] *AR* (1825): *Metaphors,*
[c] *AR* (1831): form,
[d] *AR* (1825): p 199

[34] "A regular or orderly collection of statements, propositions or doctrines, etc.": *OED*, which cites Milton *Areopagitica* (1644) 67. C's use of the term may have been prompted by the title of Gassendi's *Syntagma philosophicum*, which in a letter of 13 Feb 1824 he asked Mrs C to have checked by SC: *CL* v 328; cf *CN* IV 5123, 5125.

[35] For a long note giving many references to statements by C on the importance of understanding differences of literary form in connexion with scriptural interpretation see Barth 64 and n. See also Boulger 115–17.

[36] This distinction is referred back to in *C&S (CC)* 120.

[37] Hobbes is not endeavouring to devalue the Deity, however: ". . . when men out of the Principles of naturall Reason, dispute of the Attributes of God, they but dishonour him: For in the Attributes which we give to God, we are not to consider the signification of Philosophicall Truth; but the signification of Pious Intention, to do

him the greatest Honour we are able": Hobbes *Leviathan* pt 2 ch 31 (1651) 191; in *The English Works* ed Sir William Molesworth (11 vols 1839–45) III 354; cf III 383, 415, 672, 677; v 6. Hobbes refers particularly to "Spirit" as such an attribute.

[38] Similarly with Bolingbroke: ". . . no unprejudiced thinking man can hear, without astonishment, our perfections and our imperfections imputed to the Supreme Being . . . In a being thus constituted, they may well imagine that the moral virtues are the same as they are in our ideas: and theology may easily deduce from his attributes the characters theology has given them. But a being thus constituted is not the supreme, the All-perfect Being; and a very short analyse of the excellencies of our own nature will be sufficient to show, that they cannot be applied from man to God without profaneness, nor from God to man without the most shameful absurdity": Henry St John, 1st Viscount Bolingbroke "Fragments, or Minutes of Essays" *Works* (8 vols 1809) VII 387. Cf *Friend (CC)* I 46.

moral attributes of the Deity? Whether he regards the divine Justice, for instance, as a *metaphorical* term, a mere figure of speech? If he disclaims this, then I answer, neither do I regard the words, *born again*, or *spiritual life*, as figures or metaphors. I have only to add, that these analogies are the material, or (to speak chemically) the *base*, of Symbols and symbolical expressions; the nature of which as always *tau*tegorical (i.e. expressing the *same* subject but with a *difference*) in contra-distinction from metaphors and similitudes, that are always *alle*gorical (i.e. expressing a *different* subject but with a resemblance) will be found explained at large in the STATESMAN'S MANUAL, p. 35–38.[39]

Of *metaphorical* language, on the other hand, let the following be taken as instance and illustration. I am speaking, we will suppose, of an Act, which in its own nature, and as a producing and efficient *cause*, is transcendent; but which produces sundry *effects*, each of which is the same in kind with an effect produced by a Cause well known and of ordinary occurrence. Now when I characterize or designate this transcendent Act, in exclusive reference to these its *effects*, by a succession of names borrowed from their ordinary causes; not for the purpose of rendering the Act itself, or the manner of the Agency, conceivable, but in order to show the nature and magnitude of the Benefits received [a]from it, and thus to excite the due admiration, gratitude, and love in the Receivers;[b] in this case I should be rightly described as speaking *metaphorically*. And in this case to confound[c] *the similarity*,[d] in respect of the effects relatively to the [e]Recipients,[f] with *an identity* in respect of the causes or modes of causation relatively to the transcendent Act or the Divine Agent,[g] is a confusion of metaphor with analogy, and of figurative with literal; and has been and continues to be a fruitful source of superstition or enthusiasm in Believers, and of objections and prejudices to Infidels and Sceptics. But each of these points is worthy of a separate consideration: and apt occasions will be found of reverting to them severally in the following Aphorisms,[h] or the comments thereto attached.

[a] *AR* (1825): p 200
[b] *AR* (1825): Receivers;—
[c] COPY H: mistake
[d] *AR* (1825): *similarity*
[e-g] COPY H: *Recipients*, for an *identity* in respect of the Cause relatively to the *Agent*,
[f] *AR* (1825): Recipients
[h] *AR* (1825): Aphorisms

[39] See *SM (CC)* 28–31 and n p 30, quoting Schelling's remark to Benjamin Jowett that "Coleridge had expressed many things better than he could himself, that in one word he had comprised a whole essay, saying that mythology was not allegorical but tautegorical". For "tautegorical" see also *CN* IV 4711 and n; for "tautegory" ibid 4832 f 61ᵛ and n. For further discussions of allegory and symbol see *SM (CC)* 79, Lect 7 of 1819: *Lects 1808–1819 (CC)* II 417–18, and *CN* IV 4831–2.

APHORISM VIII[a][1]

FAITH elevates the soul not only above Sense and sensible things, but above Reason itself. As Reason corrects the errors which Sense might occasion, so supernatural Faith corrects the errors of natural Reason judging according to Sense.

COMMENT[2]

The Editor's remarks on this Aphorism[b] from Archbishop Leighton cannot be better introduced, or their purport more distinctly announced, than by the following sentence from Harrington, with no other change than was necessary to make the words express,[c] without aid of the context,[d] what from the context it is evident [e]was the Writer's meaning.[3] "The definition and proper character of Man—that, namely, which should contra-distinguish him from the Animals—is to be taken from his Reason rather than from his Understanding: in regard that in other creatures there may be something of Understanding,[f] but there is nothing of Reason." See the FRIEND, vol. i. p. 263–277:[4] and the APPENDIX (Note C.) to the STATESMAN'S MANUAL.[5]

Sir Thomas Brown, in his Religio Medici, complains, that there are not impossibilities enough in Religion for his active faith; and adopts by

[a] *AR* (1825): LEIGHTON.
[b] *AR* (1825): aphorism
[c] *AR* (1825): express
[d] *AR* (1825): context
[e] *AR* (1825): p 201
[f] *AR* (1825): Understanding

[1] See Leighton COPY C I 71: *CM (CC)* III. C changes only punctuation and accidentals. C's annotation at this point provides the germ of the discussion that follows: see below, nn 26, 32, and *Sp Aph B VIIIb* nn 2, 7, 15.

[2] In *CN* IV 5210 (May 1825) C presented "The Scheme or Argument from p. 200 to p. 242" of *AR* (i.e. pp 207–50) "subtracting the interspersed Aphorisms from 228 to 234" (i.e. pp 236–42), in schematic form: this note corresponds to a schematic discussion of reason and understanding that appears also in ms in *AR* (1825) COPIES A, C, and D in various forms and was incorporated into *AR* (1831) (p 413 below). See App D(a) below.

[3] The sentence originally appears as Aphorism 35 of James Harrington *Political Aphorisms: Oceana* ed J. Toland (1700) 516. It was copied, with changes only of punctuation and spelling, into a notebook of 1804, where it reads: "Man may rather be defined a religious than a rational Creature: in regard that in other Creatures there may be something of Reason, but there is nothing of Religion." C added: "On whom rests the onus probandi [burden of proof]?": *CN* II 2223 f 19. The quotation in *The Friend* (see next note) follows Harrington almost exactly. C's changes for *AR* hinge on the substitution of "Reason" for Harrington's "Religion", and "Understanding" for his "Reason".

[4] *Friend (CC)* I 154–61.

[5] *SM (CC)* 59–93.

choice and in free preference,[a] such interpretations of certain texts and declarations of Holy Writ, as place them in irreconcilable contradiction to the demonstrations of science and the experience of mankind, because (says he) [b]"I love to lose myself in a mystery, and 'tis my solitary re-creation to pose my apprehension with those involved enigmas and riddles of the Trinity and Incarnation"—[c]and because he delights (as thinking[d] it no vulgar part of faith) to believe a thing not only above but contrary to Reason, and against the evidence of our proper senses. For the worthy knight could answer all the objections of the Devil and Reason (!!) "with the odd resolution he had learnt of Tertullian: Certum est quia impossibile est. It is certainly true because it is quite impossible!"[6] Now this I call ULTRA-FIDIANISM.[7][*e]

* There is this advantage in the occasional use of a newly minted term or title,[f] express-ing the doctrinal schemes of particular sects or parties, that it avoids the inconvenience that presses on either side, whether we adopt the name which the Party itself has taken up [g]by which[h] to express it's peculiar tenets,[i] or that by which the same Party is designated by its opponents. If we take the latter, it most often happens that either the persons are invidiously aimed at in the designation of the principles, or that the name implies some consequence or occasional accompaniment of the principles denied by the parties them-selves, as applicable to them collectively. On the other hand, convinced as I am, that current appellations are never wholly indifferent or inert; and that, when employed to express the characteristic Belief or Object of a *religious* confederacy, they exert on the Many a great and constant, though insensible, influence; I cannot but fear that in adopting the former[j] I may be sacrificing the interests of Truth beyond what the duties of courtesy can demand or justify. In a tract published in the year 1816,[8] I have stated my objections

[a] *AR* (1825): preference

[b] *AR* (1825): I

[c] *AR* (1825): Incarnation "—

[d] *AR* (1825): thinking"

[e] *AR* (1825): ULTRA-FIDIANISM*.

[f] *AR* (1825): title

[g-h] Added in 1831

[i] *AR* (1825): tenets by,

[j] COPY H: former (that is, in adopting the Name which the Parties themselves have assumed)

[6] "I love to lose myself in a Mystery, to pursue my reason to an *Oh altitudo*! 'Tis my solitary recreation to pose my appre-hension with those involved aenigmas and riddles of the Trinity, with Incarnation, and Resurrection. I can answer all the Objec-tions of Satan, and my rebellious reason, with that odd resolution I learned of *Tertul-lian, Certum est, quia impossibile est*": Browne *Religio Medici* (1669) 17. The fi-nal translation is C's own: the Latin means, more baldly, "it is certain because it is im-possible". Many years earlier, in an anno-tation on the first sentence of this passage, C wrote: " 'Oh the Depth!' So say I: so

says dear W. W.": *CM (CC)* I 746. The quotation from Tertullian is from *De carne Christi* v (Migne *PL* II 761). See also *Sp Aph B VIIIb* n 59 below. In *AR* (1825) the inverted commas were presumably in-tended to run as here, but muddled by the compositor (see textual notes).

[7] *OED* cites this as the first use of the word, giving later examples from HC and Fitzgerald Hall.

[8] *A Lay Sermon* (1817): *LS (CC)* 176–7. C's quotation interpolates part of his note into the text and makes small alterations; it also inserts two new sentences: see below.

to the word *Unitarians:* as a name which in its proper sense can belong only to the Maintainers of the Truth impugned by the persons, who have chosen it as their designation. "For *Unity* or Unition, and indistinguishable *Unicity* or Sameness, are incompatible terms.[9] We never speak of the Unity of Attraction, or the Unity of Repulsion; but of the Unity of Attraction *and* Repulsion in each corpuscle. Indeed, the essential diversity of the conceptions, Unity and Sameness, was among the elementary principles of the old Logicians;[a] and Leibnitz,[b] in his critique on Wissowatius,[c10] has ably exposed the sophisms grounded on the confusion of the two terms. But in the exclusive sense, in which the name, Unitarian, is appropriated by the Sect, and in which they mean it to be understood, it is a presumptuous Boast and an uncharitable calumny.[11] No one of the Churches to which they on this article of the Christian Faith stand opposed, Greek or Latin, ever adopted the Term,[d] Trini—or Tri-uni-tarians as their ordinary and proper name: and had it been otherwise, yet Unity is assuredly no logical Opposite to Tri-unity, which expressly includes it. The triple Alliance[12] is a fortiori Alliance. The true designation of their characteristic Tenet, and which would simply and inoffensively express a fact admitted on all sides, is Psilanthropism,[e13] or the assertion of the *mere* humanity of Christ.''

I dare not hesitate to avow my regret, that any scheme of doctrines or tenets should be the subject of penal law: though I can easily conceive, that any scheme, however excellent in itself, may be propagated, and however false or injurious, may be assailed, in a manner and by means that would make the Advocate or Assailant justly punishable. But then it is

---

[a] *AR* (1825): Logicians: [b] *AR* (1825): Leibnitz   [c] *AR* (1825): Wissowatius

[d] *AR* (1825): term,   [e] *AR* (1825): Psilanthropism

---

[9] Under "unicity" *OED* gives an example of this distinction from R. Burthogge *An Essay upon Reason and the Nature of Spirits* (1694) 166: "Composition is Unity, but simplicity is Unicity." In *LS* C wrote "Unicity or Oneness"—*LS (CC)* 176—but in some copies changed "Oneness" to "Sameness". Cf also his citations of Spinoza's "unica substantia": *Sp Aph B II* at n 30 above, *Conc* n 52 below. In the *Logic* "sameness" becomes "negative sameness" and the word is more fully defined in C's footnote: *Logic (CC)* 250, 250–1n. For "unicism" see *CM (CC)* II 799, III 77 and nn, and *CL* IV 687.

[10] Leibniz "Defensio Trinitatis per nova reperta logica . . ." in *Opera omnia* ed L. Dutens (6 vols Geneva 1768) I 10–16. As *LS (CC)* 177n also points out, C recommended this edition in a letter of Apr 1818: *CL* IV 851.

[11] Up to here C has quoted from text and note of *LS*. He now inserts two new sentences, returning to *LS (CC)* 176–7 for the final sentence of the passage set in quotation marks.

[12] The term had been used both in 1668 and 1718 for alliances between three pow-

ers: see *OED* s.v. "triple" 5.

[13] Cf *TT* 4 Apr 1832: "What do you mean by exclusively assuming the title of Unitarians?—As if Triunitarians were not necessarily Unitarians—as much as an apple-pie must of course be a pie!'': *TT (CC)* I 279. *TT* (1836) adds: "The schoolmen would, perhaps, have called you Unicists: but your proper name is Psilanthropists—believers in the mere human nature of Christ": ibid II 161. Cf *BL* ch 10 *(CC)* I 180: ". . . I was a *psilanthropist*, one of those who believe our Lord to have been the real son of Joseph, and who lay the main stress on the resurrection rather than the crucifixion". See also *LS (CC)* 176 and n 4 and an annotation on W. E. Channing *A Discourse Delivered at the Installation of the Rev. Mellish Irving Motte . . .*: *CM (CC)* II 21–2. Cf also his coinage "psilosophy": ". . . from the Greek, psilo slender and Sophia Wisdom, in opposition to Philosophy, the Love of Wisdom and the Wisdom of Love": letter of 29 Feb 1819, *CL* IV 922; also *CN* II 3158: "A Psilosopher, i.e. a nominal Ph. without imagination, is a Coiner . . ." and *BL* chs 3, 10 *(CC)* I 67n, 185.

the *manner*, the *means*, that constitute the *crime*. The merit or demerit of the Opinions themselves depends on their originating and determining causes, which may differ in every different Believer, and are certainly known to Him alone, who commanded us,[a] Judge not, lest ye be judged.[14] At all events, in the present state of the Law,[b] I do not see where we can begin, or where we can stop, without inconsistency and consequent hardship. Judging by all that *we* can pretend to know or are entitled to infer, who among us will take on himself to deny that the late Dr. Priestley was a good and benevolent man, as sincere in his love, as he was intrepid and indefatigable in his pursuit, of Truth?[15] Now let us construct three parallel tables, the first containing the Articles of Belief, moral and theological, maintained by the venerable Hooker, as the representative of the Established Church, each article being distinctly lined and numbered; the second the Tenets and Persuasions of Lord Herbert, as the representative of the platonizing Deists;[16] and the third, those of Dr. Priestley. Let the points, in which the second and third agree with or differ from the first, be considered as to the comparative number modified by the comparative weight and importance of the several points—and let any competent and upright Man be appointed the Arbiter, to decide according to his best judgment, without any reference to the truth of the opinions, which of the two differed from the first the more widely! I say this, well aware that it would be abundantly more prudent to leave it unsaid. But I say it in the conviction, that the *liberality* in the adoption of admitted *misnomers* in the naming of doctrinal systems, if only they have been negatively legalized, is but an equivocal proof of liberality towards the *persons* who dissent from us. On the contrary, I more than suspect that the former liberality does in too many men arise from a latent pre-disposition to transfer their reprobation and intolerance from the Doctrines to the Doctors, from the Belief to the Believers. Indecency, Abuse, Scoffing on subjects dear and awful[c] to a multitude of our fellow-citizens, Appeals to the vanity, appetites, and malignant passions of ignorant and incompetent judges—these are flagrant overt-acts, condemned by the Law written in the heart of every honest man, Jew, Turk,[17] and Christian. These are points respecting which

---

[a] *AR* (1825): us;

[b] *AR* (1825): Law

[c] *AR* (1825): aweful

[14] "Judge not, that ye be not judged": Matt 7.1 (cf Luke 6.37, Rom 2.1). Cf *CN* IV 5123 f 107ᵛ.

[15] For C's praise in 1796 of Joseph Priestley (1733–1804) as ". . . Patriot, and Saint, and Sage" see *Religious Musings* line 370: *PW* (EHC) I 123, app. cr. His criticism set in early, however: see his letter of 20 Mar 1796: *CL* I 192–3; cf also below, *Sp Aph B XIX* n 104 and *Conc* n 72.

[16] Edward Herbert, 1st Baron Cherbury (1583–1648), brother to George Herbert, was soldier, statesman, and philosopher. His *De veritate*, published in Paris in 1624 and argued against by Locke, was regarded by C as a pre-Cartesian setting forth of the doctrine of innate ideas: letter of 18 Feb 1801, *CL* II 681–2. Cf C's annotation on John Smith *Select Discourses* (1660) p ⁻2, in which he sees Herbert as having been in ". . . the shaft and adit of the mine" but having then turned back and so left ". . . the honour of establishing a complete προ-

παιδεία of philosophy" to Kant: *LR* III 416, *CM (CC)*. C's characterisation of him as a "platonizing Deist" follows Thomas Halyburton, who in *Natural Religion Insufficient . . .* (4 pts 1714) iii 219 described him as ". . . the First who . . . lick'd *Deism*, and brought it to something of a Form", and John Leland, who described him as ". . . one of the first, so one of the greatest writers . . . in the deistical cause": *A View of the Principal Deistical Writers . . . in England . . .* (3 vols 1754) I 39. Sidney Lee, who cites these (var) in *DNB*, maintains, however, that "Herbert's true affinity is with the Cambridge Platonists"—which is where C groups him in the annotation on Smith. Cf also *Friend (CC)* I 426.

[17] From c 1300 the Turk was regarded as typical of the Moslem faith. Cf *OED* s.v. "Turk", citing the Collect for Good Friday in *BCP* (1548–9): "Have mercy upon all Jewes, Turkes, Infidels and Heretikes."

the humblest honest man feels it his duty to hold himself infallible, and dares not hesitate in giving utterance to the verdict of his conscience, in the Jury-box as fearlessly as by his fireside. It is far otherwise with respect to matters of faith and inward conviction: and with respect to *these* I say—Tolerate no Belief, that you judge false and of injurious tendency: and arraign no Believer. The Man is more and other than his Belief: and God only knows, how small or how large a part of him the Belief in question may be, for good or for evil. Resist every false doctrine: and call no man heretic. The false doctrine does not necessarily make the man a heretic; but an evil heart can make any doctrine heretical.

Actuated by these principles, I have objected to a false and deceptive designation in the case of one System. Persuaded*a* that the doctrines, enumerated in p. 197, 198, are not only *essential* to the Christian Religion, but those which contra-distinguish the religion as *Christian*, I merely *repeat* this persuasion in another form, when I assert, that (in *my* sense of the word, Christian) Unitarianism is not Christianity. But do I say, that those, who call themselves Unitarians, are not Christians? God forbid![18] I would not think, much less promulgate, a judgment*b* at once so presumptuous and so uncharitable. Let a friendly antagonist retort on *my* scheme of faith, in the like manner: I shall respect him all the more for his consistency as a reasoner, and not confide the less in his kindness towards me as his Neighbour and Fellow-christian. This latter and most endearing name I scarcely know how to withhold even from my friend, HYMAN HURWITZ, as often as I read what every Reverer of Holy Writ and of the English Bible ought to read, his admirable VINDICIAE HEBRAICAE![19] It has trembled on the verge, as it were, of my lips, every time I have conversed with that pious, learned, strong-minded, and single-hearted Jew, an Israelite indeed and without guile—[20]

> Cujus cura sequi naturam, legibus uti,
> Et mentem vitiis, ora negare dolis;

a *AR* (1825): Persuaded,
b *AR* (1825): judgement

An annotation (not in C's hand) to the remainder of this para in a copy of *AR* (1825) formerly belonging to Barron Field (see App D(c) 202) quotes a comment by John Wesley on an extract from *The Life of Thomas Firmin* resembling that quoted by C from Baxter at n 23 below. Thomas Firmin (1631–99) was an early Socinian; Wesley's comment is collected in his *Works* (1872) XIV 293.

[18] See C's note (BM MS Egerton 2801 f 236): "Sept 9th 1823. Found difficulty this evening, at Mr Domville's, in making Mrs Barbauld understand, how I could refuse the name of Christianity (speaking of the *System* of Christian Dogmata) to Unitarianism & yet not deny the name of Chris*tian* to a Unit*arian* . . .". Cf *TT* 4 Apr 1832 (another part of which is cited above, n 13): "I make the greatest difference between *ans* and *isms*. I should deal insincerely with you, if I said that I thought Unitarianism was Christianity . . . but God forbid that I should doubt that you, and many other

Unitarians, as you call yourselves, are, in a practical sense, very good Christians. We do not win Heaven by Logic. . . . But Unitarianism is, in effect, the worst of Atheism joined to the worst of Calvinism, like two asses tied tail to tail. They have no covenant with God . . . they look upon Prayer as a sort of self-magnetizing . . .": *TT* (*CC*) I 278–80 (1836 vn II 161–2).

[19] *Vindiciae Hebraicae; or, a Defence of the Hebrew Scriptures, as a Vehicle of Revealed Religion: Occasioned by the Recent Strictures and Innovations of Mr. J. Bellamy; and in Confutation of His Attacks on All Preceding Translations, and on the Established Version in Particular* (1820). Hyman Hurwitz (1770–1844) conducted a private academy for Jews at Highgate, where C came to know him soon after arriving there. In 1828 he was elected professor of Hebrew at University College, London (*CL* IV 784n). See also below, *Sp Aph B XXIIIa* n 20.

[20] See above, *Sp Aph B II* n 51.

Virtutes opibus, verum praeponere falso,
Nil vacuum sensu dicere, nil facere.
Post obitum vivam*[a] secum, secum requiescam,
Nec fiat melior sors mea sorte suâ!

*From a poem of Hildebert on his Master,
the persecuted Berengarius*[22]

* I do not answer for the corrupt Latin.[21]

Under the same feelings I conclude this *Aid to Reflection* by applying the principle to another misnomer not less inappropriate and far more influential. Of those, whom I have found most reason to respect and value, many have been members of the Church of Rome: and certainly I did not honor[b] those the least, who scrupled even in common parlance to call our Church a reformed Church. A similar scruple would not, methinks, disgrace a Protestant as to the use of the words, Catholic or Roman Catholic; and if (tacitly at least, and in thought) he remembered that the Romish Anti-catholic Church would more truly express the fact.—*Romish*, to mark that the corruptions in discipline, doctrine, and practice do, for the[c] larger part, owe both their origin and perpetuation to the Romish *Court*, and the local Tribunals of the *City* of Rome; and neither are or ever have been *Catholic*, i.e. universal, throughout the Roman *Empire*, or even in the whole Latin or Western Church—and *Anti*-catholic, because no other Church acts on so narrow and excommunicative a principle, or is characterized by such a jealous spirit of monopoly. Instead of a Catholic (universal) spirit,[d] it may be truly described as a spirit of Particularism counterfeiting Catholicity by a *negative* totality, and heretical self-circumscription—in the first instances cutting off, and since then cutting herself off from, all the other members of Christ's Body. For the rest, I think as that man of true catholic spirit and apostolic zeal, Richard Baxter, thought; and my readers will thank me for conveying my reflections in his own words, in the following golden passage from his Life, "faithfully published from his own original MSS. by Matthew Silvester, 1696."

"My censures of the Papists do much differ from what they were at first. I then thought[e] that their errors in the *doctrines of faith* were their most dangerous mistakes. But now I am assured that their misexpressions and misunderstanding us, with our mistakings of them and inconvenient expressing of our own opinions, have made the difference in most points appear much greater than it is; and that in some it is next to none at all. But the great and unreconcileable[f] differences lie in their Church Tyranny; in the usurpations of their Hierarchy, and Priesthood, under the name of spiritual authority exercising a tem-

[a] Asterisk and footnote added in 1831
[b] *AR* (1825): honour
[c] *AR* (1825): the far
[d] *AR* (1825): spirit
[e] *AR* (1825): thought,
[f] *AR* (1825): unreconcilable

[21] "Se" is a reflexive pronoun in classical Latin. "With him" would be "cum eo" or "cum illo"; the latter, though inelegant, would scan.

[22] C is apparently taking these lines from a notebook entry of Nov 1823–Jan 1824, in which they had been in turn copied from Tennemann VIII 106: see *CN* IV 5062 and n. Tr: "His care was to follow nature, keep the laws, ban sin from his mind, guile from his mouth, prefer virtue to wealth, truth to falsehood, to say and to do nothing without sense. . . . When I die may I live with him and rest with him, and may my lot be no better than his." See also *P Lects* Lect 9 (1949) 275n and 435–6 n 27. In 1827 C published *Lines Suggested by the Last Words of Berengarius*: *PW* (EHC) I 460–1.

poral Lordship; in their corruptions and abasement of God's Worship;[a] but above all in their systematic befriending of Ignorance and Vice.

"At first I thought that Mr. Perkins well proved, that a Papist cannot go beyond a reprobate; but now I doubt not that God hath many sanctified ones among them,[b] who have received the true doctrine of Christianity so practically,[c] that their contradictory errors prevail not against them, to hinder their love of God and their salvation: but that their errors are like a conquerable dose of poison,[d] which a healthful nature doth overcome. *And I can never believe that a man may not be saved by that religion, which doth but bring him to the true Love of God and to a heavenly mind and life: nor that God will ever cast a Soul into hell, that truly loveth him.* Also at first it would disgrace any doctrine with me,[e] if I did but hear it called popery and antichristian; but I have long learned to be more impartial, and to know that Satan can use even the names of Popery and Anti-Christ, to bring a truth into suspicion and discredit."[23]—Baxter's Life, part I. p. 131.[24]

---

[a] *AR* (1825): Worship,   [b] *AR* (1825): them   [c] *AR* (1825): practically
[d] *AR* (1825): poison   [e] *AR* (1825): me

---

[23] Baxter *Reliquiae Baxterianae* (1694) 131. For the original see App A(l) below. The first paragraph was annotated by C: see *CM (CC)* I 305. C's alterations include leaving out the "Points of Merit" specified by Baxter, expanding his word "Usurpations" to two lines, and adding "systematic" before "befriending"; and in his second paragraph the insertion of "a healthful" before "Nature", the italicisation of the middle sentence, the omission (perhaps accidental) of "and to dislike Men for bad Doctrine, rather than the Doctrines for the Men" before "and to know . . .", and the expansion of Baxter's "against a Truth" after "Antichrist,".

[24] *AR* (1825) COPY H has a long note here: "I should love my Neighbour as myself, and God above all. But tho' God may be, & ought to be, loved *above* all Creatures, yet whether we ought to strive to love him *separately from* the works, in which he has chosen to manifest his infinite Wisdom and Goodness—this is a most important question! The fearful frightful Hardness of Heart, the cold-blooded atrocious cruelty, and pitiless remorseless spiritual pride, which the long-continued effort to love, and the final self-persuasion that they actually *do* love God ~~abstractly~~ *distinctly from* all his Creatures, and therefore, as the only way in which they can prove this to their own minds, in *contra*-distinction from them,—in *opposition* to all feeling of pity or attachment to their fel-low-men, engender in Monks, Jesuits, Spanish and Portuguese Inquisitors (the Zealots of the Romish Church generally)— these facts weigh heavily on my mind on the one side/ & under this impression I would be satisfied to love the Creator in the Creatures, provided *I* love the creatures, even those most dear to me, *chiefly* in reference to the Creator, and as excitements of gratitude to him./ But probably the true answer is, that in all things the ~~Char~~ Duty must partake of the character of the Object. God is a pure Act: and it can only be in the purest Acts of the Soul that the Love of God can have its essential Being—'He that loveth me obeyeth my commandments'. Where this is, the other fit and gracious concomitants will not be wanting. . . . Lastly the answer can only be rightly sought for in Prayer.—Remove from the mind all scruple respecting the rectitude of the injunction, and the case of Abraham & Isaac is in point. '*Now* I know &c'. But here too rises the more plausible objection of the Platonic Deists to Revelations in especial Behoof of a temporal Theocracy— ex. gr. the Hebrew Church of old & the Romish Church at present.

What a deeply interesting Dialogue might be written between Spinoza and Fenelon, on the Personality of God."

On "pure Act" see below, App I Excursus Note 6 "Coleridge on God as 'pure Act' ".

The first scriptural quotation is based on

*a*Again, there is a scheme constructed on the principle of retaining the social sympathies, that attend on the *b*name of Believer, at the least possible expenditure of Belief—a scheme of picking and choosing Scripture *c*texts for the support of doctrines,*d* that had been learned beforehand from the higher oracle of Common Sense; *e*which, as applied to the truths of Religion, means the popular part of the philosophy in fashion. Of course, *f*the scheme differs at different times and in different Individuals in the number of articles excluded; but, *g*it may always be recognized by this permanent character, that its object is to draw religion down to the Believer's intellect, instead of raising his intellect up to religion. And this extreme I call MINIMI-FIDIANISM.*h*25

Now if there be one Preventive26 of both these extremes more efficacious than another, and preliminary to all the rest, it is the being made fully aware of the diversity of Reason and Understanding. And this is the more expedient, because though there is no want of *i* authorities ancient and modern for the distinction of the faculties,*i* and the distinct appropriation of the terms, yet our best writers too often confound the one with the other. Even Lord Bacon himself,27 who in his Novum Organum has so incomparably set forth the nature*j* of the difference, and the unfitness of the latter faculty for the objects of the former,28 does

a *AR* (1825): p 202
b *AR* (1825): p 203
c *AR* (1825): p 204
d *AR* (1825): doctrines
e *AR* (1825): p 205
f *AR* (1825): p 206
g *AR* (1825): p 207
h *AR* (1825): MINIMIFIDIANISM.
i *AR* (1825): faculties
j *AR* (1825): p 208 (ture)

John 14.15–24, the second is from Gen 22.12 (the Lord's speech to Abraham): ". . . now I know that thou fearest God, seeing thou hast not withheld thy son, thine only son from me". A note at the end of COPY H seems to be associated with this one: "If God, as the Absolute Will, be *a pure Act*, the love of God must partake of the same character—it must reveal itself in Actions, Abraham & Isaak—under what conditions & with what qualifications can & may the Love of God be a distinct *Feeling?*"

25 *OED* gives this as the first use of the word and also records C's apparent coinage

of "minimism" in *Bl Mag* VII (1820) 630–2. Cf "minimi-fidian": *Sp Aph B [XXIV]* n 10, below.

26 The first four sentences of this paragraph represent expansion and contraction of C's note on Leighton COPY C I 71–86 at pp 71–3: *CM (CC)* III.

27 For a long discussion of Bacon's views in this connexion and their relationship to Plato's see *Friend (CC)* I 482–95.

28 In *Novum organum* bk I §§ 41, 45–51: *Works* (1740) I 277–8, Bacon deals with the deficiencies of the understanding (*intellectus*), his "idols of the tribe": (tr) ". . . it is a false assertion, that human sense is

nevertheless in sundry places use the term Reason where he means the Understanding, and sometimes, though less frequently, Understanding for Reason. In consequence of thus confounding the two terms, or rather of wasting both words for the expression of one and the same faculty, he left himself no appropriate term for the other and higher gift of Reason, and was thus under the necessity of adopting fantastical*a* and mystical phrases,[29] ex. gr. the dry light (lumen siccum),[30] the lucific vision,[31] &c., meaning thereby nothing more than Reason in contradistinction from the Understanding. Thus too in the preceding Aphorism, by Reason Leighton means the human Understanding, the explanation annexed to it being (by a noticeable coincidence),*b* word for word,*c* the very definition which the Founder of the Critical Philosophy gives of the Understanding—namely, "the Faculty judging according to Sense."[32]

a AR (1825): fantastic
b AR (1825): coincidence)
c AR (1825): word

the measure of things; on the contrary, all perceptions, both of sense and also of mind, are referred to man as their measure, and not to the universe. And the human intellect is like an uneven mirror on which the rays of objects fall, and which mixes up its own nature with that of the object, and distorts and destroys it."

[29] Cf *Novum organum* I § 26: (tr) "For the sake of instruction we customarily call the application of human reason to nature 'Anticipations of Nature' (because it is a thing rash or premature) but that reason (rationem) which is properly elicited from facts we call 'Interpretation of Nature' ": *Works* (1740) I 276. Here Bacon seems to use *ratio* exactly in the sense in which C would use "understanding"; C had introduced a few words from this aphorism, and the words "lumen siccum" into his quotation from § 23, in the 1818 *Friend*: *Friend (CC)* I 491–2. Cf also *De Augmentis scientiarum* bk IX ch 1 on the limited function of reason (*ratio*) in relation to theology, concluding with a climactic description of his book as an offering of the human understanding (*intellectus*): *Works* (1740) I 262–7.

[30] See below, App I Excursus Note 7 "Coleridge and Bacon's 'Lumen siccum' ".

[31] "Light-making vision". The use of this phrase is also ascribed to Bacon in BM MS Egerton 2801 ff 34–6 (*Logic—CC—*283). The source is untraced, however. C may have been drawn by Bacon's quotation from his own favourite Heraclitus (see also below, *Sp Aph B VIIIb* n 14), coupled with his preference for *experimenta lucifera* ("light-bearing experiments") rather than those that bring material profit (*frugifera*): *Novum Organum* bk I §§ 70, 99: *Works* (1740) I 287, to ascribe to him a concept that is to be associated rather with the Platonists (see e.g. Plotinus *Enneads* 5.5.7) or himself. Cf also "Lux lucifica" (light-making light), a phrase from St Augustine and the Schoolmen used by C to distinguish "the Power of Light" from "the thing, Light (Lux phaenomenon)" in an annotation on Böhme: *CM (CC)* I 624 (cf *CM—CC—*III 28 and *CN* IV 4843 f 11ᵛ, 5290 f 16). C uses "lucific light" in a proposed alteration of Herbert: *CM (CC)* II 1045.

[32] See the end of the Aphorism itself at the beginning of this section. C made the same point in a marginal note on Leighton COPY C I 71–86 at p 73: ". . . word for word the same with Kant's definition of the Understanding": *CM (CC)* III. He evidently had in mind the *Critik der reinen*

*a*ON THE DIFFERENCE IN KIND OF THE REASON AND THE UNDERSTANDING[1]

SCHEME OF THE ARGUMENT*b*

On the contrary, Reason is the Power of universal and necessary Convictions, the Source and Substance of Truths above Sense, and having their evidence in themselves.[2] Its presence is always marked by the *necessity* of the position affirmed: this necessity being *conditional*, when a truth of Reason is applied to Facts of Experience,*c* or to the rules and maxims of the Understanding;*d* but *absolute*,[3] when the subject matter is itself the growth or offspring of the Reason. Hence arises a distinction in the Reason itself, derived from the different mode of applying it, and from the objects to *e*which it is directed: accordingly*f* as we consider one and the same gift, now as the ground of formal principles, and now as

---

a–b Added in 1831
c *AR* (1825): Experience
d *AR* (1825): Understanding,
e *AR* (1825): p 209
f *AR* (1825): according

Vernunft I i, in which Kant identifies the two sources of knowledge in the mind as sensibility, *Sinnlichkeit* (the capacity for receiving representations), and understanding, *Verstand* (the power of cognising by means of these representations). In 1809 C had written in *The Friend*: "By the Understanding, I mean the faculty of thinking and forming *judgements* on the notices furnished by the Sense, according to certain rules existing in itself, which rules constitute its distinct nature": *Friend (CC)* II 104n. He used Leighton's formulation, ". . . judging according to sense", again in a notebook entry of Apr 1824 (*CN* IV 5144 f 23) and in annotations on Hooker *Ecclesiastical Politie*, probably written in 1826, and on Edward Irving's tr of Manuel Lacunza (Juan Josafat Ben-Ezra) *The Coming of Messiah in Glory and Majesty* (1827) I lxxx: *CM (CC)* II 1151–2, III 423 (*LR* IV 402–3). Leighton's formulation, however, is evidently associated with Christian belief and in particular with St Paul's strictures on ". . . the carnal mind" (see below, *Sp Aph B Xa* n 31), which C follows (ibid nn 33, 41). It is by no means clear that Kant would have made or endorsed this connexion. Nor is C suggesting that Leighton had *fully* anticipated Kant: cf

his note on Leighton COPY B III 121: "How often have I found reason to regret, that Leighton had not clearly made out to himself the diversity of the reason and the understanding": *CM (CC)* III.

[1] For C's earlier discussion of reason and understanding see Editor's Introduction, above, pp lxxix–lxxxiv. The distinction continued to exercise him: see e.g. a letter of 8 Apr 1825: *CL* V 421; notes on Hooker of 1824–6: *CM (CC)* II 1131–67; a note of 1827 on Lacunza: *NED* II 337–9, *CM (CC)* III 423–4; *C&S (CC)* 58–9; *TT* 7 Jan–13 Feb 1823, 9 May and 2 Jul 1830, 14 Aug 1831, and 15 May 1833 *(CC)* I 39 and n, 129, 172–4, 244–5, 383–4 (1836 vns II 41, dated 6 Jan, 88, 111–12, 145–6, 228–9).

[2] Cf C's marginal note on Leighton COPY C I 71–86 at pp 73–4: "Reason on the contrary is the Power and the Substance of universal, necessary, self-evident & supersensual Truths": *CM (CC)* III.

[3] For cognate uses of the word "absolute" see e.g. "Man's absolute self": *To William Wordsworth* line 40: *PW* (EHC) I 405; "absolute genius": *BL* ch 2 *(CC)* I 31–2; "absolute existence": *Friend (CC)* I 514. Cf also *Logic (CC)* 35–6, 82.

the origin of *Ideas*. Contemplated distinctively in reference to *formal* (or abstract) truth, it is the *speculative* Reason; but in reference to *actual* (or moral) truth, as the fountain of Ideas[a] and the *Light* of the Conscience,[4] we name it the *practical* Reason.[5] Whenever by self-subjection to this universal Light, the Will of the Individual, the *particular* Will, has become a Will of Reason, the man is regenerate: and Reason is then the *Spirit* of the regencrated man, whereby the Person is capable of a quickening inter-communion with the Divine Spirit. And herein consists the mystery of Redemption, that this has been rendered possible for us. "And so it is written: the first man Adam was made a living soul, the last Adam a quickening Spirit." (1 Cor. xv. 45.) We need only compare the passages in the writings of the Apostles Paul and John,[b] concerning the *Spirit* and Spiritual Gifts, with those in the Proverbs and in the Wisdom of Solomon respecting *Reason*, to be convinced that the terms are synonymous.[6] In this at once most comprehensive and most appropriate

---

[a] *AR* (1825): ideas   [b] *AR* (1825): John

[4] With these images cf ". . . the fountain of truth": *P Lects* Lect 2 (1949) 108; ". . . the fontal mirror of the Idea": *C&S (CC)* 58, 70, 219, and the Church as a sunlit fountain, ibid 55. Cf also C's 1816 comment: "St Paul's Christ (as the Logos) the eternal Yea (Cor. 2.1.[i.e. 2 Cor 1.19–20]) is the fontal idea": *Friend (CC)* II 76n; ". . . my Conscience, the sole fountain of certainty": *CN* III 4005, and *TT* 15 May 1833: ". . . from the fontal light of Ideas only can a man draw Intellectual Power": *TT (CC)* I 384 (1836 vn II 229); also Beer *CV* 240.

[5] For "*practical* Reason" see *C&S (CC)* 171 on ". . . the practical and intellective". The use of the term necessarily involves a reference to Kant's *Kritik der praktischen Vernunft* (1788), in which the question of morality is dealt with; see also C's appendix below, p 413, in which C relates the practical reason to the "Will and Moral Being"; *C&S (CC)* 171, in which reason comprises ". . . both the *practical* and the intellective, not only as the light, but as the Life which is the Light of Man"; and "On the Divine Ideas": "Reason is that highest sense, in which the speculative is united with the practical": *HEHL ms* HM 8195 p 249: *C 17th C* 694.

[6] The comparison that C invites is not so immediately convincing as he suggests. In the case of St Paul he probably has in mind

passages such as Eph 4.23: "And be renewed in the spirit of your mind" and 1 Cor 14, in which those who are ". . . zealous of spiritual gifts" are urged to seek the edifying of the church as well; those who prophesy, for example, to interpret: "I will pray with the spirit, and I will pray with the understanding also" (14.12–15). Such passages suggest an intimate and necessary relationship between spirit and reason rather than synonymy, however. Similarly with St John; C may have in mind sayings such as "God is a Spirit: and they that worship him must worship him in spirit and in truth" (John 4.24) and various references to the Holy Spirit as ". . . the Spirit of truth" (John 14.17, 15.26, 16.13).

On the only occasion when the actual word "reason" appears in Proverbs (26.16 AV) it has no relation to spirit; C evidently assumes that in the AV "understanding" is often used in the sense in which he uses "reason": e.g. "The fear of the Lord is beginning of wisdom: and the knowledge of the holy is understanding" (Prov 9.10); "Understanding is a wellspring of life unto him that hath it" (16.22); ". . . a man of understanding is of an excellent spirit" (17.27). In Proverbs "wisdom" has similar associations: e.g. "I will pour out my spirit unto you, I will make known my words unto you" (1.23); "My son, if thou

acceptation of the word, Reason is pre-eminently spiritual, and a Spirit, even *our* Spirit, through an effluence of the same grace by which we are privileged to say Our Father!

On the other hand,[7] the Judgments[a] of the Understanding are binding only in relation to the objects of our Senses, which we *reflect* under the forms of the Understanding. It is, as Leighton rightly defines it, [b]"the Faculty judging according to Sense."[8] Hence we add the epithet *human*, without tautology: and speak of the *human* Understanding, in disjunction from that of Beings higher or lower than man. But there is, in this sense, no *human* Reason. There neither is nor can be but one Reason, one and the same: even the Light that lighteth every man's[9] individual Understanding (*Discursus*),[c] and thus maketh it a reasonable Understanding, *Discourse of Reason*[10]—"one only, yet manifold; it goeth through all understanding, and remaining in itself regenerateth all other powers." (Wisdom of Solomon,[d] c. viii.)[11] The same writer[e] calls it

> [a] *AR* (1825): Judgements
> [b] *AR* (1825): p 210
> [c] *AR* (1825): (*Discursus*)
> [d] *AR* (1825): Solomon
> [e] *AR* (1825): Writer

wilt receive my words . . . So that thou incline thine ear unto wisdom, and apply thine heart to understanding . . . Then shalt thou understand the fear of the Lord, and find the knowledge of God'' (2.1, 2, 5). In the case of the Wisdom of Solomon the praise of wisdom in 7.22–3: ". . . in her is an understanding spirit, holy, one only, manifold, subtil, lively, clear, undefiled, plain, not subject to hurt, loving the thing that is good, quick, which cannot be letted, ready to do good, kind to man" is akin to St Paul's ". . . the fruit of the Spirit is love, joy, peace, longsuffering, gentleness, goodness, faith, meekness, temperance . . ." (Gal 5.22–3) and his praise of charity in 1 Cor 15. Such passages again establish that there are close links between the spirit and reason in the minds of these biblical writers but not that they are identical.

[7] This and the following sentences appear to be expanded from C's comments in Leighton COPY C I 71–86 at pp 74–5: *CM (CC)* III.

[8] See above, *Sp Aph B VIIIa* n 32.

[9] See John 1.9.

[10] On discourse and intuition see above, *Sp Aph B I* n 4. C was fond of quoting this phrase from *Hamlet* I ii 150 ("A beast, that

wants discourse of reason") to enforce his distinction. Cf *SM (CC)* 61n, 69, 97; *Friend (CC)* I 156; *Op Max ms* B3 ("II") 11–12, quoted above, Editor's Introduction, at n 110. The phrase was also ascribed to Heraclitus in *SM (CC)* 97. C was equally fond of quoting the Archangel Raphael's exposition to Adam in *PL* v 482–90, where "discursive" reason was said to be the main sphere of humans, "intuitive" that of angels: see *BL* chs 10 and 13 *(CC)* I 173–4n, 295 and nn; *P Lects* Lect 12 (1949) 349; and cf *CN* IV 5089.

The term "discourse", which was associated with writers such as Hooker, Bacon, and Hobbes in both the *Friend* and "Opus Maximum" passages cited above, is further explained below at n 53. The relation of discursive thinking to understanding and reason is discussed above in *Sp Aph B II*, before n 24, and it is distinguished from intuitive below in *Sp Aph B VIIIb* after n 63 and *Xa* at n 29. John Smith is enlisted in support of C's position in *Sp Aph B Xa* at n 13 and Jeremy Taylor in *Sp Aph B XX* at n 3 (cf *XXII* at n 7). Among these John Smith comes closest to making C's distinction in its pure form.

[11] A selection of phrases from Wisd of Sol 7.22, 23, 27.

likewise "an influence from the *Glory of the Almighty*,"[12] this being one of the names of the Messiah, as the Logos, or co-eternal Filial Word. And most noticeable for its coincidence is a fragment of Heraclitus,[13] as I have indeed already noticed elsewhere.[14] "To discourse rationally it behoves us to derive strength from that which is common to all men: for all human Understandings are nourished by the one DIVINE WORD."

Beasts, we have said, partake of Understanding.[15] If any man deny this, there is a ready way of settling the question. Let him give a careful perusal to Hüber's two small volumes, on Bees and[a] Ants[16] (especially the latter), and to Kirby and Spence's Introduction to Entomology:[17] and one or other of two things must follow. He will either change his opinion as irreconcilable with the facts: or he must deny the facts, which yet I cannot suppose, inasmuch as the denial would be tantamount to the no less extravagant than uncharitable [b]assertion, that Hüber, and the several eminent Naturalists, French and English, Swiss, German, and Italian,[18]

---

[a] *AR* (1825): and on   [b] *AR* (1825): p 211

[12] Ibid 7.25.

[13] See *Sp Aph B I* n 12 above.

[14] Heraclitus Fragment 114 in Diels. See *SM (CC)* 97. C gave the original Greek there and on the front wrapper of *SM*. There too he drew attention to the similarity between the Logos of Heraclitus and St John's Gospel. He had altered the text, substituting from the beginning of the fragment νόοι ("understandings"—the plural of *nous*) for νόμοι (laws) and supplying ΛΟΓΟΥ (WORD) where "law" is to be understood in the original; yet he was, as the editor points out (*SM—CC—*95), still giving a tenable outline of Heraclitus on the λόγος. In the Greek the word for "common" is also a pun, suggesting a universal mind. See *Sp Aph A VI* n 6 above and *Sp Aph B Xa* n 29 below. For C's view of his own philosophy as "*Heraclitus Redivivus*" see his letter of Sept 1817: *CL* IV 775.

[15] Cf C's marginal note on Leighton COPY C I 71–86 at p 75: "Beasts partake of Understanding (the Dog, the Elephant, and above all the Ant) but not of reason": *CM (CC)* III. Cf also n 10 above.

[16] See also above, *Mor Aph XXXVI* nn 9, 10. In Feb 1808 C sent SH a copy of François Huber *New Observations on the Natural History of Bees* tr Dalyell (Edinburgh 1806); see his letter accompanying Chapman's Homer (1624): *CM (CC)* II 1118–19. *The Natural History of Ants* (1820) (translated from the French work

pub 1810) which C borrowed, then lent to HC (*CL* V 42), was by François's son Pierre, but C seems never to have noticed the difference in authorship or the exact orthography of the surname. For his use of the two writers in connection with the difference between reason and understanding see a note on Tennemann II in *P Lects* (1949) 461 n 9; *CL* V 137–8 (Feb 1821); his note in *SM (CC)* 19 n 1; *CN* IV 4833 (?1821) and n; 4886; and (on the State) 5059 f 57 (Nov 1823–Jan 1824).

[17] William Kirby and William Spence *Introduction to Entomology* (4 vols 1815–26). C seems to have been reading the first two volumes early in Apr 1822, making notes on them: see *CN* IV 4879–96 and nn. He quoted from vol II in his *Logic (CC)* 74–5, and recommended the work (with reservations) in *Op Max ms* B3 ("II") 186. For Emerson's interest, prompted by *AR*, see K. W. Cameron *Emerson the Essayist* (Raleigh, NC 1945) 303–19 and above, pp cxxvi–cxxvii.

[18] In a letter to the translator, J. R. Johnson (*The Natural History of Ants* pp v–vi), Pierre Huber mentions that a number of other naturalists had observed the same occurrences (specifying only French and English): "Some of these facts appear to many of so romantic a nature, that I am happy in not being the only person who has noticed them . . .". Kirby and Spence also comment on the successful experiments parallel

by whom Hüber's observations and experiments have been repeated and confirmed, had all conspired to impose a series of falsehoods and fairy-tales on the world. I see no way at least, by which he can get out of this dilemma, but by over-leaping the admitted Rules and Fences of all legitimate Discussion, and either transferring to the word, Understanding, the definition already appropriated[a] to Reason, or defining Understanding *in genere*[19] by the *specific* and *accessional* perfections which the *human* Understanding derives from its co-existence with Reason and Free-will in the same individual person; in plainer words, from its being exercised by a self-conscious and responsible Creature. And,[b] after all,[c] the supporter of Harrington's position[20] would have a right to ask him, by what other name he would designate the faculty in the instances referred to? If it be not Understanding, what is it?

In no former part of this volume has the Author[d] felt the same anxiety to obtain a patient Attention. For he does not hesitate to avow, that on his success in establishing the validity and importance of the distinction between Reason and Understanding, he rests his hopes of carrying the Reader along with him through all that is to follow. Let the Student but clearly see and comprehend the diversity in the things themselves, the expediency of a correspondent distinction and appropriation of the *words* will follow of itself. Turn back for a moment to the Aphorism, and having re-perused[e] the first paragraph of this Comment thereon, regard the two following narratives as the illustration. I do not say proof: for I take these from a multitude of facts equally striking for the one only purpose of placing my *meaning* out of all doubt.

I. Hüber[f][21] put a dozen Humble-bees under a Bell-glass along with a comb of about ten silken cocoons so unequal in height as not to be capable of standing steadily. To remedy this two or three of the Humble-bees got upon the comb, stretched themselves over its edge, and with their heads downwards fixed their forefeet on the table on which the comb stood, and so with their hind feet kept the comb from falling.

---

[a] 1831 has: "appopriated"
[b] *AR* (1825): And
[c] *AR* (1825): all
[d] *AR* (1825): Editor
[e] *AR* (1825): p 212 (perused)
[f] *AR* (1825): Huber

---

to F. Huber's by naturalists in various countries: see e.g. *Introduction to Entomology* II 133–5.
[19] "In kind". Cf C's footnote after n 29 below, and *Sp Aph B IX* at n 30.
[20] See above, *Sp Aph B VIIIa* n 3.

[21] The account is not from Huber's book but from Kirby and Spence I 374–5; here C is quoting (with only stylistic alterations) from his own notebook condensation of the latter account: see *CN* IV 4884 and n.

When these were weary, others took their places. In this constrained and painful posture, fresh bees relieving their comrades at intervals, and each working in its turn, did these affectionate little insects support the comb for nearly three days: at the end of which they had prepared sufficient wax to build pillars with. But these pillars having accidentally got displaced, the bees had recourse again to the same manœuvre (or rather *pedœuvre*[22]), till Hüber,[a] pitying their hard case, &c.

II. "I shall[23] at present describe the operations of a single ant that I observed sufficiently long to satisfy my curiosity.

"One rainy day, I observed a Laborer[b] digging the ground near the aperture which gave entrance to the ant-hill. It placed in a heap the several fragments it had scraped up, and formed them into small pellets, which it deposited here and there upon the nest. It [c]returned constantly to the same place, and appeared to have a marked design, for it labored[d] with ardor[e] and perseverance. I remarked a slight furrow, excavated in the ground in a straight line, representing the plan of a path or gallery. The Laborer,[f] the whole of whose movements fell under my immediate observation, gave it greater depth and breadth, and cleared out its borders: and I saw at length, in which I could not be deceived, that it had the intention of establishing an avenue which was to lead from one of the stories to the under-ground chambers. This path, which was about two or three inches in length, and formed by a single ant, was opened above and bordered on each side by a buttress of earth; its concavity [g]*en forme de gouttiere*[h][24] was of the most perfect regularity, for the architect had not left an atom too much. The work of this ant was so well followed and understood, that I could almost to a certainty guess its next proceeding, and the very fragment it was about to remove. At the side of the opening where this path terminated, was a second opening to which it was necessary to arrive by some road. The same ant engaged in and executed alone this undertaking. It furrowed out and opened another

[a] *AR* (1825): Huber
[b] *AR* (1825): Labourer
[c] *AR* (1825): p 213
[d] *AR* (1825): laboured
[e] *AR* (1825): ardour
[f] *AR* (1825): Labourer,
[g-h] *AR* (1825): en forme de gouttiere

[22] C's usage here is attributed to him as a nonce-word by *OED*. In *CN* iv 4884 he had substituted it for the "manoeuvre" of Kirby and Spence (see editor's note); in 1826 he resorted to it again in annotating Charles Butler *Vindication of "The Book of the Roman Catholic Church"* (1826): *CM (CC)* i 862.

[23] From Pierre Huber *Natural History of Ants* (1820) 38–41, in which the punctuation differs slightly.

[24] "In the form of a gutter".

path, parallel to the first, leaving between each a little wall of three or four lines in height. Those ants who lay the foundation of a wall,[a] chamber, or gallery, from working separately occasion now and then a want of coincidence in the parts of the same or different objects. Such examples are of no unfrequent occurrence, but they by no means embarrass them. What follows [b]proves that the workman, on discovering his error, knew how to rectify it. A wall had been erected with the view of sustaining a vaulted ceiling, still incomplete, that had been projected from the wall of the opposite chamber. The workman who began constructing it, had given it too little elevation to meet the opposite partition upon which it was to rest. Had it been continued on the original plan, it must infallibly have met the wall at about one half of its height, and this it was necessary to avoid. This state of things very forcibly claimed my attention, when one of the ants arriving at the place, and visiting the works, appeared to be struck by the difficulty which presented itself; but this it as soon obviated, by taking down the ceiling and raising the wall upon which it reposed. It then,[c] in my presence, constructed a new ceiling with the fragments of the former one.''—*Hüber's[d] Natural Hist. of Ants*, p. 38–41.

Now I assert, that the faculty manifested in the acts here narrated does not differ *in kind* from Understanding, and that it *does* so differ from Reason. What I conceive the former to be, physiologically considered, will be shown hereafter. In this place I take the understanding[e] as it exists in *Men*, and in exclusive reference to its *intelligential* functions; and it is in this sense of the word that I am to prove the necessity of contra-distinguishing it from Reason.

Premising then, that two or more Subjects having the same essential characters are said to fall under the same General Definition, I lay it down, as a self-evident[f] truth (it is, in fact, an identical proposition)[g] that whatever subjects fall under one and the same General Definition are of one and the same kind: consequently, that which does *not* fall under this definition, must differ in kind from each and all of those that *do*. Difference in degree does indeed suppose sameness in kind: and difference in kind precludes distinction from difference[h] of degree. *Heterogenea non*

[a] *AR* (1825): wall, a
[b] *AR* (1825): p 214
[c] *AR* (1825): then
[d] *AR* (1825): Huber's
[e] *AR* (1825): Understanding
[f] *AR* (1825): p 215 (evident)
[g] *AR* (1825): proposition),
[h] *AR* (1825): differences

comparari, ergo nec distingui, possunt.[25] The inattention to this rule[a] gives rise to the numerous Sophisms comprised by Aristotle under the head of Μετάβασις εἰς ἄλλο γένος,[b26] *i.e.* Transition into a new kind, or the falsely applying to X what had been truly asserted of A, and might have been true of X, had it differed from A in its degree only. The sophistry consists in the omission to notice what not being noticed will be supposed not to exist; and where the silence respecting the difference in kind is tantamou[n]t to an assertion that the difference is merely in degree. But the fraud is especially gross, where the heterogeneous subject, thus clandestinely *slipt in*, is in its own nature insusceptible of degree: such as, for instance, Certainty or Circularity, contrasted with Strength, or Magnitude.

To apply these remarks for our present purpose, we have only to describe Understanding and Reason, each by its characteristic qualities. The comparison will show the difference.

UNDERSTANDING	REASON
1. Understanding is discursive.	1. Reason is fixed.
[c]2. The Understanding in all its judgments refers to some other Faculty as its ultimate Authority.	2. The Reason in all its decisions appeals to itself, as the ground and *substance* of their truth. (*Hebrews*[d] VI.[e] 13.)[27]
3. Understanding is the Faculty of *Reflection*.	3. Reason of Contemplation. Reason indeed is much[f] nearer to SENSE than to Understanding: for Reason (says our great HOOKER)[28]

---

[a] *AR* (1825): Rule   [b] *AR* (1825): no accents or breathings in Greek
[c] *AR* (1825): p 216   [d] *AR* (1825): *Hebrews*,
[e] *AR* (1825): VI. V.   [f] *AR* (1825): far

[25] "Heterogeneous things cannot be compared, therefore cannot be distinguished". Cf *CN* IV 4945, in which C, making notes from Kant *Vermischte Schriften* (4 vols Halle 1799–1807) III 315 in Feb 1824, writes: "Again, here is the Sophism of a μεταβασις εις αλλο γενος, or a comparison between Heterogenes". See next note.
[26] "A transition into another kind"; cf *SM (CC)* 99; *CL* IV 834; *Logic (CC)* 90; *CM (CC)* I 253 and n, II 1154, III 128, 158, 211, 362, 394, note in *AR* (1825) COPY G, quoted above, *Sp Aph B II* n 78, and *Sp Aph B XIX* n 13 below. The source is Aris-

totle *Posterior Analytics* 1.7 (75[a]). Kant used the phrase in *Die Religion innerhalb der Grenzen der blossen Vernunft* (Königsberg 1794) 83n without mentioning Aristotle; see also previous note.
[27] "For when God made promise to Abraham, because he could swear by no greater, he sware by himself": Heb 6.13. C's ms for this whole tabulation and the next three paragraphs down to "of this most" is transcribed below in App B(u).
[28] In "On the Principles of Genial Criticism" this appears as ". . . 'an intuition',

is a direct Aspect of Truth, an inward Beholding, having a similar relation to the Intelligible or Spiritual, as SENSE has to the Material or Phenomenal.

The Result is: that neither falls under the definition of the other. They differ *in kind:* and had my object been confined to the establishment of this fact, the preceding Columns would have superseded all further disquisition. But I have ever in view the especial interest of my youthful Readers, whose reflective *power* is to be cultivated, as well as their particular reflections to be called forth and guided. Now the main chance of their *reflecting* on religious subjects *aright*, and of their attaining to the *contemplation* of spiritual truths *at all*, rests on their insight into the *nature* of this disparity still more than on their conviction of its existence. I now, therefore, proceed to *ᵃa brief analysis of the Understanding, in elucidation of the definitions already given.

The Understanding then (considered exclusively as an organ of human intelligence,)*ᵇ* is the Faculty by which we reflect and generalize. Take, for instance, any objects*ᶜ* consisting of many parts, a House,*ᵈ* or a group*ᵉ* of Houses: and if it be contemplated, as a Whole, *i.e.* (as many constituting a One,)*ᶠ* it forms what in the technical language of Psychology,*ᵍ* is called a *total impression.*²⁹ Among the various component parts of this,*ʰ* we direct our attention especially to such as we recollect

ᵃ *AR* (1825): p 217
ᵇ *AR* (1825): intelligence),
ᶜ *AR* (1825): Object
ᵈ *AR* (1825): House
ᵉ *AR* (1825): Group
ᶠ *AR* (1825): One),
ᵍ *AR* (1825): Psychology
ʰ *AR* (1825): this

---

says Hooker, 'that is, a direct and immediate beholding or presentation of an object in the mind through the senses or the imagination' ": *BL* (1907) ɪɪ 230. Cf also *Logic (CC)* 151: "immediate beholding"; the editor suggests as source "The greatest assurance generally with all men, is that which we have by a plain aspect and intuitive beholding" from *Of the Lawes of Ecclesiastical Politie* bk ɪɪ § 7: *Works* (1682) 119: *Logic (CC)* 151 n 1.

²⁹ "Total impression" is used also in *The Friend* 10 Aug 1809 (*CC*) ɪɪ 47. At the beginning of his *Treatise of Human Nature* (1739–40) bk ɪ pt 1 § 1 Hume draws a distinction between "simple" and "complex" impressions. Christian von Wolff *Psychologia empirica* (1736) 18–20 distinguishes between *perceptiones totales* and *perceptiones partiales*. See also his *Psychologia rationalis* (1737) 6–7, 39–40. For C's knowledge of the last-named work see *CN* ɪɪɪ 3256n. His most direct source is, however, J.G.E. Maass: see *CM (CC)* ɪɪɪ 791–2.

to have noticed in other total impressions.[a] Then, by a voluntary Act,[b] we withhold our attention from all the rest[c] to reflect exclusively on these; and these we henceforward use as *common characters*, by virtue of [d]which the[e] several Objects are referred to one and the same sort. *[f] Thus, the whole Process may be reduced to three acts, all depending on and supposing a previous impression on the Senses: first, the appropriation of our Attention; 2. (and in order to the continuance of the first) Abstraction, or the voluntary withholding of the Attention; and 3. Generalization. And these are the proper Functions of the Understanding:[g] and the power of so doing,[h] is what we mean,[i] when we say we possess Understanding, or are created with the Faculty of Understanding.

[It is obvious, that the third Function includes the act of comparing one object with another. In a note (for, not to interrupt the argument, I avail myself of this most useful contrivance,)[j] I have shown, that the act of comparing supposes in the comparing Faculty,[k] certain inherent forms,[l] that is, Modes of reflecting not referable to the Objects reflected on, but pre-determined by the Constitution and (as it were) mechanism of the Understanding itself. And under some one or other of these Forms,†[m] the Resemblances and [n]Differences must be subsumed in order

---

* Accordingly[o] as we attend more or less to the differences, the *Sort* becomes, of course, more or less comprehensive. Hence there arises for the systematic Naturalist,[p] the necessity of subdividing the Sorts into Orders, Classes, Families, &c.: all which, however, resolve themselves for the mere Logician into the conception of Genus and species,[q] *i.e.* the comprehending, and the comprehended.

† Were it not so, how could the first comparison have been possible? It would involve the absurdity of measuring a thing by itself. But if we think[r] on some one thing, the length of our own foot, or of our hand and arm from the elbow joint, it is evident that in *order* to

---

[a] COPY D: impressions: the Wall, the Roof, the Chimney, the Windows, the Door. ; COPY E: impressions: the wall, the roof, the chimney, the window, the door.

[b] *AR* (1825): Act

[c] COPIES D & E: rest ex. gr. from the carving, the color, the size.

[d-e] COPIES D & E: which

[f] *AR* (1825): sort*. ; COPY D: sort*. They are all *Houses.* Of each alike we repeat, It is *a House.* ; COPY E. sort*. They . . . Houses, Of . . . *a house.*

[g] *AR* (1825): p 218 (standing:)

[h] *AR* (1825): doing

[i] *AR* (1825): mean

[j] *AR* (1825): contrivance),

[k] *AR* (1825): Faculty

[l] *AR* (1825): Forms,

[m] *AR* (1825): Forms*,

[n] *AR* (1825): p 219

[o] *AR* (1825): According

[p] *AR* (1825): Naturalist

[q] *AR* (1825): Species,

[r] *AR* (1825): fix

do this,[a] we must have the conception of Measure. Now these antecedent and most general Conceptions are what is meant by the constituent *forms* of the Understanding: we call them *constituent* because they are not *acquired* by the Understanding, but are implied in its constitution. As rationally might a Circle be said to acquire a centre and circumference, as the Understanding to acquire these,[b] its inherent *forms*, or ways of conceiving. This is what Leibnitz meant, when to the old adage of the Peripatetics, Nihil in intellectu quod non prius in Sensu (There is nothing in the Understanding not derived from the Senses, or—There is nothing *con*ceived that was not previously *per*ceived;)[c] he replied—praeter intellectum ipsum (except the Understanding itself).[30]

And here let me remark for once and all: whoever would *reflect* to any purpose—whoever is in earnest in his pursuit of Self-knowledge, and of one of the principal means to this, an insight into the meaning of the words he uses, and the different meanings properly or improperly conveyed by one and the same word, according[d] as it is used in the Schools or the Market, according[e] as the *kind* or a high *degree* is intended (ex. gr. Heat, Weight, &c. as employed scientifically, compared with the same word used popularly)— whoever, I say, seriously proposes this as his Object, must so far overcome his dislike of pedantry, and his dread of being sneered at as a Pedant, as not to quarrel with an uncouth word or phrase, till he is quite sure that some other and more familiar one[f] would not only have expressed the *precise* meaning with equal clearness, but have been as likely to draw[g] attention to *this* meaning exclusively. The ordinary language of a Philosopher in conversation or popular writings, compared with the language he uses in strict reasoning, is as his Watch compared with the Chronometer in his Observatory. He sets the former by the Town-clock, or even, perhaps, by the Dutch clock in his kitchen, not because he believes it right, but because his neighbour's and his Cook *go* by it.[31] To afford the reader an opportunity for exercising the forbearance here recommended, I turn back to the phrase, "most general Conceptions," and observe, that in strict and severe propriety of language I should have said *generalific* or *generific*[32] rather than general, and Concipiencies[33] or Conceptive Acts[34] rather than conceptions.

It is an old Complaint, that a man[h] of Genius no sooner appears, but the Host of Dunces are up in arms to repel the invading Alien.[35] This observation would have made more

---

[a] *AR* (1825): this
[b] *AR* (1825): these
[c] *AR* (1825): *perceived*);
[d] *AR* (1825): according
[e] *AR* (1825): according
[f] Added in 1831
[g] *AR* (1825): draw his
[h] *AR* (1825): Man

---

[30] See above, *Mor Aph VI* n 15.
[31] These two sentences are developed from a notebook entry of 1815, *CN* III 4260.
[32] *OED* records these as its only examples.
[33] *OED* reports C's usage here as a nonce-word, but also relates it to "concipient", used by Horace and James Smith in *Rejected Addresses* (1812) and by C himself in a note of 1827 on App C of *SM*, on ". . . man considered as a concipient as well as a percipient being, and reason as a power supervening": *SM (CC)* 68 n 3.

[34] This also may well be a term invented by C.
[35] "When a true Genius appears in the World, you may know him by this infallible Sign, that the Dunces are all in Confederacy against him": Swift "Thoughts on Various Subjects" *Works* (4 vols Dublin 1735) I 299. In C's copy of the *Works* (13 vols Edinburgh 1768) vol V (at Texas), this appears on p 357. Beginning with this sentence, C's footnote draws heavily on an entry from N 23, *CN* IV 5435 (which is therefore presumably to be dated earlier than its position in *CN* IV suggests: see 5435n).

converts to its truth, I suspect, had it been worded more dispassionately, and with a less contemptuous antithesis. For "Dunces,"*ᵃ* let us substitute "the Many," or the "τοῦτος κόσμος"*ᵇ* (*this world*)³⁶ of the Apostle, and we shall perhaps find no great difficulty in accounting for the fact. To arrive at the *root*, indeed, and last Ground of the problem, it would be necessary to investigate the nature and effects of the sense of Difference on the human mind where it is not holden*ᶜ* in check by Reason and Reflection. We need not go to the savage tribes of North America, or the yet ruder Natives of the Indian Isles,³⁷ to learn, how slight a degree of Difference will, in uncultivated*ᵈ* minds, call up a sense of Diversity, and inward perplexity and contradiction, as if the Strangers were,*ᵉ* and yet were not,*ᶠ* of the same *kind* with themselves. Who has not had occasion to observe the effect which the gesticulations and nasal tones of a Frenchman produce on our own Vulgar? Here we may see the origin and primary import of our "*Unkindness.*" It is a sense of *Un*kind, and not the mere negation but the positive Opposite of the sense of *kind*. Alienation, aggravated now by fear, now by contempt, and not seldom by a mixture of both, aversion, hatred, enmity, are so many successive shapes of its growth and metamorphosis. In application to the present case, it is sufficient to say, that Pindar's remark on sweet Music holds equally true of Genius: as many as are not delighted by it are disturbed, perplexed, irritated.³⁸ The Beholder either recognizes it as a projected Form of his own Being, that moves before him with a Glory round its head, or recoils from it as from a Spectre.³⁹ But this

---

ᵃ *AR* (1825): "Dunces"
ᵇ *AR* (1825): no accents in Greek
ᶜ *AR* (1825): held
ᵈ *AR* (1825): uncultured
ᵉ *AR* (1825): were
ᶠ *AR* (1825): not

---

³⁶ In *AR* (1839) HNC correctly prints the first word as οὗτος. Cf *C&S (CC)* 165 and n. "Be not conformed to this world" (Rom 12.2), and cf John 18.36: "My kingdom is not of this world". C also uses "toutoukosmou" in a note on Böhme *Works: CM (CC)* I 675, and "toutoskosmos" in *C&S (CC)* 174. See also Editor's introduction above, at 110.

³⁷ No source has been found for the anthropological examples mentioned here. For C on likeness and difference more generally see *BL* ch 18 (*CC*) II 72 and n and *Prel Sp Aph* n 21 above.

³⁸ See Pindar *Pythian Ode* 1.10–14; tr Sir John Sandys (LCL 1915): ". . . thy shafts of music soothe even the minds of the deities . . . But all the beings that Zeus hath not loved, are astonied, when they hear the voice of the Pierides . . .". Typhon and his ". . . fearful founts of fire" are mentioned immediately afterwards in *Pythian Ode* 1. For the dual qualities of attraction and fear here see the discussion in Beer *CV* 123–4; for the relevance of the Typhonic in *Kubla Khan* ibid 262–5.

³⁹ *AR* (1825) COPY C has a note: "In a snow-mist or where the Air is filled with

subtle particles of Snow, a person with the Sun behind him will under certain circumstances see his Shadow projected upright at a moderate distance before him, & with a luminous Glory round the head. I have once seen it myself, and there is a case recorded in the Manchester Transactions." In COPY D the note runs: "This refers to a curious phænomenon, which occurs occasionally when the Air is filled with fine particles of frozen Snow, constituting an almost invisibly subtle Snow-mist, and a Person is walking with the Sun behind his Back. His Shadow is projected and he seems a figure moving before him with a glory round its Head. I have myself seen it twice: and it is described in the first or second Volume of the Manchester Philosophical Transactions." COPY E follows with minor variations. COPY F has: "This alludes to a Phænomenon not very uncommon in Mountainous Countries, when the Air is filled with subtle particles of frozen Snow, and the person is walking with the sun at his back, his Shadow is projected on the invisible Snow-mist, at a moderate distance before him, and leads the way with a Painter's Glory round its head. I have seen

speculation would lead us too far; we must be content with having referred to it as the ultimate ground of the fact, and pass to the more obvious and proximate causes.[40] And as the first, I would rank the Person's *not* understanding what yet he expects to understand, and as if he had a *right* to do so. An original Mathematical Work, or any other that requires peculiar and (so to say) technical marks and symbols, will excite no uneasy feelings—not in the mind of a competent Reader, for he understands it; and not with others, because they neither expect nor are expected to understand it. The second place we may assign to the *Mis*understanding, which is almost sure to follow in cases where the incompetent person, finding no outward marks (Diagrams, arbitrary signs, and the like) to inform him at first sight, that the Subject is one which he does not pretend to understand, and to be ignorant of which does not detract from his estimation as a man of abilities generally, *will* attach some meaning to what he hears or reads; and as he is out of humor[a] with the Author, it will most often be such a meaning as he can quarrel with and exhibit in a ridiculous or offensive point of view.

But above all, the whole World almost of Minds, as far as regards intellectual efforts, may be divided into two classes of the Busy-indolent and Lazy-indolent.[41] To both alike all Thinking is painful, and all attempts to rouse them to think, whether in the re-examination of their existing Convictions, or for the reception of new light, are irritating. "It *may* all be very deep and clever; but really one ought to be quite sure of it before one wrenches one's brain to find out what it is. I take up a Book as a Companion, with whom I can have an easy cheerful chit-chat on what we both know beforehand, or else matters of fact. In our leisure hours we have a right to relaxation and amusement."

Well! but in their *studious* hours, when their Bow is to be bent, when they are *apud Musas*, or amidst the Muses? Alas! it is just the same! The same craving for *amusement*, *i.e.* to be away from the Muses! for relaxation, *i.e.* the unbending of a Bow which in fact had never been strung! There are two ways of obtaining their applause. The first is: Enable them to reconcile in one and the same occupation the love of Sloth and the hatred of Vacancy![42] Gratify indolence, and yet save them from *Ennui*—in plain English, from themselves! For, spite of their antipathy to *dry* reading, the keeping company with them—

---

[a] *AR* (1825): humour

---

it twice: and it is described in the Manchester Philosophical Transactions, Vol. 1. or 2. Something of the kind, some subtle Exhalation from the Sea, gives rise, perhaps, to the upright or curtain Fata Morgana in the Straits of Messina."

For Fata Morgana see *CN* I 431 and n. C visited Messina in 1805.

The mention of a "Spectre" suggests that he was thinking also of the Brocken spectre, a similar phenomenon, which introduces the element of "fear"; he had hoped to see it when he was in Germany in 1798–9: *C Life* (C) 107–8, 113. His main reference, however, is to the "Glory", for which see below, App I Excursus Note 8 "Coleridge's interest in the 'Glory' ".

[40] At this point C returns to N 23, which he follows closely up to the word "relaxation" in the next paragraph but one below: *CN* IV 5435 ff 23v–24.

[41] For a similar observation on the

"devotees of the circulating libraries" see *BL* ch 3 *(CC)* I 48–9n (based on BM MS Egerton 2800 ff 89–90, published in *IS* 206). C's coinage "Busy-indolent" may be contrasted with Lamb's "busy-idle versions" in "Dream-Children: A Reverie" *London Magazine* v (1822) 23, reprinted in *Elia* (1823) 234.

[42] Cf the complementary sentiment in the epigraph to the first Landing-Place in *The Friend*: "Etiam *a musis* si quando animum paulisper abducamus, apud Musas nihilominus feriamur" (tr "Even if we sometimes lead our mind away *from our studious musings* for a while, let us nonetheless holiday with the Muses"): *Friend (CC)* I 127. The Latin is possibly C's. *BL* ch 3 *(CC)* I 48fn parallels the *AR* passage closely, later continuing: ". . . reconciling the two contrary yet co-existent propensities of human nature, namely; indulgence of sloth, and hatred of vacancy."

to be conceivable, and a*ᵃ* fortiori therefore in order to be comparable.*ᵇ* The Senses do not compare, but merely furnish the materials for comparison. But this the *ᶜ*Reader will find explained in the Note; and will now cast his eye back to the sentence immediately preceding this parenthesis.]*ᵈ*

*ᵉ*Now when a person speaking to us of any particular Object or Appearance refers it by means of some *ᶠ*common character to a known

---

selves is, after all, the insufferable annoyance: and the true secret of their dislike to a work of Thought and Inquiry lies in its tendency to make them acquainted with their own permanent Being. The other road to their favor*ᵍ* is, to introduce to them their own thoughts and predilections, tricked out in the *fine* language, in which it would gratify their vanity to express them in their own conversation, and with which they can imagine themselves *showing off:* and this (as has been elsewhere remarked) is the characteristic difference between the second-rate Writers of the last two or three generations, and the same class under Elizabeth and the Stuarts. In the latter we find the most far-fetched and singular thoughts in the simplest and most native language; in the former, the most obvious and common-place thoughts in the most far-fetched and motley language.[43] But lastly, and as the sine quâ non of their patronage, a sufficient arc must be left for the Reader's mind to *oscillate* in—freedom of choice,

To make the shifting cloud be what you please,[44]

save only where the attraction of Curiosity determines the line of Motion.[45] The Attention must not be fastened down: and this every work of Genius, not simply narrative, must do before it can be justly appreciated.

In former times a *popular* work meant one that adapted the *results* of studious Meditation or scientific Research to the capacity of the People, presenting in the Concrete, by instances and examples, what had been ascertained in the Abstract and by discovery of the Law. *Now,* on the other hand, that is a popular Work which gives back to the People their own errors and prejudices, and flatters the Many by creating them, under the title of THE PUBLIC, into a supreme and inappellable Tribunal of intellectual Excellence. P.S. In a continuous work, the frequent insertion and length of Notes would need an Apology: in a book of Aphorisms and detached Comments none is necessary, it being understood beforehand, that the Sauce and the Garnish are to occupy the greater part of the Dish.*ʰ*

ᵃ *AR* (1825): à
ᵇ *AR* (1825): p 220 (párable.) ; 1825 has: compárable.
ᶜ *AR* (1825): p 221
ᵈ *AR* (1825, 1831):)
ᵉ *AR* (1825): p 222
ᶠ *AR* (1825): p 223
ᵍ *AR* (1825): favour
ʰ *AR* (1825): Dish.   S. T. C.

[43] See *BL* ch 1 *(CC)* I 23.
[44] *Fancy in Nubibus* line 3 (var): *PW* (EHC) I 435.
[45] From here to "excellence" in the next paragraph the note again draws on N 23: *CN* IV 5435 f 24ᵛ. For "the public", the phrase "which has succeeded to 'THE TOWN' '' as "the infallible Judge'', see *Friend (CC)* I 125 and cf *BL* ch 3 *(CC)* I 59; for "the imaginary Word, *Public*" see *Lects 1808–1819 (CC)* I 187. In 1808 (*CL* III 112) C referred WW to his "own distinction" between People and Public, for which see *W Prose* III 84 and 106 n 7.

class[46] (which he does in giving it a Name), we say, that we understand him; *i.e.* we understand his words.[47] The Name of a thing, in the original sense of the word[a] Name,[b] (*Nomen*, Νούμενον,[c] τὸ *intelligibile*,[d] *id quod intelligitur*)[48] expresses that which is *understood* in an appearance, that which we place (or make to *stand*) *under* it, as the condition of its real existence, and in proof that it is not an accident of the Senses, or Affection of the Individual, not a phantom or *Apparition, i.e.* an Appearance that is *only* an Appearance.[49] (See Gen. ii. 19,[e] 20.[50] Thus too, in Psalm

---

[a] *AR* (1825): word,
[b] *AR* (1825): Name
[c] *AR* (1825): Νουμενον,
[d] Misprinted in *AR* (1831) as: *intelligible,*
[e] *AR* (1825): 19.

---

[46] *AR* (1825) COPY D has a note here: "Observe,—that the knowlege of Reality in genere [in kind], independent of its attribution to this or that outward Phænomenon is grounded in and derived from the Conscience or Practical Reason. The function of the *Understanding* is that ⟨of⟩ applying it to particular Phænomena, which it affirms to be *objects*."

[47] In the letter to Green of 11 Jun 1825 on his lines referring to the "Glory", mentioned below in App I Excursus Note 8, C proposed that the following sentences might be inserted at this point: "It is a most important truth, but a truth of which the Fewest are aware, that all *reality* in nature, all belief in a substance existing independently of the Perceiver (as when we say, 'Yes! it *is* a Tree'; or 'there *is* a Cloud there'—) is grounded in an act of the Understanding, not in an affection of the Sight or any other sense. The *reality* of the Image—i.e. that it is a thing and not a *thought* or *sensation*—is in all instances *Hypothesis*, Supposition, substantiation. This is the true import of the word, Understanding. It is the *substantiating*, substance-declaring, Power. When, however, we proceed under the influence of the Fancy, and not according to the rules of the Understanding, the Product or Result is an Hypo*poiēsis* not an Hypo*thesis*, a Suf*fiction* not a Supposition": *CL* v 467–8. Cf n 49, below, and, for the last phrases, *Sp Aph B XI* n 3 and *Conc* n 68.

[48] "Name, noumenon [or, an object of perception by the mind or spirit], the intelligible, that which is understood (or intellected)". C was fond of making this connexion and of adding to it the etymologically unrelated *numen*. For the relation between noumenon and understanding see particularly his letter of Jan 1824, *CL* v 325–6: "For the Νούμενον, that which is to be *understood*, that which contemplated *Objectively* and as one with the φαινόμενον, is the true Numen; and which taken subjectively, and distinctly, is the *Nomen*, or Noun, and Nominator—the Noumenon, I say, is the Logos, the WORD." Cf *CN* IV 4770 f 46. See also below, n 52 and App I Excursus Notes 1 and 4. A striking example of the *nomen–numen* connexion is found in a notebook entry of 1827: "A good Father speaks to us in nomine Dei; a Mother in *numine* [in the name of God . . . in the *power*]": N F° f 97, *CN* v.

[49] *AR* (1825) COPY D inserts here: "All *affirmation* of ⟨not merely subjective⟩ *reality*, or *objective* existence, in ~~Nature~~ every particular object is *Hypothesis, Supposition, Substantiation*: ⟨an act of the Understanding, not an affection of the Senses.⟩ When in this judicial Act we proceed by the laws of the Fancy, and not according to the rules of the Understanding, the Result is not an Hypo*thesis* but an Hypo*pœesis*, not a sub*position* but a suf*fiction*."

[50] "And out of the ground the Lord God formed every beast of the field, and every fowl of the air; and brought them unto Adam to see what he would call them: and whatsoever Adam called every living crea-

xx.[a] 1.[51] and in fifty other places of the Bible, the identity of nomen with numen,[52] *i.e.* invisible power and presence, the *nomen substantivum* of all real Objects, and the ground of their reality, independently[b] of the Affections of Sense in the Percipient). In like manner, in a connected succession of Names, as the Speaker passes from one to the other, we say that we understand his *discourse*[53] (*i.e. discursio* intellectûs, *discursus*, from discurso or discurro, to *course* or pass rapidly from one thing to another). Thus in all instances, it is words, names, or, if images, yet images used as words or names, that are the [c]only and exclusive[d] subjects of Understanding. In no instance do we [e]understand a thing in itself; but only the name to which it is referred.[54] Sometimes indeed, when several classes are recalled conjointly, we identify the words with the Object—though by courtesy of idiom rather than in strict propriety of language. Thus[f] we may say that we *understand* a Rainbow, when recalling successively the several Names for the several sorts of Colors,[g] we know that they are to be applied to one and the same Phenomenon,[h] at once distinctly and simultaneously; but even in common parlance we should not say this of a single color.[i][55] No one would say he understands

[a] *AR* (1825): xx. v.
[b] *AR* (1825): independent
[c–d] *AR* (1825): alone
[e] *AR* (1825): p 224
[f] *AR* (1825): Thus,
[g] *AR* (1825): Colours,
[h] *AR* (1825): Phænomenon,
[i] *AR* (1825): colour.

ture, that was the name thereof. And Adam gave names to all cattle, and to the fowl of the air, and to every beast of the field . . .''.

[51] ''The Lord hear thee in the day of trouble; the name of the God of Jacob defend thee . . .''.

[52] ''Substantive [i.e. under-standing] name''. See above, *Int Aph XII* n 1, and, for discussions concerning the relationship between *nomen* and *numen*, C's marginal notes on the Bible (on Ps 23.3 and Jer 13.11), on the *BCP* (on Ps 72), and on Browne *Works*: *CM (CC)* I 428, 438, 706 (cf 713), and 787; also *CN* IV 4625 f 20[v] (discussing Gen 1.5) on day as ''the manifestation, id a quo noscitur [that by which it is known], of *Light*—its natural *Name*'', and f 21; *CN* IV 4770 (on Gen 2.18–25); and cf *CL* v 325–6, VI 896. For the connexion between *nomen* and origination, and

for further texts C might have had in mind, see above, *Sp Aph B II* n 45.

[53] See above, n 10.

[54] Cf *CN* IV 5406: ''Strictly speaking, we *understand* words only.'' The subsequent discussion includes (ff 88[v]–89) a reference to the present passage in *AR* (1825).

[55] Although C's discussion here is indebted to Kant in terms of method (see n 57, below), the two write about colour differently. *Critik der Urtheilskraft* I § 14 (Berlin 1799) 39–43 (unannotated at this point in C's copy in the BM) also involves simple and complex perceptions, but whereas C's concern here is with determining the extent to which we can ''understand'' colours, Kant's is with judging their beauty: e.g. ''. . . all simple colours are regarded as beautiful so far as pure. Composite colours have not this advantage, because, not being simple, there is no

Red or Blue. He *sees* the Color,[a] and had seen it before in a vast number and variety of objects; and he understands the *word* red, as referring his fancy or memory to this his collective experience.

If this be so, and so it most assuredly is—if the proper functions of the Understanding[b] be that of generalizing the notices received from the Senses in order to the construction of *Names:*[c] of referring particular notices (*i.e.* impressions or sensations) to their proper name;[d] and, vice versâ, names to their correspondent class or kind of Notices—then it follows of necessity, that the Understanding[e] is truly and accurately defined in the words of Leighton and Kant, a Faculty judging according to Sense.

Now whether in defining the speculative Reason (*i.e.* the Reason considered abstractedly as an *intellective* Power) we call it "the source of necessary [f]and universal Principles, according to which the Notices of the Senses are either affirmed or denied;" or describe it as "the Power by which we are enabled to draw from particular and contingent Appearances universal and necessary conclusions:"*[g] it is equally [h]evident that the two definitions differ in their essential characters, and consequently (by Axiom, pp. 222–3) the Subjects differ in *kind*. Q. E. D.

---

* Take a familiar illustration. My sight[i] and touch[j] convey to me a certain impression, to which my Understanding applies its pre-conceptions (*conceptus antecedentes et generalissimi*)[56] of Quantity and Relation, and thus refers it to the Class and Name of three-cornered Bodies—We will suppose it the Iron of a Turf-spade. It compares the sides, and finds that any two measured as one are greater than the third; and according to a law of the imagination, there arises a presumption that in all other Bodies of the same figure (*i.e.* three-cornered and equilateral) the same proportion exists. After this, the senses have been directed successively to a number of three-cornered bodies of *unequal* sides—and in these too the same proportion has been found without exception,[k] till at length it becomes a fact of *experience*, that in *all* Triangles hitherto seen,[l] the two sides together[m] are greater than

[a] *AR* (1825): Colour,
[b] *AR* (1825): understanding
[c] *AR* (1825): *Names;*
[d] *AR* (1825): Name;
[e] *AR* (1825): understanding
[f] *AR* (1825): p 225
[g] *AR* (1825): conclusions*:
[h] *AR* (1825): p 226
[i] *AR* (1825): Sight
[j] *AR* (1825): Touch
[k] *AR* (1825): exception
[l] *AR* (1825): seen
[m] Added in 1831

---

standard for estimating whether they should be called pure or impure": *Critik* p 41, tr J. C. Meredith *The Critique of Aesthetic Judgement* (Oxford 1928) 67. Cf also *Logic (CC)* 78 on secondary rainbows.

[56] "Conceptions that are antecedent and of the most general order".

the third: and there will exist no ground or analogy for anticipating an exception to a Rule, generalized from so vast a number of particular instances. So far and no farther could the Understanding carry us: and as far as this "the faculty, judging according to sense," conducts many of the *inferior* animals, if not in the same, yet in instances analogous and fully equivalent.

The Reason supersedes the whole process, and on the first conception presented by the Understanding in consequence of the first sight of a tri-angular Figure, of whatever sort it might chance to be, it affirms with an assurance incapable of future increase, with a perfect *certainty*, that in all possible triangles[a] any two of the inclosing Lines *will* and *must* be greater than the third.[57] In short, Understanding in its highest form of experience[b] remains commensurate with the experimental notices of the senses, from which it is generalized. Reason, on the other hand, either predetermines Experience, or avails itself of a past Experience to supersede its necessity in all future time; and affirms truths which no Sense could perceive, nor Experiment verify, nor Experience confirm.

Yea, this is the test and character of a truth so affirmed, that in its own proper form it is *inconceivable*.[58] For *to conceive* is a function of the Understanding, which can be exercised only on subjects subordinate thereto. And yet to the forms of the Understanding all truth must be reduced, that is to be fixed as an object of reflection, and to be rendered *expressible*. And here we have a second test and sign of a truth so affirmed, that it can come forth out of the moulds of the Understanding only in the disguise of two contradictory conceptions, each of which is partially true, and the conjunction of both conceptions becomes the representative or *expression* (= the *exponent*) of a truth *beyond* conception and inexpressible. Examples:[c] Before Abraham *was*, I *am*[59]—God is a [d]Circle, the centre of which[e] is every where,[f] and circumference nowhere.[g][60] The soul[h] is all in every part.[61]

[a] *AR* (1825): Triangles

[b] *AR* (1825): Experience

[c] *AR* (1825): Examples.

[d-e] *AR* (1825): Circle whose centre

[f] *AR* (1825): where

[g] *AR* (1825): no where.—

[h] *AR* (1825): Soul

[57] The preceding discussion of the triangle follows the form of Kant's celebrated argument in the Preface to *Critik der reinen Vernunft* (2nd ed Riga 1787) xi–xii, tr Norman Kemp Smith (1929) p 19: "A new light flashed upon the mind of the first man . . . who demonstrated the properties of the isosceles triangle. The true method, so he found, was not to inspect what he discerned either in the figure, or in the bare concept of it, and from this, as it were, to read off its properties; but to bring out what was necessarily implied in the concepts that he had himself formed *a priori*, and had put into the figure in the construction by which he presented it to himself."

[58] C returned several times to the tests referred to in this paragraph: in *CN* IV 5216 he developed the conception of necessary contradiction as involving ". . . two forces of the same power" (for which phrase see Owen Barfield *What Coleridge Thought*—

1972—ch 3); in *C&S (CC)* 17 he brought it in to account for the contradictoriness of the free will; in *TT* 31 Mar 1830 *(CC)* I 98–9 (1836 vn, dated 30 Apr, II 77) it was located as an essential element in Plato's thought. For the originality of C's argument on this point see G. N. G. Orsini *Coleridge and German Idealism* (Carbondale, Ill 1969) 139–40.

[59] John 8.58. The phrase was commented on by Browne in *Religio Medici: Works* (1659) II 22; annotating this, C commented on Browne's near approach to the principle of incomprehensibility: "But the subject was too tempting for the *Rhetorician*": *CM (CC)* I 787–8. Together with the following two examples, it is repeated in *CN* IV 5046 f 89. See n 54, above.

[60] The statement (with sphere rather than circle) appeared as prop 2 in *Liber de propositionibus*, a work translated from Arabic and attributed to Aristotle: A. Va-

If this appear extravagant, it is an extravagance which no man can indeed learn from another, but which,[a] (were this possible,)[b] I might have learnt from Plato, Kepler, and Bacon; from Luther, Hooker, Pascal, Leibnitz, and Fenelon. But in this last paragraph I have, I see, unwittingly overstepped my purpose, according to which we were to take Reason as a simply intellectual power. Yet even as such, and with all the disadvantage of a technical and arbitrary Abstraction, it has been made evident—1. that there is an *Intuition* or *im*mediate Beholding,[62] accompanied by a conviction of the necessity and universality of the truth so beholden[c] not derived from the Senses,[d] [e]which Intuition,[f] when it is *construed* by *pure* Sense, gives birth to the Science of Mathematics, and when applied to Objects super*sensuous*[63] or spiritual is the Organ of Theology and Philosophy:[g]—and 2. that there is likewise a reflective and discursive Faculty, or *mediate* Apprehension which, taken by itself and uninfluenced by the former, depends on the Senses for the Materials on which it is exercised, and is contained within the Sphere of the Senses. And this Faculty it is, which in generalizing the Notices of the Senses constitutes Sensible Experience, and

[a] *AR* (1825): which
[b] *AR* (1825): possible)
[c] *AR* (1825): beheld ; COPY C: beheld—an intuition
[d] COPY C: Senses, but
[e-f] COPY C: which,
[g] *AR* (1825): Philosophy;

---

cant *Dictionnaire de théologie catholique* XII 2292. Often repeated by mediaeval theologians, e.g. Bonaventura *Itinerarium mentis ad Deum* 4. It also appears in Luther *Colloquia Mensalia* ch 6 (1652) 103 (on a page annotated by C), where it is attributed to "a philosophical and learned Heathen".

In an annotation on J. Böhme *Works* (1764–81) I i 38–9 C wrote: "As the Sun is (here conceived to be) the manifested Convergence of all the Astral Powers, subsisting from them, yet re-acting as that which is the condition of *all* being a Whole: so the Son is the omnipresent Center of that infinite Circle, whose only Circumference is in ~~his~~ its own Self-comprehension, the eternal Act of which for ever constitutes that Center": *CM (CC)* I 564. Cf also Henry More "The infinitie of Worlds" viii: *Philosophicall Poems* (Cambridge 1647) 193 and H. Steffens *Grundzüge der Philosophischen Naturwissenschaft* (Berlin 1806) 20–3. For a full account see D. Mahnke *Unendliche Sphäre und Allmittelpunkt* (Stuttgart 1966).

[61] See Plotinus *Enneads* 4.3.8 on the soul as second hypostasis and Aquinas *Summa contra gentiles* 2.77: "Quod anima sit tota in toto et tota in qualibet parte" ("That the soul is whole in the whole and whole in every part"). Cf *CN* II 2110 on "the totus in omni parte of Truth, and its

consequent non dependence on co-operation . . ." and III 4418 f 15 on "the Law of Laws deduced from the omnipresence, or Totum in omni parte, which again is deduced from the Absoluteness of the divine Acts"; also *CN* IV 4617, on God as "totus ubique", and an annotation on Donne *LXXX Sermons*: *CM (CC)* II 250. See also WW *Peele Castle* lines 30–1:

> Such Picture would I at that time have made:
> And seen the soul of truth in every part . . .

(*WPW* IV 259); Cowley *All-over Love* lines 8–10:

> For 'twas not only in my Heart,
> But like a *God* by pow'rfull Art
> 'Twas *all* in *all*, and *all* in *every Part*.

(Abraham Cowley *Works*—7th ed 1681— II 25); and Pope *Essay on Man* I 267–80.

[62] See above, *Sp Aph B I* n 4, and, for "immediate beholding", n 28 above.

[63] Cf *Friend (CC)* I 156 on conscious self-knowledge, or reason, as ". . . the organ of the Super-sensuous" (given by *OED* as first use of this word). Cf also *Sp Aph B XX* at n 2, below, *C&S (CC)* 234, and, for "super-sensual", ibid 120 and *Sp Aph B Xb* at n 23 below.

gives rise to Maxims or Rules which may become more and more *general*, but can never be raised into universal Verities, or beget a consciousness of absolute Certainty; though they may be sufficient to extinguish all doubt. (Putting Revelation out of view, take our first Progenitor in the 50th or 100th year of his existence. His experience[a] would probably have freed him from all doubt, as the Sun sank[b] in the Horizon that it would re-appear the next morning. But compare this state of Assurance with that which the same Man would have had of the 37th Proposition of Euclid, supposing him like Pythagoras to have discovered the *Demonstration*.)[c][64] Now is it expedient, I ask, or conformable to the laws and purposes of Language, to call two so altogether disparate Subjects by one and the same name? Or, having two names in our language, should we call each of the two diverse subjects by both—*i.e.* by either name, as caprice might dictate? If not, then as we have the two words, Reason and Understanding (as indeed what Language of cultivated Man has not?) what should prevent us from appropriating the former to the Power distinctive of Humanity? We need only place the derivatives from the two terms in opposition (*ex. gr.* "A and B are both rational Beings; but there is no comparison between them in point of *intelligence*," or "She always concludes *rationally*, though not a Woman of much *Understanding*") to see[d] that we cannot reverse the order—*i.e.* call the higher Gift Understanding, and the lower Reason. What *should* prevent us? I asked. Alas! that which *has* prevented us—the *cause* of this confusion in the terms—is only too obvious: viz. inattention to the momentous distinction in the *things*, and (generally) to the duty and habit recommended in the Vth Introductory Aphorism of this Volume, (*see* p. 13).[e] But the cause of this, and of all its lamentable Effects and Subcauses, "false doctrine, blindness of Heart and contempt of the Word,"[65] is best declared by the philosophic Apostle: "they did not *like* to retain God in their knowledge,"[f] (Rom. i. 28,) and though they could not *extinguish* "the Light that lighteth every man," and which "shone in the Darkness;" yet because the Darkness could not *comprehend* the Light, they refused to bear witness of it[g][66] and worshipped, instead, the shaping Mist, which the Light had drawn upward from *the Ground*[67] (i.e. from the mere Animal nature and instinct), and which that Light alone had made [h]visible, *i.e.*[i] by superinducing on the animal instinct the principle of Self-consciousness).

> [a] *AR* (1825): Experience
> [b] *AR* (1825): sunk
> [c] *AR* (1825): *Demonstration*).
> [d] *AR* (1825): see,
> [e] *AR* (1825): 2.)
> [f] *AR* (1825): knowlege,"
> [g] *AR* (1825): it, ; Corr, COPY C: the Light,
> [h-i] *AR* (1825): visible (*i. e.*

[64] See e.g. André Dacier *Life of Pythagoras, with His Symbols and Golden Verses* (1707) 81: ". . . it was he who found out and demonstrated, that the Square of the Hypothenusal Line of a rectangular Triangle is equal to the two Squares of the two Sides. Nay, 'tis said, he was so far transported at this Discovery, that he sacrificed a Hecatomb to the Muses." Proclus, who also admired those who first investigated it, had even more respect for Euclid, who demonstrated it: *Commentaries on the First Book of Euclid* (1792) II 204 (prop 47, theorem 33).

[65] Cf the Litany in *BCP*: ". . . from all false doctrine, heresy, and schism; from

hardness of heart, and contempt of thy Word and Commandment, *Good Lord deliver us*". For "blindness of heart" see Eph 4.18.

[66] See John 1.9, 5, 7.

[67] For various uses of this image see Beer *CV* 81, 153–4, 168, 236, 268–9, and nn, particularly C's interpretation of the smoke and fire on Mt Sinai as the raising of ". . . the dark and dank Stagnum into Mist" followed by fermentation until the darkness explodes into "*Ground*-Lightning": N 53 ff 10ᵛ–11: *CN* v. See also his lines, "Whene'er the mist, that stands 'twixt God and thee . . .", first published in *C&S (CC)* 184–5, *PW* (EHC) I 487.

*ª*The dependence of the Understanding on the representations of the Senses, and its consequent posteriority*ᵇ* thereto, as contrasted with the independence and antecedency of Reason, are strikingly exemplified in the Ptolemaic System (that truly wonderful product and highest boast of the Faculty, judging according to the Senses!) compared with the Newtonian, as the Offspring of a yet higher Power, arranging, correcting, and annulling the representations of the Senses according to its own inherent Laws and constitutive Ideas.⁶⁸

APHORISM IX*ᶜ¹*

In Wonder all Philosophy began: in Wonder it ends: and Admiration fills up the interspace. But the first Wonder is the Offspring of Ignorance: the *ᵈ*last is the Parent of Adoration. The First is the birth-throe of our knowledge: the Last is its euthanasy² and apotheosis.

SEQUELAE: OR THOUGHTS SUGGESTED BY THE PRECEDING
APHORISM

As in respect of the first Wonder we are all on the same Level, how

---

ª AR (1825): p 227
ᵇ AR (1825): p 228 (teriority)
ᶜ AR (1825): IV. EDITOR. ; COPIES A, C, D: IX. EDITOR. ; *AR* (1831): IV.
ᵈ AR (1825): p 229

---

⁶⁸ Cf *BL* ch 9 *(CC)* I 139.

¹ See textual note. *AR* (1825) COPIES A, C, and D corrected, properly, to "Aphorism IX", but the slip was repeated here in 1831. A notebook entry of late Feb 1824 contains three drafts of this aphorism: "In Wonder, the offspring of Ignorance, Philosophy begins: ~~in Admiration it proceeds and~~ in Wonder, the Parent of Adoration, it ends: and ever-waxing Admiration is the Line of Transit" *or* "In Surprise, that wonders, Philosophy begins: in Wonder, that adores, Philosophy ends: and Admiration is the Line of Transit.—" *or* "In Wonder Philosophy begins: in Wonder it ends: and Admiration ~~is the Line~~ marks the interspace. But the first W. is the Offspring of Ignorance: the last the Parent of Adoration: that the struggling Birth of Knowlege, this its Euthanasy and Apotheosis": *CN* IV 5131. The third draft differs only in stylistic points from the *AR* version. On the verso of the leaf (*CN* IV 5132) C quoted the

relevant passage of Aristotle *Metaphysics* 1.2 (982ᵇ), evidently taking it from Tennemann III 44; tr H. Tredennick (LCL 1933): "It is through wonder that men now begin and originally began to philosophize . . . so that if it was to escape ignorance that men studied philosophy, it is obvious that they pursued science for the sake of knowledge and not for any practical utility." C also gives Tennemann's reference to Plato *Theaetetus*: p 76 (155D); tr B. Jowett *Dialogues* (4th ed Oxford 1953) III 251: ". . . philosophy begins in wonder; he was not a bad genealogist who said that Iris the messenger of heaven is the child of Thaumas (wonder)".

Cf *Friend (CC)* I 519 for C's earlier embroidery on these two passages, referring to Aristotle for the beginning of philosophy in wonder and to Plato for its ending "in astoundment".

² "A gentle and easy death".

comes it that the philosophic mind should,*a* in all ages,*b* be the privilege of a Few? The most obvious reason is this: The Wonder takes place before the period of Reflection, and (with the great Mass of Mankind) long before the individual*c* is capable of directing his attention freely and consciously to the Feeling, or even to its exciting Causes. Surprise (the form and dress which the Wonder of Ignorance usually puts on) is worn away, if not precluded, by Custom and familiarity.*d* So is it with the Objects of the Senses, and the ways and fashions of the World around us: even as with the beat*e* of our own hearts, which we notice only in moments of Fear and Perturbation. But with regard to the concerns of our inward Being, there is yet another cause that acts in concert with the power in Custom to prevent a fair and equal exertion of reflective Thought. The great fundamental Truths and Doctrines of Religion, the existence and attributes of God, and the Life after Death, are in Christian Countries taught so early, under such circumstances, and in such close and vital association with whatever makes or marks *reality* for our infant minds, that the words ever after represent sensations, feelings, vital *f*as-surances, sense of reality—rather than thoughts, or any distinct conception. Associated, *I had almost said identified*, with the parental Voice, Look, Touch, with the living warmth and pressure of the Mother, on whose lap the Child is first made to kneel, within whose palms its little hands are folded, and the motion of whose eyes *it's* eyes follow and imitate—(yea, what the blue sky is to the Mother, the Mother's upraised Eyes and Brow are to the Child, the Type and Symbol of an invisible Heaven!)[3]—from within and*g* without, these great First Truths, these good and gracious Tidings, these holy and humanizing Spells, in the

---

a *AR* (1825): should
b *AR* (1825): ages
c *AR* (1825): Individual
d *AR* (1825): Familiarity.
e *AR* (1825): Beat
f *AR* (1825): p 230
g *AR* (1825): and from

[3] Cf *Christabel* lines 326–31, in which Christabel's "vision sweet", which may involve her mother, is associated with her assurance that "saints will aid if men will call: | For the blue sky bends over all!" (*PW*—EHC—I 226) and *CN* III 3720 (a note for *Christabel*, written in 1810): "My first cries mingled with my Mother's Death-groan . . . when I first looked up to Heaven, consciously, it was to look up after or for my Mother". See also Beer *CPI* 82–4 and 190–1 for further possible implications. C's own delight in the sky is clear from such passages as his description of Christ's Hospital days, *CL* II 791, and his rhapsodic notes in Malta, *CN* II 2346, 2453. See also above, Editor's Introduction, at n 139. In 1815–16, however, he transcribed Jean Paul's sentiment: "We all look up to the blue Sky for comfort, but nothing appears there . . .": *CN* III 4294.

preconformity[4] to which our very humanity may be said to consist, are so infused, that it were but a tame and inadequate expression to say, we all take them for granted. At a later period, in Youth or early Manhood, most of us, indeed, (in the higher and middle classes at least) read or hear certain PROOFS of these truths—which we commonly listen to, when we listen at all, with much the same feelings as a popular Prince on his Coronation Day, in the centre of a fond and rejoicing Nation, may be supposed to hear the Champion's challenge to all the Non-existents, that deny or dispute his Rights and Royalty.[5] In fact, the order of Proof is most often reversed or transposed. As far, at least[a] as I dare judge from the goings on in my own mind, when with keen delight I first read the works of Derham,[6] Niewentiet,[7] and Lyonet,[8] I should say, that the full and life-like conviction of a gracious Creator is the Proof (at all events, [b]performs the office and answers all the purpose of a Proof) of the wisdom and benevolence in the construction of the Creature.[9]

<hr>

a   *AR* (1825): least,
b   *AR* (1825): p 231

<hr>

[4] *OED* gives this as its sole example of the word; similarly with DeQ's two uses of the verb, "preconform".

[5] The first recorded appearance of the Champion was at the coronation of Richard II in 1377, the last at that of George IV in 1821. For a full account see L. G. Wickham Legg *English Coronation Records* (1901) lxv–lxvi, 359–60. No one ever accepted the challenge; at the coronation of George III the gauntlet was picked up, but by an old woman who was "reluctant that so finely dressed a gentleman should lose his glove in so great a crowd": ibid lxxvii. C is less likely to be thinking of the recent 1821 coronation than to be recalling (in a different vein) a satirical reference in the *Tatler* No 17 (17–19 May 1709) to the courage of speaking "NAKED TRUTH" when nothing is spoken that is not to the advantage of all who are mentioned: "This is just such a great Action as that of the Champion's on a Coronation-Day, who challenges all mankind to dispute with him the Right of the Sovereign, surrounded by his Guards."

[6] William Derham (1657–1735), canon of Windsor and author of many works on natural theology, including *Physico-Theology; or, a Demonstration of the Being and Attributes of God, from His Works*

of Creation (1713). C referred to him twice in the notebook entries of 1802–3: *CN* I 1147 and 1616 f 74. See also *CN* II 3074n, 3162n, 3163n, and III 3765n.

[7] Bernard Nieuwentijt (1654–1718), a Dutch disciple of Descartes, published *Het regt gebruik der Wereltbeschouwingen* (1714), tr as *The Religious Philosopher* by J. Chamberlayne (1718–19). He was quoted by Paley, who has been accused of plagiarism from him. See *EB* (11th ed 1910–11) article "Paley".

[8] Pierre Lyonnet (1707–89), naturalist and anatomist, translated F. C. Lesser *Insecto-Theologia* (1738) as *Théologie des insectes* (1742). In 1804 C cited the dissection of a wasp in this work, but it is clear that he had found the description in Reimarus. See *CN* II 2330 (and cf III 4448n).

[9] Cf the title of John Ray *The Wisdom of God Manifested in the Works of the Creation* (1691) and cf below, *Conc* n 85. Ray and Nieuwentijt both speak several times of the "wisdom and goodness" of God, but the specific term "benevolence" belongs rather to the tradition of Shaftesbury. Bp Butler questioned the idea that the only character of God was that of "simple absolute benevolence": "There may possibly be in the creation, beings, to whom the Author of Nature manifests Himself under this

Do I blame this? Do I wish it to be otherwise? God forbid! It is only one of its accidental, but too frequent[a] consequences, of which I complain, and against which I protest. I regret nothing that tends to make the Light become the Life of men, even as the Life in the eternal Word is their [b]only and single[c] true light.[10] But I do regret, that in after years— when by occasion of some new dispute on some old heresy, or any other accident, the attention has for the first time been distinctly attracted to the superstructure raised on these fundamental truths, or to truths of later revelation supplemental of these and not less important—all the doubts and difficulties, that cannot but arise where the Understanding, *"the mind of the flesh,"*[11] is made the measure of spiritual things; all the sense of strangeness and seeming contradiction in terms; all[d] the Marvel and the Mystery,[e] that belong equally to both,[f] are first thought of and applied in objection exclusively to the latter.[g] I would disturb no man's faith in the great articles of the (falsely so called) Religion of Nature. But before the man rejects, and calls on other men to reject, the revelations of the Gospel and the Religion of all Christendom, I would have him place himself in the state and under all the privations of a Simonides, when in[h] the fortieth day of his meditation the sage and philosophic Poet abandoned the Problem in despair.[12] Ever and anon he seemed to have hold of the truth; but [i]when he asked himself, what he *meant* by it,

[a] *AR* (1825): frequent,
[b-c] *AR* (1825): alone
[d] COPY C: that all
[e] *AR* (1825): Mystery ; COPIES A & C: Mystery, in short,
[f] *AR* (1825): both; ; COPY A: *both*; ; COPY C: both
[g] COPY A: *latter.*
[h] *AR* (1825): on
[i] *AR* (1825): p 232

most amiable of all characters . . . but He manifests Himself to us under the character of a righteous Governor": *Analogy of Religion* (1736) pt 1 ch 3 § 3: *Works* ed J. H. Bernard (2 vols 1900) II 47. C's most immediate source is the opening of Kirby and Spence *Introduction to Entomology*, in which the manifestation of goodness in the creation is a major theme. Several years later Kirby published his Bridgewater Treatise entitled *On the Power, Wisdom and Goodness of God as Manifested in the Creation of Animals and in Their History, Habits and Instincts* (2 vols 1835).
[10] Cf John 1.1–4. The reservation that follows had been worded more strongly

(also in relation to Derham, Nieuwentijt, and Lyonnet) in 1822: *CN* IV 4890.
[11] St Paul's φρόνημα σαρκός (Rom 8.6– 7), which C associates regularly with the "understanding". See below, *Sp Aph B Xa* nn 31, 33, 41.
[12] Simonides, asked to explain the nature and attributes of God, doubled the length of time required each time an answer was requested. Bayle (see below n 16) quotes Cicero *De natura deorum* 1.60 and Tertullian *Apologeticus* 46 (where the philosopher mentioned is Thales). The number of days is not specified by these writers nor by Minucius Felix *Octavius* 13, to whom Bayle also refers. Cf *P Lects* Lect

it escaped from him, or resolved itself into meanings, that destroyed each other. I would have the Sceptic, while yet a Sceptic only, seriously consider whether a Doctrine, of the truth of which a Socrates could obtain no other assurance than what he derived from his strong *wish* that it should be true;[13] and*[a]* which Plato found a Mystery hard to discover, and when discovered, communicable only to the fewest of men;[14] can, consonantly with History or Common Sense, be classed among the Articles, the Belief of which is ensured to all men by their mere common sense? Whether, without gross outrage to fact, they can be said to constitute a Religion of Nature, or a Natural Theology antecedent to Revelation,*[b]* or superseding its necessity?[15] Yes! in prevention (for there is little chance,

---

[a] AR (1825): or that
[b] AR (1825): Revelation

---

3 (1949) 126 and n. The present discussion may throw light on C's earlier association of WW with Simonides and Empedocles (*CN* II 1712). In 1805 WW completed the first version of *The Prelude*, in which he described how, "demanding proof", he

. . . lost
All feeling of conviction, and in fine,
Sick, wearied out with contrarieties,
Yielded up moral questions in despair. . .

(Bk 10 lines 898–901: *Prelude*—1959—418.) WW's own references to Simonides stress his piety towards the dead—*W Prose* II 52—and his tender-heartedness—*WPW* III 408, IV 100.

[13] Socrates' confident assumption as to the nature of God (or the gods, or the divine power) as benevolent ruler, creator, and source of wisdom is expressed in Xenophon *Memorabilia* 1.4. Cf also above, *Mor Aph XXI* n.

[14] The statement is made in *Timaeus* but it also appears in Tertullian, quoted by Bayle: see n 12 above and n 16 below. A copy belonging formerly to Barron Field (see below, App E 202) contains a marginal note (not in C's handwriting):

—How cam'st thou to see these truths
   so clear,
Which so obscure to Heathens did
   appear?
Not Plato these nor Aristotle found;
Nor he whose wisdom oracles
   renown'd.
Hast thou a wit so deep or so sublime,

Or can'st thou lower dive or higher
   climb?
Can'st thou by reason more of godhead
   know
Than Plutarch, Seneca or Cicero?
                                    Dryden.

See *Religio Laici* lines 72–9.
[15] AR (1825) COPY B has a note transcribed by George Grove and incorporated var by DC in *AR* (1854) 188–9: "N.B. These remarks on a Religion of Nature ⟨p. 181. 1. 24⟩ apply to the Belief in the existence, the personality and the providence of a one only God, and to the Belief of a Future State *in connection with and dependence on* the belief of God as a moral Judge—and *not* to the mere assurance of a Soul that survives the Body. This latter is, I doubt not, natural to Man. See p. 341–348: It may therefore be called a 'Faith of Nature'; but it is not a Religion of Nature—or rather it is not Religion at all." COPY C reads as follows: "It ought to have been explained, that these remarks on the 'Religion of Nature' are meant to apply to the Belief in the existence, personality and providence of a one only God, and to the Belief in a State after death in connection with, and dependence on, the Idea of God, as a moral Judge—and that the remarks are not intended to apply to the mere Assurance of a Soul that survives the Body. This latter may, I doubt not, be justly named Natural to man—a Faith of Nature (vide p. 341–348) but it is not a *Religion* of Nature—or Religion in any sense."

I fear, of a *cure*) of the pugnacious dogmatism of *partial* Reflection, I would prescribe to every man, who feels a commencing alienation from the Catholic Faith, and whose studies and attainments authorise him to argue on the subject at all, a patient and thoughtful perusal of the arguments and representations which Bayle supposes to have passed through the mind of Simonides.[16] Or I should be fully satisfied if I could induce these Eschewers of Mystery to give a patient, manly, and impartial perusal to the single Treatise of Pomponatius, De Fato.*[a]

[b]When they have fairly and satisfactorily overthrown the objections and cleared away the difficulties urged by this sharp-witted Italian against the Doctrines which they profess to retain, then let them commence their attack on those which they reject. As far as the supposed irrationality of the latter is the ground of Argument, I am much deceived if,[c] on reviewing their forces,[d] they would not find the ranks woefully thinned by the success of their own fire in the preceding Engagement— unless, indeed, by pure heat of Controversy, and to storm the lines of their Antagonists, they can bring to life again the Arguments[e] which they had themselves killed off in the defence of their own positions. In vain shall we seek for any other mode of meeting the broad facts of the scientific Epicurean, or the requisitions and queries of the all-analysing Pyrrhonist,[18] than by challenging the tribunal to which they appeal, as

---

* The Philosopher, whom the Inquisition would have burnt alive as an Atheist, had not Leo X. and Cardinal Bembo decided that the Work might be formidable to those semi-pagan Christians who regarded Revelation as a mere Make-weight to their boasted Religion of Nature; but contained nothing dangerous to the Catholic Church or offensive to a true Believer.[17]

---

[a] *AR* (1825): Fato*,
[b] *AR* (1825): p 233
[c] *AR* (1825): if
[d] *AR* (1825): forces
[e] *AR* (1825): Arguments,

---

[16] Article "Simonides" in Bayle *Dictionnaire historique et critique*: quoted from *The Dictionary Historical and Critical of Mr. Peter Bayle* (5 vols 1734–8, a tr by Pierre des Maizeaux of the 2nd ed of 1702) v 141–5n (footnote F). See also below, App I Excursus Note 9 "Bayle and Simonides". For his knowledge of Bayle, see *CN* I 277 and n, 280; BM MS Egerton 2801 ff 2ᵛ–3 (*SW&F—CC*); and *Logic (CC)* 124.

[17] C's source is likely to be Tennemann IX 81, where, after a long discussion of *De immortalitate animae*, Tennemann gives the judgement of Leo X and Cardinal

Bembo that that work contained nothing prejudicial to the Christian religion. C would have been misled by a footnote below, the first of a series of quotations from *De fato*. He was less respectful to Pomponatius in a marginal note on Tennemann IX 68, quoted in introd to *P Lects* (1949) 57.

For a brief account of *De immortalitate animae* (1516) see A. H. Douglas *The Philosophy and Psychology of Pietro Pomponazzi* (Cambridge 1910) 67–8 and, for discussion of its doctrines, the Index of References ibid 306–7.

[18] C discusses Pyrrho, the founder of

incompetent to try the question. In order to *non-suit* the infidel Plaintiff, we must remove the cause from the Faculty, that judges according to Sense, and whose judgments, therefore, are valid only on objects of Sense, to the Superior Courts of Conscience and intuitive Reason! *"The words I speak unto you, are Spirit,"* and such only *"are life,"*[19] *i.e.* have an inward and actual power abiding in them.

But the same truth is at once Shield and Bow. The Shaft of Atheism glances aside from it to strike and [a]pierce the breast-plate of the Heretic. Well for the Latter, if plucking the weapon from the wound he recognizes an arrow from his own Quiver, and abandons a cause that connects him with such Confederates! Without further rhetoric, the sum and substance of the Argument is this: an insight into the proper functions and subaltern rank of the Understanding may not, indeed, disarm the Psilanthropist[b][20] of his metaphorical Glosses, or of his *Versions* fresh from the forge,[c] and with no other stamp than the private mark of the individual manufacturer;[d] but it will deprive him of the only rational pretext for having recourse to tools so liable to abuse, and of such perilous example.

COMMENT[21]

Since the preceding pages were composed, and during an interim of depression and disqualification, I heard with a delight and an interest, that I might without hyperbole call medicinal, that the contradistinction of Understanding from Reason, for which during twenty years I have been contending, "casting my bread upon the Waters"[22] with a perseverance, which in the existing state of the public taste nothing but the deepest conviction of its importance could have inspired—has been lately adopted and sanctioned by the present distinguished Professor of Anatomy, in the Course of Lectures given by him at the Royal College of Surgeons, on the Zoological part of Natural History;[23] and, if I am

---

[a] *AR* (1825): p 234   [b] *AR* (1831): Psilanthrophist
[c] *AR* (1825): forge   [d] *AR* (1825): Manufacturer;

---

scepticism, in *P Lects* Lect 6 (1949) 196–204. For an account of Pyrrhonism in seventeenth-century thought (including that of Sir Thomas Browne—cf *Sp Aph B VIIIa* n 6 above) see Louis I. Bredvold *The Intellectual Milieu of John Dryden* (1934) esp ch 2.

[19] John 6.63.

[20] See above, *Sp Aph B VIIIa* n 13.

[21] *AR* (1825) COPY A has a note on Reason and Understanding here, reproduced below, App D(a).

[22] "Cast thy bread upon the waters: for thou shalt find it after many days": Eccles 11.1.

[23] C's friend Joseph Henry Green

rightly informed, in one of the eloquent and impressive introductory Discourses. In *a*explaining the Nature of Instinct,[24] as deduced from the actions and tendencies of animals successively presented to the Observation of the Comparative Physiologist in the ascending Scale of Organic Life—or rather, I should have said, in an attempt to determine that precise import of the *Term*, which is required by the facts*—the Profes-

* The word, Instinct, brings together a number of facts into one class by the assertion of a common ground, the nature of which ground it determines *negatively* only—*i.e.* the word does not explain *what* this common ground is, but simply indicates*b* that there *is* such a ground, and that it is different in kind from that in which the responsible and consciously voluntary Actions of Men originate. Thus, in its true and primary import, Instinct stands in antithesis to Reason; and the perplexity and contradictory statements into which so many meritorious Naturalists, and popular Writers on Natural History (Priscilla Wakefield, Kirby, Spence,[25] Hüber,[26] and even Reimarus)[27] have fallen on this subject, arise

a AR (1825): p 235
b AR (1825): indicates,

(1791–1863) was appointed Professor of Anatomy at the Royal College of Surgeons on 11 Jul 1823, and there gave four annual courses of twelve lectures (*DNB*). See H. J. Jackson "Coleridge's Collaborator, Joseph Henry Green" *SIR* XXI (1982) 167 and n. The first course began on 30 Mar 1824 and ended on 1 May 1824. (Information from Librarian.) A relevant passage from Green's *Vital Dynamics* App F (1840) 88–96 was first included by HNC in the 5th ed of *AR* (1843) II 328–34 and is reproduced as App C below. Green had described it as containing the remarks ". . . to which Coleridge refers in the Aids to Reflection" and said that ". . . whatever merit they possess must have been derived from his instructive conversation". It is clear that it was in some way the result of collaboration with C, since Green not only makes the same point about the relationship between instinct and understanding as C, but quotes the same passage from Huber on Bees (see *Sp Aph B VIIIb* at n 21 above) in a similar, though not the same, condensed form. Whether the passage appeared exactly so in the lectures of 1824 is not clear.

[24] Cf *Friend (CC)* I 155 and n.
[25] Priscilla Wakefield (1751–1832) discussed the relationship between reason and instinct in *Instinct Displayed* . . . (1811) 7–10. For Kirby and Spence see above, *Sp Aph B VIIIb* n 17. Instinct is discussed in Letter XXVII of their *Introduction to Ento-*

mology II 465–529: first negatively (495–7), then positively (512–29). "There is perhaps no surer criterion of reason than, after having tried one mode of accomplishing a purpose, adopting another more likely to succeed" (520). This, on C's terms, would be a use of the understanding. A rough draft for some lines of the text here is transcribed below in App B(u).

[26] There is little theoretical discussion of instinct in the works of either Huber (for whom see *Sp Aph B VIIIb* n 16 above). Pierre Huber touches upon the questions briefly in the Preface to his *Natural History of Ants* (1820) xx–xxiii, and in his last chapter reflects on human analogy with republicanism of ants.

[27] H. S. Reimarus (1694–1768) *Allgemeine Betrachtungen über die Triebe der Thiere* (Hamburg 1760), tr as *Observations Moral and Philosophical on the Instinct of Animals, Their Industry and Their Manners* (1770). C's reading of this in German in Malta in Dec 1804 prompted a number of notes on the nature and significance of instinct: *CN* II 2318–36 and 2544 and nn. See e.g. Dissertation vii § 7, pp 328–30, in which Reimarus discusses the instincts and continues: "On us nature has bestowed no instinct, or natural skill; the faculty of reason is all we hold of her, in order to procure many things which we cannot well be without." C would presumably argue that Reimarus's use of "reason" here corresponds to his own "understanding".

sor explained the nature of what I have elsewhere called the *Adaptive Power*,[29] i.e. the faculty of adopting*a* means to proximate ends. [N.B. I mean here a *relative* end—that which relatively to one thing is an *end*, though relatively to some other it *b*is in*c* itself a *means*. It is to be regretted, that we have no single word to express these ends, that are not *the* end: for the distinction between these and an end in the proper sense of the term is an important one.] The Professor, I say, not only explained, first, the Nature of the adaptive*d* Power *in genere*,[30] and, secondly, the distinct character of the *same* Power as it exists *specifically* and exclusively in the *human* being, and acquires the name of Understanding; but he did it in a way which gave the whole sum and substance of my convictions,[31] of all I had so long wished, and so often, but with such imperfect success, attempted to convey, free from all semblance of Paradoxy, and from all occasion of offence—omnem offendiculi* ansam praecidens.[32] It is, indeed, for the *fragmentary* reader only that I have

---

wholly from their taking the word in opposition to Understanding. I notice this,*e* because I would not lose any opportunity of impressing on the mind of my youthful readers the important truth that Language (as the embodied and articulated Spirit of the Race, as the growth and emanation of a People, and not the work of any individual Wit or Will) is often inadequate, sometimes deficient, but never false or delusive. We have only to master the true origin and original import of any native and abiding word, to find in it, if not the *solution* of the facts expressed by it, yet a finger-mark pointing to the road on which this solution is to be sought.*f* [28]

* Neque quicquam addubito, quin ea candidis omnibus faciat satis. Quid autem facias istis qui vel ob ingenii pertinaciam sibi satisfieri nolint, vel stupidiores sint quam ut satis-

---

a *AR* (1825): adapting   *b* *AR* (1825): p 236   *c* Added in 1831
d *AR* (1825): Adaptive   *e* *AR* (1825): this   *f* *AR* (1825): sought for.

---

[28] See above, *Int Aph XII* n 2, and cf *CN* III 4780 and n, *BL* ch 12 *(CC)* I 239 fn, *CN* I 354, and *CL* VI 700–1. The exact philological point at issue is not clear, but (following the Latin "instinguere") C is probably suggesting an internal stimulation or incitement which operates as much in the spiritual as the physical nature: see *BL* ch 12 *(CC)* I 242 and n. The word "finger-mark" is apparently used for "finger-post".

[29] *OED* gives the use of this term in *AR* as the earliest recorded use of "adaptive". C's use "elsewhere" has not been traced, but it is not unlikely that he invented the word for Green: see n 31.

[30] "in kind": cf above, *Sp Aph B VIIIb*

n 19, and C's footnote, ibid, after n 29.

[31] Cf Green *Vital Dynamics*: ". . . the term Instinct is only strictly applicable to the Adaptive Power, as the faculty, even in its highest proper form, of selecting and adapting appropriate means of proximate ends according to varying circumstances,—a faculty which however only differs from human understanding, in consequence of the latter being enlightened by reason,—and that the principles, which actuate man as ultimate ends, and are designed for his conscious possession and guidance, are best and most properly named Ideas": *Vital Dynamics* (1840) 96 (quoted below, at end of App C).

[32] ". . . taking away any occasion of

any scruple. In those who have had the patience to accompany me so far on the up-hill road to manly Principles, I can have no reason to guard against that disposition to hasty offence from *[a]*Anticipation of *Consequences*, that faithless and loveless spirit of fear which plunged Galileo*[b][33]* into a Prison*—a spirit most unworthy of an educated man, who ought to have learnt that the Mistakes of scientific men have never injured Christianity, while every new truth discovered by them has either added to its evidence, or prepared the mind for its reception.

---

factionem intelligant? Nam quemadmodum Simonides dixit, Thessalos hebetiores esse quam ut possint a se decipi, ita quosdam videas stupidiores quam ut placari queant. Adhuc non mirum est invenire quod calumnietur qui nihil aliud quaerit nisi quod calumnietur. (*Erasmi Epist. ad Dorpium.*) At all events, the*[c]* passing through the medium of my own prepossessions, if any fault be found with it, the fault probably, and the blame certainly, belongs to the Reporter.

* And which (I might have added) in a more enlightened age, and in a Protestant Country, impelled more than one German University to anathematize Fr. Hoffman's discovery of Carbonic Acid Gas, and of its effects on animal life, as hostile to religion, and tending to Atheism! Three or four Students at the university of Jena, in the attempt to raise a Spirit for the discovery of a supposed hidden treasure, were strangled or poisoned by the fumes of the Charcoal they had been burning in a close Garden-house of a vineyard near Jena, while employed in their magic fumigations and charms. One only was restored to Life: and from his account of the Noises and Spectres (*in* his ears and eyes) as he was losing his senses, it was taken for granted that *the bad Spirit* had destroyed them. Frederic Hoffman admitted that it was a *very bad* spirit that had *tempted* them, the Spirit of Avarice and Folly; and that a very *noxious* Spirit (Gas, or Geist, is the German*[d]* for Spirit) was the

[a] AR (1825): p 237   *[b]* AR (1825): Galilæo   *[c]* AR (1825): *german*
[d] AR (1825): the following Exposition having been received at second hand, and

---

the least offence''. Like the passage in the footnote below, from Erasmus *Epistola ad Dorpium*, in *Moriae encomium* (Oxford 1668) 257–8. This letter to Maarten Dorp (pub Antwerp 1515) was regularly included with *Moriae encomium (The Praise of Folly)* from 1516 onwards. C had copied the passage used in his footnote, with two preceding sentences, into a notebook dated Aug–Sept 1815: *CN* III 4262. Tr *CN* III 4262n: "I have no doubt that it will satisfy all sincere persons. What, however, is one to do in the case of those who either out of natural obstinacy refuse to be satisfied or are too stupid to understand their satisfaction? For as Simonides said, 'The Thessalians are too stupid to be capable of being cheated by me', so you may see some too

stupid to be capable of being placated. Besides, it is not surprising that a man who is looking only for something to criticise should find it.'' The passage was used for the epigraph to ch 23 of *BL*: *BL (CC)* II 207. The error ''Adhuc'' (still) for ''Adhaec'' (besides) is introduced into *AR* only.

[33] After having been taken into custody and tried by the Inquisition in Jun 1633, Galileo Galilei (1564–1642) was, despite his public repudiation of the Copernican system, sentenced to incarceration at the pleasure of the tribunal as being ''vehemently suspected of heresy''. He proceeded via Siena to Florence, where he fulfilled the conditions of his sentence by living in strict seclusion for the rest of his days.

*a*ON INSTINCT IN CONNEXION WITH THE UNDERSTANDING

It is evident, that the Definition of a Genus or class*b* is an *adequate* definition only of the lowest *species* of that Genus: for each higher species is distinguished from the lower by some additional character, while the General Definition includes only the characters common to *all* the Species. Consequently it *describes* the lowest only. Now I distinguish a Genus or *kind* of Powers under the name of Adaptive power,*c* and give as its generic definition—the Power of selecting, and adapting means to proximate ends; and as an instance of the lowest *species* of this genus,*d* I take the stomach of a Caterpillar.[35] I ask myself, under what words I can generalize the action of this Organ; and I see, that it selects and adapts the appropriate means (*i.e.* the assimilable part of the vegetable *congesta*) to the proximate end, *i.e.* the growth or reproduction of the Insect's Body. This we call VITAL POWER, or *vita propria*[36] of the Stomach;[37] and this being the *lowest* species, its definition is the same with the definition of the *kind*.

Well! from the Power of the Stomach,*e* I pass to the Power exerted by

---

immediate cause of their death. But he contended that this latter Spirit was the *Spirit* of Charcoal, which would have produced the same effect, had the young men been chanting psalms instead of incantations: and acquitted the Devil of all *direct* concern in the business. The Theological Faculty took the alarm: even Physicians pretended to be horror-stricken*f* at Hoffman's audacity. The Controversy and its appendages embittered several years of this great and good man's life.[34]

a AR (1825): p 238   *b* AR (1825): Class   *c* AR (1825): Power,
d AR (1825): Genus,   *e* AR (1825): Stomach   *f* AR (1825): horror-struck

[34] J. R. Partington *History of Chemistry* (1961) II 698 mentions briefly the accident at Jena in 1715 that led to Friedrich Hoffmann's (1660–1742) discoveries, published as *Gründliches Bedencken und physikalische Anmerckungen von dem tödlichen Dampf der Holtz-Kohlen* (Halle 1716). C cites Hoffmann *Opera, CM (CC)* III 374n, but his source for this information has not been found.

[35] C may well be working on from Kirby and Spence *Introduction to Entomology* I 63–4 on the butterfly: "At its first exclusion from the egg . . . it was a worm-like caterpillar . . . greedily devouring leaves with two jaws . . . Were you . . . by dissection to compare the internal conformation of the caterpillar with that of a butter-

fly, you would witness changes even more extraordinary. In the former you would find some thousands of muscles, which in the latter are replaced by others of a form and structure entirely different. Nearly the whole body of the caterpillar is occupied by a capacious stomach."

[36] "The proper life". For earlier formulations concerning "vital power" see *Friend (CC)* II (14 Sept 1808) 75–8, and C's note in a copy of *SM: SM (CC)* 19 n 1. See also *Friend (CC)* I 493–4, *TL* (1848) 26, 27, 42, and below, *Sp Aph B Xa* at n 49.

[37] For C's earlier interest in the stomach see e.g. his letter to RS 13 Jan 1804, *CL* II 1028–9; *CN* I 1826–7; and Beer *CPI* 255–7.

the whole animal. I trace it wandering from spot to spot, and plant to plant, till it finds the appropriate vegetable; and again on this chosen vegetable, I mark it seeking out and fixing on the part of the plant, bark, leaf, or petal, suited to its nourishment: or (should the animal have assumed *a*the butterfly form), to the deposition of its eggs, and the sustentation of the future Larva. Here I see a power of selecting and adapting means to proximate ends *according to circumstances:*[38] and this higher species of Adaptive Power we call INSTINCT.

Lastly, I reflect on the facts narrated and described in the preceding extracts from Hüber, and see a power of selecting and adapting the proper means to the proximate ends, according to *varying* circumstances. And what shall we call this yet higher species? We name the former, Instinct: we must call this INSTINCTIVE INTELLIGENCE.

Here then we have three Powers of the same kind;*b* Life, Instinct, and instinctive Intelligence: the essential characters that define the genus existing equally in all three. But in addition to these, I find one other character common to the highest and lowest: viz. that the purposes are all manifestly predetermined*c* by the peculiar organization of the Animals; and though it may not be possible to discover any such immediate dependency in all the Actions, yet the Actions being determined by the purposes, the *result* is equivalent: and both the Actions and the Purposes are all in a necessitated reference to the preservation and continuance of the particular Animal or of the Progeny. There is selection, but not *choice:* volition rather than Will.[39] The possible *knowledge* of a thing, or the desire to have that *thing* representable by a distinct correspondent *Thought*, does not, in the animal, suffice to render the thing an *object*, or the ground of a purpose. *d*I select and adapt the proper means to the separation of a stone from a rock, which I neither can, or desire to*e* make

---

a *AR* (1825): p 239 *b* *AR* (1825): kind,
c *AR* (1825): pre-determined *d* *AR* (1825): p 240 *e* *AR* (1825): to,

---

[38] See Green's almost identical formulation, above, n 31. "Adaptive" below is *OED*'s first example of the word.

[39] An important and long-standing distinction for C. See his note on "the generation of the Sense of Reality & Life out of us, from the Impersonation effected by a certain phantasm of double Touch . . . and thence my Hope of making out a radical distinction between this Volition & Free Will or Arbitrement, & the detection of the Sophistry of the Necessitarians as having

arisen from confounding the two . . .": *CN* I 1827 (1804). The association with his theory of double touch recurs in *Omniana* (1812) II 13–14 (reprinted in *BL* ch 12—*CC*—I 293), in an annotation on Wolfart, and in his 1819 conversation with Keats: see Beer *CPI* 81, 280; for a possible stimulus in Erasmus Darwin's comments on the "twofold use of the word 'volition' " see ibid 75–8; cf also ibid 85ff, 230, 242, and 256–7.

use of,[a] for food, shelter, or ornament: because, perhaps, I wish to measure the angles of its primary crystals, or, perhaps, for no better reason than the apparent *difficulty* of loosening the stone—stat pro ratione Voluntas[40]—and thus make a motive out of the absence of all motive, and a reason out of the arbitrary will to act without any reason.[41]

Now what is the conclusion from these premises? Evidently this: that if I suppose the Adaptive Power in its highest species,[b] or form of Instinctive Intelligence,[c] to co-exist with Reason, *Free* will, and Self-consciousness, it instantly becomes UNDERSTANDING: in other words, that Understanding differs indeed from the noblest form of Instinct, but not in itself or in its own essential properties, but in consequence of its coexistence with far higher Powers of a diverse kind in one and the same Subject. INSTINCT in a rational, responsible, and self-conscious Animal, is Understanding.[42]

Such I apprehend to have been the Professor's View and Exposition of Instinct—and in confirmation of its truth, I would merely request my Readers, from the numerous well-authenticated instances on record, to recall some one of the extraordinary actions of Dogs for the preservation of their Masters' lives,[43] and even for the avenging of their deaths. In these instances we have the third species of the Adaptive Power, in connexion with an apparently *moral* end—with an *end* in the proper sense of the word. *Here* the Adaptive[d] Power co-exists with a purpose apparently *voluntary*, and the action seems neither predetermined by the organization of the Animal, nor in any direct reference to his own preservation, or to the continuance of his race. It is united with an imposing semblance of Gratitude, Fidelity, and disinterested Love. We not only *value* the faithful Brute: we attribute *worth* to him. This, I admit, is a problem, of which I have no solution to offer. One of the wisest of un-

[a] *AR* (1825): of
[b] *AR* (1825): species
[c] *AR* (1825): Intelligence
[d] *AR* (1825): p 241 (tive)

[40] "The Will stands in the place of reason". Cf Juvenal *Satires* 6.223. C writes *stat* (stands) for Juvenal's *sit* (let it be). He often used the same tag: see e.g. BM MS Eg 2801 f 219[v] and, without a verb, *CN* IV 5241 f 30[v].

[41] The preceding sentence prompts a note in *AR* (1825) COPY G, perhaps in DC's hand: "But the motives here instanced do not seem to differ in genere [in kind] from those of the animal. Their motivity may spring from a common source with [?that]

of the motives assignable to the use. Huber." The last words are difficult to decipher: the reading is tentative.

[42] C refers back to this passage in a further notebook discussion of May 1825: see *CN* IV 5209 f 20 and n.

[43] Cf WW's poem *Fidelity*: *WPW* IV 80 (and n, p 417) and *Friend (CC)* I 156n. For some ancient parallels in Plutarch, Pliny, etc see R. H. A. Merlen *De Canibus: Dog and Hound in Antiquity* (1971) 82–3.

inspired men has not hesitated to declare the Dog a great mystery,[44] on account of this dawning of a *moral* nature unaccompanied by any the least evidence of *Reason,[a]* in whichever of the two senses we interpret the word—whether as the *practical* Reason, *i.e.* the power of proposing an *ultimate* end, the determinability of the Will by IDEAS; or as the *sciential* Reason, *i.e.* the faculty of concluding universal and necessary truths from particular and contingent appearances.[45] But in a question respecting the possession of Reason, the absence [b]of all[c] truth[d] is tantamount to a proof of the contrary. It is, however, by no means equally clear to me, that the Dog may not possess an *analogon* of WORDS, which I have elsewhere shown[46] to be the proper objects of the "Faculty, judging according to Sense."

But to return to my purpose: I intreat the Reader to reflect on any one fact of this kind, whether occurring in his own experience, or selected from the numerous anecdotes of the Dog preserved in the Writings of Zoologists. I will then confidently appeal to him, whether it is in his power not to consider the faculty [e]displayed in these actions as the same *in kind* with the Understanding, however inferior *in degree*. Or should he even in these instances prefer calling it *Instinct*, and this in *contra*-distinction from *Understanding*, I call on him to point out the boundary between the two, the chasm or partition-wall that divides or separates the one from the other. If he can, he will have done what none before him have been able to do, though many and eminent men have tried hard for it: and my recantation shall be among the first trophies of his success. If he cannot, I must infer that he is controlled by his dread of the *Consequences*, by an apprehension of some injury resulting to Religion or

[a] COPY A: *Reason*, in any other respect,
[b-c] COPY A: of
[d] *AR* (1825): proof
[e] *AR* (1825): p 242

[44] The author of this assertion has not been traced. Cf however *CN* IV 5443 (commenting on Hooker): "Love supposes Likeness.—in the very act of loving Men Dogs acquire a mysterious affinity to Man." For further reflections on dogs and reason, see *Friend (CC)* II 78n (I 112), 296–7. RS gives examples of intellectual processes in dogs in *Omniana* (1812) II 37–9.

[45] Cf above, *Sp Aph B VIIIb* n 5. "Determinability" is *OED*'s first example.

[46] See above, *Sp Aph B VIIIb*, between nn 56 and 57. A faint note, perhaps in C's hand, in COPY E at this point appears to read, "priests called χυνες [dogs] we see a harmony of moral[y] in the dog & of evil in the monkey". Cf C's mention of an order of hereditary priests called Κυνιδες ("Dog-descended"), *CN* IV 4856, with the editor's note suggesting that C might have connected them with the dog-headed Anubis, or Thoth, the Egyptian Hermes, god of wisdom, communication, introducer of writing, etc (cf *CL* I 260). Anubis was a familiar figure in contemporary mythology: standing in a priestly position, he dominated an illustration (by Blake after Fuseli) to Erasmus Darwin *The Botanic Garden* (1791) facing p 127.

Morality from this opinion; and I shall console myself with the hope, that in the sequel of this work he will find proofs of the directly*ª* contrary tendency. Not only is this view of the Understanding, as differing in *degree* from Instinct and *in kind* from Reason, innocent in its possible influences on the religious character, but it is an indispensable preliminary to the removal of the most formidable obstacles to an intelligent Belief of the *peculiar* Doctrines of the Gospel, of the *characteristic* Articles of the Christian Faith, with which the Advocates of the truth in Christ have to contend; the evil *heart* of Unbelief[47] alone excepted.[48]

*ᵇ*REFLECTIONS BY THE AUTHOR*ᶜ* INTRODUCTORY TO
APHORISM X*ᵈ*

The most *momentous* question a man can ask is, Have I a Saviour? And yet*ᵉ* as far as the individual Querist is concerned, it is premature and to no purpose, except another question has been previously put and answered,*ᶠ* (alas! too generally put after the wounded Conscience has already given the answer!) *viz.,ᵍ* Have I any need of a Saviour? For him who *needs* none,*ʰ* (O bitter irony of the evil Spirit, whose whispers[1] the proud Soul takes for its own thoughts, and knows not how the Tempter is scoffing the while!) there *is* none, as long as he feels no need. On the other hand, it is scarce possible to have answered this question in the affirmative, and not ask—first, *in what* the necessity consists? secondly, *whence* it proceeded? and, thirdly, how far the answer to this second question is or is not contained in the answer to the first? I intreat the intelligent Reader, who has taken me as his temporary guide on the straight,*ⁱ* but yet, from the number of cross roads, difficult way of religious Inquiry, to halt a moment, and consider the main points,*ʲ* that in this last division of our work have been already offered for his reflection. I have attempted then to fix the proper meaning of the words,*ᵏ* Nature

ª *AR* (1825): direct
ᵇ *AR* (1825): p 243
ᶜ *AR* (1825): EDITOR
ᵈ *AR* (1825): THE Xᵗʰ.
ᵉ *AR* (1825): yet,
ᶠ *AR* (1825): answered
ᵍ *AR* (1825): *viz.*
ʰ *AR* (1825): none
ⁱ *AR* (1825): strait,
ʲ *AR* (1825): points
ᵏ *AR* (1825): words

[47] Heb 3.12.

[48] *AR* (1825) COPY C has a note at this point: "Here a Title page should have been interposed, with an appropriate Title and Motto, and a fresh Chapter or Section have commenced."

[1] Cf the "wicked whisper" that inhibited the Ancient Mariner from praying, lines 244–7: *PW* (EHC) I 197.

and Spirit, the one being the *antithesis* to the other: so that the most general and *negative* definition of Nature is, Whatever is not Spirit; and *vice versâ* of Spirit, That which is not comprehended in Nature: or in the language of our *ᵃelder Divines, that which transcends Nature.² But Nature is the term in which we comprehend all things that are representable in the forms of Time and Space, and subjected to the Relations of Cause and Effect: and the cause of *ᵇthe existence of which, therefore,ᶜ is to be sought for perpetually in something Antecedent. The word itself expresses this in the strongest manner possible: Natura, that which is *about to be* born, that which is always *becoming.*³ It follows, therefore, that whatever originates its own acts, or in any sense contains in itself the cause of its own state, must be *spiritual*, and consequently *supernatural:*⁴ yet not on that account necessarily *miraculous*. And such must the responsible WILL in us be, if it be at all.*ᵈ

A prior step had been to remove all misconceptions from the subject; to show the reasonableness of a belief in the reality and real influence of a universal and divine Spirit; the compatibility and possible communion of such a Spirit with the Spiritual *ᵉin Principle;ᶠ⁵ and the analogy offered by the most undeniable truths of Natural Philosophy*.ᵍ

* It has in its consequences proved no trifling evil to the Christian World, that Aristotle's Definitions of Nature are all grounded on the petty and rather rhetorical than philosophical Antithesis of Nature to Art—a conception inadequate to the demands even of *his* Philosophy.⁶ Hence in the progress of his reasoning, he confounds the Natura *Naturata*

ᵃ *AR* (1825): p 244
ᵇ⁻ᶜ *AR* (1825): whose existence therefore
ᵈ *AR* (1825): all. (See p. 131—139).
ᵉ⁻ᶠ *AR* (1825): in Principle Individuals; ; Corr, COPY D: Principle in Individuals;
ᵍ *AR* (1825): Philosophy*. (See p. 67—74).

² Cf an annotation on W. M. L. De Wette *Theodor oder des Zweiflers Weihe*: "Are not the same Objections to prayer deducible from the Perfection of the Deity & the consequent immutability of his Decrees? And must not the answers that apply to Calvin, apply *here*?—Nay, Kant himself (the first who has done so since Duns Scotus and Occam) supplies the answer: viz. The Idea of God is *altogether* transcendent: what therefore we are to believe concerning him must be determined by the Conscience & the Moral Interest, under the *negative* condition ⟨only⟩ of not contradicting Reason'': *CM (CC)* II 183. For Kant see e.g. *Critik der reinen Vernunft* (2nd ed Riga 1787) 611–70. Cf also *BL* ch 12 *(CC)* I 237 and n.

³ *Natura* is the future participle feminine of the Latin *nasci*, "to be born". Cf Barfield *What Coleridge Thought* ch 2. See also *CL* IV 769 (Sept 1817): ". . . it is not of a dead machine that I speak; but I am endeavoring to trace the Genesis, the φύσις, the *Natura rerum*, the *Birth* of Things . . .".

⁴ Cf Aristotle's definition of the natural in n 6 below.

⁵ *AR* (1825) reads "in Principle Individuals;" the list of corrections "Principle in Individuals". The latter gives a better sense than the present emendation.

⁶ This contentious comment may well have been prompted by Tennemann's account of Aristotle's views on natural science: see Tennemann III 111–14 espe-

*a*These Views of the Spirit, and of the Will as Spiritual, form the ground-work of our Scheme. Among the numerous Corollaries or Appendents, the first that presented itself respects the question, Whether there is any faculty in man by which a knowledge*b* of spiritual truths, or of any truths not abstracted from Nature, is rendered possible? and an Answer is attempted in the Comment on Aphorism VIII.*c* And here I beg leave to remark, that in this Comment the only Novelty, and, if there be Merit, the only Merit is—that there being two very different Meanings, and two different Words, I have here and in former Works appropriated one meaning to one of the Words, and the other to the other—instead of using the words indifferently and by hap-hazard: a confusion, the ill effects of which in this instance are so great and of such frequent occurrence in the works of our ablest Philosophers and Divines, that I

(that is, the sum total of the Facts and Phaenomena of the Senses) with an hypothetical Natura *Naturans*,[7] a *Goddess* Nature, that has no better claim to a place in any sober system of Natural Philosophy than the Goddess *Multitudo;* yet to which Aristotle not rarely gives the name and attributes of the Supreme Being. The result was, that the Idea of God thus identified with this hypothetical *Nature* becomes itself but an *Hypothesis*, or at best but a precarious inference from incommensurate premisses*d* and on disputable Principles: while in other passages, God is confounded with (and *e*every where,*f* in Aristotle's *genuine* works, *included in*) the Universe: which most grievous error it is the great and characteristic Merit of Plato to have avoided and denounced.[8]

---

a *AR* (1825): p 245   *b* *AR* (1825): knowlege   *c* *AR* (1825): VIII*th*.
d *AR* (1825): premises   *e-f* *AR* (1825): everywhere,

---

cially. On p 112 he quotes *Physics* 2.1 (192*b*12), tr: "These things that exist by nature seem to have within themselves a cause of change, whether of local movement, or increase or decrease or of qualitative modification"; "a work of art", he continues, summarising Aristotle, "has its cause outside itself". There are, indeed, many similar comparisons, rather than definitions, in the continuing discussion in the original.

[7] See below, App I Excursus Note 10 "Coleridge on Natura Naturans and Natura Naturata".

[8] For a long critical discussion of Aristotle in Feb 1824, based probably on his reading of Tennemann, see *CN* IV 5133. On the present point C takes a different view from Tennemann, as might be expected from his frequent attacks, in his an-

notations, on Tennemann's sub-Kantian prejudices. Tennemann (III 113–14) actually objects to Aristotle's finding only a transcendental cause of change, in which he sees Plato's influence on a philosopher who was so concerned to eliminate the supernatural from natural philosophy; and he further objects to his error in finding evidence in the natural world not only of God's existence but even of his attributes. He cites *Physics* 2.7 (198*a–b*): "There are two natural causes of change (or movement), of which one is not physical; for it does not have the cause of movement within itself. Such would be anything that moves other things but is not itself moved." For a succinct discussion of the issues, see R. G. Collingwood *The Idea of Nature* (Oxford 1945) 44.

should select it before all others in proof of Hobbes's Maxim: that it is a short and downhill passage from errors in words to errors in things.[9] The difference[a] of the Reason from [b]the Understanding, and the imperfection and limited sphere of the latter, have been asserted by many both before and since Lord Bacon[10]*; but still the habit of using Reason and

* Take one passage among many from the posthumous Tracts (1660) of John Smith, not the least Star in that bright Constellation of Cambridge Men, the contemporaries of Jeremy Taylor. "While we reflect on our own idea of Reason, we know that our Souls are not it, but only partake of it; and that we have it κατὰ μέθεξιν and not κατ᾽ οὐσίην[c].[11] Neither can it be called a Faculty, but far rather a Light, which we enjoy, but the Source of which is not in ourselves, nor rightly by any individual to be denominated *mine*."[12] This *pure* intelligence he then proceeds to contrast with the *Discursive* Faculty, *i.e.* the Understanding.[13]

> [a] *AR* (1825): distinctness
> [b] *AR* (1825): p 246
> [c] *AR* (1825): no accents or breathings in Greek ; *AR* (1831): . . . ουσιήν

[9] From Hobbes *Examinatio et emendatio mathematicae hodiernae* (C's ed 1668) Dialogue II (var); tr *Opera philosophica* ed Molesworth IV 83: "Notice how easily men slip from improper use of words into errors about things themselves." C copied this into a notebook early in 1801, used it as a "text" in a letter to Josiah Wedgwood (Feb 1801), and made it a motto for Essay III in "Principles of Genial Criticism" (1814); it also appears in *BL* and *P Lects*: *CN* I 911 and n; *CL* II 691; *BL* (1907) II 228; *BL* ch 16 *(CC)* II 31 and n; *P Lects* Lect 3 (1949) 140–1; and *Op Max ms* B2 ("III") 42.

[10] For Bacon see above, *Sp Aph B VIIIa* nn 28–31.

[11] "By participation" and not "by substance". The form οὐσιήν (misaccented in 1831) reads οὐσίαν in Smith: see next note.

[12] "There is nothing whereby our own Souls are better known to us than by the Properties and Operations of *Reason:* but when we reflect upon our own *Idea* of *Pure* and *Perfect Reason*, we know that our own Souls are not it, but onely partake of it; and that it is of such a Nature that we cannot denominate any other thing of the same rank with our selves by; and yet we know certainly that it is, as finding from an inward sense of it within our selves that both we and other things else beside our selves partake of it, and that we have it κατά μέθεξιν and not κατ᾽ οὐσίαν· neither doe we or any *Finite* thing contain the source of it

within our selves: and because we have a distinct Notion of the *most Perfect Mind* and *Understanding*, we own our deficiency therein": John Smith *Select Discourses* (1660) 126–7. C's last sentence is a paraphrasing expansion from Smith: the concept of light does not occur in Smith at this point, but on p 62 he quotes Cicero in support of his contention that ". . . the best Philosophers have alwaies taught us to inquire for God within our selves . . ." and ". . . in the language of the Platonists" glosses St John's "He is that *true light which enlightens every man*" as ". . . the *Eternal Word is the light of Souls*". Cf also *CN* II 2164, in which in 1804 C quoted from p 2 of Smith: ". . . as the Eye cannot behold the Sun . . . unless it be *Sun-like* . . . so neither can the Soul of man behold God . . . unless it be *Godlike* . . .". For C's annotations on Smith see *CM (CC)*. His notes on pp 459 and 463 of C. A. Tulk's copy are dated 6 and 8 Mar 1824: *CM (CC)* I 795n, C *17th C* 365–6. C had perhaps turned back to Smith at this time for help with the problem of evil, which he was now about to embark upon. Cf also *Sp Aph B VII* n 26, above.

[13] "And therefore when we find that we cannot attain to *Science* but by a *Discursive* deduction of one thing from another . . . or that our knowledge is *Chronical* and *successive*, and cannot grasp all things at once, but works by intervals, and runs out into *Division* and *Multiplicity*; we know all

Understanding as synonymes, acted as a disturbing force. Some it led into mysticism, others it set on explaining away a clear difference *in kind* into a mere superiority in degree: and it partially eclipsed the truth for all.

In close connexion with this, and therefore forming the Comment on the Aphorism next following, is the Subject of the legitimate exercise of the Understanding and its limitation to Objects of Sense; with the errors both of unbelief and of misbelief, which[a] result from its extension beyond the sphere of possible Experience. Wherever the forms of Reasoning appropriate only to the *natural* world are applied to *spiritual* realities, it may be truly said, that the more strictly logical the Reasoning is in all its *parts*, the more irrational it is as a *whole*.

The reader[b] thus armed and prepared, I now venture [c]to present the so called mysteries of Faith, *i.e.* the peculiar tenets and especial Constituents of Christianity, or Religion in spirit and in truth. In right order I must have commenced with the Articles of the Trinity and the Apostacy, including the question respecting the Origin of Evil, and the Incarnation of the WORD. And could I have followed this order, some difficulties that now press on me would have been obviated. But (as has already been explained) the limits of the present Volume rendered it alike impracticable and inexpedient; for the necessity of my argument would have called forth certain hard though most true sayings, respecting the hollowness and tricksy sophistry of the so called "Natural Theology," "Religion of Nature," "Light of Nature," &c.,[d14] which a brief exposition could not save from innocent misconceptions, much less protect against plausible misinterpretation. And yet both Reason and Experience have convinced me, that in the greater number of our ALOGI,[15] who

[a] *AR* (1825): that
[b] *AR* (1825): Reader
[c] *AR* (1825): p 247
[d] *AR* (1825): &c.

this is from want of Reason and Understanding, and that *a Pure and Simple Mind and Intellect* is free from all these restraints and imperfections, and therefore can be no less then *Infinite*": Smith *Select Discourses* 127. Smith seems to regard the *terms* reason and understanding as of the same order; his subsequent statement, "... could we multiply Understandings into never so vast a number, yet should we be again collecting and knitting them up together in some Universal one" (127–8), is closer to, if not identical with, C's distinction. For

the "discursive" see above, *Sp Aph B VIIIb* n 10.

[14] Although C is concerned with these as terms, it may be noted that each figured in the title of a prominent book known to him, viz: Paley *Natural Theology* (1802) (*CL* I 954, etc); William Wollaston *The Religion of Nature Delineated* (1722) (*Friend— CC—*I 152); and Abraham Tucker *The Light of Nature Pursued* (1768–78), which Hazlitt earlier abridged in consultation with C: *CL* II 949 and n.

[15] "Wordless", or "without the

feed on the husks of Christianity,[16] the disbelief of the Trinity, the Divinity of Christ included, has its origin and support in the assumed self-evidence of this Natural Theology, and in their ignorance of the insurmountable difficulties which (on the same mode of reasoning) press upon the fundamental articles of their own Remnant of a Creed. But arguments, which would prove the falsehood of a known truth, must themselves be false, and can prove the falsehood of no other position in eodem genere.[17]

This *hint* I have thrown out as a *Spark* that may *a*perhaps fall where it will kindle. The Reader desirous of more is again referred to the Work already announced.[18] And worthily might the wisest of men make inquisition into the three momentous points here spoken of, for the purposes of speculative Insight, and for the formation of enlarged and systematic views of the destination of Man, and the dispensation of God. But the *practical* Inquirer (I speak not of those who inquire for the gratification of Curiosity, and still less of those who labor*b* as students only to shine as disputants; but of one, who seeks the truth, because he feels the want of it,)*c* the practical Inquirer, I say, hath already placed his foot on the rock, if he have satisfied himself that whoever needs not a Redeemer is more than human. Remove for him the difficulties and objections, that oppose or perplex his belief of a crucified Saviour; convince

---

a *AR* (1825): p 248   *b* *AR* (1825): labour   *c* *AR* (1825): it),

---

Logos'', or ''unreasonable''. The name was punningly given to a second-century sect who denied the divinity of the Holy Ghost and of the Logos, or Word of God, and were thus forerunners of Socinianism. In a notebook entry of Feb 1805 C wrote ''no ⟨*true*⟩ energies can be attributed to an Ον αλογον; the moment we conceive the divine energy, that moment we co-conceive the Λογος'': *CN* II 2446 f 21. He used the term ''Logos alogos (i.e. logos illogicus)'' in a letter of 12 Sept 1814, and the Greek form in another of 7 Oct 1815 to describe the last section of his Opus Maximum, which would deal with ''. . . modern Unitarianism, it's causes & effects'' (*CL* III 533, IV 590). See also *SM (CC)* 99–100 and n, *CM (CC)* III 141. In a more general sense he referred to ''the Alogist or Metapothecary'' and to ''our Alogology or anti-philosophical Philosophy'', calling persons who failed to interpret mythology correctly

''Alogi Amythi (. . . i.e. neither Symbol nor Sense)'': *CN* IV 4692 f 20, 4767, 4794 f 35*v*. Related words are given in *OED*: e.g. ''alogy'' to mean an absurdity or irrationality, citing Thomas Browne *Pseudo-doxia Epidemica* etc (1658) II 454: ''The Alogie of this opinion consisteth in the illation'' (cf also p 145). In George Walker's satire on Godwinianism, *The Vagabond* (1799), which includes the setting up of an ideal state in America reminiscent of C's Pantisocracy, a revolutionary character is called Dr Alogos. See also *Sp Aph B XIX* at n 59 below, and, for discussions of ''Logos'', App I Excursus Notes 1 and 4, below.

[16] For the husk image cf *C&S (CC)* 144. It may also here carry an echo of the husks that the Prodigal Son felt an urge to eat: Luke 15.16.

[17] ''In the same kind''.

[18] See above, introduction to *Sp Aph B*, n 4.

him of the reality of Sin, which is impossible without a knowledge of its true nature and inevitable Consequences; and then satisfy him as to the *fact* historically, and as to the truth spiritually, of a redemption therefrom by Christ; do this for him, and there is little fear that he will permit either logical quirks or metaphysical puzzles to contravene the plain dictate of his Common Sense, that the Sinless One that redeemed Mankind from Sin, must have been more than Man; and that He who brought Light and Immortality into the World, could not in his own nature have been an inheritor of Death and Darkness. It is morally impossible, that a man with these convictions should suffer the Objection of Incomprehensibility (and *ᵃ*this on a subject of *Faith*) to overbalance the manifest absurdity and contradiction[19] in the notion of a Mediator between God and the Human Race, at the same infinite distance from God as the Race for whom he mediates.[20]

The Origin of Evil, meanwhile, is a question interesting only to the Metaphysician, and in a *system* of moral and religious Philosophy.[21] The Man of sober mind, who seeks for truths that possess a moral and practical interest, is content to be *certain*, first, that Evil must have had a beginning, since otherwise it must either be God, or a co-eternal and co-equal Rival of God; both impious notions, and the latter foolish to boot. 2dly, That it could not originate in God; for if so, it would be at once Evil and not Evil, or God would be at once God (that is, infinite Goodness) and not God—both alike impossible positions. Instead therefore of troubling himself with this barren controversy, he more profitably turns his inquiries to *that* Evil which most concerns himself, and of which he *may* find the origin.

The entire Scheme of *necessary* Faith may be reduced to two heads,

<hr />

ᵃ AR (1825): p 249

<hr />

[19] See below, *Sp Aph B XIX* nn 102–5.
[20] Cf *CN* III 4005 ff 4ᵛ–5 and Barth 128–38 generally.
[21] C's sense of the problem of evil, sharpened by Priestley's necessitarian theories, led to a discussion of its origins in the first of his Lectures on Revealed Religion: see *Lects 1795 (CC)* 104–8 and nn. In 1798 he affirmed his belief in original sin to his brother, reserving his position on guilt, however: "Of GUILT I say nothing; but I believe most stedfastly in original Sin; that from our mothers' wombs our understandings are darkened; and even where our understandings are in the Light, that

our organization is depraved, & our volitions imperfect; and we sometimes see the good without *wishing* to attain it, and oftener *wish* it without the energy that wills & performs . . .": *CL* I 396. Subsequently he approached the problem in more psychological terms: *CN* I 1619, 1622; see also an annotation on Leibniz *Theodicee* (Hanover & Leipzig 1763) I ii 134, commenting on the "subordination of moral to physical Evill": *CM (CC)* III 505. For a long note on C's view of Satan, with references, see Barth 119n. He returns to the question below, *Sp Aph B XII* at n 4.

1. the Object and Occasion, and 2. the Fact*ᵃ* and Effect,*ᵇ* of our redemption by Christ: and to this view does the order of the following Comments correspond. I have begun with Original Sin, and proceeded in the following Aphorism to the doctrine of Redemption. The Comments on the remaining Aphorisms are all subsidiary to these, or written in the hope of making the minor tenets of general belief *ᶜ*be believed in a spirit worthy of these. They are, in short, intended to supply a febrifuge against aguish Scruples and Horrors, the hectic of the Soul! and "for servile and thrall-like fear to substitute that adoptive and chearful boldness, which our new alliance with God requires of us as Christians." (*Milton*).²² Not the Origin of Evil, not the *Chronology* of Sin, or the chronicles of the original Sinner; but Sin originant,²³ underived from without, and no passive link in the adamantine chain of Effects,²⁴ each of which is in its turn an *instrument* of Causation, but no one of them a Cause! not with Sin *inflicted*, which would be a Calamity! not with Sin (*i.e.* an evil tendency) *implanted*, for which let the Planter be responsible! But I begin with *Original* Sin. And for this purpose I have selected the Aphorism from the ablest and most formidable Antagonist of this Doctrine, Bishop Jeremy Taylor, and from the most eloquent work of this most eloquent of Divines.²⁵ Had I said, of Men, Cicero*ᵈ* would forgive me, and Demosthenes nod assent*!

* We have the assurance of Bishop Horsley, that the Church of England does not demand the literal Understanding of the Document contained in the second (from verse 8) and third Chapters of Genesis as a point of faith, or regard a different interpretation as affecting the orthodoxy of the interpreter:²⁶ Divines of the most unimpeachable orthodoxy,

ᵃ *AR* (1825): fact
ᵇ *AR* (1825): effect,
ᶜ *AR* (1825): p 250
ᵈ *AR* (1825): the Soul of Cicero

²² ". . . hence to all the Duties of evangelical Grace, instead of the adoptive and chearful boldness which our new Alliance with *God* requires, came servile, and thrall-like fear . . .": *Of Reformation in England* (1641): *A Complete Collection of the Historical, Political, and Miscellaneous Works* (2 vols 1738) I 1–2.
²³ See *Sp Aph B Xb* n 9 below.
²⁴ A favourite image with C: cf above, *Refl Mor* n 14.
²⁵ For C's views of Taylor see also *Friend (CC)* I 434, *TT* 29–30 Aug 1827 and 4 Jun 1830 *(CC)* I 91–2, 154–6 (1836 vns II 70, 104–5), *CM (CC)* I 269 and n, the annotations on Taylor in *CM (CC)* v, and

other comments collected in *C 17th C* 258–69.
²⁶ Gen 2.8–3 (end) deals with the creation of Adam and Eve and their fall. C seems to have in mind the sixteenth sermon in Samuel Horsley *Sermons* (2 vols Dundee 1812) II 32–49, which deals with possible interpretations of the serpent in Genesis as they might be expounded to a previously uninstructed heathen. In his Biblical criticism, however, Horsley accepts the Biblical account as a factual record and argues against allegorical interpretations of Genesis on the grounds that ". . . if any part be allegorical . . . every thing in every part of the whole narrative must be allegorical".

and the most averse to the allegorizing of Scripture history in general, having from the earliest ages of the Christian Church adopted or permitted it in this instance. And indeed no unprejudiced man can pretend to doubt, that if in any other work of Eastern Origin he met with Trees of Life and of Knowledge; talking and conversable Snakes;

Inque rei signum *Serpentem serpere* jussum;[27]

he would want no other proofs that it was an Allegory he was reading, and intended to be understood as such. Nor, supposing him conversant with Oriental works of any thing like the same antiquity, could it surprise him to find events of true history in connexion with, or historical personages among the Actors and Interlocutors of, the Parable. In the temple-language of Egypt the Serpent was the Symbol of the Understanding[28] in its twofold function, namely, as the faculty of *means* to *proximate* or *medial* ends, analogous to the *instinct* of the more intelligent Animals, Ant, Bee, Beaver, &c.,[a] and opposed to the practical Reason, as the Determinant of the *ultimate* End; and again,[b] as the discursive and logical Faculty possessed individually by each Individual—the LOGOS ἐν ἑκάστῳ,[c29] in distinction

---

[a] *AR* (1825): &c.

[b] *AR* (1825) Corr: again, it typifies the Understanding

[c] *AR* (1825): ἑκαστῳ,

Of the serpent he remarks there: ". . . the use of such necessary figures in the narrative of a transaction, in which a created spirit bore so principal a part, can never be supposed to turn the whole substance of the narrative into allegory and fiction": *Biblical Criticism: on the First Fourteen Historical Books of the Old Testament: also on the First Nine Prophetical Books* (4 vols 1820) I 10, 19. C's claims for the orthodoxy of the views expressed here were singled out for attack by Keats's friend Benjamin Bailey in *An Exposition of the Parables of our Lord* (1828) 24–6.

[27] "And [with] the *Serpent* commanded *to creep* into the sign of the fact". (The play on *serpens* and *serpere*, which appears also in St Augustine *De civitate Dei* 14.11 and cannot easily be translated, involves the image of a snake insinuating itself.) The source of the Latin is untraced; it may be C's own. An important stimulus to his thinking here was provided by John Webster, who maintained that the "serpent" of Moses' account in Genesis was fitted for his allegorical role "by his effectual creeping into the interiour senses, as also by infecting Mens minds with venomous perswasions". This was alluded to by C in a notebook entry as "serpens from creeping into the interior mind, say Webster & others". C then went on to cite a parallel in Virgil *Aeneid* 3.89, quoted (var) as "Da, Pater, augurium, *animisque illa-*

bere nostris" ("Give, Father, an omen *and glide into our hearts*"), and explored the symbolic possibilities further, alluding to Egyptian hieroglyphics. Cf nn 40 and 41, below; see also Webster *The Displaying of Supposed Witchcraft* (1677) 145, 146, *CN* IV 4618, and n 33, below. C had also maintained that the trees of life and knowledge and talking serpent had "all the marks of Eastern Allegory, of allegory indee[d] in genere" in a note on Herder *Briefe*: *CM (CC)* II 1053.

[28] Cf William Stukeley's letter to Roger Gale 1726–7: "A snake proceeding from a circle, is the eternal procession of the Son, from the first cause. The Egyptians frequently added wings to it, then it was the trinity properly . . .". Quoted in William Hutchinson *The History and Antiquities of Cumberland* (2 vols 1794) I 241. For C's knowledge of Hutchinson and his apparent elaboration of this image into a principal element of his philosophy, with the serpent representing both the Son as creating Word and the understanding, see the rest of C's note here and cf Beer *CV* 67–71, 109–16, 175.

[29] Cf *Sp Aph A VI* n 6, *Sp Aph B VII* n 31 and *VIIIb* n 14 above. Here again "*Logos* in each" is the understanding, the logical faculty, which must be distinguished from the Divine Logos of John 1.1–14. In COPY C (*Sp Aph A VI* n 6, above) C's use of lower case for the first letter of

from the Nous, *i.e.* Intuitive Reason, the Source of Ideas and ABSOLUTE Truths, and the Principle of the Necessary and the Universal in our Affirmations and Conclusions.[30] Without or in contra-vention to the Reason (*i.e.* "the *spiritual* mind" of St. Paul,[31] and "*the Light that lighteth every* man" of St. John)[32] this Understanding (φϱόνημα σαϱϰός,*a* or carnal mind)[33] becomes the *sophistic* Principle, the wily Tempter to Evil by counterfeit Good; the Pander and Advocate of the Passions and Appetites; ever in league with, and always first applying to, the *Desire*, as the inferior nature in Man, the *Woman*[34] in our

a AR (1825) omits Greek accents ; AR (1831): . . . σαϱϰὸς,

λόγος seems to make his point clearer; cf *Sp Aph B VIIIb* n 14, above. His practice is not totally consistent, however. See also below, App I Excursus Note 4. For the "discursive and logical faculty" see above, *Sp Aph B VIIIb* n 10.

[30] The "Nous" is the "Intuitive Reason" that transmits to each individual understanding the "light that lighteth every man", the light given by the Divine Logos. See below, App I Excursus Note 4.

[31] See Rom 8.5–7: "For they that are after the flesh do mind the things of the flesh; but they that are after the Spirit the things of the Spirit. For to be carnally minded is death; but to be spiritually minded is life and peace. Because the carnal mind is enmity against God: for it is not subject to the law of God, neither indeed can be." A crucial passage for C's argument here.

[32] John 1.9. Cf above, *Sp Aph B VIIIb* n 9.

[33] The alignment of "φϱόνημα σαϱϰός, or carnal mind", with "the understanding" was prompted partly by his reading of Webster *Displaying of Supposed Witchcraft* in Oct 1819. Webster (138) related φϱόνημα σαϱϰός to private interpretations of Scripture before going on to justify symbolic interpretations in certain cases where the literal source is absurd—as in the case of the serpent in Genesis (see n 27, above). C runs the two points together, making the serpent itself a symbol of the "carnal mind" and seeing in this an answer to Unitarian interpretations of the phrase: *CN* IV 4618 and letter of Nov 1819, *CL* VI 1049 50. Its relationship to the understanding and the serpent in Genesis is explored also in two annotations on Böhme: *CM (CC)* I 682–3, 684–5. A straightforward link with the understanding alone is more frequently made: see e.g. *LR* III 242 and IV 28–9, *CN* IV 4924, and an extract from the Opus Maximum mss quoted above, Editor's In-

troduction, p lxxxii. C's thought here was stimulated also by Leighton, who commented on the use of φϱόνημα in this phrase: ". . . the word signifies, indeed, an act of the mind, rather than either the faculty itself, or the habit of prudence in it, so as it discovers what is the frame of both those". C disagreed: "φϱονημα σαϱϰος is 'the flesh' in the act or habitude of minding—but those acts, taken collectively, are the faculty—the understanding": annotation on Leighton COPY B III 121: *CM (CC)* III. See also COPY C I 95–100: *CM (CC)* III. For the relationship with the "faculty judging according to sense" see above, *Sp Aph B VIIIa* n 32. The Greek phrase is quoted, with alternative interpretations, in Article IX, "Of Original or Birth-sin": "Articles of Religion", *BCP*.

[34] C's ideas here suggest an allegorical reading of Milton's lines concerning Adam and Eve in *PL* IV 297–9:

> For contemplation hee and valour
> form'd,
> For softness shee and sweet attractive
> Grace,
> Hee for God only, shee for God in
> him . . .

Eve's "sweet attractive Grace" corresponds to the pleasurable desire that must yet be informed by the enlightened will if it is not to be simply the "will of the flesh"; Adam's powers of "contemplation" and "valour", similarly, if truly enlightened, fit him for "Absolute rule" (line 301), transmitting the divine will, but in the fallen state become, as here, panders to the will of the flesh. C's discussion, below, of the idea that human beings were originally androgynous helps establish that his interpretation is not based primarily on gender, but applies to each human being, male or female.

Humanity; and through the DESIRE prevailing on the WILL (the *Man*hood, *Vir*tus) against the command of the Universal Reason, and against the Light of Reason in the WILL itself. (N.B. This essential inherence of an intelligential Principle (φῶς νοεϱόν*ᵃ*)³⁵ in the Will (ἀϱχὴ θελητική,)*ᵇ*³⁶ or rather the Will itself thus considered, the Greeks expressed by an appropriate word (βουλή.)*ᶜ*³⁷ This, but little differing from Origen's*ᵈ* interpretation or hypothesis,³⁸ is supported and confirmed by the very old Tradition of the *Homo androgynus*,³⁹ *i.e.* that the original Man, the Individual first created, was bi-sexual: a chimaera, of which and of many other mythological traditions the most probable explanation is, that they were originally symbolical *Glyphs* or Sculptures, and afterwards translated into *words*,⁴⁰ yet *literally*, *i.e.* into the common names of the several Figures and Images com-

ᵃ AR (1825, 1831): νοεϱὸν
ᵇ AR (1825): θελητικὴ), ; AR (1831): θελητικὴ,)
ᶜ AR (1825): βουλὴ).
ᵈ AR (1825): Origin's ; COPY C: Origen's

³⁵ "Intellectual light".
³⁶ "Willing principle"—i.e. a principle that wills—or "origination by the will".
³⁷ Often translated "counsel" or "plan". See the distinction between θέλημα and βουλή as applied to the will of God, *Sp Aph B XIX* n 82, below, and App I Excursus Note 18; and cf the distinction between *arbitrium* and *voluntas* in the discussion of the human will, *Sp Aph B Xb* at nn 20–1, above.
³⁸ Cf Origen *De principiis* 4.3.1: "What man of sense will suppose that there was a 'first', 'second', and 'third day', both evening and morning, without sun, moon, and stars? and the alleged 'first day' without even a heaven? And who is so silly as to suppose that God literally 'planted a garden', like a human farmer, in Eden towards the sun-rising, and that He made in it a visible and perceptible Tree of Life, so that one tasting of its fruit by means of his bodily teeth would receive (eternal) life? Or again, that a man could receive (the knowledge) of 'good and evil' from having chewed the fruit of the Tree so called? And if God is said to walk in the garden in the evening, and Adam to hide under the tree, no one, I imagine, will doubt that such words are meant to reveal certain mysteries metaphorically, through a seeming history, not one which happened in concrete fact." Origen believed that God had originally created a number of intellectual essences which were equal in goodness and like in status, but also capable of change and gifted with freedom of choice. Some persevered in virtue, others gave way to ". . . idleness, and weariness of the labour of

preserving goodness" or to ". . . satiety of the divine love and contemplation", so falling and becoming enmeshed in matter: *De principiis* 2.9.2, 2.8.3. In man also the power of self-determination dominates, so that the bodily appetites provide the occasion for sinful impulse, being in themselves morally neutral: ibid 1.6.2, 3. See N. P. Williams *The Ideas of the Fall and of Original Sin* (1927) 210–19 for these passages, with further references, and discussion. Origen's ideas fall between C's assertion that sin consists in contravention of the "spiritual mind" or "light that lighteth every man" and the doctrines cited from St Paul concerning the ". . . wisdom of the flesh". Cf "The fact is therefore clear that, just as in regard to things that are good the mere human will is by itself incapable of completing the good act,—for that is in all cases brought to perfection by divine help . . .": *De principiis* 3.2.2, tr G. W. Butterworth *Origen on First Principles* (1936) 214. See also pp 230ff, ch 4, and Origen's belief in a will "intermediate between the flesh and the spirit, above and beyond the will which is said to belong to the flesh or to the spirit": 3.4.2.
³⁹ This corresponds to the idea attributed to Aristophanes in Plato *Symposium* 189–93. Rees *Cyclopaedia* II, s.v. "androgynous", records the tradition that Adam was androgynous: "It is generally said, that this was a fiction of the Rabbins; but there is reason to believe that it was of more early origin." He cites Eusebius *Praeparatio evangelica* 1.10.
⁴⁰ Cf C's remark on Gen 2 in a note on Böhme *Works*: "I have sometimes conjec-

posing the Symbol, while the symbolic *meaning* was left to be decyphered as before, and sacred to the Initiate.[41] As to the abstruseness and subtlety of the Conceptions, this is so far from being an objection to this oldest *Gloss* on this venerable Relic of Semitic, not impossibly ante-diluvian, Philosophy, that to those who have carried their researches farthest back into Greek, Egyptian, Persian, and Indian Antiquity, it will seem a strong confirmation.[42] Or if I chose to address the Sceptic in the language of the Day, I might remind him, that as Alchemy went before Chemistry, and Astrology before Astronomy, so in all countries of civilized Man have Metaphysics outrun Common Sense.[43] Fortunately for us that they have so! For from all we know of the *un*metaphysical tribes of New Holland[44] and elsewhere, a Common Sense not preceded by Metaphysics is no very enviable Concern. O be not cheated, my youthful Reader! by this shallow prate! The creed of true Common Sense is composed of the *Results* of Scientific Meditation, Observation, and Experiment, as far as they are *generally* intelligible. It differs therefore in different countries and in every different age of the same country.[a] The Common Sense of a People is the movable[b] *index* of its average judgment and information. Without Metaphysics Science could have had no language, and Common Sense no materials.[45]

But to return to my subject. It cannot be impugned, that the Mosaic Narrative thus interpreted gives a just and faithful exposition of the birth and parentage and successive moments of *phaenomenal* Sin (peccatum[c] *phaenomenon*: *Crimen* primarium et com-

---

[a] *AR* (1825): Country.

[b] *AR* (1825): moveable

[c] *AR* (1825): Peccatum

---

tured that the Chapter was translated into *words* from stone Carvings, or proper Hieroglyphs.'' Nothing more was meant by the rib, he suggested (against Böhme's attempt to find a universal truth in the mythus), than ''that God made the Woman in the same mould as he had made Man'': *CM (CC)* I 684. For his general theory here see *CN* III 4325 and n. The idea of Adam and Eve as originally hieroglyphs may have been prompted partly by Erasmus Darwin *The Botanic Garden* (1791) i, Additional Notes, p 55 (citing Warburton).

[41] C enlarges on this point in his next note on Böhme: ''It is painful to observe, how this mighty but undisciplined Spirit perplexes his own intuitions by confusion of the Letter with the Life, and of the Symbolic Life with the Letter! The II Chapter of Genesis appears to be little more than a translation of Sculptured Figures into Words—the serpent being the Egyptian Symbol of intellective Invention, idolized by the Descendants of Ham, but the same, taken separately, as the φρονημα σαρκος, the wisdom of the Flesh, in St Paul. Distinctive & discursive Knowlege is was & by the fitness of the symbol remains, represented in the ramifications of a Tree, full of fruit but with the Serpent (which has here a double meaning, as being significant of poison or evil secretly working) wreathing the Boughs—Thus, the Mythos speaks to the Catechumen & to the Adept.—To the Catechumen it states the simple Fact, viz. that Man fell & falls thro' the separation and insubordination of the Fancy, the Appetence, & the discursive Intellect from the Faith or practical Reason—To the Adept it conveys the great mystery, that the origin of moral Evil is in the *Timeless*, εν τω αχρονω—in a spirit, not comprehended within the consciousness,—tho' revealed in the conscience of Man'': *CM (CC)* I 684–5. For the last point see *Sp Aph B II* n 33 above.

[42] For C's earlier interest in these antiquities see e.g. Beer *CV* Index, under each country.

[43] Cf *C&S (CC)* 167, referring back to this passage. For more on ''common sense'' see *CN* I 1700 and II 3549, *BL* ch 4 *(CC)* I 86–7n, and *Friend (CC)* I 213.

[44] A former name of Australia.

[45] Cf E. Abbott and L. Campbell *Life and Letters of Benjamin Jowett* (2 vols 1897) I 262–3: ''He often quoted the saying of Coleridge, 'The only common sense worth having is that which is based on metaphysics'; and he upheld the converse proposition, 'Metaphysics should be grounded in common sense.' ''

mune),[46] that is, of Sin as it reveals itself *in time*, and is an immediate Object of Consciousness. And in this sense most truly does the Apostle assert, that in Adam we all fell.[47] The first human Sinner is the adequate Representative of all his Successors. And with no less truth may it be said, that it is the same Adam that falls in every man, and from the same reluctance to abandon the too dear and undivorceable Eve: and the same EVE tempted by the same serpentine and perverted Understanding which, framed originally to be the Interpreter of the Reason and the ministering Angel of the Spirit, is henceforth sentenced and bound over to the service of the Animal Nature, its needs and its cravings, dependent on the Senses for all its Materials, with the World of Sense for its appointed Sphere: "Upon thy belly shalt thou go, and dust shalt thou eat all the days of thy life."[48] I have shown elsewhere, that as the Instinct of the mere intelligence differs in degree not in kind, and circumstantially not essentially from the Vis Vitae, or vital[a] Power in the assimilative and digestive functions of the stomach[b] and other organs of Nutrition, even[c] so the Understanding, in itself and distinct from the Reason and Conscience, differs in degree only from the Instinct in the Animal.[49] It is still but "a beast of the field," though "more subtle than any beast of the field," and therefore in its corruption and perversion "cursed above any"[50]—a pregnant Word! of which, if the Reader wants an exposition or paraphrase, he may find one more than two thousand years old among the fragments of the Poet Menander.[51] (See Cumberland's Observer, No. CL. vol. iii. p. 289, 290.)[52] This is the *Under-*

---

[a] *AR* (1825): Vital　　[b] *AR* (1825): Stomach
[c] *AR* (1825): that even ; COPY C: even

---

[46] "Sin as *phenomenon*: *Offence* primary and common". C is here drawing a distinction between sins as they are perceived in their effects and in the world and the original offence behind all sins, which is regarded as being in common between all mankind and committed out of the time-process altogether. The narrative in the Genesis story is seen as typifying the first, while its mythical elements hint at the nature of the second. His account of sin and evil has points of resemblance with that of Kant, who in *Die Religion innerhalb der Grenzen der blossen Vernunft* (Königsberg 1794) maintains that the problem rests upon the dualism between the phenomenal and noumenal self. Cf *Sp Aph B II* n 40, *XVIII* n 35, and App I Excursus Note 17. "Undivorceable" above is *OED*'s first example.

[47] 1 Cor 15.21–2: "For since by man came death, by man came also the resurrection of the dead. For as in Adam all die, even so in Christ shall all be made alive." Cf Rom 6.12–21.

[48] Gen 3.14.

[49] See above, *Sp Aph B IX* nn 34–6; also C's (probably late) note in a copy of *SM*: *SM (CC)* 60–1 n 2.

[50] Gen 3.1, 14.

[51] See next note.

[52] Richard Cumberland's essay on the fragments of Menander, originally No CXXXVIII of *The Observer*, contains at the outset two pieces expressing disgust at the human condition. C has in mind the first:

Suppose some God should say,—
　"Die when thou wilt,
Mortal, expect another life on earth;
And for that life make choice of all
　creation
What thou wilt be; dog, sheep, goat,
　man, or horse;
For live again thou must; it is thy fate:
Chuse only in what form; there thou art
　free—"
So help me, Crato, I would fairly
　answer—
Let me be all things, any thing but
　man!—
He only of all creatures feels affliction:
The generous horse is valued for his
　worth,
And dog by merit is preferr'd to dog;
The warrior cock is pamper'd for his
　courage,
And awes the baser brood—But what is
　man?
Truth, virtue, valour, how do they avail
　him?
Of this world's good the first and
　greatest share

standing which in its *"every thought"*[a] is to be brought *"under obedience to Faith;"*[53] which it can scarcely fail to be, if only it be first subjected to the Reason, of which spiritual Faith is even the Blossoming and the fructifying process. For it is indifferent whether I say that Faith is the interpenetration of the Reason and the Will, or that it is at once the Assurance and the Commencement of the approaching Union between the Reason and the *Intelligible Realities*, the *Living* and *Substantial* Truths, that are even in this life its most proper Objects.

I have thus put the reader in possession of my own opinions respecting the Narrative in Gen. ii. and iii. Ἔστιν οὖν δή, ὡς ἔμοιγε δοκεῖ, ἱερὸς μῦθος, ἀληθέστατον καὶ ἀρχαιότατον φιλοσόφημα, εὐσεβέσι μὲν σέβασμα, συνετοῖς τε φωνᾶν· ἐς δὲ τὸ πᾶν ἑρμηνέως[b] χατίζει.[54] Or I might ask with Augustine, Why not both?[55] Why not at once Symbol and History? or rather how should it be otherwise? Must not of necessity the FIRST MAN be a SYMBOL of Mankind, in the fullest force of the word, Symbol, rightly defined—viz. *A Symbol is a sign included in the Idea, which it represents:*[56] ex. gr. an actual *part* chosen to represent the *whole*, as a lip with a chin prominent is a Symbol of Man; or a *lower* form or species[c] of a higher in the same *kind:*[57] [d]thus Magnetism is the Symbol of Vegetation, and of the

[a] AR (1825): *Thought"*

[b] AR (1825): ... δή ... ἔμοιγε ... ἱερος ... εὐσέβεσι ... συνετοίς ... ; AR (1831): ... δή ... ἔμοιγε ... ἱερος ... εὐσέβεσι ... συνετοίς ... ἑρμήνεως

[c] AR (1825) Corr: species used as the representative ; COPY C: species, as the Representative ; COPY D: species as the representative

[d-e] AR (1825): by which definition

Is flattery's prize; the informer takes the next,
And barefaced knavery garbles what is left.
I'd rather be an ass than what I am,
And see these villains lord it o'er their betters.

C's pagination corresponds to that of the 1817 ed in A. Chalmers *The British Essayists: with Prefaces, Historical and Biographical* vol XL, in which the fragments mentioned above appear on pp 289–90, and the essay is numbered CL.

[53] 2 Cor 10.5: ". . . and bringing into captivity every thought to the obedience of Christ".

[54] "It is then indeed, as it seems to me at least, a sacred myth, a philosopheme of the highest truth and age, an object of reverence to the devout, and speaking to the wise, but for the crowd it needs an interpreter." At the end, from συνετοῖς, C is quoting, slightly adapted, a favourite tag, Pindar *Olympian Ode* 2.85–5: φωνᾶντα συνετοῖσιν· ἐς δὲ τὸ πᾶν ἑρμανέων χατίζει; tr Sir John Sandys (LCL 1915): "[I have many an arrow that is] vocal to the wise: but for the crowd they need interpreters." Cf *Lects* (1795) 310; *CN* III 4244; *LS (CC)*

126; and a letter to William Worship in 1818: *CL* IV 942. Out of five errors in accentuation in 1825 only one was corrected in 1831, another in 1839.

[55] See St Augustine *Confessions* 12.31: "So now, when one shall say; Moses meant as I do: and another; Nay the very same that I do: I suppose that with more reverence I may say: Why meant he not as you both mean, if you both mean truly?": tr William Watts (1631; LCL). This is a common theme in bk 12: see also §§ 18 and 25.

[56] Cf the characterisation of the symbol in *SM*: "It always partakes of the Reality which it renders intelligible; and while it enunciates the whole, abides itself as a living part in that Unity, of which it is the representative": *SM (CC)* 30. Cf *BL* ch 9 *(CC)* I 156 and n 1; also *CN* IV 4711.

[57] See Beer *CPI* 81 8, 242–3, 247–8, 256–7. According to C's theory of magnetism and "double touch" as reconstructed there, "single touch", magnetism in its pure form, would be related to the domination of form and growth in vegetation and in the reproductive instinct of animals. Cf also notes on J. C. Heinroth *Lehrbuch der Anthropologie*: *CM (CC)* II 1008. For a long exposition of C's theories in their later

vegetative and reproductive Power in Animals; the Instinct of the Ant-tribe or the Bee is a Symbol of the Human Understanding.[58] And this definition of the word is of great practical importance, inasmuch as[e] the Symbolical is hereby[a] distinguished *toto genere*[59] from the Allegoric and Metaphorical.[60] But, perhaps, parables, allegories, and allegorical or typical applications, are incompatible with *inspired* Scripture! The writings of St. Paul are sufficient proof of the contrary.[61] Yet I readily acknowledge, that allegorical *applications* are one thing, and allegorical *interpretation* another: and that where there is no ground for supposing such a sense to have entered into the intent and purpose of the sacred Penman, they are not to be commended. So far, indeed, am I from entertaining any predilection for them, or any favorable[b] opinion of the Rabbinical Commentators and Traditionists, from whom the fashion was derived, that in carrying it as far as our own Church has carried it, I follow her judgment and not my own.[62] But in the first place, I know but one other part of the Scriptures not universally held to be parabolical, which, not without the sanction of great authorities, I am disposed to regard as an Apologue or Parable, namely, the book[c] of Jonas; the reasons for believing the Jewish Nation collectively to be therein impersonated, seeming to me unanswerable.[63] (See the Appendix to the Statesman's Manual, Note II.)[64] Secondly, as to the[d] Chapters now in question—that such interpretation is at least tolerated by our church, I have the word of one of her most zealous[f] Champions. And lastly[g] it is my deliberate and conscientious conviction, that the proofs of such having been the inten-

---

[a] Added in 1831
[b] *AR* (1825): favourable
[c] *AR* (1825): Book
[d] Word added in 1831 and in COPY C
[f] *AR* (1825): Zealous
[g] *AR* (1825): lastly,

---

form, including discussion of ". . . the two streams of vegetation and animalization, the former characterized by the predominance of magnetism in its highest power, as reproduction, the other by electricity intensified—as irritability, in like manner", see *TL* (1848) 70–94. Cf also *CL* VI 597–9 and *C&S (CC)* 179 and n.

[58] *CN* IV 4984 f 87ᵛ, however, makes it clear that this use of "Symbol" is not to be taken further than the understanding. There C stresses the ". . . impassable chasm between the highest Orders of Animals and the Man. They are *Types* not Symbols, dim Prophecies not incipient Fulfilments." The rest of the note develops the implications of this, including the relationship between animal energies and the understanding.

[59] "Totally and in kind".

[60] Cf above, *Sp Aph B VII* n 39.

[61] C may have in mind a text such as Eph 5.30–2, cited earlier: *Int Aph XXII* at n 2, and *Refl Mor* at n 24; cf also Gal 4.24: "Which things are an allegory"; 1 Cor 10.11 (margin): ". . . these things happened to them for types".

[62] For a long note on C's attitude to mythical and allegorical interpretations of

the scriptures, with many references, see Barth 64n. See also *CN* III 4183, 4498, IV 4984.

[63] Cf C's note on Böhme *Works*: "The Book of Jonah is an Apologue—and Jonah a symbol of the Jewish Nation, and of its characteristic bigotry, spiritual pride, uncharitableness and rebellious disposition—": *CM (CC)* I 695.

[64] App B to *SM* is a comment on Matt 12.40: "For as Jonas was three days and three nights in the whale's belly; so shall the Son of man be three days and three nights in the heart of the earth", which C regarded as a later pious interpolation, taking as "an *additional* reason" the ". . . opinions and arguments of sundry doctors, rabbinical as well as christian, respecting the first and second chapter of Jonah": *SM (CC)* 57–9. Cf *CN* IV 4872 and n (1822). For the view that Jonah represented the Jewish nation collectively see James Hastings *Dictionary of the Bible* (1898–1902) article "Jonah", which adds that "Jonah", a "dove", was also the symbol of Ephraim, the northern kingdom of Israel. Cf Hos 7.11, 11.11.

^aAPHORISM X^{b1}

ON ORIGINAL SIN[2]

Is there any such Thing? That is not the question. For it is a fact^c acknowledged^d on all hands almost: and ^eeven those who will not confess it in words, confess it in their complaints. For my part I cannot but confess ^fthat *to be*, which I feel and groan under, and by which all the world is miserable.

^gAdam turned his back on the Sun, and dwelt in the Dark and the Shadow. He sinned, and brought evil ^hinto his *Supernatural* endowments, and lost the Sacrament and instrument of Immortality, the Tree of Life in the centre of the Garden.^{3*i} He then fell under the evils of a sickly Body, and a passionate and ignorant Soul. His Sin made him sickly, his Sickness made him peevish: his Sin left him ignorant, his Ignorance made him foolish and unreasonable. His sin left him to his *Nature:* and by Nature, whoever was to be born at all,^j was to be born a

---

tion of the inspired Writer or Compiler of the book of Genesis, lie on the face of the Narrative itself.[65]

  * Rom. v. 14. Query; who were they, who had *not* sinned after the similitude of Adam's transgression; and over whom notwithstanding, *death* reigned?[4]

^a *AR* (1825): p 251
^b *AR* (1825): JEREMY TAYLOR.
^c *AR* (1825): Fact
^d *AR* (1825): acknowleged
^e *AR* (1825): p 252
^f *AR* (1825): p 253
^g *AR* (1825): p 254
^h *AR* (1825): p 255
ⁱ Footnote added in 1831
^j *AR* (1825): all

[65] F. R. Tennant cites this view of C's but contends that the "face of the Narrative" does not suggest a symbolic intention: *Sources of the Doctrines of the Fall and Original Sin* (Cambridge 1903) 80–7.

[1] Adapted from Jeremy Taylor *Deus Justificatus* (1673) in Σύμβολον Θεολογικόν (1674) 869–70. For the original text see App A(m) below.

[2] For a long discussion of C's views of original sin see Barth 114–26.

[3] Taylor here reads: ". . . he sinned, and fell into God's displeasure and was made naked of all his supernatural endowments, and was ashamed and sentenced to death, and deprived of the means of long life, and of the Sacrament and instrument of Immortality, I mean the Tree of Life . . .": Σύμβολον Θεολογικόν 869. C's alterations enable him to avoid considering whether Adam was originally mortal or immortal.

[4] Rom 5.14: "Nevertheless death reigned from Adam to Moses, even over them that had not sinned after the similitude of Adam's transgression. . .". According to A. S. Peake *Commentary on the Bible* (1919) 822, the answer to C's query would be that until Moses promulgated the Ten Commandments sinners were not, like him, transgressing against *explicit* commands.

child, and to do before he could understand, and to be bred under laws to which he was always bound, but which could not always be exacted; and he was to choose when he could not reason, and had passions most strong when he had his understanding most weak; and the more need he had of a curb, the less strength he had to use it! And this being the case of all the world, what was *every* man's evil became *ᵃall* men's greater evil; and though alone it was very bad, yet when they came together it was made much worse. Like ships in a storm, every one alone hath enough to do to outride it; but when they meet, besides the evils of the Storm, they find the intolerable calamity of their mutual concussion; and every Ship that is ready to be oppressed with the tempest, is a worse Tempest to every Vessel against which it is violently dashed. So it is in Mankind. Every man hath evil enough of his own, and it is hard for a man to live up to the rule of his own Reason and Conscience.⁵ But when he hath Parents and Children, Friends and Enemies, Buyers and Sellers, Lawyers and Clients, a Family and a Neighbourhood—then it is that every man dashes against another, and one relation requires what another denies; and when one speaks another will contradict him; and that which is well spoken is sometimes innocently mistaken; and that upon a good cause produces an evil effect; and by these, and ten thousand other concurrent causes, man is made more than most miserable.

COMMENT

The first question we should put to ourselves, when we have toᵇ read a passage that perplexes us in a work of authority, is;ᶜ What does the Writer *mean* by all this? And the second question should be, What does he intend by all this? In the passage before us, Taylor's *meaning* is not quite clear.⁶ A Sin is an Evil which has its ground or origin in the Agent, and not in the ᵈcompulsion ofᵉ ᶠCircumstances. Circumstances are com-

ᵃ *AR* (1825): p 256
ᵇ Added in 1831
ᶜ *AR* (1825): is:
ᵈ⁻ᵉ Added in *AR* (1825) Corr, COPY C
ᶠ *AR* (1825): p 257

⁵ For the last twelve words Taylor reads ". . . to live soberly, temperately, and religiously".
⁶ In reading the same work C accused Taylor more roundly of Pelagianism: ". . . The truth is, J. T. was a Pelagian, believed that without Christ thousands, Jews & Heathens, lived wisely & holily, & went to

Heaven; but this he did not dare say out, probably not even to himself—and hence it is that he flounders backward & forward, now upping & now downing": annotation on *Deus Justificatus*: Σύμβολον Θεολογικόν 890: *CM (CC)* v. In annotations on his works C argued constantly with Taylor on original sin; see n 52, below.

pulsory from the absence of a power to resist or control them: and if this absence likewise be the effect of Circumstance (*i.e.* if it have been neither directly nor indirectly caused by the Agent himself) the Evil *derives* from the Circumstances; and therefore (in the Apostle's sense of the word, Sin, when he speaks of the exceeding sinfulness of Sin)[7] such *evil* is not *sin;* and the person who suffers it, or who is the compelled instrument of its infliction on others, may feel *regret,* but cannot feel *remorse.*[8] So likewise of the word origin, original, or originant.[9] The reader cannot too early be warned that it[a] is not applicable, and, without abuse of language, can never be applied, to a mere *link* in a chain of effects, where each, indeed, stands in the relation of a *cause* to those that follow, but is at the same time the *effect* of all that precede.[10] For in these cases a cause amounts to little more than an antecedent. At the utmost it means only a *conductor* of the causative influence: and the old axiom, Causa causae causa causati,[11] applies, with a never-ending regress to each several link, up the whole chain of nature. But this (as I have elsewhere shown at large) *is* Nature: and no *Natural* thing or act can be called originant, or be truly said to have an *origin*[12]* in any other.

* This sense of the word is implied even in its metaphorical or figurative use. Thus we may say of a *River* that it *originates* in such or such a *fountain;* but the water of a *Canal* is *derived* from such or such a River. The Power which we call Nature, may be thus defined: A Power subject to the Law of Continuity (*Lex Continui.*[13] *In Naturâ non datur Saltus.*[14]) which law the human understanding,[b] by a necessity arising out of its own con stitution, can *conceive* only under the form of Cause and Effect. That this *form* (or law) of Cause and Effect is (relatively to the World *without,* or to Things as they subsist indepen-

---

[a] COPY A: this word
[b] AR (1825): Understanding,

---

[7] Rom 7.13.

[8] See above, *Mor Aph XLVI* at n 1.

[9] *OED* gives a use of "originant" in 1647, but the remainder of its examples seem to derive from C's use here and at *Sp Aph B Xa* n 23, above. He meditated on the concept in Jul 1822: *CN* IV 4911; and see *HEHL ms* 113. Cf also *SM (CC)* 61: "The rational instinct . . . taken abstractedly and unbalanced, did *in itself* . . . and in its consequences . . . form the original temptation . . . and in all ages has continued to originate the same . . .", and a letter of 24 Jan 1814: ". . . original Sin—i.e. not ab Adamâ, but de *origine*—de fonte—or *originating* Sin in opposition to *derived* or *acquired*": *CL* VI 1032 (var).

[10] C is following his previous argument in *Sp Aph B Xa*, at n 23, above.

[11] "The cause of a cause is also the

cause of that which is caused". Found in Aquinas *Quaestiones disputatae de malo* 3.1.4 and elsewhere in the Schoolmen; used also by Hartley *Observations on Man* (1791 ed) II 423. A favourite point with C: see e.g. *CL* IV 549 (quoted above, Editor's Introduction at n 25) and *CM (CC)* II 299, with further references in the editor's footnote.

[12] In *CW* I 272 the editor compares *Hamlet* I iv 25–6: ". . . wherein they are not guilty, | Since nature cannot choose his origin . . .".

[13] See below, App I Excursus Note 11 "Coleridge on the Law of Continuity". C's ms for parts of this and the next sentence is transcribed below in App B(w).

[14] "In Nature there are no leaps". Discussed also in Excursus Note 11.

dently of our perceptions) only a form or mode of *thinking;*[15] that it is a law inherent in the Understanding itself (just as the symmetry of the miscellaneous objects seen by the kaleidoscope inheres in (*i.e.* results from) the mechanism of the kaleidoscope itself)[16]—this becomes evident as soon as we attempt to apply the pre-conception directly to any operation of Nature. For in this case we are forced to represent the cause as being at the same instant the effect, and vice versâ the effect as being the cause—a relation which we seek to express by the terms Action and Re-action; but for which the term Reciprocal Action or the law*[a]* of Reciprocity (*germanicè* Wechselwirkung)[17] would be both more accurate and more expressive.

These are truths which can scarcely be too frequently impressed on the Mind that is in earnest in the wish to *reflect* aright. Nature is a Line in constant and continuous evolution.[18] Its *beginning* is lost in the Super-natural: and *for our understanding*, therefore, it must appear as a continuous line without beginning or end. But where there is no discontinuity there can be no origination, and every appearance of origination in *Nature* is but a shadow of our own casting. It is a reflection from our own *Will* or Spirit. Herein, indeed, the will consists. This is the essential character by which WILL is *opposed* to Nature, as *Spirit*, and raised *above* Nature as *self-determining* Spirit—this, namely, that it is a power of *originating* an act or state.

A young friend or, as he was pleased to describe himself, *a pupil of mine, who is beginning to learn to think,*[19] asked me to explain by an instance what is meant by "*originating an act or state.*" My answer was—This morning I awoke with a dull pain, which I knew from experience the Getting up would remove; and yet by adding to the drowsiness and by weakening or depressing the *volition* (*voluntas sensorialis seu mechanica*)[20] the very

---

[a] AR (1825): Law

[15] C is still drawing on Kant's ideas (see Excursus Note 11 again).

[16] Cf *Logic (CC)* 134: ". . . little . . . can we in any particular instance detect or separate the share contributed by the mind itself, though, as in the kaleidoscope, we may have had it satisfactorily demonstrated how large a portion of all that we behold is given by the organ or machine itself". Cf also *TT* 11 Apr 1833 *(CC)* I 366 (1836 vn, dated 14 Apr, II 218).

[17] Cf an annotation on Fichte *Grundlage der Gesammten Wissenschaftslehre*, ". . . possibly, the Author has omitted a whole class of reciprocal re-actions (Wechselwirkungen) between *Life & Intelligence . . .*": *CM (CC)* II 624. *Wechselwirkung* is discussed in the third analogy of experience: Kant *Critik der reinen Vernunft* (Leipzig 1799) 256; also often in Schelling and Steffens.

[18] Cf a letter to DC 2 Feb 1826: "O if . . . Hartley could but promise himself to be a *Self* and to construct a circle by the circumvolving line . . ." and one to EC 27 Jul 1826: ". . . in Sensibility we see a power that in every instant *goes out* of itself & in the same instant retracts and falls back on itself: which the great Fountains of pure Mathesis, the Pythagorean and Platonic

Geometricians illustrated in the production or self-evolution of the Point into the Circle": *CL* VI 551, 598. Used also for *C&S (CC)* 179–80. The idea was the subject of a very long note in 1826: *CN* IV 5406. Cf also C's use of the circle image for God, above, *Sp Aph B VIIIb* n 60.

[19] The reference is probably to Charles Stutfield, Jr, whom C described in 1820 as ". . . my young Friend & Pupil . . .", rather than his companion in tuition, John Watson, whom C described to RS in May 1822 as having been ". . . for the last 18 months a House-mate of mine, as a sort of temporary Partner of Mr Gillman's rather than as an ordinary Assistant". Watson had weekly tuition from C and acted as his amanuensis; he was described in 1826 as ". . . my dear & truly filial Friend": *CL* v 31, 226–7, VI 552; cf 550, 553. In Oct 1823, however, he had gone to Berlin, where he intended to reside "for 7 or 8 months": *CL* v 303–4. Watson died in Jul 1827.

[20] "The sensory or mechanical volition". For the distinction here between *voluntas* and *arbitrium* and a likely source in Aquinas, see below, App I Excursus Note 18 "Two Words for 'Will' ".

pain seemed to *hold me back*, to fix me (as it were) to the bed. After a peevish ineffectual quarrel with this painful disinclination, I said to myself: Let me count twenty, and the moment I come to nineteen I will leap out of bed. So said, and so done.[21] Now should you ever find yourself in the same or in a similar state, and should attend to *the Goings-on* within you, you will learn what I mean by *originating* an act. At the same time you will see that it belongs *exclusively* to the Will (*arbitrium*); that there is nothing analogous to it in outward experiences; and that I had, therefore, no way of explaining it but by referring you to an *Act* of your own, and to the peculiar self-consciousness preceding and accompanying it. As we know what Life is by *Being*, so we know what Will is by *Acting*. That in *willing* (replied my young Friend) we *appear* to ourselves to constitute an actual *Beginning*, and that this seems unique, and without any example in our *sensible* experience, or in the phaenomena of Nature, is an undeniable *fact*. But may it not be an illusion arising from our ignorance of the antecedent causes? You *may* suppose this (I rejoined) That the soul of every man should impose a *Lie* on itself; and that this Lie, and the acting on the faith of its being the most important of all truths and the most real of all realities, should form the main contra-distinctive character of Humanity, and the only basis of that distinction between Things and Persons on which our whole moral and criminal Law is grounded—You *can* suppose this! I cannot, as I could in the case of an arithmetical or geometrical proposition, render it *impossible* for you to suppose it. Whether you can reconcile such a supposition with the belief of an all-wise[a] Creator, is another question. But, taken singly, it is doubtless in your power to suppose this. Were it not, the belief of the contrary would be no subject of a *Command*, no part of a moral or religious *Duty*. You would not, however, suppose it *without a reason*. But all the pretexts that ever have been or ever can be offered for this supposition, are built on certain *Notions* of the Understanding that have been generalized from *Conceptions;* which conceptions, again, are themselves generalized or abstracted from objects of Sense.[22] Neither the one or the other, therefore, have any force except in application to objects of Sense and within the sphere of sensible Experience. What but absurdity can follow, if you decide on Spirit by the laws of Matter? if you judge that which, if it be at all, must be *super*-sensual, by that faculty of your mind, the very definition of which is "the faculty[b] judging *according* to Sense?"[23] These then are unworthy the name of *reasons:* they are only pretexts. But *without* reason to contradict your own Consciousness in defiance of your own Conscience, is *contrary* to Reason. Such and such Writers, you say, have made a great *sensation*. If so, I am sorry

> [a] *AR* (1825): All-wise
> [b] *AR* (1825): Faculty

[21] Cf a notebook entry of 26 Sept 1805: "I was standing gazing at the starry Heaven, and said, I will go to bed the next star that shoots/ Observe this in counting fixed numbers previous to doing any thing, &c &c &c and deduce from man's own unconscious acknowlegement man's *dependence* on some thing *out of* him, on something more *apparently* & believedly subject to regular & certain Laws than his own Will & Reason . . .": *CN* II 2672.

[22] For the full range of distinctions involved here, together with a corresponding passage in Kant, see above, *Mor Aph VI* n 16, citing also *LS (CC)* 113.

[23] C's term can be related both to *übersinnlich*, as used by Kant and Schelling, and to his own admiration for the Platonic tradition in Renaissance philosophy. In 1817 he referred to Sir Philip Sidney as having ". . . held high converse" with Spenser ". . . on the *idea* of Supersensual beauty": *SM (CC)* 101. Cf also "Honor implies a reverence for the invisible and supersensual in our nature"—*Friend (CC)* I 426—and *Logic (CC)* 191. *OED*'s previous examples of this word are dated 1683, from E. Hooker. *OED* also records its after-life in the nineteenth century (including its use, which may well owe something to C, to translate Goethe's *übersinnlich*). See also above, *Mor Aph VI* at n 27, *Mor Aph XX* n 9, below, *Sp Aph B XIII* at n 5, and, for "supersensuous", *Sp Aph B VIIIb* n 63. For the last phrase see above, *Sp Aph B VIIIa* n 32.

The moment we *a*assume an Origin in Nature, a true *Beginning*, an actual First—that moment we rise *above* Nature, and *b*are compelled to assume a *supernatural* Power. (Gen. i.*c* 1.)²⁶

*d*It will be an equal convenience to myself and to my Readers, to let it be agreed between us, that we will *e*generalize the word Circumstance²⁷ so as to understand by it, as often as it occurs in this Comment, all and every thing not connected with the Will, past or present, of a Free Agent. Even though it were the blood in the chambers of his Heart, or his own inmost Sensations, we will regard them as *circumstantial, extrinsic,* or *from without.*

In this sense of the word Original, and in the sense before given of Sin, it is evident that the phrase, Original Sin, is a Pleonasm, the epithet

---

for it; but the fact I take to be this. From a variety of causes the more austere Sciences have fallen into discredit, and Impostors have taken advantage of the general ignorance to give a sort of mysterious and terrific importance to a parcel of trashy Sophistry, the Authors of which would not have employed themselves more irrationally in submitting the works of Rafael or Titian²⁴ to Canons of Criticism deduced from the Sense of Smell. Nay, less so. For here the Objects and the Organs are only disparate: while in the other case they are absolutely diverse. I conclude this note by reminding the reader, that my first object is to make myself *understood.* When he is in full possession of my *meaning,* then let him consider whether it deserves to be received as *the truth.* Had it been my immediate purpose to make him *believe* me as well as *understand* me, I should have thought it necessary to warn him that a *finite* Will does indeed originate an *act,* and may originate a *state* of being; but yet only *in* and *for* the Agent himself. A finite Will *constitutes* a true Beginning; but with regard to the series of motions and changes by which the free act is manifested and made *effectual,* the *finite* Will *gives* a beginning only by co-incidence with that *absolute* WILL, which is at the same time *Infinite* POWER! Such is the language of Religion, and of Philosophy too in the last instance. But I express the same truth in ordinary language when I say, that a finite Will, or the Will of a finite Free-agent, acts outwardly by confluence with the Laws of Nature.²⁵

---

a *AR* (1825): p 258   *b* *AR* (1825): p 259   *c* *AR* (1825): I. v.
d *AR* (1825): p 260   *e* *AR* (1825): p 261

²⁴ C saw original works by Raphael and Titian in Italy in 1806: see e.g. *CN* II 2844, 2840.

²⁵ *CW* I 274n here refers the reader to Kant *Critik der praktischen Vernunft,* to Jacobi *Von den göttlichen Dingen* (Leipzig 1816) 388–428 for ". . . the fullest development that has yet been made of this most fundamental and most important distinction between Nature and Spirit, or Will", and to Fichte *Die Bestimmung des Menschen* (Berlin 1800) 256ff ". . . for many forcible statements respecting the Will as *originant* in its essence". C's copy

of Fichte is unmarked at this point.

²⁶ "In the beginning God created the heaven and the earth."

²⁷ For other discussions of "circumstance" as ". . . *surrounding* influences *quotquot* STANT CIRCUM [*as many as* STAND ABOUT]"—*Logic (CC)* 9—see e.g. *Lects 1795 (CC)* 12 (written when C believed that ". . . vice originates not in the man, but in the surrounding circumstances"); 1809 *Friend (CC)* II 103–4 and n; *SM (CC)* 9–11, 19n, 64, 64a; 1818 *Friend (CC)* I 309–10 and Index s.v.

not adding to the thought, but only enforcing it. For if it be Sin, it must be *original:* and a State or Act, that has not its origin in the will, may be calamity, deformity, disease, or mischief; but a *Sin* it cannot be. It is not enough that the Act appears voluntary, or that it is intentional; or that it has the most hateful passions or debasing appetite for its proximate cause and accompaniment. All these may be found in a Mad-house, where neither Law nor Humanity permit *a*us to condemn the Actor of Sin. The Reason of Law declares the Maniac not a Free-Agent; and the Verdict follows of course—Not guilty. Now Mania, as distinguished from Idiocy,*b* Frenzy, Delirium, Hypochondria, and Derangement (the last term used specifically to express a suspension or disordered state of the Understanding or Adaptive Power)*c* is the Occultation or Eclipse of Reason, as the Power of ultimate ends.[28] The Maniac, it is well known, is often found clever and inventive in the selection and adaptation of means to *his* ends; but his *ends* are madness. He has lost his Reason. For though Reason, in finite Beings, is not the Will—or how could the Will be opposed to the Reason?—yet it is the *condition*, the *sine qua*d *non* of a *Free*-will.[29]

We will now return to the Extract from Jeremy Taylor on a theme of deep interest in itself, and trebly important from its *bearings*. For without just and distinct views respecting the Article of Original Sin, it is impossible to understand aright any one of the peculiar doctrines of Christianity. Now my first complaint is, that the eloquent Bishop, while he admits the *fact* as established beyond controversy by universal experience, yet leaves us wholly in the dark as to the main point, supplies us with no answer to the principal question—why he names it Original Sin? It cannot be said, We know what the Bishop *means*, and what matters the name? for the *nature* of the fact, and in what light it should be regarded by us, depends on the nature of our answer to the question, whether *e*Original Sin is or is not the right and proper designation. I can imagine the same quantum of *Sufferings*, and yet if I had reason to re-

a *AR* (1825): p 262
b *AR* (1825): Ideocy,
c COPY A: Power) MANIA, I say ; COPIES C & D: Power)—Mania, I say,
d *AR* (1825): *quâ*
e *AR* (1825): p 263

[28] This distinction, more fully worked out in the essay "The Soul and Its Organs of Sense" *Omniana* No 174, also occurs in a conversation with HCR in 1810: "The excess of fancy is delirium, of imagination mania . . .": CR *(BCW)* 31–2. Cf *TT* 23 Jun 1834 *(CC)* I 489–90 (1836 vn II 291–3). For further discussion and an apparent stimulus to the distinction in Erasmus Darwin *Zoonomia* (1794–6) I 432 see Beer *CPI* 76–7, 152–3.

[29] Quoted (var) in a further discussion: *CN* IV 5377 f 47.

gard them as symptoms of a commencing Change, as pains of growth, the temporary deformity and misproportions of immaturity, or (as in the final sloughing of the Caterpillar) as throes and struggles of the waxing or evolving Psyche,[30] I should think it no stoical flight to doubt, how far I was authorised to declare the Circumstance an *Evil* at all. Most assuredly I would not express or describe the fact as an evil having an origin in the Sufferers themselves, or as Sin.

Let us, however, wave*a* this objection. Let it be supposed that the Bishop uses the word in a different and more comprehensive Sense, and that by Sin he understands Evil of all kind connected with or resulting from *Actions*—though I do not see how we can represent the properties even of inanimate Bodies (of poisonous substances for instance) except as *Acts* resulting from the constitution of such bodies! Or if this sense, though not unknown to the Mystic Divines,[31] should be *too* comprehensive and remote, we will suppose the Bishop to comprise under the term Sin, the Evil accompanying or consequent on *human* Actions and Purposes:—though here too, I have a right to be informed, for what reason and on what grounds Sin is thus limited to *human* Agency? And truly, I should be at no loss to assign the reason. But then this reason would instantly bring me back to my first definition; and any other reason, than that the human Agent is endowed *b*with Reason, and with a Will which can place itself either in subjection or in opposition to his Reason—in other words, that Man is alone of all known Animals a responsible Creature—I neither know or can imagine.

Thus, then, the Sense which Taylor—and with him the Antagonists generally of this Article as propounded by the first Reformers—attaches to the words, Original Sin, needs only to be carried on into its next conse-

a *AR* (1825): waive
b *AR* (1825): p 264

[30] See below, App I Excursus Note 2 "Psyche as butterfly and soul".

[31] C is probably thinking first and foremost of Origen, whose unwillingness to find guilt as either hereditary in the will or as producing sinful acts by way of a corrupt nature he enlarges on in an annotation on Jeremy Taylor Σύμβολον Θεολογικόν 732 concerning the true meaning of guilt: "What then is it? 1. Guilt, and therefore seated in the Will. 2. Common to all men, and the beginning of which no man can determine in himself or in others. How comes this? It is a mystery, as the will itself. *Deeds* are in time & space, therefore have

a beginning. Pure *action*, i.e. the Will, is a Noumenon, & irreferable to time. Thus Origen calls it neither hereditary nor original, but universal sin": *LR* III 312–13 var: *CM (CC)* V. The terms within which C's thinking is cast also no doubt owe something to Kant, who in his *Metaphysik der Sitten* (Königsberg 1797) urged the necessity of distinguishing between the moral thinking that dealt with acts and that concerned with intentions. The first he termed *Rechtslehre* (theory of right), the second *Tugendlehre* (theory of virtue). See p l et passim. For Origen see also *Sp Aph B Xa* n 38 above.

quence, and it will be found to *imply* the sense which I have given—namely, that Sin is Evil having an *Origin*. But inasmuch as it is *evil,* in God it cannot originate: and yet in some *Spirit* (*i.e.* in some *supernatural* power) it *must*. For in *Nature* there is no origin.[32] Sin therefore is spiritual Evil: but the spiritual in Man is the Will. Now when we do not refer to any particular Sins, but to that state and constitution of the Will, which is the ground, condition,[a] and common Cause of all Sins; and when we would further express the truth, that this corrupt *Nature* of the Will must in some sense or other be considered as its own act, that the corruption must have been self-originated;—in this case and for this purpose we may, with no less propriety than force, entitle this dire spiritual evil and source of all evil, that is absolutely such, Original Sin.[33] (I have said, "the corrupt *Nature* of the Will." I might add, that the admission of a *Nature* into a spiritual essence by its own act *is* a corruption.)

Such, I repeat, would be the inevitable conclusion, *if* Taylor's Sense of the term were carried on into its immediate consequences. But the whole of his most [b]eloquent Treatise makes it certain that Taylor did not carry it on: and consequently Original Sin, according to his conception, is a Calamity which being common to all men must be supposed to result from their common Nature: in other words, the universal Calamity of Human *Nature!*

Can we wonder, then, that a mind, a heart like Taylor's should reject, that he should strain his faculties to explain away, the belief that this

[a] *AR* (1825): condition
[b] *AR* (1825): p 265

[32] A crucial point for C, related to his contention that, as ground, God transcends nature and to his use of the distinction between *natura naturata* and *natura naturans* (see above, *Sp Aph B Xa* nn 3, 7–8). Cf WW's address to C in the 1799 *Prelude,* concluding (lines 262–7):

> Hard task to analyse a soul, in which
> Not only general habits and desires,
> But each most obvious and particular
>   thought—
> Not in a mystical and idle sense,
> But in the words of reason deeply
>   weighed—
> Hath no beginning.

(*The Prelude 1799, 1805, 1850* ed J. Wordsworth, M. H. Abrams, S. Gill—New York 1979—20.) Cf *Prelude* (1805) II 232–7.

[33] *AR* (1825) COPY C has a note here: "Evil, *objectively* interpreted, has also a relative existence. Nature, or 'the Law of the Flesh', is evil by *position*. The *Being* of Evil is always *subjective*. N.B. The doctrine, attacked so vehemently by Pope in his 'Essay on Man' (that all things are made for Man) is not only tenible; but a most important Guide and Light in Natural Philosophy, especially in Comparative Anatomy & Comp. Physiology, and a necessary Idea in Moral Science." For Pope's attack see *Essay on Man* I 131–2:

> Ask for what end the heav'nly bodies
>   shine,
> Earth for whose use? Pride answers,
>   " 'Tis for mine . . ."

and the rest of the epistle.

Calamity, so dire in itself, should appear to the All-merciful God a rightful cause and motive for inflicting on the wretched Sufferers a Calamity infinitely more tremendous? nay, that it should be incompatible with Divine Justice *not* to punish it by everlasting torment? Or need we be surprised if he found nothing, that could reconcile his mind to such a belief, in the circumstance that the acts now *consequent* on this Calamity and either directly or indirectly *effects* on the same were, five or six thousand years ago in the instance of a certain Individual and his Accomplice, *anterior* to the Calamity, and the *Cause* or *Occasion* of the same? that what in all other men is *Disease*, in these two Persons was *Guilt?* that what in *us* is *hereditary*, and consequently *Nature*, in *them* was *original*, and consequently *Sin?* Lastly, might it not be presumed, that so enlightened, and at the same time so affectionate, a Divine, would even fervently disclaim and reject the pretended justifications of God grounded on flimsy analogies drawn from the imperfections of human ordinances and human justice-courts—some of very ᵃdoubtful character even as human Institutes, and all of them just only as far as they are necessary, and rendered necessary chiefly by the weakness and wickedness, the limited powers and corrupt passions, of mankind? The more confidently might this be presumed of so acute and practised a Logician, as Jeremy Taylor, in addition to his other extraordinary Gifts, is known to have been, when it is demonstrable that the most current of these justifications rests on the palpable equivocation: viz. the gross misuse of the word Right*. An ᵇinstance will explain my meaning. In as far

---

* It may conduce to the readier comprehension of this point if I say, that the Equivoque consists in confounding the almost technical Sense of the *Noun Substantive*, Right (a sense most often determined by the genitive case following, as the Right of Property, the Right of Husbands to chastise their Wives, and so forth) with the popular sense of the *Adjective*, right: though this likewise has, if not a double sense, yet a double application—the first, when it is used to express the fitness of a mean to a relative End, *ex. gr.* "the *right* way to obtain the *right* distance at which a Picture should be examined," &c.; and the other, when it expresses a perfect conformity and commensurateness with the immutable Idea of Equity, or perfect Rectitude. Hence the close connexion between the wordsᶜ righteousness and *god*liness, *i.e.* godlikeness.

I should be tempted to subjoin a few words on a predominating doctrine closely connected with the present argument—the Palëian Principle of GENERAL CONSEQUENCES; but the inadequacy of this Principle as a criterion of Right and Wrong, and above all its utter unfitness as a Moral *Guide*, have been elsewhere so fully stated (FRIEND, vol. ii. p. 216–240),³⁴ that even in again referring to the Subject, I must shelter myself under Seneca's rule, that what we cannot too frequently think of, we cannot too often be made to recol-

ᵃ AR (1825): p 266
ᵇ AR (1825): p 267
ᶜ AR (1825): words,

³⁴ *Friend (CC)* ɪ 313–25, discussing Paley *Principles of Moral and Political Phi-* *losophy* (1788) ɪ 70–81 (bk ɪɪ chs 6, 7, 8). See also below, *Conc* n 97 and references.

as, from the known frequency of dishonest or mischievous persons, it may have been found *necessary*, in so far is the Law *justifiable* in giving Landowners the Right of proceeding against a neighbour or fellow-citizen for even a slight trespass on that which the Law has made their Property:—nay, of proceeding in sundry instances criminally and even capitally. (Where at least from the known property of the Trespasser it is fore-known that the consequences will be penal.[37] Thus: three poor men were fined Twenty Pounds each, the one for knocking down a Hare, the other for picking it up, and the[a] third for carrying it off: and not possessing as many Pence, were sent to Jail.)[38] But surely, either there is no religion in the [b]world, and nothing obligatory in the precepts of the Gospel, or there are occasions in which it would be very *wrong* in the

---

lect.[35] It is, however, of immediate importance to the point in discussion, that the Reader should be made to see how altogether incompatible the principle of judging by General Consequences is with the Idea of an Eternal, Omnipresent,[c] and Omniscient Being! that he should be made aware of the absurdity of attributing *any* form of Generalization to the all-perfect Mind. *To generalize* is a faculty and function of the Human Understanding, and from the[d] imperfection and limitation [e]of the Understanding[f] are the use and the necessity of generalizing derived. Generalization is a Substitute for Intuition, for the Power of *intuitive* (that is, immediate) knowledge.[g] As a Substitute, it is a gift of inestimable Value to a finite Intelligence, such as *Man* in his present state is endowed with and capable of exercising; but yet a *Substitute* only, and an imperfect one to boot. To attribute it to God is the grossest Anthropomorphism:[36] and grosser instances of Anthropomorphism than are to be found in the controversial Writings[h] on Original Sin and Vicarious Satisfaction, the Records of Superstition do not supply.

[a] Added in 1831   [b] *AR* (1825): p 268   [c] *AR* (1825): Omnipresent
[d] *AR* (1825): its ; COPY C: the   [e-f] Added in COPY C and *AR* (1831)
[g] *AR* (1825): knowlege.   [h] *AR* (1825): writings

[35] See Robert Burton "Democritus Junior to the Reader" *Anatomy of Melancholy* (1632) 13: ". . . though Seneca bear me out, *nunquam nimis dicitur, quod nunquam satis dicitur*" ("that is never said too much which is never said enough"). The phrase appeared first in the 1632 ed; C copied it into a notebook in 1809: *CN* ii 3523 and n; cf 3502n. See also a letter to Gutch 12 Oct 1815: ". . . Seneca has said—What cannot be thought of too often, cannot be too often exprest—but he certainly would not apply this to Poetry": *CL* iv 595. In the original source, Seneca *Letters* 27.9, however, the last word is *discitur* (i.e. ". . . can never be learned too well"), which fits C's sense

here even better.
[36] Cf *SM (CC)* 90: ". . . the Almighty Goodness doth not create generalities or abide in abstractions . . .". For the intuitive, cf above, *Sp Aph B I* n 4, *IX*, at n 10, and *Xa* n 29.
[37] *AR* (1825) COPY F ends the parenthesis here (in pencil) rather than at the end of the next sentence. This gives a better reading. "Property" is here used in the sense of "character". Cf Scott *Kenilworth* ch xxi (1821) ii 231: ". . . one of whom, he would say, he knew no virtuous property save affection to his patron".
[38] The source of this example has not been found.

Proprietor to exercise the *Right*, which yet it may be highly *expedient* that he should possess. On this ground it is, that Religion is the sustaining Opposite of Law.

That Jeremy Taylor, therefore, should have striven fervently against the Article so interpreted and so vindicated, is,[a] (for me, at least,) a subject neither of Surprise nor of Complaint. It is the doctrine which he *substitutes*, it is the weakness and inconsistency betrayed in the defence of this substitute, it is the unfairness with which he blackens the established Article—for to give it, as it had been caricatured by a few Ultra-Calvinists during the fever of the (so called) *quinquarticular*[39] Controversy, was in effect to blacken it—and then imposes another scheme, to which the same objections apply with even increased force, a scheme which seems to differ from the former only by adding fraud and mockery to injustice: these are the things that excite my wonder, it is of these that I complain! For what does the Bishop's scheme amount to? God, he tells us, required of Adam a perfect obedience, and made it possible by endowing him "with perfect rectitudes and super-natural heights of grace"[40] proportionate to the obedience which he required. As a *consequence* of his disobedience, Adam lost this rectitude, this perfect sanity and proportionateness of his intellectual, moral and corporeal state, powers and impulses; and as the *penalty* of his crime, [b]he was deprived of all super-natural aids and graces. The Death, with whatever is comprised in the scriptural sense of the word, Death, began from that moment to work in him, and this *consequence* he conveyed to his offspring, and through them to all his posterity, *i.e.* to all mankind. They were *born* diseased in mind, body and will. For what less than disease can we call a necessity of error and a predisposition to sin and sickness? Taylor, indeed, *asserts*, that though perfect Obedience became incomparably more difficult, it was not, however, absolutely *impossible*. Yet he himself admits that the contrary was *universal*; that of the countless millions of Adam's Posterity, not a single Individual ever realized, or approached to the realization of, this possibility; and (if my memory*[c]

* I have since this page was written, met with several passages in the Treatise on Re-

[a] *AR* (1825): is
[b] *AR* (1825): p 269
[c] Footnote added in 1831

39 "Relating to the five articles or points of Arminian doctrine condemned by the Calvinists at the Synod of Dort, 1618": *OED*. The expression appears in the life of Hacket prefaced to *A Century of Sermons* (1675) xliii, just before the passage quoted in *Sp Aph B* II at n 6 above: *CM (CC)* II 913.

40 "*Adam* being spoiled of all the rectitudes and supernatural heights of grace": Σύμβολον Θεολογικόν (1674) 871.

does not deceive me) Taylor himself has elsewhere exposed—and if he has*a* not, yet Common Sense will do it for him—the sophistry in asserting of a whole what may be *b*true of the whole, but—is in fact*c* true only, of each of its component parts. Any one may snap a horse-hair: therefore, any one may perform the same feat with the horse's tail.[42] On a level floor (on the hardened sand, for instance, of a sea-beach) I chalk two parallel strait lines, with a width of eight inches. It is *possible* for a man, with a bandage over his eyes, to keep within the path for two or three paces: therefore, it is *possible* for him to walk blindfold for two or three leagues without a single deviation! And this *possibility* would suffice to acquit me of *injustice*, though I had placed man-traps within an inch of one *d*line, and knew that there were pit-falls and deep wells beside the other!

This *assertion*, therefore, without adverting to its discordance with, if not direct contradiction to, the tenth and thirteenth Articles of our Church,[43] I shall not, I trust, be thought to rate below its true value, if I treat it as an *infinitesimal* possibility that may be safely dropped in the calculation: and so proceed with the argument. The consequence then of Adam's Crime was, by a natural necessity, inherited by Persons who

---

pentance, the Holy Living and Dying, and the Worthy Communicant, in which the Bishop asserts without scruple the *impossibility* of total obedience; and on the same grounds as I have given.[41]

a AR (1825): have   *b-c* AR (1825): true, but is   *d* AR (1825): p 270

[41] In *AR* (1847) I 211n HNC cites a passage from *Unum Necessarium* ch 1 § 2, ¶¶ 15 and 34: Σύμβολον Θεολογικόν 580–1, in which Taylor argues that in view of man's various weaknesses and limitations, ". . . the keeping of the Commandments is morally impossible". In *Holy Dying* Taylor devotes much of ch 5 § 5 to "Considerations against unreasonable fears of not having our sins pardoned"; and § 6 to "Considerations against presumption", both of which are based on this assumption. Cf also *The Worthy Communicant* ch 5 § 3 ¶ 2 (1674) 272: ". . . it is not intended that a man must defer his Communion till he hath fully performed all his purposes of a holy life, for then he should never Communicate till he dies . . .".

[42] There is an example of such reasoning in Taylor's *XXVIII Sermons Preached at the Golden Grove* Sermon 22 § 3 (2 pts 1651) ii 277, overleaf from a passage (ii

275) that C copied into the Gutch notebook (*CN* I 177 and n): Taylor argues that if sects fall out over some of their opinions it does not follow that they are in error concerning the doctrines about which they agree. The 1825 text gives a clearer sense, suggesting an over-hasty attempt at clarification during the printing of the revised version.

For other examples of the illustration see annotation on Andrew Fuller *The Calvinistic and Socinian Systems Examined and Compared . . .* (1793): *CM (CC)* II 800, III 158, and *CN* IV 4822. In *Omniana* (1812) II 6 C includes a quotation: "Sentences in scripture (says Dr Donne) like hairs in horsetails, concur in one root of beauty and strength; but being *plucked out, one by one, serve only for springes and snares*". Although the sentiment is Donne's, this sentence has not been traced to his work.

[43] "Of Free-Will" and "Of Works before Justification": *BCP*.

could not (the Bishop affirms) in any sense have been accomplices in the crime or partakers in the guilt: and yet consistently with the divine Holiness, it was not possible that the same perfect Obedience should not be required of them. Now what would the Idea of Equity, what would the Law inscribed by the Creator in the heart of Man, seem to dictate in this case? Surely, that the supplementary Aids, the super-natural Graces correspondent to a Law above Nature, should be increased in proportion to the diminished strength of the Agents, and the increased resistance to be overcome by them! But no! not only the consequence of Adam's act, but the penalty due to his crime, was perpetuated. His descendants were despoiled or left destitute of these Aids and Graces, while the obligation to perfect obedience was continued; an obligation too, the non-fulfilment of which brought with it Death and the unutterable Woe that cleaves to an immortal Soul for ever alienated from its Creator.[a]

[b]Observe, Reader! all these *results* of Adam's Fall enter into Bishop Taylor's scheme of Original Sin equally as into that of the first Reformers. In this respect the Bishop's doctrine is the same with that laid[c] down in the Articles and Homilies of the Established Church. The only difference that has hitherto appeared, consists in the aforesaid *mathematical* possibility of fulfilling the whole Law, which in the Bishop's scheme is affirmed to remain still in human Nature,[44] or (as it is elsewhere expressed) in the Nature of the human Will*. But though it were possible

---

* Availing himself of the equivocal sense, and (I most readily admit) the injudicious use, of the word "free" in the—even on this account—*faulty* phrase, "*free only to sin*," Jeremy Taylor treats the notion of a power in the Will of determining itself to Evil without an equal power of determining itself to Good, as a "*foolery*."[45] I would this had been the only instance in his "Deus Justificatus" of that inconsiderate contempt so frequent in the polemic treatises of minor Divines, who will have Ideas of Reason, Spiritual Truths that can only be spiritually discerned, translated for them into adequate conceptions of the Understanding. The great articles of Corruption and Redemption are *propounded* to us as Spiritual Mysteries;[46] and every interpretation, that pretends to explain them into comprehensible notions, does by its very success furnish presumptive proof of its failure. The acuteness and logical dexterity, with which Taylor has brought out the falsehood or semblance of falsehood in the Calvinistic scheme, are truly admirable. Had he next concen-

---

[a] *AR* (1825): Creator!
[b] *AR* (1825): p 271
[c] *AR* (1825): layed

---

[44] HNC in *AR* (1847) I 213n cites a passage from *Unum Necessarium* ch 1 § 2 ¶ 34, just before that cited in n 41 above, ending: "In man therefore speaking naturally and of the Physical possibilities of things, there is by those assistances which are given in the Gospel, ability to keep the commandments Evangelical": Σύμβολον Θεολογικόν 580.

[45] "If it be replied, that we are free to sin, but not to good; it is such a foolery, and the cause of the mistake so evident, and so ignorant, that I wonder any man of Learning or common sence should own it": Σύμβολον Θεολογικόν 874.

[46] Cf *CN* IV 5243 and below, n 72.

to grant *a*this existence of a power in all men, which in no one man was ever exemplified, and where the *non*-actualization of such power is, a priori, so certain, that the belief or imagination of the contrary in any Individual is expressly given us by the Holy Spirit as a test, whereby it may be known that the truth is not in him! as an infallible sign of imposture or self-delusion! Though it were possible to grant this, which, consistently with Scripture and the principles of reasoning which we apply in all other cases, it is not possible to grant; and though it were possible likewise to overlook the glaring sophistry of concluding*b* in relation to a series of indeterminate length, that whoever can do any one, can therefore do all; a conclusion, the futility of which must force itself on the commonsense of every man who understands the proposition;—still the question will arise—Why, and on what principle of equity, were the unoffending sentenced to be born with so fearful a disproportion of their powers to their duties? Why were they subjected to a Law, the fulfilment of which was all but impossible, yet the penalty on the failure tremendous? Admit that for those who *c*had never enjoyed a happier lot, it was no punishment to be made to*d* inhabit a ground which the Creator had cursed, and to have been born with a body prone to sickness, and a Soul surrounded with temptation, and having the worst temptation within itself in its own *temptibility!*[49] To have the duties of a Spirit with the wants and appetites of an Animal! Yet on such imperfect Creatures, with

---

tered his thoughts in tranquil meditation, and asked himself: What then *is* the truth? If a Will *be* at all, what must a will be?*e*—he might, I think, have seen that a *Nature* in a Will implies already a *Corruption* of that Will; that a *Nature* is as inconsistent with *freedom*, as free choice with an incapacity of choosing aught but evil. And lastly, a free power in a *Nature* to fulfil a Law *above* Nature!—I, who love and honor*f* this good and great man with all the reverence that can dwell "on this side idolatry,"[47] dare not retort on this assertion the charge of *Foolery*; but I find it a Paradox as startling to my *Reason* as any of the hard sayings of the Dorp Divines[48] were to his *Understanding*.*g*

---

a *AR* (1825): p 272   *b* *AR* (1825): concluding,   *c* *AR* (1825): p 273
d Added in 1831   *e* *AR* (1825): be!   *f* *AR* (1825): honour
g *AR* (1825) adds: s. t. c.

---

[47] ". . . I lov'd the man, and doe honour his memory (on this side Idolatry) as much as any . . .": Ben Jonson (on Shakespeare) *Timber: or, Discoveries* (1646) 28: *Ben Jonson* ed C. H. Herford and P. Simpson (11 vols Oxford 1925–52) VIII 583–4.

[48] Taylor Σύμβολον Θεολογικόν 871–2. C's slip "Dorp" for "Dort" may be a re-

sult of his reference to Dorpius above, *Sp Aph B IX* n 32. It is repeated in *Sp Aph B XVII* (at n 9) below, having been originally correct in *Sp Aph B III* (at n 2).

[49] *OED* gives this (in the spelling "temptability", used in *AR*—1848) as its only example of the word.

means so scanty and impediments so numerous, to impose the same task-work that had been required of a Creature with a pure and entire nature, and provided with super-natural Aids—if this be not to inflict a penalty!—Yet to be placed under a Law, the difficulty of obeying*a* which is*b* infinite, and to have momently[50] to struggle with this difficulty, and to live in momently hazard of these consequences—if this be no punishment!—words have no correspondence with thoughts, and thoughts are but shadows of each other, shadows that own no substance for their antitype![51]

Of such an outrage on common-sense,*c* Taylor was incapable. He himself,*d* calls it a penalty; he admits that in effect it is a punishment: nor does he seek to suppress the question that so naturally arises out of this admission—On what principle of Equity were the innocent offspring of Adam *punished* at all? He meets it, and puts-in an answer. He states the problem, and gives his solution—namely, that "God on Adam's Account *was so exasperated with Mankind, that being angry he would still continue the punishment!*"[52] The case (says the Bishop)

a AR (1825): obeying and the consequences of not obeying
b AR (1825): are both   *c* AR (1825): common-sense   *d* AR (1825): himself

[50] "Moment by moment". Cf *Kubla Khan* line 19 and (for the adjectival form in the next line) a letter to Mrs C of 18 Sept 1798: ". . . a beautiful white cloud of foam at momently intervals roars & rushes by the side of the Vessel": *PW* (EHC) I 297; *CL* I 416.
[51] Cf John Smith *Select Discourses* (1660) 179 (of the visions of the prophets): ". . . the Understandings of the Prophets were alwaies kept awake and strongly acted by God in the midst of these apparitions, to see the intelligible Mysteries in them, and so in these Types and Shadows, which were Symbols of some spiritual things, to behold the Antitypes themselves . . .". For Smith see above, *Sp Aph B VII* n 26 and *Xa* nn 12–13. The word ἀντίτυπος (antitype) is translated "figure" in Heb 9.24 (AV), in which holy places made with hands are figures of heaven itself, and in 1 Pet 3.20–1, in which baptism is the figure of the saving of Noah's family by water. See also *Sp Aph B XIX* n 50. C's use of "shadow" here is slightly different.
[52] In these and the following sentences C is quoting from Taylor *Unum Necessarium, or, The Doctrine and Practice of Repentance* (1673) in Σύμβολον Θεολογικόν

711, with only minor changes. For the full text see App A(n), below. In his copy of the work C underlined "God was so exasperated with Mankind" and commented: "And such a phrase as this used by a man in a refutation of Original Sin, on the ground of its Incompatibility with God's attributes! 'EXASPERATED' with those whom Taylor declares to have been 'innocent and most unfortunate'—the two things that most conciliate Love & Pity!—"; another annotation, at "they who sinn'd not so bad" (in the following sentence) runs: "But their abandonment to a mere Nature while they were subjected to a Law above Nature, was the resistless cause that they one & all did sin. Let Taylor confute himself—& turn back, therefore, to 576–582.—If the sequel of the §§, comparing God to David in one of his worst actions, be not Blasphemy, the reason is, that the good man meant it not as such. In facto; sed non in agente[in the deed; but not in the agent].—": *CM (CC)*. Cf the 1818 *Friend (CC)* I 433–4, in which the same passage of Taylor is quoted and criticised. C is taking his text from *The Friend*, since he repeats several changes made there.

is this: "Jonathan and Michal *a*were Saul's Children. It came to pass, that seven*b* of Saul's Issue were to be hanged: all equally innocent, EQUALLY CULPABLE." [*Before I quote further, I feel myself called on to remind the Reader, that these two last words were added by Jeremy Taylor without the least ground of Scripture, according to which,*c* (2 Samuel, lxxi.)*[53]* no crime was laid to their charge, no blame imputed to them. Without any pretence of culpable conduct on their part, they were arraigned as Children of Saul, and sacrificed to a point of state-expedience. In recommencing the quotation, therefore, the Reader ought to let the sentence conclude with the words—*] "all equally innocent. David took the five Sons of Michal, for she had left him unhandsomely. Jonathan was his friend:*d* and therefore he spared *his* Son, Mephibosheth. Now here it was indifferent as to the guilt of the persons (*Bear in mind, Reader! that no guilt was attached to either of them!*) whether David should take the Sons of Michal or Jonathan's; but it is likely that as upon the kindness that David had to Jonathan,*e* he spared his son; so upon the just provocation of Michal, he made that evil fall upon them,*[54]* which, it may be, they should not have suffered,*f* if their mother had been kind. ADAM WAS TO GOD,*g* AS MICHAL TO DAVID." (Taylor's Polem. Tracts, p. 711.)

This Answer, this Solution, proceeding too from a Divine so preeminently gifted, and occurring (with other passages not less startling) in a vehement refutation of the received doctrine on the express ground of its opposition to the clearest conceptions and *h*best feelings of mankind—this it is, that surprises me! It is of this that I complain! The Almighty Father *exasperated* with those, whom the Bishop has himself in the same treatise described as "innocent and most unfortunate"—the two things best fitted to conciliate love and pity!*[55]* Or though they did not remain innocent, yet those whose abandonment to a mere nature, while they were left amenable to a law above nature, he affirms to be

---

a AR (1825): p 274
b AR (1825): Seven
c AR (1825): *which*
d AR (1825): Friend:
e AR (1825): Jonathan
f AR (1825): suffered
g AR (1825): GOD
h AR (1825): p 275

---

[53] A slip for 2 Sam 21 (given correctly in *The Friend*). C's remonstrance is well grounded: see vv 3–9.

[54] Taylor reads here in addition: ". . . of which they were otherwise capa-ble . . .".

[55] This and the next two sentences are repeated with minor changes from the 1818 *Friend: (CC)* I 434, which in turn had drawn on his annotation (n 52 above).

the irresistable cause, that they[a] one and all[b] *did* sin! And this decree illustrated and justified by its analogy to one of the worst actions of an imperfect Mortal! Let such of my Readers as possess the Volume of Polemical Discourses, or the opportunity of consulting it, give a thoughtful perusal to the pages from 869 to 893,[c] (*Third Edition enlarged,* 1674).[56] I dare anticipate their concurrence with the judgment which I here transcribe from the blank space at the end of the Deus Justificatus in my own Copy; and which, though twenty years have elapsed since it was written, I have never seen reason to recant or modify. "This most eloquent Treatise may be compared to a Statue of Janus, with the one face, which we must suppose fronting the Calvinistic Tenet, entire and fresh, as from the Master's hand:[d] beaming with life and force, witty scorn on the Lip, and a Brow at once bright and weighty with satisfying reason! the other, looking toward the '*something to be put in its place,*' maimed, featureless, and weather-bitten into an almost visionary confusion and indistinctness."[57]

[e]With these expositions I hasten to contrast the *scriptural* article respecting Original Sin, or the corrupt and sinful Nature of the Human Will, and the belief which alone is required of us, as Christians. And here the first thing to be considered, and which will at once remove a

[a] *AR* (1825): they,
[b] *AR* (1825): all,
[c] *AR* (1825): 893
[d] *AR* (1825): hand;
[e] *AR* (1825): p 276

[56] I.e. the copy mentioned above (n 52). Dating of the annotations in this volume generally suggests that they were made from 1811 onwards: *CM (CC)* v.

[57] The note, which is in Σύμβολον Θεολογικόν 893, reads: "This eloquent Treatise may be compared to a Statue of Janus, with one face fixed with on certain opponents, full of Life & Force, a witty scorn on the Lip, a brow at once bright and weighty with satisfying Reason—the other, looking at 'the something instead' of that which had been confuted, maimed, noseless, & weather-bitten into a sort of visionary confusion & indistinctness. It looks like this—aye, & very like that—but how like it is, too, [to] such another thing!—S. T. C.—'" A letter to John Kenyon of 3 Nov 1814 contains another version: "It is the masterpiece of Human Eloquence—I compare it to an old Statue of Janus, with one of the Faces, that which looks toward his Opponents, the controversial Phiz, in highest Preservation—the face of a mighty one, all Power, all Life!—the Face of a God rushing on to Battle; and in the same moment enjoying at once both Contest and Triumph. The other, that which should have been the Countenance that looks toward his Followers—that with which he substitutes his own Opinion—all weather-eaten, dim, noseless, a *Ghost in Marble*—such as you may have seen represented in many of Piranesi's astounding Engravings from Rome & the Campus Martius": *CL* III 541. When he wrote the latter C was consulting a copy in the possession of a bookseller: he either reconstructed it later from memory when he had access to a copy in which he could write or was recalling it from a note already written that he did not then have to hand. For Piranesi see *CM (CC)* II 1118n, *CN* IV 5162 and n.

world of error, is;[a] that this is no Tenet first introduced or imposed by Christianity,[b] and which, should a man see reason to disclaim the authority of the Gospel, would no longer have any claim on his attention. It is no perplexity that a man may get rid of by ceasing to be a Christian, and which has no existence for a philosophic Deist. It is a FACT, affirmed, indeed, in the Christian Scriptures alone with the force and frequency proportioned to its consummate importance; but a fact acknowledged[c] in *every* Religion that retains the least glimmering of the patriarchal faith in a God infinite,[d] yet *personal!* A Fact[e] assumed or implied as the basis of every Religion, of which any relics remain of earlier date than the last and total Apostasy of the Pagan World, when the faith in the great I AM, the *Creator*, was extinguished in the sensual polytheism, which is inevitably the final result of Pantheism or the Worship of Nature;[58] and the only form under which the Pantheistic[f] Scheme—that, according to which the World is God, and the material universe itself the one only *absolute* Being—can exist for a People, or become the popular Creed. Thus in the most ancient Books of the Brahmins, the deep sense of this Fact, and the doctrines grounded on obscure traditions of the promised remedy,[g] are seen struggling, [h]and now gleaming, now flashing, through the Mist of Pantheism, and producing the incongruities and gross contradictions of the Brahmin Mythology:[59] while in the rival Sect—in that most strange Phaenomenon, the religious Atheism of the Buddhists![i] with whom God is only universal Matter considered abstractedly from all particular forms—the Fact[j] is placed among the delusions natural to man, which, together with other superstitions grounded on a supposed *essential* difference between Right and Wrong, *the Sage* is to decompose and precipitate from the menstruum

----

[a] *AR* (1825): is:
[b] *AR* (1825): Christianity;
[c] *AR* (1825): acknowleged
[d] *AR* (1825): infinite
[e] *AR* (1825): fact
[f] *AR* (1825): pantheistic
[g] *AR* (1825): Remedy,
[h] *AR* (1825): p 277
[i] *AR* (1825): Buddheists!
[j] *AR* (1825): fact

[58] For the "final Apostacy" of Greece and Rome to "sensual polytheism" see *P Lects* Lects 6, 8 (1949) 221, 249–50.
[59] Ch 11 of Thomas Maurice *The History of Hindostan* (2 vols 1795–8) I 395–400 is devoted to parallels to the first man, the fall-story, the Flood, and the longevity, etc, in Brahmin beliefs. C was reading the first volume c 1796: *CN* I 240 and n. See also below, App I Excursus Note 12 "Indian religion and Christianity".

of *his* more refined apprehensions![60] Thus in denying the Fact,[a] they virtually acknowledge[b] it.

From the remote East turn to the mythology of Minor Asia, to the Descendants of Javan *who dwelt in the tents of Shem, and possessed the Isles.*[61] Here again, and in the usual form of an historic Solution[c] we find the same *Fact*, and as characteristic of the Human *Race,* stated in that earliest and most venerable Mythus (or symbolic Parable) of Prometheus—that truly wonderful Fable, in which the characters of the rebellious Spirit and of the Divine Friend of Mankind (Θεὸς[d] φιλάνθρωπος)[62] are united in the same Person: and thus in the most striking manner noting the forced amalgamation of the Patriarchal Tradition with the incongruous Scheme of Pantheism. This and the connected tale of Io, which is but the sequel of the Prometheus, stand alone in the Greek Mythology, in which elsewhere both Gods and Men are mere Powers and Products of Nature.[63] And most noticeable [e]it is, that soon after the promulgation and spread of the Gospel had awakened the moral sense, and had opened the eyes even of its wiser Enemies to the necessity of providing some solution of this great problem of the Moral World, the beautiful Parable of Cupid and Psyche[64] was brought forward as a *rival* FALL OF MAN:

[a] *AR* (1825): fact,
[b] *AR* (1825): acknowlege
[c] *AR* (1825): Solution,
[d] *AR* (1825): Θέος ; *AR* (1831): Θὲος
[e] *AR* (1825): p 278

[60] Maurice also describes the atheistic materialism of "Boodh, whose name the Chinese have softened into Fo", and quotes the "Bhagvat-Geeta p 177" as controverting it (I 397–400), but does not make C's ethical point.

[61] Gen 9.27: "God shall enlarge Japheth, and he shall dwell in the tents of Shem" (Gen 10.2 lists the seven sons of Japheth, of whom Javan was the fourth); Gen 10.4–5: "And the sons of Javan . . . By these were the isles of the Gentiles divided in their lands . . .". Cf Isa 66.19: ". . . I will send those that escape . . . to . . . Javan, to the isles afar off . . .". See below, App I Excursus Note 13 "Javan and the Ionians".

[62] Aeschylus *Prometheus Bound* lines 10–11: ὡς ἂν διδαχθῇ . . . φιλανθρώπου δὲ παύεσθαι τρόπου ("so that he may be taught . . . to give up his man-befriending ways"). The phrase in the text is used in connection with animal magnetism in *CN*

IV 4624.

[63] See below, App I Excursus Note 14 "Coleridge and the Prometheus myth".

[64] C borrowed the first volume of Apuleius *Opera* (Paris 1688), in which the *Metamorphoses* (or *Golden Ass*) appears, with the story of Cupid and Psyche at 4.26–6.24, from the Bristol Library 4–9 Nov 1796: *Bristol LB* 124. His interest in the myth appears in *CN* II 2588 (1805), *Friend (CC)* II 61n (I 80), I 485 and n (= *P Lects* Lect 11—1949—335–6), and Lects 3 and 11 of 1818: *Lects 1808–1819 (CC)* II 102, 192. In 1820–1 he was reading and quoting *Metamorphoses* and *Florida*, apparently in *Apuleius . . . serio castigatus* (Amsterdam 1628): *CN* IV 4694, 4743, and nn. See also below, *Conc* n 102. In *Essays* 91–100 (see above, *Sp Aph B Xb* n 30) Nares gives an abridged version of the story as told by Apuleius, the moral as unsatisfactorily explained by Fulgentius *Mythologicon* 3, and finally his own outline of the story as tell-

and the fact of a moral corruption connatural with the human race was again recognized. In the assertion of ORIGINAL SIN the Greek Mythology rose and set.

But not only was the *fact* acknowledged[a] of a Law in the Nature of Man resisting the Law of God. (And whatever is placed in active and direct Oppugnancy to the Good is,[b] ipso facto, positive Evil.) It was likewise an acknowledged[c] MYSTERY, and one which by the nature of the Subject must ever remain such—a problem, of which any other solution, than the statement of the *Fact* itself, was demonstrably *impossible*. That it is so, the least reflection will suffice to convince every man, who has previously satisfied himself that he is a responsible Being. It follows necessarily from the postulate of a responsible Will. Refuse to grant this, and I have not a word to say.[65] Concede this, and you concede all. For this is the essential attribute of a Will, and contained in the very *idea*, that whatever determines the Will acquires this power from a previous determination of the Will itself. The Will is ultimately self-determined, or it is no longer a *Will* under the law of perfect Freedom, but a *Nature* under the mechanism of Cause and Effect. And if by an act, to [d]which it had determined itself, it has subjected itself to the determination of Nature (in the language of St. Paul, to the Law of the Flesh),[66] it receives a nature into itself, and so far it becomes a Nature: and this is a corruption of the Will and a corrupt Nature. It is also a *Fall* of Man, inasmuch as his Will is the condition of his Personality; the ground and condition of the attribute which constitutes him *Man*. And

---

[a] *AR* (1825): acknowleged
[b] COPY A: becomes,
[c] *AR* (1825): acknowleged
[d] *AR* (1825): p 279

---

ing of the soul tempted to gain forbidden knowledge, fallen, subject to difficulties and trials, in which she is helped by supernatural interposition, and finally united with divine love in perfect bliss. See also C's note on HNC's reference to the myth and the NT in "Life and Writings of Hesiod" *QR* XLVII (1832) 8: "A note from the §ph in 'Aids to Ref.' would not have been amiss": *CM (CC)* II 87. See also below, App I Excursus Note 2 "Psyche as butterfly and soul" and his reference in a notebook of 1821–2 to ". . . the Prometheus and the lovely mythos of Cupid and Psyche—the one the glory of the Day-Star surmounting the Eastern Heights, the other the last soft rich gleam of the setting Orb!'":

CN IV 4839 f 120ᵛ.

[65] Cf C's annotations on De Wette *Theodor*: "Wherein but the Will, and the Intention can *Evil* exist?" and on Donne *LXXX Sermons: CM (CC)* II 199, 278–9.

[66] St Paul does not actually use the term "the Law of the Flesh"; C's statement presumably relates to Rom 7.23, 25: "But I see another law in my members, warring against the law of my mind, and bringing me into captivity to the law of sin which is in my members . . . . with the mind I myself serve the law of God; but with the flesh the law of sin." Cf Heb 7.16: ". . . the law of a carnal commandment". For the "law of perfect freedom" in this paragraph, see above, *Int Aph XXIII* n 6 and references.

the ground-work of *Personal* Being is a capacity of acknowledging[a] the Moral Law (the Law of the Spirit, the Law of Freedom, the Divine Will) as that which should, of itself, suffice to determine the Will to a free obedience of the Law, the Law working therein[b] *by its own exceeding lawfulness**[c].[68] This, and this alone, is *positive* Good;[d] good in itself, and independent of all relations. Whatever resists and, as a positive force, opposes *this* in the Will is therefore evil. But an Evil in the Will is an evil Will; and as all moral Evil (*i.e.* all evil that is evil without reference to its contingent physical consequences) is *of* the Will, this evil Will must have its source in the Will. And thus we might go back from act to act, from evil to evil, ad infinitum,[e] without advancing a step.

We call an Individual a *bad* Man, not because an action is contrary to the Law, but because it has led us to conclude from it some *Principle* opposed to the Law, some private Maxim or By-law in the Will contrary to the universal Law of right Reason in the Conscience, as the *Ground* of the action. But this evil Principle again must be grounded in some other Principle[f] which has been made determinant of the Will by the Will's own self-determination. For if not, it must have its ground in some necessity of Nature, in some instinct or propensity imposed,[g] not acquired, another's work not our own. Consequently, neither Act nor Principle could be imputed; and relatively to the Agent, not *original*, not *Sin*.

Now let the grounds, on which the fact of an Evil inherent in the Will is affirmable in the instance of any one Man, be supposed equally appli-

---

* If the Law worked *on* the Will, it would be the working of an extrinsic, alien force, and as St. Paul profoundly argues, prove the Will sinful.[67]

---

[a] *AR* (1825): acknowleging
[b] *AR* (1825): thereon
[c] Footnote added in 1831
[d] *AR* (1825): Good:
[e] *AR* (1825): infinitum
[f] *AR* (1825): p 280 (ciple)
[g] *AR* (1825): imposed

---

[67] C appears to be alluding to the argument of Rom 5–8 concerning the moral rôle of the law, e.g. Rom 5.13: "For until the law sin was in the world: but sin is not imputed when there is no law", and Rom 8.3–4: ". . . what the law could not do, in that it was weak through the flesh, God sending his own Son in the likeness of sinful flesh, and for sin, condemned sin in the flesh: That the righteousness of the law

might be fulfilled in us, who walk not after the flesh, but after the Spirit".

[68] This may be related to Rom 7.13: ". . . that sin by the commandment might become exceeding sinful". Cf C's later use of ". . . the exceeding sinfulness of Sin": *CN* IV 5243 and n 72, below. The note at this point seems to be prompted by the change from "thereon" to "therein", made for *AR* (1831).

cable in *every* instance, and concerning all men: so that the fact is asserted of the Individual, *not* because he has committed this or that crime, or because he has shown himself to be *this* or *that* Man, but simply because he is *a* Man. Let the evil be supposed such as to imply the impossibility of an Individual's referring to any particular time at which it might be conceived to have commenced, or to any period of his existence at which it was not existing. Let it be supposed, in short, that the subject stands in no relation whatever to Time, can neither be called *in* time nor*ᵃ out of* time; but that all relations of Time are as alien and heterogeneous in this question, as the relations and attributes of Space (north or south, round or square, thick or thin) are to our Affections and Moral Feelings. Let the reader suppose this, and he will have before him the precise import of the scriptural *doctrine* of Original Sin: or rather of the Fact acknowledged*ᵇ* in all Ages, and recognised,*ᶜ* but not originating, in the Christian Scriptures.

In addition to this Memento it will be well to remind*ᵈ* the Inquirer, that the stedfast conviction of the existence, personality, and moral attributes of God is pre-supposed in the acceptance of the Gospel, or required as its indispensable preliminary. It is taken for granted as a point which the hearer*ᵉ* had already decided for himself, a point finally settled and put at rest: not by the removal of all difficulties, or by any such increase of Insight as enabled him to meet every objection of the Epicurean or the Sceptic with a full and precise answer; but because he had convinced himself that it was folly as well as presumption in so imperfect a Creature to expect it; and because these difficulties and doubts disappeared at the beam, when tried against the weight and convictive power of the reasons in the other scale. It is, therefore, most unfair to attack Christianity, or any article which the Church has declared a Christian Doctrine, by arguments, which, if valid, are valid against all religion. Is there a Disputant who scorns a mere *Postulate*,⁶⁹ as the basis of any argument in support of the Faith; who is too high-minded *to beg* his ground, and will take it by a strong hand? Let him fight it out with the Atheists, or the Manichaeans; but not stoop to pick up their arrows, and then run away to discharge them at Christianity or the Church!

The only true way is to state the doctrine, believed *ᶠas well*ᵍ by Saul

---

ᵃ AR (1825): or
ᵇ AR (1825): acknowleged
ᶜ AR (1825): recognized,
ᵈ AR (1825): p 281 (mind)
ᵉ AR (1825): Hearer
ᶠ⁻ᵍ AR (1825): equally

⁶⁹ A key term for C: see above, *Prel Sp Aph* n 3.

of Tarsus, "yet breathing out threatenings and slaughter against"[70] the Church of Christ, as by Paul the Apostle "fully preaching the Gospel of Christ."[71] A moral Evil is an Evil that has its origin in *[a]*a Will. An Evil common to all must have a ground common to all. But the actual existence of moral evil we are bound in conscience to admit; and that there is an Evil common to all is a Fact; and this Evil must therefore have a common ground. Now this evil ground cannot originate in the Divine Will: it must therefore be referred to the Will of Man. And this evil Ground we call Original Sin. It is a *Mystery*, that is, a Fact, which we see, but cannot explain; and the doctrine a truth which we apprehend, but can neither comprehend nor communicate.[72] And such by the quality of the Subject (*viz.* a responsible *Will*) it must be, if it be truth at all.

A sick man, whose complaint was as obscure as his sufferings were severe and notorious, was thus addressed by a humane Stranger: My poor Friend! I find you dangerously ill, and on this account only, and having certain information of your being so, and that you have not wherewithal to pay for a Physician, I have come to you. Respecting your disease, indeed, I can tell you nothing, that you are capable of understanding, more than you know already, or can only be taught by reflection on your own experience. But I have rendered the Disease no longer irremediable. I have brought the remedy with me: and I now offer you the means of immediate relief, with the assurance of gradual convalescence, and a final perfect Cure; nothing more being required on your part, but your best endeavours to follow the prescriptions I shall leave with you. It is, indeed, too probable, from the nature of *[b]*your disease, that you will occasionally neglect or transgress them. But even this has been calculated on in the plan of your cure, and the remedies provided, if only you are sincere and in right earnest with yourself, and have your *heart* in the work. Ask me not, how such a Disease can be conceived possible! Enough for the present that you know it to be real: *and I come to cure the Disease[c] not to explain it.*

Now, what if the Patient or some of his Neighbours[d] should charge this good Samaritan with having given rise to the mischievous notion of

---

[a] *AR* (1825): p 282
[b] *AR* (1825): p 283
[c] *AR* (1825): *Disease,*
[d] *AR* (1825): Neighbors

[70] Acts 9.1.
[71] Rom 15.19 (var).
[72] For discussion of this passage in context see Boulger 160–1. Cf also above, *Sp*

Aph B Xb at n 46, and *CN* IV 5243: ". . . the actuality of Sin—'the exceeding sinfulness of Sin'—and its essential incommunicability—being my foundation stones".

an inexplicable Disease, involving the honor*a* of the King of the Country? should inveigh against *him* as the Author and first Introducer of the Notion, though of the numerous medical works composed ages before *his* arrival, and by Physicians of the most venerable Authority, it was scarcely possible to open a single volume without finding some description of the Disease, or some lamentation of its malignant and epidemic character! And, lastly, what if certain pretended Friends of this good Samaritan, in their zeal to vindicate him against this absurd charge, should assert that he was a perfect Stranger to this Disease, and boldly deny that he had ever said or done any thing connected with it, or that implied its existence?

In this Apologue or imaginary Case, Reader! you have the true bearings of Christianity on the fact and doctrine of Original Sin. The doctrine (that is, the confession of a known fact) Christianity has only in common with every Religion, and with every Philosophy,*b* in which the reality of a responsible Will and the *essential* difference between Good and Evil *c*have been*d* recognized. *Peculiar* to the Christian Religion are the Remedy and (for all purposes but those of a merely speculative Curiosity) the Solution! By the annunciation of the Remedy it affords all the solution that our *moral* interests require; and even in that which remains, and must remain, unfathomable,*e* the Christian finds a new motive to walk humbly with the Lord his God![73]

Should a professed Believer ask you whether that, which is the ground of responsible action in *your* will, could in any way be responsibly present in the Will of Adam? Answer him in these words: *You*, Sir! can no more demonstrate the Negative, than I can conceive the Affirmative. The corruption of my will may very warrantably be spoken of as a *Consequence* of Adam's Fall, even as my Birth of Adam's Existence; as a consequence, a link in the historic Chain of Instances, whereof Adam is the first. But that it is *on account* of Adam; or that this evil principle was, a priori, inserted or infused into my Will by the Will of another— which is indeed a contradiction in terms, my Will in such case being no *Will*—*this* is nowhere asserted in Scripture explicitly or by implication. It belongs to the very essence of the doctrine, that in respect of Original Sin *every* man is the adequate representative of *all* men. What wonder,

---

a AR (1825): honour
b AR (1825): p 284 (sophy,)
c–d AR (1825): were
e AR (1825): unfathomable

[73] For the last phrase see Micah 6.8,   *The Eolian Harp* line 52: *PW* (EHC) I 102. quoted above, *Sp Aph B VII* at n 15, and cf

then, that where no inward ground of preference existed, the choice should be determined by outward relations, and that the first *in time* should be *ᵃtaken as the Diagram? Even in Genesis the word, Adam, is distinguished from a ᵇproper nameᶜ by an Article before it.[74] It is *the* Adam, so as to express the *genus*, not the Individual—or rather, perhaps, I should say, *as well as* the Individual. But that the word with its equivalent, *the old man*, is used symbolically and universally by St. Paul, (1 Cor. xv. 22. 45. Eph. iv. 22. Col. iii. 9. Rom. vi. 6.)[75] is too evident to need any proof.

I conclude with this remark. The doctrine of Original Sin concerns all men. But it concerns Christians *in particular* no otherwise than by its connexion with the doctrine of Redemption; and with the Divinity and Divine Humanity of the Redeemer as a corollary or necessary inference from both mysteries. BEWARE OF ARGUMENTS AGAINST CHRISTIANITY, THAT CANNOT STOP THERE, AND CONSEQUENTLY OUGHT NOT TO HAVE COMMENCED THERE. Something I might have added to the clearness of the preceding views, if the limits of the work had permitted me to clear away the several delusive and fanciful assertions respecting the state* of our First Parents, their wisdom, science, and angelic Faculties, assertions without the slightest ground in Scripture! Or if consistently with the wants and preparatory studies of those, for whose use the Volume ᵈwas especially intended, I could have entered into the momentous sub-

---

* For a specimen of these Rabbinical Dotages I refer, not to the writings of Mystics and Enthusiasts, but to the shrewd and witty Dr. South, one of whose most elaborate Sermons[76] stands prominent among the many splendid extravaganzas on this subject.

ᵃ *AR* (1825): p 285
ᵇ⁻ᶜ *AR* (1825): Proper Name
ᵈ *AR* (1825): p 286

[74] Gen 1.26–8 refers to *'ādhām*, "mankind"; Gen 2.4–4.26 adds the article to give *hā-'ādhām*, "the man", meaning simply "the first man". See *Enc RE* article "Adam".

[75] 1 Cor 15.22: ". . . as in Adam all die, even so in Christ shall all be made alive"; 1 Cor 15.45: "The first Adam was made a living soul; the last Adam was made a quickening spirit"; Eph 4.22: "That ye put off concerning the former conversation the old man, which is corrupt . . ."; Col 3.9: ". . . seeing that ye have put off the old man with his deeds"; Rom 6.6: "Knowing this, that our old man is crucified with him, that the body of sin might be destroyed . . .".

[76] Sermon II in Robert South *Twelve Sermons Preached upon Several Occasions* (1692) 47–91, on Gen 1.27: "So God created man in his own image, in the image of God created he him", contains an elaborate panegyric on Adam's learning ("It did not so properly apprehend, as irradiate the Object . . ."): "He came into the World a Philosopher . . . he could view Essences in themselves . . . he could see Consequents yet dormant in their principles, and effects yet unborn and in the Womb of their Causes . . ." (61, 64). South concludes: "An *Aristotle* was but the rubbish of an *Adam*, and *Athens* but the rudiments of Paradise" (66–7).

ject of a Spiritual Fall or Apostacy *antecedent* to the formation of Man[77]—a belief, the scriptural grounds of which are few and of diverse interpretation, but which has been almost universal in the Christian Church. Enough, however, has been given, I trust, for the Reader to see and (as far as the subject is capable of being understood) to understand this long controverted Article in the sense, in which alone it is binding on his faith. Supposing him, therefore, to know the meaning of original sin, and to have decided for himself on the fact of its actual existence, as the antecedent ground and occasion of Christianity, we may now proceed to Christianity itself, as the Edifice raised on this ground, *i.e.* to the great Constituent Article of the Faith in Christ, as the Remedy of the Disease—The[a] Doctrine of Redemption.

But before we proceed to this momentous doctrine, let me briefly remind the young and friendly Pupil, to whom I would still be supposed to address myself, that in the [b]following Aphorisms[c] the word Science[d] is used in its strict and narrowest sense. By a Science I here mean any Chain of Truths that are either absolutely certain, or necessarily true for the human mind from the laws and constitution of the mind itself. In neither case is our conviction derived, or capable of receiving any addition, from outward Experience, or *empirical* data—*i.e.* matters-of-fact[e] *given* to us through the medium of the Senses—though these Data may have been the occasion, or may even be an indispensable condition,[f] of our reflecting on the former and thereby beoming *conscious* of the same. On the other hand, a connected series of conclusions grounded on empirical Data, in contra-distinction from Science, I beg leave (no better term occurring) in this place and for this purpose, to denominate a Scheme.

APHORISM XI[g]

In whatever age and country, it is the prevailing mind and character of the nation to regard the present life as subordinate to a Life to come, and

---

[a] *AR* (1825): the

[b-c] *AR* (1825): Aphorism to follow,

[d] *AR* (1825): Science,

[e] *AR* (1825): matter-of-fact

[f] *AR* (1825): p 287 (tion,)

[g] *AR* (1825): EDITOR.

[77] C is less likely to be referring to the fall of Satan and his angels than to his interpretation of Gen 1.1–3 as of a fall involved in the creation, an apostasis antecedent to the chaos, the state of fluidity in Gen 1.2; the creation of light then represented a return to God, an anastasis: *CN* III 4449 ff 27ᵛ–29ᵛ; cf IV 4662 ff 28ᵛ–29ᵛ.

to mark the present state, *the World of their Senses*, by signs, instruments,[a] and meme[n]tos of its connexion with a future state and a spiritual World; where[b] the Mysteries of Faith are brought within the *hold* of the people[c] at large, not by being explained away in the vain hope of accommodating them to the average of their Understanding, but by being made the objects of Love by[d] their combination with events and epochs of History, with national traditions, with the monuments and dedications of Ancestral faith and zeal, with memorial and symbolical observances, with the realizing influences of social devotion, and above all, by early and habitual association with Acts of the Will; *there* Religion is. *There,* however obscured by the hay and straw of human Will-work, the foundation is safe! In *that* country, and under the predominance of such Maxims, the national church is no mere State-*Institute*.[1] It is the State itself in its intensest federal union; yet at the same moment the Guardian and Representative [e]of all personal Individuality. For the Church is the Shrine of Morality: and in Morality alone the Citizen asserts and reclaims his personal independence, his *integrity*. Our outward Acts are efficient, and most often possible, only by coalition. As an efficient power, the Agent,[f] is but *a fraction* of Unity: he becomes an *integer* only in the recognition and performance of the Moral Law. Nevertheless it is most true (and a truth which cannot with safety be overlooked) that Morality[g] *as* Morality, has no existence for *a People*. It is either absorbed and lost in the quicksands of Prudential Calculus, or it is taken up and transfigured into the duties and mysteries of Religion. And no wonder: since Morality (including the *personal* being, the I AM,[2] as its subject) is itself a Mystery, and the ground and *suppositum*[3] of all other Mysteries, relatively to Man.

---

[a] *AR* (1825): instruments
[b] COPY C: in whatever age and country
[c] *AR* (1825): People
[d] COPY C: thro'
[e] *AR* (1825): p 288
[f] *AR* (1825): Agent
[g] *AR* (1825): Morality,

[1] On the evidence of this aphorism and a notebook entry of 1823–4, *CN* IV 5059, J. R. Barth argues that C had not at this time formulated his distinction between the National Church and the Christian Church with any clarity: Barth 160.

[2] C extends the point in *CN* IV 5243: ". . . a finite Will can become personal, an I am, only under the condition of the Eternal Logos enlightening it". For further discussion see *C Pantheist* ch 3.

[3] "Thing placed under". C has in mind the equivalent Greek word "hypothesis", defined in a notebook entry of 1809 as follows: "Hypothesis: the placing of one known fact under others as their *ground* or foundation. Not the fact itself but only its position in a ~~given~~ certain relation is imagined. Where both the position and the fact are imagined, it is Hypopœēsis not Hy-

APHORISM XII[a]

[b]PALEY NOT A MORALIST[c1]

Schemes of conduct, grounded on calculations of Self-interest; or on the average Consequences of Actions, supposing them *general*; form a branch of Political Economy, to which let all due honor[d] be given. Their utility is not here questioned. But however estimable within their own sphere,[e] such schemes, or any one of them in particular, may be, they do not belong to Moral Science, to which both in kind and purpose,[f] they are in all cases *foreign*, and when substituted for it, *hostile*. Ethics, or the *Science* of Morality, does indeed in no wise exclude the consideration of *Action;* but it contemplates[g] the same in its originating spiritual *Source*, without reference to Space or Time or Sensible Existence.[2]

---

[a] *AR* (1825): EDITOR.   [b-c] Added in 1831   [d] *AR* (1825): honour
[e] *AR* (1825): sphere   [f] *AR* (1825): purpose   [g] *AR* (1825): p 289 (templates)

---

pothesis, subfiction not supposition. That certain Bodies fall toward the Center the largest Body near them, as a stone to the Earth, is a *fact/* ponitur ā naturâ, positum est [it is laid down by nature, it has been laid down]—that this is universal and the ground of all the celestial motions is imagined—*sub*ponitur vi imaginatrici humanâ [it is *sup*posed/laid *down* as a foundation by the human imaginative power]—'': *CN* III 3587 f l[v]. Cf also *CM (CC)* I 108, 585, II 605, 886, *Friend (CC)* I 477–8 and n, suggesting a source in Abernethy *An Enquiry into the Probability and Rationality of Mr Hunter's Theory of Life* (1814 [1815]) 8–9, and *C&S (CC)* 182 (on the will as "nunquam positum, semper *suppo*nendum" [never posited, always to be *sup*posed]). The distinction between "supposition" and "subfiction" is developed with the evolution of the word "suffiction": see *Conc* n 68, below.

[1] The title was first added in 1831. For the argument in this aphorism cf *Friend (CC)* I 324–5, and for further references to Paley see *Conc* n 97, below.

[2] *AR* (1825) COPY C has a note here: "I fear, that under the influence of Ignorance self-ignored, the vainest and most conceited thing in Nature! the Disciples of

Bentham, Brougham, Jeffray and Co. would regard it as an additional proof of the *jargon*ism of this Assertion, should I quote the axiom of the great Stagyrite—Scientia non est nisi de Universalibus et Eternis. περί αχρόνων [Science or knowledge is only about Universal and Eternal things. About timeless things]. S. T. C.'' Cf e.g. Aristotle *Metaphysics* 13.9.22 (1086[b]): "without the universal it is impossible to get knowledge'', and *Nicomachean Ethics* 6.3.2 (1139[b]), tr. H. Rackham (LCL 1934): "An object of scientific knowledge, therefore, exists of necessity. It is therefore eternal [ἀίδιον], for everything existing of absolute necessity is eternal; and what is eternal does not come into being or perish.'' The former passage was twice quoted by Tennemann (III 48, 50) in a part of the work C both annotated (*CM—CC—*v) and commented on in Feb 1824 (*CN* IV 5130–3). See *Sp Aph B IX* n 1, above. The word ἄχρονος appears nowhere in Aristotle, but is used in this sense by Plotinus, 4.4.1, by Proclus in *Elements of Theology* 124, and by the Greek Fathers. Cf also *Sp Aph B XVIII* at n 17, below, *Sp Aph B II* n 33, above.

Jeremy Bentham (1748–1832), utilitarian philosopher, and Henry Brougham

Whatever springs out of "the perfect Law of Freedom,"[3] which exists only by its unity with the [a]Will of God, its[b] inherence in the [c]Word of God, and its[d] communion with the Spirit[e] of God—*that* (according to the principles of Moral Science) is GOOD—it is light[f] and Righteousness and very Truth. Whatever seeks to separate itself from the Divine Principle,[g] and proceeds from a false centre in the Agent's particular Will, is EVIL— a work of darkness and contradiction![4] It is Sin and essential Falsehood. Not the outward Deed, constructive, destructive or neutral; not the Deed as a possible Object of the Senses; is the Object of Ethical Science. For this is no Compost, Collectorium or Inventory of Single Duties: nor does it seek in the "multitudinous Sea,"[5] in the predetermined waves, tides and currents [h]of, *Nature,*[i] that freedom, which is exclusively an attribute of *Spirit.*[j] Like all other pure Sciences, whatever it enunciates, and whatever it concludes, it enunciates and concludes *absolutely.* Strictness is its essential Character: and its first Proposition is, "Whosoever shall keep the whole law, and yet offend in one point, he is guilty of all." (*James* ii. 10.)[6] For as the Will or Spirit, the Source and Substance of Moral Good, is one[k] and all,[l] in every part:[7] so must it be the totality,[m] the whole articulated Series of Single Acts, taken as Unity, that can alone, in the severity of Science, be recognized as the proper Counter- part and adequate Representative of a good Will. Is [n]it in this or that

---

[a-b] *AR* (1825): Will,

[c-d] *AR* (1825): Word, and

[e] *AR* (1825): Spirit,

[f] *AR* (1825): Light

[g] *AR* (1825): Principles, ; Corr, COPIES C & D: Principle,

[h-i] *AR* (1825): of Nature

[j] *AR* (1825): Spirit.

[k] *AR* (1825): one,

[l] *AR* (1825): all

[m] *AR* (1825): Totality,

[n] *AR* (1825): p 290

(1778–1868), later (1830) Lord Chancel- lor, were in C's mind at this time in con- nexion with the formation of the Society for the Diffusion of Useful Knowledge (the first committee of which was set up in Apr 1825) and plans for a Metropolitan Univer- sity in London. See *CL* v 445–6 and nn. Francis Jeffrey (1773–1850), critic, had taken part in the foundation of Edinburgh Academy in 1824 (*DNB*). For C's attitude to him in 1825 see *CL* v 421, 475.

[3] See above, *Int Aph XXIII* n 6. The AV reads "liberty".

[4] For C's views on evil see above, *Sp Aph B Xa* n 21.

[5] *Macbeth* II ii 64 ("multitudinous seas").

[6] In a letter to Morgan of 14 May 1814 on the guilt of his opium-taking, C cites this text, commenting: "I used to think [it] very harsh; but my own sad experience has taught me it's aweful, dreadful Truth": *CL* III 490. Cf also a letter to Wade 26 Jun 1814: *CL* III 511.

[7] See above, *Sp Aph B VIIIb* n 61 and references.

limb, or not rather in the whole body, the entire Organismus, that the Law of Life reflects itself? Much *ᵃless, then,ᵇ* can the Law of the Spirit work in fragments.

APHORISM XIII*ᶜ*

Wherever there exists a permanent* Learned Class, having authority and possessing the respect and confidence of the country;*ᵈ* and wherever*ᵉ* the Science of Ethics is acknowledged,*ᶠ* and taught in *this* class as a regular part of a learned education to its future Members generally, but as the special study and indispensable ground-work of such as are intended for Holy Orders;—*there* the Article of Original Sin will be an AXIOM of Faith in *all* Classes. Among the Learned an undisputed *truth*, and with the People a fact,*ᵍ* which no man imagines it possible to deny, the Doc-

---

* A Learned Order must be supposed to consist of three Classes. First, those who are employed in adding to the existing Sum of Power and Knowledge.*ʰ* Second, and most numerous Class, those whose office it is to diffuse through the community at large the practical Results of Science, and that kind and degree of knowledge*ⁱ* and cultivation, which for all is requisite or clearly useful. Third, the Formers and Instructors of the Second—in Schools, Halls, and Universities, or through the medium of the Press. The second Class includes not only the Parochial Clergy, and all others duly ordained to the Ministerial Office; but likewise all the Members of the Legal and Medical Professions, who have received a learned education under accredited and responsible Teachers.[1]

ᵃ⁻ᵇ AR (1825): less then
ᶜ AR (1825): EDITOR.
ᵈ AR (1825): Country;
ᵉ AR (1825): where
ᶠ AR (1825): acknowleged
ᵍ COPY A: *fact,*
ʰ AR (1825): Knowlege.
ⁱ AR (1825): knowlege

[1] In late Jun 1820 C wrote of the ". . . *Idea* of the Church" as an Estate (not to be confused with the current actuality) ". . . comprizing the interests, of ⟨1.⟩ a permanent learned Class, i.e. the Clergy; ⟨2.⟩ those of the proper, i.e. *infirm* Poor . . . and ⟨3.⟩ the adequate proportional instruction of all in all classes, by public Prayer, recitation of the Scriptures, by expounding, preaching, Catechizing, and *schooling*: and last but not least, by the example and influence of a Pastor and a School Master placed, as a germ of civilization and cultivation, in every Parish throughout the Realm": annotation on Baxter *Reliquiae Baxterianae*: *CM (CC)* I 355–6. In a letter of 12 Feb 1821 he complained that ". . . the Gentry and *Clerisy* (including all the learned & educated)" were substituting "Locke for Logic, and Paley for Morality": *CL* v 138 (cf *CN* IV 4800). The use of "clerisy" (from the German *Clerisei*, late Latin *clericia*: *C&S—(CC)*—46n) marks a move by C from his identification of the "permanent learned Class" with the clergy and towards the larger specification in the footnote here. For further discussions see *C&S (CC)* chs 5 and 6; *TT* 7 Apr 1832 *(CC)* I 284–5 (1836 vn, dated 10 Apr, II 164); *CM (CC)* I 578. For the general significance of C's concept (including its influence on thinkers such as Carlyle, Arnold, and Mill) see Ben Knights *The Idea of the Clerisy in the Nineteenth Century* (Cambridge 1978).

trine, thus inwoven in the faith of all,[a] and co-eval with the [b]consciousness of each, will for each and all,[c] possess a reality, *subjective* indeed, yet virtually equivalent to that which we intuitively give to the Objects of our Senses.

With the Learned this will be the case: because the Article is the first—I had almost said, *spontaneous*—product of the Application of Moral Science to History, of which it is the Interpreter. A Mystery in its own right, and by the necessity and essential character of its Subject—(for the Will, like the Life, in every act and product pre-supposes itself, a Past always present, a Present that evermore resolves itself into a Past!)—the Doctrine of Original Sin gives to all the other Mysteries of Religion a common Basis, a connection[d] of dependency, an intelligibility of relation, and[e] total harmony, that supersede extrinsic proof. There is here that same proof from unity of purpose, that same evidence of Symmetry, which in the contemplation of a human skeleton,[f] flashed conviction on the mind of GALEN,[g][2] and kindled meditation into a hymn of praise.

Meanwhile the People, not goaded into doubt by the lessons and examples of their Teachers and Superiors; not drawn away from the Fixed Stars of Heaven, the form and magnitude of which are the same for the naked eye of the Shepherd as for the Telescope of the Sage—from the immediate truths, I mean, of Reason and Conscience to an exercise, [h]to which[i] they have not been trained,[j] of a Faculty which has been imper-

---

[a] *AR* (1825): all
[b] *AR* (1825): p 291
[c] *AR* (1825): all
[d] *AR* (1825): connexion
[e] *AR* (1825): and a
[f] *AR* (1825): skeleton
[g] *AR* (1825): GALEN
[h-i] Added in 1831
[j] *AR* (1825): trained to,

---

[2] Discussing the marvellously apt design of the human body in *De usu partium* 3.10, Galen (129–99) described his treatise as "a true hymn of praise to our Creator". See *Galen on the Usefulness of the Parts of the Body* tr Margaret T. May (Ithaca, NY 1968) I 189. Cf Nathaniel Culverwell *An Elegant and Learned Discourse of the Light of Nature* (1652) ed R. A. Greene and H. MacCallum (Toronto 1971) 8: "*Galen* a Physician was wrought upon, by some Anatomicall observations to tune an hymne to the praise of his Creatour, though otherwise Atheist enough", and Robert South *Twelve Sermons* Sermon II (1692) 85–6: "*Galen*, who had no more Divinity, than what his Physick taught him, barely upon the consideration of this so exact frame of the Body, challenges any one upon an hundred years study, to find, how any the least fibre, or most minute particle might be more commodiously placed, either for the advantage of use, or comeliness." For C's knowledge of this sermon see above, *Sp Aph B Xb* n 76.

fectly developed, on a subject not within the ^{a}sphere of the Faculty nor in any way amenable to its judgment; the PEOPLE will need no arguments to receive a doctrine confirmed by their own experience from within and from without, and intimately blended with the most venerable Traditions common to all races, and the Traces of which linger in the latest twilight of Civilization.[3]

Among the revulsions consequent on the brute bewilderments of a godless Revolution, a great and active Zeal for the interests of Religion may be one. I dare not trust it, till I have seen what^b it is that gives Religion this interest, till I am satisfied that ^{c}it is^d not the Interests of this World; necessary and laudable interests, perhaps, but which may, I dare believe, be secured as effectually and more suitably by the Prudence of this World, and by this World's powers and motives. At all events, I find nothing in the fashion of the day to deter me from adding, that the Reverse of the preceding—that where Religion is valued and patronized as a supplement of Law, or an Aid extraordinary of Police;[4] where Moral SCIENCE is exploded as the mystic Jargon of Dark Ages; where a lax System of Consequences, by which every iniquity on earth may be (and how many *have* been!) denounced and defended with equal plausibility, is publicly and authoritatively taught as Moral Philosophy; where the Mysteries of Religion, and Truths supersensual,[5] are either cut and squared for the comprehension of the Understanding, "the faculty of^e judging according to Sense," or desperately torn asunder from ^{f}the Reason, nay, fanatically opposed to it:^{g} lastly, where Private* Interpretation

* The Author of the STATESMAN'S MANUAL must be the most inconsistent of men, if he can be justly suspected of a leaning to the Romish Church:[6] or if it be necessary for him to repeat his fervent Amen to the Wish and prayer of our late good old King,[7] that every

^{a} *AR* (1825): p 292
^{b} *AR* (1825): *what*
$^{c-d}$ *AR* (1825): they are
^{e} Added in 1831
^{f} *AR* (1825): p 293
^{g} *AR* (1825): it;

[3] *AR* (1825) COPY C inserts a heading here, "Aphorism XIII + 1", followed by the footnote, "This §ph should have been printed as a separate Aphorism. In order to save the trouble of altering all the following numbers, I have numbered it as above./" COPIES D and E follow, with minor changes.

[4] Quoted approvingly by H. J. Rose *The Commission and Consequent Duties of the Clergy; in a Series of Discourses Preached Before the University of Cambridge, in*

April 1826 (1828) 5. For Rose see *DNB* and, for his friendship with C, Indexes to *CL* IV and to *Friend (CC)*.

[5] See above, *Sp Aph B Xb* n 23.

[6] In *SM (CC)* 6 C refers to ". . . those who are still under chains of papal darkness" and to England as having ". . . like another Goshen *been severed from the plague*".

[7] When George III (1738–1820) met Joseph Lancaster in 1805 he expressed this wish concerning every child in his domin-

is every thing and the Church nothing—*there* the Mystery of Original Sin will be either rejected, or evaded, or perverted into the monstrous fiction of Hereditary Sin, Guilt inherited;[11] *a*in the Mystery of Redemption metaphors will be obtruded for the reality; and in the mysterious Appurtenants and Symbols of Redemption (Regeneration, Grace, the Eucharist, and Spiritual Communion) the realities will be evaporated into metaphors.[12]

Adult in the British Empire should be able to read his Bible, and have a Bible to read! Nevertheless, it may not be superfluous to declare, that in thus protesting against the *license*[b] of private interpretation, the Editor does not mean to condemn the exercise or deny the right of individual judgment.[8] He condemns only the pretended right of every Individual, competent and incompetent, to interpret Scripture in a sense of his own, in opposition to the judgment of the Church, without knowledge[c] of the Originals or of the Languages, the History, Customs, Opinions, and Controversies of the Age and Country in which they were written; and where the Interpreter judges in ignorance or in contempt of uninterrupted Tradition, the unanimous Consent of Fathers and Councils, and the universal Faith of the Church in all ages. It is not the attempt to form a judgment, which is here called in question; but the grounds, or rather the *no-grounds*, on which the judgment is formed and relied on—the self-willed and separative (*schismatic*) Setting-up (*haeresis*). *See note to page* 33.

My fixed Principle is: that A CHRISTIANITY WITHOUT A CHURCH EXERCISING SPIRITUAL AUTHORITY IS VANITY AND DISSOLUTION.[9] And my *belief* is, that when Popery is rushing in on us like an inundation, the Nation will find it to be so. I say *Popery*: for this too I hold for a delusion, that Romanism or *Roman* Catholicism is separable from Popery.[10] Almost as readily could I suppose a Circle without a Centre.

---

a AR (1825): p 294   *b* AR (1825): *licence*   *c* AR (1825): knowlege

---

ions, cited in *G Mag* LXXXVI pt 1 (1816) 324, as ''. . . our venerable Monarch's prayer . . . that 'every cottager in his dominions should read his Bible' ''. See *LS (CC)* 165 n 3.

[8] For a full account of C's views on authority in scriptural interpretation see Barth ch 3 (esp pp 79–84 and refs) and pp 164–5.

[9] In both the ms and COPY G of *C&S* a note before C's account of the ''. . . moral history of the last 130 years'' reads: ''With the exception of the last sentence, which is extracted from my '*Aids to Reflection*', p 293, this 'brief history' was written about the year 1808, and republished in the *Friend*, Vol. III. p. 130.'' The present sentence, from p 293 in both *AR* (1825) and (1831), is probably the one indicated, since the passage identifiable with *The Friend* ends: ''But the existence of a true philosophy, or the power and habit of contemplating particulars in the unity and fontal mirror of the idea—this in the rulers and teachers of a nation is indispensable to a

sound state of religion in all classes. In fine, Religion, true or false, is and ever has been the centre of gravity in a realm, to which all other things must and will accommodate themselves'': *C&S (CC)* 69–70. The last sentence (var) is from *The Friend (CC)* I 477; it may be that C intended to add the present sentence from *AR* to end and clinch the paragraph, but then forgot.

[10] C enlarged on this point in *C&S (CC)* 129–42.

[11] C did not totally reject the idea, however; cf his annotation on Leighton COPY C II 146: ''The Body of each man does perhaps represent & be the result of the moral qualities, good and evil, of his progenitors . . . On this Idea I ground a distinction between Original & Hereditary Sin—& believe both'': *CM (CC)* III.

[12] The point concerning realities and metaphors appears also in a letter to Samuel Mence 12 Jan 1825, for which see below, *Sp Aph B XVII* n 8.

As in great Maps or Pictures you will see the border decorated with meadows, fountains, flowers, &c. represented in it, but in the middle you have the main design: so amongst the works of God is it with the fore-ordained Redemption of Man.[2] All his other works in the world, all the beauty of the creatures, the succession of ages and the things that come to pass in them, are but as the Border to this as the Mainpiece. But as a foolish unskilful beholder, not discerning the excellency of the principal piece in such maps or pictures, gazes only on the fair Border, and goes no farther—thus do the greatest part of us[3] as to this great Work of God, the redemption of our personal Being, and the re-union of the Human with the Divine, by and through the Divine Humanity of the Incarnate Word.

APHORISM XV*b*1

It is a hard matter, yea, an impossible thing for thy human strength, whosoever thou art (without God's assistance), at such a time when

---

a *AR* (1825): LEIGHTON.   *b* *AR* (1825): LUTHER.

[1] The text here is evidently taken from a version sent by C to the printer (transcribed in App B(v) below), which had been in turn adapted from the text of Leighton COPY C I 142 (marked as a Spiritual Aphorism) and from the alterations already made by C there: *CM (CC)* III. See below, nn 2, 3.

[2] Leighton's text reads: ". . . thus is this fore-ordained redemption amongst the works of God". As altered by C in COPY C it runs: ". . . so is it with the redemption of the moral & intelligential Being in Man amongst the works of God".

[3] From here Leighton reads: "; our eyes are taken with the goodly shew of the world and appearance of earthly things; but as for this great work of God, Christ *fore-ordained*, and in time sent for our redemption, though it most deserves our attentive regard, yet we do not view and consider it as we ought." The text as altered by C in COPY C runs: ". . . as to the redemption of ~~Human~~ Personal Nature, and the re-union of the Human with the Divine by and thro' the Divine Humanity of the Word".

[1] Adapted from Martin Luther *Colloquia Mensalia* (1652) 190. For the original text see below, App A(o). C makes some important changes: see nn 2–5, below. He

annotated this paragraph in his copy, now in the BM, as follows:

"And Sin and Sorrow and the wormy Grave
Shapes of a Dream.
Religious Musings.

Yea, verily, Amen and Amen! For this short heroic Paragraph contains the sum and substance, the heighth and the depth of all true Philosophy—. Most assuredly, right difficult it is for us, while we are yet in the narrow chamber of Death with our faces to the dusky ⟨falsifying⟩ *Looking-glass* that covers the scant end-side of the blind passage from floor to ceiling, right difficult for us so wedged between its walls that we cannot turn round nor have other escape possible but by walking backward, to understand that all we behold or have any memory of having ever beheld, yea, our very selves as seen by us, are but *shadows*—and when the forms, that we loved, vanish, impossible not to feel as if real": *CM (CC)* III. For C's attitude to Luther see below, *Sp Aph B XIX* n 4. *Religious Musings* 1. 397 reads "And vice, and anguish, . . . !": *PW* (EHC) I 124.

Moses setteth on thee with the Law (see Aphorism XII.), when the holy Law written in thy heart accuseth and condemneth thee,[2] [a]forcing thee to a comparison of thy heart therewith, and convicting thee of the incompatibleness of thy Will and Nature with Heaven and Holiness and an immediate God—that then thou shouldest be able to be of such a mind[3] as if no Law nor Sin had ever been! I say it is in a manner impossible that a human creature, when he feeleth himself assaulted with trials and temptations, and the Conscience hath to do with God, and the tempted man knoweth that the root of temptation is within him, should obtain such mastery over his thoughts[4] as then to think no otherwise than that FROM EVERLASTING NOTHING HATH BEEN BUT ONLY AND ALONE CHRIST, ALTOGETHER GRACE AND DELIVERANCE![5]

COMMENT

In irrational Agents, viz. the Animals, the Will is hidden or absorbed in the Law.[6] The Law is their *Nature*. In the original purity of a rational Agent the uncorrupted Will is identical with the Law. Nay, inasmuch as a Will perfectly identical with the Law is one with the *divine* Will, we may say, that in the unfallen rational Agent the Will *constitutes* the Law[7]*[b]. But it is evident that the holy and spiritual Power and Light,

* In fewer words thus: For the Animals, their Nature is their Law—for what other third Law can be imagined, in addition to the Law of Nature, and the Law of Reason? Therefore: in irrational Agents the Law constitutes the Will. In moral and rational agents the Will constitutes, or ought to constitute, the Law: I speak of moral agents, unfallen. For the personal Will comprehends the *idea*, as a Reason, and it gives causative force to the Idea, as a *practical* Reason. But Idea + the power of realizing the same = a Law; or say:—the Spirit comprehends the Moral Idea, by virtue of it's rationality, and it gives to the Idea causative Power, as a Will: In every sense therefore, it *constitutes* the Law, supplying both the Elements of which it consists—viz. the Idea, and the realizing Power.

[a] *AR* (1825): p 295
[b] Footnote added in 1831

[2] *Colloquia Mensalia* 190 reads: ". . . (at such a time when *Moses* setteth upon thee with his Law, and fearfully affrighteth thee, accuseth and condemneth thee . . ."

[3] From "condemneth thee," to here, *Colloquia Mensalia* runs: "threatneth thee with God's wrath and death) thou shouldest as then bee of such a minde; namely . . .".

[4] From "impossible" to here, *Colloquia Mensalia* reads: ". . . that a humane creature should carrie himself in such a sort, when hee is and feeleth himself assaulted with trials and temptations, and when the conscience hath to do with

God . . .".

[5] The small capitals are C's.

[6] Cf *CN* IV 5203 (on "infra-rational" agents): "In the last, as in Animals, the Will is absorbed in the Law—or the Law constitutes the Will."

[7] Ibid: ". . . in the pure or unfallen Nature of a rational agent the Will constitutes, is identified with the Law—(we may say, constitutes the Law—for a Will identical with the Law is one with the *Divine* Will) . . .". The remainder of the notebook entry is also relevant to this paragraph.

which by a *prolepsis* or anticipation we have *named* Law, is a grace, an inward perfection, and without the commanding, binding and menacing character which belongs to a Law, acting as a Master or Sovereign distinct from, and existing, as it were, externally for, the Agent who is bound to obey it. Now *ᵃ*this is St. Paul's sense of the Word: and on this he grounds his whole reasoning. And hence too arises the obscurity and apparent paradox of several texts. That the Law is a *Law* for you; that it acts *on* the Will not *in* it; that it exercises an agency *from without*, by fear and coercion; proves the corruption of your Will, and presupposes it. Sin in this sense came by the Law:[8] for it has its essence, as Sin, in that counter-position of the Holy Principle to the Will, which occasions this Principle to be a LAW. Exactly (as in all other points) consonant with the Pauline doctrine is the assertion of John, when speaking of the re-adoption of the redeemed to be Sons of God, and the consequent resumption (I had almost said, re-absorption) of the Law into the Will (νόμον τέλειον τὸν τῆς ἐλευθερίας,*ᵇ* James i. 25. See p. 30,)[9] he says— For the law was given by Moses; but Grace and Truth came by Jesus Christ.*ᶜ*[10] That by the Law St. Paul meant only the *ceremonial* Law is a notion, that could originate only in utter inattention to the whole strain and bent*ᵈ* of the Apostle's*ᵉ* Argument.

APHORISM XVI*ᶠ*[1]

Christ's Death was both voluntary and violent.[2] There was external violence: and that was the accompaniment, or at most the occasion, of his

ᵃ AR (1825): p 296
ᵇ AR (1825): no accents or breathing in Greek
ᶜ AR (1825): Christ, P.S.
ᵈ AR (1825): gist
ᵉ AR (1825): Apostles'
ᶠ AR (1825): LEIGHTON AND ED.

[8] Cf Rom 5.13: ". . . until the law sin was in the world: but sin is not imputed when there is no law", and 7.7: "What shall we say then? Is the law sin? God forbid. Nay, I had not known sin, but by the law . . .". C is preoccupied again by St Paul's arguments in Rom 5–8: see above, *Sp Aph B Xb* at nn 66, 67.

[9] The 1831 reading, p 29, mechanically adapts to the 1831 pagination the 1825 reference, "p. 26". It is clear, however, that the latter should have read "p 16n", in which the text in question is quoted and discussed, and that the 1831 reading should therefore have been "pp 18–19". The reference was dropped altogether from the 4th ed onwards.

[10] John 1.17. See below, *Sp Aph B XXIIIb* n 47 and references.

[1] This aphorism, which corresponds to passages in Leighton COPY C II 124, 125–6, 127, but left unmarked there, is produced by a more eclectic process than usual. For the original text see below, App A(p). C's quotations and adaptations, which are not always consecutive, are reported below, nn 2–12.

[2] From Leighton COPY C II 124 lines 17–18.

Death. But there was internal willingness, the spiritual Will, the Will of the Spirit, and this was the proper cause.[3] By this Spirit he was restored from Death: neither indeed "was it *possible* for him to be holden of it." (*Acts* ii.[a] 24–27.)[b4] "Being put to death in the flesh, but quickened by the Spirit," says St. Peter.[5] But he is likewise declared elsewhere to have died by that same Spirit, which here in opposition to the violence is said to quicken him. Thus *Hebrews* ix. 14. *Through the eternal Spirit he offered himself.*[6] And even from Peter's words, and without the epithet, eternal, to aid the interpretation, it is evident that *the Spirit*, here opposed to the Flesh, Body or Animal Life, is of a higher nature and power than the individual *Soul*, which cannot of itself return to re-inhabit or quicken the Body.[7]

If these points were niceties, and an over-refining in doctrine, is it to be believed that the Apostles, John, Peter and Paul, with the Author of the Epistle[c] to the Hebrews,[8] would have laid[d] so great stress on them? But the true Life of Christians is to eye Christ in every step of his life—not only as their Rule but as their Strength: looking to him as their Pattern both in doing and in suffering, and drawing power from him for going through both: being *without him* able for nothing. Take comfort then, thou that believest! *It is he that lifts up the Soul from the Gates of Death:* [9] and he hath said, *I will raise thee up at the last day.*[10] Thou that believest *in* him, believe him and take comfort.[11] Yea, when thou art

---

[a] *AR* (1825): ii. v. (p 297 begins with "v.")

[b] *AR* (1825): 27.).

[c] *AR* (1825): Ep.

[d] *AR* (1825): layed

---

[3] These two sentences are expanded from Leighton COPY C II 125 lines 18–19, which read simply: "Thus, then, there was in His death, external violence joined with internal willingness."

[4] Based loosely on Leighton COPY C II 126, lines 1–4: "The chains of that prison are strong, but He was too strong a prisoner to be held by them; as our Apostle hath it in his sermon, (Acts ii. 24.) that it was *not possible that He should be kept by them.*"

[5] Quoted in Leighton COPY C II 125 lines 33–4 as part of the text (1 Pet 3.18) that Leighton is commenting on.

[6] Leighton COPY C II 124 lines 20–5 reads: "He therefore took our flesh, to put it off thus, and to offer it up as a sacrifice, which, to be acceptable, must of necessity be free and voluntary; and, in that sense, He is said to have died even by that same

Spirit, which here, in opposition to death, is said to quicken him. See Heb. ix. 14."

[7] After "evident that . . ." C follows Leighton COPY C II 124: "But the *Spirit*, here opposed to the *flesh* or body, is certainly of a higher nature and power than is the human soul, which cannot of itself return to re-inhabit and quicken the body."

[8] See below, *Sp Aph B XXIIIb* n 27.

[9] Leighton COPY C II 127 lines 36–8 reads: "Rest on His power and goodness, which never failed any who did so. *It is He* (as David says) *who lifts up the soul from the gates of death.*" The quotation is from Ps 9.13: ". . . thou that liftest me up from the gates of death".

[10] C is quoting from John 6.40 (= 6.44, 54): ". . . I will raise him up at the last day".

[11] Loosely based on Leighton COPY C II

most sunk in thy sad apprehensions, and he far off to thy thinking, then is he nearest to raise and comfort thee: as sometimes it grows darkest immediately before day.[12]

^aAPHORISM XVII^{b1}

Would any of you be cured of that common disease, the fear of Death?[2] Yet this is not the right name of the Disease, as a mere reference to our armies and navies is sufficient to prove: nor can the fear of death, either as loss of life or pain of dying, be justly held a *common* disease. But would you be cured of the fear and fearful questionings connected with the approach of death? Look this way, and you shall find more than you seek.[3] Christ, the Word that was from the beginning, and was made flesh and dwelt among men, died. And he, who dying conquered death in his own person, conquered Sin, and Death which is the Wages of Sin, for thee. And of this thou mayest be assured, if only thou believe in him, and love him. I need not add, keep his commandments: since where Faith and Love are, Obedience in its threefold character, as Effect, Reward, and Criterion, follows by that moral necessity which is the highest form of freedom. The Grave is thy bed of rest, and no longer the *cold* bed: for thy Saviour has warmed it, and made it fragrant.[4]

If then it be health and comfort to the Faithful that Christ descended into the grave, with especial confidence may we meditate on his return

^a *AR* (1825): p 298
^b *AR* (1825): L. AND ED.

127 lines 28–31: "Thus may a believing soul at the lowest, when, to its own sense, it is given over unto death . . . yet look up to this Divine power."

[12] This sentence is from Leighton COPY C II 127 lines 32–5.

[1] Based on Leighton COPY C II 127–8 (unmarked there). For the original text see App A(q), below. In the first paragraph only three sentences (indicated below) are from Leighton; the rest is C's own reworking of the ideas there. The next paragraph is more intimately related. For a discussion of the ideas see Barth 188.

[2] From Leighton COPY C II 127–8.

[3] This sentence is from Leighton COPY C II 128 lines 1–2 (immediately following the previous sentence quoted).

[4] Leighton COPY C II 128 lines 17–20 reads (of death): " . . . the Believer cannot

choose but embrace it. He longs to lie down in that bed of rest, since his Lord lay in it, and hath warmed that cold bed, and purified it with His fragrant body." C's more sober version is consistent with his protests against WW's lines in the Immortality Ode:

> To whom the grave
> Is but a lonely bed without the sense of
>   sight
> Of day or the warm light,
> A place of thought where we in waiting
>   lie.

In *BL* it was the specific idea of lying awake in the grave against which he inveighed: *BL* ch 22 *(CC)* II 140–1. (WW omitted the lines after 1815 as a result: see *WPW* IV 467.)

from thence, *quickened by the Spirit:* this being to those who are in him the certain pledge, yea, the effectual cause of that blessed resurrection, for which they themselves hope.[5] There is that union betwixt them and their *a*Redeemer, that they shall rise by the communication and virtue of his rising: not simply by his *power*—for so the *wicked* likewise to their grief shall be raised; but *they by his life as their life.*[6]

COMMENT

^bON THE THREE PRECEDING APHORISMS^c

To the Reader, who has consented to submit his mind to my temporary guidance, and who permits me to regard him as my Pupil or Junior Fellow-student, I continue to address myself. Should he exist only in my imagination, let the bread float on the waters! If it be the Bread of Life, it will not have been utterly cast away.[7]

Let us pause a moment, and review the road we have passed over since the Transit from Religious Morality to Spiritual Religion. My first attempt was to satisfy you, that there *is* a Spiritual principle in Man (p. 134–43), and to expose the sophistry of the arguments in support of the Contrary. Our next step was to clear the road of all Counterfeits, by showing what is *not* the Spirit, what is *not* Spiritual Religion (p. 146–53). And this was followed by an attempt to establish a difference in kind between religious truths and the deductions of speculative science; yet so as to prove, that the former are not only equally rational with the latter, but that they alone appeal to Reason in the fulness and living reality of the Power. This and the state of mind requisite for the formation of right *d*convictions respecting spiritual Truths, afterwards*e* employed our attention.*f* Having then enumerated the Articles of the Christian Faith *peculiar* to Christianity, I entered on the great object of the

^a AR (1825): p 299
^{b-c} AR (1825): On the three preceding Aphorisms.
^d AR (1825): p 300
^e Added in 1831
^f AR (1825): attention from p. 158 to 188.

[5] After "the grave" C follows Leighton COPY C II 128 lines 20–3: "But especially be looking forward to His return thence, *quickened by the Spirit*; this being to those who are in Him, the certain pledge, yea, the effectual cause, of that blessed resurrection which is in their hopes."

[6] From Leighton COPY C II 128 lines 23–7. C inserts ". . . and their Redeemer" after "them" and underlines "power", "wicked", and "they by . . . life" (substituting "their life" for "theirs").

[7] Eccles 11.1: "Cast thy bread upon the waters: for thou shalt find it after many days." John 6.35: "And Jesus said unto them, I am the bread of life . . ." (cf 6.48, 51, 58).

present work: viz. the removal of all valid Objections to these articles on grounds of right Reason or Conscience. But to render this practicable it was necessary, first, to present each Article in its true scriptural purity, by exposure of the caricatures of misinterpreters; and this, again, could not be satisfactorily done till we were agreed respecting the Faculty, entitled to sit in judgment on such questions. I early foresaw, that my best chance (I will not say, of giving an *insight* into the surpassing worth and transcendent reasonableness of the Christian Scheme; but) of rendering the very question intelligible, depended on my success in determining the true nature and limits of the human UNDERSTANDING, and in evincing its *diversity* from REASON. In pursuing this momentous subject, I was tempted in two or three instances into disquisitions, that if not beyond the comprehension, were yet unsuited to the taste, of the persons for whom the Work was principally intended. These, however, I have separated from the running text, and compressed into Notes. The Reader will at worst, I hope, pass them by as a leaf or two of waste paper, willingly given by him to those, for whom it may not be paper *wasted*. Nevertheless, I cannot conceal, that the subject itself supposes, on the part of the Reader, a steadiness in *self-questioning*, a pleasure in referring to his own inward experience for the facts *[a]*asserted by the Author, that can only be expected from a person who has fairly set his heart on arriving at clear and fixed conclusions in matters of Faith. But where this interest is felt, nothing more than a common Capacity, with the ordinary advantages of education, is required for the complete comprehension both of the argument and the result. Let but one thoughtful hour be devoted to the pages 207–38. In all that follows, the Reader will find no difficulty in *understanding* the Author's meaning, whatever he may have in *adopting* it.

The two great moments of the Christian Religion are, Original Sin and Redemption; *that* the Ground, *this* the Superstructure of our faith.[8] The former I have exhibited, first, according to the scheme of the Westminster Divines and the Synod of Dorp;[9] then, according to the* scheme

---

* To escape the consequences of this scheme, some Arminian Divines have asserted that the penalty inflicted on Adam and continued in his posterity was simply the loss of immortality, Death as the utter extinction of personal Being: immortality being regarded

---

[a] AR (1825): p 301

[8] Cf C's letter to Samuel Mence 12 Jan 1825, in which he speaks of ". . . the two great Moments of the Christian Faith, ORIGINAL SIN (i.e. Sin, as the *Source of* sinful actions) and Redemption; that the *Ground*, and this the *Superstructure*, of

Christianity": *CL* v 406. This passage would have been in proof when he wrote the letter. For discussions of C's opinions on these two issues see Barth chs 5 and 6.

[9] See Taylor Σύμβολον Θεολογικόν 871–2 for his account of the Synod of Dort and

by them (and not, I think, without good reason) as a supernatural*[a]* attribute, and its loss therefore involved in the forfeiture of super-natural graces. This theory has *its golden side;[b]* and as a private opinion, is said to have the countenance of more than one Dignitary of our Church, whose general orthodoxy is beyond impeachment. For here the *Penalty* resolves itself into the *Consequence*, and this the natural and (*naturally*) inevitable Consequence of Adam's Crime. For Adam, indeed, it was a *positive* punishment: a punishment of his guilt, the justice of which who could have dared arraign? While for the Offspring of Adam it was simply a *not* super-adding to their nature the privilege by which the Original Man was contra-distinguished from the brute creation—a mere negation,*[c]* of which they had no more right to complain than any other species of Animals. God in this view appears only in his Attribute of Mercy, as averting by supernatural interposition a consequence naturally inevitable. This is the golden side of the Theory. But if we approach to it from the opposite direction, it first excites a just scruple from the countenance it seems to give to the doctrine of Materialism. The Supporters of this Scheme do not, I presume, contend, that Adam's Offspring would not have been born *Men*, but have formed a new species of Beasts!*[d]* And if not, the notion of a rational,*[e]* and self-conscious Soul, perishing utterly with the dissolution of the organized Body, seems to require, nay, almost involves*[f]* the opinion that the Soul is a quality or Accident of the Body—a mere harmony resulting from Organization.

But let this pass unquestioned! Whatever else the Descendants of Adam might have been without the Intercession of Christ, yet (this intercession having been effectually made) they are now endowed with Souls that are not extinguished together with the material body. Now unless these Divines teach likewise the Romish figment of Purgatory, and to an extent in which the Church of Rome herself would denounce the doctrine as an impious heresy: unless they hold, that a punishment temporary and remedial the *worst* evil that the Impenitent have to apprehend in a Future State; and that the spiritual Death declared and foretold by Christ, "the Death Eternal where the Worm never dies,"[10] is

---

[a] *AR* (1825): super-natural
[b] *AR* (1825): *side:*
[c] COPY A: privation (or deprivation), ; COPY C: privation
[d] *AR* (1825): Beasts?
[e] *AR* (1825): rational
[f] *AR* (1825): involves,

---

above, *Sp Aph B III* at n 2 and onwards, for some discussion of the issues involved. For the misspelling "Dorp" see *Sp Aph B Xb* n 48 above.

[10] Not an exact quotation. In Mark 9.43–4 Christ says: ". . . it is better for thee to enter into life maimed, than having two hands to go into hell, into the fire that shall never be quenched: Where their worm dieth not, and the fire is not quenched." (Cf vv 45–8.) He also speaks of "everlasting fire" (Matt 18.8, 25.41), "everlasting punishment" (Matt 25.46), and "eternal damnation" (Mark 3.29), but the term "Death Eternal" appears nowhere in AV. In an annotation on *Eternal Punishment Proved to Be Not Suffering, But Privation* (1817) C interpreted the statements of Christ as showing that as eternal life is a

state above time, so eternal death is a state below time, and that the latter must as the contrary of the former be equally a positive state: *CM* II 559, with quotations from *CN* IV 4998 and 5076 in the editor's note. See also his comment on Isa 66.24, and Mark 9.44 etc: ibid 569–70. Even in the patristic period the biblical threats of tortures in Hell were not always taken literally: Justin Martyr and Irenaeus, for example, explained it as a state of privation. This was the destruction of the soul, referred to in Matt 10.28, 2 Thess 1.9, and Phil 3.19; cf also Rom 6.23: "The wages of sin is death, but the gift of God is eternal life." See also *Sp Aph B XIX* n 30, below, the poems *Limbo* and *Ne Plus Ultra*, *PW* (EHC) I 429–31, and App I Excursus Note 17 "Coleridge and the Abyss of Being".

of a contemporary Arminian Divine;[14] and lastly, in contrast with both schemes, I *a*have placed what I firmly believe to be the *Scriptural* Sense of this Article, and vindicated its entire conformity*b* with Reason and Experience. I now proceed to the other momentous Article—from the necessitating *Occasion* of the Christian Dispensation to Christianity itself! For Christianity and REDEMPTION are equivalent terms. And here

---

neither Death nor eternal, but a certain quantum of suffering*c* in a state of faith, hope and progressive amendment—unless they go these lengths (and the Divines here intended are orthodox Churchmen, men who would not knowingly advance even a step on the road towards them)—then I fear, that any advantage, their theory might possess over the Calvinistic Scheme in the Article*d* of Original Sin, would be dearly purchased by increased difficulties and an ultra-Calvinistic narrowness in the article of Redemption. I at least find it impossible, with my present human feelings, not to imagine otherwise, than that even in heaven it would be a fearful thing to know, that in order to my elevation to a lot infinitely more desirable than by nature it would have been, the lot of so vast a multitude had been rendered infinitely more calamitous; and that my felicity had been purchased by the everlasting Misery*e* of the majority of my fellow-men, who, if no redemption had been provided, after inheriting the pains and pleasures of earthly existence during the numbered hours, and the few and evil—evil yet *few*—days of the years of their mortal life, would have fallen asleep to wake no more, would have sunk into the dreamless Sleep of the Grave, and have been as the murmur and the plaint and the exulting swell and the sharp scream which the unequal Gust of Yesterday snatched from the strings of a Wind-Harp![11]

In another place[12] I have ventured to question the spirit and tendency of J. Taylor's Work on Repentance. But I ought to have added, that to discover and keep the true medium in expounding and applying the Efficacy of Christ's Cross and Passion, is beyond comparison*f* the most difficult and delicate point of Practical Divinity—and that which especially needs "*a guidance from above.*"[13]

---

a *AR* (1825): p 302   *b* *AR* (1825): p 303 (formity)
c *AR* (1825): Suffering   *d* *AR* (1825): article   *e* *AR* (1825): misery
f *AR* (1825): compare

[11] With the murmur and the swell cf the "murmur" of the sea and the "swell" of the wind-harp in *The Eolian Harp* lines 11, 43: *PW* (EHC) I 100–2; for a later plaintive "tender lay" and a sharp "scream | Of agony" from the wind-harp see *Dejection: an Ode* lines 117–25 and 97–9: *PW* (EHC) I 367 8. Cf also *IS* 401. For further discussion see Beer *CV* 89–92 and Geoffrey Grigson *The Harp of Aeolus and Other Essays* (1947) 24–46.

[12] See *Friend (CC)* I 433–4, concluding: ". . . I could never read Bishop Taylor's Tract on the doctrine and practice of Repentance, without being tempted to characterize high Calvinism as (comparatively)

a lamb in wolf's skin, and strict Arminianism as approaching to the reverse". Cf also C's annotation on this tract (*Unum Necessarium*) on an end-page of Σύμβολον Θεολογικόν: *LR* III 296–8, C *17th C* 290, *CM (CC)*.

[13] The locution "From above" is both Biblical and Wordsworthian. C is probably recalling the ". . . leading from above" of *Resolution and Independence* line 51: *WPW* II 237, but substituting the equally Wordsworthian "guidance" (e.g. "Urania, I shall need | Thy guidance": Preface to 1814 *Excursion* lines 25–6: *WPW* V 3).

[14] I.e. Jeremy Taylor: see *Sp Aph B X*, above.

my Comment will be comprised[a] in a few sentences:[b] for I confine my views to the one object of clearing this awful mystery from those too current misrepresentations of its nature and import, that have laid it open to scruples and objections, not to such as shoot forth from an unbelieving heart—(against these a sick bed[c] will be a more effectual Antidote than all the Argument in the world!)[15] but to such scruples as have their birth-place in the Reason and Moral Sense. Not that it is a Mystery— not that "it passeth all *Understanding!*"[16] If the doctrine be more than an hyperbolical phrase, it *must* do so. But that it is at variance with the Law revealed in the Conscience, that it contradicts our moral instincts and intuitions—*this* is the difficulty, which alone is worthy of an answer! And what better way is there of correcting the misconceptions than by laying open the source and occasion of them? What surer way of removing the scruples and prejudices, to which these misconceptions have given rise, than by propounding the Mystery itself—namely, THE REDEMPTIVE ACT, as the transcendent *Cause* of Salvation—in the express and definite words, in which it was enunciated by the Redeemer himself?

But here, in addition to the three Aphorisms preceding, I interpose a view of redemption as appropriated by faith, coincident with Leighton's,[d] though for the greater part expressed in my own words. *This* I propose as the right view. Then follow a few sentences transcribed from Field (an excellent Divine of James the First's reign, of whose work, entitled the [e]Church, it would be difficult to speak too highly)[17] containing the question to be solved, and which is numbered, as an Aphorism, rather to preserve the uniformity of appearance, than as being strictly such. Then follows the Comment: as part and commencement of which the Reader will consider the two paragraphs of p. 204–6,[18] written for this purpose and in the foresight of the present inquiry: and I entreat him therefore to begin the Comment by re-perusing[f] these.

[a] *AR* (1825): p 304 (prised)
[b] COPY C: pages:
[c] *AR* (1825): sick-bed
[d] *AR* (1825): Leighton's
[e] *AR* (1825): p 305
[f] *AR* (1825): reperusing

[15] In a letter of 11 Dec 1796 C wrote: "I have been myself sorely afflicted . . . till it pleased the Unimaginable High & Lofty One to make my Heart more tender in regard of religious feelings. My philosophical refinements, & metaphysical Theories lay by me in the hour of anguish, as toys by the bedside of a Child deadly-sick": *CL* I 267. Cf *CN* I 182 and n, in which the last phrase is traced to Jeremy Taylor.

[16] Phil 4.7: ". . . the peace of God, which passeth all understanding".

[17] Richard Field *Of the Church* (3rd ed Oxford 1635). C's copy, copiously annotated, is now in VCL: *CM (CC)* II 649–86.

[18] I.e. the distinction between analogies and metaphors.

APHORISM XVIII[1]

Stedfast by Faith. This is absolutely necessary for resistance to the Evil Principle.[2] There is no standing out without some firm ground to stand on: and this Faith alone supplies.[3] By Faith in the Love of Christ the power of God becomes ours.[4] When the Soul is beleaguered by enemies, Weakness on the Walls, Treachery at the Gates, and Corruption in the Citadel,[5] then by Faith[a] she says—Lamb of God, slain from the foundation of the World! thou art my Strength![6] I look to thee for deliverance! And thus she overcomes. The pollution (*miasma*) of Sin is precipitated by his Blood,[7] the power of Sin is conquered by his Spirit. The Apostle says not—stedfast by your own resolutions and purposes; but—*stedfast by faith.*[8] Nor yet stedfast in your Will, but *stedfast in the faith.* We are not to be looking to, or brooding over ourselves, either for accusation or for confidence, or (by a deep yet too frequent self-delusion) to obtain the latter by [b]making a *merit* to ourselves of the former. But we are to look to CHRIST and ''him crucified.''[9] The Law ''that is very nigh to thee, even in thy heart;''[10] the Law that condemneth and hath no promise; that stoppeth the guilty PAST in its swift flight,[11] and maketh it

[a] *AR* (1825): faith
[b] *AR* (1825): p 306

[1] As C suggests in his previous paragraph, he takes his starting-point here from Leighton but then proceeds in his own words. The initial sources, which are indicated in subsequent notes, are from two paragraphs in COPY C II 356, unmarked in the original (they are reproduced in App A(r)). The aphorism then moves into an affirmation of C's own conviction of the need for faith in Christ.

[2] Leighton COPY C II 356 lines 5–6 reads: ''*Stedfast*, or solid, *by faith.* This is absolutely necessary for resistance.''

[3] Ibid lines 6–9: ''A man cannot fight upon a quagmire; there is no standing out without a standing, some firm ground to tread upon; and this, Faith alone furnishes.''

[4] Ibid lines 13–14: ''The power of God, by faith becomes ours . . .''.

[5] Ibid lines 25–6: ''When the soul is surrounded with enemies on all hands, so that there is no way of escape . . .''.

[6] Rev 13.8: ''. . . the book of life of the Lamb slain from the foundation of the world''; Ps 31.1, 4: ''In thee, O Lord, do I put my trust . . . deliver me in thy righteousness . . . . for thou art my strength'';

cf Leighton COPY C II 356 lines 15–16: ''Faith lays hold there, and there finds Almighty strength.''

[7] Prompted, possibly, by Leighton's quagmire image (see n 3 above), C produces a further variant on his imagery of mists of superstition dissipated by the rising sun (see above, *Int Aph XXIX* n 5) or mists of passivity, dispersed by a gale of energy (*BL* ch 15—*CC*—II 22). Here the poisonous marsh-vapour is rendered harmless by the chemical agency of Christ's blood, turning it back into its original element.

[8] From Leighton COPY C II 356 lines 11–13.

[9] An echo of 1 Cor 2.2: ''For I determined not to know any thing among you, save Jesus Christ, and him crucified.''

[10] Deut 30.14: ''. . . the word is very nigh unto thee, in thy mouth, and in thy heart, that thou mayest do it''.

[11] An important long note distinguishing between criminal Deed and wicked Act is inserted here in *AR* (1825) COPY A, and on the end-papers of COPIES B, C, and D. For the various versions, see below, App D(b).

disown its name; the LAW will accuse thee enough. Linger not in the Justice-court, listening to thy indictment![a] Loiter not in waiting to hear the Sentence! No! Anticipate the verdict! *Appeal to Caesar!*[12] Haste to the King for a Pardon! Struggle thitherward, though in fetters;[b] and cry aloud, and collect the whole remaining strength of thy Will in the Outcry—I believe! Lord! help my unbelief![13] Disclaim all right of property in thy fetters! Say, that they belong to the *Old Man*,[14] and that thou dost but carry them to the Grave, to be buried with their Owner! Fix thy thought on what *Christ* did, what *Christ* suffered, what *Christ* is—as if thou wouldst fill the hollowness of thy Soul with Christ![15] If he emptied himself of glory[c16] to become Sin for thy salvation, must not thou be emptied of thy sinful Self to become Righteousness in and through his agony and the effective merits of his Cross*[d]? By what other means, in

* God manifested in the Flesh = Eternity in the form of Time. But Eternity to Time = the absolute to the conditional, or the Real to the Apparent Redemption must partake of both, always perfected, for it is a Fiat of the Eternal;—continuous, for it is a process in relation to man; the former, the alone objectively, and therefore universally, true.[17] That Redemption is an *opus perfectum*, a finished Work, the claim to which is conferred in Baptism; that a Christian cannot speak or think as if his Redemption by the Blood, and his Justification by the Righteousness of Christ alone, were future or contingent events, but must both say and think, I *have been* redeemed, I am justified; lastly, that for as many as are received into his Church by baptism, Christ has condemned Sin in the Flesh,[18] has made it *dead in law, i.e.* no longer imputable as *Guilt*, has destroyed the *objective reality* of Sin: —(See p. 299, 300, Aph. xv.) These are Truths, which all the Reformed Churches, Swedish, Danish, Evangelical, (or Lutheran,) the Reformed, (the Calvinistic in mid-Germany, France, and Geneva, so called,) lastly, the Church of England, and the Church of Scotland—nay, the best and most learned Divines of the Roman Catholic Church have united in upholding as most certain and necessary Articles of Faith, and the effectual preaching of which Luther declares to be the appropriate criterion, *stantis vel cadentis, ecclesiae*.[19] The Church is standing or falling, according as this doctrine is supported, or

[a] *AR* (1825): indightment!   [b] *AR* (1825): fetters:
[c] *AR* (1825): Glory   [d] Footnote added in 1831

[12] Cf St Paul's action in Acts 25.11 and chs 25–8 generally.

[13] Mark 9.24, a favourite text of C's in 1814: cf his letters to Morgan 15 May 1814 and Cottle 27 May 1814: *CL* III 491, 499; and his 1814 annotation on Leighton COPY A I 82: "Lord I believe! help thou my unbelief. My natural reason acquiesces. I believe enough to *fear*—& grant me the Belief that brings sweet Hope": *CM (CC)* III.

[14] Rom 6.6; Eph 4.22; Col 3.9.

[15] For a forceful reiteration of the point, referring back to this passage, see a note on Bunyan *Pilgrim's Progress*: *CM (CC)* I 813.

[16] Cf Phil 2.7, relating how Christ ". . . made himself of no reputation, and took upon him the form of a servant, and was made in the likeness of men". The first clause is a translation of the Greek ἑαυτὸν ἐκένωσε, "he emptied himself"; hence the Christian doctrine of "kenosis".

[17] For C's view of time here, and its relation to redemption and baptism, see above, *Sp Aph B II* n 33. C may have intended a stop after "Apparent".

[18] Rom 8.3.

[19] See Luther's comment on the "first and chief" of the Schmalkaldic Articles concerning Christ: "That Jesus Christe

overlooked, or countervened. Nor has the contrary Doctrine, according to which the Baptized are yet, each individually, to be called, converted, and chosen, with all the corollaries from this assumption, the watching for signs and sensible assurances, ''the frames,'' and ''the states,'' and ''the feelings,'' and ''the sudden conversions,'' the contagious Fever-boils of the (most unfitly, so called) Evangelicals, and Arminian Methodists of the day,[20] been in any age taught or countenanced by any known and accredited Christian Church, or by any Body and Succession of learned Divines. On the other hand it has rarely happened, that the Church has not been troubled by pharisaic and fanatical Individuals, who have sought, by working on the fears and feelings of the weak and unsteady that celebrity, which they could not obtain by learning and orthodoxy: and alas! so subtle is the Poison, and so malignant in its operation, that it is almost hopeless to attempt the cure of any person, once infected, more particularly when, as most often happens, the Patient is a Woman: Nor does Luther in his numerous and admirable Discourses on this point, conceal or palliate the difficulties, which the carnal mind, that works under many and different disguises, throws in the way to prevent the laying firm hold of the Truth.[21] One most mischievous and very popular mis-belief must be cleared away in the first instance—the presumption, I mean, that whatever is not *quite* simple, and what any plain body can understand at the first hearing, cannot be of necessary belief, or among the fundamental Articles or Essentials of Christian Faith. A docile child-like mind, a deference to the authority of the Churches, a presumption of the truth of doctrines that have been received and taught as true by the whole Church in all times,[22] reliance on the positive declarations of the Apostle—in short all the convictions of the truth of a Doctrine that are previous to a perfect *insight* into its truth, because these convictions with the affections and dispositions accompanying them are the very means and conditions of attaining to that insight—and their attention, study, quiet meditation, gradual growth of spiritual knowledge, and earnest prayer for its increase; all these, to each and all of which the young Christian is so repeatedly and fervently exhorted by St. Paul, are to be superseded, because forsooth, truths needful for all men, must be quite simple and easy, and adapted to the capacity of all, even of the plainest and dullest understanding! What cannot be poured all at once on a man, can only be supererogatory Drops from the emptied shower-bath of Religious Instruction! But surely, the more rational inference would be, that the Faith, which is to save

---

oure God and Lorde, suffered death for oure synnes, and rose agayne for oure Justification'': ''And upon this Article standeth all whatsoever we teache and spue agaynst the Pope, devill and worlde'': *The Chief and Pryncypall Articles of the Christen Faythe . . .* (1548) [10–12]. For the Latin see his exposition of Ps 130.4: ''quia isto articulo stante stat ecclesia, ruente ruit ecclesia''. The phrase appears to have passed into common theological usage in the seventeenth century: see Alister E. McGrath *Luther's Theology of the Cross* (Oxford 1985) 23 n 43. Cf *CM (CC)* III 31.

[20] *OED* gives several examples of ''frame'' in this sense, including Cotton Mather *Magnalia Christi Americana* (1702) III xvi 117: ''He would compose himself unto a most heavenly frame in all things.'' For instances of extreme Methodist behaviour see R. A. Knox *Enthusiasm* (1950) ch xxi. C had recently come across

such matters in reading RS's *Life of Wesley* (1820), which he annotated heavily: *CM (CC)*.

[21] In his *Colloquia Mensalia* (1652) Luther often dwells on the difficulties besetting Christians: see particularly ch 37 ''Of Tribulation and Temptation''. For C's annotations on this volume see *CM (CC)* III.

[22] C's prime reference is to Lactantius' principle of ''*universal and unanimous testimony of people and nations* through all course of time, *who* (otherwise differing in language, custom, and conceit) *only have agreed in this one matter of opinion*'', as cited by Isaac Barrow in one of his sermons: see *CN* IV 5124 and n. Cf also the canon of St Vincent of Lérins (d c 950): ''What is always, what is everywhere, what is by all believed'': *Commonitorium* ii, quoted by C in an annotation on Taylor Σύμβολον Θεολογικόν 168: *CM (CC)* V.

what other form, is it *possible* for thee to stand in the presence of the Holy One? With *what* mind wouldst thou come before God, if not with the Mind of Him, in whom *alone* God loveth the World? With good advice, perhaps, and a little assistance, thou wouldst rather cleanse and patch up a mind of thy own, and offer it as thy *admission-right*, thy *qualification*, to him who "charged ᵃhis angels with folly!"²⁴ Oh!ᵇ take counsel of thy Reason! It will show thee how impossible it is, that even a World should merit the love of Eternal Wisdom and all-sufficing Beatitude, otherwise than as it is contained in that all-perfect Idea, in which the Supreme Spiritᶜ comtemplateth itself and the plenitude of its infinity—the only-begotten before all Ages! the beloved Son, in whom the Father is indeed well pleased!²⁵

And as the Mind, so the Body with which it is to be clothed! as the Indweller, so the House in which is to be the Abiding-place*! There is

---

the whole man, must have its roots and justifying grounds in the very depths of our being!²³ And he who can read the Writings of the Apostles, John and Paul, without finding in almost every page a confirmation of this, must have looked at them, as at the sun in an eclipse, through blackened Glasses.

* St. Paul blends both forms of expression, and asserts the same doctrine when speaking of the "celestial body" provided for "the New Man" in the spiritual Flesh and Blood,²⁶ (*i.e.* the informing power and vivific life of the incarnate Word: for the Blood is the Life, and the Flesh the Power)—when speaking, I say, of this "celestial body,"²⁷ as a "house not made with hands, *eternal in the heavens*," yet brought down to us, made appropriable by faith, and *ours*—he adds,ᵈ "For in this earthly house (*i.e.*,ᵉ this mortal life, as the inward principle or energy of our Tabernacle, or outward and sensible Body) we groan, earnestly desiring to be *clothed upon with* our house which is from heaven;ᶠ not that we would be unclothed, but *clothed upon*, that Mortality might be swallowed up of life." 2 Cor.ᵍ v.1–4.

ᵃ *AR* (1825): p 307   ᵇ *AR* (1825): Oh,   ᶜ *AR* (1825): Mind
ᵈ *AR* (1825): adds: ᵉ *AR* (1825): i. e.   ᶠ *AR* (1825): heaven: ᵍ *AR* (1825): *Cor.*

---

²³ For a discussion of this in relation to the doctrine of justification by faith see Boulger 60.
²⁴ Job 4.18: "Behold . . . his angels he charged with folly".
²⁵ Matt 3.17 etc.
²⁶ 1 Cor 15.40: "There are also celestial bodies, and bodies terrestrial . . ." and vv 42, 44: "So also is the resurrection of the dead . . . It is sown a natural body; it is raised a spiritual body." For the "new man" see Eph 4.24, Col 3.10. C's imagery does not follow exactly that of St Paul, who associates the "celestial body" specifically with the resurrection from physical death.

The phrase "flesh and blood", as such, is normally used by St Paul in contradistinction to the spirit (1 Cor 15.50; Gal 1.10); C's usage here looks rather to Christ's words at Capernaum (John 6.53–6), concluding "He that eateth my flesh, and drinketh my blood, dwelleth in me, and I in him" and the implications of being "members of his body, of his flesh, and of his bones" (Eph 5.20).
²⁷ The term "celestial body" is taken over from 1 Cor 15 (see n 26, above): the quotations from 2 Cor 5 which follow do not make explicit reference to the "celestial body".

The four last words of the first verse (*eternal in the heavens*) compared with the conclusion of v. 2[a] (*which is from heaven,*)[b] present a coincidence[c] with *John* iii.[d] 13, "And no man hath ascended up to heaven,[e] but he that came down from heaven, even the Son of Man which is in heaven." (Qy. Whether the coincidence[f] would not be more apparent, if the words of John had been rendered word for word, even to a disregard of the English Idiom, and with what would be servile and superstitious fidelity in the translation of a common Classic? I can see no reason why the οὐδείς,[g] so frequent in St. John, should not be rendered literally, *no one;*[28] and there may be a reason why it should. I have some doubt likewise respecting the omission of the definite articles τόν, τοῦ, τῷ[h29]—and a greater, as to the ὁ ὤν, both in this place and in *John* i.[i]18,[30] being *adequately* rendered by our "*which is.*" P.S. What sense some of the Greek Fathers attached to, or inferred from, St. Paul's "*in the Heavens*," the Theological Student (and to Theologians is this note principally addressed) may find in WATERLAND's Letters to a Country Clergyman[31]—a Divine, whose Judgment and strong sound Sense are as unquestionable as his Learning and Orthodoxy. A Clergyman,[j] in full Orders, who has never read the works of Bull[32] and Waterland, has[k] a duty yet to perform.)

[a] *AR* (1825): 2
[b] *AR* (1825: *heaven*),
[c] *AR* (1825): cöincidence
[d] *AR* (1825): iii. v.
[e] *AR* (1825): heaven
[f] *AR* (1825): cöincidence
[g] *AR* (1825): ουδεις, ; *AR* (1831): οὐδεὶς,
[h] *AR* (1825): τον, του, τῳ ; *AR* (1831): τὸν, τοῦ, τῶ
[i] *AR* (1825): i. v.
[j] *AR* (1825): Clergyman
[k] *AR* (1825): has—

[28] E.g. John 1.18 AV: "No man [οὐδείς] hath seen God at any time . . .". A verse of great importance to C: in *CN* IV 5262 (Nov 1825) he interpreted it as declaring "the *essential* invisibility of God . . . God is necessarily *super*-essential". See also ibid 5297–8 and nn.

[29] By translating the definite articles in John 1.13 C would read "the heaven" all three times. (AV "in the heavens" and "from heaven" in 2 Cor 5.1, 2 is strictly accurate.)

[30] In John 1.18, which continues: ". . . the only begotten Son, which is in the bosom of the Father, he hath declared him", C would translate ὁ ὤν as "the Being" or "the I Am". He had it in mind that ὁ Ὤν was the name of God in Exod 3.14 in the Septuagint version. See above, *Sp Aph B II* n 74. C developed his interpretation of John 1.18 in notebook entries of Dec 1825 and in letters to DC of 11 Jan and to EC of 27 Jul 1826: *CN* IV 5078, 5256, 5297–8, *CL* VI 537, 600. It appears again in *C&S*

(CC) 182, in which the letter to EC was worked up as an appendix. For the same point, made in relation to Rom 9.5, see *CM (CC)* I 460 and n.

[31] See Daniel Waterland (1683–1740) *A Vindication of Christ's Divinity . . . in Answer to a Clergyman in the Country.* C's annotated copy of the 2nd ed (Cambridge 1719) is in the BM: *CM (CC)* V. (Perhaps, also, C alludes to *A Second Vindication of Christ's Divinity . . . in Answer to the Country Clergyman's Reply*—1723: see below, App I Excursus Note 18.) For a discussion of the precise point in Waterland that C may have had in mind see below, App I Excursus Note 15 "Coleridge, Waterland, and 'St Paul's "in the Heavens" ' ".

[32] George Bull (1634–1710), author, among other works, of the *Defensio Fidei Nicaenae* (1685), a standard work on trinitarian doctrine. Cf *CN* III 3934 f 69 and C's recommendation of Waterland and Bull on the Trinity to Mr Pryce: *CL* IV 850.

Let it not be objected, that,[a] forgetful of my own professed aversion to allegorical inter-pretations,[b] *see* p.[c] 39,)[d] I have,[e] in this note,[f] fallen into "the fond humor[g] of the Mystic Divines,[h] and *Allegorizers* of Holy Writ."[33] There is, believe me! a wide difference be-tween *symbolical* and *allegorical*.[34] If I say[i] that the Flesh and Blood (Corpus *noumenon*)[35] of the Incarnate Word are[j] Power and Life, I say likewise that this mysterious Power and Life are *verily* and *actually* the Flesh and Blood of Christ. *They* are the Allegorizers, who turn the 6th chapter[k] of the Gospel according to St. John,[l]—*the hard saying*,[m]—*who can hear it? After* which *time many* of (Christ's) Disciples, who had been eye-witnesses of his mighty Miracles, who had heard the sublime Morality of his Sermon on the Mount, had glorified God for the Wisdom which they had heard, and had been prepared to acknowl-edge,[n] "this is indeed the Christ,"[o][36]—went back and walked no more with him![37]—the hard sayings, which even THE TWELVE were not yet competent to understand farther than that they were to be spiritually understood; and which the Chief of the Apostles was con-tent to receive with an implicit and anticipative faith!—*they*, I repeat, are the Allegorizers who moralize these hard sayings, these high words of Mystery, into a[p] hyperbolical Met-

[a] *AR* (1825): that
[b] *AR* (1825): interpretations
[c] *AR* (1825): *p*.
[d] *AR* (1825): 24)
[e] *AR* (1825): have
[f] *AR* (1825): note
[g] *AR* (1825): humour
[h] *AR* (1825): Divines
[i] *AR* (1825): say,
[j] *AR* (1825): is
[k] *AR* (1825): c.
[l] *AR* (1825): John
[m] *AR* (1825): *saying*
[n] *AR* (1825): acknowlege,
[o] *AR* (1825): Christ"
[p] *AR* (1825): an

[33] See above, *Int Aph XXIX* n 18.
[34] Cf *Sp Aph B VII* n 39, above.
[35] "*Noumenal* Body". C again applies his own version of Kantian terminology to Christianity: cf above, *Sp Aph B II* n 40, *VIII* n 5, *Xa* n 46. Cf also an annotation of late 1823 on Burnet *History of the Refor-mation*: "In the Appendix to Strype's Life of Cranmer is to be found an excellent pa-per of Bucer's on the Eucharist, in a spirit very superior to the metaphysics of his age. The result is that the Body & Blood are the Corpus νουμενον, or actual, substantial Body, and therefore spiritual; not the Cor-pus φαινομενον. And that in the former or noumenal sense the doctrine of the *real* (as opposed to phænomenal) presence is agree-able *with* Reason and *to* Scripture—οὖτος ἀρτος νοεῖ σωμα ἐμον ['. . . this bread means—or is noumenally—my body', in-terpreting the NT 'This is my body']": *CM*

(CC) I 839, cf II 670–2, 1184–6. C returns to this paper of Bucer's below: see *Sp Aph B XIX* n 97.
[36] John 4.42.
[37] John 6.66. See below, *Conc* n 13.
[38] "Through Catachresis"—i.e. by us-ing words with incorrect meanings. Cf above, *Sp Aph B I* at n 11, and 1809 *Friend (CC)* II 250. In an annotation of 1826 on Charles Butler *Vindication of "The Book of the Roman Catholic Church"* C wrote: "The Eucharistic Act as instituted by Christ is a Symbol, i.e.—a part, or partic-ular instance selected as representative of the whole, of which whole however it is it-self an actual, or real part. Now the Sacra-mentaries degrade the Symbol into a Met-aphor, and that too, a Catachresis, while the Romish Superstition makes the Symbol representant, the whole thing represented, and in consequence, equally with the for-

but one Wedding-garment,[a][43] in which we can sit down at the marriage-

---

aphor *per Catachresin*,[38] that only means a belief of the Doctrines which Paul believed, an obedience to the Law, respecting which Paul "was blameless,"[39] before the Voice called him on the road to Damascus![40] What every Parent, every humane Preceptor, would do when a Child had misunderstood a Metaphor or Apologue in a literal sense, we all know. But the meek and merciful Jesus suffered *many* of HIS Disciples to fall off from eternal life, when,[b] to retain them,[c] he had only to say,[d]—O ye Simple ones! why are ye offended? My words,[e] indeed,[f] sound strange; but I mean no more than what you have often and often heard from me before,[g] with delight and entire acquiescence!—Credat Judaeus! Non ego.[41] It is sufficient for me to know that I have used the language of Paul and John,[h] as it was understood and interpreted by Justin Martyr, Tertullian, Irenaeus, and (if he does not lie) by the whole Christian Church then existing.[42]

---

[a] *AR* (1825): p 308 (garment,)   [b] *AR* (1825): when
[c] *AR* (1825): them   [d] *AR* (1825): say   [e] *AR* (1825): words
[f] *AR* (1825): indeed   [g] *AR* (1825): before   [h] *AR* (1825): John

---

mer, destroys the *Symbol*": *CM (CC)* I 862. Cf also *TT* 13 May 1830 *(CC)* I 135 (1836 vn, dated 20 May, II 92): "The former [the Sacramentaries] have volatilized the Eucharist into a Metaphor; the latter [the Romanists] have condensed it into an Idol."

[39] Phil 3.6: ". . . touching the righteousness which is in the law, blameless".

[40] Acts 8.1–9.9.

[41] "Credat Judaeus Apella, | Non ego". Horace *Satires* 1.5.100; tr H. R. Fairclough (LCL 1926): "Apelles the Jew may believe it, not I". A favourite tag of C's from Bristol days onwards: see *Lects 1795 (CC)* 309.

[42] C's authority here is very probably again Waterland. The sixth chapter of his *A Review of the Doctrine of the Eucharist* (1737) 136–96 is devoted to ancient interpretations of Christ's words on "*eating* his *Flesh* and *drinking* his *Blood*", John 6, of which he remarks (p 137): "His strong way of expressing Himself, and his emphatic repeating the same Thing . . . are alone Sufficient to persuade us that some very *important* Mystery, some very *significant* Lesson of Instruction is contained in what he said." In the following chapter, "Concerning Sacramental or Symbolical Feeding in the Eucharist", Waterland cites Justin Martyr (217–21), Irenaeus (221–5), and

Tertullian (230–3) among his eight major ancient authorities; he further invokes 1 Cor 10.16 and 11.27, 29 as he attempts to safeguard the symbolic reality (the symbol does not, he says, merely represent, but effectuates) against the extreme exponents, respectively, of transubstantiation and of a merely memorial function. According to Waterland, Justin "supposes a *Divine* Power, the Power of the *Logos* Himself (which implies his *Spiritual* Presence) to be necessary for making the elements become such Symbolical *Flesh* and *Blood*" (219). Irenaeus is quoted as saying that the elements "by the Divine Wisdom serve for the use of Man, and receiving the *Logos* [Word] of God, become the Eucharist which is the Body and Blood of Christ" (223). For another possible echo from Waterland's *Review*, see *CN* IV 5126 f 104n.

If by "he" C means one of the ancient authorities cited it is probably Justin Martyr, who speaks of "we" throughout the passage quoted from him (ibid 217–18). But it is likely that (overlooking his failure to repeat his name) C refers to Waterland, who writes of his interpretation of the sacrament (204): ". . . it appears to have been the antient Notion of all the Christian Churches for six Centuries or more".

[43] Although the immediate source is Matt 22.11, the story of the man who wore

feast of Heaven: and that is the Bridegroom's[a] own [b]Gift, when he gave himself for us that we might live in him and he in us. There is but one robe of Righteousness,[44] even the Spiritual Body, formed by the assimilative power of faith for whoever eateth the flesh of the Son of Man and drinketh his blood.[45] Did Christ come from Heaven, did the Son of God leave the Glory which he had with his Father before the World began,[46] only to *show* us a way to life, to *teach* truths, to *tell* us of a resurrection? Or saith he not, I *am* the way, I *am* the truth, I *am* the Resurrection and the Life![47]

APHORISM XIX[c1]

The *Romanists* teach that sins committed after [d]baptism (*i.e.* for the immense majority of Christians having Christian Parents, all their sins from the Cradle to the Grave)[2] are not so remitted for Christ's sake, but that we must suffer that extremity of punishment which they deserve: and therefore either we must afflict ourselves in such sort and degree of extremity as may answer the demerit of our Sins,[3] or be punished by God here or in the world to come, in such degree and sort that his Justice may be satisfied. [N.B.[e] *As the encysted venom, or poison-bag, beneath*

---

[a] *AR* (1825): Bride-groom's
[b] *AR* (1825): p 309
[c] *AR* (1825): FIELD.
[d] *AR* (1825): p 310
[e] *AR* (1825): N. B.

---

no wedding-garment at a marriage feast, it may have been brought into C's mind, coming after the word "Abiding-place" and its association with clothing in the footnote, by a link between the "Wedding Garment" in the *Letter to Sara Hutchinson* line 298 and the "*abiding* Home" of the Wordsworths in the same poem, line 135: *CL* II 797, 793.

[44] See Isa 61.10, quoted below, *Sp Aph B [XXIV]* n 33; cf also above, *Int Aph XXIII* at n 11.

[45] Cf a later annotation on Bunyan *Pilgrim's Progress*: "Purity and Beneficence are the Epidermis, Faith = Love the Cutis vera [i.e. the true skin beneath] of Christianity—Morality is the outward Cloth, Faith the Lining—both together form the Wedding-Garment, given to the true Believer by Christ—even his own Garment of Righteousness, which like the Loaves & Fishes he mysteriously multiplies": *CM*

(CC) I 814–15.

[46] John 17.5: ". . . the glory which I had with thee before the world was".

[47] A conflation of John 11.25: "I am the resurrection, and the life" and John 14.6: "I am the way, the truth, and the life". See also below, *Sp Aph B XXIII* at n 11 and Conc at n 79.

[1] Selected and adapted from Field *Of the Church* (Oxford 1635) 58. See above, *Sp Aph B XVII* n 17, and, for the original text, App A(s), below. C introduces a long parenthesis but, except as indicated below, makes only trivial changes in Field's text. His own annotation forms the basis of the Comment that follows it: see below, nn to pp 318–33. For discussion of the general argument see Boulger 59–70.

[2] Parenthetical statement is C's.

[3] Field writes: ". . . the desert of our sinne".

the Adder's fang, so does this doctrine lie beneath the tremendous power of the Romish Hierarchy. The demoralizing influence of this dogma, and that it curdled the very life-blood in the veins of Christendom, it was given to Luther beyond all men since Paul to see, feel, and promulgate.[4] *And yet in his large Treatise on Repentance, how near to the spirit of this doctrine—even to the very walls and gates of Babylon—was Jeremy Taylor driven, in recoiling from the fanatical extremes of the opposite error!*][5] But they[a] that are orthodox, teach that it is injustice to require the payment of one debt twice.***[6] It is no less absurd to say, as the Papists do, that *our* satisfaction is required as a condition, without which *Christ's*[7] satisfaction is not applicable unto us, than to say, Peter hath paid the debt of John, and He, to whom it was due, accepteth of the same payment on the condition that John[8] pay it himself also.*** The satisfaction of Christ is communicated and applied unto us without suffering the punishment that Sin deserveth, [*and essentially involveth*,][b9] upon the condition of our Faith and Repentance. [To which I[c] would add: Without faith there is no power of repentance: without a commencing

---

[a] *AR* (1825): they,
[b] *AR* (1825): *involveth*, ED.] (p 311 begins with "ED.")
[c] *AR* (1825): the Editor

[4] In his letter to Mence of Jan 1825 the passage concerning original sin (quoted above, *Sp Aph B XVII* n 8) is followed by discussion of the relation between "Realities" and "Metaphors" in this context and then continues: "Luther indeed was a mighty Wrestler: and the very *Halt* on the Thigh bears witness of the Manfulness of his Struggles. But Luther had no Elisha to succeed him": *CL* v 406. With the image cf that in a note of 1800: "Luther—a hero, one fettered indeed with prejudices; but with those very fetters he would knock out the Brains of a modern Fort Esprit": *CN* I 864. For C's admiration of Luther see also his annotations on *Colloquia Mensalia*: *CM (CC)* III.

[5] The whole of this parenthesis is by C. In *Unum Necessarium* Taylor discusses the question of sin after baptism centrally in ch 9 §§ 1–3: Σύμβολον Θεολογικόν (1674) 800–8. C has a line in the margin alongside the relevant passage (807): "For after great crimes, the state of a sinner is very deplorable by reason of his uncertain pardon; not that it is uncertain whether God will pardon the truly penitent, but that it is uncertain

who is so . . . nor can they estimate which is greater, the example of the sin, or the example of the punishment. And therefore in such great cases the Church had reason to refuse to give pardon, which she could minister neither certainly, nor prudently, nor . . . safely or piously." He also marked a passage on p 806: "Although the Criminal must do penance to his dying day . . . the Church will not absolve, or admit him to her communion yet he must not be without hope of pardon, which yet is not to be hop'd for from the Church, but from him, who is so rich in mercy, that no man may despair . . .". For C on purgatory see Barth 194.

[6] For "teach" Field's text reads "teach, first,". C's asterisks indicate that he is now passing to the fourth of these teachings, as given by Field.

[7] The emphases on "our" and "Christ's" are C's.

[8] For ". . . on the condition that John", Field's text reads ". . . conditionally if hee". The asterisks indicate that C is now reverting to the third of the "teachings".

[9] C's parenthesis, as *AR* (1825) shows.

repentance no power to faith:[a] and that it is in the power of the will either to repent or to have faith[b] in the Gospel Sense of the words, is itself a Consequence of the Redemption of Mankind, a free gift of the Redeemer: the guilt of its rejection, the refusing to avail ourselves of the power, being all that we can consider as exclusively attributable to our own Act.][10] FIELD'S CHURCH, p. 58.

COMMENT[11]

[c](CONTAINING AN APPLICATION OF THE PRINCIPLES LAID DOWN
IN P.[d] 204–6)

Forgiveness of Sin, the Abolition of Guilt, through the redemptive power of Christ's Love, and of his perfect Obedience during his voluntary assumption of Humanity, is expressed, on account of the resemblance of the Consequences in both cases, by the payment of a Debt for another, which Debt the Payer had not himself incurred. Now the *impropriation* of this Metaphor—(*i.e.* the taking it *literally*) by transferring the sameness from the Consequents to the Antecedents, or inferring the identity of the causes from a resemblance in the effects—this is the point on which I am at issue:[12] and the View or Scheme of Redemption grounded on this confusion I believe to be altogether unscriptural.

Indeed, I know not in what other instance I could better exemplify the species of sophistry noticed in [e]p. 223, as the Aristotelean μετάβασις εἰς ἄλλο γένος,[f] or clandestine passing over into a diverse kind.[13] The purpose of a Metaphor is to illustrate a something less known by a partial

---

[a] *AR* (1825): faith;
[b] *AR* (1825): faith,
[c–d] *AR* (1825): (*Containing an application of the principles laid down in p.*
[e] *AR* (1825): p 312
[f] *AR* (1825): no accents or breathings in Greek

---

[10] As indicated at the outset, the whole parenthesis is by C. For discussion of C's views on grace and free will see Boulger 63 and Barth 153 and n.

[11] The long discussion that follows is expanded from C's much briefer annotation at this point in Field (see above, n 1). This annotation, which appears in full in *CM (CC)* II 657–9, is also reproduced piecemeal in the notes that follow.

[12] C's annotation on Field begins: "This *propriation* of a *metaphor*, viz. forgiveness of Sin and abolition of guilt thro' the redemptive Power of Christ's Love and ⟨of

his⟩ perfect Obedience during his voluntary assumption of Humanity expressed, on account of the sameness of the consequences in both cases by the payment of a *Debt* for another, which ⟨Debt⟩ the Payer had not himself incurred—the *propriation* of this, I say, by transferring the *sameness* from the consequents to the Antecedents is the one point of Orthodoxy (so held, I mean) in which I still remain at Issue".

[13] C's annotation on Field continues, simply, "it seems to be so evidently a μεταβασις εις αλλο γενος". For the last phrase see above, *Sp Aph B VIIIb* n 26.

identification of it with some other thing better understood, or at least more familiar.[14] Now the article of Redemption may be considered in a two-fold[a] relation—in relation to the *Antecedent*, *i.e.* the Redeemer's Act, as the efficient cause and condition of Redemption; and in relation to the *Consequent*, *i.e.* the effects in and for the Redeemed. Now it is the latter relation, in which the Subject is treated of, set forth, expanded, and enforced by St. Paul. The Mysterious Act, the Operative Cause is *transcendent*—FACTUM EST[15]: and beyond the information contained in the enunciation of the FACT, it can be characterized only by the *Consequences*. It is the *Consequences* of the Act of Redemption, that the zealous Apostle would bring home to the minds and affections both of Jews and Gentiles. Now the Apostle's Opponents and Gainsayers were principally of the former class. They were Jews: not only Jews unconverted, but such as had partially received the Gospel, and who, sheltering their national prejudices under the pretended authority of Christ's Original Apostles and the Church in Jerusalem, set themselves up against Paul as followers[b] of Cephas. Add too, that Paul himself was "a Hebrew of the Hebrews;" intimately versed "in the Jews'[c] religion above many, his equals, in his own nation, and above measure zealous of the traditions of his fathers."[16] It might, therefore, have been anticipated, that his reasoning would [d]receive its outward forms and language, that it would take its predominant colors,[e] from his own *past*, and his Opponents' present, habits of thinking; and that his figures, images, analogies, and references would be taken preferably from objects, opinions, events, and ritual observances ever uppermost in the imaginations of his own countrymen. And such we find them: yet so judiciously selected, that the prominent forms, the figures of most frequent recurrence, are drawn from points of belief and practice, forms,[f] laws, rites and customs, that then prevailed through the whole Roman World, and were common to Jew and Gentile.

[a] *AR* (1825): twofold
[b] *AR* (1825): Followers
[c] *AR* (1825): Jew's
[d] *AR* (1825): p 313
[e] *AR* (1825): colours,
[f] *AR* (1825): from

[14] C's annotation on Field continues: "A metaphor is an illustration of something less known by a more or less *partial* identification of it with something better understood." See also above, pp 205–6 and 267n.

[15] "It has been done" or "it is (now) fact". C's treatment of a corresponding Greek expression, though without this etymological pun, is relevant: see *Mor Aph XV* and n 7, above.

[16] Phil 3.5; Gal 1.14 (var), where St Paul begins by saying that he ". . . profited in the Jews' religion"; for "and above measure" AV reads "being more exceedingly".

Now it would be difficult if not impossible to select points better suited to this purpose, as being equally familiar to all,[a] and yet having a special interest for the Jewish Converts, than those are from which the learned Apostle has drawn the four principal Metaphors, by which he illustrates the blessed *Consequences* of Christ's Redemption of Mankind. These are: 1. Sin-offerings, sacrificial expiation. 2. Reconciliation, Atonement, Καταλλαγή*[b]. 3. Ransom from slavery, Redemption,

* This word occurs but once in the New Testament, viz. Romans v. 11,[17] the marginal rendering being[c] reconciliation. The personal Noun, καταλλακτής,[d] is still in use with the modern Greeks for a money-changer, or one who takes the debased Currency, so general in countries under despotic or other dishonest governments, in exchange for sterling Coin or Bullion; the purchaser paying the *catallage*, i.e. the difference. In the elder Greek writers,[e] the verb means *to exchange for an opposite*, as,[f] κατηλλάσσετο τὴν ἔχθρην τοῖς στασιώταις.[g]—He exchanged within himself enmity for friendship,[h] (that is, he reconciled himself) with his party[i18]—or as we say, *made it up* with them, an idiom which (with whatever loss of dignity) gives the exact force of the word. He made it *up the difference*. The Hebrew word of very frequent occurrence in the Pentateuch, which we render by the substantive, atonement, has its radical or visual image, in *copher*, pitch. Gen. vi. 14, *thou shalt pitch it within and without with pitch*. Hence, to unite, to fill up a breach, or leak, the word expressing both the *act*, viz. the bringing together what had been previously separated, and the *means*, or material, by which the re-union is effected, as in our English verbs, *to caulk, to solder, to poy* or *pay* (from *poix*, pitch), and the French, *suiver*. Thence, metaphorically, *expiation*, the *piacula* having the same root, and being grounded on another property or use of Gums and Resins,[j] the supposed *cleansing* powers of their fumigation.[19] Numbers viii. 21: "made *atonement* for the Levites to *cleanse* them."—Lastly (or if we are to believe the Hebrew Lexicons, *properly* and most *frequently*) Ransom.[20]

[a] *AR* (1825): all
[b] *AR* (1825): Καταλλαγη* ; *AR* (1831): Καταλλαγὴ*
[c] *AR* (1825): being,
[d] *AR* (1825): no accent in Greek
[e] *AR* (1825): writers
[f] *AR* (1825): as
[g] *AR* (1825): no accents or breathing in Greek
[h] *AR* (1825): friendship
[i] *AR* (1825): Party
[j] *AR* (1825): Rosins,

[17] Incorrect: καταλλαγή occurs also in Rom 11.15 and 2 Cor 5.18, 19, and the related verb six times. The Anglicised form "catallage" is not in *OED*, but "catallactic" is found there.

[18] Herodotus 1.61. C quotes exactly, except for the dialect endings of the last two words, and translates accurately, giving the force of the middle voice by "within himself".

[19] *OED* does not record "poy" as an alternative to "pay". *Piaculum* (plural *piacula*), an expiatory offering, used five times in the Vulgate, is not thought by modern etymologists to have any connexion with *pix* (pitch).

[20] It is true that the noun *kopher* is commonly translated "ransom", so appearing nine times. The equivalent verb "*kophar*" however, is commonly translated "to make atonement", appearing 69 times. Hebrew lexicons available in C's time as well as modern ones all, apparently, give the general meaning as "cover". No source has been found for C's information here. Perhaps he was consulting Hyman Hurwitz (see above, *Sp Aph B VIIIa* n 19) or his successor at the school in Highgate, L. Neumegen (cf e.g. *CN* III 4418 f 11, IV 4667n, 5321n, and *CL* V 135).

*^a*the buying back again, or being bought back, from *re* and *emo*. 4. Satisfaction of a Creditor's claims by a payment of the debt.²³ To one or other of these four heads all the numerous forms and exponents of Christ's Mediation in St. Paul's writings may be referred. And the very number and variety of the words or periphrases used by him to express one and the same thing furnish *^b*the strongest presumptive proof, that all alike were used *metaphorically*. [In the following notation, let the small letters represent the *effects* or *consequences*, and the Capitals the efficient *causes* or *antecedents*. Whether by Causes we mean Acts or Agents, is indifferent. Now let X signify a *Transcendent,*²⁴ *i.e.* a Cause beyond our Comprehension and not within the sphere of sensible experience;*^c* and on the other hand, let A, B, C, and D represent*^d* each some one known and familiar cause,*^e* in reference to some single and characteristic effect: viz. A in reference to k, B to l, C to m, and D to n. Then I say X + k l m n is in different places expressed by (or as =) A + k; B + l; C + m; D + n. And these I should call *metaphorical* Exponents²⁵ of X.]

Now John, the beloved Disciple, who leant on the Lord's Bosom, the

---

But if by *proper* the Interpreters mean *primary* and *radical*, the assertion does not need a confutation: all radicals belonging to one or other of three classes. 1. Interjections, or sounds expressing sensations or passions. 2. Imitations of sounds, as splash, roar, whiz, &c. 3. and principally, visual images, objects of sight.²¹ But as to *frequency*, in all the numerous (fifty, I believe,)*^f* instances of the word in the Old Testament, I have not found one in which it can, or at least need, be rendered by Ransom: though beyond all doubt Ransom is used in the Epistle to Timothy,²² as an *equivalent* term.

---

^a *AR* (1825): p 314   *^b* *AR* (1825): p 315   *^c* *AR* (1825): experience:
^d *AR* (1825): represent,   *^e* *AR* (1825): cause   *^f* *AR* (1825): believe)

²¹ For all its conciseness, this is perhaps C's most complete statement on a principle of great importance to him, as his footnote to *Int Aph XII*, above, indicates. Cf *CN* IV 5136 ff 135ᵛ–133ᵛ, written Mar 1824 for James Gillman, Jr, and *CN* III 4210, associated with his own attempt at compiling a Greek–English lexicon (*CN* III 3422). See also *Logic (CC)* 24, *CM (CC)* I 354.

²² 1 Tim 2.5–6: ". . . Christ Jesus; Who gave himself a ransom for all, to be testified in due time".

²³ C's annotation on Field continues: "Thus Sᵗ Paul illustrates the *consequences* of the act of Redemption by four different metaphors drawn from things most familiar to those, for whom, it was to be illustrated—viz. Sin-offerings or sacrificial ex-

piations 2. Reconciliation. 3. Ransom from Slavery. 4. Satisfaction of a first Creditor by vicarious payment of the Debt.—These all refer to the consequences of Redemption." Cf also C's annotation on Bahrdt *Glaubens Bekänntniss: CM (CC)* I 200 and n.

²⁴ For a distinction between "transcendent" and "transcendental", based on Kant *Critik der reinen Vernunft* (2nd ed Riga 1787) 330, see *Logic (CC)* 147.

²⁵ With C's use of "Exponents" here and earlier in the paragraph, cf *Omniana* (1812) II 12 (cited by *OED* as its first example of the substantive). See also *CN* IV 4530 and n and *Logic (CC)* 39, 90, 114, 216, 307.

Evangelist κατὰ πνεῦμα,[a] i.e. according to the *Spirit*, the inner and substantial truth of the Christian Creed[26]—John, recording the Redeemer's own words, enunciates the fact[b] itself, to the full extent in which it is enunciable for the human mind, simply and *without any metaphor*, by identifying it[c] *in kind* with a fact of hourly occurrence—*expressing* it, I say, by a familiar fact the same *in kind* with that intended, though of a far lower *dignity*;—by a fact of every man's experience, *known* to all, yet not better *understood* than the fact described by it. In the Redeemed it is a re-*generation*, a *birth*, a spiritual seed impregnated and evolved, the germinal principle of a higher and enduring Life, of a *spiritual* Life—that [d]is, a Life, the actuality of which is not dependent on the material body, or limited by the circumstances and processes indispensable to its organization and subsistence.[27] Briefly, it is the *Differential* of Immortality, of which the assimilative power of Faith and Love is the *Integrant*, and the Life of Christ the *Integration*.[28]

But even this would be an imperfect statement, if we omitted the awful[e] truth, that besides that dissolution of our earthly tabernacle which we call death,[29] there is another death, not the mere negation[f] of Life,[g]

----

[a] *AR* (1825): no accents in Greek
[b] *AR* (1825): Fact
[c] *AR* (1825): *it*
[d] *AR* (1825): p 316
[e] *AR* (1825): aweful
[f] COPIES A, C, D, E: privation
[g] *AR* (1825): life,

[26] John himself is traditionally identified with the disciple who "was leaning on Jesus' bosom . . . whom Jesus loved": John 13.23. C regularly described John's Gospel as "according to the spirit" and the others as "according to the flesh". See *CN* IV 5323 f 29, below, *Sp Aph B [XXIV]* n 3, and, for the special character of John, *TT* 29 Dec 1822 and 6 Jun 1830 *(CC)* I 23–4, 158 (1836 vn II 39, dated 6 Jan 1823, 106–7).

[27] C's annotation continues: "Now Sᵗ John without any metaphor declares the mode by and in which it is effected—for he identified it with a *fact*, not with a Consequence, and a fact too not better understood in the one case than in the other—namely, by generation and birth". C has in mind the reference in John 1.13 to those who are ". . . born . . . of God", followed by many others: e.g. John 3.3–7, and 1 John 3.9, 4.7, 5.1, 4, 18.

[28] The present sentence was added after the ms drafting: see App B(y¹) below. *OED* cites this as its first example of "integrant" as a substantive; for the use of "Differential" and "Integration" here cf *Logic (CC)* 223: "The student, if acquainted with fluxions and the processes of integration and of differentials, will find the happiest and most perfect exemplification of the relations which the two forms of the outer and inner sense, that is, of space and time, are capable of bearing to each other." For a caveat concerning his own mathematical knowledge, see ibid 224 and his note on Böhme *Works: CM (CC)* I 615; cf *CM (CC)* III 349.

[29] Cf 2 Cor 5.1: "For we know that if our earthly house of this tabernacle were dissolved, we have a building of God, an house not made with hands, eternal in the heavens." (Cf also 2 Pet 1.13–14.)

but its positive Opposite.[30] And as there is a mystery of Life and an assimilation to the Principle of Life, even to him who is *the* Life; so is there a mystery of Death and an assimilation to the Principle of Evil ἀμφιθαλὴς θανάτῳ[a]![31] a fructifying of the corrupt seed, of which Death is the germination.[32] Thus the regeneration to spiritual life is at the same time a redemption from the spiritual death.

Respecting the redemptive act itself, and the Divine Agent, we know from revelation that he "was made a quickening (ζωοποιοῦν, *life-making*) Spirit:"[33] and that in order to this it was necessary, that God should be manifested in the flesh,[34] that the eternal Word, through whom and by whom the World (κόσμος,[b][35] the Order, Beauty, and sustaining Law of visible natures) was and is,[36] should be made flesh,[37] assume our humanity personally, fulfil all righteousness,[38] and so suffer and so die for us as in dying to conquer Death for as many as should receive him.[39]

---

[a] *AR* (1825): αμφιθαλης θανατῳ ; *AR* (1831): ἀμφιθαλὴς θανάτῳ
[b] *AR* (1825): no accent in Greek

[30] The closest parallel in C's own writing is perhaps in the poem *Limbo* (1811), which ends: "Hell knows a fear far worse, | A fear, a future fate. Tis *positive Negation!*": *CN* III 4073 f 149. Making notes for his last philosophical lecture in 1819, C feared an omen of his "second death", but neither this nor the "second death" of Rev 21.8 (cf *CN* IV 4504 and n) is necessarily relevant here, where the reference is rather to a spiritual death during this mortal life. See also above, *Sp Aph B XVII* n 10, and below, App I Excursus Note 17 "Coleridge and the Abyss of Being".

[31] For C's Greek oxymoron "blossoming on all sides with death", cf Aeschylus *Agamemnon* 1144: ἀμφιθαλὴς κακοῖς. C borrowed the latter phrase in his Greek prize ode on the slave-trade in 1792: *PW* (JDC) 476. ἀμφιθαλής is also used, by contrast, to describe Love (Eros) in the marriage hymn at the conclusion of Aristophanes *Birds*, line 1737. The Greek was omitted in *AR* (1839), perhaps as unbiblical.

[32] Cf Rom 7.5: "For when we were in the flesh, the motions of sins, which were by the law, did work in our members to bring forth fruit unto death".

[33] 1 Cor 15.45: ". . . The first man Adam was made a living soul; the last Adam was made a quickening spirit." The Greek is as here. C's ms for the first five

sentences here is transcribed below in App B(y[2]).

[34] 1 Tim 3.16: ". . . God was manifest in the flesh . . .".

[35] C points, as often, to the multiple meanings of this word. It meant "order", "beauty", or "adornment" before Pythagoras (as it was supposed) applied it to the world, or universe. In the NT it also, and usually, means mankind in general, but cf John 1.10, in the next note, where κόσμος is repeated three times.

[36] John 1.3 (of the Word): "All things were made by him; and without him was not any thing made that was made." C's "through whom and by whom" reflects the use of the preposition διά (primarily "through") in both verses; and with his "was and is" cf the objection to "was made" above, *Int Aph XXIII* n 3. See also John 1.10: "He was in the world, and the world was made by him, and the world knew him not."

[37] John 1.14: "And the Word was made flesh, and dwelt among us . . .". But see above, *Int Aph XXIII* n 3 again.

[38] Matt 3.15 (Jesus to John the Baptist): ". . . it becometh us to fulfil all righteousness".

[39] John 1.12: "But as many as received him, to them gave he power to become the sons of God . . ."; see also text at n 44, below. Throughout the preceding para-

More than this, the mode, the possibility, we are not competent to know.[40] It is, as [a]hath been already observed concerning the primal Act of Apostacy, a mystery by the necessity of the subject—a mystery, which at all events it will be time enough for us to seek and expect to understand, when we understand the mystery of our *Natural* life, and *its* conjunction with mind and will and personal identity. Even the truths, that are given to us to know, we can know only through faith in the spirit.[41] They are spiritual things that must be spiritually discerned.[42] Such, however, being the means and the effects of our Redemption, well might the fervent Apostle associate it with whatever was eminently dear and precious to erring and afflicted Mortals, and (where no expression could be commensurate, no single title be other than imperfect) seek from similitude of *effect* to describe the superlative boon by successively transferring to it, as by a superior claim, the name of each several Act and Ordinance, habitually connected in the minds of *all* his Hearers with feelings of joy, confidence, and gratitude.

Do you rejoice when the Atonement made by the Priest has removed the civil stain from your name, restored you to your privileges as a Son of Abraham, and replaced you in the respect of your Brethren?—Here is an atonement which takes away a deeper, worser stain, an eating Canker-spot[43] in the very heart of your personal Being! This, to as many as receive it, gives the privilege to become Sons of God (*John[b]* i. 12),[44] this will admit you to the society of Angels, and [c]insure to[d] you the rights of Brotherhood with [e]Spirits made perfect! (*Heb.[f]* xii. 22.)[45] Here is a

---

[a] *AR* (1825): p 317   [b] *AR* (1825): John   [c–d] *AR* (1825): ensure
[e] *AR* (1825): p 318   [f] *AR* (1825): Heb.

---

graph C conflates the teaching of John 1 (which is much simpler) with that in other parts of the NT.

[40] Cf "Rem credimus, modum nescimus" ["We have faith in the thing, we do not understand the means"], a sentiment often repeated by C in similar contexts, e.g. *CN* IV 4599, approving of Luther's attitude, and on Taylor Σύμβολον Θεολογικόν 227, *CM (CC)* V, concerning transubstantiation; in c 1831–2, however, he wrote of it as "a poor evasion": *CM (CC)* II 281; cf also *CM (CC)* III 934.

[41] The paragraph up to this point is an expansion of C's annotation, which continues: "There remains therefore only the Redemptive *Act* itself—and this is transcendent, ineffable, and a fortiori therefore

inexplicable—here the act of primal Apostacy, it is in its own nature a *Mystery*, known only thro' faith in the Spirit." On the "primal Act of Apostasy" see *Sp Aph B Xb* at n 77.

[42] 1 Cor 2.14: "But the natural man receiveth not the things of the Spirit of God . . . neither can he know them, because they are spiritually discerned." See above, p 77. C's ms insertion for the next sentence is transcribed below in App B(y[1V]).

[43] See also above, at n 32.

[44] In *SM* also C thought "privilege" a better translation: *SM (CC)* 96; in 2 Cor 10.8 he preferred "prerogative" to "authority": *CM (CC)* I 462.

[45] Heb 12.22–3: "But ye are come unto

Sacrifice, a Sin-offering[46] for the whole world:[47] and a[a] High Priest,[48] who is indeed a Mediator,[49] who not in type or shadow[50] but in very truth and in his own right stands in the place of Man to God, and of God to Man; and who receives as a Judge[51] what he offered as an Advocate.[52]

Would you be grateful to one who had ransomed you from slavery under a bitter foe, or who brought you out of Captivity? Here is redemption from a far direr slavery, the slavery of Sin unto Death![53] and he, who gave himself for the ransom, has taken Captivity Captive.[b][54]

Had you by your own fault alienated yourself from your best, your only sure Friend? Had you, like a Prodigal, cast yourself out of your Father's House?[55] Would you not love the good Samaritan,[56] who should reconcile you to your Friend? Would you not prize above all price the intercession,[57] that had brought you back from Husks and the tending of Swine, and restored you to your Father's Arms, and seated you at your Father's Table?

Had you involved yourself in a heavy DEBT for certain gew-gaws, for

---

[a] *AR* (1825): an
[b] *AR* (1825): Captive!

---

mount Sion . . . to an innumerable company of angels . . . to God the Judge of all, and to the spirits of just men made perfect.''

[46] Heb 7.26–7 (of Christ): "For such an high priest became us . . . who needeth not daily, as those high priests, to offer up sacrifice, first for his own sins and then for the people's: for this he did once, when he offered himself up." Cf e.g. Heb 10.18 and Eph 5.2.

[47] 1 John 2.2: "And he is the propitiation . . . for the sins of the whole world".

[48] The rôle of Christ as high priest is a constant theme in Heb: see e.g. 2.17, 3.1, 4.14–15, 5.1–10, 6.20, and the whole of chs 7–10; and again in 13.10–11.

[49] Heb 2.17, 9.15, 12.24; and cf 1 Tim 2.5: ". . . there is one God, and one mediator between God and men, the man Christ Jesus".

[50] See *CN* IV 5269 and *Sp Aph B Xb* n 51, above. Shadow (σκιά) and type (τύπος: tr as "pattern" in AV) are found close together in the Greek of Heb 8.5. The author of Hebrews (see below, *Sp Aph B XXIIIb* n 27) used the language and practice of typology ("figure", "pattern", "example", "shadow", etc in AV) more concentratedly than any other biblical writer, finding foreshadowings of Christ in Melchizedek

(cf *CN* IV 5269 again and above, *Int Aph XXIX* n 19), and in Moses. See also *Sp Aph B XXIIIb* n 42 below, and *Enc RE* s.v. "Typology". Cf also Milton *PL* XII 232–3: "informing them, by types | And shaddows . . .", and WW *Excursion* VII 526–7: "That to the imagination may be given | A type and shadow of an awful truth . . .": *WPW* v 248.

[51] Acts 10.42 (of Christ): ". . . it is he which was ordained of God to be the Judge of quick and dead" (cf 2 Tim 4.1; 1 Pet 4.5).

[52] 1 John 2.1: "And if any man sin, we have an advocate with the Father, Jesus Christ the righteous".

[53] Rom 7.23: ". . . I see another law in my members . . . bringing me into captivity to the law of sin which is in my members".

[54] Matt 20.28: ". . . the son of Man came . . . to give his life a ransom for many"; cf 1 Tim 2.6: "Who gave himself a ransom for all . . ."; Eph 4.8: ". . . When he ascended up on high, he led captivity captive . . .".

[55] Luke 15.11–32.

[56] Luke 10.29–37.

[57] Heb 7.25 (of Christ): ". . . he ever liveth to make intercession for them".

*a*high seasoned*b* meats, and intoxicating drinks, and glistering apparel, and in default of payment had made yourself over as a bondsman to a hard Creditor, who*c* it was foreknown, would enforce the bond of Judgment*d* to the last tittle![58] With what emotions would you not receive the glad tidings, that a stranger, or a friend whom in the days of your wantonness you *e*had neglected and reviled, had paid the DEBT for you, had made SATISFACTION to your Creditor? But you have incurred a debt of Death to the EVIL NATURE! you have sold yourself over to SIN! and relatively to *you*, and to all *your* means and resources, the Seal on the Bond is the Seal of necessity!*f* Its stamp is the *Nature* of Evil. But the Stranger has appeared, the forgiving friend*g* has come, even the Son of God from heaven: and to as many as have faith in his name, I say—the Debt is paid*h* for you! The Satisfaction has been made.

Now to simplify the argument and at the same time to bring the question to the test, we will confine our attention to the figure *i*last mentioned,*j* viz. the satisfaction of a Debt. Passing by our modern Alogi[59] who find nothing but metaphors in either Apostle, let us suppose for a moment with certain Divines that our Lord's Words, recorded by John, and which in all places repeat and assert the same Analogy,[60] are to be regarded as metaphorical; and that it is the varied expressions of St. Paul that are to be literally interpreted: *ex. gr.* that Sin is, or involves an infinite Debt, (in the proper and law-court sense of the word, debt)—a debt owing by us to the vindictive Justice of God the Father, which can only be liquidated by the everlasting misery of Adam and all his posterity, or by a sum of suffering equal to this. Likewise, that God the Father by his absolute decree, or (as some Divines teach)[61] through the neces-

---

a–b   *AR* (1825): high-seasoned
c   *AR* (1825): who,
d   *AR* (1825): Judgement
e   *AR* (1825): p 319
f   *AR* (1825): Necessity!
g   *AR* (1825): Friend
h   *AR* (1825): payed
i–j   *AR* (1825): last-mentioned,

[58] Matt 5.18: ". . . Till heaven and earth pass, one jot or one tittle shall in no wise pass from the law, till all be fulfilled''. C's ms for this paragraph down to "Seal on the Bond" is transcribed below in App B(y²ᵛ).

[59] See above, *Sp Aph B Xa* n 15.

[60] The reference here is not clear, since the metaphor of debt is not found in St John's Gospel. C perhaps has in mind the First Epistle of John: ". . . he is the pro-

pitiation for our sins: and not for ours only, but also for the sins of the whole world'': 1 John 2.2; cf 4.10. The phrase ". . . our Lord's Words recorded by John" might then refer to 1 John 1.5: "This then is the message which we have heard of him, and declare unto you . . .". He may also be recalling the parables of the unforgiving servant, Matt 18.21–35, and of the two debtors, Luke 7.37–50.

[61] See e.g. Hooker *Ecclesiastical Politie*

sity of his unchangeable Justice, had determined to exact the full sum; which must, therefore, *a*be paid either by ourselves or by some other in our name and behalf. But besides the Debt which *all* Mankind contracted in and through Adam, as a Homo Publicus,[62] even as a Nation is bound by the Acts of its Head or its Plenipotentiary, every man (say these Divines) is an insolvent Debtor on his own score. In this fearful predicament the Son of God took compassion on Mankind, and resolved to pay the debt for us, and to satisfy the divine Justice by a perfect equivalent. Accordingly, by a strange yet strict *consequence,* it has been holden*b* by more than one of these Divines, that the agonies suffered by Christ were equal in amount to the sum total of the torments of all mankind*c* here and hereafter, or to the infinite debt, which in an endless succession of instalments*d* we should have been paying to the divine Justice, had it not been paid in full by the Son of God incarnate!

It is easy to say—O but I*e* do not hold this, or *we* do not make this an article of our belief! The true question is: Do you take any *part* of it: and can you reject the rest without being *inconsequent*? Are Debt, Satisfaction, Payment in full, Creditor's*f* *Rights,* &c. nomina *propria,*[63] by which the very nature of Redemption and its occasion is expressed? or are they, with several others, figures of speech for the purpose of illustrating the nature and extent of the consequences and effects of the redemptive Act, and to excite in the receivers a due sense of the magnitude and manifold operation of the Boon, and of the Love and gratitude due to the Redeemer? If still you reply, *g*the former: *then,* as your whole theory is grounded on a notion of *Justice,* I ask you—Is this Justice a *moral* Attribute? But morality*h* commences with, and begins in, the sacred distinction between Thing and Person:[64] on this distinction all Law human and divine is grounded: consequently, the Law of Justice. If you

a *AR* (1825): p 320
b *AR* (1825): held
c *AR* (1825): Mankind
d *AR* (1825): installments
e *AR* (1825): *I*
f *AR* (1825): Creditors'
g *AR* (1825): p 321
h *AR* (1825): Morality

(1593–1662) bk vi 5.2: *Works* (1682) 350 ff, John Pearson *Exposition of the Creed* (1659) art iv, "Dead", and, more generally, J. K. Mozley *The Doctrine of the Atonement* (1915) esp 156–7. At the end of the paragraph C may be thinking of the above passage from Hooker and, in particular, of Richard Baxter *Methodus*

theologiae Christianae pt 3 ch 1 §§ 5–15.
[62] "A Public Man", that is, "a representative human being".
[63] "*Proper* nouns"; i.e. used in a non-metaphorical sense. Cf C's n 6 to *Int Aph XII* and n 21 in the present section.
[64] See *Mor Aph VI* n 11, above.

attach any meaning*a* to the term Justice, as applied to God, it must be the same *b*to which you refer*c* when you affirm or deny it of any other personal Agent—save only, that in its attribution to God, you speak of it as unmixed and perfect. For if not, what *do* you mean? And why do you call it by the same name? I may, therefore, with all right and reason, put the case as between man and man. For should it be found irreconcilable*d* with the Justice, which the Light of Reason, made *Law* in the Conscience, dictates to *Man*, how much more must it be incongruous with the all-perfect Justice of God!—Whatever case I should imagine would be felt by the Reader as below the dignity of the subject, and in some measure jarring with his feelings: and in other respects the more familiar the case, the better suited to the present purpose.

A sum of £1000 is owing from James to Peter,[65] for which James has given a Bond.*e* He is insolvent, and the Bond is on the point of being *f*put in suit against him,*g* to James's utter ruin. At this moment Matthew steps in, pays Peter the thousand pounds*h* and discharges the Bond. In this case, no man would hesitate to admit, that a complete *satisfaction* had been made to Peter. Matthew's £1000 is a perfect equivalent*i* for*j* the sum which*k* James was bound to have paid,*l* and*m* which Peter had lent. *It is the same thing*: and this is*n* altogether a question of *Things*. Now instead of James's being indebted to Peter for a sum of money, which (he having become insolvent) Matthew pays for him, we will put the case, that James had been guilty of the basest and most hard-hearted ingratitude to *o*a most*p* worthy and affectionate Mother, who had not only *q*performed all*r* the duties and tender offices of a mother, but whose whole heart was bound up in this her only child—who had *s*foregone all*r* the pleasures and amusements of life in watching over his sickly child-

a AR (1825): idea

b–c AR (1825): which you refer to

d AR (1825): irreconcileable

e AR (1825): Bond in Judgement.

f–g AR (1825): carried into effect,

h AR (1825): pound

i AR (1825): p 322 (valent)

j AR (1825): of

k Added in 1831

l AR (1825): payed,

m AR (1825): and for the sum

n Added in 1831

o–p COPIES A, C, D, E, G: a

q–r COPY G: performed in

s–t COPIES A, C, D, E, G: foregone

[65] The argument of the next two paragraphs is based on a single short paragraph in C's 1819 annotation on Field 58–69, which presents in brief the issue of the difference between a debt in money and a debt in affection: *CM (CC)* II 658.

hood, had sacrificed her health and the far greater part of her resources to rescue him from the consequences of his follies and excesses during his youth and early manhood; and to procure for him the means of his present Rank and Affluence*[a]*—all which he had repaid*[b]* by neglect, desertion, and open profligacy. Here the mother*[c]* stands in the relation of the creditor: and here too we will suppose the same generous Friend to interfere, and to perform with the greatest tenderness and constancy all those duties of a grateful and affectionate Son, which James ought to have performed. Will this satisfy the Mother's claims on James, or entitle him to her Esteem, Approbation, and Blessing? Or what if Matthew, the vicarious Son, should at length address her in words to this purpose: "Now, I trust, you are appeased, and will be henceforward reconciled to James. I have satisfied all your claims on him. I have paid*[d]* his Debt in full: and you *[e]*are too just to require the same debt to be paid*[f]* twice over. You will therefore regard him with the same complacency, and receive him into your presence with the same love, as if there had been no difference between him and you. For I have *made it up.*" What other reply could the swelling heart of the Mother dictate than this? "O misery! and is it possible that *you* are in league with my unnatural child to insult me? Must not the very necessity of *your* abandonment of your proper sphere form an additional evidence of *his* guilt? Must not the sense of your goodness teach me more fully to comprehend, more vividly to feel, the evil in him? Must not the contrast of your merits magnify his Demerit in his Mother's eye, and at once recall and embitter the conviction of the canker-worm in his soul?"

If indeed by the force of Matthew's example, by persuasion or by additional and more mysterious influences, or by an inward co-agency, compatible with the existence*[g]* of a personal will, James should be led to repent; if through admiration and love of this great goodness gradually assimilating his mind to the mind of his benefactor, he should in his own person become a grateful and dutiful child—*then* doubtless the mother would be wholly satisfied! But then the case is no longer a question of *Things**, or a matter of *Debt* payable*[h]* by another. Nevertheless, the *Ef-*

* On a subject, concerning which we have so deep an interest in forming just and

[a] *AR* (1825): Affluences ; COPIES C, D, E: Affluence
[b] *AR* (1825): repayed
[c] *AR* (1825): Mother
[d] *AR* (1825): payed
[e] *AR* (1825): p 323
[f] *AR* (1825): payed
[g] *AR* (1825): idea
[h] *AR* (1825): p 324 (able)

distinct conceptions, no serious Inquirer after religious truth; much less any man dedicated to its pursuit, and who ought to be able to declare with the Psalmist, it is "more desirable to me than thousands of gold and silver;*a* therefore do I hate every false way;"[66] will blame my solicitude to place a notion, which I regard not only as a misbelief, but as a main source of unbelief—at all events, among the most frequent and plausible pretexts of Infidelity—in all the various points of view, from which this or that Reader may more readily see, and see *into*, its falsity. I make therefore no apology for adding one other illustration of the whimsical Logic by which it is supported, in an Incident of recent occurrence, which will at the same time furnish an instance in proof of the contrariety of the Notion itself to the first and most obvious principles of morality, and how spontaneously Common Sense starts forward, as it were, to repel it.

Let it be imagined, that the late Mr. Fauntleroy[67] had, in compliance with the numerous petitions in his behalf, received a pardon—that soon after some other Individual had been tried and convicted of forging a note for a Hundred Pounds*b*—that on application made for the extension of mercy to the culprit it should be declared that in a commercial country like this it was contrary to all Justice to grant a pardon to a man convicted of Forgery—and that in invalidation of this dictum, the Applicants having quoted, as they naturally would quote, the case of Mr. Fauntleroy, the Home Secretary should reply, Yes! but Mr. Fauntleroy forged to the amount of Two Hundred Thousand Pounds!*c*—Now it is plain, that the Logic of this reply would remain the same, if instead of comparative Criminality I had supposed a case of comparative Purity from Crime: and when the Reader has settled with himself, what he would think of such Logic, and by what name he would describe it, let him peruse the following extract:[68]

MANSION HOUSE.

Monsieur Edmund Angelini, Professor of the La[n]guages, and *la morale*, whose fracas with the Austrian Ambassador was reported on Wednesday, came before the Lord Mayor, and presented his Lordship with a Petition, of which the following is a translation:—

"My Lord—He who has violated the law ought to perish by the sword of Justice.*d* Monsieur Fauntleroy ought to perish by the sword of Justice.*e* If another takes his place, I think that justice ought to be satisfied. I devote myself for him. I take upon myself his crime, and I wish to die to save him.

(Signed)   Edmund Angelini,

18, Ossulston-street, Somers-town.   of Venice."

---

a   *AR* (1825): silver:

b   *AR* (1825): Pound

c   *AR* (1825): Pound!

d   *AR* (1825): justice.

e   *AR* (1825): justice.

[66] Ps 119.72: "The law of thy mouth is better unto me than thousands of gold and silver"; ibid v 104: "Through thy precepts I get understanding: therefore I hate every false way" (and cf v 128).

[67] Henry Fauntleroy (1785–1824), a banker, was arrested for forgery on 11 Sept 1824, condemned to death on 2 Nov, and executed on 30 Nov. The case, which involved very large sums of money, aroused considerable interest and the execution was watched by a crowd estimated at 100,000: Arthur Griffiths *The Chronicles of Newgate* (2 vols 1884) II 294–300. As the subse-

quent newspaper cutting shows, C must have been writing shortly after 4 Dec. He had referred to a report of the trial in a letter to Gillman of 2 Nov 1824: *CL* v 392.

[68] From *Baldwin's London Weekly Journal* 4 Dec 1824 p 3. The original text of the second paragraph continues, "He is a father, he is a citizen; his life is useful, mine a burden to the world. I am in good health—my mental faculties are perfect. I do not make this request merely to get myself spoken of, but in the earnest hope that what I seek may be granted me as a favour."

fect,—and the reader will remember, that it is the *effects* and *consequences*^a of Christ's mediation, on which St. Paul is dilating—the Effect to *James* is similar in both cases, *i.e.* in the case of James, the Debtor, and of James, the undutiful Son. In both cases, James is liberated from a grievous burthen:^b and in both cases, he has to attribute^c his liberation to the Act and free grace of another. The only *difference* is, that in the former case (viz. the payment of the debt) the beneficial Act is, *singly* and without requiring any re-action or co-agency on the part of James, the efficient *cause* of his liberation; while in the latter case (viz. that of Redemption) the beneficial Act is, the^d *first*, the indispensable *Condition*, and *then*, the *Co*-efficient.

The professional Student of Theology will, perhaps, understand the different positions asserted in the preceding Argument more readily if they are presented *synoptically*, i.e. brought at once within his view, in the form of Answers to four Questions, comprising the constituent parts

---

The Lord Mayor expressed his surprise at the application; and Mr. Angelini was informed that it was contrary to all justice that the life of an innocent person should be taken to save that of one who was guilty, even if an innocent man chose to devote himself.[69]

Angelini exclaimed that our Saviour died as an atonement for the sins of the guilty, and that he did not see why he should not be allowed to do so.

But in answer to this, doubts were expressed whether Monsieur Angelini was sufficiently pure to satisfy justice.[70]

*   *   *   *   *

From *Baldwin's London Weekly Journal,*
Saturday, Dec. 4th,^e *1824.*

The Reader is now, I trust, convinced, that though the *Case* put by me, introductory to this extract, was imaginary, the *Logic* was not of my invention. *It is contrary to all Justice, that an* INNOCENT *person should be sacrificed,* &c. &c.; *but a person* ALTOGETHER innocent—Aye! that is a different question!

---

^a *AR* (1825): p 325 (*quences*)   ^b *AR* (1825): burthen;
^c *AR* (1825): p 326 (bute)   ^d Added in 1831   ^e *AR* (1825): 4,

[69] The first part of this sentence condenses the original: "He began to speak in support of this Petition with all his native energy of manner, and an external manifestation of sincerity. The Lord Mayor expressed his surprise at the application, and his doubts whether the petitioner was not mistaken in his assertion as to his faculties being in good order.

"Angelini exclaimed with fervour, 'Accordez moi cette grace j'ai tante ma tete'."

[70] Instead of this paragraph the original continues: "Doubts were expressed whether M. Angelini was in a proper state of purity himself to become an atonement. He, however, supplicated that he might be accepted.

"The Lord Mayor was inclined to consider the offer as a fit of mad benevolence.

"M. Angelini, after the refusal, became calmer, but said that he was willing to die . . .".

of the Scriptural Doctrine of Redemption. And I trust that my Lay Readers of both sexes will not allow themselves to be scared from the perusal of the following short catechism by half a dozen Latin words, or rather words with Latin endings, that translate themselves into English, when I dare assure them, that they will encounter no other obstacle to their full and easy comprehension of the contents.

Synopsis[71] *of the Constituent Points in the Doctrine of Redemption, in Four Questions, with Correspondent Answers*

Questions

Who (or What) is the
1. Agens Causator?
2. Actus Causativus?
3. Effectum Causatum?
4. Consequentia ab Effecto?[72]

[a]Answers

I. The Agent and Personal Cause of the Redemption of Mankind is—the co-eternal Word and [b]only begotten[c] Son of the Living God, incarnate, tempted, agonizing (*Agonistes* ἀγωνιζόμενος),[73] crucified, submitting to Death, resurgent, communicant of his Spirit, ascendent, and obtaining for his Church the Descent,[d] and Communion of the Holy Spirit, the Comforter.[74]

II. The Causative Act is—a spiritual and transcendent Mystery, ''that passeth all understanding.''[75]

III. The Effect caused is—the being born anew: as before in the *flesh* to the World, so now born in the *spirit* to Christ.[76]

IV. The Consequences[e] from the Effect are—Sanctification from Sin, and Liberation from the inherent and penal consequences of Sin in the World to come, with all the means and processes of Sanctification by

[a] *AR* (1825): p 327
[b-c] *AR* (1825): only-begotten
[d] *AR* (1825): Descent
[e] *AR* (1825): Consequents

[71] This synopsis is based on a final section of the annotation on Field *Of the Church* 58–69 (*CM—CC*—II 658–9), written in ink rather than the pencil of the earlier part of the annotation and evidently at a later date. Some important additions for the text of *AR* (1825) are noted below.

[72] ''1. The Acting Cause? 2. The Causative Act? 3. The Effect Caused? 4. The Consequents from the Effect?''

[73] Perhaps ''the agonist agonising'' or ''the champion contending''. The possible connotations are too extensive for adequate translation, as is often the case when C has recourse to another language. See below, App I Excursus Note 16 ''Coleridge and the word 'Agonistes' ''.

[74] The ms annotation has a shorter list.

[75] See above, *Sp Aph B XVII* n 16.

[76] The ms annotation continues with an explanatory point that adds little.

the Word and the Spirit: these Consequents being the same for the Sinner relatively to God and his own Soul, as the satisfaction of a debt for a Debtor relatively to his Creditor; as the sacrificial atonement made by the Priest for the Transgressor of the Mosaic Law; as the reconciliation to an alienated Parent for a Son who had estranged himself from his Father's house and presence; and as a redemptive Ransom for a Slave or Captive.[77]

Now I complain, that this metaphorical *Naming* of the transcendent Causative Act through the medium of its proper effects from Actions and Causes of familiar occurrence connected with the former by similarity of [a]Result, has been mistaken for an intended designation of the essential character of the Causative Act itself; and that thus Divines have interpreted *de omni* what was spoken *de singulo*[78], and magnified a *partial equation* into a *total identity*.

I will merely hint, to my more *learned* readers, and to the professional Students of Theology, that the origin of this error is to be sought for[79] in the discussions of the Greek Fathers, and (at a later period) of the Schoolmen, on the obscure and *abysmal*[80] subject of the Divine *A-seity*,[81] and the distinction between the θήλημα[b] and the βουλή,[c][82] i.e.[d] the

----

[a] *AR* (1825): p 328
[b] A slip, for θέλημα, repeated from *AR* (1825) (where the word is unaccented)
[c] *AR* (1825): βουλη, ; *AR* (1831): βουλὴ,   [d] *AR* (1825): *i. e.*

[77] This paragraph mostly paraphrases the ms annotation, but omits the example of a subject and an offended sovereign.

[78] "As concerning the whole . . . concerning a particular case". The present paragraph expands and explains the corresponding one in the ms annotation.

[79] The expression from this point is perhaps over-compressed: the intended meaning appears to be that the error arises in the discussion of profound but difficult truths.

[80] If there is a jocular, self-deprecating overtone here (cf *BL* ch 10—*CC*—ɪ 181: "O . . . the anticlimax, the abysmal bathos, of that *four-pence*") it lightly masks a serious interest in the idea of abyss as a symbol of God's being. See below, App I Excursus Note 17 "Coleridge and the Abyss of Being".

[81] "Underived or independent existence". See *OED*, which cites John Norris *An Essay Towards the Theory of the Ideal or Intelligible World* pt 1 ch 1 (2 vols 1701) ɪ 7: ". . . the *Natural* WORLD, or Universe . . . is not a self Existent, Eternal, Immu-

table Nature . . . and for any self stability, Aseity, or Essential Immutability of its own, may again cease to be". (Norris's chapters on the "Divine Ideas" may have been the inspiration for the title of the ms by C, now *HEHL ms* HM 8195. Cf J. H. Muirhead *Coleridge as Philosopher*—1930—269.) C uses the word to convey the idea of God as containing the ground of his existence (see preceding note and ref). In a letter to Tulk of 12 Feb 1818 he spoke of the danger for Swedenborgians of ". . . utterly demerging the tremendous incompatibilities with an evil will that arise out of the essential Holiness of the abysmal Aseity in the Love of the eternal *Person*": *CL* ɪᴠ 837. He listed, possibly in 1825 (*CN* ɪᴠ 5256), "*Ase*itatis principium ineffabile" (the ineffable principle of aseity), as a synonym for the Absolute Will, along with βυσσος αβυσσος (tr by him "deepless Depth" in *CN* ɪɪɪ 4418 f 13; used again in *CN* ɪᴠ 5249 f 40 and in *CL* ᴠɪ 583). *Aseitas* appears also in *Op Max ms* B3 ("II") 252.

[82] Two words for "will" (the first being

absolute Will, as the universal *Ground* of *all* Being, and the Election and purpose of God in the personal Idea, as the Father. And this view[a] would have allowed me to express (what I believe to be) the true import and scriptural idea of Redemption in terms much more nearly resembling those used ordinarily by the Calvinistic Divines, and with a conciliative *show* of coincidence.[83] But this motive was outweighed by the reflection, that I could not rationally have expected to be understood by those, to whom I most wish to be intelligible: et si non vis intelligi, cur vis legi?[84]

N.B. Not to countervene the purpose of a Synopsis, I have detached the confirmative or explanatory remarks from the Answers to Questions II[b] and III.,[c] and place them below as Scholia. A single glance of the eye will enable the reader to re-connect each with the sentence it is supposed to follow.

[a] *AR* (1825): View
[b] *AR* (1825): II.
[c] *AR* (1825): III.

---

a slip for θέλημα). For C's sources see below, App I Excursus Note 18 "Two words for 'Will' ". His own views are given in the note that follows here.

[83] Cf *Prel Sp Aph* n 14, *Sp Aph B Xa* nn 36–7 above, and, especially, C's annotation to Field *Of the Church* (1635) commenting on God's permitting men to do evil: after outlining the situation in ancient Greece, where the existence of "moral and intelligent Shapers" was admitted, but not that of one "intelligent Ground" to the universe, C continued, "The Leibnitzian distinction of the eternal Reason or Nature of God (= τό Θεῖον) from the Will or Personal Attributes of God (= θέλημα καί βουλησιν . . .) planted the Germ of the only possible Solution . . .": *CM (CC)* II 665. His point is prompted primarily by his tetradic doctrine (see above, *Sp Aph B II* n 64), where the personal Father is the synthesis in a process which springs ultimately from the unknowable Absolute Ground. In the Father, the θέλημα is that illuminated element in the Will which is related back to the Original Ground, while the βουλή corresponds to his active will, particularly as it is directly experienced in the world in

moral terms. For C's version of the distinction between these two words for "will" and its relation to that between God's absolute will and his election see also above, *Sp Aph B Xa* n 37. For this "absolute Will"—which again is coloured by his own thought—see annotations recorded in *LS (CC)* 67n and *Friend (CC)* I 515n; also an annotation on De Wette *Theodor* in *CM (CC)* II 198 and on Hooker, ibid 1137; *CN* IV 4517, 4728, 5249, 5256, *Op Max ms* B3 ("II") 166 ("the Absolute Will which is one with the Supreme Reason"), and *C&S (CC)* 182. See also Barth 107–12 and Boulger 127–40, including also (226) a quotation from N 26 (*CN* v): ". . . in the Almighty Creator Infinite Intelligence was one with Absolute Will . . .".

[84] "And if you do not wish to be understood, why do you wish to be read?" C may here be recalling Locke: "Si non vis intelligi, debes negligi": "If you do not wish to be understood, you ought to be neglected." See John Locke *An Essay Concerning Human Understanding* III ix 10 ed P. H. Nidditch (Oxford 1975) 481, where the source is stated to be untraced.

*^a*SCHOLIUM TO *^b*ANS. II*^c*

Nevertheless, *the fact or actual truth having been assured to us by Revelation,* it is not impossible, by stedfast meditation on the idea and super-natural character of a personal WILL, for a mind spiritually disciplined to satisfy itself, that the redemptive act *supposes* (and that our redemption is even negatively *conceivable* only on the supposition of) an Agent who can at once act *on* the Will as an exciting cause, *quasi ab extra;*[85] and *in* the Will, as the *condition^d* of its potential, and the *ground^e* of its actual, Being.

*^f*SCHOLIUM TO ANS. III*^g*

Where two subjects, that stand to each other in the relation of *antithesis* (or contradistinction) are connected by a middle term common to *both*, the sense of this middle term is indifferently determinable by *either;^h* the preferability of the one or the other in any given case being decided by the circumstance of our more frequent experience of, or greater familiarity with, the Term in *this* connexion. Thus, if I put Hydrogen and Oxygen Gas, as opposite Poles, the term *Gas* is common to both; and it is a matter of indifference, by which of the two bodies I ascertain the sense of the Term. But if for the conjoint purposes of connexion and contrast, I oppose transparent chrystallized Alumen to opake derb[86] (*unchrystallized*) Alumen;[87]—it may easily happen to be far more *convenient* for me to show the sense of the middle term, *i.e.* Alumen, by a piece of Pipe-clay *ⁱ*than by a Sapphire or Ruby;*^j* especially, if I should be describing the beauty and preciousness of the latter to a *^k*Peasant Woman,*^l* or in a District, where a Ruby was a rarity which the fewest*^m*

^a AR (1825): SCHOLIUM (p 329)

^{b-c} AR (1825): ANS. II.

^d COPIES A, C, D, E, G: ground

^e COPIES A, C, D, E, G: condition

^{f-g} AR (1825): SCHOLIUM TOA NS. III.

^h AR (1825): *either:*

ⁱ AR (1825): p 330

^j AR (1825): Ruby:

^{k-l} AR (1825): female Peasant,

^m AR (1825): Fewest

[85] "As if from outside".

[86] "Rough, uncrystallized, massive". *OED* derives from the German *derb* and regards C's use of it here as possibly a nonce-word in English.

[87] W. T. Brande *A Manual of Chemistry* (1819) 328–9 begins: "The earth alumina constitutes some of the hardest gems, such as the sapphire and ruby, and it gives a peculiar softness and plasticity to some earthy compounds, such as the different kinds of clay"; it goes on to compare crystallised hydrated alum with its amorphous derivative (p 329).

only had an opportunity of seeing. This is a plain rule of common Logic directed in its application by Common Sense.

Now let us apply this to the case in hand. The two opposites *here* are Flesh and Spirit, *this* in relation to *Christ, that* in relation to the *World;*[a] and these two Opposites are connected by the middle term, *Birth,* which is of course common to both. But for the same reason, as in the instance last-mentioned, the interpretation of the common term is to be ascertained from its known sense, in the more familiar connexion—Birth, namely, in relation to our natural life and to the Organized Body, by which we belong to the present World. Whatever the word signifies in this connexion, the same *essentially* (in *kind* though not in dignity and value) must be its signification in the other. How else could it be (what yet in this text it undeniably *is*), the *punctum indifferens,* or *nota communis,*[88] of the Thesis (Flesh: the World) and the Antithesis (Spirit: Christ)? We might therefore, supposing a writer to have been speaking of River-water in distinction from Rain-water, as rationally pretend that in the latter phrase the term, Water, was to be understood metaphorically, as that the word, Birth, is a *metaphor,* and "means only" so and so, in the Gospel according to St. John.

There is, I am aware, a numerous and powerful [b]Party in our church, so numerous and powerful as not seldom to be entitled *the* Church, who hold and publicly teach, that "Regeneration is only Baptism."[89] Nay, the Writer of the Article on the Lives of Scott and Newton in our ablest and most respectable Review is but one among many who do not hesitate to brand the contrary opinion as heterodoxy, and schismatical superstition.[90] I trust, that I think as seriously, as most men, of the evil of Schism; but with every disposition to pay the utmost deference to an

---

[a] *AR* (1825): *World:*   [b] *AR* (1825): p 331

[88] "Point of indifference" (see above, *Sp Aph B II* n 61); "note in common".

[89] In a note on *Reliquiae Baxterianae* C ascribes this view to George Pretyman and William Magee: *CM (CC)* I 262–3. Cf also *CN* III 4401 f 55.

[90] In *AR* (1839) HNC refers at this point to *QR* XXXI (Apr 1824) 26–52; there "Mr Potter" (see W. E. Houghton ed *Wellesley Index to Victorian Periodicals*—1966—I 703), reviewing J. Scott *Life of the Rev. Thomas Scott* and two memoirs of the Rev John Newton, comments (p 27) on the error that arises from "not attending to the

distinction . . . between the extraordinary and the ordinary operations of the Spirit"; continuing, "The first species of this error which we shall mention, is the attributing to a supernatural influence, feelings and conduct, which may be referred to the *effects of very early education.* We heard much, a short time since, of regeneration being distinct from baptism, and without doubt cases like the one which we are about to quote from Mr. Scott's life of his father, had their weight with the supporters of that heterodoxy."

acknowledged[a] majority including, it is said, a very large proportion of the present Dignitaries of our Church, I cannot but think it a sufficient reply, that if Regeneration means Baptism,[b] Baptism must mean Regeneration:[c] and this too, as Christ himself has declared, a Regeneration[d] in the Spirit. Now I would ask these Divines this simple question. Do they believingly suppose a spiritual regenerative power and agency inhering in or accompanying the sprinkling a few drops of water on an infant's face? They cannot evade the question by saying that Baptism is a *type* or *sign*. For this would be to supplant their own assertion, that Regeneration means Baptism, by the contradictory admission, that Regeneration is the significatum,[91] of which Baptism is the significant.[92] Unless, indeed, they would incur the absurdity of saying, that regeneration is a type of regeneration, and Baptism a type of itself—or that Baptism only means Baptism! And this indeed is the plain consequence, to which they might be driven, should they answer the above question in the Negative.

[e]But if their answer be, Yes! we do suppose and believe this efficiency in the baptismal act—I have not another word to say. Only, perhaps, I might be permitted to express a hope, that for consistency's sake they would speak less slightingly of the *insufflation*,[93] and *extreme unction*,[94] used in the Romish Church: notwithstanding the not easily to be answered arguments of our Christian Mercury,[95] the all-eloquent Jeremy Taylor, respecting the latter,—"which, since it is used when the man is above half dead, when he can exercise no act of understanding, *it must needs be nothing. For no rational man can think, that any ceremony can make a spiritual change without a spiritual act of him that is to be*

---

[a] *AR* (1825): acknowleged   [b] *AR* (1825): baptism,
[c] *AR* (1825): regeneration: [d] *AR* (1825): regeneration   [e] *AR* (1825): p 332

[91] "Signified".

[92] See *OED* for other uses of "significant" as a noun meaning "that which signifies".

[93] "Blowing or breathing upon a person or thing to symbolize the influence of the Holy Spirit and the expulsion of evil spirits; a rite of exorcism used in the Roman, Greek, and some other churches": *OED*, which also cites Taylor *Liberty of Prophesying* (1647) v 87.

[94] A sacrament in which the sick who are in danger of death are anointed by a priest.

[95] C apparently alludes to two of Mercury's numerous functions: he was god of eloquence and leader of souls (as well as being divine messenger in general). The source of his usage here is an engraving in certain eds of Taylor's *Holy Living and Holy Dying* (e.g. 1652–4, 1663, 1680), showing the author pointing to heaven, and standing on a pedestal that bears the inscription "Mercurius Christianus". (A common formulation: C's early favourite Böhme was called "Mercurius Teutonicus" and Joseph Hall "Mercurius Britannicus".)

changed; nor that it can work by way of nature, or by charm, but morally and after the manner of reasonable creatures."

TAYLOR's *Epist. Dedic. to his Holy Dying,* p. 6.[96]

It is too obvious to require suggestion, that these words here quoted apply with yet greater force and propriety to the point in question: as the Babe is an unconscious subject, which the dying man need not be supposed to be. My avowed convictions, respecting Regeneration with the spiritual baptism, as its Condition and Initiative, (Luke iii. 16; Mark i. 8; Matt. iii. 11), and of which the sacramental Rite, the Baptism of John, was appointed by Christ to remain as the Sign and Figure; and still more, perhaps, my belief respecting the Mystery of the Eucharist, (concerning which I hold the same opinions as Bucer (Strype's Life of Archb. Cranmer, Appendix),[97] Peter Martyr, [a]and presumably Cranmer himself[98])[b]—these convictions and this belief will, I doubt not, be deemed by the Orthodox *de more Grotii,*[99] who improve the *letter* of Arminius[100] with the *spirit* of Socinus,[c][101] sufficient data to bring me in guilty of irrational and Superstitious[d] Mysticism. But I abide by a maxim, which I learnt at an early period of my theological studies, from Benedict Spinoza.[102] Where the Alternative lies between the Absurd[103]

---

[a] *AR* (1825): p 333
[b] No parenthesis in *AR* (1825) or *AR* (1831)
[c] *AR* (1825): the Socini,
[d] *AR* (1825): superstitious

---

[96] Taylor, Dedication to *The Rule and Exercises of Holy Dying* (1652) [vii] (C's typography suggests a seventeenth- rather than an eighteenth-century ed). The exact ed used by C is unidentified; the 1652 ed differs only in accidentals and in C's insertion of "that it can".

[97] See John Strype, Appendix XLVI: "The Sentencious Sayings of Master Martin Bucer upon the Lordes Supper" *Memorials of the Most Reverend Father in God, Thomas Cranmer* (2 pts 1694) 124–33: ". . . these heavenly misteries do passe all mens capacityes" (§ 25); "the bread and wyne . . . be *signes exhibityve*" (§ 45). C refers to this Appendix in a note of 1823 on Burnet *History of the Reformation*: *CM (CC)* I 839, and returns to it in a note of Dec 1825 on Blanco White *The Poor Man's Preservative Against Popery*: *CM (CC)* I 509. C also annotated the Appendix itself, noting that "the whole N° evinces a superior mind"; see *CM (CC)* IV.

[98] Pietro Martire Vermigli (1500–62)

and Martin Bucer (1491–1551) both settled in England and worked on the Book of Common Prayer together with Cranmer: see *DNB* under both names and e.g. C. W. Dugmore "The First Ten Years, 1549–59" in Michael Ramsay et al *The English Prayer Book 1549–1662* (1963) 19–22.

[99] "In the manner of Grotius". See above, *Sp Aph B II* n 14.

[100] See above, *Sp Aph B II* n 13.

[101] See above, *Mor Aph L* n 4.

[102] Cf *CN* IV 4618: "Axiom.—Where ever the Choice lies between the Incomprehensible (praeter intellectum, sive intelligentiam *definientem* [beyond intellect, or the *defining* intelligence]) the Absurd (rationi contrarium [contrary to reason]) and a palpable Shuffle (nihilismus turpis [a base nihilism]) to choose the former."

C was reading Spinoza in late 1799 (*CL* I 534, 551) and annotated the *Opera* (Jena 1802–3) in 1812–13: *CM (CC)*. He may here be thinking of his *Tractatus theologico-politicus* ch 15, on belief in the scrip-

and the Incomprehensible,[104] no wise man can be at a loss which of the two to prefer.[105] To be *called* irrational, is a trifle: to *be* so, and in matters of religion, is far otherwise: and whether the irrationality consists in men's believing (*i.e.* in having persuaded themselves that they believe) *against* reason, or *without* reason, I have been early instructed to consider it as a sad and serious evil, pregnant with mischiefs, political and moral. And by none of my numerous Instructors so impressively, as by that great and shining Light of our Church in the aera of her intellectual splendor,[a] Bishop Jeremy Taylor: from one of whose works, and that of especial authority for the safety as well as for the importance of the principle, inasmuch as it was written expressly ad populum, I will now, both for its own intrinsic worth, and to relieve the attention, wearied, perhaps, by the length and argumentative character of the preceding *discussion*, interpose the following Aphorism.

[b]APHORISM XX[c][1]

Whatever is against right reason, that no faith can oblige us to believe.

[a] *AR* (1825): splendour,
[b] *AR* (1825): p 334
[c] *AR* (1825): JER. TAYLOR.

---

tures, in which Spinoza attacks the view of Rabbi Alpakhar that Scripture never in express words contradicts affirmatively or negatively in one place what it affirms or denies in another. He points out e.g. that when God comes down on Mt Sinai (Exod 19.20) this is contrary to Solomon's statement that God is infinite and cannot be contained even in the heaven of heavens (1 Kgs 8.27), contending that such instances are enough to show "what absurdities follow from the rule of interpretation suggested by the author quoted"; C might not have accepted without question his further position, "that theology is neither subject or subordinate to reason, nor reason subject to theology. . . . the sphere of reason being truth and knowledge, while that of theology is piety and obedience . . .": Spinoza *Tractatus theologico-politicus* tr R Willis (1862) 260–5. See also above, *Sp Aph B II* n 30.

[103] Cf *Friend (CC)* I 430: ". . . the human mind has no predilection for absurdity".

[104] Cf C's letter of 20 Mar 1796: "Has not Dr Priestly forgotten that *Incomprehensibility* is as necessary an attribute of the First Cause, as Love, or Power, or Intelligence?—": *CL* I 193. C's point emerges also in *The Eolian Harp* line 59, especially in the second draft, and, by implication, in the poem *To Mr. Pye*: *PW* (EHC) I 102, II 1023, 959. See also below, *Conc* n 72.

[105] In *CN* IV 5243 (Sept 1825) C used this argument in relation to the redemption and incarnation: "an incomprehensible Mystery/ to the belief of which we can *intellectually* supply one indirect argument, viz. an exposure of the Absurdity of every comprehensible Substitute, that has been imagined".

[1] This aphorism is transcribed from Taylor *Worthy Communicant* ch 3 § 5 par 2 (1674) 176. Apart from the insertion of "*(speculative)*" before "reason" in the second sentence and the omission of "true" before it in the third, the changes are stylistic. For the original text see App A(t), below.

For though Reason is not the positive and affirmative measure of our faith, and our faith ought to be larger than our *(speculative)* Reason, *(see* p. 188*ᵃ*) and *take* something into her heart, that Reason can never take into her eye; yet in all our creed there can be nothing *against* reason. If Reason justly contradicts an article, it is not *of the household of Faith.* In this there is no difficulty, but that in practice we take care that we do not call *that* Reason, which is not so *(see* p. 168, 169*ᵇ*; p. 224*ᶜ*). For although Reason is a right judge*ᵈ**, yet it ought not to pass sentence in an inquiry of faith, until all the information be brought in; all that is within, and all that is without, all that is above, and all that is below; all that concerns it in experience and all that concerns it in act:*ᵉ* whatsoever is of pertinent observation and whatsoever is revealed. For else Reason may argue very well and yet conclude falsely. It may conclude well *ᶠ*in Logic, and yet infer a false proposition in Theology *ᵍ*(p. 168, line 24– 169, line 7*⁵*).*ʰ* But when our Judge is fully and truly informed in all that, whence she is to make her Judgment,*ⁱ* we may safely follow her whithersoever she invites us.

APHORISM XXI*ʲ¹*

He that speaks against his own Reason, speaks against his own Conscience: and therefore it is certain, no man serves God with a good conscience, who serves him against his reason.

---

* Which it could not be, in respect of spiritual truths and objects super-sensuous,² if it were the same with, and merely another name for "the Faculty judging according to Sense"—*i.e.* the Understanding, or (as Taylor most often calls it in distinction from Reason) *Discourse*³ *(Discursus* seu *Facultas discursiva* vel *discursoria).*⁴ N.B. The Reason, so instructed and so actuated as Taylor requires in the sentences immediately following, is what I have called the Spirit.*ᵏ*

ᵃ AR (1825): *p.* 179   *ᵇ AR* (1825): *p.* 161, 162
ᶜ AR (1825): *p.* 216   *ᵈ AR* (1825): Judge   *ᵉ AR* (1825): act;
ᶠ AR (1825): p 335   *ᵍ⁻ʰ AR* (1825): *(p.* 161, *lines* 16—28).
ⁱ AR (1825): Judgement,   *ʲ AR* (1825): JER. TAYLOR.
ᵏ AR (1825): Spirit. *Vide p.* 208, 209.

² For this word see above, *Sp Aph B VIIIb* n 63.
³ See e.g. Taylor *Worthy Communicant* (1674) 160, cited in *Sp Aph B XXIIIa* n 7, below.
⁴ "*Discourse,* or the *discursive,* or else discoursing, *Faculty*". See above, *Sp Aph B VIIIb* n 10.
⁵ *AR* (1831) cites, wrongly, "p 165".
¹ From Taylor *Worthy Communicant* ch 3 § 5 par 2 (1674) 177 with minimal changes: see App A(u), below.

APHORISM XXII[a1]

By the eye of Reason through the telescope of Faith, *i.e.* Revelation, we may see what without this telescope we could never have known to exist.[2] But as one that shuts the eye hard, and with violence curls the eyelid, forces a phantastic fire from the crystalline humor, and espies a light that never shines, and sees thousands of little fires that never burn; so is he that blinds the eye of Reason, and pretends to see by an eye of Faith. He makes little images of Notions, and some atoms dance before him; but he is not guided by the light, nor instructed by the proposition, but sees like a man in his sleep.[3] IN NO CASE CAN TRUE REASON AND A RIGHT FAITH OPPOSE EACH OTHER.[4]

NOTE PREFATORY

TO

APHORISM XXIII.—Less on my own account, than in the hope of forearming my youthful friends, I add [b]one other Transcript from Bishop Taylor, as from a Writer to whose name no taint or suspicion of Calvinistic or schismatical tenets can attach, and for the purpose of softening the offence which, I cannot but foresee, will be taken at the positions asserted in paragraph the first of Aphorism VII. p. 196, and the documental proofs of the same in p. 199–202: and this by a formidable party composed of men ostensibly of the most dissimilar Creeds, *regular* Church-Divines, voted orthodox by a great majority of suffrages, and the so called Free-thinking Christians, and Unitarian Divines. It is the *former* class alone that I wish to conciliate: so far at least as it may be done by removing the aggravation of *novelty* from the offensive article.

[a] *AR* (1825): THE SAME.
[b] *AR* (1825): p 336

[1] Apart from the first sentence, for which see the next note, the text is taken from Taylor p 177 just before and, with an omission, after, the sentence in *Aph XXI*, with minimal changes. See App A(v), below.

[2] Cf Jebb *Works* (2 vols 1787) II 137: "Reason is analogous to the naked eye; revelation to the sight, assisted by the telescope." (For Jebb see above, *Mor Aph VI* n 32.) C picks up this analogy in his annotation on Harvey *The Synagogue* (1673): "Reason is to Faith, as the Eye to the Telescope"—*CM (CC)* II 1046—and repeats it

in *P Lects* Lect 9, in which faith is defined as ". . . the energies of our moral feelings": *P Lects* (1949) 269. For different telescope metaphors see *CN* I 1798 and III 4065, both quoted in *CM (CC)* I 170, and cf *SM (CC)* 24.

[3] Some remarks on lycanthropy, annotated by C, follow this sentence in Taylor. See *CM (CC)* V.

[4] This sentence is taken from one in Taylor immediately after that quoted in *Aph XXI*: see n 1 above and App A(u) below.

And surely the simple re-assertion of one of "the two great things," which Bishop TAYLOR could assert as a fact, which, he took for granted, no Christian would think of controverting, should at least be controverted without bitterness by his successors in the Church. That which was perfectly safe and orthodox in 1657, in the judgment[a] of a devoted Royalist and Episcopalian, must be at most but a venial heterodoxy in 1825.[1] For the rest, I am prepared to hear in answer—what has already been so often, and with such theatrical effect dropt, as an *extinguisher*,[2] on my arguments—the famous concluding period of one of the chapters in Paley's Moral and Political Philosophy,[3] declared by Dr. Parr to be the *finest* prose passage in English Literature.[4] Be it so! I bow to so great an authority. But if the learned Doctor would impose it on me as [b]the *truest* as well as the finest, or expect me to admire the Logic equally with the Rhetoric—ἀφίσταμαι.[c5] I start off! As I have been *un-English[d]* enough to find in Pope's tomb-epigram on Sir Isaac Newton[6] nothing better than a gross and wrongful falsehood conveyed in an enormous and irreverent hyperbole; so with regard to this passage in question, free as it is from all faults of taste, I have yet the hardihood to confess, that in the sense in which the words *discover* and *prove,* are here used and intended, I am not convinced of the truth of the principle, (that he alone discovers who proves), and I question the correctness of the particular case, brought as instance and confirmation. I *doubt* the validity of the

---

[a] *AR* (1825): judgement
[b] *AR* (1825): p 337
[c] *AR* (1825): ἀφίσταμαι·
[d] *AR* (1825): *unenglish*

---

[1] The mention of "1825" might mean that the year had already turned when C first wrote; but the date may have been given so in order to accord with the year in which *AR* would be published.

[2] An extinguisher was a hollow conical cap for extinguishing a candle or light (*OED*), large metal ones being set up outside houses for link-boys to put out their torches. If the reference is literal, it might be to a comic theatrical performance in which a giant extinguisher fell upon a person or group of people.

[3] The passage was in fact reprinted at the end of *AR* in 1825 (and from then on): see p 411–12, below. Notes in *AR* (1825) COPIES A, D, and E record the fact. The crucial sentence for what follows is the last: "He alone discovers, who *proves*; and no man can prove this point, but the teacher

who testifies by miracles that his doctrine comes from God."

[4] Samuel Parr (b 1747) died on 6 Mar 1825, near to the time when this written. The source of the opinion cited here is not traced.

[5] "I recoil": Pindar *Olympian Odes* 1.52—at the story of the serving of his son's flesh by Tantalus to the gods, his guests.

[6] Pope *Epitaph Intended for Sir Isaac Newton, in Westminster-Abbey* (1730):

Nature, and Nature's Laws lay hid in Night.
God said, *Let Newton be*! and all was Light.

Poems (Twickenham ed) VI, *Minor Poems* ed N. Ault and J. Butt (1954) 317–18.

assertion as a *general* rule; and I *deny* it, as applied to matters of *faith,* to the verities of religion, in the belief of which there must always be somewhat of moral election, "an act of the *Will* in it as well as of the Understanding, as much *love* in it as discursive power. True Christian Faith must have in it something of in-evidence, something that must be made up by duty and by obedience."—Taylor's Worthy Communicant, p. 160.[7] But most readily do I admit, and most fervently do I contend, that the Miracles worked by Christ, both as miracles and as fulfilments of prophecy, both as signs and as wonders, made plain discovery, and gave unquestionable proof, of his divine character and authority; that they were to the whole Jewish nation true and appropriate evidences, that HE was indeed come who had promised and declared to their Forefathers, Behold[a] your God will come with vengeance, (*Matth.* x. 34, *Luke* xii. 49).[b8] even God a recompense! HE will come and save you! (*Isaiah* xxxv. 4,[9] compared with *Matth.* x. 34, and *Luke* xii. 49.)[10] I receive them as proofs, therefore, of the truth of every word, which he taught who was himself THE WORD: and as sure evidences of the final victory over death and of the life to come, in that they were manifestations of HIM, who said: I am the Resurrection and the Life![11]

The obvious inference from the passage in question, if not its express import, is: Miracula *experimenta[c] crucis* esse, *[d]quibus solis[e]* probandum erat, Homines non, pecudum instar, omnino perituros esse.[12] Now this

---

[a] *AR* (1825): Behold, (p 338 begins)
[b] *AR* (1825): 49),
[c] *AR* (1825): *experimento*
[d-e] *AR* (1825): quo solo

---

[7] The two sentences here appear in successive paragraphs of *Worthy Communicant* ch 3 § 4.1 (1674) 160. In addition to one or two stylistic changes, C writes "discursive power" for Taylor's "discourse"; and "in-evidence" (= want of clearness: cf *OED* and *BL—CC*—I 276n) for Taylor's "obscurity".

[8] These references were probably included in error, since they serve no purpose here and are made otiose by their appearance in the next parenthesis.

[9] Isa 35.4 ends ". . . behold, your God will come *with* vengeance, even God *with* a recompence; he will come and save you". C's omission of the second "with" is authorised by the AV italic, signifying that they are not in the original Hebrew.

[10] Matt 10.34: "Think not that I am come to send peace on earth: I came not to send peace, but a sword." Luke 12.49: "I am come to send fire on the earth; and what will I, if it be already kindled?"

[11] John 11.25. See also above, *Sp Aph B XVIII*, at n 47.

[12] "That miracles are the *crucial tests*, by which alone it was to be proved that Men were not, like cattle, wholly to perish"; the reading in 1825 is good idiomatic Latin, and seems to make better sense: "That miracles serve as the crucial test by which . . .". Perhaps in revising for *AR* (1831) C, or HNC, detected a misprint, as he thought, in the idiomatic dative singular, *experimento*, and changed it to nominative plural, altering the relative pronoun accordingly. C's ms for the first four sentences of this paragraph is transcribed below in App B(z), where the differing Latin includes "quiddam *experimentum crucis*".

doctrine I hold to be altogether alien from the *spirit*, and without authority in the *letter*, of Scripture. I can recall nothing in the history of human Belief, that should induce me, I find nothing in my own moral Being that enables me, to understand it. I can, however, perfectly well understand, the readiness of *those* Divines in hoc PALEII Dictum oro pleno, jurare, qui nihil aliud in toto Evangelio invenire posse profitentur.[13] The most unqualified admiration of this superlative passage I find perfectly in character for those, who while Socinianism and Ultra-Socinianism[14] are spreading like the roots of an Elm, on and just below the surface, through the whole land, and *here and there* at least have even dipt under the garden-fence of the Church, and blunt the edge of the Laborer's[a] spade in the gayest *parterres* of our Baal-hamon, (*Sol. Song,* viii. 11.)[b][15]—who, while Heresies, to which the Framers and [c]Compilers of our Liturgy, Homilies and Articles would have refused the very name of Christianity, meet their eyes on the List of Religious Denominations for every City and large Town throughout the kingdom—can yet congratulate themselves with Dr. Paley (in his Evidences) that *the Rent has not reached the foundation*[16]—*i.e.*[d] that the Corruption of Man's Will; that the responsibility of man in any sense in which it is not equally predicable of Dogs and Horses; that the Divinity of our Lord, and even his pre-existence; that Sin, and Redemption through the merits of Christ; and Grace; and the especial aids of the Spirit; and the efficacy of Prayer![e] and the subsistency of the Holy Ghost; may all be extruded without breach or rent in the essentials[f] of Christian Faith!—that a Man may deny and renounce them all, and remain a *fundamental* Christian, notwithstanding! But there are many that cannot keep up with Latitudi-

[a] *AR* (1825): Labourer's

[b] *AR* (1825): 11)

[c] *AR* (1825): p 339

[d] *AR* (1825): i. e.

[e] *AR* (1825): Prayer;

[f] *AR* (1825): Essentials

[13] ". . . to swear heartily to the truth of the PALEYAN Maxim, who profess that they can find nothing else in the entire Gospel''.

[14] C's point here is elaborated more clearly in a note of May 1825: *CN* iv 5213.

[15] Song of Sol 8.11: "Solomon had a vineyard at Baal-hamon; he let out the vineyard unto keepers; every one for the fruit thereof was to bring a thousand pieces of silver."

[16] In his *A View of the Evidences of Christianity* pt 3 ch 7 (3 vols 1794) Paley argued that the essence of Christianity lies in the facts of Christ's life, the steadfastness of his disciples, and their witness as to his resurrection. "Other articles of the Christian faith[, although of infinite importance when placed beside any other topic of human inquiry,] are only the adjuncts and circumstances of this'': iii 241. The passage in parentheses was added in later editions. Paley's statement that the rent has not reached the foundation appears on iii 226.

narians of such a stride: and I trust*[a]* that the majority of serious Believers are in this predicament. Now for all these it would seem more in character to be of Bishop Taylor's opinion, that the Belief in question is *presupposed* in a convert to the Truth in Christ—but at all events not to circulate in the great whispering gallery of the religious*[b]* Public suspicions and hard thoughts of those who, like myself, *are* of this opinion! who do not dare decry the religious instincts of Humanity as a baseless dream;[17] who hold, that to excavate the ground under the faith of all mankind, is a very questionable method of building up our faith, as Christians; who fear, that *[c]*instead of adding to, they should detract from, the honor of the Incarnate Word by disparaging the light of the Word, that was in the beginning, and which lighteth *every* man;[18] and who, under these convictions, can tranquilly leave it to be disputed, in some new "Dialogues in the shades,"*[d]*[19] between the fathers of the Unitarian Church on the one side, and Maimonides, Moses Mendelsohn, and Lessing on the other,[20] whether the famous passage in Paley[21] does or does

[a] *AR* (1825): trust,
[b] *AR* (1825): religious
[c] *AR* (1825): p 340
[d] *AR* (1825): Shades,"

[17] Cf *The Tempest* IV i 151: ". . . the baseless fabric of this vision".

[18] John 1.1, 9.

[19] Lucian's *Dialogues of the Dead* were imitated by various English writers, such as George, Lord Lyttelton (1760). A title close to C's is *Dialogues in the Shades, Between General Wolfe, General Montgomery, David Hume, George Grenville, and Charles Townshend* (1777) in BM.

[20] Moses Maimonides (1135–1204); Moses Mendelssohn (1729–86); Gotthold Ephraim Lessing (1729–81). The latter two were known as broadminded religionists; Maimonides, though more narrow and dogmatic, believed that evil was no more than the absence of good, and probably influenced Spinoza. C, who at one time planned to write a life of Lessing (see e.g. *CL* I 518–19), drew on the latter's work for the 1818 *Friend* (see Index to *CC* ed) and annotated it (*CM—CC*—III). He evidently groups the three as thinkers—two Jewish, the other very sympathetic to Judaism—each of whom had at least some liberal opinions. C first spoke highly of Mendelssohn in a letter to Thelwall 17 Dec 1796: *CL* I 284; see also his 1799 reference to him and Lessing: *CN* I 377 f 13ᵛ. His annotated copies of Mendelssohn's *Morgenstunden* (Frankfurt & Leipzig 1790) and *Jerusalem* (Frankfurt & Leipzig 1791) are now in the BM: he quoted from *Jerusalem* in 1809: *CN* III 3548 and n; *Friend* (*CC*) I 96n reprints a note on toleration. See also *EOT* (*CC*) III 235, Alice D. Snyder "Coleridge's Reading of Mendelssohn's 'Morgenstunden' and 'Jerusalem' " *JEGP* XXVIII (1929) 503–17, and *CM* (*CC*) III. His interest in both Maimonides and Mendelssohn was renewed by his friendship with Hyman Hurwitz (see above, *Sp Aph B VIIIa*, n 19), whom he described in 1825 as "the English MENDELSSOHN" (*CL* V 440). In a letter to him of 4 Jan 1820 he spoke of the thirteen articles of Hurwitz's "Maimonidean" creed, ". . . not one of . . . which a Christian is not bound to believe", and pointed to the sharp disparity between the views of Maimonides and Mendelssohn on the question of the Messiah: *CL* V 2–4. For C's use of Mendelssohn in the *Logic* see *Logic* (*CC*) Index. C was thinking of him and Lessing in connexion with these issues at other times; see his letter to RS of 2 Sept 1802: "Lessing very sensibly con-

not contain the three dialectic flaws, Petitio principii, Argumentum in circulo, and Argumentum contra rem a premisso rem ipsam includente.[22]

Yes! fervently do I contend, that to satisfy the Understanding, that there is a Future State, was not the *specific* Object of the Christian Dispensation; and that neither the Belief of a Future State, nor the *Rationality* of this belief, is the *exclusive* Attribute of the Christian Religion. An *essential,* a *fundamental,* Article of *all* Religion it is, and therefore of the Christian; but otherwise than as in connexion with the salvation[a] of Mankind from the *terrors* of that State, among the essential Articles *peculiar* to the Gospel Creed (those, for instance, by which it is *contra*-distinguished from the Creed of a religious Jew) I do not place it. And before sentence is passed against me, as heterodox, on this ground, let not my Judges forget, who it [b]was that[c] assured us, that if a man did not believe in a state of retribution after death, previously and on other grounds, "neither would he believe, though a man should be raised from the dead."[23]

[d]Again, I am questioned as to my *proofs* of a future state, by men who are so far, and *only* so far, professed believers, that they admit a God, and the existence of a Law from God: I give them:[e] and the Questioners turn from me with a scoff or incredulous smile.[f] Now should others of a less scanty Creed infer the weakness of the reasons assigned by me from their failure in convincing *these* men; may I not remind them, Who it was, to whom a similar question was proposed by men of the same class? But at all events it will be enough for my own support to remember it; and to know that He held such Questioners, who could

---

[a] *AR* (1825): Salvation
[b-c] COPY A: was,
[d] *AR* (1825): p 341
[e] COPY A: my proofs: ; COPIES D, E: these proofs: ; COPY G: the proofs:
[f] *AR* (1831) misprints: simle

---

siders Grotius as the greatest Enemy that Xtianity ever had" (*CL* II 861); and cf a note of Aug 1805 (*CN* II 2640 and n); also his letter to George Fricker 4 Oct 1806: "Even as Christ did, so would I teach; that is, build the miracle on the faith, not the faith on the miracle" (*CL* II 1190); and his note of Sept 1807: "Prophetiae veritas non confirmatur miraculis [the truth of prophecy is not confirmed by miracles], is the maxim of Maimonides & all the Jews.—": *CN* II 3137. See also *CM (CC)* III 699.

[21] I.e. the one mentioned above, at n 3,

and quoted at the end of *AR* (1825).

[22] "Begging the question, Arguing in a circle, and Arguing against a thing from a premise that includes the thing itself".

[23] At the end of Jesus's story of Dives and Lazarus (Luke 16.19–31) Lazarus asks Abraham to let him return to his brothers and warn them of the retribution that awaits them, but Abraham refuses (v 31): "If they hear not Moses and the prophets, neither will they be persuaded, though one rose from the dead."

not find a sufficing proof of this great all-concerning verity in the words, ''The God of Abraham, the God of Isaac, and the God of Jacob,'' unworthy of any other answer![24] men not to be satisfied by *any* proof!—by any such proofs, at least, as are compatible with the ends and purposes of all religious conviction! by any proofs, that would not destroy the faith they were intended to confirm, and reverse the whole character and quality of its effects and influences! But if, notwithstanding all here offered in defence of my opinion, I must still be adjudged heterodox and in error,—what can I say, but malo cum Platone errare,[25] and take refuge behind the ample shield of BISHOP JEREMY TAYLOR.

APHORISM XXIII[a1]

In order to his own glory, and for the manifestation of his goodness, and that the accidents of this world [b]might not overmuch trouble those good men who suffered evil things, God was pleased to do TWO GREAT THINGS. The one was: that he sent his Son into the World to take upon him our Nature, that every man might submit to a necessity, from which God's own Son was not exempt, when it behoved even *Christ to suffer,* and so to enter into glory. The other great thing was: that God did *not only by Revelation* and the Sermons of the Prophets *to his Church;* but even to ALL MANKIND *competently* teach, and *effectively* persuade, that the Soul of Man does not die; that though things were ill here, yet to the good who usually feel most of the evils of this life, they should end in honor and advantages. And therefore Cicero had reason on his side to conclude, that there is a time and place after this life, wherein the wicked shall be punished,[c] and the virtuous rewarded; when he consi-

---

[a] *AR* (1825): TAYLOR.
[b] *AR* (1825): p 342
[c] *AR* (1825): punished

[24] In the Gospels the Sadducees, who denied the existence of a resurrection from the dead (see also above, *Sp Aph B VII* n 22), tried to trap Jesus by putting the case of a wife who had seven husbands and asking which was her husband in the resurrection. Jesus in reply proclaimed that God was the god of the living not the dead, reminding them that when he spoke to Moses out of the burning bush (Exod 3.6) he called himself ''. . . the God of Abraham, and the God of Isaac, and the God of Jacob'' (Mark 12.18–27; cf Matt 22.23–32, Luke 20.27–38). Cf Acts 3.13, 7.32; see also above, *Sp Aph B II* at n 52, and *Conc*

at n 79 below. For a less reverent reference to the formula see *TT* 7 Jul 1830 *(CC)* I 176–7 (1836, vn, dated 8 Jul, II 113–14).

[25] ''Errare . . . malo cum Platone . . . quam cum istis vera sentire'': Cicero *Tusculan Disputations* 1.17.39; tr J. E. King (LCL 1927): ''I prefer . . . to go astray with Plato . . . rather than hold true views with those [his opponents]''. C quotes only the first part.

[1] From Jeremy Taylor ''A Sermon at the Funeral of . . . Sir George Dalston'' (1657) in *The Worthy Communicant* (1674) 416–17. See App A(w), below.

dered[a] that Orpheus and Socrates, and how many others, just men and benefactors of mankind, were either slain or oppressed to death by evil men.[2] (*Compare* Heb. xi.[b] 36–39.) *"And all these received not the promise."* But when Virtue made men poor; and free speaking of brave truths made the wise to lose their liberty; when an excellent life hastened an opprobrious death, and the obeying Reason and our Conscience lost us our lives,[c] or at least all the means and conditions of enjoying them: it was but time to look about for *another* state of things, where Justice should rule,[d] and Virtue find her own portion. And therefore Men cast out every line, and turned every stone,[e] and tried every argument: [f]*and sometimes proved it well, and when they did not, yet they believed strongly; and* THEY WERE SURE OF THE THING, EVEN WHEN THEY WERE NOT SURE OF THE ARGUMENT.—(*Sermon at the Funeral of Sir George Dalston, 28th Sept.* 1657, p. 2.)[3]

COMMENT

A fact may be truly stated, and yet the Causes or Reasons assigned for it mistaken; or inadequate; or *pars pro toto,*[4] one only or few of many that might or should have been adduced. The preceding Aphorism is an instance in point. The Phenomenon[g] here brought forward by the Bishop, as the ground and occasion of men's belief of a future state— viz. the frequent, not to say ordinary, disproportion between moral worth and worldly prosperity—must, indeed, at all times and in all countries of the Civilized World have led the observant and reflecting Few, the men of meditative habits and strong feelings of natural equity, to a nicer consideration of the current Belief, whether instinctive or traditional. By forcing the Soul in upon herself, this Enigma of Saint and Sage from Job,[5] David[6] and Solomon[7] to Claudian[8] and Boetius,[9] this

[a] *AR* (1825): considered,
[b] *AR* (1825): ch. xi. v.
[c] *AR* (1825): Lives,
[d] *AR* (1825): rule
[e] *AR* (1825): stone
[f] *AR* (1825): p 343
[g] *AR* (1825): Phænomenon

[2] Taylor may be thinking of *Tusculan Disputations* 1.41.98, in which Cicero quotes Socrates (Plato *Apology* 40) on the great value of an afterlife if it affords the opportunity of conversing with Orpheus, Musaeus, Homer, Hesiod, and others.

[3] C's reference probably indicates not that he is using an original edition of the sermon (which is not known to exist separately) but simply that his extract begins on the second page.

[4] "A part for the whole".

[5] See e.g. Job 21.7–15, beginning "Wherefore do the wicked live, become old, yea, are mighty in power?" and concluding "What is the Almighty, that we

perplexing disparity of success and desert, has, I doubt not, with such men been the occasion of a steadier and more distinct consciousness of a *Something* in man different *in kind,* and which not merely distinguishes but contra-distinguishes, him from animals—at the same time that it has brought into closer view an enigma of yet harder solution— the fact, I mean, of a *Contradiction*[a] in the Human Being, of which no traces are observable elsewhere, in animated or inanimate Nature*!*[b]* A struggle of jarring impulses; a mysterious diversity between the injunctions of the mind and the elections of the will; and (last not least) the utter incommensurateness and the unsatisfying qualities of the things around us, that yet are the only objects which our senses discover or our appetites require us to pursue. Hence for the finer and more contempla-

---

* I trust, that my *Age* will exempt me from the charge of presumption, when I avow, that the forty lines here following are retained as a specimen of *accumulative* reasoning,[c] and as an *Exercise,* on which my supposed Pupil may try and practice the power of sustaining the[d] attention up the whole ascent of a "piled Argument."[10] The most magnificent Example of a Sorites[11] in our—perhaps in *any*—Language, the Reader may find in the FRIEND, vol. ii. p. 157, transcribed from J. Taylor's *Dissuasive from Popery.*[12]

[a] *AR* (1825): p 344 (*diction*)
[b] *AR* (1825): Nature!*
[c] *AR* (1825): reason, ; COPY A: reasoning,
[d] COPY A: his

---

should serve him? and what profit should we have, if we pray unto him?"

[6] See e.g. Ps 73.3–11, beginning "For I was envious at the foolish, when I saw the prosperity of the wicked" and concluding "And they say, How doth God know? and is there knowledge in the most High?"

[7] Since C regarded Ecclesiastes as the work of Solomon (cf *LS—CC*—145–6) he may have in mind Eccles 8.14: "There is a vanity which is done upon the earth; that there be just men, unto whom it happeneth according to the work of the wicked; again, there be wicked men, to whom it happeneth according to the work of the Righteous . . .". Cf also Eccles 9.2: "All things come alike to all: there is one event to the righteous, and to the wicked . . .".

[8] See Claudian *In Rufinum* 1.12–14: "Sed cum res hominum tanta caligine volvi | Adspicerem laetosque diu florere nocentes | Vexarique pios . . ."; tr M. Platnauer (LCL 1922): "But when I saw the impenetrable mist which surrounds human affairs, the wicked happy and long prosper-

ous and the good discomforted . . .".

[9] Boethius *De consolatione philosophiae* 4.1 opens with the narrator saying to Philosophy (tr S. J. Tester, LCL 1918): ". . . this is the chiefest cause of my sorrow, that since the governor of all things is so good, there can either be any evil at all, or that it pass unpunished . . . But there is another greater than this; for wickedness bearing rule and sway, virtue is not only without reward, but lieth also trodden under the wicked's feet, and is punished instead of vice."

[10] Another term for a sorites (see next note). Cf Addison's witticism, *Spectator* No 239, 4 Dec 1713 (III 396): "These Disputants convince their Adversaries with a *Sorites* commonly called a Pile of Faggots."

[11] "A series of propositions, in which the predicate of each is the subject of the next, the conclusion being formed of the first subject and the last predicate": *OED,* after Mansel. Cf *CM (CC)* II 800n.

[12] See *Friend (CC)* I 283–7.

tive spirits the ever-strengthening suspicion, that the two Phenomena[a] must some way or other stand in close connexion with each other, and that the Riddle of Fortune and Circumstance is but a form or effluence of the Riddle of Man![13] And hence again, the persuasion, that the solution of both problems is to be sought for—hence the pre-sentiment, that this solution will be found—in the *contra*-distinctive constituent[b] of Humanity, in the *Something* of Human Nature which is exclusively human;[c] And as the objects discoverable by the senses, as all the Bodies and Substances that we can touch, measure, and weigh, are either mere Totals, the unity [d]of which results from the parts, [e]and is of course[f] only apparent; or Substances, [g]the Unity of Action of which[h] is owing to the nature or arrangement of the partible bodies which they actuate or set in motion; [i](Steam[j] for instance, in a steam-engine;)[k] as on one hand the conditions and known or conceivable properties of all the objects, that [l]perish and utterly[m] *cease* to be, [n]together with[o] all[p] the properties[q] that we ourselves have in common [r]with these[s] perishable things, differ *in kind* from the acts and properties peculiar to our Humanity,[14] so that the former cannot even be conceived, cannot without a contradiction in terms be predicated, of the proper and immediate subject of the latter—for who would not smile at an ounce of Truth, or a square foot of Honor?—[t]and as, on the other hand,[u] whatever things in visible nature

[a] *AR* (1825): Phænomena

[b] *AR* (1825): Constituent

[c] *AR* (1825): human!

[d] *AR* (1825): p 345

[e–f] *AR* (1825): often *accidental*, as that of a pebble, and always

[g–h] *AR* (1825): whose Unity of Action

[i–j] *AR* (1825): Steam,

[k] *AR* (1825): steam-engine, or the (so called) imponderable fluids;—

[l–m] Added in 1831; COPY G: utterly perish and ; COPY H: , we know,

[n–o] *AR* (1825): and whose whole of existence is *then* a detached and completed Past, that links on to no Present; as ; COPIES G & H: read as in 1831

[p] COPY A: Present, together with all ; COPY C: Present; as these, together with all ; COPIES D & E: Present—as these, together with all ; COPY G: deleted

[q] *AR* (1825): properties,

[r–s] COPIES D & E: with

[t–u] *AR* (1825): and as ; COPIES A & E: and as on the other hand ; COPIES C & D: and as, on the other hand, ; COPY G: while, on the other hand, ; COPY H: while on the other hand

[13] On man as the ". . . riddle of the world" see the opening to Epistle 2 of Pope's *Essay on Man*. The underlying "contradiction" has to do with the middle state of human beings, between the divine and the beasts, which is discussed in e.g. Plotinus *Enneads* 3.2.8.9 and (in a trinitarian context) by St Augustine: *De Trinitate* 12.11, 16.

[14] Cf *Human Life* line 1: "If dead, we cease to be . . ." (*PW*—EHC—I 425); and note of 1829, N 39 f 36v (*CN* v): "The moment that the Soul affirms, I am, it asserts, I cannot cease to be"; Barth 187.

have the character of Permanence, and endure amid continual flux un-changed[a] like a Rainbow in a fast-flying[b] shower,[15] (ex. gr. Beauty, Or-der, Harmony, Finality, Law,)[c] are all akin to the *peculia*[16] of Humanity, are all *congenera*[d17] of Mind and Will, without which indeed they would not only exist in vain, as pictures[e] for Moles, but actually not *exist* at all: hence, finally, the conclusion, that the Soul of Man, as the subject of Mind and Will, must likewise possess a principle of permanence, and be destined to endure! And were these grounds lighter than they are, yet as a small weight will make a Scale descend, where there is nothing in the opposite[f] Scale, or[g] *painted* Weights, that have only an illusive relief or prominence; so in the Scale of Immortality slight Reasons are in effect weighty, and sufficient to determine the Judgment,[h] there being no counter-weight, no reasons against them, and no facts in proof of the contrary, that would not prove equally well the cessation of the eye on the removal or diffraction of the Eye-glass, and the dissolution or inca-pacity of the Musician on the fracture of his instrument or its strings.

But though I agree with Taylor so far,[18] as not to doubt that the[i] mis-allotment of worldly goods and fortunes was one principal occasion, exciting well-disposed and spiritually awakened Natures by reflections and reasonings, such as I have here supposed, to mature the presenti-ment of immortality into full consciousness, into a principle of action and a well-spring of strength and consolation; I cannot concede to this circumstance any thing like the importance and *extent* of efficacy which he in this passage attributes to it. I am persuaded, that as the belief of all mankind, of all* tribes, [j]and nations, and languages, in all ages,[k] and in

* I say, *all*: for the accounts of one or two travelling French *Philosophes,* professed

[a] *AR* (1825): unchanged,
[b] *AR* (1825): fast flying
[c] *AR* (1825): Law)
[d] *AR* (1825): *congeners*
[e] *AR* (1825): Pictures
[f] *AR* (1825): p 346
[g] COPY A: or at best but
[h] *AR* (1825): Judgement,
[i] COPY A: the (perhaps too* hastily) presumed ; COPY C: the assumed (perhaps mistakenly* presumed) [Footnote reads: *See FRIEND, Vol. III. p. 271.272.]
[j] *AR* (1825): p 347
[k] *AR* (1825): ages

[15] C may be recalling the description of such a rainbow in MS W of *The Prelude* (compiled in Jan–Mar 1804). See *Prelude* (1959) 623–4.
[16] "Particular properties".
[17] "Things of the same kind with".
[18] See textual note *i* above, COPY C, for a reference by C to *The Friend* (= *Friend—CC—*I 527–9).

all states of social union, it must be referred to far deeper grounds, common to man as man: and that its fibres are to be traced to the *tap-root* of Humanity. I have long entertained, and do not hesitate to avow, the conviction, that the argument,[a] from Universality of Belief,[21] urged by

Atheists and Partizans of Infidelity, respecting one or two African Hordes, Caffres,[b] and poor outlawed Boschmen hunted out of their humanity,[19] ought not to be regarded as exceptions. And as to Hearne's Assertion respecting the non-existence and rejection of the Belief among the Copper-Indians,[20] it is not only hazarded on very weak and insufficient grounds, but he himself, in another part of his work, unconsciously supplies data, from whence the contrary may safely be concluded. Hearne, perhaps, put down his friend Motannabbi's *Fort*-philosophy for the opinion of his tribe; and from his high appreciation of the moral character of this murderous Gymnosophist,[c] it might, I fear, be inferred, that Hearne himself was not the very person one would, of all others, have chosen for the purpose of instituting the inquiry.

[a] *AR* (1825): argument   [b] *AR* (1825): Caffres   [c] *AR* (1825): Gymnosophist

[19] It is not clear which French *philosophes* C has in mind. François Levaillant e.g. says of the "Caffrees", "They entertain a very high opinion of the Supreme Being, and of his power; believe in a future state, where the good will be rewarded and the wicked punished; but have no idea of the creation, thinking the world had no beginning, and will ever continue its present state. . . .": *Travels from the Cape of Good-Hope into the Interior Parts of Africa* . . . tr Elizabeth Helme (2 vols 1790) ii 344. C's use of "Boschmen" (= bushmen, from the Dutch) here (as also in 1826, *CN* iv 5387) predates by some thirty years the first usage recorded in *OED*.

[20] Hearne's "Assertion" is evidently found in a passage annotated by C: "Matonabbee, without one exception, was a man of as clear ideas in other matters as any that I ever saw: he was not only a perfect master of the Southern Indian language, and their belief, but could tell a better story of our Saviour's birth and life, than one half of those who call themselves Christians; yet he always declared to me, that neither he, nor any of his countrymen, had an idea of a future state": Samuel Hearne *A Journey . . . to the Northern Ocean* (1795) 344. C annotated pp 344–5: *CM* (*CC*) ii 985–7. Questioning Hearne's account there he commented: "An instance of speculative Religion occurs in the very page preceding, 343—as respectable a cosmogony, as that of the E. Indians, and the

allegory more intelligible" and concluded: "Hearne should have questioned the old men, and the women." Matonabbee was Hearne's chief Indian guide and associate during his voyage. Examples of his murderous actions include his stabbing the former husband of one of his wives; his beating one of his wives to death for making a joke against him; and his leading an unprovoked massacre of Esquimaux: ibid 103, 265, 151–9. For C's use of Hearne see *Friend* (*CC*) ii 89 and i 431; *PW* (EHC) i 269 (quoted *IS* 34); *RX* 127, 493; and *CN* i 1637 and n, ii 2297 and n. C's misspelling of Matonabbee, though corresponding to that in his annotation, suggests that he may not have had the book in front of him when writing *AR*, and it is not altogether clear where he located the data "unconsciously" supplied, from which a belief in immortality could be concluded; he may be thinking of the evidence of belief in supernatural phenomena generally that occurs in ch 9, or of the belief among some Indians that ". . . when the *Aurora Borealis* is remarkably bright . . . their deceased friends are very merry" (p 346n). Yet this refers to the Southern Indians, and could be ascribed to the Northern Indians only by way of their respect for that phenomenon—which, however, they associate rather with deer. See Beer *Wordsworth and the Human Heart* (1978) 68–9.

[21] A note in *AR* (1825) COPY A runs: "This remark was occasioned by the wild

Barrow[22] and others in proof of the *first* Article of the Creed, is neither in point of *fact*—for two very different objects may be intended, and two (or more) diverse and even contradictory conceptions may be expressed, by the same *Name*—nor in legitimacy of conclusion as strong and unexceptionable, as the argument from the same ground for the continuance of our personal being after death. The Bull-calf *buts* with smooth and unarmed Brow.[23] Throughout animated Nature, of each characteristic Organ and Faculty there exists a pre-assurance, an instinctive and practical Anticipation: and no Pre-assurance common to a whole species does in any instance prove delusive*[a]. All other prophecies of Nature have their exact fulfilment—in every other "ingrafted word" of Promise Nature is found true to her Word, and is it in her noblest Creature, that she tells her first Lie?[25]—(The Reader will, of course, understand, that I am here speaking in the assumed character of a mere Naturalist, [b]to whom no light of revelation had been vouchsafed; one, who

* See Baron Field's Letters from New South Wales.[24] The poor Natives, the lowest in the Scale of Humanity, evince no symptom of any Religion, or the belief of any Superior Power as the Maker of the World; but yet have no doubt that the Spirits of their Ancestors survive in the form of Porpoises, and mindful of their descendants with imperishable affection, drive the Whales ashore, for them to feast on.

[a] Footnote added in 1831
[b] *AR* (1825): p 348

game I have seen & still see played with Pope's Jehovah, Jove or Lord. Nay a recent Tourist in Hindostan and a warm advocate for the Baptist Missions too, gravely assures us that the prayers offered in the Temples of India & those in the Churches of Christendom are . . ." [last line cut away by the binder]. The reference to Pope is to the first stanza of *The Universal Prayer* line 4. The "Tourist" may have been one of the contributors to the *Periodical Accounts* cited in *Int Aph XVIII* nn 1, 3–5, above. *AR* (1825) COPY C has a note, "See p 232" (i.e. pp 240–1 above).

[22] See Isaac Barrow *A Brief Exposition of the Creed* (1697) 28–32.

[23] C uses this and other illustrations to develop the same point in *Op Max ms* B3 ("II") 63. See also *CN* IV 4604 f 42[v].

[24] Barron Field (1786–1846), a friend of Lamb's, was in New South Wales from 1817 to 1824. His papers on his voyage there and back were published as an appendix to *Geographical Memoirs on New South Wales* (1825), which he edited, but

C may well have known them from the *London Magazine*, where they first appeared. (In the first, describing the voyage out, Field included a critique of C's use of the albatross.) Field does not describe the religious beliefs of the natives as such, but refers to the irredeemable backwardness of the Indian natives at Bathurst, including their absence of shame at their nakedness: *London Magazine* VIII (Nov 1823) 467. The anecdote of the coastal natives' belief concerning the porpoises is from his journal of the following year: ibid X (Aug 1824) 183. For Field's copy of *AR*, see App E 202, below.

[25] James 1.21: ". . . and receive with meekness the engrafted word, which is able to save your souls". For the question concerning Nature's truthfulness see *Mor Aph XXXVI* n 13 above, quoting from *CN* III 4378, and citing *CN* III 4438, IV 4692 f 21[v]. C refers back to the beliefs on this page, giving page-reference to *AR* (1825), in an annotation on Baxter *Reliquiae Baxterianae*: *CM (CC)* I 283.

―――――with gentle heart
Had worshipp'd Nature in the Hill and Valley,
Not knowing what he loved, but loved it all!)[26]

Whether, however, the introductory part of the Bishop's argument is to be received with more or less qualification, the *Fact* itself, as stated in the concluding sentence of the Aphorism, remains unaffected, and is beyond exception true.

If other argument and yet higher authority were required, I might refer to St. Paul's Epistle to the Romans, and to the Epistle to the Hebrews, which whether written by Paul or, as Luther conjectured, by Apollos,[27] is out of all doubt the work of an Apostolic Man filled with the Holy Spirit, and composed while the Temple and the Glories of the Temple Worship were yet in existence. Several of the Jewish and still Judaizing Converts had begun to vacillate in their faith, and to "stumble at the stumbling-stone"[28] of the contrast between the pomp and splendor of the Old Law and the simplicity and humility of the Christian Church. To break this sensual charm, to unfascinate these bedazzled brethren, the Writer to the Hebrews institutes a comparison between the two religions, and demonstrates the superior spiritual grandeur, the greater intrinsic worth and dignity of the Religion of Christ. On the other hand, at Rome where the Jews formed a numerous, powerful, and privileged class (many of *[a]*them, too, by their proselyting zeal and frequent disputations with the Priests and Philosophers trained and exercised Polemics) the recently-founded Christian Church was, it appears, in greater danger from the reasonings of the Jewish Doctors and even of its own Judaizing Members, respecting the *use* of the new revelation. Thus the object of the Epistle to the Hebrews was to prove the *superiority* of the Christian Religion; the object of the Epistle to the Romans to prove its *necessity*.

[a] *AR* (1825): p 349

[26] *Osorio* I 244–6 (var) (cf *Remorse* I ii 243–5): *PW* (EHC) II 529, 830–1. Quoted again (var): *Conc* at n 79.

[27] Preaching in 1537 on 1 Cor 3.4ff, Luther said, "This Apollos is a man of high intelligence. The Epistle to the Hebrews is certainly by him." He repeated the assertion in his commentary on Gen 48.20 in 1545, the last year of his life. See P. E. Hughes *A Commentary on the Epistle to the Hebrews* (Grand Rapids, Mich 1977) 23. C refers to Apollos as probable author of the Epistle in annotations on the Bible, *CM (CC)* I 466, on Fleury, ibid II 706, and on Kant *Die Religion innerhalb der Grenzen der blossen Vernunft* (Königsberg 1794) 210–11, printed by H. Nidecker *Revue de littérature comparée* VII (1927) 144: *CM (CC)* III. His source of information was no doubt J. G. Eichhorn *Einleitung in das Neue Testament* (3 vols Leipzig 1804–14) III 477. See *CM (CC)* I 467 and n. The epistle had also been attributed to Barnabas, as C mentioned in 1826: *CN* IV 5352–3 and n.

[28] "Israel . . . hath not attained to the law of righteousness. Wherefore? Because they sought it not by faith, but as it were by the works of the law. For they stumbled at that stumbling-stone . . .": Rom 9.31–2. "Unfascinate" below is *OED*'s sole example.

Now there was one argument extremely well calculated to stagger a faith newly transplanted and still loose at its roots, and which, if allowed, seemed to preclude the *possibility* of the Christian Religion, as an especial and immediate revelation from God—on the high grounds, at least, on which the Apostle of the Gentiles placed it, and with the exclusive rights and *superseding* character, which *he* claimed for it. You admit (said they) the divine origin and authority of the Law given to Moses, proclaimed with thunders and lightnings and the Voice of the Most High heard by all the people from Mount Sinai, and introduced, enforced, and perpetuated by a series of the most stupendous miracles! Our Religion then was given by God: and can God give a perishable, imperfect religion? If not perishable, how can it have a successor? If perfect, how can it need to be superseded? The entire argument is indeed comprised in the latter attribute of our Law. We know, from an authority which you yourselves acknowledge[a] for divine, that our Religion is perfect. "He is the [b]Rock, and his *Work* is perfect." (*Deuter.* xxxii. 4.)[29] If then the Religion revealed by God himself to our Forefathers is *perfect*, what need have we of another?—This objection, both from its importance and from its (for the persons at least, to whom it was addressed) extreme plausibility, [c]required an answer[d] in both epistles. And accordingly, the answer is included in the one (Hebrews) and it is the especial purpose and main subject of the other. And how does the Apostle answer it? Suppose—and the case is not impossible*—a man of sense, who had

* The case here supposed actually occurred in my own experience in the person of a Spanish Refugee,[30] of English Parents, but from his tenth year resident in Spain, and bred

[a] *AR* (1825): acknowlege
[b] *AR* (1825): p 350
[c-d] *AR* (1825): behoved to be answered

[29] "He is the Rock, his work is perfect . . .": Deut 32.4.
[30] This probably refers to Joseph Blanco White (1775–1841), who, though not yet known to C when he produced *AR* (1825), was a friend of RS, but if so C's biographical information, which presumably derives from RS, is not entirely accurate: White, the grandson of an Irish Roman Catholic, was born in Seville. He was christened José María Blanco y Crespo and ordained priest in 1800, but was beset by many doubts and scruples. In 1810, when the French were advancing on Seville, he fled to England and abandoned the priesthood. After four years he signed the Thirty-nine Articles of the Church of England and became a friend of RS. After procuring a copy of *AR*, White secured an introduction to C and visited him at Highgate on 14 Jul 1825: *CL* v 476–7, 481, etc. The two men remained friends for several years, and C annotated some of his books: see *CM (CC)* I 500–25. A year after C's death White left the Anglican Church and died a Unitarian in Liverpool, where his copy of *AR*, with a few annotations by him, is preserved in the University Library (See App E, item 201). For biographical notices see *CM (CC)* I 500, *DNB*, J. H. Thom *The Life of the Rev. Joseph Blanco White* (3 vols 1845), and Martin Murphy *Blanco White: the Self-banished Spaniard* (New Haven, Conn 1989).

studied the evidences of Priestley and Paley with Warburton's Divine Legation,[31] but who should be a perfect stranger to the Writings of St. Paul: and that I put *this* question*ᵃ* to him:—What*ᵇ* do *you* think, will St. Paul's answer be? Nothing, he would reply, can be more obvious. It is in vain, the Apostle will urge, that you bring your notions of probability and*ᶜ* inferences from the arbitrary interpretation of a word in an absolute rather than a relative sense, to invalidate a known *fact*. It is a *fact*, that your Religion is (in *your* sense of the word) *not* perfect: for it is deficient in one of the two essential Constituents of all true Religion, the Belief of a Future State on solid and sufficient grounds. Had the doctrine indeed been revealed, the stupendous Miracles, which you most truly affirm to have accompanied and attested the first promulgation of your Religion, would have supplied the requisite proof. But the doctrine was not revealed; and your belief of a future state rests on no solid grounds. You believe it (as far as you believe it, and as many of you as profess this belief) without revelation, and without the only proper and sufficient evidence of its truth. Your Religion, therefore, though of divine Origin is, (if taken in disjunction from the new revelation, which I am commissioned to proclaim) but a Religio *dimidiata*;[32] and the main pur-

---

in a family of wealthy,*ᵈ* but ignorant and bigotted,*ᵉ* Catholics. In mature manhood he returned to England, disgusted with the conduct of the Priests and Monks, which had indeed for some years produced on his mind its so common effect among the better-informed Natives of the South of Europe—a tendency to Deism. The results, however, of the infidel system in France, with his opportunities of observing the effects of irreligion on the French officers in Spain, on the one hand; and the undeniable moral and intellectual superiority of Protestant Britain on the other; had not been lost on him: and here he began to think for himself and resolved to *study* the subject. He had gone through Bishop Warburton's Divine Legation, and Paley's Evidences; but had never read the New Testament consecutively, and the Epistles not at all.

ᵃ AR (1825): p 351 (tion)   ᵇ AR (1825): What,
ᶜ COPY A: , or your   ᵈ AR (1825): wealthy   ᵉ AR (1825): bigotted

[31] Priestley *Discourses on the Evidence of Revealed Religion* (1794) and *Discourses Relating to the Evidences of Revealed Religion* (Philadelphia 1796, 1797): *Works* ed J. T. Rutt (1820) xv, xvi; Paley *A View of the Evidences of Christianity* (1794); and Warburton *The Divine Legation of Moses* (1738–41; completed 1765). Cf below, *Conc* nn 83–7. For Priestley see also ibid nn 70 and 82 and for Warburton above, *Mor Aph VI* n 24.

[32] "*Divided into two halves*". C had similar recourse to Latin with the phrase "homo dimidiatus" when discussing love and marriage in a letter of 1819 (*CL* iv 914); cf *CN* iv 4730 ff 9ᵛ–10 (Oct 1820). See also *CN* iv 5348 f 37ᵛ (Apr 1826) on ideal marriage: "Dimidia in totum concurrunt [the halves run together into a whole], like two opposite Mirrors . . ."; also *CN* iv 5377 f 47. Cf also Horace *Odes* 1.3.8: "animae dimidium meae" ("Half of my soul").

pose, the proper character, and the paramount object*ᵃ* of Christ's Mission and Miracles, is to supply the missing Half by a clear discovery of a future state; and (since *"he alone discovers who proves"*)³³ by proving the truth of the doctrine, now for the first time declared with the requisite authority, by the requisite, appropriate, and alone satisfactory *evidences.ᵇ*

*ᶜ*But *is* this the Apostle's answer to the Jewish Oppugners, and the Judaizing false brethren, of the Church of Christ? It is *not* the Answer, it does not resemble the Answer returned by the Apostle. It is neither parallel nor corradial³⁴ with the line of Argument in either of the two Epistles, or with any one line; but it is a *chord* that traverses them all, and only touches where it cuts across. In the Epistle*ᵈ* to the Hebrews the directly*ᵉ* contrary position is repeatedly *asserted:* and in the Epistle*ᶠ* to the Romans it is every where *supposed.* The death to which the Law sentenced all Sinners (and which even the Gentiles without the *revealed* Law had announced to them by their consciences, "the judgment*ᵍ* of God having been made known even to them")³⁵ must be the same death, from which they were saved by the faith of the Son of God, or the Apostle's reasoning would be senseless, his antithesis a mere equivoque, a play on a word, quod *idem sonat, aliud vult.*³⁶ Christ "redeemed mankind from the curse of the Law" (*Galatiansʰ* iii. 11):³⁷ and we all know, that it was not from temporal death, or the penalties and afflictions of the present life, that Believers have been redeemed. The Law, of which the inspired Sage of Tarsus is speaking, from which no man can plead excuse; the Law miraculously delivered in thunders from Mount Sinai, which was inscribed on tables of stone for the *Jews,* and

---

ᵃ AR (1825): object,
ᵇ AR (1825): *evidences."*
ᶜ AR (1825): p 352
ᵈ AR (1825): Epist.
ᵉ AR (1825): direct
ᶠ AR (1825): Epist.
ᵍ AR (1825): judgement
ʰ AR (1825): *Galatians,*

---

³³ A quotation from the passage from Paley referred to above, *Sp Aph B XXIIIa* n 3, and reproduced at the end of *AR*.

³⁴ "Radiating to or from the same centre": *OED*, which gives this as its only example.

³⁵ Probably referring to Rom 2.14–15: "For when the Gentiles, which have not the law, do by nature the things contained in the law, these, having not the law, are a law unto themselves: Which shew the work of the law written in their hearts, their conscience also bearing witness . . .". The last phrase may be a verbal reminiscence from Prov 22.19: ". . . I have made known to thee . . . even to thee".

³⁶ "Which *sounds the same, but means something other*".

³⁷ Gal 3.13: "Christ hath redeemed us from the curse of the law . . .".

written in the hearts of *all* men (*Rom.* xi. 15.)[a38]—the Law "holy and *spiritual!*"[39] what was the great point, of which this Law, in its own name, offered no solution? the mystery, which it left behind[b] the veil,[40] or in the cloudy tabernacle of types[41] and figurative sacrifices?[42] Whether there was a Judgment[c] to come, and Souls to suffer the dread sentence? Or was it not far rather—what are the Means of escape? Where may Grace be found, and redemption? St. Paul says, the latter. The Law brings condemnation: but the conscience-sentenced Transgressor's question, What shall I do to be saved?[43] Who will intercede for

a AR (1825): 15)
b AR (1825): p 353 (hind)
c AR (1825): Judgement

[38] A slip for Rom 2.15: see above, n 35.

[39] Rom 7.12: "Wherefore the law is holy"; Rom 7.14: "For we know that the law is spiritual".

[40] Heb 6.19: "Which hope we have as an anchor of the soul . . . and which entereth into that within the veil". It is possible that C's phrase here, "behind the veil", provided, indirectly or directly, a source for Tennyson's famous "Behind the veil, behind the veil": *In Memoriam* st lvi line 28. Tennyson's editors note the biblical source, but have been able to trace the word "behind" only in Hallam's sonnet to Emily Tennyson:

> Who in my Sais-temple was a light
> Behind all veils of thought . . .

where the reference is to the veil of Isis. See *The Poems of Tennyson* ed C. B. Ricks (1969) 912. Although Tennyson ". . . never much cared" for C's prose (Hallam, Lord Tennyson *Tennyson: A Memoir*—1897—I 50), he and Hallam probably read *AR*, which was well known in the Cambridge of their time (see above, Editor's Introduction, at nn 241–6); Hallam visited C at Highgate and in 1829 wrote of him in his poem "Timbuctoo" (*Memoir* 50n). C's phrase would provide a natural link between Isis and the more obvious source of Tennyson's phrase in Hebrews. See also n 42, below.

[41] See above, *Sp Aph B XIX* n 50.

[42] After his reference to entry into "that within the veil", the author of the Epistle to the Hebrews goes on, "Whither the forerunner is for us entered, even Jesus, made an high priest for ever after the order of Melchisedec" (6.20). He goes on to describe (9.3–10, 25) how behind the second veil in the Temple lay ". . . the tabernacle which is called the Holiest of all", where the high priest would enter once a year, alone, to make a blood-sacrifice for the sins of the people. By this, however, the Holy Ghost had signified that ". . . the way into the holiest of all was not yet made manifest"; it was ". . . a figure for the time then present". Christ as the ultimate high priest then offered the sacrifice of his own blood once and for all, "By a new and living way, which he hath consecrated for us, through the veil, that is to say, his flesh" (10.20). St Paul's reference to the veil of Moses ". . . which vail is done away in Christ" (2 Cor 3.13–16) is sometimes invoked in this connexion; C's use of the phrase "cloudy tabernacle" suggests further links in his mind. The pillar of cloud that guided the children of Israel in the wilderness (Exod 13.21 etc), and which, when the Tabernacle was constructed, covered it, filling it with the glory of the Lord (Exod 40.34–8), was viewed figuratively by St Paul: ". . . all our fathers were under the cloud" (1 Cor 10.1). There may also be a looser link with the transfiguration, when, after Peter proposed that three tabernacles should be made for Moses, Elias, and Jesus, ". . . there was a cloud that overshadowed them: and a voice came out of the cloud, saying, This is my beloved Son: hear him": Mark 9.5–7; cf Matt 17.4–5, Luke 9.33–5.

[43] Acts 16.30: ". . . what must I do to be saved?"

me?[44] she dismisses as beyond the jurisdiction of her Court, and takes no cognizance thereof, save in prophetic murmurs or mute out-shadowings[45] of mystic ordinances and sacrificial types. Not, therefore, *that* there is a Life to come, and a future state; but *what* each individual Soul may hope for itself therein; and on what grounds; and that this state has been rendered an object of aspiration and fervent desire, and a source of thanksgiving and exceeding great joy; and by whom, and through whom, and for whom, and by what means and under what con-ditions—*these* are the *peculiar* and *distinguishing* fundamentals of the Christian Faith![46] These are the revealed Lights and obtained Privileges of the Christian Dispensation! Not alone the knowledge[a] of the Boon, but the precious inestimable Boon itself, is the "Grace and Truth that came by Jesus Christ!"[47] I believe Moses, I believe Paul; but I believe *in* Christ.[48]

[b]APHORISM [XXIV][c1]

ON BAPTISM

"In those days came John the *Baptist,[d] preaching.*"—It will suffice for our present purpose, if by these* words we direct the attention to the

* By certain biblical Philologists of the Teutonic School[2] (Men distinguished by Learn-

[a] AR (1825): knowlege
[b] AR (1825): p 354
[c] AR (1825): LEIGHTON.
[d] AR (1825): Baptist

[44] Isa 53.12 (of the suffering servant): ". . . he bare the sin of many, and made intercession for the transgressors"; Rom 8.34: "It is Christ that died . . . who also maketh intercession for us." Cf also Heb 7.25.

[45] A formation from "shadow": see above, *Sp Aph B XIX* n 50. "Shadow out" is a common form, but this is *OED*'s only recorded example of "out-shadow".

[46] For an extended discussion see Barth 187ff.

[47] "For the law was given by Moses, but grace and truth came by Jesus Christ": John 1.17. Cf above, *Int Aph XXIII* n 3, *Sp Aph B VII* at n 12 and *XV* at n 10.

[48] Implicitly, but not quite explicitly, a NT distinction: cf John 5.46: ". . . had ye believed Moses, ye would have believed me", and 14.1: ". . . ye believe in God, believe also in me"; also St Paul's question

in 1 Cor 1.13: "Is Christ divided? Was Paul crucified for you? or were ye baptized in the name of Paul?"

[1] C here returns to Leighton COPY C III 20 for his final aphorism, this being the only occasion when he draws on vol III. The two paragraphs are taken from the third of Leighton's "Lectures on the first nine chapters of St Matthew's Gospel". The first sentence corresponds to Matt 3.1, cited by Leighton on p 18; for the first sentence, up to "BAPTISM", Leighton has "I will not here speak of the nature of Baptism . . .". In the last sentence but one C reads "see" for Leighton's "use"; apart from this the changes are only stylistic. For the original text see *CM (CC)* III. From the 5th ed onwards this aphorism, unnumbered till then, was taken into sequence with the others to become "Aphorism XXIV" of *AR*.

[2] C refers primarily to J. G. Eichhorn,

origin,[a] or at least first Scriptural Record, of BAPTISM, and to the combinement of PREACHING therewith; their aspect each to the other, and their concurrence to one excellent end; the Word unfolding the Sacrament, and the Sacrament sealing the Word; the Word as a Light, informing and clearing the sense of the Seal, and this again, as a Seal, confirming and ratifying the truth of the Word:[b] as you see some significant Seals, or engraven Signets, have a word about them expressing their Sense.

But truly the Word is a Light[4] and the Sacraments have in them of the same Light illuminating them. This (*sacrament*) of Baptism, the An-

---

ing, but still more characteristically by hardihood in conjecture and who suppose the Gospels to have undergone several successive *revisions and enlargements* by, or under the authority of, the Sacred Historians) these words are contended to have been, in the first delivery, the common commencement of all the Gospels κατὰ σάρκα[c] (i.e. *according to the Flesh,*) in distinction from St. John's, or the Gospel κατὰ πνεῦμα[d] (i.e. *according to the Spirit*).[e3]

[a] *AR* (1825): Origin,   [b] *AR* (1825): word:
[c] *AR* (1825): no accents in Greek; *AR* (1831): κατὰ σαρκὰ
[d] *AR* (1825): no accents in Greek   [e] *AR* (1825): *Spirit*). EDITOR.

---

who in 1794 published his theory that the Gospels of Mark, Matthew, and Luke derived their common material from a single, lost "Urevangelium", which had begun with an account of John the Baptist's preaching: *Allgemeine Bibliothek der biblischen Litteratur* v 763–996. In *Einleitung in das Neue Testament* he argued both from the absence of mention in the early Fathers and from internal evidence that the accounts in Matt 1 and 2 and Luke 1.5–2.52 could not be as early as the apostolic age, and that these Gospels must, like Mark's, have begun with John the Baptist. See especially I 142–3, 422–34, 630. At I 426 he gave a list of earlier discussions of the first chapters of Matthew, mostly by Germans. In an annotation on I 430–1—*CM (CC)* II 446—C argued against Eichhorn's views but acknowledged "great, very great Difficulties", which he discussed also in Dec 1823 and on several subsequent occasions: see *CN* IV 5075 and e.g. 5228, 5240. For Eichhorn's view of St John's Gospel see *Conc* n 12, below. C had known his work as early as 1799: *CM (CC)* II 369.

[3] For the characterisation of St John's Gospel see also above, *Sp Aph B XIX* n 26. The form "according to" alludes, in both

Greek and English, to the titles of the Gospels ("The Gospel According to St Matthew", etc); C elsewhere sought to distinguish further the first three Gospels as having been written "according to" their authors rather than by them: *CN* IV 5069 f 23, cf *CM (CC)* II 436. The term "according to the flesh" is here descriptive, as in Rom 1.3, 4: ". . . Jesus Christ our Lord, which was made of the seed of David according to the flesh; And declared to be the son of God with power, according to the spirit of holiness . . ."; the overtones of St Paul's use of κατὰ σάρκα elsewhere (see e.g. Rom 8 as cited in *Sp Aph B Xa* n 31, above) are absent. C believed nevertheless that the Gospels needed to be reconciled "*doctrinally*" with the Pauline Letters, *CM (CC)* I 512, and indeed, so far as the resurrection of the body was concerned, was "almost tempted to conjecture . . . that the Church preferred the sensuous and therefore more popular belief of the Evangelists κατα σαρκα to the ⟨more⟩ intelligible faith of the spiritual Sage of 'the other Athens' ", or Tarsus: *CM (CC)* II 918–19.

[4] Cf Ps 119.105: "Thy word is a lamp unto my feet, and a light unto my path."

cients do particularly express by *Light*. Yet are they both nothing *ᵃbut darkness to us, till the same light shine in our Hearts; for till then we are nothing but darkness ourselves, and therefore the most luminous things are so to us. Noonday is as midnight to a blind man.⁵ And we see these ordinances, the word and the sacrament, without profit or comfort for the most part, because we have not of that Divine Light within us. And we have it not, because we ask it not.⁶

A born and bred Baptist, and paternally descended from the old ortho-dox Non-conformists, and both in his own and in his father's right a very dear Friend of mine,⁷ had married a member of the National Church. In consequence of an anxious wish expressed by his Lady for the baptism of their first child, he solicited me to put him in possession of my Views respecting this controversy: though principally as to the degree of importance which I attached to it. For as to the point itself, his natural pre-possession in favor of the Persuasion*ᵇ* in which he was born, had been confirmed by a conscientious examination of the Arguments on both sides. As the Comment on the preceding Aphorism, or rather as an Expansion of its *ᶜsubject matter,ᵈ* I will give the substance of the con-versation: and amply shall I have been remunerated, should it be read with the interest and satisfaction with which it was heard. More partic-ularly, should any of my Readers find themselves under the same or similar Circumstances.

*ᵉ*COMMENT,*ᶠ*

*Or Aid to Reflection in the forming of a sound Judgementᵍ respecting the purport and purpose of the Baptismal Rite, and a just appreciation of its value and importance.*⁸

Our discussion is rendered shorter and more easy by our perfect agree-ment in certain preliminary points. We both disclaim alike every attempt

---

ᵃ *AR* (1825): p 355   *ᵇ* *AR* (1825): Persuasion,   *ᶜ⁻ᵈ* *AR* (1825): subject-matter,
ᵉ *AR* (1825): p 356   *ᶠ* *AR* (1825): COMMENT.   *ᵍ* *AR* (1825): *Judgement*

⁵ Deut 28.29: ". . . thou shalt grope at noonday, as the blind gropeth in dark-ness".

⁶ James 4.2: ". . . ye fight and war, yet ye have not, because ye ask not".

⁷ The friend was Launcelot Wade, son of C's old Bristol friend Josiah Wade, to whom a letter of 8 Jan 1819 on marriage was apparently addressed (*CL* IV 903–9, V 182n) and who came to Highgate to consult Gillman about his health in Nov 1820: *CN*

IV 4740. After the discussion on infant bap-tism described here C set down in a note-book some points of agreement between them, which provided a starting-point for the ensuing Comment, as noted below. See *CN* IV 4750 and III 4462 (an entry which seems therefore—along with a few others, including two extracts from Baxter—to be dated a little too early there).

⁸ C referred back to this "disquisition on Baptism" in a note of May 1825: *CN* IV

to explain any thing *into* Scripture, and every attempt to explain any thing *out of* Scripture. Or if we regard either with a livelier aversion, it is the latter,[a] as being the more fashionable and prevalent. I mean the practice of both high and low *Grotian* Divines to *explain away* positive assertions of Scripture on the pretext, that the *literal sense* is not agreeable to Reason, that is, THEIR *particular* Reason.[9] And inasmuch as,[b] (in the only right sense of the word) there is no such thing as a *particular* Reason, they must, and in fact they *do*, mean, that the literal sense is not accordant to their *Understanding*, *i.e.* to the *Notions* which *their* Understandings have been taught and accustomed to form in *their* school of philosophy. Thus a Platonist[c] who should become a Christian, would at once, even in texts susceptible of a different interpretation, recognize, because he would expect to find, several doctrines which the disciple of the Epicurean or Mechanic School will not receive on the most positive declarations of the Divine Word. And as we agree in the opinion, that the *Minimi-fidian*[10] Party (p. 214) err grievously [d]in the latter point, so I must concede to you, that too many Paedo-baptists (*Assertors of Infant Baptism*) have erred, though less grossly, in the former.[11] I have, I confess, no eye for these smoke-like Wreaths[12] of Inference, this ever widening spiral *Ergo*[13] from the narrow aperture of perhaps a single Text: or rather an interpretation forced into it by construing an idiomatic

[a] *AR* (1825): latter
[b] *AR* (1825): as
[c] *AR* (1825): Platonist,
[d] *AR* (1825): p 357

5215 f 24 (see also below, n 95), and in a letter of Mar 1826 to Lady Beaumont reported that in Jeremy Taylor's *Holy Living* he had found a passage ". . . completely co-inciding with & so far sanctioning the view of Infant Baptism" expressed in it: ". . . viz. that the assertion of regeneration in the Baptismal Service is symbolical & prospective . . .": *CL* VI 572. He refers back to *AR* in an annotation on Blomfield *Charge . . . to the Clergy of His Diocese* (1830), *CM (CC)* I 532, and in N Q f 41 (on Thomas Fuller *The Infants Advocate* ch 8—1653—71): *CN* V, cf *C 17th C* 236. In 1828 C wrote a further note to explain his views, which HNC included in *AR* (1843), I 301–3. See below, n 94 and App D(d). An earlier view of baptism may be found in a letter to Godwin of 22 Sept 1800: *CL* I 624–5. It was a topic to which he frequently returned in later life: for an extended discussion, with further references,

see Barth 171–5.

[9] The preceding four sentences are a reworking of the first one agreed with Wade in *CN* IV 4750.

[10] Cf *Sp Aph B VIIIa* n 25, above, and C's use of this adjective in a note of 21 Jul 1825 on Blanco White *Practical Evidence Against Catholicism*: *CM (CC)* I 512.

[11] The previous two sentences correspond closely with the second and third agreed with Wade in *CN* IV 4750; the next ones elaborate a point made simply at the beginning of the fourth.

[12] The evidence in the *OED* entry under "Wreath" suggests that WW may have brought into favour this term for smoke, following Milton's ". . . smoke . . . in duskie wreathes": *PL* VI 58. Cf *Tintern Abbey* line 17, etc.

[13] "Therefore" (particularly as used in logic to mark the conclusion of a syllogism).

phrase in an artless Narrative with the same absoluteness, as if it had formed part of a mathematical problem! I start back from these inverted Pyramids, where the apex is the base! If I should inform any one that I had called at a friend's house, but had found nobody at home, the Family having all gone to the play;*a* and if he*b* on the strength of this information, should take occasion to asperse my friend's wife for unmotherly conduct in taking an infant, six months old, to a crowded theatre; would you allow him to press on the words, *nobody* and *all* the family, in justification of the slander? Would you not tell him, that the words were to be interpreted by the nature of the subject, the purpose of the speaker, and their ordinary acceptation? And that he must,*c* or might have known, that Infants of that age would not be admitted into the Theatre? Exactly so, with regard to the words, "he and all his Household,"[14] Had Baptism of Infants at that early period of the Gospel been a known practice, or had this been previously demonstrated—then indeed the argument, that in all probability there was one or more infants or young children in so large a family, would be no otherwise objectionable than as *d*being superfluous, and a sort of anticlimax in Logic. But if the words are cited as *the* proof, it would be a clear *petitio principii*,[15] though there had been nothing else against it. But when we turn back to the Scriptures preceding the narrative, and find Repentance and Belief demanded as the terms and indispensable Conditions of Baptism—*then* the case above imagined applies in its full force. Equally vain is the pretended analogy from circumcision, which was no sacrament at all; but the means and mark of national distinction. In the first instance it was, doubtless, a privilege or mark of superior rank conferred on the Descendants of Abraham. In the patriarchal times this rite was confined (the first Governments being Theocracies) to the Priesthood, who were set apart to that office from their Birth. At a later period this Token of the *premier class* was extended to Kings. And thus, when it was re-ordained by Moses for the whole Jewish Nation,[16] it was at the same time said—Ye are *all* Priests and Kings[17]—Ye are a consecrated People.[18] In addition to this, or rather

---

a *AR* (1825): Play;
b *AR* (1825): he,
c *AR* (1825): must
d *AR* (1825): p 358

[14] Of Lydia: ". . . she was baptized, and her household": Acts 16.15; of the prison-keeper: ". . . and was baptized, he and all his, straightway": ibid v 33.

[15] See above, *Sp Aph B XXIIIa* n 23.

[16] C's point here is not clearly supported in the biblical record. According to Joshua 5.2–9, Joshua circumcised the people of Is-

rael a second time, since those who were born in the wilderness had not undergone the rite; there is no mention of a re-ordaining by Moses. C might, however, be thinking of his injunction to Israel, "Circumcise therefore the foreskin of your heart . . .": Deut 10.16 (and cf 30.6).

[17] In Exod 19.6 the Lord says to Moses:

in aid of this, Circumcision was intended to distinguish the Jews by some indelible sign: and it was, no less necessary,[a] that Jewish children should be recognizable as Jews, than Jewish Adults—not to mention the greater safety of the rite in infancy. Nor was it ever pretended that any Grace was conferred with it, or that the Rite was significant of any inward or spiritual Operation. In short, an unprejudiced and competent Reader need only peruse the first 33 Paragraphs of the 18th Section of Taylor's Liberty of [b]Prophesying; and then compare with these the remainder of the Section added by him after the Restoration: those, namely, in which he *attempts* to overthrow his own arguments.[19] I had almost said, *affects*: for such is the feebleness, and so palpable the sophistry, of his Answers, that I find it difficult to imagine, that Taylor himself could have been satisfied with them. The only plausible arguments apply with equal force to Baptist and Paedo-baptist; and would prove, if they proved any thing, that both were wrong,[c] and the Quakers only in the right.

Now, in the first place, it is obvious, that nothing conclusive can be drawn from the silence of the New Testament respecting a practice, which, *supposing* it already in use, must yet,[d] from the character of the first Converts, have been of comparatively rare occurrence; and which from the predominant, and more concerning, Objects and Functions of the Apostolic Writers (1 *Corinth.* i. 17.)[e][20] was not likely to have been mentioned otherwise than incidentally, and very probably therefore might not have occurred to them to mention at all. But, secondly, admitting that the practice was introduced at a later period than that in which the Acts of the Apostles and the Epistles were composed: I should yet be fully satisfied, that the Church exercised herein a sound* discre-

---

* That every the least *permissible* form and ordinance, which at different times it might be expedient for the Church to enact, are pre-enacted in the New Testament; and that

---

[a] *AR* (1825): necessary
[b] *AR* (1825): p 359
[c] *AR* (1825): wrong
[d] *AR* (1825): yet
[e] *AR* (1825): 17)

". . . ye shall be unto me a kingdom of priests, and an holy nation". Cf Rev 1.6: "And hath made us kings and priests unto God and his Father . . .". Cf 5.10.

[18] "Then Hezekiah answered and said, Now ye have consecrated yourselves unto the Lord . . .": 2 Chron 29.31.

[19] See Taylor *Liberty of Prophesying* sect xviii §§ 1–33 in Σύμβολον Θεολογικόν

(1674) 1040–50, and the Answers, pp 1052–68. Taylor gives a brief account of his additions to these original arguments in his Epistle Dedicatory to the whole volume, p [iv]. In his annotation on p 1053 C writes: "All mere sophistry: I doubt whether T. himself believed it a sufficient Reply to his own Argument."

[20] "For Christ sent me not to baptize,

tion. On either supposition,[a] therefore, it is never without regret that I see a Divine of our Church attempting to erect forts on a position so evidently commanded by the strong-hold of his Antagonists. I dread the use which the Socinians may make of their example, and the Papists of their failure. Let me not, however, deceive you. (*The Reader understands, that I suppose myself conversing with a Baptist.*) I am of opinion, that the Divines on your side are chargeable with a far more grievous mistake, that of giving a carnal and *Judaizing* interpretation to the various Gospel Texts in which the terms, baptism and baptize, occur, contrary to the express and earnest admonitions of the Apostle Paul. And this I say without in the least retracting my former concession, that the Texts appealed to, as commanding or authorizing Infant Baptism, are all without exception made to bear a sense [b]neither contained nor deducible:

whatever is not to be found *there,* ought to be allowed *no where*—this has been *asserted.* But that it has been *proved;* or even rendered plausible; or that the Tenet is not to be placed among the *revulsionary*[21] Results of the scripture-slighting Will-worship of the Romish Church; it will be more sincere to say, I disbelieve, than that I doubt. It was chiefly,[c] if not exclusively,[d] in reference to the extravagances built on this tenet, that the great SELDEN ventured to declare, that the words, *Scrutamini* SCRIPTURAS,[22] had set the world in an uproar.[23]

N.B. Extremes *appear* to generate each other;[24] but if we look steadily, there will most often be found some common error, that produces both as its Positive and Negative Poles. Thus Superstitions go *by Pairs,* like the two Hungarian Sisters, always quarrelling[e] and *inveterately averse,* but yet joined at the Trunk.[25]

[a] *AR* (1825): p 360 (position)   [b] *AR* (1825): p 361   [c] *AR* (1825): chiefly
[d] *AR* (1825): exclusively   [e] *AR* (1825): quarreling

but to preach the gospel: not with wisdom of words, lest the cross of Christ should be made of none effect.''

[21] *OED* gives this as its first example of the adjective, from "revulsion", and "preenacted", above, as its only example.

[22] "*Search* the SCRIPTURES". From John 5.39 (Vulgate).

[23] See *Table Talk: Being the Discourses of John Selden Esq* "Bible" § 4 (1689) 3: "*Scrutamini Scripturas.* These two Words have undone the World, because Christ spake it to his Disciples, therefore we must all, Men, Women, and Children, read and interpret the Scripture." It is sometimes pointed out that both the Latin word and the Greek version, ἐρευνᾶτε, may be read as a present indicative: "Ye search . . .".

[24] A development from C's favourite proverb, "Extremes meet". See above, *Int Aph I* n 2.

[25] The sisters Helena and Judith were born at Szony in Hungary in 1701, with bodies joined together at the small of the back. They spent their earliest years being exhibited in fairs across England, Holland, Germany, and Italy, but at the age of nine were placed in a convent, surviving until the age of twenty-two. According to Buffon *De l'homme* (1749) and M. Duchet (Paris 1971) 403–4, their arguments arose only over the need to pass urine, which overtook each at different times, their excretory organs being, however, in common; apart from this they loved one another very tenderly. Several accounts of them were brought together in *Phil Trans RS* L pt i (1757) 311–22.

and likewise that (historically considered) there exists no sufficient *positive* evidence, that the Baptism of Infants was instituted by the Apostles in the practice of the Apostolic age.[26]*

Lastly, we both coincide[a] in the full conviction, that it is neither the outward ceremony of Baptism, under any form or circumstance, nor any other ceremony; but such a faith in Christ as tends to produce a conformity to his holy doctrines and example in heart and life,[31] and which faith is itself a declared mean and condition of our partaking of his spiritual Body,[32] and of being "cloathed upon" with his righteousness;[33] that[b] properly makes us Christians, and can alone be enjoined as an Article of

* More than this I[c] do not consider as necessary for the[d] argument. And as to Robinson's assertions in his History of Baptism,[27] that Infant Baptism did not commence till the time of Cyprian, who condemning it as a general practice, allowed it in particular cases by a dispensation of Charity; and that it did not actually become the ordinary rule of the Church, till Augustin in the fever of his anti-pelagian Dispute had introduced the Calvinistic interpretation of Original Sin, and the dire state of Infants dying unbaptized—I am so far from acceding to them, that I reject the whole statement as rash, and not only unwarranted by the Authorities he cites, but unanswerably confuted by Baxter,[28] Wall,[29] and many other learned Paedo-baptists before and since the publication of his Work. I confine myself to the assertion—not that Infant Baptism was *not*; but—that there exist no sufficient proofs that it *was*, the practice of the Apostolic Age.[30]

> [a] *AR* (1825): co-incide
> [b] COPY A: that it is this fact alone which
> [c] *AR* (1825): we
> [d] *AR* (1825): our

[26] The preceding sentence corresponds with the one spanning *CN* IV 4750 f 50–50[v].

[27] Robert Robinson *History of Baptism* (1790) 182–295—esp on Cyprian, pp 182–201, and on Augustine, pp 202–22. See also below, nn 60 and 63.

[28] See Richard Baxter *Plain Scripture Proof of Infants Church-membership and Baptism* (1651); but C may be thinking rather of *Reliquiae Baxterianae* (1696) I 141, where Baxter says, "And I found in all Antiquity, that though Infant Baptism was held lawful by the Church, yet some with *Tertullian* and *Nazienzen*, thought it most convenient to make no haste, and the rest left the time of Baptism to every ones liberty . . . So that in the Primitive Church some were Baptized in Infancy, and some at ripe Age, and some a little before their Death; and none were forced, but all left free." C annotated this passage, though making a different point: see *CM (CC)* I 245.

[29] W. Wall *A Conference between Two*

Men that had doubts about Infant-Baptism (1795) 69–80. See below, n 76.

[30] The preceding footnote corresponds to the paragraph comprising the "P.S." of *CN* IV 4750 ff 50[v]–51.

[31] ". . . to be conformed to the image of his Son . . .": Rom 8.29.

[32] See the conditions of faith realised in works, implicitly attached in 2 Pet 1.3–7 to becoming "partakers of the divine nature"; the phrase, as used by C, had occasioned a remonstrance from CL in Oct 1796: *CL* I 239, *LL* (M) I 53–4, 56. Cf also Heb 3.14: "For we are made partakers of Christ, if we hold the beginning of our confidence stedfast unto the end."; and Phil 3.21.

[33] "For in this we groan, earnestly desiring to be clothed upon with our house which is from heaven": 2 Cor 5.2, cf v 4, also 7: "For we walk by faith". "He hath clothed me with the garments of salvation, he hath covered me with the robe of righteousness": Isa 61.10. Cf above, *Int Aph XXIII* at n 11, *Sp Aph B XVIII* at nn 44, 45.

Faith necessary to Salvation,[34] *a*so that the denial thereof may be denounced as "a damnable heresy."[35] In the strictest sense of essential, this alone is the essential in Christianity, that the same spirit should be growing in us which was in the fulness*b* of all perfection in Christ Jesus.[36] Whatever else is named essential is such because, and only as far as, it is instrumental to this,*c* or evidently implied herein. If the Baptists hold the *visible Rite* *d*to be*e* indispensable to Salvation, with what terror must they not regard every disease that befel their children between Youth and Infancy! But if they are saved by the faith of the Parent, then the outward rite is not essential to Salvation, otherwise than as the omission should arise from a spirit of disobedience: and in this case it is the cause, not the effect, the wilful and unbaptized Heart, not the unbaptizing hand,*f* that perils it. And surely it looks very like an *inconsistency* to admit the vicarious faith of the Parents and the therein implied promise, that the child shall be christianly bred up, and as much as in them lies prepared for the communion of saints—to admit this, as safe and sufficient in their own instance, and yet to denounce the same belief and practice as hazardous and unavailing in the Established Church—the same, I say, essentially, and only differing from their own by the presence of two or three Christian Friends as additional Securities, and by the promise being expressed![37]

But you, my filial Friend! have studied Christ under a better Teacher[38]—the Spirit of Adoption,[39] even the spirit that was in Paul, and which still speaks to *g*us out of his writings. You remember and admire the saying of an old Divine, that a ceremony duly instituted was a Chain

a *AR* (1825): p 362
b *AR* (1825): fullness
c *AR* (1825): this
d-e Added in 1831
f *AR* (1825): Hand,
g *AR* (1825): p 363

[34] Cf 1 Pet 1.7–9: ". . . Jesus Christ: Whom having not seen, ye love; in whom, though now ye see him not, yet believing, ye rejoice with joy unspeakable and full of glory: Receiving the end of your faith, even the salvation of your souls." Cf also perhaps Luke 10.42.

[35] 2 Pet 2.1: ". . . there shall be false teachers among you, who privily shall bring in damnable heresies, even denying the Lord that bought them . . .".

[36] Eph 4.13–15: "Till we all come in the unity of the faith, and of the knowledge of the Son of God, unto a perfect man, unto the measure of the stature of the fulness of Christ: That we henceforth be no more children . . . But speaking the truth in love, may grow up into him in all things, which is the head, even Christ . . .". Cf also Phil 2.5: "Let this mind be in you, which was also in Christ Jesus."

[37] This paragraph is based on a shorter one in *CN* IV 4750, ending at the top of f 51ᵛ.

[38] Eph 4.20: "But ye have not so learned Christ".

[39] "For ye have not received the spirit of bondage again to fear; but ye have received the Spirit of adoption, whereby we cry, Abba, Father": Rom 8.15.

of Gold around the Neck of Faith;[40] but if in the wish to make it co-essential and consubstantial, you draw it closer and closer, it may strangle the Faith[a] it was meant to deck and designate. You are not so unretentive a Scholar as to have forgotten the "pateris et auro" of your Virgil:[41] or if you were, you are not so inconsistent a reasoner, as to translate the Hebraism, Spirit and Fire, in one place by spiritual fire, and yet refuse to translate Water and Spirit by Spiritual Water in another place:[42] or if, as I myself think, the different position marks a different sense, yet that the former must be ejusdem generis[43] with the latter—the Water of Repentance,[44] reformation in *conduct;* and the Spirit that which purifies the inmost *principle* of action, as Fire purges the metal substantially and not cleansing the surface only![45] (See Aph. xxiii. p. 28–31.)

But in this instance, it will be said, the ceremony, the outward and visible sign, is a Scripture Ordinance. I will not reply, that the Romish Priest says the same of the anointing of[b] the sick with oil and the imposition of hands.[46] No! my answer is: that this is a very sufficient reason for the continued observance of a ceremonial Rite so derived and sanc-

---

[a] *AR* (1825): Faith,
[b] Added in 1831

[40] A source for this saying has not been found.

[41] Virgil *Georgics* 2.192; tr "[we pour offerings] from golden bowls" (literally, "from bowls and gold"). C misquoted the Virgil when commenting on a similar Hebrew idiom in a later note on the Bible: see *CM (CC)* I 471.

[42] C is thinking of John 3.5: ". . . Except a man be born of water and of the Spirit, he cannot enter into the Kingdom of God". See also his annotation of 1810 on Sedgwick *Hints . . . on the Nature and Effect of Evangelical Preaching: LR* IV 336–7, *CM (CC)* IV. "Spiritual fire" does not appear in either form in the OT. C's point does, however, provide a plausible interpretation for a text such as Mic 2.11: "If a man walking in the spirit and falsehood . . ." For his interest in Hebrew generally see also above, *Sp Aph B XIX* n 20.

[43] "Of the same kind".

[44] Cf John the Baptist's statement, "I indeed baptize you with water unto repentance . . .": Matt 3.11.

[45] The immediate reference here is to Matt 3.11–12, in which John the Baptist says, ". . . he that cometh after me . . . shall baptize you with the Holy Ghost, and with fire: Whose fan is in his hand, and he will throughly purge his floor, and gather his wheat into the garner . . .". Cf Luke 3.16. The reference to purification of metal, however, looks back to OT imagery, e.g. Isa 4.4: ". . . When the Lord . . . shall have purged the blood of Jerusalem from the midst thereof by the spirit of judgment, and by the spirit of burning"; Mal 3.3: "And he shall sit as a refiner and purifier of silver: and he shall purify the sons of Levi, and purge them as gold and silver . . .".

[46] The rite of extreme unction (see above, *Sp Aph B XIX* at n 94) finds scriptural authority in James 5.14, while the laying on of hands in certain ceremonies is supported by Acts 8.18, 1 Tim 4.14, and Heb 6.2. With C's opinion here cf Taylor *The Worthy Communicant* ch 1 § 3 (1674) 43: "Thus we find that the grace of God is given by the imposition of hands, and yet as *St. Austin* rightly affirms, God alone can give his holy spirit, and the Apostles did not give the holy Ghost to them upon whom they laid their hands, but prayed that God would give it, and he did so at the imposition of their hands."

tioned, even though its own beauty, simplicity, and natural significancy had pleaded less strongly in its behalf! But it is no reason why the Church should forget, that the perpetuation of a thing does not alter the nature of the thing, and *a*that a ceremony to be perpetuated is to be perpetuated as a *Ceremony*. It is no reason why, knowing and experiencing even in the majority of her own Members the proneness of the human mind to* Superstition, the Church might not rightfully and piously adopt the measures best calculated to check this tendency, and to correct the abuse, to which it had led in any particular Rite. But of superstitious notions respecting the baptismal ceremony, and of abuse resulting, the instances were flagrant and notorious. Such, for instance, was the frequent deferring of the baptismal rite to a late period of Life, and even to the death-bed, in the belief that the mystic water would cleanse the baptized person from all sin and (if he died immediately after the performance of the ceremony,)*b* send him pure and spotless[48] into the other world.*c*[49]

Nor is this all. The preventive remedy applied by the church is legitimated as well as additionally recommended by the following consideration. Where a ceremony answered and was intended to answer several

---

* Let me be permitted to repeat and apply the *Note* in page 192. Superstition may be defined as *Super*stantium (cujusmodi sunt Cerimoniae*d* et Signa externa quae, nisi in significando, nihili sunt et paene nihil) *Sub*stantiatio.[47]

---

a *AR* (1825): p 364
b *AR* (1825): ceremony)
c *AR* (1825): World.
d *AR* (1825): Cærimoniæ ; *AR* (1831): Cerimoniæ

[47] "The *Sub*stantiation of things that stand *over* (of which kind are Ceremonies and external Signs that, apart from their signifying, amount to nothing and are almost nothing)". (The note in *AR*—1825—gives p 194 in error for 184.) Cf above, *Sp Aph B IV* n 8.
[48] Cf Spenser *Teares of the Muses* I 387–8: "Sweete Love . . . pure and spotles". The common NT form is "without spot".
[49] The best-known example of a death-bed baptism was that of Constantine the Great (c 288–337). See also Rees *Cyclopaedia* s.v. "Baptism": "The catechumens [in primitive times] were not forward in coming to baptism: St. Ambrose was not baptized before he was elected bishop of Milan: and some of the fathers not till the time of their death. Some deferred it out of a tender conscience; and others out of too

much attachment to the world; it being the prevailing opinion of the primitive times, that baptism, whenever conferred, washed away all antecedent stains and sins." C's point is derived from discussion by Taylor of the effectiveness of late repentance in *Unum Necessarium*, towards the end of which Taylor affirms that "new-converted persons, heathens newly giving up their names to Christ and being baptized, if they die in an hour, and were baptized half an hour after they believe in Christ, are heirs of salvation": ch 5 § 5 par 64. C agrees with this: "I would rather be *durus pater infantum* [harsh father of infants], like Austin, than *durus pater aegrotantium* [harsh father of the sick]": annotation on *Polemicall Discourses* pt i 681, *LR* III 304–5, *CM (CC)* V. For the Latin see below, n 63.

purposes, which purposes at its first institution were blended in respect of *the time*, but which afterwards by change of circumstances (as when, for instance, a large and ever-increasing proportion of the members of the Church, or those who at least bore the Christian name, were of Christian Parents) were necessarily dis-united*ᵃ*—*then* either the Church has no power or authority delegated to her (which is shifting the ground of controversy)—or she must be authorized to choose and determine, to which of the several purposes the ceremony should be attached. Now one of the purposes of Baptism was—the making it *publicly manifest*, first, what Individuals were to be regarded by the *World* (*Phil*. ii. 15.)*ᵇ*⁵⁰ as belonging to the visible Community of Christians: inasmuch as by their demeanour and apparent condition,*ᶜ* the general estimation of "the City set on a hill and not to be hid" (*Matth*. v. 14.)*ᵈ* could not but be affected—the City that even "in the midst of a crooked and perverse nation" was bound not only to give no cause, but by all innocent means to prevent every occasion,⁵¹ of "Rebuke." Secondly*ᵉ* to mark *ᶠ*out, for the Church itself,*ᵍ* those that were entitled to that *especial* Dearness, that watchful and disciplinary Love and Loving-kindness, which *over and above* the affections and duties of Philanthropy and Universal Charity, Christ himself had enjoined, and with an emphasis and in a form significant of its great and especial importance. A NEW COMMANDMENT I give unto you, that ye love *one another*.⁵² By *ʰ*a Charity wide as sunshine, and comprehending the whole human race,*ⁱ* the Body of Christians was to be placed in contrast with the proverbial*ʲ* misanthropy and bigotry of the Jewish Church and People: *ᵏ*while yet they were to be distinguished and known to all men, by the peculiar love and affection displayed by them towards the members of their own community; thus exhibiting the intensity of sectarian attachment, yet by the no less notorious and ex-

---

ᵃ *AR* (1825): p 365 (united)
ᵇ *AR* (1825): 15)
ᶜ *AR* (1825): condition
ᵈ *AR* (1825): 14)
ᵉ *AR* (1825): Secondly,
ᶠ⁻ᵍ *AR* (1825): out
ʰ⁻ⁱ *AR* (1825): the former
ʲ *AR* (1825): notorious
ᵏ⁻ˡ *AR* (1825): and thus without *draw-back*, and precluding the objection so commonly made to Sectarian Benevolence, to be distinguished and known to all men by their fervid fulfilment of the latter.

⁵⁰ "That ye may be blameless and harmless, the sons of God, without rebuke, in the midst of a crooked and perverse nation, among whom ye shine as lights in the world".

⁵¹ Cf 1 John 2.10: "He that loveth his brother abideth in the light, and there is none occasion of stumbling in him."
⁵² John 13.34.

emplary practice of the duties of Universal Benevolence,[53] secured from the charge so commonly brought against it, of being narrow and exclusive.[1] How *kind*[a] these Christians[b] are to the poor and afflicted,[54] without distinction of religion or country! But how they *love*[c] *each other!*[55]

Now combine with this the consideration before urged—the duty, I mean, and necessity of checking the superstitious abuse of the baptismal rite: and I then ask, with confidence, in what way could the Chu[r]ch have exercised a sound discretion more wisely, piously, or effectively, than by affixing, from among the several ends and purposes of Baptism, the outward ceremony to the purposes here mentioned? How could the great Body of Christians be more plainly instructed as to the true nature of all outward ordinances? What can be conceived better calculated to prevent the ceremony from being regarded as other and more than a ceremony, if not the administration of the same on an *object,* (yea, a dear and precious *object*) of spiritual duties, [d]though the *conscious* subject[e] of spiritual operations and graces only by anticipation and in hope;—a subject[f] unconscious as a flower[g] of the dew falling on it,[h] or the early rain, and thus emblematic of the myriads who (as in our Indian Empire, and henceforward, I[i] trust, in Africa) are temporally and even morally benefited by the outward existence of Christianity, though as yet ignorant of its saving truth! And yet, on the other hand, what more reverential than the application of this, the common initiatory rite of the East sanctioned and appropriated by Christ—its application, I say, to the very subjects, whom he himself commanded to be *brought* to him—

----

[a] *AR* (1825): kind   [b] *AR* (1825): p 366 (tians)
[c] *AR* (1825): love   [d-e] *AR* (1825): but a *subject*
[f] *AR* (1825): subject,   [g] *AR* (1825): Flower   [h] *AR* (1825): it
[i] *AR* (1825): we

----

[53] For an early definition of benevolence as "Natural Sympathy made permanent by an acquired Conviction, that the interests of each and of all are one and the same", or, "in fewer words", "Natural Sympathy made permanent by enlightened Selfishness", see *Watchman (CC)* 132. C's developing usage of this favourite word may be traced via the Indexes to successive volumes of *CC*. See also above, *Refl Mor* at n 6.

[54] Cf Ps 82.3: "Defend the poor and fatherless: do justice to the afflicted and needy." This has its NT counterpart in Jas 1.27.

[55] This famous phrase is traced first to Tertullian: "Vide, inquiunt, ut invicem se diligant" ("See, they say, how they love one another")—*Apologeticus adversus Gentes pro christianis* ch 39: Migne *PL* I 471. Tertullian continues: "for [they] themselves [i.e. the opponents of the Christians] are animated by mutual hatred": *The Writings of Tertullian* ed A. Roberts and J. Donaldson (Edinburgh 1869) I 119. The saying has often been quoted satirically against Christians, but C is following Tertullian's original meaning, which echoes John 13.34 and 1 Pet 1.22.

the children *in arms*, respecting whom "Jesus *a*was much displeased with his disciples, who had rebuked those that brought them!'"[56] What more expressive of the true character of that originant[57] yet*b* *generic* Stain, from which the Son of God, by his mysterious incarnation and agony and death and resurrection, and by the baptism of the Spirit, came to cleanse the Children of Adam, than the exhibition of the outward element to Infants free from and incapable of *crime*, in whom the evil principle was *c*present only as *potential* being,*d* and whose outward semblance represented the Kingdom of Heaven? And can it—to a man, who would hold himself deserving of *Anathema Maranatha* (1 *Cor.* xvi. 22.)*e* if he did not *"love* the Lord Jesus'"[58]—can it be nothing to such a man, that the introduction and commendation of a new Inmate, a new spiritual Ward, to the assembled Brethren in Christ (—and this, as I have shown above, was *one* purpose of the baptismal Ceremony) does in the baptism of an Infant recall our Lord's own presentation in the temple on the eighth day after his birth?[59] Add to all these considerations the known fact of the frequent exposure and the general light regard of Infants, at the time when Infant Baptism is by the Baptists supposed to have been first *ruled* by the Catholic Church, not overlooking the humane and charitable motives, that influenced Cyprian's decision in its favor![60] And then make present to your imagination, and meditatively

---

a AR (1825): p 367
b AR (1825): and
c–d COPY A: only potentially present,
e AR (1825): 22,)

[56] "And they brought young children to him, that he should touch them: and his disciples rebuked those that brought them. But when Jesus saw it, he was much displeased . . .": Mark 10.13–14.

[57] See *Sp Aph B Xb* n 9 above.

[58] "If any man love not the Lord Jesus Christ, let him be Anathema Maranatha", 1 Cor 16.22. "Anathema" means "accursed". "Mara natha", "The Lord is come", is now commonly read separately but was formerly regarded as an intensification of the curse. *OED* cites Nathan Bailey's 1721 *Dictionary*: "Maranatha, the highest Degree of Excommunication".

[59] C conflates Christ's Presentation in the Temple with his circumcision, which, following the law of Moses, was carried out after eight days. The mother was then to ". . . continue in the blood of her purifying three and thirty days" before bringing offerings to the temple (Lev 12.1–8); according to Luke 2.21–4 this procedure was followed exactly. The feast of the Presentation is celebrated in the Christian Church on 2 Feb.

[60] Robinson *History of Baptism* 182–97 stressed the savagery of the Africans at that time and their practice of sacrificing children or selling them for that purpose; he suggested that by persuading them to dedicate their children to God at birth the bishops might have hoped to save their lives, though he admits there is no support for his theory in the letter of Cyprian, bp of Carthage, to Fidus, who was a bishop in such a country place. Fidus had consulted Cyprian as to the desirability of postponing baptism to the eighth day, following the Jewish custom. Cyprian's reply, given through a church council in A.D. 255, included the words "If baptism should be de-

contemplate the still continuing tendency, the profitable, the *beautiful* effects, of this ordinance *now* and for so many centuries back, on the great Mass of the *a*Population throughout Christendom—the softening, elevating exercise of Faith and the Conquest over the senses, while in the form of a helpless crying Babe the Presence, and the unutterable Worth and Value, of an Immortal Being made capable of everlasting bliss are solemnly proclaimed and carried home to the mind and heart of the Hearers and Beholders! Nor will you forget the probable influence on the future Education of the Child, the opportunity of instructing and impressing the friends, relatives, and parents in their best and most docile mood! These are, indeed, the *mollia tempora fandi*.[61]

It i[s] true, that by an unforeseen accident, and through the propensity of all Zealots to caricature partial truth into total falsehood—it is too true, that a Tree the very contrary in quality of that shown to Moses (*Exod.* xv. 25.)[b] was afterwards "cast into the sweet waters from this fountain," and made them like "the waters of Marah," too bitter to be drunk.[62] I allude to the Pelagian Controversy, the perversion of the Article of Original Sin by Augustine, and the frightful conclusions which this *durus pater infantum*[63] drew from the Article thus perverted.[64] It is

---

[a] *AR* (1825): p 368
[b] *AR* (1825): 25)

---

ferred it should be to adults who have committed great crimes, but if they should be admitted to repentance, how much rather should infants be baptised, who have not committed such crimes and come into the world crying for baptism". The letter is in Migne *PL* III 1014–19, these words at 1018. For a further quotation and interpretation see N. P. Williams *The Ideas of the Fall and of Original Sin* (1927) 295–6.

[61] "Favourable times of speaking"; cf "Mollissima fandi | Tempora" ("the most favourable times of speaking"): Virgil *Aeneid* 4.293.

[62] "And . . . they could not drink of the waters of Marah for they were bitter . . . . and the Lord shewed him a tree, which when he had cast into the waters, the waters were made sweet . . .": Exod 15.23, 25.

[63] "Harsh father of infants". See above, n 49. The phrase appears in Jeremy Taylor Σύμβολον Θεολογικόν 897: ". . . it having been affirmed by *S. Austin* that Infants dying unbaptized are damn'd, he is deserv-

edly called *Durus Pater Infantum* and generally forsaken." C annotated the opposite page: *CM (CC)*. In a note on Luther *Colloquia Mensalia* (1652) 315 C gives it (again in connection with Augustine) as "crudelis pater infantum" (cruel father of infants). William Wall *History of Infant Baptism* pt ii ch vi § 6 (1705) ii 139 claims for St Augustine that it was the treatise by Fulgentius *De Fide ad Petrum* that "being commonly join'd to his works, and taken for his . . . fixed on him in after Ages the title of *Durus infantum Pater*" so that it was Fulgentius who "most deserv'd that name". See next note, however.

[64] Robinson *History of Baptism* (see above, n 27) gives a summary account, with many digressions, of the Pelagian controversy. See especially pp 209–10, 217–18. He does not quote Augustine's own pronouncements on the fate of unbaptised infants, which vary from "the lightest possible damnation of all" to "why should you be surprised that [the babe] who is not allowed to enter into the kingdom of God

not, however, to the predecessors of this African, whoever they were that authorized Paedo-baptism, and at whatever period it first became general—it is not to the Church at the time being, that these consequences are justly imputable. She had done her best to preclude every superstition, by allowing in urgent cases any and every Adult, Man, and Woman, to administer the ceremonial part, [a]the outward rite, of baptism:[b] but reserving to the highest Functionary of the Church (even to the exclusion of the Co-presbyters) the most proper and spiritual purpose, viz. the declaration of Repentance and Belief, the free Choice of Christ, as his Lord, and the open profession of the Christian Title by an individual in his own name and by his own deliberate [c]act. *This*[d] office of Religion, the essentially moral and spiritual nature of which could not be mistaken, this most *solemn* office the Bishop alone was to [e]perform.

Thus[f]—as soon as the *purposes* of the ceremonial Rite were by change of circumstances divided, that is, took place at different periods of the Believer's Life—to the *outward* purposes, where the effect was to be produced on the Consciousness[f] of others, the Church continued to affix the *outward rite*; while to the substantial and spiritual purpose, where the effect was to be produced on the Individual's own mind, she gave its beseeming dignity by an ordinance not figurative, but standing in the direct cause and relation of *means* to the *end*.

In fine, there are two great Purposes to be answered, each having its own subordinate purposes, and desirable consequences. The Church answers both, the Baptists one only. If, nevertheless, you would still prefer the union of the baptismal rite with the Confirmation, and that the Presentation of Infants to the assembled Church had formed a separate in-

---

[a] *AR* (1825): p 369
[b] *AR* (1825): baptism;
[c-d] *AR* (1825): act. The admission, and public reception of the Believer into the name of the Father, the Son, and the Holy Ghost—*this*
[e-f] *AR* (1825): perform. Thus
[g] *AR* (1825): minds

---

will be with the devil in eternal fire?'': *Contra Julianum Pelagianum* 5.44; *Opus Imperfectum contra Julianum* 3.199: Migne *PL* XLIV 809, XLV 1333. C may have in mind a further point, again unmentioned by Robinson: Augustine repeatedly supported his argument against Pelagius and his party by reference to Rom 5.12 ἐφ' ᾧ πάντες ἥμαρτον, translated in the usual Latin versions (and by Jerome in the Vulgate) as ''. . . in quo omnes peccaverunt'',

which he interpreted as meaning ''in whom [i.e. Adam] all [including newborn babies] have sinned''. The Pelagians more correctly translated ἐφ' ᾧ as ''quia'' or ''propter quod'', ''because'' or ''because of which''. AV gives ''for that'', with ''in whom'' as alternative in the margin. See further Williams *Ideas of the Fall and of Original Sin* 308–9, 377–80 and Gerald Bonner *St. Augustine of Hippo* (1963) 371–4.

stitution, avowedly prospective—I answer: first, that such for a long time ^{a}and to a late period was my own Judgment.^{b65} But even then it seemed to me a point, as to which an indifference would be less inconsistent in a lover of Truth, than a zeal to separation in a professed lover of Peace. And secondly, I would revert to the History of the Reformation, and the calamitous accident of the Peasants' War: when the poor ignorant multitude, driven frantic by the intolerable oppressions of their feudal Lords, rehearsed all the outrages that were acted in our own times by the Parisian Populace headed by Danton, Marat, and Robespierre; and on the same outrageous Principles, and in assertion of the same RIGHTS OF BRUTES[66] to the subversion of all the DUTIES OF MEN.[67] In our times, most fortunately for the interests of Religion and Morality, or of their prudential Substitutes at least, the Name of Jacobin was every

^{a} *AR* (1825): p 370
^{b} *AR* (1825): Judgement.

[65] Cf Rees *Cyclopaedia* (1819) s.v. "Confirmation": "The ancients called it *chrisma* and *unction*; amongst them it was conferred immediately after baptism; and was esteemed, in some measure, a part thereof: whence the fathers call it the *accomplishment* of baptism. . . . Among the Greeks, and throughout the east, it still accompanies baptism; but the Romanists make it a distinct independent sacrament." For general references to confirmation see C's notes on Taylor *Of the Sacred Order and Offices of Episcopacy* (1642) § xxi and *A Discourse of Confirmation* (1673): Σύμβολον Θεολογικόν (1674) 184, ii 1–33: *LR* III 212–14, 381–9, *CM (CC)*. Cf also notes on Baxter *Reliquiae Baxterianae*: *CM (CC)* I 263–4, 266.

[66] *La Déclaration des droits de l'homme et du citoyen* was voted by the *assemblée constituante* on 27 Aug 1789; Mary Wollstonecraft's *A Vindication of the Rights of Men* was published in 1790, Thomas Paine's *The Rights of Man* in 1791–2, and Wollstonecraft's *A Vindication of the Rights of Woman* in 1792. In the same year Thomas Taylor the Platonist, a great animal-lover, published anonymously *A Vindication of the Rights of Brutes*, based on the Neoplatonic view of the subject. The BM Catalogue records also *The Rights of Asses*, signed A Dull Ass, N.P. (Edinburgh 1793) and *The Rights of Swine, An Address*

to the Poor*, sold by Citizen Lee (London ?1795).
[67] An oblique reference to *The Whole Duty of Man* (1659), a popular work attributed to Thomas Allestree (1619–82), which went into many editions. Cf *CN* IV 4931 f 101^v. The distinction was always important for C, but his emphasis varied. In 1795 he urged that he who would diffuse Truth "should be *personally* among the Poor, and teach them their *Duties* in order that he may render them susceptible of their *Rights*": *Lects 1795 (CC)* 43; cf *Watchman (CC)* 122n. The question was crucial to his discussion of political philosophy in 1809: see e.g. *Friend (CC)* II 78–82, 126, and 131. In his 3rd letter "To Mr. Justice Fletcher", 21 Oct 1814, he called attention to the "seditious spirit which still clamours of RIGHTS and RIGHTS, while it conceals, or tramples on, all the correlative DUTIES, the co-presence of which could alone substantiate them": *EOT (CC)* II 387. In 1832, however, he added: "But in truth and candor it should be said, that the Working Classes did not substitute Rights for Duties . . . till the higher Classes, their natural Protectors, had subordinated *Persons* to *Things* . . .": ibid 393n. See also *TT* 20 Nov and 17 Dec 1831, 8 Jun 1833 *(CC)* I 255, 260, 286 (1836 vns II 151–2, 153–4, dated 18 Dec, 232); and above, *Mor Aph VI* n 11; cf also *CM (CC)* III 960.

where associated with that of Atheist and Infidel. Or rather, Jacobinism and Infidelity were the two Heads of the Revolutionary Geryon[68]—connatural[69] misgrowths of the same Monster-trunk. In the German Convulsion, on the contrary, by a mere but most unfortunate *accident*, the same Code of *Caliban*[70] Jurisprudence, the same sensual and murderous Excesses, were connected with the name of Anabaptist. The Abolition of Magistracy, Community of Goods, the Right of Plunder, Polygamy, and whatever else was fanatical, were comprised in the word, Anabaptism![71] It is not to be imagined, that the Fathers of the Reformation could, without a miraculous influence, have taken up the question of Infant Baptism with the requisite calmness and *[a]*freedom of Spirit. It is not to be wished, that they should have entered on the discussion. Nay, I will go farther. Unless the Abolition of Infant Baptism can be shown to be involved in some fundamental article of Faith, unless the Practice could be proved fatal or imminently perilous to Salvation, the Reformers would not have been justified in exposing the yet tender and struggling cause of Protestantism to such certain and violent prejudices as this Innovation would have excited. Nothing less than the whole substance and efficacy of the Gospel Faith was the prize, which they had wrestled for and won; but won from enemies still in the field, and on the watch to re-take, at all costs, the sacred Treasure, and consign it once again to darkness and oblivion.[72] If there be a time for all things,[73] this

---

[a] *AR* (1825): p 371

[68] Geryon, in Greek mythology, was a three-headed monster.

[69] Either "congenital" or "agreeing in nature". Cf Satan's reference to "som connatural force": *PL* x 246, quoted in *Friend (CC)* i 471.

[70] "The character of Caliban, as an original and caricature of Jacobinism, so fully illustrated at Paris during the French Revolution, he described in a vigorous and lively manner, exciting repeated bursts of applause": report of C's Lect 4 of 6 Feb 1818 in *The Courier*: *Lects 1808–1819 (CC)* ii 124. Caliban had "mere understanding without moral reason" and did not have "the instincts which belong to mere animals": Lect 9 of 16 Dec 1811: ibid i 364. In his political comparison C no doubt had in mind the speech at the end of *The Tempest* ii ii, in which Caliban sings that he will no longer do menial tasks, concluding "Freedom, hey-day! hey-day,

freedom! freedom, hey-day, freedom!"

[71] Cf *Friend (CC)* ii 106 (i 180); *BL* ch 10 *(CC)* i 197–8. The refusal to admit civil rulers into their communion, or allow their members to perform the functions of magistracy, was general among Anabaptists: see J. L. Mosheim *Ecclesiastical History* tr A. Maclaine (1774) iv 154. For the rest C has in mind events of 1525 during the Peasants' War in South Germany, which became under Thomas Münzer an attempt to establish by force his ideal Christian commonwealth with absolute equality and community of goods; and from 1532 to 1535 in Münster, where Johann Bockholdt legalised polygamy and himself took four wives, one of whom he publicly beheaded with his own hand in a fit of frenzy. See *EB* (11th ed 1910–11) i 904a.

[72] Cf Pope *The Temple of Fame* line 351: "Be all your acts in dark oblivion drowned": *Poems of Alexander Pope* ed J.

was not the time for an innovation, that would and must have been followed by the triumph of the enemies of scriptural Christianity, and the alienation of the Governments, that had espoused and protected it.

Remember, I say this on the supposition of the question's not being what you do not pretend it to be, an Essential of the Faith, by which we are saved. But should it likewise be conceded, that it is a *disputable* point—and that in point of fact it is and has been disputed by Divines, whom no pious Protestant of any denomination will deny to have been faithful and eminent servants of Christ—should it, I say, be likewise conceded that the question of Infant Baptism is a point, on which two Christians, who perhaps differ on this point only, may differ without giving just ground for ᵃimpeaching the piety or competence of either— in this case I am obliged to infer, that the Person who *at any time* can regard this difference as *singly* warranting a separation from a religious Community, must think of Schism under another point of View, than I have been taught to contemplate it by St. Paul in his epistles to the Corinthians.[74]

Let me add a few words on a diversity of doctrine closely connected with this: the opinions of Doctors Mant and D'Oyly*ᵇ*[75] as opposed to those of the (so called) Evangelical Clergy. ''The Church of England (says WALL*) does not require assent and consent''*ᶜ* to either opinion

---

* Conference between Two Men that had Doubts about Infant Baptism. By W. Wall, Author of the ᵈHistory of Infant Baptism,*ᵉ* and Vicar of Shoreham in Kent.[76] A very sensible little Tract, and written in an excellent spirit: though it failed, I confess, in satisfying my mind as to the existence of any decisive proofs or documents of Infant Baptism having been an Apostolic Usage, or specially intended in any part of the New Testament: though

---

ᵃ *AR* (1825): p 372
ᵇ *AR* (1825): D'Oyley
ᶜ *AR* (1825): p 373 (sent'')
ᵈ⁻ᵉ *AR* (1825): Hist. of Inf. Bapt.

Butt (1963) 183; also ''. . . dark forgetfulness and deep oblivion'': *Richard III* III vii 129.

[73] The exact form ''There is a time for all things'' is recorded first in Shakespeare *Comedy of Errors* II ii 65. The idea behind it is proverbial, and expressed memorably in the Bible: see Eccles 3.

[74] See esp 1 Cor 1.10–31; 3.1–23; 11.17–19; 12.4–31.

[75] Richard Mant, bp of Down and Connor and Dromore, and George D'Oyly produced a Bible ''for the use of Families'' with notes revised by C's friend Middleton:

1st ed 1814, 2nd 1817. See H. K. Bonney's memoir in T. F. Middleton *Sermons and Charges* (1824) xvi. For their views on the present question see below, App I Excursus Note 19 ''Mant and D'Oyly on Baptism'', and, for a more general comment on their ''System'', *CN* IV 5281.

[76] *A Conference Between Two Men That Had Doubts About Infant Baptism* (6th ed 1795) 6. C's account of the title-page establishes that he was reading not the first (1706), but a later edition, such as this 6th ed of 1795, since Wall's qualifications were not given in the early ones.

deducible *generally* from many passages, and in perfect according with the *spirit* of the whole.

P.S. A mighty Wrestler[77] in the cause of Spiritual Religion and *Gospel* morality,[a] in whom more than in any other Contemporary I seem to see the Spirit of LUTHER revived,[78] expressed to me his doubts whether we have a right to deny that an infant is capable of a spiritual influence. To such a man I could not feel justified in returning an answer *ex tempore*, or without having first submitted my convictions to a fresh revisal. I owe him, however, a deliberate answer; and take this opportunity of discharging the debt.

The Objection supposes and assumes the very point which is denied or at least disputed—viz. that [b]Infant Baptism[c] is specially injoined in the Scriptures. *If* an express passage to this purport *had* existed in the New Testament, the other passages, which evidently imply a spiritual operation under the condition of a preceding spiritual act on the part of the person baptized, remaining as now—*then* indeed, as the only way of removing the apparent contradiction, it *might* be allowable to call on the Anti-paedobaptist to prove the negative—namely, that an Infant a week old is not a Subject capable or susceptible of spiritual agency.—And vice versâ, should it be made known to us, that Infants are not without reflection and self-consciousness—*then*, doubtless, we should be entitled to infer that they were capable of a spiritual operation, and consequently of that which is signified in the baptismal rite administered to Adults. But what does this prove for those, who (as DD. Mant and D'Oyly)[d][79] not only cannot show, but who do not themselves profess to believe, the self-consciousness of a New-born Babe; but who rest the defence of [e]Infant Baptism[f] on the *assertion*, that God was pleased to affix the performance of this rite to his offer of Salvation, as the indispensable, though arbitrary, condition of the Infant's salvability?—As Kings in former ages, when they conferred Lands in perpetuity, would sometimes, as the condition of the Tenure, exact from the Beneficiary a hawk, or some trifling ceremony, as the putting on or off of their Sandals, or whatever else royal caprice or the whim of the moment might suggest.[80] But *you*, honored IRVING, are as little disposed, as myself, to favor *such* doctrine!

> Friend pure of heart and fervent! we have learnt
> A different lore! We may not thus profane
> The Idea and Name of Him whose absolute Will
> *Is* Reason—Truth Supreme!—Essential Order![81]

[a] *AR* (1825): Morality,
[b-c] *AR* (1825): Infant-baptism
[d] *AR* (1825): D'Oyley)
[e-f] *AR* (1825): Infant-baptism

[77] I.e. Edward Irving (1792–1834). See below, App I Excursus Note 20 "Coleridge and Edward Irving".

[78] For a reference in Jan 1825 to Luther as a "mighty Wrestler" and more on him, see above, *Sp Aph B XIX* n 4.

[79] See above, n 75.

[80] Thomas Blount *Fragmenta Antiquitatis: antient tenures of Land, and jocular customs of some Mannors* (1679) includes many examples of such token payments and ceremonies, including a yearly "Mued Sparhawk" (p 10). The putting on or off of sandals suggests some other tradition, possibly Oriental. Cf also Blake *Milton* 8.11: *Complete Writings* ed G. Keynes (Oxford

1966) 488.

[81] These lines of poetry were first collected from their place here by JDC, who noted that their opening was adapted from *The Nightingale* lines 40–3:

> My Friend, and thou, our Sister! we
>   have learnt
> A different lore: we may not thus
>   profane
> Nature's sweet voices, always full of
>   love
> And joyance!

PW (JDC) 465; *PW* (EHC) II 1008 and I 265.

"in order to *lay* communion." But I will suppose the person a *Minister;* but Minister of a Church which has expressly disclaimed all pretence to infallibility, a Church which in the construction of *ᵃ*its liturgy and articles is known to have worded certain passages for the purpose of rendering them subscribable by both A and Z—*i.e.* the opposite parties as to the points in controversy.[82] I suppose this person's convictions those of Z, and that out of five passages there are three, the more natural and obvious sense of which is in his favor; and two, of which,*ᵇ* though not absolutely *precluding* a different sense, yet the more probable interpretation is in favor of A,*ᶜ i.e.* of those who do not consider the Baptism of an Infant as *prospective,* but hold it to be an *Opus Operans et in praesenti.*[83] Then I say, that if such a person regards these two sentences or single passages as obliging or warranting him to abandon the Flock entrusted to his charge, and either to join such, as are the avowed Enemies of the Church on the double ground of its particular Constitution and of its being an Establishment, or to set up a separate Church for himself—I cannot avoid the conclusion, that either his Conscience is morbidly sensitive in one speck to the exhaustion of the sensibility in a far larger portion; or that he must have discovered some mode, beyond the reach of my conjectural powers, of interpreting the scriptures enumerated in the following Excerpt from the popular Tract before cited,[84] in which the writer expresses an opinion, to which I assent with my whole heart: *viz.*

> *ᵃ AR* (1825): p 374
> *ᵇ AR* (1825): which
> *ᶜ AR* (1825): A

[82] The articles were originally designed to combat two forms of error: "Medievalism" on the one hand and Anabaptism on the other, according to E. C. S. Gibson *The Thirty Nine Articles* (2 vols 1896) I 20–6. C's rather different assertion here may be based on Gilbert Burnet's assurance: ". . . an Article being conceived in such general Words, that it can admit of different literal and grammatical Senses, even when the Senses given are plainly contrary one to another, yet both may subscribe the Article with a good Conscience, and without any Equivocation": *An Exposition of the Thirty-nine Articles of the Church of England* (5th ed 1746) 8. (For Burnet see also above, *Int Aph XIII* n 3.) Burnet's view was to be cited by J. H. Newman in Tract Ninety (1841) in *Tracts for the Times* as supporting his view that the Articles would bear a "Catholic" interpretation. The title-page, as Burnet records, includes words "For the avoiding of diversities of Opinions, and for the establishing consent touching true Religion".

[83] "A Rite Efficacious also in the present".

[84] From Wall *A Conference Between Two Men That Had Doubts About Infant-Baptism* (1795) 6–8. After ". . . separating for them" Wall has some further dialogue, following which, instead of "And in support of this tenet, I will refer you . . .", he reads "And, to show you they are in the right in thinking so, I will (because you seem not to have considered this matter so well as some others) refer you . . .". Between "Rom. xv." and "Are not these passages . . ." there is also some dialogue; other changes are purely stylistic.

"That all Christians in the world that hold the same fundamentals ought to make one church, though differing in lesser opinions; and that the sin, the mischief, and danger to the souls of men, that divide into *ᵃ*those many sects and parties among us, does (for the most of them) consist not so much in the opinions themselves, as in their dividing and separating for them. And in support of this tenet, I will refer you to some plain places of Scripture, which if you please now to peruse, I will be silent the while. See what our Saviour himself says, *John* x. 16. *John* xvi. 11.*⁸⁵* And what the primitive Christians practised, *Acts* ii. 46, and iv. 32. And what St. Paul says, 1 *Cor.ᵇ* i. 10, 11, 12, and 2, 3, 4,*⁸⁶* also the whole 12th chapter: *Eph.* ii. 18, &c. to the end. Where the Jewish and Gentile Christians are showed to be *one body, one household, one temple fitly framed together:* and yet these were of different opinions in several matters. Likewise chap. iii. 6. iv. 1–13.*ᶜ Phil.* ii. 1, 2. where he uses the most solemn adjurations to this purpose. But I would more especially recommend to you the reading of *Gal.* v. 20, 21.*ᵈ Phil.* iii. 15, 16. The 14th chapter to the *Romans,ᵉ* and part of the 15th, to ver. 7, and also *Rom.* xv. 17.*⁸⁷*

"Are not these passages plain, full, and earnest? Do you find any of the controverted points to be determined by scripture in words nigh so plain or pathetic?"*ᶠ*

Marginal Note written (in 1816) by the Authorᵍ in his own Copy of Wall's Workʰ⁸⁸

This and the two following pages are excellent. If I addressed the ministers recently seceded,*⁸⁹* I would first prove from Scripture and Reason the justness of their doctrines concerning Baptism and Conversion. 2. I would show, that even in respect *ⁱ*of the Prayer-

ᵃ AR (1825): p 375
ᵇ AR (1825): Cor.
ᶜ AR (1825): 1, to 13,
ᵈ AR (1825): 21,
ᵉ AR (1825): Romans,
ᶠ AR (1825): pathetic?
ᵍ AR (1825): *Editor*
ʰ AR (1825): *work.*
ⁱ AR (1825): p 376

⁸⁵ "John xvi. 11" is a misprint for Wall's John xvii. 11.

⁸⁶ Probably a misprint by Wall for "iii. 2, 3, 4."

⁸⁷ A misprint in later eds of Wall: the 1708 ed, p 8, reads "16. 17".

⁸⁸ The copy containing C's marginal comment had not been traced when the present volume went to press. See also *CM*

(CC) v.

⁸⁹ The secession of antipaedobaptist ministers from the Anglican Church in the seventeenth century was continuing during Wall's lifetime. See Thomas Crosby *History of the English Baptists* ch 4 (4 vols 1738–40) I 259–382 for some notable early examples.

book, Homilies, &c. of the Church of England, taken as a whole, their opponents were comparatively as ill off as themselves, if not worse. 3. That the few mistakes or inconvenient phrases of the Baptismal Service did not impose on the conscience the necessity of resigning the pastoral office. 4. That even if they did, this would by no means justify schism from Lay-membership: or else there could be no schism except from an immaculate and infallible Church. Now, as our Articles have declared that no Church is or ever was such, it would follow that there is no such sin as that of Schism—*i.e.* that St. Paul wrote falsely or idly.[90] 5. That the Escape through the Channel of Dissent is from the Frying-Pan[a] to the Fire—or to use a less worn and vulgar simile, the Escape of a Leech from a glass-jar of Water into the naked and open Air.[91] But never, never, would I in one breath allow my Church to be fallible, and in the next contend for her absolute freedom from all error—never confine inspiration and perfect truth to the Scriptures, and then scold for the perfect Truth of each and every word in the Prayer-book. Enough for me, if in my Heart of Hearts, free from all fear of man and all lust of preferment, I believe (as I do) the Church of England to be the *most* Apostolic Church; that its doctrines and ceremonies contain nothing dangerous to Righteousness or Salvation;[92] and that the imperfections in its Liturgy are spots indeed, but spots on the sun,[93] which impede neither its Light nor its Heat, so as to prevent the good seed from growing in a good soil and producing fruits of Redemption.[94]

⁎⁎⁎ The author had written and intended to insert a similar exposition on the Eucharist. But as the leading view has been given in the Comment on Redemption, its length induces him to defer it, together with the Articles[b] on Faith and the philosophy of Prayer, to a small supplementary Volume.[95]

> [a] *AR* (1825): Frying Pan
> [b] *AR* (1825): articles

[90] C has in mind the passages from St Paul cited by Wall above; e.g. 1 Cor 1.10: "Now I beseech you brethren . . . that there be no divisions among you . . ." and ibid 12.25: ". . . That there should be no schism in the body . . .".

[91] The means by which leeches respired was a subject of experimental interest in C's day. See Rees *Cyclopaedia* (1819) xx s.v. "Leech".

[92] Modelled perhaps on Art 6 of the "Articles of Religion" in *BCP*: "Holy Scripture containeth all things necessary to salvation."

[93] Spots on the sun were reported by at least three astronomers before Galileo's *Istoria . . . intorno alle macchie solari* (Rome 1613). They were thought by some to impair its perfection and incorruptibility, hence the image in *Paradise Lost* bk III 588–90. See *Poems of John Milton* ed John Carey and Alastair Fowler (1968) 597 and n. Cf also *CM (CC)* I 630 and n.

[94] From *AR* (1843) onwards, HNC omitted the following paragraph and inserted a passage from a notebook dated 8 May 1828. This is reproduced below in App D(d). See Barth 171–2 and n.

[95] In a letter to Hessey of 7 May 1825 C included these three among the six disquisitions which he proposed for publication as a separate volume: *CL* v 434. See Editor's Introduction above, at n 185. In a note at about the same time he wrote, ". . . this I have attempted in my disquisitions on Baptism & the Eucharist—viz. to retain the truth symbolized, so as to guard the Symbol from being rarified into a Metaphor . . .": *CN* IV 5215 f 24. For an account of C's views on the Eucharist see Barth 133–4, 175–8. In 1827 C received the sacrament again for the first time after more than thirty years. See below, *Conc* n 13. The disquisition on faith would perhaps have been based on the material in *Op Max ms* B2 ("III") 106–52 and B3 ("II") 1–25: cf its rewritten form, the "Essay on Faith", published in *LR* IV 425–38. See Barth 29n and Index for references to discussions of faith in C's works. For references to prayer see *CM (CC)* I 702, 713 and nn, and Barth Index again. The latter question engaged C particularly in 1827 and after: see Barth 181–5.

^aCONCLUSION

I AM not so ignorant of the temper and tendency of the age in which I live, as either to be unprepared for the *sort* of remarks which the literal interpretation of the Evangelist will call forth, or to attempt an answer to them. Visionary Ravings, Obsolete Whimsies, Transcendental Trash, &c. &c.,^b I leave to pass at the price current^c among those who are willing to receive abusive phrases as substitutes for argument. Should any Suborner of anonymous Criticism have engaged some literary Bravo or Buffoon beforehand, to vilify this work, as in former instances,[1] I would give a friendly hint to the operative Critic that he may compile an excellent article for the occasion, and with very little trouble, out of Warburton's Tract^d on Grace and the Spirit, and the Preface to the same.[2]—There is, however, one—objection, shall I say? or accusation? which will so often be heard from men, whose talents and reputed moderation must give a weight to their words, that I owe it both to my own character and to the interests of my readers, not to leave it unnoticed. The charge will probably be worded in this way:—There is nothing new

^a *AR* (1825): p 377
^b *AR* (1825): &c.
^c *AR* (1825): current,
^d *AR* (1825): Brochure

[1] In the *Examiner* of 8 Sept 1816 (reprinted in *CH* 248–53) Hazlitt published a "review" of *The Statesman's Manual*, which had so far been only advertised, commenting "We see no sort of difference between his published and his unpublished compositions. It is just as impossible to get at the one as the other": *CH* 249. This was followed by two further attacks attributed to him, one in the *Examiner* 29 Dec 1816 and one in *Ed Rev* Dec 1816: they formed part of a hostile campaign, the history of which is summarised in *CL* IV 668. The episode of the anticipatory review evidently rankled particularly: cf *BL* ch 24 *(CC)* II 241–2 and *LS (CC)* xxxviii–xxxix.

[2] Warburton *The Doctrine of Grace: or, the Office and Operations of the Holy Spirit* (2nd ed 1763) contains long attacks on enthusiasm and pretensions to inspiration, the Preface being largely devoted to the best way of ". . . answer[ing] a Fool according to his Folly". Elsewhere in the tract Wesley's account of Böhme's *Mysterium Magnum* as ". . . most sublime nonsense, inimitable bombast, fustian not to be paralleled" is quoted with approval and Böhme's "illuminated Disciple" William Law described as one ". . . who obscured a good understanding by the fumes of the rankest enthusiasm, and depraved a sound judgment, still further, by the prejudices he took up against all Sobriety in Religion . . ." (116 and n, 29–30n). For Warburton see also above, *Mor Aph VI* nn 21, 24.

in all this! (*as if novelty were any merit in questions of Revealed Religion!*) It is *Mysticism,*[3] all taken out of WILLIAM LAW, after he had lost his senses, poor Man! in brooding over the Visions of a delirious German Cobbler, Jacob Behmen.[4]

Of poor Jacob Behmen I have delivered my sentiments[a] at large in another work.[5] Those who have condescended to look into his writings must know, that his characteristic errors are;[b] first, the mistaking the accidents and peculiarities of his own over-wrought mind for realities and modes of thinking common to all minds: and secondly, the confusion of Nature, *i.e.* the active powers communicated to matter, with God, the Creator.[6] And if the same persons have done more than merely looked into the present volume, they must have seen, that to eradicate, and, if possible, to preclude[c] both the one and the other stands prominent among its avowed objects. (See p. 142–53: 177–84).

Of William Law's Works I am acquainted with the SERIOUS CALL;[7] and besides this I remember to have read a small tract, on Prayer, if I mistake not,[8] as I easily may, it being at least six-and-twenty years since

---

[a] *AR* (1825): p 378 (ments)
[b] *AR* (1825): are:
[c] *AR* (1825): preclude,

---

[3] For an extended discussion of mysticism, which also throws light on the next pages, see *C&S (CC)* 165–85; and cf Boulger 48–9.

[4] On Böhme and Law see *BL* ch 9 *(CC)* I 151 and n 5.

[5] C is probably referring to *Biographia Literaria*: see *BL* ch 9 *(CC)* I 146–7, 161. There is also, however, a longer discussion of Böhme in the then unpublished lectures on the history of philosophy: *P Lects* Lect 11 (1949) 327–31. In both these works, as in some of his marginal annotations, he is more complimentary to Böhme than here. See next note for a balanced view from him.

[6] Cf an annotation on Böhme *Works*: "Frequently does he mistake the dreams of his own over-excited Nerves, the phantoms and witcheries from the cauldron of his own seething Fancy, for parts or symbols of a universal Process; but frequently likewise does he give incontestible proofs, that he possessed in very truth 'The Vision and Faculty divine!' ": *CM (CC)* I 558. Another annotation reads: ". . . the Errors of this extraordinary Man fall under two

heads. The first . . . is the occasional substitution of the Accidents of his own peculiar acts of association (for instance, his exemplification of the language of Nature) for the laws and processes of the creaturely Spirit in universo. The second, componental and dissolved thro' the whole, which it requires a spiritual Chemistry, and the addition of a new ingredient to decombine and precipitate—the confusion of the creaturely spirit in the great moments of its renascence . . . thro' the Breath and Word of Comforter and Restorer for deific energies in Deity itself": *CM (CC)* I 601–2. See also *P Lects* Lect 11 (1949) 330–1 and *CN* IV 4793.

[7] William Law *A Serious Call to a Devout and Holy Life* (1728). Samuel Johnson reported that it was ". . . the first occasion of my thinking in earnest of religion, after I became capable of rational inquiry": Boswell *Life of Johnson* ed Hill rev Powell (Oxford 1934–50) I 68.

[8] Presumably *The Spirit of Prayer; or, The Soul Rising out of the Vanity of Time, into the Riches of Eternity* 2 pts (1749–50). See next note.

I saw it.[9] He may in this or in other tracts have quoted the same passages from the fourth Gospel as I have done.[10] But surely this affords no presumption that my conclusions are the same with his; still less, that they are drawn from the same premisses;[a] and least of all, that they were adopted from his writings.[b] Whether Law has used the phrase, assimilation by faith, I know not; but I know that I should expose myself to a just charge of an idle parade of my Reading,[c] if I recapitulated the tenth part of the Authors,[d] Ancient and Modern, Romish and Reformed, from Law to Clemens Alexandrinus and Irenaeus, in whose works the same phrase occurs in the same sense.[11] And after all, on [e]such a subject how worse than childish is the whole dispute!

[a] *AR* (1825): premises;
[b] *AR* (1825): Writings.
[c] *AR* (1825): Reading
[d] *AR* (1825): Authors
[e] *AR* (1825): p 379

[9] C's insistent and detailed self-defence here is puzzling, since hardly any public accusations of plagiarism had yet been made, and none relating to Law or other specified writers. It may reflect his response to "Noctes Ambrosianae", No XII, an article by John Wilson in *Bl Mag* XIV (Oct 1823) 500, in which "The Opium-Eater" is made to say of C, ". . . I have traced him through German literature, poetry, and philosophy; and he is, sir, not only a plagiary but, sir, a thief, a *bonâ fide* most unconscientious thief". Although he continues, "Strip him of his stolen goods, and you will find good clothes of his own below", the virulence of the negative phrasing may have set C on his guard.

His references also suggest that the pamphlets mentioned did have a strong effect upon him when first read. This is not surprising, since *The Spirit of Prayer* contains many things that would be likely to appeal to the young C, including its opening sentence, "The greatest Part of Mankind, nay of Christians, may be said to be asleep; and that particular Way of Life, which takes up each Man's Mind, Thoughts, and Affections, may very well be called his particular Dream." For further examples see below, App I Excursus Note 21 "Coleridge and William Law's *Spirit of Prayer* and *Spirit of Love*".

[10] In the *Spirit of Prayer* Law refers to (without necessarily quoting exactly) the passage from St John's Gospel concerning Christ as the vine (i 45); ". . . the Light that lighteth every Man" (i 56); "I am the Light of the World"; "I am the Way, the Truth and the Life" (ii 53); "I am the door of the sheep" (ibid). One of the characters claims to have found ". . . that Christ is always within me; that he is the inward *Light* and *Life* of my Soul, a *Bread* from Heaven, of which I may always eat, a *Water* of eternal *Life* springing up in my Soul, of which I may always drink" (ii 4). C used some of these texts in *AR*, and may generally owe more to his original reading of Law than he is willing to acknowledge here—but this would still fall far short of plagiarism.

[11] Another puzzle, since the phrase appears neither in *The Spirit of Prayer* nor in *AR*; C must be referring rather to the idea, which is found above in e.g. *Sp Aph B I*, "Comment", and which permeates *The Spirit of Prayer*: see e.g. i 45, in which Law is discussing the parable of the vine, and ii 172 (of the soul): "It is now come so near to God, has found such Union with him, that it does not so much pray as live in God."

The early Greek Fathers were inevitably concerned with the possibility of realising Plato's ideal of ὁμοίωσις τῷ Θεῷ ["becoming like/assimilation to God"] by means of the Christian faith. Cf Clement of Alexandria *Stromateis* 2.19. The doctrine is im-

Is the fourth Gospel authentic? And is the interpretation, I have given, true or false? These are the only questions which a wise man would put, or a Christian be anxious to answer. I not only believe it to be the true sense of the texts; but I assert that it is the only true, rational, and even *tolerable* sense. And this position alone I conceive myself interested in defending. I have studied with an open and fearless spirit the attempts of sundry learned Critics of the Continent, to invalidate the authenticity of this Gospel, before and since Eichhorn's Vindication.[12] The result has been a clearer assurance, and (as far as this was possible) a yet deeper conviction of the genuineness of *all* the writings, which the Church has attributed to this Apostle. That those, who have formed an opposite conclusion, should object to the use of expressions which they had ranked among the most obvious marks of spuriousness, follows as a matter of course. But that men, who with a clear and cloudless assent receive the sixth chapter of this Gospel[13] as a faithful, nay, *inspired* Record of an actual discourse, should take offence at the repetition of words which

---

plicit in e.g. John 1.9–14, quoted by C in an annotation on *BCP* (*CM—CC—*i 713), in Gal 3.26–7 and Eph 3.17–19. Irenaeus bp of Lyons (c 130–200), who expounded the manner in which God draws up the life of human beings into himself through the Incarnation, laid great stress on strict orthodoxy, Clement on the recognition that Greek philosophy was not irreconcilable with the Christian faith. The doctrine of the Logos held a paramount place in the thinking of both Fathers.

[12] Eichhorn decided on internal evidence that St John's Gospel could well have been written in the first century, summarised the early references to it, and dismissed the arguments of modern critics who attacked its authenticity: *Einleitung in das Neue Testament* ii 223–54. C remarked that although unable to deny its authenticity, Eichhorn "*would* not admit its obvious meaning" (that is, the meaning of John 1, on the Logos). See his annotation on p 253: *CM (CC)* ii 464.

[13] The sixth chapter of St John's Gospel contains the discourse on the bread of life, including Christ's description of himself as ". . . that bread which came down from heaven", at which many of his disciples commented, "This is an hard saying; who can hear it?" He then asked, "What and if ye shall see the Son of man ascend up

where he was before?"—after which, it is recorded, ". . . many of his disciples went back, and walked no more with him" (v 66). Cf C's annotation on Böhme *Works*: "These—the whole VIth of John to wit— are indeed hard sayings, alike for the disciples of the crude or dead *Letter*, and for the Doctors of abstractions & mere moral meanings. The former swallow all as it comes untasted, neither masticating nor ruminating: the latter expound the highest and for the outward Man the most intolerable Assertions of Christ . . . into the baldest Truisms or most familiar ethical Common-places . . . . Almost miraculous, however, must be the influence of Prejudice, if their way of interpreting Scripture is not rendered ludicrous even to themselves in its application to this Chapter— the manifest object of which is to reveal to us that Spiritual Things differ from Objects of Sense by their *greater reality*, by being more truly and more literally *living substances*—ex gr. that *the* Flesh & Blood of Christ, which his Redeemed must eat and drink, are far more properly Flesh and Blood, than the phænomena of the visible Body so called": *CM (CC)* i 673. C evidently intended to take his speculations on John 6 further: see his note on Böhme: ". . . the affinity of the Arterio-muscular System, and of the Flesh and Blood gener-

the Redeemer himself, in the perfect foreknowledge[a] that they would confirm the disbelieving, alienate the unsteadfast, and transcend the present capacity even of his own Elect, had chosen as the *most* appropriate; and which,[b] after the most decisive proofs, that they *were* misinterpreted by the greater number of his Hearers, and [c]not understood by any, he nevertheless repeated with stronger emphasis and *without comment,* as the *only* appropriate symbols of the great truth he was declaring, and to realize which ἐγένετο σάρξ;[d][14]*—that in their own discourses

---

* Of which our *he was made flesh,* is perhaps the best, that our language admits, but is still an inadequate translation. See the Note to p. 29 of this Volume.[15] The Church of England in this as in other doctrinal points, has preserved the golden mean between the superstitious reverence of the Romanists, and the avowed contempt of the Sectarians, for the Writings of the Fathers, and the authority and unimpeached traditions of the Church during the first three or four Centuries. And how, consistently with this honorable characteristic of our Church, a minister[e] of the same could, on the sacramentary scheme now in fashion, return even a plausible answer to Arnauld's great Work on Transubstantiation,[16] (not without reason the Boast of Catholicism,)[f] exceeds my powers of conjecture.[g]

[a] *AR* (1825): foreknowlege
[b] *AR* (1825): which
[c] *AR* (1825): p 380
[d] *AR* (1825): no breathing or accents in Greek ; *AR* (1831): ἐγένετο σάρξ;
[e] *AR* (1825): Minister
[f] *AR* (1825): Catholicism)
[g] *AR* (1825): conjecture!

---

ally to Light I trust that I shall make evident in my Commentaries on the first and sixth Chapters of the Gosp. of John. Hence in the Logos (distinctive Energy) is *Light,* and the Light became the *Life* of Man . . .'': *CM (CC)* I 624. See also *CM (CC)* II 1084–5 and *CN* IV 4909, referring also to an annotation on Leighton COPY B I 2: *CM (CC)* III. When C took the sacrament on Christmas Day 1827 (noting that it was the first time since his first year at Cambridge), he referred to "that masterful Mystery revealed in John VI, of which the Eucharist is at once Symbol and instance": N 36 ff 32ᵛ–33 (*CN* V), quoted Barth 178–9n. See also *TT* 13 May 1830 (*CC*) I 135–6 (1836 vn, dated 20 May, II 92), and cf his annotations on the Bible: *CM (CC)* I 469, and on Sedgwick *Hints on the Nature and Effect of Evangelical Preaching: LR* IV 375–7, *CM (CC)* IV.
[14] John 1.14.
[15] The "p 118" of *AR* (1831) is a misprint for "18", i.e. C's 2nd footnote to *Int Aph XXIII.* For further discussion of the

phrase see also *Sp Aph B XIX* nn 36–7 above.
[16] Antoine Arnauld *La Perpétuité de la foi de l'église catholique touchant l'Euchariste* first appeared in 1664; the edition read by C is not known. Cf his note of 1824–6: "The Reading of Arnold's Great work did not shake but rather confirm the opinion, I had deduced from the Scripture, and have since then found in Bucer's Exposition, printed in the Appendix to Strype's Life of Cranmer. But if I had known no other scheme of the Eucharist but that of Transubstantiation, and the scheme of Bishop Hoadly and the modern Sacramentaries, I could not have hesitated in preferring the former, spite of its logical unstateability": *CN* IV 5161. See also *C&S (CC)* 134 and n, *TT* 13 May 1830 (*CC*) I 136 (1836 vn, dated 20 May, II 92). Arnauld cited chiefly Chrysostom (c 347–407) and later theologians. For Bucer's "Exposition" see above, *Sp Aph XIX* at n 97.

these men should hang back from all express reference to these words, as if they were afraid or ashamed of them, though the earliest recorded ceremonies and liturgical forms of the primitive Church are absolutely inexplicable, except in connexion with this discourse, and with the *mysterious* and *spiritual*, not allegorical and merely ethical, import of the same; and though this import is solemnly and in the most unequivocal terms asserted and taught by their own Church, even in her Catechism, or compendium of doctrines necessary for all her Members; *this* I may, perhaps, *understand;* but *this* I am not able to vindicate or excuse!

There is, however, one opprobrious phrase which *ª*it may be profitable for my younger Readers that I should explain, viz. Mysticism. And for this purpose I will quote a sentence or two from a Dialogue which, had my prescribed limits permitted, I should have attached to the present Work; but which with an Essay on the Church, as instituted by Christ, and as an Establishment of the State,[17] and a series of Letters on the right and the superstitious use and estimation of the Bible,[18] will appear in a small volume by themselves, should the reception given to the present volume encourage or permit the publication.

MYSTICS AND MYSTICISM[19]

"Antinöus.—What do you call Mysticism? And do you use the word in a good or in a bad sense?"

"Nöus.[20]—In the latter only: as far, at least, as we are now concerned

ª AR (1825): p 381

[17] In preparing this text for *AR* (1831) C and HNC seem to have overlooked this reference to a work that had by then already appeared. The title-page of the 1st edition of *C&S* bears the date 1830; it was included, however, by *Bent's Literary Advertiser* in a list of new books published in 1829. See also note 96 below.

[18] I.e. the material eventually published after C's death as *Confessions of an Inquiring Spirit* (1840). An early draft, watermarked 1822, is in the BM (Add MS 34225). Either this or a later version was sent to Hessey for inclusion in *AR*, but omitted on account of its length, whereupon it lay in a desk until 1826, when Hessey returned it. See Hessey's letter of 30 Jun 1826: *The Keats Circle* ed H. E. Rollins (Cambridge, Mass 1948) II 463–4. *CIS* will be published in *SW&F (CC)*; for con-

temporary references by C see *CL* v 285n, 372, 434–5 and nn, 444, 455, 486 and n; *CL* vi 622n, 738 and n, 967n. See also *CN* iv 5323 f 28ᵛ (Feb 1826), in which C mentions that a reason for suspending their publication was his fear that it might prejudice the favourable reception of *AR*.

[19] The dialogue from which this excerpt is taken runs over eighteen pages of N 25 and was first published in 1892: see *CN* iv 4931, where it is reproduced in full, and 4931n, giving details of earlier publication. The present excerpt, drawing on f 100ᵛ to f 99ᵛ of *CN* iv 4931, includes many minor alterations from the notebook text. For the last sentence see n 22 below.

[20] In naming his characters C was, no doubt, influenced by Berkeley's *Three Dialogues Between Hylas and Philonous* (1713), but was also bent on making a fur-

with it. When a Man refers to *inward feelings* and *experiences,* of which Mankind at large are not conscious, as evidences of the truth of any opinion—such a Man I call a A MYSTIC: and the grounding of any theory or belief on accidents and anomalies of individual sensations or fancies, and the use of peculiar terms invented or perverted from their ordinary significations, for the purpose of expressing these *idiosyncracies,* and pretended facts of interior consciousness, I name MYSTICISM. Where the error consists simply in the Mystic's attaching to these anomalies of his individual temperament the character of *Reality,* and in receiving them as Permanent[a] Truths, having a subsistence in the Divine Mind, though revealed[b] to himself alone; but entertains this persuasion without demanding or expecting the same faith in his neighbours—I should regard it as a species of ENTHUSIASM,[21] always indeed to be deprecated,[c] but yet capable of co-existing with many excellent qualities both of Head and Heart. But when the Mystic by ambition or still meaner passions, or (as sometimes is the case) by an uneasy and self-doubting state of mind that seeks confirmation in outward sympathy, is led to impose his faith, as a duty, on mankind generally: and when with such views he asserts, that the same experiences would be vouchsafed,[d] the same truths revealed, to *every man* but for his secret wickedness and unholy will— such a Mystic is a FANATIC, and in certain states of the public mind a dangerous Member of Society. And most so in those ages and countries in which Fanatics of elder standing are allowed to persecute the fresh competitor. For under these predicaments, Mysticism, though originating in the singularities of an individual Nature, and therefore essentially anomalous, is nevertheless highly *contagious*. It is apt to collect a swarm and cluster *circum fana*, around the new *Fane:* and therefore

[a] AR (1825): permanent
[b] AR (1825): p 382 (vealed)
[c] AR (1825): deprecated
[d] AR (1831): vouschafed,

ther distinction. The names "Nöus" and "Antinöus" seem to mean "Mind" and "Antimind" in a special sense: i.e. one who subscribes to the idea of the "Intuitive Reason" (see Epigraph to *Sp Aph A* n 2 and *Sp Aph B Xa* at n 29, above) and one who does not. At the end of the dialogue Antinöus (whose favourite motto is "The proper Study of Mankind is Man") is sufficiently swayed by Nöus's arguments to promise a sympathetic reading of his book, which is to be entitled "The Science of Transcendental Logic".

[21] Cf the comments on Edward Irving quoted in App I Excursus Note 19 below and those on Böhme in nn 6, 29, and 30 of the present section. The attempt to desynonymise "enthusiasm" and "fanaticism" that follows appears elsewhere in C's writing, notably in a long annotation on Birch *Sermon: CM (CC)* I 495. For further examples see App I Excursus Note 22 "Coleridge on Enthusiasm and Fanaticism".

merits the name of FANATICISM, or as the Germans say, Schwärmerey, i.e. *Swarm-making.*''[22]

We will return to the harmless species—the enthusiastic Mystics: a species that may again be subdivided into two ranks. And it will not be other than germane to the subject, if I endeavour to describe them [a]in a sort of allegory, or parable.[23] Let us imagine a poor pilgrim[b] benighted in a wilderness or desart, and pursuing his way in the starless dark with a lantern[c] in his hand. Chance or his happy genius leads him to an Oasis or natural Garden, such as in the creations of my youthful fancy I supposed Enos* the Child of Cain to have found. And here, hungry and

---

* Will the Reader forgive me if I attempt at once to illustrate and relieve the subject by annexing the first stanza of the Poem[d] composed in the same year in which I wrote the Ancient Mariner and the first book of Christabel?

> "Encinctur'd with a twine of Leaves,
> That leafy twine his only Dress!
> A lovely Boy was plucking fruits
> In a moonlight wilderness.
> The Moon was bright, the air was free,
> And Fruits and Flowers together grew
> On many a Shrub and many a Tree:
> And all put on a gentle hue,
> Hanging in the shadowy air
> Like a Picture rich and rare.
> It was a Climate where, they say,
> The Night is more belov'd[e] than Day.
> But who that beauteous Boy beguil'd,
> That beauteous Boy! to linger here?

> [a] *AR* (1825): p 383
> [b] *AR* (1825): Pilgrim
> [c] *AR* (1825): lanthorn
> [d] *AR* (1825): Poem,
> [e] *AR* (1825): beloved

---

[22] For this sentence, not in the original notebook version, cf the annotation on Baxter: "The Field-Methodists are fanatics, *i.e. circâ fana densâ turbâ concalefacti*; those who catch heat best by crowding together round the same *Fane*"; and on Birch *Sermon*: "*Fanatici—qui circum fana furorem mutuo contrahunt et afflant*—those who in the same conventicle, or before the same shrine, relique or image, heat and ferment by coacervation": *CM (CC)* I 270, 496. See also *BL* ch 2 *(CC)* I 30, where the additional point concerning "Schwärmerey" occurs.

[23] C may have found the first germ of this allegory in Henry More *Enthusiasmus Triumphatus* § LIV: *A Collection of Several Philosophical Writings* (1662) 38–9, in which More urges the importance of taking reason as guide by the contrary image of a ". . . company of men travailing by night with links, torches and lanthorns" who, persuaded by an orator of the wretchedness of their condition by comparison with daylight, "beat out their lights and stumble on in the dark". For the full passage see App A(x) below.

thirsty, the way-wearied Man rests at a fountain; and the *a*Taper of his Lantern*b* throws its Light on an over-shadowing Tree, a Boss of snow-white Blossoms, through which the green and growing Fruits peeped, and the ripe golden Fruitage glowed. Deep, vivid, and faithful are the impressions, which the lovely Imagery comprised within the scanty Circle of Light, makes and leaves on his Memory! But scarcely has he eaten of the fruits and drunk*c* of the fountain, ere scared by the roar and howl from the desart he hurries forward: and as he passes with hasty steps through grove and glade, shadows and imperfect beholdings and vivid fragments of things distinctly seen blend with the past and present shapings of his Brain. Fancy modifies Sight. His Dreams transfer their forms to real Objects;[25] and these lend a substance and an *outness*[26] to his

---

Alone, by night, a little child,
In place so silent and so wild—
Has he no friend, no loving mother near?''
WANDERINGS OF CAIN*d*[24]

---

a *AR* (1825): p 384   *b* *AR* (1825): Lanthorn   *c* *AR* (1825): drank
d *AR* (1825): CAIN, *a MS. Poem.*

[24] This extract, first included in a letter to Byron of 22 Oct 1815 (*CL* IV 602 and n), was reprinted in the Prefatory Note for *The Wanderings of Cain* when it was finally published in the 1828 ed of *Poetical Works*: *PW* (EHC) I 287. In that ed line 4 reads "By moonlight, in a wilderness".

[25] Cf C's comments in *Int Aph XXIX*, at n 2, above, and his note on pp 98–9 of *AR* (1825) COPIES C, D, and E (*Mor Aph IX* n 9, above). See also *Lects 1808–1819 (CC)* I 135–6 and nn and *Friend (CC)* II 117, 119–20 (I 139–42); also next note.

[26] See C's note of Dec 1802: "Take away from sounds &c the sense of out-ness—what a horrid disease every moment would become/ the driving over a pavement &c—apply this to sympathy—& disclosure of Feeling": *CN* I 1307. The following summer he wrote, "Language & all *symbols* give *outness* to Thoughts/ & this the philosophical essence & purpose of Language": *CN* I 1387. *OED* ascribes the first use of the word to Berkeley, citing *Essay Towards a New Theory of Vision* (1709) § 46 and *Principles of Human Knowledge* (1710) § 43. In a note of 1808

C wrote about the yearning for vividness of symbol, which "something . . . that has the property of *Outness* . . . can alone fully gratify", and contended that Berkeley used the term in preference to "Externality": *CN* III 3325 and n (cf 3592, 3605, 4058 and nn). His most vivid use of the term comes in the account of Luther's vision of the Devil: ". . . a brain-image of the Devil, vivid enough to have acquired apparent *Outness*": *Friend (CC)* II 117 (I 140 and n). In *Bl Mag* X (1821) he wrote (p 249): ". . . outness is but the feeling of *other-ness* (alterity) rendered intuitive, or alterity visually represented". See also his note in Gillman's copy of *SM* on the "outness" of the impressions possibly created by departed spirits (*SM—CC*—81n), his mention of "that chasm between the Subjective and the Objective which *visual* sunshiny Outness in the latter gives . . ." (*CN* IV 5281), and the note (dated 1827) added to the 1839 ed of *SM*: ". . . but for the confidence which we place in the assertions of reason and conscience, we could have no certainty of the reality and actual outness of the material world": *SM (CC)* 18n. On the further

Dreams. Apparitions greet him; and when at a distance from this enchanted land, and on a different track, the Dawn of Day discloses to him a Caravan, a troop of his fellow-men, his memory, which is itself half fancy, is interpolated afresh by every attempt to recall, connect, and *piece out* his recollections. His narration is received as a Madman's Tale.[27] He shrinks from the rude Laugh and contemptuous Sneer, and retires into himself. Yet the craving for Sympathy, strong in proportion to the intensity of his Convictions, impels him to unbosom himself to abstract Auditors; and the poor Quietist becomes a Penman, and, all too poorly stocked for the Writer's trade, he borrows his phrases and figures from the only Writings to which [a]he has had access, the sacred Books of his Religion. And thus I shadow out the enthusiast Mystic of the first sort; at the head of which stands the illuminated Teutonic Theosopher[b][28] and Shoemaker, honest JACOB BEHMEN,[29] born near Gorlitz, in Upper Lusatia, in the 17th of our Elizabeth's Reign, and who died in the 22nd[c] of her Successor's.[30]

<hr>

[a] *AR* (1825): p 385
[b] *AR* (1825, 1831): Thelosopher ; *AR* (1825) COPY A: Theosopher
[c] *AR* (1825): 22d

<hr>

implications see e.g. *BL* ch 12 *(CC)* I 258–62 (building on, but not identical with, Schelling), *Friend (CC)* I 171, and his note on Kant *Logik*: ". . . the sense of outwardness as a sense of reality, is a law of our nature, and no conclusion of our judgment": H. Nidecker *Revue de littérature comparée* VII (1927) 137, *CM (CC)* III. Some of these, along with others and an important discussion, may be found in ch 5, "Outness", of Owen Barfield *What Coleridge Thought* (Oxford 1972) 59–68. For "uttering" as "outering" see *CN* IV 4954 f 109–109[v].

[27] The paradox of the visionary whose true version of reality is received as madness is a favourite of C's: see e.g. ". . . honoured with the name of madman": *Lects 1795 (CC)* 19; the end of the Fable of the Maddening Rain, *Friend (CC)* II 12 (I 9); and his joke about a philosophy that ". . . distinguishes truth from illusion only by the majority of those who dream the same dream": " '*I* asserted that the world was mad,' exclaimed poor Lee, 'and the world said, that I was mad, and confound them, they outvoted me' ": *BL* ch 12 *(CC)* I 262.

[28] The misprint "Thelosopher" (see textual note) was corrected in *AR* (1825) COPY A by C, but not changed in print until the 4th ed.

[29] See above, nn 5, 6. The image of Böhme as pilgrim with taper-lantern is foreshadowed and further interpreted by C's annotation on his *Works*: ". . . being but a poor unlearned Man he contemplated Truth and the forms of Nature thro' a luminous Mist, the vaporous darkness rising from his Ignorance and accidental peculiarities of fancy and sensation, but the Light streaming into it from his inmost Soul. . . . The true wonder is, that in so many places it thins away almost into a transparent Medium, and Jacob Behmen, *the Philosopher* surprizes us in proportion as Behmen, the Visionary, had astounded or perplexed us": *CM (CC)* I 558.

[30] C has turned for his information to "The Life of Jacob Behmen": Böhme *Works*, in which the date and place of his birth (1575) and death (1624) are given, and to his own ms note there, which begins: "Elizabeth began to reign 1558—Shakspere born 1564/ about 11 years before Behmen: ⟨who was⟩ born in 17th of

To delineate a Mystic of the second and higher order, we need only endow our Pilgrim with equal gifts of Nature, but these developed and displayed by all the aids and arts of Education and favorable Fortune. *He* is on his way to the Mecca of his ancestral and national Faith, with a well-guarded and numerous Procession of Merchants and Fellow-pilgrims, on the established Track.[31] At the close of Day the Caravan has halted: the full moon rises on the Desart: and he strays forth alone, out of sight, but to no unsafe distance; and Chance leads *him* too,[a] to the same Oasis or Islet of Verdure on the Sea of Sand.[32] He wanders at leisure in its maze of Beauty and Sweetness, and thrids his way through the odorous and flowering Thickets into open "Spots of Greenery,"[33] and discovers statues and memorial characters, grottos, and refreshing Caves. But the Moonshine, the imaginative Poesy of Nature,[34] spreads its soft shadowy charm over all, conceals distances, and magnifies heights, and modifies relations; and fills up vacuities with its own whiteness, counterfeiting substance; and where the dense shadows lie, makes solidity imitate Hollowness; and gives to all objects a tender visionary hue and [b]softening. Interpret the Moonlight and the Shadows as the peculiar genius and sensibility of the Individual's own Spirit: and here you have the other sort: a Mystic, an Enthusiast of a nobler Breed—a FE-NELON.[35] But the residentiary, or the frequent visitor of the favored spot,

[a] *AR* (1825): too
[b] *AR* (1825): p 386

Eliz.—Shakspere died in 1616, in the 14th year of James I. Behmen in the 22nd year . . .": *CM (CC)* I 559. Cf below, n 43.

[31] There is a touch of irony here, C's specific reference turning out to be to Fénelon and so to the Roman Catholic Church.

[32] For the image cf C's letter of 1798: "Laudanum gave me repose, not sleep: but YOU, I believe, know how divine that repose is—what a spot of inchantment, a green spot of fountains, & flowers & trees, in the very heart of a waste of Sands!": *CL* I 394.

[33] *Kubla Khan* line 11: ". . . Enfolding sunny spots of greenery": *PW* (EHC) I 297. The imagery of this sentence, "maze", "odorous and flowering Thickets", "Caves", is reminiscent of the opening stanzas of that poem: there is also a resemblance to elements in the landscape of *The Wanderings of Cain* (see above, n 24),

which was projected at the time (1797) when C says that he wrote *Kubla Khan*. See *PW* (EHC) I 295 and M. L. Reed *Wordsworth: the Chronology of the Early Years, 1770–99* (Cambridge, Mass 1967) 208–9n.

[34] Cf *BL* ch 14 *(CC)* II 5–7, in which "The sudden charm, which accidents of light and shade, which moon-light or sunset diffused over a known and familiar landscape" offered to C and WW the possibility of combining "faithful adherence to the truth of nature" with "the modifying colours of the imagination"—C's role (p 6) corresponding more to that of moonlight, apparently.

[35] François de Salignac de la Mothe-Fénelon (1651–1715), French theologian and abp of Cambrai, who adopted the quietism of Mme Guyon and supported it in his *Explication des maximes des saints* (1697). In 1796 C referred to ". . . almost

who has scanned its beauties by steady Day-light, and mastered its true proportions and lineaments, he will discover that both Pilgrims have indeed been there! *He* will know, that the delightful Dream, which the latter tells, is a Dream of Truth; and that even in the bewildered Tale of the former there is Truth mingled with the Dream.

But the source, the Spring-head, of the Charges which I anticipate, lies deep. Materialism, conscious and avowed Materialism, is in *ª*ill re-pute:*ᵇ* and a confessed Materialist therefore a rare character. But if the faith be ascertained by the fruits:*ᶜ* if the predominant, though most often unsuspected, persuasion is to be learnt from the influences, under which the thoughts and affections of the Man move and take their direction; I must reverse the position. ONLY NOT ALL ARE MATERIALISTS. Except a few individuals, and those for the most part of a single Sect: every one, who calls himself a Christian, holds himself to have a Soul as well as a Body. He distinguishes Mind from Matter, the *Subject* of his conscious-ness from the *Objects* of the same. The former is his MIND: and he says, it is immaterial. But though *Subject* and *Substance* are words of kindred roots, nay, little less than equivalent terms,[36] yet nevertheless it is *ᵈ*ex-clusively to sensible OBJECTS, to Bodies, to modifications of Matter, that he habitually attaches the attributes of reality, of substance. Real and Tangible, Substantial and Material, are Synonymes*ᵉ* for him. He never indeed asks himself, what he means by MIND? But if he did, and tasked himself to return an honest answer—as to what, at least, he had hitherto meant by it—he would find, that he had described it by nega-tives, as the opposite of Bodies, *ex. gr.* as a somewhat opposed to solid-ity, to visibility*ᶠ* &c. as if you could abstract the capacity of a vessel, and conceive of it as a somewhat by itself, and then give to the emptiness

---

ª⁻ᵇ AR (1825): ill-repute:
ᶜ AR (1825): fruits;
ᵈ AR (1825): p 387
ᵉ AR (1825): Synonimes
ᶠ AR (1825): visibility,

---

all the followers of Fénelon" as believing in a state of pre-existence (*CL* I 246), and in 1805, expounding his belief that ". . . the truly Beloved is the symbol of God to whomever it is truly beloved by", he re-marked, "By some such feeling as this I can easily believe the mind of Fénelon & Madame Guyon to have coloured its faith in the Worship of Saints—but that was most dangerous . . .": *CN* II 2540. See also *CN* III 3922 and n, 3972 and n. C an-notated an untraced work by Fénelon on charity hostilely, see *CM (CC)* II 590–2, but apart from this his reading of him has not been traced.

[36] C appears to be connecting the ety-mology of "substance" as "standing un-der" (always important to him: see above, *Int Aph XII* n 1) with that of "subject" as "cast under". Cf annotation on RS *Life of Wesley* (Oxford 1820) I 434: *CM (CC)* V.

the properties of containing, holding, being entered, and so forth. In short, though the proposition would perhaps be angrily denied in words, yet *in fact* he thinks of his *Mind,* as a *property,* or *accident* of a something else, that he calls a *Soul* or *Spirit:* though the very same difficulties must recur, the moment he should attempt to establish the difference. For either this Soul or Spirit is nothing but a thinner Body, a finer Mass of Matter: or the attribute of Self-subsistency vanishes from the Soul on the same grounds, on which it is refused to the Mind.

I am persuaded, however, that the dogmatism of the Corpuscular School,[37] though it still exerts an influence on men's notions and phrases, has received a mortal blow from the increasingly *dynamic* spirit of the physical Sciences now highest in public estimation. And it may safely be predicted, that the results will extend beyond the intention of those, who are gradually[a] effecting this revolution. It is not Chemistry alone that will be indebted to the Genius of Davy, Oersted,[38] and their compeers: and not as the Founder of Physiology and philosophic Anatomy alone, will Mankind love and revere the name of John Hunter.[39] These men have not only *taught,* they have compelled us to admit, that the immediate objects of our *senses,* or rather the grounds of the visibility and tangibility of all Objects of Sense, bear the same *relation* and

---

[a] *AR* (1825): p 388 (ally)

[37] The words "corpuscle" and "corpuscular" became fashionable in English in the seventeenth century, when the ancient atomic theory, revived in France by Pierre Gassendi (1592–1655), came into favour. *OED*'s first example of the adjective is a title by Robert Boyle: "Origine of Formes and Qualities (According to the corpuscular philosophy)" (1667). In *The True Intellectual System of the Universe* (1678) Ralph Cudworth asserted that the "Atheistical System of the World" was "Built upon a peculiar physiological *Hypothesis* . . . which is called by some *Atomical* or *Corpuscular*, by others *Mechanical* . . .": (2nd ed 2 vols 1743) I 7.

[38] C's relationship with Sir Humphry Davy (1778–1829) had in youth been one of admiring friendship. In private, however, he came to entertain reservations: see e.g. his note in Böhme *Works*: "Alas! Since I wrote the preceding note, H. Davy is become Sir Humphry Davy, and an *Atomist*!": *CM (CC)* I 572 and his charge in 1820 of ". . . continued plagiarisms . . . from the Discoveries of Steffens and oth-

ers": *CL* v 130. In 1823, nevertheless, he referred to Davy's "March of Glory as the Chemical Lecturer, a Glory not brighter or filling a larger space to my mind now that I look back on it, than it did at Bristol, in his 20th year, when I had to look forward to it": *CL* v 309. He also communicated with him on business in Feb 1825: *CL* v 410.

Hans Christian Oersted (1777–1851), Danish physicist. C's annotated copy of his *Ansicht der chemischen Naturgesetze* (Berlin 1812) is in the BM. See *CN* III 4454n, *CM (CC)* IV, and T. Levere *Poetry Realized in Nature* (Cambridge 1981) 64, 79, 220, 256 n 44.

[39] John Hunter (1728–93). C's major statement in this connexion is a note in the 1818 *Friend (CC)* I 493–4, but he was already aware of Hunter's view of life in 1796: *CL* I 295. See also *Friend (CC)* I 473–5 and nn, *TL* (1848) 17–18, *CM (CC)* I 550 and n, 624, and *L&L* 16–23. For further discussion see Barfield *What Coleridge Thought* 45, 130, 206–7 and Levere *Poetry Realized in Nature* esp pp 46–52, 92–4, 205–10.

similar proportion to the *intelligible* object—*i.e.* to the Object, which we actually *mean* when we say, *"It is such or such a thing,"* or *"I have seen this or that,"*—as the paper, ink, and differently combined straight and curved lines of an Edition of Homer bear to what we understand by the words, Iliad and Odyssey. Nay, nothing would be more easy than so to construct the paper, ink, painted Capitals, &c. of a printed disquisition on the Eye, or the Muscles and Cellular Texture (*i.e.* the Flesh) of the human Body, as to bring together every one of the sensible and ponderable *Stuffs* or Elements, that are *sensuously* perceived in the Eye itself, or in the Flesh itself. Carbon and Nitrogen, Oxygen and Hydrogen, Sulphur, Phosphorus, and one or two Metals and Metallic Bases, constitute the whole. It cannot be these, therefore, that we mean by an *Eye*, by our *Body*. But perhaps it may be a particular *Combination* of these? But here comes a question: In this term do you or do you not include the *Principle,* the *Operating Cause,* of the Combination? If *not,* then detach this Eye from the Body! *a*Look steadily at it—as it might lie on the Marble Slab of a dissecting Room. Say it were the Eye of a Murderer, a Bellingham:[40] or the Eye of a murdered Patriot, a Sidney![41]—Behold it, handle it, with its various accompaniments or constituent parts, of Tendon, Ligament, Membrane, Blood-vessel, Gland, Humors; its Nerves of Sense, of Sensation, and of Motion. Alas! all these names, like that of the Organ itself, are so many Anachronisms, figures of Speech, to express that which has been: as when the Guide points with his finger to a heap of Stones, and tells the Traveller, "That is Babylon, or Persepolis."—Is this cold Jelly "the Light of the Body?"[42] Is this the Micranthropos[43] in the marvellous Microcosm? Is this what you *mean*

a *AR* (1825): p 389

[40] John Bellingham (d 1812), a deranged man, murdered the Prime Minister, Spencer Perceval (b 1762), on 11 May 1812. Horrified by the event, C cancelled his lecture for that day and hurried to the *Courier* office to offer his services: *CL* III 409–10 and n, 416. The obituary of Perceval that appeared on 14 May is attributed to him on the basis of style and occasion: *EOT (CC)* II 347–9 (and cf III 130–2, a conjectural attribution).

[41] Cf *Friend*: "But when we reverse the iniquitous sentence passed on Algernon Sidney, during our perusal of his work on Government, at the moment we deny it to have been a traitrous Libel, our beating Hearts declare it to have been a benefaction to our Country, and under the circum-

stances of those times, the performance of an heroic Duty." See also the reference to ". . . the infamy of those, who misled an English Jury to the murder of Algernon Sidney!": *Friend (CC)* II 60 (I 79), II 67 (I 92). Sidney (1622–83), a grandson of Sir Philip Sidney, was tried for conspiracy in the Rye House Plot, convicted, and executed on Tower Hill; the charges included one of treasonable libel for his authorship of *Discourses Concerning Government,* then as yet unpublished.

[42] "The light of the body is the eye . . .". Matt 6.22; cf Luke 11.34.

[43] "Little human being". *OED* cites this as a nonce-word. This and the next sentence, together with an earlier one, are based on an annotation of 20 Jul 1822 on

when you well define the Eye as the Telescope and the Mirror of the Soul, the Seat and Agent of an almost magical power?

Pursue the same inquisition with every other part of the Body, whether integral or simply ingredient; and let a *Berzelius* or a *Hatchett*[44] be your interpreter, and demonstrate to you what it is that in each actually meets your Senses. And when you have heard the scanty catalogue, ask yourself if *these* are indeed the living *Flesh*, the *Blood* of Life? Or not far rather—I speak of what, as a Man of Common Sense, you really *do*, not what, as a philosopher, you *ought* to believe—is it not, I say, far rather the distinct and individualized Agency that by the given combinations utters and bespeaks its Presence? Justly and with strictest propriety of language may I say, *Speaks.* [a]It is to the coarseness of our Senses, or rather to the defect and limitation of our percipient faculty, that the *visible* Object appears the same even for a moment. The characters, which I am now shaping on this paper, abide. Not only the forms remain the same, but the particles of the coloring stuff are fixed, and, for an indefinite period at least, remain the same. But the particles that constitute the *size*, the visibility of an organic structure (see p. 75) are in perpetual flux. They are to the combining and constitutive Power as

---

[a] *AR* (1825): p 390

Böhme *Works*: "Eye! the Micranthrope thou in the marvellous Microcosmos! Even bodily comprizing Bone, Tendon, Ligament, Membrane, ⟨Blood-⟩ vessel, Gland, with the 3 forms of the Nervous Systems, Nerves of Sense, Nerves of Motion, and the gangliac Nerves—at once the Telescope and the Mirror of the Soul, and even more *imperiously* than the Hand & Touch the Seat and Agent of ⟨the⟩ Magical Power—!'' The annotation continues with the lines, also relevant, on Berkeley Coleridge's death (which employ the same metre as that in the first sentence): *CM (CC)* I 671, 672 (cf *PW*—EHC—I 305). Cf the satiric lines *To a Critic*: *PW* (EHC) II 962. See also Aristotle *De anima* 2.1 (412[b]) tr W. S. Hett (LCL 1936): "If the eye were a living creature, its soul would be its vision . . . . and if vision fails there is no eye, except in an equivocal sense, as for instance a stone or painted eye.''

[44] Baron Jöns Jacob von Berzelius (1779–1848), analytical chemist. In 1814 and 1815 he was publishing impressively accurate analyses of organic compounds;

he also listed the constituents of blood. See Levere *Poetry Realized in Nature* 33, 53, 79, 182. In a ms note of 1817 (BM Add MS 36532) C referred to him in connexion with Davy: *IS* 49.

Charles Hatchett (1765–1847) was perpetual president of the Society for Animal Chemistry, founded in 1812. C's chief tribute to him comes in the 1818 *Friend*, in which he described Hatchett's recent paper on the egg and its analogies, published in *Phil Trans RS* CVI (1816) 301–10, as being ''. . . in the proper sense of the term, the development of a FACT in the history of physiology'' and as exhibiting ''. . . a luminous instance of what we mean by the discovery of a *central phænomenon*''. In BM MS Egerton 2800 f 78 he referred to it as possibly ''. . . among the seminative *Ideas* of the Age, one of its most *scientific* as well as *essential* Births'': *Friend (CC)* I 474–5 and n. See also *CN* IV 4580 f 71[v], 4645, 4646 f 4[v], 4929 f 32n; and Levere *Poetry Realized in Nature* Index s.v. ''Hatchett''.

the pulses of air to the Voice of a Discourser; or of one who sings a roundelay. The same words may be repeated; but in each second of time the articulated air hath passed away, and each act of articulation appropriates and gives momentary form to a new and other portion. As the column of blue smoke from a cottage chimney in the breathless Summer Noon,[45] or the stedfast-seeming Cloud on the edge-point of a Hill in the driving air-current, which momently condensed and recomposed is the common phantom of a thousand successors;—such is the flesh, which our *bodily* eyes transmit to us; which our *Palates* taste; which our Hands touch.

But perhaps the material particles possess this combining power by inherent reciprocal attractions, repulsions, and elective affinities; and are themselves the joint Artists of their own combinations? I will not reply, though well I might, that this would be to solve one problem by another, and merely to shift the mystery. It will be sufficient to remind the thoughtful [a]Querist, that even herein consists the essential difference, the contra-distinction, of an Organ from a Machine; that[b] not only the characteristic Shape is evolved from the invisible central power, but the material Mass itself is acquired by assimilation. The germinal power of the Plant transmutes the fixed air and the elementary Base of Water into Grass or Leaves; and on these the Organific[46] Principle in the Ox or the Elephant exercises an Alchemy still more stupendous. As the unseen Agency weaves its magic eddies,[47] the foliage becomes indifferently the Bone and its Marrow, the pulpy Brain, or the solid Ivory. That what you see *is* blood, *is* flesh, is itself the work, or shall I say, the translucence, of the invisible Energy, which soon surrenders or abandons them to inferior Powers, (for there is no pause nor chasm in the activities of Nature) which repeat a similar metamorphosis according to *their* kind;—[c]These are not fancies, conjectures, or even hypotheses, but *facts;* to deny which is impossible, not to reflect on which is ignominious. And we need only reflect on them with a calm and silent spirit to learn the utter emptiness and unmeaningness of the vaunted Mechanico-corpuscular

---

[a] *AR* (1825): p 391
[b] COPY D: that in the former
[c] *AR* (1825): kind.

---

[45] This image of cottage-smoke for form constant in flux appears also in an annotation on G. Schubert *Ansichten von der Nachtseite der Wissenschaft* (Dresden 1808) 268: *CM (CC)* IV.

[46] Cf C's letter to Gillman 22 Nov 1825: ". . . it is some *specific* sensibility, having it's seat and source in some special energy of the organic and organific Life . . .": *CL* v 517. *OED* gives as its first example the use of "organific" by C's disciple J. H. Green in *Vital Dynamics* (1840) 36.

[47] For other uses of this central image of eddying see Beer *CPI* 214–17.

Philosophy,[48] with both its twins, Materialism on the one hand, and Idealism, rightlier named *Subjective Idolism*[49] on the other: the one obtruding on us a World of Spectres and Apparitions; the other a mazy Dream! Let the Mechanic or corpuscular Scheme, which in its absoluteness and strict consistency was first introduced[a] by DES CARTES, be judged by the results. *By its fruits shall it be known.*[50]

In order to submit the various phenomena[b] of moving bodies to geometrical construction, we are under the necessity of abstracting from corporeal substance all its *positive* properties, and obliged to consider Bodies as differing from equal portions of Space∗ only by [c]figure and

> ∗ Such is the conception of Body in Des Cartes' own system.[51] *Body* is [d]every where[e] confounded with *Matter*, and might in the Cartesian sense be defined, Space or Extension with the attribute of Visibility. As Des Cartes at the same time zealously asserted the existence of intelligential Beings, the reality and independent Self-subsistence of the Soul, Berkleianism or Spinosism was the immediate and necessary Consequence. Assume a *plurality* of self-subsisting Souls, and we have Berkleianism; assume one only, (unam et unicam Substantiam),[52] and you have Spinosism, *i.e.*[f] the Assertion of one infinite Self-subsistent,[g] with the two Attributes of Thinking and Appearing. "Cogitatio infinita sine centro, et omniformis Apparitio."[53] How far the Newtonian Vis inertiae[54] (interpreted any

---

[a] *AR* (1825): p 392 (duced)   [b] *AR* (1825): phænomena
[c] *AR* (1825): p 393   [d-e] *AR* (1825): everywhere
[f] *AR* (1825): i. e.   [g] COPY A: Subsistent,

---

[48] Cf "The Mechanico-corpuscular Theory raised to the Title of the Mechanic Philosophy": *C&S (CC)* 64, 217. *OED* cites the present as the first usage, with no further examples.

[49] A pun on "subjective idealism", the term commonly used to characterise (not necessarily from the same points of view) the philosophies of Berkeley and Fichte. *OED* gives no example of "subjective idealism" in English before 1887, but the term had been at least latent from the turn of the century: see e.g. F. W. J. von Schelling: "Fichte . . . könnte den idealismus in völlig subjektiver, ich dagegen in objektiver Bedeutung gedacht haben" (tr "Fichte . . . could have thought of Idealism with a fully subjective, I on the contrary with an objective, meaning"): *Darstellung meines Systems der Philosophie* (1801): *Sämmtliche Werke* (14 vols Stuttgart 1859) IV 109.

[50] Matt 7.20: ". . . by their fruits ye shall know them".

[51] For C's views on Descartes's dualism, and further discussion, see also *BL* ch 8 *(CC)* I 129–30 and nn, *P Lects* Lect 13 (1949) 376–9 and nn, and K. M. Wheeler *Sources, Processes and Methods in Coleridge's "Biographia Literaria"* (Cambridge 1980) 33–4 and nn.

[52] For the Latin phrase see above, *Sp Aph B II* n 30. C's most succinct critique of Spinozism is in a letter to R. H. Brabant of 10 Mar 1815, quoted at length in the Editor's Introduction above, p xlviii–xlix.

[53] "Infinite thought without a center, and omniform Appearance". A source for this has not been found and the full Latin may be C's: cf *CN* IV 4728: ". . . an infinite Power without Personality or Consciousness, . . . infinita cogitatio sine centro—Spinoza . . ." and *CM (CC)* I 566, III 78.

[54] "Power (or force) of inertia". *OED* (s.v. "Inertia"; see also *OED* s.v. "Vis") quotes Newton's *Principia* (1687) 2, Definitio III ("Materiae vis insita est potentia resistendi . . . . neque differt quicquam ab

mobility. And as a *Fiction of Science*,[58] it would be difficult to overvalue this invention. It possesses the same merits in relation to Geometry that the atomic theory has in relation to Algebraic Calculus. But in contempt of Common Sense, and in direct opposition to the express declarations of the inspired Historian (Genesis I.), and to the tone and spirit of the Scriptures throughout, Des Cartes propounded it as *truth of fact:*[59] and instead of a World *created* and filled with productive forces by the Almighty Fiat,[60] left a lifeless Machine whirled about by the dust of its

---

otherwise than as an arbitrary term = x y z, to represent the unknown but necessary supplement or integration of the Cartesian Notion of Body) has patched up the Flaw, I leave for more competent Judges to decide. But should any one of my Readers feel an interest in the speculative principles of Natural Philosophy, and should be master of the German Language, I warmly recommend for his perusal the earliest known publication of the Great Founder of the Critical Philosophy, (written in the twenty-second Year of his Age!) on the then eager controversy between the Leibnitzian and the French and English Mathematicians, respecting the Living Forces—"Gedanken von der wahren Schätzung der lebendigen Kräfte: 1747''[55]—in which Kant demonstrates the *right reasoning* to be with the latter; but the Truth of *Fact*, the evidence of *Experience,*[a] with the former; and gives the explanation, namely: Body, or Corporeal Nature, is something else and more than geometrical extension, even with the addition of a Vis inertiae. And Leibnitz, with the Bernouillis,[56] erred in the attempt to demonstrate geometrically a problem not susceptible of geometrical construction.—This Tract, with the succeeding Himmels-system, may with propriety be placed, after the Principia of Newton, among the striking instances of early Genius; and as the first product of the Dynamic Philosophy in the Physical Sciences, from the time, at least, of Giordano Bruno, whom the Idolaters burnt for an Atheist, at Rome, in the year 1600.—See the FRIEND, Vol. I. p. 193–197.[57]

---

[a]   AR (1825): *experience,*

---

inertia massae''), finding its first example of precise usage in England in E. Phillips *New World of English Words* ed J. Kersey (6th ed 1706). In a note of 1821 C used the term in connexion with a more positive sense, by which nature is ''. . . the same with the power of Gravity'', and so ''=*Natura* NATURABILIS'': *CN* IV 4843 f 117^v, a continuation of the ms later used for ''*Prometheus*'': see below, n 71. Hartley discussed the *vis inertiae* of matter in relation to the immateriality of God: *Observations on Man* (3 vols 1791) II 31; see III 508–10 for Pistorius' reply. For C's attitude in earlier years see *Lects 1795 (CC)* 156n.

[55] Kant *Gedanken von der wahren Schätzung der lebendigen Kräfte* [''Thoughts on the True Estimation of the Living Forces''] (1747), in *Vermischte Schriften* (Halle 1799) I 1–282. C refers to this also in *Logic (CC)* 194 and fn. Kant was born in 1724.

[56] In a notebook entry of 14 May 1805 C discussed one kind of possible afterlife: ''. . . in the next State to meet with the Luthers, Miltons, Leibnitzs, Bernouillis, Bonnets, Shakesperes, etc/ and to live a longer & better Life, the good & wise entirely among the good & wise, as a step to break the abruptness of an immediate Heaven'': *CN* II 2584. Jean Bernouilli (1667–1748) corresponded with Leibniz and shared his mathematical and philosophical interests, but other members of his family were also distinguished in these fields; see *CN* II 2584n. See also *TL* (1848) 89 for Bernouilli on magnetism.

[57] *Friend (CC)* I 114–18 (cf II 79–82).

[58] Cf C's note in App C of *SM (CC)* 99.

[59] See n 51, above

[60] See above, *Refl Mor* n 29.

own Grinding: as if Death could come from the living Fountain of Life;[61] Nothingness and Phantom from the Plenitude of Reality![a][62] the Absoluteness of Creative Will![63]

Holy! Holy! Holy! let me be deemed mad by all men, if such be thy ordinance: but, O! from *such* Madness save and preserve me, my God! When, however, after a short interval, the Genius [b]of Kepler,[64] expanded and organized in the soul of Newton, and there (if I may hazard so bold an expression) refining itself into an almost celestial Clearness, had expelled the Cartesian Vortices[65]*; then the necessity of an active

* For Newton's own doubtfully suggested Ether,[66] or *most* subtle Fluid, as the Ground and immediate Agent in the phenomena[c] of universal Gravitation, was either not adopted

[a] COPY H: Reality! from
[b] *AR* (1825): p 394
[c] *AR* (1825): phænomena

[61] For the centrality of this image in C's thinking and writing see Beer *CPI* 30–7.

[62] Related, by contrast, to *The Destiny of Nations* lines 23–6:

> Infinite Love,
> Whose latence is the plenitude of All,
> Thou with retracted beams, and self-eclipse
> Veiling, revealest thine eternal Sun.

PW (EHC) I 132.

[63] For the "absolute will" see above, *Sp Aph B XIX* nn 81, 82.

[64] Johannes Kepler (1571–1630), the German astronomer who succeeded Tycho Brahe at the Prague observatory. C translated an epigram on him in 1799 (*CN* I 432 f 49ᵛ: *PW*—EHC—II 1004), but other references are later: e.g. *SM (CC)* 51; letter of 28 Jul 1817: *CL* IV 760; and 1818 *Friend (CC)* I 485–6. The suggestion that Newton was anticipated by Kepler in the matter of gravitation is not there in *SM* and seems later still: see *TT* 8 Oct 1830 *(CC)* I 210–11 (1836 vn II 125–6): "The Laws of the Planetary System are due to Kepler. Gravitation he had fully conceived, but because it seemed inconsistent with some received observations on Light &c. he gave it up in allegiance, as he says, to Nature." C's preceding comment in *TT* "It is in the order of Providence that the inventive, generative, constitutive mind—the Kepler—should come first; and then the patient and collective mind—the Newton—should follow and elaborate the pregnant Queries and il-

lumining Guesses of the former" may owe something to his reading of Schubert *Ansichten von der Nachtseite der Naturwissenschaft* on the subject in 1818. See *CN* III 4457 and n. Kepler's near anticipation of Newton and Newton's own doubts about gravity as a force acting at a distance are discussed in A. Koestler *The Sleepwalkers* (Harmondsworth, Middx 1968) 341–5, 505–7. Koestler quotes from Kepler's introduction to *Astronomia nova*.

[65] For an account of Descartes's theory of vortices and Newton's criticisms, see Charles Hutton *A Mathematical and Philosophical Dictionary* (2 vols 1795–6) II 662–3 and Priestley *History and Present State of Discoveries Relating to Vision, Light and Colours* (1772) 126. See also Marie Boas "The Establishment of Medieval Philosophy" *Osiris* x (1952) 442–60; E. J. Aiton "The Vortex Theory of the Planetary Motions" *Annals of Science* XIII (1957) 249–64, XIV (1958) 132–47, 157–72. Cf *TT* 29 Jun 1833 *(CC)* I 394 and nn (1836 vn II 234–5).

[66] Newton's concept of ether was taken up by Hartley in *Observations on Man* (1749; new ed 1791) I 13–16 as a model for the medium in which he believed association of ideas to take place. Earlier, however, Andrew Baxter, in his *Enquiry into the Nature of the Human Soul* (2nd ed 1737) I 34n, had taken issue with the whole concept. C reprinted and adapted Baxter's note (with insufficient acknowledgment) in a long note to line 34 of *Joan of Arc* (1796)

power, of positive forces present in the Material Universe, forced itself on the conviction. For as a Law without a Lawgiver is a mere abstraction; so a *Law* without an Agent to realize it, a *Constitution* without an abiding Executive, is, in fact, not a Law but *an Idea*! In the profound Emblem of the Great Tragic Poet, it is the powerless Prometheus fixed on a barren Rock.[71] And what was the result? How was this necessity provided for? God himself—my hand trembles as I write! Rather, then, let me employ the word, which the religious Feeling, in its perplexity,

---

or soon abandoned by his Disciples; not only as introducing, against his own Canons of Right Reasoning, an Ens imaginarium[67] into physical Science, a Suf*fiction* in the place of a legitimate Sup*position*;[68] but because the Substance (assuming it to exist) must itself form part of the Problem, it was meant to solve. Meantime Leibnitz's Pre-established Harmony,[69] which originated in Spinosa,[70] found no acceptance; and, lastly, the Notion of a corpuscular Substance, with Properties *put* into it, like a Pincushion hidden in the Pins, could pass with the unthinking only for any thing more than a Confession of ignorance, or technical terms expressing a hiatus of scientific insight.

---

bk II 41–2: *PW* (EHC) II 1112. See also Beer *CPI* 60, 71–2 and *Wordsworth in Time* (1979) 165–7.

[67] "Imaginary Being": cf *CM (CC)* III 43.

[68] The basic distinction, between "supposition" and "sub-fiction", or "hypothesis" and "hypopœēsis", is found in a notebook entry of 1809, quoted above, *Sp Aph B XI* n 3 with further references. For use of it in connexion with Kant see *CM (CC)* III 328; with Newton *CM (CC)* I 108 and n, and with Newton's "ether" *TT* 29 Jun 1833 *(CC)* I 393–4 (1836 vn II 234). The form "suffiction" is used similarly in *BL* chs 5, 12 *(CC)* I 101–2, 258, *CL* IV 760, *P Lects* Lect 12 (1948) 361, *CN* IV 4910 f 73ᵛ, and *LR* II 343; *OED* gives no example of the word outside C's writings. For "sufficta" see *CM (CC)* II 445, and for God as the ground, and therefore by contrast "subfaciens" (making, rather than positing, from beneath), *CL* IV 770. Cf "substance": *Int Aph XII* n 1 and *Sp Aph B IV* n 8 above.

[69] See e.g. Leibniz's assertion that the monads received their nature "from . . . a universal and supreme cause", since otherwise it would have been impossible for them "ever to have produced this order, this harmony, this beauty that we find in nature. This argument, which appears to have only a moral certainty, is brought to a state of absolute metaphysical necessity by the new kind of harmony which I have introduced, namely the pre-established harmony": *Nouveaux essais* bk 4 ch 10 § 10: *Œuvres philosophiques* (1765) 407; tr P. Remnant and J. Bennet (Cambridge 1981). In this § Leibniz pointed out that Locke had *almost* anticipated his pre-established harmony. See also *CM (CC)* II 555–6, III 243, 790.

[70] For C's belief that the doctrine was ". . . certainly borrowed from Spinoza" see *BL* ch 8 *(CC)* I 130 and n; cf 131. In an annotation of uncertain date on Descartes's "De passionibus animae", however, C challenged such an assertion (ascribing it there to "Brucker and the German Manualists"), and asked "What is this XVIᵗʰ Article if not a clear and distinct statement of the Theory?": *CM (CC)* II 172. The concept of a "supersensual essence, which, being at once the *ideal* of the reason and the cause of the material world, is the pre-establisher of the harmony in and between both", can be found in *Friend (CC)* I 463. C may first have encountered Leibniz's scheme in Priestley *Disquisitions relating to Matter and Spirit* § 7 (2nd ed 1782) I.

[71] C developed this reading of the myth of Prometheus in terms of a dialectic between *nomos* (law) and *idea* in his lecture "On the *Prometheus* of Aeschylus", delivered on 18 May 1825. See below, App I Excursus Note 14 "Coleridge and the Prometheus myth".

suggested as the substitute—the *Deity itself* was declared to be the real Agent, the actual [a]Gravitating Power! The Law and the Law-giver were identified. God (says Dr. Priestley) not only does, but *is* every thing.[72] Jupiter est quodcunque vides.[73] And thus a system, which commenced by excluding all life and immanent activity from the visible Universe and evacuating the natural World of all Nature, ended by substituting the Deity, and reducing the Creator to a mere Anima Mundi:[74] a scheme that has no advantage over Spinosism but its inconsistency, which does indeed make it suit a certain Order of Intellects, who, like the Pleuronectae (or Flat Fish) in Ichthyology that have both eyes on the same side,[75] never see but half of a subject at one time, and forgetting the one before they get to the other are sure not to detect any inconsistency between them.

And what has been the consequence? An increasing unwillingness to contemplate the Supreme Being in his *personal* Attributes: and thence a Distaste to all the peculiar Doctrines of the Christian Faith, the Trinity, the Incarnation of the Son of God, and Redemption. The young and ardent, ever too apt to mistake the inward triumph in the detection of error for a positive love of truth, are among the first and most frequent

----

[a] *AR* (1825): p 395

[72] Cf C's letter to John Edwards 20 Mar 1796: "How is it that Dr. Priestley is not an atheist?—He asserts in three different Places, that God not only *does*, but *is*, every thing.—But if God *be* every Thing, every Thing is God—: which is all, the Atheists assert—. An eating, drinking, lustful God—with no *unity* of *Consciousness*—these appear to me the unavoidable Inferences from his philosophy . . .": *CL* I 192–3. (For the next sentence in this letter see *Sp Aph B XIX* n 104 above.) C returns to the point repeatedly: cf *BL* ch 8 *(CC)* I 136, *P Lects* Lect 12 (1949) 352, notes on Sedgwick *Hints on Evangelical Preaching* (1808) i 102, ii 37: *LR* IV 331–2, 340–1, *CM (CC)* IV, and *Op Max ms* B3 ("II") 55. See also Boulger 12–15.

[73] Lucan *De bello civili* [*Pharsalia*] 9.580: "Jupiter est quodcumque vides, quodcumque moveris" ("Jupiter is everything that you see, every motion that you make"). C's tone was more favourable in 1807 when he cited this in a letter to DW to indicate the culmination he looked for from Davy's researches: "all human Knowlege will be Science and Metaphysics

the only Science". He continued there, however, "Yet after all, unless all this be identified with Virtue, as the ultimate and supreme Cause and Agent, all will be a worthless Dream": *CL* III 38. He quoted it also in *HEHL ms* 201.

[74] "Soul of the World". In a note on *Reliquiae Baxterianae* C comments: "No man in his senses can deny *God* in some sense or other, as *anima mundi, causa causarum*, &c., but it is the *personal, living, self-conscious* God, which it is so difficult, except by faith of the Trinity, to combine with an infinite being infinitely and irresistibly causative": *CM (CC)* I 242. See also *CM (CC)* I 180, *P Lects* Lect 2 (1949) 92, *Friend (CC)* I 505, and *Int Aph IX* n 1 above, citing lines from *The Eolian Harp*.

[75] C may first have met the scientific name (Linnaeus *Systema naturae*, 1758) in Oliver Goldsmith *An History of the Earth and Animated Nature* (new ed 1805) v 127, on "The Pleuronectes or Flat-Fish". He was using it in 1824: *CN* IV 5144 f 25ᵛ, 5174. Cf *CM (CC)* III 132. Earlier he transposed the Cyclops into an example of one-eyed backward vision: *LS (CC)* 43 and n.

victims to this epidemic *fastidium*.[76] Alas! even the sincerest seekers after light are not safe from the contagion.[77] Some have I known, constitutionally religious—I speak feelingly; for I speak of that which for a brief period was my own state—who under this unhealthful influence have been so estranged from the heavenly[a] *Father*, the *Living* God, as even to shrink from the personal [b]pronouns as applied to the Deity.[78] But many do I know, and yearly meet with, in whom a false and sickly *Taste* co-operates with the prevailing fashion: many, who find the God of Abraham, Isaac, and Jacob,[79] far too *real*, too substantial; who feel it more in harmony with their indefinite sensations

> "To worship NATURE in the hill and valley,
> Not knowing what they love:—"

and (to use the language, but not the sense or purpose[c] of the great Poet of our Age) would fain substitute for the Jehovah of their Bible

> "A sense sublime
> Of something far more deeply interfused,
> Whose dwelling is the Light of setting suns,
> And the round Ocean and the living Air;
> A Motion and a Spirit, that impels
> All thinking things, all objects of all thought,
> And rolls through all things!"
>
> WORDSWORTH[80]

And this from having been educated to understand the Divine Omni-

---

a   *AR* (1825): Heavenly
b   *AR* (1825): p 396
c   *AR* (1825): purpose,

---

[76] "Distaste".

[77] From the beginning of the next sentence to the words "rude and barbarous race!" in the next paragraph C draws heavily for his wording on a passage in *Op Max ms* B3 ("II") 51–2 which includes the passages from his own poetry and WW's, along with the mention of Priestley cited above in n 72.

[78] See C's letter to Matthew Coates 5 Dec 1803: ". . . you were the first man, from whom I heard that article of Faith distinctly enunciated, which is the nearest to my Heart, the pure Fountain of all [my] moral & religious Feelings & [C]omforts—I mean, the absolute Impersonality of the [D]eity. The Many would deem me an Atheist; alas! I know them to be Idolaters—": *CL* II 1022–3. He appears to have solved the problem, however (then or later), by making a distinction between the absolute Deity, who must be impersonal, and the personal Father and personal Son with whom human beings can enter into personal relationships. See above, *Sp Aph B XIX* nn 80–3, and below, App I Excursus Notes 17 and 18.

[79] See above, *Sp Aph B XXIIIa* n 24.

[80] From *Osorio*—see above, *Sp Aph B XXIIIb* n 26 and WW *Tintern Abbey* lines 95–102: *WPW* II 262. Line 99: "And the blue sky, and in the mind of man", omitted here, is inserted in COPY A.

presence in any sense rather than the alone safe and legitimate one, the presence of all things to God![81]

Be it, however, that the number of such men is *comparatively* small! And be it (as in fact it often *is*) but a brief stage, a transitional state, in the process of intellectual Growth! Yet among a numerous and increasing class of the higher and middle Ranks, there [a]is an inward withdrawing from the Life and Personal Being of God, a turning of the Thoughts exclusively to the so called physical Attributes, to the Omnipresence in the counterfeit form of Ubiquity,[82] to the Immensity, the Infinity, the Immutability!—the attributes of space[b] with a notion of Power as their Substratum!—A FATE, in short, not a Moral Creator and Governor! Let intelligence be imagined, and wherein does the conception of God differ essentially from that of Gravitation (conceived as the Cause of Gravity) in the understanding of those, who represent the Deity not only as a necessary but as a *necessitated* Being! those, for whom Justice is but a scheme of General Laws; and Holiness, and the divine Hatred of Sin, yea and Sin itself, are words without meaning or accommodations to a rude and barbarous race! Hence, I more than fear, the prevailing taste for Books of Natural Theology,[83] Physico-theology,[84] Demonstrations of God from Nature,[85] Evidences of Christianity,[86] &c. &c. *Evidences of Christianity!* I am weary of the Word.[87] Make a man feel the *want of*

---

[a] *AR* (1825): p 397
[b] *AR* (1825): Space

[81] For discussion of this passage see F. D. Maurice *The Kingdom of Christ* pt 2 ch 4 § 2 (2 vols 1843) II 104.

[82] C may be thinking of Priestley, who discusses a theory of God's omnipresence as his "power of *acting every where* though he *exists no where*": *Disquisitions relating to Matter and Spirit* (1777) 54.

[83] Cf William Paley *Natural Theology; or, Evidences of the Existence and Attributes of the Deity, Collected from the Appearances of Nature* (1802). See below, n 97.

[84] Cf William Derham *Physico-Theology; or, a Demonstration of the Being and Attributes of God, from His Works of Creation* (1713). For C's "keen delight" when he first read Derham's work and for his knowledge of it, see *Sp Aph B IX* at n 6.

[85] Cf John Ray on the Cartesian hypothesis: "This Opinion . . . supersedes and cassates the best *medium* we have to demonstrate the Being of a Deity . . .": *The Wisdom of God Manifested in the Works of the Creation* (1691) 22–3. For C's knowledge see *CN* I 1147 and n, 1616 f 74; III 4029. Cf also *Sp Aph B IX* n 9, above.

[86] Cf Paley *A View of the Evidences of Christianity* (1794).

[87] Cf *SM (CC)* 110 and n, in which the editor points out that in his Unitarian days C had relied on such evidences, *Lects 1795 (CC)* 169–90, and even helped J. P. Estlin with his *Evidences of Revealed Religion* (1796). By 1810 C was writing, "O it is a sad Symptom this perpetual Bustle about *evidences* . . .": *CN* III 3754 f 22ᵛ; cf 3817; but a few years later he dictated to Dr Brabant a piece (collected by HNC, *LR* I 386–9: *SW&F—CC*) instancing "Evidences of Christianity". In a notebook entry of Dec 1823 (*CN* IV 5065) C acknowledged a utility in such "forensic Defence" but "in the prevention of Infidelity rather than the re-

it; rouse him, if you can, to the self-knowledge of his *need* of it; and you may safely trust it to its own Evidence—remembering only the express declaration of Christ himself: No man cometh to me, unless the Father leadeth him![88] Whatever more is desirable—I speak now with reference to Christians generally, and not to professed[a] Students of Theology— may, in my judgment, be far more safely and profitably taught, without controversy or the supposition [b]of infidel antagonists, in the form of Ecclesiastical History.

The last fruit of the Mechanico-corpuscular Philosophy, say rather of the mode and direction of feeling and thinking produced by it on the educated class of society; or that result, which as more immediately connected with my present theme I have reserved for the last—is the habit of attaching all our conceptions and feelings, and of applying all the words and phrases expressing reality, to the objects of the Senses:[c] more accurately speaking, to the images and sensations by which their presence is made known to us.[89] Now I do not hesitate to assert, that it was one of the great purposes of Christianity, and included in the process of our Redemption, to rouse and emancipate the Soul from this debasing Slavery to the outward Senses, to awaken the mind to the true Criteria of Reality, viz. Permanence, Power, Will manifested in Act, and Truth

[a] *AR* (1825): profest
[b] *AR* (1825): p 398
[c] *AR* (1825): Senses;

moval''; in another, written after Jul 1824 (iv 5159), he again stressed rather that "the full, *positive* and satisfying Evidence of Christianity is by Grace and the influence of the Holy Ghost''. The impatience of the present entry was echoed in 1825 when he commented on the difference between speaking to simple straightforward Christians and to ''. . . the *educated* Blair-Sermon People, or the Clergy, with Evidences, Natural Theologies, and Bishop Prettyman alias Tomkins or the like on their Library Table . . .'': *CN* iv 5240 f 26ᵛ. On C and Paley see also n 97, below. Cf also *CN* iv 5067, 5158, 5264 and n. C's disparagement of ''evidences'' was approved by many subsequent readers; for an opposing view see E. J. Whately *Life and Correspondence of Richard Whately* (1866) ii 154–6. It was warmly endorsed, on the other hand, by Baden Powell in the essay ''On the Study of the Evidences of Christianity'' which he contributed to *Es-*

says and Reviews (1860; 10th ed 1862) 163–4.

[88] ''No man can come to me, except the Father which hath sent me draw him . . .'': John 6.44.

[89] This range of distinctions seems to have evolved early in C's thought, perhaps in response to Priestley's discussion of God's omnipresence (see above, n 82). See the lines (38–40) in *Reflections on Having Left a Place of Retirement* on a landscape: ''It seemed like Omnipresence! God, methought, | Had built him there a Temple: the whole World | Seem'd *imag'd* in its vast circumference . . .''. *PW* (EHC) i 107; also the theory in *The Destiny of Nations* (lines 44–7) of ''. . . one all-conscious Spirit, which informs | With absolute ubiquity of thought . . . | All his involved Monads . . .''. Particularly relevant is the phrase, derived from Cudworth, ''counterfeit infinity'': see *CN* i 273, *CL* i 349, and Beer *CPI* 155–6.

operating as Life. "My words," said Christ, "are Spirit:^{a} and they (*i.e.* the spiritual powers expressed by them) are Truth;"[90]—*i.e. very* Being. For this end our Lord, who came from Heaven to "take Captivity captive,"[91] chose the words and names, that designate the familiar yet most important Objects of Sense, the nearest and most concerning Things and Incidents of corporeal nature:—Water, Flesh, Blood, Birth, Bread! But he used them in Senses,^{b}[92] that could not without absurdity be supposed to respect the mere *phaenomena*, Water, Flesh, &c., ^{c}in senses that by no possibility could apply to the colour,^{d} figure, specific mode of Touch or Taste produced on ourselves, and by which we are made aware of the presence of the Things, and *understand* them—Res, quae *sub* apparitionibus istis *statuenda* sunt.[93] And this awful Recalling of the drowsed soul from the dreams and phantom world of sensuality to *actual* Reality,—how has it been evaded! These words, that were Spirit! these Mysteries, which even the Apostles must wait for the Paraclete, (*i.e.* the Helper, the Strengthener) in order to comprehend![94] these spiritual things which can only be *spiritually* discerned,[95]—were mere Metaphors, Figures of Speech, Oriental Hyperboles!^{e} "All this means *only* MORALITY!" Ah! how far nearer to the truth would these men have been, had they said that Morality means all this!

The effect, however, has been most injurious to the best interests of our Universities, to our incomparably constituted Church, and even to our National Character. The few who have read my two Lay-Sermons

^{a} *AR* (1825): Spirit;
^{b} *AR* (1825): senses,
^{c} *AR* (1825): p 399
^{d} *AR* (1825): Color,
^{e} *AR* (1825): Hyperboles.

[90] ". . . the words that I speak unto you, they are spirit, and they are life": John 6.63. Cf also John 4.24: "God is a Spirit: and they that worship him must worship him in spirit and in truth."

[91] Eph 4.8 (of Christ): "When he ascended up on high, he led captivity captive", a quotation from Ps 68.18.

[92] In a note in *C&S* C referred back to the discussion here in aid of his point that ". . . as the mistaking of symbols and analogies for metaphors . . . has been a main occasion and support of the worst errors in Protestantism; so the understanding the same symbols in a literal *i.e. phaenomenal* sense . . . was the rank wilding, on which . . . the lust of power and worldly aggrandizement, was enabled to graft, one by one, the whole branchery of papal superstition and imposture": *C&S (CC)* 120.

[93] "The Things, which are *to be stood under* those appearances". See above, *Int Aph XII* n 1.

[94] Cf John 14.16, quoted above as an epigraph to *Prel Sp Aph*. The Greek word translated as "Comforter" is παράκλητος, "intercessor". It is also rendered as "advocate" in 1 John 2.1; see above, *Sp Aph B XIX* n 52.

[95] "But the natural man receiveth not the things of the Spirit of God . . . neither can he know them, because they are spiritually discerned": 1 Cor 2.14. See above, p 77.

are no strangers to my opinions on this head; and in my Treatise on the Church and Churches, I shall, if Providence vouchsafe, submit them to the Public, with their grounds and historic evidences in a more systematic form.[96]

I have, I am aware, in this present work furnished occasion for a charge of having expressed myself with slight and irreverence of celebrated Names, especially of the late Dr. Paley.[97] O, if I were fond and ambitious of literary Honor, of public Applause, how well content [a]should I be to excite but one third of the admiration which, in my inmost Being, I feel for the head and heart of PALEY! And how gladly would I surrender all hope of contemporary praise, could I even approach to the incomparable grace, propriety, and persuasive facility of his writings! But on this very account I believe[b] myself bound in conscience to throw the whole force of my intellect in the way of this triumphal Car, on which the tutelary Genius of modern Idolatry is borne, even at the risk of being crushed under the wheels! I have at this moment before my eyes the 343d—344th pages of his Posthumous Discourses: the amount of which is briefly this,—that all the words and passages in the New Testament which express and contain the *peculiar* doctrines of Christianity, the paramount objects of the Christian Revelation, "all

---

[a] *AR* (1825): p 400
[b] *AR* (1825): believed

[96] See above, n 17, for another reference overtaken, in part at least, by the publication of *C&S* in 1829.

[97] See above, *Sp Aph B Xb* at n 34, *XXIIIa* at nn 3, 16, 21, and *XXIIIb* at n 31; also *Conc* at nn 83, 86–7. C attacked Paley's doctrines only rarely in his published work but hostile references appeared in his private writings from an early date. Although in 1793, as an undergraduate, he had been willing to call Paley "that great and good man" (*CL* I 48) and in 1795 to use his *Evidences* (1794) for his lectures (*Lects 1795—CC—*169–73 etc), his opposition to Paley's defence of "secret influences" in the same year (*Lects 1795—CC—*69, 222) was followed by many attacks on his doctrines: see e.g. his early plan to write "Strictures on Godwin, Paley &c &c" (*CN* I 161) and his view of him in 1801 as one of the ". . . corrupters & poisoners of all moral sense & dignity" (*CL* II 720), followed by attacks on the ethical doctrines as ". . . vile cowardly selfish calculating" (*CN* II 2627) and as degrading ". . . the spirit of honor into a mere club-

law among the higher classes originating in selfish convenience": *Friend (CC)* I 425. Cf also the 1809 *Friend (CC)* II 72, 103, 313; *SM (CC)* 110; *LS (CC)* 186–7; *C&S (CC)* 68, and, for a general discussion, Boulger 20–36. The Indexes of *CL* and *CN* s.v. Paley lead to many more such references. For respectful comments see e.g. *CL* II 949, *Logic (CC)* 198. Increasingly C made his prime argument against Paley the point on the previous page concerning "spiritual discernment": for example, in a later note on 1 Cor 12.3 (which ends ". . . no man can say that Jesus is the Lord, but by the Holy Ghost") he remarks, "How little have our latter Divines, of the School of Paley & Watson, meditated on the last clause of this verse. If only by the Spirit, then assuredly not by arguments of the common Understanding grounded on miracles, which may indeed attest the historic manifestation of the great Idea of Christ's Divinity, but can never *give* it": *CM (CC)* I 462. Cf an annotation on Böhme, ibid 683. This idea dominates C's view of "thinking" as developed below.

those which speak so strongly of the value, benefit, and efficacy, of the Death of Christ,'' assuredly mean *something:*[a] but *what* they mean, nobody, it seems[b] can tell! But doubtless we shall discover it, and be convinced that there is a substantial sense belonging to these words—in a future state![98] Is there an enigma, or an absurdity, in the Koran or the Vedas which might not be defended on the same pretence? A similar impression, I confess, was left on my mind by Dr. Magee's statement or exposition (*ad normam Grotianam*) of the doctrine of Redemption;[99] and deeply did it disappoint the high expectations, sadly did it chill the fervid sympathy, which his introductory chapter, his manly and masterly [c]disquisition on the sacrificial rites of Paganism, had raised in my mind.[100]

And yet I cannot read the pages of Paley,[101] here referred to, aloud,

---

[a] *AR* (1825): *something;*
[b] *AR* (1825): seems,
[c] *AR* (1825): p 401

---

[98] Paley *Sermons on Several Subjects* (1815) 343–4: "We may be assured, that these expressions mean something real; refer to something real: though it be something, which is to take place in that future dispensation, of which we have been speaking. It is reasonable to expect, that, when we come to experience what that state is, the same experience will open to us the distinct propriety of these expressions, their truth, and the substantial truth which they contain; and likewise show us, that however strong and exalted the terms are which we see made use of, they are not stronger nor higher than the subject called for. But for the present we must be, what I own it is difficult to be, content to take up with very general notions, humbly hoping, that a disposition to receive and to acquiesce in what appears to us to be revealed, be it more or be it less, will be regarded as the duty which belongs to our subsisting condition, and the measure of information with which it is favoured: and will stand in the place of what, from our deep interest in the matter, we are sometimes tempted to desire, but which, nevertheless, might be unfit for us, a knowledge, which not only was, but which we perceived to be, fully adequate to the subject." Paley's statements refer primarily to knowledge of the future dispensation, but he also states on p 343, just before the above quotation, "Of this kind are many, if not all, of those ex-pressions, which speak so strongly of the value, and benefit, and efficacy of the death of Christ; of its sacrificial, expiatory, and atoning nature."

[99] For the work by William Magee (1766–1831) "on the Grotian pattern" see *Discourses and Dissertations on the Scriptural Doctrines of Atonement & Sacrifice* (2 vols Dublin 1809). In 1826 C again discussed Magee's theory of the Redemption as "an arbitrary act, as one way chosen out of many, by which the same result might have been secured": *CN* IV 5389 f 69ᵛ; cf 5215 f 25.

[100] In his *Logic* C commented in relation to Hume: ". . . to such an *exposure* of the fallacy of his *conclusions* by a fair *exposition* of the assertions on which they are grounded, as the Archbishop of Dublin (Dr Magee) has given in his work on redemption I have paid my full tribute of applause": *Logic (CC)* 192n. The reference is to vol II pt i pp 265–97. In BM MS Egerton 2801 f 260 (watermark 1820), nevertheless, he is described as a "Prig of Preferment" and a "modern Episcopal Arminian" (cf N 35 f 30ᵛ: *CN* v). See also *CM (CC)* I 262, and the "Mageeites" of *CL* VI 902. He might be the "Dʳ M" of *CN* III 4140, also: see the editor's note. The "disquisition" referred to is probably No V, I 96–129.

[101] For the whole of this paragraph C draws on a notebook of 1824: *CN* IV 5195.

without the liveliest sense;[a] how plausible and popular they will sound
to the great majority of Readers! Thousands of sober, and in their way
pious, Christians, will echo the words, together with Magee's kindred
interpretation of the Death of Christ, and adopt the doctrine for their
Make-faith![102] And why? It is feeble. And whatever is feeble is always
plausible: for it favors[b] mental indolence. It is feeble: and feebleness in
the disguise of confessing and condescending Strength is always popular. It flatters the Reader, by removing the apprehended distance between him and the superior Author; and it flatters him still more by enabling him to transfer to himself, and to appropriate, this superiority:
and thus to make his very weakness the mark and evidence of his
strength. Ay, quoth the *rational*[c] Christian—or with a sighing, self-
soothing sound between an Ay and an Ah!—*I* am content to think, with
the *Great* Dr. Paley, and the learned Archbishop of Dublin——

Man of Sense! Dr. Paley *was* a great Man, and Dr. Magee *is* a learned
and exemplary Prelate; but You do not *think* at all!

With regard to the convictions avowed and enforced in my own work,
I will continue my address to the Man of Sense in the words of an old
Philosopher:—"Tu vero[d] crassis auribus et obstinato corde respuis quae
forsitan vere[e] perhibeantur. Minus hercule[f] calles, [g]pravissimis opinio-
nibus *ea putari mendacia, quae vel auditu nova, vel visu rudia, vel
certe*[h] *supra captum cogitationis extemporaneae tuae ardua videan-
tur:* quae si paulo accuratius exploraris,[i] non modo compertu evidentia,
sed etiam factu facilia, senties." APUL: 1.1.[j103]

  [a] *AR* (1825): sense:
  [b] *AR* (1825): favours
  [c] COPY D: *rational, sensible*
  [d] *AR* (1825): verò
  [e] *AR* (1825): verè
  [f] *AR* (1825): herculè
  [g] *AR* (1825): p 402
  [h] *AR* (1825): *certè*
  [i] *AR* (1825): exploràris,
  [j] *AR* (1825): On line below: S. T. COLERIDGE.

[102] *OED* cites as nonceword.

[103] Apuleius *Metamorphoses* 1.3; tr W.
Adlington (1566) rev S. Gaselee (LCL
1915): "You, perhaps, that are of gross
ears and an obstinate mind, mock and contemn those things which are perchance
really the truth; know you not, i' faith, that
those things are accounted untrue by the
false opinion of men, which are either seldom heard or rarely seen, or are so high
that they pass the capacity of [your unpre-
pared] reason? The which if you scan them
more narrowly, you shall not only find
them evident to the understanding, but
even very easy to be brought to pass." For
editions used by C see above, *Sp Aph B Xb*
n 64. He inserted the words "extemporaneae tuae" and substituted "sed" for
"verum".

^{a}IN compliance with the suggestion of a judicious friend, the celebrated conclusion of the fourth Book of Paley's Moral and Political Philosophy, cited in p. 342 of this Volume, is here transprinted[104] for the convenience of the Reader:—

"Had Jesus Christ delivered no other declaration than the following— 'The hour is coming, in the which all that are in the grave shall hear his voice, and shall come forth: they that have done good, unto the resurrection of life; and they that have done evil, unto the resurrection of damnation;'[105]—he had pronounced a message of inestimable importance, and well worthy of that splendid apparatus of prophecy and miracles with which his mission was introduced, and attested: a message in which the wisest of mankind would rejoice to find an answer to their doubts, and rest to their inquiries. It is idle to say, that a future state had been discovered already:—it had been discovered as the Copernican System was;—it was one guess among many. He alone discovers, who *proves;* and no man can prove this point, but the teacher who testifies by miracles that his doctrine comes from God."

Paedianus says of Virgil,—"Usque adeo^b expers invidiae, ut siquid erudite^c dictum inspiceret alterius, non minus gauderet ac si suum esset."[106] My own heart assures me, that this is less than the truth: that Virgil ^{d}would have read a beautiful passage in the work of another with

^{a} *AR* (1825): p 403
^{b} *AR* (1825): adeó
^{c} *AR* (1825): eruditè
^{d} *AR* (1825): p 404

[104] In a letter to Taylor and Hessey, dated by the editor "early May 1825", presumably on the basis of its contents, C asks for the second half of a previous letter to be sent ". . . with the *second* Volume of Paley and the corrected Proof" to the printer: *CL* v 432. The reference to the second volume and the punctuation of the quotation suggest that the 1814 ed, where this is at II 106–7, or an equivalent, was sent. The word "fourth" should read "fifth" (i.e. bk v ch 9). "Transprint" here is *OED*'s only example of the verb.

[105] John 5.28–9, which reads "graves" for "grave".

[106] This is from the Life of Virgil attributed to Aelius Donatus, usually prefixed to editions of his works. Tr: "[Pedianus also reporteth] that if he sawe any thing done, or spoken learnedly by any, he reioyced thereat, none other-wise than if it were his owne . . .": *XII Bookes of Aeneidos* tr T. Phaer and T. Twine (1593). In 1811 C wrote it down in a notebook, applying it to himself in the same terms as here: "I dare say more of myself—that I more delighted; because I was more free from the fear that Self-partiality might blind me, more free from that inward Sympathy of Shame from the suspicions that I might be so blinded": *CN* III 4125 and n. He had probably turned back to his notebook before reworking his idea here. For another quotation from this Life of Virgil see *BL* ch 2 *(CC)* I 46 and n.

a higher and purer delight than in a work of his own, because free from the apprehension of his judgment being warped by self-love, and without that repressive modesty akin to shame, which in a delicate mind holds in check a man's own secret thoughts and feelings, when they respect himself. The cordial admiration with which I peruse the preceding passage as *a master-piece of Composition* would, could I convey it, serve as a measure of the vital importance I attach to the convictions which impelled me to animadvert on the same passage as *doctrine.*[a][107]

THE END

<hr>

[a] *AR* (1825): On line below: S. T. C.

[107] *AR* (1825) COPY K contains a note on the blank space remaining at this point, beginning "Is a Mad *Soul* a possible conception? Is Madness (a *Mania*, not rabies or frenzy) conceivable in an unsouled Body? . . .", going on to discuss madness in animals ("Sir Samuel Raffles's Uran Utan was the only Beast, I have ever heard of, who went mad—melancholy-mad and hung itself . . .") and concluding, "Ought any man, tho' he could go into public with as enormous a *tail* as Dr. Granville, to write a Book on Insanity, unless he has devoted a full year at least to the meaning of words? . . .": transcribed Christie's Sale Catalogue 29 Nov 1978. The note is cancelled with a pen-stroke. For Sir Stamford Raffles (1781–1826) see *TT* 7 May 1830 *(CC)* I 123 and n (1836 vn, dated 11 May, II 86) and *CN* IV 4833n. His pet monkey is mentioned in the *Memoir* (1830) written by his widow (pp 447, 476–7), but the source of this anecdote has not been traced.

The reference to the "tail" of Dr Granville (A. B. Granville, 1783–1872, physician) is to the number of letters after his name, as on the title-page of his *The Catechism of Health* (3rd ed 1832): "F.R.S., F.L.S., F.A.S., F.G.S., M.R.I., &c, &c, &c". For the usage cf Title–page n 1, above.

^{a}APPENDIX^1

A SYNOPTICAL SUMMARY OF THE SCHEME OF THE ARGUMENT TO
PROVE THE DIVERSITY IN KIND, OF THE REASON AND THE UNDER-
STANDING. SEE P. 236.

The Position to be proved is the *difference in kind* of the Understanding
from the Reason.

The Axiom, on which the Proof rests, is: Subjects, that require essentially different General Definitions, differ *in kind* and not merely *in degree*. For difference *in degree* forms the ground of *specific* definitions,
but not of *generic* or general.

Now Reason is considered either in relation to the Will and Moral
Being, when it is termed the * Practical Reason = A: or relatively, to
the intellective and Sciential Faculties, when it is termed Theoretic or
Speculative Reason = *a*. In order therefore to be compared with the
Reason; the Understanding must in like manner be distinguished into
The Understanding as a Principle of *Action,* in which relation I call it
the Adaptive Power, or the faculty of selecting and adapting Means to
Medial or proximate ends = B: and the Understanding, as a mode and
faculty of Thought, when it is called REFLECTION = *b*. Accordingly, I
give the General Definitions of these four: that is, I describe each severally by its *essential characters:* and I find, that the Definition of
A differs *toto genere* from that of B, and the Definition of *a* from that
of *b*.

Now subjects that require essentially different &c. do themselves differ in kinds. But Understanding, and Reason, require ess. diff. &c.
Therefore Understanding and Reason differ in kind. Q.E.D.^{b}

* N.B. The Practical Reason alone *is* Reason in the full and substantive sense. It is
reason in its own Sphere of *perfect freedom;* as the source of IDEAS, which *Ideas,* in their
conversion to the responsible Will, become Ultimate Ends. On the other hand, Theoretic
Reason, as the ground of the Universal and Absolute in all Logical *Conclusion,* is rather
the *Light* of Reason in the *Understanding,* and known to be such by its contrast with the
contingency and particularity which characterize all the proper and indigenous growths of
the Understanding.

$^{a-b}$ Added in 1831

^{1} For the provenance of this "Appendix", which was not in *AR* (1825), see below, App D(a).

413

EDITOR'S APPENDIXES

PRINTED SOURCES OF
AIDS TO REFLECTION

PRINTED SOURCES OF
AIDS TO REFLECTION

THIS SECTION gathers together passages from printed works which Coleridge reproduced in some form for his work on *Aids to Reflection* and which are too long to be given conveniently in the footnotes to the text above. Other passages, including some from his own work used again for *Aids to Reflection* and his markings and notes in volumes of the 1820 edition of Leighton's *Whole Works* now in the British Library, are simply cross-referenced in the main text, since they can be found in other volumes of the *Collected Coleridge*: the marked Leighton passages, for example, form part of a long and complex entry in volume III of the *Marginalia*. The passages from Leighton reproduced here are ones which were not marked by Coleridge in the original volumes. (In some cases it is possible that he used James Gillman's copy of Leighton—COPY B in *CM(CC)* III—to make transcripts for the later extracts, but the evidence from the small textual variants between the two editions, while not conclusive, suggests that COPY C was used throughout.)

Passages from Coleridge's manuscript which were used by the printer and are extant appear in the following section, Appendix B.

(a) Leighton COPY C IV 190. See above, *Int Aph VI*.

From Introduction to Theological Lectures.

But that you may be capable of this supernatural light and heavenly instruction, it is, first of all, absolutely necessary, that your minds be called off from foreign objects, and turned in upon themselves; for, as long as your thoughts are dispersed and scattered in pursuit of vanity and insignificant trifles, he that would lay before them the principles and precepts of this spiritual wisdom, would commit them, like the sibyl's prophecies, that were written on loose leaves of trees, to the mercy of the inconstant winds, and thereby render them entirely useless.

(b) Ibid 190, 191. See above, *Int Aph VIII*.

It is certainly a matter of great difficulty, and requires uncommon art, to fix the thoughts of men, especially of young men and boys, and turn them in upon themselves. We read in the parable of the Gospel concerning the prodigal son, that, first of all, *he came to himself*, and then returned to his father. It is certainly a very considerable step towards conversion to God, to have the mind fixed upon itself, and disposed to think seriously of its own immediate concerns . . .

It is the advice of the Psalmist, that we should *converse much with ourselves*: an advice, indeed, which is regarded by few; for the greatest part of mankind are no where greater strangers than at home.

(c) Henry More *An Explanation of the Grand Mystery of Godliness*, in *Theological Works* (1708) 372. See above, *Prel Sp Aph* at n 27.

These things I could not forbear to write, as being very much pressed in Spirit thereunto. For *the Light within me*, that is, *my Reason and Conscience*, does assure me that the Ancient and Apostolick Faith according to the *Historical* Meaning thereof is very solid and true; and that the Offices of Christ are never to be antiquated till his visible Return to Judgment according to the *literal* Sense of the Creed; and that *Familism* is a mere Flam of the Devil, a smooth Tale to seduce the Simple from their Allegeance to Christ.

(d) Ibid 368. See above, *Sp Aph A I*.

For that *tedious Buz and Noise of the Spirit* has now, I think, made it self so ridiculous and contemptible, that no prudent Man will listen to such lazy Impostures. Every one is *to give a Reason of his Faith*; but Priests or Ministers more punctually than any; their Province being to make good every Sentence of the Bible to a rational Enquirer into the Truth of those Oracles. Who therefore can sufficiently attend these things, and be to seek for Bread for himself and his Family? How unjust and sordid a Temper therefore are those Persons of, that could be content to leave the Clergy to work for their Living? Any inferiour Fellow may talk and prate Phrases and make Faces, but when a sober Man would be satisfied of the Grounds from whence they speak, he shall not have one Syllable or the least Tittle of an Answer, only they will talk big of the *Spirit*, and inveigh against *Reason* with bitter Reproaches, calling it *carnal* though it be indeed no soft Flesh but hard and penetrant Steel, and such as pierces them to the very Heart, for all their Contempt and slighting of it.

(e) Ibid 368. See above, *Sp Aph A II*.

And verily while I consider the Unreasonableness and ill Consequence of this Kind of *Enthusiasm*, I cannot but think the Vigilancy of the Christian Magistrate should extend to this also amongst other things, namely, to suppress and keep under all Sects and Religions that hold of so fanatick a Tenour, that is to say, that profess they believe against the Christian Faith from the Illumination of such a Spirit as they can give no Account of, *viz*. such as does not *illuminate* their Reason, whereby their Doctrine may be *accountable* and *intelligible* to others, but only *heat* them and make them furious against the Christian Church. For besides the hazarding of making a whole Nation mad (for seriously it is an infectious Disease, if not the very possession of the Devil) there may some dam-nable Plot lie under it against Christianity and the State. For it is a more easie thing to *heat the Fancies* of the Vulgar, than to *inform their Judgments*; though this tends to sober Edification, that to Confusion and Destruction. In brief, there are these two very bad things in this resolving of Matters into *the immediate Suggestion of the Spirit* not acting upon our Understandings. First, it defaces and makes useless that Part of the Image of God in us which we call *Reason*: and secondly, it takes away that special Advantage that Christianity has above all other Religions, that she dare appeal to so solid a Faculty. And therefore he that takes away the Use of *Reason* in Religion, treacherously undermines Christianity, and laies it as low as the basest Superstition that ever appeared in the World.

(f) Ibid 369. See above, *Sp Aph A IV*.

For tell me, O ye high-flown *Perfectionists*, and ye great Boasters of the *Light within you*, Could the highest Perfection of your inward Light every shew to you the histories of past Ages, the Universal State of the World at present, the Knowledge of Arts and Tongues, without any external Helps of either Books or Teachers? How then can you understand the Providence of God, the Purpose of Prophecies and the authority of that Religion which God has peculiarly ap-pointed us to walk in, without external Assistances? How can you make a due Judgment of the Truth of Christianity, without a rational Explication of the Prophecies that foretold the coming of Christ, without weighing what may be said concerning the Authentickness and Uncorruptedness of his History in the Gospels, and without considering the reasonableness of all those miraculous Matters there recorded concerning him, and of what is behind for him to perform at his visible Return to judge the quick and the dead? No *Light within you*, unassisted of *Helps without*, and of the knowledge of History, Tongues, and Sciences, and careful Exercise of Reason, that excellent Gift of God to Man-kind, can ever make you competent Judges of this Matter.

(g) Ibid 372–3. See above, *Sp Aph A V* and *Sp Aph A VI* n 8.

And therefore I beseech every Man in these Days of Liberty to take Heed how they turn in thither, especially those that are of an *Enthusiastick* Temper, such as are most of the honester and beter-meaning *Quakers*. For if in their bewildred Wandrings they take up their Inn here, let them look to it that they be not robbed of all the Articles of the Christian Faith, and be stripped into naked Infidelity and Paganism, and (which is worst of all) be so intoxicated with the Cup of this Inchantress, as to think this Injury their Gain, and to prefer false Liberty before their Christian Simplicity, and those gaudy and phantastick Titles of being *Dei-fied* and *begodded* before the real Possession of Christian Truth and Godliness.

. . . for mine own Part, I have ever had so right a Sense and touch upon my Spirit of their Condition, that I think none more worthy of a man's best Direc-tions than they; the most imperious Sects having put such unhandsom Vizards upon Christianity, that they have frighted and driven away these Babes that seem to me very desirous of the sincere Milk of the Word. Which having been every where so sophisticated by the Humours and Inventions of Men, it has driven these anxious Melancholists to seek for *a Teacher within*, and to cast themselves upon him who they know will not deceive them, the Voice of the Eternal Word within them; to which if they be faithful, they assure themselves he will be faithful to them again. Which is no groundless Presumption of theirs, it supposing nothing but what is very closely consistent with the Nature of God and his Providence. And truly as many of them as do persist in that serious and impartial Desire of such Knowledge as tends to Life and Godliness, I do not question but that God will in his due time lead them into the Truth, and that they will be *more confirmed Christians* than ever.

10. Which Success of theirs will be more speedy and sure, if (as they set themselves against other Vices, so) they mainly bend their Force against Spiritual *Pride* and Affectation of Peculiarity in Religion, and of finding themselves wiser in the Mysteries thereof than the best of Christians have pretended to. And above all things if they beware of *Enthusiasm* either in themselves or others, or of thinking that the Gift of the Spirit can be any Revelation that is contrary to Reason or the acknowledged History of Christ, the Truth thereof being so rationally evincible to all such as apply themselves without Prejudice to examine it to the Bottom. If in Pursuance of their sincere Intentions they keep off from these Rocks, I doubt not but they will at length return safe again to *Jesus Christ* the great Pastor and Bishop of their Souls.

(h) John Hacket *A Century of Sermons* (1675) 449. See above, *Sp Aph A VI.*

When every man is his own end, all things will come to a bad end. Blessed were those days, when every man thought himself rich and fortunate by the good success of the publick wealth and glory. We want publick souls, we want them, I speak it with compassion, there is no sin or abuse in the world that afflicts my thought so much. Every man thinks that he is a whole Commonwealth in his private Family. *Omnes quae sua sunt quaerunt*; All seek their own. Did St. *Paul* write it against us, or against the *Philippians*? *Chap*.ii.21. Can the Publick be neglected and any mans Private be secure. It is all one whether the mischief light upon him or his Posterity. There are some, says *Tully*, that think their own Gardens and Fishponds shall be safe when the Commonwealth is lost. Doth he not call them fools by craft? Away with this *bonum nobis*, to intend our own good rather than the general, it was the greatest error that St. *Peter* committed.

(i) Thomas Plume *Life of Hacket*, prefixed to John Hacket *A Century of Sermons* (1675) xliii–xliv. See above, *Sp Aph B II* at n 6.

In the *Quinquarticular* Controversie he was ever very moderate, but being bred under *Bishop Davenant*, and *Dr. Ward* in *Cambridge*, was addicted to *their Sentiments*. *Bishop Usher* would say *Davenant* understood those Controversies better than ever any man did since *St. Austin*; but He used to say, he was sure he had *three* excellent men of his mind in *this Controversie*. 1. *Padre Paulo*, whose Letter is extant to *Heinsius Anno* 1604. 2. *Thomas Aquinas*. 3. *St. Austin*;

but besides and above them all, he believed in his conscience *St. Paul* was of the same mind likewise; yet would profess withal, he disliked no *Arminian*, but such a one as reviled and defamed every one that was *not so*, and would often commend *Arminius* himself for his excellent wit and parts, but only tax his want of reading and knowledg in Antiquity, and ever held it was the foolishest thing in the world to say the *Arminians* were *Papists*, when so many *Dominicans* and *Jansenists* were no *Arminians*; and so again to say the *Anti-Arminians* were *Puritans*, or *Presbyterians*, when *Ward*, and *Davenant*, and Prideaux, and *Brownrig* were Anti-Arminians, and also stout Champions for *Episcopacy*; and *Arminius* himself was ever a *Presbyterian*, and therefore much commended the moderation of our *Church*, which made not any of these nice and doubtful Opinions the *resolved Doctrin* of the *Church*; this he judg'd was the great fault of the *Tridentine* and late *Westminster* Assemblies: But our *Church* was more ingenuous, and left these dark and curious points to the several apprehensions of learned men, and extended equal Communion to both.

(j) G. Burnet *History of the Reformation* II (1683) xviii. See above, *Sp Aph B III*.

From the Preface.

That Religion is chiefly designed for perfecting the nature of Man, for improving his Faculties, governing his Actions, and securing the Peace of every Mans Conscience, and of the societies of Mankind in common, is a truth so plain, that without further arguing about it all will agree to it. Every part of Religion is then to be judged by its Relation to the main ends of it; and since the Christian Doctrine was revealed from Heaven, as the most perfect and proper way that ever was, for the advancing the good of Mankind, nothing can be a part of this holy Faith but what is proportioned to the end for which it was designed.

(k) Richard Hooker *Works* (1682) 521. See above, *Sp Aph B VI*.

What is Virtue, but a Medicine, and Vice, but a Wound? Yet we have so often deeply wounded our selves with Medicine; that God hath been fain to make wounds medicinable; to cure by Vice where Virtue hath strucken; to suffer the just man to fall, that being raised, he may be taught what Power it was which upheld him standing: I am not afraid to affirm it boldly with St. *Augustine*, That men puffed up through a proud opinion of their own Sanctity and Holiness, receive a benefit at the hands of God, and are assisted with his Grace, when with his Grace they are not assisted, but permitted, and that grievously to transgress; whereby, as they were in over-great liking of themselves supplanted, so the dislike of that which did supplant them, may establish them afterwards the surer. Ask the very Soul of *Peter*, and it shall undoubtedly make you it self this Answer; my eager Protestations, made in the glory of my ghostly strength, I am ashamed of; but those Crystal tears wherewith my sin and weakness was bewailed, have procured my endless joy; my Strength hath been my Ruine, and my Fall my Stay.

(l) Richard Baxter *Reliquiae Baxterianae* (1696) pt i 131–2. See
above, *Sp Aph B VIIIa* at n 23.

My Censures of the Papists do much differ from what they were at first: I then
thought that their Errours in the *Doctrines of Faith* were their most dangerous
Mistakes, as in the Points of Merit, Justification by Works, Assurance of Salvation, the Nature of Faith, &c. But now I am assured that their mis-expressions,
and mis-understanding us, with our mistakings of them, and inconvenient expressing our own Opinions, hath made the difference in these Points to appear
much greater than they are; and that in some of them it is next to none at all. But
the great and unreconcilable Differences lye, in their Church Tyranny and Usurpations, and in their great Corruptions and Abasement of God's Worship, together with their befriending of *Ignorance* and *Vice*. At first I thought that Mr.
Perkins well proved that a Papist cannot go beyond a Reprobate: but now I doubt
not but that God hath many sanctified Ones among them, who have received the
true Doctrine of Christianity so practically, that their contradictory Errours prevail not against them, to hinder their Love of God, and their Salvation: but that
their Errours are like a conquerable Dose of Poyson which Nature doth overcome. And I can never believe that a Man may not be saved by that Religion,
which doth but bring him to the true Love of God, and to a heavenly Mind and
Life: nor that God will ever cast a Soul into Hell that truly loveth him. Also at
first it would disgrace any Doctrine with me, if I did but hear it called Popery
and Antichristian: but I have long learned to be more impartial, and to dislike
Men for bad Doctrine, rather than the Doctrines for the Men; and to know that
Satan can use even the Names of Popery and Antichrist, against a Truth.

(m) Jeremy Taylor *Deus Justificatus* (1673) in Σύμβολον Θεολογικόν,
or a Collection of Polemicall Discourses (1674) 869–70. See
above, *Sp Aph B Xb*.

But first (Madam) be pleased to remember that the question is not whether
there be any such thing as *Original Sin*; for it is certain, and confessed on all
hands almost. For my part, I cannot but confess that to be which I feel, and
groan under, and by which all the World is miserable.

Adam turned his back upon the Sun, and dwelt in the dark and the shadow; he
sinned, and fell into Gods displeasure, and was made naked of all his supernatural endowments, and was ashamed and sentenced to death, and deprived of the
means of long life, and of the Sacrament and instrument of Immortality, I mean
the Tree of Life; he then fell under the evils of a sickly body, and a passionate,
ignorant, uninstructed soul; his sin made him sickly, his sickness made him
peevish, his sin left him ignorant, his ignorance made him foolish and unreasonable: His sin left him to his nature, and by his nature, who ever was to be born
at all, was to be born a child, and to do before he could understand, and be bred
under Laws, to which he was always bound, but which could not always be
exacted; and he was to chuse, when he could not reason, and had passions most
strong, when he had his understanding most weak, and was to ride a wild horse
without a bridle, and the more need he had of a curb, the less strength he had to
use it, and this being the case of all the World, what was *every mans* evil, became all mens greater evil; and though alone it was very bad, yet when they

came together it was made much worse; like Ships in a storm, every one alone hath enough to do to out-ride it; but when they meet, besides the evils of the storm, they find the intolerable calamity of their mutual concussion, and every Ship that is ready to be oppressed with the tempest, is a worse tempest to every vessel, against which it is violently dashed. So it is in mankind, every man hath evil enough of his own; and it is hard for a man to live soberly, temperately, and religiously; but when he hath Parents and Children, Brothers and Sisters, Friends and Enemies, Buyers and Sellers, Lawyers and Physicians, a Family and a Neighbourhood, a King over him, or Tenants under him, a Bishop to rule in matters of Government spiritual, and a People to be ruled by him in the affairs of their Souls; then it is that every man dashes against another, and one relation requires what another denies; and when one speaks, another will contradict him; and that which is well spoken, is sometimes innocently mistaken, and that upon a good cause produces an evil effect, and by these, and ten thousand other concurrent causes, man is made more than most miserable.

(n) Jeremy Taylor *Unum Necessarium* in Σύμβολον Θεολογικόν 711. See above, *Sp Aph B Xb* at n 52.

. . . and therefore it was no wonder that upon the sin of *Adam* death entred upon the world, who generally sinn'd like *Adam*, since it passed on and reigned upon less sinners. It reigned upon them whose sins therefore would not be so imputed as *Adams* was, because there was no law with an express threatning given to them as was to *Adam*; but although it was not wholly imputed upon their own account, yet it was imputed upon theirs and *Adams*. For God was so exasperated with Mankind, that *being angry* he would still continue that punishment even to the lesser sins and sinners, which he only had first threatned to *Adam*: and *so Adam brought it upon them*. They indeed in rigour did themselves deserve it, but if it had not been for that provocation by *Adam*, they who sinn'd not so bad, and had not been so severely and expresly threatned, had not suffer'd so severely. The case is this. *Jonathan* and *Michal* were *Sauls* children; it came to pass that seven of *Sauls* issue were to be hanged, all equally innocent, equally culpable. *David* took the five sons of *Michal*, for she had left him unhandsomly. *Jonathan* was his friend, and therefore he spar'd his son *Mephibosheth*. Here it was indifferent as to the guilt of the persons, whether *David* should take the sons of *Michal*, or of *Jonathan*; but it is likely that as upon the kindness which *David* had to *Jonathan* he spar'd his son, so upon the just provocation of *Michal* he made that evil to fall upon them, of which they were otherwise capable, which it may be they should not have suffered, if their Mother had been kind. *Adam was to God, as Michal to David.*

(o) Luther *Colloquia Mensalia* (1652) 190. See above, *Sp Aph B XV*.

That it is a difficult thing in trials and temptations, to contemn the curs and the burthen of the Law.

I T is (said *Luther*) a very hard matter; yea, an unpossible thing for thy humane strength, whosoëver thou art (without God's assistance) that (at such a time when *Moses* setteth upon thee with his Law, and fearfully affrighteth thee, accuseth and condemneth thee, threatneth thee with God's wrath and death) thou shouldest as then bee of such a minde; namely, as if no Law nor sin had ever been at anie time; I saie, it is in a manner a thing unpossible, that a humane creature should carrie himself in such a sort, when hee is and feeleth himself assaulted with trials and temptations, and when the conscience hath to do with God, as then to think no otherwise, then that from everlasting nothing hath been, but onely and alone Christ, altogether Grace and deliverance.

(p) Leighton COPY C II 124; 125–6; 127. See above, *Sp Aph B XVI*.

From commentary on 1 Peter 3.18.

"For Christ also hath once suffered for sins, the just for the unjust, (that he might bring us to God,) being put to death in the flesh, but quickened by the Spirit."

. . . The whole man suffers death, a dissolution, or taking to pieces, and the soul suffers a separation, or dislodging; but death, or the privation of life and sense, belongs particularly to the flesh or body. But the *Spirit*, here opposed to the *flesh* or body, is certainly of a higher nature and power than is the human soul, which cannot of itself return to re-inhabit and quicken the body.

Put to death.] His death was both voluntary and violent. That same power which restored His life, could have kept it exempted from death; but the design was for death. He therefore took our flesh, to put it off thus, and to offer it up as a sacrifice, which, to be acceptable, must of necessity be free and voluntary; and, in that sense, He is said to have died even by that same Spirit, which here, in opposition to death, is said to quicken him. See Heb. ix. 14. . . .

Thus, then, there was in His death, external violence joined with internal willingness. But what is there to be found but complications of wonders in our Lord Jesus? Oh! high inconceivable mystery of godliness! *God manifested in the flesh!* Nothing in this world so strange and sweet as that conjuncture, *God Man, humanitas Dei!* What a strong foundation of friendship and union betwixt the person of man and God, that their natures met in so close embraces in one Person! And then, look on, and see so poor and despised an outward condition through His life, yet, having hid under it, the majesty of God, *all the brightness of the Father's glory!* And this is the top of all, that He was *put to death in the flesh;* the Lord of life dying, the Lord of glory clothed with shame! But it quickly appeared what kind of person it was that died, by this, *He was put to death, indeed, in the flesh, but quickened by the Spirit.*

Quickened.] He was indeed too great a morsel for the Grave to digest. For all its vast craving mouth and devouring appetite, crying, *Sheol, Give, give,* yet was it forced to give Him up again, as the fish to give up the Prophet Jonah, who, in that, was the figure of Christ. The chains of that prison are strong, but He was too strong a prisoner to be held by them; as our Apostle hath it in his sermon, (Acts ii. 24.) that it was *not possible that He should be kept by them.* . . .

Ref. 2. Thus may a believing soul at the lowest, when, to its own sense, it is given over unto death, and swallowed up of it, as it were *in the belly of hell,* yet look up to this Divine power. He whose soul was not left there, will not leave

thine there. Yea, when thou art most sunk in thy sad apprehensions, and far off
to thy thinking, then is He nearest to raise and comfort thee; as sometimes it
grows darkest immediately before day. Rest on His power and goodness, which
never failed any who did so. *It is He* (as David says) *who lifts up the soul from
the gates of death.* Psal. ix. 13.

(q) Leighton COPY C II 127–8. See above, *Sp Aph B XVII*.

On the same text.

Would any of you be cured of that common disease, the fear of death? Look
this way, and you shall find more than you seek; you shall be taught, not only
not to fear, but to love it. Consider, 1. His death: *He died.* By that, thou who
receivest Him as thy life, mayest be sure of this, that thou art, by that His death,
freed from the second death. *Descendit huc vita nostra, et tulit mortem nostram,
et occidit eam de abundantia vitae suae*: He who is our life, says Augustine,
descended hither, and bore our death, killing it by the abounding of His life.
And that is the great point. Let that have the name which was given to the other,
the most terrible of all terrible things; and, as the second death is removed, this
death which thou art to pass through, is, I may say, beautified and sweetened;
the ugly visage of it becomes amiable, when ye look on it in Christ, and in His
death: that puts such a pleasing comeliness upon it, that whereas others fly from
it with affright, the Believer cannot choose but embrace it. He longs to lie down
in that bed of rest, since his Lord lay in it, and hath warmed that cold bed, and
purified it with His fragrant body. 2. But especially be looking forward to His
return thence, *quickened by the Spirit*; this being to those who are in Him, the
certain pledge, yea, the effectual cause, of that blessed resurrection which is in
their hopes. There is that union betwixt them, that they shall rise by the communication, and virtue of His rising; not simply by His power, for so the wicked
to their grief shall be raised, but they by His life, as theirs.

(r) Leighton COPY C I 356. See above, *Sp Aph B XVIII*.

On 1 Peter 5.9: "Whom resist stedfast in the faith".

Stedfast, or solid, *by faith*. This is absolutely necessary for resistance. A man
cannot fight upon a quagmire; there is no standing out without a standing, some
firm ground to tread upon; and this, Faith alone furnishes. It lifts the soul up to
the firm advanced ground of the promises, and fastens it there; and there it is
sure, even *as Mount Sion, that cannot be removed*. He says not, stedfast by your
own resolutions and purposes, but, *stedfast by faith*. The power of God, by faith
becomes ours; for that is contained and engaged in the word of promise. Faith
lays hold there, and there finds Almighty strength. *And this is our victory*, says
the Apostle St. John, *whereby we overcome the world, even our Faith*. 1 John
v. 4. So Faith is our victory, whereby we overcome *the prince of this world*.
Whom resist, stedfast in the faith. And, universally, all difficulties, and all
enemies, are overcome by *faith*. Faith sets the stronger *Lion of the tribe of Ju-
dah*, against this *roaring lion* of the bottomless pit; that delivering Lion, against
this devouring lion.

When the soul is surrounded with enemies on all hands, so that there is no way of escape, Faith flies above them, and carries up the soul to take refuge in Christ, and is there safe. That is the power of Faith; it sets a soul in Christ, and there it looks down upon all temptations, as at the bottom of the rock, breaking themselves into foam. When the floods of temptations rise and gather, so great and so many, that the soul is even ready to be swallowed up, then, by faith, it says, Lord Jesus, thou art my strength, I look to thee for deliverance; now appear for my help! And thus it overcomes. The guilt of sin is answered by His blood, the power of sin is conquered by His Spirit; and afflictions that arise, are nothing to these: His love and gracious presence makes them sweet and easy.

(s) Richard Field *Of the Church, five bookes* (Oxford 1635) 58. See above, *Sp Aph B XIX.*

The *Romanists* teach, that sins committed after baptisme, are not so remitted for Christs sake, but that wee must suffer that extremity of punishment which they deserve, & therefore either we must afflict our selves in such sort & degree of extremity as may answer the desert of our sinne, or bee punished by God heere or in the world to come, in such degree and sort that his justice may bee satisfied. But they that are Orthodoxe teach, first, That it is injustice to require the payment of one debt twice. Secondly, That Christ suffered the punishment due to all sinnes committed before and after Baptisme, and therefore so satisfied the justice of God, that they are partakers of the benefit of his satisfaction, so farre forth as they are made partakers of it, are freed from the guilt of punishment. Thirdly, That the satisfaction of Christ is applied and communicated unto us upon the condition of our faith and repentance without suffering the punishment that sinne deserveth. Fourthly, That it is no lesse absurd to say, as the Papists doe, that our satisfaction is required as a condition, without which Christs satisfaction is not appliable unto us; then to say, *Peter* hath paid the debt of *John*, and hee to whom it was due accepteth of the same payment, conditionally if hee pay it himselfe also. Fiftly, that as one man payeth an other mans debt, and the payment of it is accepted upon condition of his dislike of former evill courses, and promise of amendment, and not otherwise: so it may be truely said, that neither Christ hath paid our debt, or God the Father accepted the payment of it for us, but upon condition of our sorrowfull conversion and repentance.

(t) Jeremy Taylor *Worthy Communicant* ch 3 § 5 par 2 (1674) 176. See above, *Sp Aph B XX.*

2. Whatsoever is against right reason, that no faith can oblige us to believe. For although reason is not the positive and affirmative measures of our faith, and God can do more than we can understand, and our faith ought to be larger than our reason, and take something into her heart that reason can never take into her eye; yet in all our Creed there can be nothing against reason. If true reason justly contradicts an article, it is not *of the houshold of faith.* In this there is no difficulty, but that in practice we take care that we do not call that reason which is not so: for although a mans reason is a right Judge, yet it ought not to pass

sentence in an inquiry of faith, until all the Information be brought in; all that is within, and all that is without, all that is above, and all that is below; all that concerns it in experience, and all that concerns it in act; whatsoever is of pertinent observation, and whatsoever is revealed: for else reason may argue very well, and yet conclude falsly; it may conclude well in Logick, and yet infer a false Proposition in Theology: but when our Judge is fully and truly informed in all that where she is to make her judgment, we may safely follow it, whithersoever she invites us.

(u) Ibid 177. See above, *Sp Aph B XXI* and end of *XXII*.

He that speaks against his own reason, speaks against his own conscience, and therefore it is certain, no man serves God with a good conscience, that serves him against his reason. For though in many cases reason must submit to faith, that is, natural reason must submit to supernatural, and the imperfect informations of art, to the perfect revelations of God; yet in no case, can true reason and a right faith oppose each other; and therefore in the article of the Sacrament, the impossible affirmatives concerning Transubstantiation, because they are against all the reason of the world, can never be any part of the faith of God.

(v) Ibid 176–7. See above, *Sp Aph B XXII* (followed there by preceding extract (u)).

If therefore any society of men calls upon us to believe in our Religion what is false in our experience, to affirm that to be done, which we know is impossible it ever can be done; to wink hard that we may see the better; to be unreasonable men, that we may offer to God a reasonable sacrifice; they make Religion so to be seated in the will, that our understanding will be useless, and can never minister to it. But as he that shuts the eye hard, and with violence curles the eye lid, forces a phantastick fire from the crystalline humor, and espies a light that never shines, and sees thousands of little fires that never burn; So is he that blinds the eye of his reason, and pretends to see by an eye of faith, he makes little images of notion, and some atoms dance before him; but he is not guided by the light, nor instructed by the proposition, but sees like a man in his sleep, and grows as much the wiser as the man that dreamt of a *Lycanthropy*, and was for ever after wisely wary not to come near a River.

(w) Jeremy Taylor *The Worthy Communicant* (1674) 415 17. Cf above, *Sp Aph B XXIIIb*.

From ''A Sermon Preached at the Funeral of that Worthy Knight Sir George Dalston of Dalston in Cumberland, September 28, 1657''.

WHEN God, in his infinite and eternal wisdom, had decreed to give to Man a Life of Labour, and a Body of Mortality, a state of Contingen[c]y, and a Composition of fighting Elements; and having designed to be glorified by a free obedience, would also permit sin in the World, and suffer evil Men to go on in their wickedness, to prevail in their impious Machinations, to vex the Souls, and grieve the Bodies of the Righteous, he knew that this would not only be very hard to be suffered by his Servants, but also be very difficult to be understood by them who know God to be a *Law-giver* as well as a *Lord*, a *Judge* as well as a *King*, a *Father* as well as a *Ruler*; and that in order to his own Glory, and for the manifestation of his Goodness he had promised to reward his Servants, to give good to them that did good: therefore to take off all prejudices and evil resentments and temptations which might trouble those good Men who suffered evil things, he was pleased to do two great things which might confirm the Faith, and endear the Services, and entertain the hopes of them who are indeed his Servants, but yet were very ill used in the accidents of this World.

1. The one was, That he sent his Son into the World to take upon him our nature, and him being the *Captain of our Salvation he would perfect through sufferings*; that no man might think it much to suffer, when God spared not his own Son; and every Man might submit to the necessity, when the Christ of God was not exempt; and yet that no Man should fear the event which was to follow such sad beginnings, when *it behoved* even *Christ to suffer, and so to enter into glory*.

2. The other great thing was, that God did not only by revelation, and the Sermons of the Prophets *to his Church*, but even *to all Mankinde* competently teach, and effectively perswade, that the Soul of Man does not Die; but that although things were ill here, yet they should be well hereafter; that the evils of this Life were short and tollerable, and that to the good who usualy feel most of them, they should end in honour and advantages. And therefore *Cicero* had reason on his side to conclude, that there is to be a time and place after this Life, wherein the wicked shall be punished, and the virtuous well rewarded, when he considered that *Orpheus* and *Socrates, Palamedes* and *Thraseas, Lucretia* and *Papinian* were either slain or oppressed to death by evil Men. But to us Christians εἰ μὴ ἐπαχθὲς εἰπεῖν ἐστι πάνυ ἱκανῶς ἀποδέδεικται (as Platoes expression is) we have a necessity to declare and a demonstration to prove it, when we read that *Abel* died by the hands of *Cain*, who was so ignorant, that though he had *malice* and *strength*, yet he had scarce *art* enough to kill him; when we read that *John* the *Baptist*, Christ himself and his Apostles, and his whole Army of Martyrs, died under the violence of evil Men; when vertue made good Men poor, and free speaking of brave truths made the wise to lose their liberty; when an excellent life hastned an opprobrious death, and the obeying God destroyed our selves; it was but time to look about for another state of things, where justice should rule, and vertue find her own portion: where the Men that were like to God in mercy and justice, should also partake of his felicity: and therefore Men cast out every line, and turned every stone, and tried every argument, and sometimes proved it well, and when they did not, yet they believed strongly, and they were sure of the thing, even when they were not sure of the argument.

(x) Henry More *Enthusiasmus Triumphatus* (1656) 38–9. See above, *Conc* at n 23.

From ''A brief Discourse of Enthusiasm''.

And those that talk so loud of that higher Principle, *The Spirit*, with exclusion of these, betray their own ignorance; and while they would by their wilde Rhetorick disswade men from the use of their *Rational* faculties under pretence of expectation of an higher and more glorious Light, do as madly, in my mind, as if, a company of men travailing by night with links, torches and lanthorns, some furious Orator amongst them should by his wonderful strains of Eloquence so befool them into a misconceit of their present condition, comparing of it with the sweet and chearful splendor of the day, as thereby to cause them, through impatience and indignation, to beat out their links and torches, and break a-pieces their lanthorns against the ground, and so chuse rather to foot it in the dark with hazard of knocking their noses against the next Tree they meet, and tumbling into the next ditch, then to continue the use of those convenient lights that they had in their sober temper prepared for the safety of their journey.

But the *Enthusiast's* mistake is not onely in leaving his present Guide before he has a better, but in having a false notion of him he does expect. For assuredly that *Spirit of illumination* which resides in the Souls of the faithful, is a Principle of the *purest Reason* that is communicable to the humane Nature. And what *this Spirit* has, he has from Christ (as Christ himself witnesseth) who is the Eternal λόγος, the all-comprehending Wisdome and Reason of God, wherein he sees through the Natures and *Ideas* of all things, with all their respects of Dependency and Independency, Congruity and Incongruity, or whatever Habitude they have one to another, with one continued glance at once.

MANUSCRIPTS
AND AN EARLY PROOF

MANUSCRIPTS
AND AN EARLY PROOF

A S H A S been pointed out in the Editor's Introduction above, the copy which Coleridge submitted to his publisher in 1823 took two forms, comprising sections of straightforward manuscript to provide the framework of the volume together with a volume of Leighton with manuscript annotations from which the printer was expected to print indicated extracts. In these early pages, moreover, the manuscript matrix took a different form from that eventually adopted: the unattractive appearance of the first proofs when they began arriving prompted several changes, notably the separation of previously continuous text into briefer "Aphorisms" and "Comments".

The surviving pieces of early manuscript reproduced here can be seen to form part of that original, continuous writing, as does the one extant piece of proof reprinted at the end of the appendix. The close correspondences in detail between these fragments and the 1825 text suggest, moreover, that Coleridge's work at proof-stage was primarily devoted to improving the presentation on the page; the piece of proof makes it clear, however, that there was some rearrangement of the order as well.

The early material extends to passage (k) below; after this some heavily corrected material, drafted for pages in the middle of the volume, bears witness to the difficulties Coleridge found in dealing with the section to be known as "Spiritual Aphorisms". The state of the copy that has survived for the later part, on the other hand, suggests that by then the composition of the volume had become more straightforward. The full range of sources available for study comprises the present appendix, the preceding one, and the annotations of Leighton to be published in *CM (CC)* III. On some later occasions, at least, the compositor was working from a transcript of Leighton rather than from the printed volume: see e.g. *Sp Aph B XIV* n 1, above.

The manuscript material in the present appendix is arranged in the order of its use in the 1825 edition.

For the light it throws on the use of capitals in the volume, see the headnote to the Index.

(a) 　　　　　　　MS Harvard Eng 1094 f 68
　　　　　　　　AR (1825) 5; *Int Aph IX* above.

On a page numbered 6, inserted in Elizabeth Aders's album.

of our becoming conscious of certain Truths and Realities for the Truths and
Realities themselves) a House gloriously furnished. Nothing is wanted but the
Eye, which is the Light of this House, the Light which is the Eye of this Soul.
This *seeing* Light, this *enlightening* Eye is Reflection. It is more indeed than is
ordinarily meant by that word; but it is what a *Christian* ought to mean by it,
and to know too, ~~from whom it all~~ [. . . .] whence it first came, and still continues to come—of what Light even this Light is but a Reflection. This too is
THOUGHT—and all Thought is but unthinking that does not flow out of this or
tend towards it.

(b) 　　　　　　　MS Yale, Osborn Collection, recto
　　　　　　　　AR (1825) 5; *Int Aph X* above.

Self-superintendence! that any thing should overlook itself! Is not this a paradox, and hard to understand? It is indeed difficult, and to the imbruted Sensualist a direct contradiction. And yet, most truly does the Poet exclaim,

　　　　　　—Unless *above* himself He can
　　　　　　Erect himself, how mean a thing is Man!

(c) 　　　　　　　MS Yale, Osborn Collection, verso
　　　　　　　　AR (1825) 6n; *Int Aph XII* above at n 1.

Quod stat subtus, that which ~~lies~~ ⟨stands⟩ *beneath* and ⟨(as it were)⟩ supports,
the appearance. In a Language, ~~such as our own, w~~ ⟨like ours', where so many⟩
words are derived from other Languages, there a few modes of instruction more
useful or more amusing than that of accustoming young People to seek for the
etymology, or primary meaning, of the words they use. There are cases, in
which more knowlege & of more value may be conveyed by the History of a
word, than by the History of a Campaign.

(d) 　　　　　　　MS BM Egerton 2801 f 162
　　　　　　　　AR (1825) 8; *Int Aph XIII* (Comment) above.

Continuous with next extract.

　　　　　　　　　　　　　　　　　　　　　　　　　　　　　9

of *Certainty*; but—for that calm Assurance, the very means and conditions of
which it supersedes; if a Belief that seeks the Darkness and yet strikes no Root,
immoveable as the Limpet from the Rock, and like the Limpet fixed there by
mere force of Adhesion;—if these suffice to make men Christians, in what sense
could the Apostle affirm, that Believers receive, not indeed ~~the~~ worldly wisdom
~~of this world~~ that comes to nought, but the wisdom of God, *that we might know
and comprehend* the things that are freely given to us of God? On what grounds

could he denounce the sincerest *fervor* of Spirit, as *defective* where it does not likewise bring forth fruits in the UNDERSTANDING?

In our present state, it is little less than impossible that the Affections should be kept constant to an Object, which gives no employment to the Understanding, ~~while yet it transcends the senses~~ and yet cannot be made manifest to the Senses. The Exercise of the reasoning and reflecting Powers, increasing Insight, and enlarging Views, are requisite to

(e)   MS Cornell Healey 2632, 21 f 1
              AR (1825) 9; *Int Aphs XIV–XV* above.

Transcript by SC, with her note: "Copy ~~of~~ from a scip [for scrap or slip?] of paper found in Coleridge's room; such scaps [for scraps] and these ~~thrown~~ scattered about he used to call his fly catchers—"; and at the end, "sad pity that paper here broke off".

keep alive the substantial faith in the heart—

In the state of perfection, perhaps, all other faculties may be swallowed up in Love, or superseded by immediate Vision; but it is, on the wings of the CHERU-BIM i e (according to the interpretation of the ancient Hebrew Doctors) the *intellectual* Powers & energies, that we must first be borne up to the "pure Empyrean". It must be seraphs, and not the Hearts of imperfect mortals, that can burn unfuelled and *self*-fed. Give me *understanding* (is the prayer of the Royal Psalmist) and I shall observe thy Law with my *whole* heart. Thy Law is exceeding *broad*—that is comprehensive, pregnant, containing far more than the apparent import of the words on a first perusal. It is my *meditation* all the day—

It is worthy of especial observation, that the Scriptures are distinguished from all other writings pretending to Inspiration, by the strong and

(f)   MS Sotheby 1971
        AR (1825) 11; *Int Aphs XVIII* (Comment)–*XIX* above.

Beginning of ms leaf numbered 13 mounted on an album leaf, together with a letter from James Gillman presenting the fragment to his unidentified correspondent; sold at Sotheby's 26 October 1971, Lot 421. Text from catalogue.

. . . see and bear witness to these advantages in the conduct, the immunities and the superior powers of the Possessors. Were they attainable by Pilgrimages the most toilsome or Penances the most painful, we should assuredly have as many Pilgrims and ~~as~~ Self-tormentors in the service of true Religion as now exist under the tyranny of Papal or Brahman Superstition. In

(g)   MS BM Egerton 2801 f 163
              AR (1825) 13–14; *Int Aphs XX–XXI* above.

∧ ∧ *insert*

The Requisites for the execution of this high Intent may be comprized under three Heads, the Prudential; the Moral; and the Spiritual.

First, PRUDENCE.—What this is, will be best explained by its effects and operations. It consists then in the Prevention or Abatement of Hindrances and Distractions; and consequently in avoiding, or removing from, all such Circumstances as, by diverting the attention of the Workman retard the progress and hazard the safety of the Work. It is likewise (we deny not) a part of this unworldly Prudence to place ourselves, as much and as often as it is in our power so to do, in circumstances directly favorable to our great Design; and to avail ourselves of all the *positive* Helps and Furtherances, which these Circumstances [ma]y afford. But neither dare we, as Christians, forget, whose and under what dominion the Things are, quæ nos *circum stant*, i.e. that *stand around* us. We are to remember, that it is the World, that constitutes our outward circumstances; that in the Form of the World, which is evermore at variance with the Divine Form (or Idea) that they are cast and moulded; and that ~~not only~~ of the Means and Measures, which Prudence requires in the forming anew of the Divine Image in the Soul, the far greater

(h) MS BM Egerton 2801 f 164
First draft for *AR* (1825) 15–18;
see *Int Aphs XXIII–XXIV* above.

16

Ancient Religion, the ceremonial Rites and Vestments of the Old Law, had morality ~~as~~ for their Substance and Spirit. They were pregnant Enigmas, of which Morality was the Solution. But ~~in~~ the Scheme of Grace and Truth that †*became* ~~(ἐγένετο, began to exist, not ne was made to exist~~ thro' Jesus Christ, ~~in~~ the ~~Faith~~ Faith that I I looks down into the perfect Law of Liberty, ⟨has "Light for its Garment": its very "*Robe* is Righteousness".⟩ Morality itself is the Divine Service and Ceremonial of the Christian Religion. ~~Herein the Apostle ma places its~~ pre-eminence, its distinguishing Excellence, that its ~~indicative Exterior partake~~ is of the same kind, tho' not of the same order, with itself; ~~an~~ not accidental or arbitrary, as an Hieroglyphic in relation to the Truth or Object, which it expresses, but inseparable and partaking therefore of the same Life, Permanence and intrinsic Worth. As the Body to the Soul, ~~such~~ so is Morality to the Religion in Christ—but there are Bodies *celestial* as well as ~~transitory~~ Bodies transitory and terrestrial. And such a Body—on the earth indeed (i.e. our ~~state~~ present state and condition in this world) and both the Form and the Instrument of Communion therewith, yet not earthly, but capable of being transfigured from Glory to Glory according to the new relations, in which its Soul and abiding Principle may

(i) MS NY Univ Fales Library 65.6.6-426
AR (1825) 19–20; *Int Aphs XXV* (Comment)–*XXVIII* above.

A single leaf. The four footnotes signalled on the recto (numbered page "18") of this leaf were evidently given on the verso of page "17" on the previous leaf (now missing), with the quotation from Donne, begun in the fourth note there (see *AR*—1825—20n; *Int Aph XXVIII* at n 1), continuing on to the verso of the present one.

18

[h]ollowness: or I would have recommended the following ~~aphorism~~ ~~among~~ as the first exercise.

It is a ~~weak~~ dull and ~~obtuse~~ obtuse Mind, that must divide in order to distinguish; but it is a still worse, that (except in the case of Right and Wrong) distinguishes in order to divide. In the former we may contemplate the source of Superstition, and * Idolatry; in the latter of Schism, Heresy ‡; and a seditious and sectarian Spirit. II

Exclusive of the abstract Sciences, the ~~greatest~~ largest and worthiest portion of our Knowlege consists of *Aphorisms*: and the ~~best~~ greatest and ~~worthiest~~ best of Men is but an *Aphorism*.

We ~~enter not~~ meddle not with the Dispute respecting *Conversion*, whether and in what sense necessary in all Christians. It is sufficient for the present purpose, what no ~~Christian~~ Believer will deny, that a very large number of men even in Christian Countries need to be converted, and that not a few, we trust, have been. The Tenet becomes fanatical and dangerous only when rare and extraordinary Exceptions are made the general Rule—when what was vouchsafed to the Apostle of the Gentiles by especial grace and ~~purpose~~ for an especial purpose, viz. a Conversion begun ‡ and completed in the same moment,

[verso]

note ‡ continued

melted and the Mold that received and shaped him. Donne's Sermons—*quoted from Memory*.

~~Notes to p. 19~~

S. T. Coleridge

(j)   MS BM Egerton 2801 ff 165–166ᵛ

Prud Aphs VI, VII, and *VIII* (Comment) *AR* (1825) 36–7, 38–40;

cf *Prud Aphs I* (Comment, end) and *II* (Comment), above.

Showing the state of *AR* ms, before ''Aph VIII'' (1825) = *Prud Aph II* (1831) was inserted from later in the first proof: see end of this Appendix and Editor's Introduction, pp lxiii–lxiv. From marks in the ms it appears that p 42 in the original proof began at ''without it. . .'' below.

3

of the Many by technical terms, ~~alike q~~ hard to be remembered, and alike quarrelsome to the ear & the tongue. In the business of moral and religious reflection, in the acquisition of clear and distinct Conceptions ~~respecting~~ of our Duties, and of the relations, in which we stand to God, our Neighbour, and our selves, no such difficulties occur. We have at best only to rescue words already existing and familiar from the false or vague meanings imposed on them by Carelessness, ~~and~~ or the clipping and debasing Misusage of the Market. And surely Happiness, Duty, Faith, Truth, and final Blessedness are matters of ~~higher~~ deeper & dearer Interest for all men, than Circles to the Geometrician, or the characters of Plants to the Botanist, or the affinities & combining principle of ⟨the⟩ elementary of Bodies to the Chemist, or even the fearful & wonderful Mechanism of the perishable Organ of the Soul to the Anatomist.—~~One and a~~ Among the *aids to*

Reflection place the following maxim prominent— Let distinctness in Expression ~~ma~~ advance side by side with Distinction in Thought. For one useless Subtlety in our elder Divines and Moralists I will ~~shew~~ produce ten ~~dangerous~~ Sophisms of Equivocation in the Writings of our modern Preceptors:

[*f 165ᵛ*] 4
and for one ~~mischief inconvenience~~ error resulting from excess in *distinguishing* the indifferent, I would shew ten mischievous delusion from the habit of *confounding* the diverse.

~~7. Make it a rule~~ Whether you are reflecting for yourself or reasoning with another, make it a rule, to ask yourself the precise meaning of the ~~words~~, on which the Point in question ~~mainly~~ appears to turn; & if it may be (i.e. ~~has~~ by writers of authority *has been*) used in several senses, then ask which of these the word is at present intended to convey. By this mean and scarcely without it, you will ~~gr~~ at length acquire a facility in detecting the Quid pro quo. And believe me, in so doing you will enable yourself to disarm and expose four fifths of the main arguments of our most renowned ~~Epicurean~~ irreligious Philosophers, ancient and modern. For the Quid pro Quo is ~~the~~ at once the Rock and Quarry, on and with which the Strongholds of ~~Infidelity~~ Disbelief, Materialism, and ~~the yet~~ (more pernicious still) Epicurean Morality are built.

8. In the works of Moralists, both Christian and Pagan, ~~it is a (few) commonplaces are of more frequent occurrence than~~

[*f 166*] 5
it is often asserted—indeed few Common-places of more frequent recurrence— that ⟨the⟩ Happiness ~~in~~ even of this Life consists solely, or principally, in Virtue; that Virtue is the only Happiness of this life; (Leighton, V. ɪᴠ. 319.) that Virtue is the truest *Pleasure*; &c. ~~the like/~~ I doubt not that the meaning, which the Writers intended to convey by these ~~and equivalent~~ and the like Expressions, was true and wise. But I deem it safer to say— ~~and~~ nor do I doubt, that in diverting men from ~~a~~ sensual and dishonest courses it will often be expedient to say—that in all the outward relations of this life, in all ⟨our⟩ outward conduct and Actions, ~~whether in doing~~ both in what we should do, and in what we should abstain from, the Dictates of Virtue are the very same with those of Self-interest; that tho' the Incitements of Virtue do not proceed *from* the same point, yet they ~~move~~ tend *to* the same point with the Impulses of a reflecting and consistent Selfishness; that the ⟨outward⟩ Object of Virtue being the greatest producible sum of Happiness of all men must needs include the object of an intelligent Self-love which is the greatest possible Happiness of ~~a man~~ one individual: for what is true of all, must be true of each. Hence, you cannot

[*f 166ᵛ*] 6
become better, (i.e. more virtuous) ~~without~~ but you will ~~be~~ become happier: and you cannot become worse (i.e. more vicious) ~~but you~~ without an increase of Misery, or at the best a proportional Loss of Enjoyment as the Consequence. If the ~~act~~ thing were not inconsistent with our Well-being, and ~~proved by~~ known to be so, it would not have been classed as a *Vice*. Thus what in an enfeebled and disordered mind is called Prudence is the voice of Nature in a healthful

State: as is proved by the known fact, that the prudential duties, (i.e. those actions ~~or~~ which are commanded by Virtue *because* they are prescribed by Prudence) the Animals fulfil by natural instinct.

The pleasure that accompanies or depends on a healthy and vigorous Body will ~~follow~~ be the consequence and reward of a temperate Life and Habits of active Industry, whether this Pleasure were or were not the chief or only deter-min~~ing~~ning *motive* thereto. Virtue may, possibly add to this pleasure a good of another kind, a higher good, perhaps, than the worldly mind is capable of understanding,

(k) MS BM Egerton 2801 f 167–167ᵛ
Prud Aph VIII AR (1825) 41–2; cf *Prud Aph II*
(Comment) at nn 10–16 above.

The insertion of ''D49'' as shown, along with a crotchet splitting ''it'' from ''self'' in the previous line (both presumably by the printer), indicates the page-numbering of the proof: see Editor's Introduction pp lxiv–lxv above. Another crotchet after ''even'', five lines above, may indicate an earlier paging.

9

disputandum. No man can judge for another.

This, I repeat, appears to me a safer language, than the Sentences quoted above, that Virtue alone is Happiness; that Happiness consists in Virtue, &c.— ~~positions~~ Sayings which I find it hard to reconcile with other positions of still more frequent occurrence in the same Divines, ~~and (which weighs far more with me)~~ or with the declarations of Sᵗ Paul—If in this life only we have hope, we are of all men most miserable. And such language, as this, the soundest Moralists were obliged to employ, before Grace and Truth were brought into the world by Jesus Christ. And such language may, I doubt not, even now be profitably addressed both to individuals and to classes of men: tho' in what *proportion* ⟨it should be dwelt on,⟩ & to what extent it is likely to be efficacious, a Review of the different Epochs memorable for the turning of Many from their evil ways, and of the ~~principal~~ Means, by which this Reformation of Life ~~was~~ has been principally effected, renders me scrupulous in deciding: and tho' I should rely ~~with~~ far more confidently on the converse—viz. that to be vicious is to be *miserable*. Few men are so utterly reprobate, so imbruted by their vices,

(f 167ᵛ) 10
as not to have some lucid, or at least quiet and sober, intervals: and in such a moment, *dum desæviunt iræ*, few can stand up unshaken against the Appeal to their own Experience—What have been the wages of Sin? What has the Devil done for you? What sort of Master have you *found* him? and then in the befitting *detail*, and by a series of questions that ask no loud, and are secure against any *false*, answer, urging home the proof of the Position, that to be vicious is to be wretched—and adding the fearful corollary, that if even in th~~ise~~ ~~life~~ body which, as long as life is in it, can never be *wholly* bereaved of pleasurable sensations, Vice is found to be Misery, in the world to come where the criminal Acts, and much more the momentary gratifications, ~~that~~ are no longer possible,

and nothing ⟨of it⟩ remains but the Guilt and its consequences, Vice must be Misery itself, all and utter Misery.—

D 49

So best, if I err not, may the motives of Prudence be held forth, and the Impulses of Self-love be awakened, in alliance with Truth, and free from the danger of confounding things which it

(l) MS BM Egerton 2801 f 168–168ᵛ

AR (1825) 87–9; *Mor Aphs XII–XIV* above.

Opposite the heading to Aphorism XIII there is a transverse note (probably by the printer): "87–7ᵗʰ G", which corresponds to *AR* (1825) 87 (the 7th page of signature G, where this appears in the middle of the page).

12

more fruitful, perhaps more solid, inference from the fact would be, that there is some thing in the human mind which makes it know (as soon as it is sufficiently awakened to reflect on its own thoughts & notices) that in all finite Quantity there is an Infinite, in all measures of Time an Eternal; that the latter are the basis, the substance, the true and abiding *reality* of the former; and that as we truly *are*, ~~because~~ only as far as God is with us, so neither can we truly possess (i.e. enjoy) our Being or any thing real Good, but by living in the sense of his holy presence.

A Life of Wickedness is a Life of Lies: and an Evil Being or the Being of Evil the last and darkest mystery

Aphor. XIII

THE WISEST USE OF THE IMAGINATION.

It is not altogether————fight in earnest, p. 55.

Aphorism XIV.

THE LANGUAGE OF SCRIPTURE.

The Word of God speaks to Men, and therefore it speaks the Language of the Children of Men. Gen. XXII. 12.

~~to the concerning sensible~~.

(*f 168ᵛ*) 13

—On moral subjects in the language of the Affections, they excite in us; on sensible Objects, neither metaphysically, as they are known by superior intelligences, nor theoretically, as they would be seen by us, were we placed in the Sun, but as they are represented by our human senses in ~~their~~ our present relative position. Lastly, from no vain or worse than vain Ambition of seeming "to walk on the ~~Waters" of the Deep in Twilight, understand the immediate~~ ⟨Sea" of⟩ Mystery in my way to Truth, but ~~in the hope (desirous)~~ in the hope of removing ⟨a⟩ difficulty that ~~weighs~~ presses heavily on the ~~many~~inds of many ~~Hearts~~ believers in Heart and Desire, and which long pressed on my own mind, I venture to add that on *Spiritual* things, and ~~with~~ allusion ~~allu~~sively to the mysterious union ~~and~~ or conspiration of the Divine with the Human in the Spirits of the Just, spoken of in Romans VII. 27., the Word of God attributes the language of the Spirit sanctified to the Holy One, the Sanctifier.

Now the Will (—or Spirit in Man) ~~can~~ knows it only in and by its Acts: even as in geometry, the Mind knows its constructive power in the act of constructing; and contemplates its purpose in the product (the

(m)   MS BM Egerton 2801 ff 174ᵛ–174, 175
                     AR (1825) 144–5, 148–9;
            Sp Aphs A III–VI (Comment) above, inc *Aph VI* n 8.

See *Sp Aph A VI* n 8. Above the heading to Aphorism IV is a note ''145 L'', corresponding to its position in *AR* (1825), beginning signature L at p 145. The ms of this section is continuous with the next (n).

3

Charter and the Christian Constitution, that its Author and Head is the Spirit of Truth, Essential Reason as well as Absolute and Incomprehensible Will. Like a just Monarch, he refers ~~the~~ ⟨even his⟩ own causes ~~of his subjects~~ ⟨to the Judgement⟩ to his ~~own~~ high Courts.—⟨He⟩ his King's Bench in the Reason, his Court of Equity in the Conscience; ⟨that the representative of his Majesty and universal Justice, this the⟩ ~~the Decrees highest in dignity and~~ nearest to the King's heart, and ⟨the Dispenser of his⟩ ~~his secret and~~ particular Decrees. He has ⟨likewise⟩ his Court of Common Pleas in the Understanding, his Court of Exchequer in the Prudence. The Laws are *his* Laws, ~~those ⟨Laws⟩ of the Mind and Laws of Nature~~. And tho' by Signs and Miracles he has mercifully condescended ⟨to interline here and there with his own hand⟩ the great Statute-book, he had dictated to ~~his Amanuensis~~ his Amanuensis, Nature, yet has he been graciously pleased to forbid our receiv~~ing~~ing as the *King's* Mandates ~~whatever~~ aught that ~~has~~ is not stamped with the Great Seal of ~~his~~ the Conscience & Countersigned by the Reason.

[*f 174*] 4
    Aphorism IV.
    On an unlearned Ministry, under pretence of a *Call* of the Spirit, and inward *Graces* superseding outward Helps.
    H. More, Theol. Works, p. 368. The transcript will be sent with the next parcel.
    Note. This and the three preceding Extracts ~~in addition to the Preliminary~~ will suffice as precautionary Aphorisms. And here again the Reader may exemplify the great advantages ~~which~~ to be obtained from the habit of tracing the *proper* Meaning and history of Words. We need only recollect the common and idiomatic phrases, in which the word ''Spirit'' occurs ~~ex. gr. the~~ in a physical or material sense (ex. gr. fruit has lost its *spirit* and flavor.)~~&c~~ to be convinced that the natural meaning is to improve, enliven, actuate some other thing, not to be or constitute a thing ~~un~~ in its own name.—~~He~~ The enthusiast may find one exception to this—where the material itself is called *Spirit*. And when he calls to mind, ~~the ⟨its⟩ qualities and properties~~ how its acts when taken *alone* ~~and~~ by the unhappy persons who in their first exultation will boast that

[*f 175*]   5
it is ~~Fire, Food, and ⟨Drink⟩~~ Meat, Drink, Fire and Clothing to them all in one— that its properties are to inflame, intoxicate, madden, with exhaustion, lethargy

and atrophy for ~~an~~ the Sequels—~~that man~~ well for him if in some lucid interval he should ~~ask hims~~ fairly put the question to his own mind—How far this is *analogous* to his own case, and whether the exception does not confirm the Rule. The *Letter* without the Spirit killeth; but does it follow, that the Spirit is to kill the Letter? To kill that which it is its appropriate Office to enliven?

However, where the Ministry is not invaded, and the plain sense of the Scriptures is left undisturbed, and the Believer looks for the suggestions of the Spirit only or chiefly in applying ~~the~~ particular passages to his own individual case and exigencies, tho' in this there may be much weakness, and confused notions and wandering in twilight, some Delusion and ~~more~~ imminent Danger of more—I can not but join with ~~the~~ Henry More in avowing, that "for my own part——confirmed Christians than ever."—P. 372, 373.

(n) MS BM Egerton 2801 ff 175^v–177^v, 265
AR (1825) 150–2; opening to *Sp Aph B* above.

[*f 175^v*] 6

Aphorisms
on that which is indeed Spiritual Religion. ~~and~~

NOTICE. In the selection of the Extracts that form the remainder of this Volume and of the Comments affixed, the Editor ~~proposed to him~~ had the following Objects principally in view. First, to exhibit the true ⟨and scriptural⟩ meaning and intent of several Articles of Faith, that are rightly classed among the Mysteries and peculiar Doctrines of ~~So~~ Christianity. Secondly, to shew the perfect rationality of these Doctrines, and their freedom from all just objection when examined by their proper Organ, the Reason and Conscience of Man. Lastly, to exhibit from the Works of Leighton, who perhaps

[*f 176*] 7
of all our learned protestant Theologians best deserves the title of a Spiritual Divine, an instructive and affecting picture of the contemplations, reflections, conflicts, consolations and monitory experiences of a philosophic, and richly-gifted Mind, amply stored with all the knowlege that Books and long intercourse with men of the most discordant characters can give, under the convictions, impressions, and habits of a Spiritual Religion.

To obviate ~~any~~ a possible disappointment in any of my Readers, who may chance to be engaged in theological studies, ~~I think it well to~~ it may be well to notice—that among the ~~Myster doctrines~~ peculiar tenets of our Faith, I have not adverted to the ~~Mystery~~ Doctrine of the Trinity, or to the still profounder Mystery of

[*f 176^v*] 8
the Origin of Moral Evil—and this for the reasons following. ~~Neither of~~
1. These Doctrines are ⟨not (strictly speaking)⟩ subjects of *Reflection*, in the proper sense of this word: and ~~to~~ both of them ~~re~~ demand a power and persistency of Abstraction, and a previous discipline in the highest forms of human

Thought, which it would be unwise, ~~and~~ if not presumptuous, to expect from ~~those~~ any, who require "*Aids* to Reflection" or would be likely to seek them in the present Work. 2. In ~~my~~ ⟨my⟩ intercourse ~~of many years with serious and~~ with ~~persons~~ men of various ranks and ages I have found the far larger number of serious and inquiring ~~Men, lovers of Truth, undecided (Persons in ma every)~~ Persons little if at all disquieted by doubts respecting Articles of Faith, that are simply above their comprehension. It is only where the Belief required of them jars with their *moral* feelings, where a Doctrine in the sense, in which

[*f 177*]   9
they have been taught to receive appears to contradict their clear notions of Right and Wrong, or to be ~~palpably~~ at variance with the divine Attributes of Goodness and Justice, that these men are surprized, perplexed, and alas! not seldom offended and alienated. Such are the Doctrines of Arbitrary Election and Reprobation; the Sentence to ever-lasting Torment by an eternal and necessitating Decree; vicarious Atonement, and the necessity of the Abasement, Agony and ignominious Death of a most holy and meritorious Person to appease the Wrath of God/—and the like. Now it is more especially for such Persons, ~~Sceptics~~ unwilling Sceptics who believing earnestly ask help for their unbelief, that this Volume was compiled and the Comments &c written: and therefore to the Scripture Doctrines, *intended* by the above-mentioned, my principal

[*f 177ᵛ*]   10
attention has been directed.

But lastly, the whole Scheme of the Christian Faith, including *all* the Articles of Belief common to the Greek and Latin, the Roman and the Protestant Church, ~~an~~ with the three fold proof, that it is *ideally* true (or true in the Idea); that it is *actually* true (correspondent to the practical reason and moral necessities of mankind, and ~~capable of~~ of existing *actually* in the will and spirit); and that it is *really* true/ true as *fact* of history—is contained in a proportionally larger Work, the principal Labor of ~~the~~ my Life since Manhood, and which ~~is~~ I am now preparing for the Press under the title—Assertion of Religion, as necessarily involving Revelation; and of Christianity,

[*f 265*]   11
as the only Revelation of permanent and universal validity.''

———————

———

(o)   MS BM Egerton 2801 f 262

Cf *AR* (1825) 152 = end of opening to *Sp Aph B* above: this passage may have been written as a draft for *AR*, or for the "Assertion of Religion" as described there.

The ~~several~~ Plans, on which ~~the~~ hitherto the Advocacy of the Christian Faith has been ~~or may be~~ undertaken, may be brought under two Classes or main Divisions: the ~~Defence~~ Proof of the Religion by the Revelation, and the ~~Defence~~ Proof of the Revelation ~~by~~ from the Religion—each ~~of wh~~ containing several species

(p)   MS BM Egerton 2801 ff 178–179ᵛ
                       AR (1825) 152–5: *Sp Aph B I* above.

Slip VI p. 11   11 7

⟨Preliminary.⟩
~~Aphorisms~~
~~on~~
~~Spiritual Religion~~.

⟨Aphorism I.⟩
~~Aphorism I~~

Where ~~⟨⟨says Leighton⟩⟩~~ if not in Christ, is the Power that can persuade a
Sinner to return, that can *bring home a Heart to God?*—Vol. II. p. 120, 121.

Note. By the phrase *"in Christ"* I mean all the supernatural Aids vouchsafed
and conditionally promised in the Christian Dispensation: ⟨and among them the
Spirit of Truth, which the world cannot receive, were it only that ⟨the knowlege
of⟩ *spiritual* Truth is of necessity immediate and *intuitive*: and the World or
Natural Man possesses no higher intuitions than those of the pure *Sense*, which
are the subjects of *Mathematical* Science.⟩ But *Aids*, observe! Therefore, not *by*
the Will of man alone; but neither *without* the Will. The doctrine of modern
Calvinism, as layed down by Jonathan Edwards and the late Dʳ Williams, which
represents a Will absolutely passive, clay in the hands of a Potter, destroys all
Will, takes away its essence & definition, as effectually as ~~if I should say~~ in
saying—This Circle is square—I should deny the

[*f 178ᵛ*]   8 12
figure to be a Circle at all. It was in strict consistency therefore, that these Writers supported the ~~mater~~ Necessitarian Scheme, and made the relation of Cause
and Effect the Law of the Universe, [. . .] subjecting to its mechanism the moral
World no less than the material or physical. It follows, that all is Nature. Thus,
tho' few Writers use the term, Spirit, more frequently, they in effect deny its
existence, and evacuate the term of all its proper meaning. With such a system
⟨not⟩ the Wit of Man nor all the Theodices ever framed by human ingenuity
before and since the attempt of the celebrated Leibnitz, can reconcile the sense
of Responsibility, nor the fact of the difference *in kind* between REGRET and
REMORSE. The same compulsion of Consequence drove the Fathers of Modern
(or Pseudo-) Calvinism to the origination of Holiness in Power, of Justice in
Right of Property,

[*f 179*]   13 9
and whatever other outrages on the common sense and moral feelings of Mankind they have sought to cover under the fair name of *Sovereign Grace.*

I will not take on me to defend ~~any~~ sundry harsh and inconvenient Expressions
in the Works of Calvin. ⟨Phrases equally strong and Assertions not less rash and
startling are no rarities in the Writings of Luther: for⟩ Catachresis was the favorite Figure of Speech in that Age. But ~~far different was the purpose~~ let not the
opinions of either on this most fundamental Subject be confounded with the
New-England System, now entitled Calvinistic. The fact is simply this. ~~Both~~
Luther ~~and with~~ considered the Pretensions to Free Will *boastful,* ~~and better~~

suited to & better suited to the "budge Doctors of the Stoic Fur" than to the Preachers of the Gospel, whose great Theme is the Redemption of the Will from Slavery; in order to its final

[*f 179ᵛ*]   10 14

the restoration of the Will to perfect Freedom being the *end*, and Consummation of the redemptive Process, and the same with the entrance of the Soul into Glory—i.e. its union with Christ, "GLORY" ⟨(John XVII. 5.)⟩ being one of the Names of the Spiritual Messiah. Prospectively to this ⟨we are to understand the words of⟩ our Lord, prayed that as "As I am in the Father, even so ye may be in me." John XIV. 20: " At that day ye shall know, that I am in my Father & ye in me: & XVII. 5. the freedom of a finite will being possible under this one only condition, that it has become one with the Will of God. Now as the difference of a captive and enslaved Will, and *no* will at all, such is the difference between the *Lutheranism* of Calvin and the Calvinism of Jonathan Edwards.

It has been before remarked, that the Will is ⟨in a peculiar and pre-eminent sense⟩ the *Spiritual* Part of our Humanity: and without clear conceptions respecting this & some acquaintance with the ⟨prevalent⟩ errors that in regard to it, our inquiries into all questions respecting the existence and our all reflections on the Truths, of Spiritual Religion will remain perplexed and unsafe. To place the Reader on this requisite Vantage-ground is the purpose \

(q)   MS BM Egerton 2801 ff 171ᵛ, 171, 172
                       AR (1825) 158–9; *Sp Aph B II* at nn 22–5.

First drafted, probably, as the comment on COPY B I 9–10: see *Sp Aph B II* n 22 above. The passage deleted is replaced by a further draft, section (r) below; for continuation of f 172 see section (s).

Spiritual

        Aphorism II. L.

Vol. I. p. 9, 10.

Comment

    Leighton gives an example in this passage well worthy the attention and imitation of all Ministers of the Gospel. Here (and indeed throughout his work) he avoids all metaphysical views of Election, relatively to God, and confines himself to the Doctrine in its relation to Man: and in that sense too, in which every Christian may judge, who is strives to be sincere with his own heart. The following may, I think, be taken as a safe and useful Rule in religious inquiries. Ideas, that have derive their origin and substance from the *Moral* Being, and to the reception of which as true *objectively* (i.e. having u as corresponding *reality* to a *reality* out of the Believer's own human mind) we are determined by a *practical* interest exclusively, may not, like theoretical or speculative Positions, be pressed onward into all their possible *logical* consequences. The Law of Conscience, and not the Canons of discursive Reasoning, must decide in

[*f 171*]   2

such cases. At least, the latter has no validity, which the single *Veto* of the former is not sufficient to nullify. The most pious Conclusion is here the most legitimate. ~~This holds good even of the Ideas (Forms and Principles) which the Reason forms for in proof of its own Needs and from a speculative interest, whenever they are applied to a moral or religious purpose: without which they would remain, like the Circles and Asymptots of Geometry, mere *Ideas* (or Theorems rather) subsisting wholly and exclusively in and for the mind that contemplates them.~~ Take an instance. It is the office & necessity of the Reason to bring a unity into all our conceptions ⟨of Nature.⟩ But this is possible ~~and~~ only under the idea of a One supreme Being as the Ground [and] Cause of the Universe, and as such the subject neither of Time or Change. The One must be contemplated as eternal and immutable. The Conscience and Religion demand the same Idea, but with additional Attributes—namely, Holiness, Love, Providence, Justice and Mercy: and

[*f 172*] ~~3~~ 5

together with these ~~the~~ extramundane, ~~ex~~ and ~~real~~, existence and personality of this Being, as our Creator, Lord & Judge.

(r)   MS BM Egerton 2801 ff 169–170
AR (1825) 159–61; *Sp Aph B II* above at nn 24–6.

Taking up the argument from before the passage deleted in the previous section.   2

legitimate.

It is too seldom considered, tho' most worthy of consideration, how far even those Ideas or Theories of pure Speculation, that ~~seem~~ bear the same ~~as~~ name with the Objects of Religious Faith, are indeed the same. Out of the principles necessarily presumed in all discursive Thinking, and which being, in the first place, *universal*, and, secondly, antecedent to ~~all~~ every particular exercise of the Understanding, are therefore referred to the Reason, the human Mind (wherever its powers are sufficiently developed, and its attention strongly directed to speculative or theoretical inquiries) forms certain ~~Notional~~ Ideas, to which by the necessity of its own constitution it gives a relative and notional *Subsistence*. Hence they are called *Entia rationalia*: the conversion of which into Entia *realia* or real Objects by aid of the Imagination has in all times been the fruitful Stock of empty Theories and mischievous Superstitions, of surreptitious Premises and extravagant Conclusions. For as these substantiated Notions were

[*f 169ᵛ*]   3

in many instances expressed by the same terms, as the objects of religious Faith; as in most instances they were applied, ⟨tho' deceptively,⟩ to the explanation of ~~outward~~ real experiences; and lastly, from the ⟨gratifications, which the⟩ pride and ambition of Man received from the supposed extension of human Knowlege & Insight; it was too easily forgotten or overlooked, that the stablest and most indispensable of these notional Beings were but the necessary *forms* of Thinking, taken abstractly: and that like the breadthless Lines, depthless Surfaces, and perfect Circles of Geometry, they subsisted wholly and solely in and for the Mind, that contemplates them. ~~Beyond~~ Where the ~~precincts~~ evidence of the Senses fails us, and beyond the precincts of sensible †experiences, there is no *Reality* attributable to any Idea, but what is given to it by Revelation, or the Law of Conscience, or the necessary interests of Morality.

Take an instance. It is the office, and, as it were, the instinct of Reason to bring a unity

† How far even ⟨these, how far even⟩ the phænomena of Sense, or as the materials of Experience are ⟨rightful⟩ exceptions, will be found considered at large in the Chapter on Faith in the "Assertion of Religion &c, already spoken of.

[*f 170*]   4
into all our conceptions and several knowleges. On this all system depends: and without this we could reflect connectedly neither on Nature or [our/own] minds. Now this is possible only on the assumption or hypothesis of a ONE as the Ground and Cause of the Universe, and which in all succession and thro' all changes is the subject neither of Time or Change. The ONE must be contemplated as Eternal and Immutable.

Well! The Idea, which is the basis of Religion, commanded by the Conscience and required by Morality, contains the same truths or at least Truths that can be expressed in no other terms; but this Idea presents itself to our Mind with additional Attributes, and these too not formed by mere Abstraction and Negation—with the Attributes of Holiness, Providence, Love, Justice and Mercy. It comprehends, moreover, the independent (*extra-mundane*) existence and personality of the Supreme ONE, as our Creator, Lord, and Judge.

(s)   MS BM Egerton 2801 ff 172–173ᵛ
           AR (1825) 161–3; *Sp Aph B. II* at nn 27–31 above.

In the ms the opening of this section is continuous with the cancelled end of section (q) above, which also forms part of f 172. The sentence beginning "No man . . ." on f 173 is the long sentence which C wished the publisher to change (*CL* v 321), and which he evidently did. After ". . . to God only but. . ." the printer has marked "M 161", indicating the original opening to signature M (see *CL* v 321 again); in *AR* (1825) the sentence is on p 163. See above, Editor's Introduction pp xcix, ci. The footnote quotation is from the 1818 *Friend*: see *Friend (CC)* i 317.

The ~~Idea~~ Principle of a one ground and principle of the Universe is raised into the Idea of ⟨the LIVING⟩ GOD, ~~as~~ the ⟨supreme⟩ Object of our Faith, Love, Fear and ~~exclusive~~ Adoration. Religion and Morality ~~no less than Reason~~ do indeed, constrain us to declare him Eternal and Immutable. But if from the former attribute ~~we~~ a Reasoner should deduce the impossibility of a Creation; or ⟨conclude⟩ with Aristotle, that the creation was Co-eternal; or, like the later Platonists, turn it into an *emanation* from Deity as the Rays from the Sun; or if from the latter ⟨he should infer,⟩ that all Prayer and Supplication must be vain and superstitious: then ~~let the inference~~ however evident & logically necessary such conclusions may appear ⟨from the Principle premised,⟩ it is scarcely worth our while to examine, ~~into~~ whether ~~there is or is not a flaw in the Argument~~ it is so or not. ~~For~~ †The Positions so deduced *must* be false. For were they true, the Idea would ~~have every~~ lose the sole ground of its *reality*.

[*f 172ᵛ*] 6
It would be no longer the Idea intended ⟨by the Believer in *his* premise—⟩ in the

Premise, with which alone Religion and Morality were concerned. The very subject of the discussion would be changed. It would no longer be the GOD, in whom we *believe*; but a stoical FATE, or the superessential ONE of Plotinus, to whom ~~not even Being, much less~~ neither Intelligence, or Self-consciousness, or Life, or even *Being* dare be attributed; or lastly, the World itself, ~~considered~~ the indivisible one and only substance (*Substantia una et unica*) of Spinoza, ~~the~~ of which all the phænomena, all particular and individual Things, Lives, Minds, Thoughts and Actions are modifications.

Let the religious inquirer never be alarmed by any objections to his faith, or to any article of it, that are built wholly on speculative grounds, ~~and on which~~ when they are either alien or repugnant to the dictates of Conscience and the interests of Morality. For to baffle the Objector he has only to demand of him, by what right and under what authority he converts a Thought into

[*f 173*] 7

a Substance, or asserts ~~a reality~~ the existence of of a real somewhat in exact correspondence to a Notion, ~~that does not refer to any~~ not derived from the experience of his Senses. It will be of no purpose for him to answer, that it is a *legitimate* Notion. The *Idea* may originate in the Speculative Reason; but its realization ~~can bet~~ must be the work of the FANCY.

A reflecting Reader will easily apply these remarks to the subject of Election, one of the stumbling stones in the ordinary conceptions of the Christian Faith, ~~on~~ to which the Infidel points in scorn, and which far better men pass by in silent perplexity. Yet surely, from mistaken conceptions of the Doctrine. No man who is fully and earnestly convinced of a future existence, and that a state of perfect and enduring Bliss is attainable by man under certain conditions, declared by Scripture and attested by the Conscience; and who knows, that the conditions so prescribed are of such ⟨a⟩ kind ~~that~~ as to render it impossible that the true and faithful *performance* of them should not have certain *Consequences*, some of which may indeed be visible

[*f 173ᵛ*] 8   M 161

to God only, but others (and these plainly stated and distinctly described in the New Testament) of such a nature that they *may* (and ⟨if⟩ there be no fault in the will, ~~must~~ cannot but) be *ascertained* by every Individual, in relation to *himself*; and †*negatively* in ~~relation to the~~ the case of other men; and that these latter consequences are sure *Marks* and *taken collectively* (that is, where the consciousness of the inward life is in harmony with the outward Conduct, where the Conscience bears witness to the principle, and the principle is manifested in the actions) safe *Pledges*, that he is at the time in the right road to the Life promised to him on the continued performance of the Conditions;—no such man, I say, however fervent his Charity, and however deep his humility, may be, ~~can attentively reflect on the facts, knowlege learnt from history and his own experience,~~ can ~~have~~ peruse the records of History with a reflecting spirit or "look round the

† "In this world a good life is a presumption of a good Man; his virtuous *actions* are for other men the only possible, tho' still ambiguous, manifestations of his virtue. *But the absence of a good life is not only a presumption but a proof of the Contrary, as long as it continues.*" FRIEND, Vol. II. p. 224.

(t)   MS BM Egerton 2801 f 187–187ᵛ
                 Cf *AR* (1825) 163; *Sp Aph B II* n 31 above.

Another attempt to clarify the long sentence in ms (s) above. In view of the opening it is more likely to be the missing one referred to in C's letter to Hessey, *CL* v 321, than the one enclosed in that letter. This one was not used; that one may have been: see p 170, lines 17–22 above. The "Judicious Friend" may well have been C himself: cf *BL* ch 13 *(CC)* ɪ 300 and n.

   To the Printer.
P. 160: last line but 8 to line 12 of p. 161. "this long and complex Sentence would require the Author himself to read it out, with all the nice shades of emphasis, and nicely measured pauses and semi-cadences, in order to be intelligible." So writes a Judicious Friend. I have in consequence of this remark cast the passage anew, into several independent periods; but despair of correcting it by means of marginal alterations, so as not to confuse and perplex the Compositor. Therefore, as the lesser evil, I write the whole, as it is to stand. Turn over leaf.

[*f 187ᵛ*]
~~The conditions (rules) in scripture, (Certain rules are prescribed) as the~~ conditions under which
~~A state of enduring Bliss~~. I
   I suppose the mind already convinced that a state of enduring Bliss is attainable under certain conditions; the compliance, to ~~with~~, with the rules prescribed and the directions given in the Christian Scriptures: These Rules ~~are~~ being such, ~~in themselves~~ that a full and faithful compliance therewith by the very law & constitution of human

(u)   MS Univ Iowa Library c 693 com
                AR (1825) 215–18; *Sp Aph B VIIIb* at nn 27–9.

Sold by Blackwell in 1950. Folio lᵛ is used for the fair copy of the footnote to *AR* (1825) 226, first drafted in a deleted passage on f 1, and for an instruction in relation to the last lines on that page: "OBSERVE, to print the sentences within the crotchets as a separate paragraph; but yet retaining the crotchet [at the beginning and end of the paragraph." A mark, before the words "a brief analysis . .", is evidently by the printer and corresponds to the beginning of p 217 in *AR* (1825).

UNDERSTANDING	REASON
1. Understanding is discursive.	1. Reason is fixed.
2. The Understanding in all its judgements refers to some other Faculty as its ultimate Authority.	2. Reason in all its decisions appeals to itself, as the ground and *substance* of their truth. (*Hebrews*, VI. v. 13.)
3. Understanding is the Faculty of *Reflection*.	3. Reason of Contemplation. Reason indeed is far nearer to SENSE than to Understanding: for Reason (says our great HOOKER) is a direct Aspect of Truth, an

inward Beholding, having a
similar relation to the
Intelligible or Spiritual, as
SENSE has to the Material or
Phænomenal.

~~It is impossible to~~ The Result is: that neither falls under the definition of the other. They differ *in kind*: and had my object been confined to the ~~proof~~ establishment of this fact, the preceding Columns would have superseded all further disquisition. But I have ever in view the especial interests of my youthful Readers, whose reflective *power* is to be cultivated, as well as their particular reflections to be called forth and guided. Now the main chance of

[*f* 2]

their *reflecting* on religious subjects *aright*, and of their attaining to the *contemplation* of spiritual truths *at all*, rests on their insight into the *nature* of this disparity still more than on their conviction of its existence. I now, therefore, proceed to a brief analysis of the Understanding, in elucidation of the definitions already given.

The Understanding then, (considered exclusively as an organ of human intelligence) is the Faculty by which we reflect and generalize. Take, for instance, any Object consisting of many parts, a House or a Group of Houses: and if it be contemplated, as a Whole, i.e. as many constituting a One) it ~~in~~ forms what in the technical language of Psychology is called a *total impression*. Among the various component parts of this we direct our attention especially to such as we recollect to have noticed in other total impressions. ~~and~~ Then, by a voluntary Act we withhold our attention from all the rest to reflect exclusively on these ~~which henceforth, (are thus considered) and called~~ And these we henceforward use as *common characters*, ~~of~~ by virtue of which the several Objects are referred to one and the same * sort. ~~(*(This parenth to be printed as a Note.) According as we attend more or less to the differences, the *Sort* becomes of course more or less comprehensive: and hence the necessity, in the more comprehensive (Zoology, Botany and) other Departments (for the systematic Naturalists) of natural history, of distinguishing the Sorts into Orders, Classes, Families, &c: all which, however, resolve themselves for the Logician into the Conception of Genus and Species, i.e. comprehending and comprehended.)~~ Thus, the whole Process may be reduced to three acts, all depending on and ~~pre~~ supposing a previous impression on the Senses: first, the appropriation of our Attention; 2. (and in order to the continuance of the first) Abstraction, or the voluntary withholding of the Attention; and 3. Generalization. And these are the proper Functions of the Understanding: and the power of so doing is what we mean when we say, we possess Understanding, or are created with the Faculty of Understanding.

[It is obvious, that the third Function includes the act of comparing one object with another: and in Note II (for, not to interrupt the argument I ~~have removed this part of the enquiry~~ avail myself of this most

[*f* 1ᵛ]

*According as we attend more or less to the differences, the *Sort* becomes, of course, more or less comprehensive. Hence there arises for the systematic Naturalist the necessity of subdividing the Sorts into Orders, Classes, Families, &c: all which, however, resolve themselves for the mere Logician into the conception of Genus and Species, i.e. the comprehending, and the comprehended.

(v)   MS BM Egerton 2801 f 155

See *AR* (1825) 235–6 (cf *Sp Aph B IX* (Comment) after n 24), for which this is a rough first draft.

10

which is required by the * facts, the Professor explained the nature of *the adaptive power* (= the faculty of adapting means to relative ends) *generally*, and the ~~specific character~~ nature of of ~~the human~~ the Understanding ⟨in Man⟩ as differenced from Instinct in Animals, *in specie*, in a form which ~~retaining~~ giving the substance of ~~my~~ what ~~convictions prevented~~ freed ~~them from even the semblance of paradox, omnem offendiculi ansam praecidens. I mean and had long been trying to convey &c~~.

(w)   MS Sotheby 1990
            AR (1825) 257n–258n; *Sp Aph B Xb* at nn 13–14 above
                 (pp 267fn lines 7–8, 268fn lines 4–6).

Part of a leaf containing the beginning of C's footnote to *AR* (1825) 257 (signature S), evidently from a packet sent for insertion at proof stage: see also next section. Sold at Sotheby's 13 Dec 1990. Text from a transcription made while in possession of a previous owner. A transverse note in Gillman's hand identifies the writing as Coleridge's.

Continuation of the Comment on Aph. IX (Original Sin) from last line of p. 6 of Slip 2nd.—As but a few lines only of the Comment have been written in p. 6 I page this as *page the first* and distinguish the papers by K.
    S,257
[*the rest of the sheet is cut away*]

(*verso*)
P. 5. *insert*
        (relatively to the World *without*, or to Things as
        they [. . .] subsist independently of our perceptions)

Note * continued

to the Law of Continuity (*Lex Continui. In Natura non datur Saltus*) which Law [. . .] the human understanding [*words cut away*] of its own constitution can

(x)   MS VCL S MS F 1.16
                AR (1825) 294–5; *Sp Aphs B XIV–XV*.

The cancelled numbering of the Aphorisms as "V" and "VI" suggests that they were originally intended to appear earlier. The "K" at the beginning probably identifies this as belonging to some additional papers beginning with Fragment (w) above: see C's explanation there. The filling in of the blank space in Aphorism "VI" as "XII" in *AR* (1825) is correct, though this does not follow the comment on Original Sin immediately, as C's footnote might suggest. The verso accommodates an overflow from the next page of C's copy for the printer: see *AR* (1825) 296 and end of *Sp Aph B XV* above.

K   20

The Printer must add the numbers of
the Aphorisms—

APH. ~~V~~   Leighton

As in great Maps or Pictures you will see the borders decorated with meadows, fountains, flowers, &c represented in it; but in the middle you have the main design: so amongst the works of God is it with the fore-ordained Redemption of Man. All his other works in the world, all the beauty of the creatures, the succession of ages and the things that come to pass in them, are but as the Border to this as the Main-piece. But as a foolish unskilful beholder, not discerning the excellency of the principal piece in such maps or pictures, gazes only on the fair Border, and goes no farther—thus do the greatest part of us as to this great Work of God, the redemption of our personal Being and the re-union of the Human with the Divine by and thro' the Divine Humanity of the Incarnate Word.

APH. ~~VI~~   LUTHER.

It is a hard matter, yea an impossible thing for thy human strength whosoever thou art (without God's assistance) at such a time when Moses setteth on thee with the Law (see Aphorism   *), when the holy Law written in thy heart accuseth and condemneth thee, forcing thee to a comparison of thy heart therewith, and convicting thee of the incompatibleness of thy Will and Nature with Heaven and Holiness and ~~the~~ an immediate God—that then thou should~~stest~~ be ~~of~~ able to be of such a mind as if no Law nor Sin had ever been! I say it is in a manner impossible that a human creature when he feeleth himself assaulted with trials and temptations

*⟨to the Printer⟩ I mean the aphorism on Moral *Science*, that which follows the comment on Original Sin./

[*verso*]
meant only the *ceremonial* Law is a notion, that could originate only in utter inattention to the whole strain and gist of the Apostle's Argument.

(y¹)   MS Penn State Univ Library CoS 840
AR (1825) 316; *Sp Aph B XIX* at nn 27–32.

This extract and the next, (y²), originally formed a single leaf, numbered "10". See also entries (y¹ᵛ) and (y²ᵛ) below.

on the material body, or limited by the circumstances and processes indispensable to its organization and subsistence.

But even this would be an imperfect statement, if we omitted the aweful truth, that besides that ~~passing absence~~ dissolution of ~~the~~ our earthly tabernacle which we call death, there is another death, not the mere negation of life, but its positive Opposite. And as there is a mystery of Life and an assimilation to the Principle of Life, even to him who is *the* Life; so is there a mystery of Death and an assimilation ⟨to⟩ the Principle of Evil ἀμφιθαλής θανάτῳ, a fructifying of the corrupt Seed, of which Death is the germination. Thus the regeneration to Spiritual life is at the same time a redemption from the spiritual death.

(y²)   MS Blackwell 1980
          AR (1825) 316–17; *Sp Aph B XIX* at nn 33–42.

See headnotes to sections (y¹), (y¹ᵛ) and (y²ᵛ). Sold by Blackwell in 1980. Transcribed while in possession of a former owner.

Respecting the redemptive act itself, and the Divine Agent, we know from revelation that he "was made a quickening (Ζωοποιοῦν, *life-making*) Spirit": and that in order to this it was necessary, that God should be manifested in the flesh, that the eternal Word, through whom and by whom the World (κοσμος, the Order, Beauty, and sustaining Law of ~~the~~ visible natures) was and is, should be made flesh, assume our humanity personally, and fulfil all righteousness, and suffer and so die for us as in dying to conquer Death ~~and~~ ⟨for⟩ as many as should receive him. More than this, the mode, the possibility, we ~~have no faculty~~ are not competent to know. It is, as hath been already observed concerning the primal Act of Apostacy, a mystery by the necessity of the Subject—a mystery, which ~~we may~~ at all events it will time enough ⟨for us⟩ to seek and expect to understand, when we understand the mystery of our *Natural* life, and its conjunction with mind and will and personal identity. Even the truths, that are given to us to know, we can know only thro' faith in the Spirit. They are spiritual things that must be spiritually discerned.

(y¹ᵛ)   MS Penn State Univ Library CoS 840 verso
          AR (1825) 317 lines 13–15; *Sp Aph B XIX* after n 42.

An insertion for the (missing) opposite recto page of C's copy for the printer. See headnote to (y¹) above.

(where no ~~description title~~ Expression could be commensurate, no single title be other than imperfect) seek from simi &c

(y²ᵛ)   MS Blackwell 1980 verso
          AR (1825) 318–19; *Sp Aph B XIX* at n 58.

An insertion for the same opposite page of printer's copy. Written under that on (y¹ᵛ). See headnote to section (y¹) above.

∧   Had you involved yourself in a heavy debt for certain gew-gaws, for high-seasoned meats and intoxicating drinks, and glistering apparel, and in default of a paper had made over yourself as a bondsman, to a hard Creditor, who, ~~was~~ it was foreknown, would enforce the bond of Judgement to the last tittle! With what emotions would you receive the glad tidings, that a stranger, or a friend whom in the days of your wantonness you had neglected and reviled, had payed the debt for you, had made satisfaction to your Creditor. But you have incurred a debt of Death ⟨to the EVIL NATURE!⟩ you have sold yourself over to SIN! and relatively to *you* and to all your means and resources, the Seal on the Bond

(z)   MS BM Egerton 2801 f 224
Cf *AR* (1825) 338; *Sp Aph B XXIIIa* at n 12.

Copy for the printer, probably used but then changed in proof. The Latin, where differing from that in *AR* (1825) and *AR* (1831), means ''(I speak in Latin to reduce the acrimony)'' and ''miracles were nothing other than a kind of acid test by which it was proved . . .''

The commencement of this last §ph. to stand thus.—
The plain inference from the passage in question is: ~~this:~~ (ad invidiam compescendam Latinè loquor) *miracula* nihil aliud esse quam quiddam *experimentum crucis* quo probatum fuit, Homines non, pecudum instar, omnino perituros esse. Now this doctrine appears to me without authority in the *letter*, and alien from the spirit, of the Scripture. I see nothing without, I find nothing within, that enables me to understand it. I can, however, perfectly well understand, why *those* should be ready ore pleno jurare in hoc Paleyii Dictum, qui nihil aliud in ⟨toto⟩ Evangelio invenire posse profitentur.

A FRAGMENT FROM THE EARLIEST PROOF, 1823

A leaf from the earliest proof, printed off before Coleridge made his changes to the design and order of the volume late in 1823, has survived bound into a volume which he annotated and which is now in the BM (C 43 e 24): W. G. Tennemann *Geschichte der Philosophie* (Leipzig 1798–1817) VIII i, between pages 346 and 347. The two sides of the fragment are reproduced following this page in the present edition. For an account of its significance, and the revisions made for the 1825 edition, see above, Editor's Introduction at n 57. The first two paragraphs were omitted in 1831, having appeared in *AR* (1825) on pp 37–8 (see App G(i) below). The third and fourth (*AR*—1825—37–8) are on p 48 above.

5. Two pages from the first proof of *Aids to Reflection* (1825),
showing the earlier proposed format and Coleridge's original corrections
British Library; reproduced by kind permission

or hurried hither and thither, and sometimes, flying high, are ensnared by pride, sometimes brought down and caught by pleasure? But, as it is shameful for him who rules over nations, to be a slave at home, and for the man who sits at the helm of the state, to be meanly subjected to the beck of a contemptible harlot, or even of an imperious wife; will it not be, in like manner, disgraceful for you, who exercise dominion over the beasts that are without you, to be subject to a great many, and those of the worst sort, that roar and domineer in your distempered mind*?"

LEIGHTON, vol. iv. p. 268.

"* There is a settled friendship, nay, a near relation and similitude between God and good men; he is even their father; but, in their education, he inures them to hardships. When, therefore, you see them struggling with difficulties, sweating, and employed in up-hill work; while the wicked, on the other hand, are in high spirits, and swim in pleasures; con-

---

* Θεῷ ἂν ὅμοιÓ· ἰσὶ διὰ τῆς χρηςότητος, διὰ τὸ ἀνεξικακίας· διὰ καὶ, γνησίας, μισοπονηρὸς ὢν καὶ κατάκατον τῶν παθῶν τῶν ἐνδον ἄρχε Θηρίων· τί οὖν ἐρεῖς; ἐγὼ Θηρία ἐχὼ ἐν ἐμαυτῷ; καὶ μυρία πάλιν ὄχλον ἐν σοὶ Θηρίων ἔχεις, καὶ μὴ ὑβοῦν νομίσας εἶναι τὸ λεγόμενον. Πόσον Θηρίον ἐςὶν ὁ θυμος ὅταν ὑλακῇ τῇ καρδίᾳ, &c.

sider, that we are pleased with modesty in our
children, and forwardness in our slaves: the
former we keep under by severe discipline,
while we encourage impudence in the latter.
Be persuaded, that God takes the same method.
He does not pamper the good man with delicious fare, but tries him; he accustoms him
to hardships, and, (which is a wonderful expression in a heathen) PREPARES HIM FOR
HIMSELF*." LEIGHTON, p. 274, 275.

"And if we seriously consider this subject
but a little, we shall find the saying of the wise
king Solomon concerning this wisdom, to be
unexceptionably true: *Her ways are ways of
pleasantness, and all her paths are peace.*

"Doth religion require any thing of us more
than that we live *soberly, righteously, and
godly in this present world?* Now what, I
pray, can be more pleasant or peaceable than

* Inter bonos viros ad DEUM est amicitia, imo neces-
situdo, et similitudo, imo ille eorum pater, sed durius eos
educat, cum itaq; eos videris laborare, sudare, et ardum
ascendere, malos autem lascivire, et voluptatibus fluere,
cogita, filiorum nos modesta delectare, vernularum
licentia: illos disciplina tristiori contineri, horum ali
audaciam. Idem tibi de DEO liqueat, bonum virum
deliciis non innutrit, experitur, indurat, et SIBI ILLUM
PRÆPARAT.

APPENDIX C

J. H. GREEN'S
DISCUSSION OF INSTINCT

J. H. GREEN'S DISCUSSION
OF INSTINCT

THE FOLLOWING extract from J. H. Green *Vital Dynamics* (1840)
App F, pp 88–96, which is closely related to the discussion of instinct in *Aids to Reflection* (see above, *Sp Aph B IX* nn 23, 31, and 38;
and cf *Mor Aph XV* n 13), was first reprinted by HNC as an appendix to
the fifth edition of *AR* (1843) II 328–34.

What is Instinct? As I am not quite of Bonnet's opinion "that philosophers will in vain torment themselves to define instinct until they have
spent some time in the head of the animal without actually being that
animal," I shall endeavour to explain the use of the term. I shall not
think it necessary to controvert the opinions which have been offered on
this subject, whether the ancient doctrine of Descartes, who supposed
that animals were mere machines; or the modern one of Lamark, who
attributes instincts to habits impressed upon the organs of animals, by
the constant efflux of the nervous fluid to these organs to which it has
been determined in their efforts to perform certain actions, to which their
necessities have given birth. And it will be here premature to offer any
refutation of the opinions of those who contend for the identity of this
faculty with reason, and maintain that all the actions of animals are the
result of invention and experience;—an opinion maintained with considerable plausibility by Dr. Darwin.

   "Perhaps the most ready and certain mode of coming to a conclusion
in this intricate inquiry will be by the apparently circuitous route of determining first, what we do not mean by the word. Now we certainly do
not mean, in the use of the term, any act of the vital power in the production or maintenance of an organ: nobody thinks of saying that the
teeth grow by instinct, or that when the muscles are increased in vigour
and size in consequence of exercise, it is from such a cause or principle.
Neither do we attribute instinct to the direct functions of the organs in
providing for the continuance and sustentation of the whole co-organized body. No one talks of the liver secreting bile, or of the heart acting

459

for the propulsion of the blood, by instinct. Some, indeed, have maintained that breathing, even voiding the excrement and urine, are instinctive operations; but surely these, as well as the former, are automatic, or at least are the necessary result of the organization of the parts in and by which the actions are produced. These instances seem to be, if I may so say, below instinct. But again, we do not attribute instinct to any actions preceded by a will conscious of its whole purpose, calculating its effects, and predetermining its consequences, nor to any exercise of the intellectual powers, of which the whole scope, aim, and end are intellectual. In other terms, no man who values his words will talk of the instinct of a Howard, or of the instinctive operations of a Newton and Leibnitz, in those sublime efforts, which ennoble and cast a lustre, not less on the individuals than on the whole human race.

"To what kind or mode of action shall we then look for the legitimate application of the term? In answer to this query, we may, I think, without fear of the consequences, put the following cases as exemplifying and justifying the use of the term, Instinct, in an appropriate sense. First, when there appears an action, not included either in the mere functions of life, acting within the sphere of its own organismus; nor yet an action attributable to the intelligent will or reason: yet at the same time, not referable to any particular organ, we then declare the presence of an Instinct. We might illustrate this in the instance of a bull-calf butting before he has horns, in which the action can have no reference to its internal economy, to the presence of a particular organ, or to an intelligent will. Secondly, likewise if it be not indeed included in the first, we attribute Instinct where the organ is present, if only the act is equally anterior to all possible experience on the part of the individual agent, as for instance, when the beaver employs its tail for the construction of its dwelling; the tailor-bird its bill for the formation of its pensile habitation; the spider its spinning organ for fabricating its artfully woven nets, or the viper its poison fang for its defence. And lastly, generally, where there is an act of the whole body as one animal, not referable to a will conscious of its purpose, nor to its mechanism, nor to a habit derived from experience, nor previous frequent use. Here with most satisfaction, and without doubt of the propriety of the word, we declare an Instinct; as examples of which, we may adduce the migratory habits of birds, the social instincts of the bees, the construction of their habitations, composed of cells formed with geometrical precision, adapted in capacity to different orders of the society, and forming storehouses for containing a supply of provisions; not to mention similar instances in wasps, ants, termites; and the endless contrivances for protecting the future progeny.

"But if it be admitted that we have rightly stated the application of the term, what we may ask is contained in the examples adduced, or what inferences are we to make as to the nature of Instinct itself, as a source and principle of Action? We shall, perhaps, best aid ourselves in the inquiry by an example, and let us take a very familiar one of a caterpillar taking its food. The caterpillar seeks at once the plant, which furnishes the appropriate aliment, and this even as soon as it creeps from the ovum; and the food being taken into the stomach, the nutritious part is separated from the innutritious, and is disposed of for the support of the animal. The question then is, what is contained in this instance of instinct? In the first place what does the vital power in the stomach do, if we generalize the account of the process, or express it in its most general terms? Manifestly it selects and applies appropriate means to an immediate end, prescribed by the constitution; first of the particular organ, and then of the whole body or organismus. This we have admitted is not instinct. But what does the caterpillar do? Does it not also select and apply appropriate means to an immediate end prescribed by its particular organization and constitution? But there is something more; it does this according to circumstances; and this we call Instinct. But may there not be still something more involved? What shall we say of Hüber's humble-bees? A dozen of these were put under a bell glass along with a comb of about ten silken cocoons, so unequal in height as not to be capable of standing steadily; to remedy this, two or three of the humble-bees got upon the comb, stretched themselves over its edge, and with their heads downwards, fixed their forefeet on the table on which the comb stood, and so with their hindfeet kept the comb from falling: when these were weary others took their places. In this constrained and painful posture, fresh bees relieving their comrades at intervals, and each working in its turn, did these affectionate little insects support the comb for nearly three days; at the end of which time they had prepared sufficient wax to build pillars with it. And what is still further curious, the first pillars having got displaced, the bees had again recourse to the same manœuvre. What then is involved in this case? Evidently the same selection and appropriation of means to an immediate end as before; but observe! according to varying circumstances.

"And here we are puzzled; for this becomes Understanding. At least no naturalist, however predetermined to contrast and oppose Instinct to Understanding, but ends at last in facts in which he himself can make out no difference. But are we hence to conclude that the instinct is the same, and identical with the human understanding? Certainly not; though the difference is not in the essential of the definition, but in an addition to, or modification of, that which is essentially the same in both. In such cases, namely, as that which we have last adduced, in which instinct assumes the semblance of understanding, the act indicative of instinct is not clearly prescribed by the constitution or laws of the animal's peculiar organization, but arises out of the constitution and previous circumstances of the animal, and those habits, wants, and that predetermined sphere of action and operation which belong to the race, and beyond the limits of which it does not pass. If this be the case, I may venture to assert that I have determined an appropriate sense for instinct: namely, that it is a power of selecting and applying appropriate means to an immediate end, according to circumstances and the changes of circumstances, these being variable and varying; but yet so as to be referable to the general habits, arising out of the constitution and previous circumstances of the animal considered not as an individual, but as a race.

"We may here, perhaps, most fitly explain the error of those who contend for the identity of Reason and Instinct, and believe that the actions of animals are the result of invention and experience. They have, no doubt, been deceived, in their investigation of Instinct, by an efficient cause simulating a final cause; and the defect in their reasoning has arisen in consequence of observing in the instinctive operations of animals the adaptation of means to a relative end, from the assumption of a deliberate purpose. To this freedom or choice in action and purpose, instinct, in any appropriate sense of the word, cannot apply, and to justify and explain its introduction, we must have recourse to other and higher faculties than any manifested in the operations of instinct. It is evident, namely, in turning our attention to the distinguishing character of human actions, that there is, as in the inferior animals, a selection and appropriation of means to ends—but it is (not only according to circumstances, not only according to varying circumstances, but it is) according to varying purposes. But this is an attribute of the intelligent will, and no longer even mere understanding.

"And here let me observe that the difficulty and delicacy of this investigation are greatly increased by our not considering the understanding (even our own) in itself, and as it would be were it not accompanied with and modified by the co-operation of the will, the moral feeling, and that faculty, perhaps best distinguished by the name of Reason, of determining that which is universal and necessary, of fixing laws and principles whether speculative or practical, and of contemplating a final purpose or end. This intelligent will,—having a self-conscious purpose, under the guidance and light of the reason, by which its acts are made to bear as a whole upon some end in and for itself, and to which the understanding is subservient as an organ or the faculty of selecting and appropriating the means—seems best to account for that progressiveness of the human race, which so evidently marks an insurmountable distinction and impassable barrier between man and the inferior animals; but which would be inexplicable, were there no other difference than in the degree of their intellectual faculties.

"Man doubtless has his instincts, even in common with the inferior animals, and many of these are the germs of some of the best feelings of his nature. What, amongst many, might I present as a better illustration, or more beautiful instance, than the *storge* or maternal instinct? But man's instincts are elevated and ennobled by the moral ends and purposes of his being. He is not destined to be the slave of blind impulses, a vessel purposeless, unmeant. He is constituted by his moral and intelligent will, to be the first freed being, the master-work and the end of nature; but this freedom and high office can only co-exist with fealty and devotion to the service of truth and virtue. And though we may even be permitted to use the term instinct, in order to designate those high impulses which in the minority of man's rational being, shape his acts unconsciously to ultimate ends, and which in constituting the very character and impress of the humanity reveal the guidance of Providence; yet the convenience of the phrase, and the want of any other distinctive appellation for an influence *de supra*, working unconsciously in and on the whole human race, should not induce us to forget that the term instinct is only strictly applicable to the adaptive power, as the faculty, even in its highest proper form, of selecting and adapting appropriate means to proximate ends according to varying circumstances,—a faculty which however, only differs from human understanding in consequence of the latter being enlightened by reason, and that the principles which actuate man as ultimate ends, and are designed for his conscious possession and guidance, are best and most properly named Ideas."

FOUR EXTENDED NOTES ON
AIDS TO REFLECTION (1825)

FOUR EXTENDED NOTES ON
AIDS TO REFLECTION (1825)

FOUR LONG notes by Coleridge concerning matters in *Aids to Reflection* to which he attached especial importance, made after its first publication in presentation copies and notebooks, are reproduced here, with variant readings where appropriate. Full details are given in the headnotes to the individual entries.

In subsequent years all four passages found their way from manuscript into editions of the work. The discussion of consciousness (*c*) was incorporated into *AR* (1831) after *Moral Aphorism XV*, while the discussion of reason and understanding (*a*) appeared as the Appendix to the same edition. The note on baptism (*d*) was inserted by HNC in square brackets into the fifth edition (1843) after the long discussion of that topic, while in the seventh edition (1854) the distinction between criminal deed and sinful act (*b*) was introduced at the appropriate point by DC as a footnote. Once published all four passages were retained by HNC and DC in subsequent editions.

Some further notes, gathered by DC from manuscript into the seventh edition, are noticed briefly in Appendix H below.

(a) The distinction between Reason and Understanding

(i) From *AR* (1825) Copy 1(a) (COPY A in the *CC* notes: see App E below). JDC notes croppings of the text in both annotations, indicated here by "[. . . .]".

(1) An annotation indicated at p viii, line 18 (= *Pref* at n 7, above):

Reason may be considered, either in relation to intelligence, i.e., either as the *Speculative* or *Theoretic* Reason = A
or, in relation to our moral being, i.e., as the Practical Reason = a

I [. . . .] the understanding is taken, either as a mode or faculty of *thinking*, i.e. as Reflection = B or as a mode or principle of *Acting* = b
I define each of the four, that is, describe it by its *Essential Characters*: and, I find the definition of A differs in toto [. . . .] B [. . . .] of b. Therefore the Subjects are diverse by the axiom
Subjects that fall under the same general Definition are of the same kind: et vice versâ.   S. T. C.

467

(2) An annotation marked at p 234, line 14 (= *Sp Aph B IX* at n 21, above):

§ Observe, my position is, the diversity of the Understanding from the Reason.

My axiom is—Subjects that fall under the same general definition are of the same Genus & vice versâ; Subjects that cannot be brought under the same General Definition are not Eiusdem Generis [. . . .] I took it in two senses, i.e. I ~~contemplated~~sidered Reason under two points of view—1. as theoretic & contemplative and 2. as practical: and gave the definition of each. Of course, I was bound to consider the understanding 1. as cogitative, i.e. as the reflective faculty and [2.] as active. The first has been examined in comparing it with the theoretic [. . . .] demonstrating the same diversity in respect of its general definition completes the Proof.

(ii) From COPY C pp ⁻2 to ⁻1.

The Scheme of Argument from p. 200 to 242, the pages interposed between 228 and 234 being subtracted, may be thus given:—

The Position is—the Diversity or Difference *in kind*, of THE UNDERSTANDING from THE REASON.

The Axiom, on which the Proof is to rest, is, that

Subjects, which require essentially different General definitions, differ in kind.

Now Reason must be considered, either in relation to the Will or Moral Being, when it is termed the Practical Reason = A;

or relatively to Intelligence, and as a *sciential* Power, when it is termed the Theoretic or Speculative Reason = *a*

The Understanding, therefore, in order to be compared with the Reason, must in like manner be distinguished into

the Understanding as a Principle of ACTION, in which case I term it the ADAPTIVE POWER, or Faculty of adapting means to relative ends = B:

~~or~~ and the U. as a faculty and mode of THINKING, when it is called Reflection = *b*.

Accordingly, I give the General Definitions: that is, I describe each of the four by its *essential* characters: and I find, that

~~A~~ The Definition of A differs *toto genere* from that of B: and

The Definition of *a* from that of *b*

But Subjects, that require essentially different general Definitions, differ *in kind*. Q.E.D.

P.S. In ~~a~~ the larger Work, announced and described at p. 152, in which I proceed *synthetically* from the Idea of the Absolute ~~and then from~~ to the Idea of the Tri-une God, it was in my power to give in a more satisfactory because more positive form the Idea and Genesis of Reason, as it exists for Man, than was possible in the present Volume, in which I was obliged to proceed *analytically* and *a posteriori*/ or rather, *a ~~D~~ datis*. But ~~if~~ taking it as analytic, the unprejudiced and competent Inquirer will, I dare assure myself, find the reasoning legitimate, and the demonstration compleat.

(iii) See *CN* IV 5210. This seems to be a polished version of the previous note, copied into the notebook perhaps for future reference.

(iv) From COPY D, two leaves before title-page preserved separately in BM copy: pp $^-$2 to $^-$1, with last paragraph of footnote written at head of title-page (p 1). COPY I contains a similar note in another hand, differing in details, such as underlinings and ampersands, sometimes corrected in C's hand and reading at the end in his hand after "209": "i.e. as the Opposites of Contingency and Particularity. S. T. Coleridge".

Preparative notice, to facilitate the understanding of the Disquisition, beginning at p. 228: or Scheme of the Argument.

The Position to be proved is—the *difference in kind* of the Understanding from the Reason.

The Axiom, on which the Proof rests, is: Subjects, that require essentially different General Definitions, differ *in kind* and not merely *in degree*. For difference *in degree* forms the ground of *specific* definitions; but not of *generic* or general.

Now Reason is considered either in relation to the Will and Moral Being, when it is termed the * Practical Reason = A:

or relatively to the intellective and sciential Faculties, when it is termed Theoretic or Speculative Reason = *a*.

In order therefore to be compared with the Reason, the Understanding must in like manner be distinguished into

The Understanding as a Principle of ACTION, in which relation I call it the Adaptive Power, or the faculty of selecting and adapting Means to *medial* or *proximate* ends = B:

and the Understanding, as a mode and faculty of Thought, when it is called REFLECTION = *b*.

Accordingly, I give the General Definitions of these four: that is, I describe each severally by its *essential characters*: and I find, that the Definition of A differs *toto genere* from that of B, and the Definition of *a* from that of *b*.

Now Subjects, that require essentially different &c, do themselves differ in kind.

But U. and R. require ess. diff. &c

Therefore U and R. differ in kind. Q.E.D.

* N.B. The Practical Reason alone *is* Reason in the full and substantive Sense. It is Reason in its own sphere of *perfect freedom*, as the source of *IDEAS*, which *Ideas* in their conversion to the responsible Will become *Ultimate* Ends. On the other hand, Theoretic Reason, as the ground of the Universal and Absolute in all Logical *Conclusion*, is rather the *Light* of Reason in the Understanding and known to be such by its contrast with the contingency and particularity which characterize all the proper & indigenous growths of the Understanding.

Hence like an Alien in an inferior Sphere, the Light of Reason, known only by contrast, must *appear* as Necessity and Universality. See p. 168 §2. and p. 208, 209.

(v) C's *Appendix* to *AR* (1831) above. Along with the prefatory note to *AR* (1831) entitled *To the Reader*, this was taken either from COPY D or from a transcript closely associated with it; it has been edited from the ms in ways which may not represent C's considered wishes. See p 413 above.

(b) The distinction between criminal Deed and wicked Act

(i) From a slip inserted in Copy 1(a) (COPY A in the *CC* notes), at p 306, line 5 (= *Sp Aph B XVIII* at n 11, above).

Observe: it is not the criminal *Deed* (Factum noxium) but the wicked *Act* (*Facinus*) that wounds the Conscience. But the Act is inseparable from—say rather, it is *one with*—the Sinful Will as its source. *The Act* is one with the Agent. The Self-deceiving Sinner, however, would fain confound the guilty *Act*, which is always present in its source with the *Deed* which indeed is past. The Act assumes the name and attribute of the *Deed*. But the LAW (i.e. the knowlege of the Law) in the conscience working Remorse, detects & exposes this imposture—compels the Act, (i.e. the Agent in reference to this, his Guilt) to know & confess its continual *present* being: as long as the Will continues unregenerate. But the regenerate Will, which St Paul rightly calls the *New Man*, is by *Grace* not by the *Law*. Does not experience show the same? Remorse can torment, but Remorse without Hope never yet *reformed*, a sinner. Now, there is no true Hope, but in & thro' Christ.

The reader will be pleased to bear in mind that the Author's motive but [?both] for the Note on this slip & for the language of the printed Text is to be found in his desire to initiate the Student into St Paul's views and mode of reasoning—especially in the Epistle to the Romans & the Galatians.

S. T. C.

(ii) From a ms transcript by George Grove of annotations in Southey's copy (COPY B in the *CC* notes: see App E 2(a) below). "Detachability" here is *OED*'s first example of the word.

1. Note on the Fly leaf at the end of the Book—referring to p. 306, line 5.

This and one or two other similar passages were written for the purpose of accustoming the young Student to St Paul's style of Thought and expression. The Impersonation of the Act is in imitation of the Apostle's impersonations of Sin, Law, &c. and the following remarks may show that they are more than mere Hebraisms or Figures of Rhetoric—

It is not the criminal DEED (= *Factum*) but the sinful ACT (= *Facinus*) that wounds the *Conscience*. But the *Act* is inseparable from its spiritual source. See Aph. XII. It is one *with* the sinful Will, *one* therefore *with* the *Agent*, the Man himself *sensu eminenti*. As long as the Will remains the same (in ~~scripture~~ ⟨theological⟩ language as long as the Man is unregenerate) the Act is evermore present *in* the Will even when thro' spiritual lethargy it is not present *to* the Conscience. It is the *Deed* only that can be rightly spoken of as *the past*, id quod factum fuit. Still, however among the tricks and devices of self-delusion, the *Act* (=*the Agent thus abstracted*) would fain lose itself in the *Deed*: and under this impulse it usurps the name, and transfers to itself the predicates, or proper characters of the *Deed*: ex. gr. its singleness, its *detachability* for the imagination, its particularity, and, above all, its *past*ness. In the language of the Day we should express all this by saying, that the Sinner cheats himself by transferring his attention from the corrupt *State* of his Moral Being, to some one or more contingent *result*, *product*, or *symptom* of that State.

Now the Law in the Conscience working *remorse*, detects and unmasks this imposture: compelling the Act (i.e. the Sinner considered abstractly in relation to the Sin) to feel and confess its continuing and abiding *present*ness. In the very act of Remorse, the guilty person *finds* and is made to *know*, that the Act is present in its abiding Principle and *as one with* its Principle. Even to the inmost mind the guilty Act is constrained by the Law to disown its name, as past: as long as the corrupt source remains unregenerate. But the regenerate Will (which the Apostle aptly calls the *New Man*) is by *Grace* and not by the Law. Does not Experience confirm and bear witness to the truth of this doctrine? Remorse can torment, but Remorse without Hope never yet *reformed*, a Sinner. Remorse is no Purgatory Angel. It is a light that *burns*. Now there is no true Hope but in and thro' Christ.—

(iii) From COPY C pp +1 to +2.

NOTE on lines 5, 6 in page 306.

This with similar passages was intended to accustom the readers to Sᵗ Paul's manner of reasoning and expressing his thoughts. And the object of this note is to convince them that the Apostle's impersonations of Sin, Law, &c as of which the Editor's impersonation of the Act in this passage ⟨is an imitation⟩ is are something more than ⟨figures of⟩ rhetoric or Hebraisms.

First. It is not the criminal DEED (*Factum*) but the sinful ACT (*Facinus*) that wounds the Conscience. But the *Act* is inseparable from its spiritual *Source*. See Aph. XII. p. 288. It is *one with* the sinful WILL, *one* therefore *with* the AGENT, with the MAN *himself sensu eminenti*. As long as the Will remains the same— i.e. as long as the Man is unregenerate—the Act is evermore present *in* the Will, even when thro' spiritual lethargy it is not present *to* the Conscience. It is the Deed only that can be attrib rightly spoken of, as the Past—id quod factum *fuit*. (The Regenerate alone can truly say, "Fui*mus* Troes" ["*We* were Trojans"].) Still however, in the tricks and devices of Self-delusion, the Act would fain lose itself in the *Deed*, or confound itself with therewith. ⟨The *Act*⟩ usurps the name and takes on transfers to itself the ⟨predicates,⟩ ex. gr. the singleness, the particularity, and above all the *past*ness, of the Deed. In the language of our times, we should express this by saying, that the Sinner cheats himself by transferring his attention from the corrupt *state* of his Moral Being to some one (or more) contingent *result*, *product*, or *symptom* of the same.

Now the LAW—(that is, the Knowlege of the Law—) in the conscience working remorse detects and exposes this imposture: and compels the ACT (i.e. the Agent, the Sinner considered abstractly in reference to this his Sin) to know and confess its abiding *present*ness. In the very pang of Remorse the guilty person *finds* and is made to *feel*, that the Act is present in its abiding Principle and as one with its Principle. Even to his own the inmost mind "the guilty Act disowns its name as Past": as long as the *Principle*, the corrupt *Will*, remains unregenerate. But the regenerate Will, which the Apostle aptly and significantly calls the *New Man*, is by Grace and not by the Law. Does not our ordinary Experience confirm this, and bear witness to the truth of Sᵗ Paul's doctrine? REMORSE may suffice to *torment*, but Remorse without Hope never yet *reformed*, a Sinner. Remorse is no *Purgatory Angel*. Now there is no true Hope but in and thro' Christ.

S. T. C.

(iv) From COPY D, two leaves preserved separately in BM copy: pp 404 $^{+}$1 to $^{+}$3. COPY I contains a similar note in another hand, differing in details, such as underlinings and ampersands, and sometimes corrected in C's hand. This version includes the footnote (missing in COPY D) indicated by the asterisk after "factum" in both copies: "The Regenerate alone are privileged to say, *Fuimus* Troes" ["*We were* Trojans"]. The reference, as with the corresponding parenthesis in (iii) above, is to Vergil *Aeneid* 2.325.

Note to Lines 5, 6, page 306.

The ACT is here personified in imitation of St Paul's impersonations of LAW and SIN: and for the purpose of accustoming the Biblical Student to the Apostle's mode of thinking and expressing his thoughts. The following remarks may, perhaps, incline the Reader to the opinion that these impersonations are more than Hebraisms or Figures of Rhetoric.—I say, *perhaps*: for this result depends on his insight into the positions layed down on p. 286–296: and his persuasion of their validity. What I am about to add, he may find in his own heart: and then the truth of the said positions will follow as a necessary Consequence. Or he admits the positions, as true in themselves: and then these additional reflections will be the Corollary—

Reflections.

It is not the criminal DEED (*Factum*) but the sinful ACT (*Facinus*) that wounds the Conscience. But the Act is inseparable from its spiritual Source. See Aphorism XII. p. 288. It is *one with* the evil WILL, *one* therefore with the *Agent*, with the *Man himself* sensu eminenti [in an eminent sense]. As long as the Will remains the same—i.e. as long as the Man is unregenerate—the Act is evermore PRESENT *in* the Will, even where thro' spiritual lethargy it is not present *to* the Conscience. It is the *Deed* only that can be rightly described as the Past, as id quod factum **fuit* [that which, having been done, *was*]. Still, however, among other tricks and devices of Self-delusion the Act (i.e. the Agent considered *in abstracto*) would fain lose itself in the *Deed*—: It sinks its own name in that of the particular offence; and while it usurps the Appellation, transfers to itself clandestinely the predicates of the *Deed*, ex. gr. the singleness, the particularity, the *detachability*; but above all, the *past*ness: ~~that~~ all which belong exclusively to the Deed. In the language of ~~the day~~ our times, we ~~should~~ express ~~this by sayinge~~ same thing when we say, that the Sinner cheats himself by transferring his attention from the corrupt *state* of his Moral Being to some one (or more) contingent consequence, product or symptom of this state.

Now the Law in the Conscience—i.e. the Conscience awakened to or by the knowlege of the Law—working *remorse* detects this imposture, and compels the ACT—i.e. the ~~Agent~~ Sinner considered abstractly in reference to this his Sin—to feel and know its own abiding *presentness*. In the very pang of remorse the guilty Person *finds* that the Act is still present in its abiding Principle and as one with the corrupt Will which is its Source. In the inmost mind the Guilty ACT is constrain'd by the LAW in the conscience to disown its usurped name of PAST, as long as its principle continues unregenerate. But the regenerate Will, which ~~the Apostle~~ St Paul aptly denominates *the New Man*, is by Grace and not by the Law. Does not Experience confirm this, and bear witness to the truth of the Apostle's doctrine? Remorse can *torment*, but Remorse without Hope never yet *reformed*, a Sinner. (Remorse is no *Purgatory* Angel. Its Light is a Light that *burns*—a specimen of the unquenchable Fire, from which the Fury's torch had kindled her torch.) Now there is no true Hope but in and thro' Christ.

This is the substance and spirit of the Apostle's Argument. But no one can be th more thoroughly aware than myself, that this and all the other reasonings in the Epist. to the Romans, and to the Galatians, must appear mere jargon to those who substitute this or that scheme of Social and Political Economy for the Science of Ethics, and the calculations of worldly Prudence for the MORAL LAW.

S. T. Coleridge

(c) On the proper role of Consciousness

From *AR* (1825) COPY F p ⁻2. Incorporated, with many slight variations, into *AR* (1831): see *Mor Aph XV* at nn 2–12, above, for further details.

Corollaryies to Aphorism XV. p. 91.

1. The more *consciousness* in your Thoughts and Words, and the less in your Impulses and general Actions—the better and more healthful the state of your both of Head & Heart. As the Flowers from an Orange tree in its time of Blossoming, that burgeon forth, expand, fall and are momently replaced, such is the sequence of hourly and momently Charities in the pure and gracious Soul. The modern Fiction, which depictures the Son of Cytherea with a bandage round his eyes, is not without a Christian spiritual meaning. There is a sweet and holy Blindness in Christian LOVE, even the as there is a Blindness of Life; ⟨yea,⟩ and of Genius ⟨too⟩ in the moment of productive Energy.

Ειργασται: ιδε δ' αυ· εστι γαρ αγαθον.

2. Motives are symptoms of weakness, and Supplements for the deficient Energy for of the living PRINCIPLE, the LAW within us. Let them then be reserved for those momentous Acts and Duties, in which the Strongest and best-balanced Natures must feel themselves deficient, and where Humility, no less than Prudence, prescribes Deliberation. We find a similitude of this, I had almost said a remote analogy, in Organized Bodies. The lowest class of Animals or Protozoa, the Polyps for instance, are without nerves & have neither Brain nor Nerves. Their motive powers all are all from without. The Sun-light, the Warmth, the Air, are their Nerves and Brain. As Life ascends, Nerves appear; but still as only the Instruments Conductors of an *external* Influence. Next are seen the Knots or Ganglions, as so many Foci of *instinctive* Agency, that imperfectly imitate the yet wanting *Center*. ⟨And now the Sign Promise and Token of a true Individuality are disclosed:⟩—It is as both the Reservoir of Sensibility, and the Initiative Power that sets actuates the organs of Motion (the Muscles) with all with the network of conductors, are ⟨all⟩ taken inward, and appropriated: the Spontaneous rises into the Voluntary: and finally, after various steps and a long Ascent the material and animal Means and Conditions are prepared for the manifestation of a Free Will, having its Law within itself and its Motive in the Law—and thus bound to originate its own Acts, not only without but even against the influence of alien Stimulants.

That in our present state we have only the Dawning of this inward Sun, (Noμος αυτονομος "the perfect Law of Liberty") will sufficiently limit and qualify the preceding Position, if only it have been allowed to produce its two-fold Consequences—the excitement of Hope, and the Repression of Vanity.

(d) A further note on Baptism, 1828

From N 37 ff 80–78: BM Add MS 47517 (*CN* v). Incorporated (var) in *AR* (1843) I 301–3 and later editions: see *Sp Aph B [XXIV]* nn 8 and 94, above.

8 May 1828.

I see the necessity of greatly expanding and clearing up the Chapter on Baptism in the Aids to Reflection—/ and of proving the substantial accordance of my Scheme with that of our Church—I still say that an Act of the Spirit *in Time*, as that it might be asserted, the moment of the uttering the words, I baptize thee in the Name &c, *Now* the Spirit *begins* to act—is false in Philosophy and contrary to Scripture—and that our *Church*-service needs no such hypothesis/ Further, I still say—that the Communication of the Spirit as of a power in principle not yet possessed, to an unconscious Agent by human Ministry, ~~is (can) not to be justified by~~ is without precedent in Scripture, and that there is no Scripture Warrant for ~~such a~~ the doctrine—and that the ⟨nature of the *Holy*⟩ Spirit communicated by the Apostles by laying on of hands is a very difficult question— and that the reasons for supposing it to be certain miraculous *gifts* of the Spirit [*f 79ᵛ*] peculiar to the first Age of Christianity and *during* the formation of the CHURCH are neither few nor insignificant—

—Further, I say, that in itself it might be indifferent, whether the outward Rite of Baptism formed the Initiation into the Baptismal Period, εις το φωτι-ζειν [into the process of enlightening], or the Finale and Coronation/ That from the necessity of the Circumstances, viz. the non-existence of the *Church*, as the Sponsor and Security for the undertaking of the enlightening Process, and the adult age of the Persons to be baptized, the latter was & could not but be the practice of the Apostolic Age—but that in after times both the Commencement & the Close were ritually solemnized— In the first the Church confers all the privileges of Christianity, in the second the Donee acknowleges the Gift & declares his consent to the Conditions; and the Church confirms the Gift & receives the Individual as [*f 79*]—ηδη πεφωτισμενον [already enlightened], and no long[er] εν τω φωτιζεσθαι [in the process of being enlightened], as one *being* enlightened, or a Catechumen—/ —Now it is notorious, that during the two first Centuries the Catechumens *generally* were not baptized—and that their Baptism was immediately followed by ~~the~~ admission to the Eucharist— And such was the force of Custom that when the Baptism of Infants became the Rule of the Church, the Eucharist was administered to *them*/ a Practice which greatly obscured, if it did not destroy, the beautiful harmony and distinct significancy of the two Rules, as symbolic, the one of the *Light* of the Word, the other of the *Life*—and therefore with great reason was the Practice discontinued.

Observe. I do not deny (God forbid!) the possibility or the reality, of the influence of the Spirit on the Soul of the Infant— His first smile bespeaks a Reason (the *Light* from the Life of the Word) [*f 78ᵛ*] as already existent—and where the Word is, there will the Spirit *act*. Still less do I think lightly of the Grace which the Child receives as a living Part of the Church, and whatever flows from the Communion of Saints, and the περιχωρησις [intercommunion] of the Spirit— Our Ch~~ild~~urch most wisely and scripturally precludes all the mischievous fanaticism of *moments* of Conversion. Except the time* when the Church receives the Subject into her own Body, and co-organizes the person/ therewith, no time dare be specified for the Spirit's descent & in-coming.—.

[*] The true import is this. The operations of the Spirit are as little referable to Time as to Space/ but in reference to our principles of Conduct ⟨toward⟩ and Judgement concerning, our neighbors, the Church declares, that *before* the ⟨time of the⟩ baptism~~al Rite~~ there is no authority for asserting, and that *since* the time there is no authority for denying, that gift and regenerative presence of the Holy Spirit, promised ⟨by an especial covenant⟩ to the Members of Christ's mystical Body—consequently, no just pretence for expecting or requiring another new Init[iat]ion, [*f 78*] or Birth into the state of Grace./

ANNOTATED, INSCRIBED, AND ASSOCIATION COPIES OF *AIDS TO REFLECTION* (1825)

ANNOTATED, INSCRIBED, AND ASSOCIATION COPIES OF *AIDS TO REFLECTION* (1825)

THIS SECTION contains details of (*a*) the various copies which Coleridge is known to have annotated for friends and (*b*) those which he is known to have inscribed for presentation. A further section (*c*) notices three copies which have particularly apposite associations with his work and with the volume. In the case of Section (*a*), copy 12 is known only by a description at second hand claiming that it contains annotations in Coleridge's hand; it is possible that it contains no more than corrections in accordance with the List of Corrections and Amendments, or annotations not in his hand. It is equally possible that some of the unlocated copies in Section (*b*) may contain hitherto unknown annotations.

(A) ANNOTATED COPIES

1. Gioacchino de' Prati's copy.

> Not located. At one time in the possession of J. Pearson & Co., booksellers.
> See 1(a) below for text.

1(a). Copy formerly belonging to J. Dykes Campbell (COPY A in the *CC* notes) into which he copied notes from Copy 1.

> Harvard *EC85.R7358.Zz825c (formerly 19476.390.3).
> Inscribed "The Houghton Library | 13 June 1925".
> On a flyleaf preceding the title-page JDC has copied the inscription: "Dr De Prati | with affectionate | regards of the | Author | S. T. Coleridge | 1 June 1825" followed by a note of his own: "The copy from [which] the notes corrections &c marked 'P' are taken was lent me by J. Pearson & Co Booksellers, Pall Mall Place London S W | March 1891 | J Dykes Campbell." A further note records that W. M. Rossetti bought the present copy in 1904 for 4*s* at JDC's sale and states the handwriting in the book to be JDC's. On a previous flyleaf JDC has noted several page-references, partly in connection with his edition of the *Poetical Works*, published in 1893. C's acquaintance with Prati from Apr 1825 onwards is summarised in *CL* v 452n. See below, Index, for references to the changes and additions given in the notes to the *CC* text.

479

2. Robert Southey's copy.

Present location unknown. Formerly in the possession of Sir George Grove; listed in Rosenbach sale catalogues of 1931, 1937, and 1947.

The title-page is inscribed "Robert Southey, from S.T.C. London, 6 June 1825": see Rosenbach SC, which also mentions annotations and a long note at end. Further details under 2(a), 2(b), 2(c), and 2(d) below.

2(a). MS transcript of notes from Copy 2. (COPY B in the *CC* notes.)

VCL LT 55.

Transcript of two notes from Southey's copy, then in the possession of George Grove. He adds references to the fifth edition and notes at the end, "A great many of the errours of the press, in this copy, have been corrected by the Master himself. G.G." He also notes that the Erratum for page 177 line 2 has not been corrected even in the fifth edition and appends his signature, "George Grove | May 13th 1844". A note on the back reads "Aids Southey's Copy (copied S.D.)". See below, Index, for reference to the changes and additions given in the notes to the *CC* text.

2(b). MS transcript of notes from Copy 2.

VCL BT 33 (Pt i).

A further transcript of the notes in 2(a). It is not clear whether this was an independent transcription from Copy 2 or made from 2(a), but the form suggests the latter.

2(c). MS transcript of notes from Copy 2.

VCL LT 56.

A further transcript, in the hand of Mrs H. N. Coleridge.

2(d). Copy of the third edition (1836) into which EHC copied the notes from Copy 2.

University of Indiana Libraries, Lilly Collection; Quaritch 1926, Blackwell 1950.

The front flyleaf is inscribed as follows: "The marginalia etc. are transcribed from a copy of The Aids to Reflection—1825—inscr: 'Robert Southey from S.T.C. London 6 June 1825'— in Southey's handwriting, and now in the possession of Sir George Grove D.C.L. | E.H.C. May 10 1890". The note on the flyleaf at the end of the book, referring to page 306, line 5, is inscribed: "Note. This concluding note is in S.T.C.'s best late handwriting. The doctrine is eminently characteristic, and the fact that his subtle analysis of *Remorse* should have been appended to a copy intended to be presented to *Southey* lends an additional interest to the note. | E.H.C. *May 10* 1890." EHC copied notes from pages 2, 13, 194, 232–3, 306, 345, and on a back flyleaf; he also made notes of his own in pencil, criticising some of C's statements in *AR*.

3. John Taylor Coleridge's copy. (COPY C in the *CC* notes.)

BM C 126 d 3. Bookplate of Bernard Lord Coleridge.

Inscribed by C on the title-page: "To John Coleridge Esqre | with the best regards | of the Author." The copy was sent to JTC with a letter of c 13 Jun 1825 (*CL* v 468). See below, Index, for references to the changes and additions given in the notes to the *CC* text. Some pencil notes (probably not by C) are not included.

4. Daniel Stuart's copy. (COPY D in the *CC* notes.)

BM C 134 c 10 (formerly Add MS 34047). Bequeathed by Miss Mary Stuart.
Inscribed by C on a front flyleaf (p ⁻4, now preserved separately in BM copy): "To Daniel Stuart Esqʳᵉ | from his | obliged Friend | S. T. Coleridge". A letter of c 8 Jul 1825 directs his attention to particular points in the volume (*CL* v 474–5). Many of the notes are similar to those in COPY C. See below, Index, for references to the changes and additions given in the notes to the *CC* text.

5. J. H. Frere's copy. (COPY E in the *CC* notes.)

NY Public Library, Berg Collection accession No 178385B. Bookplate of "Rᵗ. Honᵇˡᵉ J. H. Frere, Roydon". Also inscribed by John Drinkwater, 1920.
Inscribed by C on p ⁻2 "To J. H. Frere, Esqʳᵉ | most respectfully | from the Author, | S. T. Coleridge." In Jan 1826 C sent Frere a copy of *AR* for transmission to Lord Liverpool (Copy No 13 below). This one had presumably been sent some time previously. See below, Index, for references to the changes and additions given in the notes to the *CC* text.

5(a). Miss Frere's copy.

Harvard 19476.390.4*.
Inscribed by J. H. Frere on the title-page: "Given to Miss Frere from her affectionate brother, May 21, 1829." J. H. Frere has transcribed into this copy the notes from COPY E.

6. Edward Coleridge's copy. (COPY F in the *CC* notes.)

Pierpont Morgan Library, PML 41029. Given by F. B. Adams, Jr, 1949.
An autograph letter of 15 Jul 1825 from C presenting this volume to his nephew and describing it further, which is also in the Pierpont Morgan Library, is printed in *CL* v 478–82. Receipt of the copy as a gift was recorded as follows on the title-page by EC: "Edward Coleridge. Eton. 1825. E Dono S.T.C."; he also wrote on a preceding flyleaf, p ⁻3: "This Volume, given to me by my Uncle, Samuel Taylor Coleridge, and enriched by his Autograph notes, is not to go out of my family. *E. C.*" A further inscription reads "Charles Edw. Coleridge. Jan. 24. 1875." and another "Oct. 9. 1879. I now give this Volume to my dear daughter | H.E. Shadwell | E.C." See below, Index, for references to the changes and additions given in the notes to the *CC* text.

7. Derwent Coleridge's copy. (COPY G in the *CC* notes.)

Mrs N. F. D. Coleridge. Bookplate of Rev Derwent Coleridge.
Inscribed by C on the title-page: "Derwent Coleridge | from his affectionate | Father | S. T. Coleridge." A note on another flyleaf reads "I will send you another Copy with the MSS. Addenda—At present I am preparing one for Lord Liverpool—". Sent to DC January 1826: *CL* vi 533; see also Copies 13 and 104 below. A badly rubbed pencil note, evidently by DC, reads "January [. . .] 1826, when staying with my [. . .] friend Tom Macaulay, at Plymouth—Brought [?from London] by Mʳ Edwᵈ Lowndes." See below, Index, for references to the changes and additions given in the notes to the *CC* text.

8. Sir Thomas Grey's copy. (COPY H in the *CC* notes.)

Yale University Library, Chauncey Brewster Tinker collection No 705.
Flyleaf inscribed "Jane Sayer 1835".
The title-page is inscribed in C's hand "To Sir Thomas Gray | in testimony of sincere Respect and regard | from his obliged Friend | S. T. Coleridge." When at Ramsgate C

dined on occasion with Sir Thomas and Lady Grey (whose name he spelt in both ways): see *CL* v 374–5, 377, 394, 397, 515, vi 707. Annotated throughout: see Textual Notes and below, Index, for references to the changes and additions given in the notes to the *CC* text.

9. Unidentified copy. (COPY I in the *CC* notes.)

Owned by Mary Anne Perkins.
Inscribed on flyleaf: "A. G. K. Woodgate staying at Pembury Vicarage for Xmas *Dec. 22. 1871*".
Arthur George Kennedy Woodgate was a grandson of Rev Stephen Woodgate MA, Vicar of Pembury. The copy probably came back into the possession of his aunt Louisa Margaret (née Shaw), who married Rev George Stephen Woodgate MA and lived at Pembury Hall.
This copy contains annotations throughout, transcribed either directly from COPY D or from another associated closely with it. Most of the variants, being in another hand, are not recorded in the present volume; for corrections and additions in C's hand to the long notes at the beginning and end of the volume see Appendix D above.

10. Sophia Gillman's copy. (COPY J in the *CC* notes.)

Not located. Clemens Sale Catalogue. Sold by Christie, Manson and Woods, NY, on 16 Nov 1985.
Inscribed on the title-page "Sophia Gillinan" according to Clemens SC. The Christie SC ascribes the ownership to "Sarah Gillman", as the "daughter" of James Gillman, Sr, but Gillman had no daughter. The Clemens SC reading, though evidently containing a misreading for "Gillman", is probably correct as to the first name. The owner is less likely to have been Sophia, wife of James Gillman, Jr, who married him in 1837 after C's death and predeceased her husband, than James's daughter Sophia Raby (b 1851), who was still alive at her father's death.
The Christie SC reports "annotations and corrections to the text on 29 pages", including (in addition to items from the printed "Corrections and Amendments") "word substitutions" at pp 21, 22, 23, etc, "renumbering of paragraphs" (pp 23, 24), and "the insertion of explanatory notes (as at pp. 244–245, where some 60 words are written in the margins)". Like the Clemens SC it records a note pasted to the front endpaper (see *Sp Aph B VII* n 4 above).

11. Unidentified copy. (COPY K in the *CC* notes.)

Not located; one page sold at Christie's 29 Nov 1978.
For C's annotation, beginning "Is a Mad *Soul* a possible conception? . . .", see above, *Conc* at n 106.

12. Thomas Tylecote's copy.

Not located. Clemens Sale Catalogue.
Inscribed on the title-page "T. Tylecote, St John's".
Thomas Tylecote (1798–1882) was admitted to St John's College, Cambridge, in 1816 and was a Fellow from 1824 to 1838. There is a good chance that he knew DC, therefore.
Annotations, notes, and corrections throughout in STC's hand, according to Clemens SC.

13. Lord Liverpool's copy.

Not located or described.

From 1825 to 1827 C was endeavouring to procure financial help through the good offices of Lord Liverpool (1770–1828), who had been Prime Minister since 1812. In a note in Copy 7 above, sent to Derwent in Jan 1826, C wrote, "I will send you another Copy with the MSS. Addenda—At present I am preparing one for Lord Liverpool—". At about the same time he wrote a letter to J. H. Frere, beginning, "With this you will receive the copy of the Aids to Reflection, which I had been mustering courage to send to Lord Liverpool. It came like a Breeze in one of our hot soundless Summer-noons, which one *sees* rustling in a Tree, and in the next moment feels on one's forehead, when you were so good as to say that you would present it yourself to his Lordship" (*CL* VI 539). In September Frere received a letter from Liverpool returning the copy and promising to do something for C when he had the means (*CL* VI 539n). Liverpool, however, suffered a paralytic stroke before the matter could be settled, and died on 4 Dec 1828.

(B) INSCRIBED COPIES

101. James Gillman Senior's copy.

Not located.

It is unlikely that Coleridge did not present a copy of *Aids to Reflection* to Gillman, who had shown constant concern about its progress. It is possible that the poem and address transcribed in Copy 101(a) below originally formed a presentation inscription for that copy, though one might have expected Coleridge to say more about the volume itself. The only known copy of the poem and address in Coleridge's autograph appears on a separate leaf in Yale University Library, written in a transverse direction untypical of Coleridge's inscriptions and annotations:

The Three Sorts of Friends

Tho' Friendships differ endless *in degree*,
The *Sorts*, methinks, may be reduced to Three:
*A*cquaintance many; and *Con*quaintance few;
But for *In*quaintance I know only two,
The Friend, I've mourn'd with, and the Maid, I woo!

My dear Gillman,

The ground and "matériel" of this division of one's friends into *Ac-* *Con-* and *In*quaintance was given by Hartley Coleridge, when he was scarcely five years old. On some one asking him, if Anny Sealy (a little girl, he went to school with) was an Acquaintance of his, he replied very fervently, pressing his right hand on his heart—No! She is an *In*quaintance—"Well! 'tis a Father's Tale!"—& the recollection soothes your old
Friend & *In*quaintance—
S. T. Coleridge

The words "My dear Gillman" appear to have been squeezed in after the paragraph below them had been written. The ms is printed in *CL* V 466. The version printed in an article in *Fraser's Magazine* for Jan 1835, XI 54, and reprinted from there in *PW* (EHC) II 1012, may well derive from this ms.

A copy of *AR* (1825) listed in Harry Bache Smith *A Sentimental Library* (privately printed 1914) p 59 is described as being the one presented to James Gillman, Sr, and as containing the poem and address in Coleridge's hand, along with other corrections and additions. It is very likely, however, that that copy was in fact Copy 101(a) below, in which case the version of the ms that appears in Smith's description (which differs from all known versions) was a mistranscription. It is unclear, in other words, that the poem and address were ever written by Coleridge into any copy of *AR*. It might, for example, have been written to Gillman on an occasion when they had been mourning together. See also below.

101(a). H. H. Carwardine's Copy.

NY Public Library, Berg Collection accession No 178384B. Bookplate of W. Van R. Whitall.

Inscribed on front flyleaf with a variant version of the Yale ms poem "The Three Sorts of Friends" above, in Carwardine's handwriting. A further inscription reads "H. H. Carwardine Colne Priory The gift of his Friend Jaˢ Gillman Junʳ". Further ms additions and corrections in Carwardine's hand, some probably by Carwardine himself.

It is possible that James Gillman, Jr, allowed Carwardine to copy the lines from a copy of *AR* presented to his father (see Copy 101 above). It is equally possible, however, that they were transcribed, with variations, from the leaf now in Yale University Library (described under Copy 101) or from some other source.

As explained above, this copy seems to be the one described by Harry Bache Smith in *A Sentimental Library*. Smith's version reads "Anne Sealy" and "pressing his hand", which follows Copy 101(a) rather than the Yale ms ("Anny Sealy" and "pressing his right hand"); on the other hand it does follow the punctuation of the Yale ms in reading "he replied very fervently, pressing . . ." rather than that of Copy 101(a): "he replied, very fervently pressing . . .".

102. Edward Bather's copy.

NY Public Library, Berg Collection accession No 110144B.

Inscribed "Grove, Highgate. To the Reverend F. Bather in testimony of warm Regard and reverential Esteem from the Author, S. T. Coleridge | 21, July 1825."

Since there is no other Bather in the clergy lists of the time, the recipient was presumably Edward Bather (1779–1847), a friend of the schoolmaster of Cholmeley's Free Grammar School at Highgate from 1816, Rev Samuel Mence (1781–1860) (see *CL* v 41 and n). Bather was vicar of Meole Brace, Salop, and helped with the placing of Henry Gillman at Shrewsbury School in 1826, after his departure from Eton (*CL* vi 647). In 1828 he was collated to the archdeaconry of Salop. He also enjoyed a high reputation as a preacher (see *DNB*): in 1829 C heard from him "the very best sermon the best delivered, I ever heard" (*CL* vi 816).

Some corrections and amendments (all from the Errata), not in C's hand.

103. John Keate's copy.

Eton College Library Gaᵃ 4.20. Heraldic bookplate of John Keate DD.

Inscribed by C on the title-page: "To the Reverend Dʳ Keate | in testimony of high respect (et parvum quoque μνημοσυνη colluctationis academicae "juvenilibus annis"") ["and also a small remembrance of an academic struggle 'in youthful years' "] from the Author | S. T. Coleridge | July 1825". See illustration 2, above.

John Keate (1773–1852) was Headmaster of Eton from 1809 to 1834 and famous, among other things, for his floggings: on 30 Jun 1832 he flogged more than 80 boys, after which he was cheered. From 1820 to 1824 he held the living of Nether Stowey. C probably presented him with this copy in late July 1825, when he conducted Henry Gillman to Eton to take his entrance examination and so made contact with him again after many years. He wrote that the Provost, Dr Keate, and the Fellows had received him with "flattering attentions'' (*CL* v 487). In Jan 1793 Keate and C had ranked equally among the best four in the competition for the Craven Scholarship (awarded in the event to the youngest, Samuel Butler) and later C had been beaten by Keate in the competition for one of the Browne Medals—a competition in which Keate scored successes in the following two years as well.

104. John Macaulay's copy.

Not located.
On 4 Jan 1826 C wrote to Derwent, who was in Plymouth staying with the Macaulays, ''I send the Aids of Reflection by Mr Edward Lowndes—The Father, and not the Author, earnestly intreats that you will give a fair and (as far as is in your own power) an unprejudiced attention to it's contents.'' On 2 Feb 1826 C wrote again to Derwent, who was by then back in Cambridge, ''The two copies of the Aids were dispatched on the day after your departure—the one with Mr J. Macauley's Name & mine, the other with mine as in acknowlegement of friendship to my Son, D. Coleridge—I understood Mr Whiteford to say, that they *had been* forwarded to Plymouth'' (*CL* vi 533, 552). Derwent had probably asked him to send the copies during his visit to Highgate in late January (*CL* vi 548).

105. Thomas Macaulay's copy.

Not located.
See previous entry. The second of the two copies sent to Plymouth was presumably for Thomas Babington Macaulay, a close friend of Derwent's during and after their years at Cambridge. In February 1824 C had expressed anxiety concerning the influence on Derwent of Macaulay's and Austin's religious opinions, but had later been reassured (*CL* v 330, 336, 340, and above, Editor's Introduction at nn 76–8).

106. John Watson's copy.

Not located.
The *Carlisle Patriot* for 6 Sept 1834 published a copy of a letter from Coleridge ''to a dear young friend upon the blank leaf of his 'Aids to Reflection', with which the author had presented him on his leaving London in a hopeless state of consumption.'' The letter (of which another version—probably a draft—is published in *CL* vi 693 from a ms leaf) was addressed to John Watson and is dated 24 Jun 1827 in the 1834 version. Watson, who had studied with C for some years, died on 9 Jul 1827, aged 28.

(c) Association Copies

201. Joseph Blanco White's copy.

Liverpool University Library, Blanco White collection 82.2.6.
In a letter to EC of 15 Jul 1825 C wrote ''The Bishop of London has been pleased to express a MOST favorable Opinion of my Work—in consequence of which the celebrated Mr Blanco White procured the Volume, and a few days after the Friend. He then procured an introduction to me. . .'' (*CL* v 481). This copy, apparently the one in question, contains two annotations, presumably by Blanco White himself, on pp 16n and 364, concerning Coleridge's discussions of θρησκεία and of death-bed baptism. White was evidently the ''Spanish Refugee'' described in a footnote to p 350 of *AR* (1825): see *Sp Aph B XXIIIb* n 30, above.

202. Barron Field's copy.

Owned by the editor. Bookplate of Barron Field.

A footnote on p 349 of *AR* (1831), and not in *AR* (1825), refers to Barron Field's "Letters from New South Wales": see above, *Sp Aph B XXIIIb* n 23. Field was a friend of Lamb's (through whom he came to know Wordsworth, Coleridge, Hazlitt, and Leigh Hunt) and appears twice in the *Essays of Elia*. He returned to England from New Zealand in July 1824; in 1830 he became chief justice in Gibraltar, where he remained for several years.

This copy contains three relevant annotations, presumably in Field's hand, which are mentioned in the notes to the text above (*Int Aph XXXI* n 2, *Sp Aph B VIIIa* n 17, *IX* n 14).

203. E. H. Coleridge's copy of the third edition.

University of Indiana Libraries, Lilly Collection. See above, Copy 2(d) of the Annotated Copies, for details.

PRELIMINARY ESSAY TO
AIDS TO REFLECTION
(BURLINGTON, VERMONT 1829)

BY JAMES MARSH

PRELIMINARY ESSAY TO
AIDS TO REFLECTION
(BURLINGTON, VERMONT 1829)

BY JAMES MARSH

SEE ABOVE, Editor's Introduction, pp cxiv–cxxiii. The text of the essay as reprinted here corresponds to that which was included in the fourth English edition of 1839, edited by H. N. Coleridge. It differs from the original American edition of 1829 in excluding some references to further material which was cited and reprinted from works such as the *Lay Sermons* and *The Friend* in that edition. (Reprinting of the works themselves in America made such further citing unnecessary in later editions there.) HNC's version was adopted whenever the Essay was subsequently reprinted in America: see Appendix H below.

Three mottoes which appeared at the beginning of the 1829 edition but were never reprinted are reproduced overleaf.

Ταυτα ὁ ΝΟΜΟΘΕΤΗΣ ΝΟΥΣ διαθεσμοθεται ταις ψυχαις. ὁ δε υποδεξα-
μενος αυτα ΛΟΓΙΣΜΟΣ, δικαστης αγρυπνος ἑαυτου γινεται. Πη παρεβην; τι
δ' ερεξα; και εν ταξει την μνημην αναλαμβανων αρετης ἑνεκα ειτα ἑυρων ἑαυτον
συμφωνως τοις προκειμενοις ὁροις διημερευσαντα, της θειας ευφροσυνης τοις
καρποις αναδει. παρα μελος δε τι πραξαντα φωρασας ωσπερ τισι φαρμακοις
ταις εκ της μετανοιας νουθετησεσιν επιστυφει.

Hierocles, as quoted by Renatus Vallinus in notes on Boethius.[1]

Neque esse mens divina sine RATIONE potest, nec RATIO divina non hanc vim
in rectis pravisque sanciendis habere. Erat enim RATIO profecta a rerum naturâ,
et ad recte faciendum impellens, et a delicto avocans; quae non tum denique
incipit lex esse, cum scripta est, sed tum cum orta est. Orta autem simul est cum
mente divinâ.   *Cicero de Legibus, Lib.* ii. c. 4.[2]

Hardly do we guess aright at things that are upon earth, and with labour do
we find the things that are at hand; but the things that are in heaven who hath
searched out? And thy counsel who hath known, except thou give WISDOM, and
send thy HOLY SPIRIT from above? For *so* the ways of them which lived on the
earth were reformed, and men were taught the things that are pleasing unto thee,
and were saved through wisdom.   Wisdom of Solomon, ix. 16, 17, 18.

---

[1] "These laws the LAW-GIVING MIND imposes on souls; and the REASONING POWER, receiving them, becomes her own unsleeping judge. 'Where have I transgressed? What have I done?' and if, running over her memories in order, with virtue as her concern, she finds that she has passed the day consistently with the prescribed limits she crowns herself with the fruits of divine bliss. But if she detects herself as having acted unfittingly she applies, like certain astringent medicines, the admonishments of repentance.'' See Boethius *Consolationis Philosophiae libri* v (1556) Notes, 79.

[2] See *De legibus* 2.4.10 (reading "habet'' for "habere''); tr C. W. Keyes (LCL 1928): "For the divine mind cannot exist without reason, and divine reason cannot but have this power to establish right and wrong . . . For reason did exist, derived from the Nature of the universe, urging men to right conduct and diverting them from wrong-doing, and this reason did not first become Law when it was written down, but when it first came into existence; and it came into existence simultaneously with the divine mind.''

PRELIMINARY ESSAY.

BY THE REV. JAMES MARSH. D.D.

WHETHER the present state of religious feeling, and the prevailing topics of theological inquiry among us, are particularly favorable to the success of the Work herewith offered to the Public can be determined only by the result. The question, however, has not been left unconsidered; and however that may be, it is not a work, the value of which depends essentially upon its relation to the passing controversies of the day. Unless I distrust my own feelings and convictions altogether, I must suppose, that for some, I hope for many, minds, it will have a deep and enduring interest. Of those classes, for whose use it is more especially designated in the Author's Preface, I trust there are many also in this country, who will justly appreciate the object at which it aims, and avail themselves of its instruction and assistance. I could wish it might be received, by all who concern themselves in religious inquiries and instruction especially, in the spirit which seems to me to have animated its great and admirable author; and I hesitate not to say, that to all of every class, who shall so receive it, and peruse it with the attention and thoughtfulness, which it demands and deserves, it will be found by experience to furnish, what its title imports, "AIDS TO REFLECTION" on subjects, upon which every man is bound to reflect deeply and in earnest.

What the specific objects of the Work are, and for whom it is written, may be learned in few words from the Preface of the Author. From this, too, it will be seen to be professedly didactic. It is designed to aid those who wish for instruction, or assistance in the instruction of others. The plan and composition of the Work will to most readers probably appear somewhat anomalous; but reflection upon the nature of the objects aimed at, and some little experience of its results, may convince them that the method adopted is not without its advantages. It is important to observe, that it is designed, as its general characteristic, to aid REFLECTION, and for the most part upon subjects which can be learned and understood only by the exercise of reflection in the strict and proper sense of that term. It was not so much to teach a speculative system of doctrines built upon established premisses, for which a different method

491

would have been obviously preferable, as to turn the mind continually back upon the premises themselves—upon the inherent grounds of truth and error in its own being. The only way in which it is possible for any one to learn the science of words, which is one of the objects to be sought in the present Work, and the true import of those words especially, which most concern us as rational and accountable beings, is by reflecting upon and bringing forth into distinct consciousness, those mental acts, which the words are intended to designate. We must discover and distinctly apprehend different meanings, before we can appropriate to each a several word, or understand the words so appropriated by others. Now it is not too much to say, that most men, and even a large proportion of educated men, do not reflect sufficiently upon their own inward being, upon the constituent laws of their own understanding, upon the mysterious powers and agencies of reason, and conscience, and will, to apprehend with much distinctness the objects to be named, or of course to refer the names with correctness to their several objects. Hence the necessity of associating the study of words with the study of morals and religion; and that is the most effectual method of instruction, which enables the teacher most especially to fix the attention upon a definite meaning, that is, in these studies, upon a particular act, or process, or law of the mind—to call it into distinct consciousness, and assign to it its proper name, so that the name shall thenceforth have for the learner a distinct, definite, and intelligible sense. To impress upon the reader the importance of this, and to exemplify it in the particular subjects taken up in the Work, is a leading aim of the Author throughout; and it is obviously the only possible way by which we can arrive at any satisfactory and conclusive results on subjects of philosophy, morals, and religion. The first principles, the ultimate grounds, of these, so far as they are possible objects of knowledge for us, must be sought and found in the laws of our being, or they are not found at all. The knowledge of these, terminates in the knowledge of ourselves, of our rational and personal being, of our proper and distinctive humanity, and of that Divine Being, in whose image we are created. "We must retire inward," says St. Bernard, "if we would ascend upward."[3] It is by self-inspection, by reflecting upon the mysterious grounds of our own being, that we can alone arrive at any rational knowledge of the central

[3] Cf St Bernard *Meditations on Knowledge of the Human Condition* 1.1: ". . . ab exterioribus redeam ad interiora, et ab inferioribus ad superiora ascendam: ut possim cognoscere unde venio aut quo vado; quid sum, vel unde sum"; tr: ". . . may I return from external things to internal, and rise from lower to higher: so that I may know whence I come or whither I am going; what I am, and whence I am": Migne *PL* CLXXXIV 485.

and absolute ground of all being. It is by this only, that we can discover that principle of unity and consistency, which reason instinctively seeks after, which shall reduce to an harmonious system all our views of truth and of being, and destitute of which all the knowledge that comes to us from without is fragmentary, and in its relation to our highest interests as rational beings but the patch-work of vanity.

Now, of necessity, the only method, by which another can aid our efforts in the work of reflection, is by first reflecting himself, and so pointing out the process and marking the result by words, that we can repeat it, and try the conclusions by our own consciousness. If he have reflected aright, if he have excluded all causes of self-deception, and directed his thoughts by those principles of truth and reason, and by those laws of the understanding, which belong in common to all men, his conclusions must be true for all. We have only to repeat the process, impartially to reflect ourselves, unbiassed by received opinions, and un-deceived by the idols of our own understandings, and we shall find the same truths in the depths of our own self-consciousness. I am persuaded that such, for the most part, will be found to be the case with regard to the principles developed in the present Work, and that those who, with serious reflection and an unbiassed love of truth, will refer them to the laws of thought in their own minds, to the requirements of their own reason, will find there a witness to their truth.

Viewing the Work in this manner, therefore, as an instructive and safe guide to the knowledge of what it concerns all men to know, I can not but consider it in itself as a work of great and permanent value to any Christian community. Whatever indeed tends to awaken and cherish the power and to form the habit, of reflection upon the great constituent principles of our own permanent being and proper humanity, and upon the abiding laws of truth and duty, as revealed in our reason and con-science, can not but promote our highest interests as moral and rational beings. Even if the particular conclusions, to which the Author has ar-rived, should prove erroneous, the evil is comparatively of little impor-tance, if he have at the same time communicated to our minds such powers of thought, as will enable us to detect his errors, and attain by our own efforts to a more perfect knowledge of the truth. That some of his views may not be erroneous, or that they are to be received on his authority, the Author, I presume, would be the last to affirm; and al-though in the nature of the case it was impossible for him to aid reflec-tion without anticipating, and in some measure influencing, the results, yet the primary tendency and design of the Work is, not to establish this or that system, but to cultivate in every mind the power and the will to seek earnestly and steadfastly for the truth in the only direction, in which it can ever be found. The work is no further controversial, than every work must be, "that is writ with freedom and reason" upon subjects of the same kind; and if it be found at variance with existing opinions and modes of philosophizing, it is not necessarily to be considered the fault of the writer.

In republishing the Work in this country, I could wish that it might be received by all, for whose instruction it was designed, simply as a didactic work, on its own merits, and without controversy. I must not, however, be supposed ignorant of its bearing upon those questions, which have so often been, and still are, the prevailing topics of theological controversy among us. It was indeed incumbent on me, before inviting the attention of the religious community to the Work, to consider its relation to existing opinions, and its probable influence on the progress of truth. This I have done with as severe thought as I am capable of bestowing upon any subject, and I trust too with no want of deference and conscientious regard to the feelings and opinions of others. I have not attempted to disguise from myself, nor do I wish to disguise from the readers of the Work, the inconsistency of some of its leading principles with much that is taught and received in our theological circles. Should it gain much of the public attention in any way, it will become, as it ought, an object of special and deep interest to all, who would contend for the truth, and labor to establish it upon a permanent basis. I venture to assure such, even those of them who are most capable of comprehending the philosophical grounds of truth in our speculative systems of theology, that in its relation to this whole subject they will find it to be a Work of great depth and power, and, whether right or wrong, eminently deserving their attention. It is not to be supposed that all who read, or even all who comprehend it, will be convinced of the soundness of its views, or be prepared to abandon those which they have long considered essential to the truth. To those, whose understandings by long habit have become limited in their powers of apprehension, and as it were identified with certain schemes of doctrine, certain modes of contemplating all that pertains to religious truth, it may appear novel, strange, and unintelligible, or even dangerous in its tendency, and be to them an occasion of offence. But I have no fear that any earnest and single-hearted lover of the truth as it is in Jesus, who will free his mind from the idols of preconceived opinion, and give himself time and opportunity to understand the Work by such reflection as the nature of the subject renders unavoidable, will find in it any cause of offence, or any source of alarm. If the Work become the occasion of controversy at all,

I should expect it from those, who, instead of reflecting deeply upon the first principles of truth in their own reason and conscience and in the word of God, are more accustomed to speculate—that is, from premisses given or assumed, but considered unquestionable, as the constituted point of observation, to look abroad upon the whole field of their intellectual vision, and thence to decide upon the true form and dimensions of all which meets their view. To such I would say with deference, that the merits of this Work can not be determined by the merely relative aspect of its doctrines, as seen from the high ground of any prevailing metaphysical or theological system. Those on the contrary who will seek to comprehend it by reflection, to learn the true meaning of the whole and of all its parts, by retiring into their own minds and finding there the true point of observation for each, will not be in haste to question the truth or the tendency of its principles. I make these remarks because I am anxious, as far as may be, to anticipate the causeless fear of all, who earnestly pray and labor for the promotion of the truth, and to preclude that unprofitable controversy, which might arise from hasty or prejudiced views of a Work like this. At the same time I should be far from deprecating any discussion which might tend to unfold more fully the principles which it teaches, or to exhibit more distinctly its true bearing upon the interests of theological science and of spiritual religion. It is to promote this object, indeed, that I am induced in the remarks which follow to offer some of my own thoughts on these subjects, imperfect I am well aware, and such as, for that reason, as well as others, worldly prudence might require me to suppress. If, however, I may induce reflecting men, and those who are engaged in theological inquiries especially, to indulge a suspicion that all truth, which it is important for them to know, is not contained in the systems of doctrine usually taught, and that this Work may be worthy of their serious and reflecting perusal, my chief object will be accomplished. I shall of course not need to anticipate in detail the contents of the Work itself, but shall aim simply to point out what I consider its distinguishing and essential character and tendency, and then direct the attention of my readers to some of those general feelings and views on the subjects of religious truth, and of those particulars in the prevailing philosophy of the age, which seem to me to be exerting an injurious influence on the cause of theological science and of spiritual religion, and not only to furnish a fit occasion, but to create an imperious demand, for a Work like that which is here offered to the public.

In regard then to the distinguishing character and tendency of the Work itself, it has already been stated to be didactic, and designed to aid reflection on the principles and grounds of truth in our own being; but in another point of view, and with reference to my present object, it might rather be denominated A PHILOSOPHICAL STATEMENT AND VINDICATION OF THE DISTINCTIVELY SPIRITUAL AND PECULIAR DOCTRINES OF THE CHRISTIAN SYSTEM. In order to understand more clearly the import of this statement, and the relation of the Author's views to those exhibited in other systems, the reader is requested to examine in the first place, what he considers the *peculiar doctrines of Christianity*, and what he means by the terms *spirit* and *spiritual*. A synoptical view of what he considers peculiar to Christianity as a revelation is given in Aph. vii. on Spiritual Religion, and, if I mistake not, will be found essentially to coincide, though not perhaps in the language employed, with what among us are termed the Evangelical doctrines of religion. Those who are anxious to examine further into the orthodoxy of the Work in connection with this statement, may consult the articles on ORIGINAL SIN and REDEMPTION, though I must forewarn them that it will require much study in connection with the other parts of the Work, before one unaccustomed to the Author's language, and unacquainted with his views, can fully appreciate the merit of what may be peculiar in his mode of treating those subjects. With regard to the term *spiritual*, it may be sufficient to remark here, that he regards it as having a specific import, and maintains that in the sense of the New Testament, *spiritual* and *natural* are contradistinguished, so that what is spiritual is different in kind from that which is natural, and is in fact *super*-natural. So, too, while morality is something more than prudence, religion, the spiritual life, is something more than morality.

In vindicating the peculiar doctrines of the Christian system so stated, and a faith in the reality of agencies and modes of being essentially spiritual or supernatural, he aims to show their consistency with reason and with the true principles of philosophy, and that indeed, so far from being irrational, CHRISTIAN FAITH IS THE PERFECTION OF HUMAN REASON. By reflection upon the subjective grounds of knowledge and faith in the human mind itself, and by an analysis of its faculties, he develops the distinguishing characteristics and necessary relations of the natural and the spiritual in our modes of being and knowing, and the all-important fact, that although the former does not comprehend the latter, yet neither does it preclude its existence. He proves, that "the scheme of Christianity, though not discoverable by reason, is yet in accordance with it—that link follows link by necessary consequence—that religion passes out of the ken of reason only where the eye of reason has reached its own horizon—and that faith is then but its continuation.''[4] Instead of adopting, like the popular metaphysicians of the day, a system of philosophy at war with religion, and which tends inevitably to undermine our belief in the reality of any thing spiritual in the only proper sense of that word, and then coldly and ambiguously referring us for the support of our faith to the authority of Revelation, he boldly asserts the reality of something distinctively spiritual in man, and the futility of all those modes of philosophizing, in which this is not recognized, or which are incompatible with it. He considers it the highest and most rational purpose of any system of philosophy, at least of one professing to be Christian, to investigate those higher and peculiar attributes, which distinguish us from the brutes that perish—which are the image of God in us, and constitute our proper humanity. It is in his view the proper business and the duty of the Christian philosopher to remove all appearance of contradiction between the several manifestations of the one Divine Word, to reconcile reason with revelation, and thus to justify the ways of God to man. The methods by which he accomplishes this, either in regard to the terms in which he enunciates the great doctrines of the Gospel, or the peculiar views of philosophy by which he reconciles them with the subjective grounds of faith in the universal reason of man, need not be stated here. I will merely observe, that the key to his system will be found in the distinctions, which he makes and illustrates between *nature* and *free-will*, and between the *understanding* and *reason*. It may meet the prejudices of some to remark farther, that in philosophizing on the grounds of our faith he does not profess or aim to solve all mysteries, and to bring all truth within the comprehension of the understanding. A truth may be mysterious, and the primary ground of all truth and reality must be so. But though we may believe what *passeth all understanding*, we *can not* believe what is *absurd*, or contradictory to *reason*.

Whether the Work be well executed, according to the idea of it, as now given, or whether the Author have accomplished his purpose, must be determined by those who are capable of judging, when they shall have examined and reflected upon the whole as it deserves. The inquiry which I have now to propose to my readers is, whether the idea itself be a rational one, and whether the purpose of the Author be one which a wise man and a Christian ought to aim at, or which in the present state of our religious interests, and of our theological science, specially needs to be accomplished.

[4] See *BL* conc *(CC)* II 247.

No one, who has had occasion to observe the general feelings and views of our religious community for a few years past, can be ignorant, that a strong prejudice exists against the introduction of philosophy, in any form, in the discussion of theological subjects. The terms *philosophy* and *metaphysics*, even *reason* and *rational*, seem, in the minds of those devoted to the support of religious truth, to have forfeited their original, and to have acquired a new import, especially in their relation to matters of faith. By a philosophical view of religious truth would generally be understood a view, not only varying from the religion of the Bible in the form and manner of presenting it, but at war with it; and a rational religion is supposed to be of course something diverse from revealed religion. A philosophical and rational system of religious truth would by most readers among us, if I mistake not, be supposed a system deriving its doctrines not from revelation, but from the speculative reason of men, or at least relying on that only for their credibility. That these terms have been used to designate such systems, and that the prejudice against reason and philosophy so employed is not, therefore, without cause, I need not deny; nor would any friend of revealed truth be less disposed to give credence to such systems, than the Author of the Work before us.

But, on the other hand, a moment's reflection only can be necessary to convince any man, attentive to the use of language, that we do at the same time employ these terms in relation to truth generally in a better and much higher sense. *Rational*, as contradistinguished from *irrational* and *absurd*, certainly denotes a quality, which every man would be disposed to claim, not only for himself, but for his religious opinions. Now, the adjective *reasonable* having acquired a different use and signification, the word *rational* is the adjective corresponding in sense to the substantive *reason*, and signifies what is conformed to reason. In one sense, then, all men would appeal to reason in behalf of their religious faith; they would deny that it was irrational or absurd. If we do not in this sense adhere to reason, we forfeit our prerogative as rational beings, and our faith is no better than the bewildered dream of a man who has lost his reason. Nay, I maintain that when we use the term in this higher sense, it is impossible for us to believe on any authority what is directly contradictory to reason and seen to be so. No evidence from another source, and no authority could convince us, that a proposition in geometry, for example, is false, which our reason intuitively discovers to be true. Now if we suppose (and we may at least suppose this), that reason has the same power of intuitive insight in relation to certain moral and spiritual truths, as in relation to the truths of geometry, then it would be equally impossible to divest us of our belief of those truths.

Furthermore, we are not only unable to believe the same proposition to be false, which our reason sees to be true, but we can not believe another proposition, which by the exercise of the same rational faculty we see to be incompatible with the former, or to contradict it. We may, and probably often do, receive with a certain kind and degree of credence opinions, which reflection would show to be incompatible. But when we have reflected, and discovered the inconsistency, we can not retain both. We can not believe two contradictory propositions, knowing them to be such. It would be irrational to do so.

Again, we can not conceive it possible, that what by the same power of intuition we see to be universally and necessarily true should appear otherwise to any other rational being. We can not, for example, but consider the propositions of geometry as necessarily true for all rational beings. So, too, a little reflection, I think, will convince any one, that we attribute the same necessity of reason to the principles of moral rectitude. What in the clear daylight of our reason, and after mature reflection, we see to be right, we can not believe to be wrong in the view of other rational beings in the distinct exercise of their reason. Nay, in regard to those truths, which are clearly submitted to the view of our reason, and which we behold with distinct and steadfast intuitions, we necessarily attribute to the Supreme Reason, to the Divine Mind, views the same, or coincident, with those of our own reason. We can not (I say it with reverence and I trust with some apprehension of the importance of the assertion), we *can not* believe that to be right in the view of the Supreme Reason, which is clearly and decidedly wrong in the view of our own. It would be contradictory to reason, it would be irrational, to believe it, and therefore we can not do so, till we lose our reason, or cease to exercise it.

I would ask, now, whether this be not an authorized use of the words reason and rational, and whether so used they do not mean something. If it be so—and I appeal to the mind of every man capable of reflection, and of understanding the use of language, if it be not—then there is meaning in the terms *universal reason*, and *unity of reason*, as used in this Work. There is, and can be, in this highest sense of the word, but one reason, and whatever contradicts that reason, being seen to do so, can not be received as matter either of knowledge or faith. To reconcile religion with reason used in this sense, therefore, and to justify the ways of God to man, or in the view of reason, is so far from being irrational, that reason imperatively demands it of us. We can not, as rational beings, believe a proposition on the grounds of reason, and deny it on the authority of revelation. We can not believe a proposition in philosophy, and deny the same proposition in theology: nor can we believe two incompatible propositions on the different grounds of reason and revelation. So far as we compare our thoughts, the objects of our knowledge and faith, and by reflection refer them to their common measure in the universal laws of reason, so far the instinct of reason impels us to reject whatever is contradictory and absurd, and to bring unity and consistency into all our views of truth. Thus, in the language of the Author of this Work, though "the word *rational* has been strangely abused of late times, this must not disincline us to the weighty consideration, that thoughtfulness, and a desire to rest all our convictions on grounds of right reason, are inseparable from the character of a Christian."[5]

But I beg the reader to observe, that in relation to the doctrines of spiritual religion—to all that he considers the peculiar doctrines of the Christian revelation, the Author assigns to reason only a negative validity. It does not teach us what those doctrines are, or what they are not, except that they are not, and can not be, such as contradict the clear convictions of right reason. But his views on this point are fully stated in the Work, and the general office of reason in relation to all that is proposed for our belief, is given with philosophical precision in other parts of his Works.[6]

If then it be our prerogative, as rational beings, and our duty as Christians, to think, as well as to act, *rationally*,—to see that our convictions of truth rest on the grounds of right reason; and if it be one of the clearest dictates of reason, that we should endeavor to shun, and on discovery should reject, whatever is contradictory to the universal laws of thought, or to doctrines already established, I know not by what means we are to avoid the application of philosophy, at least to some extent, in the study of theology. For to determine what *are* the grounds of right reason, what are those ultimate truths, and those universal laws of thought, which we can not rationally contradict, and by reflection to compare with these whatever is proposed for our belief, is in fact to philosophize; and whoever does this to a greater or less extent, is so far a philosopher in the best and highest sense of the word. To this extent we are bound to philosophize in theology, as well as in every other science. For what is not rational in theology, is, of course, irrational, and can not be of the

---

[5] See above, *Int Aph XVI*.

[6] *LS (CC)* 103–5 (quoted by Marsh at   this point in his ed).

household of faith; and to determine whether it be rational in the sense already explained or not, is the province of philosophy. It is in this sense that the Work before us is to be considered a philosophical work, namely, that it proves the doctrines of the Christian Faith to be rational, and exhibits philosophical grounds for the *possibility* of a truly spiritual religion. The *reality* of those experiences, or states of being, which constitute experimental or spiritual religion, rests on other grounds. It is incumbent on the philosopher to free them from the contradictions of reason, and nothing more; and who will deny, that to do this is a purpose worthy of the ablest philosopher and the most devoted Christian? Is it not desirable to convince all men that the doctrines, which we affirm to be revealed in the Gospel, are not contradictory to the requirements of reason and conscience? Is it not, on the other hand, vastly important to the cause of religious truth, and even to the practical influence of religion on our own minds, and the minds of the community at large, that we should attain and exhibit views of philosophy and doctrines in metaphysics, which are at least compatible with, if they do not specially favor, those views of religion, which, on other grounds, we find it our duty to believe and maintain? For, I beg it may be observed, as a point of great moment, that it is not the method of the genuine philosopher to separate his philosophy and religion, and adopting his principles independently in each, to leave them to be reconciled or not, as the case may be. He has, and can have, rationally but one system, in which his philosophy becomes religious, and his religion philosophical. Nor am I disposed in compliance with popular opinion to limit the application of this remark, as is usually done, to the mere external evidences of revelation. The philosophy which we adopt will and must influence not only our decision of the question, whether a book be of divine authority, but our views also of its meaning.

But this is a subject, on which, if possible, I would avoid being misunderstood, and must, therefore, exhibit it more fully, even at the risk of repeating what was said before, or is elsewhere found in the Work. It has been already, I believe, distinctly enough stated, that reason and philosophy ought to prevent our reception of doctrines claiming the authority of revelation only so far as the very necessities of our rational being require. However mysterious the thing affirmed may be, though *it passeth all understanding*,[7] if it can not be shown to contradict the unchangeable principles of right reason, its being incomprehensible to our understandings is not an obstacle to our faith. If it contradict reason, we

---

[7] Phil 4.7.

can not believe it, but must conclude, either that the writing is not of divine authority, or that the language has been misinterpreted. So far it seems to me, that our philosophy ought to modify our views of theological doctrines, and our mode of interpreting the language of an inspired writer. But then we must be cautious, that we philosophize rightly, and "do not call *that* reason which is not so. Otherwise we may be led by the supposed requirements of reason to interpret metaphorically, what ought to be received literally, and evacuate the Scriptures of their most important doctrines." But what I mean to say here is, that we can not avoid the application of our philosophy in the interpretation of the language of Scripture, and in the explanation of the doctrines of religion generally. We can not avoid incurring the danger just alluded to of philosophizing erroneously, even to the extent of rejecting as irrational that which tends to the perfection of reason itself. And hence I maintain, that instead of pretending to exclude philosophy from our religious inquiries, it is very important that we philosophize in earnest—that we should endeavor by profound reflection to learn the real requirements of reason, and attain a true knowledge of ourselves.

If any dispute the necessity of thus combining the study of philosophy with that of religion, I would beg them to point out the age since that of the Apostle's, in which the prevailing metaphysical opinions have not distinctly manifested themselves in the prevailing views of religion; and if, as I fully believe will be the case, they fail to discover a single system of theology, a single volume on the subject of the Christian religion, in which the author's views are not modified by the metaphysical opinions of the age or of the individual, it would be desirable to ascertain, whether this influence be accidental or necessary. The metaphysician analyzes the faculties and operations of the human mind, and teaches us to arrange, to classify, and to name them, according to his views of their various distinctions. The language of the Scriptures, at least to a great extent, speaks of subjects that can be understood only by a reference to those same powers and processes of thought and feeling, which we have learned to think of, and to name, according to our particular system of metaphysics. How is it possible then to avoid interpreting the one by the other? Let us suppose, for example, that a man has studied and adopted the philosophy of Brown,[8] is it possible for him to interpret the 8th chapter of Romans, without having his views of its meaning influenced by

---

[8] Thomas Brown (1778–1820), metaphysician, who studied under Dugald Stewart at Edinburgh and taught with him there, was noted for a philosophy which seemed to find no place for free will. See also Marsh's letter to C of 23 Mar 1829, Duffy 80.

his philosophy? Would he not unavoidably interpret the language and explain the doctrines, which it contains, differently from one, who should have adopted such views of the human mind as are taught in this Work? I know it is customary to disclaim the influence of philosophy in the business of interpretation, and every writer now-a-days on such subjects will assure us, that he has nothing to do with metaphysics, but is guided only by common sense and the laws of interpretation. But I should like to know how a man comes by any common sense in relation to the movements and laws of his intellectual and moral being without metaphysics. What is the common sense of a Hottentot on subjects of this sort? I have no hesitation in saying, that from the very nature of the case, it is nearly, if not quite, impossible for any man entirely to separate his philosophical views of the human mind from his reflections on religious subjects. Probably no man has endeavored more faithfully to do this, perhaps no one has succeeded better in giving the truth of Scripture free from the glosses of metaphysics, than Professor Stuart. Yet, I should risk little in saying that a reader deeply versed in the language of metaphysics, extensively acquainted with the philosophy of different ages, and the peculiar phraseology of different schools, might ascertain his metaphysical system from many a passage of his Commentary on the Epistle to the Hebrews.[9] What then, let me ask, is the possible use to the cause of truth and of religion, from thus perpetually decrying philosophy in theological inquiries, when we can not avoid it if we would? Every man, who has reflected at all, has his metaphysics; and if he reads on religious subjects, he interprets and understands the language, which he employs, by the help of his metaphysics. He can not do otherwise.— And the proper inquiry is, not whether we admit our philosophy into our theological and religious investigations, but whether our philosophy be right and true. For myself, I am fully convinced that we can have no right views of theology, till we have right views of the human mind; and that these are to be acquired only by laborious and persevering reflection. My belief is, that the distinctions unfolded in this Work will place us in the way to truth, and relieve us from numerous perplexities, in which we are involved by the philosophy which we have so long taken for our guide. For we are greatly deceived, if we suppose for a moment that the systems of theology which have been received among us, or even the theoretical views which are now most popular, are free from the entanglements of worldly wisdom. The readers of this Work will be

[9] Moses Stuart *A Commentary on the Epistle to the Hebrews* (2 vols Andover,   Mass 1827).

able to see, I think, more clearly the import of this remark, and the true bearing of the received views of philosophy on our theological inquiries. Those who study the Work without prejudice, and adopt its principles to any considerable extent, will understand too how deeply an age may be ensnared in the metaphysical webs of its own weaving, or entangled in the net which the speculations of a former generation have thrown over it, and yet suppose itself blessed with a perfect immunity from the dreaded evils of metaphysics.

But before I proceed to remark on those particulars, in which our prevailing philosophy seems to be dangerous in its tendency, and unfriendly to the cause of spiritual religion, I must beg leave to guard myself and the Work from misapprehension on another point of great importance in its relations to the whole subject. While it is maintained that reason and philosophy, in their true character, *ought* to have a certain degree and extent of influence in the formation of our religious system, and that our metaphysical opinions, whatever they may be, *will* almost unavoidably, modify more or less our theoretical views of religious truth *generally*, it is yet a special object of the Author of the Work to show that the spiritual life, or what among us is termed experimental religion, is, in itself, and in its own proper growth and development, essentially distinct from the forms and processes of the understanding; and that, although a true faith can not contradict any universal principle of speculative reason, it is yet in a certain sense independent of the discursions of philosophy, and in its proper nature beyond the reach "of positive science and theoretical *insight*." "Christianity is not a *theory* or a *speculation*; but a *life*. Not a *philosophy* of life, but a life and a living process."[10] It is not, therefore, so properly a species of knowledge, as a form of being. And although the theoretical views of the understanding, and the motives of prudence which it presents, may be, to a certain extent, connected with the development of the spiritual principle of religious life in the Christian, yet a true and living faith is not incompatible with at least some degree of speculative error. As the acquisition of merely speculative knowledge can not of itself communicate the principle of spiritual life, so neither does that principle, and the living process of its growth, depend wholly, at least, upon the degree of speculative knowledge with which it co-exists. That religion, of which our blessed Saviour is himself the essential Form and the living Word, and to which he imparts the actuating Spirit, has a principle of unity and consistency in itself distinct from the unity and consistency of our theoretical views.

[10] See above, *Sp Aph B VII* at n 26.

Of this we have evidence in every day's observation of Christian character; for how often do we see and acknowledge the power of religion, and the growth of a spiritual life in minds but little gifted with speculative knowledge, and little versed in the forms of logic or philosophy! How obviously, too, does the living principle of religion manifest the same specific character, the same essential form, amidst all the diversities of condition, of talents, of education, and natural disposition, with which it is associated; everywhere rising above nature, and the powers of the natural man, and unlimited in its goings on by the forms in which the understanding seeks to comprehend and confine its spiritual energies. *There are diversities of gifts, but the same Spirit*; and it is no less true now than in the age of the Apostles, that in all lands, and in every variety of circumstances, the manifestations of spiritual life are essentially the same; and all who truly believe in heart, however diverse in natural condition, in the character of their understandings, and even in their theoretical views of truth, are *one* in *Christ Jesus*. The essential faith is not to be bound in the understanding or the speculative theory, but "the *life*, the *substance*, the *hope*, the *love*—in one word, the *faith*— these are derivatives from the practical, moral, and spiritual nature and being of man."[11] Speculative systems of theology indeed have often had little connection with the essential spirit of religion, and are usually little more than schemes resulting from the strivings of the finite understanding to comprehend and exhibit under its own forms and conditions a mode of being and spiritual truths essentially diverse from their proper objects, and with which they are incommensurate.

This I am aware is an imperfect, and I fear may be an unintelligible, view of a subject exceedingly difficult of apprehension at the best. If so, I must beg the reader's indulgence, and request him to suspend his judgment, as to the absolute intelligibility of it, till he becomes acquainted with the language and sentiments of the Work itself. It will, however, I hope, be so far understood, at least, as to answer the purpose for which it was introduced—of precluding the supposition that, in the remarks which preceded, or in those which follow, any suspicion was intended to be expressed, with regard to the religious principles or the essential faith of those who hold the opinions in question. According to this view of the inherent and essential nature of Spiritual Religion, as existing in the *practical reason* of man, we may not only admit, but can better understand the possibility of what every charitable Christian will acknowledge to be a fact, so far as human observation can determine facts

[11] See above, end of *Sp Aph B II*, Comment.

of this sort—that a man may be truly religious, and essentially a believer at heart, while his understanding is sadly bewildered with the attempt to comprehend and express philosophically, what yet he feels and knows spiritually. It is indeed impossible for us to tell how far the understanding may impose upon itself by partial views and false disguises, without perverting the will, or estranging it from the laws and the authority of reason and the divine word. We can not say to what extent a false system of philosophy and metaphysical opinions, which in their natural and uncounteracted tendency would go to destroy all religion, may be received in a Christian community, and yet the power of spiritual religion retain its hold and its efficacy in the hearts of the people. We may perhaps believe that in opposition to all the might of false philosophy, so long as the great body of the people have the Bible in their hands, and are taught to reverence and receive its heavenly instructions, though the Church may suffer injury from unwise and unfruitful speculations, it will yet be preserved; and that the spiritual seed of the divine word, though mingled with many tares of worldly wisdom and philosophy falsely so-called, will yet spring up, and bear fruit unto everlasting life.

But though we may hope and believe this, we can not avoid believing, at the same time, that injury must result from an unsuspecting confidence in metaphysical opinions, which are essentially at variance with the doctrines of Revelation. Especially must the effect be injurious, where those opinions lead gradually to alter our views of religion itself, and of all that is peculiar in the Christian system. The great mass of the community, who know little of metaphysics, and whose faith in revelation is not so readily influenced by speculations not immediately connected with it, may, indeed, for a time, escape the evil, and continue to *receive with meekness the ingrafted word.* But in the minds of the better educated, especially those who think and follow out their conclusions with resolute independence of thought, the result must be either a loss of confidence in the opinions themselves, or a rejection of all those parts of the Christian system which are at variance with them. Under particular circumstances, indeed, where both the metaphysical errors, and the great doctrines of the Christian Faith, have a strong hold upon the minds of a community, a protracted struggle may take place, and earnest and long-continued efforts may be made to reconcile opinions which we are resolved to maintain, with a faith which our consciences will not permit us to abandon. But so long as the effort continues and such opinions retain their hold upon our confidence, it must be with some diminution of the fulness and simplicity of our faith. To a greater or less degree, according to the education and habits of thought in different individuals, the word of God is received with doubt, or with such glozing modifications as enervate its power. Thus the light from heaven is intercepted, and we are left to a shadow-fight of metaphysical schemes and metaphorical interpretations. While one party, with conscientious and earnest endeavors, and at great expense of talent and ingenuity, contends for the Faith, and among the possible shapings of the received metaphysical system, seeks that which will best comport with the simplicity of the Gospel,—another more boldly interprets the language of the Gospel itself in conformity with those views of religion to which their philosophy seems obviously to conduct them. The substantial being and the living energy of the WORD, which is not only the light but the life of men, is either misapprehended or denied by all parties; and even those who contend for what they conceive the literal import of the Gospel, do it—as they must to avoid too glaring absurdity—with such explanations of its import as to make it to become, in no small degree, the *words of man's wisdom*, rather than a simple *demonstration of the Spirit and of power*. Hence, although such as have experienced the spiritual and life-giving power of the Divine Word, may be able, through the promised aids of the Spirit, to overcome the natural tendency of speculative error, and, by *the law of the spirit of life* which is in them, may at length be made *free from the law of sin and death*, yet who can tell how much they may lose of the blessings of the Gospel, and be retarded in their spiritual growth when they are but too often fed with the lifeless and starveling products of the human understanding, instead of that *living bread which came down from heaven*? Who can tell, moreover, how many, through the prevalence of such philosophical errors as lead to misconceptions of the truth or create a prejudice against it, and thus tend to intercept the light from heaven, may continue in their ignorance, *alienated from the life of God*, and groping in the darkness of their own understandings?

But however that may be, enlightened Christians, and especially Christian instructors, know it to be their duty, as far as possible, to prepare the way for the full and unobstructed influence of the Gospel, to do all in their power to remove those natural prejudices, and those errors of the understanding, which are obstacles to the truth, that the word of God may find access to the heart, and conscience, and reason of every man, that it may have *free course, and run, and be glorified*. My own belief, that such obstacles to the influence of truth exist in the speculative and metaphysical opinions generally adopted in this country, and that the present Work is in some measure at least calculated to remove them, is pretty clearly indicated by the remarks which I have already made. But, to be perfectly explicit on the subject I do not hesitate to express my conviction, that the natural tendency of some of the leading principles of our prevailing system of metaphysics, and those which must unavoidably have more or less influence on our theoretical views of religion, are of an injurious and dangerous tendency, and that so long as we retain them, however we may profess to exclude their influence from our theological inquiries, and from the interpretation of Scripture, we can maintain no consistent system of Scriptural theology, nor clearly and distinctly apprehend the spiritual import of the Scripture language. The grounds of this conviction I shall proceed to exhibit, though only in a very partial manner, as I could not do more without anticipating the contents of the Work itself, instead of merely preparing the reader to peruse them with attention. I am aware, too, that some of the language, which I have already employed, and shall be obliged to employ, will not convey its full import to the reader, till he becomes acquainted with some of the leading principles and distinctions unfolded in the Work. But this also is an evil which I saw no means of avoiding without incurring a greater, and writing a book instead of a brief essay.

Let it be understood, then, without further preface, that by the prevailing system of metaphysics, I mean the system, of which in modern times Locke is the reputed author, and the leading principles of which, with various modifications, more or less important, but not altering its essential character, have been almost universally received in this country. It should be observed, too, that the causes enumerated by the Author, as having elevated it to its "pride of place" in Europe, have been aided by other favoring circumstances here. In the minds of our religious community, especially, some of its most important doctrines have become associated with names justly loved and revered among ourselves, and so connected with all our theoretical views of religion, that a man can hardly hope to question their validity without hazarding his reputation, not only for orthodoxy, but even for common sense. To controvert, for example, the prevailing doctrines with regard to the freedom of the will, the sources of our knowledge, the nature of the understanding as containing the controlling principles of our whole being, and the universality of the law of cause and effect, even in connection with the arguments and the authority of the most powerful intellect of the age, may even now be worse than in vain. Yet I have reasons for believing there are some among us, and that their number is fast increasing, who are willing to revise their opinions on these subjects, and who will contemplate the views presented in this Work with a liberal, and something of a prepared feeling of curiosity. The difficulties in which men find themselves involved by the received doctrines on these subjects, in their most anxious efforts to explain and defend the peculiar doctrines of spiritual religion, have led many to suspect that there must be some lurking error in the premises. It is not that these principles lead us to mysteries which we can not comprehend; they are found, or believed at least by many, to involve us in absurdities which we can comprehend. It is necessary indeed only to form some notion of the distinctive and appropriate import of the term spiritual, as opposed to natural in the New Testament, and then to look at the writings, or hear the discussions, in which the doctrines of the Spirit and of spiritual influences are taught and defended, to see the insurmountable nature of the obstacles, which these metaphysical dogmas throw in the way of the most powerful minds. To those who shall read this Work with any degree of reflection, it must, I think, be obvious, that something more is implied in the continual opposition of these terms in the New Testament, than can be explained consistently with the prevailing opinions on the subjects above enumerated; and that through their influence our highest notions of that distinction have been rendered confused, contradictory, and inadequate. I have already directed the attention of the reader to those parts of the Work, where this distinction is unfolded; and had I no other grounds than the arguments and views there exhibited, I should be convinced that so long as we hold the doctrines of Locke and the Scotch metaphysicians respecting power, cause and effect, motives, and the freedom of the will, we not only can make and defend no essential distinction between that which is *natural*, and that which is *spiritual*, but we can not even find rational grounds for the feeling of *moral obligation*, and the distinction between *regret* and *remorse*.

According to the system of these authors, as nearly and distinctly as my limits will permit me to state it, the same law of cause and effect is the law of the universe. It extends to the moral and spiritual—if in courtesy these terms may still be used—no less than to the properly natural powers and agencies of our being. The acts of the free-will are predetermined by a cause *out of the will*, according to the same law of cause and effect which controls the changes in the physical world. We have no notion of power but uniformity of antecedent and consequent. The notion of a power in the will to act freely is therefore nothing more than an inherent capacity of being acted upon, agreeably to its nature, and according to a fixed law, by the motives which are present in the understanding. I feel authorized to take this statement partly from Brown's Philosophy, because that work has been decidedly approved by our highest theological authorities; and indeed it would not be essentially varied, if expressed in the precise terms used by any of the writers most usually quoted in reference to these subjects.

I am aware that variations may be found in the mode of stating these doctrines; but I think every candid reader, who is acquainted with the metaphysics and theology of this country, will admit the above to be a fair representation of the form in which they are generally received. I am aware, too, that much has been said and written to make out, consistently with these general principles, a distinction between natural and moral causes, natural and moral ability, and inability, and the like. But I beg all lovers of sound and rational philosophy to look carefully at the general principles, and see whether there be, in fact, ground left for any such distinctions of this kind as are worth contending for. My first step in arguing with a defender of these principles, and of the distinctions in question, as connected with them, would be to ask for his definition of nature and *natural*. And when he had arrived at a distinctive general notion of the import of these, it would appear, if I mistake not, that he had first subjected our whole being to the law of nature, and then contended for the existence of something which is not nature. For in their relation to the law of moral rectitude, and to the feeling of moral responsibility, what difference is there, and what difference can there be, between what are called natural and those which are called moral powers and affections, if they are all under the control of the same universal *law* of cause and effect? If it still be a mere nature, and the determinations of our will be controlled by causes out of the will, according to our nature, then I maintain that moral nature has no more to do with the feeling of responsibility than any other nature.

Perhaps the difficulty may be made more obvious in this way. It will be admitted that brutes are possessed of various natures, some innocent or useful, otherwise noxious, but all alike irresponsible in a moral point of view. But why? Simply because they act in accordance with their natures. They possess, each according to its proper nature, certain appetites and susceptibilities which are stimulated and acted upon by their appropriate objects in the world of the senses; and the relation—the law of action and reaction—subsisting between these specific susceptibilities and their corresponding outward objects, constitutes their nature. They have a power of selecting and choosing in the world of sense the objects appropriate to the wants of their nature; but that nature is the sole law of their being. Their power of choice is but a part of it, instrumental in accomplishing its ends, but not capable of rising above it, of controlling its impulses, and of determining itself with reference to a purely ideal law, distinct from their nature. They act in accordance with the law of cause and effect, which constitutes their several natures, and can not do otherwise. They are, therefore, not responsible—not capable of guilt, or of remorse.

Now let us suppose another being, possessing, in addition to the susceptibilities of the brute, certain other specific susceptibilities with their correlative objects, either in the sensible world, or in a future world, but that these are subjected, like the other, to the same binding and inalienable law of cause and effect. What, I ask, is the amount of the difference thus supposed between this being and the brute? The supposed addition, it is to be understood, is merely an addition to its nature; and the only power of will belonging to it is, as in the case of the brute, only a capacity of choosing and acting uniformly in accordance with its nature. These additional susceptibilities still act but as they are acted upon; and the will is determined accordingly. What advantage is gained in this case by calling these supposed additions moral affections, and their correlative stimulants moral causes? Do we thereby find any rational ground for the feeling of moral responsibility, for conscience, for remorse? The being acts according to its nature, and why is it blameworthy more than the brute? If the moral law existing out of the will be a power or cause which, in its relation to the specific susceptibility of the moral being, produces under the same circumstances uniformly the same result, according to the law of cause and effect; if the acts of the will be subject to the same law, as mere links in the chain of antecedents and consequents, and thus a part of our nature, what is gained, I ask again, by the distinction of a moral and a physical nature? It is still only a nature under the law of cause and effect, and the liberty of the moral being is under the same condition with the liberty of the brute. Both are free to follow and fulfil the law of their nature, and both are alike bound by that law, as by an adamantine chain. The very conditions of the law preclude the possibility of a power to act otherwise than according to their nature. They preclude the very idea of a free-will, and render the feeling of moral responsibility not an enigma merely, not a mystery, but a self-contradiction and an absurdity.

Turn the matter as we will—call these correlatives, namely, the inherent susceptibilities and the causes acting on them from without, natural, or moral, or spiritual—so long as their action and reaction, or the law of reciprocity, which constitutes their specific natures, is considered as the controlling law of our whole being, so long as we refuse to admit the existence in the will of a power capable of rising above this law, and controlling its operation by an act of absolute self-determination, so long we shall be involved in perplexities both in morals and religion. At all events, the only method of avoiding them will be to adopt the creed of the Necessitarians entire, to give man over to an irresponsible nature as a better sort of animal, and resolve the will of the Supreme Reason into a blind and irrational fate.

I am well aware of the objections that will be made to this statement, and especially the demonstrated incomprehensibleness of a self-determining power. To this I may be permitted to answer, that, although the power to originate an act or state of mind may be beyond the capacity of our understandings to comprehend, it is still not contradictory to reason; and that I find it more easy to believe the existence of that, which is simply incomprehensible to my understanding, than of that which involves an absurdity for my reason. I venture to affirm, moreover, that however we may bring our understandings into bondage to the more comprehensible doctrine, simply because it is comprehensible under the forms of the understanding, every man does, in fact, believe himself possessed of freedom in the higher sense of self-determination. Every man's conscience commands him to believe it, whenever for a moment he indulges the feeling of moral self-approbation, or of remorse. Nor can we on any other grounds justify the ways of God to man upon the supposition that he inflicts or will inflict any other punishment than that which is simply remedial or disciplinary. But this subject will be found more fully explained in the course of the Work. My present object is merely to show the necessity of some system in relation to these subjects different from the received one.

It may perhaps be thought, that the language used above is too strong and too positive. But I venture to ask every candid man, at least every one who has not committed himself by writing and publishing on the subject, whether in considering the great questions connected with moral accountability and the doctrine of rewards and punishments, he has not felt himself pressed with such difficulties as those above stated; and whether he has ever been able fully to satisfy his reason, that there was not a lurking contradiction in the idea of a being created and placed under the law of its nature, and possessing at the same time a feeling of moral obligation to fulfil a law above its nature. That many have been in this state of mind I know. I know, too, that some whose moral and religious feelings had led them to a full belief in the doctrines of spiritual religion, but who at the same time had been taught to receive the prevailing opinions in metaphysics, have found these opinions carrying them unavoidably, if they would be consequent in their reasonings, and not do violence to their reason, to adopt a system of religion which does not profess to be spiritual, and thus have been compelled to choose between their philosophy and their religion. In most cases indeed, where men reflect at all, I am satisfied that it requires all the force of authority, and all the influence of education, to carry the mind over these difficulties; and that then it is only by a vague belief that, though we can not see how, there must be some method of reconciling what seems to be so contradictory.

If examples were wanting to prove that serious and trying difficulties are felt to exist here, enough may be found, as it has appeared to me, in the controversy respecting the nature and origin of sin, which is at this moment interesting the public mind. Let any impartial observer trace the progress of that discussion, and after examining the distinctions which are made or attempted to be made, decide whether the subject, as there presented, be not involved in difficulties, which can not be solved on the principles to which, hitherto, both parties have adhered; whether, holding as they do the same premises in regard to the freedom of the will, they can avoid coming to the same conclusion in regard to the nature and origin of sin; whether in fact the distinctions aimed at must not prove merely verbal distinctions, and the controversy a fruitless one. But in the September number of the Christian Spectator, the reader will find remarks on this subject, to which I beg leave to refer him, and which I could wish him attentively to consider in connection with the remarks which I have made. I allude to the correspondence with the editors near the end of the number.[12] The letter there inserted is said to be, and obviously is, from the pen of a very learned and able writer; and I confess it has been no small gratification and encouragement to me, while laboring to bring this Work and this subject before the public, to find such a state of feeling expressed, concerning the great question at issue, by such a writer. It will be seen by reference to p. 545, of the C. S., that he places the "*nucleus* of the dispute" just where it is placed in this Work and in the above remarks. It will be seen, too, that by throwing authorities aside, and studying his own mind, he has "come seriously to doubt," whether the received opinions with regard to *motives*, the law of *cause and effect*, and the *freedom of the will*, may not be erroneous. They appear to him "to be bordering on fatalism, if not actually embracing it." He doubts whether the mind may not have within itself the adequate cause of its own acts; whether indeed it have not a self-determining power, "for the power in question involves the idea of originat-

---

[12] See the letter from "Pacificus" concerning a review of works by N. W. Taylor and J. Harvey on Human Depravity in the previous issue (pp 343–84): *Quarterly Christian Spectator* NS I (New Haven, Conn Sept 1829) 536–47.

ing volition. Less than this it can not be conceived to involve, and yet be *free* agency." Now this is just the view offered in the present Work; and, as it seems to me, these are just the doubts and conclusions which every one will entertain, who lays aside authority, and reflects upon the goings on of his own mind, and the dictates of his own reason and conscience.

But let us look for a moment at the remarks of the editors in reply to the letter above quoted. They maintain, in relation to original sin and the perversion of the will, that from either the *original* or the *acquired* strength of certain natural appetites, principles of self-love, &c., "left to themselves," the corruption of the heart will certainly follow. "In every instance the will does, in fact, yield to the demands of these. But whenever it thus yielded, *there was power to the contrary*; otherwise there could be no freedom of moral action." Now I beg leave to place my finger on the phrase in italics, and ask the editors what they mean by it. If they hold the common doctrines with regard to the relation of cause and effect, and with regard to power as connected with that relation, and apply these to the acts of the will, I can see no more possibility of conceiving a *power to the contrary* in this case, than of conceiving such a power in the current of a river. But if they mean to assert the existence in the will of an *actual* power to rise above the demands of appetite, &c., above the law of nature and to decide *arbitrarily*, whether to yield or not to yield, then they admit that the will is not determined *absolutely* by the extraneous *cause*, but is in fact *self*-determined. They agree with the letter-writer; and the question for them is at rest. Thus, whatever distinctions may be attempted here, there can be no real distinction but between an irresponsible nature and a will that is self-determined. The reader will find a few additional remarks on this topic in a note, and for the general views of the Work is again referred to a former note and the references there made. To the subject of that note, and to the great distinction between nature and the will, between the natural and the spiritual, as unfolded in the Work, I must beg leave, also, again to request the special and candid attention of the reader. I must beg, too, the unprejudiced attention of every reader, friendly to the cause of practical and spiritual religion, to the tendency of this part of the Author's system, and of the remarks hazarded above.

I cannot but be aware, that the views of the Will here exhibited will meet with strong prejudices in a large portion, at least, of our religious community. I could wish that all such would carefully distinguish between the Author's views of the doctrines of religion and the philosophical grounds on which he supposes those doctrines are to be defended.

If no one disputes, and I trust no one will dispute, the substantial orthodoxy of the Work, without first carefully examining what has been the orthodoxy of the Church in general, and of the great body of the Reformers, then I should hope it may be wisely considered, whether, as a question of philosophy, the metaphysical principles of this Work are not in themselves more in accordance with the doctrines of a spiritual religion, and better suited to their explanation and defence, than those above treated of. If on examination it can not be disputed that they are, then, if not before, I trust the two systems may be compared without undue impartiality, and the simple question of the truth of each may be determined by that calm and persevering reflection, which alone can determine questions of this sort.

If the system here taught be true, then it will follow, not, be it observed, that our religion is necessarily wrong, or our essential faith erroneous, but that the *philosophical grounds*, on which we are accustomed to defend our faith, are unsafe, and that their *natural tendency* is to error. If the spirit of the Gospel still exert its influence; if a truly spiritual religion be maintained, it is in *opposition* to our philosophy, and not at all by its aid. I know it will be said, that the practical results of our peculiar forms of doctrine are at variance with these remarks. But this I am not prepared to admit. True, religion and religious institutions have flourished: the Gospel, in many parts of our country, has been affectionately and faithfully preached by great and good men; the word and the Spirit of God have been communicated to us in rich abundance; and I rejoice with heartfelt joy and thanksgiving, in the belief, that thereby multitudes have been regenerated to a new and spiritual life. But so were equal or greater effects produced under the preaching of Baxter, and Howe,[13] and other good and faithful men of the same age, with none of the peculiarities of our theological systems. Neither reason nor experience indeed furnish any ground for believing that the living and life-giving power of the Divine Word has ever derived any portion of its efficacy, in the conversion of the heart to God, from the forms of metaphysical theology, with which the human understanding has invested it. It requires, moreover, but little knowledge of the history of philosophy, and of the writings of the 16th and 17th centuries to know, that the opinions of the Reformers, and of all the great divines of that period, on subjects of this sort, were far different from those of Mr. Locke and his

---

[13] The first volume of Marsh *Select Practical Theology of the Seventeenth Century* (Burlington Vt, 1830) included ''The blessedness of the righteous'' etc and ''The vanity of man as mortal'' by John Howe (1630–1705). No more volumes were published.

followers, and were in fact essentially the same with those taught in this Work. This last remark applies not only to the views entertained by the eminent philosophers and divines of that period on the particular subject above discussed, but to the distinctions made, and the language employed by them, with reference to other points of no less importance in the constitution of our being.

It must have been observed by the reader of the foregoing pages, that I have used several words, especially *understanding* and *reason*, in a sense somewhat diverse from their present acceptation; and the occasion of this I suppose would be partly understood from my having already directed the attention of the reader to the distinction exhibited between these words in the Work, and from the remarks made on the ambiguity of the word "reason" in its common use. I now proceed to remark, that the ambiguity spoken of, and the consequent perplexity in regard to the use and authority of reason, have arisen from the habit of using, since the time of Locke, the terms understanding and reason indiscriminately, and thus confounding a distinction clearly marked in the philosophy and in the language of the older writers. Alas! had the *terms* only been confounded, or had we suffered only an inconvenient ambiguity of language, there would be comparatively little cause for earnestness upon the subject; or had our views of the things signified by these terms been only partially confused, and had we still retained correct notions of our prerogative, as rational and spiritual beings, the consequences might have been less deplorable. But the misfortune is, that the powers of understanding and reason have not merely been blended and confounded in the view of our philosophy;—the higher and far more characteristic, as an essential constituent of our proper humanity, has been as it were obscured and hidden from our observation in the inferior power, which belongs to us in common with the brutes which perish. According to the old, the more spiritual, and genuine philosophy, the distinguishing attributes of our humanity—that *image of* God in which man alone was created of all the dwellers upon earth, and in virtue of which he was placed at the head of this lower world, was said to be found in the *reason* and *free-will*. But understanding these in their strict and proper sense, and according to the true *ideas* of them, as contemplated by the older metaphysicians, we have literally, if the system of Locke and the popular philosophy of the day be true, neither the one nor the other of these— neither reason nor free-will. What they esteemed the image of God in the soul, and considered as distinguishing us specifically, and so vastly too, above each and all of the irrational animals, is found, according to this system, to have in fact no real existence. The reality neither of the free-will, nor of any of those laws or ideas, which spring from, or rather constitute reason, can be authenticated by the sort of proof which is demanded, and we must therefore relinquish our prerogative, and take our place with becoming humility among our more unpretending companions. In the ascending series of powers, enumerated by Milton, with so much philosophical truth, as well as beauty of language, in the fifth book of Paradise Lost, he mentions

> *Fancy* and *understanding*, whence the soul
> REASON receives. And reason is her *being*,
> Discursive or intuitive.

But the highest power here, that which is the being of the soul, considered as any thing differing in kind from the understanding, has no place in our popular metaphysics. Thus we have only the *understanding*, ''the faculty judging according to sense,'' a faculty of abstracting and generalizing, of contrivance and forecast, as the highest of our intellectual powers; and this we are expressly taught belongs to us in common with brutes. Nay, these views of our essential being, consequences and all, are adopted by men, whom one would suppose religion, if not philosophy, should have taught their utter inadequateness to the true and essential constituents of our humanity. Dr. Paley tells us in his Natural Theology, that only ''CONTRIVANCE,'' a power obviously and professedly belonging to brutes, is necessary to constitute *personality*.[14] His whole system both of theology and morals neither teaches, nor implies, the existence of any specific difference either between the understanding and reason, or between nature and the will. It does not imply the existence of any power in man, which does not obviously belong, in a greater or less degree, to irrational animals. Dr. Fleming, another reverend prelate in the English Church, in his ''Philosophy of Zoology,'' maintains in express terms, that we have no faculties differing in kind from those which belong to brutes.[15] How many other learned, and reverend, and wise men adopt the same opinions, I know not: though these are obviously not the peculiar views of the individuals, but conclusions resulting from the essential principles of their system. If, then, there is no better *system*, if this be the genuine philosophy, and founded in the nature of things, there is no help for us, and we must believe it—*if we can.* But most certainly it will follow, that we ought, as fast as the prejudices of education will permit, to rid ourselves of certain notions of

---

[14] See William Paley *Natural Theology* ch 23 (14th ed 1813) 408.

[15] John Fleming *Philosophy of Zoology* (Edinburgh 1822) I 303–14. Fleming's arguments rest on the superior use of faculties by human beings.

prerogative, and certain feelings of our own superiority, which somehow have been strangely prevalent among our race. For though we have indeed, according to this system, a little *more* understanding than other animals—can abstract and generalize and forecast events, and the consequences of our actions, and compare motives *more* skilfully than they; though we have thus *more* knowledge and can circumvent them; though we have *more* power and can subdue them; yet, as to any *distinctive* and *peculiar* characteristic—as to any inherent and essential *worth*, we are after all but little better—though we may be better off—than our dogs and horses. There is no essential difference, and we may rationally doubt—at least we might do so, if by the supposition we were rational beings—whether our fellow animals of the kennel and the stall are not unjustly deprived of certain *personal rights*, and whether a dog charged with trespass may not *rationally* claim to be tried by a jury of his *peers*. Now however trifling and ridiculous this may appear, I would ask in truth and soberness, if it be not a fair and legitimate inference from the premises, and whether the *absurdity* of the one does not *demonstrate* the utter falsity of the other. And where, I would beg to know, shall we look, according to the popular system of philosophy, for that *image of God* in which we are created? Is it a thing of *degrees*? And is it simply because we have something *more* of the same faculties which belong to brutes, that we become the objects of God's special and fatherly care, the *distinguished* objects of his Providence, and the *sole* objects of his Grace?— *Doth God take care for oxen*? But why not?

I assure my readers, that I have no desire to treat with disrespect and contumely the opinions of great or good men; but the distinction in question, and the assertion and exhibition of the higher prerogatives of reason, as an essential constituent of our being, are so vitally important, in my apprehension, to the formation and support of any rational system of philosophy, and—no less than the distinction before treated of—so pregnant of consequences to the interests of truth, in morals, and religion, and indeed of all truth, that mere opinion and the authority of names may well be disregarded. The discussion, moreover, relates to facts, and to such facts, too, as are not to be learned from the instruction, or received on the authority, of any man. They must be ascertained by every man for himself, by reflection upon the processes and laws of his own inward being, or they are not learned at all to any valuable purpose. We do indeed find in ourselves then, as no one will deny, certain powers of intelligence, which we have abundant reason to believe the brutes possess in common with us in a greater or less degree. The functions of the understanding, as treated of in the popular systems of metaphysics, its faculties of attention, of abstraction, of generalization, the power of forethought and contrivance, of adapting means to ends, and the law of association, may be, so far as we can judge, severally represented more or less adequately in the instinctive intelligence of the higher orders of brutes. But, not to anticipate too far a topic treated of in the Work, do these, or any and all the faculties which we discover in irrational animals, satisfactorily account to a reflecting mind for all the *phenomena* which are presented to our observation in our own consciousness? Would any supposable addition to the *degree* merely of those powers which we ascribe to brutes, render them *rational* beings, and remove the sacred distinction, which law and reason have sanctioned, between things and persons? Will any such addition account for our having— what the brute is not supposed to have—the pure *ideas* of the geometrician, the power of ideal construction, the intuition of geometrical or other necessary and universal truths? Would it give rise, in irrational animals, to a *law of moral rectitude* and *to conscience*—to the feelings of moral *responsibility* and *remorse*? Would it awaken them to a reflective self-consciousness, and lead them to form and contemplate the *ideas* of the *soul*, of *free-will*, of *immortality*, and of God? It seems to me, that we have only to reflect for a serious hour upon what we mean by these, and then to compare them with our notion of what belongs to a brute, its inherent powers and their correlative objects, to feel that they are utterly incompatible—that in the blessing of these we enjoy a prerogative, which we can not disclaim without a violation of reason, and a voluntary abasement of ourselves—and that we must therefore be possessed of some *peculiar* powers—of some source of ideas *distinct* from the understanding, differing *in kind* from any and all of those which belong to us in common with inferior and irrational animals.

But what these powers are, or what is the precise nature of the distinction between the understanding and reason, it is not my province, nor have I undertaken, to show. My object is merely to illustrate its necessity, and the palpable obscurity, vagueness and deficiency, in this respect, of the mode of philosophizing, which is held in so high honor among us. The distinction itself will be found illustrated with some of its important bearings in the Work, and in the notes and Appendix attached to it; and can not be too carefully studied—in connection with that between nature and the will—by the student who would acquire distinct and intelligible notions of what constitutes the truly spiritual in our being, or find rational grounds for the possibility of a truly spiritual religion. Indeed, could I succeed in fixing the attention of the reader upon this distinction, in such a way as to secure his candid and reflecting perusal of the Work, I should consider any personal effort or sacrifice abundantly recompensed. Nor am I alone in this view of its importance. A literary friend, whose opinion on this subject would be valued by all who knew the soundness of his scholarship, says in a letter just now received,—"If you can get the attention of thinking men fixed on his distinction between the reason and the understanding, you will have done enough to reward the labor of a life. As prominent a place as it holds in the writings of Coleridge, he seems to me far enough from making too much of it."[16] No person of serious and philosophical mind, I am confident, can reflect upon the subject, enough to understand it in its various aspects, without arriving at the same views of the importance of the distinction, whatever may be his conviction with regard to its truth.

But indeed the only grounds, which I find, to apprehend that the reality of the distinction and the importance of the consequences resulting from it, will be much longer denied and rejected among us, is in the overweening assurance, which prevails with regard to the adequateness and perfection of the system of philosophy which is already received. It is taken for granted, as a fact undisputed and indisputable, that this is the most enlightened age of the world, not only with regard to the more general diffusion of certain points of practical knowledge; in which, probably, it may be so, but *in all respects*; that our whole system of the philosophy of mind as derived from Lord Bacon, especially, is the only one, which has any claims to common sense; and that all distinctions not recognized in that are consequently unworthy of our regard. What those Reformers, to whose transcendent powers of mind, and to whose characters as truly spiritual divines, we are accustomed to look with feelings of so much general regard, might find to say in favor of their philosophy, few take the pains to inquire. Neither they nor the great philosophers with whom they held communion on subjects of this sort, can appear among us to speak in their own defence; and even the huge folios and quartos, in which, though dead, they yet speak—and ought to be heard—have seldom strayed to this side of the Atlantic. All our information respecting their philosophical opinions, and the grounds on which they defended them, has been received from writers, who were confessedly advocating a system of recent growth, at open war with every thing more ancient, and who, in the great abundance of their self-complacency, have represented their own discoveries as containing the sum and substance of all philosophy, and the accumulated treasures of

---

[16] Letter from Ebenezer Tracy of Andover, 28 Oct 1829: see Duffy 97.

ancient wisdom as unworthy the attention of "this enlightened age." Be it so—yet the *foolishness* of antiquity, if it be *of God*, may prove *wiser than men*. It may be found that the philosophy of the Reformers and their religion are essentially connected, and must stand or fall together. It may at length be discovered, that a system of religion essentially spiritual, and a system of philosophy which excludes the very idea of all spiritual power and agency, in their only distinctive and proper character, can not be consistently associated together.

It is our peculiar misfortune in this country, that while the philosophy of Locke and the Scottish writers has been received in full faith, as the only rational system, and its leading principles especially passed off as unquestionable, the strong attachment to religion, and the fondness for speculation, by both of which we are strongly characterized, have led us to combine and associate these principles, such as they are, with our religious interests and opinions, so variously and so intimately, that by most persons they are considered as necessary parts of the same system; and from being so long contemplated together, the rejection of one seems impossible without doing violence to the other. Yet how much evidence might not an impartial observer find in examining the theological discussions which have prevailed, the speculative systems which have been formed and arrayed against each other, for the last seventy years, to convince him that there must be some discordance in the elements, some principle of secret but irreconcilable hostility between a philosophy and a religion, which, under every ingenious variety of form and shaping, still stand aloof from each other and refuse to cohere. For is it not a fact, that in regard to every speculative system which has been formed on these philosophical principles,—to every new shaping of theory which has been devised and has gained adherents among us,—is it not a fact, I ask, that, to all, except those adherents, the *system*—the philosophical *theory*—has seemed dangerous in its tendency, and at war with orthodox views of religion—perhaps even with the attributes of God? Nay, to bring the matter still nearer and more plainly to view, I ask, whether at this moment the organs and particular friends of our leading theological seminaries in New England, both devotedly attached to an orthodox and spiritual system of religion, and expressing mutual confidence as to the *essentials* of their mutual faith, do not each consider the other as holding a philosophical *theory* subversive of orthodoxy? If I am not misinformed, this is the simple fact.

Now, if these things be so, I would ask again with all earnestness, and out of regard to the interests of truth alone, whether serious and reflecting men may not be permitted, without the charge of heresy in RELI-

GION, to stand in doubt of this PHILOSOPHY *altogether*; whether these facts which will not be disputed, do not furnish just grounds for suspicion, that the principles of our philosophy may be erroneous, or at least induce us to look with candor and impartiality at the claims of another and a different system?

What are the claims of the system, to which the attention of the public is invited in this Work, can be understood fully, only by a careful and reflecting examination of its principles in connection with the conscious wants of our inward being—the requirements of our own reason and consciences. Its purpose and tendency, I have endeavored in some measure to exhibit; and if the influence of authority, which the prevailing system furnishes against it, can and must be counteracted by any thing of a like kind—(and whatever professions we may make, the influence of authority produces at least a predisposing effect upon our minds)— the remark which I have made, will show, that the principles here taught are not wholly unauthorized by men, whom we have been taught to reverence among the great and good. I can not but add, as a matter of simple justice to the question, that however our prevailing system of philosophizing may have appealed to the authority of Lord Bacon, it needs but a candid examination of his writings, especially the first part of his *Novum Organum*, to be convinced that such an appeal is without grounds; and that in fact the fundamental principles of his philosophy are the same with those taught in this work. The great distinction especially, between the understanding and the reason, is fully and clearly recognized; and as a philosopher he would be far more properly associated with Plato, or even Aristotle, than with the modern philosophers, who have miscalled their systems by his name. For further remarks on this point, the reader is requested to refer to the notes.[17] In our own times, moreover, there is abundant evidence, whatever may be thought of the principles of this Work here, that the same general views of philosophy are regaining their ascendency elsewhere. In Great Britain there are not few, who begin to believe that the deep-toned and sublime eloquence of Coleridge on these great subjects may have something to claim their attention besides a few peculiarities of language. In Paris, the doctrines of a rational and spiritual system of philosophy are taught to listening and admiring thousands by one of the most learned and eloquent philosophers of the age;[18] and

---

[17] In the 1829 ed Marsh draws attention to two long notes containing relevant extracts from C's works, including *Friend* (*CC*) I 467–8nn, 492–3, 154–61, and 177n.

[18] I.e. Victor Cousin (1792–1867): see Marsh's letter to Joseph Torrey, 14 Feb 1829: Duffy 69, 70, and other refs there. By 1841 he was warning Nancy Smith of the pantheism in some of his works: Duffy

in Germany, if I mistake not, the same general views are adopted by the serious friends of religious truth among her great and learned men.

Such—as I have no doubt—must be the case, wherever thinking men can be brought distinctly and impartially to examine their claims; and indeed to those who shall study and comprehend the general history of philosophy, it must always be matter of special wonder, that in the Christian community, anxiously striving to explain and defend the doctrines of Christianity in their spiritual sense, there should have been a long-continued and tenacious adherence to philosophical principles, so subversive of their faith in every thing distinctively spiritual; while those of an opposite tendency, and claiming a near relationship and correspondence with the truly spiritual in the Christian system, and the mysteries of its sublime faith, were looked upon with suspicion and jealousy, as unintelligible or dangerous metaphysics.

And here I must be allowed to add a few remarks with regard to the popular objections against the system of philosophy, the claims of which I am urging, especially against the writings of the Author, under whose name it appears in the present Work. These are various and often contradictory, but usually have reference either to his peculiarities of language, or to the depth—whether apparent or real,—and the unintelligibleness, of his thoughts.

To the first of these it seems to me a sufficient answer, for a mind that would deal honestly and frankly by itself, to suggest that in the very nature of things it is impossible for a writer to express by a single word any truth, or to mark any distinction, not recognized in the language of his day, unless he adopts a word entirely new, or gives to one already in use a new and more peculiar sense. Now in communicating truths, which the writer deems of great and fundamental importance, shall he thus appropriate a single word old or new, or trust to the vagueness of perpetual circumlocution? Admitting for example, the existence of the important distinction, for which this writer contends, between the understanding and reason, and that this distinction when recognized at all is confounded in the common use of language by employing the words indiscriminately, shall he still use these words indiscriminately, and either invent a new word, or mark the distinction by descriptive circumlocutions, or shall he assign a more distinctive and precise meaning to the words already used? It seems to me obviously more in accordance with the laws and genius of language to take the course which he has

---

264. For Emerson's changing view of Cousin see K. W. Cameron *Emerson the*   *Essayist* (Raleigh, NC 1945) 303–19.

adopted. But in this case and in many others, where his language seems peculiar, it can not be denied that the words had already been employed in the same sense, and the same distinctions recognized, by the older and many of the most distinguished writers in the language. But the reader will find the Author's own views of the subject in the Work.[19]

With regard to the more important objection, that the *thoughts* of Coleridge are *unintelligible*, if it be intended to imply, that his language is not in itself expressive of an intelligible meaning, or that he affects the appearance of depth and mystery, while his thoughts are common-place, it is an objection, which no one who has read his Works attentively, and acquired a feeling of interest for them, will treat their Author with so much disrespect as to answer at all. Every such reader *knows* that he uses words uniformly with astonishing precision, and that language becomes, in his use of it—in a degree, of which few writers can give us a conception—a living power, "consubstantial" with the power of thought, that gave birth to it, and awakening and calling into action a corresponding energy in our own minds. There is little encouragement, moreover, to answer the objections of any man, who will permit himself to be incurably prejudiced against an Author by a few peculiarities of language, or an apparent difficulty of being understood, and without inquiring into the cause of that difficulty, where at the same time he can not but see and acknowledge the presence of great intellectual and moral power.

But if it be intended by the objection to say simply, that the thoughts of the Author are often difficult to be apprehended—that he makes large demands not only upon the attention, but upon the reflecting and thinking powers, of his readers, the fact is not, and need not be, denied: and it will only remain to be decided, whether the instruction offered, as the reward, will repay us for the expenditure of thought required, or can be obtained for less. I know it is customary in this country, as well as in Great Britain—and that too among men from whom different language might be expected—to affect either contempt or modesty, in regard to all that is more than common-place in philosophy, and especially "Coleridge's Metaphysics," as "too deep for them." Now it may not be every man's duty, or in every man's power, to devote to such studies the time and thought necessary to understand the deep things of philosophy. But for one who professes to be a scholar, and to cherish a manly love of truth for the truth's sake, to object to a system of metaphysics because

[19] In the 1829 ed Marsh referred specifically to C's statements in the "Selection from Mr Coleridge's Literary Correspondence", Letter II etc in *Bl Mag* Oct 1821, which he reprinted as his first Appendix to that volume.

it is "too *deep* for him," must be either a disingenuous insinuation, that its depths are not worth exploring—which is more than the objector knows—or a confession that—with all his professed love of truth and knowledge—he prefers to "sleep after dinner." The misfortune is, that men have been cheated into a belief, that all philosophy and metaphysics worth knowing are contained in a few volumes, which can be understood with little expense of thought; and that they may very well spare themselves the vexation of trying to comprehend the depths of "Coleridge's Metaphysics." According to the popular notions of the day, it is a very easy matter to understand the philosophy of mind. A new work on philosophy is as easy to read as the last new novel; and superficial, would-be scholars, who have a very sensible horror at the thought of studying Algebra, or the doctrine of fluxions, can yet go through a course of moral sciences, and know all about the philosophy of the mind.

Now why will not men of sense, and men who have any just pretensions to scholarship, see that there must of necessity be gross sophistry somewhere in any system of metaphysics, which pretends to give us an adequate and scientific self-knowledge—to render comprehensive to us the mysterious laws of our own inward being, with less manly and persevering effort of thought on our part, than is confessedly required to comprehend the simplest of those sciences, all of which are but some of the *phaenomena*, from which the laws in question are to be inferred?—Why will they not see and acknowledge—what one would suppose a moment's reflection would teach them—that to attain true self-knowledge by reflection upon the objects of our inward consciousness—not merely to understand the motives of our conduct as conscientious Christians, but to know ourselves scientifically as philosophers—must, of necessity, be the most deep and difficult of all our attainments in knowledge? I trust that what I have already said will be sufficient to expose the absurdity of objections against metaphysics in general, and do something towards showing, that we are in actual and urgent need of a system somewhat deeper than those, the contradictions of which have not without reason made the name of philosophy a terror to the friends of truth and of religion. "False metaphysics can be effectually counteracted by true metaphysics alone; and if the reasoning be clear, solid, and pertinent, the truth deduced can never be the less valuable on account of the depth from which it may have been drawn." It is a fact, too, of great importance to be kept in mind, in relation to this subject, that in the study of ourselves—in attaining a knowledge of our own being,—there are truths of vast concernment, and living at a great depth, which yet no man can draw for another. However the depth may have been fathomed, and the same truth brought up by others, for a light and a joy to their own minds, it must still remain, and be sought for by us, each for himself, at the bottom of the well.

The system of philosophy here taught does not profess to make men philosophers, or—which ought to mean the same thing—to guide them to the knowledge of themselves, without the labor both of attention and of severe thinking. If it did so, it would have, like the more popular works of philosophy, far less affinity than it now has, with the mysteries of religion, and those profound truths concerning our spiritual being and destiny, which are revealed in the *things hard to be understood* of St. Paul and of the beloved disciple. For I cannot but remind my readers again, that the Author does not undertake to teach us the philosophy of a human mind, with the exclusion of the truth and influences of religion. He would not undertake to philosophize respecting the being and character of man, and at the same time exclude from his view the very principle which constitutes his proper humanity: he would not, in teaching the doctrine of the solar system, omit to mention the sun, and the law of gravitation. He professes to investigate and unfold the being of man *as man*, in his higher, his peculiar, and distinguishing attributes. These it is, which are hard to be understood, and to apprehend which requires the exercise of deep reflection and exhausting thought. Nor in aiming at this object would he consider it very philosophical to reject the aid and instruction of eminent writers on the subject of religion, or even of the volume of Revelation itself. He would consider St. Augustine as none the less a philosopher, because he became a Christian. The Apostles John and Paul were, in the view of this system of philosophy, the most rational of all writers, and the New Testament the most philosophical of all books. They are so because they unfold more fully, than any other, the true and essential principles of our being; because they give us a clearer and deeper insight into those constituent laws of our humanity, which as men, and therefore as philosophers, we are most concerned to know. Not only to those, who seek the practical self-knowledge of the humble, spiritually-minded Christian, but to those also, who are impelled by the "heaven descended γνῶθι σεαυτόν"[20] to study themselves as philosophers, and to make self-knowledge a science, the truths of Scripture are a light and a revelation. The more earnestly we reflect upon these and refer them, whether as Christians or as philosophers, to the movements of our inward being—to the laws which reveal themselves

---

[20] See *BL* ch 12 *(CC)* I 252 and n. The quotation on p 525 above is from ibid I 291.

in our own consciousness, the more fully shall we understand, not only the language of Scripture, but all that most demands and excites the curiosity of the genuine philosopher in the mysterious character of man. It is by this guiding light, that we can best search into and apprehend the constitution of that "marvellous microcosm," which, the more it has been known, has awakened more deeply the wonder and admiration of the true philosopher in every age.

Nor would the Author of this Work, or those who have imbibed the spirit of his system, join with the philosophers of the day in throwing aside and treating with a contempt, as ignorant as it is arrogant, the treasures of ancient wisdom. *He*, says the son of Sirach, *that giveth his mind to the law of the Most High, and is occupied in the meditation thereof, will seek out the wisdom of all the ancient.*[21] In the estimation of the true philosopher, the case should not be greatly altered in the present day; and now that two thousand years have added such rich and manifold abundance to those ancient "sayings of the wise," he will still approach them with reverence, and receive their instruction with gladness of heart. In seeking to explore and unfold these deeper and more solemn mysteries of our being, which inspire us with awe, while they baffle our comprehension, he will especially beware of trusting to his own understanding, or of contradicting, in compliance with the self-flattering inventions of a single age, the universal faith and consciousness of the human race. On such subjects, though he would call no man master, yet neither would he willingly forego the aids to be derived, in the search after truth, from those great oracles of human wisdom—those giants in intellectual power, who from generation to generation were admired and venerated by the great and good. Much less could he think it becoming, or consistent with his duty to hazard the publication of his own thoughts on subjects of the deepest concernment, and on which minds of greatest depth and power had been occupied in former ages, while confessedly ignorant alike of their doctrines and of the arguments by which they are sustained.

It is in this spirit, that the Author of the work here offered to the public has prepared himself to deserve the candid and even confiding attention of his readers, with reference to the great subject of which he treats.

And although the claims of the Work upon our attention, as of every other work, must depend more upon its inherent and essential character, than upon the worth and authority of its Author, it may yet be of service to the reader to know, that he is no hasty or unfurnished adventurer in

---

[21] Ecclus 39.1, reading "ancients".

the department of authorship, to which the Work belongs. The discriminating reader of this Work can not fail to discover his profound knowledge of the philosophy of language, the principles of its construction, and the laws of its interpretation. In others of his works, perhaps more fully than in this, there is evidence of an unrivalled mastery over all that pertains both to logic and philology. It has been already intimated, that he is no contemner of the great writers of antiquity and of their wise sentences; and probably few English scholars, even in those days when there were giants of learning in Great Britain, had minds more richly furnished with the treasures of ancient lore. But especially will the reader of this Work observe with admiration the profoundness of his philosophical attainments, and his thorough and intimate knowledge, not only of the works and systems of Plato and Aristotle, and of the celebrated philosophers of modern times, but of those too much neglected writings of the Greek and Roman Fathers, and of the great leaders of the Reformation, which more particularly qualified him for discussing the subjects of the present Work. If these qualifications, and—with all these, and above all—a disposition professed and made evident seriously to value them, chiefly as they enable him more fully and clearly to comprehend and illustrate the truths of the Christian system,—if these, I say, can give an Author a claim to serious and thoughtful attention, then may the Work here offered urge its claim upon the reader. My own regard for the cause of truth, for the interests of philosophy, of reason, and of religion, lead me to hope that they may not be urged in vain.

Of his general claims to our regard, whether from exalted personal and moral worth, or from the magnificence of his intellectual powers, and the vast extent and variety of his accumulated stores of knowledge, I shall not venture to speak. If it be true indeed that a really great mind can be worthily commended only by those who adequately both appreciate and *comprehend* its greatness, there are few who should undertake to estimate, and set forth in appropriate terms, the intellectual power and moral worth of Samuel Taylor Coleridge. Neither he, nor the public, would be benefited by such commendations as I could bestow. The few among us who have read his works with the attention which they deserve, are at no loss what rank to assign him among the writers of the present age; to those who have not, any language, which I might use, would appear hyperbolical and extravagant. The character and influence of his principles as a philosopher, a moralist, and a Christian, and of the writings by which he is enforcing them, do not ultimately depend upon the estimation in which they may now be held; and to posterity he may safely intrust those ''productive ideas'' and ''living words''—those

> ——truths that wake
> To perish never,[22]

the possession of which will be for their benefit, and connected with which, in the language of the Son of Sirach,—*His own memorial shall not depart away, and his name shall live from generation to genera-tion.*[23]   J. M.

[22] Wordsworth ''Ode: Intimations of Immortality . . .'' lines 156–7: *WPW* iv 284.
[23] Ecclus 39.9.

APPENDIX G

PASSAGES OMITTED FROM THE 1825 TEXT IN *AIDS TO REFLECTION* (1831)

PASSAGES OMITTED FROM
THE 1825 TEXT IN
AIDS TO REFLECTION (1831)

AS RECORDED in the Editor's Introduction above, Coleridge at first planned to carry out a much more sweeping revision of his text for the second edition than he was eventually able to complete; in the event, the last stages of the revision were largely left to H. N. Coleridge. The passages omitted from the 1825 edition include some which were no longer relevant, considering the manner in which the volume had developed in its later sheets, and some which were probably omitted in order to reduce the proportion of Leighton's writing in the early part. All cutting of this kind ceased after page 58 of the text of the first edition, to be succeeded (apart from a long addition at page 92) by minor alterations. Up to that page the overwhelming majority of the deletions had been from the "Prudential Aphorisms", which were effectively reduced from eighteen pages to ten. The sections omitted in 1831 were as follows.

(a)

ADVERTISEMENT.

In the bodies of several species of Animals there are found certain Parts, of which neither the office, the functions, nor the relations could be ascertained by the Comparative Anatomist, till he had become acquainted with the state of the Animal before birth. Something sufficiently like this (for the purpose of an illustration, at least) applies to the Work here offered to the Public. In the introductory portion there occur several passages, which the Reader will be puzzled to decypher, without some information respecting the original design of the Volume, and the Changes it has undergone during its immature and embryonic state. On this account only, I think myself bound to make it known, that the Work was proposed and begun as a mere Selection from the Writings of Archbishop Leighton, under the usual title of The Beauties of Archbishop Leighton, with a few notes and a biographical preface by the Selector. Hence the term, *Editor*, subscribed to the notes, and prefixed alone or conjointly to the Aphorisms, accordingly as the Passage was written entirely by myself, or only modified and (*avowedly*) interpolated. I continued the use of the word on the plea of uniformity: though like most other deviations from propriety of language, it would probably have been a wiser choice to have omitted or exchanged it. The various Reflections, however, that pressed on me while I was considering the motives for selecting this or that passage; the desire of enforcing, and as it were integrating, the truths contained in the Original Author, by adding those which the words suggested or recalled to my own mind; the conversation with men of eminence in the Literary and Religious Circles, occasioned by the Objects which I had in view; and lastly, the increasing disproportion of the Commentary to the Text, and the too marked difference in the frame, character, and colors of the two styles; soon induced me to recognize and adopt a revolution in my plan and object, which had in fact actually taken place without my intention, and almost unawares. It would indeed be more correct to say, that the present Volume owed its accidental origin to the intention of compiling one of a different description, than to speak of it as the same Work. It is not a change in the child, but a changeling.

Still, however, the selections from Leighton, which will be found in the prudential and moral Sections of this Work, and which I could retain consistently with its present form and matter, will both from the intrinsic excellence and from the characteristic beauty of the passages, suffice to answer two prominent purposes of the original plan; that of placing in a clear light the principle, which pervades all Leighton's Writings—his sublime View, I mean, of Religion and Morality as the means of reforming the human Soul in the Divine Image (*Idea*); and that of exciting an interest in the Works, and an affectionate reverence for the name and memory, of this severely tried and truly primitive Churchman.

S. T. C.[1]

(b)

In Greek, Logos (Anglicé,[2] Word), means likewise the Understanding. If the same idiom existed in our own language, only with the substitution of the *practical* for the intellectual, I would say : THE WORD* (*i. e.* Practical Rectitude), has Virtue (or Morality) for its Consonants and Prudence for the Vowels. Though the former can scarcely be pronounced without the latter, yet we ought to acquaint ourselves with their true nature and force. But this we can do only by a distinct knowledge of the latter, that is, what they are of themselves, and sounded separately from the consonants. In like manner, to understand aright what morality is, we must first learn what prudence is, and what acts and obli-

---

* LOGOS in Greek, signifies an intelligible *word* as distinguished from ῥῆμα, a flowing or articulate *sound*; and it likewise signifies *the understanding,* in distinction from Νοῦς (the pure reason) in one direction, and from αἰσθῆσις (the sense) in the other.[3]

[1] *AR* (1825) iii–iv.
[2] "In English".
[3] For the distinction between logos and ῥῆμα see below, App I Excursus Note 1, and for that between logos and Νοῦς, ibid, Excursus Note 4. Αἴσθησις is the normal Greek word for sense perception.

gations are *prudential*; and having removed these to a class of their own, we shall find it comparatively easy to determine what acts and duties belong to morality.[4]

(c)

I have now, I trust, effected the two purposes of this introductory chapter, viz.

1. That of explaining the true nature and evincing the necessity of reflection in the constitution of a Christian character.

2. That of assigning my reasons, why having proposed to select from Archbishop Leighton's Works the most striking prudential, moral, and spiritual maxims, I have separated the prudential from the two following, and interpolated the extracts with mementos of my own.[5]

(d)

PRUDENTIAL APHORISMS.

APHORISM I.   L. & ED.

You will not be offended, nor think I intend to insult you, if once and again, with great earnestness and sincerity, I wish you and myself a sound and serious temper of mind; for, if we may represent things as they really are, very few men are possessed of so valuable a blessing. The far greater part of them are intoxicated either with the pleasures or the cares of this world; they stagger about with a tottering and unstable pace; and, as Solomon expresses it, *The labour of the foolish wearieth every one of them; because he knoweth not how to go to the city*: Eccl. x. 15:—the heavenly city, and the vision of peace, which very few have a just notion of, or are at pains to seek after. Nay, they know not what it is they are seeking. They flutter from one object to another, and live at hazard. They have no certain harbour in view, nor direct their course by any fixed star. But to him that knoweth not the port to which he is bound, no wind can be favourable; neither can he who has not yet determined at what mark he is to shoot, direct his arrow aright.

I assert, then, that there is a proper object to aim at; and if this object be meant by the term happiness, (though I think that not the most appropriate term for a state, the perfection of which consists in the exclusion of all *hap* (*i. e.* chance), and should greatly prefer the Socratic *Εὐπραξy*, as expressing the union of well-being and well-doing,)[6] I assert that there is such a thing as human happiness. This is indeed implied in the belief of an infinitely wise Author of our being.[7]

---

[4] *AR* (1825) 25.

[5] *AR* (1825) 28.

[6] See above, *Prud Aph I* n 1.

[7] *AR* (1825) 31–2, from Leighton COPY c IV 198: *CM (CC)* III.

APHORISM II. LEIGHTON.

The whole human race must have been created in misery, and exposed to unavoidable torments, from which they could never have been relieved, had they been formed not only capable of a good, quite unattainable and altogether without their reach, but also with strong and restless desires towards that impossible good. Now, as this is by no means to be admitted, there must necessarily be some full, permanent, and satisfying good, that may be attained by man, and in the possession of which he must be truly happy.[8]

(e)

APHORISM IV. LEIGHTON.

It is the wisdom of mankind to know God, and their indispensable duty to worship Him. Without this, men of the brightest parts and greatest learning seem to be born with excellent talents only to make themselves miserable; and according to the expression of the wisest of kings, *He that increaseth knowledge increaseth sorrow*, Eccl. i. 18. We must, therefore, first of all, consider this as a sure and settled point, that religion is the sole foundation of human peace and felicity. This, even the profane scoffers at religion are, in some sort, obliged to own, though much against their will, even while they are pointing their wit against it; for nothing is more commonly to be heard from them, than that the whole doctrine of religion was invented by some wise men, to encourage the practice of justice and virtue through the world. Surely then, religion, whatever else may be said of it, must be a matter of the highest value, since it is found necessary to secure advantages of so very great importance. But, in the mean time, how unhappy is the case of integrity and virtue, if what they want to support them is merely fictitious, and they cannot keep their ground but by means of a monstrous forgery! But far be it from us to entertain such an absurdity! For the first rule of righteousness cannot be otherwise than right, nor is there any thing more nearly allied or more friendly to virtue, than truth.[9]

APHORISM V. LEIGHTON.

And it is, indeed, very plain, that if it were possible entirely to dissolve all the bonds and ties of religion, yet, that it should be so, would certainly be the interest of none but the worst and most abandoned part of mankind. All the good and wise, if the matter was freely left to their own choice, would rather have the world governed by the Supreme and Most Perfect Being, mankind subjected to His just and righteous laws, and all the affairs of men superintended by His watchful providence, than that it should be otherwise. Nor do they believe the doctrines of religion with aversion or any sort of reluctancy, but embrace them with pleasure, and are excessively glad to find them true. So that, if it was possible, to abolish them entirely, and any person, out of mere good-will to them, should attempt to do it, they would look upon the favour as highly prejudicial to

[8] *AR* (1825) 32, from Leighton COPY C IV 201: *CM (CC)* III.

[9] *AR* (1825) 33–4, from Leighton COPY C IV 243–4: *CM (CC)* III.

their interest, and think his good-will more hurtful than the keenest hatred. Nor would any one, in his wits, choose to live in the world, at large, and without any sort of government, more than he would think it eligible to be put on board a ship without a helm or pilot, and, in this condition, to be tossed amidst rocks and quicksands. On the other hand, can any thing give greater consolation, or more substantial joy*, than to be firmly persuaded, not only that there is an infinitely good and wise Being, but also that this Being preserves and continually governs the universe which Himself has framed, and holds the reins of all things in His powerful hand; that He is our father, that we and all our interests are His constant concern; and that, after we have sojourned a short while here below, we shall be again taken into His immediate presence? Or can this wretched life be attended with any sort of satisfaction, if it is divested of this divine faith, and bereaved of such a blessed hope?[11]

* Φεῦ τι τούτων χάρμα μεῖζον ἂν λαβοίς.[10]

(f)

Vices seize upon men with the violence and rage of furies; but the Christian virtues replenish the breast which they inhabit, with a heavenly peace and abundant joy, and thereby render it like that of an angel. The slaves of pleasure and carnal affections, have within them, even now, an earnest of future torments; so that, in this present life, we may truly apply to them that expression in the Revelations, *They that worship the beast have no rest day nor night.*[12] "There is "perpetual peace with the humble," says the most devout A Kempis;[13] "but the "proud and the covetous are never at rest."[14]

(g)

[a]Such language the soundest moralists were obliged to employ,[b] before grace and truth were brought into the world by Jesus [c]Christ.[15] And[d] such language may, I doubt not, even now be profitably addressed both to individuals and to classes of [e]men; though in what *proportion*[f] it should be dwelt on, and to what extent it is likely to be efficacious, a review of the different epochs memorable for the turning of many from their evil ways, and a review of the means by which

[a-b] COPIES D & E: It is not only a safer language, but it is such language as the soundest moralists were *obliged* to employ

[c-d] COPIES D & E: Christ: and

[e-f] COPIES D & E: men. In what *proportion*, though,

---

[10] Stobaeus *Florilegium* 59.12; Sophocles fragment 636 (Pearson). Tr: "Ah, what greater joy than these could you obtain?"

[11] *AR* (1825) 34–5, from Leighton COPY C IV 245–6: *CM (CC)* III.

[12] Rev 14.11.

[13] Thomas à Kempis *De imitatione Christi* 1.7.3.

[14] *AR* (1825) 38, from Leighton COPY C IV 319–20: *CM (CC)* III.

[15] John 1.17: "Grace and truth came by Jesus Christ".

this reformation of life has been principally effected, renders me scrupulous in deciding.[16]

(h)

Dissertations on the profitableness of righteousness, that "her ways are ways of pleasantness,"[17] we possess many and eloquent, and in our most popular works. Many such passages, and of great beauty, occur in the volumes of Archbishop Leighton; but they are not particularly characteristic of his mind and genius. For these reasons therefore, in addition to the scruples avowed in the preceding pages, I have confined my selection to a few specimens; and shall now conclude what I have thought expedient to observe in my own person, by guarding against any possible misinterpretation of my sentiments by the two following aphorisms:[18]

(i)

APHORISM XII.   LEIGHTON.

What, you will say, have I beasts within me? Yes, you have beasts, and a vast number of them. And that you may not think I intend to insult you, is anger an inconsiderable beast, when it barks in your heart? What is deceit, when it lies hid in a cunning mind; is it not a fox? Is not the man who is furiously bent upon calumny, a scorpion? Is not the person who is eagerly set on resentment and revenge, a most venomous viper? What do you say of a covetous man; is he not a ravenous wolf? And is not the luxurious man, as the prophet expresses it, a neighing horse? Nay, there is no wild beast but is found within us. And do you consider yourself as lord and prince of the wild beasts, because you command those that are without, though you never think of subduing or setting bounds to those that are within you? What advantage have you by your reason, which enables you to overcome lions, if, after all, you yourself are overcome by anger? To what purpose do you rule over the birds, and catch them with gins, if you yourself, with the inconstancy of a bird, or hurried hither and thither, and sometimes flying high, are ensnared by pride, sometimes brought down and caught by pleasure? But, as it is shameful for him who rules over nations, to be a slave at home, and for the man who sits at the helm of the state, to be meanly subjected to the beck of a contemptible harlot, or even of an imperious wife; will it not be, in like manner, disgraceful for you, who exercise dominion over the beasts that are without you, to be subject to a great many, and those of the worst sort, that roar and domineer in your distempered mind?[19]

---

[16] *AR* (1825) 41 (from *Prud Aph* "VIII").

[17] Prov 3.17 (of Wisdom). See above, *Prud Aph II* at n 2.

[18] *AR* (1825) 44 (from *Prud Aph* "IX").

[19] *AR* (1825) 45–6, from Leighton COPY C IV 268: *CM (CC)* III.

APHORISM XIII. LEIGHTON.

There is[a] a settled friendship, nay, a near relation and similitude between God and good men; he is even their father; but, in their education he inures them to hardships. When, therefore[b], you see them struggling with difficulties, sweating, and employed in up-hill work; while the wicked, on the other hand, are in high spirits, and swim in pleasures; consider, that we are pleased with modesty in our children, and forwardness in our slaves: the former we keep under by severe discipline, while we encourage impudence in the latter. Be persuaded, that God takes the same method. He does not pamper the good man with delicious fare, but tries him; he accustoms him to hardships, and, (which is a wonderful expression in a heathen) PREPARES HIM FOR HIMSELF.[20]

APHORISM XIV. LEIGHTON.

If what we are told concerning that glorious city, obtain credit with us, we shall cheerfully travel towards it, nor shall we be at all deterred by the difficulties that may be in the way. But, however, as it is true, and more suitable to the weakness of our minds, which are rather apt to be affected with things present and near, than such as are at a great distance, we ought not to pass over in silence, that the way to the happiness reserved in heaven, which leads through this earth, is not only agreeable because of the blessed prospect it opens, and the glorious end to which it conducts, but also for its own sake, and on account of the innate pleasure to be found in it, far preferable to any other way of life that can be made choice of, or, indeed, imagined. Nay, that we may not, by low expressions, derogate from a matter so grand and so conspicuous, that holiness and true religion which leads directly to the highest felicity, is itself the only happiness, as far as it can be enjoyed on this earth. Whatever naturally tends to the attainment of any other advantage, participates, in some measure, of the nature of that advantage. Now, the way to perfect felicity, if any thing can be so, is a means that, in a very great measure, participates of the nature of its end; nay, it is the beginning of that happiness, it is also to be considered as a part of it, and differs from it, in its completest state, not so much in kind, as in degree.[21]

APHORISM XV. LEIGHTON.

"We are always resolving to live, and yet never set about life in good "earnest*."[22] Archimedes was not singular in his fate; but a great part of mankind die unexpectedly, while they are poring upon the figures they have de-

* Victuros agimus semper, nec vivimus unquam.

[a] COPY E: is (says Seneca) ; COPY G: is (says SENECA)
[b] AR (1825) Corr: therefore (says Seneca)

[20] *AR* (1825) 46, from Leighton COPY C IV 274–5: *CM (CC)* III. The text follows the original exactly, but before C's opening Leighton reads: "Seneca tells us," placing the rest in inverted commas, and thus explaining the final parenthesis (see also the Textual Notes at this point for an amend- ment by C himself). The passage is adapted from Seneca *De providentia* 1.5– 6.

[21] *AR* (1825) 46–7, from Leighton COPY C IV 317–18: *CM (CC)* III.

[22] Manilius *Astronomica* 4.5.

scribed in the sand.[23] O wretched mortals! who, having condemned themselves, as it were, to the mines, seem to make it their chief study to prevent their ever regaining their liberty. Hence, new employments are assumed in the place of old ones; and, as the Roman philosopher truly expresses it, "one hope succeeds "another, one instance of ambition makes way for another; and we never desire "an end of our misery, but only that it may change its outward form*."[24] When we cease to be candidates, and to fatigue ourselves in soliciting interest, we begin to give our votes and interest to those who solicit us in their turn. When we are wearied of the trouble of prosecuting crimes at the bar, we commence judges ourselves; and he who is grown old in the management of other men's affairs for money, is at last employed in improving his own wealth. At the age of fifty, says one, I will retire, and take my ease; or the sixtieth year of my life shall entirely disengage me from public offices and business. Fool! art thou not ashamed to reserve to thyself the last remains and dregs of life? Who will stand surety that thou shalt live so long? And what immense folly is it, so far to forget mortality, as to think of beginning to live at that period of years, to which a few only attain![25]

* Spes spem excipit, ambitionem ambitio, et miseriarum non quaeritur finis, sed schema tantum mutatur.

(j)

Again, I would impress it on the reader, that in order to the full understanding of any Whole, it is necessary to have learnt the nature of the component parts, of each severally and, as far as is possible, abstracted from the changes it may have undergone in its combination with the others. On this account I have deferred in order to give effectually the more interesting and far more cheering contemplation of the same Subjects in the reverse order; Prudence, namely, as it flows out of Morality, and Morality as the natural Overflowing of *a*Religion;*b* always the true though sometimes the hidden*c* Spring and Fountain-head of all true Morality.

I have hitherto considered Prudence and Morality as two Streams from different sources, and traced the former to its supposed confluence with the latter. And if it had been my present purpose and undertaking to have placed Fruits from my own Garden before the Reader, I should in like manner have followed the course of Morality from its Twin Sources, the Affections and the Conscience, till (as the main Feeder into some majestic Lake rich with hidden Springs of its own) it flowed into, and became one with, the Spiritual Life.[26]

a–b AR (1825) Corr: Religion: for the religious *principle* is

a–c COPIES C, D, F: Religion; true religion being always the actual, though sometimes the hidden, ; COPY G: Religion: the religious sense being the always present, though sometimes hidden,

[23] Archimedes (c 288–212 B.C.) was killed by a soldier at the capture of Syracuse while deeply absorbed in a demonstration which involved drawing a mathematical figure in the sand. See Valerius Maximus *Facta et dicta memorabilia* 8.7.

[24] Seneca *De brevitate vitae* 17.5.

[25] AR (1825) 47–8, from Leighton COPY C IV 372: *CM (CC)* III.

[26] For variant examples of this favourite strain of imagery see e.g. letter to RS of 13 Nov 1795, expressing a faith that "how-

But without a too glaring Breach of the promise, that the Banquet for the greater part should consist[a] of Choice Clusters from the Vineyards of Archbishop Leighton, this was not practicable, and now, I trust, with the help of these introductory pages, no longer neccessary.

Still, however, it appears to me of the highest use and of vital importance to let it be seen, that Religion or the Spiritual Life is a something in itself, for which mere Morality, were it even far more perfect in its kind than experience authorises us to expect in unaided human Nature, is no *Substitute*, though it cannot but be its Accompaniment. So far, therefore, I have adapted the arrangement of the extracts to this principle, that though I have found it impossible to separate the Moral from the Religious, the morality and moral views of Leighton being every where taken from the point of Christian Faith, I have yet brought together under one head, and in a separate Chapter, those subjects of Reflection, that *necessarily* suppose or involve the faith in an eternal state, and the probationary nature of our existence under Time and Change.

These whether doctrinal or *ascetic* (*disciplinary, from the Greek* ασκεω, *to exercise*), whether they respect the obstacles to the attainment of the Eternal, irremoveable by the unrenewed and unaided Will of Man; or the removal of these Obstacles, with its Concurrents and Consequents; or, lastly, the Truths, necessary to a rational belief in the Future, and which alone can interpret the Past, or solve the Riddle of the Present; are[b] *especially* meant in the term Spiritual.

Amply shall I deem myself remunerated if either by the holy Charm, the good Spell of Leighton's Words, than which few if any since the Apostolic age better deserve the name of *Evangelical*, or by my own notes and interpolations, the reflecting Reader should be enabled to *apprehend*—for we may rightly *apprehend* what no finite mind can fully *comprehend*—and attach a distinct meaning to, the Mysteries into which his Baptism is the initiation; and thus to feel and know, that CHRISTIAN FAITH IS THE PERFECTION OF HUMAN REASON.[27]

---

[a] COPY F (in the margin): See the ADVERTISEMENT
[b] COPY A: all these, I say, are ; COPY C: all *these* are

---

ever foul your Stream may run here, yet that it will filtrate & become pure in it's subterranean Passage to the Ocean of Universal Redemption'': *CL* I 168, and *Reli-gious Musings* line 204 on Property as a "twy-streaming fount": *PW* (EHC) I 116.

[27] *AR* (1825) 56–8.

EDITIONS AND REPRINTINGS OF
AIDS TO REFLECTION
FROM 1825 ONWARDS

EDITIONS AND REPRINTINGS OF
AIDS TO REFLECTION
FROM 1825 ONWARDS

DETAILS of editions and reprints in this section are from various sources, including *Samuel Taylor Coleridge: An Annotated Bibliography* ed (vol I) R. Haven, J. Haven, and M. Adams; (vol II), W. B. Crawford and E. S. Lauterbach (Boston, Mass 1976–83).

The first edition (London: Taylor and Hessey 1825)
> For differences between this and the present edition see Textual Notes and App G above. The "Corrections and Amendments" printed on pp xv–xvi are also recorded in the Textual Notes.

James Marsh's first American edition (Burlington, Vt: Chauncy Goodrich, 1829)
> Edited by James Marsh with a Preliminary Essay, reprinted in App F above. See also Editor's Introduction, pp cxvi–cxxiii above.

The second edition (London: Hurst, Chance, & Co. 1831)
> The copy-text for the present edition. Seen through the press by HNC. See Editor's Introduction, pp cxxvii–cxxxiii above.

The third edition (London: William Pickering 1836)
> A new printing, based on the second ed.

The fourth edition (London: William Pickering 1839)
> For this edition the subtitles on the title-page were dropped, to be replaced by "Aids to Reflection | By Samuel Taylor Coleridge | Fourth Edition with the Author's Last Corrections | Edited by | Henry Nelson Coleridge Esq. M.A." HNC also removed some elements from the 1831 text. This was the first English edition to include James Marsh's Preliminary Essay (from 1829 ed above). It also contained a new "Advertisement" by HNC, commending the volume as

>> supported by the authority of almost every one of our great divines, before the prevalence of that system of philosophy, (Locke's), which no consistent reasoner can possibly reconcile with the undoubted meaning of the Articles and Formularies of the English Church . . .

> and concluding,

>> The Editor had intended to offer to the reader a few words by way of introduction to some of the leading points of philosophy contained in this volume. But he has been delighted to find the work already done to his hand, in a manner superior to anything he could have hoped to accomplish himself, by an affectionate disciple of Coleridge on the other side of the Atlantic. The following Essay was written by the Rev. James

Marsh, President of the University of Vermont, United States of America, and pre-fixed by him to his edition of the Aids to Reflection, published at Burlington in 1829. The Editor has printed this Essay entire;—as well out of respect for its author, as believing that the few paragraphs in it, having a more special reference to the state of opinion in America, will not be altogether without an interest of their own to the attentive observers of the progress of Truth in this or any other country.

A third motto was added to the two in previous editions: see above, pp 4–5n.

John McVickar's American edition (New York: Swords, Stanford & Co. 1839)

Title-page begins: "AIDS TO REFLECTION | by | Samuel Taylor Coleridge, | with the | Author's Last Corrections | edited by | Henry Nelson Coleridge, Esq. M.A. | To which is prefixed | A Preliminary Essay, | By John McVickar, D.D. | Professor of Moral Philosophy in Columbia College, New-York" and concludes: "London; | Pub-lished by William Pickering. | New-York: | Swords, Stanford & Co. | 1839." For the background to this edition and subsequent reactions to it, see Editor's Introduction, pp cxx–cxxiii above.

Reprinted 1844, 1845, 1847, 1830, 1854, 1863, 1872.

James Marsh's second edition (Burlington, Vt: Goodrich 1840)

Probably identical with that issued in New York by Gould, Norman and Saxton in the same year.

The fifth edition, two volumes (London: William Pickering 1843)

Title-page begins: "Aids to Reflection | By Samuel Taylor Coleridge | Edited by | Henry Nelson Coleridge". This edition was further enlarged by two new items: the discussion of Instinct by J. H. Green from *Vital Dynamics* (App C above) and the long essay "On Rationalism" by SC. It was originally to have opened with a new "Advertisement" by HNC, paying tribute to the work's continuing power as a confutation of "the evil side of modern Germanism in religion,—its Pantheistic spirit—", lamenting the death of James Marsh, and justifying the inclusion of Sara's essay. After his death on 26 Jan 1843, the work of seeing the new edition through the press was undertaken by DC, who (as he described in the new Advertisement which he now prefixed to the one just mentioned, written in the previous year) decided that some rearrangement was necessary. Accordingly, he took the existing appendix on Reason and Understanding and added Marsh's essay, Green's discussion, and SC's Essay as new appendixes, making the four items into a second volume.

The sixth edition, two volumes (London: William Pickering 1848)

For the most part a reprint of the fifth ed: again credited to the editorship of HNC but seen through the press by DC. In vol II the essay "On Rationalism" by SC was enlarged and divided into sections; a further piece by SC, "Extracts from a New Treatise on Regeneration", occupying a further 74 pages, was also included, which in turn concluded with a footnote: "It is with regret that for want of room, I withhold the remainder of the Treatise, especially the part which considers in detail the Scrip-tural evidence. It is my hope for a future edition to remodel the original Essay, and bring the whole subject within the compass of the volume in a better form than the present."

W. G. T. Shedd's American edition, seven volumes (New York: Harper and Bros. 1853)

The Complete Works of Samuel Taylor Coleridge ed W. G. T. Shedd; includes *AR*, with Marsh's essay and HNC's appendixes, as vol I.

Reprinted several times to 1884.

The seventh edition (London: Edward Moxon 1854)

Title-page begins: "Aids to Reflection | By Samuel Taylor Coleridge | Edited by | The Rev. Derwent Coleridge, M.A." Having suffered a breakdown of health in

1850, SC died in 1852. Producing a new edition for Edward Moxon soon afterwards, DC decided to shorten the work: he therefore cut out both Marsh's essay and Sara's Essay on Rationalism, expressing a hope that the latter would be "reproduced as an independent treatise with the other literary remains of the lamented writer". He also introduced, as "additional notes" to the text, several annotations which C had made in copies presented to EC (COPY G) and to RS (COPY B). They are located as follows: pp 15 (from COPY G: *Int Aph XXIII* n 10 above); 133 (from COPY G: *Sp Aph B II* n 57 above); 138–9 (from COPY G: *Sp Aph B II* n 78 above); 188–9 (*from* COPY B: *Sp Aph B IX* n 15 above); 254–6 (from COPY B, App D(*b*)(ii) above). For the last two items the presentation suggests that he may have been using the Grove transcript (Copy 2(a) in App E above), where they appear together.

Reprinted as "Eighth edition " 1859; "Ninth edition" 1861; "Tenth edition" 1864; "Eleventh edition" 1866; and "Twelfth edition" 1867. (No copy of the tenth ed has been located: its date is inferred from the fact that Moxon's list for December 1863—in Cambridge University Library copy of R. Buchanan *Undertones* (1863)—gives the ninth ed, while that for August 1864—in CUL copy of W. M. Praed *Poems* (1864)—gives the tenth.)

Thomas Fenby's edition (Liverpool: Edward Howell 1873)

The text follows that of the 1831 edition, including the appendix on Reason and Understanding. None of the matter inserted by HNC from the fourth ed onwards finds a place; instead Fenby has contributed a number of expository notes of his own, amplifying various points, which are distinguished from Coleridge's by being placed in square brackets. A new system of numbering is adopted for this edition: the aphorisms appear throughout in a continuous sequence from I to CXXIV, a Comment by C being given the same number as the preceding aphorism, followed by a small "c"; sections which were not originally aphorisms are either made into aphorisms or are notionally numbered in the same sequence. The Conclusion is numbered notionally as CXXV, the two final addenda in arabic numerals as 126 and 127. Within individual sections, all paragraphs are numbered from 1 onwards in arabic numerals. The editor has provided an index using this notation in place of page-numbers.

Reprinted (Liverpool) 1874, 1877, 1883; (Edinburgh: John Grant) 1896, 1900, 1905, 1915; also in New Universal Library (London: Routledge and New York: Dutton) 1905.

Thomas Ashe's Bohn edition (London: George Bell and Sons 1884)

Title-page begins "Aids to Reflection | and | The Confessions of an Inquiring Spirit. | By | Samuel Taylor Coleridge. | To which are added | His Essays on Faith and the Book of | Common Prayer, Etc."

As part of the reprinting of Coleridge's Works in Bohn's Standard Library, Thomas Ashe undertook a new editing of *AR*, along with other religious writings of his. He records in a prefatory note that he has relied mainly on the fourth ed; "In some points, however, the earlier editions, which have been carefully consulted throughout, have been followed." James Marsh's Preliminary Essay is included, as in the fourth ed, but Ashe records that he is taking his text from Marsh's second ed of 1840 (which, however, differs little if at all from that reproduced by HNC). An original index is provided.

Reprinted Bohn's Standard Library 1890, 1893, 1901, 1904, 1913; reissued also in York Library 1904, Bohn's Popular Library 1913. Some, at least, of the printings were issued also in New York. The 1884 text was reissued by Chelsea House in 1983.

Two further reissues of *AR* are recorded in the *Annotated Bibliography* (see opening paragraph above): one by 1912 in Coleridge *Essays* (3 vols) (item C1006) and another based on the fourth ed (Port Washington, NY: Kennikat Press 1971) (item C209).

APPENDIX I
EXCURSUS NOTES

EXCURSUS NOTES

Note 1. *"Logos" and related words (Pref n 4)*

Logos rarely appears in Greek as meaning a single, separate word, but rather as speech or utterance in general; by contrast ἔπος is the normal term for a single word in an etymological or grammatical context. C no doubt chose λόγος for its further connotations, particularly as conveying meaningfulness. Cf a note of 1808 in which ἔπος does mean a single word (*CN* III 4401); and a note of c 1822–3 in which "words . . . are not words (λόγοι) without a corresponding accuracy of conceptions" (*CN* IV 4932). The opposition between the two terms here depends on the then commonly accepted derivation of ἔπος from ἔπομαι (Latin *sequor*), "I follow", which suggested the meaning "connected speech", as in epic. This, with λόγος and its verb λέγω, "I speak, or say", as implying "laying out the particular [*das Einzelne*] in number and so in words" and with ῥῆμα as flowing speech, from ῥέω, "I flow", was given by G. F. Creuzer in ch 2 of *Symbolik und Mythologie der alten Völker* (4 vols Leipzig 1810–12) I 51–4. C used this work from Dec 1818 onward in connexion with his lectures on the history of philosophy and in notebook entries. (He also used the expanded edition of 1819–23.) See *P Lects* (1949) 90n, 98n, and *CN* IV 4831n; and, esp, *CN* IV 4832 f 60. None of these etymologies is now considered valid, but C was able to use them creatively. See also, for an extended discussion of the derivation and meaning of λόγος, *Logic (CC)* 24–37, for the "higher meaning", reason as opposed to understanding, *Logic (CC)* 169, and for a summary history of the word in BM MS Egerton 2800 ff 34–6, *Logic (CC)* 282–3. For St John's use see *TT* 7 Jan–13 Feb 1823 *(CC)* I 34–6 and nn; 1836 vn, dated 6 Jan, II 40–1. C used the distinction between λόγος and ῥῆμα in an allusion to Swedenborg's interpretation of the Bible by "correspondences": see *CL* v 326 (Jan 1824): ". . . the Noumenon, I say, is the Logos, the WORD. The Phaenomenon, or visual and literal Apprehension is ῥῆμα—a fluxion." Cf also *CM (CC)* I 669, II 881; *CN* IV 4765 f 42ᵛ, 4771, 5338. The distinction appears in *AR* (1825) 25 in a passage omitted in 1831: see App G(b) above. For Λόγος in relation to Νοῦς see Excursus Note 4 below. Cf also Epigraph to *Sp Aph A* n 2, *Sp Aph B VII* n 31, *VIIIb* n 14, *Xa* n 29.

Note 2. *Psyche as butterfly and soul (Mor Aph XXXVI at n 5, Sp Aph B Xb at n 30)*

In *Biographia Literaria* C wrote "In Greek Psyche is the common name for the soul, and the butterfly": *BL* ch 4 *(CC)* I 78. There is no overt allusion in ancient literature, apparently, to this duality, and only two examples of the latter

551

meaning appear to survive, in Aristotle and Plutarch. C had probably read about the representations of Cupid with Psyche in the form of a butterfly in Greek art in Joseph Spence *Polymetis*: see the 3rd ed (1774) 71; the book, edition unspecified, was in the Christ's Hospital "English Library" first established in 1787 (MS catalogue). Cf Leigh Hunt *Autobiography* (1928) 100–1. The connection was also made by Robert Nares in his "Remarks on the Favourite Ballet of Cupid and Psyche", first published 1788: *Essays* (1810) I 101–2; and by Jacob Bryant *A New System of Ancient Mythology* (1744–6) II 388: for his borrowing of Bryant in May 1792 see J. C. C. Mays "Coleridge's Borrowings from Jesus College Library, 1791–94" *Transactions of the Cambridge Bibliographical Society* VIII (1985) 566. In early years C sometimes explores this imagery in terms of nature and human experience. Between two notes on the relationship between Body and Soul in Dec 1803 there appears the single sentence "The paradise of Flowers' and Butterflies' Spirits"; in the next year he wrote: "I addressed a Butterfly (on a Pea-blossom) thus—Beautiful Psyche, Soul of a Blossom that art visiting & hovering o'er thy former friends whom thou hadst left—": *CN* I 1736, II 2317. The image was used in 1808 for his love of SH: see his projected emblem, *CL* III 101, and the Latin verses in *CN* III 3264 and n. *CM (CC)* I 175 records a distinction by C between ψυχή as *"animal life"* and πνεῦμα as "the immortal *Spirit"*. The imagery of "Youth and Age", first drafted 10 Sept 1823, is also relevant: *CN* IV 4993, 4996, *PW* (EHC) I 439–41 (with account of mss), II 1084–5. The moral implications were never far away, however: the note of 1804 addressing a butterfly quoted above continues: "Had I forgot the Caterpillar or did I dream like a mad metaphysician the Caterpillars hunger for Plants was Self-love—recollection-feeling, & a lust that in its next state refined itself into Love?" (*CN* II 2317). They are developed also in the poem *Psyche: BL* ch 4 *(CC)* I 78n, *PW* (EHC) I 412 (in which it is dated 1808); also ms versions in *C&SH* 17 and *CN* IV 4832 f 61ᵛ; his comment in 1829, concerning DC's early "free-thinking": ". . . I felt sure, that it was not the true IMAGO of the PSYCHE, but only one of the Larvae that he would soon *slough"*, *CL* VI 797; and a similar comment in 1830 on Shelley's atheism: *CL* VI 849–50. Cf also *BL* ch 12 *(CC)* I 242. C's analogical use of "Imago" seems to derive from W. Kirby and W. Spence *Introduction to Entomology* (1815–26) I 71: the double meaning of "psyche" as soul and butterfly is used there as an image of the Resurrection on pp 75–8.

Note 3. *"Sneers at Verbal Criticism by the contemporaries of Bentley"* (*Mor Aph XLIII* n 86)

The most famous occasion for such attacks on Richard Bentley (1662–1742) was his publication of *A Dissertation on the Epistles of Phalaris* [and others] (1697) and the much expanded *Dissertation on the Epistles of Phalaris* [only] (1699), in which he insultingly, wittily, and eruditely proved that the letters were not the work of that sixth-century B.C. ruler of Acragas and declared them to be without merit. His principal victims and opponents, Charles Boyle, the editor of these letters (1685), and Sir William Temple, who had singled them out as among the "most ancient and the best of the books that we know" in his *Reflections on Ancient and Modern Learning* (1694), were joined by many others, including Swift in *A Tale of a Tub* and *The Battle of the Books* (1704). Though Bentley was eventually seen to have had the best of this argument, the taunts against his "verbal criticism" continued, mingled with attacks on his religious orthodoxy. See also *TT* 15 Jun 1830 *(CC)* I 167–8; II (1836 vn) 110 and n. Relevant facts and more names are given in Francis Wrangham's rather unreliable *Life of Richard Bentley* (nd) 5–15, published also in *The British Plutarch* ed Wrangham (6 vols 1816) v 369–79. C frequently mentioned the attacks on Bentley for doubting the date and authorship of the book of Daniel: e.g. c Oct 1819 in *CN* IV 4615; in a note of Jul 1828: "Was this not the *dirk* they struck into Bentley's side?" N 40 f 24ᵛ: *CN* v; and a marginal note on Wrangham *Life* 5. C's copy presented by Wrangham is in the BM (*CM—CC—*v). See *CL* IV 802. There was a story that Bentley's project to publish a revised text of the NT was frustrated in 1716 by a pamphlet of Conyers Middleton—or "by the caustic remarks . . . made upon his projects by his keen and implacable enemies": Wrangham *Life* 20 (384). Wrangham cites Robert Lowth's description of Bentley as "a mere verbal critic" as well as the "slashing Bentley" of Pope (cf *CN* II 2120) and quotes from Bentley's *Remarks upon Collins on Freethinking* a passage relevant to the defence of verbal criticism, both biblical and classical: *Life* 34–5, 38–45 (398–9, 402–9). Pope's fullest attack mentions Bentley's editions of Horace (1711) and Milton (1732), and the digamma which he intended to introduce into the text of Homer: *Dunciad* IV 201–44 (*Poems* ed J. Butt— 1963—777–9).

Note 4. Coleridge on Nous and Logos (Sp Aph A Epigraph n 2)

Coleridge's belief that the *nous* and the ideas of ancient wisdom were a foreshadowing of St Paul's "Spirit" may perhaps be associated with his interpretation of a fragment of Speusippus (Plato's successor in the Academy, d 338 B.C.) preserved by Stobaeus. This (quoted by Tennemann III 9n) runs "The Nous is not the same as the One or the Good, but has a nature of its own." C's gloss on it is that "the intelligential powers, by the Pythagoreans and Anaxagoras called the *Nous*, (the *Logos* or the *Word* of Philo and St John) is indeed invisibly united with, but not the same as the absolute principle of causation, THE PATERNAL One, the super-essential Will . . .": *P Lects* (1949) 175. (See also *CM—CC—*I 557 and n and *Logic—CC—*33–4 and nn, in which further links are made by C.) For Heraclitus see above, *Sp Aph B XVIIIb* n 14. While C was fond of exploring such possible links between "reason" and ancient wisdom concerning the mind, however, he gave Christian terminology precedence.

Given the high valuation C affords to the Divine Logos, the signification of the word λόγος is at first sight confusing, since at the human level he often equates it with the "understanding", in contradistinction to νοῦς, his "reason". Examination of his usages indicates that a further distinction was at work, however, and that when he equated λόγος with "understanding" it was as the discursive and logical faculty in human beings in its higher form. See the important passage quoted from the Opus Maximum ms in the Editor's Introduction above, p xxxii, which makes clear the distinction between the subordinate understanding (his λόγος) as "discourse of reason", whose work it is to bring out "the necessary & universal truths in the infinite into distinct contemplation", and the "*un-*

subordinated understanding", his φϱόνημα σαϱκός, or "mind of the flesh", which is seen as the antagonist of reason. The resulting variations of emphasis in his use of λόγος are well illustrated by two annotations in 1827: when he finds Claude Fleury equating Nous with Understanding he annotates emphatically: "No! Nous = Reason, *Logos* is *understanding.*" Six pages before, however, he refines further: "N.B. Nous = the pure Reason; Logos = intelligential Imagination or Reason manifesting itself in forms; Phronesis = the Understanding": *CM (CC)* II 715, 713. It seems likely that this refinement of his thought took place from about 1819 (it was used in its simple form in an annotation on Leighton COPY C IV 267: *CM—CC—*III) and that when he quoted his 1816 translation from Heraclitus above (see *Sp Aph B VIIIb* at n 14) he overlooked the fact that there it had been the human νόοι, translated then by him as "Understandings", that were said to be nourished by the Λόγος, the "one DIVINE WORD". For the relation between the λόγος in human beings and the universal Λόγος, see also above, *Sp Aph A VI* n 6, *Sp Aph B VII* n 31 and *Xa* n 29.

A close parallel to C's relating of Noῦς and Λόγος is furnished by John Norris, who, writing about the divine ideas, refers to the "one undivided essence of God . . . whom the *Christian* Philosophy has long since decypher'd by the signal title of νοῦς or the *Mind*, and who in the Holy Scripture is known by the more expressive name of λόγος and set forth as the Wisdom of God, and the Brightness of his Glory. . . . And who also is said to be the Light of the World, that enlightens every Man that comes into it, and even Truth itself": *Essay Towards the Theory of the Ideal or Intelligible World* (2 vols 1701–4) I 240; cf above, Editor's Introduction, pp lxxxix–xc. Both λόγος and νοῦς were firmly distinguished from the Father (τὸ ἕν) by Berkeley in *Siris* §§ 341–62; he pointed out, nevertheless, that they were generated by him, but "not . . . in respect of time, . . . only in respect of order, as an eternal and necessary emanation" (§ 362). Cf Excursus Note 10, below. For a useful note on the two terms, see W. R. Inge *Christian Mysticism* (1899) 94–5. For the Trinity as Noῦς, Λόγος, and Σοφία, see *CM (CC)* II 430 and n; for "the Noυς as uttering in the same act the Logos and the πνευμα, the word and the breath", *CN* IV 4907; and for the relation between "*Logos*, or *manifested* Intelligence, *Outerance* of the Divine mind or Will" and Ruach Elohim, "the Breath of God, αλη θεια", *CN* IV 4830, *CM (CC)* III 23. The relationship between Nous and intuition is discussed above, *Sp Aph B I* n 4. For C's uses of the term "Logos" throughout his career, see M. A. Perkins "The Logos Reconciler" (unpub PhD thesis, University of London 1991).

Note 5. *Coleridge on the Cosmological Proof (Sp Aph B II* n 75)

Coleridge's latest position on the "cosmological proof" of God's existence appears in *TT* 22 Feb 1834 *(CC)* I 462–3 (1836 vn II 276): "Assume the existence of God—and then the harmony and fitness of the physical creation may be shown to correspond with and support such an assumption; but to set about *proving* the existence of a God by such means is a mere circle—a delusion. It can be no proof to a good reasoner, unless he violates all syllogistic logic, and presumes his conclusion." Yet while the ontological proof could be said to violate syllogistic logic in the same way, C was drawn to the spirit behind it, finding Tennemann's "detection of the illusion" in it no more than a "Counter-assertion" of his own. See the annotation on a front flyleaf of Tennemann VIII pt i referring to p 139, which is quoted in *P Lects* (1949) 436–7. He presumably found the "great light" with which Anselm saw the idea of God as "the only idea of which man was capable which involved the necessity of its existence" (ibid Lecture 9 p 277) akin to that which dawned on Pythagoras when he perceived the true nature, generating its own certainty, of number (see *Sp Aph B II* n 65 above). While acknowledging, in a further note on Anselm's proof, on the back flyleaves of Tennemann VIII pt i, addressed explicitly to J. H. Green (who owned the annotated copy), the "heavy difficulties that weigh on the doctrine of Ideas, or Knowledges that are super-sensuous and yet truly objective" (ibid 437), he quoted with approval in Lecture 9 the contention that Anselm's idea was "something so near to human nature it could not be given up—without falling into scepticism and an utter distrust of anything in external reality coincident with our clear perception of truth" (ibid 277–8). See also Barth 96–7.

His attitude to the cosmological proof links with his distrust of Paley's reasoning: see his example of the watch (above, pp 186–7n) and the opening chapters of William Paley *Natural Theology* (1802). *OED* cites C's use of "cosmological" on p 185 as its first example.

Note 6. *Coleridge on God as "pure Act" (Sp Aph B VIIIa n 24)*

C's references to God as "pure Act", or as "actus purissimus" (purest act) include *CL* II 1195 (13 Oct 1806), *CM (CC)* I 232 and n, II 1186, III 710, *BL* ch 9 *(CC)* I 143, *CN* IV 4644 f 25, 4907, 4998 f 12ᵛ, 5143 f 21, 5241 f 30, N 26 ff 125ᵛ–126 (*CN* v), quoted Boulger 152–3, and *HEHL ms* 39–43, quoted Barth 112 and nn. The term was much used by the Schoolmen: for Aquinas see *CM (CC)* I 232n. It also appears in John Norris *Essay Towards the Theory of the Ideal or Intelligible World* (2 pts 1701–4) II 151 and J. Priestley *Disquisition on Matter and Spirit* (2nd ed 2 vols 1782) I 230. An association with human genius is suggested by *CN* II 2026 f 7: ". . . a Shakspere, a Milton, a Bruno, exist in the mind as *pure Action*, defecated of all that is material & passive" (1804) and a relevance to humanity generally in *TT* 24 Jul 1830 *(CC)* I 183 (1836 vn, dated 29 Jul, II 116): ". . . every act . . . is truly the act of the entire man". See also Barfield *What Coleridge Thought* (1972) ch 1 et passim.

Note 7. *Coleridge and Bacon's "Lumen siccum" (Sp Aph B VIIIa n 30)*

C also alluded to Bacon's "lumen siccum" in an annotation on Luther *Colloquia Mensalia* 7: *LR* IV 7, *CM (CC)* III. His strongest affirmation appeared in *The Friend*: "But that there is, potentially, if not actually, in every rational being, a somewhat, call it what you will, the pure reason, the spirit, lumen siccum, νοῦς, φῶς νοερόν, intellectual intuition, &c. &c.; and that in this are to be found the indispensible conditions of all science, and scientific research . . . is often expressed, and every where supposed, by Lord Bacon": *Friend (CC)* I 491.

For Bacon's "expression" of this see e.g. the beginning of *Novum organum* bk I § 49: "Intellectus humanus luminis sicci non est, sed recipit infusionem a voluntate et affectibus", literally: "The human understanding is not of a dry light but receives an infusion from the will (*voluntate*) and the affections (*affectibus*)": *Works* (1740) I 279. This, if taken as a statement strictly about the "understanding", could be read by C in the further light of *The Advancement of Learning* I 3: ". . . all knowledge and wonder (which is the seed of knowledge) is an impression of pleasure in it self: but when men fall to framing conclusions out of their knowledge, applying it to their particular, and ministring to themselves thereby weak fears or vast desires there groweth that carefulness and trouble of mind which is spoken of: for then knowledge is no more *Lumen siccum*, whereof *Heraclitus* the profound said, *Lumen siccum optima anima* [a dry light is the best soul]; but it becometh *Lumen madidum*, or *maceratum*, being steeped and infused in the humours of the affections": *Works* (1740) II 417.

The phrase *lumen siccum* was derived by Bacon from Plutarch *De esu carnis: Moralia* 995E. (Cf Heraclitus Fragment 118 in Diels.) F. J. A. Hort treated with scepticism C's assertions in *The Friend* concerning the Platonic element in Bacon's thought, "a doctrine, which might have been expected to make its presence felt throughout the *Novum Organum*, had it been held by Bacon with any firmness": "Coleridge" *Cambridge Essays* (2 vols 1856) II 335. C had probably drawn support for his view from a passage in *The Advancement of Learning* I § 3, immediately after the one just quoted: ". . . if any man shall think by view and enquiry into these sensible and material things, to attain that light whereby he may reveal unto himself the nature or will of God; then indeed is he spoiled by vain philosophy . . . it was most aptly said by one of *Plato's* school, That the sense of man carrieth a resemblance with the sun, which (as we see) openeth and revealeth all the terrestrial globe; but then again it obscureth and concealeth the stars and celestial globe: so doth the sense discover natural things, but it darkneth and shutteth up divine": *Works* (1740) II 417 (cf I 30).

Despite such references, however, Bacon's eye was on nature, and on distortion in our view of natural phenomena: i.e. the loss of "dryness" when knowledge (or the understanding) is "steeped", "infused" or "drenched" in the affections, or emotions. C's less assertive comments in *AR*, in which the terms retailed with reverence in *The Friend* have become "fantastical and mystical phrases", suggest a shift in his perception of Bacon, whose stress on the psychological rather than the metaphysical emerges clearly in a comment on Heraclitus' *lumen siccum* in his Essay xxvii, "Of Friendship", *Works* (1740) III 340: "And certain it is, that the Light, that a man receiveth, by Counsell from Another, is Drier, and purer, than that which cometh from his owne Understanding, and Judgement; which is ever infused and drenched in his Affections and Customes." C stated, perhaps in 1826, that Bacon's comment was "no doubt a pertinent Corollary from the adage/ but the immediate Sense is incomparably deeper—S‹ John would have been a truer interpreter—Vide Ch. I. v. 4." His use of the word "drench" elsewhere in this notebook entry suggests that this passage was in his mind: *CN* IV 5379.

Note 8. *Coleridge's interest in the "Glory" (Sp Aph B VIIIb n 39)*

In the Gutch Notebook C copied out the description of a Glory from a piece by John Haygarth in *Memoirs of the Literary and Philosophical Society of Manchester* (1790) III 463, which also has an illustration. See *CN* I 258 and n. Lowes, who quotes it, *RX* 470–1, compares the description of a glory around the sun in *The Three Graves*: *PW* (EHC) I 284 and C's use of the phenomenon in *Constancy to an Ideal Object* (see below).

In a letter of 11 Jun 1825 to J. H. Green, C inquired: "Could you procure me a Copy of those Lines which a long time ago I sent to Mrs Green by you, on constancy to the *Idea* of a beloved Object—ending, I remember, with a Simile of a Woodman following his own projected Shadow?—In my Supplementary Volume I should like to publish it, as a Note to the sentence, last line but 13, in p. 220 of the Aids to Reflection": *CL* v 467. The lines in question were first printed as *Constancy to an Ideal Object* in *Poems* (1828), in which C referred to it as ". . . this phenomenon, which the Author has himself experienced" and quoted the present passage from *AR*. The closing lines read:

> . . . The woodman winding westward up the glen
> At wintry dawn, where o'er the sheep-track's maze
> The viewless snow-mist weaves a glist'ning haze,
> Sees full before him, gliding without tread,
> An image with a glory round its head;
> The enamoured rustic worships its fair hues,
> Nor knows he makes the shadow, he pursues!
> Lines 26–32: *PW* (EHC) I 455–6

Note 9. *Bayle and Simonides* (*Sp Aph B IX* nn 12 and 16)

In his *Dictionary, Historical and critical* (5 vols 1734–8), Bayle was concerned to defend Simonides against the likes of Tertullian, who, as Bayle points out (*Dictionary* v 142n [col 2]), was himself so unreflecting as to believe that God was corporeal and who yet could write, in *Apologeticus* 46,

> For what certain answer did Thales, the chief of natural Philosophers, give to Croesus asking him concerning the Deity; when he had often found that the time he required for the considering of it, was not sufficient? Any Christian tradesman can both discover and declare what GOD is, and from thence can impart to others a full and satisfactory answer: though Plato affirms, that the Maker of the universe neither can easily be discovered, nor, when discovered, can be easily described to all men.

For Leighton's citation of this passage and C's comment on it see above, *Int Aph XII*.

Bayle's reconstruction of Simonides' arguments included (*Dictionary* v 142n [col 1]): "It is not sufficient to say, that GOD is a being distinct from the bodies which compose the universe. They will desire to know . . . whether he is extended . . . . I do not find myself able to make them understand, that there are two kinds of extension, one corporeal, the other incorporeal . . . If I say that GOD is not extended . . . [it will be asked] How can he act where he is not? . . . But supposing it should be granted me, that GOD is an immaterial and unextended substance, a spirit infinite and omnipotent . . . [it will be said] Is not his power an attribute as necessary as his knowledge? Therefore he does not act freely, taking freedom to be the power of acting or not acting . . . . I shall be told that I entirely destroy religion . . ."

Later, *Dictionary* v 143 n [col 1], Bayle puts Simonides into confrontation with the Christian tradesman and adds that "these Christians . . . are beholden for their great knowledge to their . . . being educated in a Church, where they obtained an historical and even sometimes a justifying faith of revealed truths. This convinces them of the existence of several things which they do not comprehend. Our greatest divines, if . . . [like Simonides] they affirmed nothing for certain concerning the nature of GOD but what by the light of reason appeared to them undeniable, evident, and proof against all objections, would have continually demanded farther delays of all the Hieroes in the world." And later: "The powers of reason . . . go no farther than to hold us in suspence and to keep us in fear of erring, whether we affirm or whether we deny . . . Either the Grace of GOD, or education must come necessarily to their assistance . . . [The mysteries of certain Christian doctrines] would have furnished Simonides with greater doubts, than his imagination did ever suggest to him."

The often quoted Tertullian passage presumably stimulated C's assertion elsewhere that through the unobtrusive working of the established Church, truths hard for a Plato to discover or express had become "the almost hereditary property of childhood and poverty, of the hovel and the workshop . . ." See *BL* ch 11 *(CC)* I 226–7, repeated *C&S (CC)* 75, and cf *Op Max ms* B3 ("II") 26, where they are referred to as "the truths of which a Simonides despaired, and which a Plato deemed scarcely discoverable and still more difficultly communicated."

Note 10. *Coleridge on Natura Naturans and Natura Naturata* (*Sp Aph B Xa* at n 7)

Coleridge distinguishes the two terms thus in his Philosophical Lectures of 1819: ". . . in speaking of the world without us as distinguished from ourselves, the aggregate of phenomena ponderable and imponderable, is called nature in the passive sense,—in the language of the old schools, *natura naturata*—while the sum or aggregate of the powers inferred as the sufficient causes of the former (which by Aristotle and his followers were called the substantial forms) is nature in the active sense, or *natura naturans*": *P Lects* Lect 13 (1949) 370.

The strange word *naturatum* is first found used c 1200 in the Latin versions of Aristotle *Physics* 2.1 (193[b]17)—translating φυόμενον, "what is born, or produced naturally"—and of Averroes' commentary on Aristotle *De caelo* 1.1; the precise terms were used in conjunction by Michael Scott (or Scot, c 1175–c 1234), for whom see *CN* IV 4642, 4690, and *TT* 16 Feb 1833 *(CC)* I 336–43 (1836 vn II 197–200); but C would more probably be thinking of Thomas Aquinas, e.g. in *Summa theologica* 1.2.85.6. For discussion of the history of the terms and further references see *Historisches Wörterbuch der Philosophie* (Basle 1971–) VI 504.

In *P Lects* Lect 13 (1949) 371 C identified the *natura naturans* with God, "in Berkeley's language", recalling perhaps *De motu* 32. Berkeley related the two terms to Osiris and Isis in *Siris* § 299. See *Works* (1784) II 133–4, 599 (the edition borrowed by C in 1796: *Bristol LB* 77); *Siris* (1774), annotated by him, *CM (CC)* I 409–10; and Beer *CV* 109–10. C knew the terms in addition from Spinoza (e.g. *Ethics* pt 1 prop 29 scholium): see BM MS Egerton 2801 f 1; also, no doubt, from Bruno. In 1829 he mentioned them in connexion with Bacon's philosophy: *C&S (CC)* 13 and n, referring perhaps to *Novum organum* bk II § 1. See also *BL* ch 12 *(CC)* I 240fn and n 5, giving references in Schelling; *CN* III 4397 f 50ᵛ and n; *Lects 1808–1819 (CC)* II 148; *Logic (CC)* 45 and n; and *CN* IV 4521 f 89ᵛ and n, 4646 f 4, 4796, 4843, and 5150.

Note 11. Coleridge on the Law of Continuity ("In Nature there are no leaps") (Sp Aph B Xb at nn 13–15)

Important references by C to this law include *CN* III 4237 f 41 (Oct 1814): "Incarnation deduced from the *Lex Continui*—the errors arising from the consideration of God, as a vague Exponent of blind powers, instead of adoring him as the *Wisdom* which is the Creator of the Universe"; *CN* III 4455: ". . . The action of the Lex Continui on the Lex quâ omne tendit in formam, or Lex manifesti?" ("Law by which everything takes on form, or Law of Manifestation"); and a letter to Tulk Sept 1817 (*CL* IV 769): "Observe too, that the two great poles of manifestation are Continuity (Lex Continui) and Individuation—the latter being the final cause of nature, or her object . . . yet so as that the whole process is cyclical tho' progressive, and the Man separates from Nature only that Nature may be found again in a higher dignity in the Man." See also *CN* IV 4814 f 54ᵛ. Making a point similar to the present one in *AR* about the limitations of the human understanding, C inserted the term *lex continui* into a passage from Kant that he quoted in *BL* ch 12 *(CC)* I 288–9. Though not wishing to plead the cause of the concepts of continuity and infinity, Kant pointed out that many rejected such ideas simply because they were not amenable to the forms of sensuous evidence: *De mundi sensibilis et intelligibilis forma et principiis* (1770) in *Vermischte Schriften* (Halle 1799) II 439–40. (The passage is also quoted in *Logic—CC—*244 and in part in BM MS Egerton 2801 f 159.) Kant stated and discussed the law later in the same work (3.14): *Vermischte Schriften* II 457, and, with the statement of the law as "in Nature there are no leaps", in *Kritik der reinen Vernunft* (Riga 1787) 281: tr J. M. D. Meiklejohn: "The principle of continuity forbids any leap in the series of phaenomena regarded as changes (*in mundo non datur saltus*)". (C annotated the 1799 edition, with the same pagination, but not at this point.) Leibniz is credited with the first statement of this as a law; he wrote of it as "mon axiome" in a letter to the Canon of Foucher c 1692: *Opera omnia* ed L. Dutens (6 vols Geneva 1768) II i 238. (See also *BL* ch 7—*CC*—I 123 and n 3, in which the *concept* is traced back to Aristotle.) C would have met it in the Preface to *Nouveaux essais*: Leibniz *Œuvres philosophiques* (Amsterdam & Leipzig 1765) 11: "Nothing takes place suddenly and it is one of my great and best confirmed maxims that *nature never makes leaps*. I called this the Law of Continuity . . . .": tr Peter Remnant and Jonathan Bennet (Cambridge 1981) § 56. Cf also *Nouveaux essais* bk IV ch 16: *Œuvres philosophiques* 440, tr (Cambridge 1981) § 473. Cf also Leibniz *Essais de théodicée* § 348 (see *Sp Aph B I* n 9 above). In Apr 1818 C had recommended Kant *De mundi . . . forma et principiis* (with *Nouveaux essais* and other works) to a Mr Pryce: *CL* IV 851, and in a marginal note on one of the copies of *Vermischte Schriften* called it a "Masterwork of profundity and precision": *CM (CC)* III

318. For C's reading of Leibniz see also *Mor Aph VI* n 15 above. The Latin phrase, a traditional one and so an earlier, looser version of the "law", is also a well-known form. See e.g. Linnaeus *Philosophia botanica* § 77 (Stockholm 1751) 36.

Note 12. Indian religion and Christianity (Sp Aph B Xb n 59)

As well as in Maurice, discussion of the parallels between the Brahmin and Christian accounts of evil, and the possible relation to the doctrine of metempsychosis, can be found in J. Z. Holwell *A Review of the Original Principles, Religious and Moral of the Ancient Brahmins* (1779) 9–12 and esp ch 8. Cf *P Lects* Lect 3 (1949) 127–9, quoting the *Bhagavat-Geeta* tr Charles Wilkins (1785) 91–3 as an example of the excesses of pantheism or polytheism. A transcript of the same passage in the hand of John Watson is followed by C's comment that with the exception of some parts of the *Sakuntala* (tr Sir Wiliam Jones 1799) all the Sanskrit writings he had yet seen, including *Ramayana* tr William Carey (3 vols 1806–10), were of the same character: VCL MS LT 32. In a notebook entry of, perhaps, 1821 he quoted other lines from the *Bhagavadgita* from Creuzer *Symbolik und Mythologie der alten Völker* (4 vols Leipzig 1810–12), which Creuzer had taken from F. Schlegel *Über die Sprache und Weisheit der Indier* (Heidelberg 1808): *CN* IV 4832 f 61ᵛ. There seems to be no evidence that C read the latter work, but much that he used Schlegel's *Geschichte der alten und neuen Litteratur* (2 vols Vienna 1815), in which the fifth lecture is devoted to Indian literature and religion, Brahmin and Buddhist. Creuzer's work (which C had used in the 1810–12 ed for the preparation of *P Lects* and in that and the enlarged 1819–23 ed for various notebook entries: *CN* IV 4831, 4832, 4839, 4856) contained a discussion of Indian religion in *Symbolik* bk II ch 2 (1819–23) I 533–649.

In a notebook entry of c Oct 1820 C discussed the "Pantheistic Scheme of Theomonism of the Persian and Indian Philosophers" as described by Sir William Jones in the sixth of his *Dissertations . . . Relating to the History and Antiquities, the Arts, Sciences and Literature of Asia* (1793): *CN* IV 4737. See also his discussion in the part of *HEHL ms* printed in J. H. Muirhead *Coleridge as Philosopher* (1930) 225, 283–4. For his annotations on J. A. Dubois *Description of the . . . People of India* (1817) see *Int Aph XVIII* n 5 above and *CM (CC)* III 339–49.

Note 13. Javan and the Ionians (Sp Aph B Xb n 61)

The descent of the Ionians (as Greeks in general were called in Hebrew) from Javan ('Ιωυαν) was in C's time a commonplace, needing no further explanation. See his annotation on G. S. Faber *Mysteries of the Cabiri* (1803), *CM (CC)* II 578, with a further reference to the Scottish Iona; cf *CN* IV 4507 and n, and, for more extended discussion of racial origins as implied in Genesis, *CN* III 4384, IV 4548, and a marginal note on Blumenbach: *CM (CC)* I 539–41. The Biblical account was ignored by Kant, Blumenbach, and Steffens, but F. Schlegel considered it a recognised basis of all historical truth: Lect 4 in *Geschichte der alten und neuen Litteratur* (1815). The connexion between Javan and Ionia was made in a work read by C as a schoolboy (see above, *Refl Mor* n 19): John Potter *Antiquities of Greece* bk I ch 1; and (among other works known to him) Samuel Bochart *Geographia sacra* (Frankfurt 1681) and the *Universal History* (1799) I 144–5n, v 5 (see above, *Sp Aph B VII* n 22). Hastings *Dictionary of the Bible* s.v. "Javan" adds references to the Ionians in Persian, Assyrian, and Egyptian inscriptions not known in C's time.

Note 14. Coleridge and the Prometheus myth (*Sp Aph B Xb* n 63)

Coleridge's interest in the Prometheus myth as told by Aeschylus (then the undisputed author) in *Prometheus Bound* seems to have been strong around 1820–1, when HC was working on a poem on the subject. C had used phrases from the play in the Sapphic ode for which he won a prize at Cambridge in 1792; he was apparently reading it in 1806 and taking an interest in the metre and in Prometheus himself: *CN* II 2900, 2913. In 1817 he wrote two notes in Cary's copy of Blomfield's edition on the interpretation of words in lines 13 and 17: *CL* IV 781, *CM (CC)* I 26–7. In 1821 he sent HC "a small volume almost" of his own ideas on the subject: letter to DC 16 May, *CL* v 142–3. HC found these beyond him, and his poem remained a fragment: HC *Poems* ed DC (2nd ed 1851) II 257–85; see also *Letters of Hartley Coleridge* ed E. L. Griggs (1936) 29 and n. He did, however, publish a piece, "On the Poetical Use of the Heathen Mythology", in the *London Magazine* XXVI (Feb 1822) 113–24. At least part of the material evidently written for HC has survived in a transcript by John Watson, with revisions in C's hand, now at Duke University. Most of this was used in his lecture to the RSL on 18 May 1825, which was published in their *Transactions* II (1834) 384–404 (the preferable text) and later edited (with variations) by HNC in *LR* II 323–59. The main use of the Duke University ms (to be pub in *SW&F—CC*) begins at pp 389 and 333 respectively. See S. W. Reid "The Composition and Revision of Coleridge's Essay on Aeschylus' *Prometheus*" *SB* XXIV (1971) 176–83 and *CN* IV 4834 and n; also Excursus Note 16, below.

In the play Prometheus, one of the older race of Titans, is punished for bringing fire and civilisation to mankind, in defiance of Zeus, the new tyrant. The arrival of Io (line 561), loved by Zeus and changed into a cow, fleeing gadfly-tormented from the wrath of Hera, leads to prophecies of her future wanderings (705–35, 790–814) through Asia to Egypt, where she is to bear a son, the ancestor of Prometheus' liberator, Heracles (846–73). Under C's interpretation, Jupiter, or Jove (Zeus), represented Law, or Nature, Prometheus, Idea, in the mysteries the content of which Aeschylus was revealing. Isis (or Io) represented productive nature and later the mundane religion, grounded on the worship of nature: *Transactions* II 386. The Duke University ms includes a slightly fuller statement where Io is in the same relation to Juno (Hera) as Prometheus to Jove, representing a foreign, persecuted religion, a crude Christianity before Christ, and (like Prometheus) "the efforts of the Spirit of the World to achieve by its own powers . . . the predicted synthesis of the human and the rational, the mundane and the positive, religion". A brief reading of the Prometheus myth as symbolising "the chaos, the Fall or Degeneracy of man, and the Deluge" can be found in *CN* IV 4841 f 120ᵛ. See also *TT* 8 May 1824 *(CC)* I 58 (1836 vn II 52).

At the end of his lecture C promised a further communication concerning ". . . the persecutions, wanderings, and migrations of the Io, the mundane religion", but this never emerged: the Society perhaps held up publication of the existing lecture in the hope of receiving it. The lecture is discussed in G. Whalley "Coleridge's Lecture on the Prometheus of Aeschylus" *Proceedings and Transactions of the Royal Society of Canada* LIV (1960) 13–24 and (set against a larger context) in N. J. Leask *The Politics of Imagination in Coleridge's Critical Thought* (1988) esp 147–219. See in addition Beer *CV* 68, 129–31 (relevant also to *Sp Aph B Xb* n 64) and above, *Conc* n 71.

Note 15. Coleridge, Waterland, and "St Paul's 'in the Heavens' " (Sp Aph B XVIII n 31)

No specific discussion of "St Paul's *in the Heavens*" has been found in any of Waterland's works. But if by "eternal in the Heavens" C implies Christ's divinity and co-eternity, it is relevant that both his *Vindication* (1719) and *Second Vindication* (1723) are devoted to proving, by the evidence from the Bible and from the tradition surviving in the early Fathers, that Christ as the Son and the Logos was one God with the Father, co-eternal and not created, was himself described as Creator in Col 1.16, 17 and Heb 1.10, and was similarly given all the characteristics that are applied to God the Father, apart from his sonship. Waterland refers to Justin Martyr's description of the Logos and Son as "ὁ ὤν, in his own proper right" in *Vindication* 153–4. The Greek fathers are hardly quoted on the subject of the body of Christ incarnate and resurrected when it is discussed in *Vindication* 96–8 and *Second Vindication* 225–31; fuller treatment is given in *A Review of the Doctrine of the Eucharist* (see above, *Sp Aph B XVIII* n 42).

The actual phrase "in the Heavens" does occur in Warburton's *Vindication*, on p 95: "Barnabas, speaking of the Sun in the Heavens, calls it ἔργον χειρῶν αὐτου, meaning Christ, tho' there's some dispute about the Reading." If this is what C has in mind, it must be supposed that he creatively misread the text at this point, being led back by the phrases "the sun in the Heavens" and "meaning Christ" to an earlier speculation of his, where the sun "apparently suspended" in the sky, or Aether, and the reflection of both in the Mediterranean, were seen as presenting a great symbol of Logos proceeding from Being: "Λογος ab *Ente* at once the existent Reflexion and the Reflex Act—at once actual and real & therefore filiation not creation . . .": *CN* II quoted above, Editor's Introduction at n 139. In these terms the sun apparently suspended in the heavens becomes a sublime symbol for the Father, linking with C's interpretation of the phrase in John 1.18 which he often quoted as ὁ ὤν ἐν (for εἰς) τῷ κόλπῳ τοῦ πατρός as, literally, "*the Being* in the bosom of the Father"; see *Sp Aph B XVIII* n 30 and the main text at that point. In presenting a reflection of this relationship to humanity (as the Mediterranean reflection of the sun in the heavens gives it actual "substance") the Son is truly "Λογος ab *Ente*"; and as the believer takes on the "informing power and vivific life of the incarnate Word" he or she is in turn initiated into a version of this relationship, becoming also "eternal in the heavens". The possibility that C was speculating boldly (if also aberrantly, so far as Waterland's actual text is concerned) in this fashion is further suggested by his assertion immediately afterwards that he is addressing a select audience, his insistence on Waterland's "orthodoxy" and "strong sound sense", and his ensuing defence of symbolic interpretations.

Note 16. *Coleridge and the word "Agonistes" (Sp Aph B XIX n 73)*

Ἀγών meant, in classical times, competition, game, match (wrestling or boxing), or race. The word and its derivatives, used already for mental struggle or suffering in classical times, were applied specifically to Christ's agony (ἀγωνία) in the garden in Luke 22.44 (though only later to the agony on the cross) and to Christians in e.g. St Paul's injunction "fight (ἀγωνίζου) the good fight (ἀγῶνα)" (1 Tim 6.12). Christ or the Christian or Milton's Samson were all fighting and suffering in the struggle against sin and unbelief. In the second century the noun ἀγωνιστής was applied to Christ by Theodotus, according to Clement of Alexandria and Origen: Migne *PG* IX 688, XI 789. On at least three occasions C considered including the word in a title, surely with *Samson Agonistes* in mind: "Λόγος ἀγωνιστής" was to deal with the "Pantheists and Mystics . . . Giordano Bruno, Jacob Behmen, George Fox, and Benedict Spinoza", *CL* IV 589 (Sept 1815); "Homo Agonistes" was to be the title of his projected play on Michael Scott, the magician (see above, Excursus Note 10); and "Prometheus, or Nous Agonistes" was suggested as an appropriate title for "in the language of the first reviewers of the Drama in the middle ages" for HC's poem: *CN* IV 4642 (1820) and Duke ms (c 1821), for which see above, *Sp Aph B Xb* n 63. The tradition is discussed further in F. M. Krouse *Milton's Samson and the Christian Tradition* (Princeton, NJ 1949) 108–33; see also Milton *The Poems* ed J. Carey and A. Fowler (1968) 331n.

Note 17. *Coleridge and the Abyss of Being (Sp Aph B XIX n 80)*

Some of C's speculations on this subject may date from his reading in 1803 (*CN* I 1006n, 1369, 1382) of Johannes Scotus Erigena's commentary on the history of the creation, when "tenebrae erant super faciem abyssi", and on God as the "fons et origo" ("fountain and source"): *De divisione naturae* (Oxford 1681) 57–73; he wrote an annotation concerning "Creation e nihilo" on his copy (*CM—CC—*III 138–9). (St Augustine *Confessions* 12.7–8 is another relevant text.) In 1818 he contended that in the relevant passage of the Bible, Gen 1.2 ("And the earth was without form, and void; and darkness was upon the face of the deep"), the ". . . writer of this divine Hymn" was referring to ". . . the byssus abyssus, the deepless Depth": *CN* III 4418 f 13, cf IV 5249, 5256; also *HEHL ms* 73 and *CM (CC)* III 12. Annotating Böhme at about the same period he used the same phrase to describe the nature of God: "In all Living there is ever an aliquid *sup*positum [a something placed *under*], which can never [be] lifted up into the intelligible—it is the Darkness that is the Bearer of all Light. But it is peculiar to God that he hath the ground of *his* Existence within himself . . .": *CM (CC)* I 585. "I AM in that I AM, is God's self-affirmation, and ⟨that⟩ God verily *is*, is all we can affirm of him; ⟨that,⟩ to which no addition can be made, when we speak of *the total God*, Θεος αβυσσος": *CM (CC)* I 618; cf I 636; also *CN* IV 5466: "The Personality, the I AM, of the

Abysmal Will & Absolute Reason''. Despite C's joking reference to the Gnostic belief that Intelligence and Truth were the offspring of ''Abyss and Silence'' (following Priestley: *Lects 1795*—*CC*—199 and n), the existence by 1796 of a note based on Böhme that ended by quoting Böhme's phrases ''Well-spring—total God'' (*CN* I 262) (coupled, conceivably, with philological speculations on the element of ''abyss'' in Abyssinia, location of the Nile springs) suggests that he may have been exploring the idea seriously at a much earlier stage. See also *TT* 7 Jan–13 Feb 1823 *(CC)* I 35–6 and nn (1836 vn, dated 6 Jan, II 40). (A reference to ''the Living God'' as ''. . . not only the Abyss of Life in Himself, but the Fountain of Life to Us'' may be found in so orthodox a work as William Beveridge *An Exposition of the XXXIX Articles of the Church of England*—Oxford 1710—2.) This would throw light on the ''. . . caverns measureless to man . . .'' in *Kubla Khan* and the similar idea in WW *The Prelude* (1805) III 246–7, coupled with WW's association of the imagination with ''. . . the mind's abyss . . .'' and ''. . . the dark abyss . . .'': *Prelude* (1850) VI 594 and XIV 72. The suggestion would be that that which is in man an unfathomable depth is in God a self-renewing fountain: knowledge of the one is a dark key to knowledge of the other. In an annotation on Irving the ''Holy Will'' is the ''Abysmal good'': *CM (CC)* III 30.

In some ms notes on Edward Williams *Essay on the Equity of Divine Government* (see above, *Sp Aph B I* nn 7, 10), sent to Dr R. H. Brabant in Mar 1815, and published in the *Westminster Review* XCIII (1870) 349–54, on the other hand, the spiritual state of ''Death'' also is characterised by C as ''abyss'', ''. . . most fearful, and the greatest of possible evils''. This ambiguity of the abyss is consonant with his subsequent affirmation that ''both Scripture and the profoundest philosophy conspire to teach us that to man is given but one positive act, that of opening out his nature either to the Author of all Good or to the Prince of Darkness'', an act ''not in time'', known ''by and through the Φαινο-μενα in our consciousness, of which that supersensual act is the νουμενον, or intelligible ground'' (pp 350–1). Either act in his eyes, evidently, commits one to the abyss, but in the one case also to knowledge of the fountainous creativity and mercy of God, in the other only to the ''state below time'' of his 1817 annotation (see *CM*—*CC*—II 559 and *Sp Aph B XVII* n 10 above), the ''eternity without time, and as it were below it, God present without manifestation of his presence . . . depths which we dare not linger over'' of *Biographia Literaria*: *BL* ch 24 *(CC)* II 235. It is the ''positive Opposite'' of life, as described in *Sp Aph B XIX* at n 30, above—an abyss with no awareness of a fountain, as it were.

In a further ms note on Edwards C seeks to show that misunderstanding of the nature of causality when the term ''First Cause'' is applied to God—the failure, that is, to appreciate that ''God alone has the *ground* of his own existence in himself''—has led to ''the doubts and supposed contradictions in the idea of creation *e nihilo*''. ''The ancients who deemed God the First Cause did none of them admit of absolute creation, a doctrine . . . peculiar to divine revelation'': *Westminster Review* p 352. In his view, presumably, apprehension of absolute creation transforms one's idea of the abyss.

Note 18. Two words for ''Will'' (Sp Aph B XIX n 82)

An annotation on Field *Of the Church* (*CM*—*CC*—II 664–6) shows that C found the phrase θέλημα καὶ βούλησιν (with many others) in Waterland *A Second*

Vindication of Christ's Divinity (1723) 282, where it appears on p 282. Water-land also points out that Athanasius described Christ as βουλὴ καὶ θέλημα τοῦ πατρός as part of his evidence to prove that Christ is one God with the Father, and that this was necessarily the case. Though the Fathers could not accept that God was subject to necessity they did in fact tacitly acknowledge it in this sense; the later Schoolmen were the first to speak of God's existence as necessary. Waterland himself distinguishes ''Will'' in the sense in which God wills his own existence, or wills the eternal generation of the Son, from ''Arbitrary Will'', or choice of what otherwise might not take place: *Vindication* (1719) 125–9 and *passim*. There is no sign in Waterland's numerous quotations of any distinction in meaning between θελ- and βουλ- (except their use in conjunction in various passages) and he does not claim that the Fathers made any distinction.

Patristic and scholastic theology distinguished between the antecedent will of God, e.g. that all men should be saved, and the consequent, that nevertheless sinners should be damned, and between absolute will, e.g. that the world should be created, and that sinners should be punished, and conditional will, that there should be sin in the world, and that men exercising free will should refuse to be saved. Clement of Alexandria appears to use θέλημα of absolute and βούλησις of consequent will in this sense in *Stromata* 4.12. Christ and the persecuted Christians did not suffer by the βούλησις of the Father and of God, but nothing happens without the θέλημα of the Ruler of the universe. Aquinas (*Summa theologica* 1.83.4) distinguishes between *voluntas* as θέλησις, and *electio* or *liberum arbitrium* as βούλησις. For C's own views see above, *Sp Aph B XIX* n 83, and, for his distinction between *voluntas* and *arbitrium*, *Int Aph XXIX* at n 7 and *Sp Aph B Xb* at nn 20–1.

Note 19. *Mant and D'Oyly on Baptism* (*Sp Aph B [XXIV]* n 75)

In an annotation on Leighton COPY C II 53 C wrote ''Messrs Mant and D'oyly entertain no doubt that there are myriads of Christians baptized in infancy who pass from the cradle to the grave without any remorse of conscience, or act of special Conversion toward God & without any reason or occasion for such— They cannot deny the temptibility, *supposing* (alas! what a supposition!) nothing worse—but this they hold guiltless, blameless, on the same footing with the body's sensibility to pain . . .'': *CM (CC)* III. C seems to be referring to the second edition of their Family Bible (2 vols in 3 Oxford 1817–18) III at Rom 6.9–11, in which the note quotes from Abp Thomas Secker (1693–1768): ''When the infants of believers are baptized, they are, by the solemnity which Heaven hath appointed, 'born again of water and the Spirit,' John iii.5, into a better state than that of nature. And till either sort of persons forfeit their claim by wilful wickedness, which it may be hoped some never do, though 'in many things we offend all', James iii.2, they continue heirs of everlasting life.'' C's awareness of Mant's ideas on this subject dates, however, from his reading of a ''tract'' by him in 1815: see his discussion in a letter of 2 Aug 1815 to T. A. Methuen, concluding, ''What had been said of Baptism during the times when few, if any, but adult, tried, and *built-up* Christians were baptized, was incautiously (*as appears to me*) applied in these one or two passages to the baptism of infants; which (if we will not contradict the most positive commands and determinations of the Gospel, 'Repent and believe,' and 'thou mayest be baptized,') we must regard as a sacrament of *conditional promise* and as a *means* of grace, but not as a sacrament of *effect*, and an immediate *conveyance* of grace": *CL* IV 581. Cf R. Mant *Two Tracts, Intended to Convey Correct Notions of Regeneration and Conversion* (1815) 10: ". . . I shall venture to show by the adduction of several passages in her Liturgy . . . that the doctrine of regeneration by baptism is most clearly asserted by [the Church]" and examples following, pp 11–17.

Note 20. *Coleridge and Edward Irving (Sp Aph B [XXIV] n 77)*

Edward Irving, who had been a friend of Thomas Carlyle in Scotland and helped introduce him to C, came to a Scottish chapel in Hatton Garden in 1822 and achieved an extraordinary fashionable success as a preacher. In the summer of 1823 C went to hear this ". . . super-Ciceronian, ultra-Demosthenic Pulpiteer" (*CL* v 280) and met him soon afterwards (ibid 284). He then described him as ". . . the greatest *Orator*, I ever heard"—making a distinction however between oratory and eloquence as equivalent to that ". . . between the Mouth + Windpipe & the Brain + Heart"; he also described him as ". . . a man of great simplicity, of overflowing affections and enthusiastically in earnest": *CL* v 286–7. His error, he remarked in a contemporary note, was to use "Declamation", i.e. "high & passionate Rhetoric not introduced & pioneered by calm and clear Logic": *CN* IV 4963. C continued to see him, often with Basil Montagu, in 1824 and after. Irving dedicated to him his first book, *For Missionaries after the Apostolical School* (1825), the preface being dated Jan 1825. In Jul C said that he had ". . . a vigorous & (what is always pleasant) a *growing* mind: and his character is *manly* throughout": *CL* v 474. But from early in 1826, when Irving became intimate with Hatley Frere (1779–1866), a writer ". . . quite swallowed up in the quicksands of conjectural prophecy" (*CL* VI 557), C had increasing reservations, and at a breakfast party with WW and Aders on 18 Jun 1828 went so far as to say that he thought him mad: *C Talker* 344–5. "Noble but erring" was his main judgment: see *TT (CC)* II 400, 430, I 127–8.

For C's later considered view of Irving see *C&S (CC)* 142–3: "Well then! I have no faith in his prophesyings; small sympathy with his fulminations; and in certain peculiarities of his *theological* system, as distinct from his religious principles, I cannot see my way. But I hold withal, and not the less firmly for these discrepancies in our moods and judgments, that EDWARD IRVING possesses more of the spirit and purpose of the first Reformers, that he has more of the Head and Heart, the Life, the Unction, and the genial power of MARTIN LUTHER, than any man now alive; yea, than any man of this and the last century. . . . I look forward with confident hope to a time when his soul shall have perfected her victory over the dead letter of the senses and its apparitions in the sensuous understanding; when the Halcyon IDEAS shall have alit on the surging sea of his conceptions . . ." (The first part appears also in BM MS Egerton 2801 f 207: see *IS* 298.) For more on Irving see the notes and references in *C&S (CC)* 142–3; *CN* IV 4963n, 5293; *CL* v 280n and VI Index; Sterling's record, *C Talker* 343–4; Beer "Some Transatlantic and Scottish Connections" in *The Coleridge Connection* ed R. Gravil and M. Lefebure (1990) 321–32; and the entries on Irving in *CM (CC)* III. For longer accounts of the relationship see A. L. Drummond *Edward Irving and His Circle* (1937) 65–9 and Index under "'Coleridge'", and ch 2 of W. B. Elliott "The Uses of Coleridge" (unpub PhD thesis, University of London 1978), in which the present passage is discussed, pp 74–6.

Note 21. *Coleridge and William Law's* Spirit of Prayer *and* Spirit of Love *(Conc* n 9)

In the opening pages of *The Spirit of Prayer* (i 15) Law has a *bravura* passage in which he describes the delights of the unfallen angels: "Perpetual Scenes of Light, and Glory, and Beauty, were rising and changing through all the Heighth and Depth of their *glassy Sea*, merely at their Will and Pleasure. But finding what wonders of Glory and Light they could perpetually bring forth; how all the *Powers* of Eternity, treasured up in their *glassy Sea*, unfolded themselves, and broke forth in ravishing Forms of Wonder and Delight, merely in Obedience to their Call; they began to admire and even adore themselves, and to fansy that there was *some Infinity of Power hidden* in themselves; which they supposed was kept under, and suppressed, by that Meekness, and Subjection to God, under which they acted." Their subsequent abjuring of such meekness and submission precipitated the fall, which is then, in the case of Adam, read symbolically as a raising up of the bestial life in him (i 21; cf C's footnote to *Sp Aph B Xa*, after n 25, above). Law also describes (e.g. in i 42) how regenerate Man could become a "*Partaker* of the Divine Nature", a phrase that Lamb rebuked C for using, urging that though admittedly scriptural (2 Pet 1.4) it might be dangerous to those who were ". . . tinctured . . . with mystical notions and the pride of metaphysics". See *CL* I 239; *LL* (M) I 53–4, 56. This suggests that he may have heard C expounding the phrase in mystical terms. In the same treatise (ii 39) Law goes on to claim that "No other Religion can be right but that which has it[s] foundation in Nature". His exploration of analogies from the vegetable world for the growth of the soul (taking in Christ's description of himself as the vine) resembles C's: cf also the analogy of the butterfly above, Excursus Note 2.

In addition to *The Spirit of Prayer* it is likely that C knew *The Spirit of Love* (2 pts 1752–4), since Law, in addition to using some of the same analogies, maintains that Newton ". . . plowed with *Behmen's* Heifer" when he brought forth his ". . . *three* great Laws of *Matter* and *Motion*" (i 37), a point that seems to lie behind C's assertion that Böhme ". . . by the result of his own meditations presented the Newtonian system in a clearness which it certainly had never before appeared in": *P Lects* Lect 11 (1949) 329. Law also speaks of a "*Sabbath* of the Soul*", ii 231, a phrase used by C in the 1809 *Friend (CC)* II 173.

Note 22. *Coleridge on Enthusiasm and Fanaticism (Conc* n 21)

For a use of the two terms in 1802 see *EOT (CC)* I 382. Cf also C's note on Kant *Vermischte Schriften* (Halle 1799) II 426n: *CM (CC)* III, in which Kant distinguishes the two terms but on different grounds: *IS* 143. C's version follows his favourite light/heat distinction, as in "Socinianism moonlight—Methodism a Stove! O for some Sun to unite heat & Light!"': *CN* I 1233.

Fanaticism also resembles the warmth generated by damp hay or by bees in a hive: *BL* ch 2 *(CC)* I 30. Cf also his comment in 1814: ". . . Speeches like these . . . substitute the feverish heat of fanaticism for the vital warmth of an intelligent faith": *EOT (CC)* II 398. C had more hope for enthusiasm, on the other hand: *Friend (CC)* I 432 contains a call for restoration of ". . . the true Christian *enthusiasm*", drawing attention to the original Greek meaning: ". . . the influence of the divinity such as was supposed to take possession of the priest during the performance of the services at the altar"; cf also *P Lects* Lect 6 (1949) 216n. At the same time he attacked the unreasoning faith into which it commonly degenerated. In the Opus Maximum ms he condemns those who "boast of having sacrificed their reason to their faith" equally with those heated emotionalists who pretend to "sensible raptures, transports of pain or pleasure", comparing the one group to "moths in moonshine" and the other to "crickets chirping in darkness and having for their vital element warmth without light, & this too the warmth of the kitchen", Op Max ms B3 ("II") 201. (In 1808 he had used similar imagery to compare the different ways in which love, the "genial Sun of human nature", affected Sara Hutchinson (". . . cold, as the tropic Firefly") and himself, "the Cricket in hot ashes": *CN* III 3379.) The benevolent but false light of such enthusiasm is reflected also in the moonlight of the illustrations that follow in *AR*. His ideal of a sun that reconciles heat and light, on the other hand, prompts an annotation on Bunyan *Pilgrim's Progress*: "No two qualities more contrary than Genius and Fanaticism/ Enthusiasm indeed—θεος εν ἡμιν [*God in us*] is almost a Synonime of Genius—the moral *Life* in the intellectual *Light*, the Will in the Reason: and without it, says Seneca, nothing truly great was ever atchieved by Man": *CM (CC)* I 818. See also C's note on Baxter *Reliquiae Baxterianae*: "Fanaticism is the *fever* of *superstition*. Enthusiasm, on the contrary, implies an undue (or when used in a good sense, an unusual) vividness of ideas, as opposed to perceptions, or of the obscure inward feelings": *CM (CC)* I 270. Cf *BL* chs 2, 9 *(CC)* I 31, 147, *SM (CC)* 23 and n, *CM (CC)* III 1079, and *CN* IV 4924.

INDEX

q = quoted
fn = C's footnotes

ed = edited by
tn = textual notes
n = editorial footnotes

rev = revised
anon = anonymous

GENERAL PRINCIPLES

All works appear under the author's name; anonymous works, newspapers, periodicals, etc., are listed under titles.

Frequently recurring names and titles are abbreviated according to the List of Abbreviations (e.g., Samuel Taylor Coleridge = C; Henry Nelson Coleridge = HNC; Henry Crabb Robinson = HCR; *Quarterly Review* = *QR*).

Where multiple cross-references are given in the notes, individual items are not necessarily indexed, nor are the recipients of letters necessarily included. Titles and authors of annotated books are included in the Index only where specifically given in the notes.

Where necessary for clarity, the entry is abbreviated within its subentries by first letter plus a period (e.g. power = p.).

Entries may have up to three parts, general references preceding more specific subentries (arranged alphabetically), which in turn take precedence over works. For example, under Shakespeare, "C's lectures on" precedes *Hamlet, King Lear*, etc. The arrangement of subentries under *Aids to Reflection* and Coleridge, Samuel Taylor, is indicated at the head of those entries.

Where possible, subentries are given in Coleridge's own words. His capitalization of certain nouns, a particularly distinctive feature in *Aids to Reflection* after p 48 of the 1825 edition, when he evidently noticed from the proofs that they were not always being reproduced by the compositor from his manuscript (see Appendix B (a) to (k) above), is not necessarily carried on into such subentries.

A page number in parentheses indicates an Appendix source for text on the page indicated immediately before it.

Dates of persons believed to be alive in 1992 are not given. Dates of persons living earlier are given where determinable.

A selected list of Greek terms (the "Greek Index" in the main Index below) has been appended to this index. English transliterations, if they occur, are to be found in the main index. Extended Biblical and classical quotations are not included. Greek titles of books (including books in English) are listed in the index by author.

Abbott, Evelyn (1843–1901), and Lewis Campbell (1830–1908) *Life and Letters of Benjamin Jowett* 261n q
Abel (Bible) 430
Aberglaube lii

Abernethy, John (1764–1831) 151n
An Enquiry into . . . Mr Hunter's Theory of Life 293n
abiding words, original import of 244fn
abiding-place 312

AIDS TO REFLECTION

I GENERAL REFERENCES

xlix–li; project for "Beauties of Archbishop Leighton" sent to Murray and refused lii–lvi; project for "Aids to Reflection" sent to Taylor and Hessey and accepted lvi–lvii; first work lvii–lxvi; status of "Comments" in *AR* lxiii, lxiv; developing conception lxvi–lxxviii; reason and understanding distinction elaborated lxxix–lxxxiv; doctrines of original sin and redemption lxxxiv–lxxxviii; question of reflection lxxxviii–xcvi;

problems of composition, 1823–5 xcvi–cvi; publication of 1st ed cvi; further discussion of issues, 1825–8 cvi–cx, 64n–5n; early English reception cx–cxvi; American reception cxvi–cxxxiii, cxlix; "Synoptical Summary" cxxxii; "Corrections and Amendments" cxxxiii; later English reception cxxxiii–cxlix; lasting significance cxlix; preface, explaining for whom intended 5–10

II EDITIONS

1st edition (1825) 2n, 4n, 12n, 37n, 40n, 42n, 43n, 46n, 48n, 51n, 53n, 55n, 64n, 65n, 69n, 70n, 88n, 89n, 91n, 97n, 99n, 112n, 139n, 157n, 195n, 200n, 208n, 211n, 231n, 251n, 301n, 317n, 332n, 342n, 346n, 353n, 355n, 369n, 413n, 435–56 *passim*, 479–86, 533–41, 545; *see also* textual notes to this ed, *passim* "Advertisement" xli n, cxxxi, 3n; first plans sent to Taylor and Hessey lvi–lvii; work on planned Life of Leighton (later dropped) lvii–lx; annotations on Leighton prepared for press lix; first part sent to publisher lx–lxi; first version submitted in continuous prose lxiv–lxv; C troubled by appearance of proofs lxi; changes format lxi–lxv; adopts aphoristic method lxi–lxiii, lxvi–lxvii; detailed method of working lxvii–lxviii; themes of "Moral and Religious Aphorisms" lxviii–lxxi; development of "Spiritual Aphorisms" lxxi–lxxviii; work "growing and new-forming itself" under his hand xcvi–xcviii; problems raised by having to refer to COPY B xcvii; changes during composition, early 1824 xcvii–civ; hopes to complete in late November civ; work on original sin and redemption in early 1825 civ–cv; "last sheet of my work now going to press", 16 Feb cv; "on eve of publication", late April cv; passage rewritten, mottos added, early May cvi, 4; Corrections and Amendments added cvii; *AR* (1825) published, late May cvi; copies sent to Stuart, EC, Blanco White and DC with major issues indicated cviii; further annotated volumes sent to friends cviii–cix; C considers effect of volume cix–cx. For C's use of capitals in *see* Headnote to Index

James Marsh's 1st American edition (1829) cxvi–cxxviii and n
Marsh's enthusiasm for C's thought in *BL* cxvii–cxviii; impressed further by *AR* in 1826 cxviii; writes introduction for American edition cxviii; plans 2nd American ed if C produces a revised text cxx

2nd English edition (1831) ed C and HNC 3n, 33tn, 43n, 55n, 64n, 94n, 96n, 97n, 180n, 207n, 236n, 286n, 293n, 298n, 301n, 343n, 387n, 388n, 467, 469, 473–4, 545; textual variants 4tn, 10tn, 12tn, 14tn, 15tn, 17tn, 18tn, 26tn, 27tn, 28tn, 29tn, 30tn, 38tn, 39tn, 45tn, 49tn, 52tn, 58tn, 72tn, 76tn, 81tn, 84tn, 87tn, 94tn, 95tn, 96tn, 107tn, 132tn, 136tn, 142tn, 149tn, 162tn, 167tn, 169tn, 170tn, 171tn, 180tn, 183tn, 185tn, 192tn, 194tn, 198tn, 201tn, 202tn, 205tn, 208tn, 212tn, 216tn, 220tn, 226tn, 230tn, 232tn, 236tn, 244tn, 253tn, 259tn, 260tn, 263tn, 264tn, 265tn, 266tn, 275tn, 276tn, 279tn, 284tn, 286tn, 293tn, 296tn, 297tn, 300tn, 304tn, 313tn, 320tn, 323tn, 328tn, 331tn, 333tn, 338tn, 346tn, 350tn, 360tn, 367tn, 368tn, 369tn, 387tn, 389tn, 392tn, 413tn
C floats idea of republishing *AR*, "considerably improved", 1828 cxxix; draft agreement sent to Hurst, Jan 1829 cxxix–cxxx; task suspended, Feb cxxx; proposes to work on new ed with HNC, Sept 1829 cxxx; offers 1st half to Hurst, 2nd to be revised if possible cxxx–cxxxi; problems created by amendments cxxxi–cxxxii; C's work on contents page cxxxii; small extent of major revisions cxxxiii; reasons for adoption as copy text

III ANNOTATED COPIES
(for details see Appendix E).

air lxix, lxxxviii, 75, 98 (473), 398
living A. 404; pulses of 398; driving a.-current 398
Aiton, Eric John "The Vortex Theory of the Planetary Motions" 401n
alchemy lxxxviii, 261fn, 398
Alcott, Amos Bronson (1799–1888) *The Journals of Bronson Alcott* cxxv n; *Ralph Waldo Emerson, Philosopher and Seer* cxxv n
Alford, Henry (1810–71) *Life* cxi n
algebra 525
algebraic calculus 400
alienation 278
Alism cxliii n
alkalis 181fn
all
a.-analysing Pyrrhonist 241; a.-conscious Spirit 406n; a.-merciful God 274; a.-perfect and supreme Reason 141; Will or Spirit as a., in every part 233fn, 294
allegorical 206, 314fn
import of Christ as Bread of Life not a. 388; a. interpretations 314fn; mythical and a. interpretations of scriptures 264n; mythology not a. but tautegorical 206n
allegorizers of Holy Writ 39, 314fn
allegory/-ies cxxii, 79, 82, 97n, 142, 258fn, 264fn, 264n, 390
Eastern a. 258n; and metaphor 141n; and symbol 206n
Allegri, Antonio (Correggio) (c 1494–1534) lvi
Allen, George (1808–76) cxxii, cxxiii, cxxiv
Allen, Peter *The Cambridge Apostles* cxiv n, cxvi, cxvi n, cxxxvi n
Allestree, Thomas (1619–82) *The Whole Duty of Man* 375n
Allsop family cii

Allsop, Thomas (1795–1880) cv
Letters, &c. of S. T. Coleridge 108n
Almighty
A. Fiat 400; A. Goodness 275n; glory of A. 219
Alogi 254, 326
alogi amythi 255n
alogist 255n
alogology (RS's coinage) 255n
Alogos, Dr 255n
Alpakhar, Rabbi 339n
alterity 391n
alumen 335
ambassadors 69
Ambrose, St (340?–397), bp of Milan 369n
amendment
faith, hope and progressive a. 307fn
America, United States of cxiii, 177
metaphysics and theology of 510; reception of Marsh's ed of *AR* cxvi–cxxviii and n
American
A. Congregationalists 158n; A. woodmen 122–3
amphoteric 180n
amphotericum 179fn–180fn
amusement 228fn
Anabaptist 376
anachronisms 396
analogy/-ies lxxxvi, 88, 104, 185n, 205, 206, 319, 326
a. fails 186n; and metaphors 308n; mistaking of symbols and a. for metaphors 407n; psychological a. xci
analogon
dog may possess an a. of words 249
analogous 205
analytic procedure *a posteriori* 468
anastasis 291n
Anathema Maranatha 158n, 372, 372n

COLERIDGE, SAMUEL TAYLOR (1772-1834)

I BIOGRAPHICAL AND GENERAL:
(1) Biographical (2) Self-descriptions (in chronological order),
(3) Observations, opinions, ideas (in order of first appearance in text),
(4) Relationships (other than family), (5) Word-coinages
II POETICAL WORKS   III PROSE WORKS
IV CONTRIBUTIONS TO NEWSPAPERS AND PERIODICALS
V ESSAYS   VI LECTURES   VII MSS   VIII PROJECTED WORKS
IX COLLECTIONS AND SELECTIONS   X LETTERS
XI MARGINALIA   XII NOTEBOOKS

I BIOGRAPHICAL AND GENERAL

anxious interrogations, Feb 1825 cv; remaining copy ''ready'', 16 Feb 1825 cv; meets Dr Prati, spring 1825 cvi, 4n; ''Advertisement'' in proof, 5 May 1825 cvi; meets bp of London, 20 May 1825 197n; *AR* (1825) pub, c 23 May 1825 cvi; *AR* sent to Prati, 1 Jun 1825 cvi, to Southey, 6 Jun 1825 cvi, to J. T. Coleridge, 13 Jun 1825 cvi, to Stuart, July 1825 3n; *AR* praised by bp of London, July 1825 cx, 197n; C visited by Blanco White, July 1825 cx, 355n; C conducts Henry Gillman to Eton College and gives copy of *AR* to Keate, late July 1825 484; Lamb reports C's better health, Aug 1825 cvii; plans ''Six Disquisitions'', supplementary to *AR*, 1825–6 cxxix; takes sacrament again, 25 Dec 1827 387n; visited by Hallam, 1828 358n; new ed of *Poetical Works* 1828 557; plans 2nd ed of *AR*, 1828–9 cxxix; new ed of *PW*, 1829 cxxx; ailments and depression, 1829 cxxx; visited by Spurzheim, 1829 151, and by John Wheeler, 1829 cxxvii; working on *C&S*, 1829 cxxx; does not answer letter from James Marsh, 1830 cxx; HNC collaborating, late 1830 cxxx; offers 1st half of *AR* 2nd ed to Hurst, Aug 1830 cxxx; visited by McVickar, 1830 cxxi; *AR* 2nd ed pub c June 1831 cxxxiii; meets Trench, 1832 cxv; visited by Emerson, 1833 cxxvi; fortitude in face of death, 1834 57n; lifelong concern with language xii; unacknowledged borrowings commented on more sharply, 1840 cxvi and n, cxxxii

(2) *Self-descriptions* (in chronological order)

''cold hollow spot in heart'' in boyhood 24n; forced to look into himself by sorrows and ill health, c 1802–5 xliv; moral being untranquil, passion after an earthly good withheld, 1806 xlv; new world opened in infinity of his own spirit, 1813 xlv; feeling of infinite worthlessness, 1814 xlvi; recognition of own failings in Leighton's descriptions, 1814 xlvi–xlvii; own philosophy ''Heraclitus Redivivus'', 1817 219n; believes in certain doctrines until explanation is attempted, 1819 lxxiv; would not resent another's editing Leighton instead, 1823 liv; wishes for proof he has not lived in vain, 1823–4 lv, lxxxiv; identifies foundations

of his own moral nature, 1824 lxix; little wish to be admired as a fine writer in *AR*, 1825 3; no fondness for letters after name, 1825 2; uncertainty and restiveness of his ''Beast-body'', 1830 cxxx

(3) *Observations, opinions and ideas* (in order of appearance in *AR—CC*)

miracles ''extra essential'', 1806 xliv; fruits of prayer spiritual, 1814 xlvi; Leighton's writing almost as inspired as Bible xlvi; Leighton's power to convince xlvii; virtues and shortcomings of Spinoza xlviii–xlix; will acted on by shocks of sickness li; working of providential aids li; objection to publishing ''Beauties'', Leighton an exception lvi; attack on ''immethodological aphorisming Eclectics'' lxii; disturbed by rationalist movements in theology and reliance on ''evidences'' lxviii; view of nature of ''being'' in humans lxviii; analogy from nature lxix; importance of loving Truth above all lxix, cxlvi; necessary relationship between will and moral universe lxix; antecedent unity in moral and natural universe lxx; ascent inherent in Creation lxx; attacks chronological evolution lxx, cxlviii; crucial role of godly fear lxxii; ideas of reason not addressed primarily to intellect lxxiv; attacks modern Calvinism lxxv; need to guard against both superstition and enthusiasm lxxv; Methodist accent on self lxxvi; need to distinguish personëity from personality lxxvi; distinction between reason and understanding lxxix–lxxxiv, can be elucidated from animal instinct lxxx; understanding associated with wisdom of flesh lxxxi–lxxxii, lxxxiv; discursive distinguished from intuitive lxxxii; reason as light lxxxiii; rôle of wonder in philosophy lxxxiii–lxxxiv; view of original sin and redemption lxxxiv–lxxxviii; views of Taylor and Field on hereditary guilt criticized lxxxv, civ; doctrine of election lxxxv; two kinds of will distinguished lxxxvi; relation of Word and Sacrament lxxxvi; view of baptism lxxxvi–lxxxvii; defence of his ''mysticism'', interpretation of fourth Gospel lxxxvii; enthusiasts and fanatics alike dismissed lxxxvii–lxxxviii; advocacy of dynamic philosophy lxxxviii; attack on reliance on ''evidences'' lxxxviii; call to

II POETICAL WORKS

XII NOTEBOOKS

Griffiths, Arthur George Frederick (1838–1908) *The Chronicles of Newgate* 330n

Griggs, Earl Leslie (1899–1976) lxii, xcix, c, cxxxi; ed *Letters, see* S. T. Coleridge x

Grigson, Geoffrey (1905–85) *The Harp of Aeolus and Other Essays* 307n

Grotianism/Grotians 163fn, 164

Grotius, Hugo (Hugo de Groot) (1583–1645) xliv, l, 164, 164n, 338, 338n

Christianity according to 164; enemy of Christianity 346n; high and low Grotian divines 362

Annotationes in Libros Evangeliorum 200n q; *De veritate Christiana* 164n

grottos 393

ground/Ground cv, 125, 223 (451), 227fn, 235fn, 286, 305, 305n, 401fn

absolute/Absolute g. 139, 334n; absolute G. of all being 140n; evil g. cannot originate in Divine Will 288; of formal principles 216; God has G. of his Existence within himself xlix, 333n, 563; infinite omnipresent Mind as the G. of the universe 86; intelligent G. 334n; intelligible g. 564; One as g. and cause of Universe 168 (449); one supreme Being as G. and Cause of Universe 448; and origin of election 172; and *suppositum* of all other Mysteries 292; ultimate g. 228fn; universal G. of all Being 334

Ground-lightning 235n

grounded in act of understanding 230n

groundwork of Christianity 196

Grove of Academus 191

Grove, Sir George (1820–1900) 240n, 470, 480

grow

conclusion from things made to things that g. 185n

growing mind 566

growth/Growth 246

form and g. in vegetation 263n; language the g. and emanation of a people 244fn; moral g. 103n; principle of g. and individual form 179fn, 179n

guardian spirit 146n

The Guardian cxlv n

guile 112, 178n

"Israelite without g." (Hurwitz) 211fn

guilt/Guilt lxxvi, 53, 256n, 267n, 272n, 274, 281, 310fn, 318, 329, 470, 511

abolition of 318; annals of 62; inherited g. 298

guilty 128, 294

g. act 472; atonement for sins of 331fn; g. men 127; g. past 309

gunpowder, white 111

Guyon, Jeanne-Marie Bouverie de la Mothe (1648–1717) 164n, 393n

gymnosophist, murderous 352fn

Habich, Robert D. *Transcendentalism and the Western Messenger* cxxvi n

habit of referring actions and opinions to fixed laws 151

Hacket, John (1592–1670) lviii, lx

life of 163fn, 163n

A Century of Sermons 150 (422), 150n, 163n, 276n

Hackwood, Frederick William (b 1857) *William Hone* cxi n

Hadleigh Rectory Conference cxxxvii n

haeresis 298fn

Haggren, M. 62n

halcyon ideas 566

Halifax, George Savile, 1st Marquis of (1633–95) "Of Punishment" 137n

Hall, Joseph (1574–1656), bp of Norwich 164, 164n

Hall, Robert (1764–1831) xlv

Hallam, Arthur Henry (1811–33) cxv, cxxviii, cxxxiv, cxxxvi

sonnet to Emily Tennyson 358n q; "Timbuctoo" cxv, cxxxvi, cxlvi q and n, 358n; *The Writings of Arthur Hallam* cxv n

Halyburton, Thomas (1674–1712) *Natural Religion Insufficient* 210n

Ham (Bible), descendants of 261n

hand(s) 397n, 398

imposition of 368, 368n

Hannas, Linda *The English Jigsaw Puzzle* 32n

hap 45, 50n, 535

happiness/Happiness 46, 47 (439), 48 (440), 49 (440), 50, 51 (441), 70, 116

eternal h. 140; way to h. reserved in Heaven 539

happy lxxi

higher good to make one h. 118–19; h. man's ideas and impressions 118n

hard

heart growing h. 157; h. saying 314fn

Harding, Anthony John "Coleridge and Transcendentalism" cxvi and n; "James Marsh as Editor of Coleridge" cxvi and n, cxvii and n, cxviii n, cxxi n

362n, 365n, 372n, 391n, 395n, 396n, 398n, 399n, 402n, 555; *see also* S. T. Coleridge I (5) *Word-coinages*
Oxlee, John (1779–1854) *The Christian Doctrines of the Trinity and Incarnation* 21n
oxygen 182fn, 335, 396

"Pacificus" 513n
Paddy, hot-blooded 173n
Padre Paolo *see* Paolo Sarpi
Paedianus *see* Asconius Pedianus
Paedo-baptism, authorized 374
Paedo-baptist(s) 362
  Anti-p. 378fn; Baptist and 364
pagan(s)
  modern P. 195; P. Moralists 129; P. Philosophers 129; p. philosophy 8, 18fn
paganism/Paganism
  night of 191; philosophic 195; sacrificial rites of 409
pain xlv, 49, 57, 58
  eternal pleasure or p. 140; experience of p. on arising 268fn
Paine, Thomas (1737–1809) *The Rights of Man* 375n
painted
  p. eye 397n; p. weights 351
painter's glory 227n
palace, council-chamber of 34fn
Palace-Yard, mob in 34fn
palates, flesh tasted by 398
Paley, William (1743–1805) xliv, lxviii, lxxxviii, cvi, cxiii, 238n, 295n, 344 (456), 345, 356, 357n, 408n, 410
  head and heart of 408; not a moralist 293; Palëian principle of general consequences 274fn
  Beauties of Paley lvii n; *Natural Theology* 254n, 405n, 517n, 555; *Principles of Moral and Political Philosophy* 274n, 342, 411; *Sermons on Several Subjects* 409n; *View of the Evidences of Christianity* 344n, 356fn, 356n, 405n, 408n
palpable shuffle 338n
Panofsky, Erwin (1892–1968), "Blind Cupid" 97n
Pantheism cxvii, cxxvii, 87n, 181fn, 283, 284, 522n
pantheist xlii
pantheistic spirit 546
Pantheon 187n
Pantisocracy 255n

papal superstition 23 (437)
  and imposture 407n
Papists 212fn (424), 317 (428)
  sanctified ones among 213fn
parable 264fn, 390
  of Cupid and Psyche 284; symbolic p. 284
Paraclete 407
paradise/Paradise 290n
  of flowers' and butterflies' spirits 552
Paradise Lost see Milton
paradox 16 (436), 17, 279fn
paradoxy 244
parakupsas 30fn
parallel strait lines 277
pardon 310
parental Voice, Look, Touch 237; *see also* father, maternal, mother
parents 367
  Christian p. 370
Paris 522
  Parisian populace 375; Sorbonne 164n
Parkhurst, John (1728–97) *A Greek and English Lexicon to the New Testament* 34n; *Hebrew and English Lexicon* 21n
Parr, Samuel (1747–1825) 342, 342n
pars pro toto 348
part
  soul is all in every p. 233fn; whole in every p. 234n
partaker(s) of Divine Nature 366n, 567
participle 180fn
particles 397
particular and contingent appearances 249
Particularism, spirit of 212fn
parties, sects and 380
Partington, James Riddick (b 1886) *History of Chemistry* 246n
partisans of infidelity 352fn
parts, unity and 350
Pascal, Blaise (1623–62) lxii, lxvii n, 164, 234fn
  Lettres provinciales 164n; *Pensées* 164n
Pasquin, Anthony (John Williams) (1761–1818) *Memoirs of the Royal Academicians* 62n
"passeth all understanding" 332
passion(s)/Passion(s) 16, 19, 266 (424)
  anxiety to be admired is loveless p. 193; malignant 210fn; nature and irrational passions 195; for new and striking thoughts 113; p. no friend to truth 123; pander and advocate of 259fn; truth needs not the service of p. 123

INDEX OF GREEK TERMS